W9-CHL-150

Advertising
PRINCIPLES *&* PRACTICE

Advertising
PRINCIPLES & PRACTICE

FOURTH EDITION

William Wells
UNIVERSITY OF MINNESOTA

John Burnett
UNIVERSITY OF DENVER

Sandra Moriarty
UNIVERSITY OF COLORADO

PRENTICE-HALL, UPPER SADDLE RIVER, NEW JERSEY 07458

Acquisitions Editors: Donald J. Hull and Gabrielle Dudnyk
Associate Editor: John Larkin
Editorial Assistant: Jim Campbell
Vice President/Editorial Director: James Boyd
Marketing Manager: John Chillingworth
Associate Managing Editor: Linda DeLorenzo
Managing Editor: Dee Josephson
Production: Progressive Publishing Alternatives, Inc.
Manufacturing Supervisor: Arnold Vila
Manufacturing Manager: Vincent Scelta
Design Manager: Patricia Smythe
Interior Design: Ox & Company
Cover Design: Ox & Company

Copyright © 1998, 1995, 1992, 1989 by Prentice-Hall, Inc.
A Simon & Schuster Company
Upper Saddle River, New Jersey 07458

All rights reserved. No part of this book may be reproduced, in any form or by any means, without written permission from the Publisher.

Library of Congress Cataloging-in-Publication Data
Wells, William, 1926–
    Advertising: principles & practice / William Wells, John Burnett,
Sandra Moriarty.—4th ed.
       p.   cm.
    Includes bibliographical references and index.
    ISBN 0-13-597881-5
    1. Advertising. I. Burnett, John,   II. Moriarty,
Sandra E. (Sandra Ernst)   III. Title.
HF5823.W455   1998
659.1—dc21   97-40898
                                                  CIP

Prentice-Hall International (UK) Limited, London
Prentice-Hall of Australia Pty. Limited, Sydney
Prentice-Hall Canada, Inc., Toronto
Prentice-Hall Hispanoamericana, S.A., Mexico
Prentice-Hall of India Private Limited, New Delhi
Prentice-Hall of Japan, Inc., Tokyo
Simon & Schuster Asia Pte. Ltd., Singapore
Editora Prentice-Hall do Brasil, Ltda., Rio de Janeiro

Printed in the United States of America

10 9 8 7 6 5 4 3 2 1

OVERVIEW

PART VI MISCELLANEOUS ADVERTISING

CONTENTS

vii

 **PART IV CREATING ADVERTISING**

*P*ART **V** **ADVERTISING OPERATIONS**

PART VI   MISCELLANEOUS ADVERTISING

PREFACE

Advertising: Principles & Practice, Fourth Edition, is a comprehensive textbook and teaching package that breathes life into advertising. This text's strengths are many. First, the voices of *real practitioners* are interwoven with the practical and theoretical lessons throughout the book. Second, today's *integrated marketing communications* approach has been incorporated in a meaningful way. Third, the book is *complete* and *current*. Fourth, content, organization, and writing style offer students an appealing and thorough introduction to the field of advertising. Fifth, the teaching package provides the instructor with the tools needed to engage and hold student interest. Finally, the book provides an objective portrayal of the role advertising can play in a modern business.

Today, the world of advertising is going through dramatic changes. No longer is winning awards for creativity a sufficient reason for spending millions of dollars on advertising. Modern advertising is led by objectives and implemented through carefully designed strategies. Accountability is the byword as we approach the twenty-first century. Finally, constant improvements in technology may require major adjustments in how advertising delivers messages. *Advertising: Principles & Practice* is guided by and reflects these changes.

ADVERTISING AND THE REAL WORLD

Advertising professionals often question whether this field can be taught from a book. Although nothing compares with the experience of *being there*, it is a fact of life that all college students who want an introduction to advertising will not work in an advertising agency. How does this book help solve this problem? Simply by creating a textbook and a teaching package that will bring the real-world experience of advertising alive using paper, ink, pictures, overheads, audiotapes, and videotapes.

PROFESSIONAL VOICES

To provide a real-life view of advertising for a student who wants an introduction to the field, we have consulted specialists from the different areas of advertising and brought their stories to life. Much of the narrative in the text reflects advertising as those working in the field see it—their theories, their styles and approaches, their rules of thumb, their hindsight and foresight, and their visions. Of course, not everyone in the field agrees, so this book presents a variety of theories, styles, and approaches.

An approach upon which advertising professionals seem to agree is presented in this book as a *principle*. Advertising is still a young field, so these principles are evolving and changing as the field develops. In particular, the notion of *integrating* advertising with the other tools of marketing communication is in its infancy. Many of the integration principles posited in this text are original.

FOCUS ON EFFECTIVENESS

All the various professionals working in the field—artists, producers, performers, composers and arrangers, researchers, accountants, salespeople, and managers, to name a few—are important to getting the job done. The focus of all their efforts, regardless of their area of expertise, is on the *most effective way to present a sales message to a potential consumer.* This is the focus of advertising departments and advertising agencies, of media sales departments and consumer behavior researchers, of huge global mega-agencies and small creative boutiques. All of these activities are ultimately directed at producing a message that helps sell something to someone, which is the focus of this book.

ART AND SCIENCE

Advertising is a combination of specialized skills and professions that incorporate a number of approaches and philosophies, including those of a scientific or numbers oriented, strategic or problem/solution oriented, and artistic or aesthetically oriented nature. An introduction to advertising is an introduction to all sides of the advertising field and to the processes—quantitative, strategic, and aesthetic—by which the sales message is planned and produced. This text covers both the art and the science of advertising.

REALISTIC SCOPE

Advertising includes a variety of disciplines and specialties, including research, media buying and planning, copywriting, art direction, print and broadcast production, media sales, sales promotion and product publicity, strategic planning, personnel management, budgeting, scheduling, negotiating, and even business presentations. Because advertising is a major element in a company's marketing plan, it works in conjunction with a firm's overall corporate marketing practices. As we will describe, this edition has been rewritten to reflect more effectively today's *integrated marketing communications approach.*

INTEGRATED MARKETING COMMUNICATION

Advertising is a business, and advertising is part of business. Businesses whose goal is profit from the sales of products and services use the tool called advertising to carry a message to the consumer. Advertising is the voice, the expression of marketing. It is *communication.*

STRATEGY

The big picture in business includes a marketing strategy that begins with research, adds a thorough understanding of consumer behavior, runs realistic cost-benefit analyses, and emphasizes communication and problem solving. The advertising created and produced to support a firm's marketing strategy communicates through traditional print and broadcast advertising, sales promotion, and well-known media such as direct response, out-of-home and directory media—and increasingly—through alternative media such as interactive forms, advanced cable or telecommunications technology, or unique demand-based media. This book emphasizes how *new methods of communication are central to marketing communication.*

INFORMATION AND CHANGE

In turn, additional research and tight budgeting in today's economy provide the data and feedback that support the growth of marketing into new areas and away from other areas. In today's age of information, we have come to know this complete decision-making process as *integrated marketing communication* (IMC). The incorporation of IMC into this text has broadened in this edition. *Advertising: Principles & Practice* addresses this contemporary view as it applies to each specific area of advertising.

PROFESSIONALS AND BASIC PHILOSOPHIES

David Ogilvy, founder of Ogilvy & Mather and one of the true giants in the advertising world, opens his classic book *Ogilvy on Advertising* with a new well-known gem:

> I do not regard advertising as entertainment or an art form, but as a medium of information. When I write an advertisement, I don't want you to tell me that you find it 'creative.' I want you to find it so interesting that you *buy the product*. When Aeschines spoke, they said 'how well he speaks.' But when Demosthenes spoke, they said 'Let us march against Philip.'[1]

This is one of several basic philosophies that guided the direction of this book; not surprisingly, many of these philosophies touch on the same theses. For another example, the bottom line of advertising, according to Lou Hagopian, chairman of the N.W. Ayer agency, is *to sell more of something*. And according to John O'Toole, of the American Association of Advertising Agencies in New York, advertising is an important factor in our economic freedom of choice. In earlier editions of this book, this basic and practical sense of the business climate underlined the book's message that advertising is not only a business itself, but it is an important aspect of business in general.

Bill Bernbach, a founder of Doyle, Dane, and Bernbach (now DDB Needham Worldwide) insisted that *what is said is only the beginning*. "How you say it makes people look and listen." When it is done well—and admittedly not all advertising is done well—advertising touches common chords in all of us with carefully composed messages. So, an important premise of this book is that although *what is said is important, how it is said is equally as important*. Insights into human behavior and respect for people are absolutely fundamental to good advertising. Unfortunately, not all advertising is good, and not all advertising respects the people it tries to reach, but that is still the goal of the true professionals in the business—and another premise of this book.

John O'Toole explains it best in his book *The Trouble with Advertising* when he says you have to respect the critical faculties of the contemporary consumer. He points to the fact that 66 percent of new products do not make it. They are purchased and evaluated by the public and not bought again, no matter how powerful the advertising may be. He calls the public "these formidable folks whose wrath is so fearful." He describes the implicit contract, or at least understanding, between the advertiser and the public that makes advertising work:

> I promise you this. My advertising won't lie to you, or it will not deliberately try to mislead you. It won't bore the hell out of you or treat you as though you were a fool or embarrass you or your family. But remember, it's a salesman. Its purpose is to persuade you to trade your hard-earned cash for my product or service.[2]

So this is the real world of advertising—and this book is a medium of information to help the reader experience it in as lively and focused a fashion as possible.

ACKNOWLEDGMENTS

Advertising: Principles & Practice, Fourth Edition, has benefited from an outstanding team of authors and contributors. We wish to acknowledge the assistance of many academics and professionals in bringing the real world of advertising into the text.

---

[1]David Ogilvy, *Ogilvy on Advertising* (New York: Crown Publishers, Inc., 1983);7.
[2]John O'Toole, *The Trouble with Advertising* (New York: Times Books, 2nd ed. 1985).

Various experts in the industry contributed to the development of the text and supplements package. We are indebted to Peter Turk of the University of Akron and Norval Stephens of the Norval Stephens Company for their contributions to earlier editions, and also to Mark Green of Simpson College for his development of various video cases throughout the text. Special thanks to Lois J. Smith for preparing the Instructor's Manual and Robert Field for preparing the Test Item File. We would also like to thank Richard Gist for preparing the Transparency Package.

No text can be successfully developed without a supportive publisher. The team at Prentice Hall helped to develop both the text and the supplementary package, and we thank Don Hull and Gabrielle Dudnyk for overseeing the project; Linda DeLorenzo for patience during the production process; Mary Motiff at The Permissions Group for researching ads and photos, and procuring text permissions, John Larkin and Jim Campbell for handling the supplements; and John Chillingworth and Patti Arneson for developing the promotional program.

Many reviewers provided helpful comments on the drafts of the chapters. Their team and thoughtful comments are appreciated:

Edd Applegate
Middle Tennessee State University

Richard Behrman
Elon College

Charles Armstrong
Kansas City Kansas Community College

William Claypoole
Texas A&M University

Joel Davis
San Diego State University

Sue Anne Davis
University of California at Berkeley

George R. Franke
Virginia Polytechnic Institute & State University

Vicki Griffis
University of South Florida

Charles S. Gulas
Wright State University

James B. Hunt
University of North Carolina at Wilmington

Bart Kittle
Youngstown State University

Tina Lowery
Rider University

Patricia M. Manninen
North Shore Community College

James M. Maskulka
Lehigh University

Mary Ann McGrath
Loyola University of Chicago

Anita M. Olson
North Hennepin Community College

Stephen P. Phelps
Southern Illinois University at Carbondale

Scott D. Roberts
University of Texas

Allen Schaefer
Southwest Missouri State

L. J. Shrum
Rutgers University

James R. Smith
State University of New York at New Paltz

Shelly R. Tapp
St. Louis University

John P. Thurin
University of Notre Dame

Donna Uchida
Colorado State University

D. Joel Whalen
DePaul University

Kurt Wildermuth
University of Missouri at Columbia

ABOUT THE AUTHORS

WILLIAM WELLS One of the industry's leading market and research authorities, Bill Wells is Professor of Advertising at the University of Minnesota's School of Journalism and Mass Communication. Former Executive Vice President and Director of Marketing Services at DDB Needham Chicago, he is, in fact, the only representative of the advertising business elected to the Attitude Research Hall of Fame. He earned a Ph.D. from Stanford University and was formerly Professor of Psychology and Marketing at the University of Chicago. He joined Needham, Harper, Chicago as Director of Corporate Research. Author of the Needham Harper Lifestyle study as well as author of more than 60 books and articles, Dr. Wells also published *Planning for R.O.R.: Effective Advertising Strategy* (Prentice Hall, 1989).

JOHN BURNETT A Professor of Marketing at the University of Denver, he holds a D.B.A. degree in Marketing from the University of Kentucky. Dr. Burnett is author of *Promotion Management*, now in its third edition. In addition, he has had numerous articles and papers in a wide variety of professional and academic journals. In particular, his research has examined the effectiveness of emotional appeals in advertising and how various segments respond to such strategies. He is an active consultant in marketing and advertising and has served as a consultant for AT&T, the Dallas Mart, the AAFES organization, and Scott & White Hospitals. Dr. Burnett has won several teaching awards and serves as faculty advisor for student chapters of the American Marketing Association.

SANDRA MORIARTY A Professor in the Integrated Marketing Program at the University of Colorado-Boulder, she holds a Ph.D. in instructional communication from Kansas State University. Before moving into full-time teaching, she owned her own public relations and advertising agency. In addition to the present text, Dr. Moriarty has written or co-written several books, including *Marketing, The Creative Package, Creative Advertising* and most recently, *Driving Brand Value* with Tom Duncan. She is also author of numerous professional articles and scholarly research reports. Her current research interests include the analysis of changing marketing practice and the development of new theoretical approaches in marketing communications.

AND THEY SAID WE COULDN'T GIVE IT AWAY.

FREE
ARCH DELUXE

with this coupon and purchase of large fries and medium soft drink. With or without bacon.

It's the burger with the grown up taste.

As any kid can tell you, McDonald's new Arch Deluxe is the burger with the grown up taste. So try one today. It's big. It's sophisticated. It's everything kids hate. You'll love it.

CHAPTER

Introduction to Advertising

CHAPTER OUTLINE

- Refurbishing the Golden Arches
- What Makes an Ad Great?
- The World of Advertising
- The Four Players
- The Evolution of Advertising

CHAPTER OBJECTIVES

When you have completed this chapter, you should be able to:

- Define advertising and discuss its component parts
- Understand the elements of great advertising
- Identify the eight types of advertising
- Explain the four roles of advertising
- Identify the four players in the advertising world
- Explain the impact on advertising of the invention of media forms such as print, radio, and television
- Relate key figures in the history of advertising to their contributions to the field
- Comprehend the future direction of advertising

REFURBISHING THE GOLDEN ARCHES

McDonald's is still the leading fast-food restaurant in the world. Yet, the trends were not promising. Hundreds of new competitors, aging baby boomers, and the move toward low-fat dining all suggested to McDonald's that a strategic change was necessary.

The answer was the Arch Deluxe—a quarter-pound patty with bakery roll, cheese, tomato, lettuce, onions, ketchup, seasoned sauce, and optional bacon. The price is $2.39 with bacon and $1.99 without. The new burger was aimed squarely at adults, including the national advertising that used kiddie icon Ronald McDonald in a parody-style campaign without a theme line. "McDonald's owns the kids market, but the core, heavy fast-food user is late teen/early adult," noted Prudential Securities analyst Janice Meyer. "It's always about getting the heavy user to come [to McDonald's] more." While the chain has a big share of adult breakfast traffic, adults don't choose the golden arches for lunch or dinner.

The Arch Deluxe advertising campaign began with teaser promotions featuring an aging Ronald McDonald. On launch day, May 9, 1996, ads appeared on the four major networks, plus cable channels ESPN, Lifetime, Black Entertainment Television, and Spanish-language Univision and Telemundo. There were also simultaneous live media events in New York, Los Angeles, and Toronto. The print campaign featured a peel-off coupon positioned where a child's tongue would be. The estimated cost of the campaign was $100 million.

The big question is whether or not it worked. McDonald's maintains that Arch Deluxe has "exceeded expectations" by more than 30 percent, and that the product is among the most successful in its history, with more than 100 million served during the first two months. What McDonald's won't say is what its expectations were, and how much of the total served included discounted or free burgers—one expert put the number at 20 percent—or whether or not Arch Deluxe is cannibalizing its other burgers.[1]

The situation facing McDonald's is indicative of the business climate of the 1990s. Growth industries, such as soft drinks, computer technology, athletic ware, and fast food, tend to be dominated by one or two companies—Coke and Pepsi, Apple and IBM, Nike and Reebok, and McDonald's and Burger King, respectively. Relatively minor players such as Diet Dr Pepper, Compaq, Adidas, and Wendy's are faced with the inevitable task of attacking head on or pursuing a flanking strategy. Wendy's, for example, realizes that targeted advertising, in respect to both message and media, is the only way to compete.

WHAT MAKES AN AD GREAT?

Is the "Always and Only Coca-Cola" ad campaign great? Clearly, there are many critics in the industry who contend it is not great, it's not even good. Yet, defining what is great advertising is not easy. Experience has shown that greatness is not based solely on a popularity contest. If that were true, Pepsi has produced great ads for many years (see Ad 1.1). Table 1.1 lists the television ads of 1995 deemed most popular with consumers. Pepsi's number-three position would seem to support this point. But note the two products ahead of Pepsi's ad of a little boy getting sucked into a Pepsi bottle. What do you think of the Budweiser frogs and

---

[1]Judann Pollack, "McDonald's to Aim Its Arch at Grown-ups," *Advertising Age*, April 8, 1996, p. 3; Richard Gibson, "McDonald's Plays Catch-Up with BLT Burger," *The Wall Street Journal*, May 2, 1996, p. B1; Judann Pollack, "Burger King Sizzles in Wake of Arch Deluxe," *Advertising Age*, June 17, 1996, p. 3; Richard Gibson, "Arch DeFunct: A Big Mac Loses Where Old McDonald's Survives," *The Wall Street Journal*, August 2, 1996, p. B1.

AD 1.1

THIS COLLECTION OF PEPSI ADS
ILLUSTRATES THE CREATIVE
PHILOSOPHY OF PEPSI-COLA
OVER A 30-YEAR PERIOD.

TABLE 1.1	TOP TELEVISION CAMPAIGNS OF 1995

Omnicom's ad agencies had six of the 15 most popular commercials

1995 RANK	1994 RANK	BRAND	AGENCY
1	12	Budweiser	DDB Needham[†]
2	4	McDonald's	Leo Burnett
3	4	Pepsi	BBDO[†]
4	2	Little Caesars	Cliff Freeman & Partners
5	1	Coca-Cola	Creative Artists Agency
6	11	Pizza Hut	BBDO Worldwide[†]
7	6	AT&T	FCB/Leber Katz/N.W. Ayer & Partners/ McCann-Erickson, Young & Rubicam
8	26–50	Milk	Goodby, Silverstein & Partners[†]
9	5	Bud Light	DDB Needham[†]
10	26–50	Edy's/Dryers	Goldberg Moser O'Neill
11	9	Nike	Wieden & Kennedy
12	26–50	Doritos	BBDO[†]
13	26–50	Taco Bell	Bozell/Salvati Montgomery Sakoda
14	15	Diet Coke	Lowe & Partners/SMS
15	—*	Jeep	Bozell

*Not in the top 100 last year.

[†]Owned by Omnicom.

Source: From "Omnicom Menagerie Tops Poll of Most Popular TV Ads" by Sally Goll Beatly. Reprinted by permission of *The Wall Street Journal* (March 11, 1996):B1; Video Storyboard Tests. Copyright © 1996 Dow Jones & Company, Inc. All rights reserved worldwide.

ants ads? What makes them more appealing than Pepsi's ad? Furthermore, these popularity rankings have nothing to do with sales. Do sales follow great ads?

Clearly, the Coke ads produced in the 1960s were great. The "I'd like to buy the world a Coke" mountaintop ad is considered a classic. These ads won many industry awards and contributed significantly to brand awareness and increased sales. When did Coke ads stop being great? Some would argue that it began with the introduction of Diet Coke. The creative focus initiated by McCann-Erickson for Coke somehow was dissipated with the efforts of Lintas, the agency assigned to Diet Coke. Consumers couldn't discern if Coke was "it" or not. But others contend that many other factors in addition to advertising played a critical role in the relative success of the Coca-Cola franchise. Marketing decisions have been questioned. Was Diet Coke positioned too closely to regular Coke, so that one product cannibalized the other? Did Coke interpret the changing demographics correctly? How about new and better competitors? Finally, the emphasis of price discounting as a way of life in the soft-drink industry dramatically changed the relative importance of advertising in the industry. Essentially, advertising—even the greatest advertising—cannot counter so many powerful factors. Still, what *is* great advertising?

Often the determination of great advertising is reduced simply to determining what people like best in advertisements. We all have our favorite ads. Which television commercials do you remember? Which radio commercials? Magazine ads? Why are they your favorites? If you are like most people, your favorite ads are either funny or have a clever execution. As we will see, the reasons why people like certain ads and the effectiveness, or greatness, of the ads are often based on the same qualities.

Several companies ask people questions that get to the "whys" of advertising preferences. *Advertising Age*, working with the SRI Research Center, conducts a monthly "Ad Watch" survey of advertising awareness. Video Storyboard Tests asks consumers to list the most outstanding print advertisements and television commercials. *Advertising Age* also regularly interviews top creative people to identify those ads that professionals think are most effective. The advertising industry evaluates its work through such award programs as the Clios, the EFFIES, and the Addy Awards. Just as achieving consumer recognition does not make an ad great, neither does winning industry prizes. Many agencies that have developed award-winning campaigns have been dropped by their clients because the ads did not increase sales for the company.

Although awards are still considered a necessary morale booster for creative staffs, a survey of advertising agencies shows that many agencies have pulled back from entering advertising competitions, reserving entries for those shows that have greater acclaim, such as the Clios, the New York Art Directors, the One Show, and the International Advertising Film Festival in Cannes, France. For example, BBDO, which annually enters 14 shows, is getting pickier about its choices. "The rising costs are outrageous and I don't think they're warranted," says creative administrator June Baloutine.

Agencies are not entering competitions for other reasons as well. In these days of awards proliferation, awards no longer seem to impress clients. Michael Lollis, executive vice president and executive creative director at J. Walter Thompson in Atlanta, states, "As there are more and more shows, they become less meaningful. If you enter often enough, you can win something someplace."[2]

The situation was cogently summarized by David Ogilvy, interviewed at his Chateau Touffou in France: "If I could persuade the creative lunatics to give up their pursuit of awards, I would die happy. . . . Down with advertising that forgets to promise the consumer any benefit. Down with the creative show-offs. Too clever by half."[3]

So, if awards, popularity, and longevity are not reliable measures of great advertising, then what is?

CLASSICS

There are few ads that have stood the test of time. This chapter will discuss the objective and subjective criteria for greatness that these ads have consistently met. Certain ads are simply outstanding; they are classics. Some are from campaigns that have been running for a long time; others are single ads or campaigns that have been around for only a short time. What do all these ads have in common? Good ads work on two levels: *They engage the mind of the consumer and at the same time deliver a selling message.*

The California Raisins "I Heard It Through the Grapevine" commercials, for example, dominated the AdWatch awareness studies in the late 1980s (see Ad 1.2). The catchy music and the parody of a rhythm-and-blues singing group performing a 1960s hit have made this campaign a favorite of consumers and professionals alike.

The campaigns for Obsession, Nike, and Levi's 501 have each achieved a considerable level of success. Targeted primarily at young men, these ads reflect this group's interests and needs. Moreover, they have used a variety of techniques, such as humor, action, and sex, effectively enough to attract the attention of young males and keep it.

Spokespersons and celebrities have been an important part of many classic ads. Bill Cosby is a successful presenter for a number of companies, and his long-standing relationship with Jell-O has produced a number of winning ads. Ed and Frank, two invented but believable characters for Bartles and Jaymes Wine Coolers, became well-loved stars in their own continuing miniseries. Their "Baseball Tips" commercial, which ran for two weeks around the time of the 1988

---

[2]Kathy Ruehle and Barbara Holsonback, "Some Agencies Deciding Awards Not Worth the Cost," *Adweek* (April 30, 1990):1, 10.

[3]Noreen O'Leary, "Waiting for the Revolution," *Adweek* (June 15, 1992):30–34.

AD 1.2

THIS "I HEARD IT THROUGH THE GRAPEVINE" AD SPONSORED BY CALIFORNIA RAISINS WAS ONE OF THE FIRST TO USE CLAYMATION ALONG WITH NOSTALGIC '60S MUSIC—QUITE COMMON TODAY.

AD 1.3

THE LITTLE CAESARS® PIZZA! PIZZA! CHARACTER PROVIDES A SILLY BUT LOVABLE IMAGE THAT IS SOMEHOW EASY FOR US TO RELATE TO.

World Series, reached and affected three times as many people as the average commercial.

Michael Jordan, the premier spokesperson of the 1990s, delivers believable commercials for Diet Coke, Wheaties, and Nike, to name but a few. His animated Coke ads, with a variety of cartoon characters, shown during the 1992 and 1993 Super Bowls produced awareness scores five times higher than the norm.[4]

These campaigns are widely remembered, not only because they are entertaining, but also because they involve viewers and make them wonder what the campaigns' creators will come up with next. The campaigns also use humor, ranging from soft and gentle to outrageous. Humor is an important part of some of the other all-time great ads, such as the Federal Express ad featuring the fast-talking executive. Underneath the funny characterizations, however, the Federal Express ads carry a hard-hitting message of dependability: "When it absolutely, positively has to be there overnight." The silly Little Caesars® Roman character strikes our funny bone in a way that evokes a smile and he is easy to remember and associate with the product; he's effective—he can prompt a trip to Little Caesars for a purchase (Ad 1.3).

Great ads often touch emotions other than humor. The AT&T/Long-Distance Service "Reach Out and Touch Someone" campaign has been touching emotions since 1979. The messages are warm and sentimental, but more than that, they communicate the idea that it is easy and rewarding to call friends and family at any time.

Children, cats, and puppy dogs are lovable and give a product warm associations. The Oscar Mayer kids have been singing the product's theme song since 1973. The sing-along music contributes to the Oscar Mayer success story.

Often the characters are fictional, like Ed and Frank. Some of these characters, like Charlie the Tuna and the Jolly Green Giant, are total fantasy. But all of them capture the "inherent drama" of the product. Imagine yourself an advertiser who wants to position vegetables to make them acceptable to children. Why not use a cartoon character like a giant to promote them? But giants are fearsome, you think, so how do I make this character appealing to kids? Make him "Jolly." Leo

---

[4]An *awareness* or *recall* score determines how well a consumer can remember all or parts of an advertisement. More will be said about awareness in Chapter 21.

Burnett, creative genius behind this campaign and others, such as Exxon's Tony the Tiger, had a real penchant for animal mascots, which have come to be called "critters" in the advertising industry. Burnett was able to take complex messages and embody them in a single cartoon character.

Drama is often an important aspect of successful advertising. One of the most dramatic advertisements ever produced was a commercial for the launch of the Apple Macintosh computer that took on Apple's most serious competitor, IBM. The stark images of the classic George Orwell novel *1984* (Ad 1.4) came alive in this commercial, which only ran once, on the 1984 Super Bowl before 100 million viewers. Not only was this ad a captivating drama, it also demonstrated the power of a timely media buy. As noted in the Issues and Controversies box, the "1984" ad almost did not run. It was considered outrageous and too abstract.

Significant images are another important part of advertising. Nike, with their "Just do it!" campaign has provided the intended audience—young athletic men and women, or athletic "wannabes"—with rewarding praise for the physically fit and consistent inspiration for the unfit to chuck their lethargy, to stop the tendency to accept the societal norm, and *just do it*. These images of men and women committed to "no pain—no gain," both inspire and challenge. This imagery is heightened through excellent photography, the use of celebrities, and dramatic situations. It is a type of advertising called, rather literally, *image advertising*.

Perhaps the most successful image advertising of all time, however, is the Marlboro campaign, which has been running since 1955. With overwhelming single-mindedness the campaign has focused on western imagery with cowboys, horses, and ranching. The cowboy myth is a strong and compelling image. This campaign has been successful both as communication and as a marketing effort. It has helped to make Marlboro the best-selling cigarette in the world. However, this seems to be changing.

Because Marlboro feels that the Marlboro Man is losing its effectiveness, several modifications have been made. The traditional cowboy image has been replaced by a more abstract interpretation, including a print campaign that displays nothing but his blue-jeaned groin with a strategically positioned carton of Marlboros. Still, there is a dilemma: Its fortunes are so tied to the Marlboro Man that the company can't afford to remake him too drastically for fear of alienating existing smokers.

AD 1.4

THE 1984 APPLE MACINTOSH COMPUTER COMMERCIAL PLAYED ONLY ONE TIME, BUT IS CONSIDERED BY SOME AS THE GREATEST AD OF ALL TIME.

Issues and Controversies

BIG BROTHER ALMOST MISSED THE BOAT

The Apple "1984" ad recently won the Advertisement of the Century award, but few people realize how close it came to not being aired. In the third quarter of the National Football League's Super Bowl game on January 22, Apple introduced the Mac with a 60-second Orwellian epic in which a youthful woman hurled a mallet at a big screen to kill Big Brother, from George Orwell's classic novel *1984*. The commercial changed advertising; the product changed the ad business; the technology changed the world.

"1984" was a creative and media-buying achievement, a teaser spot with the pretension of a serious film that cost $400,000 to produce and $500,000 to broadcast in its single national paid airing.

It turned the Super Bowl from a football game into advertising's Super Event of the year. And it ushered in the era of advertising as news: The three major television networks replayed parts or all of the spot as a story on nightly news programs.

"What '1984' as a commercial for Apple really signified was the first time somebody could put a great deal of production money into a single commercial and run it only once and get tremendous benefit from running it only once," noted John O'Toole, president of the American Association of Advertising Agencies. "It took great coordination with PR. It was really event marketing, with sales promotion and PR built in. That was the beginning of the new era of integrated marketing communications."

"1984" initially was pegged to air on a New Year's Day college football game but was pushed back to the Super Bowl to be closer to Macintosh's official introduction to Apple's January 24 annual shareholders' meeting. Apple bought two minutes of time. Even then, "1984" did come to an abrupt, albeit temporary, halt after a screening for Apple's directors. "At the end of the 60-second commercial, the room was silent," says Michael Murray, then Macintosh director of marketing and now a vice president at Microsoft Corp. "Phil Schlein [a former director] had his head on the table, and he was pounding a fist on the table in slow motion. The first comment came from Mike Markkula," then an outside director. "He says, 'Steve [Mr. Jobs], I can't believe you want to show this ad.' All of a sudden, the meeting takes on a very funeral tone, as in my own funeral. We were instructed by the board to sell the time that Chiat/Day had purchased." Chiat sold off the first minute, but the second minute, for reasons unknown, was never sold.

Someone at Apple—it's not clear who—gave the go-ahead to fill the other Super Bowl minute with "1984," and the story of Macintosh reached the millions of Americans who had the good graces not to be in the bathroom or kitchen during that particular commercial break. Mr. O'Toole recalls that before "1984," he tuned into the Super Bowl for football. "From '84 on, I watched the Super Bowl to see the commercials," he says.

Source: Bradley Johnson, "10 Years After '1984,'" *Advertising Age* (January 10, 1994):1, 12–14. Reprinted with permission from *Advertising Age*. Copyright Crain Communications Inc.

CHARACTERISTICS OF GREAT ADS

What do you think makes an ad great? And what turns great ads into classics? What makes certain ads stand out in people's minds? And why do some ad campaigns continue to run for years, sometimes even for decades? From this discussion it should be clear that great advertising employs a variety of techniques: celebrities and spokespersons, fantasy characters, children and puppies, music, drama, significant imagery, and creative media buying. Advertising is the complex voice of marketing, and the rest of this book will try to explain how all of these factors are interwoven to create great advertising. The premise of this book, however, is that three broad dimensions characterize great advertising: strategy, creativity, and execution (see Ad 1.5). This book is built around these three dimensions.

STRATEGY

Every great ad is strategically sound. In other words, it is carefully directed to a certain audience, it is driven by specific objectives, its message is crafted to speak to that audience's most important concerns, and it is run in media that will most effectively reach that audience. The measure of an ad's success is how well it achieves its goals, whether they be increased sales, memorability, attitude change, or brand awareness.

Ally & Gargano

CLIENT: FEDERAL EXPRESS CORP.
PRODUCT: AIR FREIGHT
TITLE: "FAST PACED WORLD"
COMMERCIAL NO.: QFAS 1326 (:30)
DATE APPROVED: 7/14/81

1. MR. SPLEEN: (OC) Okay Eunice,travelplans,Ineedtobein NewYorkonMonday,LAon Tuesday,NewYorkon Wednesday,LAonThursday,

2. andNewYorkonFriday. Gotit? Soyouwanttoworkhere,well whatmakesyouthinkyoudeserve ajobhere?

3. GUY: Wellsirlthinkonmyfeet, I'mgoodwithfiguresandIhavea sharpmind.

4. SPLEEN: Excellent,canyou startMonday?

5. (OC): Andinconclusion,Jim, Bill,BobandTed,

6. businessisbusinesssolet'sgetto work. Thankyoufortakingthis meeting.

7. (OC): Peteryoudidabang-up job,I'mputtingyouinchargeof Pittsburgh.

8. PETER: (OC) Pittsburgh's perfect. SPLEEN: Iknowit's perfect,Peter,that'swhyIpicked Pittsburgh. Pittsburgh'sperfect Peter,MayIcallyouPete?

9. (OC): Congratulationson yourdealinDenverDavid.

10. I'mputtingyoudowntodealin Dallas. ANNCR: (VO) In this fast moving, high pressure, get-it-done yesterday world,

11. aren't you glad there's one company that can keep up with it all?

12. Federal Express. (SFX) When it absolutely, positively has to be there overnight.

AD 1.5

THE FAST-TALKING EXECUTIVE ADS FOR FEDERAL EXPRESS ARE EXAMPLES OF GREAT ADVERTISING.

The crazy characters and situations in the Federal Express ads bring to life a very important selling premise about the essence of dependability. Mikey likes Life, so it must be good. See the Concepts and Applications box for an example of how the National Fluid Milk Processor Promotion Board has repositioned its products for the adult target market.

CREATIVITY

The *creative concept* is a central idea that gets your attention and sticks in your memory. Every one of the ads we've discussed has a Big Idea that is creative and original. Frank and Ed are unique characters, as is the Jolly Green Giant. Isuzu took the stereotype of the untrustworthy car salesman and created the unforgettable Joe Isuzu, who retired in 1993.

A concern for creative thinking drives the entire field of advertising. Planning the strategy calls for creative problem solving; the research efforts are creative; the buying and placing of ads in the media are creative. Advertising is an exciting field because of the constant demand for creative solutions to media and message problems.

*C*ONCEPTS AND *A*PPLICATIONS

DRINK MILK—FOREVER

Who would have thought that beautiful women would ever be plastered on the pages of magazines sporting mustaches? Milk mustaches, that is. But the milk industry is trying to make its product as hip as the leading—not to mention slim—ladies of fashion, entertainment, and sports. The "Milk, What a Surprise!" campaign, created by the New York agency Bozell for the National Fluid Milk Processor Promotion Board, represents one of several multimillion-dollar efforts now under way from different segments of the industry.

Milk ads don't lack creativity. Besides the mustache advertising, the "Got Milk" campaign that Goodby, Silverstein & Partners, San Francisco, created for the California Milk Processor Board has won a Clio and two Obies. It has also boosted grocery sales of milk by 7 percent in California while the rest of the United States stayed flat.

However, consistently moving the sales needle will be a bigger feat since several problems stubbornly plague the industry:

- Milk sales have been going sour for decades.
- Controversy has ranged from fat content to the hormones farmers use to stimulate production.
- The producers are reluctant to push their hottest product, 2 percent milk, because of questions about its "low-fat" designation.

"Milk has been taking a drubbing for the past 30 years," said Jay Schulberg, chief creative officer at Bozell. "People's attitudes and perceptions have to be changed."

The $52 million milk mustache campaign recognizes the diverse tastes of milk drinkers. Celebrities like Christie Brink-

ley, Mary Lou Retton, and Joan Lunden praise different kinds of milk for various nutritional reasons. "All milk advertising before this has basically been generic," said Charles Decker, executive director of the promotion board's Milk Processing Promotion Program. "This time around, the goal is to debunk the myths consumers have about milk. The current health debate focuses on fat. Estimates of whole milk's fat content, which is 3.5 percent, have been 'blown out of proportion' and its nutritional value has been disregarded," said George Harmon, senior vice president, Strategic Information Group at Dairy Management, Inc.

Dairy Management's $50 million in "Milk, Help Yourself" spots from J. Walter Thompson USA, and Goodby's $28 million campaign for the California group promote milk as a beverage that consumers can't do without in certain situations, like eating cereal.

According to Kurt Graetzner, executive director of the Milk Processor Education Program, the campaign has been a huge success. "Our reach and frequencies are amazing with women 18–44. Just five months into the all-magazine campaign, we placed fifth among the Top Ten ad campaigns . . . Ten months into the ad campaign, we saw dramatic improvements—with significant attitude shifts in the four major areas that concerned us."

Sources: Andrew Wallenstein, "Milk Producers Fight Fat Fatalism," *Advertising Age* (May 22, 1995):2, 12; Barbara Lippert, "Lip Service," *Adweek* (February 6, 1995):38.

EXECUTION

PRINCIPLE Great ads are creative, strategically sound, and perfectly executed.

Finally, every great ad is well executed. That means the craftsmanship is impressive. The details, the techniques, and the production values have all been fine-tuned. Many of these techniques are experimental, such as the Intel Computer commercial that uses ADOBE, a contemporary computer graphic software package. There is more to execution than technology, however. The warm touch in the AT&T commercials is a delicate emotional effect. It is sensitive without being overly sentimental or manipulative.

Good advertisers know that how you say it is just as important as what you say. *What you say* comes from strategy, whereas *how you say it* is a product of creativity and execution. The great ads, then, are ads that (1) are strategically sound, (2) have an original creative concept, and (3) use exactly the right execution for the message. Strategy, creativity, and execution—these are the qualities that turn great ads into classics.

*T*HE *W*ORLD OF *A*DVERTISING

DEFINING ADVERTISING

What is advertising? What are its important dimensions? The standard definition of advertising includes six elements. Advertising is a *paid form of communication*, although some forms of advertising, such as public service, use donated space and

Advertising: Paid nonpersonal communication from an identified sponsor using mass media to persuade or influence an audience.

time. Not only is the message paid for, but the *sponsor is identified*. In some cases the point of the message is simply to make consumers aware of the product or company, although most advertising tries to *persuade or influence* the consumer to do something. The message is conveyed through many different kinds of *mass media* reaching a large *audience* of potential consumers. Because advertising is a form of mass communication, it is also *nonpersonal*. A definition of **advertising**, then, would include all six of those features.

> **Advertising** is *paid nonpersonal communication* from an identified *sponsor* using *mass media* to *persuade or influence* an *audience*.

In an ideal world every manufacturer would be able to talk one-on-one with every consumer about the product or service being offered for sale. Personal selling approaches that idea, but it is very expensive. Calls made by salespeople can cost well in excess of $150 per call.

It should be noted that advertising delivered through interactive technology might be considered personal communication rather than mass communication. However, as will be noted in later chapters, although advertisers can provide more customization through interactive media, it is still a far cry from personal selling. There the costs, for *time* in broadcast media and for *space* in print media, are spread over the tremendous number of people that these media reach. For example, $1.1 million may sound like a lot of money for one ad on the Super Bowl, but when you consider that the advertisers are reaching over 500 million people, the cost is not extreme.

TYPES OF ADVERTISING

Advertising is complex because so many diverse advertisers try to reach so many different types of audiences. There are eight basic types of advertising.

BRAND ADVERTISING

The most visible type of advertising is *national consumer advertising*. Another name for this is *brand advertising*, which focuses on the development of a long-term brand identity and image. It tries to develop a distinctive brand image for a product.

RETAIL ADVERTISING

In contrast, *retail advertising* is local and focuses on the store where a variety of products can be purchased or where a service is offered. The message announces products that are available locally, stimulates store traffic, and tries to create a distinctive image for the store. Retail advertising emphasizes price, availability, location, and hours of operation.

POLITICAL ADVERTISING

Political advertising is used by politicians to persuade people to vote for them and therefore is an important part of the political process in the United States and other democratic countries that permit candidate advertising. Although it is an important source of communication for voters, critics are concerned that political advertising tends to focus more on image than on issues.

DIRECTORY ADVERTISING

Another type of advertising is called directory because people refer to it to find out how to buy a product or service. The best-known form of *directory advertising* is the Yellow Pages, although there are many different kinds of directories that perform the same function.

DIRECT-RESPONSE ADVERTISING

Direct-response advertising can use any advertising medium, including direct mail, but the message is different from that of national and retail advertising in that it tries to stimulate a sale directly. The consumer can respond by telephone or mail, and the product is delivered directly to the consumer by mail or some other carrier. Interactive falls under this heading.

BUSINESS-TO-BUSINESS ADVERTISING

Business-to-business advertising includes messages directed at retailers, wholesalers, and distributors, as well as industrial purchasers and professionals such as lawyers and physicians. Business advertising tends to be concentrated in business publications or professional journals.

INSTITUTIONAL ADVERTISING

Institutional advertising is also called *corporate advertising*. The focus of these messages is on establishing a corporate identity or on winning the public over to the organization's point of view.

PUBLIC SERVICE ADVERTISING

Public service advertising (PSA) communicates a message on behalf of some good cause, such as stopping drunk driving (MADD) or preventing child abuse. These advertisements are created for free by advertising professionals, and the space and time are donated by the media.

As you can see, there isn't just one kind of advertising; in fact, advertising is a large and varied industry. All of these areas demand creative, original messages that are strategically sound and well executed. In the chapters to come, all of these types of advertising will be discussed in more depth.

ROLES OF ADVERTISING

Advertising can also be explained in terms of the roles it plays in business and in society. Four different roles have been identified for advertising:

1. Marketing
2. Communication role
3. Economic role
4. Societal role

THE MARKETING ROLE

Marketing is the strategic process a business uses to satisfy consumer needs and wants through goods and services. The particular consumers at whom the company directs its marketing effort constitute the *target market*. The tools available to marketing include the product, its price, and the means used to deliver the product, or the place. Marketing also includes a mechanism for communicating this information to the consumer, which is called *marketing communication*, or promotion. These four tools are collectively referred to as the *marketing mix* or the *4 Ps*. Marketing communication is further broken down into four related communication techniques: advertising, sales promotion, public relations, and personal selling. Thus, advertising is only one element in a company's overall marketing communication program, although it is the most visible. The marketing role will be discussed in depth in Chapter 3.

THE COMMUNICATION ROLE

Advertising is a form of mass communication. It transmits different types of market information to match buyers and sellers in the marketplace. Advertising both informs and transforms the product by creating an image that goes beyond straightforward facts. Specific suggestions about how to accomplish these tasks will be discussed in later chapters on creating messages.

PRINCIPLE Advertising provides information that helps match buyers and sellers in the marketplace.

THE ECONOMIC ROLE

The two major schools of thought concerning the effects of advertising on the economy are the market power school and the market competition school.[5] According to the market power school, advertising is a persuasive communication tool used by marketers to distract consumers' attention from the price of the product. In contrast, the market competition school sees advertising as a source of information that increases consumers' price sensitivity and stimulates competition.

Actually, little is known about the true nature of advertising in the economy. Charles Sandage, an advertising professor, provides a different perspective. He sees the economic role of advertising as "helping society to achieve abundance by informing and persuading members of society with respect to products, services, and ideals."[6] In addition, he argues that advertising assists in "the development of judgment on the part of consumers in their purchase practices."

THE SOCIETAL ROLE

Advertising also has a number of social roles. It informs us about new and improved products and teaches us how to use these innovations. It helps us compare products and features and make informed consumer decisions. It mirrors fashion and design trends and contributes to our aesthetic sense.

Advertising tends to flourish in societies that enjoy some level of economic abundance, that is, in which supply exceeds demand. It is at this point that advertising moves from being a simple informational service (telling consumers where they can find the product) to being a message designated to create a demand for a particular brand.

The question is: Does advertising follow trends or does it lead them? At what point does advertising cross the line between *reflecting* social values and *creating* social values? Critics argue that advertising has repeatedly crossed this line and has evolved into an instrument of social control. Although these concerns are not new, the increasing power of advertising, both in terms of money (we spend more annually educating consumers than we spend educating our children) and in terms of communication dominance (the mass media can no longer survive without advertising support), has made these concerns more prominent than ever.

Can advertising manipulate people? Some critics argue that advertising has the power to dictate how people behave. They believe that, even if an individual ad cannot control our behavior, the cumulative effects of nonstop television, radio, print, and outdoor ads can be overwhelming.

Although certain groups of people, such as young children, the less educated, and the elderly, might be more susceptible to certain kinds of advertising, it is hard to conclude that a particular ad or series of ads caused, tricked, or coerced anyone into making a particular buying decision. There is no solid evidence for the manipulative power of advertising because so many other factors contribute to the choices we make. Although advertising does attempt to persuade, most people are aware that advertisers are biased in favor of their own products and learn how to handle persuasive advertising in their daily lives. Manipulation and other ethical issues will be discussed in more detail in Chapter 2.

FUNCTIONS OF ADVERTISING

Not all advertising attempts to accomplish the same objectives. Although each ad or campaign tries to reach goals unique to its sponsor, there are two basic functions that advertising performs, along with several subfunctions.

---

[5]John M. Vernon, "Concentration, Promoting, and Market Share Stability in the Pharmaceutical Industry," *Journal of Industrial Economics* (July 1971):146–266.

[6]Charles H. Sandage, "Some Institutional Aspects of Advertising," *Journal of Advertising*, Vol. 1, No. 1 (1973):9.

Product advertising aims to inform or stimulate the market about the sponsor's product(s). The intent is clearly to sell a particular product, to the exclusion of competitors' products. Conversely, *institutional advertising* is designed to create a positive attitude toward the seller. The intent is to promote the sponsoring organization rather than the things it sells.

DIRECT ACTION VERSUS INDIRECT ACTION

Product advertising may be either direct-action or indirect-action advertising. *Direct-action advertising* is intended to produce a quick response. Ads that include a coupon with an expiration date, or a sale with an expiration date, or an 800 number, or a mail-in order blank fall under this heading. *Indirect-action advertising* is designed to stimulate demand over a longer period of time. These advertisements inform customers that the product exists, indicate its benefits, state where it can be purchased, remind customers to repurchase, and reinforce this decision.

PRIMARY VERSUS SELECTIVE

Product advertising can also be primary or selective. *Primary advertising* aims to promote demand for a generic product. Thus, ads by the Beef Industry Council promote beef; it really doesn't matter to the council which brand of beef you purchase. *Selective advertising* attempts to create demand for a particular brand. It typically follows primary advertising, which more or less sets the stage for selective advertising.

COMMERCIAL VERSUS NONCOMMERCIAL

Finally, product advertising can serve either a commercial or a noncommercial function. *Commercial advertising* promotes a product with the intent of making a profit. Most of the advertising you see in the mass media falls under this heading. In contrast, *noncommercial advertising* tends to be sponsored by organizations that are not in business to make money. Charities and nonprofit organizations such as museums produce this type of advertising. Although the goal may be to raise money for a particular cause, it could just as easily be the donation of time or ideas.

As noted, rather than selling a particular product, institutional advertising aims to establish a high level of goodwill. *Public relations institutional advertising* attempts to create a favorable image of the firm among employees, customers, stockholders, or the general public. Texaco Petroleum, for example, runs ads that highlight the company's attempts to protect the environment.

THE FOUR PLAYERS

In addition to the types of advertising and their various roles and functions, advertising can be defined in terms of those who play important roles in bringing ads to the consumer. The four primary players in the advertising world are:

1.   The advertiser
2.   The advertising agency
3.   The media
4.   The vendor

THE ADVERTISER

Advertiser: The individual or organization that initiates the advertising process.

Advertising begins with the **advertiser**—the individual or organization that usually initiates the advertising process. The advertiser also makes the final decisions about whom the advertising will be directed to, the media in which it will appear, the size of the advertising budget, and the duration of the campaign.

We can only estimate how much money is spent annually by advertisers. Even then, the estimates seem to be less accurate as the expenditure categories become more complicated. For example, Robert J. Coen, senior vice president/director of forecasting at McCann-Erickson Worldwide, who is considered the most reliable source of advertising expenditures, acknowledges that it's a guessing game.[7] Nonetheless, he reports that expenditures on U.S. advertising in 1995 were $161 billion, with an expected increase in 1996 of at least 7 percent, or a total of approximately $173 billion. Much of this 1996 growth comes as a result of the Olympics.[8]

TYPES OF ADVERTISERS

There are a number of different types of advertisers. Some manufacture the product or service; others sell manufacturers' products to the ultimate consumer; some use advertising to represent themselves and the services they provide; and others provide a service to the public. The various businesses that perform these tasks fall into four categories: manufacturers, resellers, individuals, and institutions.

MANUFACTURERS *Manufacturers* actually make the product or service and distribute it to resellers or ultimate users for a profit. They usually build their advertising around a product brand name. Because so much advertising is sponsored by manufacturers, we are most familiar with this type of advertising.

Clearly, manufacturers spend more money on mass advertising than any other category. Note in Table 1.2 that only one nonmanufacturer, retailer Sears, Roebuck & Co., was in the top ten companies by ad spending in 1992.

RESELLERS *Resellers* are wholesalers and retailers who distribute the manufacturers' products to other resellers or to the ultimate user. Wholesalers promote their goods through personal selling and possess little expertise in advertising. Conversely, retailers advertise a great deal, either cooperatively with manufacturers or independently.

INDIVIDUALS An *individual* advertiser is a private citizen who wishes to sell a personal product for a profit, to request a particular need, or to express a perspective or an idea. For example, a college student selling a motorcycle would place a classified ad in the school newspaper. This same student may advertise for collector baseball cards in a hobby magazine. Politicians often advertise to voters to express their position on certain issues.

INSTITUTIONS The last group of advertisers includes *institutions, government agencies,* and *social groups.* They are distinguished from the other categories in that their primary objective is not to sell a product or generate profits but rather to raise issues, influence ideas, affect legislation, provide a social service, or alter behavior in ways that are seen as socially desirable. Examples are Mothers Against Drunk Drivers (MADD), the Southern Baptist Convention, the Metropolitan Museum of Art, a local school board, the U.S. Army, the Teamsters Union, and a government-sponsored campaign telling us to "get out and vote."

---

[7] Gary Levin, "Coen's Crystal Ball," *Advertising Age* (August 10, 1992):16.

[8] Robert J. Coen, " '96 Expected to Deliver Energetic Ad Growth," *Advertising Age* (May 20, 1996):22.

TABLE 1.2 ADVERTISING SPENDING TOTAL FOR 1995: COMPANIES, PRODUCT CATEGORIES, AND MEDIA

Top 10 companies by 1995 ad spending

RANK	COMPANY	TOTAL MEASURED AD SPENDING			AD SPENDING BY BRANDS IN 200			NUMBER OF BRANDS
		1995	1994	% CHG	1995	1994	% CHG	
1	Procter & Gamble Co.	$1,507.4	$1,463.7	3.0	$515.8	$423.8	21.7	7
2	General Motors Corp.	1,499.6	1,398.8	7.2	1,382.5	1,313.8	5.2	8
3	Philip Morris Cos.	1,398.7	1,295.5	8.0	907.5	796.3	14.0	8
4	Chrysler Corp.	954.7	758.7	25.8	935.0	743.3	25.8	5
5	Ford Motor Co.	891.8	920.3	−3.1	859.0	884.6	−2.9	4
6	Walt Disney Co.	777.6	587.1	32.4	622.8	438.4	42.1	4
7	PepsiCo	730.2	669.7	9.0	608.8	555.2	9.6	4
8	Time Warner	692.6	571.1	21.3	412.5	318.8	29.4	3
9	AT&T Corp.	674.9	700.4	−3.7	673.4	698.4	−3.6	1
10	Johnson & Johnson	594.0	478.5	24.1	417.2	289.3	44.2	4

Notes: Dollars are in millions.

Source: Competitive Media Reporting. Reprinted with permission from *Advertising Age.* Copyright Crain Communications Inc.

Top 10 categories by 1995 ad spending

RANK	CATEGORY	MEASURED AD SPENDING			AD SPENDING BY MEDIA			NUMBER OF BRANDS
		1995	1994	% CHG	PRINT	BROADCAST	OUTDOOR	
1	Automotive	$5,261.5	$4,976.0	5.7	$1,658.8	$3,567.1	$35.6	31
2	Retail	2,992.8	2,774.3	7.9	1,572.1	1,415.8	4.9	26
3	Food	2,563.6	2,491.5	2.9	302.4	2,254.6	6.5	24
4	Entertainment and Movies	2,561.2	1,909.8	34.1	1,208.6	1,330.8	21.8	21
5	Restaurants and Fast Food	1,805.6	1,583.1	14.1	21.7	1,743.2	40.7	12
6	Personal Care and Remedies	1,693.1	1,370.7	23.5	376.8	1,315.5	0.7	23
7	Telephone	1,658.9	1,570.9	5.6	367.6	1,276.0	15.2	10
8	Financial Services, Securities	937.1	917.3	2.2	291.8	639.5	5.7	11
9	Computers and Electronics	665.2	425.5	56.3	353.8	310.4	0.9	6
10	Beer	503.3	490.6	2.6	10.1	455.2	37.9	4

Notes: Dollars are in millions. Totals include only brands from the Top 200.

Source: Competitive Media Reporting. Reprinted with permission from *Advertising Age.* Copyright Crain Communications Inc.

Total measured media spending for 1995

RANK	MEDIA	TOTAL MEASURED AD SPENDING			AD SPENDING BY BRANDS IN 200		
		1995	1994	% CHG	1995	1994	% CHG
1	Newspaper	$13,338.6	$11,744.6	13.6	$3,107.7	$2,583.6	20.3
2	Spot TV	13,017.2	12,718.8	2.3	4,574.4	4,430.3	3.3
3	Network TV	12,402.2	11,893.2	4.3	7,827.8	7,215.6	8.5
4	Magazine	10,057.8	8,980.2	12.0	3,193.4	2,851.3	12.0
5	Cable TV Networks	3,418.8	2,970.2	15.1	1,447.1	1,269.7	14.0
6	Syndicated TV	2,316.8	2,358.1	−1.8	1,050.2	968.3	8.5
7	National Spot Radio	1,352.3	1,272.3	6.3	425.4	340.3	25.0
8	National Newspaper	1,136.5	1,092.1	4.1	309.0	328.6	−6.0
9	Outdoor	1,114.9	909.8	22.5	262.0	196.5	33.3
10	Sunday Magazine	955.5	999.9	−4.4	377.1	364.5	3.5
11	Network Radio	776.5	599.8	29.5	355.0	255.0	39.2
	Total	59,886.9	55,539.1	7.8	22,929.0	20,803.8	10.2

Notes: Dollars are in millions.

Source: Competitive Media Reporting. R. Craig Endicott, "Top 200 Brands," *Advertising Age* (May 16, 1996):34. Reprinted with permission from *Advertising Age.* Copyright Crain Communications Inc.

THE ADVERTISING AGENCY

PRINCIPLE The agency-client partnership is the dominant organizational arrangement in advertising.

The second key player in the advertising world is the advertising agency. Advertisers hire independent agencies to plan and implement part or all of their advertising effort. The agency-client partnership is the dominant organizational arrangement in advertising. There are approximately 10,000 advertising agencies in the United States.

Ongoing mergers, acquisitions, and agency casualties are continually changing the rankings, but McCann-Erickson Worldwide was the top agency worldwide in 1995, with worldwide gross income of $1.2 billion, followed by BBDO Worldwide and Young & Rubicam (see Table 1.3). Rankings change when you look at the agency "mega groups," which are actually holding companies that include the

TABLE 1.3	TOP AD AGENCIES FOR 1995

Top 10 ad organizations

RANK	ORGANIZATION	WORLDWIDE GROSS INCOME	% CHG
1	WPP Group	$3,129.7	12.7
2	Omnicom Group	2,576.7	16.7
3	Interpublic Group of Cos.	2,337.2	9.9
4	Dentsu	1,998.6	21.8
5	Cordiant	1,377.8	11.5
6	Young & Rubicam	1,197.5	14.4
7	Hakuhodo	958.6	23.8
8	Havas Advertising	909.4	11.8
9	Grey Advertising	896.5	10.9
10	Leo Burnett Co.	803.9	18.7

Top 10 consolidated agencies

RANK	U.S.-BASED AGENCY	WORLDWIDE GROSS INCOME	% CHG
1	McCann-Erickson Worldwide	$1,195.7	11.7
2	BBDO Worldwide	1,139.5	16.3
3	Young & Rubicam	1,122.0	15.4
4	J. Walter Thompson Co.	1,048.5	13.7
5	DDB Needham Worldwide	1,047.0	19.6
6	Ogilvy & Mather Worldwide	892.5	16.1
7	Grey Advertising	826.9	10.3
8	Leo Burnett Co.	803.9	18.7
9	Saatchi & Saatchi Advertising*	767.2	11.1
10	Foote, Cone & Belding Communications	758.7	12.4

Top 10 U.S. agency brands

RANK	AGENCY	U.S. GROSS INCOME	% CHG
1	Leo Burnett Co.	$370.6	15.1
2	J. Walter Thompson Co.	347.0	9.3
3	Grey Advertising	326.7	7.3
4	DDB Needham Worldwide	284.7	9.2
5	McCann-Erickson Worldwide	279.6	9.2
6	Saatchi & Saatchi Advertising*	275.5	14.1
7	BBDO Worldwide	259.5	5.5
8	Foote, Cone & Belding Communications	244.2	2.9
9	Ogilvy & Mather Worldwide	209.5	20.6
10	Young & Rubicam	205.8	9.1

Notes: Dollars are in millions for calendar 1995.

*AA estimate. AA charts: Kevin Brown

Source: R. Craig Endicott, "Shops Soar on Growth of 9.2%, to $17 Billion," *Advertising Age* (April 15, 1996):S-2.

parent agency and all of its subsidiaries. As listed in Table 1.3, WPP Group was ranked first with 1995 worldwide gross income of $3.1 billion. The top 500 U.S. agencies and the nearly 1,000 foreign shops linked in the global networks of the 20 largest returned gross income of $17 billion, up 9.2 percent.[9]

An advertiser uses an outside agency because it believes the agency will be more effective and efficient in creating an individual commercial or a complete campaign. The strength of an agency is its resources, primarily in the form of creative expertise, media knowledge, and advertising strategy. Chapter 4 will discuss agencies in more detail.

Large advertisers—either companies or organizations—are involved in the advertising process in one of two ways: (1) through their advertising department or (2) through their in-house agency.

THE ADVERTISING DEPARTMENT

The most common organizational arrangement in a large business is the *advertising department*. The primary corporate responsibility for advertising lies with the *advertising manager*, or *advertising director*, who usually reports to the *director of marketing*. In the typical multiple-brand, consumer-products company, responsibility is divided by brand, with each brand managed by a *brand manager*. The brand manager is the business leader for the brand and has the ultimate responsibility for sales, product development, budget, and profits, as well as for advertising and other promotions. The brand manager, or advertising director, along with the advertising agency, develops the advertising strategy.

The advertising is usually presented by the agency to the brand manager and the director of advertising. The director of advertising, a specialist in recognizing and supporting effective advertising, advises the brand manager. Frequently the advertising director is responsible for approving advertising before it undergoes preliminary testing with real consumers.

PRINCIPLE The advertiser's ad manager is in charge of the total advertising program.

The advertising manager organizes and staffs the advertising department, selects the advertising agency, and coordinates efforts with other departments within the company and businesses outside the organization. The advertising manager is also in charge of advertising control, which involves checking on such things as: Have the ads been run? At the right time, the right size, and in the right place? Was the ad produced exactly the way the company wanted? Was the work done within the budget? Most importantly, did the advertisement reach its objectives?

Who performs these tasks varies within the industry and the size of the business. The small retailer, for example, might have one person (often the owner) laying out the ad, writing the copy, and selecting the media. Physical production of the ad may be farmed out to freelancers or to the local media. Large retailers have more complete advertising departments and may have specialists on staff to do much of the work in house. Manufacturers tend to rely more on ad agencies to perform these tasks, with the advertising manager acting as a liaison between the company and the agency.

THE IN-HOUSE AGENCY

In-House Agency: An advertising department on the advertiser's staff that handles most, if not all, of the functions of an outside agency.

Companies that need closer control over the advertising have their own in-house agencies. Large retailers, for example, find that doing their own advertising provides cost savings as well as the ability to make fast-breaking local deadlines. An **in-house agency** performs most, and sometimes all, of the functions of an outside advertising agency. According to the American Association of Advertising Agen-

[9]R. Craig Endicott, "Shops Soar on Growth of 9.2%, to $17 Billion," *Advertising Age* (April 15, 1996):S-2.

cies (AAAA), the percentage of total business handled by in-house agencies remained fairly constant in the late 1980s at about 5 percent.[10]

Most in-house agencies are found in retailing, for several reasons. First, retailers tend to operate under small profit margins and find they can save money by doing their own advertising. Second, retailers often receive a great many advertising materials either free or at a reduced cost from manufacturers and trade associations. Local media, for example, will provide creative and production assistance for free. Third, the timetable for retailing tends to be much tighter than that for national advertising. Retailers often create complete campaigns in hours, whereas advertising agencies may take weeks or months.

PRINCIPLE An in-house agency provides more control for the advertiser over the costs and the time schedule.

THE MEDIA

The third player in the advertising world is the media used by advertisers. The **media** are the channels of communication that carry the messages from the advertiser to the audience. Media organizations are organized to sell space (in print media) and time (in broadcast media). A media representative meets with the agency media buyers to convince them that the medium is a good advertising vehicle for their client's message. The most frequently used advertising media are newspapers, television, radio, magazines, out-of-home media such as outdoor and transit, and direct response. The primary media used in advertising are shown in Table 1.4.

Media: The channels of communication used by advertisers.

Media must deliver advertising messages in a way that is consistent with the creative effort. Media staffs gather relevant information about their audiences so the message can be matched with the medium. Media also need to sell the product to prospective advertisers. Media representatives negotiate directly with the advertiser or work through the agency and its media department. They usually initiate the selling effort and personally call on the decision makers.

PRINCIPLE Media provide information necessary to match the medium with the message.

VENDORS

The final player in the world of advertising is the collective variety of service organizations that assist advertisers, advertising agencies, and the media—the **vendors.** Members of this group are also referred to as freelancers, consultants, and self-employed professionals. The list of possibilities is quite extensive and examples include freelance copywriters and graphic artists, photographers, music studios, computer service bureaus, printers, market researchers, direct-mail production houses, marketing consultants, telemarketers, and public relation consultants.

Vendors: Institutions that provide certain expertise that advertisers and agencies cannot perform.

Why would one of the other advertising players hire a vendor? Common reasons might be that the advertisers have no expertise in that area, they're overloaded, or they wish to gain a fresh perspective. Often, vendors simply can do the job less expensively. Today the trend is clearly toward doing less in house or with agencies and more through freelancers. Several experts note that the main advantage to using freelancers over in-house departments or agencies is access to a broad range of specialized talent on an as-needed basis. The main idea is to utilize the talents and skills of individuals who are uniquely suited to particular projects.

Using freelancers provides broader, more flexible access to the best creative talent and a broader range of ideas than you can get either in house or through an agency. Discussion of vendors will be interlaced throughout the text.

---

[10]R. Craig Endicott, "Sales Surge 11% for Media Giants," *Advertising Age* (June 29,1987):S-1.

TABLE 1.4 | U.S. ADVERTISING VOLUME

McCann-Erickson's U.S. advertising volume report represents all expenditures by U.S. advertisers—national, local, private individuals, etc. The expenditures, by medium, include all commissions as well as the art, mechanical and production expenses that are part of the advertising budget for each medium.

MEDIUM	1994 EXPENDITURES (MILLIONS)	% OF TOTAL	1995 EXPENDITURES (MILLIONS)	% OF TOTAL	CHANGE
NEWSPAPERS					
National	$3,906	2.6%	$3,996	2.5%	+2.3%
Local	$30,450	20.3%	$32,321	20.1%	+6.1%
Total	$34,356	22.9%	$36,317	22.6%	+5.7%
MAGAZINES					
Weeklies	$3,140	2.1%	$3,347	2.1%	+6.6%
Women's	$2,106	1.4%	$2,236	1.4%	+6.2%
Monthlies	$2,670	1.8%	$2,997	1.8%	+12.2%
Total	$7,916	5.3%	$8,580	5.3%	+8.4%
FARM PUBLICATIONS	$262	0.2%	$283	0.2%	+8.0%
TELEVISION					
Four Networks	$10,942	7.3%	$11,600	7.2%	+6.0%
Big 3 Minus Fox	$9,959	6.6%	$10,263	6.4%	+3.1%
Cable Networks	$2,321	1.5%	$2,670	1.7%	+15.0%
Syndication	$1,734	1.2%	$2,016*	1.2%	+16.3%
Spot (National)	$8,993	6.0%	$9,119	5.7%	+1.4%
Spot (Local)	$9,464	6.3%	$9,985	6.2%	+5.5%
Cable (Non-Network)	$713	0.5%	$856	0.5%	+20.0%
Total	$34,167	22.8%	$36,246	22.5%	+6.1%
RADIO					
Network	$463	0.3%	$480	0.3%	+3.7%
Spot (National)	$1,902	1.3%	$1,959	1.2%	+3.0%
Spot (Local)	$8,164	5.4%	$8,899	5.5%	+9.0%
Total	$10,529	7.0%	$11,338	7.0%	+7.7%
YELLOW PAGES					
National	$1,314	0.9%	$1,410	0.9%	+7.3%
Local	$8,511	5.7%	$8,826	5.5%	+3.7%
Total	$9,825	6.6%	$10,236	6.4%	+4.2%
DIRECT MAIL	$29,638	19.7%	$32,866	20.4%	+10.9%
BUSINESS PAPERS	$3,358	2.2%	$3,559	2.2%	+6.0%
OUTDOOR					
National	$648	0.4%	$701	0.4%	+8.2%
Local	$519	0.4%	$562	0.4%	+8.2%
Total	$1,167	0.8%	$1,263	0.8%	+8.2%
MISCELLANEOUS					
National	$13,928	9.3%	$15,041	9.4%	+8.0%
Local	$4,884	3.2%	$5,191	3.2%	+6.3%
Total	$18,812	12.5%	$20,232	12.6%	+7.6%
National Total	$87,325	58.2%	$94,280	58.6%	+8.0%
Local Total	$62,705	41.8%	$66,640	41.4%	+6.3%
Grand Total	$150,030	100.0%	$160,920	100.0%	+7.3%

*Includes UPN and WB. Prepared for *Advertising Age* by Robert J. Coen, McCann-Erickson Worldwide.

Source: Robert J. Coen, "'96 Expected to Deliver Energetic Ad Growth," *Advertising Age* (May 20, 1996):22.

THE EVOLUTION OF ADVERTISING

PRINCIPLE Information rather than persuasion was the objective of early commercial messages.

Now that we have discussed the factors of great advertising and introduced the roles and functions of advertising, advertisers, agencies, and the media, let's look at how these roles and players developed historically.[11] The key players and events that influenced the development of advertising are listed in Figure 1.1.

THE ANCIENT PERIOD

Persuasive communication has been around since early times. Inscriptions on tablets, walls, and papyrus from ancient Babylonia, Egypt, and Greece carry messages listing available products and upcoming events and announcing rewards for the return of runaway slaves.

Because of widespread illiteracy before the age of print, most messages were actually delivered by *criers* who stood on street corners shouting the wares of the sponsor. Stores, and the merchandise they carried, were identified by signs. Information rather than persuasion was the objective of the early commercial messages.

THE AGE OF PRINT

PRINCIPLE The invention of movable type ushered in mass literacy, mass communication, and, ultimately, advertising.

The invention of movable type by Johannes Gutenberg around 1440 moved society toward a new level of communication—mass communication. No longer restricted by the time required by a scribe to hand-letter a single message, advertising could now be mass-produced. The availability of printed media to a greater number of people increased the level of literacy, which, in turn, encouraged more businesses to advertise. In terms of media, the early printed advertisements included posters, handbills, and classified advertisements in newspapers. Ad 1.6 is an example of an early print ad from the fifteenth century. The first printed advertisements in English appeared in London around 1472 tacked to church doors. The product advertised was a prayer book for sale.

The word *advertisement* first appeared around 1655. It was used in the Bible to indicate notification or warning. Book publishers, for example, headed most of their announcements with the term, and by 1660 it was generally used as a heading for commercial information, primarily by store owners. The messages continued to be simple and informative through the 1700s and into the 1800s.

The culmination of the age of print was the development of the newspaper. The very first U.S. newspaper was titled *Public Occurrences both Forreign and Domestick;* it appeared in 1690 and only lasted one issue. In 1704 the *Boston Newsletter* was the first paper to carry an ad, which offered a reward for the capture of a thief. James and Benjamin Franklin, early colonial printers, started the *New England Courant* in 1721. By the time of the American Revolution, there were over 30 newspapers in the United States. The first daily newspaper was *The Pennsylvania Evening Post and Daily Advertiser,* which appeared in 1783.

THE FORMATIVE YEARS

The mid-1800s marked the beginning of the development of the advertising industry in the United States. The emerging importance and growth of advertising during this period resulted from a number of social and technological developments associated with the industrial revolution.

THE AGE OF MASS MARKETING
Because of inventions that increased productivity, such as the internal combustion engine and the cotton gin, manufacturers were able to mass-produce goods of uni-

---

[11]Much of this historical review was adapted from Stephen Fox, *The Mirror Makers* (New York: Vintage Books, 1985).

FIGURE 1.1

THE EVOLUTION OF ADVER-
TISING.

	People	Time	Events	People	Time	Events
Ancient Period			Signs	E.E. Calkins	1895	Image Copy
			Criers	John B. Kennedy	1904	Hard-Sell Copy
			Sequis	Claude Hopkins	1910	Reason-Why Copy
	Johannes Gutenberg	1441	Movable Type	Albert Lasker	1904 to 1944	Great Advertising Executive
	Wm. Claxton	1477	First Ad in English	Thoedore MacManus	1910	Atmosphere Advertising
					1914	FTC Act Passed
		1625	First Ad in English Newspaper		1917	Am. Assoc. of Advt. Formed
		1655	Term Advertising Introduced	Stanley/Helen Resor	1920	Intro. Psych./Res.
Modern Period		1704	First U.S. Newspaper to Carry Ads	Raymond Rubicam	1923	Y&R Formed
	Volney Palmer	1841	First Ad Sales Agent		1926	Commercial Radio
	George Rowell	1850	First Ad Wholesaler		1940	Selling Strategems
	Charles Bates	1871	First Formal Agency		1947	Commercial Television
Formative Period	Francis Ayer	1875	Fixed Commission	Rosser Reeves Marion Harber	1950s	Mergers, Research and Hard-Sell
	John Powers	1880	First Great Copywriter	Leo Burnett David Ogilvy	1960s	High Creativity
	E.C. Allen	1887	Magazine Advertising	William Bernbach	1970s	Back to the 50s
					1980s	Mergers and Creativity
	J. Walter Thompson	1891	First Account Executive		1990s	Accountability, Globalization, Integrated Marketing Communications, and Online Media

AD 1.6

AN EARLY ENGLISH AD
WRITTEN BY WILLIAM CAXTON
IN 1477.

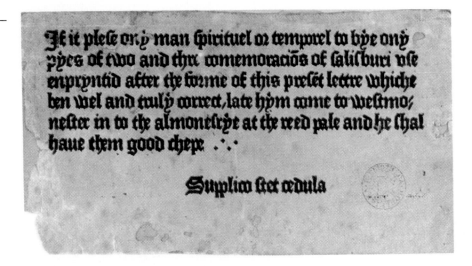

form quality. The resulting excess production, however, could be profitable only if it attracted customers living beyond the local markets. Fortunately, the long-distance transportation network of rivers and canals was being replaced in mid-century by a much speedier system of roads and railroads.

All that remained for modern advertising to do was to devise an effective and efficient communication system that could reach a widely dispersed marketplace. National media developed as the country's transportation system grew. At about the same time a number of new technologies emerged that greatly facilitated mass marketing and mass communications. Most notably, the telegraph, the telephone, and the typewriter provided dramatic improvements in mass-message delivery. The early advertising experts, such as Volney Palmer, the first "adman," functioned strictly as *media brokers*. Palmer established himself as an "agent" in 1841 in Philadelphia, and opened a branch office in Boston in 1845 and New York in 1849, charging a commission for placing ads in newspapers. Thoroughly familiar with all the periodicals and their rates, these early media brokers had a keen ability to negotiate. They received their commissions out of the fees paid by publishers. The messages were prepared primarily by the advertisers or writers they hired directly and often featured exaggerated and outrageous claims.

By the late nineteenth century the advertising profession was more fully developed. Agencies had taken on the role of convincing manufacturers to advertise their products. Ads had assumed a more complete informational and educational role. Copywriting had become a polished and reputable craft. Ad 1.7 is an example of an ad for an early advertising agency.

THE GROWTH OF THE RETAILER

In the late 1800s John Wanamaker revolutionized retailing. Before the Civil War there were no set prices for merchandise sold in retail outlets. As a result, store owners bartered and changed prices depending on the perceived wealth of the customer being served or on their own need for cash that day. Wanamaker, who owned a dry-goods store in Philadelphia, changed this tradition by standardizing the prices on all the merchandise he sold. Furthermore, he established even greater credibility by offering a money-back guarantee. This strategy of honest dealings and straight talk was so successful that Wanamaker built two more outlets and the huge Philadelphia Grand Depot department store.

Wanamaker also hired the first well-known copywriter, John E. Powers. In 1880 Powers was hired to communicate Wanamaker's philosophy to the public. Powers "journalized" advertising by writing ads that were newsy and informationally accurate. He also made the ad more up to date with new copy every day. "My discovery," as Powers explained it, was to "print the news of the store."[12]

---

[12]*Printer's Ink* (October 23, 1895).

AD 1.7

IN AN 1869 ADVERTISEMENT
FOR ITSELF, GEORGE P.
ROWELL'S AD-WHOLESALING
AGENCY MADE USE OF A TESTI-
MONIAL FROM A SATISFIED
CUSTOMER—AN ADVERTISING
DEVICE AS POPULAR NOW AS IT
WAS THEN.

With Powers's assistance, the sales volume in Wanamaker's stores doubled in just a few years.

THE ADVENT OF MAGAZINES

During the 1800s most advertising was placed in newspapers or appeared on posters and handbills. Until the late 1880s magazines were a medium strictly for the wealthy and well educated, containing political commentaries, short stories, and discussions of art and fashion. This changed with the introduction of the *People's Literary Companion* by E. C. Allen, which appealed to a large group of general readers. Also, about this time Congress approved low postage rates for periodicals, which allowed magazines to be distributed economically by mail. The first magazine advertising appeared in July 1844 in the *Southern Messenger,* which was edited for a short time by Edgar Allan Poe.

Magazines offered a medium for longer, more complex messages. They also had enough lead time to permit the production of art such as engravings to illustrate articles and ads. As the production processes improved, photographs were introduced, and magazine advertisements became highly visual. Some of the earliest magazines to contain advertising are still around today, including *Cosmopolitan, Ladies' Home Journal,* and *Reader's Digest.*

MODERN ADVERTISING

By the beginning of the twentieth century the total volume of advertising had increased to $500 million from $50 million in 1870. The industry had become a major force in marketing and had achieved a significant level of respect and esteem.[13]

---

[13]*Printer's Ink* (October 23, 1953).

THE ERA OF PROFESSIONALISM

CALKENS AND GRAPHICS   The twentieth century also witnessed a revolution in advertising. Earnest Elmo Calkens of the Bates agency created a style of advertising that resembled original art and adapted beautifully to the medium of magazines. Calkens's ads not only attracted the viewer's attention but also increased the status and image of the advertiser. His work represented the first venture into image advertising.

LORD & THOMAS SALESMANSHIP   Advertising took a dramatic detour when John E. Kennedy and Albert Lasker formed their historic partnership in 1905 at the powerful Lord & Thomas agency. Lasker was a partner in the firm and the managerial genius who made Lord & Thomas such a force in the advertising industry. Ads that sold the product were all that mattered to him. Because of Lasker's philosophy, the agency was able to make a profit when others were losing money. (See Ad 1.8.)

In 1905 Lasker was pondering the question: What is advertising? Like Powers, he had been approaching advertising as news. John E. Kennedy, who had worked for a variety of retailers and patent-medicine clients, responded with a note that said, "I can tell you what advertising is." When the two met, Kennedy explained, "Advertising is salesmanship in print."[14]

PRINCIPLE "Advertising is salesmanship in print."

Thus was born the "sales" approach to advertising copy. Kennedy's style was simple and straightforward, based on the belief that advertising should present the same arguments a salesperson would use in person. This "reason-why" copy style became the hallmark of Lord & Thomas ads. Lasker, referring to his meeting with Kennedy in 1905, said, "The whole complexion of advertising for all America was changed from that day on."

HOPKINS AND TESTING   At the height of his career in the early 1930s Claude Hopkins was Lord & Thomas's best-known copywriter and made the unheard-of-salary of $185,000. Sometimes called the greatest copywriter of all time, he was also the most analytical.

Hopkins worked with direct mail and used that medium to test and refine his techniques. In his 1923 book *Scientific Advertising,* he discussed the principles

---

[14]Merrill DeVoe, Effective Advertising Copy (New York: Macmillan Co., 1956):21.

CLAUDE HOPKINS, CONSIDERED BY SOME PEOPLE TO BE THE GREATEST COPYWRITER OF ALL TIMES.

COPYWRITER JOHN E. KENNEDY EXPLAINED THAT "ADVERTISING IS SALESMANSHIP IN PRINT."

 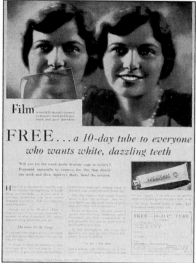 

AD 1.8

LORD & THOMAS ADS FROM THE 1920s.

and laws he had discovered as a result of his constant copy testing: "One ad is compared with another, one method with another. . . . No guesswork is permitted. One must know what is best. Thus mail-order advertising first established many of our basic laws."[15]

MACMANUS AND SOFT-SELL   Theodore F. MacManus was a copywriter for the young General Motors company, where he produced an image style of advertising resembling that of Calkens. He felt that a "soft-sell" rather than a "hard-sell" copy style would better create the long-term relationship considered necessary between a car manufacturer and its customers. Image was everything. The only way to penetrate the subconscious of the reader was through a slow accumulation of positive images.[16] The positive illusions created by MacManus for Cadillac and Buick had much to do with their early successes.

PRINCIPLE Soft-sell advertising creates messages through a slow accumulation of positive images.

WAR AND PROSPERITY

With the outbreak of World War I, the advertising industry offered its services to the Council of National Defense. The Division of Advertising of the Committee of Public Information was formed. This volunteer agency created advertising to attract military recruits, sell Liberty Bonds, and support the Red Cross and the war effort in general (see Ad 1.9). Thus was born public service advertising that relied on volunteer professionals and donated time and space.

J. WALTER THOMPSON AND THE POSTWAR BOOM   After the war consumers were desperate for goods and services. New products were emerging constantly (see Ad 1.10). A great boom in advertising was led by the J. Walter Thompson agency (JWT) through the innovative copy and management style of the husband-and-wife team Stanley and Helen Resor. Stanley administered the agency and developed the concept of account services.

The JWT agency was known for many innovations in advertising. The Resors coined the concepts of *brand names* to associate a unique identity with a particular product. They also developed the status appeal by which they persuaded nonwealthy people to imitate the habits of richer people. JWT advertising introduced modern marketing research to advertising. Stanley Resor also built a network of agencies, including some outside the United States.

---

[15]DeVoe, *Effective Advertising Copy*, p. 22.
[16]*Printer's Ink* (January 31, 1918).

AD 1.9

UNCLE SAM APPEARED ON U.S.
ARMY RECRUITMENT POSTERS
IN 1917, SUPPORTING THE WAR
EFFORT IN WORLD WAR I.

DEALING WITH THE DEPRESSION

Advertising diminished drastically after the October stock market crash and the onset of the Great Depression in 1929. Advertising budgets were slashed in an attempt to cut costs, and advertisers and consumers alike began to question the value and legitimacy of advertising. Clients demanded more service and special deals. The Depression brought back the hard-sell, reason-why copy approach of Lasker and Hopkins and gave rise to the consumer movement and tighter government regulation.

For example, 60 years ago, General Electric needed to convince suspicious consumers that its newfangled refrigeration device was "as durable and dependable as the icebox." That's probably why the company felt it prudent to point out that the refrigerator never needed oiling (see Ad 1.11). The Federal Trade Commission (FTC), which was established in 1914 to prevent unfair or anticompetitive business practices, amended guidelines at this time to give the agency more consumer-oriented power. The Wheeler-Lea Amendment gave the FTC the power to curb "deceptive" or "unfair" advertising. The FTC was also given authority over false advertising of food, drugs, cosmetics, and therapeutic devices.

AD 1.10
FOLLOWING WORLD WAR I, "I WANT TO BE HAPPY" WAS THE CALL OF CONSUMERS, AND JAZZ AND DANCING BECAME POPULAR, AS THIS 1922 AD FOR THE VICTOR TALKING MACHINE COMPANY ILLUSTRATES.

PRINCIPLE The value of an idea is measured by its originality.

RUBICAM AND ORIGINALITY   During and after the Depression Raymond Rubicam emerged as one of the giants of advertising. In the spring of 1923 he launched his own agency with John Orr Young, a Lord & Thomas copywriter. Young & Rubicam created unique ads with intriguing headlines. Rubicam emphasized fresh, original ideas. He also hired the researcher George Gallup and made research an essential part of the creative process. Research became an important part of advertising as research organizations founded by Daniel Starch, A.C. Nielsen, and George Gallup gave rise to the research industry.

CAPLES AND HEADLINES   John Caples, a vice president of Batten, Barton, Durstine and Osborn (BBDO), made a major contribution to the field in 1932 when he published *Tested Advertising Methods.* His theories about the "pulling power" of headlines were based on extensive mail-order and inquiry testing. Caples was also known for changing the style of advertising writing, which had been wordy and full of exaggerations. He used short words, short sentences, and short paragraphs.[17]

THE ADVENT OF RADIO

Radio offered the Depression-weary consumer an inexpensive form of entertainment. The tremendous potential of radio created two serious problems for advertising, however. First, it meant that advertising agencies had to find or train staff employees who could write copy for the ear. The second problem was financial. In the early days of radio, sponsors underwrote the programming, which involved a much greater financial commitment than a single ad. The growth of radio, however, was phenomenal. Twelve years after its first commercial broadcast, radio surpassed magazines as the leading advertising medium.

---

[17]DeVoe, *Advertising Copy,* pp. 25–26.

AD 1.11

THIS 60-YEAR-OLD AD FOR
GE REFRIGERATORS HAD TO
INCLUDE A GREAT DEAL OF
PERSUASIVE COPY.

WORLD WAR II

During World War II the advertising industry once again served as mass communicator for America. The War Advertising Council (WAC) used advertising to enlist recruits, sell war bonds, and encourage the planting of victory gardens and the sending of V-mail letters. Ad 1.12 is an example of a 1944 ad encouraging the purchase of war bonds. Over $1 billion was spent on the most extensive advertising campaign ever created. The effort was so successful that after the war, instead of disbanding, the WAC simply changed its name to the Advertising Council and has remained a very effective public service effort to this day.

PRINCIPLE For many products, differentiation is created by advertising.

POSTWAR ADVERTISING

During the 1950s markets were inundated with "me too" products with similar features. "Keeping up with the Joneses" was the attitude among consumers, and many products stressing style, luxury, and social acceptance were forced to compete. The primary difference between many of these products was the image created by the advertising.

ROSSER REEVES AND THE USP   One person who was able to cut through this clutter of products was Rosser Reeves of the Ted Bates agency. Reeves proposed that an effective ad had to offer a "unique selling proposition" (USP) containing a benefit that was important to consumers and that no other competitor offered. "M&M's melt in your mouth, not in your hands" and "Double your pleasure, double your fun" are two USPs made famous by Reeves.

BEDELL AND SELLING STRATEGEMS   Like Caples, Clyde Bedell was a student and a master of mail-order copy. In a 1940 book *How to Write Advertising That Sells* he expressed his philosophy of advertising, which focused on the selling aspects. He developed a set of "31 Proved Selling Strategems" that defined the relationship between product features and selling points.[18]

---

[18]DeVoe, *Advertising Copy*, p. 27.

JOHN MAYNER, ACCOUNT COORDINATOR, *Dally Advertising, Dallas*

If you are interested in pursuing a career in advertising, the door is wide open for almost anyone from any background. Although I had no formal training in advertising, my eclectic background, education, and work experiences have served me well in this field.

As an undergraduate at the University of Texas at Austin, I had an extremely diverse and well-rounded liberal arts education—I was one or two classes short of a double major in history and English. While I was going to school, I worked at the state capitol as Assistant Sergeant-at-Arms in the House of Representatives. I worked for 3-1/2 years for a large corporate law firm, and I also worked as an au pair for an Austin family. After graduation, I landed a job as a kitchen assistant in a gourmet restaurant. After that, I proceeded to work in a Catholic lay apostolate that works with the poor, and then began a year-and-a-half stint as a legal assistant. While I was trying to figure out "what I wanted to be when I grew up," I took my GMAT, got accepted into Texas A&M University's MBA program, got a concentration in marketing, and began to get familiar with a lifestyle that is very similar to someone who works in the advertising field.

During my first semester in graduate school, I contacted Leo Burnett, asked if I could go to Austin for their presentation at the University of Texas, and it was there that I became hooked on the idea of working for an agency. I still remember listening to a gentleman named Bill Haljun, a senior vice president who had worked at Burnett for over 20 years. He made it sound like the most exciting career imaginable. From that first campus visit with Leo Burnett, I decided that I was going to pursue a career in advertising in account services.

Even for those people who are lucky enough to find employment quickly, job searches are really stressful. I never would have imagined that it would take me ten months, 225 résumés and cover letters, and two trips to New York to land my first job in advertising.

My first job was working as an assistant media planner at a large agency (Bloom FCA, with approximately $200 million in billings and 250 employees). Although I am grateful for the experience and the exposure that a larger agency was able to provide, the job itself was not a really good experience. The second-to-last pay period I was there I worked 212 hours in a two-week pay period (with no overtime or comp time) and was told by my planner when we left at 6:45 A.M. that we needed to be back at work by 9:00 A.M. to finish up our project. I soon began to reconsider what I was doing, and whether or not it was at all worthwhile.

It didn't take a genius to know that something was definitely wrong with my quality-of-life professional outlook equation. I was making $14,000 a year, I rarely got to spend any time with my wife (we thought that nothing could be worse than graduate school, silly us), and my professional advancement opportunities were virtually nonexistent. In addition, work had become so oppressive that I started to get sick as I pulled into the parking garage each morning. That should be an obvious sign to anyone that something is definitely wrong or unhealthy with such a work environment.

In what proved to be the most wonderful solution to my predicament, on my last day of work at that big agency, I received a phone call from my brother-in-law saying that his agency, a much smaller creative shop in Fort Worth that I had interviewed with a year and a half earlier, had called him to see if I might still be interested. Not only did they have a job opening, but it was in account services. Six weeks later, I started working at Dally Advertising as an account coordinator.

Going to work for a much smaller agency has been a very positive experience for me personally. Due to the limitations of size, a smaller agency will force you to become a more well-rounded generalist, because you always pitch in on other accounts, new business prospects, and help out in other departments in a crunch. In my first week at Dally, I was able to help prepare for one of the largest pitches that our agency had ever been in on—that type of opportunity would never have been available to me at a much larger shop. In addition, when we had difficulty selling a very controversial public service campaign to one of our clients, I voiced my opinion that I thought we would have a much better opportunity selling that campaign to another group. I was then given the chance to "give away" my first campaign, less than six months into my job. Within 24 hours, I had my first appointment, and by the close of the week, I had sold my first campaign. That campaign went on to win Dally a National Addy Award, and I was able to be the account executive on that particular piece of business.

Although the hours are still long, and I still struggle from time to time with maintaining a balance between my personal and professional lives, I am much happier doing what I am now doing, and where I am doing it, than I was before. If you are patient and capable of measuring your success on your own terms and not on what others think it should be, then a career in advertising can offer you excitement, variety, and the strange pleasure that comes from knowing not any two days will ever be alike.

AD 1.12

MANY COMPANIES OPENLY SUP-
PORTED THE WORLD WAR II
EFFORT THROUGH THEIR
ADVERTISEMENTS.

THE ADVENT OF TELEVISION

In 1939 NBC became the first television network to initiate regular broadcasting. Not until the 1950s, however, did television become a major player in advertising. By the end of that decade television was the dominant advertising medium. Its total advertising revenues grew from $12.3 million in 1949 to $128 million in 1951.[19] Ad 1.13 is an example of a popular ad from the 1950s.

THE ERA OF CREATIVITY

The 1960s saw a resurgence of art, inspiration, and intuition in advertising. This revolution was inspired by three creative geniuses: Leo Burnett, David Ogilvy, and William Bernbach.

BURNETT AND MIDDLE AMERICA   Leo Burnett was the leader of the "Chicago School" of advertising. He believed in finding the "inherent drama" in every product and then presenting it as believably as possible. The Leo Burnett agency created mythical characters who represented American values, such as the Jolly

---

[19]Stephen Fox, The Mirror Makers: A History of American Advertising and Its Creators (New York: Vintage Books, 1985):211.

AD 1.13

THE SUBTLE APPROACH TO THIS
FEMININE PRODUCT IS TYPICAL
OF THE 1950S.

AD 1.14

THIS HIGHLY CREATIVE AD BY
BILL BERNBACH REFLECTS THE
1960S.

Green Giant, Tony the Tiger, Charlie the Tuna, and Morris the Cat. The most famous campaign is the Marlboro Man, which has built the American cowboy into the symbol of the best-selling cigarette in the world. Burnett never apologized for his common-touch approach. He took pride in his ability to reach the average consumer.

OGILVY: DISCIPLINE AND STYLE   David Ogilvy, founder of the Ogilvy & Mather agency, is a paradox because he represents both the "image" school of MacManus and Rubicam and "claim" school of Lasker and Hopkins. Although Ogilvy believed in research and mail-order copy with all of its testing, he had a tremendous sense of image and story appeal. He created enduring brands with campaign symbols like the eyepatch on the Hathaway man. Among the other products he handled were Rolls-Royce, Pepperidge Farm, and Guinness.

THE ART OF BERNBACH   Doyle, Dane, and Bernbach opened in 1949. From the beginning, William Bernbach was the catalyst for the agency's success. A copy writer with an acute sense of design, he was considered by many to be the most innovative advertiser of his time. His advertising touched people by focusing on feelings and emotions. He explained: "There are a lot of great technicians in advertising. However, they forget that advertising is persuasion, and persuasion is not a science, but an art. Advertising is the art of persuasion."[20] (See the Dreyfus Lion, Ad 1.14.)

THE ERA OF ACCOUNTABILITY   The Vietnam War and the economic downturn of the 1970s led to a reemphasis on hard-sell advertising. Clients wanted results, and agencies hired MBAs who understood strategic planning and the elements of

[20]Printer's Ink (January 2, 1953).

marketing. A great deal of advertising moved away from the 1950s "formula ads"—vignettes and slice-of-life commercials showing people enjoying the product. This is not to suggest, however, that this period was void of creative geniuses. On the contrary, Hal Riney, creator of the well-known Henry Weinhard's Private Reserve beer commercials, Bartles & Jaymes's Frank and Ed, and most recently, the award-winning Saturn commercials, has been at work since the early 1970s. Charlotte Beers was the creative genius behind the American Express, "Cardholder since. . . ." campaign. Bill Backer is the man who created the legendary Coca-Cola hilltop singers commercial. He also came up with the "Tastes great, less filling" spots that turned Miller Lite beer into a major player. Finally, Jane Maas, who learned her craft from David Ogilvy, was the person responsible for the "I love New York" campaign, Prell shampoo, and Safeguard soap. Perhaps no campaign better reflects this era than the Xerox campaign featuring Brother Dominic. This is just a very small sample of the creative firepower that produced good advertising while running profitable businesses. It wasn't easy, yet 11 agencies, led by Y&R at $2.3 billion, had reached the billion-dollar mark by the end of the decade, compared to none in 1970.[21]

In response to the intense emphasis on performance and profit in the 1970s and 1980s, many consumer-product companies shifted their budgets from traditional media to *sales promotion*, which uses strategies such as coupons, rebates, and sweepstakes to generate short-term sales gains. Agencies either learned to create sales promotions or acquired firms that specialized in doing so.

THE FUTURE OF ADVERTISING

What advertising will be like in the 1990s and into the twenty-first century is still unclear. The advertising industry has come to realize just how vulnerable it is to the outside world, however. Many agencies closed when poor economic conditions in the late 1980s and early 1990s severely reduced advertising budgets.

A more important influence on the fate of advertising than economic conditions, however, is the changing demographics. The typical consumer will be older and wiser. Furthermore, these individuals will have a great acceptance of divergent views and lifestyles, increased acceptance of technology, and increased concern for social issues and for the environment. In addition, they will not accept trade-offs. Their view will be "Maximize. Don't compromise." For advertisers, this will mean a creative strategy that is more pointed and fact based, delivered at the moment when the consumer needs the information (see Xerox Ad 1.15). The latter requirement will be provided by media technology, such as interactive cable, which allows the consumer to customize the advertising message. As we move closer to cable and satellite systems capable of delivering hundreds of choices, messages will become more and more customer specific.

Marketers are expecting a great deal more from advertising than they did a decade ago. Advertising must pay its own way—and quickly. Sales promotions, which directly affect sales, have replaced advertising in many cases. Moreover, clients are demanding more value-added services from agencies, at no extra charge. To cope with these new demands agencies have reduced staff size and carefully pruned services that are not cost-effective. They have also placed tremendous pressure on media companies to reduce their rates and to provide better measures of effectiveness. Thanks to ongoing technological advances, media will be able to report on how a particular ad affects actual purchase, brand switching, and customer retention. Accountability will be both expected and verifiable.

Undoubtedly the biggest trend in the 1990s is and will continue to be the continued growth in **integrated marketing communication.** According to Northwestern advertising professor Don E. Schultz, "The concept of integrated

Integrated Marketing Communication: The concept or philosophy of marketing that stresses bringing together all the variables of the marketing mix, all the media, all the actions with which a company reaches its publics, and integrating the company's strategy and programs.

---

[21]Fox, *Mirror Makers*, p. 262.

AD 1.15

THIS AD FOR XEROX REPRE-
SENTS A NEW TYPE OF
MESSAGING

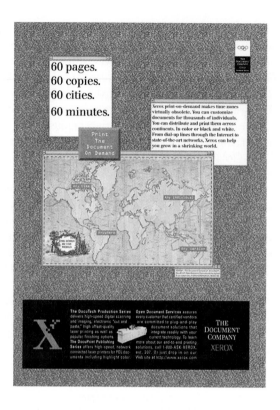

marketing communication (IMC) follows basically the concept of marketing: we start with the consumer needs and wants, and work back to the brand."[22] He contends this approach is now possible because of the tremendous improvements made in capturing data about who actually buys products. The assumption in the past was that the world was a mass market, and that standardized marketing communication was appropriate. The result was *inside-out planning*, where marketing and advertising planning was predetermined by the marketers. This strategy focuses on what the marketer wants to say, when the marketer wants to say it, about things the marketer believes are important about the brand, and in media forms the marketer wants to use.

IMC is the practice of unifying all marketing communication tools—from advertising to packaging—so they send a consistent, persuasive message to target audiences that promotes company goals. In companies that use IMC, marketers coordinate all marketing communication tools to create synergy, which means each individual tool has more impact working jointly to promote a product than it would working on its own.

Today, advertisers are able to do *outside-in planning*. Employing base amounts of data about customers and prospects, the advertiser can measure what customers have done over time, assess which promotional efforts customers responded to and those they did not, and determine when customers change their responses.

IMC means that the relationship between the advertisers and the agency will also change. Timm Crull, chairman-CEO of Nestlé USA, succinctly described this relationship in a recent speech at the American Association of Advertising Agencies annual meeting: "Agencies must help clients develop compelling advertising concepts that will serve as launching pads for the broad range of other marketing tools available. That list includes packaging, in-store promotions, direct

---

[22]Don E. Schultz, "Integration Helps You Plan Communication from Outside-In," *The Marketing News* (March 15, 1993):12.

mail, direct response, product 800 numbers, data base marketing, coupon redemption programs, cable programming—to name a few."[23]

Another trend that is sure to continue is the globalization of advertising. In the early 1990s the trade barriers throughout much of Europe came down, making it the largest contiguous market in the world. Eastern Europe, Russia, and China have at least partially opened their markets to Western businesses. Advertisers are moving into these markets, and ad agencies are forming huge multinational agencies with international research and media-buying capabilities. The advertising challenge, however, will not be global versus local. The objective will be to practice global and local advertising simultaneously. Standardizing ads or customizing ads will become a major strategic question.

Along with the trend toward globalization is a move toward tighter and tighter *niche marketing* to market segments and even to individuals. Mass advertising, as we know it, will change. New technologies will permit advertisers to reach select groups of consumers with selective media. Marketers will search for and implement media and marketing plans aimed at special selective markets.

Although the information will continue to expand, the use of interactive television and online services may not grow as rapidly as expected. In one survey of 1,000 cable television subscribers, almost two-thirds of the respondents had not heard of interactive television.[24] Furthermore, survey participants were willing to pay only limited amounts for interactive services. Industry experts are beginning to provide reality checks about the emerging technology, following much hype. The direct-marketing chapter (Chapter 16) chronicles this move from mass marketing to individualized or personalized marketing.

Increasing trade concentration and increasing retailer sophistication will require a changing approach to advertising. Knowledge is power. The power is shifting from the marketer to the retailer, and the source of that power is information. In the future, the retailer will take a more active role in the communication effort. With increased concentration and sophistication, getting closer to the retailer will be critical. The advertiser and the ad agency must both play a more active role in local retail marketing.

The bywords for advertising in the future will be *accountability* and *adaptability*. Advertising will be forced to walk the precarious tightrope between creativity and profitability, and survival will go to the fittest.

---

[23]Timm Crull, "Nestlé to Agencies: 'Shake Mindset,'" *Advertising Age* (May 3, 1993):26.
[24]*Broadcasting and Cable*, "Interactive Television and the New Media," 1995, unpublished research report.

SUMMARY

- Classic ads that have stood the test of time work on two levels: they engage the mind of the consumer and at the same time deliver a selling message.

- The characteristics of a great ad are as follows: (1) It is strategically sound in that it is directed at a certain audience, driven by specific objectives, its message is crafted to speak to that audience's most important concerns, and it is placed in media that will most effectively reach that audience. (2) A great ad has a creative concept that gets the audience's attention and is remembered. (3) It employs the right execution for the message and the audience.

- The definition of advertising has six elements: (1) paid communication, (2) that is nonpersonal, (3) from an identified sponsor, (4) using mass media, (5) to persuade or influence (6) an audience.

- There are eight types of advertising, each appropriate for certain distinct strategies: (1) brand advertising, (2) retail advertising, (3) political advertising, (4) directory advertising, (5) direct-response advertising, (6) business-to-business advertising, (7) institutional advertising, and (8) public service advertising.

- Advertising fulfills (1) a marketing role, (2) a communication role, (3) an economic role, and (4) a societal role.

- Advertising has three basic functions: (1) advertising may be either direct-action or indirect-action advertising, (2) advertising can be primary or secondary, and (3) advertising can serve a commercial or noncommercial function.

- The four key players in the advertising industry are: (1) advertisers, (2) advertising agencies, (3) media, and (4) vendors.

- A firm's advertising can be handled either internally by an in-house agency or externally by an advertising agency. Companies often have advertising departments to either handle their own work or interface with an agency.
- The evolution of advertising has gone through many creative peaks and valleys, largely influenced by soci-

etal factors and the creative capabilities of the individuals working in advertising at the time.
- The future of advertising will be strongly affected by new organizational patterns both within the field itself and in the business community, globalization, integrated marketing communication, and online media.

Questions

1. Critics charge that advertising seeks to manipulate its audience, whereas advertising's supporters claim that it merely seeks to persuade. Which interpretation do you agree with? Why?

2. "I'll tell you what great advertising means," Bill Slater said during a heated dorm discussion. "Great advertising is the ability to capture the imagination of the public—the stuff that sticks in the memory, like Dancing Raisins, or Levi's jeans commercials, or that rabbit with the drum—that's what great is," he says. "Bill, you missed the point," says Phil Graham, a marketing major. "Advertising is a promotional weapon. Greatness means commanding attention and persuading people to buy something. It's what David Leisure did for Isuzu. No frills, no cuteness—great advertising has to sell the public and keep them sold," he adds. How would you enter this argument? What is your interpretation of "great advertising?"

3. Walt Jameson has just joined the advertising department faculty in a university after a long professional career. In an informal talk with the campus advertising club, Jameson is put on the spot about career

choices. The students want to know which is the best place to start in the 1990s—with an advertiser (a company) or with an advertising agency. How should Jameson respond? Should he base his answer on the current situation or on how he reads the future?

4. A strong debate continues at Telcom, a supplier of telephone communication systems for business. The issue is whether the company will do a better communication job with its budget of $15 million by using an in-house advertising agency or by assigning the business to an independent advertising agency. What are the major issues that Telcom should consider?

5. The chapter discussed a number of creative approaches that are honored in the history of advertising. When you think of Reeves, Burnett, Ogilvy, and Bernbach, do any of their styles seem suited to the 1990s? Do the years ahead seem to require hard-sell or soft-sell advertising strategies? Explain your reasons.

6. Identify five major figures in the history of advertising and explain their contributions to the field.

7. How did the advertising field change after the invention of movable type, radio, and television?

Suggested Class Project

Form small groups of five or six students. Have a spokesperson contact one or two advertising agencies. Question one or more key individuals about the changes that have taken place in their agency and the

industry during the last five years. (Prepare a list of questions ahead of time.) What kinds of changes do they expect in the next five years? Get together to write a report that is three to five pages long.

Further Readings

Aaker, David A., and John G. Meyers, *Advertising Management* (Englewood Cliffs, NJ: Prentice Hall, 1975).

Bogart, Leo, *Strategies in Advertising*, 2nd ed. (Lincolnwood, IL: NTC Business Books, 1990).

Fox, Stephen, *The Mirror Makers: A History of American Advertising and Its Creators* (New York: Vintage Books, 1985).

"How Advertising Is Reshaping Madison Avenue," *Business Week* (September 15, 1986):147.

Jaffe, Andrew, "Entrepreneurs Fashion Lean, Mean Shops," *Adweek* (January 19, 1987):34.

Ogilvy, David, *Ogilvy on Advertising* (New York: Vintage Books, 1985).

Ornstein, Stanley I., *Industrial Concentration and Advertising* (Washington, DC: American Enterprise Institute, 1977).

Rotzell, Kim B., and James E. Haefner, *Advertising in Contemporary Society* (Cincinnati, OH: South-Western Publishing Co., 1986).

In November 1996, the Distilled Spirits Council lifted a voluntary industry ban that had kept liquor ads off American television and radio for nearly half a century. The trade group's action came after the American subsidiary of Joseph E. Seagram & Sons defied the ban and began running television ads for Royal Crown whiskey during the summer of 1996. The ads were seen as an effort to halt the declining consumption of spirits, especially among consumers between the ages of 25 and 35. According to figures compiled by the council, overall sales of hard liquor fell 28 percent over a 14-year period, from 450 million gallons in 1981 to 325 million gallons in 1995. Distillers have watched in frustration as the brewing industry spends more than half a billion dollars each year on television advertising. The council's action did not affect a network ban; ABC, NBC, CBS, and Fox still refuse to air liquor ads. However, managers at local television affiliates and radio stations can sell air time to liquor advertisers if they wish to do so.

Some industry observers complained that the Seagram ads represented the first wave of a new advertising assault on America's children, and negative reaction to the council's move came from both the government and private advocacy groups. Reed Hundt, chairperson of the Federal Communications Commission (FCC), said, "This decision is disappointing for parents, and dangerous for our kids." The FCC is empowered to make sure broadcasters serve the public interest, and Hundt favors some form of restriction on liquor ads. Karolyn Nunallee, president-elect of Mothers Against Drunk Driving, declared that "this will open a floodgate to alcohol ads on TV." George Hacker, director of alcohol policies at the Center for Science in the Public Interest, was more blunt. "This means open season on America's kids," he said.

Fred Meister, CEO of the Distilled Spirits Council, defended the decision to end the self-imposed ban. "There is simply no justifiable, social, political or scientific basis for treating spirits differently from other beverage alcohol," Meister said. Responding to critics who believe distillers are targeting children, Meister noted, "Distilled spirits advertisements will continue to be responsible, dignified and tasteful messages for adults, and will avoid targeting those under the legal purchase age, regardless of the medium." Rather than rush out new ads, some of Seagram's competitors are adopting a wait-and-see attitude. Jack Shea, a spokesperson for Heublein, which markets Smirnoff vodka and Jose Cuervo tequila, said, "It may make sense for some of our brands, but we want to make sure if it's done, that it's done responsibly and tastefully."

Some advertising experts have even questioned whether or not liquor advertising would substantially increase consumer demand for alcohol. According to this view, advertising does not persuade nondrinkers to start using alcohol. Instead, advertising helps one brand take market share away from another. Indeed, nearly a decade ago, the Federal Trade Commission issued a report stating that there is "no reliable basis to conclude that alcohol advertising significantly affects consumption, let alone abuse." The report went on: "Absent such evidence, there is no basis for concluding that rules banning or otherwise limiting alcohol advertising would offer significant protection to the public." In any event, it is likely that only a handful of distillers can afford the expense of advertising on a national basis.

Video Source: "Hard Liquor TV Ads," *Nightline* (November 11, 1996). *Additional Sources:* Bruce Horovitz, "Distillers Indulge Anew in TV Ads," *USA Today* (November 8, 1996):1B, 2B; Sally Goll Beatty, "Seagram Again Challenges a Ban on TV Ads Invoked By Industry," *The Wall Street Journal* (November 24, 1996):B12; Catherine Yang, "The Spirited Brawl Ahead Over Liquor Ads on TV," *Business Week* (December 16, 1996): 47; Doug Bandow, "Liquor Ads on the Rocks," *The Wall Street Journal* (December 31, 1996):6.

𝒬UESTIONS

1. Explain Seagram's objectives in terms of the functions of advertising discussed in the chapter.

2. Do you believe that consumption of spirits in the United States will increase substantially if distillers follow Seagram's lead and advertise on television and radio?

3. As a representative of the distilled spirits industry, how would you respond to criticism that liquor ads on television represent "liquor profiteering at the expense of America's children"?

Dramatization

Testing done by an independent Engineering Consultant

Volvo 850 Turbo Sportswagon vs Automatic BMW 320i Sedan

Advertising and Society: Ethics and Regulation

CHAPTER OBJECTIVES

When you have completed this chapter, you should be able to:

- Discuss the major issues that advertisers must address
- Explain the current judicial position concerning the First Amendment rights of advertisers
- Comprehend the role of the FTC in regulating advertising
- List and understand the characteristics of other federal agencies governing advertising
- Explain the remedies available to different groups when an ad is judged deceptive or offensive
- Discuss the self-regulatory opportunities available to advertisers and agencies

Has Volvo Done It Again?

Six years after being banged up by the "monster truck" ad scandal, Volvo Cars of North America is on a collision course with BMW, which claims a recent Volvo television spot is deceptive and is trying to get it yanked off the air. That collision course, if it draws in the Federal Trade Commission, could end up costing Volvo $10,000 in fines for every time it runs the commercial.

The commercial is a dramatization of Volvo's 850 Turbo Sportswagon accelerating faster than BMW's 328i sedan in a zero-to-60-miles-per-hour test. BMW of North America claims Volvo's testing is invalid and conflicts with BMW's own test and those of independent outsiders, including automotive buff books.

The charges raise the specter of a 1990 commercial in which a reinforced Volvo was the only car not crushed by a "monster truck" rolling over a line of vehicles. The FTC penalized the automaker for using deceptive advertising methods, and the scandal led to the dismissal of Volvo's agency at the time—Scali, McCabe, Sloves, New York.

Volvo denies BMW's allegations. "BMW came here to us calling the ad deceptive, misleading, inaccurate and biased," noted Bob Austin, Volvo communications director. "We disagree wholeheartedly." He indicated that BMW had filed a complaint about the advertising with the National Advertising Division of the Council of Better Business Bureaus. Mr. Austin also said that BMW had its media-buying service, DeWitt Media, New York, ask television networks to yank the Volvo spot.

Jay Durante, the agency's partner-account director on Volvo, said that "our position is we developed advertising to explain the results of independent research that found the Volvo 850 Turbo Sportswagon was faster than the 328i in acceleration. The results are quite unexpected, which is the whole point of the commercial." Mr. Durante noted that Volvo hired freelance auto journalist Peter Allerecht to conduct the test and brought his test results to the agency. Actor Donald Sutherland does the voice-over in the spot, saying: "The ultimate driving machine, outdone by a Volvo. Is nothing sacred?"

BMW is apparently upset with Volvo's testing methods. The German automaker is said to be upset that the Swedish car's engine may have benefited because it was more broken in—with 9,150 miles on the odometer—than the 328i with 1,091 miles. The BMW's transmission was tested in economy mode, while the Volvo was in sport mode. The Volvo was driven twelve times versus BMW's five. None of these qualifications were mentioned in the Volvo commercial. Mr. Austin said he's confident Volvo will prevail against any FTC scrutiny.[1]

After a thorough investigation, and after hearing from both parties, NAD's decision was that the Volvo advertisement was properly substantiated. They found that the test procedures used by Mr. Allerecht were the same as those used by the leading automotive magazines and this data is frequently used as substantiation in advertising. By the time the decision was released Volvo had completed the commercial's flight. The commercial would not be aired again as both Volvo and BMW had entered new model years.

Chapter 1 outlined some of the major social criticisms of advertising. Because advertising is so visible, it draws a great deal of attention from citizens and government. This chapter will examine in detail the ethical questions advertisers face as well as the regulations imposed by government and by the industry itself.

---

[1]Jean Holliday, "Volvo's Ad Claims Questioned—Again," *Advertising Age* (June 10, 1996):1, 44.

ADVERTISING ETHICS

Advertising is a dynamic public forum in which business interests, creativity, consumer needs, and government regulation meet. Advertising's high visibility makes it particularly vulnerable to criticism.

An annoyance with advertising in general is also expressed by the population at large. In one survey, cosponsored by *Advertising Age* and the Roper Organization, both consumers and marketing executives were queried about their attitudes toward advertising. The findings indicated that ad executives are getting fed up with the bad ads produced by their trade—and, importantly, that they're becoming more and more concerned about advertising clutter. "The quality of advertising is really lousy. [Marketing people] feel the bad stuff compromises their work," notes Allison Cohen, president of People Talk, a marketing consultancy in New York. On another note, a large number of consumers in the Roper poll said they "don't care one way or the other" about several types of advertising. Many research experts believe such ambivalence could be an indication of doom for the ad industry. "People care less because there is too much advertising—they're just getting overwhelmed," People Talk's Cohen notes. "They are subject to so much that they tune it out." Perhaps most surprising was the fact that 42.5 percent of the people who work in advertising could not recall an ad seen during the past 24 hours. Only 17 percent of all consumers were able to recall a specific brand name.[2]

In a nationwide survey recently conducted for *Adweek* magazine, people were asked: Do you feel commercials talk down to you? Overall, 42 percent of respondents answered yes to this question, while 54 percent said no. There was very little gender gap. The survey found 44 percent of female respondents feel commercials talk down to them while 39 percent of male respondents put themselves in that category. On the other hand, youthful respondents played closer to supposed form on this issue. Among those in the notoriously ad-resistant 18–24 age group, 56 percent said they feel commercials talk down to them, while just 35 percent in the 25–34 age group answered affirmatively.[3]

It is doubtful that negative attitudes toward advertising will ever disappear, so it is worthwhile to be aware of the social issues facing advertisers. Each of these issues is complex, and each involves the public welfare as well as freedom of speech. The collective advertising industry, including agencies, advertisers, and the media, has an important stake in how these social issues are viewed both by the public and by those in a position to pass legislation to regulate the industry.

ETHICAL CRITERIA

Although advertisers face extensive regulation, every issue is not covered by a clear, written rule. Many advertising-related issues are left to the discretion of the advertiser. Decisions may be based on a variety of considerations, including the objective of the advertising campaign, the attitudes of the target audience, the philosophies of the agency and the advertiser, and legal precedent. Many decisions are based on ethical concerns. Three issues are central to an ethical discussion of advertising: advocacy, accuracy, and acquisitiveness.[4]

ADVOCACY

The first issue is *advocacy*. Advertising, by its very nature, tries to persuade the audience to do something. Thus, it is not objective or neutral. This fact disturbs

---

[2]Adrienne Ward Fawcett, "Even Ad Pros Hate Ad Clutter," *Advertising Age* (February 8, 1993):33.

[3]"Do You Feel Commercials Talk Down to You?" *Adweek* (March 13, 1995):16.

[4]John Crichton, "Morals and Ethics in Advertising," in *Ethics, Morality & the Media*, Lee Thayer, ed. (New York: Hastings House, 1980):105–15.

critics who think that advertising should be objective, informative, and neutral. They want advertising to provide information and to stop there. Most people, however, are aware that advertising tries to sell us something, whether it be a product, a service, or an idea.

ACCURACY

The second issue is *accuracy*. Beyond the easily ascertainable claims in an advertising message (for example, does the advertised automobile have a sun roof and an AM/FM radio, and is it available in different colors?) are matters of perception. Will buying the automobile make me the envy of my neighbors? Will it make me more attractive to the opposite sex? Such messages may be implied by the situations pictured in the advertisements.

Ad 2.1 for Toyota's MR2, for example, has fun with this accuracy issue by including notes from the various people who would review it, commenting on important features overlooked in the preliminary version of the ad. This type of ad would appeal to a more upscale, intelligent consumer.

Most of us are realistic enough to know that buying a car or drinking a certain brand of scotch won't make us a new person, but innuendos in the messages

AD 2.1

SOMETIMES THE ACCURACY ISSUE CAN BE TURNED INTO A HUMOROUS CREATIVE STRATEGY.

IFESTYLES

"ADVERTISING PRINCIPLES OF AMERICAN BUSINESS" OF THE AMERICAN ADVERTISING FEDERATION (AAF)

1.   TRUTH Advertising shall reveal the truth, and shall reveal significant facts, the omission of which would mislead the public.

2.   SUBSTANTIATION Advertising claims shall be substantiated by evidence in possession of the advertiser and the advertising agency prior to making such claims.

3.   COMPARISONS Advertising shall refrain from making false, misleading, or unsubstantiated statements or claims about a competitor or its products or services.

4.   BAIT ADVERTISING Advertising shall not offer products or services for sale unless such offer constitutes a bona fide effort to sell the advertised products or services and is not a device to switch consumers to other goods or services, usually higher priced.

5.   GUARANTEES AND WARRANTIES Advertising of guarantees and warranties shall be explicit, with sufficient informa-tion to apprise consumers of their principal terms and limitations or, when space or time restrictions preclude such disclosures, the advertisement shall clearly reveal where the full text of the guarantee or warranty can be examined before purchase.

6.   PRICE CLAIMS Advertising shall avoid price claims which are false or misleading, or savings claims which do not offer provable savings.

7.   TESTIMONIALS Advertising containing testimonials shall be limited to those of competent witnesses who are reflecting a real and honest opinion or experience.

8.   TASTE AND DECENCY Advertising shall be free of state-ments, illustrations, or implications which are offensive to good taste or public decency.

Source: Courtesy of the American Advertising Federation.

---

we see cause concern among advertising critics. The subtle messages coming across are of special concern when they are aimed at particular groups with limited experiences, such as children and teenagers.

ACQUISITIVENESS

The third issue is *acquisitiveness.* Some critics maintain that advertising is a symbol of our society's preoccupation with accumulating material objects. Because we are continually exposed to an array of changing, newer-and-better products, critics claim we are "corrupted" into thinking that we must have these products. The rebuttal of this criticism is that advertising allows a progressive society to see and choose among different products. Advertising gives us choices and incentives for which we continue to strive. For the most part, advertising simply tells consumers about goods and services that they implicitly demand. It is a part of the integrated marketing program that helps produce a satisfied, well-informed consumer.

Ultimately, it is the consumer who makes the final decision. If advertising for a product is perceived as violating ethical standards, consumers can exert pressure by refusing to buy the product or by complaining to the company and to a variety of regulatory bodies. However, decisions about advertising campaigns start with the advertiser.

THE PROBLEM OF BEING ETHICAL

Although advertisers can seek help in making decisions about questionable advertising situations from such sources as codes of ethics (see the Lifestyles box entitled "Advertising Principles of American Business"), these codes provide only general guidance. When advertising decisions are not clearly covered by a code, a rule, or a regulation, someone must make an ethical decision. That person must weigh the pros and cons, the good and the bad, the healthy and harmful effects, and make a value judgment about an unfamiliar situation. These kinds of decisions are complex because there is no clear consensus about what constitutes ethical behavior and also because of the potential conflict between personal ethics and what might be good for the business. Even though it might increase sales of your product, do you use copy that has an offensive double meaning? Do you use illustrations that portray people in stereotypical situations? Do you stretch the truth when making a claim about the product? Do you malign the competitor's product even though you know it is basically the same as your own?

The complexity of ethical issues requires us to make a conscious effort to deal with each situation. We should develop personal standards of what is right and wrong so that we will be less likely to behave unethically. Remember, it is people who create the ethical atmosphere of the organization. Advertising people in particular must address the following questions:

- Who should, and should not, be advertised to?
- What should, and should not, be advertised?
- What should, and should not, be the content of the advertising message?
- What should, and should not, be the symbolic tone of the advertising message?
- What should, and should not, be the relationship between advertising and the mass media?
- What should, and should not, be advertising's conscious obligation to society?[5]

Unfortunately, answers to these questions are not always straightforward. Rather, the advertiser must consider a number of related factors, such as the nature of the company, mission, marketing objectives, reputation, available resources, and competition. Even then, what is or is not ethical is still a judgment call made by imperfect individuals. Mistakes are made, and some companies pay for them for a very long time.

ETHICAL ISSUES IN ADVERTISING

Advertising involves many ethical issues. The predominant issues concern puffery, taste, stereotyping, advertising to children, advertising controversial products, and subliminal advertising. Engaging in any of these techniques is always a matter of choice for the advertiser. Just because it is not illegal does not mean it is right. Moreover, concerned consumers may make choices for or against the products of one advertiser as opposed to another based on ethical issues.

PUFFERY

Because the federal government does not pursue cases involving obviously exaggerated, or "puffing," claims, the question of puffery has become an ethical issue rather than a legal one.

Virtually everyone is familiar with a variety of puffery claims made for different products. Sugar Frosted Flakes are "great," Burger King serves "the best darn burgers in the whole wide world," people buy Hallmark cards when they "want to send the very best," and so on. Such puffery claims are legally viewed as patently different from other advertising claims. The legal logic assumes that consumers expect exaggerations and inflated claims in advertising and therefore know that certain statements ("puffs") are not to be believed as literal facts.

Puffery: Advertising or other sales representation that praises the item to be sold using subjective opinions, superlatives, and similar mechanisms that are not based on specific fact.

Puffery is defined as "advertising or other sales representations which praise the item to be sold with subjective opinions, superlatives, or exaggerations, vaguely and generally, stating no specific facts."[6] Critics contend that puffery is misleading and should be regulated by the Federal Trade Commission (FTC).

---

[5]Kim B. Rotzoll and James G. Haefner, "Advertising and Its Ethical Dimensions," in *Advertising in Contemporary Society* (Cincinnati, OH: South-Western Publishing Co., 1986):137–49.

[6]"The Image of Advertising," *Editor and Publisher* (February 9, 1985).

Defenders counter that reasonable people know puffery is just a way of showing enthusiasm for a product and consumers understand this aspect of selling.

Unfortunately, the empirical evidence supporting one position or the other is quite mixed. For example, studies supporting the critics found that audience members often draw inferences beyond the manifest content of an advertised statement, by reading the ad in terms of what the advertiser might have liked to have said. Rotfeld and Rotzoll produced results indicating that some consumers might in fact expect advertisers to be able to prove the truth of superlative claims.[7] Conversely, a study by Etzel and Knight found that inclusion of claim documentation did not influence consumers' response to particular ads.[8]

The Uniform Commercial Code (UCC), a relatively standard law that has been adopted by states across the country to govern sales and other commercial matters, draws a distinction between mere "puffing" and statements made about the performance or qualities of a product that can form an "express warranty." Under the UCC, a statement affirming the value of a product or purporting to be the seller's opinion or commendation of a product does not create an express warranty. More concrete representations, however, might do so.

The UCC long has recognized that advertisers cannot be expected to prove or live up to every general, glorifying statement made about a product. After all, it's only a company's opinion that its product is the "best" on the market. No one would want to, or could, prove the reasonableness or rationality of opinions.

However, the National Conference of Commissioners on Uniform State Laws is attempting the first-ever redraft of the UCC provisions regarding sales. The currently proposed revision of the section of the UCC relating to the creation of express warranties would make all statements about a product part of the sale agreement. This could mean that all statements about a product will create an express warranty, which could transform advertising as we know it.[9]

TASTE AND ADVERTISING

We all have our own ideas as to what constitutes good taste. Unfortunately, because these ideas vary so much, creating general guidelines for good taste in advertising is difficult. Different things offend different people. What is in good taste to some people is objectionable to others. Calvin Klein ads have become famous for their provocative appeals. In one *Vanity Fair* issue, there was a 116-page insert sponsored by Klein. It began with a photograph of a beautiful young male torso who is rubbing his soaking wet Calvins against his crotch. Altogether, we get four nudes of him under the water in the white-tiled stall. Although individuals in the 16–24 age group find such ads exciting and appealing, most older consumers view them with dismay.[10] More is said about Calvin Klein in the Issues and Controversies box.

PRODUCT CATEGORIES AND TASTE

One dimension of the taste issue concerns the product itself. Television advertising for certain products, such as designer jeans, pantyhose, bras and girdles, laxatives, and feminine hygiene aids, produces higher levels of distaste than do ads for other product categories.[11] The fact that television has the ability to bring a spokesperson into our living rooms to "talk" to us about such "unmentionables"

---

[7]Herbert J. Rotfeld and Kim B. Rotzoll, "Is Advertising Puffery Believed?" *Journal of Advertising*, 9, 3 (1980):16–20, 45.

[8]Michael J. Etzell and E. Leon Knight, Jr., "The Effect of Documented versus Undocumented Advertising Claims," *Journal of Consumer Affairs*, 10 (Winter 1976):233–38.

[9]Barry R. Shapiro, "Beyond Puffery," *Marketing Management*, 4, no. 3 (Winter 1995):60–62.

[10]Barbara Lippert, "Calvin Klein, Masturbation and Jeans," *Adweek* (September 16, 1991):39.

[11]Bill Abrams, "Poll Suggests TV Advertisers Can't Ignore Matters of Taste," *The Wall Street Journal* (July 23, 1981):25.

ℐSSUES AND ℭONTROVERSIES

THE SHOCK APPROACH OF CALVIN KLEIN

In the Water Tower Place Mall in Chicago, Jennifer Marks and her mother Clara had a Calvin Klein problem. His ads were "absolutely pornographic," said Clara, 41. "They're exploiting children." It was the day after Klein had announced that he was pulling his controversial ad campaign, and Jennifer and Clara were debating one of the posters. Against the backdrop of cheap paneling and purple pile carpet, the ad showed a very young-looking girl in a skimpy tank top, her jeans pushed below her bellybutton. "Where are the parents who are allowing their children to do this?" asked Clara. They had come to the mall together, Clara and Jennifer, and now here they were—in the juniors department of Marshall Field's—at opposite sides of a cultural divide. "I wouldn't allow my daughter to dress like that," said Clara. "And she knows it."

But to Jennifer, 15, the image had a different meaning. "I think she looks cute there," Jennifer said. "All my friends wear pants down past their underwear." In her school, she said, Calvin Klein was the most popular designer, though boys were always stealing her Victoria's Secret catalog. "I don't think they're exploiting her at all," Jennifer said of the girl in the ad. "She's got the body to wear it. Why not? I can't believe there's a controversy over this."

To veteran watchers of Calvin Klein, Inc., it had seemed like just another marketing splash. For the last 15 years, Klein has built a fashion empire largely by tapping both the charge and the cultural unease about youthful sexuality. In the early '80s, when feminists like Gloria Steinem protested his crotch shots of a 15-year-old Brooke Shields cooing that nothing came between her and her Calvins, some television stations refused to air the spots. Klein simply banked the controversy. "F—k off," he said to Steinem. With Brooke's pouting, his jean sales nearly doubled. Since then, as he eroticized the nubile bodies of Marky Mark and Kate Moss, Klein refined the formula. When the current ads for CK jeans rolled out in August 1995—discomfittingly intimate snapshots of very young men and women in provocative states of undress—they carried the shock of the old. When interviewed, Klein said matter-of-factly: "I'm sure they're going to be controversial."

But as the free publicity mounted, the circus took a different turn. In September 1995, the FBI and U.S. Department of Justice launched an investigation of the controversial jeans campaign. "I can't remember, in the 30 years I've been in this business, any case where the FBI has investigated an advertisement," said Felix Kent, a lawyer specializing in advertising. The government is trying to determine whether or not Calvin Klein, Inc. ran afoul of federal pornography laws.

In addition, some retailers rebelled. Dayton Hudson, the giant midwestern retail conglomerate, urged Klein to pull the ad campaign. "Our company's point of view is that the ads were offensive," said Dayton Hudson vice president Mary Hughes. "This is the '90s. We just culturally don't deal with children." Protesters threatened to picket department stores like Macy's and Wal-Mart. One New York City councilman even called for a boycott of the designer's products.

Sources: Pat Sloan and Jennifer DeCoursey, "Gov't Hot on Trail of Calvin Klein Ads," *Advertising Age* (September 1, 1995):1, 8; Michele Ingrassia, "Calvin's World," *Newsweek* (September 11, 1995):60–66.

embarrasses many people, who then complain that the advertisements are distasteful. Although certain ads might be in bad taste in any circumstances, viewer reactions are affected by such factors as sensitivity to the product category, the time the message is received (for example, in the middle of dinner), and whether the person is alone or with others when viewing the message. There is also the issue of matching questionable ads with certain media or programs. Parents, for example, may object to a racy ad in *Sports Illustrated* or one that is seen by children in a prime-time family program.

In addition, taste changes over time. What is offensive today may not be considered offensive in the future. In 1919 a *Ladies Home Journal* deodorant advertisement that asked the question, "Are you one of the many women who are troubled with excessive perspiration?" was so controversial that 200 readers immediately canceled their subscriptions.[12] By today's standards that advertisement seems pretty tame. Ad 2.2 is an example of a current ad that once would have been considered offensive.

CURRENT ISSUES

Today's questions of taste center around the use of sexual innuendo, nudity, and violence. Although the use of sex in advertising is not new, the blatancy of its use

---

[12]Julian Lewis Watkins, *100 Greatest Advertisements. Who Wrote Them and What They Did* (New York: Moore Publishing Co., 1949):201.

AD 2.2

IF IT AIN'T BROKE: CHRISTIAN DIOR'S DIOR SVELTE HAS BEEN SO SUCCESSFUL WITH ITS GLAMOROUS ADS THAT IT HAS NOT CHANGED THEM SINCE THE ANTI-CELLULITE CREAM WAS INTRODUCED IN 1993.

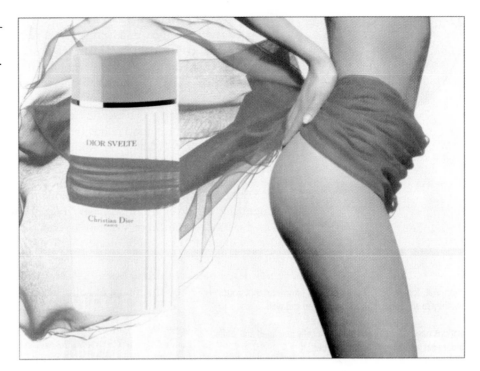

is. The fashion industry has often been criticized for its liberal use of sex in advertising. There are experts in the fashion industry who feel that outrageous ads are necessary in order to appeal to the MTV generation. In response to the Calvin Klein insert discussed earlier, Larry Burstein, publisher of *Elle*, had the following to say: "Maybe it is a trend. I think people are trying very hard to come up with new ways of talking to their audiences . . . If people aren't getting what they want by doing things as usual, they're going to look for new and interesting ways to make things happen." Carl Portale, publisher of *Harper's Bazaar*, added, "What this does is force guys like me to try to think of alternative methods to get [fashion and cosmetic marketers] to stand out."[13] The fashion industry is also a leader in the use of *infomercials*, which are 30- or 60-minute ad programs. There are certainly consumers who find this program format objectionable as well, seeing it as an attempt to fool the consumer.

It is to the advantage of the advertiser to be aware of current standards of taste. The safest way to make sure that you are not overlooking some part of the message that could be offensive is to pretest the advertisement. Pretest feedback should minimize the chances of producing distasteful advertising.

STEREOTYPING IN ADVERTISING

Stereotyping: Presenting a group of people in an unvarying pattern that lacks individuality and often reflects popular misconceptions.

Stereotyping involves presenting a group of people in an unvarying pattern that lacks individuality. Critics claim that many advertisers stereotype large segments of our population, particularly women, minorities, and the elderly. The issue of stereotyping is connected to the debate about whether advertising shapes society's values or simply mirrors them. Either way, the issue is very important. If you believe that advertising has the ability to shape our values and our view of the world, you will believe it essential that advertisers become aware of how they portray different groups. Conversely, if you believe that advertising mirrors society, you will think that advertisers have a responsibility to ensure that what is portrayed is accurate and representative. Advertisers struggle with this issue every time they use people in an ad.

PRINCIPLE Debates about advertising ethics begin with the question: Does advertising shape society's values or simply mirror them?

---

[13]Pat Sloan and Scott Donaton, "Klein 'Outsert': New Trend?" *Advertising Age* (September 9, 1991):12.

WOMEN IN ADVERTISEMENTS

The portrayal of women in advertisements has received much attention over the years. Initially, critics complained that ads showed women as preoccupied with beauty, household duties, and motherhood. Advertising executives were accused of viewing women as zealous homemakers who were

> in endless pursuit of antiseptic cleanliness. Television ads for Lysol, Spic and Span, and Lemon Pledge, for example, show these ladies frantically spraying and polishing everything in sight—from refrigerator doors to dining-room tables to kitchen floors.[14]

Although there is still concern about this stereotype, more advertisers are recognizing the diversity of women's roles. However, with the effort to portray women as more than obsessive housewives came a different problem. Suddenly advertisements focused on briefcase-toting professional women (see Ad 2.3). Consider the commercial where a women discusses the benefits of serving her children a powdered breakfast drink. She is a NASA engineer. The image of "Supermom" has been displaced by the image of "Superwoman."[15]

---

[14]William Miles, *The Image Makers* (Metuchen, NJ: Scarecrow Press, 1979).

[15]Jim Auchmutey, "Graphic Changes Charted in the Middle Class," Special Report: Marketing to Women, *Advertising Age* (September 12, 1985):15–17.

AD 2.3

THIS AD PORTRAYS WOMEN AS THE SUCCESSFUL EXECUTIVE.

One industry that is attempting to appeal to women without offending is the realm of high-tech marketers. Technology companies haven't given up hope of attracting more women customers: If anything, the desire is even stronger today. With the home personal computer (PC) market booming and women controlling more household budgets, high-tech companies realize they have to look beyond their hard-core male base. Link Resources Corp., a New York consulting concern, found in a recent survey that 26 percent of the households with computers count women as their primary users. That comes out to about 8.3 million households, up sharply from the 4.4 million reported in 1989. So far, Compaq Computer Corp. has led the latest marketing push. The PC giant has taken a direct approach with television commercials aimed squarely at work-at-home moms. One spot shows a woman putting her child to bed, then heading to her Compaq PC for some late-night work. Unfortunately, some women say they're offended that computer ads in fashion and home-and-garden magazines focus on how easy the systems are to use. Others say the focus on children's software—considered by marketers to be a surefire way to women's pocketbooks—ignores the army of female managers who long ago mastered the most complex spreadsheets and engineering software.[16]

The challenge facing advertisers today is to portray woman realistically, in diverse roles, without alienating any segment of women. Experts agree that today's woman wants to see women portrayed with a new freedom, but also as mature, intelligent people with varied interests and abilities.[17]

RACIAL AND ETHNIC STEREOTYPES

Racial and ethnic groups also complain of stereotyping in advertising. The root of most complaints is that certain groups are shown in subservient, unflattering ways. Many times minorities are the basis of a joke or, alternatively, consigned to a spot in the background. There is also the suggestion that advertising perpetuates some of the myths associated with certain minorities.

Other critics complain about underrepresentation of minorities in advertisements. A review of magazine and television advertising determined that blacks account for between 2 and 6 percent of models in print ads and about 13 percent in television advertisements. (Blacks constitute about 13 percent of the total U.S. population.)[18]

SENIOR CITIZENS

Another group frequently mentioned with regard to stereotyping is senior citizens, a growing segment of the population with increasing disposable income (see Chapter 5). Critics often object to the use of older people in roles that portray them as slow, senile, and full of afflictions. Although Clara Peller achieved success in the Wendy's hamburger commercials, some critics charged that these ads were too cutesy.[19] Others were offended by the shrill "Where's the beef?" and felt that the tone of the commercial portrayed older people as hard to get along with, obstinate, and unattractive.

In contrast, the Quaker Oats ad (Ad 2.4) portrays senior citizens as a healthy, intelligent, forward-looking group in society.

---

[16]Kyle Pople, "High-Tech Marketers Try to Attract Women Without Causing Offense," *The Wall Street Journal* (March 17, 1994):B1.

[17]Lynn Folse, "Workers Labor to Raise Women's Status," Special Report: Marketing to Women, *Advertising Age* (September 12, 1985):36–38.

[18]Lynette Unger and James M. Stearns, "The Frequency of Blacks in Magazine and Television Advertising: A Review and Additional Evidence," *Southern Marketing Association Proceedings*, Robert L. King, ed. (1986):9–13.

[19]Laurie Freeman and Nancy Giges, "Ads Giving Older Consumers Short Shrift," *Advertising Age* (November 3, 1986):92.

AD 2.4

THIS AD IS A VERY POSITIVE PORTRAYAL OF THE ELDERLY.

Name: George (Junior)

Age: A state of mind.

Weight: Welterweight

Cholesterol Level: The envy of others.

Blood Pressure: Right in the ballpark.

Diet: Just say no to donuts.

Goal: To sail around the world.

Motto: Never wear someone else's hair.

Experts say that cholesterol, high blood pressure and excess body weight are three risk factors for heart disease. Delicious Quaker® Oatmeal is low in saturated fat, low in sodium and naturally cholesterol free, so it fits into the kind of diet that may lower your cholesterol and high blood pressure. Which may help reduce your risk of heart disease. And it's satisfying, so you won't be tempted to indulge before lunch.

As for its ability to stimulate hair follicles, no comment.

Oh, what those oats can do.™

http://www.quakeroatmeal.com

BABY BOOMERS

Few groups in our society have been more extensively stereotyped than baby boomers. Born between 1946 and 1964, these 76 million people represent the largest of all markets. Of the original baby boomers, approximately 68 million are still alive, and they represent over one-fourth of the total population of the United States. Although the total bulk of the economic resources possessed by this group is impressive, the assumption that all baby boomers are wealthy and seek material possessions is inaccurate. Though nurtured through prosperous times, the baby boomers are considered an unlucky generation. Their unprecedented large numbers had to compete for college admission, interesting jobs, and housing. In a reversal of historic trends, boomers so far have experienced lower economic status than their parents.

Nevertheless, advertising has often been blamed for perpetuating the baby boom myth of the "American Dream." The American Dream is to have it all; a beautiful car, a fancy home, a swimming pool, a beautiful body, and the money to travel and entertain. Clearly, it is a dream attainable for a very small percentage of baby boomers.

ADVERTISING TO CHILDREN

Advertising to children was one of the most controversial topics of the 1970s and led to a regulatory policy for the industry. In 1977 experts estimated that the aver-

"I CAN'T COME RIGHT NOW, MOM...
I'M WATCHING A COMMERCIAL
SPECIFICALLY TARGETED AT MY
DEMOGRAPHIC SEGMENT OF
THE POPULATION."

age child watched more than 1,300 hours of television annually, which resulted in exposure to over 20,000 commercials.[20] Proponents of regulating children's advertising were concerned that children did not possess the skills necessary to evaluate advertising messages and to make purchase decisions. They also thought that certain advertising techniques and strategies appropriate for adults were confusing or misleading to children. Two groups in particular, Action for Children's Television (ACT) and the Center for Science in the Public Interest (CSPI), petitioned the FTC to evaluate the situation.

In 1978 the FTC initiated proceedings to study possible regulation of children's television. Several regulations were suggested, including the banning of some types of advertising directed at children. Opponents of the proposed regulations argued that many self-regulatory mechanisms were already in place and that, ultimately, the proper place for restricting advertising to children was in the home.[21]

After years of debate over the issue, the proposed FTC regulations were abandoned. This did not mean, however, that advertisers to children had unlimited freedom. Advertising to children was carefully monitored by self-regulation. The National Advertising Division (NAD) of the Council of Better Business Bureaus, Inc. set up a group charged with helping advertisers deal with children's advertising in a manner sensitive to children's special needs. (The NAD is discussed in more detail later in the chapter.) The Children's Advertising Review Unit

---

[20]National Science Foundation, *Research on the Effects of Television Advertising on Children* (1977):45.

[21]"The Positive Case for Marketing Children's Products to Children," comments by the Association of National Advertisers, Inc., American Association of Advertising Agencies and the American Advertising Federation before the Federal Trade Commission (November 24, 1978).

GUIDELINES FOR CHILDREN'S ADVERTISING

The controversy surrounding the issue of children's advertising has encouraged the advertising industry to regulate this practice carefully. In the 1970s the industry issued written guidelines for children's advertising and established the Children's Advertising Review Unit within the Council of Better Business Bureaus to oversee the self-regulatory process. The unit revised the written guidelines in 1977 and again in 1983. The following are the five basic principles on which guidelines for advertising directed at children are based.

1. Advertisers should always take into account the level of knowledge, sophistication, and maturity of the audience to which their message is primarily directed. Younger children have a limited capability for evaluating the credibility of what they watch. Advertisers, therefore, have a special responsibility to protect children from their own susceptibilities.

2. Realizing that children are imaginative and that make-believe play constitutes an important part of the growing up process, advertisers should exercise care not to exploit that imaginative quality of children. Unreasonable expectations of product quality or performance should not be stimulated either directly or indirectly by advertising.

3. Recognizing that advertising may play an important part in educating the child, information should be communicated in a truthful and accurate manner with full recognition by the advertiser that the child may learn practices from advertising which can affect his or her health and well-being.

4. Advertisers are urged to capitalize on the potential of advertising to influence social behavior by developing advertising that, wherever possible, addresses itself to social standards generally regarded as positive and beneficial, such as friendship, kindness, honesty, justice, generosity, and respect for others.

5. Although many influences affect a child's personal and social development, it remains the prime responsibility of the parents to provide guidance for children. Advertisers should contribute to this parent-child relationship in a constructive manner.

Source: "Self-Regulatory Guidelines for Children's Advertising," 3rd ed. Children's Advertising Review Unit, National Advertising Division, Council of Better Business Bureaus, Inc. (1983):4–5.

(CARU) was established in 1974 to review and evaluate advertising directed at children under the age of 12.

Then, on October 2, 1990, the House of Representatives and the Senate approved the Children's Television Advertising Practice Act, which restored 10.5-minute-per-hour ceilings for commercials in weekend children's television programming and 12-minute-per-hour limits for weekday programs. The act also restored rules requiring that commercial breaks be clearly distinguished from programming and barring "host selling," tie-ins, and other practices that involve the use of program characters to promote products.

Advocates for children's television continue to argue that many stations are making little real effort to comply with the 1990 act and petitioned the FCC to increase the required number of hours of educational programming to be shown daily. The FCC was ready to make a ruling in 1995 but delayed doing so because of lobbying efforts on the part of the broadcasters.[22]

---

[22] Cheryl Heuton, "FCC Again Defers Ruling on Kid Shows," *Adweek* (March 13, 1995):10.

ADVERTISING CONTROVERSIAL PRODUCTS

ALCOHOL AND TOBACCO

One of the most heated advertising issues in recent years is the proposed restrictions on advertising such product categories as alcohol and tobacco. Restrictions on products thought to be unhealthy or unsafe are not new. Cigarette advertising on television and radio has been banned since January 1, 1971. In 1987 the issue was the advisability of a total ban of every form of media advertising of tobacco and alcohol products. A 1986 Tobacco-Free Young American Project poll of 1,025 Americans—70 percent nonsmokers and 30 percent smokers—found that most respondents favored tougher restrictions on public smoking and tobacco-related promotional activities.[23]

Proponents of such a ban argued that advertising tobacco or alcohol products might result in sickness, injury, or death for the user and possibly others. Restricting advertising of those products would result in fewer sales of the products and consequently would reduce their unhealthy effects.

Opponents of an advertising ban countered that banning truthful, nondeceptive advertising for a legal product is unconstitutional. As attorney and First Amendment authority Floyd Abrams pointed out, "Censorship is contagious and habit-forming . . . even for commercial speech. . . . What we need is more speech, not less. There would be a precedential effect for all other lawful products . . . that are said to do harm." Opponents also cited statistics demonstrating that similar bans in other countries had proved unsuccessful in reducing sales of tobacco and alcohol.[24]

The tobacco and alcohol industries have maintained that their intent is to advertise only to those who have already decided to use their products and not to persuade nonusers to try them. Adolph Coors Company sponsored a "Gimme the Keys" television commercial intended to remind people to be responsible drinkers. They also developed a public service campaign using the movie character E.T. to deliver the message, "If you go beyond your limit, please don't drive. Phone home." More recently, Coors ran a television commercial for Coors' Light that used the tag line "right beer now—but not now" to depict safe times for drinking, such as a social gathering, and unsafe times, such as before getting into a car.

Still, the negative publicity seems to supersede the positive. Joe Camel, an advertising spokesanimal for R. J. Reynolds, has clearly caused the greatest controversy. It all began with a series of studies reported in the *Journal of the American Medical Association*. In the first study, involving 229 preschool children, researchers determined that, by age six, children recognize Joe Camel as readily as they do Mickey Mouse. By high school, according to the second study, nearly half the students think Joe "is cool." The third study looked at 5,040 California teenagers, ages 12 to 17, and found that Camel's increasing popularity with the 131 smokers among them paralleled, the buildup of the Joe Camel campaign. The authors allege that illegal sales of Camels to minors have skyrocketed from $6 million to $476 million a year, since the inception of the campaign.[25] Although R. J. Reynolds has vehemently rejected these findings, it appears the damage to Joe and the industry has been done.

In 1996, the Food and Drug Administration, with the support of President Clinton, laid down a set of recommendations that would greatly restrict tobacco advertising. Specifically, the FDA proposed banning outdoor ads within 1,000 feet

---

[23]Joe Agnew, "Trade Groups Align to Counter Public, Government Ban Efforts," *Marketing News* (January 30, 1987):1, 18.

[24]Steven W. Colford, "Tobacco Ad Foes Press Fight," *Advertising Age* (February 23, 1987):12; and "Strict Ad Bans Not Effective," *Advertising Age* (August 8, 1986).

[25]"Camels for Kids," *Time* (December 23, 1991):52.

of a school or playground; restricting tobacco companies to black-and-white, text-only advertising in magazines with more than 55 percent readership by those under 18; eliminating giveaways of merchandise with tobacco symbols; limiting tobacco symbols in many sports sponsorships to black-and-white text only; and placing $150 million in a fund for antismoking messages targeted toward children. As expected, the tobacco industry has challenged this ruling.[26]

The outcome of the proposed advertising bans has far-reaching implications for advertisers, advertising agencies, and the general public. For example, magazine publishers could be financially devastated if print tobacco ads were banned. According to one report, as many as 165 magazines would fold without tobacco advertising.[27]

CONDOMS

Another topic of controversy is whether or not condoms should be advertised and, if so, in what media. Magazines have been more receptive to condom ads than television. Even though the National Association of Broadcasters repealed its ban on the broadcast of contraceptive ads in 1982, the major networks have hesitated to accept condom ads because of the sensitive nature of the product. Supporters of such advertising contend that the growing number of sexually transmitted diseases, including AIDS, makes such advertising necessary. They further argue that such messages can be done in good taste and at appropriate times, so that few groups would be offended. This issue raises difficult questions that will not be easily resolved.

An interesting example of condom advertising occurred in 1994 with the introduction of the first female condom. Wisconsin Pharmacal's Reality female condom was advertised through an initial education campaign, through ten magazines targeted to 18- to 24-year-old females. Mary Anne Leeper, president and chief executive of Wisconsin Pharmacal, summarizes its strategy as follows: "Reality isn't competing against perception. My issue isn't competition. My issue is introducing a whole new concept . . . This is a serious product and humor has no place in our effort." This low-key approach appears to be acceptable to most female consumers.[28]

SUBLIMINAL ADVERTISING

Subliminal Message: A message transmitted below the threshold of normal perception so that the receiver is not consciously aware of having viewed it.

Generally when we think of messages we consider symbols that are consciously seen and heard. However, it is possible to transmit symbols in a manner that puts them below the threshold of normal perception. These kinds of messages are termed *subliminal*. A **subliminal message** is one that is transmitted in such a way that the receiver is not consciously aware of receiving it. This usually means that the symbols are too faint or too brief to be clearly recognized. The furor over subliminal perception began with a 1958 study by James Vicary in a movie theater in Fort Lee, New Jersey, where the words "Drink Coke" and "Eat Popcorn" were flashed on the screen, allegedly resulting in increased sales of popcorn and Coke.

The issue was further publicized by Vance Packard in his book *The Hidden Persuaders*, and more recently, Wilson Bryan Key discussed the subject in his books *Subliminal Seduction* and *Media Sexploitation*. Key maintains that subliminal "embeds" are placed in ads to manipulate purchase behavior, most frequently through appeals to sexuality. For example, he suggests that 99 percent of ads for alcoholic beverages employ subliminal embeds. Key contends that the messages

---

[26]Ira Teinowitz, "White House Studies Final Rules on Tobacco Ads," *Advertising Age* (August 19, 1996):3, 29.

[27]Scott Donaton, "Publishers Bracing for Smoke-Free Pages," *Advertising Age* (March 12, 1990):3.

[28]Kevin Goldman, "Company Faces Challenge in Marketing Female Condom," *The Wall Street Journal* (July 27, 1994):B6.

are buried so skillfully that the average person does not notice them unless they are pointed out. He believes the subliminal embeds are the work of airbrush touch-up artists.[29] Ad 2.5 sponsored by the American Association of Advertising Industries, reflects the industry's opinion of the subliminal advertising theory.

Whether or not subliminal stimuli can cause some types of minor reactions has never been the advertising issue. In tightly controlled laboratory settings subliminal stimuli have been shown to produce some reactions, such as a "like/dislike" response. The advertising issue is whether or not a subliminal message is capable of affecting the public's *buying behavior.*

Research in this field has uncovered several practical difficulties with the theory that subliminal embeds can be used to influence buying behavior. To begin with, perceptual thresholds vary from person to person and from moment to moment. Symbols that are subliminal to one person might be consciously perceived by another. A message guaranteed to be subliminal to an entire audience would probably be so weak that any effect would be limited. Another problem is the lack of control that the advertiser would have over the distance and position of the message receiver from the message. Differences in distances and position could affect when the stimulus is subliminal and when it is recognizable. The third problem comes from the effect of recognizable (supraliminal) material, such as the movie or commercial, used in conjunction with the subliminal message. The supraliminal stimulus might overpower the subliminal material.

Besides the physiological limitations that make it questionable that subliminal messages can cause certain behaviors, there are several pragmatic issues. Most

---

[29]Walter Weir, "Another Look at Subliminal Facts," *Advertising Age* (October 15, 1984):46.

AD 2.5

THE ADVERTISING INDUSTRY CONSIDERS ACCUSATIONS OF SUBLIMINAL ADVERTISING TO BE BOTH DAMAGING AND TOTALLY UNTRUE.

PEOPLE HAVE BEEN TRYING TO FIND THE BREASTS IN THESE ICE CUBES SINCE 1957.

The advertising industry is sometimes charged with sneaking seductive little pictures into ads.

Supposedly, these pictures can get you to buy a product without your even seeing them.

Consider the photograph above. According to some people, there's a pair of female breasts hidden in the patterns of light refracted by the ice cubes.

Well, if you really searched you probably *could* see the breasts. For that matter, you could also see Millard Fillmore, a stuffed pork chop and a 1946 Dodge.

The point is that so-called "subliminal advertising" simply doesn't exist. Overactive imaginations, however, most certainly do.

So if anyone claims to see breasts in that drink up there, they aren't in the ice cubes.

They're in the eye of the beholder.

ADVERTISING
ANOTHER WORD FOR FREEDOM OF CHOICE.
American Association of Advertising Agencies

importantly, consumers normally will not buy products they don't need or can't afford to purchase, regardless of the advertising message and whether it is presented subliminally or directly. There will always be freedom of choice. Furthermore, there are many factors besides the advertising message itself that induce consumers to purchase a product. (These influences will be discussed in more detail in Chapter 5.)

Nonetheless, many people still believe subliminal advertising is used frequently, widely, and successfully. Little evidence exists to support this belief, however. A survey of advertising agency art directors found that over 90 percent claimed no personal knowledge of the use of subliminal advertising. Timothy Moore concluded after his overview of the subliminal area, "In general, the literature on subliminal perception shows that the most clearly documented effects are obtained in only highly contrived and artificial situations. These effects, when present, are brief and of small magnitude. . . . These processes have no apparent relevance to the goals of advertising."[30]

ADVERTISING AND THE LAW

Few elements of business have been more heavily legislated than advertising. This section discusses the most important federal legislation as well as advertisers' attempts at self-regulation (see Figure 2.1).

ADVERTISING AND THE FIRST AMENDMENT

PRINCIPLE Recent interpretations of the First Amendment find that commercial information should not be prohibited, but the "right" of expression for advertisers is still being defined.

Freedom of expression in the United States is protected from government control by the Bill of Rights to the Constitution. In particular, the First Amendment states that Congress shall make no law "abridging the freedom of speech, or of the press; or the right of people peaceably to assemble, and to petition the Government for a redress of grievances." Initially, the Court ruled that freedom of expression is not absolute, although only the most compelling circumstances justify prior restraint on the spread of information. Specifically the Court held that the First Amendment applied to most media, including newspapers, books, magazines, broadcasting, and film. However, since Congress adopted the amendment in 1791, the

[30]Timothy Moore, "Subliminal Advertising: What You See Is What You Get," *Journal of Marketing* (Spring 1982):38–47.

FIGURE 2.1

REGULATORY FACTORS AFFECTING ADVERTISING.
(Courtesy of American Advertising Federation.)

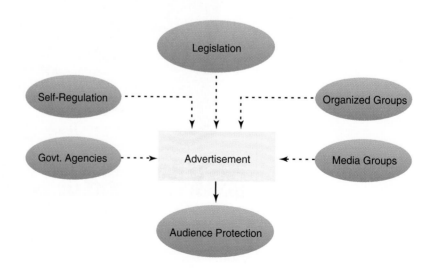

Supreme Court has continued to reinterpret it as it applies to different situations. Table 2.1 lists some of the important First Amendment legislation.

The First Amendment has been used to strike down many statutes prohibiting commercial expression. For example, as a result of the *Virginia Pharmacy* ruling, states no longer can bar attorneys from advertising the prices of "routine" legal services, homeowners from advertising their houses by placing "For Sale" signs in their yards, drugstores from advertising contraceptives, or utilities from promoting the use of electricity.[31]

Can advertisers now assume they are free from government regulation? Hardly. Essentially, the Court has ruled that the scope of the commercial-speech guarantee is limited. Only truthful and not misleading or deceptive commercial speech is protected. By contrast, the Court secures both false and misleading news reports if published without malice, that is, with no intention to deceive and not made recklessly. In fact, until two critical rulings in 1993, there was considerable question about how strong First Amendment protection for advertising was. In the first case, *Cincinnati* v. *Discovery Network*, the city had revoked the permits issued to companies that publish magazines consisting principally of advertising to place 62 free-standing newsracks on public property. In the Cincinnati case, the Court decided the fit between the newsrack ban and the enforcement of safety and appearance (the reasons for the ban) was not tight enough to justify the city's action. In the second case, the Court ruled that Fane, a CPA, was entitled to solicit prospective clients through telemarketing.[32] Both these rulings are encouraging for advertising, suggesting that the Supreme Court will continue to view the First Amendment as protection for commercial speech.

The Supreme Court's May 13, 1996 decision in *44 Liquormart, Inc.* v. *Rhode Island* marked an acknowledgment that may afford companies greater protection under the First Amendment. In this case, the Court struck down two Rhode

---

[31]Ivan L. Preston, "A Review of the Literature on Advertising Regulation," in *Current Issues and Research in Advertising* (1983), James H. Leigh and Claude L. Martin, eds. (Ann Arbor: University of Michigan Press, 1983):2–37.

[32]Alan Pell Crawford, "Getting an Edge," *Adweek* (May 10, 1993):24; Bernard H. Seegan, "High Court Revives 1st Amendment for Ads," *Advertising Age* (April 26, 1993):22.

TABLE 2.1   FIRST AMENDMENT LEGISLATION
Valentine v. *Christensen* (1942)   First Amendment does not protect purely commercial advertising because that type of advertising does not contribute to decision making in a democracy.
Virginia State Board of Pharmacy v. *Virginia Citizens Consumer Council* (1976)   States cannot prohibit pharmacists from advertising prices of prescription drugs because the free flow of information is indispensable.
Central Hudson Gas & Electric Corporation v. *Public Service Commission of New York* (1980)   Public Service Commission's prohibition of promotional advertising by utilities is found to be unconstitutional, placing limitations on government regulation of unlawful, nondeceptive advertising.
Posadas de Puerto Rico Associates v. *Tourism Company of Puerto Rico* (1986)   Puerto Rican law banned advertising of gambling casinos to residents of Puerto Rico.
Cincinnati v. *Discovery Network* (1993)   Court ruled that the Cincinnati City Council violated the First Amendment's protection of commercial speech when it banned newsracks of advertising brochures from city streets for aesthetic and safety reasons, while permitting newspaper vending machines.
Edenfield v. *Fane* (1993)   Court ruled that Florida's prohibition of telephone solicitation by accountants to be unconstitutional.
44 Liquormart, Inc. v. *Rhode Island* (1996)   Court ruled that two Rhode Island statutes that banned advertising for alcohol prices were unconstitutional.

Island statutes that banned the advertisement of alcohol prices in an attempt to advance the state's interest in temperance. The first statute prohibited advertising alcohol prices in the state except via signs within the store. The second statute prohibited the "publication or broadcast" of alcohol price ads. The Supreme Court held that Rhode Island's statutes are invalid because the ban abridged the First Amendment's guarantee of freedom of speech.[33]

The Federal Trade Commission

Federal Trade Commission (FTC): A federal agency responsible for interpreting deceptive advertising and regulating unfair methods of competition.

The **Federal Trade Commission (FTC)** is the government agency responsible for regulating much of American business. It was established in 1914 to prevent business activities that were unfair or anticompetitive. Its original mission was to protect business rather than the consumer, and its enabling act contained no statement about advertising. In 1922, a Supreme Court ruling placed deceptive advertising within the scope of the FTC's authority, giving the agency the right to regulate false labeling and advertising as unfair methods of competition. Figure 2.2 shows the organization of the Federal Trade Commission.

The Wheeler-Lea Amendment, passed in 1938, extended the FTC's powers, and the agency became more consumer oriented. This amendment added "deceptive acts and practices" to the list of "unfair methods of competition." In addition, the Wheeler-Lea Amendment gave the FTC authority to (1) initiate investigations against companies without waiting for complaints, (2) issue cease-and-desist orders, and (3) fine companies for not complying with cease-and-desist orders. The FTC was also given jurisdiction over false advertising of foods, drugs, cos-

FIGURE 2.2

ORGANIZATION OF THE FEDERAL TRADE COMMISSION.
(*Source:* Office of the Federal Register National Archives and Records Administration, *The United States Government Manual 1989/90*)

---

[33]Stephen P. Durchslag, "Score One for Commercial Free Speech," *Promo* (August 1996):27.

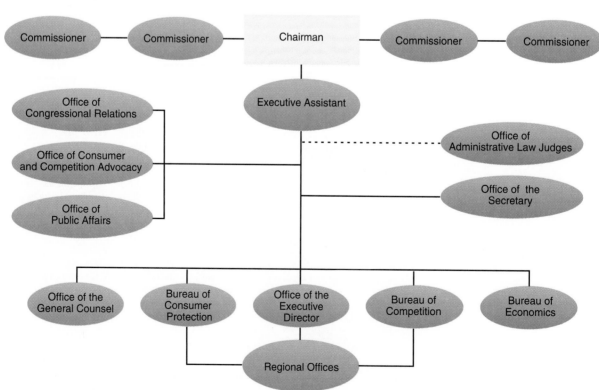

metics, and therapeutic devices. False advertising was defined as "any false representation, including failure to reveal material facts."[34]

The FTC acquired increased authority during the late 1960s and mid-1970s through a series of important acts, which are listed in Table 2.2, along with other advertising legislation. An issue of high concern to the advertising industry was winning congressional reauthorization of the FTC, a feat last accomplished in 1982. The U.S. Senate passed the reauthorization bill in 1989. In addition to appropriating a substantial budget increase, the Senate also commissioned a study identifying those areas under the FTC's jurisdiction that might be appropriate for state enforcement and eliminate the agency's ability to make new rules regulating commercial advertising on the basis of unfairness. Unfortunately, the House and Senate have been unable to reconcile differences over the FTC's ability to use unfairness as the basis for rule-making, and as of early 1993, there was still debate about a reauthorization bill.

In addition, the laissez-faire political climate of the 1980s resulted in new appointees to the FTC who were less aggressive in regulating advertising. The Reagan administration's position was that regulation was justifiable only if it produced economic benefits that outweigh the costs. However, when George Bush succeeded Reagan as president in 1989, the FTC once again became more rigorous in enforcing business trade regulations. The FTC of the Bush administration was especially aggressive in enforcing regulation on advertising, including health claims or promotions for alcohol and tobacco products.[35]

Some people think that the end of the Reagan era signaled a change in the hands-off attitude that insulated marketers from regulation. In her coming-out speech in 1990, FTC chairperson Janet Steiger warned agencies that they will be held accountable for ads or practices deemed unfair or deceptive. The response of one advertising executive was typical of the industry: "We haven't heard that from the FTC for years, and I think a lot of agencies don't understand their liability."

---

[34]*Bates* v. *State Bar of Arizona*, 433 U.S. 350 (1977); *Linmark Associates, Inc.* v. *Township of Willingboro*, 431 U.S. 85 (1977); *Carey* v. *Population Services International*, 431 U.S. 678 (1977); *Central Hudson* v. *Public Services Commission*, 6 Med. L. Reptr. 1497 (U.S. 1980).

[35]Steven W. Colford, "Bush FTC May Clamp Down on Ads," *Advertising Age* (April 17, 1989):63.

TABLE 2.2   IMPORTANT ADVERTISING LEGISLATION
Pure Food and Drug Act (1906)   Forbids the manufacture, sale, or transport of adulterated or fraudulently labeled foods and drugs in interstate commerce. Supplanted by the Food, Drug, and Cosmetic Act of 1938; amended by Food Additives Amendment in 1958 and Kefauver-Harris Amendment in 1962.
Federal Trade Commission Act (1914)   Establishes the commission, a body of specialists with broad powers to investigate and to issue cease-and-desist orders to enforce Section 5, which declares that "unfair methods of competition in commerce are unlawful."
Wheeler-Lea Amendment (1938)   Prohibits unfair and deceptive acts and practices regardless of whether competition is injured; places advertising of foods and drugs under FTC jurisdiction.
Lanham Act (1947)   Provides protection for trademarks (slogans and brand names) from competitors and also encompasses false advertising.
Magnuson-Moss Warranty/FTC Improvement Act (1975)   Authorizes the FTC to determine rules concerning consumer warranties and provides for consumer access to means of redress, such as the "class action" suit. Also expands FTC regulatory powers over unfair or deceptive acts or practices and allows it to require restitution for deceptively written warranties costing the consumer more than $5.
FTC Improvement Act (1980)   Provides the House of Representatives and Senate jointly with veto power over FTC regulation rules. Enacted to limit FTC's powers to regulate "unfairness" issues in designing trade regulation rules on advertising.

Reprinted with permission from *Advertising Age*, Copyright Crain Communications Inc.

In June 1995, Bill Clinton's candidate, Robert Pitofsky, was appointed as the new chairperson of the FTC. Pitofsky is former Georgetown University Law School dean and former director of the commission's Bureau of Consumer Protection. At his first address to the American Advertising Federation, Pitofsky proclaimed himself generally satisfied with the state of national advertising, and talked of other commission initiatives and interests, including global advertising, monitoring the news media, and fraudulent financial schemes.[36]

Another outcome of the soft FTC years was the development of the National Association of Attorneys General, an organization determined to regulate advertising at the state level. Members of this organization have been successfully bringing suits in their respective states against such advertising giants as Coca-Cola, Kraft, and Campbell Soup.[37] Most recently, a number of attorneys generals have led the way against the tobacco industry and supporting the advertising restrictions discussed earlier.

THE FTC AND ADVERTISERS

Regardless of the philosophy of a given administration, the very existence of a regulatory agency like the FTC influences the behavior of advertisers.

Although most cases never reach the FTC, advertisers prefer not to run the risk of a long legal involvement with the agency. Advertisers, are also conscious that competitors, with a lot of consumer dollars at stake, may be quick to complain to an appropriate agency about a questionable advertisement. As was suggested in an editorial in *Advertising Age:*

> We've long since agreed that lies, deception, and fraud are beyond debate. No, ethics in advertising goes far beyond that. To the study of fine-linesmanship of what constitutes "weasel-wording" and what constitutes the whole truth. . . . If the copy stretches the truth even by a hair, or can be misinterpreted by anyone exposed to it, find another way. Chances are you'll end up with a stronger, more believable, more persuasive product presentation. And isn't that what good advertising is all about anyway?[38]

Ultimately, most advertisers want their customers to remain happy and pleased with their products and advertising, so they take every precaution to make sure their messages are not deceptive.

FTC CONCERNS WITH ADVERTISING

DECEPTION

PRINCIPLE Data must be on file to substantiate claims made by advertisers.

Deceptive advertising is a major focus of the FTC. Some of the activities that the commission has identified as deceptive are deceptive pricing, false criticisms of competing products, deceptive guarantees, ambiguous statements, and false testimonials. Until recently, the legal standard of deceptiveness involved judging only that an advertisement had the *capacity* to deceive consumers, not that it had actually done so. In 1983 the FTC changed the standard used to determine deception. The current policy contains three basic elements:

1. Where there is representation, omission, or practice, there must be a high probability that it will mislead the consumer.

---

[36]Rance Crain, "Pitofsky's FTC Enlists Ad Execs," *Advertising Age* (June 19, 1995):1, 8.

[37]Steven W. Colford, "FTC Warns Agencies; Eyes Tobacco, Cable," *Advertising Age* (March 12, 1990):6; "Attorney General's Office Investigates Advertising Claims," *Marketing News* (February 29, 1988):16.

[38]Win Roll, "A Valuable Lesson in Integrity," *Advertising Age* (May 25, 1987):18.

2. The perspective of the "reasonable consumer" is used to judge deception. The FTC tests "reasonableness" by looking at whether the consumer's interpretation or reaction to an advertisement is reasonable.

3. The deception must lead to material injury. In other words, the deception must influence consumers' decision making about products and services.[39]

This new policy makes deception more difficult to prove. It also creates uncertainty for advertisers, who must wait for congressional hearings and court cases to discover what the FTC will permit.

In March 1995, the FTC charged that the Home Shopping Network, Inc. was broadcasting deceptive claims about several vitamin and stop-smoking products. In its first charge ever against a television shopping channel, the FTC posited that a 1993 program on the Home Shopping Network made health claims about avoiding colds, curing hangovers, and stopping smoking that were not backed by scientific evidence. The charges followed unsuccessful negotiations toward an out-of-court settlement.

Home Shopping Network said it refused to settle the case because it feels it's being treated differently than other retail companies. Manufacturers, and not retailers, should bear primary responsibility for the kind of rigorous scientific testing required by the FTC's complaint, the company noted.[40]

REASONABLE BASIS FOR MAKING A CLAIM

The advertiser should have a reasonable basis for making a claim about product performance. This involves having data on file to substantiate any claims made in the advertising.

Determining the reasonableness of a claim is done on a case-by-case basis. The FTC has suggested that the following factors be examined:

1. Type and specificity of claim made
2. Type of product
3. Possible consequences of the false claim
4. Degree of reliance by consumers on the claims
5. The type and accessibility of evidence available for making the claim[41]

RICO SUITS

One of the most serious legal issues facing advertisers has been the recent application of the Racketeer Influenced and Corrupt Organizations Act (RICO) to false advertising lawsuits. Originally designed in 1970 to help curb fraud and organized crime, the broadly worded statute became an increasingly attractive legal weapon against advertisers in late 1989 after it was used in a false advertising suit against Ralston-Purina. Because losing a RICO suit means triple damages, legal costs, and the stigma of being labeled a "mobster," Ralston-Purina agreed to settle.

In early 1991 there were at least six RICO suits pending against companies. Coors was charged with falsely advertising Coors beer as being made from Rocky Mountain spring water, and CPC International was charged with false claims that Mazola corn oil products could lower serum cholesterol. Mobil Corporation was charged with false package labeling, advertising and promoting Hefty trash bags as biodegradable, and using sales proceeds to continue a faulty marketing campaign. The charge was dismissed, as was the claim that the relationship between

---

[39]"Letter to Congress Explaining FTC's New Deception Policy," *Advertising Compliance Service* (Westport, CT: Meckler Publishing, November 21, 1983) and Ivan Preston, "A Review of the Literature":2–37.

[40]Bob Drummond, "Home Shopping Charged With False Advertising by FTC," *The Denver Post* (March 4, 1995):C8.

[41]*Federal Trade Commission v. Raladam Company*, 283 U.S. 643 (1931).

Mobil and its ad agency Wells, Rich, Greene, New York (WRG) was unlawful. According to the RICO criterion, it is unlawful for someone employed or associated with an enterprise affecting interstate commerce to participate in the enterprise's affairs through racketeering activity. Mobil's relationship with WRG did not satisfy the definition of an enterprise.

A more recent application of RICO occurred in 1994 when seven antitobacco congressmen asked the Justice Department to examine whether or not tobacco markets, perhaps aided by their advertising and public relations agencies, trade associations, and lobbyists, knowingly misled the public and Congress about the health hazards of tobacco. The prospect of a Justice Department investigation into possible criminal or racketeering conduct silenced the tobacco industry. This investigation continues today.[42]

RICO was enacted to prevent organized crime from taking illegal money and putting it into a legal enterprise and the taking of control of an innocent enterprise by racketeers. The *Mobil* ruling may be an indication that the proliferation of such suits may be decreasing. The concern over RICO suits is that they may reduce advertisers' inclination to settle regulatory disputes with federal or state agencies through consent decrees. Advertisers fear that the terms and admissions from these settlements will be used against them in subsequent RICO suits. Congress has attempted to stem the use of RICO suits with legislation, based on the shakiness of the argument that the ads in question, and only the ads, caused the consumers to purchase the product or service.[43] Legislation to reduce the application of RICO was introduced by Representative William J. Hughes in 1991. Critics were concerned, however, that reducing the power of RICO in any way would also reduce its ability to affect organized crime. The bill did not pass.[44] Although courts dismissed the spate of RICO lawsuits major advertisers faced in the early 1990s, the threat remains, if for no other reasons than the cost of losing—treble damages, all attorney fees, and the stigma of a racketeering conviction.

COMPARATIVE ADVERTISING

PRINCIPLE Comparative advertising is supported as a means of providing more information to consumers.

The FTC supports comparative advertising as a way of providing more information to consumers. A substantial percentage of all television commercials use a comparative strategy. The commission requires that comparative claims, like other claims, be substantiated by the advertiser. Comparative advertising is considered deceptive unless the comparisons are based on fact, the differences advertised are statistically significant, the comparisons involve meaningful issues, and the comparisons are to meaningful competitors (see Table 2.3).

ENDORSEMENTS

A popular advertising strategy involves the use of a spokesperson who endorses the brand (see Chapter 8). Because consumers often rely on these endorsements when making purchase decisions, the FTC has concentrated on commercials that use this approach. Endorsers must be qualified by experience or training to make judgments, and they must actually use the product. If endorsers are comparing

---

[42]Steven W. Colford, "Nicotine Fit," *Advertising Age* (June 27, 1994):1.

[43]Steven W. Colford, "Mobil's RICO Victory Bolsters Ad Industry," *Advertising Age* (December 10, 1990):1, 59; Steven W. Colford and Ira Teinwitz, "Coors, CPC to Fight RICO Ad Charges," *Advertising Age* (October 22, 1990); and Barbara Hobsonback, "RICO Suit Looms: Volvo Probes Slow," *Adweek* (December 3, 1990):21.

[44]Jonathan M. Moses, "Guiliani Works Other Side of RICO Street," *The Wall Street Journal* (September 16, 1992):B8.

TABLE 2.3	AMERICAN ASSOCIATION OF ADVERTISING AGENCIES' TEN GUIDELINES FOR COMPARATIVE ADVERTISING

1. The intent and connotation of the ad should be to inform and never to discredit or unfairly attack competitors, competing products, or services.

2. When a competitive product is named, it should be one that exists in the marketplace as significant competition.

3. The competition should be fairly and properly identified but never in a manner or tone of voice that degrades the competitive product or service.

4. The advertising should compare related or similar properties or ingredients of the product, dimension to dimension, feature to feature.

5. The identification should be for honest comparison purposes and not simply to upgrade by association.

6. If a competitive test is conducted, it should be done by an objective testing service.

7. In all cases the test should be supportive of all claims made in the advertising that are based on the test.

8. The advertising should never use partial results or stress insignificant differences to cause the consumer to draw an improper conclusion.

9. The property being compared should be significant in terms of value or usefulness of the product to the consumer.

10. Comparisons delivered through the use of testimonials should not imply that the testimonial is more than one individual's thought unless that individual represents a sample of the majority viewpoint.

Source: James B. Astrachan, "When to Name a Competitor," *Adweek* (May 23, 1988):24. Copyright American Association of Advertising Agencies. Reprinted by permission.

competing brands, they must have tried those brands as well. Those who endorse a product improperly may be liable if the FTC determines there is a deception. Determining whether or not the endorsement is authentic is not easy. Is Michael Jordan a regular Coke drinker? Does Shaquille O'Neill really crave Pepsi? Are either qualified to judge the quality of the product? There is also the problem of implicit endorsement when a celebrity does a voice-over for a television commercial. Tom Selleck is the voice behind AT&T, Demi Moore speaks for Keds shoes, and Jack Lemmon represents Honda.

DEMONSTRATIONS

Product demonstrations in television advertising must not mislead consumers. A claim that is demonstrated must be accurately shown. This mandate is especially difficult for advertisements containing food products because such factors as hot studio lights and the length of time needed to shoot the commercial can make the product look quite unappetizing. For example, because milk looks gray on television, advertisers often substitute a mixture of glue and water. The question is whether or not the demonstration falsely upgrades the consumer's perception of the advertised brand. The FTC evaluates this kind of deception on a case-by-case basis.

One technique some advertisers use to sidestep restrictions on demonstrations is to insert disclaimers or supers, verbal or written words that appear in the ad that indicate exceptions to the claim being made. One recent example is a 30-second spot for Chrysler's Jeep Cherokee that starts out cleanly and concisely, with bold shots of the vehicle and music swelling in the background. Suddenly the message is less clear; for several seconds five different, often lengthy disclaimers flash on the screen in tiny, eyestraining type, including "See dealers for details and guaranteed claim form" and "Deductibles and restrictions apply."[45]

---

[45]Thomas R. King, "More Fine Print Clouds Message of Commercials," *The Wall Street Journal* (July 12, 1990):B1.

REMEDIES FOR DECEPTIVE AND UNFAIR ADVERTISING

The most common sources of complaints concerning deceptive or unfair advertising practices are competitors, the public, and the FTC's own monitors. If a complaint is found to be justified, the commission can follow several courses of action. Until 1970 cease-and-desist orders and fines were the FTC's major weapons against deception, but the commission has developed alternative remedies since then, including corrective advertising, substantiation of advertising claims, and consumer redress.

CONSENT DECREES

Consent Decree: An order given by the FTC and signed by an advertiser, agreeing to stop running a deceptive ad.

A **consent decree** represents the first step in the regulation process after the FTC determines that an ad is deceptive. The FTC simply notifies the advertiser of its finding and asks the advertiser to sign a consent decree agreeing to stop the deceptive practice. Most advertisers do sign the decree, thereby avoiding the bad publicity and the possible fine of $10,000 per day for refusing to do so.

CEASE-AND-DESIST ORDERS

Cease-and-Desist Order: A legal order requiring an advertiser to stop its unlawful practices.

When the advertiser refuses to sign the consent decree and the FTC determines that the deception is substantial, a **cease-and-desist order** will be issued. The process leading to an issuance of a cease-and-desist order is similar to a court trial. An administrative law judge presides, FTC staff attorneys represent the commission, and the accused parties are entitled to representation by their lawyers. If the administrative judge decides in favor of the FTC, an order is issued requiring the respondents to "cease-and-desist" their unlawful practices. The order can be appealed to the full five-member commission.

CORRECTIVE ADVERTISING

Corrective Advertising: A remedy required by the FTC in which an advertiser that produced misleading messages is required to issue factual information to offset these messages.

PRINCIPLE Corrective advertising is required when the FTC determines that an ad has created lasting false impressions.

Corrective advertising is required by the FTC when consumer research determines that lasting false beliefs have been perpetuated by an advertising campaign. Under this remedy, the offending firm is ordered to produce messages that correct any deceptive impressions created in the consumer's mind. The purpose of corrective advertising is not to punish a firm but to prevent that firm from continuing to deceive consumers. The FTC may require a firm to run corrective advertising even if the campaign in question has been discontinued.

The landmark case involving corrective advertising was *Warner-Lambert* v. *FTC* in 1977. According to the FTC, Warner-Lambert's 50-year-old campaign for Listerine mouthwash had been deceiving customers into thinking that Listerine was able to prevent sore throats and colds or to lessen their severity. The company was ordered to run a corrective advertising campaign, mostly on television, for 16 months at a cost of $10 million. Interestingly, even after the corrective campaign ran its course, 42 percent of Listerine users continued to believe the mouthwash was being advertised as a remedy for sore throats and colds, and 57 percent of users rated cold and sore throat effectiveness as a key reason for purchasing the brand.[46] These results raised doubts about the effectiveness of corrective advertising, as consumers may continue to remember earlier advertising claims without integrating the "details" corrective advertising may supply. However, the *Warner-Lambert* case remains significant because for the first time the FTC was given the

---

[46]William Wilke, Dennis L. McNeil, and Michael B. Mazis, "Marketing's 'Scarlett Letter': The Theory and Practice of Corrective Advertising," *Journal of Marketing* (Spring 1984):26.

Inside Advertising

Suzanne Makowsky, Worldwide Recruitment Manager, McCann-Erickson Worldwide, New York

It all began the first day of my MBA in the advertising campaign class at George Washington University. I took the class as a last resort; it was the only marketing course I had not already taken as an undergraduate. Professor Maddox informed the class that we had to do a group project, or join her advanced advertising campaign class as an alternative.

I eagerly signed up for the extra class as I was going to be a participant in the General Motor's National Student Marketing Competition. I also figured it would look good on my résumé. I found that working as a member of a dedicated team at all hours around the clock was something I thoroughly enjoyed. The most exciting part was that GWU won the competition nationally. This was it, I made up my mind; I'm going to be in advertising; New York here I come!

I began my career at McCann-Erickson in a part of the advertising business that not too many students think of—as an international assistant media planner on Coca-Cola. I then became the international media planner on RJ Reynolds, and shortly thereafter, the account executive. RJR was the perfect account, as it provided me with the opportunity to travel to the various McCann offices in Europe and become familiar with the McCann worldwide network. After two years, I worked on USAir to provide me with a more rounded experience by adding a domestic account to my international background.

I briefly left McCann to work as an account supervisor at a mid-sized agency, then returned as the worldwide recruitment manager. I felt that my personality and experience were better suited to work in human resources at an international level. I have three primary functions that receive my undivided attention on a daily basis.

As the worldwide recruiter, my first role is to provide the agency with access to a wide range of talent both in the United States and in other countries for assignments throughout the McCann network. I work with our general managers and human resources managers around the world to locate executives (internally and externally) who have what it takes to work in various markets. For example, last year we located and hired several executives to work in Russia, Poland, Vietnam, Belgium, and Colombia. It is important to keep in mind that McCann-Erickson has over 200 offices in over 100 countries, with over 43 global advertising clients handled in ten or more countries. It is essential that we have the ability to locate and relocate talent efficiently and effectively.

Second, I am the human resources person for the international groups (media, account, creative) that are based in New York. Basically, this is a function of recruiting, interviewing, hiring, sometimes firing, and making evaluations and salary reviews. These groups work primarily on Coca-Cola, Lucent Technologies, AT&T, UPS, Gillette, International Ferrero, Chesebrough-Ponds International, and Reckitt & Coleman to name just a few.

I also supervise and coordinate the Eugene Kummel Scholarship Program. This program is designed to provide our future leaders with experience outside their home country so that they may better serve our agency portfolio of global clients. This program enables our young professionals, from any McCann agency, to work for a four- to six-month period in a different country. Through this learning experience, scholars develop greater sensitivity to foreign cultures, an appreciation of the McCann network, and a more global advertising perspective. It is our hope that Kummel Scholars will go on to develop long and successful careers as leaders of our company.

Through this program, we try to move scholars between developing markets and key developed centers, with particular attention to major accounts. For instance, in 1996 I had a media planner from Seoul, Korea work as a planner on AT&T in New York. It was through this experience that she is now able to educate her office in Seoul on media planning in the United States. Other interesting movements included Prague to San Francisco to work on Nestlé, Melbourne, Australia to Detroit to work on General Motors, and New York to Bucharest, Romania to work on Vaseline Intensive Care.

Each day begins with calls to Europe followed by afternoon calls to Latin America, and evening calls to AsiaPacific for updates on current issues and movements around the world. My day revolves around all of these areas, with small breaks in between to reply to applicants and meet with our employees. At the end of the day, I return calls, faxes, and e-mails from around the world and start over again the next morning.

Nominated by Professor Lynda Maddox, George Washington University

power to apply retrospective remedies and to attempt to restrict future deceptions. In addition, the Supreme Court rejected the argument that corrective advertising violates the advertiser's First Amendment rights.

$\mathcal{FTC\ H}$INTS

It should be obvious by now that creating ads that are FTC-proof is not easy. In 1993 the FTC published a bulletin titled "Law Enforcement Achievements and Ongoing Projects." It represents a compilation of ads that prompted action by the commission during the period from October 1, 1989 through March 31, 1993. Among the FTC's targets: an antibaldness product employing the impressive-sounding "Helsinki Formula"; another company claiming to have cures for baldness and cellulite; yet another firm proffering cures for baldness and impotence; a marketer of bulletproof vests claiming certification under government standards; a grapefruit marketer making health claims for the fruit; and weight-loss claims for bee pollen.[47]

THE LEGAL RESPONSIBILITY OF THE AGENCY

With the resurgence of the FTC has come a new solution for deception—making the ad agency liable. To quote former FTC Chairperson Janet Steiger, "An agency that is involved in advertising and promoting a product is not free from responsibility for the content of the claims, whether they are express or implied. You will find the commission staff looking more closely at the extent of advertising agency involvement."[48] Essentially an agency is liable for deceptive advertising along with the advertiser when the agency was an active participant in the preparation of the ad and knew or had reason to know that it was false or deceptive.

Three recent examples point to the extent to which the FTC has taken this warning seriously. In 1990 the FTC slapped sanctions on Lewis Galoob Toys and its agency for ads that the FTC said showed toys doing things they really couldn't do. Under terms of the consent agreement, Galoob and its agency, Towne, Silverstein, Rotter, New York, are prohibited from misrepresenting a toy's ability to move without human assistance. In addition, future ads must disclose that assembly is required when such a toy is shown fully assembled in a commercial.[49]

In 1991 a group of state attorney generals reached a settlement with Pfizer and ad agency Ally & Gargano. Pfizer and Ally agreed to stop making a number of deceptive claims in their advertising about the plaque-reducing qualities of Pfizer's Plax mouthwash, and Pfizer agreed to pay the states a total of $70,000 in investigative costs.[50]

In 1992 Judge Kimba Wood found that Wilkinson, the maker of the Ultra Glide shaving system, intended to make misleading claims and enjoined the campaign. The court awarded Gillette damages of nearly $1 million, and then it assessed matching damages against Wilkinson's agency, Friedman Benjamin.[51]

---

[47]"How to Get Yourself on the Wrong Side of the FTC," *Adweek* (May 10, 1993):18.

[48]Steven W. Colford, "FTC Warns Agencies; Eyes Tobacco, Cable," *Advertising Age* (March 12, 1990):6.

[49]Steven W. Colford, "FTC Hits Galoob, Agency for Ads," *Advertising Age* (December 10, 1990):62.

[50]"Ally in Plax Settlement," *The Wall Street Journal* (February 12, 1991):B4.

[51]Stephen P. Durchslag, "Agency Liability Extends to False Advertising Claims," *PROMO* (October 1992):17.

The following is a list of tips to avoid legal pitfalls in advertising that one law firm offers agencies:

1.   Early in the creative process, get written permission from the appropriate people if an ad carries the potential to violate copyright and/or privacy laws.
2.   During production, make sure no one hires a person to sound like, look like, or otherwise represent a celebrity.
3.   Before the shoot, get the producers' affidavit signed to substantiate that demonstrations are not mockups.
4.   Have regular seminars with a lawyer to update staff on specifically how to stay within the limits of advertising law.[52]

SUBSTANTIATING ADVERTISING CLAIMS

In 1971 the FTC initiated a policy that required advertisers to validate any claims when requested by the commission. Advertisers must have a "reasonable basis" for making a claim. It is the responsibility of the advertiser to show the reasonableness of claim; it is *not* up to the FTC to disprove a claim's validity. Documentation may be based on a variety of sources, including scientific research and the opinions of experts.

CONSUMER REDRESS

The Magnuson-Moss Warranty-FTC Improvement Act of 1975 empowers the FTC to obtain consumer redress in cases where a person or a firm engages in deceptive practices. The commission can order any of the following: cancellation or reformation of contracts; refund of money or return of property; payment of damages; and public notification.

FOOD AND DRUG ADMINISTRATION

Food and Drug Administration (FDA): A federal regulatory agency that oversees package labeling and ingredient listings for food and drugs.

Federal Communications Commission (FCC): A federal agency that regulates broadcast media and has the power to eliminate messages, including ads, that are deceptive or in poor taste.

Two other major government agencies deal with advertising-related concerns: the **Food and Drug Administration (FDA)** and the **Federal Communications Commission (FCC).** The FDA is the regulatory division of the Department of Health and Human Services. It oversees package labeling and ingredient listings for food and drugs and determines the safety and purity of foods and cosmetics. Although not directly involved with advertising, the FDA provides advice to the FTC and has a major impact on the overall marketing of food, cosmetics, and drugs.

FEDERAL COMMUNICATIONS COMMISSION

The FCC was formed in 1934 to protect the public interest with regard to broadcast communication. It has limited control over broadcast advertising through its authority to issue and revoke licenses to broadcasting stations. The FCC is concerned with radio and television stations and networks, and it has the power to eliminate messages, including ads, that are deceptive or in poor taste. The agency monitors only those advertisements that have been the subject of complaints and works closely with the FTC with regard to false and deceptive advertising. The FCC takes actions against the media, whereas the FTC is concerned with advertisers and agencies.

---

[52] Barbara Holsomback, "Ad Agencies Feel Piercing Glare of Watchdogs," *Adweek* (December 3, 1990):18.

OTHER FEDERAL AGENCIES

Other federal agencies are involved in the regulation of advertising, although most are limited by the type of advertising, product, or medium. For example, the Postal Service regulates direct-mail and magazine advertising and has control over the areas of obscenity, lottery, and fraud. Consumers who receive advertisements in the mail that they consider sexually offensive can request that no more mail be delivered from that sender. The postmaster general also has the power to withhold mail that promotes a lottery. Fraud can include any number of activities that are questionable, such as implausible get-rich-quick schemes.

The Bureau of Alcohol, Tobacco, and Firearms (BATF) within the Treasury Department both regulates deception in advertising and establishes labeling requirements for the liquor industry. This agency's power comes from its authority to issue and revoke annual operating permits for distillers, wine merchants, and brewers. Because there is a danger that public pressure could result in banning all advertisements for alcoholic beverages, the liquor industry strives to maintain relatively tight control on its advertising.

In one recent case, the BATF investigated whether or not Miller Brewing Co. is basing the marketing of an ice beer—Molson Ice—on the product's higher alcohol content. It is against federal law to trumpet a beer's alcoholic kick in advertising.

The Patent Office, under the Lanham Trade-Mark Act of 1947, oversees registration of trademarks, which include both brand names and corporate or store names as well as their identifying symbols. This registration process protects unique trademarks from infringement by competitors. Because trademarks are critical communication devices for products and services, they are important in advertising.

Finally, the Library of Congress provides controls for copyright protection. Legal copyrights give creators a monopoly on their creations for a certain time. Advertising is a competitive business where "me too" ads abound. Copyrighting of coined words, illustrations, characters, and photographs can offer some measure of protection from other advertisers who borrow too heavily from their competitors.

Certain state laws also regulate unfair and deceptive business practices. These laws are important supplements to federal laws because of the sometimes limited resources and jurisdiction of the FTC and the Justice Department. Because these laws are so numerous and diverse, we cannot begin to examine them in this chapter.

$\mathscr{S}$ELF-$\mathscr{R}$EGULATION

Societal Marketing Concept: A concept that requires balancing the company, consumer, and public interest.

Based on the discussion thus far, it would appear that all advertising and advertisers must be carefully governed because without that control all ads would be full of lies. Nothing could be further from the truth, however. For the great majority of advertisers, a societal marketing approach is followed. Philip Kotler defines the **societal marketing concept** as follows: The organization's task is to determine the needs, wants, and interests of target markets and to deliver the desired satisfactions more effectively and efficiently than its competitors in a way that preserves or enhances the consumer's and society's well-being. This requires a careful balance between company profits, consumer-want satisfaction, and public interest.[53]

PRINCIPLE Self-regulation encourages voluntary withdrawal of deceptive advertising.

Admittedly, this is not an easy balance to maintain. Yet, advertisers realize that everything they do is carefully scrutinized by millions of consumers and a

---

[53]Philip Kotler, *Marketing Management: Analysis, Planning, Implementation, and Control*, 7th ed. (Upper Saddle River, NJ: Prentice Hall, Inc. 1991):25–26.

host of agencies. Therefore, it has become necessary for advertisers to regulate themselves even more stringently than do the government agencies discussed earlier. Using this system of self-regulation ensures that societal marketing is more likely to become a reality.

J.J. Boddewyn offers a classification for different levels of self-regulation: (1) self-discipline—norms are developed, used, and enforced by the firm itself, (2) pure self-regulation—norms are developed, used, and enforced by the industry itself, (3) co-opted self-regulation—the industry, on its own volition, involves nonindustry people (for example, consumer and government representatives, independent members of the public, experts) on the development, application, and enforcement of norms, and (4) negotiated self-regulation—the industry voluntarily negotiates the development, use, and enforcement of norms with some outside body (for example, government department or a consumer association).[54] We will discuss examples of the first two categories.

SELF-DISCIPLINE

Virtually all major advertisers and advertising agencies have in-house mechanisms to review ads for both ethical and legal problems. A number of U.S. advertisers (Colgate-Palmolive, General Foods, AT&T) have developed their own codes of behavior and criteria for the acceptance of advertisements. This practice is accepted internationally as well. In the Netherlands, industry has encouraged the appointment in all agencies, advertisers, and media of an "ethical officer" responsible for overseeing the application of the Dutch Advertising Code as well as general principles of ethical behavior. In Swedish advertising agencies, an executive trained and experienced in marketing law and known as the "responsible editor" reviews for acceptability all the advertisements and other materials produced.

At a minimum, advertisers and agencies will have every element of a proposed ad evaluated by an in-house committee, or lawyers, or both. When one considers how closely every word, picture, and intonation is critiqued, it is somewhat amazing that any ads still get in trouble.

NATIONAL AGENCIES

In the case of both advertisers and advertising agencies, the most effective attempts at self-regulation have come through the Advertising Review Council and the Better Business Bureau. In 1971 the National Advertising Review Council was established by several professional advertising associations in conjunction with the Council of Better Business Bureaus. The main purpose of the council is to negotiate voluntary withdrawal of national advertising that professionals consider to be deceptive. The National Advertising Division (NAD) of the Council of Better Business Bureaus and the National Advertising Review Board (NARB) are the two operating arms of the National Advertising Review Council.

NAD

The NAD is a full-time agency made up of people from the field of advertising. It evaluates complaints that are submitted by consumers, consumer groups, industrial organizations, and advertising firms. The NAD also does its own monitoring. After a complaint is received, the NAD may ask the advertiser in question to substantiate claims made in the advertisement. If such substantiation is deemed inadequate, the advertiser is requested either to change or to withdraw the offending ad. When a satisfactory resolution cannot be found, the case is referred to the NARB.

---

[54]J.J. Boddewyn, "Advertising Self-Regulation: Private Government and Agent of Public Policy," *Journal of Public Policy and Marketing* (1985):129–41.

Occasionally, the NAD refers a case to the FTC. This happened recently in the dispute between Johnson & Johnson's Tylenol and American Home Products Corp.'s Advil. It was passed on to the FTC because Johnson & Johnson did not feel the NAD was the appropriate forum for settling the dispute.

NARB

The NARB is a 50-member regulatory group that represents national advertisers, advertising agencies, and other professional fields. When a case is appealed to the NARB, a five-person panel is formed that consists of three advertisers, one agency person, and one public representative. This panel reviews the complaint and the NAD staff findings and holds hearings to let the advertiser present its case. If the case remains unresolved after the process, the NARB can (1) publicly identify the advertiser and the facts about the case and (2) refer the complaint to the appropriate government agency (usually the FTC). Although neither the NAD nor the NARB has any real power other than threatening to invite governmental intervention, these groups have been relatively effective in controlling cases of deception and misleading advertising.

LOCAL REGULATION: BBB

At the local level self-regulation has been supported by the Better Business Bureau (BBB). The BBB functions much like the national regulatory agencies, and in addition provides local businesses with advice concerning the legal aspects of advertising. The origin of the bureau can be traced to the truth-in-advertising campaign sponsored by the American Advertising Federation in 1911. Since that time more than 240 local and national bureaus, made up of advertisers, agencies, and media, have screened hundreds of thousands of advertisements for possible violation of truth and accuracy. Although the BBB has no legal power, it does receive and investigate complaints and maintain files on violators. It also assists local law enforcement officials in prosecuting violators.

MEDIA REGULATION AND ADVERTISING

PRINCIPLE Media can refuse to accept advertising that violates standards of truth or good taste.

The media attempt to regulate advertising by screening and rejecting ads that violate their standards of truth and good taste. For example, *Reader's Digest* does not accept tobacco and liquor ads, and many magazines and television stations will not show condom ads. Each individual medium has the discretion to accept or reject a particular ad. In the case of the major televisions networks, the ARC's advertising standards and guidelines serve as the primary standard. The Concepts and Applications Box details self-regulation of the newest medium — interactive.

A FINAL CONSIDERATION

It is clear that advertising, as a high-profile industry, will remain extremely susceptible to controlling legislation and the criticisms of the general public. Rather than lamenting such scrutiny and becoming defensive, advertisers would be wise to take the initiative and establish individual ethical parameters that anticipate and even go beyond the complaints. Such a proactive stance will facilitate the creative process and avoid the kind of disasters that result from violating the law or offending certain publics.

In addition, as advertisers, agencies, and media become more and more global, it will be imperative that the players understand the ethical standards and laws in which they operate. For example, in Hungary tobacco ads have been banned since the Communist occupation and are still on the books. Advertisers who violate the code of conduct in Brazil can be fined up to $500,000 or given up

CONCEPTS AND APPLICATIONS

ROPING IN THE WORLD WIDE WEB

One of the most serious debates raging these days is the control of the various online media—especially the World Wide Web. The question is: should the FTC or the industry itself govern this evolving media?

Recently, FTC chairperson Robert Pitofsky suggested that there should be voluntary industry codes rather than FTC rules. "We are not shying away from regulations, but what happens if [a Web site's communication] is not deceptive or unfair?" asked Mr. Pitofsky, noting the FTC's legal areas and extending them would require congressional legislation. He further noted that he saw an apparent consensus among consumer and industry groups that worry about privacy—together with those about convincing the public of the Web's viability as a commercial medium—necessitate adoption of new ethical standards for Web sites. Furthermore, new technology will allow consumers to restrict their own access to sites that don't comply.

Major industry groups proposed including significant restrictions in the way marketers use the Web to get information from consumers and the information they can get. Among them:

- A ban on unsolicited e-mail that can't be automatically screened out.
- Full and prominent disclosure of both the marketer's identity and the use for which information is being gathered in every communication.
- Rights of consumers to not only bar marketers from selling or sharing information collected but to review the personal information collected.

These recommendations are aimed at adults. Much of the most controversial suggestions seek to restrict marketers' actions when the sites or pages are aimed at children. The Center for Media Education, in partnership with the Consumer Federation of America, urged guidelines that would require marketers to get verifiable parental consent before seeking any information used to identify a child. Marketers who clearly identified themselves could sell aggregate information without parental consent under the proposal.

Source: Ira Teinowitz, "FTC Chairman Seeking Voluntary Web Rules," *Advertising Age* (June 10, 1996):42. Reprinted with permission from *Advertising Age*. Copyright Crain Communications Inc.

to a five-year prison sentence. This would certainly prompt an advertiser to be very careful. The smart advertiser follows the advice given by David Ogilvy, founder of Ogilvy & Mather: Never run an advertisement you would not want your family to see.

SUMMARY

- In general, the public and many advertisers feel advertising is unethical and hold a low opinion of advertising.
- Ethical questions about advertising revolve around three criteria: advocacy, accuracy, and acquisitiveness.
- The primary ethical issues facing advertising are: puffery, taste, stereotyping (of women, racial and ethnic groups, senior citizens, and baby boomers), communicating with children, controversial products, and subliminal advertising.
- The primary legal protection available to advertising is the First Amendment, and the level of protection has varied over time.
- The Federal Trade Commission is the most important government agency affecting advertising.
- The Federal Trade Commission deals with the following advertising legal issues: deception, reasonable basis for making a claim, RICO suits, comparative advertising, endorsements, and demonstrations.

- The FTC can initiate the following remedies for deceptive and unfair advertising: consent decrees, cease-and-desist orders, and corrective advertising.
- An ad agency can be held legally liable if the agency was an active participant in the preparation of the ad and knew or had reason to know that it was false or deceptive.
- A number of other government agencies influence advertising, including: the Food and Drug Administration, Federal Communications Commission, the Postal Service, the Bureau of Alcohol, Tobacco, and Firearms, and others.
- Advertising engages in a great deal of self-regulation, and at various levels: self-discipline, pure self-regulation, co-opted self-regulation, and negotiated self-regulation.

QUESTIONS

1. Two local agencies are in fierce contention for a major client in Hillsboro. The final presentations are three days away when Sue Geners, an account executive for the Adcom Group, learns from her sister-in-law that the creative director for the rival agency has serious personal problems. His son has entered a drug rehabilitation program and his wife has filed for a divorce. Because this information comes from inside the clinic, Sue knows it's very unlikely that anyone in the business side of Hillsboro has any knowledge of this. Should she inform Adcom management? If she does, should Adcom warn the prospective client that a key person in the rival's agency's plans will be seriously limited for months to come?

2. Sue Geners, our account executive from the preceding question also has a quandary of her own. Adcom keeps very strict hourly records on its accounts for billing and cost accounting purposes. Sue has an old friend with an Adcom client that needs some strong promotional strategy. The client, however, is very small and cannot afford the hours that Sue would have to charge. Should Sue do the work and charge those hours to one of her large clients? Should she turn down her friend? What should she do?

3. Zack Wilson is the advertising manager for the campus newspaper. He is looking over a layout for a promotion for a spring break vacation package. The headline says "Absolutely the Finest Deal Available This Spring—You'll Have The Best Time Ever If You'll Join Us in Boca." The newspaper has a solid reputation for not running advertising with questionable claims and promises. Should Zack accept or reject this ad?

4. The Dimento Game Company has a new video game on basketball. To promote it, "Slammer" Aston, an NBA star is signed to do the commercial. In it Aston is shown with the game controls as he speaks these lines: "This is the most challenging court game you've ever tried. It's all here—zones, man-to-man, pick and roll, even the alley oop. For me, this is the best game off-the-court." Is Aston's presentation an endorsement or is he a spokesperson? Should the FTC consider a complaint if Dimento uses this strategy?

5. What are the central issues in ethical decision making? Write a short evaluation of a current ad campaign utilizing three ethical criteria.

6. Think of an ad you have found deceptive or offensive. What bothered you about the ad? Should the media have carried it? Is it proper for the government or the advertising industry to act in cases like this? Why or why not?

7. There is a great deal of controversy surrounding subliminal advertising. Do you think subliminal advertising exists? If so, what do you believe are risks associated with this technique?

SUGGESTED CLASS PROJECT

Select three print ads that you feel contain one or more of the ethical issues discussed in this chapter. Ask five people (making sure they vary by gender, age, or background) how they feel about the ads. Conduct a mini-interview with each of your subjects; it would be helpful to have a list of questions prepared. Write a report on these opinions that follows the format of your questionnaire. Don't be afraid to draw your own conclusions. What differences or similarities do you see across the different target groups?

FURTHER READINGS

Armstrong, Gary M., and Judith L. Osanne, "An Evaluation of NAD/NARB: Purpose and Performance," *Journal of Advertising,* 12(1983):15–26.

Buchanan, Bruce, and Doron Goldman, "U.S. vs. Them: The Mindfold of Comparative Ads," *Harvard Business Review* (June 1989):38–50.

Rotzell, Kim G., and James E. Haefner, *Advertising in Contemporary Society* (Cincinnati, OH: South-Western Publishing, 1990).

Schudson, Michael, *Advertising: The Uneasy Persuasion* (New York: Basic Books, 1984).

Throughout the health-conscious 1990s, consumers continue to exhibit a preference for products that contain less fat, less salt, and less sugar. Comparing the nutritional value of food products has become easier since Congress passed the Nutrition and Labeling Act of 1990. Unfortunately, the mere presence of the proper label on a product doesn't necessarily guarantee that the package contains what the label says it does. In one recent case, executives of a Midwest orange juice manufacturer were found guilty of defrauding consumers over a period of more than ten years. The company added beet sugar and preservatives to the juice, even though the label said "pure orange juice from concentrate." The Food and Drug Administration launched an investigation after a government inspector saw an employee adding something to a vat of juice. The president of the company was ultimately fined $100,000 and sentenced to five years in prison.

The FDA's discovery was fortuitous because, until recently, it was very hard to detect whether or not a liquid food product contained illegal or unadvertised ingredients. In a more recent case, high technology helped finger the culprit. A new, highly accurate form of chemical analysis permits researchers to determine whether a juice sample is 100 percent juice or a combination of juice plus sugar and other additives. The test showed that apple juice marketed by the Mott's subsidiary of Cadbury Schweppes as "100% real fruit juice" actually contained at least 10 percent sugar water. The test also indicated that Cadbury's Holland House cooking wine was a blend of two parts sugar water and one part wine. When he learned of the findings, Dr. Michael Johnson of the Center for Science in the Public Interest said, "You would assume that it's really 100 percent red cooking wine. Cadbury's is cheating people on a massive scale."

Cadbury spokesperson Catherine Van Evans said that the company had recalled all of the suspect apple juice products from its warehouses. The recall did not extend to retailers, and the FDA had no evidence of health hazards to anyone who consumed the adulterated juice. Van Evans also blamed the problem on European suppliers that had put sugar in the apple juice without authorization from Cadbury's. Dr. Jacobson was skeptical of the spokesperson's claim. "These are multimillion dollar companies. It's their job to watch for this kind of thing," he said. Cadbury's woes were not over, however; several class action lawsuits have been filed against the company on behalf of consumers seeking compensation for being defrauded.

Video Source: "Gotcha! New Tests Detect Food Fraud," *20/20* (March 1, 1996). *Additional Sources:* Don Dzikowski, "Cadbury Recalls Apple Juice, Faces Lawsuit Over Wine," *Fairfield County Business Journal* (April 29, 1996):1; Kevin Ropp, "Juice Maker Cheats Consumers of $40 Million," *FDA Consumer* (January 1, 1994):35.

QUESTIONS

1. Do you believe the manufacturer's claim that the company was unaware of the deceptive practices of its European suppliers?

2. What should Cadbury's and other manufacturers do in the future to ensure that their food products are not adulterated? Do they need to take any additional steps to reassure consumers about product ingredients?

Advertising and the Marketing Process

CHAPTER OUTLINE

- Paring Down at P&G
- The Marketing Concept
- The 4Ps of Marketing
- Advertising and the Marketing Mix

CHAPTER OBJECTIVES

When you have completed this chapter, you should be able to:

- Understand the concept of marketing, and the role of advertising within the marketing strategy
- Appreciate the concept of the market and the four types of markets
- Explain the marketing concept and its evolution
- Explain and define the 4Ps of marketing and how they interface with advertising

$\mathcal{P}$ARING $\mathcal{D}$OWN AT $\mathcal{P}$&$\mathcal{G}$

Does the world really need 31 varieties of Head & Shoulders shampoo? Or 52 versions of Crest? Procter & Gamble Co., the world's preeminent marketer, has decided that the answer is no. After decades of spinning out new-and-improved this, lemon-freshened that, and extra-jumbo-size the other thing, P&G has decided that it sells too many things. Now, it has started doing the unthinkable: It's cutting back. P&G's U.S. product roster is a third shorter today than it was at the start of the decade. In hair care alone, it has slashed the number of items almost in half. Fewer shapes, sizes, packages, and formulas mean less choice for consumers. So sales went down, right? Wrong. Market share in hair care grew by nearly five points, to 56.5 percent, over the past five years. P&G's overall sales, powered by international expansion, have grown by a third in the same period.

P&G's drive to trim its product list is just one piece of a larger strategy of simplification. The company is now taking an ax to many of its marketing practices, hacking away at layers of complexity in a drive to cut costs, serve customers better, and expand globally. Besides just saying no to runaway product proliferation, it's standardizing formulas and packaging worldwide, selling marginal brands, cutting inefficient promotions, and curbing new-product launches. P&G is even putting its sacrosanct ad budget under the microscope to help shrink overall marketing costs from 25 percent today to 20 percent of revenues by the year 2000.

But although the drive to simplicity began as an exercise in old-fashioned cost cutting, P&G is looking for other benefits. It knows the thousands of supermarket products leave shoppers staggering down aisles in sensory overload, increasingly immune to marketing messages, indifferent to brands, and suspicious of pricing. Since so many of the 30,000 items in a typical supermarket offer niggling differences from each other, shoppers face numbing selection—but little in the way of real variety.

The upshot: Stores have been crammed with things that people never buy. Here are the startling statistics of that waste: Almost a quarter of the products in a typical supermarket sell fewer than one unit a month. On the other hand, just 9.6 percent of all personal care and household products account for 84.5 percent of sales. A lot of the rest go almost unnoticed by consumers.

As usual, P&G is something of a bellwether for the packaged-goods industry. The Cincinnati-based company is leading a broad movement among marketers as executives realize complexity alienates consumers and generates expensive and error-prone operations. "Complex processes are the work of the devil," in the words of reengineering guru Michael Hammer.[1]

The paring down at P&G points to the dynamic nature of marketing. It also suggests two other important ideas. First, advertising is just a part of the total marketing effort. Second, marketing strategies, including advertising, are not easily transferred from one culture to another. The purpose of this chapter is to provide a perspective on the marketing function and how it influences the advertising effort. This relationship underlies at a basic level the integrated marketing communication strategy introduced in Chapter 1. It also serves as a foundation for the rest of this book.

Marketing: Business activities that direct the exchange of goods and services between producers and consumers.

The American Marketing Association defines **marketing** as "the process of planning and executing the conception, pricing, promotion, and distribution of ideas, goods, and services to create exchanges that satisfy individual (customer) and organizational objectives."[2] Marketing can also be defined in terms of its ulti-

[1]Zachary Schiller, Gary Burns, and Karen Lowry Miller, "Make It Simple," *Business Week* (September 9, 1996):96–103.
[2]"AMA Board Approves New Marketing Definition," *Marketing News* (March 1, 1985):1.

mate business objectives; that is, marketing is a process intended to find, satisfy, and retain customers, while the business makes a profit. Although the exchange itself is the focus of the effort, marketing is a complicated process operating in a complex business environment. There are general principles that suggest how to best perform a marketing task, but every business customizes marketing to fit its particular situation.

The success of a given marketing effort depends on whether or not a *competitive advantage* for a product can be established in the minds of consumers. A competitive advantage is attributed to a product when a consumer makes the judgment that the product comes closer to satisfying his or her needs than does a competitor's product. A human need is a state of felt deprivation, such as hunger, shelter, a need for affection, knowledge, or self-expression. These needs can be rational or irrational. Harley-Davidson sells a great many motorcycles in Japan because of the irrational need of many Japanese to own any product made in the United States. Sometimes the consumer decides that none of the choices provided by marketers is acceptable and so makes no purchase. Often you go to a mall looking for a particular style of clothing and come home empty-handed. At other times, one choice is perceived to be superior, and the consumer does make a purchase. That's what happened when you selected the college you are currently attending. This is referred to as an **exchange**—the act of obtaining a desired object from someone by offering something of value in return. The process began with a simple barter system, when a farmer exchanged corn for salt, for example, and continues today when we purchase shoes in exchange for a credit card payment (a promise to pay). Today, more than ever, the process of creating an exchange is not random, and it requires a great deal of marketing effort—in other words, for the marketer the process revolves around a marketing plan.

As we will discuss in Chapter 7, a *marketing plan* involves different stages: a research stage, during which the marketing environment, including the consumer, is analyzed; a strategic stage, during which objectives are developed, along with the enduring strategy for achieving them; an implementation stage, which involves the coordination of the marketing strategy with actual marketing activities; and the evaluation stage, when it is determined to what extent the objectives were achieved. Figure 3.1 is a sample marketing plan. Figure 3.2 illustrates advertising's place in the marketing plan.

Marketing is a part of the overall business plan, and advertising is an integral but relatively small part of the marketing plan. Traditionally, the hierarchy of strategies employed by businesses starts with the marketing mix, which involves activities such as designing the product, including its package; pricing of the product, as well as terms of sale; distribution of the product, including placing it in outlets accessible to customers; and promoting or communicating about the product. This last element, promotion or marketing communication, is the home base for advertising, along with public relations, sales promotion, personal selling, packaging/point of sale, and direct marketing. Each of these promotional techniques has its own set of capabilities, some of which complement one another, some of which duplicate each other's efforts. For example, advertising is capable of reaching a mass audience simultaneously and repeatedly. It is also an excellent device for informing customers about new products or important changes in existing products. Reminding customers to buy and reinforcing past purchases are two other strengths of advertising. Finally, advertising can persuade customers to change their attitudes, beliefs, or behavior. Public relations possesses several of these same strengths. Sales promotion, personal selling, and direct marketing are all similar in that they prompt behavior in a timely manner.

Superior advertising cannot save an inferior marketing plan or rescue a bad product—at least not for long—but inferior advertising can destroy an excellent plan or product. (This is illustrated in the Issues and Controversies box.) Therefore, it is as important for the advertising director to have a thorough understand-

Exchange: The process whereby two or more parties give up a desired resource to one another.

FIGURE 3.1

CONSUMER SERVICES AND PRODUCTS STRATEGIC PLAN.
(Courtesy of The Conference Board, The Marketing Board in the 1990s, *Report No. 951 (1990):34–35). Reprinted by permission of The Conference Board.*

Mission

To become the premiere source of residential and commercial services and products to consumers in the United States and selected international markets. These services and products will be ones that improve the quality of life and assist the consumers in maintaining their property and surrounding.

Objectives

1. To develop the [Company] Quality Service Network, which will be made up of several service companies, each being specialists in their own field, which the consumer can access through one source.
2. To build market share in each of the operating units.
3. To maintain a minimum of X% annual increase in both revenues and profits.

The operational objectives are:

1. To make available the entire range of consumer services in a profitable and timely manner in all major markets in the United States.
2. To establish and enforce quality standards among all the operating units.
3. To introduce some of the services into selected foreign markets.

The major marketing objectives of the [Company] Quality Service Network are:

1. Cross sell to existing customers of one [Company] operating unit the services of the other operating units.
2. Expand the customer base of the [Company] Network to include customers who have no services with any operating unit.
3. Increase customer loyalty and retention.
4. Expand the number of services available through the [Company] Quality Service Network.

Strategy

1. Each operating unit will continue to build brand awareness for its own service or product. [X], [Y], and [Z] will be promoted under their respective brand names.
2. All the different services and products will be linked together by the 1-800-XXX-XXXX number and the Partners Logo Block.
3. Channels of distribution will be increased by expansion of the services into all markets. Certain segments of the business may be more suitable to franchising while others should be company owned.
4. Foreign markets will be pursued with a minimum investment strategy. A foreign partner will be selected to license the know-how from [Company]. [X] will be the entering brand in the [foreign] markets.
5. The *Partners Pledge* will represent the minimum standards by which all operating units are measured. All [Company] service centers must agree to abide by the pledge before they will be certified to operate under the [Company] Quality Service Network umbrella. This Partners Pledge will be the network's guarantee to the customer that service will be delivered on time and that the job will be done right.

Summary of Mission and Objectives by Operating Units

[Company] currently provides the following services:
Residential and commercial cleaning of carpets, upholstery, and drapes; residential disaster restoration; contract cleaning services; residential home cleaning service, lawn care service; termite and pest control; home system care; and consumer products.

The Marketing Plan

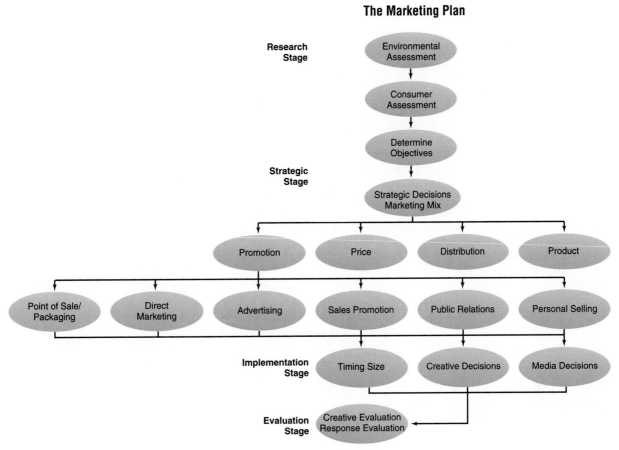

FIGURE 3.2

THE PLACE OF ADVERTISING IN
THE MARKETING PLAN.

ing of marketing and all its facets as it is for the marketing manager to understand how advertising works. This mutual awareness and understanding is the underlying premise of integrated marketing communication.

This chapter provides only a simple overview of marketing. In the real world of advertising a much deeper understanding of the entire marketing process, as well as of the specific marketing strategy employed by the client, would be required. (Readers who wish to understand marketing at a deeper level are referred to the reading list at the end of this chapter.) The starting point for our overview is the market itself.

THE IDEA OF A MARKET

The word *market* originally meant the place where the exchange between seller and buyer took place. The term has taken on several additional meanings. Today we speak of a **market** as either a region where goods are sold and bought or a particular type of buyer.

The term implies that the buyer and seller are not paired at random but rather are engaged in negotiation because each has evaluated the likelihood that the other will be able to satisfy his or her needs and wants. How is this accomplished? Businesses are able to locate the best market for an existing or potential product through experience and market research. Likewise, customers rely on experience, market information, and many other factors (including advertising) to identify markets where they believe they will find the best value.

Market: An area of the country, a group of people, or the overall demand for a product.

TYPES OF MARKETS

When marketing strategists speak of markets they are generally referring to groups of people or organizations. The four primary types of markets are (1) con-

Issues and Controversies

RENOVA — NOT THE SUCCESS PROMISED

Johnson & Johnson's Ortho Pharmaceuticals unit bet close to $50 million in marketing money that it can outsell the wrinkle warriors of department stores with its prescription skin cream Renova. Given the approval of the FDA, J&J introduced a print and television campaign in July 1996. Both the print and television ads use a 40-something model, but the television spot is said to be less cheeky and more emotional. The talking head in the spot speaks of wrinkles and aging and what they mean, what they say to people, and how she feels about them. There is no theme line, and the product's name isn't disclosed. Indeed, at the close of the spot, viewers are invited to talk to their doctors and are given an 800 number to call for more information. The print campaign consists of four-page inserts and spreads with the theme "Companies were forever selling me hope-in-a-bottle. What a relief to find a tube of truth."

Renova was also promoted in a line of Renova-compatible skin care products from J&J beauty subsidiary Neutrogena.

If the brand is as successful as J&J hopes, it will almost certainly impact alpha hydroxy acid skin treatments, the fastest-growing category segment, up an estimated 35 percent in 1995 to about $500 million in sales in the $3 billion U.S. skin care market. Alpha hydroxy acid products cannot claim to do anything but affect the skin's surface. Renova can say it works on all layers of the skin, reducing wrinkles, brown spots, and the natural aging process when used in conjunction with a comprehensive skin care and sun avoidance program.

Department store marketers like Elizabeth Arden Co. are already working on alternatives that may not be able to make the same claims as a drug but also do not sensitize skin

the way Renova can. The sensitivity is a well-known side effect of Retin-A, Renova's predecessor.

Renova's first-year sales were expected to hit $100 million if enough consumers spend $60 for a tube that lasts four to six months. However, Renova's sales hit just $10.9 million at the end of August. Executives close to J&J acknowledge the marketer is disappointed but, in the words of one, "not yet panicked."

Behind the slow start, some experts say, are both a reluctance on the part of doctors to prescribe Renova, given its tendency to cause sun-sensitive reactions in some users, and the lack of initial advertising. Although Renova was launched in February, advertising from DDB Needham Worldwide, New York, didn't start until June because of the necessary clearance from the FDA. Consequently, J&J spent only $5 million of its ad budget in June, July, and August.

At least one consultant thinks Renova's slow start is only a temporary wrinkle. "I'm surprised it's sold that much, since advertising just started," says Gary Stibel, partner at the New England Consulting Group. "J&J has managed it to be a slow start by new intent. Women have been lied to over and over again in this category, and they want to be sure people aren't overpromised . . . It will grow and be much more successful in a year or two because it will do better after trial, unlike many other products." We'll see.

Sources: Pat Sloan, "J&J Unleashing $50 Million to Launch Renova Skin Cream," *Advertising Age* (June 3, 1996):27, 57; Pat Sloan and Michael Wilke, "Initial Sales Tally for J&J's Renova Disappointing," *Advertising Age* (September 2, 1996):4.

sumer, (2) business-to-business (industrial), (3) institutional, and (4) reseller (see Figure 3.3).

CONSUMER

Consumer markets consist of people who buy products and services for their own personal use or for the use of others in the household. As a student, you are considered a member of the market for companies that sell jeans, sweatshirts, pizza, textbooks, backpacks, and bicycles, along with a multitude of other products.

BUSINESS-TO-BUSINESS (INDUSTRIAL)

Industrial markets consist of companies that buy products or services to use in their own businesses or in making other products. General Electric, for example, buys computers to use in billing and inventory control, steel and wiring to use in the manufacture of its products, and cleaning supplies to use in maintaining its buildings.

INSTITUTIONAL

Institutional markets include a wide variety of profit and nonprofit organizations, such as hospitals, government agencies, and schools, which provide goods and services for the benefit of society at large. Universities, for example, are in the market for furniture, cleaning supplies, computers, office supplies, groceries and food products, audio-visual materials, and tissue and toilet paper, to name just a few.

FIGURE 3.3

THE FOUR PRINCIPAL TYPES OF MARKETS.

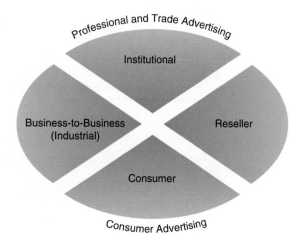

RESELLER

The reseller market includes what we often call the *middlemen*. These are wholesalers, retailers, and distributors who buy finished or semifinished products and resell them for a profit. Resellers are considered a market by companies that sell such products and services as trucks, cartons, crates, and transportation services (airlines, cruise ships, and rental car agencies).

Of the four markets, the consumer market is probably the largest in terms of dollars spent on advertising. Marketing to this group is generally done through mass media such as radio, television, newspapers, general consumer magazines, and direct-response advertising media. The other three markets—industrial, institutional, and reseller—are reached through trade and professional advertising in specialized media such as trade journals, professional magazines, and direct mail.

THE MARKETING CONCEPT

PRINCIPLE Integrated marketing communication requires a thorough understanding of all the components of marketing, including the facets that must be communicated to consumers.

The historical evolution of marketing is not only interesting, but it also provides important insights as to why marketing is the way it is in the decade of the 1990s. Although a simplification, from the industrial revolution in the 1860s until the 1950s, marketing emphasized two activities: mass production and efficient product delivery. The heroes of the 1800s were larger-than-life financiers and empire builders, such as Morgan, Rockefeller, and Carnegie, who built enormous factories to make new products and transportation networks to deliver these products. This was followed in the 1900s by geniuses such as Ford and Watson, who opened the door to mass production with new technologies. The Roaring Twenties were followed by the Great Depression, a time of significant suffering and deprivation; there was very little cause for marketing. World War II converted U.S. factories to war production: tanks and jeeps, artillery and ammunition, and fighters and bombers. Following the war, there was a greater demand for products after four years of ration coupons and sacrifice. The economy picked up as soldiers went to work, married, and had children. Marketing had not been formalized as a concept, and with the increased demand for goods, sales efforts were not as important. Getting the product out to consumers was paramount, making efficient manufacturing the most important function of the decade.

By the late 1950s, the initial surge of demand had been satisfied and the economy had begun to shift, yet production-oriented companies sought to maintain profitability by either taking cash out of the manufacturing process or selling more product. Mass marketing was invented to sell standardized, mass-produced

AD 3.1

HONDA'S APPEAL TO THE CON-
SUMER'S DESIRE FOR QUALITY
AND COMMITMENT COMES
ACROSS IN THIS AD ADDRESSING
OWNER LOYALTY.

products to a similarly standardized, undifferentiated mass of consumers. The role of marketing was to sell. The role of advertising was to reflect the stereotypical values and mores that were in the popular culture (through television and other media) and to create formula-driven ads, over and over again. During the 1960s, the term *marketing concept* was introduced. It suggested that everything started with the needs and wants of the customer. Although it was a noble sentiment, it was mostly lip service, and business went on as usual. There is a handful of businesses, such as L.L. Bean and United Parcel Service (UPS), who appeared to adopt this perspective, but they are the exception.

Many business historians posit that it was not until the late 1980s that the marketing concept was truly embraced by business. More than likely, business had no choice. Consumers are now better educated, wiser, and empowered with opinions and dollars. World trade barriers have come down and we are introduced to a global society, with new competitors and more and better choices. Me-too products, although very profitable, are no longer always acceptable to most consumers. There is no homogeneous American culture, and people are not buying products exclusively to "keep up" with others. Today, marketers know that in order to compete effectively, they must focus on consumer problems and try to develop products to solve them. Performing this task well promises the ultimate competitive advantage. The marketing concept states: First determine what the customer needs and wants, and then develop, manufacture, market, and service the goods and services that fill those particular needs and wants.

Once a company has accepted the marketing concept, the natural evolution is to develop a strategic approach by which to implement the marketing concept.

Integrated marketing has emerged as the strategic approach with the greatest potential. Essentially, integrated marketing is taking the same ideas and principles we discussed for integrated marketing communication and applying them to the marketing mix instead of just the communication/promotion mix. That is, how is product, price, distribution, and promotion blended in a way so that the needs of the customer are prominent and a synergy is created between the elements? All the marketing mix elements must be in harmony and the competitive advantage offered by the company should address a primary need of the target market. Every element of the marketing strategy is influenced by this integrated approach to marketing.

Adopting integrated marketing affects advertising as well. Primarily, advertising is employed as a mechanism for delivering information. Through research, the marketer understands how the consumer makes decisions most efficiently and satisfactorily. This information is then incorporated within advertising messages. The intent is for advertising to facilitate decision making. More importantly, the goal is to create advertising that is honest, useful, and matches the needs of the customer so that the customer is satisfied with the choices made. When advertising is guided by the marketing concept, there is a central goal—satisfying the customer—that helps coordinate advertising with the other marketing functions and increases the likelihood that a particular advertisement will be successful.

This is exactly the philosophy that has made Honda so successful in the American market. When consumers wanted fuel efficiency, Honda was there with the Civic. When they wanted roominess, comfort, and performance, Honda was ready with the Accord. Ad 3.1 shows how Honda has maintained this high level of quality and integrity.

THE 4PS OF MARKETING

In his book *Basic Marketing* Jerome McCarthy popularized the classification of the various marketing elements into four categories that have since been known in the marketing industry as the "4Ps"[3] (see Figure 3.4). They are:

1.   *Product:* Includes product design and development, branding, and packaging.
2.   *Place* (or Distribution): Includes the channels used in moving the product from the manufacturer to the buyer.

---

[3]E. Jerome McCarthy and William D. Perreault, Jr., *Basic Marketing* (Homewood, IL: Irwin, 1987):37.

FIGURE 3.4

THE 4PS OF MARKETING.

Product

- Design and
  Development
- Branding
- Packaging

Place

- Distribution Channels
- Market Coverage

Price

- Price Copy
- Psychological Pricing
- Price Lining

Promotion

- Personal Selling
- Advertising
- Sale Promotion
- Direct Marketing
- Public Relations
  and Publicity
- Point of Sale /
  Packaging

3.   *Price:* Includes the price at which the product or service is offered for sale and establishes the level of profitability.

4.   *Promotion* (or Marketing Communication): Includes personal selling, advertising, public relations, sales promotion, direct marketing, and point-of-sales/packaging.

It is the job of the marketing or product manager to manipulate these elements to create the most efficient and effective *marketing mix.*

PRODUCT

The product is both the object of the advertising and the reason for marketing. Marketing begins by asking a set of questions about the product offered. These questions should always be asked from the consumer's perspective: What product attributes and benefits are important? How is the product perceived relative to competitive offerings? How important is servicing? How long do they expect the product to last?

Customers view products as "bundles of satisfaction" rather than just physical things. For example, in the United States, some car buyers perceive automobiles made in Germany and Japan as offering superior quality, better gas mileage, and less costly service and maintenance than American cars. At the luxury level, cars such as Porsche, BMW, Audi, and the Mazda RX-7 now offer the status and prestige once associated with Cadillac and Lincoln (see Ad 3.2). Thus, the intangible, symbolic attributes foreign-made automobiles now possess over and above the

AD 3.2

THE COPY IN THIS AD FOR
THE PORSCHE 911 TURBO
DESCRIBES THE COMMITMENT
TO QUALITY THAT MAKES IT A
LUXURY CAR.

tangible ones perform psychological and social functions for the buyer. Figure 3.5 portrays both tangible and intangible product characteristics.

To have a practical impact on consumers, managers must translate these product characteristics into concrete attributes with demonstrable benefits. In other words, they must develop message strategy. Consider packaged cookies. The physical ingredients might include sugar, flour, chocolate, and baking powder. The intangible features might be an implied return policy and a reputable brand name. However, these characteristics are too far removed from the real attributes or benefits customers perceive. A customer looks for descriptive phrases such as "tastes like homemade" or "a great afternoon snack," so these are the real pieces of information the marketer desires to communicate. Stressing the most important attributes is the key to influencing customer choices and serves as the foundation for much of advertising.

PRODUCT LIFE CYCLE

The concept of *product life cycle* was introduced by Theodore Levitt in an article in the *Harvard Business Review* in 1965.[4] It is based on a metaphor that treats products as people and assumes they are born (introduced), develop (grow), age (mature), and die (decline).

A newly developed product is first presented to its market during the introductory stage. Operations are characterized by high costs, low sales volume, and limited distribution. If the product is a true innovation (that is, unknown to the consumer group), marketing communication must stimulate *primary demand* rather than *secondary demand*. That is, the type of product rather than the seller's brand is emphasized. The role of advertising might be to educate or carry sales promotion inducements such as coupons or samples.

One of the most difficult decisions for a marketer to make at the introductory stage of the life cycle is determining whether the product being introduced is a trend or a fad. A *trend* suggests that the new product has tapped into an ongoing need of the consumer and that the product will likely go through the rest of the life cycle. Investing in a trend makes strategic sense. A *fad* is a product that has a very uncertain future and its development and introduction is based on a tempo-

---

[4]Theodore Levitt, "Exploit the Product Life Cycle," *Harvard Business Review* (November–December 1965):81–84.

FIGURE 3.5

TANGIBLE AND INTANGIBLE CHARACTERISTICS OF A PRODUCT.

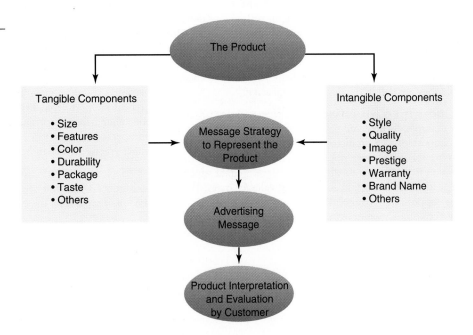

rary need. An entirely different strategy would be employed. More is said about fads in the Concepts and Applications box.

The second stage of the product life cycle is the growth stage. By this stage, the product has received a general acceptance, previous purchasers continue their purchasing, and new buyers enter in large numbers. The success of the new product attracts competitors. The aim of advertising often shifts from building brand awareness to creating a clear brand position and illiciting conviction and purchase. Advertising expenditures are based on those of competitors. Premium athletic shoe marketers such as Nike, Inc. and Reebok find themselves currently in this position.

In maturity, the company shares the market with successful and rigorous competitors. This stage is characterized by continued sales increases, but the rate

---

*C*ONCEPTS AND *A*PPLICATIONS

TREND OR FAD? THAT IS THE QUESTION

Distinguishing between fads and trends at an early stage can make or break a business career. The first company to identify a trend and act on it gains a powerful competitive advantage. It happened to Starbucks coffee, which capitalized on a new consumer desire for higher quality and greater variety in coffee. It's working for Snackwell's cookies and crackers, which did the best job of combining good taste with reduced fat. And when Taco Bell first recognized the power of value pricing, it gained a powerful competitive advantage.

On the other hand, companies that miss a trend will spend their time playing catch-up to the competition. The American auto industry has spent decades paying the cost of ignoring early signs that consumers wanted cars to be smaller, higher in quality, and more fuel efficient. IBM let Apple take a big chunk of the personal computer market.

Correctly identifying a fad has its own benefits. Aggressive marketers can make a lot of money by reaping the short-term rewards of a fad and abandoning it just as it begins to lose its impact. More conservative companies can safely ignore a short-lived fad and concentrate on opportunities with longer-term potential. But can you really tell whether a new development will be a fad or a trend?

The following checklist can help you analyze changes while they are still in the developmental stage:

1.   DOES IT FIT WITH BASIC LIFESTYLE CHANGES?
For example, divorce and delayed childbearing have made age less important as a predictor of behavior, while life stage has become relatively more important. For this reason, a critical question is the degree to which a new development is consistent with these important lifestyle and value changes. Which ones support the change? Which ones conflict with it? If a new development complements other important changes, it is much more likely to be a trend. If it conflicts with those basic lifestyle changes, it is almost certainly a fad.

2.   WHAT ARE THE BENEFITS?
What benefits do consumers receive from the new product or service? How many benefits does it have, and how strong are

they? Do consumers feel good about the new product, or are they reluctantly being forced to change? Will making the change improve their lives in important ways? The more diverse and immediate a product's benefits, the more likely the new development will be a trend.

3.   CAN IT BE PERSONALIZED?
We should ask whether or not the new product or service can be modified or expressed in different ways by different people. The more adaptable it is, the greater chance it has of becoming a trend.

4.   IS IT A TREND OR A SIDE EFFECT?
We should distinguish between a basic trend and the specific expressions of that trend. The expressions will emerge and be replaced by other expressions of the basic theme, while the trend continues to grow. In other words, a good market researcher must separate the forest from the trees.

5.   WHAT OTHER CHANGES HAVE OCCURRED?
Is the new development supported by developments in other areas? If it stands alone, it is more likely to be a fad.

6.   WHO HAS ADOPTED THE CHANGE?
It is always important to determine which consumers have changed their behavior. Two questions are particularly valuable in determining whether or not a new development will become a trend: support from unexpected sources and the degree of support from key market segments. If a change in consumer behavior or another development comes from an unexpected source (for example, working women), it has a much greater chance of being a trend.

Separating trends from fads is an inexact science. With consumers' wants and needs changing more rapidly than ever, the job of separating the two can only grow more difficult.

Source: Martin G. Letscher, "How to Tell Fads from Trends," *American Demographics* (December 1994):38–41, 44–45. Reprinted with permission. Copyright © 1994, American Demographics, Ithaca, New York.

of increase continually moderates and toward the end of the period becomes almost negligible. Marginal producers are forced to drop out of the market, and price competition becomes increasingly severe. Advertising often becomes more image based, attempting to protect and reinforce the equity the brand holds. Also, advertising may become more a responsibility shared with intermediaries, especially retailers through cooperative advertising programs. With cooperative advertising, the cost of advertising is shared by the advertisers and the intermediaries. Soft-drink marketers, as well as beer manufacturers and fast-food retailers, find themselves at this stage.

Finally, many products face a period of obsolescence when they no longer sell as well as they previously did. Example of products in decline include wine coolers, window air conditioners, push lawn mowers, and typewriters. During this stage of decline, advertising may be reduced or eliminated altogether. Not all products have to decline, however; a product may be reformulated or turned around, and the product life cycle begins again. This tactic is called *take-off strategy*.

A classic example of a product category that has engaged in a take-off strategy is premium cigars. This product—handmade with long, not chopped, filler leaf—retails from $1 to $10 each. After growing at 2.4 percent since 1976, consumption on a compound annual growth rate rose to 8.9 percent from 1991 to 1994 and zoomed to 30.6 percent from 1994 to 1995. And thanks to the rise of cigar bars, cigar magazines, and Hollywood's preoccupation with stogies, there's no letup in sight.[5]

BRANDING

When you think of bread, what product name comes to mind? When you think of facial tissues, what product name occurs to you? What product name comes to mind when you picture a copy machine? Do you think of a product name when you think of salt?

Branding: The process of creating an identity for a product using a distinctive name or symbol.

Wonder Bread, Kleenex, Xerox, and Morton's have been extensively advertised over many years. **Branding** makes a product distinctive in the marketplace, just as your name makes you unique in the society in which you live. However, there are subtle differences. A *brand* is the name, term, design, symbol, or any other feature that identifies the goods, service, institution, or idea sold by a marketer. The *brand name* is that part of a brand that can be spoken, such as words, letters, or numbers. Hershey's is a brand name, as is K2R. The *brand mark*, also known as the *logo*, is that part of the brand that cannot be spoken. It can be a symbol, picture, design, distinctive lettering, or color combination. When a brand name or brand mark is legally protected through registration with the Patent and Trademark Office of the Department of Commerce, it becomes a *trademark*.

The importance of the brand cannot be overestimated. When we talk about *brand equity*, we are referring to the reputation that name or symbol connotes. It is on every important message and becomes synonymous with the company. Losing brand equity, through excessive discounting, producing substandard products, or poor service has proven disastrous for many companies.

PACKAGING

The package is another important communication device. In today's marketing environment a package is much more than a container. The self-service retailing phenomenon means that the consumer in the typical grocery store or drugstore is faced with an endless array of products. In such a situation the package is the mes-

---

[5]Gail DeGeorge and Ivette Diaz, "I'm Rolling as Fast as I Can," *Business Week* (September 9, 1996):46.

sage. When the package works in tandem with consumer advertising, it catches attention, presents a familiar brand image, and communicates critical information. Many purchase decisions are made on the basis of how the product looks on the shelf.

An article in *Advertising Age* explained the importance of the package as a communication medium: "Even if you can't afford a big advertising budget, you've got a fighting chance if your product projects a compelling image from the shelf."[6] For products that are advertised nationally, the package reflects the brand image developed in the advertising. It serves as a very important reminder at that critical moment when the consumer is choosing among several competing brands. As an advertising medium, the package has to be an eye-catcher as well as an identifier. Most of us carry around in our minds some kind of visual image of our most familiar products. That image is usually the package.

> **PRINCIPLE** The package stimulates the purchase at the critical moment when the consumer is making a choice.

In sum, packaging is an important part of the advertising strategy. It is the constant communicator. Packages that are colorful, cleverly designed, functional, and complementary to the product enhance the advertising effort. Such a package facilitates the association between the package and the brand name. Finally, the package is an effective device for carrying advertising messages.

PLACE (CHANNEL OF DISTRIBUTION)

It does little good to manufacture a fantastic product that will meet the needs of the consumer unless there is a mechanism for delivering and servicing the product and receiving payment. Those individuals and institutions involved in moving products from producers to customers make up the **channel of distribution.** Resellers, or intermediaries, are primary members of the channel who may actually take ownership of the product and participate in its marketing. Wholesalers, retailers, and modes of transportation are typical channel members. Each is capable of influencing and delivering advertising messages.

> **Channel of Distribution:** People and organizations involved in moving products from producers to consumers.

For example, the primary strength of wholesalers is personal selling. Wholesalers do not advertise often. There are, however, instances when special types of advertising strategies are employed. For instance, regional wholesalers are apt to use direct mail, trade papers, or catalogs. Local wholesalers may use newspapers or local radio. The copy tends to be simple and straightforward with few pictures or illustrations. Conversely, retailers are quite good at advertising, especially local advertising. The retailers' main concern is that the advertising be directed at their own customers. The media used, the copy employed, and the size and frequency of ads, and so on will vary from one retailer to another. The ad for Famous Footwear is a typical retail ad. (See Ad 3.3).

Other channel-related decisions influence advertising as well. Part of the channel nomenclature includes the idea of a "channel captain," or the dominant member in a channel of distribution. Historically, the channel captain tended to be the manufacturer. This pattern has been reversed during the last two decades, and today retailers such as Wal-Mart and Mervyns tend to dominate. Consequently, the leverage possessed by the channel captain often extends into the realm of advertising. For example, Sears may strongly influence the advertising strategy of its product suppliers, for example, General Electric and Texas Instruments. General Electric may have similar power over a small appliance chain.

Is the channel direct or indirect? Companies that distribute their products without the use of a reseller engage in *direct marketing*. Companies such as Lands' End, Spiegel, and Burpee Seeds all use direct-marketing channels. In place of

---

[6]Lori Kesler, "Shopping Around for a Design," *Advertising Age* (December 28, 1981):2–4, 2–8.

Cooperative Advertising: A form of advertising in which the manufacturer reimburses the retailer for part or all of the retailer's advertising expenditures.

AD 3.3

THIS AD FOR FAMOUS FOOTWEAR IS A TYPICAL RETAIL AD, WITH A FOCUS ON PRICE AND INFORMATION.

stores or personal salespeople, direct marketing relies on advertising media to inform and stimulate customer purchase responses. Direct marketing will be discussed in more detail in Chapter 16.

In *indirect marketing* the product is distributed through a channel structure that includes one or more resellers. A key decision in indirect marketing concerns resellers' involvement in advertising. Wholesalers and especially retailers are often expected to participate in the advertising programs offered by producers. Through **cooperative advertising** allowances the producer and reseller share the cost of placing the advertisement. This activity not only saves money (because lo-

cal advertising rates are less expensive than national rates); it also creates an important tie-in with local retailers, who often have a much greater following than the producer's brand does.

Wholesalers and retailers also initiate their own advertising campaigns, which often highlight the items of various manufacturers. Few manufacturers can match the advertising impact of retailers such as Sears, J.C. Penney, or Federated Stores. Rather, manufacturers attempt to penetrate these outlets in order to take advantage of their advertising strength.

Another channel-related factor that may influence advertising is whether a push or a pull strategy is being employed. (See Figure 3.6.) A *pull strategy* directs marketing efforts to the ultimate consumer and attempts to "pull" the product through the channel; the process is fueled by consumer demand. There is usually a large emphasis on consumer advertising, along with incentives to buy such as coupons, rebates, free samples, or sweepstakes. Little is expected from resellers other than to stock the product. In contrast, a *push strategy* directs marketing efforts at resellers, and success depends greatly on the ability of intermediaries to market the product, including the use of advertising. Thus, advertising may be first targeted at resellers in order to gain their acceptance; then it is targeted at ultimate users through joint manufacturer-reseller advertising.

A final channel-related decision influencing advertising concerns the *market coverage* desired. Three strategies are possible: exclusive distribution, selective distribution, and intensive distribution. With *exclusive distribution*, only one distributor is allowed to sell the brand in a particular market. Two examples of companies that employ exclusive distribution are Rolls-Royce and Ethan Allen Furniture. The retailer is expected to provide a strong personal selling effort, effective merchandising, and heavy participation in cooperative (co-op) advertising. *Selective distribution* expands the number of outlets but restricts participation to those outlets that prove most profitable to the manufacturer.

FIGURE 3.6

PUSH, PULL, AND COMBINATION STRATEGIES.

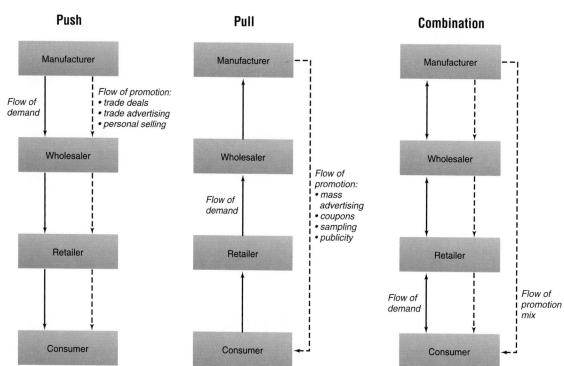

Florsheim Shoes, Farrah Fashions, and Timex all engage in selective distribution. The role of advertising is quite varied under this arrangement, but normally the manufacturer does some mass advertising and offers co-op possibilities. *Intensive distribution* involves placing the product in every possible outlet (including vending machines) in order to attain total market coverage. Intensive distribution is used to market soft drinks, candy, and cigarettes. Advertising is paramount in this situation. Because little personal selling can be expected from the retailer, it is up to mass advertising to create brand awareness and preference.

Market coverage also dictates the geographic distribution of the product. This may influence both the creative strategy and the media strategy. In the case of the former, an ad for a product distributed in the Pacific Northwest and Florida (for example, rain gear) may require significant changes in copy and illustration. In terms of media, the selection of media is clearly a function of a product's geography. An ad placed in *The New York Times* makes no sense for a product sold only in Utah. Of course, there also are instances when national marketers change their copy or illustration for different parts of the country. Ford has done this with its truck advertising. Healthy Choice also modifies its copy depending upon geographic location.

PRICING

The price a seller sets for a product is based not only on the cost of making and marketing the product but also on the seller's expected level of profit. Certain psychological factors also affect the price. For example, it has long been assumed that price suggests quality in the consumer's mind.

Ultimately, the price charged is simply based on what the traffic will bear, given what the competition is doing, the economic well-being of the consumer, the relative value of the product, and the ability of the consumer to gauge that value.

With the exception of price information delivered at the point of sale, advertising is the primary vehicle for telling the consumer about the price and associated conditions of a particular product. The term *price copy* has been coined to designate advertising copy devoted primarily to this information.

In turn, there are a number of pricing strategies that influence the specific creative strategy employed in a particular ad. For example, *customary* or *expected* pricing involves the use of a single well-known price for a long period of time. Movie theaters, the U.S. Post Office, and manufacturers of candy and other products sold through vending machines use this pricing strategy. Only price changes would be made explicit in advertising.

Psychological pricing techniques are intended to manipulate the judgment process employed by the customer. A very high price—for example, prestige pricing, where a high price is set to make the product seem worthy or valuable—would be accompanied by photographs of an exceptional product or a copy platform consisting of logical reasons for this high price. Conversely, a dramatic or temporary price reduction is translated through terms such as *sale, special,* and *today only*.

Finally, *price lining* involves offering a number of variations of a particular product and pricing them accordingly. Sears Roebuck, for example, offers many of their products on a "good," "better," and "best" basis. Price lining requires that the ad show the various products so that consumers can assess the relative differences.

It is important that advertising clearly and consistently reflects the product's pricing strategy. For many consumers, this ad-price tandem represents the initial decision to purchase.

INSIDE ADVERTISING

CHRISTY CLOUGHLEY, ADVERTISING TEAM MANAGER,
Western Auto Supply Company

After four years at Kansas State University, I graduated from the School of Journalism and Mass Communications with a degree in advertising and an outside emphasis in graphic design. I then left the United States for a year of study and travel in southern France. Upon my return from France, I decided I was finally ready to dive into the "real world." After about 80 résumés and cover letters and 20 interviews, I landed my first job at Western Auto Supply Company's corporate office in Kansas City in its in-house advertising department.

Western Auto is an automotive retailer with stores in 45 states, Puerto Rico, and the U.S. Virgin Islands. During my first two years at Western Auto, I worked as an advertising coordinator, electronically producing print advertising from start to finish. I am now one of four advertising team managers in our department, and I oversee a team of four advertising coordinators.

It is my responsibility to initiate and delegate all new projects for the team, see that deadlines are met, arrange printing with outside vendors, as well as assist my team in meeting all established goals and objectives. In my position I have been exposed to various sides of the retail automotive business. Some experiences include communicating with merchandising and operations, producing in-house projects for human resources and other departments, coordinating the production of promotions with the marketing department, helping to promote our company-sponsored NASCAR and NHRA drivers through advertising, and meeting with outside vendors and print agencies.

My typical day looks like this:

8:00 A.M.   I arrive at work and check all voice mail and e-mail messages. I read over the status report that I compile weekly for my team, which describes all projects we have scheduled for the upcoming weeks and deadlines to meet. I then make a list of my day's top priorities and check my calendar for any meetings I have scheduled for the day.

8:30 A.M.   I attend our weekly staff meeting, which is led by the vice president of marketing and advertising. All direct reports from the marketing, advertising, and art departments attend (about 15 people). The weekly sales reports are discussed for the retail and wholesale sides of the business. A motorsports report is given updating us on the standings of our company-sponsored NHRA and NASCAR drivers. Then each person discusses current events and brings up any issues that need to be resolved immediately.

9:30 A.M.   I return to my office and clean out my in-box. I fill out production requests for any new projects needing to be put into production and distribute them to the appropriate team member (advertising coordinator).

10:00 A.M.   I attend the advertising production meeting led by the director of advertising. All four advertising team managers attend as well as the network manager and art director. Issues specific to production and current projects are discussed.

11:30 A.M.   One of my team members and I meet with a local printer to discuss the specs of a companywide newsletter being printed for us. We give the newsletter to the printer on removable disk with hard copies and a purchase order memorandum. In the next few days the printer will send me

PROMOTION

Promotion: That element in the marketing mix that communicates the key marketing messages to target audiences. Also called *marketing communication*.

Advertising, personal selling, sales promotion, public relations, direct marketing, and point-of-sales/packaging represent the primary techniques available to the marketer for communicating with target markets. These combined techniques are referred to as **promotion** or **marketing communication.** Marketing promotion is defined as "persuasive communication designed to send marketing-related messages to a selected target audience." With the refocusing of commerce from product-centered to consumer-centered strategies, the revolution in marketing brought together a group of activities that had existed on the fringe of the manufacturing process. Bogart explains that "when American business was reorganized in the postwar years, marketing emerged as a major function" that coordinated previously separate specialties—such as product development, sales promotion,

bluelines of the newsletter to be proofed. I will then make a trip out to the printer for a press O.K. on the job. This is a final chance to look over the job before it goes to press. It is also an opportunity to verify that colors are printing and trapping correctly.

12:00 P.M. I meet a local printer for lunch and take a tour of the printing plant. I explore other printing resources available here and we discuss the option of the printer taking on a future project.

1:30 P.M. I call a team meeting. I pass on any important information from the day's staff meeting and production meeting. We run through the status report to verify upcoming deadlines for the week and clear up any pending questions regarding team projects. An electronic publishing report is given by one of the team members to update the rest of the team on any new software or hardware in the department, and I make note of any upcoming vacation time that team members might be taking.

2:15 P.M. I return an e-mail message from our Internet provider. I am one of six people in the department who helps to update and maintain our Web site. One of our artists e-mails me an updated piece of artwork and I forward this along with an updated text file to our Internet provider.

2:30 P.M. I proof a seasonal signage package that one of my team members has produced. The package consists of all signs that will hang in the retail stores for the spring season. I discuss any changes and corrections with the team member and ask him to pass a copy of the signage package on to the marketing and merchandising departments to proof.

3:15 P.M. I meet with a coworker in the marketing department to discuss a magazine advertisement my team will produce that will run in a national motorsports magazine. The ad congratulates one of the drivers we sponsor for a recent win. We discuss the specs for the ad, and I pass the production request on to a team member. I ask the team member to fax a proof of the finished ad to our motorsports public relations agency.

3:45 P.M. A courier drops off the bluelines for a brochure we have produced for the human resources department. I proof the bluelines and call our account representative at the printer with a correction.

4:00 P.M. The director of advertising (my supervisor) comes by with a "hot" project—a direct-mail flyer for our Nashville market. We discuss color, size, and quantity and I immediately run through the specs with the appropriate team member.

4:15 P.M. I meet with a committee to discuss our upcoming companywide fundraiser to benefit the United Way. I have volunteered to coordinate all communications to the company relating to fundraiser events.

5:00 P.M. I return to my office and return any e-mail or voice mail. I sift through my in-box and attempt to regain some order in my office. Before leaving for the day, I review my calendar for any appointments or meetings I have the next day and I make a list of tomorrow's priorities. The day has once again proven that there is never a dull moment in the world of advertising.

Nominated by Prof. Charles Pearce, Kansas State University.

Promotion Mix: The combination of personal selling, advertising, sales promotion, and public relations to produce a coordinated message structure.

merchandising, advertising, and market research; "great emphasis was placed on the integrated marketing plan."[7]

The idea of coordination suggests that there are a number of elements involved in the marketing process, including the product, the distribution channel, the sales force, and the marketing communication program. These elements can also be viewed as *activities*, such as product design and development, branding, packaging, pricing, distribution, personal selling, advertising, sales promotion, and public relations. Combining these four communication devices in a way that produces a coordinated message structure is called the **promotion mix.**

Implementing the promotion mix in a coordinated manner is integrated

[7]Leo Bogart, *Strategy in Advertising*, 2nd. ed. (Lincolnwood, IL: NTC Business Books, 1990):3.

marketing communication, a topic introduced in Chapter 1. The basic elements of the promotion mix—personal selling, advertising, sales promotion, public relations, direct marketing, and point-of-sales/packaging—appear in most marketing plans. These elements differ in terms of their intended effect, the type of customer contact, and the time element of response. (See Figure 3.7.)

PERSONAL SELLING

Personal selling is face-to-face contact between the marketer and a prospective customer. The intention is to create both immediate sales and repeat sales. There are several different types of personal selling, including sales calls at the place of business by a field representative (field sales), assistance at an outlet by a sales clerk (retail selling), and calls by a representative who goes to consumers' homes (door-to-door selling). Personal selling is most important for companies that sell products requiring explanation, demonstration, and service. Such products tend to be higher priced.

ADVERTISING

PRINCIPLE Advertising helps the salesperson by laying the groundwork and preselling the product.

Advertising has already been defined in Chapter 1, and several of its key characteristics were discussed at the beginning of this chapter. It differs from the other promotional elements in several ways. Although advertising has a greater ability to reach a larger number of people simultaneously than do the other elements, it has less ability to prompt an immediate behavioral change. Furthermore, the contact between the advertiser and the audience is indirect, and it takes a longer period of time to deliver information, change attitudes, and create a rapport or trust between the two parties.

SALES PROMOTION

PRINCIPLE Sales promotion activities are used to generate immediate sales.

Sales promotion includes a number of communication devices offered for a limited period of time in order to generate immediate sales. Simply stated, sales promotion is an extra incentive to buy *now*. Examples are price discounts, coupons, product sampling, contests or sweepstakes, and rebates. Sales promotion will be discussed in greater detail in Chapter 18.

Advertising is used to promote sales promotion activities such as sweepstakes and contests. Sales promotions can also be used in support of advertising campaigns. Advertising and sales promotion can work together to create a *synergy* in which each makes the other more effective.

PUBLIC RELATIONS

Public relations encompasses a set of activities intended to enhance the image of the marketer in order to create goodwill. Public relations includes publicity (stories in the mass media with significant news value), news conferences, company-sponsored events, open houses, plant tours, donations, and other special events.

FIGURE 3.7
PROMOTIONAL-MIX COMPARISON.

Promotion Type	Intended Effect	Customer Contact	Timing
Personal Selling	Sales	Direct	Short
Advertising	Attitude Change Behavior Change	Indirect	Moderate-Low
Sales Promotion	Sales	Semidirect	Short
Direct Marketing	Behavior Change	Semidirect	Short
Public Relations	Attitude Change	Semidirect	Long
Point of Sale/ Packaging	Behavior Change	Direct	Short

Rather than attempt to sell the product, public relations seeks to influence people's attitudes about the company or product. In most cases the lag effect associated with public relations is quite long, making any relationship between promotion and sales difficult to determine.

Advertising interacts with public relations in several ways. A public relations event or message can serve as part of an advertising campaign. Product publicity can also be used in support of an advertising campaign. For example, Kingsford charcoal sponsors a Ribfest cooking contest in Chicago that includes giving free charcoal to all contestants. This event reinforces the association between Kingsford and outdoor activities. Public relations is discussed in greater detail in Chapter 19.

DIRECT MARKETING   Direct marketing is a rapidly changing field and its definition is evolving. However, it does have some basic characteristics: (1) it is an interactive system that allows two-way communication; (2) it provides a mechanism for the prospect to respond; (3) it can occur at any location; (4) it provides a measurable response; and (5) it requires a database of consumer information. Direct marketing is the fastest growing element in marketing because it provides the consumer with the three things he or she wants most—convenience, efficiency, and compression of decision-making time.[8] For example, when a consumer buys shirts from Lands' End, every step of the process is smoothly executed, from the toll-free conversation with the order taker to prompt delivery of well-made, fully guaranteed shirts, billed to a Visa card at a cost lower than many retail stores charge. Unfortunately, not all direct-marketing techniques are viewed as viable product sources for consumers. A great deal is still viewed as junk mail; especially in disfavor is unsolicited material that advertises cheap merchandise or implies high risks.

Messages delivered for direct-marketing products are usually called *direct-response advertising*. It is designed to motivate customers to make some sort of response, either an order or an inquiry. Direct-response advertising is directed to target groups through vehicles such as direct mail, telemarketing, print, broadcast, catalogs, and point-of-purchase displays. More will be said about this topic in Chapter 16.

POINT-OF-SALE/PACKAGING   Point-of-sale (POS) and packaging encompass all the communication devices and marketing messages found at the place where the product is sold. The message-delivery capabilities of the package discussed earlier come into play here. POS materials include signage, posters, displays, and a variety of other materials designed to influence buying decisions at the point of purchase. Estimates vary, depending upon the product category, that from 30 percent to 70 percent of our purchases are unplanned. This marketing material is intended to take advantage of that fact, along with fulfilling other basic communication objectives, such as product identification, product information, and product comparisons.

The role advertising plays in this context may vary as well. Often the POS materials are an extension of the ad. Michael Jordan posters and cut-outs are found in every store that sells a product sponsored by Michael Jordan. Seasonal events, such as Fourth of July or Christmas, may produce matching ads and posters.

ADVERTISING AND THE MARKETING MIX

Having examined the elements that make up the marketing mix, you are now better prepared to understand how advertising and marketing interact. As noted at the beginning of this chapter, advertising is a subset of marketing that relies on

---

[8]John J. Burnett, *Promotion Management* (Boston: Houghton Mifflin Company, 1993):652–53.

the evaluation and coordination of product-centered and consumer-centered strategies. The product must come first. Its characteristics, its strengths and weaknesses, and its position in the marketplace all dictate the rest of the marketing mix. Advertising must account for all these factors as well as reflect the price of the product and the way it is distributed. For a highly technical product, advertising will probably take a backseat to personal selling and support services. Such advertising would tend to be laden with facts and restricted to trade magazines targeted at a very well-defined audience. For a product such as Peter Pan peanut butter, it is critical to create brand awareness and provide basic product information through mass advertising; advertising would play a much more important role. A wide range of media would be used. Advertising copy would attempt to instill an emotional appeal for a product that is inherently unexciting. Because price is important to consumers who buy peanut butter, print ads would probably carry coupons.

Even products that have a similar marketing mix may use very different advertising strategies. A case in point is found in the computer industry. When Apple Computer entered the market, they realized that they faced a serious competitive disadvantage. They attacked IBM through their product innovations and breakthrough advertising. IBM and Apple followed very different creative strategies to achieve comparable objectives. Both were driven by their own unique marketing mix.

*S*UMMARY

- Understanding how marketing works and the role advertising plays within the marketing strategy is mandatory for successful advertising.

- The success of marketing is dependent upon whether a business can create a competitive advantage that results in an exchange.

- Exchange takes place within a market; there are four types of markets: (1) consumer, (2) business-to-business (industrial), (3) institutional, and (4) reseller.

- The marketing concept focuses on the needs of the consumer rather than the predetermined goals of the marketer.

- The marketing mix identifies the most effective combination of the four primary marketing functions: product, price, place (or distribution), and promotion (or marketing communication).

- The product consists of a bundle of tangible and intangible components that satisfies the needs of the customer.

- It is assumed that a product goes through a predictable life cycle (i.e., introduction, growth, maturity, and decline) and that advertising plays a different role at each stage.

- A product also has a branding strategy that makes the product distinctive in the marketplace.

- An effective package not only holds the product but is an important communication device.

- A channel of distribution is the basic mechanism for delivering the product to the customer, receiving payment, and servicing the product.

- The two primary types of channel institutions are wholesalers and retailers, each of which employ advertising in a unique manner.

- Several other channel-related factors influence advertising: Who is the channel captain? Is the channel direct or indirect? Is a push or pull strategy being followed? Is the market coverage exclusive, selective, or intensive?

- Price includes the cost, profit, and value expectations. Factors that influence advertising include the need for price copy, the customary or expected price, psychological pricing, and price lining.

- Promotion or mass communication includes advertising, sales promotion, public relations, personal selling, point-of-sale/packaging, and direct marketing; together these are called the promotion mix.

- Each element of the promotional mix contributes to the ability of the company to communicate in a special way.

QUESTIONS

1. Find examples of three advertisements that demonstrate the marketing concept. What elements of these ads reflect this approach?

2. How would you advertise a toothpaste at the four different stages in its life cycle?

3. Imagine you are starting a company to manufacture fudge. Consider the following decisions:

   A. Describe the marketing mix you think would be most effective for this company.

   B. Describe the promotion mix you would recommend for this company.

   C. How would you determine the advertising budget for your new fudge company?

   D. Develop a plan for a brand image for this fudge.

4. Professor Baker tells his advertising class that advertising's relationship to marketing is like the tip of an iceberg. As the class looks puzzled he explains that most (80 percent) of the iceberg cannot be seen. "It's the same with consumer's perception of how much of marketing is advertising-related," Baker explains. What is Baker trying to illustrate with the iceberg analogy?

5. In the 1980s marketers began to look for short-run marketing strategies. This often meant investment in activities other than advertising. Advertising professionals warned companies about ignoring the need for long-run investment through advertising. What activities would marketers use for short-run results? What is the connection between advertising and long-run marketing objectives?

6. The chapter stressed integration of advertising with other components of the marketing mix. If you were in marketing management for Kellogg cereals how would you see advertising supporting product, price, and place? Could advertising improve each of these functions for Kellogg? Explain your answer.

7. Angie Todd, an account assistant at a local advertising agency, is upset at the comments of a marketing consultant during a media reception. The consultant is telling listeners that consumer advertising has lost its edge and does not have credibility. He claims consumers pay no attention to glitter or glitz (advertising); they just want a deal on price. "I'll bet none of you can name even two consumer products last year with ad campaigns that made any difference to the target consumer," he challenged. If you were Angie how would you respond?

SUGGESTED CLASS PROJECT

Interview the manager of a large retail outlet store in your area, such as Target, K-Mart, or Wal-Mart. Assess how the various elements of the promotion mix are used. Study a few diverse products such as food items, blue jeans, and small appliances. You might even talk to the automotive service department. Write a report, making conclusions about how advertising comes into play.

FURTHER READINGS

Aaker, David A., Rajeev Batra, and John L. Myers, *Advertising Management*, 3rd ed. (Upper Saddle River, NJ: Prentice Hall, Inc., 1992).

Bly, Robert, *Advertising Manager's Handbook* (Upper Saddle River, NJ: Prentice Hall, 1993).

Hardy, Kenneth G., and Allan J. Magrath, *Marketing Channel Management* (Glenview, IL: Scott, Foresman, 1988).

Lodish, Leonard M., *The Advertising and Promotion Challenge* (New York: Oxford University Press, 1986).

Monroe, Kent B., *Pricing: Making Profitable Decisions* (New York: McGraw-Hill, 1979).

Shimp, Terence, *Promotion Management and Marketing Communications* (Chicago: Dryden, 1993).

Wind, Yoram J., *Product Policy: Concepts, Methods, and Strategy* (Reading, MA: Addison-Wesley, 1982).

In the mid-1980s, New York businessman Richard Worth set out to develop a cookie sweetened with fruit juice rather than sugar. By 1987, Worth had created R. W. Frookies, a product that he hoped would find great success with health-conscious American snackers. However, when Worth tried to get a regional grocery store chain to stock the product, he was asked to pay $1,000 per store—a total of $1 million—to introduce R. W. Frookie cookies in the chain's 100 stores. Worth rejected the deal because it would have forced him to raise the price of his product by 50 cents a package.

In the grocery industry, payments demanded by grocers in return for stocking new products in warehouses and finding *slots* for them on supermarket shelves are known as slotting fees. The fees were originally developed as a response to line extensions—new flavors or variations of existing products that manufacturers can create with very little expenditure. As industry consultant Paul Kelly notes, "Originally, there were good intentions: Making companies put up the money to ensure that the product was worthwhile. But the costs inhibit entrepreneurs, and hurt innovation."

The product categories for which fees are most often demanded include cake mixes, cereals, frozen dinners, dog food, ice-cream novelties, pasta, and pickles. A typical grocery store carries only about 25,000 of 100,000 different items available. One industry newsletter notes that only about 5 percent of new-product introductions are truly new from the consumer's point of view; rather, most are line extensions of questionable value. Moreover, most new products fail due to inadequate test marketing and advertising. According to industry studies, only about one product in ten is a success. Grocers must thus absorb the costs of warehousing, pricing, shelving, and removing all of these failed products. Large packaged-goods marketers such as Procter & Gamble and General Mills can usually avoid paying slotting fees because they have good track records for product introductions, which they back with multimillion-dollar promotion campaigns. This puts the burden of paying slotting fees on smaller, regional companies— such as Richard Worth's—that lack a solid track record for successful product launches.

Slotting fees are one indication of a new balance of power between food retailers and manufacturers. Whereas food companies once had the power to dictate terms to grocers, now—due largely to consolidations and mergers—the groceries, particularly grocery chains, have much more power. In addition to slotting allowances, grocers have started making further demands. Annual renewal fees

(also known as *pay to stay*) are sometimes required before a store will continue to stock an item. Some buyers have even started charging *presentation fees*—as much as $500— before they will even grant an appointment with a manufacturer's representative. Finally, there is the *failure fee*— an *additional* charge above and beyond the slotting fee for products that don't sell as well as expected and must be removed from store shelves.

Not surprisingly, this proliferation of fees angers Richard Worth and many other manufacturers. Worth notes, "There are a thousand vendors who feel like I do. When you're confronted by imposing fees, if you don't have the money, you don't get the space." A disturbing aspect of the practice is that most of the people involved are reluctant to discuss it. Many of the deals are conducted behind closed doors, and payments are sometimes made in cash. Worth has formed an advocacy group called Crossroads in an effort to help eliminate fees and enable manufacturers and retailers to share profits. Fortunately, there are some parts of the country where slotting fees haven't taken hold. One food industry executive told *Advertising Age*, "Salesmen would give their eyeteeth to have a nice, clean territory like Des Moines or Denver, where the person on the other side of the table would get fired if even a hint of an incentive payment was made."

The questionable legality of slotting fees has prompted investigations and reports by CBS's *60 Minutes* and ABC's *20/20*. Although the fees themselves are not illegal, if retailers in the same market area are requesting fees from some but not all manufacturers, the parties may be in violation of the Robinson-Patman Act for discriminatory distribution of advertising and merchandising allowances. The FTC appears not to regard the slotting fee issue as a pressing one: Slotting allowances are not addressed in the agency's recent revision of guidelines pertaining to Robinson-Patman compliance. In the words of New York attorney Linda Goldstein, "It is clear that [the FTC] does not care about the issue."

Video Source: "Money Talks: Grocery Industry Manufacturers' Fees," *20/20* (November 11, 1995). *Additional Sources:* Allison Lucas, "Shelf Wars," *Sales and Marketing Management* (March 1996):121; Todd Hyten, "Slotting Fees Pose Market Barriers," *Boston Business Journal* (December 30, 1994):1; Christine Donahue, "Conflict in the Aisles," *Adweek's Marketing Week* (September 4, 1989):20–21; Tim Hammonds and Helmut Radtke, "Two Views on Slotting Allowances," *Progressive Grocer* (February 1990):46, 48; David Kiley, "California Probes Slotting Fees," *Adweek's Marketing Week* (October 8, 1990):6.

QUESTIONS

1. Do you approve of slotting fees? Why or why not?

2. Evaluate Richard Worth's response to the practice of slotting fees. Do you agree with his approach?

3. If you were a supermarket vice president of marketing, what would be your policy on slotting fees? Explain your answer.

Don't buy an Aurora simply because you go for that tight, muscular body and the way its

dual-overhead-cam V8 glides you past that cute little V6 Lexus ES 300

because the Aurora tends to stand out from the crowd

and you wouldn't want to stand out.

Or would you?

AURORA

LEO BURNETT COMPANY, INC.
35 W. Wacker Drive
Chicago, Illinois 60601

 Oldsmobile
1 800 718 7778 www.oldsmobile.com

CHAPTER

Advertising Agencies

CHAPTER OUTLINE

- Managing a Lasting Relationship
- Essence of the Business: Value-Adding Ideas
- Why Hire an Agency?
- The Agency World
- Trends in Advertising and Marketing Communication

- How Agencies Are Organized
- How Agencies Are Paid
- The Future: Efficiency, Effectiveness, and Accountability

CHAPTER OBJECTIVES

When you have completed this chapter, you should be able to:

- Understand the functions of an advertising agency
- Explain how an agency is organized
- Recognize the pressures for change in the business
- Understand how agencies are paid
- Comprehend the impact of technology in this sector as in other business sectors

MANAGING A LASTING RELATIONSHIP

A client switching an account from one agency to another is important news in the advertising business. When Subaru, for example, dumped Levine, Huntley, Schmidt & Beaver, its agency of 18 years, the story was chronicled in Randy Rothenberg's book, *Where the Suckers Moon.*[1] The agency subsequently went out of business.

A variation on the agency switch story occurs when a client reviews its agency assignment and decides to stay (this happens in roughly 20 percent of cases). This is the story of how the Leo Burnett Company retained General Motors' Oldsmobile account in a category (automobiles) that has seen a great deal of turmoil in the 1990s. In the period from 1987 to 1992, 67 percent of the clients of the 50 largest agencies moved some or all of their business to another agency. The agency that fared best during this period was Leo Burnett, which had a loss rate of 24 percent, or six out of 25 clients listed in 1987.[2]

In September 1992, after years of declining sales and market share, the Oldsmobile Division of General Motors announced that it was putting its advertising business up for review. A team of Oldsmobile executives and dealers reviewed a long list of agencies, visited more than a dozen, and asked for presentations from a short list of finalists.

In the midst of this review, other market factors intruded. As often happens, a change of management at Oldsmobile triggered the advertising review. But as General Motors suffered a string of quarterly losses, the business press began to suggest that Oldsmobile would be discontinued. Division management faced the now exacerbated problem of selling cars to a public beginning to wonder if Oldsmobile would soon be extinct.

This called for drastic and radical action. A crisis team including Oldsmobile and Burnett personnel was established at Oldsmobile to guide the marketing effort, to focus on the strengths of Oldsmobile, to get dealer morale up, and to get sales moving. Instead of offering more rebates, the decision was made to select one or two best-selling models, load them with options, and "value price" them to sell. The market crisis and the urgent need to get a strong program into the market forced client and agency management to take personal charge of the rescue effort. And that made the difference.

Meanwhile, agency chairperson Richard (Rick) Fizdale took personal control of the Oldsmobile account. Marketing strategy direction moved from the Burnett office in Detroit to Burnett headquarters in Chicago. When Oldsmobile announced in mid-1993 that it was retaining Burnett, both sides agreed that the grueling hours spent together, objectively facing the problems each had with the other, showed them that they could work together under pressure. Oldsmobile was convinced that Burnett was the right agency.

Furthermore, in the late 1990s the Burnett/Olds relationship became a testing ground for a new kind of commissionless compensation system. Recognizing that nonmeasured media (brochures, events, CD-ROMs, and so forth) are the fastest-growing part of the budget, Philip Guarascio, vice president and general manager for GM's North American marketing and advertising, proposed compensating agencies for their thinking and work, rather than the amount of media placed, which has been the standard in the past.

Olds is a GM division that is adopting many of the successful business practices pioneered by GM's Saturn Corp., and one of those practices involves a com-

---

[1]Randall Rothenberg, *Where the Suckers Moon: An Advertising Story* (New York: Alfred A. Knopf, 1994).

[2]Adapted from Raymond Serafin, "GM Tests Fee-Based Compensation System," *Advertising Age* (February 19, 1996):3; Joanne Lipman, "Study Shows Clients Jump Ship Quickly," *The Wall Street Journal* (May 21, 1992):B8.

missionless compensation system for Saturn's agency, San Francisco-based Hal Riney & Partners. Former Saturn marketing executive Steve Shannon was named Oldsmobile general manager in 1995 and he is believed to be instrumental in carving out a new relationship with its agency. Saturn's revolutionary approach involves a negotiated set fee with incentives built in for exceeding advertising and marketing goals. Such a system can only work when there is a solid relationship of trust between agency and client.

ESSENCE OF THE BUSINESS: VALUE-ADDING IDEAS

PRINCIPLE The role of the agency is to add value to its clients' products.

This chapter will deal with the organization of an advertising agency. Before understanding what an advertising agency does, let's consider why agencies exist. Advertisements can be written for clients by individuals outside of agencies and even sometimes by the clients themselves. Media can be bought through media-buying companies or by clients directly, and research projects can be carried out by research companies. So what does the advertising agency do that has caused this type of organization to dominate the industry worldwide?

When functioning at their best, advertising agencies *create value* for their clients in ways lawyers and accountants simply do not. When an agency clearly interprets to its client what customers want and expect and then communicates information about the client's product or service so meaningfully, so uniquely, or so consistently that customers reward that brand or product or service with their loyalty, then the value of the agency comes most sharply into focus.

Perceived Value: The value that a customer or buyer intrinsically or subjectively attaches to a brand or service. It is the image or personality that differentiates one product from a virtually identical competitor.

The essence of the agency business, the goal each agency strives to achieve, is to add **perceived value** to the product or service of its client. This is done by giving the product a personality, by communicating in a manner that shapes the basic understanding of the product, by creating an image or memorable picture of the product, and by setting the product apart from its competitors.

But basic marketing wisdom and business intuition tell us that, to do this effectively, communication (not just advertising) must do more than merely transmit information. Rather it must "tailor the product story to a potential customer."[3] Communication at this level converts information into perceptions that are memorable and motivating. Perceptions then become key facts in differentiating between brands.

The perceived value of a brand was raised to new heights when British companies and then others began to recognize on their balance sheets the value, presumably the market value or value to another corporate buyer, of brands that they owned. This *brand equity* was largely due to the contribution of advertising in the building of the brand. Campbell's red and white imagery, for example, has tremendous impact because of the consistency of the advertising over the years. (See Ad 4.1.)

What follows in this chapter is the story of how advertising agencies organize to accomplish the goal of adding value to brands. And most clients recognize the value that advertising delivers for their brands. As Edwin L. Artzt, retired chairperson-CEO of Procter & Gamble, put it: "We believe in advertising. We believe it is our most effective marketing tool—the very lifeblood of our brands."[4]

The success of advertising agencies in serving their clients is attested to by the amount of money spent on advertising. Published in *Advertising Age* in 1996, Table 4.1 includes the 1995 spending for the leading U.S. brands, companies, and categories in the United States. These charts give you some idea of the size of the industry and its major players.

---

[3]*The Value Side of Productivity*. Committee on the Value of Advertising, American Association of Advertising Agencies (1989).
[4]Edwin L. Artzt, "The Lifeblood of Brands," *Advertising Age* (November 4, 1991):32.

AD 4.1

THE "NEVER UNDERESTIMATE
THE POWER OF SOUP" CAM-
PAIGN BY BBDO HAS CONTIN-
UED TO HELP THE BRAND MAIN-
TAIN ITS DOMINANCE OF THE
SOUP CATEGORY.

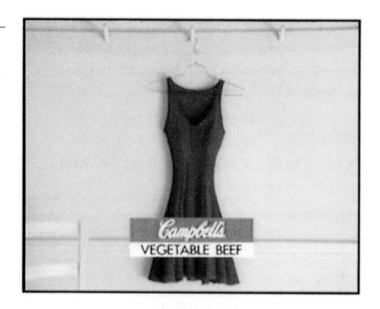

TABLE 4.1	TEN TOP BRANDS

Megabrands by 1995 ad spending

RANK		BRAND, PRODUCT OR SERVICE	PARENT COMPANY	TOTAL MEASURED AD SPENDING		
1995	1994			1995	1994	% CHG
1	1	AT&T telephone svcs	AT&T Corp.	$673,386.9	$698,413.2	−3.6
2	2	Ford cars & trucks	Ford Motor Co.	564,866.4	565,183.2	−0.1
3	4	Sears stores	Sears, Roebuck & Co.	540,052.5	471,813.1	14.5
4	5	McDonald's restaurants	McDonald's Corp.	490,549.9	425,698.8	15.2
5	3	Kellogg breakfast foods	Kellogg Co.	488,205.1	483,693.7	0.9
6	6	Chevrolet cars & trucks	General Motors Corp.	477,599.5	419,941.0	13.7
7	15	Dodge cars & trucks	Chrysler Corp.	414,530.6	233,893.2	77.2
8	7	Toyota cars & trucks	Toyota Motor Corp.	384,074.0	374,502.2	2.6
9	8	MCI telephone svcs	MCI Communications Corp.	320,955.9	325,366.4	−1.4
10	19	Warner Bros. movies	Time Warner	294,003.7	204,452.4	43.8

Top 10 companies by 1995 ad spending

RANK	COMPANY	TOTAL MEASURED AD SPENDING			AD SPENDING BY BRANDS IN 200			NUMBER OF BRANDS
		1995	1994	% CHG	1995	1994	% CHG	
1	Procter & Gamble Co.	$1,507.4	$1,463.7	3.0	$515.8	$423.8	21.7	7
2	General Motors Corp.	1,499.6	1,398.8	7.2	1,382.5	1,313.8	5.2	8
3	Philip Morris Cos.	1,398.7	1,295.5	8.0	907.5	796.3	14.0	8
4	Chrysler Corp.	954.7	758.7	25.8	935.0	743.3	25.8	5
5	Ford Motor Co.	891.8	920.3	−3.1	859.0	884.6	−2.9	4
6	Walt Disney Co.	777.6	587.1	32.4	622.8	438.4	42.1	4
7	PepsiCo	730.2	669.7	9.0	608.8	555.2	9.6	4
8	Time Warner	692.6	571.1	21.3	412.5	318.8	29.4	3
9	AT&T Corp.	674.9	700.4	−3.7	673.4	698.4	−3.6	1
10	Johnson & Johnson	594.0	478.5	24.1	417.2	289.3	44.2	4

Notes: Dollars are in millions.
Source: Competitive Media Reporting. *Advertising Age*, May 6, 1996, p. 36.

Top 10 companies by 1995 ad spending

RANK	CATEGORY	MEASURED AD SPENDING			AD SPENDING BY MEDIA			NUMBER OF BRANDS
		1995	1994	% CHG	PRINT	BROADCAST	OUTDOOR	
1	Automotive	$5,261.5	$4,976.0	5.7	$1,658.8	$3,567.1	$35.6	31
2	Retail	2,992.8	2,774.3	7.9	1,572.1	1,415.8	4.9	26
3	Food	2,563.6	2,491.5	2.9	302.4	2,254.6	6.5	24
4	Entertainment & movies	2,561.2	1,909.8	34.1	1,208.6	1,330.8	21.8	21
5	Restaurants & fast-food	1,805.6	1,583.1	14.1	21.7	1,743.2	40.7	12
6	Personal care & remedies	1,693.1	1,370.7	23.5	376.8	1,315.5	0.7	23
7	Telephone	1,658.9	1,570.9	5.6	367.6	1,276.0	15.2	10
8	Financial services, securities	937.1	917.3	2.2	291.8	639.5	5.7	11
9	Computers & electronics	665.2	425.5	56.3	353.8	310.4	0.9	6
10	Beer	503.3	490.6	2.6	10.1	455.2	37.9	4

Notes: Dollars are in millions. Totals include only brands from the Top 200.
Source: Competitive Media Reporting. *Advertising Age*, May 6, 1996, p. 34.

WHY HIRE AN AGENCY?

Agencies are retained to plan and execute client advertising efforts. But, as mentioned, each segment of these plans can be purchased separately. Why should an advertiser sign a long-term contract with an agency? What extra benefit comes from hiring such an agency? What comfort level does a client achieve by appointing an agency? Does it cost more or less to use an agency than to buy services separately?

The answers vary from client to client and from agency to agency, but generally the agency-client relationship is carefully established and maintained. Although the trade press reports the comings and goings of notable clients from one agency to another, the fact is that the average tenure of a client with an agency is between seven and ten years. Some have lasted 50 years. The following is a discussion of the reasons why advertisers establish long-term relationships with agencies. First, outside agencies bring expertise, objectivity, and dedication and, second, they handle the staffing and management requirements needed to achieve the communication objectives.

EXPERTISE, OBJECTIVITY, AND DEDICATION

An established agency has gained expertise through years of experience and can offer objective advice to its clients. Agencies are committed to solving problems for and delivering service to their clients.

An agency acquires expertise by working with a variety of clients; agency professionals can apply lessons learned with one client to another. Applying a broad perspective through the varied backgrounds and skills of employees often is the key to solving difficult advertising problems. This perspective is often lacking in smaller in-house agencies or limited departments. Just as a company may hire an outside law firm even if it has an attorney on staff, so too a company may hire an agency to work for its advertising department in order to benefit from the agency's professional expertise. (See Ad 4.2.)

Clients expect an agency to tell them when they are misreading the market or are out of step with consumers. Agency objectivity is a necessary part of the relationship. Someone from outside the client company is more likely to speak up

AD 4.2

A BOOK PUBLISHED BY THE LEO BURNETT AGENCY CONTAINS THE SAYINGS OF THE AGENCY'S FOUNDER AND DEMONSTRATES HOW THIS AGENCY HAS LEARNED FROM ITS EXPERIENCES WITH ADVERTISING FOR VARIOUS CLIENTS.

and is better able to maintain an independent and detached view of the marketplace and the consumer. Advertising people are experts in their field, whereas few clients feel competent to approve, as well as create, advertisements. They depend on the agency for professional judgment.

Clients, especially those who nurture the relationship, expect and receive dedication and commitment from their agencies. The agency becomes very much a part of the client team. This client-agency relationship serves as an incentive for the agency to produce an extra effort, an interest in every aspect of the client's business, and a drive never to be satisfied with "good enough." The commitment to a client's business and the need to remain objective can produce some of the most difficult decisions in the business. Agencies that hold fast to their point of view may lose a client but not their own self-respect.

STAFFING AND MANAGEMENT

Agencies provide the human resources and management skills necessary to accomplish the communication task. Usually clients lack the resources to create and produce advertising strategies and quality advertisements. They look to an outside agency to provide them with the expertise they don't have on staff. Even the largest clients might have need for a statistician, a network negotiator, a television producer, or a special-events coordinator only once a year. Only large agencies that have multiple accounts needing these kinds of services can afford to employ these specialists full time. Most recently, agencies have been designing home pages for their clients who are creating a presence on the Internet. (See Ad 4.3.)

MANAGING THE CREATIVE PROCESS

Creative people who work for advertising agencies may not be at all like the employees of a corporation. Artists, writers, and television producers might not fit easily into the culture of the corporate environment. Stated work hours, dress

AD 4.3

CKS IS AN AGENCY THAT SPE-CIALIZES IN NEW MEDIA. ONE OF ITS PROJECTS WAS TO BUILD A HOME PAGE FOR GM. THIS IS A PAGE FROM THE AGENCY BROCHURE THAT DEMON-STRATES ITS WORK FOR GM.

TABLE 4.2	TOTAL INCOME BY U.S. AGENCIES

Ten-year gross income and volume review

	TOTAL GROSS INCOME OF U.S.-BASED AGENCIES					
YEAR	**W'WIDE**	**% CHG**	**U.S.**	**% CHG**	**NON-U.S.**	**% CHG**
1995	$17.26	9.2	$10.10	7.7	$7.15	11.4
1994	15.80	9.1	9.38	10.7	6.42	6.9
1993	14.48	−0.4	8.48	3.8	6.00	−5.7
1992	14.54	7.2	8.17	6.8	6.37	7.6
1991	13.57	4.7	7.65	2.9	5.92	7.0
1990	12.96	13.4	7.43	6.2	5.53	24.9
1989	11.43	1.7	7.00	2.5	4.43	0.4
1988	11.24	16.9	6.83	9.8	4.41	29.9
1987	9.61	11.1	6.22	−4.4	3.40	58.2
1986	8.65	5.8	6.50	3.8	2.15	12.3

Notes: Gross income and capitalized volume are in billions of U.S. dollars. Change is computed from previous years figures, including 1985, not shown. All figures are constant, representing reporting by the Top 500 U.S.-based agencies in the year given. *Advertising Age*, April 15, 1996, p. 515.

codes, and limitations on overtime would be difficult to enforce among the creative "free spirits" who tend to work in advertising. Pay scales may vary widely: It might be difficult to explain why a brilliant writer who has odd work habits is paid more than a department head. Advertising agencies provide a supportive environment for these people. Agencies can organize their skills, maintain morale, and build spirit more effectively among creative people than corporations can.

FLEXIBILITY IN STAFFING

Client advertising budgets go up and down, and as the budget level increases or decreases, so does the employment level. Because agencies handle a number of clients, they are better able to adjust the comings and goings of clients. Clients might find it difficult to accommodate their staffing levels to the condition of the marketplace. A company with a commitment to employee loyalty (or a very liberal termination policy) might find it difficult to deal with hiring and firing employees whose positions depend on the advertising budget. Clients have decided it is better to let the agency deal with staffing, spreading the effects among a roster of clients and building personnel policies that adjust to and compensate for these risks.

The size of agency staffs has been declining in recent years. Between October 1992 and October 1993, advertising-related jobs with the top 16 U.S. agencies decreased by 3.1 percent. These top 16 agencies employ 22 percent of all agency workers. Total U.S. employment in agencies for the same period was down by 0.8 percent to 152,700, but off 3.9 percent from 1990. Total U.S. advertising spending began a slow recovery after 1991, dropped in 1993, and then increased dramatically in 1994 and 1995 (see Table 4.2).[5] The general downward trend in employment opportunities, however, is expected to continue as agencies try to service more business with smaller staffs in order to maintain profitability. According to the American Association of Advertising Agencies, the average number of people per million dollars in billings continued its long decline by dropping from 2.37 in 1984 to 1.57 in 1992. The reasons for this decrease in advertising staffing in the large agencies are due to increased pressures from clients on compensation paid to agencies and a desire by the agen-

[5]Melanie Wells, "Burnett, Others Feed Staff-Cutting Trend," *Advertising Age* (December 6, 1993):5–8.

TOTAL CAPITALIZED VOLUME OF U.S.-BASED AGENCIES					
W'WIDE	**% CHG**	**U.S.**	**% CHG**	**NON-U.S.**	**% CHG**
$130.50	11.1	$78.75	9.6	$51.75	13.4
117.49	9.5	71.84	10.4	45.65	8.1
107.29	3.7	65.07	8.9	42.22	−3.4
103.45	7.4	59.76	6.4	43.69	8.7
96.34	4.1	56.16	3.1	40.18	5.5
92.57	15.5	54.47	8.9	38.10	26.6
80.13	2.8	50.03	3.6	30.10	1.4
77.99	18.7	48.30	12.4	29.69	30.6
65.70	10.8	42.97	−4.0	22.73	55.9
59.32	6.3	44.74	8.1	14.58	1.0

cies for greater efficiency and productivity by reducing corporate overhead and support staffs.

The reason total employment in the industry has dropped less is reflected in the trend for small and medium-sized agencies to add services in public relations, database management, direct response, Yellow Pages or directory advertising, recruitment advertising, and in taking over the production of newsletters, annual reports, and employee communications.

THE AGENCY WORLD

Advertising agencies range in size from small shops to giant businesses that employ thousands. In any major market in the United States you will find dozens of advertising agencies. The smallest agencies usually have up to a dozen employees and bill up to $10 million. Medium-sized agencies bill $10 million to $100 million. The top 20 U.S. and world agencies are given in Table 4.3.

In addition to these local agencies, there are also large agency networks that are national or international in focus (see Tables 4.3 and 4.4). In any major market there is probably a local agency that is affiliated with a large group such as BBDO, Bates, Young & Rubicam, Ogilvy & Mather, and DDB Needham. The J. Walter Thompson agency, for example, has 218 offices worldwide. There are also groups of independent agencies such as Advertising Agencies Affiliated International (3AI), an association with worldwide headquarters in Denver that has a member agency in most major markets. These independent agencies affiliate among themselves in order to be competitive with the large network agencies.

To make the picture even more complex, there are also holding companies such as Interpublic, WPP, and Omnicom, which own several agency networks. Omnicom, for example, owns both the BBDO and DDB Needham advertising conglomerates as well as smaller agencies Goodby, Silverstein and Partners, and Diversified Services (DAS), a network of what is called *below-the-line agencies* that specialize in other marketing communication areas such as public relations, sales promotion, direct marketing, and events. Table 4.4 (on page 114) gives the top ten advertising organizations in the world market.

TABLE 4.3 TOP 20 U.S. AND WORLD AGENCIES

U.S. agency brands ranked by gross income

RANK 1995	RANK 1994	AGENCY	HEADQUARTERS	GROSS INCOME 1995	GROSS INCOME % CHG	VOLUME 1995
1	1	Leo Burnett Co.	Chicago	$370.6	15.1	$2,484.8
2	2	J. Walter Thompson Co.	New York	347.0	9.3	2,419.9
3	3	Grey Advertising	New York	326.7	7.3	2,178.9
4	4	DDB Needham Worldwide	New York	284.7	9.2	2,546.0
5	5	McCann-Erickson Worldwide	New York	279.6	9.2	1,865.0
6	7	Saatchi & Saatchi Advertising*	New York	275.5	14.1	2,204.1
7	6	BBDO Worldwide	New York	259.5	5.5	2,621.8
8	8	Foote, Cone & Belding Communications	Chicago	244.2	2.9	2,827.0
9	11	Ogilvy & Mather Worldwide	New York	209.5	20.6	2,091.7
10	10	Young & Rubicam	New York	205.8	9.1	2,142.6
11	12	Bozell Worldwide	New York	200.3	25.6	1,585.0
12	9	D'Arcy Masius Benton & Bowles	New York	191.4	−5.5	1,960.4
13	13	Bates Worldwide*	New York	152.1	−2.5	1,217.1
14	15	TMP Worldwide	New York	137.4	16.7	915.9
15	14	TBWA Chiat/Day	New York	130.7	0.1	1,046.5
16	16	Ammirati Puris Lintas	New York	113.8	0.1	870.0
17	18	Gage Marketing Group	Minneapolis	108.5	13.4	723.8
18	21	Wunderman Cato Johnson	New York	101.0	25.8	842.6
19	17	N.W. Ayer & Partners	New York	94.1	−4.8	851.9
20	19	Wells Rich Greene BDDP	New York	89.2	−3.9	850.3

Notes: Figures are in millions of U.S. dollars. Each worldwide agency brand excludes U.S. branded subsidiary shops ranked elsewhere in this report. Included are international networks associated with the agency. *Advertising Age*, April 15, 1996, p. s8.

World's top 20 agency brands

RANK 1995	RANK 1994	AGENCY	WORLDWIDE GROSS INCOME 1995	WORLDWIDE GROSS INCOME 1994	WORLDWIDE GROSS INCOME % CHG	WORLDWIDE CAPITALIZED VOLUME 1995	WORLDWIDE CAPITALIZED VOLUME 1994	WORLDWIDE CAPITALIZED VOLUME % CHG
1	1	Denstu	$1,930.0	$1,583.7	21.9	$13,933.8	$11,609.4	20.0
2	2	McCann-Erickson Worldwide	1,153.9	1,037.0	11.3	7,658.9	6,917.2	10.7
3	3	J. Walter Thompson Co.	1,007.1	887.7	13.4	6,771.7	6,045.8	12.0
4	4	Hakuhodo	958.6	774.2	23.8	6,909.3	5,766.5	19.8
5	5	BBDO Worldwide	857.5	736.5	16.4	6,748.6	5,832.3	15.7
6	7	Leo Burnett Co.	803.9	677.5	18.7	5,373.6	4,592.0	17.0
7	8	DDB Needham Worldwide	785.7	661.7	18.7	6,199.8	5,157.0	20.2
8	6	Grey Advertising	777.3	703.0	10.6	5,190.9	4,704.2	10.3
9	9	Ogilvy & Mather Worldwide	714.1	611.4	16.8	6,391.9	5,304.6	20.5
10	10	Foote, Cone & Belding Communications	679.0	605.2	12.2	5,751.4	5,056.1	13.8
11	11	Saatchi & Saatchi Advertising	676.9	602.7	12.3	5,415.7	4,821.7	12.3
12	12	Euro RSCG	643.4	568.6	13.2	4,879.6	4,310.1	13.2
13	14	Publicis Communication	606.3	543.2	11.6	4,139.7	3,694.6	12.0
14	15	Bates Worldwide	575.2	510.3	12.7	4,601.6	4,082.2	12.7
15	13	Ammirati Puris Lintas	568.3	545.7	4.1	3,904.9	3,657.1	6.8
16	16	Young & Rubicam	555.8	498.1	11.6	5,289.2	4,177.0	26.6
17	17	D'Arcy Masius Benton & Bowles	497.0	483.5	2.8	4,549.0	4,300.9	5.8
18	18	TBWA International	318.2	287.3	10.7	2,330.8	2,041.7	14.2
19	19	Lowe Group	310.3	280.9	10.5	2,174.3	1,959.8	10.9
20	21	Bozell Worldwide	279.9	224.7	24.6	2,085.0	1,717.0	21.4

Notes: Figures are in millions of U.S. dollars. Each worldwide agency brand excludes U.S. branded subsidiary shops ranked elsewhere in this report. Included are international networks associated with the agency. *Advertising Age*, April 15, 1996, p. s8.

INSIDE ADVERTISING

MICHELLE STETZ, ACCOUNT EXECUTIVE, *The Leffler Agency, Baltimore, Maryland*

Throughout your college career, you will learn many lessons. The most valuable lesson I learned as a mass communications major was the importance of internships. In fact, when I began my pursuit for a career in advertising, it was my internship experience that helped me get my foot in the door.

As an undergraduate at Towson State University, I was highly aware of the competition to break into the advertising field, but I did not let that discourage me. In addition to my advertising courses, I joined the American Advertising Federation (AAF) during my sophomore year. The AAF provided me the opportunity to participate in a national advertising campaign competition against other East Coast AAF chapters. Although our chapter did not win, the experience I gained from working on that campaign was invaluable. During my junior year, I became eligible to apply for an internship at an advertising agency. I interviewed with the Leffler Agency and, although it was small, I knew I would have more flexibility with my responsibilities than I would at a larger agency. Choosing to intern at a small agency was probably the best decision I ever made because I did more than just answer phones and fax traffic. I had the opportunity to write radio and television copy for two major clients, I assisted an account executive with a campaign proposal, and I attended a photo shoot. Another advantage of interning at a small agency is the ability to establish a good relationship with the staff. It is much easier to get acquainted with eleven employees than with five hundred!

When my internship ended, I decided that advertising was definitely the career for me. I was particularly interested in the position of account executive because I saw it as the most versatile position. An account executive not only maintains client relations but can do everything from writing copy to buying media. Every day can offer a new and exciting project, so there is little monotony. Since account executive positions are high in demand, I knew I had to distinguish myself from the other candidates. To broaden my educational background, I chose to pursue a minor in English literature. I also enrolled in public relations and marketing courses, since they are integrated with advertising. During my senior year, I became chief financial officer of the AAF and was inducted into the AAF's honor fraternity, Alpha Delta Sigma.

As my graduation day approached, I made a list of local agencies to contact for informational interviews, which are a great opportunity to differentiate yourself from applicants who mail or fax their résumés. The first agency on my list was the Leffler Agency. I figured interning there proved to be a good experience, and if the agency could not offer me a job, perhaps it could offer me another internship. I contacted the account supervisor to schedule an interview. She remembered who I was, and to my surprise, the agency needed a junior account executive. After my second interview, I was offered the position. Within two months, I was promoted to account executive.

I have been an account executive for almost a year now, but I'm beginning to understand that being a *22-year-old* account executive is not an easy task. For example, I never considered my age to be a hindrance until I started working. I sometimes experience what I like to call "reverse ageism." Some new clients often feel uncomfortable with someone so "young" in charge of their account, so I have to work extra hard to prove that I am just as competent as someone ten years my senior. This leaves very little room for mistakes, but I accept the challenge willingly. Nothing is more satisfying than having a client who once doubted you complement your work.

Looking back, I was very fortunate to find a job prior to my graduation, but it may not have happened if I hadn't taken advantage of the opportunities my internship had to offer. Internships provide a real-world experience that you will never find in a classroom. If your school has an internship program, apply! If not, find a list of agencies and call them yourself. (Tip: If you do not know a supervisor's name, speak to the human resources department.) Above all, remember that a proactive attitude is an absolute must for success in the world of advertising. Only *you* can make it happen.

Nominated by Professor Richard Gist, Towson State University.

In smaller markets, small agencies tend to offer a range of services for specialized markets. For example, Lewis Advertising in Mobile, Alabama, has its own public relations department, a collateral production unit, and a department that specializes in hospital and health care advertising. To deal with special situations, employees develop special skills. Hood, Light & Geise agency in Harrisburg, Pennsylvania, billing less than $5 million, has three divisions: advertising, public relations, and association management. Marketing Resources of America near Kansas City focuses on strategic marketing for clients and then bundles the skills needed for a client; these skills include advertising but also could include such activities as in-store promotions and dealer training. In larger markets, local independent agencies usually specialize either in a type of service, such as creative work or collateral (brochures, reports, newsletters), or in a particular type of market, such as health care, agribusiness, or the upscale market.

TABLE 4.4	TOP AD ORGANIZATIONS		

Top 10 ad organizations

RANK	ORGANIZATION	WORLDWIDE GROSS INCOME	% CHG
1	WPP Group, London	$3,129.7	12.7
2	Omnicom Group, New York	2,576.7	16.7
3	Interpublic Group of Cos., New York	2,337.2	9.9
4	Dentsu, Tokyo	1,998.6	21.8
5	Cordiant, London	1,377.8	11.5
6	Young & Rubicam, New York	1,197.5	14.4
7	Hakuhodo, Tokyo	958.6	23.8
8	Havas Advertising, Paris	909.4	11.8
9	Grey Advertising, New York	896.5	10.9
10	Leo Burnett Co., Chicago	803.9	18.7

Advertising Age, April 15, 1996, p. s2.

The forms, services provided, and types of agencies are in constant change. The boundary of what is included is restricted by what is affordable within the revenue the agency receives; conversely, services are expanded to the extent an agency can negotiate a fee for special service. The following types, while not an exhaustive list, are described to show the variety found in the advertising agency business.

FULL-SERVICE AGENCY

Full-Service Agency: An agency that handles all of a client's advertising efforts and offers four major staff functions—account management, creative services, media planning and buying, and research.

In advertising, a **full-service agency** is one that has on staff the four major staff functions—account management, creative services, media planning and buying, and research. A full-service advertising agency will also have its own accounting department, a traffic department to handle internal tracking on completion of projects, departments for broadcast and print production (usually organized within the creative department), and a human resources department.

Typically, an agreement between a full-service agency and a client will determine that the agency, for the commission received on media and production services or for an agreed fee, will analyze market data, propose a strategy, prepare a recommendation, produce the advertising, place it in approved media, verify the advertising's appearance as ordered, invoice the client against the approved budget, collect funds from the client, and disburse those funds to media and suppliers. The Price-McNabb ad (Ad 4.4) focuses on this agency's research and strategy capabilities.

Normally not included in the basic agreement and not covered by the revenue the agency receives are public relations work, research projects, direct marketing, event marketing, and sales promotion. Some agencies offer these services to clients through departments or subsidiaries that deliver the specific service, or clients may use specialty agencies for these activities. The largest full-service agencies are shown in Table 4.3.

SPECIALIZED AGENCIES

There are many agencies that do not follow the traditional full-service agency approach. They either specialize in certain functions (creative or media buying), audiences (minorities, youth), or certain industries (health, computers, agriculture, or business-to-business communication). In addition, of course, there are specialized agencies in all the various marketing communication areas, such as direct marketing, sales promotion, public relations, events and sports marketing, packaging and corporate design, and so forth. Furthermore, there are one-client agencies such as the Focus agency in Dallas that served only GTE, in-house agencies operated by the advertiser itself, and freelancers.

Business-to-business agencies, for example, specialize in trade communication. Their clients are selling to other manufacturers or service providers rather than to consumers. These agencies understand trade promotion and trade shows, as well

AD 4.4

THESE ILLUSTRATIONS FROM
A PRICE/MCNABB BROCHURE
DEMONSTRATE IN A HUMOROUS
WAY HOW THE AGENCY USES
INSIGHTS FROM RESEARCH AS
A PLATFORM FOR BUILDING
STRATEGIES.

as business-to-business advertising. Direct advertising is an important tool in business-to-business marketing and the advertising objectives are often directed at supporting the efforts of personal sales. Because business-to-business marketing uses so many communication tools, these agencies are often integrated marketing communication (IMC) agencies.

INDUSTRY-FOCUSED AGENCIES

There are a number of agencies that concentrate on certain fields or industries, such as agriculture, medicine and pharmaceuticals, health care, and computers. These agencies handle a variety of clients from within that field so they are able to bring their particular expertise to the service of their clients.

To better understand these specialist agencies, let's look at a type of agency that concentrates on advertising for pharmaceutical companies such as Abbott, Merck, Pfizer, Hoffman-LaRoche, and Upjohn. Medical agencies require staff members with detailed knowledge of chemistry and pharmacology as well as an understanding of medical practices and laws relating to health care advertising. People with advanced scientific degrees are often hired or retained by these agencies as consultants. This type of agency carries out most of the functions a full-service agency performs but concentrates in the medical field. Seminars, symposia, and the writing and publication of technical papers relating to the business are often planned and managed by pharmaceutical agencies. These agencies may be small such as Durot, Donahoe & Purohit of Rosemont, Illinois, with 12 employees, or large, such as Kallir Phillips Ross, Sudler & Hennessey, and Medicus Intercom of New York City, each with well over 100 employees.

These medical agencies have been growing more rapidly than the total industry, as prescription drugs have been released for over-the-counter sale as part of a government effort to reduce health care costs. Many full-service agencies and holding companies have responded by buying medical agencies. Eight of the top ten medical shops are now owned by full-line agencies. It is difficult to predict how America's changing health care system will affect these agencies, but managed competition and drug-buying cooperatives will probably reduce the market for medical agencies.

MINORITY AGENCIES

Agencies that focus on an ethnic group, or minority agencies, grew substantially in the 1980s as marketers realized that African-Americans and Hispanic-Americans, the two largest minorities, had different preferences and buying patterns from the general market. These agencies are organized much the same as full-service agencies, but they are specialists in reaching and communicating with their market. When Texaco, for example, settled a charge of racial bias in the winter of 1996, it responded among other things by hiring a black-owned agency, UniWorld Group, to create ads aimed at boosting its image among minorities.

Burrell Advertising in Chicago is one of the largest and most successful African-American agencies. Tom Burrell worked for several general-market agencies before starting his agency. With over 100 employees, Burrell Advertising represents such clients as Brown-Forman Beverage Co., Ford Motor Company, McDonald's, Polaroid, Procter & Gamble, Coca-Cola, Stroh's Brewery, and Sony Corporation.

Conill Advertising founded in 1968 is representative of Hispanic agencies. Conill handles national accounts and is minority managed. This New York agency is now owned by Saatchi & Saatchi and has 45 employees. Clients include Helene Curtis, Procter & Gamble, and Toyota. The market for Hispanic advertising has attracted agencies from outside the continental United States. Noble & Asociados of Mexico City (now owned by DMB&B) opened an office in Irving, California, and is billing over $20 million. Premier Maldonado, the leading independent agency in San Juan, Puerto Rico, opened an office in Miami in the late 1980s to capitalize on its Hispanic marketing experience to serve its clients in the "upper 48."

The 1990 U.S. census counted more than 24 million foreign language households, many of which are bilingual. The largest foreign language group is Hispanic, 71 percent of the total at 17.3 million households, followed by German at 1.5 million, Italian at 1.3 million, and Chinese at 1.2 million.

Targeting minorities is not without problems. African-American groups in New York and Chicago have tried to remove billboards advertising alcohol and cigarettes from their neighborhoods. R.J. Reynolds was forced by public pressure, touched off by criticism from Health and Human Services Secretary Louis Sullivan, to withdraw Uptown cigarettes from test. The brand was aimed at African-Americans. Operation PUSH boycotted Nike shoes in 1990 when the organization felt Nike was presumably marketing to the African-American community but not returning enough of its revenue to that community. Nike had used African-American athletes extensively in its advertising but did not use a minority advertising agency. It has since appointed one.

African-American and Hispanic advertising agencies have been vocal in criticizing the infringement of free speech implied by the attempted removal of advertising material from ethnic neighborhoods while maintaining the wisdom and the right of the advertisers to segment markets. The ethical side of the issue is that so-called sin products, alcohol and tobacco, which can lead to addiction and health problems, are more heavily advertised in these neighborhoods than to the population in general. Advertising follows usage patterns. Activists argue this focus is leading to greater usage of the products.

CREATIVE BOUTIQUES

Creative boutiques are organizations, usually relatively small agencies (two or three people to a dozen or more) that concentrate entirely on preparing the creative execution of client communications. A creative boutique will have one or more writers and artists on staff. The organization typically is capable of preparing advertising to run in print media, outdoor, radio, and television. The focus of the organization is entirely on the idea, the creative product. There is no staff for media, research, strategic planning, or annual plan writing. Creative boutiques usually are hired by clients but are sometimes retained by an advertising agency when it is "stuck" or has an overload of work.

Creative boutiques are not as long-lived as full-service agencies. They depend on a small group of individuals, frequently organized as a partnership. If a key individual leaves, the creative boutique may disband. Some of the most successful boutiques, on the other hand, have become full-service agencies. Grace and Rothchild in New York started as a creative service and has grown to over $75 million in capitalized billing—hardly a boutique anymore.

MEDIA-BUYING SERVICES

Media-Buying Service: A company that offers to buy media directly for advertisers and performs basically only this service.

Media-buying services first flowered in the 1970s, as media experts in advertising agencies felt they could make more money on their own than in an agency. They were probably correct, and media salaries have increased substantially since the late 1970s. Media services called on advertisers to propose buying media at rates as low as 1 percent of spending for network television, 2 percent to 3 percent for national magazines, and somewhat more for local newspapers and radio on a nationwide basis.

The relative popularity of the creative boutique, especially in New York and Chicago at the same time, augmented the breakup of services normally provided by full-service agencies. As mentioned, a creative boutique does not plan or buy media. The client might turn that assignment over to a media-buying service or plan the media internally and pay a buying service to execute the plan.

As media became more and more complex with additional media choices, the growth of cable, the segmentation of magazines, and the wide variety of radio stations, the cost to maintain a competent media department caused some smaller agencies to use media-buying services. Clients, introduced to media-buying services either on their own or through agencies that had dropped media, found the services competent, professional, and often possessing substantial buying power. Media buyers with these services, often buying in more markets or in greater quantities than some advertising agencies, delivered media at greater efficiency. Although the media-buying services seldom can beat the top 25 agencies in buying clout, they can usually better small and medium-sized agencies, especially in spot television and spot radio buying in markets with which the smaller agencies are not familiar.

Western International Media Corporation, with more than $900 million in annual media buying, is the largest of the group. It opened in 1970 in Los Angeles after an earlier attempt by its founder, Dennis Holt, in New York and now has offices in more than 20 cities in the United States and Canada. Western Media works almost exclusively for advertising agencies and services only one advertiser directly. It has expanded its services to agencies by offering market research; print, outdoor, Yellow Pages, television, and radio production; Hispanic media and marketing; premiums and employee incentives; syndication and promotional broadcast placement.

CPM, founded by Norman Goldring in 1969 in Chicago, is typical of the media-buying services that work for agencies and for advertisers. Clients include Walgreen's, Ralston, Kinko, and Turtle Wax. CPM employs 55 people and handles more than $100 million in media annually. In 1993 it split off its direct-response unit, CPO (for cost per order), into a separate company. Its clients include Nordic-Track, Montgomery Ward, and Cancer Treatment Centers of America.

IN-HOUSE AGENCIES

In-house agencies are advertising agencies owned and supervised by the companies that advertise. A large retailer like Macy's, for example, may have its own in-house advertising department or agency because its daily advertising budget would overwhelm most outside agencies. In-house agencies are organized like independent agencies but can take a variety of forms. The advertising director of the company is usually the chief executive officer of the agency. The director supervises account managers responsible for brands or business groups. The in-house agency has writers and artists as needed, traffic personnel, media specialists, all of whose functions will be explained later in this chapter. If the company has a research department, this specialty will probably not be duplicated in the in-house unit. The in-house agency may do its own billing, paying, and collecting, but it is more likely to use the company's accounting department. Why use an in-house agency? Here are the reasons:

- *Savings.* To the extent that the agency duplicates the staffing of a client or has counterparts in the client's firms, this expense can be eliminated. Probably the most appealing reason is that every agency seeks to make a profit on a client's business, and by taking the work in-house that profit can be saved. A failure to realize this profit is the reason many return to the use of an outside agency.
- *Specialization.* Clients in a highly technical field often find it difficult to get scientifically correct copywriting from an agency. They watch a copywriter master the field and then get promoted or transferred to another account. Better to have someone who knows the business on staff in the in-house agency. The disadvantage to this solution is the burn-out a person may experience working in one field without any variety.
- *Priority Service.* Clearly the in-house agency works only for the client and is

available immediately for high-priority projects. There are no conflicts with other clients for the use of key personnel or the time of agency management.

- *Minimum Staffing.* The in-house agency attempts to staff for minimum requirements and engages freelance staff to handle peak workloads. Freelance operators may not always be available and may not possess the requisite knowledge, although management of freelance services is a function built into the in-house agency's role, and problems certainly can be controlled with good planning. The need for flexibility cuts both ways. When problems arise, as noted in the previous section, some clients may again employ ad agencies so that the peaks and valleys of workloads may be spread out.

FREELANCERS

A freelance creative person differs from a creative boutique chiefly by the nature of employment and extent of service. Freelancers are in business for themselves; they have a variety of agency clients but usually do not work exclusively for any one. Many work at home, although some have their own offices. A freelance creative writer may work with a freelance artist as a team and bring each other business. Together, they might present their creative recommendation to a client. But they are each individual practitioners.

VIRTUAL AGENCIES

A recent phenomenon is the agency that operates like a group of freelancers. The trend toward virtual agencies also sees the abandonment of conventional office space. Los Angeles-based Chiat/Day chief operating officer, Adelaide Horton, says that at any time, one third to one half of an agency's offices are empty as people are out calling on clients or at meetings. Why pay for space that isn't being used? Chiat/Day has pioneered an approach dubbed "team workroom" or a virtual office. In a virtual agency like Chiat/Day, staff members do not have fixed offices—they work at home, in their cars, or at their clients' offices. Modern technology allows team members to work outside the office. They conduct meetings by video conferencing or electronic mail. When they need to come into the office, they can use any cubicle that's free and check out a computer to work on. Their personal things are stored in lockers on wheels, which they retrieve from storage and move to their workspace. Under the team workroom concept, walled-off or partitioned workspace is done away with in favor of an open area with room for staffers, computers, fax machines, and telephones that the team members bring with them into the room.

AGENCY PHILOSOPHIES

Regardless of the focus or size of an agency, most of them have a philosophy of business that separates one agency from another. Agencies use these statements in making client pitches, as well as in orienting their employees to the corporate culture. In some cases, such as Leo Burnett, the agency philosophies have remained stable for many years. Other agencies try to adapt their philosophy statements to the times or to their management. For example, "brand stewardship" became an important concept at Ogilvy & Mather after Charlotte Beers was named chairperson and CEO in 1992. Jon Bond, chief executive of New York-based Kirshenbaum Bond & Partners, explains that philosophies also change with the times. He points to the impact of relationship marketing on traditional advertising approaches. "There's a new paradigm forming. It's all about defining who is the client. With the traditional model, it was the client [advertiser]; with the creative model, [it's] the consumer."[6]

The following is a collection of agency philosophies that we have compiled from agency brochures to give you some idea how agencies position themselves in the marketplace.

---

[6]Noreen O'Leary, "Suits," *Adweek* (April 22, 1996):21–28.

AGENCY PHILOSOPHIES

The following statements come from agency brochures. They represent big traditional advertising agencies (Leo Burnett, Ogilvy & Mather, McCann-Erickson, BBDO, Bozell) as well as agencies that are more focused on either integration or specialized services (Price/McNabb and CKS).

Leo Burnett and Integrity, Chicago: Every new employee of the Chicago-based agency sits down on his or her first day to view the film of one of Leo Burnett's last talks to the troops, given on December 1, 1967. A collection of midwestern values and admonishments, it's called "When to Take My Name Off the Door." Burnett told people that they should remove his name when "you spend more time trying to make money and less time making advertising," when "you compromise your integrity," when "you lose your humility and become big-shot weisenheimers . . . a little too big for your boots." In 1991 when the agency was pitching the $35 million Sony advertising account, it screened this film. Leo Burnett got the account and runner-up, Jerry Della Femina, said: "I walked in there at the end, as chairman of my agency, and explained to them how much I really wanted their business, and how closely involved I would be, personally. And then the Burnett people came in and popped in this video of Leo talking. It was just Leo talking about his philosophy of advertising. And he beat me. Sony would rather work with Leo dead than me alive. That's how powerful he is—he's one of the few people in this business who started an agency who really got to live forever." Burnett's slogan is to "reach for the stars," an idea illustrated in its logo, which shows a hand reaching for stars with the legend, "When you reach for the stars, you may not always get one, but you won't come up with a handful of mud either."

Ogilvy & Mather's Brand Stewardship, New York: Goal: "To be most valued by those who most value brands." The following are selections from O&M's mission statement on shared values:

> We work not for ourselves, not for the company, not even for the client. We work for brands. We work with the clients as Brand Teams. We encourage individuals, entrepreneurs, inventive mavericks: with such members, teams thrive. We value candor, curiosity, originality, intellectual rigor, perseverance, brains—and civility. We prefer the discipline of knowledge to the anarchy of ignorance. We respect the intelligence of our audiences: "The consumer is not a moron." We expect our clients to hold us accountable for our Stewardship of their Brands. Only if we have built, nourished, and developed prosperous Brands, only if we have made them more valuable both to their users and to their owners, may we judge ourselves successful.

McCann-Erickson and Managing the Beast, New York: A brand is a curious beast. On the one hand, it has a genuine life of its own. Its own personality. Its own presence and impor-

tance. And as with People, a brand must evolve and grow over time. On the other hand, as a brand evolves, it may not stray too far from "who" it is and what it stands for. Otherwise, it will face the charge of not remaining true to itself, of violating the expectation of trust it has built; of abandoning its roots.

BBDO and Advertising that Touches Emotions, New York: The common thread that runs through everything we do is humanity. It's not one particular emotion, but real people in real situations who get through to you. And that ingredient of humanity can come out in several ways. It can be drama, it can be comedy or something whimsical, but as long as it has the element, that is our trademark. It's advertising that connects with people on an emotional level. It makes you feel something. It might make you feel happy or melancholy or it might make you laugh. But it will make you feel something relative to the product.

Bozell and Creative Advertising, New York: Creativity in advertising is often the only point of difference as products and services become more alike. Which makes it all the more important that ads stand out by attracting attention and holding it. At Bozell, we believe that for many products people respond to emotions more readily than to reason. And that the emotional connection must be made before the rational selling message will be absorbed. Emotional connections that follow from both perspiration and inspiration: solid strategic thinking and hard work, coupled with ingenuity, imagination, taste and good judgment. We always strive to create ads that cannot be ignored.

Price/McNabb and Relationships, Charlotte, NC: In 1995 we became the first agency to re-invent itself around relationship marketing principles. Our team mission is to set the standard for understanding and building relationships with the individual customers and prospects of our clients, and to use that knowledge to create communications that are recognized for extraordinary business results.

CKS, IMC, and New Media, Cupertino, CA: CKS Group's overall mission is to consistently deliver integrated marketing communication programs and products to its clients through the creative use of advanced technology, breakthrough design, and superior account management. CKS Group's core strengths include leadership in new media communications, an ability to provide a full range of marketing communication services to its clients and a high level of creative expertise and technological sophistication, which enable CKS to provide marketing communication services and products quickly and efficiently.

DISCUSSION QUESTION

Study these statements and identify an agency where you think you would like to work. Explain what viewpoints in the statement attract your interest.

TRENDS IN ADVERTISING AND MARKETING COMMUNICATION

The advertising agency business, as well as advertising as an industry, is periodically subject to short-term fads and long-term trends. It is difficult in the early stage to distinguish what may be a passing fancy and what may be a significant change in the way business is conducted.

The traditional approach during the period from the late 1950s until the middle to late 1980s was the *marketing plan concept*. Developed out of the packaged-goods category, this reflected a marketing approach based on identifying a target market or audience, stating a clear and measurable objective, developing a strategy on how to achieve that objective, and finally crafting specific plans to carry out that strategy.

Beginning in London in the late 1970s, Boase Massini Pollett (now BMP DDB Needham) refined this system by adding *account planning*. The account planner is a person or department responsible for gathering all available intelligence on the market and the consumer and preparing a comprehensive recommendation centering on the consumer. The account planner is a strategic specialist who speaks on behalf of the consumer based upon his or her comprehensive understanding of the consumer's wants and needs.

At the same time account planning was changing the research function, the computer was expanding the ability to collect, collate, and analyze data. *Single-source data* are now available for many households that identify their purchase patterns in the retail store relative to the advertising messages they have seen. The industry is becoming flooded with more information than it can analyze.

Changes in the media industry also have impacted upon the advertising industry. For one thing, the available media have multiplied in number, specificity, and type. But more importantly, interactive and personalized media are becoming more efficient and effective in delivering messages one-on-one, which is beginning to move advertising away from its mass-media base.

Computers have also changed how the creative people operate, with most of these people now writing and designing their ads on computers and sharing their ideas as they develop with others in the agency, and sometimes even the client, through online networks.

INTEGRATED MARKETING COMMUNICATION

One change that is having great impact on advertising agencies and their relationships with their clients is *integrated marketing communication* (IMC). As clients become more focused on efficiency, effectiveness, and accountability, the issue has become how to coordinate all of the various messages being delivered to all the various stakeholder groups. The investor relations department might be explaining a severe downsizing to the financial community; public relations might be showcasing the qualifications of the chief executive to the media; human resources may be trying to motivate employees to do an excellent job delivering a new service; the marketing department may be announcing the latest price or value-pack promotion. Do all these parts work together? Is there a complementary impact? Not likely.

From this condition arose the concept of integrated marketing communications (IMC), which was introduced in Chapter 1. Professor Don Schultz of the Medill School of Journalism at Northwestern University was the first to recognize the lack of integration of marketing efforts and was a pioneer in enunciating the principles of IMC. Even at Northwestern, public relations and copywriting were taught at Medill, while marketing and advertising strategy were offered at the Kellogg School of Management, a few hundred unconnected yards away. Tom Duncan at the University of Colorado was another IMC pioneer and the program he developed for his university was able to tie these educational efforts together by creating an interdisciplinary master's degree that involved the marketing department as well as journalism and mass communication.

Problem solved? Hardly. These breakthroughs are happening at the educational level but there are still problems to be solved in practice. A number of studies showed that IMC was found to be difficult to install at client organizations because of what has been called "functional silos," really turf wars among departments. These studies have also found that clients generally want to adopt a more integrated program; however, they don't know how to do it.[7] Until the Northwestern, Colorado, and other university programs that teach IMC have a substantial number of graduates, leadership is lacking in the industry.

Furthermore, clients often do not understand how the advertising agency fits into the integrated marketing plan. Often even the advertising agencies are not sure how to best organize themselves to manage an integrated communication program nor how to bill for it. According to a study commissioned by the Promotion Marketing Association of America among 100 senior-level marketing executives, 60 percent rated IMC as the most important strategy factor in the next three to five years (see Table 4.5), but meeting IMC needs via an advertising agency was hard to envision. As few as 10 percent believed that their company would find its IMC needs met by an advertising agency. The pressure to integrate increases as options proliferate and the business becomes more complex. As Professor Schultz put it:

> Technology is what makes IMC possible, and the more rapidly technology diffuses, the faster IMC grows and matures. Because technology drives and supports IMC, it is not just another passing marketing fad or hot communications topic that will fade and die. Instead, IMC is likely the future of all marketing communications.[8]

Since the 1980s, advertising agencies have struggled to figure out their place in an IMC environment. Young & Rubicam touted its "whole egg" concept. Ogilvy & Mather, highly regarded for its rigorous internal training, educated its employees on "orchestrating" client efforts. While chairperson of the American Association of Advertising Agency (4As), DDB Needham chairperson Keith Reinhard tried to lead the industry to adopt IMC but his efforts were repudiated by his

[7] Tom Duncan and Steve Everett (1993), "Client Perceptions of Integrated Marketing Communications," *Journal of Advertising Research*, 33, 3 (May/June):30–39; Clarke Caywood, Don Schultz, and Paul Wang, "Integrated Marketing Communications: A Survey of National Consumer Goods Advertisers," Northwestern University Report (June 1991).

[8] Don E. Schultz, *Marketing News* (February 15, 1993):20.

TABLE 4.5	FACTORS INFLUENCING MARKETING STRATEGIES
FACTOR	**IMPORTANCE RANK (%)**
Integrated marketing communications	60
Consumer lifestyle changes	55
Economic trends	45
Everyday low-pricing strategies	32
New retail formats	29
Integration of consumer/trade promotion	27
Globalization	26

Source: NPO Group. Reprinted with permission from *Advertising Age* (March 22, 1993):3. Copyright, Crain Communications, Inc., 1993.

successor. The former Saatchi & Saatchi group acquired several specialty companies in an array of fields from public relations to sales promotion to product design as it strove to satisfy perceived or anticipated client needs—only to sell off many of these new divisions to avoid bankruptcy in the early 1990s.

Many large advertising agencies with subsidiary companies in several marketing areas are organized around the profit center concept. Each division, department, or affiliated agency must manage its own resources independently. Therefore, it is often the case that one profit center, even a department within an agency, is reluctant to let a client get away to another agency subsidiary. Small and medium-sized agencies have fewer organizational problems to solve as they attempt to move into IMC because they are less likely to have developed specialized functions that operate in isolation.

The Leo Burnett Company, a monolithic agency that never bought subsidiaries in other categories, led the way in integrating services within the agency. Another smaller agency, Price/McNabb in Asheville, North Carolina, also adopted IMC. Price/McNabb, cited by *PR Magazine* as one of the five best integrated agencies, abolished profit centers by department and by city among its four offices. It promotes its planning, advertising, and public relations services to clients as one coordinated effort.

Other agencies using an integrated approach include Campbell-Mithun of Minneapolis and San Francisco's CKS Group, a technology-focused integrated agency that offers its clients advertising, trade shows, packaging, brochures, corporate design, virtual stores, and even interactive kiosks. What makes CKS different is its focus on technology. The CKS system uses a computer-stored database, communication, and imagery system that can be shared across many applications. A proposed logo can be presented in everything from signage to packaging; team members working on a coordinated communication program can share ideas and review work in progress from their computers.

Integration very definitely impacts upon the structure and organization of an agency and demands partnership relationships with other agencies, which provide specialized services that the agency can't do. Some clients are of the opinion that integrated marketing is probably not a service to be bought from an advertising agency because they fear that an agency might be strong in advertising but weak in other areas, such as direct marketing. The Interpublic Group sought to overcome this by adopting a "general contractor" approach. For a fee of 1.5 percent of the billing, an Interpublic agency will develop the overall strategy and retain the specialist agencies needed to carry out the plan, be it advertising, public relations, direct-response marketing, event marketing, database marketing, or design development—either within the IPG agency group or outside of it. (Commissions and fees are discussed in detail later in this chapter.)

An example of how the general contractor approach might work is Leo Burnett's work in the interactive area. The agency's interactive group has designed a number of Web sites for its clients (Maytag at http://www.maytag.com, for example), but it also can line up a specialist agency as it did for McDonald's "McFamily" area on the Microsoft Network and America Online. Burnett recommended the developer, Organic Online, and then backed off, letting the client and Organic work together. Doug Ryan, codirector of the interactive group, explains that "our goal is to keep the client happy, and we're not crazy enough to assume we'll do everything." Being "solution neutral" is central to Burnett's philosophy of client management and the client's needs always come first.[9]

As mentioned earlier, smaller agencies or agencies without the resources of giants like Interpublic, Omnicom, and WPP, or the huge international agencies, such as Young & Rubicam, Grey, and Leo Burnett, are competitive in the IMC

---

[9]Kim Cleland, "Where Old Brands and New Thinking Merge," *Advertising Age* (February 26, 1996): Interactive p. 1.

arena because they usually don't have the functional silos. Cross-functional planning is much easier for them. In smaller companies, people typically do several jobs and the company either does whatever is needed to meet its clients' needs or it finds partners who can help. In other words, smaller agencies often compete for IMC business by using *strategic alliances*. Strategic alliances are agreements between firms of different marketing specialties to complement each others' services and provide referrals. Basically, a strategic alliance is a plan to cooperate, not compete.

Experience at Price/McNabb with strategic alliances to augment the agency's ability to work in integrated marketing has taught the agency that it needs to have established relationships with more than one specialist company in a field. Price/McNabb has found strategic partners in research and database marketing but finds sales promotion agencies still look upon themselves as complete purveyors of service and often don't understand the long-range principle of brand building through IMC.

How Agencies Are Organized

As the agency grows larger, a division of labor occurs. Most full-service agencies offer specific functions handled by specialists. Smaller agencies offer the same basic functions, but they employ fewer people who are less specialized and may perform more than one function. For the purpose of giving a full explanation, the following description of agency organization is based on larger agencies. Figure 4.1 offers a humorous look into the inner workings of an advertising agency.

Because employment at large agencies has not been growing, there are more entry-level employment opportunities in smaller agencies or in smaller markets. For that reason, profiles of the workday for employees of small as well as large agencies will be included in this book (see Day in the Life box). Major corporations are focused on one or a cluster of product lines, brands, or services called **business units.** Advertising agencies use a similar structure but have a variety of clients and product lines. The agency's products, however, are ideas rather than goods. These ideas are manifested in advertisements and plans for campaigns and media programs.

Business Unit: A cluster of related products or services that functions as if it were a company within a larger corporation.

Rather than organizing around a business unit, an agency organizes around a client's account. Because clients come and go and account needs change, agencies must be adaptable. The agency must encourage new ideas and protect them as they are refined. Openness and flexibility are more important than organizational structure in most agencies. Furthermore, agencies must organize internally to function as a business as well as externally to work with their clients.

Unlike corporations, agencies often change structure to accommodate the needs of new clients or the talents of their people. For example, an agency might have one client that advertises a leading brand on a national basis using primarily television and national magazines. For this client, the emphasis in staffing might be in the creative and research departments. Another client in the fast-service restaurant field, which has local cooperatives of owner-operators or franchisees in major markets, would need field service account executives to work with the co-ops and the franchisees.

There are, however, standard functions around which most large and small agencies organize. The following are the four primary functions of most agencies:

1. Account management
2. Creative services
3. Media services
4. Research

124

FIGURE 4.1

THE AD GAME.

(*Source: Advertising Age*, December 21, 1987:18. Copyright Crain Communications, Inc.) Reprinted with permission from *Advertising Age*. Copyright Crain Communications, Inc.

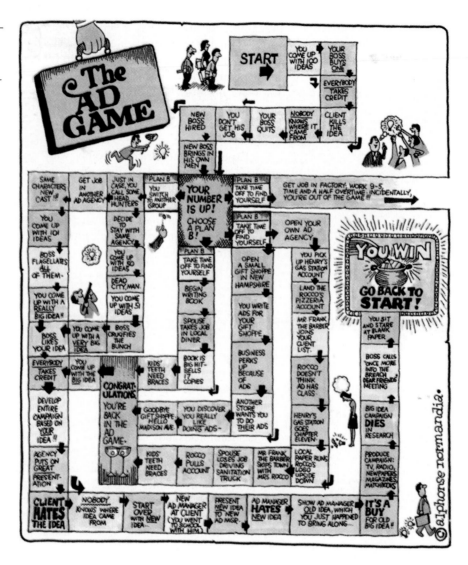

In addition to these major functional areas, most agencies offer support services, such as traffic, print production, financial services, personnel, and, increasingly, direct marketing. Some are beginning to offer account planning services, as well. Figure 4.2 illustrates the organization of one advertising agency.

ACCOUNT MANAGEMENT

Account Management: The function within an advertising agency that acts as liaison with the client and supervises day-to-day work and development of recommendations and plans.

The role of **account management** is to serve as a liaison between the client and the agency in order to ensure that the agency focuses its resources on the needs of the client. At the same time, the agency also develops its own point of view, which is presented to the client. Once the client (or the client and the agency together) establishes the general guidelines for a campaign or even one advertisement, the account management department supervises the day-to-day development of recommendations within these guidelines. These guidelines answer the following questions:

1. What is the purpose of the advertising?
2. Who is the target audience?
3. What promise does the advertising make?

4.   What is the support for this promise? Are there secondary support points for specific target audiences or models of the product?

5.   What media will deliver the message?

6.   What is the tone or personality of the advertising?

7.   Are there unique opportunities in terms of timing, competitive weaknesses, technological leadership, customer loyalties, or brand equities that must be considered?

Chapter 3 discusses brand names and their dominance in product marketing. A company's brand is assigned to a *brand manager*. The brand manager at the client firm is typically the contact for the account manager from the agency. This person is responsible for supervising all aspects of the brand's marketing: manufacturing, packaging, distribution, improvements, changes occasioned by environmental or safety laws, trade relations, promotions, public relations, profits, and advertising. This person is variously boss, tyrant, friend, partner, and guardian of the relationship with the agency.

Providing service to the brand manager and the client in general can be a difficult role for the account manager. Deadlines can sometimes be missed. An ad may not produce anticipated results. Agency profitability requirements may cause conflicts in levels of staffing a client may want. The agency recommendation may be unusually blunt or even critical. But the agency must maintain its independence and an honest point of view. Paul Harper, chairperson emeritus of DDB Needham, put the role in perspective this way in a "Memorandum to All Our Account Executives":

FIGURE 4.2

ORGANIZATION CHART FOR A MEDIUM-SIZE AGENCY: ELKMAN ADVERTISING AND PUBLIC RELATIONS HANDLES $50 MILLION IN BILLINGS ANNUALLY.

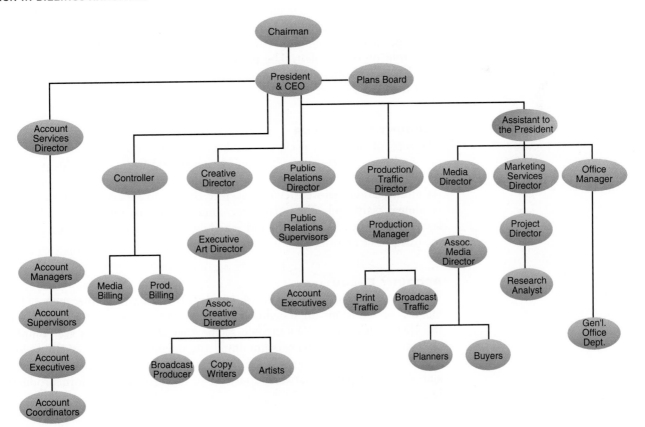

Most good clients have strong views of their own. You will win client respect for yourself and the agency mainly for two things: (1) for forthrightness and thoroughness in presenting the agency's views, and (2) for respectful knowledge of the problems the client faces as he makes his own often difficult decisions. When his answer is "No," as it will sometimes be, this may be a professional defeat. But it will never be a moral defeat if the agency's position has been well presented and stoutly defended.

The account management function is becoming even more stressful as more clients are asking for integrated marketing communications and as more agencies organize around multidisciplinary team efforts to better serve client needs. A number of agencies such as Leo Burnett and the New York offices of Saatchi & Saatchi and DDB Needham have reorganized around brand teams. As an *Adweek* article that reported that trend noted, "Selecting the means of communication is one of the biggest factors changing the way account execs ply their trade." This trend toward teams and integration increases the pressure for ad execs to be familiar with marketing disciplines ranging from public relations and direct marketing to promotions. Mullen agency CEO, Joe Grimaldi, observes that "It's not enough anymore to think just in terms of advertising."[10]

Account management in a major agency typically has four levels: management representative or supervisor, account supervisor, account executive, and assistant account executives. Sometimes a fifth level may exist, the account director, who is above the account supervisor. A smaller agency will combine some of these levels and probably have only two or at most three levels.

MANAGEMENT SUPERVISOR

The management supervisor reports to the upper management of the agency. This person provides leadership on strategic issues, looks for new business opportunities, helps guide personnel growth and development within the account team, keeps agency management informed, and ensures that the agency is making a realistic profit on the account. The position normally carries the title of senior vice president and is offered to someone who has been working in account management for 10 to 15 years.

ACCOUNT SUPERVISOR

The account supervisor usually is the key working executive on the client's business and the primary liaison between the client and the agency. This person directs the preparation of strategic plans, assigns priorities, reviews and approves all recommendations before they are taken to the client, supervises the presentation of annual plans and other major recommendations to the client, and ensures agency adherence to deadlines and schedules. Account supervisors usually carry the title of vice president.

ACCOUNT EXECUTIVE

The account executive is responsible for day-to-day activities that include keeping the agency team on schedule and delivering the services as promised to the client. Other functions include seeing that all assignments are completed on time and within budget, maintaining the operating records of the account, preparing status and progress reports, supervising the production of materials, and securing legal or network approval of all advertising before production begins.

---

[10]Noreen O'Leary, "Suits," *Adweek* (April 22, 1996):21–28.

CREATIVE DEVELOPMENT AND PRODUCTION

To some people creative organization is an oxymoron—they believe that creativity can only occur in an unstructured environment. In an agency, however, management must take into consideration how people work together and what assignments are flowing through the agency. The wisest agency managers are flexible in terms of organization but strict in terms of quality and deadline control. Young & Rubicam stated its creative point of view in Ad 4.5.

PRINCIPLE Creative management is flexible in organization but is strict in quality and deadline control.

The creative members of the agency typically hold one of the following positions: creative director, creative department manager, copywriter, art director, or producer. In addition to these positions, the broadcast production department and the art studio are two other areas where creative personnel can apply their skills.

CREATIVE DIRECTOR

Most agencies have one senior executive called the creative director, or executive creative director, who serves as the agency's creative conscience. Other comparable titles include executive creative director or director of creative services. This person stimulates the department to improve its creative work and approves all ideas before they are presented outside the department. Because of the importance of the creative product, the creative director may be a member of the agency's board of directors or senior management group.

CREATIVE DEPARTMENT MANAGER

Another person may oversee the internal management process, the administrative activities needed to keep the department running. Referred to as the creative department manager, this person handles budgeting, salary administration, office assignments, hiring and supervising secretarial and support staff,

AD 4.5

YOUNG & RUBICAM USED THIS
"HOUSE AD" TO HIGHLIGHT ITS
PHILOSOPHY OF SERVICE AND
CREATIVE STRATEGY.

You can really fly
once you know where you're going.

We believe the sharpest advertising strategies provide the greatest creative freedom. Only when you know exactly where you're going can the imagination soar free, without fear or formulas.

YOUNG & RUBICAM INC.

recruiting professional staff, and internal accounting. Practitioners may refer to the creative department manager as "house mother," "warden," "priest," "rabbi," "confessor," "crying towel," or "punching bag," acknowledging the parental and instructive nature of the job. Creative directors can survive the loss of a senior staff member more easily than the loss of the creative department manager.

THE CREATIVE GROUP

Two types of people are generally found within the creative department. One is the brilliant and sometimes eccentric creator who conceives, writes, and produces innovative advertising. A staff is often built around this person as an extension of his or her skills. The second-type is the coach, who delegates assignments, works with the staff to find an idea, and then molds, improves, nurtures, and inspires the staff. Agencies organize teams around these people, who may be called creative group heads or associate creative directors. Both the creator and the coach can coexist within the creative department. In fact, many people possess characteristics of both types, but the coach typically supervises the larger team of people.

A *creative group* includes people who write (*copywriters*), people who design ideas for print ads or television commercials (*art directors*), and people who translate these ideas into television or radio commercials (*producers*). In many agencies an art director and copywriter who work well together are teamed, and a support group is built around them. Art directors and copywriters are discussed in more detail in Chapter 13.

BROADCAST PRODUCTION

In some cases the broadcast production department is a separate department (as the print production department usually is), but more often it will be a part of the creative department. Because the execution of the tone and action of broadcast advertising is so central to its success, the creative team usually works with a broadcast producer, who is directly involved in the filming or videotaping and editing of a commercial.

THE ART STUDIO

An art studio is another part of the creative department. The studio includes artists who specialize in presentation pieces, lettering, and paste-up. (Presentation pieces are discussed in more detail in Chapter 14.) Beginning art directors often start in an agency studio. The computer is increasingly doing the work once done in the studio and in some agencies it has replaced the studio and some of the print production functions.

THE COMPUTER

Graphics capabilities of today's computers, particularly the Apple Macintosh, have brought them into everyday use in creative departments. The computer commonly is used for fast rough layouts, quick changes on storyboards, and even finished production for some black-and-white newspaper ads. In broadcast, computer applications are increasingly promising with the advent of CD-ROM and sound capabilities.

An exciting new area of business for many agencies is creating home pages for their clients on the World Wide Web. Agencies such as Ogilvy & Mather, Saatchi & Saatchi, and Foote, Cone & Belding among many others have appointed new-media gurus to move their agencies and their clients onto the electronic superhighway. There has also been a growth of new agencies that specialize in helping clients with Web advertising. Ad 4.6 is for DoubleClick, an internet advertising company.

AD 4.6

AGENCIES SUCH AS
DOUBLECLICK HAVE COME ON
THE SCENE SPECIFICALLY TO
DESIGN INTERNET PAGES.

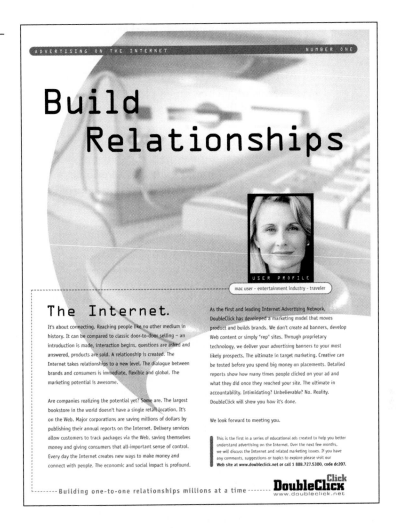

MEDIA PLANNING AND BUYING

The media department performs one of the most complex functions in an advertising agency. It must recommend the most efficient means of delivering the message to the target audience. Most media departments basically break down into three functions: planning, buying, and research. These functions will be outlined here and discussed in more detail in Chapters 9 and 12.

THE MEDIA PLANNER

Developing a media plan is a creative skill that involves determining which medium or media to use, when, for what length of time, and at what cost. The *media planner* must be involved in the overall strategy and creative development of the advertising campaign. Most media and creative plans are prepared concurrently so the message and the medium will work together.

THE MEDIA BUYER

The *media buyer* determines what media coverage is likely to be available at what costs. Buying involves ordering media on behalf of the client according to the plan approved by the client. Once the client approves the plan, the media buyer acts quickly to place orders. There is no point in recommending a plan calling for advertising on specific network television programs if those programs are already sold. (Chapter 9 details the media-buying process.)

Rapid changes in market conditions triggered by timely research (from scanners in retail outlets or daily inventory control by computer) have caused frequent adjustments in media plans and schedules. Without computers and laser printers, these changes would have been difficult to plan and track and very expensive in terms of agency time. The computer has not only made rapid response possible, its capabilities have driven change.

MEDIA RESEARCH

In addition to planning and buying, most media departments have a media research section that gathers and evaluates media data. The department's forecasts of future prices, ratings of television programs, and audience composition are prepared by the media research manager. Media research often provides entry-level positions in clerical and data gathering for computer-literate newcomers.

RESEARCH DEPARTMENT

Full-service agencies in the United States usually have a separate department specifically devoted to research. The emphasis in agency research is on assisting the development of the advertising message. Most major agencies conduct research before the advertising is prepared to make the advertising more focused and appropriate to the target audience. They also purchase research from companies that specialize in this area. The leading research firms in each country work on projects both for clients and agencies.

Most European advertising agencies either do not have a research department or have only a research director, who is responsible for commissioning outside research projects and interpreting the results for the agency. These are often called *account planners*. This European pattern is becoming more common in North America.

Whether composed of a single person in a small agency or teams of professionals in a large agency, the research department has a number of duties besides helping creative development. It ensures that the agency has reliable information, screens all new research findings to determine if they change the body of information about a brand, company, industry, or market, and provides the agency with accurate information about consumer behavior. When conducting original research, the agency almost always concentrates on consumer attitudes and behavior. Advertising research will be discussed in more detail in Chapters 6 and 21.

PRINCIPLE Research should be a partner with the creative side in the development of great advertising, not a scorekeeper or judge of the creative department.

An important philosophical consideration is how the research function is positioned in the agency. It should not be the judge of the creative department. It should be the scout, the eyes, and ears of the agency. By concentrating on precreative research and on evaluating consumer reaction to creative alternatives, the research department contributes to the development of new ways to think about the consumer. Most agencies ask clients to conduct postresearch studies to evaluate the advertising after it has made its contribution.

INTERNAL SERVICES

The departments in an agency that serve the very important "backroom" operations are called internal service departments. They get the work produced, get it to the media, handle the finances, and manage relationships with employees. These include the traffic department, print production, financial services, and human resources or personnel.

TRAFFIC DEPARTMENT

The traffic department is responsible for internal control and tracking of projects to meet deadlines. The account executive works closely with the assigned traffic coordinator or traffic manager to review deadlines and monitor progress. The

PRINCIPLE The traffic department is the lifeline of the agency.

traffic department is the lifeblood of the agency, and its personnel keep track of everything that is happening in the agency.

Traffic requires diligence, tact, and great attention to detail. Diligence is needed to keep track of the progress of elements of a campaign as they come together to ensure that the key jobs, the ones upon which other departments depend to meet deadlines, are not allowed to slip. Tact is needed to negotiate with creative people who complain they never have enough time and have too many jobs to complete, but who appreciate a traffic manager to push the critical assignments and buy a day or two on ones with a cushion in the schedule. Attention to detail is needed because it is the task of the traffic coordinator to get the job finished, assemble all the bills and charges, and deliver the proper signatures to financial services for billing to the client. Although computers now can help trace and program projects (and have reduced the size of traffic departments), nothing can replace the persistent traffic coordinator who has heard every excuse for delay.

PRINT PRODUCTION

Taking a layout, a photograph or an illustration, and a page of copy and turning these elements into a four-color magazine page or a full-page newspaper advertisement is the work of the print production department.

Because of the technical nature of making the printing plates, adjusting and matching color, and achieving reproduction, print production is not handled within the creative department. In contrast, television and radio production usually are part of creative development. In print production the art director on the account normally supervises the illustrator or photographer and approves the work but does not supervise the production of the material sent to the publication. The use of computers and the increasing power and definition of computer graphics are moving some print production to the art director's computer terminal, but most production for four-color ads and brochures is still done in the print production department.

FINANCIAL SERVICES

Whether large or small, the agency must send its invoices out on time, pay its bills on time, control its costs, ensure that expenses incurred on behalf of a client are properly invoiced to that client, meet its payroll, pay its taxes, and make a profit within its budget. The chief financial officer manages these functions. In a large agency the treasurer is responsible for cash management, seeing that funds are invested until needed, bills are paid just before they are due, cash discounts are taken, and cash reserves are available for peak billing periods. The comptroller is charged with internal procedures, for example, conducting internal audits to prevent misuse of agency resources, making sure that money is not spent without authority, large checks are countersigned, and invoices are not paid unless approved.

HUMAN RESOURCES

An operation of any size requires keeping personnel files and records. The larger the agency, the more likely it will have a professional human resources or personnel staff. These people handle the hiring and firing of clerical, secretarial, and support staff. Recruitment of professional staff, although conducted by the head of the department in which the person will work, is normally coordinated by the human resources department. Both the financial services and human resources departments of advertising agencies function the same way as do comparable departments in corporations.

OTHER SPECIALIST DEPARTMENTS

With the increasing demand for integrated marketing programs, agencies are often adding internal departments that provide the specialized functions they regularly use. Public relations, sales promotion, direct marketing, and event marketing are areas that may be set up as departments within an agency. An agency handling a major car account may have a separate department to produce collateral materials such as brochures and other product information and work with dealer groups.

How Agencies Are Paid

Agencies derive their revenues and, therefore, their profits from two main sources—commissions and fees. As discussed in the Concepts and Applications box, compensation is a critical factor in agency-client relationships. To understand these processes, we must first understand the word *agent.* An agent is someone who acts for another. In this case, an advertising agency acts for a client in creating and placing advertising.

THE COMMISSION SYSTEM

Commission: A form of payment in which an agent or agency receives a certain percentage (historically 15 percent) of media charges.

Early advertising agents acted on behalf of the medium rather than on behalf of the client. Well into the nineteenth century advertising agents acted as representatives for newspapers, magazines, and handbill printers. If the agent brought advertising to the publisher, the publisher paid the agent a **commission,** which was justified by the work the agent did in bringing the publisher the business and preparing the advertisement for publication. The agent might write the copy, prepare the layout, set the type, and arrange for any drawings or plates

Concepts and Applications

ACCOUNTABILITY: THE HEART OF THE AGENCY-CLIENT RELATIONSHIP

Performance-based compensation is a notion whose time has come. DDB Needham's chief executive, Keith Reinhard, has sounded the call for more performance-based accountability systems. Since then a number of agency reviews and new business pitches have revolved around this new way to structure the agency-client relationship. The opening story about Oldsmobile and its agency, Leo Burnett, concluded that a new effort to negotiate a performance-based compensation system was a sign of the health of the agency-client relationship.

Red Dog, one of the most profitable new-product launches in the 1990s, was managed by BBDO-Toronto in an agreement with its client, first Molson of Canada and then Molson's parent company, Miller Brewing Company, that the agency would only be paid for its expenses until the brand's marketing goals were met. At that point, a bonus system would kick in. Howard Breen, head of the BBDO-Toronto, and chief engineer of the launch campaign, says the agency has made more money on the business under this novel performance-based agreement than it would have under a traditional commission or straight fee system. And the brand has done well, too, being tagged as Miller's most successful new-product launch and named Marketer of the Year in 1996 by *Brandweek.*

Rance Crain, editor-in-chief of *Advertising Age,* lauded Reinhard's leadership on this issue but said Young & Rubicam (Y&R) may have moved farther in figuring out how to do it. Y&R's Peter Georgescu says, "If we are really serious about being our clients' partners, we have to be as accountable for our results as our clients are for their results—sharing in the rewards and risks." Y&R doesn't try to isolate the agency's contribution to overall brand objectives, which is extremely difficult and frequently leaves the agency in a nickle-and-dime argument with its client. Instead Y&R uses a combination of measurements—some that are specific to advertising and others that broadly gauge its clients' overall market performance. If its clients do well, Y&R does well.

Both Reinhard and Georgescu believe that this new approach to compensation is crucial to their agencies' fiscal well-being. As Georgescu explains, "Performance-based compensation is the most powerful expression of accountability for an agency or for a client executive."

Sources: Rance Crain, "First Trust, Then Accountability," *Advertising Age* (April 22, 1996):18; Gerry Khermouch, "Marketers of the Year, Beverages, Rich Lalley," *Brandweek's Superbrands '96* (October 1995):68, 72.

that were part of the advertisement. These efforts saved the publisher time and work.

As advertising grew in importance, advertisers began to work with fewer and fewer agents and eventually signed with one agent exclusively. In 1901, Clarence Curtis of Curtis Publishing granted a 15 percent commission to advertising agencies—10 percent for preparation of material and 5 percent for prompt payment. This practice changed the entire advertising industry. Instead of representing one medium to many advertisers, the agent now acted on behalf of one client and placed ads with many media. The commission system remains, however, as a legacy of the early years of advertising.

A 15 percent commission long has been considered standard even though it is now observed more in the breach (see Table 4.6). As Timm Crull, chairperson-CEO of Nestlé USA, pointed out, the battle is more fierce now because of:

1. Intense and increasing competition
2. Rapidly changing demographics
3. An explosion of new media

Crull stated, "If advertising is to continue to serve as the anchor in the overall marketing plan, agencies must come up with more than clever messages. . . . I believe that major advertising agencies are understandably reluctant to abandon the lucrative comfort of traditional broadcast media to explore the full range of media alternatives."[11]

It is standard in the sense that most media allow agencies a 15 percent commission. (Outdoor is 16.67 percent.) For example, if it costs $100,000 to run a television commercial, the agency commission at 15 percent is $15,000. Stated another way, the agency bills the client $100,000 but pays the station $85,000.

In the 1980s, starting first in Great Britain, clients began to squeeze the 15 percent commission in an attempt to reduce expenses. When advertising accounts were opened for presentation, the client might indicate it intended to pay, say, 12 percent commission. When agencies accepted that commission, it undercut the 15 percent commission standard. Negotiated commission rates, especially for the largest budgets of $10 million and up, are common. Confidential sources indicate that the largest agencies averaged about 12 percent commission in 1992 on commission clients.

Although the 15 percent commission system is common, it is not universal. In New Zealand, for example, the commission allowed by media is 20 percent.

---

[11]Timm Crull, "Nestlé to Agencies: 'Shake Mindset,'" *Advertising Age* (May 3, 1992):26.

TABLE 4.6	HOW CLIENTS COMPENSATE AGENCIES		
	PERCENTAGE OF ADVERTISERS CHOOSING EACH OPTION, BY ACCOUNT SIZE		
ACCOUNT SIZE	**STANDARD 15% COMMISSION**	**SLIDING-SCALE OR LOWER COMMISSION**	**LABOR-BASED FEE**
Under $10 million	36	4	47
$10 million–$49 million	31	28	35
$50 million+	29	50	13
All advertisers	33%	26%	32%

All figures may not add up to 100 percent because some advertisers gave other responses or no answer.

Source: Association of National Advertisers. Reprinted with permission from *Advertising Age* (May 11, 1992):26. Copyright, Crain Communications, Inc., 1992.

TABLE 4.7	COMMISSION SYSTEM COMPONENTS		
		PERCENTAGE OF BILLING	**PERCENTAGE OF REVENUE**
Billings placed in media	$5,000,000	100%	
15% commission (agency revenue)	750,000	15.0	100%
Expenses			
Direct salaries*	250,000	5.0	33.3
Indirect salaries*	165,000	3.3	22.0
Social security, health benefits	125,000	2.5	16.7
Rent	45,000	0.9	6.0
Travel	10,000	0.2	1.3
Telephone, postage, etc.	10,000	0.2	1.3
Supplies	10,000	0.2	1.3
All other	20,000	0.4	2.7
Profit sharing	50,000	1.0	6.7
Gross profit	65,000	1.3	8.6
Tax	20,000	0.4	2.7
Net profit after tax	45,000	0.9	6.0

*Direct salaries apply to people who work directly on client business.

**Indirect salaries apply to people who do not work directly on client business: senior management, accounting, telephone operators, studio, mailroom, receptionist.

The argument for this higher rate is that New Zealand is a small country and its agencies have to do as much work to prepare a campaign to reach 3.5 million New Zealanders as would, say, a U.S. agency to reach a much larger audience. In Australia, five times as populous, the commission allowed by media is 16 percent. Throughout the world, while the commission rate allowed by media is most commonly 15 percent, clients are increasingly negotiating to get some of that commission back. Very large clients frequently negotiate sliding scales on commission: for example, 15 percent up to $10 million, 12 percent from $10 million to $25 million, and 10 percent above that.

Table 4.7 shows how the commission system works and how agencies derive their profits. In this example, 15 percent will be used, but the principle will be the same regardless of the percent commission used.

The percentages shown are within a range the industry considers typical. In the late 1980s, the rate of profit of the publicly held agencies was slightly below 6 percent. In 1992, the six largest public agencies (Foote, Cone & Belding (FCB); Grey; Interpublic; Omnicom; Saatchi, and WPP) had combined after-tax profits of 2.4 percent, with a high of 6.1 percent for FCB and 6.0 percent for Interpublic but losses of under 2 percent on revenue for WPP and Saatchi (see Table 4.8).

TABLE 4.8	PUBLIC AGENCY RESULTS (1992 FISCAL YEAR)		
AGENCY	**REVENUE ($ MILLION)**	**NET INCOME ($ MILLIONS)**	**AFTER-TAX PROFITS (%)**
Foote, Cone & Belding	353.3	21.7	6.1
Grey Advertising	564.5	16.5	2.9
Interpublic Group	1,856.0	111.9	6.0
Omnicom Group	1,356.0	65.5	4.7
Saatchi & Saatchi	1,120.2	(18.9)	(1.7)
WPP Group	1,927.9	(23.3)	(1.2)

Source: Annual Reports

What happens when the commission is lower than 15 percent and how is the rate set? The rate is negotiated between client and agency. What work will be done by the agency and what will be charged for separately are included in the negotiation. Here are examples:

INCLUDED	SOMETIMES INCLUDED	CHARGED SEPARATELY FROM THE COMMISSION
Analysis of client research	Layouts	Advertising production
Preparation of overall strategy	Telephone	Television production
	Duplicating	Travel not related to client contact
Creation of advertising	Test market plans	
Media planning	Travel directly related to client contact	Shipping
Media buying		Postage
Payment of suppliers	Alternate campaigns	Delivery charges
Billing to client	IMC coordination	Market research
Research in support of recommendation		Direct marketing
		Public relations
Discounts for prompt payment		Sales promotion
		Event planning
Syndicated media services		Interest for late payment

Advertising agencies are asking clients to pay for services that can be said to be intangible. Marketing strategies, for instance, are costly services when provided by marketing consultancies. Martin Sorrell, chief executive of WPP Group, argues agencies should charge for them.[12]

If the agency agrees to a commission of 10 percent, here is how that works:

Billing placed in media	$5,000,000
15 percent commission from media	750,000
10 percent commission rate	500,000
Rebated to client	250,000

The media accepts the order for $5 million and bills the agency $4.2 million. The agency charges the client $4.7 million instead of $5 million and makes a commission of 10 percent on the theoretical $5 million budget. A full 15 percent commission as shown in Table 4.6 is the practice in only one-third of the cases.

To the degree that the agency does not charge for items in the sometimes included column or for items usually charged separately from commission, the agency effectively lowers its rate of commission.

Some media and most production houses—those that make printing plates or produce television commercials—do not allow agency commissions. The agency then will gross up the outside charge to reflect the commission. Here is how that works:

		NET	GROSSED UP
Media cost	$100,000		
15% commission	15,000		
Net cost to agency	85,000	85%	100.%
Equivalent commission	15,000		17.65%

---

[12]Martin Sorrell interview, *Advertising Age* (March 19, 1990):1.

If the $85,000 cost of service to the agency has no commission allowance, and a 15 percent commission is agreed upon with the client, the agency adds $15,000 (17.65 percent) to the $85,000 when billing the client. If the agreed-upon commission is 10 percent, the $85,000 represents 90 percent of what the agency charges the client. The agency adds $9,444 (11.1 percent) to gross up the amount so that its final charge to the client ($94,444) contains a 10 percent ($9,444) commission.

THE FEE SYSTEM

Fee: A mode of payment in which an agency charges a client on the basis of the agency's hourly rates.

An alternative form of compensation is the fee system. This system is comparable to the means by which advertisers pay their lawyers and accountants. The client and agency agree on an hourly **fee,** or charge. This fee can vary according to department or levels of salary within a department. In other cases, a flat hourly fee for all work is agreed upon regardless of the salary level of the person doing the work. Charges are also included for out-of-pocket expenses, travel, and the items normally charged separately under a commission system. These are charged net, without any markup or commission. All media are billed to the client net of any commission.

Trust is the critical element in a fee system. The client must believe that each person in the agency is keeping track of his or her time accurately and charging that time correctly to a particular brand or project. In addition, the client must believe that the agency's hourly charge for salary, overhead, and profit is fair.

How is the agency fee calculated? The agency assigns costs for salary, rent, telephone, postage, internal operations, equipment rentals, taxes, and other expenses, and then determines what hourly charge will recover all of these costs and also provide the agency with a profit. A common rule of thumb in setting a fee is to charge three times the person's annual salary divided by the number of hours that person worked.

Here is how the agency profit and loss statement might look compared to the commission system. In this example, there is equivalent billing of $5 million and 1.7 people per million dollars of billing working on the business. The client, therefore, has the services of 8.5 people, approximately five of whom would work directly on the account. Since the agency using the fee system would be seeking substantially the same revenue ($750,000) and is charging only for the five people who work on the business (direct salaries), the fee would be three times the direct salaries ($750,000 ÷ $250,000). Assume an 1,800-hour work year and an average of $50,000 per year for those working on the account:

Average salary	$ 50,000
Divided by 1,800 hours, direct cost per hour	$ 27.77
Multiplied by 3, fee charge per hour	$ 83.33
9,000 hours times $83.33 per hour	$750,000

If the other costs remain the same, the agency will achieve a profit after tax of $45,000. With the 15 percent commission system now being regularly discounted, agencies are under pressure to reduce operating costs and waste. No matter what the level of commission or fee is, the agency seeks to achieve a profit of approximately 6 percent of revenue received by the agency from each client.

An interesting difference appears between the commission and fee systems when a client decides to cut the advertising budget. Under the commission system, when the client cancels advertising to save money, whatever is canceled is saved. Under the fee system, the client saves the amount of the schedule that is canceled but will have to pay the agency for the hours and expense required to contact the media, revise the media plan, and redo the billing.

The fee system has many supporters within the field. Those who favor it believe that an agency's payments should not be based on the price a medium charges. The commission system has survived, however, because it is simple, easy to understand, and puts pressure on an agency to keep its costs down.

A variation on the fee system is incentive-based agency compensation. Under this system, the agency performance is judged by a combination of objective and subjective standards. Seldom does even outstanding performance produce much more than the equivalent of 15 percent of billings, and acceptable performance will often pay less than 15 percent. If media buying is removed from the agency, the base commission will almost certainly be in a range of 10 percent to 13 percent, with a bonus of 1 percent to 2 percent for high performance.

The agencies have not just supinely accepted reductions in commissions and fees. In 1993, Margeotes, Fertitta & Weise fired Remy Martin. "More and more ad agencies are walking away from low-margin accounts, rather than struggle to stick by them."[13]

$\mathscr{T}$HE $\mathscr{F}$UTURE: $\mathscr{E}$FFICIENCY, $\mathscr{E}$FFECTIVENESS, AND $\mathscr{A}$CCOUNTABILITY

As the 1990s unfold, we are seeing trends in the business toward merging, heightened competition, and integrated marketing that reflect clients' demands for increased accountability. Agencies struggle to make the argument that their marketing communication plans are more efficient or more effective than the plans of their competitors. Clients ask them to put their money on the line and agree to be compensated based on whether or not the work accomplishes its objectives.

This performance mentality has changed the entire field. The proportion of client marketing budgets declined from over 60 percent in advertising in the 1970s to less than 35 percent in 1992 as clients switch money to areas that provide immediate, easy-to-measure impact, such as sales promotion.[14] The recession from 1991 to 1992 even saw total advertising spending decrease in 1991, the first time this phenomenon had occurred in three decades. Agencies restructured, closed branch offices, expanded by acquiring agencies in nearby markets to secure a client and achieve economies of scale, dropped departments (usually research and even media) and replaced them with strategic partners, and in some cases closed their doors.

Two defining events occurred in the early 1990s that reflect the client thrust for greater efficiency and effectiveness: (1) the appointment of Creative Artists Agency (CAA) by Coca-Cola and (2) the formation of Pentacom by BBDO, an agency of the Omnicom Group, to buy all the media for all agencies serving the Chrysler Corporation. CAA is a talent service and served as a major new source of creative ideas and their production, especially for television commercials. Chrysler adopted the proposal by BBDO to form a separate media-

---

[13]Kevin Goldman, "Poor Payoffs Push Agencies to Drop Clients," *The Wall Street Journal* (November 17, 1993):B1.

[14]Joe Cappo, "Agencies: Change or Die," *Advertising Age* (December 7, 1992):26.

*I*SSUES AND *C*ONTROVERSIES

CONFLICTS AND LOYALTY

The standard industry contract states that the agency agrees not to handle different products or companies in the same category or industry. For example, an agency that represents Coca-Cola will not represent Pepsi. In contrast to lawyers or accountants, who may specialize in a sector or an industry and handle a number of clients in the same field, advertising agencies agree not to work for a competing product or company because this would cause a *conflict of interest.* ("How can you work for a competitor and assure me I am getting your best ideas and the best media buys?") In theory, the conflict clause is simple. In practice, it has become one of the major controversies in the industry for several reasons: mergers of clients, internationalization of agencies, and the megamergers of agencies.

Likewise, the basic principles of the agency-client relationship, as defined in *The Encyclopedia of Advertising,* states that "It is understood that the client agrees not to engage a second agency to handle part of the advertising of the product without the consent of the first agency." Unfortunately, in the late 1990s, that practice is also being tested. Advertisers like Hardee's, Boston Market, and even Coca-Cola are engaging a variety of agencies as if they were free agents in their continuing search for home-run creative ideas. The à la carte approach is thought to be a better way by clients like Samsung, which doles out its assignments to a horde of freelancers and small shops with teams pitching against each other.

As clients have merged, agencies and clients are confronted with new conflict issues. A client might acquire a new division and want the agency to take on the new assignment—but the agency already might be representing the leading product in the category from another very important client. Either way, the agency would risk offending one client. In a worst-case scenario, both clients insist that the agency resign the other company because only one of the company's many divisions compete with the client. Usually, goodwill and loyalty resolve these problems of how conflict is interpreted. Clients often will agree that the agency can handle divisions of competing companies as long as the agency keeps the people working for one multidivision client from working on any division of another multidivision client. For example, the 1987 merger of Doyle Dane Bernbach, the agency for Weight Watchers International, with Needham Harper Worldwide, the agency for the Mrs. Paul product line, created a potential conflict because both companies produced frozen fish. However, the Campbell Soup Company, which owns the Mrs. Paul line, did not ask the new agency to drop either product. (Later, DDB Needham lost the business in a product alignment among Campbell agencies.)

Client nationalities even come into play in sorting out conflicting policies. One case involved a Japanese client's U.S. division and a U.S. company. Inquiring about the Japanese client's reaction to the agency soliciting a U.S. company would be taken by the Japanese company as a lack of loyalty, even though the U.S. company was comfortable that the inquiry be made.

Out of loyalty to a client, an agency might keep itself free of direct conflicts (product-to-product) anywhere in the world and avoid indirect conflicts (where two companies have similar divisions but the agency avoids the second company altogether). Companies rewarded this loyalty by avoiding agencies serving their competitors anywhere. This was especially true with soap and detergent products (Procter & Gamble, Colgate, Lever, and Henkel); automobiles (General Motors, Ford, Chrysler, Toyota, and Nissan); beer (Anheuser-Busch, Miller, and Stroh's), and is increasing in food (Nestlé, Kraft General Foods, RJR Nabisco, and Mars). Agencies that have one client in each of these categories will not accept, or be cleared to accept, another client in this category.

Internationalization creates a second problem. Suppose a client has no European distribution nor plans to enter Europe. Could its U.S. agency safely take a competitive product in its client's category in Germany? Usually the answer is yes, but in one recent instance the U.S. client was bought by a European company, and the agency found itself with an unanticipated conflict problem in Europe. Mergers in the United States and continuing acquisition of companies by the large global corporations have created a need for agencies and clients to maintain communication on what the policy is and how it will be interpreted. This requires a central clearing mechanism at agency headquarters, which includes new-product assignments.

These are particularly nettlesome problems. What if two clients the agency has successfully kept separate decide the same week to ask the agency to begin work in the same new-product area? The agency suddenly is in possession of a valuable piece of competitive intelligence. The best solution is to keep the decision at the highest level and make an informed judgment quickly.

Loyalty is important in sorting out these difficult conflict questions. Agencies develop loyalties to clients and vice versa. Marketing scholar, David Aaker, for example, argues that a brand needs a single architect, someone who will implement and coordinate a cohesive strategy across multiple media and markets for the long term and notes that the advertising agency is often the best candidate for this brand architect role. Loyalty sounds old-fashioned, however, in these days of throw-away relationships.

Sources: Keith Gould, "Limited Partners," *Adweek* (July 22, 1996); David A. Aaker, "The Agency as Brand Architect," *American Advertising* (Spring 1996):18–21.

buying company, which became an independent subsidiary of BBDO functioning exclusively as the media management for Chrysler and the media department for each agency involved in the Chrysler business.[15] By the end of the year, General Motors, after a review, consolidated $800 million in media buying in a new media operation to be formed as a subsidiary of Lintas within the Interpublic Group.[16]

What are the implications of these two radical developments amid the other trends in the business? In the past, clients had gone to outside suppliers for research projects and not used agency research departments, or they had used both outside and agency research. Clients had used media-buying services but had never established their own. Clients had used creative boutiques or other agencies for creative concepts in competition with the appointed agency but had never gone to a talent agency for an entire campaign.

To bring this discussion back to the essence of the business—value-adding ideas—advertising agencies are responding to these many new challenges by becoming generalists in strategy while developing work in specific areas of expertise, especially creative execution. If an agency is competitive in media, research, sales promotion, public relations, or other areas related to the business, the agency will offer these services as part of a complete plan. Through integrated marketing communication, the agency will seek to guide strategy and coordinate execution, using its own departments or strategic partners to provide additional specialized services needed by the client.

---

[15]Richard Brunelli, "Chrysler Sets Up Agency Buying Unit," *Brandweek* (May 10, 1993):5.
[16]"GM Merging Media Buying at Interpublic," *The Wall Street Journal* (December 8, 1993):B5.

$\mathcal{S}$UMMARY

- When functioning at their best, advertising agencies develop campaigns that enhance the value of the brands they handle.

- Agencies usually have four basic functions: account management, creative development and production, media planning and buying, and research.

- Support departments typically include traffic, print production, financial services, and human resources. Many agencies also develop other services as sources of profit.

- The account management function acts as the primary liaison between the agency and the client.

- Computerization has had a significant effect on the advertising agency business since the 1980s.

- Agencies typically have received a 15 percent commission from media placed, although this rate is increasingly being negotiated and will vary from country to country. Under the fee system, agencies' charges are computed on the basis of actual time and services provided.

- The economic climate of the late 1980s and early 1990s provoked many changes in the world of advertising agencies, including megamergers and increased competition.

$\mathcal{Q}$UESTIONS

1. This chapter says that the chief purpose of an advertising agency is to create value for its clients. What does that mean? What kind of value does it add to a product or service?

2. What impact has integrated marketing communications had on advertising agencies?

3. Why does the organizational chart for an agency remain flexible?

4. What is the symbiotic relationship between creative boutiques and media-buying services?

5. Why has the 15 percent commission system weakened as the industry standard? Why do many agencies prefer the fee system to the commission system?

6. Why has the growth of ethnic agencies and media targeting of minorities brought these two into conflict with activists?

7. How do agencies separate the internal management function from the creative process in the creative department?

8. Why are agencies under such pressure that their structure and form may change?

9. State two essential differences between the commission and the fee systems of compensation.

10. Name two events that reflect major change in the agency business.

11. Why do clients sometimes create in-house agencies?

12. Why has employment decreased in the largest agencies and grown in the rest in recent years?

13. Has the percentage of advertising in client marketing budgets grown or decreased in recent years? Why?

14. Give examples of how technology has had an impact on the agency business.

Suggested Class Project

1. Advertising is a discipline. Creation of advertising requires background information, often unavailable to a class. But advertising as a business practice can be understood by reversing the process. Divide the class into groups of four or five. Collect one or two print advertisements or tape one or two commercials for the same brand or company. Then work back to formulate the creative platform:

A. What is the purpose of the advertising?

B. Who is the target audience? Be as specific as possible in terms of age, income, occupation, habits, and attitudes.

C. What is the promise of the advertising? Is it a claim from the advertiser or a benefit to the user?

D. What is the support for the promise?

E. What media were used and why?

F. What is the tone being used and the personality being conveyed?

2. Form three or four "agencies" within the classroom. Form one smaller "client" group. (Drawing names might be best.) Each group needs to structure itself for job responsibilities. The client group provides an assignment (the same) for everyone to "produce," by gathering the elements of a current campaign. Candidates could include a car brand (for which material would be available at a local dealership), a fast-food outlet, or a brand of clothes (Levis, Dockers, J. Crew, Gap). The agencies would be given a copy platform and samples of the existing campaign, asked to critique the campaign, and to suggest new executions and a new slogan within the deadline. How would each agency delegate work responsibilities to complete the campaign? For fairness, each agency receives the same fee, and each has the same resources or access to the same resources, including computers. The client group decides which agency best meets the objective.

3. All advertising assignments can be reduced to a simple question: "How do we sell this thing?" Imagine this "thing" is an extra goat you have around, and the job is to sell it.

The following is a progression of ten headline ideas from ten copywriters, each with a different approach.

A. *Goat for Sale.* This is pure, simple marketing. An announcement of the availability of a product.

B. *Buy a Goat.* This adds urgency with a call to action.

C. *Buy a Great Goat.* Some hard sell, introducing the idea that all members of this product category may not be alike.

D. *Buy a Goat Instead of a Sheep.* Breaking out of the envelope, expanding the potential category. Sowing the seeds of discontent among sheep users, hoping to raise the category development index of goats.

E. *Save on a Goat.* A nice retail feel to this one.

F. *Goat. Guaranteed.* There may be some buyers out there who lack confidence in their ability to know a good goat when they see one. This should ease their concerns.

G. *Buy a Cheap Labor-Saving Device.* Aha! The Theodore Levitt school: You aren't buying a product, you're buying the solution to a problem. The rational benefit to the buyer is spelled out.

H. *Buy an Affectionate Labor-Saving Device.* Even better: an emotional benefit. You can't wait to read the body copy.

I. *Give a Goat a Home.* The ultimate cop-out, a shameless appeal to guilt. But it could work, depending on the illustration.

J. *Don't Let Someone Else Get Your Goat.* A cutesy pun with no meaning, but the approach most favored by lazy writers.

Rank each of these approaches, in descending order of expected effectiveness. The criterion is which will sell the goat, not which will win an award or make you feel good. You might suggest alternatives, but don't give it away, as in "Free Goat."

Class project 3 was suggested by George Lemmond, Lemmond Associates, Roswell, Georgia.

FURTHER READINGS

David A. Aaker, "The Agency as Brand Architect," *American Advertising* (Spring 1996):18–21.

Mayer, Martin, *Whatever Happened to Madison Avenue?* (New York: Little Brown & Co., 1991).

Randall Rothenberg, *Where the Suckers Moon: An Advertising Story* (New York: Alfred A. Knopf, 1994).

Honda faces the new century with a garage full of new car projects. It plans to introduce an experimental electric car in 1997 and a new minivan in 1998. Also on the roll is a new hybrid vehicle with the off-road capabilities of a sport utility but the comfort and handling of a passenger car, which should be on the highways in early 1997. Why so much activity?

Honda is one of the most competitive automakers because of its continued reliance on consumer insight research to spot trends and meet the needs of its customers. Its success is also the product of a company philosophy known as "The Honda Way," which promotes a consistent, yet flexible, marketing and advertising strategy.

Honda's story in the United States began in the fall of 1969 when Honda produced the top-selling motorcycle in America. Honda automobiles, however, had not yet appeared in this country. Over 7,000 miles away at Honda corporate headquarters in Tokyo, plans were being made to change that.

The plans were successful. By the 1980s Honda cars were some of the most popular in the United States, and in 1989 the Honda Accord was the number-one selling car in America. What took the company from zero to 717,000 cars a year in record time? It was a combination of engineering prowess, technological innovation, commitment, and good timing, all driven by "The Honda Way" corporate philosophy.

From the beginning, Honda's marketing philosophy stressed supplying high-efficiency products at a reasonable price. The company has continually emphasized customer satisfaction. Honda Associates were encouraged to be ambitious and daring, to develop fresh ideas, to embrace challenges, and to respond quickly to unforeseen changes and opportunities. In 1969 Honda engineers set the ambitious goal of developing a "world car." This project took them to the center of a profoundly changing automotive marketplace.

At that time over 88 percent of all automobiles sold in the United States came from Detroit. Moreover, the majority of imported cars were European, not Japanese. Toyota was the leading Japanese import followed by Datsun (now Nissan). Mazda and Subaru were just making plans to enter the U.S. market.

The popularity of the Volkswagon Beetle convinced Honda executives that a market for a quality small car existed in the United States. In 1970 Honda introduced its first car to America—the N600. Sales were modest. Only a few thousand were sold. Then, in 1973, the company introduced its "world car," the innovative Honda Civic. The Civic was nearly 8 inches longer than the 600 model, and it featured an advanced four-cylinder engine and front-wheel drive. Available in both a two-door sedan and a three-door hatchback, it was priced at only $2,150.

Although the Civic was well received by the automotive press and the American public, it was still considered too small. At that point, however, international politics intervened. In October 1973 the Arab oil-producing countries banned oil imports to the West. As gasoline lines grew and prices skyrocketed, Detroit's large engines—some delivering under 12 miles per gallon—began to lose their appeal. Sales of small, fuel-efficient automobiles like the Honda Civic grew rapidly. By the end of 1974 Civic sales had climbed to over 43,000.

Meanwhile, the OPEC embargo produced tough new federal fuel economy regulations. The Environmental Protection Agency (EPA) issued strict new emissions standards. As Detroit carmakers scrambled to meet the new regulations, Honda engineers had already developed their next big idea: the 1975 Civic CVCC. With its fuel-efficient new engine, the Civic not only met the EPA clean air standards, it also ran on any grade of fuel. At 42 miles per gallon, the Civic was promoted as both the most fuel-efficient and the lowest-priced car in America. The advertising campaign for the Civic positioned the car in the forefront of the move toward economical transportation. The Honda advertising slogan, "What the World Is Coming To," stressed the innovative philosophy behind the Civic. More than 100,000 Civics were sold.

Then Honda's research indicated that the market was about to change once again. As both fuel shortages and gasoline prices eased somewhat, car buyers began to favor values like quality, roominess, performance, and comfort. Honda developed a car to meet this need and in June 1976 launched what would become its most popular model—the Accord.

Honda advertising emphasized the roominess and lively performance of the Accord. The automotive press praised its clean design and advanced engineering. The public reception was remarkable: By the end of 1978 Honda sales had climbed to over 274,000 cars.

During this time, car buying had become more complex. There was a growing number of manufacturers and car models. Financing was more complicated, and Detroit was offering an expanded array of optional equipment. Amid this confusion, Honda's marketing approach was clear and simple: Honda builds quality cars that are simple to drive, simple to park, simple to understand, and simple to own. The message was summed up in Honda's slogan, used in print ads, brochures, on television, and even on shopping bags, "We Make It Simple" (see Exhibit A). It was The Honda Way—and it worked.

By the end of 1978 Honda was number three in import car sales, behind Toyota and Nissan. Over the next few years, the company increased its momentum by refining and expanding its product line. Honda's third series, the Prelude, was introduced in 1979. In 1980, the second-generation Civic was named *Motor Trend* magazine's "Import Car of the Year." Annual sales were now well over 375,000. In 1984 Honda launched its newest idea—the CRX. Conceived as a sporty commuter car with high gas mileage, it too was named *Motor Trend*'s "Import Car of the Year." In addition, the Honda Prelude and Civic Hatchback captured the first and second runner-up spots, making it the first time ever that a single manufacturer had won the top three spots in the long history of this prestigious competition.

Honda was now selling 12 different models in the United States, at the rate of over half a million cars per year. For the first time, Honda advertising began to focus on the particular personality of each model instead of using a unifying corporate slogan. Honda portrayed its luxury Accord as the benchmark in its class and the Prelude Sports Coupe as "a sports car for adults." Its second-generation Civics were marketed as being larger and more stylish than their predecessors while still keeping earlier fuel economy and value. Ironically, "We Make It Simple" was no longer the way to advertise an increasingly sophisticated product line, which now appealed to a wide variety of buyers.

Customer satisfaction has always been emphasized as part of The Honda Way. In 1986 Honda outperformed Mercedes-Benz to become number one in overall customer satisfaction, based on owners' ratings of both the quality of their cars and of the dealerships that service them. Honda spotlighted this success by announcing in print advertising, "We're Happy You're Happy."

When it came time for *Motor Trend*'s 1988 "Import Car of the Year" competition, Honda once again captured the top three spots. The redesigned CRX Si won the top honors, followed by the Prelude Si with four-wheel steering and the Civic four-door sedan. In typical Honda fashion, advertisements announcing the award stated simply, "Who says it's lonely at the top?" (see Exhibit B).

One reason for Honda's consistently strong performance in customer satisfaction is its dealer network. Honda works closely with its dealers to ensure that their operations—sales, service, parts, and accessories—reflect the quality of the cars themselves. Honda provides its dealers with support materials, from sales training and service manuals to full-line product brochures and videos.

Part of Honda's corporate philosophy is to be a good corporate citizen. In this spirit, Honda began another important campaign: saving lives. For three consecutive years—long before it became fashionable to do so—Honda sponsored a multimillion-dollar advertising effort to persuade drivers to use their seat belts. The company placed ads designed to convince drivers of the importance of seat belts in saving lives on television and in print media.

Responsible corporate citizenship took another form as well. By 1980, with the desire to manufacture products in the market in which they are sold, Honda began work on a new automobile plant in Marysville, Ohio. The decision posed both problems and opportunities. Research indicated that prospective buyers might perceive an Ohio-built Honda as inferior to one made in Japan. However, many Americans who felt uncomfortable buying an imported car would now consider buying an Accord built in the United States.

Honda decided to use advertising and marketing campaigns to help sell the idea of its Ohio-made cars.

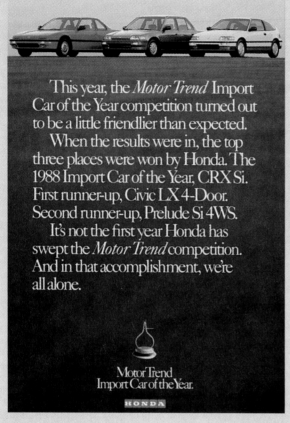

Who says it's lonely at the top?

This year, the *Motor Trend* Import Car of the Year competition turned out to be a little friendlier than expected.

When the results were in, the top three places were won by Honda. The 1988 Import Car of the Year, CRX Si. First runner-up, Civic LX 4-Door. Second runner-up, Prelude Si 4WS.

It's not the first year Honda has swept the *Motor Trend* competition. And in that accomplishment, we're all alone.

Motor Trend
Import Car of the Year.

HONDA

EXHIBIT B

People won't be the only Americans building Hondas in our new plant.

HONDA

EXHIBIT C

These campaigns described the contribution that Honda was making to the U.S. economy (see Exhibit C). The company also ran a series of ads in key business publications, such as *The Wall Street Journal*, emphasizing the quality of Ohio-built Accords.

When the Marysville plant opened in November 1982, the Honda state of mind had been successfully imported to Ohio. Impartial road tests gave the American-built Accord and the imported Accord equal marks on fit, finish, and overall quality. Moreover, Honda began to implement a new five-part strategy for the future of Honda's operations in the United States, which called for Honda's total manufacturing involvement in this country to reach $1.7 billion. The recently completed manufacturing plant in nearby East Liberty, Ohio, is now producing Civic four-door sedans at a rate of 150,000 per year. Other facets of the strategy called for an increase in research and development activities, the expansion of production engineering, the increase of domestic content in American-made Hondas to 75 percent, and the export of U.S.-built Honda products.

By the end of 1990 many of these goals had been reached. The Marysville plant was operating ahead of capacity, producing over 360,000 cars per year, and

Honda was selling more American-built cars than imported cars in the United States. The Anna, Ohio, engine facility had produced its one-millionth Honda engine. In December 1990, building off of the success of its top-selling Accord model, Honda introduced the Accord Wagon. This vehicle was the first Honda completely designed, engineered, and manufactured in the United States.

Before the introduction of the Accord Wagon, the Accord Coupe, first introduced in 1988, had been the first Honda to be manufactured exclusively in the United States. A special edition of this Accord became the first Japanese nameplate ever exported back to Japan where it immediately became a much sought-after status symbol among the upwardly mobile Japanese. In 1991 Honda planned to export 70,000 automobiles to Japan and other countries. The new Accord Wagon was the first U.S.-built Japanese car to be exported to Europe, where Honda sold about 5,000 units in 1991.

The automotive market of the 1990s has changed dramatically. The selling environment for automobiles has become increasingly difficult. There has been a proliferation of the number of car models that compete within Honda's core volume segments. American manufacturers are producing automobiles that are now approaching the quality levels of the Japanese brands. In

Introducing the Passport from Honda. It's the one with a 175-horsepower V-6 engine. It's the one with four-wheel drive. It's the one on top.
The Passport HONDA

this new, dynamic sales environment, Honda's advertising effort has quietly evolved to respond to the demands of the 1990s' marketplace.

The role of Honda national advertising is to continue to maintain the positive image of the brand. To make Honda brand advertising efforts more effective, Rubin Postaer and Associates, Los Angeles now includes planning in its development process to glean additional insight to the consumer. This insight is used to help develop ad programs that are extremely effective in talking to the consumer. This has helped make successful introductory campaigns for new Honda products such as the all-new 1994 Accord and the sport utility vehicle, the Passport (see Exhibit D).

On the retail level, Honda consolidated its dealer association advertising, formerly done by 51 separate regional agencies, with RPA in a new agency named RP alpha. This unified effort helps Honda provide a consistent retail image while continuing to support its overall brand/model image strategies. With this new organization, Honda regional dealer advertising works in concert with the Honda national image effort. This move effectively focuses Honda's advertising effort on breaking through the clutter and boosting overall image and sales with a single voice.

From the beginning, perhaps the key factor in Honda's success has been consistency. Honda products have consistently been of the highest quality and value, and they have continued to evolve in terms of engineering innovations, performance, styling, and comfort. Throughout the years Honda has also maintained a consistent image through its advertising and marketing. Honda advertising has always appealed to the intelligence and common sense of its customers. Consistently clever and subtle, often lighthearted and whimsical, but

always honest and confident, Honda's advertising treats the buying public with respect by presenting a message that allows consumers to think for themselves and draw their own conclusions.

Honda's advertising created by Rubin Postaer and Associates has received high praise from industry au-

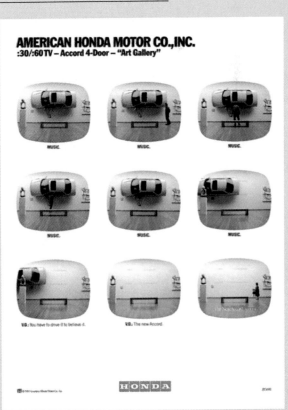

AMERICAN HONDA MOTOR CO., INC.
:30/:60 TV – Accord 4-Door – "Art Gallery"

HONDA

NOTHING PICKS UP DIRT FASTER.

If you can see beyond the Passport's rugged good looks, you will appreciate
its shift-on-the-fly 4-wheel drive and 190-horsepower V6 engine. HONDA

EXHIBIT F

thorities. A commercial for the 1990 Accord called "Art
Gallery" (see Exhibit E) emulated the engineering magic
that allowed Fred Astaire to dance on the ceiling in
the movie *Royal Wedding.* In this spot, a new Accord is
driven off the wall of a museum with the line, "You have
to drive it to believe it," as the only copy. *Adweek* advertising critic Barbara Lippert stated, "Rubin Postaer en-
dows Honda with another masterpiece." She went on to
say that, "Since 1980 few things have been as consistently engaging as Honda commercials. Honda spots are
thinking people's car commercials; they're clever, beautifully shot, and never obvious."

This praise was, perhaps, best summed up by automotive expert Chris Cedergren, who said, "Honda's
strength is in the fact that they don't radically change
their advertising every 6 months like others do. Honda
definitely won't tamper with success."

Source: Adapted from "The Honda Way: The Marketing of Honda
Automobiles in America." (Courtesy of Sanford Edelstein, Rubin
Postaer and Associates.)

QUESTIONS FOR DISCUSSION

1. What themes in Honda's advertising and marketing reflect what you know of
social needs and issues in the 1990s?
2. How does Honda identify its desired audience for these cars and how can the
company reach them? Would you recommend any changes in Honda's targeting?
3. What advertising strategy could be used to position Honda cars in a more
competitive market at the turn of the century?

Founded in 1968 by Jay Chiat and Guy Day, Chiat/Day has been responsible for some of the most memorable advertising ever produced by an American agency. That success was due in no small part to the efforts of creative director Lee Clow. Yet, even as the agency's reputation grew, it confronted many of the painful challenges facing the advertising industry as a whole. Chiat/Day's ups and downs during its first quarter century have been chronicled in *Inventing Desire*, a 1993 book by Karen Stabiner.

Chiat/Day started out as a small California boutique operation and quickly began producing eye-catching work for major clients. By the time the agency's Orwellian television ad for Macintosh computers aired during the Super Bowl broadcast in January 1984, Chiat/Day was on a roll. *Advertising Age* magazine heralded the Macintosh ad as "Commercial of the Decade"; Chiat/Day went on to create the memorable "Energizer Bunny" campaign for Eveready. Then, in 1987, Nissan Motor Corporation awarded its U.S. advertising account to Chiat/Day.

Even though the Nissan account more than doubled Chiat/Day's billings, the agency's founders continued to pursue an aggressive program of acquisition and expansion. The company added packaging, graphics, public relations, and direct-mail firms to its operations. Then Chiat/Day merged with an Australian agency; the new organization was named Chiat/Day/Mojo. The merger proved to be a disaster due to geographic and cultural differences as well as an economic downturn in Australia. Back in the United States, the early 1990s were lackluster years, in part because Lee Clow seemed to have lost his creative touch. Typical of this era was the Nissan "Built for the Human Race" campaign, which did little to boost Nissan's fortunes. In 1995, the Omnicrom Group bought Chiat/Day, then merged it with TBWA.

Since 1996, TBWA Chiat/Day, as the new company is called, has been back in top form. The agency received glowing notices for its new Nissan campaign, keyed to the slogan "Life is a Journey. Enjoy the Ride." Nissan budgeted $200 million for the campaign, a record for the company; the company's instructions to the agency were "to create advertising that everybody would be talking about." Recalling the origins of the campaign, Clow told *The New York Times*, "People don't really like car advertising. It's all the same; it's all sheet metal, features, and usually some kind of deal at the end. We're changing the rules of how car advertising can be done."

Each ad in the television campaign features a cameo by a Japanese-American actor modeled on Yutaka Katayama, Nissan's U.S. executive in the company's early export days. In "Toys," one of the campaign's most memorable spots, stop-motion animation is set against a music bed of Van Halen's version of "You Really Got Me." In the 60-second spot, a GI Joe-like doll drives a 300ZX to pick up a Barbie lookalike, much to the dismay of a third, preppy figure. Production costs for the "Toys" spot alone totaled $1 million, twice as much as Nissan usually spends on a commercial.

Chiat/Day's work for Nissan appears to be succeeding on several levels. In *USA Today's* Ad Track poll between May 1995 and November 1996, the Nissan spots scored higher in popularity than any other car ad. Dottie Enrico, who writes about advertising and marketing for *USA Today*, described the campaign this way: "Car advertising as it should be: cool, cooler, coolest. 'Toys' is a masterpiece—a boomer-targeted ad disguised as a Beavis & Butthead daydream. These spots push every one of my buttons: dead-on marketing strategy, engaging visuals and story, a good beat and a heroic Asian spokesfigure." It remains to be seen whether or not the campaign can help boost Nissan's share of the U.S. car and truck market above its current level of 4 percent. Sales appear to be up slightly; explains auto industry analyst George Peterson, "These ads are making the cars more top of mind. The campaign is pretty effective at getting people to at least consider Nissan."

Sources: Melanie Wells, "Nissan Scores with Curious Character," *USA Today* (February 10, 1997):4B; Wells, "Ad Man Lee Clow Has Nothing Left to Prove," *USA Today* (November 11, 1996):5B; David Barboze, "Nissan Is Changing the Rules for Car Ads by Rolling Out Entertaining Spots Using Toy Characters," *The New York Times* (October 24, 1996):D11.

$\mathcal{Q}$UESTIONS

1. Chiat/Day has produced some of the most memorable advertising created in the United States, as well as some notable failures. Why do you think it is possible for an agency to produce both brilliant work and work that flops?

2. Many of the hottest creative agencies in the country did not exist 20 years ago. Why would the age of an agency influence its creative ability?

CHAPTER

5

The Consumer Audience

CHAPTER OBJECTIVES

When you have completed this chapter, you should be able to:

- Understand the different factors that affect the responses of consumers to advertisements
- Define the concept of culture and subculture as it applies to advertising and consumers
- Distinguish between psychographics and demographics and explain how advertisers use each
- Relate such concepts as family, reference groups, race, and VALS to the practice of advertising

Settling Kids' Tummies

"My mommy said Mylanta." Looking to protect its struggling Mylanta franchise during a shakeout of the stomach remedies market, Johnson & Johnson/Merck rolled out a children's extension of the brand in May.

An estimated $5 million to $7 million television and print campaign began on May 7 for the line's rollout. J&J spent $36 million on the entire brand in 1995, according to Competitive Media Reporting through Saatchi & Saatchi Advertising's Healthcare Connection, New York.

Bubble gum and fruit flavors in both chewable and liquid forms are available. The retail price is in the $4.50 range, but as part of the promotional package, $4 in-store rebates were provided.

The notion of such adult problems as acid indigestion, sour stomach, and heartburn in children amused some industry observers. "I never thought there was a need. I wonder if this is an idea asking for a home," said Don Stuart, a partner at Cannondale Associates. "It is breaking new ground. However, with all the changes in the category, traditional products are under some heavy competition; I see this as a tactic to relieve that." Marketing spending of more than $300 million by acid blockers vying for share has sent the category skyrocketing 20 percent while upsetting older brands. Mylanta recently yielded the top spot to its new sibling brand, acid blocker Pepcid AC, barely a year old and already generating sales of $180 million.

There was an increasing interest in extending adult brands into children's products during 1995 and 1996. Warner-Lambert Co. went that route in late 1995 with allergy brands Benadryl and Sudafed, while J&J's McNeil Consumer Products Co. did the same with Motrin. Sales for the children's version of Benadryl were $40 million for the first year, while Sudafed Pediatric had $11 million, gathering respective market shares of 1.6 percent and 0.4 percent in the overall cough-cold category.

"They've tried to do children's extensions for a long time, but it has always been difficult," said Paul Kelly, president of Silvermine Consulting. "There have only been two very successful [kids] brands over the last 40 years—St. Joseph and Tylenol."[1]

Consumer Behavior

The situation for Mylanta is difficult. Advertisers not only have to understand what motivates children to take a product such as Mylanta, they must also understand the thought processes the parents engage in as well as the considerations of the family doctor. Understanding the behavior of customers to the best of your ability is the goal of any successful business.

The goal of advertising is to persuade the consumer to do something, usually to purchase a product. If advertising is to attract and communicate to audiences in a way that produces this desired result, advertisers must first understand their audiences. They must acquaint themselves with consumers' ways of thinking, with those factors that motivate them, and with the environment in which they live.

This difficult task is further complicated by the fact that the elements advertisers must take into account are constantly changing. Information that is appropriate to consumers today is often invalid tomorrow. Furthermore, advertisers must appeal to a complex consumer audience that is affected by many factors. In other words, the breadth of coverage is challenging. Advertisers must draw on input available from fields such as psychology, anthropology, and sociology to learn all they need to know about people.

---

[1]Michael Wilke, "Mylanta Targets Children," *Advertising Age* (May 27, 1996):1, 46. Reprinted with permission from *Advertising Age*. Copyright Crain Communications Inc.

Furthermore, there will be exceptions to every pattern or behavior. It is important to be prepared for these exceptions but not to assume that they negate the observed pattern. Finally, as target markets get larger and businesses move into other countries, finding general patterns of consumer behavior will become more difficult because each culture must be assessed separately.

In this chapter we will restrict our coverage to the specific behaviors people engage in as consumers. At the same time, we recognize that a great deal of what a person does outside the role of consumer is also relevant to advertising.

THE CONSUMER AUDIENCE

Consumers: People who buy or use products.

Consumers are people who buy or use products in order to satisfy needs and wants. There are actually two types of consumers: those who shop for and purchase the product, and those who actually use the product. This distinction is important because the two groups can have different needs and wants. In the case of children's cereals, for example, parents (the purchasers) look for nutritional value, whereas children (the users) look for a sweet taste and a game on the back of the package. Have you ever noticed that many cereals are advertised as *both* fun and "low sugar"? Because of the consumer orientation in marketing, consumer behavior is a very important field. Companies need to understand how consumers think and make decisions about products. In order to do this they conduct sophisticated research into consumer behavior. Companies must know who their consumers are, why they buy, what they buy, and how they go about buying certain products. (Consumer research will be discussed in Chapter 6.)

PRINCIPLE Marketers look at people as consumers who buy products; advertisers look at people as an audience for messages.

Figure 5.1 depicts a general model of consumer behavior, including the most relevant components and the relationship between these variables. It serves as the framework for this chapter.

MARKET SEGMENTATION/TARGET MARKETING

The advertising manager is responsible for answering many questions about the consumer or industrial customer. This would be an insurmountable task without the framework provided by market segmentation. Kotler and Armstrong define *market segmentation* as the process of dividing a market into distinct groups of buyers who might require separate products or marketing mixes.[2] Market segmentation divides potential consumers of a particular product into several submarkets or segments, each of which tends to share one or more significant characteristics.

For example, a 1995 study by Porsche Cars North America indicated that the average Porsche owner is a 40-something male college graduate earning over $200,000 per year. However, when they looked at market segments within this general profile, the five segments that follow were identified.

Top Guns (27%)	Driven, ambitious types. Power and control matter. They expect to be noticed.
Elitists (24%)	Old-money blue bloods. A car is just a car, no matter how expensive. It is not an extension of personality.
Proud Patrons (23%)	Ownership is an end in itself. Their car is a trophy earned for hard work, and who cares if anyone sees them in it.
Bon Vivants (17%)	Worldly jet setters and thrill seekers. Their car heightens the excitement in their already passionate lives.
Fantasists (9%)	The car is an escape. Not only are they uninterested in impressing others with it, they feel guilty owning one.[3]

[2]Philip Kotler and Gary Armstrong, *Marketing: An Introduction*, 4th ed. (Upper Saddle River, NJ: Prentice Hall, 1996):208.

[3]Alex Taylor III, "Porsche Slices Up Its Buyers," *Fortune* (January 16, 1995):24. Copyright ©1995 Time Inc. All rights reserved. Reprinted by permission of Fortune Magazine.

FIGURE 5.1

A MODEL OF CONSUMER

DECISION MAKING.

Reprinted with permission. Copyright
© 1995, *American Demographics,*
Ithaca, New York.

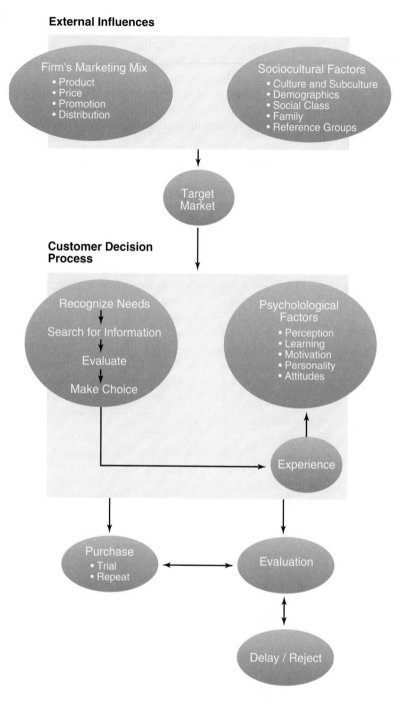

As this example illustrates, segmentation enables organizations to design a
marketing strategy that matches the market's needs and wants. Advertising, in particular, can be more focused. However, most firms do not have the capabilities to
market their product effectively to all viable segments, so they select one or more
target markets from the available market segments. The *target market* is a group of
people (segment) who are most likely to respond favorably to what the marketer
has to offer.

Market segments and target market(s) are based on the consumer characteristics and behaviors discussed in this chapter. (A more complete list of characteristics and behaviors is shown in Table 5.1.) A market segment can be based

on geography (domestic versus foreign), usage level of the product (heavy versus light), brand loyalty (disloyal versus highly loyal), and type of customer (ultimate user versus business user or industrial user). There are a great many characteristics that can be used to separate people into segments and target markets.

The segmentation process begins after the advertiser understands how and why the consumer generally thinks, feels, and behaves in a particular manner. Only then can the advertiser design a campaign that will effectively reach the fade-resistant laundry detergent market, the premium ice cream market, or the frequent business traveler market.

TABLE 5.1	MAJOR SEGMENTATION VARIABLES FOR CONSUMER MARKETS
VARIABLE	**TYPICAL BREAKDOWNS**
Geographic	
Region	Pacific, Mountain, West North Central, West South Central, East North Central, East South Central, South Atlantic, Middle Atlantic, New England
County size	A, B, C, D
City size	Under 5,000; 5,000–20,000; 20,000–50,000; 50,000–100,000; 100,000–250,000; 250,000–500,000; 500,000–1,000,000; 1,000,000–4,000,000; 4,000,000 or over
Density	Urban, suburban, rural
Climate	Northern, southern
Demographic	
Age	Under 6, 6–11, 12–19, 20–34, 35–49, 50–64, 65+
Sex	Male, Female
Family size	1–2, 3–4, 5+
Family life cycle	Young, single; young, married, no children; young, married, youngest child under 6; young, married, youngest child 6 or over; older, married, with children; older, married, no children under 18; older, single; other
Income	Under $10,000; $10,000–$15,000; $15,000–$20,000; $20,000–$30,000; $30,000–$50,000; $50,000 and over
Occupation	Professional and technical; managers, officials, and proprietors; clerical, sales; craftsmen, foremen; operatives; farmers; retired; students; homemakers; unemployed
Education	Grade school or less; some high school; high school graduate; some college; college graduate
Religion	Catholic, Protestant, Jewish, other
Race	White, black, Asian, Hispanic
Nationality	American, British, French, German, Scandinavian, Italian, Latin American, Middle Eastern, Japanese
Psychographic	
Social class	Lower lowers, upper lowers, working class, middle class, upper middles, lower uppers, upper uppers
Lifestyle	Belongers, achievers, integrateds
Personality	Compulsive, gregarious, authoritarian, ambitious
Behavioristic	
Purchase occasion	Regular occasion, special occasion
Benefits sought	Quality, service, economy
User status	Nonuser, ex-user, potential user, first-time user, regular user
User rate	Light user, medium user, heavy user
Loyalty status	None, medium, strong, absolute
Readiness stage	Unaware, aware, informed, interested, desirous, intending to buy
Attitude toward product	Enthusiastic, positive, indifferent, negative, hostile

Source: Philip Kotler and Gary Armstrong, *Marketing: An Introduction*, 4e (Upper Saddle River, NJ: Prentice Hall, 1997):217. Reprinted by permission of Prentice-Hall, Inc.

*I*NFLUENCES ON *Y*OU AS A *C*ONSUMER

Your responses to an advertising message are affected by many factors. Study yourself. You are going to be the subject of our field research for this chapter. You are a product of the culture and the society in which you were raised. Many of your values and opinions were shaped by your social environment. Likewise, you are a product of the family in which you were raised, and many of your habits and biases were developed within the family environment.

You are also an individual. As you matured and began to think for yourself, you developed your own individual way of looking at the world, based on such factors as your age, income, sex, education, occupation, and race. Deep within you are factors that influence every decision you make—such things as how you perceive events and other people, how you learn from experience, your basic set of attitudes and opinions, your internal drive and motivation, and the whole bundle of characteristics called your "personality."

CULTURAL AND SOCIAL INFLUENCES

Cultural and Social Influences: The forces that other people exert on your behavior.

The forces that other people exert on your behavior are called **cultural and social influences.** They can be grouped into four major areas: (1) culture, (2) social class, (3) reference groups, and (4) family.

CULTURE

Culture: The complex whole of tangible items, intangible concepts, and social behaviors that define a group of people or a way of life.

Norms: Simple rules for behavior that are established by cultures.

Culture is defined as a complex of tangible items (art, literature, buildings, furniture, clothing, and music) called *material culture*, along with intangible concepts (knowledge, laws, morals, and customs) that together define a group of people or a way of life. The concepts, values, and behaviors that make up a culture are learned and passed on from one generation to the next. The boundaries each culture establishes for behavior are called **norms.** Norms are simple rules that we learn through social interaction that specify or prohibit certain behaviors.

Customs are overt modes of behavior that constitute culturally approved ways of behaving in specific situations. For example, taking one's mother out for dinner and buying her presents on Mother's Day is an American custom that Hallmark and other card companies support enthusiastically. However, customs do vary from region to region and from country to country. For example, sending your child to college is a custom adopted by many Americans who want their children to do well (Ad 5.1).

Values: The source for norms, which are not tied to specific objects or behaviors.

The source for norms is our **values.** An example of a value is personal security. Possible norms expressing this value range from bars on the window and double-locked doors in Brooklyn, New York, to unlocked cars and homes in Eau Claire, Wisconsin. Values are few in number and are not tied to specific objects or situations. For several decades researchers have attempted to identify *core values* that characterize an entire culture. One simplified list consists of nine core values: (1) a sense of belonging, (2) excitement, (3) fun and enjoyment in life, (4) warm relationships, (5) self-fulfillment, (6) respect from others, (7) a sense of accomplishment, (8) security, and (9) self-respect. Advertisers often refer to core values when selecting their primary appeals. Because values are so closely tied to human behavior, private research firms attempt to monitor values and look for groupings of values and behavioral patterns. Values are discussed in more detail later in the chapter. Ad 5.2 reports on a research study sponsored by *Good Housekeeping* magazine, titled "Family Values in the '90s."

Cultural influences have broad effects on buying behavior. For example, the busy working mother of today is not as devoted to meal preparation and household cleaning as was the full-time homemaker of the past. Food marketers have changed their promotional strategies to reach these women, and we now see more advertising for fast foods, convenience foods, and restaurants.

AD 5.1

THIS AD REFLECTS A CORE
CULTURAL VALUE—SENDING
YOUR CHILD TO COLLEGE.

A cultural trend prevalent in the United States for the last decade or so has been eating low-calorie, low-fat foods in order to be slim or for good health.

How does culture affect you as a consumer? Can you think of any cultural factors that influence your behavior? How about patriotism and sacrificing for the good of others? Can you see yourself signing up for the Peace Corps? How about materialism? How do you feel about acquiring possessions and making money?

SUBCULTURES   A culture can be divided into *subcultures* on the basis of geographic regions or human characteristics such as age, values, or ethnic background. More specific criteria have also been suggested: (1) an economic system, or the way in which benefits are distributed; (2) social institutions, or participation in an identified institution; (3) belief systems, which include religious and political affiliations; (4) aesthetics, or art, music, dance, drama, and folklore; and (5) language, including dialects, accents, and vocabulary.

In the United States, for example, we have many different subcultures: teenagers, college students, retirees, southerners, Texans, blacks, Hispanics, athletes, musicians, and working single mothers, to list just a few. Within subcultures there are similarities in people's attitudes and secondary values.

AD 5.2

THIS AD ADDRESSES THE
CHANGE IN TRADITIONAL
AMERICAN FAMILIES.

THE NEW TRADITIONALIST FAMILY.

ITS STRUCTURE MAY BE CHANGING,
BUT ITS STRENGTH IS NOT.

Here's the traditional family portrait–circa 1993. Sandra Manzke, a single mother and successful business woman, and six boys between 12 and 16. Two are her own. Four were added when Sandra became engaged to their father, who recently died. They're still close. They still spend weekends with her and her boys.

It may sound confusing, but anyone who has seen them ski together, play together, or just hang around the house together will never doubt that this is "family" in every sense of the word.

They're living proof that family values are as strong as ever, even though the family "structure" is changing.

We found overwhelming evidence of that fact in the latest Good Housekeeping/Roper survey: "Family Values in the '90s." We asked over 1,500 parents and children about their life, their family, their values.

The study reveals the highest level of optimism about the family and family values that we have seen in ten years.

Obviously that's good news for Good Housekeeping. For four generations, Good Housekeeping – the Magazine, the Institute, and the Seal – have been dedicated to the values of the American family.

For a copy of Good Housekeeping's "Family Values in the '90s" study – contact your Good Housekeeping account manager.

AMERICA BELIEVES IN GOOD HOUSEKEEPING

What subcultures do you belong to? Look at your activities. Do you do anything on a regular basis that might identify you as a member of a distinctive subculture?

SOCIAL CLASS

Social Class: A way to categorize people on the basis of their values, attitudes, lifestyles, and behavior.

A **social class** is the position that you and your family occupy within your society. Social class is determined by such factors as income, wealth, education, occupation, family prestige, value of home, and neighborhood.

Every society has some social class structure. In a rigid society you are not allowed to move out of the class into which you were born. In the United States we like to think we have a classless society because it is possible for us to move into a different class regardless of what social class our parents belonged to. However, even in the United States we speak of an upper class, a middle class, and a lower class.

Marketers assume that people in one class buy different goods from different outlets and for different reasons than people in other classes. Advertisers can get a feel for the social class of a target market by using marketing research or available census data.

In what class do you see yourself? Does social class affect what you buy and how you respond to advertising? Do you know people you would consider to be upper- or lower-class? Do they buy different products than you do? Do they look at products differently in terms of price or quality?

REFERENCE GROUPS

Reference Group: A group of people that a person uses as a guide for behavior in specific situations.

A **reference group** is a collection of people that you use as a guide for behavior in specific situations. General examples of reference groups are political parties, religious groups, racial or ethnic organizations, clubs based on hobbies, and informal affiliations such as fellow workers or students.

For consumers, reference groups have three functions: (1) they provide information; (2) they serve as a means of comparison; and (3) they offer guidance. Sometimes the group norms have the *power* to require the purchase or use of certain products (uniforms, safety equipment). The reference group members may be so *similar* to you that you believe that any product or service the group members use is right for you too. Ads that feature typical users in fun or pleasant surroundings are using a reference-group strategy. You also may be *attracted* to a particular reference group and wish to be like the members of that group out of respect or admiration. Advertisers use celebrity endorsements to tap into this desire.

Think about all the groups you belong to, both formal and informal. Why do you belong to these groups? How do other members influence you or keep you informed? Have you ever bought anything specifically because it was required by a group you belonged to?

THE PROLIFERATION OF FAST-FOOD RESTAURANTS IS AN EXAMPLE OF THE INFLUENCE OF CULTURE ON CONSUMER BEHAVIOR.
(Courtesy of Dennie Cody/FPG)

Family: Two or more people who are related by blood, marriage, or adoption and live in the same household.

Household: All those people who occupy one living unit, whether or not they are related.

Lifestyle: The pattern of living that reflects how people allocate their time, energy, and money.

FAMILY

A **family** consists of two or more people who are related by blood, marriage, or adoption and live in the same household. A **household** differs from a family in that it consists of all those who occupy a living unit, whether they are related or not.

Your family is critical to how you develop as an individual. It provides two kinds of resources for members: *economic*, such as money and possessions; and *emotional*, such as empathy, love, and companionship. The family is also responsible for raising and training children and establishing a lifestyle for family members. Your **lifestyle** determines how you spend your time and money and the kinds of activities you value. More will be said about lifestyles later.

It is important for advertisers to understand the structure and workings of the family. For example, the U.S. family structure is changing because of an increase in divorces, later marriages, one-parent and two-family households, and other alternative family systems. (These changing family structures are discussed in more detail later in the chapter.) Advertisers must create messages that appeal to the needs and lifestyles of these consumers. A family's purchase and consumption patterns offer some interesting challenges as well. For instance, most families have members, such as parents, who screen and evaluate product information. Other members, such as children, strongly influence which product or brand is purchased, although they are not necessarily the actual decision makers. The family is our most important reference group because of its longevity and intensity. Other reference groups, such as peers, coworkers, and neighbors, tend to change as we age and switch occupations or residency. Advertisers respond to the family in various ways. As reflected in the Sony ad, some companies attempt to portray the family in a realistic manner, including the positives and the negatives (Ad 5.3).

How has your family influenced you in your choice of schooling, lifestyle, and the way you spend your time and money? Now think about your best friend. Are the two of you different in any ways that can be traced to family differences?

AD 5.3

SONY PORTRAYS FAMILIES IN A MORE REALISTIC WAY.

PERSONAL INFLUENCES

Every consumer is a product of culture and society, social class, and family. Ultimately, however, a consumer is an individual. Individual characteristics strongly influence the way you think, decide, and behave as a consumer. These characteristics can be divided into two categories: demographic variables and psychographic variables. *Demographics* are the statistical representations of social and economic characteristics of people, including age, sex, income, occupation, and family size. In contrast, *psychographics* refer to people's psychological variables, such as attitudes, lifestyles, opinions, and personality traits.

DEMOGRAPHICS

Demography: The study of social and economic factors that influence human behavior.

Demography is the study of those social and economic factors that influence how you behave as an individual consumer. These factors serve as the basis for much of the advertising strategy. Knowing the age, sex, occupation, and race of the members of the target audience assists advertisers in message design and media selection. On May 31, 1996, the U.S. population reached 265 million. What do we know about these people?

AGE

People in different stages of life have different needs. An advertising message must be understandable to the age group to which the product or service is targeted and should be delivered through a medium used by members of that group. How old are you? What products did you use five or ten years ago that you don't use now? Look ahead five or ten years—what products will you be in the market for then? What products do your parents buy that you don't? Do you read different publications and watch different programs than your parents do? If you were in the market for a car, would you look at the same features that your parents look at? In the United States several trends with respect to age have a direct bearing on advertising.

As noted in Figure 5.2, the U.S. population will continue to age, with the 65 and over age group representing our largest age group by 2030.

FIGURE 5.2

THIS BAR GRAPH SHOWS THAT THE PERCENTAGE OF PEOPLE 65 AND OLDER IS INCREASING IN THE UNITED STATES.
Source: U.S. Census Bureau, 1990. Reprinted with permission. Copyright © 1994, *American Demographics*, Ithaca, New York.

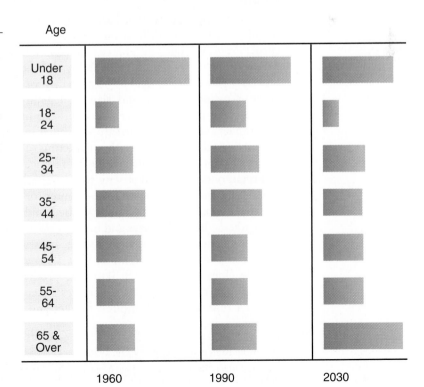

Age

	1960	1990	2030
Under 18			
18-24			
25-34			
35-44			
45-54			
55-64			
65 & Over			

BABY BOOMERS The baby boom includes all U.S. citizens born between 1946 and 1964. During that period 76.4 million people were born in the United States of whom approximately 68 million are still alive.[4] We have already described some of the characteristics of the baby boomers in Chapter 2. Recall that the majority of baby boomers are in blue-collar occupations, and they have fallen short of reaching the American Dream. Despite having a better education, higher-paying jobs, and more family members in the work force, baby boomers are experiencing a crisis of expectations due to increasing costs and excessive competition for higher-paying jobs. Younger baby boomers (ages 29 to 37), however, are enjoying the hard work of the older members of the group. This younger group is somewhat smaller and has found career opportunities and job advancement to be much easier and more readily available because the older boomers have expanded the size of the job market. It is this group that has been able to obtain many of the material possessions associated with the American Dream.[5]

THE ELDERLY As the baby boomers become more frustrated, the elderly market is growing in size and importance. By the turn of the century one person in eight will be 65 or older.

The importance of senior citizens to the advertiser, however, is not just the tremendous growth in their numbers. Rather, the opportunities offered by seniors are found in their differences. For instance, the "young old"—those who chose early retirement and those in their seventies—are healthier and wealthier than those who formerly filled this slot. Marketers have responded to the new elderly population by introducing a host of products that appeal to affluent, healthy people who have free time. Advertisers often portray the elderly as attractive and active. Even products difficult to advertise, such as adult diapers, have been positively portrayed through testimonials by former movie star June Allyson. In addition, several new media that are directed to the elderly have emerged. Examples are the Silver Pages directory, telemarketing, and magazines such as *Modern Maturity*, *New Choices*, and *Extended Vacations*.

GENDER

Gender, or sex, is an obvious basis for differences in marketing advertising. When we talk about gender differences, we consider both primary and secondary differences. *Primary* gender differences are physical or psychological traits that are inherent to males or females. The ability to bear children is a primary female trait. *Secondary* gender traits tend to be primarily associated with one sex more than the other. Wearing perfume and shaving legs are secondary traits associated with women. The primary gender characteristics of men and women create demands for products and services directly associated with a person's sex. In the past there were many taboos regarding the marketing of such products. For example, marketers of tampons or sanitary pads were once restricted to advertising in media and retail outlets devoted strictly to women; and condoms, purchased almost exclusively by men, were behind-the-counter (or perhaps under-the-counter) items. Today these barriers have all but vanished, and primary female and male products are marketed in similar ways and in comparable media.

Marketing products related to secondary sexual characteristics has become more complicated. For example, hair, skin, and body type have long provided reliable clues to marketers. Skin-care products were the exclusive domain of women, and erotic magazines were restricted to men. Now skin-care products for men represent a $60 million market and *Playgirl* magazine is popular with women.

---

[4]"Growing Pains at 40," *Time* (May 19, 1986):22–41.

[5]Alan L. Otten, "Baby Boomer People Make Less But Make Do," *The Wall Street Journal* (July 5, 1990):B1.

𝓘SSUES AND 𝓒ONTROVERSIES

GAYS AND LESBIANS AS CONSUMERS

There is a marketplace revolution—serious, multifaceted, and destined to reorganize customer landscapes in consumer product and service industries across the country. Gay and lesbian consumerism, and the spectacular developments it is spawning, is already affecting much of America's commercial media imagery. What is coming specifically is a cataclysmic change in the spending patterns of millions of American consumers—gay and lesbian as well as heterosexual. For many companies, the entire way of doing business will alter significantly as a direct result of gay and lesbian buying power and its indirect commercial influence.

Gay and lesbian buying power is now recognized as such a commercial and economic force that it is affecting decision making at Hill and Knowlton Public Relations, American Express, Nike, Calvin Klein, Revlon, AT&T, Time Warner, Continental, NBC News, Home Box Office, IKEA, and General Motors. These and other companies are pondering all the social nuances and marketing opportunities that are being brought about by this new age of racial and sexual diversity.

Gay and lesbian market segments exist in much the same way heterosexual market segments exist. And determining the size and breakdown of each of these gay and lesbian segments requires the same kind of approach that has been used to determine the demographics, human values, needs, wants, fears, and dreams in the segments of what were once assumed to be all straight consumers.

The 1994 Yankelovich MONITOR Gay and Lesbian report is the most important and accurate study conducted to date. The research was collected by means of a 90-minute personal interview conducted in the homes of a representative national sample of 2,500 consumers over the age of 16. The following list reflects the more important differences identified:

- The gay/lesbian population is more likely to have attended graduate school, be self-employed, and live in large metropolitan areas.
- The gay/lesbian population is less likely to be Protestant, live in the South, be married, be parents, or to live in a household where children under 18 are present.
- Approximately 6 percent of the population identify themselves as gay/lesbian.
- The gay/lesbian sample is more concerned about understanding themselves and their motivations, and has a stronger interest in keeping up with the latest in fashion.
- Gays and lesbians are more interested in new products and services.
- Gays and lesbians feel a higher level of personal stress and the need to resolve this stress.
- Gays and lesbians feel less than trusting of their environment—both socially and economically.
- Due to their strong feeling of alienation and victimization, gays and lesbians have a stronger need for self-understanding, association with people like themselves, emotional and physical security, and independence.

The overriding point for marketers is that many gays and lesbians view the world through a prism of cynicism toward business, are quick to interpret actions as attempts at victimization, and feel alienated from the dominant culture.

Source: Grant Lukenbill, "Untold Millions," *Harper Business* (1995).

As prevalent as this crossover effect appears, many consumers will consider certain brands masculine or feminine. It is unlikely that men would use a brand of after-shave called White Shoulders. The Gillette Company found that women would not purchase Gillette razor blades, so they introduced new brands with feminine names such as Daisy and Lady Gillette. Marketers of products formerly associated with one sex who want to sell them to both sexes find it necessary to offer "his and her" brands or even different product names for the same basic goods. What products do you buy that are unisex? What products do you use that are specifically targeted to your sex?

During the last decade, gay and lesbian consumers have become a salient target market. As indicated in the Issues and Controversies box, this gender-complex segment has important implications for advertisers.

FAMILY STATUS

Your purchasing patterns are affected by your family situation. People living alone buy different products, in different sizes, than do people living in families. Has your family's spending patterns changed since you went to college? Unless your parents were able to start a college fund when you were born, they have probably had to reduce their purchases of luxury items, vacations, and new cars to help send you to school.

TABLE 5.2	THE FUTURE OF THE FAMILY			
HOUSEHOLD TYPE	1990	1995	2000	PERCENTAGE CHANGE 1990–2000
Total Households	92,257	98,769	104,977	13.8%
Single-Person Families	23,112	25,184	27,903	20.7%
Married With Children under 18	23,808	24,354	24,520	3.0%
Married—No Children	27,500	29,073	31,020	12.8%
Lone Parent	7,477	8,409	8,882	18.9%
Other Households	10,360	11,749	12,404	19.7%

Note: Other Households include unmarried couples, unmarried couples with children, single-parents with children over the age of 18, roommates, and couples raising children who are not their own.

Source: Joint Center for Housing Studies, Harvard University, 1993; "Percentage Changes," *Sales & Marketing Management*, April 1994. Reprinted by permission of Bill Communications.

Although the most common arrangement among U.S. families remains two parents with children, a number of alternative family arrangements have become more common. The prevalence of divorce—the number of divorces granted each year more than doubled from 1977 to 1990, although most divorces are followed by remarriage—has enlarged three other family categories: divorced with no children, single parent with children, and the blended family, or "his, hers, and ours" family with children from different marriages living together in the same home with remarried parents. Each family system has its unique problems and offers special marketing opportunities. Table 5.2 depicts summary information about the American family.[6]

In addition, not everyone wishes to get married; at least, not right away. Today the median age of first marriages is at a historic peak of 26.7 years for men and 24.5 years for women. In 1994, there were more than 44.2 million never-married adults in the United States—more than twice the number that existed in 1970. Furthermore, singles are living alone in greater numbers. Between 1970 and 1994, the number of men older than 15 living alone mushroomed from 3.5 million to 9.4 million, and for women over 18 a whopping six in ten are living alone.[7]

The final factor strongly affecting the American family is the increase in the number of women in the work force. More than half of all women between the ages of 15 and 64 now work outside the home, and women comprise one third of the world's work force.[8] The two-income couple has caused a substantial realignment of family spending and role responsibilities. Families with two wage earners eat out more often, own more expensive cars, take more expensive vacations, and wear more expensive clothes. Men in many of these families participate in child care, housecleaning, food shopping and preparation, and laundry responsibilities. Do both of your parents work? Do you have friends whose families are headed by only one wage earner? Do you see a difference in your lifestyles? How have your parents divided the family responsibilities?

EDUCATION

The level of education you have attained also influences your behavior as a consumer. Advertisers know they must market products differently to better-educated consumers than to the less educated. Consumers with higher educations are often more responsive to technical-scientific appeals, prefer informative ads, and are better able to judge the relationship between the price and quality of a product. The trend toward a better-educated consumer is expected to continue through the

---

[6]Melissa Healy, "Americans Waiting Longer to Marry," *The Denver Post* (March 13, 1996):D-2.

[7]Berna Miller, "Household Futures," *American Demographics* (March 1995):4, 6.

[8]William B. Johnston, "Global Work Force 2000: The New World Labor Market," *Harvard Business Review* (March–April 1991):117.

1990s. By the year 2000 nearly 30 percent of all Americans over age 25, male and female, will have a college degree.[9] As indicated in Figure 5.3, level of education has direct bearing on how consumers view shopping.

OCCUPATION

Most people identify themselves by what they do. Even nonwage earners such as homemakers and students identify themselves this way. There has been a gradual movement from blue-collar occupations to white-collar occupations during the last three decades. There have also been shifts within white-collar work from sales to other areas, such as professional specialty, technical, and administrative positions. Furthermore, the number of service-related jobs is expected to increase, especially in the health care, education, and legal and business-service sectors. Much of this transition is a direct result of advanced computer technologies, which have eliminated many labor-intensive blue-collar occupations.[10] This shift has affected advertising in a number of ways. Most notably, blue-collar jobs are seldom portrayed in advertisements anymore, and ad copy tends to be more technical. Also, women are being depicted increasingly in professional roles.

Another interesting trend in occupation status is the increase in people who work at home. In 1995, this category contained 40.6 million U.S. households or about 4.1 percent of all U.S. households.[11]

You belong to the student occupational category, but you are also in training for some other profession. Why did you choose that career objective? Obviously, your decision to go to college was affected by occupational considerations, as well as by the geographical area in which you live. What other decisions have you made on the basis of your occupation or profession—either past, present, or intended?

---

[9]Shannon Dortch, "Colleges Come Back," *American Demographics* (May 1995):4.

[10]Walter Kiechel III, "How Will We Work in the Year 2000?" *Fortune* (May 17, 1993):38–52.

[11]"Numbers for the '90's," *Advertising Age* (September 4, 1995):3.

FIGURE 5.3

SHOPPING SENSIBILITIES.
Source: Diane Crispell, "The Real Middle America," *American Demographics* (October 1994):30. SRI Consulting. Reprinted by permission.

People with different levels of education have different outlooks on shopping.

(index* of adults aged 25 and older who mostly agree with selected statements, by education, 1993)

* *100 equals U.S. average; an index above 100 indicates that a group is more likely than average to agree; an index below 100 indicates it is less likely.*

INCOME

Discretionary Income: The money available for spending after taxes and necessities are covered.

You are only meaningful to a marketer if you have the resources to buy the product advertised. That means you must possess money and credit. It also means you must have some **discretionary income,** the money available to a household after taxes and basic necessities such as food and shelter are paid for. As your total income increases, the proportion that is considered discretionary income grows at a much faster rate. Some 26 million American households are thought to have significant discretionary income. Although this group represents only 29 percent of all households, it receives 53 percent of all consumer income before taxes.[12]

The distribution of the income among the population has a great impact on marketers. The average before-tax income for all U.S. households in 1995 was $34,950, according to the Bureau of Labor Statistics. The poverty threshold for a four-person family in 1995 was about $15,000; this represents 30 percent of U.S. households. Over 60 percent of U.S. households earn between $15,000 to $75,000, and less than 10 percent earn over $75,000. Evidence suggests that, indeed, the rich are getting richer and the poor are getting poorer.[13] Yet, in a recent survey conducted for *Adweek*, when asked the question, "Are you living better than your parents?," 68 percent of the respondents answered "yes."[14]

Can you think of any product that you wanted to buy recently but could not afford? Do you have a "wish list" of purchases you would like to make "someday"?

RACE AND ETHNICITY

The United States has long been considered the "melting pot" of the world—an image implying that the diverse peoples who have settled here have adopted the same basic values and norms. This idea is probably less true than most people imagine. Race and ethnic background might not influence the consumer behavior of most white Anglo-Saxon Americans, simply because such considerations are not very important in their daily lives. However, there is evidence that this group actually has a strong tendency to adopt the tastes of others. Witness the tremendous growth in the consumption of ethnic foods, especially Mexican, Chinese, Thai, Indian, and Vietnamese cuisines.

Racial and ethnic identities affect both self-image and consumer behavior of nonwhites and people with strong ethnic backgrounds. This is a complex area, however, because race and ethnicity are difficult to separate from such factors as family, language, and reference groups. For example, although in the United States we use the label *Hispanic* to identify members of many different ethnic groups, members of these groups do not identify with this umbrella term, but differentiate themselves as distinct cultures. Using the same ad in the Cuban community in Miami, the Puerto Rican community in New York, and the Mexican-American community in San Antonio could therefore prove disastrous for an advertiser. A similar confusion exists for the African-American market.

Together, ethnic Americans now account for more than $500 billion in purchasing power. From 1980 to 1990, the Hispanic market grew by 53 percent to 22 million people, African Americans by 13.2 percent to 32 million, and Asians by 107 percent to 7 million, compared with a growth rate of 9.8 percent for the total population. (See Table 5.3).

Because of its tremendous growth in the near future, a great deal of research has been conducted on the Hispanic market. "The Hispanic market today resembles the general market of the 1950's," says Karin McGinley-Urquiza, vice president of promotions at BDS Marketing. Hispanic Americans, she says, lack the cynicism about offers and product claims because "they want to be educated about what they

---

[12]Bickley Townsend, "This Is Fun Money," *American Demographics* (October 1989):39–41.

[13]Paula Mergenhagen, "What Can Minimum Wage Do?" *American Demographics* (January 1996):32–36.

[14]"Are You Living Better Than Your Parents Did?" *Adweek* (June 26, 1995):20.

TABLE 5.3	A POPULATION SHIFT

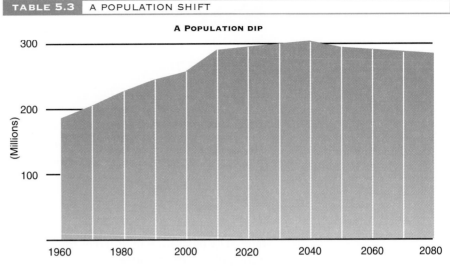

A POPULATION SHIFT

GROUP	1990	2040 (PERCENT OF TOTAL POPULATION)	2080
White*	84.1	76.9	72.6
Black	12.4	15.3	16.3
Other†	3.5	7.8	11.1
Over 65	12.6	22.6	24.5
Under 35	53.5	40.8	39.2

*Includes Hispanics, currently 7.5 percent of all whites.

†Mainly Asian, Pacific Islanders, and American Indians.

Source: U.S. Census Bureau. From *Sales & Marketing Management*, April 1993, p.53. Reprinted by permission of Bill Communications.

buy." Because Hispanic consumers are more image and quality conscious, she adds, they tend to be more brand loyal than non-Hispanic neighbors. Product quality is the Hispanic consumer's overriding consideration in any purchase.[15]

One of the serious problems associated with race and ethnicity is the fact that the Census Bureau sees race and ethnicity as two different demographic characteristics and has separate questions on census forms and surveys. But the people who fill out the forms sometimes find the two concepts impossible to separate. People, especially young people, do not accept the racial categories in the census, and tend to check the "other race" category. For example, over 40 percent of the nation's 22 million Hispanics aren't willing to identify themselves as black or white.[16]

GEOGRAPHIC LOCATION

Knowing where people live is important to advertisers. Marketers study the sales patterns in different regions of the country to discover variations in the purchase behavior of consumers. People residing in different regions of the country have different needs for certain products or services. Someone living in the Midwest or Northeast is more likely to purchase products for removing snow and ice, for example, whereas a Floridian would be more apt to buy suntan lotion or beach attire. There are also differences between urban areas and suburban or rural areas. Swimming pools that sell well in a residential suburban neighborhood would not be very much in demand in an urban neighborhood filled with apartment buildings.

[15]Kerry J. Smith, "Marketers Target the New Majority," *PROMO* (January 1993):171–74.

[16]Gabrielle Sandor, "The Other Americans," *American Demographics* (June 1994):36–42.

TABLE 5.4	POPULATION AND CHANGE IN POPULATION BY REGION, 1980–1990			
	1990 POPULATION	**1980 POPULATION**	**CHANGE**	**PERCENT CHANGE**
			1980–90	
United States	249,870	226,546	23,324	10.3%
Northeast	50,911	49,135	1,776	3.6%
Midwest	59,939	58,866	1,073	1.8%
South	87,012	75,372	11,640	15.4%
West	52,008	43,172	8,836	20.5%

Source: Adapted from *American Demographics* (January 1990):24. Reprinted with permission. Copyright ©1990, *American Demographics,* Ithaca, New York.

In addition, marketers analyze different markets by population and growth rates. The population of different states and regions of the country will affect the weight of advertising placed in specific areas. For example, according to the 1990 census, the Northeast had become the least populous region of the country, whereas the South, with 87 million people, had the highest population.[17]

The 1990 census also showed that states in the South and West accounted for nearly 90 percent of the nation's ten-year population gain. Although the Midwest was the slowest-growing region, it was still the second most populous area in the nation. California gained more people than any other state—over 5 million since 1980. Texas and Florida gained more than 3 million residents each during the 1980s, and Georgia gained over 1 million. In contrast, the populations of West Virginia, Iowa, and the District of Columbia decreased.[18] This kind of information is valuable to an advertiser in deciding where and to whom to target specific advertising messages. Table 5.4 illustrates the changes in the U.S. population from 1980 to 1990.

A system employed to combine geographic location with other demographic traits is called *geodemographic* cluster systems. More is said about this segmentation technology in the Concepts and Applications box.

PSYCHOGRAPHICS

Psychographics: All the psychological variables that combine to shape our inner selves, including activities, interests, opinions, needs, values, attitudes, personality traits, decision processes, and buying behavior.

We have analyzed you as a member of social and reference groups and have looked at your personal characteristics. Now let's look at the internal elements that make you an individual. The variables that shape your inner self are referred to as your *psychological makeup.*

Advertisers use the term **psychographics** to refer to all the psychological variables that combine to shape our inner selves. Psychographics goes beyond demographics in attempting to explain complex behavior patterns. For example, why does one mother with a newborn infant use disposable diapers whereas another mother chooses reusable cloth diapers? And why does she use Pampers when others use generic brands or the brand for which they have a coupon? Why does one person drive a brand-new BMW, whereas a neighbor in the identical condo next door drives an old Ford?

To explain these "true" motivations for behavior, advertisers look at a variety of dimensions, including activities, interests and hobbies, opinions, needs, values, attitudes, and personality traits. Taken together, these elements give a much broader picture of a person than do demographic data.

Although hundreds of different dimensions are: encompassed under *psychographics,* the areas with the most relevance to advertising are: perception, learning, motives, attitudes, personality, lifestyles, and buying behavior.

[17]Waldrop and Exter, "What the 1990 Census Will Show," p. 24.
[18]Ibid., p. 24.

*C*ONCEPTS AND *A*PPLICATIONS

IT'S WHERE YOU LIVE THAT COUNTS

One of the most sophisticated tools for capturing customers is the geodemographic segmentation system. Products like Claritas PRIZM, Strategic Mapping's Cluster 2000, NDS/Equifax's MicroVision, and CACI's ACORN use data from the decennial census and other sources to separate the nation's neighborhoods into similar groups known as clusters.

Cluster systems are based on the premise that birds of a feather tend to flock together. Look at your own neighborhood. The homes and cars are probably of similar size and value. If you could look inside the mailboxes and cupboards, you'd probably find many of the same magazines and cereals.

The idea behind geodemographic cluster systems is the same. Each system divides neighborhoods into groups based on similarities in income, education, and household type, as well as attitudes and product preferences. But each of the four major cluster systems is dynamic and changeable, and the 1990 census gave them an enormous infusion of new data. Two of the players used census data to completely overhaul their systems in 1994, creating new sets of clusters organized in new ways.

Merging new data into an existing or updated cluster system is no mean feat. Geodemographic segmentation systems start with millions of raw statistics. They divide the nation's households into groups based on similarities, much as biologists divide living things into orders, families, and so on.

Marketers use cluster systems to find new customers, locate sites for stores, buy advertising, target direct mail, and develop new products. If a direct-mail campaign gets a strong response from one zip code, for example, a cluster system can locate other zip codes with similar characteristics.

Cluster systems can reveal niches of potential customers in unlikely places. Equally important, they can show that some favorite groups are in reality poor prospects. "There are some surprises that can let the air out of your notion of who your customers are," says Jim Keryan, GTE's staff administrator of market assessment. Joe Darling of Isuzu used Cluster-PLUS 2000 to find the target market for the launch of the 1989 Amigo convertible. What he found went against his expectations. "Chicago wasn't the first place we imagined a soft-top car would sell," says Darling. "But the system predicted it. Sure enough, the top two dealers in sales were in Chicago."

Clusters sell advertising, too. Cable Networks, Inc. sells time on cable television systems. It uses cluster system maps to "show our customers where the big purchasers of certain items are located within cable system geographies," says director of marketing research Laura James. Advertisers are far more impressed by a cluster-coded map than they would be with a page of basic statistics, she says.

Not every business needs the full resources of a major geodemographic segmentation system. To effectively use geodemographic segmentation systems, businesses should have a minimum of 2,000 customers. The systems work best with a minimum of 5,000 to 10,000 customers.

Source: Susan Mitchell, "Birds of a Feather," *American Demographics* (February 1995):40–48. Reprinted with permission. Copyright ©1995, *American Demographics*, Ithaca, New York.

PERCEPTION

Each day you are bombarded by stimuli—faces, conversations, buildings, advertisements, news announcements—yet you actually see or hear only a small fraction. Why? The answer is perception. **Perception** is the process by which we receive information through our five senses and assign meaning to it. Perceptions are shaped by three sets of influences: the physical characteristics of the stimuli, the relation of the stimuli to their surroundings, and conditions within the individual. It is this last set of influences that makes perception a personal trait. Each individual perceives a given stimulus within a personal frame of reference. Factors that influence this frame of reference include learning experiences, attitudes, personality, and self-image. The process is further complicated by the fact that we are exposed to a great number of stimuli. Some of these stimuli are perceived completely, and some partially, some correctly, and some incorrectly. Ultimately, we select some stimuli and ignore others because we do not have the ability to be conscious of all incoming information at one time.

Perception: The process by which we receive information through our five senses and acknowledge and assign meaning to this information.

SELECTIVE PERCEPTION   The process of screening out information that does not interest us and retaining information that does is called **selective perception.** Think about the route you take when driving to school every day. How many stimuli do you perceive? If you're like most people, you perceive traffic signals, what's going on in your car, other traffic, and pedestrians crossing in front of you. This is selective perception. This same process is repeated when we watch television or read a magazine. It also occurs when we look at an ad and perceive only the headline, a photograph, or a famous spokesperson. In addition to our ten-

Selective Perception: The process of screening out information that does not interest us and retaining information that does.

Perception.

Reality.

To a new generation of Rolling Stone readers, pigs live on farms. You'll find the cops living in Beverly Hills or on Hill Street, now heralded instead of hated. If you're looking for an 18 to 34 year old market that is taking active part instead of active protest, you'll have a riot in the pages of Rolling Stone.

Rolling Stone

AD 5.4

THIS CLASSIC AD FOR *ROLLING STONE* ILLUSTRATES OUR TENDENCY TO DISTORT.

Selective Exposure: The ability to process only certain information and avoid other stimuli.

Selective Distortion: The interpretation of information in a way that is consistent with the person's existing opinion.

Selective Retention: The process of remembering only a small portion of what a person is exposed to.

dency to select stimuli that are of interest to us, we also perceive stimuli in a manner that coincides with our reality. That is, your world includes your own set of experiences, values, biases, and attitudes. It is virtually impossible to separate these inherent factors from the way you perceive. For example, we naturally tend to seek out messages that are pleasant or sympathetic with our views and to avoid those that are painful or threatening. This is called **selective exposure.** Consumers tend to selectively expose themselves to advertisements that reassure them of the wisdom of their purchase decisions. Similarly, when we are exposed to a message that is different from what we believe, we engage in **selective distortion.** For example, a consumer may "hear" that an automobile gets good gas mileage, even though the salesperson has clearly indicated this is not so, because the consumer perceives other features of the car as perfect and therefore wants very much to buy it. (See Ad 5.4.)

Advertisers are interested in these selective processes because they affect whether consumers will perceive an ad and, if so, whether they will remember it. Selective perception is also strongly influenced by our attitudes toward the person, situation, and idea. If we hold a strong positive attitude toward safety, for example, we will tend to perceive messages that deal with this subject. In turn, we will tend to remember details about the message, such as product features and the brand name, when perception is intense. More will be said about attitudes later in the chapter.

Our response to a stimulus has a direct bearing on advertising. A large part of what the brain processes is lost after only an instant. Even when we try very hard to retain information, we are unable to save a lot of it. **Selective retention** describes the process we go through in trying to "save" information for future use. Advertising can facilitate this process by using repetition, easily remembered brand or product names, jingles, high-profile spokespeople, music, and so forth. Its ability to stimulate and assist the consumer in selective retention often determines the success of an individual ad.

Cognitive Dissonance: A tendency to justify the discrepancy between what a person receives relative to what he or she expected to receive.

PRINCIPLE An ad will be perceived only if it is relevant to the consumer.

COGNITIVE DISSONANCE   Another possible response to selective perception is a feeling of dissatisfaction or doubt. Seldom does a purchase produce all the expected positive results. According to the theory of **cognitive dissonance,** we tend to compensate or justify the small or large discrepancy between what we actually received and what we perceived we would receive. Research on this phenomenon has shown that people engage in a variety of activities to reduce dissonance.[19] Most notably, they seek out information that supports their decision and they ignore or distort information that does not. Advertising can play a central role in reducing dissonance. For example, car manufacturers anticipate where dissonance is likely to occur and provide supportive information, IBM uses testimonials by satisfied customers, and restaurants include discount coupons with their print ads.

The next time you watch television, study yourself as you view the ads. What do you select to pay attention to? Why? When do you "tune out"? Why? Did you find yourself disagreeing with a message or arguing with it? Can you see how your own selection processes influence your attention and response to advertising?

LEARNING

Perception leads to learning—that is, we cannot learn something unless we have accurately perceived the information and attached some meaning to it. Because people often associate attempts at learning with formal education, they tend to think of it as a conscious, deliberate, tedious, and painful process. In fact, learning is typically an unconscious activity; consumers don't usually even know when it's happening. It does happen, however, starting early in life and continuing throughout. If advertisers understand how learning takes place, they can design ads to optimize the learning of the key elements in the ad, such as brand name, location, product features, price, and so forth. Understanding how learning takes place is important for other reasons as well. Most notably, we can learn different attitudes, beliefs, preferences, values, and standards, all of which may lead to changes in purchase behavior. As you might recall from our discussion on corrective advertising in Chapter 2, occasionally we learn something so well, such as "Listerine prevents colds," that we cannot unlearn it.

COGNITIVE LEARNING   Various theories have been developed to explain different aspects of learning. Typically, two schools of learning are considered. The first is called the *cognitive* school. Cognitive interpretations emphasize the discovery of patterns and insight. Cognitive theorists stress the importance of perception, problem solving, and insight. They contend that most learning occurs not as a result of trial-and-error or practice but of discovering meaningful patterns that enable people to solve problems. These meaningful patterns are called *gestalts,* and cognitive theories of learning rely heavily on the process of insight to explain the development of gestalts. This is comparable to the "ah ha" effect that occurs when we finally figured out how calculus worked.

When confronted with a problem, we sometimes see the solution instantly. More often we need to search for information, carefully evaluate what we learn, and make a decision. Cognitive learning characterizes people as problem solvers who go through a complex process of mentally processing information. Advertisers employing this perspective concentrate on the role of motivation in decision making and the mental processing consumers do when making decisions.

CONNECTIONISTS   The second school of learning, the connectionists, argues that people learn connections between stimuli and responses. The connectionists school is further divided into classical conditioning and instrumental condition-

---

[19]Leon Festinger, *A Theory of Cognitive Dissonance* (Evanston, IL: Row, Peterson, 1957):83.

ing. Essentially, *classical conditioning* pairs one stimulus with another that already elicits a given response. Classical conditioning is often associated with experiments of Ivan Pavlov, in which a dog was taught to salivate at the sound of a bell.

Instrumental or *operant* conditioning depends on the voluntary occurrence of behaviors that are then rewarded, punished, or ignored. The greatest practical development of instrumental conditioning is attributed to B.F. Skinner and his followers. According to Skinner, most learning takes place in an effort to control the environment—that is, to obtain favorable outcomes. Control is gained by means of a trial-and-error process during which one behavior results in a more favorable response than do other behaviors. The reward received is instrumental in teaching the person about a specific behavior that provides more control. For advertisers, this process requires emphasizing repetition and discrimination in order to convince consumers that their brand provides greater rewards than do other brands.

For example, learning would include a stimulus such as needing a new pair of shoes. This stimulus—worn-out shoes—is called a *need*. Next, a cue addresses that particular need, such as a local department store that is having a shoe sale. You may respond to this cue in a positive way because you have purchased shoes there before and have been very satisfied. Finally, *reinforcement* of learning occurs when the response is followed by satisfaction. Positive reinforcement strengthens the relationship between the cue and the response and therefore increases the probability that the response will be repeated.

HABIT   When we have repeated a process many times and continue to be satisfied with the outcome, we reach a point called *habit*. Habit is a limitation on or total absence of information seeking and evaluation of alternative choices. Purchasing by habit provides two important benefits to the consumer: (1) it reduces risk; and (2) it facilitates decision making. Buying the same brand time and again reduces the risk of product failure and financial loss for important purchases. Habit also simplifies decision making by minimizing the need for information search. Obviously, advertisers would like consumers to be habitual users of their product. Achieving that requires a powerful message backed by a superior product. American automakers learned a hard lesson when they assumed that American consumers would continue habitually to purchase cars built in the United States even though they were inferior to Japanese cars. Once a habit is formed, the role of advertising is to reinforce that habit through reminder messages, messages of appreciation, and actual rewards, such as coupons, premiums, and rebates. Breaking a consumer's habit is very difficult. Attacking a well-entrenched competitor may only make consumers defensive and reinforce their habit. Offering the consumer new relevant information about yourself or your competition is one successful approach. Providing an extra incentive to change, such as coupons, or free samples, has also proved effective. Certainly consumers who are price sensitive tend to habitually purchase items of the lowest cost. This deal-prone individual has a habit that is difficult to break.

Advertisers use a number of techniques to improve learning. Music and jingles improve learning because they intensify the repetition. Creating positive associations with a brand also enhances learning. Testimonials by well-liked celebrities and scenes of attractive people in attractive settings are used to intensify positive associations. Humor is employed because it gives the audience some reward for paying attention. Ad 5.5 is an example of advertising that creates a positive association with a product.

MOTIVATION AND NEEDS

Motive: An unobservable inner force that stimulates and compels a behavioral response.

A **motive** is an internal force that stimulates you to behave in a particular manner. This driving force is produced by the state of tension that results from an unfulfilled need. People strive—both consciously and subconsciously—to reduce this tension through behavior they anticipate will fulfill their needs and thus relieve the stress they feel.

AD 5.5

THE HUMOR ASSOCIATED WITH
THE ENERGIZER BUNNY® HAS
RUBBED OFF ON THE BRAND
ITSELF.

At any given point you are probably being affected by a number of different motives, some of which may be contradictory. Some motives are stronger than others, but even this pattern changes from time to time. For example, your motivation to buy a new suit will be much higher when you start going out on job interviews.

What are your buying motives? Think back over all your purchases during the past week. Did you have a reason for buying those products that you might tell your mother or an interviewer, but also a hidden reason that you will keep to yourself? You can see how important the concept of buying motives is to an understanding of consumer behavior.

Needs: Basic forces that motivate you to do or to want something.

Needs are the basic forces that motivate you to do something. Each person has his or her own set of unique needs; some are innate; others are acquired. *Innate needs* are physiological and include the needs for food, water, air, shelter, and sex. Because satisfying these needs is necessary to maintaining life, they are referred to as *primary needs. Acquired needs* are those we learn in response to our culture or environment. These may include needs for esteem, prestige, affection, power, and learning. Because acquired needs are not necessary to our physical survival, they are considered *secondary needs* or motives. Abraham Maslow noted that needs exist in a hierarchy, and that we tend to satisfy our primary needs before our secondary needs. He identified five different need categories that can be arranged vertically, with the most primary at the bottom: (1) physical or biological needs, (2) safety and security needs, (3) love and affiliation needs, (4) prestige and esteem

| **TABLE 5.5** | CONSUMER NEEDS |

Achievement
The need to accomplish difficult feats; to perform arduous tasks; to exercise your skills, abilities, or talents.

Exhibition
The need to display yourself, to be visible to others; to reveal personal identity; to show off or win the attention and interest of others; to gain notice.

Dominance
The need to have power or to exert your will on others; to hold a position of authority or influence; to direct or supervise the efforts of others; to show strength or prowess by winning over adversaries.

Diversion
The need to play; to have fun; to be entertained; to break from the routine; to relax and abandon your cares; to be amused.

Understanding
The need to learn and comprehend; to recognize connections; to assign causality; to make ideas fit the circumstances; to teach, instruct, or impress others with your expertise; to follow intellectual pursuits.

Nurturance
The need to give care, comfort, and support to others; to see living things grow and thrive; to help the progress and development of others; to protect your charges from harm or injury.

Sexuality
The need to establish your sexual identity and attractiveness; to enjoy sexual contact; to *receive* and to *provide* sexual satisfaction; to maintain sexual alternatives without exercising them; to avoid condemnation for sexual appetites.

Security
The need to be free from threat of harm; to be safe; to protect self, family, and property; to have a supply of what you need; to save and acquire assets; to be invulnerable to attack; to avoid accidents or mishaps.

Independence
The need to be autonomous, to be free from the direction or influence of others; or have options and alternatives; to make your own choices and decisions; to be different.

Recognition
The need for *positive* notice by others; to show your superiority or excellence; to be acclaimed or held up as exemplary; to receive social rewards or notoriety.

Stimulation
The need to experience events and activities that stimulate the senses or exercise perception; to move and act freely and vigorously; to engage in rapid or forceful activity; to saturate the palate with flavor; to engage the environment in new or unusual modes of interaction.

Novelty
The need for change and diversity; to experience the unusual; to do new tasks or activities; to learn new skills; to be in a new setting or environment; to find unique objects of interest; to be amazed or mystified.

Affiliation
The need for association with others; to belong or win acceptance; to enjoy satisfying and mutually helpful relationships.

Succorance
The need to *receive* help, support, comfort, encouragement, or reassurance from others; to be the *recipient* of nurturant efforts.

Consistency
The need for order, cleanliness, or logical connection; to control the environment; to avoid ambiguity and uncertainty; to predict accurately; to have things happen as you expect.

Source: Adapted from Robert B. Settle and Pamela L. Alreck, *Why They Buy* (New York: John Wiley & Sons, 1986):26–28.

needs, and (5) self-fulfillment needs. Although it's very useful to examine this hierarchy, looking at needs from a cross-sectional point of view is also helpful. From a cross-sectional perspective, no one category of needs consistently takes precedence over the others. A list of general consumer needs is shown in Table 5.5.

Although basic need categories tend to be somewhat stable over time, the way we satisfy our individual needs appears to change over time. In recent research, for example, the ever-expanding desire for more is taking off again. They'll take the pool, the summer house on the Cape, and the home-entertainment center. Not the exact same things they wanted in the '80s—the population is older, with different wants and needs—but the bottom line is the same. They want more. Far from simplifying, Americans are interested in acquiring. The biggest increases since 1991 are having a vacation home (up nine points to 44 percent), having a lot of money (up eight points to 63 percent), and having a swimming pool (up eight points to 37 percent).[20]

[20]Jon Berry, "At Mid-Decade, Just Call the Consumer: Frustrated Inc.," *Superbrands* (October 9, 1995):31–33.

ATTITUDES

Attitude: A learned predisposition that we hold toward an object, person, or idea.

An **attitude** is a learned predisposition, a feeling that you hold toward an object, a person, or an idea that leads to a particular behavior. An attitude focuses on some topic that provides a focal point for your beliefs and feelings. Attitudes also tend to be enduring. You can hold an attitude for months or even years.

We develop and learn attitudes, we are not born with them. Because attitudes are learned, we can change them, unlearn them, or replace them with new ones. Attitudes also vary in direction and in strength. That is, an attitude can be *positive* or *negative*, reflecting like or dislike. (See Figure 5.4.)

Attitudes are important to advertisers because they influence how consumers evaluate products. A strong positive attitude might be turned into brand preference and loyalty. For example, most American consumers over the age of 50 know that test pilot Chuck Yeager is one of our national heroes. An ad such as the one shown hopes that the readers will transfer their positive attitude toward such a hero to the sponsoring product—Rolex. (See Ad 5.6.) A weak attitude, even if it is positive, might not be enough to convince you to act. Changing an attitude is not impossible, but it is difficult.

Attitudes also reflect consumers' values. They tell the world what we stand for and identify the things and ideas we consider important. They also track our positive and negative reactions to things in our life. Opinion research is used to check how people feel about other people, products, brands, appeals, and contemporary trends. One of the most important areas for opinion research in advertising is product and brand perception. It is important to know how the consumer sees the product before developing an advertising strategy. Furthermore, advertisers must be aware of the factors with which the product is associated in the consumer's mind.

The results of a survey commissioned by Lifetime network to Yankelovich Partners might prove a point about attitudes. The study attempted to segment women cable subscribers according to their viewing preferences and attitudes toward television. The five groups that emerged were: Companions, Dreamers, Contemporaries, Realists, and Traditionalists. Companions use television as their connection to the world and support in managing their home lives. Dreamers use television for entertainment and escape. Contemporaries use television in their role as modern women and for relaxation. Traditionalists want television to provide reassurance for traditional values. Realists want television to provide information and to keep them up-to-date. The biggest and most concentrated Lifetime viewing groups are Contemporaries, career women concerned with women's issues.[21]

---

[21]Rebecca Pürto, "New Markets for Cable TV," *American Demographics* (June 1995):40–47.

FIGURE 5.4
American Demographics (June 1995):55.

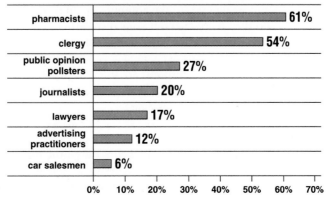

Who's Trusted, Who's Not
Most Americans don't trust lawyers, but they trust advertisers even less.

(percent of adults who rate the honesty and ethical standards of practitioners in selected fields as high or very high, 1994)

pharmacists	**61%**
clergy	**54%**
public opinion pollsters	**27%**
journalists	**20%**
lawyers	**17%**
advertising practitioners	**12%**
car salesmen	**6%**

0%   10%   20%   30%   40%   50%   60%   70%

Source: The Gallup Poll Monthly, Princeton, NJ

AD 5.6

OLDER CONSUMERS HOLD
STRONG POSITIVE ATTITUDES
TOWARD CHUCK YEAGER—AND
HOPEFULLY ANY PRODUCT HE
RECOMMENDS.

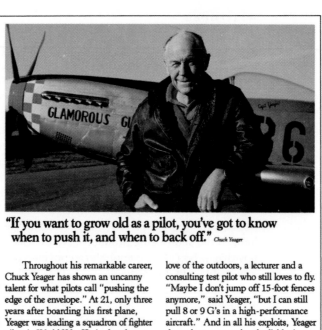

Personality: Relatively long-lasting personal qualities that allow us to cope with, and respond to, the world around us.

PERSONALITY

All of these personal and psychological factors interact to create your own unique personality. A **personality** is a collection of traits that makes a person distinctive. How you look at the world, how you perceive and interpret what is happening around you, how you respond intellectually and emotionally, and how you form your opinions and attitudes are all reflected in your personality. Your personality is what makes you an individual.

SELF-CONCEPT   Self-concept refers to how we look at ourselves. Our self-image reflects how we see our own personality and our individual pattern of strengths and weaknesses. Take a minute to think of the traits that best describe you. What do they tell you about your own self-concept? Are they basically positive or negative? Do you have high or low self-esteem? What image of yourself do you see?

Now consider yourself as a consumer. Explain how these same characteristics affect your response to different products, to advertising, and to your behavior as a consumer. Can you see how understanding personality is important in developing a relevant message?

LIFESTYLES

Lifestyle factors are often considered the mainstay of psychographic research. Essentially, lifestyle research looks at the ways people allocate time, energy, and money. Marketers conduct research to measure and compare people's activities, interests, and opinions—in other words, what they usually do or how they behave, what intrigues or fascinates them, and what they believe or assume about the world around them. One very popular research tool that clusters lifestyle characteristics is VALS 2.

Value and Lifestyle Systems (VALS): Classification systems that categorize people by values for the purpose of predicting effective advertising strategies.

VALS   The firm of SRI International is famous for its **Values and Lifestyles Systems (VALS)** conceptual models that categorize people according to their values and then identify the consumer behaviors associated with those values. VALS systems are used to show clients how consumer groups are changing and how these changes will affect the client's advertising strategy. The first model, VALS, was introduced in 1978 and contained nine categories that divided the American population along a hierarchy of needs. In 1989, SRI modified VALS to better serve the business world. The firm dropped social values as the basis for its psychographic segmentations scheme, having determined that the link between social values (for example, federal funding of abortions should be prohibited) and purchasing choices was less strong than it once was. The new system—VALS 2—is based on psychological characteristics about oneself (for example, I am often interested in theories) that were found to be indicative of purchase behavior (see Figure 5.5). The psychographic groups in VALS 2 are arranged in a rectangle. They are stacked vertically by resources (minimal to abundant) and horizontally by self-orientation (principle, status, or action oriented). Resources include income, education, self-confidence, health, eagerness to buy, and energy level.

A person's position along the resource/self-orientation axis determines which of eight classifications he or she falls into; Actualizers, Fulfilleds, Achievers, Experiencers, Believers, Strivers, Makers, or Strugglers. Members of each group hold different values and maintain different lifestyles. Actualizers, located above the rectangle, have the highest resources including income, self-esteem and energy. Actualizers are difficult to categorize by self-orientation because their high resources allow them the freedom to express many facets of their personalities. Image is important to these people. Because of their wide range of interests and openness to change, actualizers' purchases are directed at "the finer things in life."[22] Obviously, knowing the psychographic orientation of consumers is a valuable asset to an advertiser in deciding to whom messages should be targeted.

Even more important, however, is that these VALS 2 categories correspond to consumer behaviors that are useful to the advertiser. This relationship is illustrated in Table 5.6, where the eight categories correspond with the frequency of certain activities.

Also on the horizon is i VALS, a project that focuses on the attitudes, preferences, and behaviors of online service and Internet users. Early results of i VALS reinforce the idea of a dual-tiered society, but one based on knowledge, not income. People who are out of the information highway loop are excluded more because of their limited education than because of the lower income less educated people tend to have. Education is the crucial factor in who participates in the Internet and to what degree.[23]

BUYING BEHAVIOR

The information we have discussed thus far is used by advertisers to understand how the consumer decision-making process works—in other words, how the consumer goes about buying the product. Although at first it sounds like an individual process that cannot be generalized across consumers, there is evidence that most people engage in a similar decision process. Our understanding is also enhanced if we view decision making as either a low-involvement or high-involvement process.

---

[22]Martha Farnsworth Riche, "Psychographics for the 1990s," *American Demographics* (July 1989):25.

[23]Rebecca Pürto Heath, "The Frontier of Psychographics," *American Demographics* (July 1996):38–43.

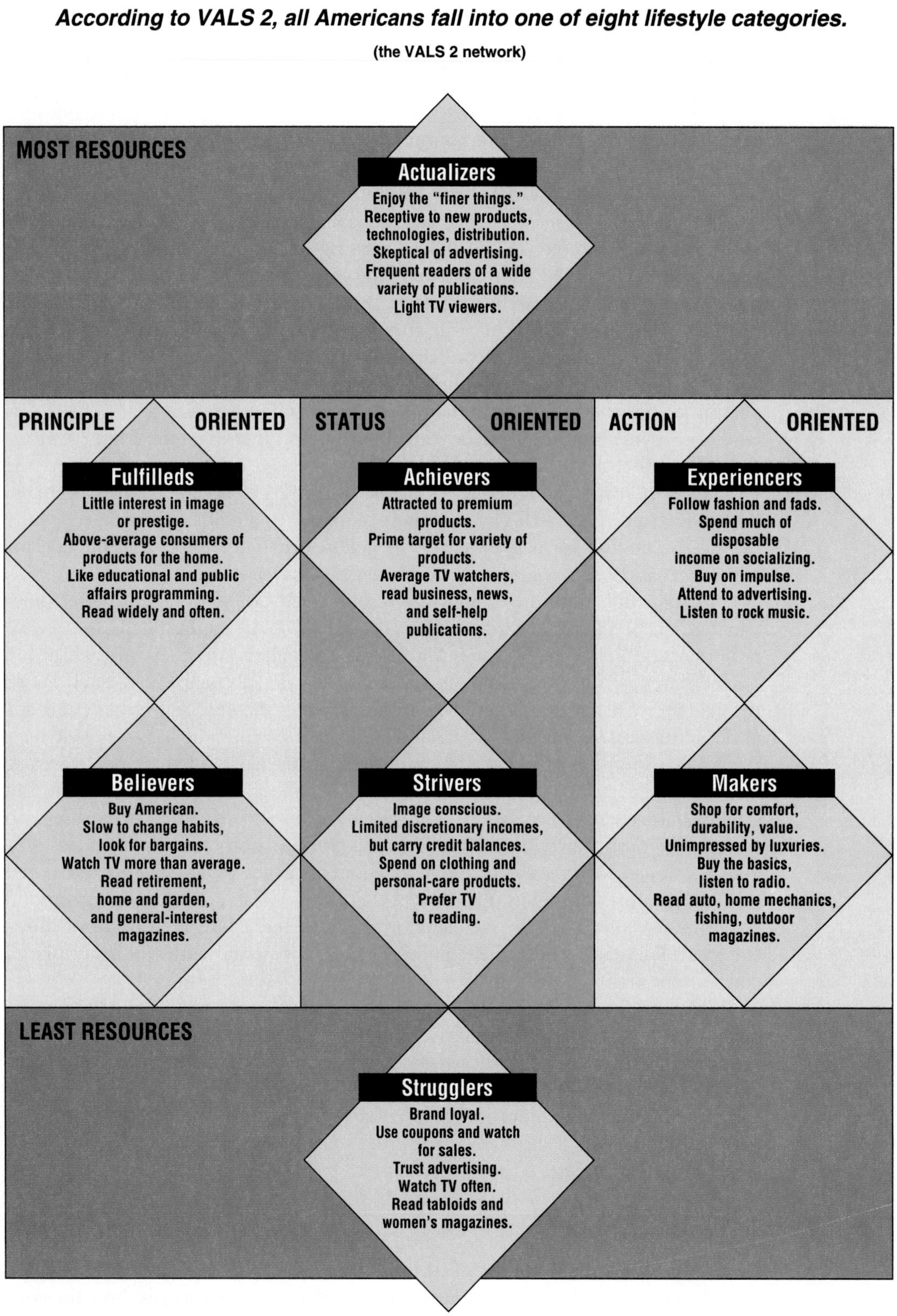

According to VALS 2, all Americans fall into one of eight lifestyle categories.

(the VALS 2 network)

MOST RESOURCES

Actualizers
Enjoy the "finer things."
Receptive to new products,
technologies, distribution.
Skeptical of advertising.
Frequent readers of a wide
variety of publications.
Light TV viewers.

PRINCIPLE ORIENTED   **STATUS ORIENTED**   **ACTION ORIENTED**

Fulfilleds
Little interest in image
or prestige.
Above-average consumers of
products for the home.
Like educational and public
affairs programming.
Read widely and often.

Achievers
Attracted to premium
products.
Prime target for variety of
products.
Average TV watchers,
read business, news,
and self-help
publications.

Experiencers
Follow fashion and fads.
Spend much of
disposable
income on socializing.
Buy on impulse.
Attend to advertising.
Listen to rock music.

Believers
Buy American.
Slow to change habits,
look for bargains.
Watch TV more than average.
Read retirement,
home and garden,
and general-interest
magazines.

Strivers
Image conscious.
Limited discretionary incomes,
but carry credit balances.
Spend on clothing and
personal-care products.
Prefer TV
to reading.

Makers
Shop for comfort,
durability, value.
Unimpressed by luxuries.
Buy the basics,
listen to radio.
Read auto, home mechanics,
fishing, outdoor
magazines.

LEAST RESOURCES

Strugglers
Brand loyal.
Use coupons and watch
for sales.
Trust advertising.
Watch TV often.
Read tabloids and
women's magazines.

FIGURE 5.5

THE VALS 2 SYSTEM.
Source: American Demographics
(July 1994):25.

TABLE 5.6	VALS 2 SEGMENT ACTIVITIES							
ITEM	**ACTUALIZER**	**FULFILLED**	**BELIEVER**	**ACHIEVER**	**STRIVER**	**EXPERIENCER**	**MAKER**	**STRUGGLER**
Buy hand tools	148	65	105	63	59	137	170	57
Barbecue outdoors	125	93	82	118	111	109	123	50
Do gardening	155	129	118	109	68	54	104	80
Do gourmet cooking	217	117	96	103	53	133	86	47
Drink coffee daily	120	119	126	88	87	55	91	116
Drink domestic beer	141	88	73	101	87	157	123	50
Drink herbal tea	171	125	89	117	71	115	81	68
Drink imported beer	238	93	41	130	58	216	88	12
Do activities with kids	155	129	57	141	112	89	116	32
Play team sports	114	73	69	104	110	172	135	34
Do cultural activities	293	63	67	96	45	154	63	14
Exercise	145	114	69	123	94	143	102	39
Do home repairs	161	113	85	82	53	88	171	58
Camp or hike	131	88	68	95	84	156	158	33
Do risky sports	190	48	36	52	59	283	171	7
Socialize weekly	109	64	73	90	96	231	94	62

Note: Figures under each segment are the index for each segment (100 = Base rate usage).

Source: SRI Consulting. Reprinted by permission.

High-Involvement Decision Process: Decisions that require an involved purchase process with information search and product comparison.

Low-Involvement Decision Process: Decisions that require limited deliberation; sometimes purchases are even made on impulse.

LOW- AND HIGH-INVOLVEMENT DECISION MAKING When we think about the thought process we go through in making product decisions, it is fairly safe to say that for the more expensive, personal, or emotion-laden products (such as automobiles, medical care, clothes, and vacations), we expend a great deal of effort, whereas for the inexpensive, less exciting products that are purchased regularly, such as those found at supermarket checkout counters, we exert very little thought and effort. The former is called a complex, **high-involvement decision process,** whereas the latter is labeled a simple, **low-involvement decision process.** Table 5.7 shows how this involvement level and the decision-making process relate to one another.

This concept of involvement originated in the research conducted on hemispheral lateralization, that is, right-brain–left-brain functioning. The left hemisphere of the brain specializes in cognitive activities, such as reading and speaking.

TABLE 5.7	CONSUMER DECISION PROCESS FOR HIGH- AND LOW-INVOLVEMENT PURCHASE DECISIONS	
	LOW-INVOLVEMENT PURCHASE DECISIONS	**HIGH-INVOLVEMENT PURCHASE DECISIONS**
Problem recognition	Trivial to minor	Important and personally meaningful
Information search	Internal to limited external search	Extensive search
Alternative evaluation	Few alternatives evaluated on few performance criteria	Many alternatives considered using many performance criteria
Store choice, purchase	One-stop shopping where substitution is very possible	Multiple store visits with substitution less likely
Postpurchase activities	Simple evaluation of performance	Extensive performance evaluation, use, and disposal

Source: D. Hawkins, R. Best, and K. Coney, *Consumer Behavior,* 5th ed. (Homewood, IL: Irwin, 1992):21.

FIGURE 5.6

THE MAJOR STAGES OF THE
CONSUMER PURCHASE PROCESS.

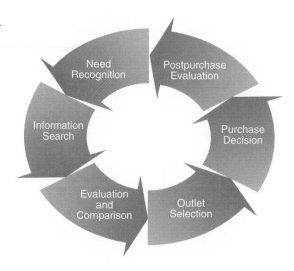

People who are exposed to verbal information cognitively analyze the information through left-brain processing and form mental images. Conversely, the right hemisphere of the brain is concerned with nonverbal, timeless, and pictorial information. This scheme can be applied to product decision making. Product decisions that have high personal relevance and contain a high perceived risk are called high-involvement purchases, and they necessitate complex decision making. Products at the opposite end of the relevance/risk continuum are low-involvement purchases that require simple decision making. Simple decision making requires very little information and virtually no evaluation. We discuss complex decision making next.

DECISION PROCESS

The process consumers go through in making a purchase varies considerably between low-involvement and high-involvement situations. There are some generally recognized stages, however, and these are highlighted in Figure 5.6. The stages are (1) need recognition, (2) information search, (3) evaluation and comparison, (4) outlet selection, (5) purchase decision, and (6) postpurchase evaluation.

NEED RECOGNITION   The first stage, *need recognition*, occurs when the consumer recognizes a need for a product. This need can vary in terms of seriousness or importance. The goal of advertising at this stage is to activate or stimulate this need. For example, the Burger King "Aren't you hungry?" campaign appeals to people's appetites and nutritional needs.

INFORMATION SEARCH   The second stage is the *information search*. This search can be casual, such as reading ads and articles that happen to catch your attention, or formal, such as searching for information in publications like *Consumer Reports*. Another type of informal search is recalling information you have seen previously. Advertising helps the search process by providing information in the advertisement itself.

EVALUATION AND COMPARISON   The third stage is *evaluation and comparison*. Here we begin to compare various products and features and reduce the list of options to a manageable number. We select certain features that are important and use them to judge our alternatives. Advertising is important in this evaluation process because it helps sort out products on the basis of features.

OUTLET SELECTION AND PURCHASE DECISION   The fourth stage is *outlet selection*. Is this product available at a grocery store, a discount store, a hardware store, a boutique, a department store, or a specialty store? Will the consumer select the brand first and then try to find a store that carries it, or will he or she select a store first and then consider the available brands? Instore promotions such as packaging, point-of-purchase displays, price reductions, banners and signs, and coupon displays affect these choices. (Sales promotion techniques will be discussed in more detail in Chapter 18). The outlet is the site of the fifth stage, which is the actual *purchase*.

POSTPURCHASE EVALUATION   The last step in the process is the point where we begin to reconsider and justify our purchase to ourselves. As soon as we purchase a product, particularly a major one, we begin to engage in postpurchase evaluation. Is the product acceptable? Is its performance satisfactory? Does it live up to our expectations? This experience determines whether we will repurchase the product or even return it to the store.

Even before you open the package or use the product, you may experience doubt or worry about the wisdom of the purchase. This doubt is called *postpurchase dissonance*. Many consumers continue to read information even after the purchase in order to justify their decision to themselves. Advertising, such as copy on package inserts, helps reduce postpurchase dissonance by restating the features and confirming the popularity of the brand or product.

THE KEY TO EFFECTIVE ADVERTISING: UNDERSTANDING THE AUDIENCE

Once a year, DDB Needham Worldwide mails questionnaires to a sample of 4,000 U.S. adults, covering various lifestyle topics from eating habits to attitudes toward neatness. The data are used to create in-depth profiles of client's target consumers. Betty Crocker wants to know who buys cake mixes, Wrigley's would be interested to know that 40 percent of Americans think people shouldn't chew gum in public, and Listerine and Scope want to know what percentage of the population thinks people should use mouthwash to ameliorate bad breath.

The detailed profiles DDB Needham compiles are passed on to the creative people working on the specific accounts. A person responsible for the National Dairy Board campaign, for example, needs to know who are the heavy users of cheese. These Lifestyle studies provide data on demographics, attitudes, beliefs, habits, needs, and opinions on all sorts of topics, from religion, family, and morals to the economy, law enforcement, and volunteerism—all the information necessary for developing and appropriately targeting campaigns.

Some of the questions asked may seem irrelevant, such as asking respondents to agree or disagree with the statement, "I like the look of a large lamp in a picture window," or "I would do better than average in a fistfight." These responses are valuable, however, and help to determine whether a person has traditional values, how he or she feels about sex roles, and help round out the profiles.

The Lifestyle studies also help to disprove some of the popular myths of so-called "trends" that seem to be appearing. For example, although it is believed that families don't eat together anymore, the Lifestyle data show that 75 percent of respondents say their whole family usually eats dinner together.[24]

Although it is impossible for us to know everything about the people with whom we communicate, the more we do know, the more likely our message will be understood. This same assumption is true for advertisers, although at a much broader level. Fortunately, advertisers have the resources to conduct extensive research that taps this information. Such research must not only be accurate, it must also be conducted constantly because people are always changing.

[24]Joseph M. Winski, "Lifestyle Study: Who We Are, How We Live, What We Think," *Advertising Age* (September 24, 1990):25.

In this chapter we identified several key audience traits and behaviors that are relevant to the advertiser. There are more traits and behaviors that we have not discussed. Furthermore, those involved in the design and implementation of an advertisement may interpret these traits differently. We all have our own perceptions of things. The key to successful advertising is staying sensitive to the consumer. If all you know about your audience is what the computer printout tells you, you are unlikely to be an effective communicator. Creative advertising requires both basic awareness and empathy. In the next chapter we will turn to the specific research and planning strategies involved in achieving this kind of consumer awareness.

SUMMARY

- The social and cultural influences on consumers include society and subcultures, social class, reference groups, and family.
- Personal influences on consumers include age, gender, family status, education, occupation, income, and race.
- Psychological influences on the individual as a consumer include perception, learning, motivation, attitudes, personality, and self-concept.
- Advertisers identify audiences in terms of demographics and psychographics.
- Demographic profiles of consumers include information on population size, age, gender, education, family situation, occupation, income, and race.

- Psychographic profiles on consumers include information on attitudes, lifestyles, buying behavior, and decision processes.
- Your personality reflects how you look at the world, how you perceive and interpret what is happening, how you respond, and how you form opinions and attitudes.
- The decision process involves six stages: need recognition, information search, evaluation and comparison, outlet selection, purchase decision, and postpurchase evaluation.

QUESTIONS

1. How must advertisers adjust to the elderly? Do you think different adjustments will be required when the baby boomers enter this group? What kind?

2. Choose four VALS 2 categories and find one or more print advertisements that appear to be targeted to individuals in each category. Explain why you think the ad addresses that audience.

3. What are the six stages in the consumer decision process? Give examples of how advertising can influence each stage. Find an ad that addresses the concern of consumers in each stage.

4. Sean McDonnell is the creative director for Chatham-Boothe, an advertising agency that has just signed a contract with Trans-Central Airlines (TCA). TCA has a solid portfolio of consumer research and has offered to let the agency use it. McDonnell needs to decide whether demographic, psychographic, or attitude/motive studies are best for developing the creative profile of the TCA target audience. If the choice were yours, which body of research would you base a creative strategy on? Explore the strengths and weaknesses of each.

5. Look at the social class segments illustrated in Table 5.1. State which two class segments would be most receptive to these product marketing situations:
  A. Full line of frozen family-style meals (for microwaving) that feature superior nutritional balances.
  B. Dairy product company (milk, cheese, ice cream) offering an exclusive packaging design that uses fully degradable containers.

6. If the projected U.S. age shifts forecasted for the next 20 years happen, what impact would these changes have on our current advertising practices (creative and media selection influences)?

7. Avon Products has established an admirable reputation for residence-to-residence personal selling. Now the corporation has seriously modified its marketing approach. What changes in consumer lifestyles have happened to prompt Avon's shift? How can Avon change with the times without giving up personal salesmanship?

Suggested Class Project

Posing as a customer, visit one or more stores that sell stereo systems. Report on the sales techniques used (check on advertising, point-of-purchase displays, store design, and so forth). What beliefs concerning consumer behavior appear to underlie these strategies?

Further Readings

Bard, B., "The Eighties Are Over," *Newsweek* (January 4, 1988):40–45.

Mullen, Brian, and Craig Johnson, *The Psychology of Consumer Behavior* (Hillsdale, NJ: Lawrence Erlbaum Associates, 1990).

Popcorn, Faith, *The Popcorn Report* (New York: Currency and Doubleday, 1991).

Prus, Robert C., *Pursuing Customers: An Ethnography of Marketing Activities* (New York: Sage Publications, 1989).

Robertson, Thomas S., and Harold H. Kassarjian, *Handbook of Consumer Behavior* (Upper Saddle River, NJ: Prentice Hall, 1991).

Schiffman, Leon G., and Leslie Lazar Kanuk, *Consumer Behavior* (Upper Saddle River, NJ: Prentice Hall, 1987).

Settle, Robert B., and Pamela L. Albeck, *Why They Buy: American Consumers Inside and Out* (New York: John Wiley & Sons, 1986).

ABCNEWS

$\mathcal{V}$IDEO $\mathcal{C}$ASE   HOW HEALTHY IS HEALTH FOOD?

Consumers looking for organic produce, fresh juices, whole grains, and other natural foods often find what they seek in health food stores. Although the phrase *health food* may conjure up images of 60s-era hippies selling bulk grains out of small stores, health food retailing has evolved considerably over the past three decades. Today large health food stores comprise a viable—and growing—part of the U.S. retail grocery industry. The reason is simple: Increasing numbers of consumers want to eat food that is free of artificial ingredients and grown by farmers who don't use pesticides and herbicides. Revenues from natural food sales quadrupled between 1980 and 1994. Regional supermarket chains such as Whole Foods Markets, Fresh Fields, Mrs. Gooch's, and Bread & Circus have been established in recent years to capitalize on the health food trend. In 1994, the chain stores rang up $186.5 million in sales of organic produce alone, four times the amount sold by small health food stores. Overall U.S. sales of organic foods are expected to exceed $6.5 billion by the year 2000.

Today's health food stores provide copious amounts of product information, plus cooking seminars, and tips on food preparation and healthy eating. Health food chains also have developed considerable buying power; as a result, the prices at many health food stores are on a par with those in conventional supermarkets. Nor are modern health food stores catering only to vegetarians. Bruce Perlstein, whose Wild By Nature store is located in New York, notes, "Their other mission is to provide products for people with special diets, so they offer lots of salt-free, wheat-free, dairy-free, gluten-free, and yeast-free items." Meat is also often available, although it is likely to be from animals that have not been fed growth hormones or treated with antibiotics.

In short, health food stores are no longer specialty shops; many can accommodate "one-stop shopping." Chris Anderson, editor of *Gourmet News*, says, "Places like Whole Foods Markets appeal to people who used to shop at a health food store for certain items, then went to finish their shopping at supermarkets. Now they can do it all under one roof."

Some industry observers have expressed concerns that the growing number of consumers who shop at health food stores may not always be getting what they are paying for. For example, some "healthy" foods made without artificial ingredients or refined sugar may actually contain as much fat as comparable products sold in conventional supermarkets. The U.S. Food and Drug Administration (FDA) recently ruled that any food bear-ing the word *healthy* on the label can contain no more than 3 grams of fat. The Federal Trade Commission (FTC) recently stepped up efforts to see that food advertising conforms to the same standards established by the FDA for food labeling. The FTC is adopting standards governing the use of words like *low* and *lean* in descriptions of nutritional content. Advertisers will also be required to indicate specific percentage differences—"10 percent less," for example—when making comparative claims such as "less," "reduced," and "more." In addition, solid scientific research must be used to substantiate health claims used in advertising.

For years, the integrity of the organic agriculture and marketing was protected by both state legislation and private industry standards. Iowa and other states restrict use of the word *organic* to crops grown on land that has been free of synthetic chemicals for three years or more. Independent crop certifiers such as the Organic Crop Improvement Association inspect and certify crops grown by individual farmers. Now the U.S. Department of Agriculture (USDA) is joining in. The Organic Food Production Act, part of the 1990 farm bill passed by Congress, set the stage for the USDA to create a National Organic Standards Board (NOSB). In 1997, the NOSB prepared to issue standards that are expected to boost sales of organic food. There is a catch, however; the government standards will be the *only* standards, and farmers will not be able to claim certification to a higher, private standard. Some observers fear that the result will be a lower standard.

Above and beyond present and pending legislation, many health food stores are acting independently to safeguard the well-being of their customers. For example, Fresh Fields has a policy calling for 99 percent of the products it sells to be free of hydrogenated oil and saturated fat. Still, Fresh Fields stores also offer Ben & Jerry's Homemade, a superpremium ice cream with an elevated butterfat content. In an interview with *Food & Wine* magazine, Linda Boardman, marketing coordinator at Massachusetts-based Bread & Circus, explained, "It is not our position to tell you what you can or can't eat. We give you options, then let you choose."

Video Source: "Misconceptions About Health Food," *PrimeTime Live* (June 23, 1994). *Additional Sources:* Neil Hamilton, "Rules May Determine Future of 'Organic' Foods," *The Des Moines Register* (January 20, 1997):7A; Julia Califano, "Natural Born Shoppers: Consumers Are Flocking to New Health Food Megamarkets," *Food & Wine* (June 1, 1996):37; Scott Kilman, "Major Companies in the Food Industry Have Little Taste for Organic Products," *The Wall Street Journal* (January 10, 1992):B1, B8.

1. Do you agree that some shoppers may have the misconception that all the food products sold in health food stores are, in fact, healthy?

2. Do you believe the FTC and FDA regulations are sufficient to prevent deceptive or misleading product labeling and advertising?

3. Will new standards set by the USDA for organic foods help or hurt the industry?

Several years ago, Betty Crocker adopted the "Sweet Talker" advertising campaign to provide a fresher, more contemporary, less traditional image to its line of baked goods. This image "makeover" was necessary in order to reflect the current lifestyle of Betty Crocker's target audience more accurately.

When long-term trends indicated that time-pressed consumers couldn't afford the time to get their houses neat and clean, Rubbermaid designed an advertising campaign around a line of new products that were durable and highly effective in easing the burden and drudgery of housework.

As these two examples suggest, major decisions about manufacturing, marketing, and advertising products to American consumers are based in part on assumptions about how consumers' attitudes, beliefs, and behaviors are changing. In other words, business decisions are often predicated on assumptions about *trends* in American values and lifestyles.

SPOTTING TRENDS

Advertisers spot trends in values in at least four ways:

1. PERSONAL OBSERVATION Some advertising executives believe that spotting trends is simply a matter of observing what others are doing. They ask friends, neighbors, and acquaintances what they think, buy, read, watch, and listen to. In addition, they comb the popular press, books, and other literature to see what others say is happening.

2. QUALITATIVE RESEARCH Qualitative research, such as focus group discussions and in-depth interviews with "real people," is an extremely popular way for business to monitor what's going on in society.

3. TREND EXPERTS Another approach is to let trend experts identify trends. These "gurus" often use personal observation and qualitative research for much of their "expertise."

4. PERIODIC MEASUREMENT The fourth approach is to survey large and representative samples of the population over time. These surveys typically include a lengthy battery of questions about people's attitudes, interests, and behavior on a wide range of subjects.

AD 5A.2

THE RUBBERMAID "WORKOUT" CAMPAIGN.

One such survey is the Lifestyle Study conducted by the advertising agency DDB Needham Worldwide. This survey, conducted annually since 1975, has a sample of 4,000 men and women nationwide.

Respondents are asked over 1,000 questions on their attitudes and opinions on diverse topics such as the activities in which they participate, the kinds of products and services they use, their media habits, and demographics.

REAL TRENDS, IMAGINARY TRENDS

The first three approaches to spotting trends—personal observation, qualitative research, and trend experts or gurus—have one important element in common. All three depend on *stories*. Trend spotters who employ their own personal obser-

AD 5A.1

THE BETTY CROCKER "SWEET TALKER" CAMPAIGN.

vations depend on stories they tell to themselves. Moderators of focus groups and in-depth interviews, as well as trend gurus, depend mostly on stories others have told to them.

The benefit of stories is that they produce fascinating ideas and hypotheses that are easy to believe. For example, here's a brief excerpt from a *Newsweek* (December 19, 1988) story about the Midwest:

> Kathy and Jack Ellis were not thrilled about moving to the Midwest from suburban New Jersey three years ago. Besides being separated from family and friends, there was the culture shock to consider. "My image was bib overalls," says Kathy, "that sort of thing."
>
> Now, Kathy and Jack can hardly say a bad word about Kansas City. When Jack returns home from a business trip back East, he feels as if he were going on vacation. "I take a big breath. I make a big sigh. It's just so wonderful to be back home."

On the basis of this and other stories, *Newsweek* concluded that the HEARTLAND IS HOT! This type of coherent detail makes us believe that the story must be true. We may even know people like Kathy and Jack. We are ready to believe that there is a trend toward people moving to the Midwest and embracing heartland values and lifestyles.

The trouble with relying solely on stories to spot trends, however, whether from personal observation, qualitative research, or trend gurus, is that such stories often cannot distinguish real trends from imaginary trends. As convincing as the story is of Kathy's and Jack's love of Kansas City, it hardly constitutes a trend toward Midwest migration. A careful and systematic analysis of population changes conducted by the U.S. Census Bureau indicates that at the time the story was written metropolitan areas were growing everywhere *except* in the Midwest. Thus, the news magazine provided an excellent example of what might be called an imaginary trend.

Stories cannot help us distinguish real trends from imaginary trends because the samples are small and unrepresentative, and there is no reliable history to compare with current findings. Sometimes an observation which appears to be a trend is just a unique and impressive case. Other times, the trend has been present all along but has gone unnoticed.

Compared to stories, periodic measurement has one unquestionable benefit: *accuracy*. Trends reported from periodic measurement rely on data drawn from large, representative samples of the population. Unfortunately, data with tables of percentages and clinical-looking trend lines are less exciting and memorable than a well-told story. Nevertheless, it is periodic measurement that provides the degree of accuracy advertising decision makers need.

Here are some other examples of trends generated from stories and posited by trend experts. Some of them are supported by periodic measurement; some are not.

Many trend experts have said that today's family is so abuzz with activity that, as one trend expert put it, "it is nearly impossible for families to sit down together for dinner." Accordingly, some advertisers have portrayed family dinners as hit-and-miss affairs and have positioned their products as catering to this on-the-go lifestyle.

Unfortunately, such advertising and product positioning may miss the mark.

According to the DDB Needham Lifestyle Study, 76 percent of married Americans currently say their family "usually eats dinner together." Similar results have been obtained from surveys conducted by *The New York Times/CBS News* and *Los Angeles Times*. While this percentage has declined since 1975, the decline has not been as dramatic, nor is the level as low, as some trend experts would have us believe.

Another supposedly widespread trend is *grazing*, that is, eating small, quick meals on the run. Often these meals consist of foods normally thought of as snacks or appetizers. Sometimes grazing means skipping meals altogether and simply snacking during odd moments of the day. Many products positioned in advertising as "meals-on-the-run" for the time-pressed consumer are attempting to cash in on this trend. But can advertisers take this trend to the bank? Perhaps not.

First, the percentage of people who regularly eat breakfast, lunch, and dinner is pretty much the same today as it was in the early and mid-1980s.

Looking more closely at lunch, a time when grazing is said to be quite popular, the percentage of people who say they often skip lunch or just have a light snack at noon is not increasing sharply. In fact, it is not increasing at all; it is *declining*.

GRAPH 1

OUR WHOLE FAMILY USUALLY EATS DINNER TOGETHER (MARRIED RESPONDENTS).

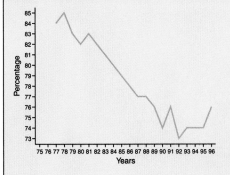

GRAPH 2

AT NOONTIME, I OFTEN SKIP LUNCH OR JUST HAVE A LIGHT SNACK.

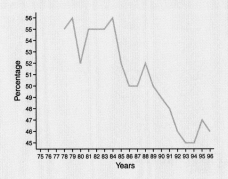

No doubt some people are grazing. Some people may even graze a lot. But grazing hardly appears to be as large a social phenomenon as we have heard.

Finally, only about one person out of three admits to eating mini-meals made up of snacks and appetizers.

Advertising strategy and advertising copy based on assumptions about trends can easily go wrong. Inaccurate estimates of the magnitude and direction of a trend can produce advertising campaigns that don't "ring true" to the target customer. Conversely, accurate estimates of the magnitude and direction of trends can greatly improve the chances of a successful advertising campaign.

DETAILS, DETAILS

The preceding cases do not mean that all trends reported by the news media or offered up by trend gurus are imaginary. Many are real. For example, the news media and many trend experts have frequently highlighted the effects of inflation on consumer attitudes. In the DDB Needham Lifestyle Study, this effect also is easy to see.

As inflation grew in the late 1970s and early 1980s, people expressed deep concern about making ends meet. As inflation cooled during the remainder of the 1980s and throughout the 1990s, so too have people's worries about losing their nest egg.

When trends are relatively easy to detect, periodic measurement can add important details on exactly how and among whom they are at work. For example, many media discussions have remarked on how women's employment outside the home has affected the time available to prepare meals at home. The DDB Needham Lifestyle Study also has uncovered this trend, as shown by the steady increase among women in agreement with the statement that "meal preparation should take as little time as possible."

Much of the media focus on this subject assumes that the increase in this sentiment is due solely to the increase in the number of working women who must meet the demands of both their families and their jobs.

Yet, when we separate working women from homemakers, we see that sharply increasing proportions of women in *both* segments are seeking to reduce the amount of time spent on preparing meals.

THE UNNOTICED TREND

Possibly the most important contribution of periodic measurement is in revealing a trend that was previously unnoticed but is both important and real. An advertiser that discovers such a trend has a decided advantage over the competition.

Let's put ourselves in the shoes of an advertising agency executive in charge of advertising a client's new line of healthy, microwavable entrées. We have heard that consumer concern about food and its relationship to health has grown dramatically. As such, we are developing an advertising campaign that emphasizes the line's all-natural, vitamin-rich, protein-rich, low-sodium food.

However, an unnoticed but real trend we may have missed is that some of the food concerns that were growing dramatically are now temporarily on hold or, in some instances, moving in reverse.

The proportion of people who say they try to avoid foods with a high salt content reached its peak in the mid-1980s and has since declined somewhat.

Similarly, additive-free foods have lost some of their appeal, while the proportion of people who try to select foods that are fortified with vitamins, minerals, and protein has been in decline since the second half of the 1980s. Even the public's concern about fat and cholesterol, while high, has abated somewhat since the beginning of the decade.

Therefore, an advertising campaign based on the assumption that concerns about salt, fat, additives, and vitamins are increasing would not accurately reflect what is really going on.

GRAPH 4

I TRY TO AVOID FOODS WITH A HIGH SALT CONTENT.

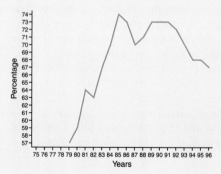

GRAPH 3

NO MATTER HOW FAST OUR INCOME GOES UP, WE NEVER SEEM TO GET AHEAD.

GRAPH 5

I TRY TO AVOID FOODS THAT HAVE ADDITIVES IN THEM.

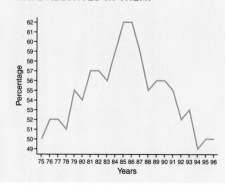

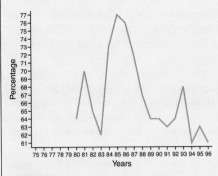

GRAPH 6

I TRY TO SELECT FOODS THAT
ARE FORTIFIED WITH VITAMINS,
MINERALS AND PROTEIN.

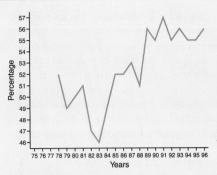

GRAPH 8

I TRY TO AVOID PREPARED
DEEP-FRIED FOODS.

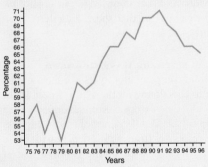

GRAPH 7

I TRY TO AVOID FOODS THAT
ARE HIGH IN CHOLESTEROL.

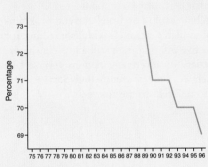

GRAPH 9

I TRY TO AVOID FOODS
THAT ARE HIGH IN FAT.

All this is not to say that health and nutrition are no longer important issues for Americans. They still are.

However, with a clearer insight into how diet and nutrition trends are unfolding, an advertiser may decide to shift the emphasis from health-oriented claims to some other appropriate product characteristics, such as "superb taste."

These various advertising strategies might also change the advertiser's competitive frame of reference and future source of business. The competition for an advertiser whose product emphasizes its low-fat, low-cholesterol benefits may be other "diet" meals. If the advertiser's strategy shifts to a focus on taste, the competition may be premium-priced, "nondiet" meals. Likewise, different strategies would call for different target audiences for the advertising. A nutrition advertising strategy might focus on older consumers who are concerned about their intake of fat and cholesterol. A taste strategy might be aimed at middle-aged consumers who are fussy about the taste of microwavable entrées.

BEWARE OF PITFALLS

It is important to emphasize that trend watching is not a solution for all advertising problems. Even when the trend data being analyzed are drawn from periodic measurement, which is the preferred choice, the marketer must beware of certain pitfalls.

GRAPH 10

I MAKE A SPECIAL EFFORT TO
GET ENOUGH FIBER (BRAN)
IN MY DIET.

First, the advertiser must realize that *attitudes can be put into action in many different ways.* Specific behaviors, such as buying a particular product, do not always follow general attitudes or values. For example, even though a large majority of Lifestyle Study respondents say they "like to buy new and different things," new-product success rates are only about 10 percent. Simply being new isn't enough; the product has to satisfy a real consumer need.

A second point to which the advertiser must be sensitive is that *many things can come between an attitude and behavior.* The growing consumer interest in dietary fiber has not translated into huge market shares for those cereals that are *very* high in fiber. Although possessing the specific property that consumers seem to want, in this case, a lot of fiber, many high-fiber cereals simply do not taste as good as lower-fiber, sweeter cereals. Thus, taste has come between the attitude (a desire for high-fiber foods) and the behavior (the purchase of high-fiber cereals).

Finally, the advertiser should be aware that *trends can reverse at any time.* We have already seen a reversal of major trends in diet and nutrition. Yesterday's trends are no guarantees of tomorrow's product triumphs.

Another example of a reversing trend is interest in television. From 1975 to 1987; the percentage of Americans who said "television is my primary form of entertainment" grew steadily. Since then, that percentage has plummeted.

Will the impending explosion from current programming to hundreds of available channels with "something for everyone" and interactive offerings that will allow consumers to choose from a variety of advertising options reverse this decline? Systems such as Time Warner's Full Service Network are now being tested to learn the answer.

GRAPH 11

I LIKE TO BUY NEW AND DIFFERENT THINGS.

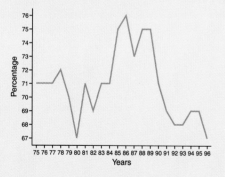

GRAPH 12

TELEVISION IS MY PRIMARY FORM OF ENTERTAINMENT.

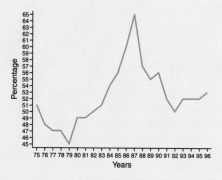

If specific behaviors do not always follow trends in attitudes, or if social trends do not always parallel business trends, why do advertisers think it still is important to monitor trends?

The reason is simple. The savvy advertiser knows how to avoid, or at least be sensitive to, the pitfalls listed previously. Having solid trend information at one's disposal, even with its limitations, is a much more desirable alternative to having no trend information. Even worse is having trend misinformation that is largely or even partly wrong.

Almost all facets of marketing—including advertising, promotion, packaging, and price—are a form of communicating to a target consumer. The better the advertisers know their targets, the more effectively they can communicate with them. Trend information about consumers' values and lifestyles provides advertisers with a much more detailed and thorough understanding of the target market than unaided judgment could provide. And that knowledge can greatly increase the chances for campaigns that speak directly to what is on consumers' minds.

RESEARCH REVEALS: MOTHERS HAVE CHANGED

How should a baby-food company modify its products and its advertising to attract today's young mothers? Or should it not make any changes at all? One company commissioned a mail survey of women typical of Middle America; the study was designed to compare responses from a 1980 survey with those of 1989 and 1996. Each participant in the research had at least one child 2 years of age or younger.

In contrast to the 1980 respondents, the 1996 mothers did not feel that their family income was sufficient to satisfy most of their important desires. In fact, just over one half of these mothers asserted that their families were already too heavily in debt. Fortunately, the newer mothers were optimistic that their family finances would improve markedly within five years.

Newer mothers say that children are the most important element in a marriage, and in making family decisions, the children's needs should come first. This was a distinct difference from mothers in the prior decade. Compared to the mothers of 1980, the newer mothers weren't such fervent cooks and preferred that meal preparation require as little time as possible. The mothers themselves seemed to have healthier eating patterns than did the women in the earlier study. They were less likely to skip lunch, for example.

In general, the mothers of 1980 were seeking interesting, even adventurous personal lives. Since then, new mothers were more likely to see themselves as people who would "try anything once." They bought on impulse and relished the fun of purchasing new products or different things for themselves and their families. However, they were about as concerned as the earlier mothers with checking on prices, shopping for specials, and making shopping lists before they set out. The newer mothers were also far less partial to store brands and instead tried to stick to well-known brand names. Unlike the earlier mothers, they did not feel that advertising insults the purchaser's intelligence, although both the 1980 and 1996 mothers thought that advertising provides information that shapes better buying decisions.

The mothers of 1996 were just as concerned with creating a distinctive appearance as were the earlier set of mothers, and they definitely wanted to feel attractive to males.

The women in the later survey were also more apt to feel that they worked hard and operated under a good deal of pressure. They didn't find much spare time in their days, and they were less likely to establish neighborhood friendships. Perhaps this was because a majority expected to be moving at least once within the next five years. All in all, they were not entirely content with their lives and would do things differently, given the chance.

EXERCISE

Now that you know something about how recent consumers feel about their lives, as compared to those of a decade earlier, what kinds of research do you think might help you sharpen your advertising message?

CHAPTER

Strategic Research

CHAPTER OUTLINE

- Understanding Europe's Generation X
- Research: The Quest for Intelligence
- Strategic Research versus Evaluative Research
- The Strategy Document
- Message Development Research
- The Future of Advertising Research

CHAPTER OBJECTIVES

When you have completed this chapter, you should be able to:

- Explain the difference between qualitative and quantitative research
- Identify sources of exploratory research in government departments, trade associations, secondary and primary research suppliers, and advertisers' and agencies' research departments
- Develop a research program using the five parts of a strategy document
- Distinguish between primary and secondary research
- Understand how and when to use the six basic research methods: surveys, experiments, observation, content analysis, in-depth interviews, and focus groups
- Understand how research is used in the development of the creative message

Understanding Europe's Generation X

Marketers are trying new tactics to reach the lucrative but often elusive youth market in Europe. To keep up with the tastes and styles of 15- to 25-year-olds who are hip and trendy but also cynical and fickle about brands, marketers are attacking on three fronts. They're spending more on in-house research, turning to a new breed of youth research agencies, and diversifying their use of youth-oriented media.

According to a 1994 report by Yankelovich Partners for Viacom's MTV Europe, there are more than 100 million young, affluent, media-literate, music-loving Europeans. Youth in the mid- to late 1990s are considered more realistic and sensible about their buying power than the previous generation. They are less rebellious and, therefore, more desirable for marketers. But they are much less definable, which frustrates advertisers trying to reach them.

"There is nothing to support what the overall concept of youth is," said Yann Tardif, PepsiCo International's marketing director for Europe. "The youth market is volatile. Their behavior can vary in a single country, but you'll find similarities in different countries. All of them are very selective. They will not listen to [a marketer's message] again if you do not get their attention first time around. Youth are easy to research. For traditional [TV audience] monitoring methods, they are not ideal. Sitting still at home is not what they're about."[1]

Increasingly, advertisers are commissioning their own research. PepsiCo carries out surveys continuously, and Mr. Tardif suggests that marketing executives of any age can benefit from mixing with young consumers to gauge what's hot and what's not. PepsiCo's own research for its European launch of Pepsi Max, a sugar-free beverage, helped focus its campaign. "We had evidence that the youth market was ready for a different cola," Mr. Tardif said. "It just happened to be one that didn't have sugar."[2]

The problem, though, was getting young people, especially males, to drink what they considered a diet drink. Pepsi Max ads needed to show that diet drinks are not only for people who want to lose weight; they needed to show that it's trendy and cool to drink sugar-free cola.

The end result was the vibrant "Live Life to the Max" campaign, part of the $80 million to $100 million television campaign outside the United States by BBDO Worldwide, in which Pepsi Max drinkers perform death-defying stunts.[3] Throughout this chapter we will refer to research on this segment.[4]

Research: The Quest for Intelligence

PRINCIPLE Understanding can come from research as well as from experience.

If an advertising agency were a factory, the products coming out the back door would be advertisements and media purchases. The raw material going in the front door would be information. Information is the basic ingredient from which all advertisements and all media purchases are made.

This information comes from two major sources. The first and most important source is the collective business and personal experience of the advertiser and the advertising agency. In the Pepsi Max campaign, for example, all the advertising and marketing executives had extensive experience in the soft-drink industry. They also spent a great deal of their time traveling to Europe, talking to their personnel working in the targeted countries, as well as spending time with the youth

---

[1]Excerpt, "Young Fogies," by Kindall Hamilton and J. Trent Gegax. From *Newsweek*, 10/28/96. Copyright © 1996, Newsweek, Inc. All rights reserved. Reprinted by permission.

[2]Ibid.

[3]Juliana Koranteng, "Tracking What's Trendy, Hot Before It's Old News," *Advertising Age International* (May 1996):130.

[4]Lori Bongiorno, "Fiddling with the Formula at Pepsi?" *Business Week* (October 14, 1996):42.

market consumer. Every effort was made to immerse themselves within the cultures that they would have to market.

Every advertising campaign has similar personal input. For example, Shirley Polykoff, the copywriter who created the classic, award-winning "Does She or Doesn't She?" campaign for Clairol hair coloring, recounted this experience:

> In 1933, just before I was married, my husband had taken me to meet the woman who would become my mother-in-law. When we got in the car after dinner, I asked him, "How'd I do? Did your mother like me?" and he told me his mother had said, "She paints her hair, doesn't she?" He asked me, "Well do you?" It became a joke between my husband and me; anytime we saw someone who was stunning or attractive we'd say, "Does she or doesn't she?" Twenty years later, I was walking down Park Avenue talking out loud to myself, because I have to hear what I write. The phrase came into my mind again. Suddenly I realized, "That's it. That's the campaign.[5]

The second source of information is formal research—surveys, in-depth interviews; **focus groups,** which are like in-depth interviews but involve a group rather than individuals, and all types of primary and secondary data. **Marketing research** is used to identify consumer needs, develop new products, evaluate pricing levels, assess distribution methods, and test the effectiveness of various promotional strategies. One type of marketing research, called **market research,** is much more specific and is used to gather information about a particular market. Although information of this sort plays a major role in every major advertising campaign, it is always assimilated into, combined with, altered by, and sometimes even overwhelmed by the professional and personal experiences of the writers, producers, and art directors who create the advertising and by the business and personal experiences of the marketing executives who approve that advertising. Advertising is never the product of personal experience alone, however. Even as brilliant an inspiration as Shirley Polykoff's recollection of a 20-year-old experience was no doubt checked against the experiences of others and subjected to various forms of testing before it ever appeared in a magazine. All advertising campaigns are complex blends of fact and fiction, judgment, experience, inspiration, speculation, science, magic, and art.

Focus Group: A group interview that tries to stimulate people to talk candidly about some topics or products.

Marketing Research: Research that investigates all the elements of the marketing mix.

Market Research: Research that gathers information about specific markets.

Strategic Research versus Evaluative Research

Strategic Research: All research that leads to the creation of the ad.

Evaluative Research: Research that determines how you did.

In addition to the two sources of research information, advertising research also varies in respect to its purpose. **Strategic research,** the topic of this chapter, deals with all the advertising research issues considered that lead to the actual creation of advertising. Think of strategic research as collecting all relevant background information needed to make a decision. You engaged in strategic research when you were looking for an acceptable college to attend. **Evaluative research** deals with an assessment of your efforts. This is the topic covered in Chapter 21. The creation of an advertisement goes through various stages of development and evaluation takes place at each stage. Although strategic and evaluative research share some common research tools and processes, there are differences. These differences will be highlighted in each chapter.

Another way to think about strategic versus evaluative research is through the results of a recent survey conducted by the Advertising Research Federation. In the study, a large sample of advertisers and agency managers was asked to indicate how much they used five types of advertising research. Clearly, advertisers do far more research than agencies, and advertisers consider strategic research to be more important than the four types of evaluative research listed.

Next, we discuss exploratory research, the beginning of all strategic research.

---

[5]Paula Champa, "The Moment of Creation," *Agency* (May–June 1991):32.

EXPLORATORY RESEARCH

Exploratory Research: Informal intelligence gathering, backgrounding.

Exploratory research is informal intelligence gathering. When advertising people get new accounts or new assignments, they start by reading everything that is available on the product, company, and industry: sales reports, annual reports, complaint letters, and trade articles about the industry. What they are looking for with exploratory research is a new insight, an insight that ultimately might demand more formal research and, perhaps, the development of a new strategy.

In an advertising agency the end users of exploratory research are the writers, art directors, and producers who create the advertisements and the media planners and buyers who select the media through which those advertisements reach the public. Before these end users begin their tasks, however, a great many other professionals play important roles in gathering, editing, and organizing research information. Among the most important of these professionals are researchers who work for government departments, trade associations, secondary research suppliers, primary research suppliers, and the research departments of advertisers and advertising agencies.

GOVERNMENT ORGANIZATIONS

Through its various departments the U.S. government provides an astonishing array of statistics that can be of great importance in making advertising and marketing decisions. Those statistics include census records and estimates of the U.S. population's size and geographical distribution, as well as highly detailed data on the population's age, income, occupational, educational, and ethnic segments. Demographic information of this kind is fundamental to decision making about advertising targets and market segmentation. An advertiser cannot aim its advertising at a target audience without knowing that audience's size and major dimensions. (See Figure 6.1 for an example that relates to the introduction).

In addition to basic population statistics, the U.S. government issues thousands of reports on topics of great interest to advertisers. For instance, the government publishes reports on food labeling and advertising, regulation of alcohol and tobacco marketing, auto safety, and sales and marketing of farm products and financial services. Figure 6.2 offers a sampling of reports that can be obtained from the U.S. government.

Many state governments issue reports on the status of in-state business as well as trend data on business development, construction, tourism, education, retailing, and medical services. These reports, which would include information on tourism, ski resorts, and recreational facilities, would help any ski resort measure its performance against the performance of its competitors.

Foreign governments provide information roughly parallel to the information issued by the U.S. government. In other countries that information is just as useful as it is in the United States and is essential in planning and executing multinational advertising.

TRADE ASSOCIATIONS

Many industries support trade associations that gather and distribute information of interest to association members. For instance, the American Association of Advertising Agencies (AAAA) issues reports on *The Advertising Agency of the Future, Patterns of Agency Compensation, Case Studies in Effective Advertising, Managing Your Agency for Profit, Executive Compensation and Employee Benefits, Analysis of Agency Costs,* and *Types of Insurance Carried by Agencies.* The major consumers of such reports are advertising agencies themselves, which use them in making salary and staffing decisions, monitoring their own performance, and keeping tabs on competitors. However, much of this information would also be useful to research suppliers, personnel recruiters, advertising media companies, and anyone else to whom advertising agencies are important customers. In a direct-marketing program designed to sell a service to agency executives, for example, basic knowledge of the industry would guide selection of the executives to be addressed, the pricing and design of the service itself, and even the choice of words used to describe the offer.

Counting the young, hip

Marketers want young consumers. Here is where they are:

Country	Total Population	% 15- to 24-year-olds
France	57,526,521	14.4%
Germany	79,364,504	13.7%
Ireland	3,525,719	17.1%
Italy	57,746,163	15.8%
Netherlands	15,184,138	14.7%
Poland	38,309,226	14.4%
Sweden	8,692,013	12.9%
United Kingdom	57,998,400	13.7%

FIGURE 6.1

Source: U.N. Demographic Yearbook, 1993.

FIGURE 6.2

**U.S. GOVERNMENT REPORTS
OF INTEREST TO ADVERTISERS**

Survey of Current Business: Basic operational statistics on U.S. business. (Bureau of Economic Analysis of the U.S. Department of Commerce)

Requirements of Laws and Regulation Enforced by the U.S. Food and Drug Administration: Laws and regulations affecting food and beverage advertising. (U.S. Department of Health and Human Services, Food and Drug Administration)

Economic Issues: How Should Health Claims for Foods Be Regulated? Regulation of health claims in food advertising. (Bureau of Economics, Federal Trade Commission)

Children's Information Processing of Television Advertising: How children react to television commercials. (National Technical Information Service, U.S. Department of Commerce)

Food Consumption: Households in the United States, Seasons and Year 1977–78, released in 1983: Detailed data on consumption of a wide range of foods. (Human Nutrition Information Service, U.S. Department of Agriculture)

Guidelines for Relating Children's Ages to Toy Characteristics: Rules that govern toy advertising. (U.S. Consumer Product Safety Commission)

Vital and Health Statistics: Smoking and Other Tobacco Use: Consumption of tobacco products. (U.S. Department of Health and Human Services, National Center for Health Statistics)

Franchising in the Economy: Statistical review of franchised businesses. (U.S. Department of Commerce International Trade Administration)

Other major trade associations include the Radio Advertising Bureau, which publishes *Radio Facts*, an overview of the commercial radio industry in the United States; the Association of Home Appliance Manufacturers, which conducts research and reports industry statistics; the American Meat Institute, which publishes *Meat Facts*, an annual statistical review of the industry; the American Paper Institute, which gathers, compiles, and disseminates current information on the paper industry; and the National Soft Drink Association, which publishes *NSDA News* every month, covering legislative issues affecting soft-drink bottlers and suppliers to the soft-drink industry.

SECONDARY RESEARCH SUPPLIERS

Considering the overwhelming amount of information available from government reports, trade associations, and other sources of marketing data, it is not surprising that a mini-industry has sprung up to gather and organize this information around specific topic areas. Because this information was originally collected by some other organization (and usually for some other purpose), the research is called **secondary research,** and the firms that collect and organize the information are called *secondary research suppliers.* The two most important secondary research suppliers are FIND/SVP and Off-The-Shelf Publications, Inc.

In addition to firms that provide written reports, a new breed of secondary research supplier now provides information via computer terminal. Among the most important of these on-line vendors are Dialog Information Services, Inc., Lexis/Nexis, Dow Jones News/Retrieval, and Market Analysis and Information Database, Inc. With a connection to Dialog Information Service, Copper Mountain's managers could have used Dialog's Marketing and Advertising Information Service to access information on competitors' sales, market shares, and marketing activities. They could have used the Donnelley Demographics database to retrieve mobility, housing, education, income, population, and household information for the local area and for other areas that might be sources of customers. The Prompt database could have been used to identify hot trends in the leisure market in general and in the skiing industry in particular.

Secondary Research: Information that has been compiled and published.

PRIMARY RESEARCH SUPPLIERS

Primary Research: Information that is collected from original sources.

Much of the information that ultimately appears in the form of advertisements or media purchases is gathered by research firms that specialize in interviewing, observing, and recording the behavior of those who purchase, or influence the purchase of, industrial and consumer goods and services. Firms that collect and analyze this kind of **primary research** are called *primary research suppliers.*

The primary research supplier industry is extremely diverse. The companies range from A.C. Nielsen, which employs more than 45,000 workers in the United States alone, to several thousand one-person entrepreneurs who conduct focus groups and individual interviews, prepare reports, and provide advice on specific advertising and marketing problems. The most comprehensive listing of primary research suppliers is the *International Directory of Marketing Research Companies and Services,* published by the American Marketing Association (AMA).

PRINCIPLE Secondary research is information that has already been compiled for you; primary research is information you find out yourself.

PepsiCo has relied heavily on primary research information that is proprietary. Most of this research is conducted by an independent research firm specializing in the youth market and is directed by a market research manager.

Many advertising agencies subscribe to very large-scale surveys conducted by the Simmons Market Research Bureau (SMRB) or by Mediamark Research, Inc. (MRI). The surveys conducted by these two organizations employ large samples of American consumers (approximately 30,000 for each survey) and include questions on consumption or possession of a very wide range of products and services and usage of all the major advertising media. The products and services covered in the MRI survey range from toothbrushes and dental floss to diet colas and bottled water to camping equipment and theme parks.

Strictly speaking, both SMRB and MRI are secondary data sources; they are primarily intended to be used in media planning, which will be discussed in detail in Chapter 9. Because these surveys are so comprehensive, however, they can be mined for consumer information. Through a computer program called Golddigger, for example, an MRI subscriber can select a consumer target and ask the computer to find all the other products and services and all the media that members of the target segment use more than do consumers in general. The resulting profile provides a vivid and detailed description of the target as a person—just the information agency creatives need to help them envision their audiences.

ADVERTISERS' RESEARCH DEPARTMENTS

Almost all large advertisers maintain marketing research departments of their own. These departments collect and disseminate secondary research data and conduct concept tests, product tests, test markets, package and pricing tests, and attitude and usage studies—all types of large- and small-scale consumer explorations. The immediate "clients" of advertisers' marketing research departments are the top offices of their respective companies and the line-product managers who are responsible for the pricing promotion, advertising, distribution, sales, and profit of their brands. As we will discuss later in this chapter, much of this information ultimately finds its way into advertising.

The marketing research department of the Oscar Mayer Foods Corporation provides a good example. Oscar Mayer's marketing research department is divided into two groups: brand research and marketing systems analysis. The brand research group conducts primary and secondary consumer research and sales analysis, serves as a marketing consultant to product managers, reports and interprets broad consumer trends, and works on projects intended to improve marketing research methods. The marketing systems analysis group performs sales analyses based on shipment and store scanner data, supports computer users within the marketing and sales departments, and manages Oscar Mayer's marketing information center.[6]

---

[6]Charlie Etmekjian and John Grede, "Marketing Research in a Team-Oriented Business: The Oscar Mayer Approach," *Marketing Research: A Magazine of Management Applications,* 2, no. 4 (December 1990):6–12.

The product's performance, the performance and marketing activities of competing products, and the needs, wants, values, and attitudes of consumers are essential input to the strategy document described later in this chapter. For many advertising campaigns, the advertiser's marketing research department is the key source of such intelligence. Often this department is also responsible for one other activity that directly affects the marketer's advertising: It either conducts or supervises the testing procedures that determine whether an advertising campaign should run. These testing procedures, often called *copy tests*, are discussed in detail in Chapter 21. Copy tests are of great importance to the advertiser because they determine which advertising messages do and do not reach the public. They are therefore directly responsible for the success or failure of the advertising program.

Copy tests are possibly even more important to the advertising agency. In the course of developing a campaign an agency will create many alternatives, some or all of which may be tested by the advertiser's testing system. If that system rejects much of the work submitted, the account can require so much extra work that the agency cannot make a profit on it. Even more importantly, the agency's creative reputation (and the careers of its writers, art directors, and producers) depends on the ads that get through the testing system. Any system that persistently rejects the agency's "best" creative efforts is certain to become an object of bitter controversy.

Even when an advertiser is not large enough to support a marketing research department of its own, the information generated in the course of marketing activities can play an important part in determining how that firm will communicate with the public. For example, while revising the marketing program for its line of plant containers, the Weathashade division of the Gale Group—a manufacturer of outdoor lawn and garden supplies based in Apopka, Florida—conducted focus groups with potential customers, in-store observations of plant container purchasers, and both in-person and telephone interviews with retailers and distributors. This research led to the following recommendations:

- Integrate the indoor and outdoor offering under one umbrella, but develop a brand, name, and merchandising system in which either brand can stand alone.
- Take advantage of the planned purchase behavior and develop emotional appeals to both the novice and the expert gardener.
- Emphasize size, durability, and fade resistance in the outdoor offering. Emphasize size, color, style, value, and quality in the indoor offering. Emphasize lifestyle and performance convenience for both lines.
- Because of the potential opportunity, Weathashade should be the first company to create major brand recognition in this product category.
- The packaging and merchandising system will increase sales by creating excitement, attracting attention, stimulating interest with product ideas, and suggesting lifestyles. Information should be provided to maintain interest and aid purchase but this information should avoid being highly technical.
- The system should create a selling environment to take advantage of space through efficient stacking, to display the product, and to increase brand presence and awareness. A small on-product label denoting pot size and usage should be explored to reinforce brand awareness in the absence of the full merchandising system. Unique free-standing merchandisers could be incorporated into the design. The merchandising system must be flexible enough to allow use of one component, of multiple components, or of any combination.[7]

When these recommendations were followed, sales increased over 200 percent, surpassing even the most optimistic expectations. Thus strategic research,

---

[7]"Growing Indoors: Research Helps Makers of Gardening Containers Expand," *Quirk's Marketing Research Review* (October 1990):6–7, 33–35.

*I*NSIDE *A*DVERTISING

MARTY HORN, SENIOR VP, GROUP DIRECTOR, *Strategic Planning & Research, DDB Needham, Chicago*

So you want to be in advertising.

You're probably wondering "What courses should I take?" "Do I need a graduate degree?" "How do I break into a business that wants experienced people?" "Should I work at a large agency or a small one?"

I was asking these and other questions in the early 1970s when I was graduating from the University of Connecticut, armed with a B.A. and M.A. in Communications (a relatively new degree at the time).

I'll tell you what I did to help me get into the business—which doesn't mean it's what you should do. But it may aid you in whatever decisions you finally make.

1.   START WITH THE END IN MIND. When I was ready to graduate, I had a pretty good idea of what I wanted to do with my degree. With a major in communications and its emphasis on questionnaire design, statistics and analysis, along with a minor in marketing, I knew I wanted to do consumer research. So, I set my sights on applying to marketing research firms or to companies, including advertising agencies, that had marketing research departments. It didn't make a difference to me what type of company it was, as long as they did what I wanted to do—marketing research. Although I had an interest in advertising, my priority was landing a job in consumer research, irrespective of where that happened to be.

But if you know you want advertising, try to get a good idea of what advertising agencies do and how your skills mesh with them. I mention this only because a lot of college graduates I talk to say they "want to get into advertising" but have, at best, a fuzzy idea of what an agency does and what the role in it would be. Do you want account work? Media? Creative? Planning & research?

So, it pays to do a little research on the workings of an agency and how your educational skills and, perhaps more importantly, who you are as person, match up with the various disciplines within the organization. Once you have a vision in mind, it makes the search a lot more productive.

By the way, I got a job at Burke Marketing Research in Cincinnati right out of graduate school. I didn't get any offers from agencies. More on that later. Within a year, though, I moved to Chicago to what is now DDB Needham, the country's largest advertising agency.

2.   GET AN ADVANCED DEGREE—MAYBE. Some of the smartest, most innovative and most successful people I know in advertising never got a college degree, let alone a Master's or Ph.D. Conversely, I've come across some folks with terrific academic credentials who turned out to be duds. So, a lack of an advanced degree is not a guarantee of failure, nor is the accumulation of degrees a ticket to success.

However, "all things being equal," an advanced degree does help. First, you gain an added measure of training in your selected field. Second, you gain additional maturity, which counts for a lot. Third, the marketplace, rightly or wrongly, uses academic "credentialism" as a screening device. Often, the first people to get weeded out are those who "only" have a four year degree.

How far should you go? Should you stop at a Master's Degree? Go on for a Ph.D.? I know a lot of people who have done both, and, again, some have done spectacularly well, others haven't. Success and failure are often independent of what it says on your sheep skin.

In my case, I thought there was a lot of value in getting a Master's Degree but a diminishing return to getting a Ph.D. But that's me. It may be different for you. Frankly, there's no right or wrong answer.

One more thing for those seriously contemplating a doctorate. Don't be intimidated by the "you'll be over-qualified to get a job" naysayers. A lot of companies value a Ph.D. and encourage employees to include it on their business cards and letterhead because it confers status and brains (whether it's true or not!).

3.   POUND THE PAVEMENT. Perhaps the most frustrating thing the would-be ad person faces after graduation is getting their proverbial foot in the door. Inevitably, you will run across a company that is looking for people with experience, which, of course, you don't have if you're fresh out of college and which, obviously, the company is unwilling to provide you. This is small consolation, but that problem has always existed and always will. I know I faced it in the mid-1970s when the economy was going to hell in a hand basket.

This bit of advice may not be terribly profound, but all you can do is keep trying. Hard though it may be to believe, lots of companies don't require that you have worked in the "real world" before they hire you. As long as you have the smarts, skills and personality they're looking for, they'll hire you if a position is open.

There are a million self-help books out there on how to put together a resumé, and how to target the companies, people and locations where you want to work. Pick one up. Pick up a few. They're helpful.

translated into effective communication, produced impressive results even in the absence of a budget that could support advertising in national magazines or on network television.

ADVERTISING AGENCY RESEARCH DEPARTMENTS

In the 1950s all the major advertising agencies featured large, well-funded, highly professional research departments. Agencies highlighted their research power in new-business presentations, and had a list been made of the most respected

While these books all take a different tact, one thing they almost always recommend is identifying exactly who in the company you need to contact for an interview and then calling that person in addition to (or instead of) sending a resumé. That's sage advice. I wish I had done it when I was first applying for a job! I probably wasted a lot of time and money sending out resumés to everyone and anyone who had a marketing research department and then waiting around for all those companies to contact me, impressed by my awesome resumé. Well, if they got back to me at all, which was rare, it was with a TBNT (thanks but no thanks) letter. So, in this case, don't do what I did!

Once you've identified the right people in the companies in which you have an interest, then work to get an interview. Even if they don't have any positions open at the time, ask for a brief informational interview, ask them if it's OK to chat with them in person for a short while to learn more about the company and the business. It's a great way to meet people and make connections, to get them to know you as a person rather than as a disembodied voice, to get advice, and to get a firmer handle on what agencies do.

One of the reasons I got my job at Burke was I did a lot of follow up calls with them after getting an initial job application to fill out. If I didn't make myself a bit of a pest (a pleasant one, though, I like to think!), I may never have gotten the interview in the first place—an interview which eventually led to a job offer.

As it so happens, I got my job at DDB Needham (then Needham, Harper & Steers) because my graduate school advisor decided to leave academia. He got a job at Needham when the research department was undergoing a transformation; they were looking for entry level people (experience was *not* needed) and I fit the bill. A little luck doesn't hurt!

When my advisor-cum-colleague described to me what the research department did—a broad spectrum of qualitative and quantitative research with consumers that help develop advertising strategies and executions—my interest was piqued. It sounded like the perfect combination of the kind of research I enjoyed doing with my interest in advertising.

4. WORK AT THE AGENCY THAT'S RIGHT FOR YOU. People ready to embark on an advertising career often ask me whether they should work at a small agency or a large one. Here's the answer I give them: "I don't know." I've worked at a large agency my entire career. It's a lot bigger now than it was when I started, but it's always been on the big side. So I can't speak

from direct experience. Large agencies definitely have their advantages, such as top notch resources and support services. Small agencies definitely have their advantages, too, such as fewer layers of bureaucracy and greater camaraderie. That said, plenty of small agencies have top-notch resources and support services, and lots of big agencies have restructured themselves to eliminate wasteful managerial layers. So go figure!

What you shouldn't do is go in with the mind set that "I'll work for a small agency first because that'll make it easier to get a job at a big agency." First, it's demeaning and suggests a lack of true commitment to that small agency. Second, what makes you think a large agency will be better?!

So, don't worry about size so much as "feel." Ask yourself, "Is this the kind of place where I would want to work?" Do they have the kinds of people I would like to work with? Do they have the resources and talent that will help me to grow professionally and personally. Do they have the kinds of client businesses on which I'd enjoy working? (OK, go ahead and ask how well they pay and what their benefits are!)

I hope these suggestions will help you answer the question "How do I get into advertising?" In parting, however, let me give you one more suggestion: don't ask this question at all—or at least don't make it the first question you want answered!

While it's a perfectly reasonable question to ask, the answer only addresses a short-term issue. The key is not just to "get into advertising." Ultimately, you should enter the field with an eye towards *success over the long haul*.

What does it take to succeed? Frankly, I don't have any magic formula. But if I can deal in some glittering generalities for a minute, I'd say it's a combination of things: You need "street smarts" and a large dose of common sense; "book smarts" will only get you so far. You have to have an ability to work with a diverse range of people, personalities and egos. You must clearly and compellingly communicate ideas; advertising is a communications business so you have to be articulate and you have to write well. You need to be creative and innovative, no matter which department of an agency you work in; "creativity" is not the sole purview of the Creative Department. You have to be entrepreneurial people who succeed in this business take a few chances and risks if they have an idea they want to champion. And you have to know how to listen and not just talk.

In sum, it really helps to be nice and good. Niceness alone won't cut it if you can't do the job. Being a jerk can only be tolerated for so long, even if you are competent. So be both. You, advertising and the world will be better off!

leaders in the advertising research field at that time, many of the names on that list would have been found on agency research department payrolls.

One of the reasons for this prominence was that profit margins in the 1950s allowed the agencies to provide expensive and impressive advertising and marketing research at no extra cost to their clients. Another was that many advertisers' own marketing research departments were relatively underdeveloped. In some cases, such as the Maxwell House Division of General Foods, the advertising agency research department supplied *all* the research used by the client.

In the 1960s both of these conditions began to change. Agency profit margins shrank to the level where agencies found it increasingly difficult to provide research at no extra cost. At the same time, partly as a result of agencies' declining research role, advertisers' own marketing research departments began to grow. By the end of the decade most major advertisers had developed effective research departments that bore primary responsibility for marketing research. In most cases, they took over the evaluative testing of advertisements as well.

Those trends continue today. Although some of the largest agencies, including Young and Rubicam, Grey Advertising, and the Leo Burnett Company, still invest heavily in their own research departments, others have sharply curtailed internal research activities and some have turned the research function over to account managers. Smaller agencies, which never had large research departments to begin with, now hire outside research suppliers on a case-by-case basis.

In those agencies that still have internal research departments, efforts now focus on projects that contribute directly to the development of advertising. These projects may range from two or three group interviews intended to show how consumers talk about a product or a brand, through small- or medium-scale surveys of consumers' opinions and attitudes concerning a specific product or service category, to relatively large-scale surveys, like the annual DDB Needham Lifestyle Study, intended to identify and measure activities, interests, and opinions within segments of the consumer population.

Those agencies that are too small to sustain internal research departments usually employ outside research suppliers when they need help. In some cases, these agency-supplier relationships become so productive that the supplier fulfills most of the roles of an internal research department.

INFORMATION CENTERS

All large advertising agencies, and even some relatively small ones, maintain specialized libraries (often called *information centers*) that provide access to reference volumes, such as dictionaries, encyclopedias, atlases, cookbooks, books of famous quotations, and trade and general newspapers and magazines. Writers, art directors, and producers use these sources when they need more information about a client, a product, or a brand, and when they are browsing in search of creative ideas. The information center is one of the most important features of the advertising agency research department. Even agencies that are not large enough to support a full-fledged research department usually have an information center of some kind. For a sample of the questions that come in to an information center, see Figure 6.3.

Many information centers also maintain subject and picture files. Subject files contain clippings from magazines, newspapers, and government and trade reports, all classified by subject matter. The subjects may range from "advertisers," "airlines," "animal food," "auto care," and "baby market" to "video," "watch industry," "water softeners," "wine," and "women." Picture files may include "Americana," "amusements," "animals," "architecture," "art," "water," "waterfalls," "witches," "X-rays," and "zodiacs." The subject files provide quick synopses of subjects that may suddenly become important. The picture files provide images that jog creative work. Some of the pictures spark creative ideas and eventually inspire other pictures that finally appear in ads.

Many information centers are wired into Lexis, the Dow Jones Retrieval Service, and other computerized utilities that provide instant access to information in the general and trade press. To take just one example, a Lexis search on key words "Visa" and "Olympics Sponsorship" might produce seven pages abstracting current articles on those related topics from *Mediaweek, Adweek's Marketing Week, Advertising Age, Euromarketing, ABA Banking Journal, Campaign, Bank Advertising News,* and *Tour and Travel News.* This file would give anyone interested in Visa's role in the Olympics a quick and current rundown on what is being written on the topic.

FIGURE 6.3

A SAMPLE OF QUESTIONS AN-
SWERED BY A TYPICAL ADVER-
TISING AGENCY INFORMATION
CENTER.

- Compile trends of the 1990s as they relate to diet and salt and the impact of salt on the environment.
- We plan to shoot in Sydney and northern Australia. What is the average temperature and rainfall there for mid-July? What are the famous places and landmarks?
- What information regarding the Fourth of July is available at the Information Center? I need both historic and fun ideas.
- I need pictures of birds flying in a flock, teens walking on a sandy beach, a close-up of shells on the beach, a close-up of a red rose, sand dunes with dramatic effect, and pictures of brightly dressed ladies—right away.
- Who are the leading marketers of frozen dinners and entrées? I need sales and market shares.
- Give me the number of families with children under 5 years old, the number of households with heads 25 to 45 years old, and the number of households with incomes over $25,000.
- What was the average Dow Jones Industrial Average in 1993?
- How much did Michael Jordan get for the Nike and Wheaties commercials? What was the package deal?
- Are people concerned about cholesterol in pancakes? Are people aware that pancakes have cholesterol?
- How many breakfast foods containing oats were introduced during the last 5 years?
- What is the weight of a hockey puck?
- How big is the foot-powder market?
- We need pictures of Simon and Garfunkel, the cast of *The Mary Tyler Moore Show*, President Jimmy Carter and his family, and the 1980 U.S. National Hockey Team. We also need their bios.
- We need pictures of brand characters—the original look and the revised ones. Examples: Betty Crocker, the Campbell Soup children, and the Morton Salt girl.

WHO ORGANIZES THE FACTS?

A typical advertising campaign might be influenced, directly or indirectly, by information from many sources, including the advertiser's marketing research department, one or more of the primary or secondary outside research suppliers, and the agency's research department itself. Surprisingly, the problem usually is not too little information, but too much. Someone must sift through the **qualitative data,** which seek to understand how and why consumers behave as they do, and the **quantitative data**—the numerical data such as exposures to ads, purchases, and other market-related events—that are available. This person must also separate the potentially relevant from the irrelevant material and put the outcome into a format that decision makers and creatives can use.

In advertising agencies with internal research departments that task usually falls to the research department staff. Indeed, the ability to organize huge amounts of information and to deliver that information in a useful form is one of the most important skills members of an advertising agency research department can have. In agencies without research departments the task of collecting and organizing information usually falls to members of the account group. Even in agencies with research departments members of the account group are likely to be highly involved in the final decisions as to what information will be passed on to those who will create the campaign. An account manager who is doing his or her job effectively will play a major role in every facet of the agency's work on his or her brand.

ACCOUNT PLANNING

Boase Massimi Pollitt (BMP), an advertising agency in London, England, originated the concept of the **account planner,** a new way of thinking about the role of research within an advertising agency. Partly because of the consistently high

Qualitative Data: Research that seeks to understand how and why people think and behave as they do.

Quantitative Data: Research that uses statistics to describe consumers.

Account Planner: The person responsible for the creation, implementation, and modification of the strategy on which creative work is based.

recognition accorded to BMP's creative work, this concept has spread to other London agencies as well as to agencies in Europe, Asia, and the United States.

Charles Cannon, director of Studies at the Institute of Practitioners in Advertising, in London, defined account planning this way:

> The account planner is responsible for the creation, implementation, and modification of the strategy on which creative work is based. The planner will therefore be responsible for the generation, selection, and interposition of the research evidence at each stage of the advertising process, namely, in strategy development (such as the creation of the strategy), and in creative development (such as the implementation of the strategy), and in market evaluation (such as the assessment of effectiveness in the marketplace with a view to the maintenance or modification of the strategy for future work).

He went on to elaborate:

> (a) The core craft skill of planning is the translation of research evidence into advertising judgment.
> (b) In this sense, account planning is the integration of the research function into the account team.
> (c) Research relevant to advertising almost never speaks for itself and almost always requires interpretation which must be based on knowing about research *and* knowing about advertising, not one or the other on its own.[8]

When confronted with definitions of this kind, members of research departments of U.S. advertising agencies usually say, "That's what we've been doing all the time!" Indeed, if an advertising agency research department has not been performing many of these functions, it has probably ceased to exist.

Whether the information providers are called researchers, planners, or members of the account group, the most effective agency research parallels the planner model. Under one name or another, account planning is here to stay. The person who can pick out the most useful information from the suffocatingly large amount of data available, and who can make that information instantly relevant to the problem at hand, will always have an important role in the creative process.

THE STRATEGY DOCUMENT

The outcome of strategic research usually reaches agency creative departments in the form of a *strategy document* or *creative brief*. Although the exact form of this document differs from agency to agency and from advertiser to advertiser, most have five major parts: the marketing objective, the product, the target audience, the promise, and the brand personality.

MARKETING OBJECTIVE

The section of the document that presents the marketing objective reviews the competitive situation and establishes a goal for the campaign. It includes both past and present sales figures; market shares of the brand and of its major competitors; competitors' advertising and promotional resources, tactics, and practices; and any other information about the brand that may lead to a prediction of early success or risk of failure. Although advertisers and agencies are acutely aware that marketing success depends on many factors besides advertising, advertisers do expect advertising to help them meet their marketing goals. It is therefore important that everyone involved in the development of the campaign understand exactly what those goals are. If the advertiser has an unspecified but totally unreasonable marketing objective, and the agency, through ignorance, implicitly agrees to meet that objective, the agency has unknowingly put itself in an extremely vulnerable posi-

---

[8]Charles Cannon, "The Role of the Account Planner," paper presented at the Conference of the Institute of Canadian Advertising, London, England (June 1986).

tion. In the strategy document the marketing objective should be specific; it should be agreed to at the outset.

THE PRODUCT

The product section of the strategy document includes the results of product tests, consumers' perceptions of the brand and its major competitors, and tests of or reactions to the brand's and its competitors' advertisements, promotions, retail displays, and packaging. In other words, any facts, opinions, perceptions, or reactions to the product that might fuel an advertising campaign are presented in this section of the strategy document.

THE TARGET AUDIENCE

PRINCIPLE Learn everything you can about how consumers think, feel, decide, and act.

The next section of the document provides a demographic and psychographic description of the campaign's target audience. The demographic data come from secondary sources or from surveys that reveal the age, income, education, gender, and geographical distribution of the consumers who might be persuaded to adopt the brand. The psychographic information comes from attitude and opinion surveys, individual in-depth interviews, or focus groups, all of which help paint a portrait of the target as a person. The Lifestyle box examines how an advertiser uses research to attract a specific target audience. Ad 6.1 for MTV is an example of an ad that is targeted at a specific audience.

Both the creative team, who must create communication, and the media planners, who must decide how and when to contact targets most efficiently, need to know as much as they can, in as much depth and detail as possible, about the people they are trying to reach.

OLD-TIMERS AT HEART

Alex Klenert may only be 22 years old, but he's already acquired a taste for the finer things in life. He loves big-band music, a bracing round on the links, and all-night card games with the guys. And when it's time for a haircut, Klenert knows just the place. Up a short flight of granite steps, just a few blocks off New York's Wall Street, lies John Allen's, a dark-paneled paradise. Young Alex settles back in a green leather chair, leafing through the latest issue of the glossy cigar monthly *Smoke*, as Mary Ann, an attractive stylist in a very short skirt, runs her fingers through his hair, snipping it just so. Another woman holds his hand, administering a glistening manicure. Yet a third brings him a glass of beer, fresh from the tap, and sits it atop a svelte black metal stand. "You kind'a get hooked on it," says Klenert, a marketing writer who clears barely $20,000 a year, but finds the budgetary headroom to fund a haircut, manicure, shoeshine, and hot-towel treatment at John Allen's every six weeks. It's $44 plus tip—but, hey, it's worth it. "With the hot towel, you just lose yourself in the heat, it just radiates through your body."

Mary Ann's proximity may have something to do with that particular sensation, but the appeal of a place like John Allen's extends far beyond the boundaries of Klenert's leather chair. In every corner of the culture, it seems, people in their twenties—and not just men—are embracing the good life, old style. Indeed, if Generation Xers skipped the Clinton-Dole debates, it's because they're too busy immersing them-

selves in the accouterments of the Eisenhower era. There are the precious connoisseurs, like Klenert, with their cigars, single malts, and men's club mentality. Others seek high style in the low culture of yore. Cocktail-happy "lounge" devotees, with their rat-packy, Foster Grant esthetic and irony as dry as their martinis, trade bons mots on banquettes from New York to L.A. On most golf courses, you can't swing a club without smacking into somebody's grandson. Even bridge is finding a toehold among those who still have all their teeth. Gen X? It's more like the Young Fogies.

Nowadays a Scotch-swilling, stogie-chomping guy stands an even chance with the ladies—as long as he's willing to share. "I've been smoking cigars for a while," says Allison Weinbaum, a 26-year-old teacher unwinding with her pal Lee Tomkin, 29, one recent night at Hudson Bar & Books. "Smoking cigars and having a good Scotch—all my friends do that." And golf? "It's a big dating thing," says Weinbaum. Tomkin pipes up: "I have a friend whose boyfriend took her to a golf camp in the Catskills after they'd been dating a while."

For a good part of Gen X, something that merely represents high living might have to suffice forever. All the numbers suggest that Gen Xers will never experience the economic well-being of their parents. Oh well. Light up.

Source: Kindall Hamilton and J. Trent Gegax, "Young Fogies," *Newsweek* (October 28, 1996):64–66.

AD 6.1

RESEARCH HAS FOUND THAT
TWO-THIRDS OF MTV'S AUDI-
ENCE ARE 18- TO 34-YEAR-
OLDS, A FACT THAT CHANNEL
USES IN ITS ADS TO ATTRACT
ADVERTISERS INTERESTED
IN REACHING A YOUNGER
AUDIENCE.

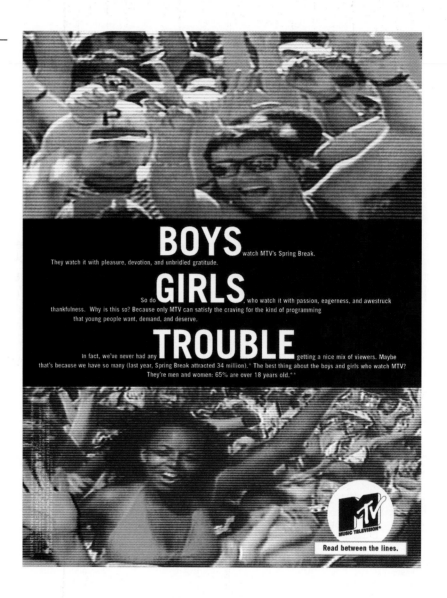

PROMISE AND SUPPORT

Advertising always promises some sort of reward the customer can obtain by buying or using the advertised product or service. The promise section of the strategy
document tells writers and art directors which reward, out of many possibilities,
the advertising should promise. The support section of the strategy document indicates which facts about the product and its users are likely to make that promise
most acceptable. Such insights into consumer motivations and purchasing decisions help solve the often difficult puzzle of selecting the most motivating promise
and deciding how that promise will be supported.

BRAND PERSONALITY

Brands, like people, have personalities. When a brand has a winning personality,
its advertising should perpetuate and reinforce that personality. When a brand
has a less than desirable personality, advertising should work to remedy the problem. Research that asks potential customers what the brand and its competitors
would be like if they were people supplies the information needed to specify the
brand's present personality and identifies the kind of improvements that are
needed.

PRINCIPLE Know your product
intimately.

STRATEGY STATEMENT

A strategy document is usually prefaced by a brief *strategy statement* that distills the document's main points. Following the strategy statement, the document itself presents the highlights of the most relevant research. Figure 6.4 is an example of a typical strategy statement.

Although formats vary considerably from advertiser to advertiser and from agency to agency, some way of conveying in writing what is known about the product, the brand, the competitive situation, and the prospective customer is as essential to an advertising campaign as a blueprint is to a construction project.

MESSAGE DEVELOPMENT RESEARCH

For the sake of orderly exposition, it is convenient to speak as though research contributes to advertising in a logical, systematic, and linear way. Someone in the agency research department or the account group collects and organizes a vast array of facts, distills those facts into a strategy document, and hands that document over to previously uninformed writers and art directors, who then go off and create some advertising.

That impression is almost entirely wrong. Although facts do indeed play an important role in many advertising campaigns, they are always filtered through and evaluated against a system of ideas, experiences, prejudices, memories of past successes and failures, hierarchical relationships, and tastes and preferences within the advertiser's own company and within the advertising agency. Decisions as to what facts find their way into advertisements are never cut and dried.

Furthermore, as writers and art directors begin working on a specific creative project, they almost always conduct at least some informal research of their own. They may talk to friends—or even strangers—who might be in the target audience.

FIGURE 6.4

A STRATEGY STATEMENT FOR MILK.

---

1. Marketing Objective

Increase consumption of milk by members of the target audience by 10 percent.

2. The Product

Although milk is considered to be among the healthiest of beverages, milk drinking drops off sharply in the teenage years. Part of the problem is concern about fat and calories, part has to do with taste, and part has to do with milk's childish and unexciting image. Advertising can have its most direct effect on the image problem.

3. The Target Audience

Males and females 16 to 30 years old. Milk is a beverage they had to drink as children, and although they are still drinking it, they are choosing more often to drink other beverages. Milk has become less relevant to their lifestyle. They believe milk doesn't go as well with foods they like, such as pizza, Mexican cooking, and Oriental dishes.
Females in particular are concerned about the calories and fat in milk.
Other beverages, such as soft drinks, are of greater interest to this group. Soft drinks are an exciting, versatile, and socially acceptable alternative to milk, which is practical, unexciting, and conservative.
These people are active and energetic. They want very much to be popular with their peers, to be attractive, and to look and feel fit.

4. Promise and Support

Today's milk can help you become the attractive, fun, dynamic person you want to be (promise). Milk has the nutrition your body needs to look and feel terrific. Today's most attractive and dynamic people drink milk. Ice-cold milk tastes great (support).

5. Brand Personality

Personality now: childish, practical, conservative. Needed personality: exuberant, contemporary, young adult.`1`

They may visit retail stores, talk to salespeople, and watch people buy. They may visit the information center, browse through reference books, and borrow subject and picture files. They will conjure up old memories, as Shirley Polykoff did when thinking about the Clairol campaign. They will look at previous advertising (especially the competition's) to see what others have done, and in their heart of hearts they will become absolutely convinced that they are able to create something better than, and different from, anything that has been done before. This informal, personal research has a powerful influence on what happens later on.

DIAGNOSTIC RESEARCH AND EARLY FEEDBACK

Diagnostic Research: Research used to identify the best approach from among a set of alternatives.

Early Feedback: Preliminary reactions to alternative creative strategies.

Diagnostic research is used to choose the best approach from among a set of alternatives. As creative ideas being to take shape, writers and art directors bounce their ideas off each other and discuss them with their supervisors in the creative group. At this point, they may request some feedback from consumers, just to help them decide whether they are on the right track. **Early feedback** is the target audience's evaluation of alternative creative strategies. This feedback usually takes the form of loose, unstructured conversations with members of the target audience, either in individual interviews or in focus groups. Sometimes the people working on the advertising participate in these conversations; sometimes they only watch.

When advertising begins to approach a more finished form, diagnostic research becomes more clearly defined. Creative concepts are translated into rough comprehensives and storyboards—presentation pieces that show the artwork and print to be used in the final ad. Ideas begin to look more like print ads and television commercials. Consumers now have something specific to look at, and their reactions and evaluations to the concepts presented are taken more seriously.

Consumers aren't the only source of input at this stage, however. Supervisors within the creative department react favorably or unfavorably to early versions. Creative directors—the executives who are ultimately responsible for the agency's creative product—exercise editorial control. Creative review boards—groups of senior executives—might have the final word concerning what may and may not be submitted to the client.

In most cases, the advertiser also plays a part. Brand managers or their assistants review and comment on rough executions of the ad. They might request major changes. They might also pass the advertisement up the line so that higher-level executives can make contributions.

PRINCIPLE Concept testing helps creatives decide which ideas are worth pursuing and which are not.

Whether from the agency or the client, these evaluations are all based on guesses about how consumers ultimately will react to the advertising. This is where diagnostic research can help. Instead of *guessing* how prospects will interpret an advertisement, the agency and the advertiser can *hear* what real consumers think.

CONTACT METHODS

Message development research may use any combination of methods to contact customers. The contact can be in person, by telephone, or by mail. In a personal interview the researcher asks questions of the respondent directly. The questions can be either tightly structured in a questionnaire or they can be presented in an open-ended format. These interviews often are conducted in malls or downtown areas.

A telephone survey is used when the questions are relatively simple and the questionnaire is short. It is efficient and, depending on the number of interviewers, can reach many people quickly and easily. A mail survey can be longer and more in-depth than a telephone survey; however, it has to be absolutely clear because no interviewer is present to explain procedure or ambiguous questions.

Verbatims: Spontaneous comments by people who are being surveyed.

Primary research data can be reported *quantitatively* in tables of numbers. For example, a survey might find out how many people prefer two-ply toilet paper. The results would be expressed quantitatively as a number and as a percentage of the total. If the survey also reported spontaneous comments, or **verbatims,** it would include *qualitative* data.

Survey Research: Research using structured interview forms that ask large numbers of people exactly the same questions.

Population: Everyone included in a designated group.

Sample: A selection of people who are identified as representative of the larger population.

True Experiments: A research method that manipulates a set of variables to test hypotheses.

Randomization: Everyone has a known and equal chance of being selected.

Manipulation: Control of the variable of interest.

Control Group: A control group does not receive the treatment.

SURVEY RESEARCH

Several types of quantitative research are important in marketing and advertising. **Survey research** uses structured interview forms to ask large numbers of people the same questions. The questions can deal with personal characteristics, such as age, income, behavior, or attitudes. The people can be from an entire group, or **population,** or they can be a representative **sample** of a much larger group. Sampling uses a smaller number of people to represent the entire population.

EXPERIMENTAL RESEARCH

In **true experiments** researchers meet two criteria: randomization and manipulation. **Randomization** means that everyone in the experiment has a "known and equal chance" of being selected. For example, if you started with 100 subjects, each would have a 1-out-of-100 chance of being selected. If we put 100 names in a hat and drew them out one at a time, each would have the same chance of being selected as long as each name drawn was placed back into the hat. **Manipulation** refers to a variable (referred to as an independent variable or causal variable) that can be modified (controlled) in order to create an effect (measure of success). For example, an agency might want to know which of three emotional appeals (independent variable) produces the highest amount of information (the effect). People would be randomly assigned to one of the three emotional appeals. Those that were not exposed to any of the three messages are called a **control group.** Because it is so difficult to organize and implement a true experiment, few advertisers engage in this type of research.

DIRECT OBSERVATION

Direct observation is a type of field research that takes researchers into natural settings where they record the behavior of consumers. Researchers might, for example, conduct an *aisle study* in a supermarket. The assignment would be to note how people buy a particular product or brand. Do they deliberate or just grab a product and run? Do they compare prices? Do they read the labels? How long do they spend making the decision?

A pioneering study of the direct-observation technique concluded that "direct observation has the advantage of revealing what people actually do, as distinguished from what people say [they do]. It can yield the correct answer when faulty memory, desire to impress the interviewer, or simple inattention to details would cause an interview answer to be wrong."[9] The biggest drawback to direct observation is that it shows *what* is happening, but not *why.* The results of direct observation are, therefore, often combined with the results of personal interviews to provide a more complete and more understandable picture of attitudes, motives, and behavior.

CONTENT ANALYSIS

In preparation for a new campaign, agency researchers or account executives often conduct systematic audits of competitors' advertisements. These audits might include only informal summaries of the slogans, appeals, and images used most often, or they might include more formal and systematic tabulation of competitors' approaches and strategies. The basic question always is: "What are competitors doing, and how can we do it better?" By disclosing competitors' strategies and tactics, analysis of the content of competitive advertisements provides clues to how competitors are thinking, and suggests ways to develop new and more effective campaigns to argue against and possibly even overcome their efforts.

IN-DEPTH INTERVIEWS

A common type of qualitative research is the in-depth one-on-one interview. This technique is used to probe feelings, attitudes, and behaviors such as decision making. The insights can be instructive about how typical members of the target audi-

[9]William D. Wells and Leonard A. Lo Sciuto, "Direct Observation of Purchasing Behavior," *Journal of Marketing Research* (August 1966):227–33.

FOCUS GROUPS HAVE BECOME
INCREASINGLY IMPORTANT
WITHIN THE CREATIVE PROCESS.

ence respond to the product, to competitors' products, to the advertiser's marketing efforts, and to competitors' advertising and marketing activities.

FOCUS GROUPS

A *focus group* is another method used to structure qualitative research. As we mentioned earlier, the focus group is like an in-depth interview, except that it involves a group rather than an individual. The objective is to stimulate people to talk candidly about some topic with one another. The interviewer sets up a general topic and then lets conversation develop as group interaction takes over. (See the following Concepts and Applications box.)

PERILS OF QUALITATIVE DIAGNOSIS

Although in-depth interviews and focus groups provide valuable feedback at early stages in the creative process, they are not without problems. The samples of consumers are usually very small, and they may not be truly representative of the whole audience.

Because the advertising ideas submitted to early qualitative evaluation are usually in very rough form, they might omit some important element that would make them work very well in the context of a full campaign.

A third problem specific to focus groups is that sometimes a small minority of respondents dominates the group, imposing their opinions on everyone else. Although a skilled interviewer can moderate this kind of behavior, the loudest and most authoritative respondents often contribute more than their fair share. Furthermore, when interested parties witness qualitative interviews, they cannot help but single out and remember comments that support their special points of view. With a few off-

CONCEPTS AND APPLICATIONS

FOCUS GROUPS

In a typical focus group, members of the target audience are invited to attend a group discussion at a central interviewing location.

When the group has been assembled and seated around a conference table, the "moderator" introduces the group members to one another and tries to make them feel at home. The moderator then leads the group through a preset list of topics, encouraging responses and attempting to make sure that all members of the group have opportunities to express what they think and how they feel.

Most focus group facilities provide a viewing room where observers can watch and listen to the discussion from behind a "one-way" mirror. Although respondents are told about the observers, they soon forget that they are there.

Focus groups are valuable because they bring decision makers into direct contact with consumers. Most marketing executives, and most members of advertising agency creative departments, live so differently from their customers that they have little direct day-to-day contact with how consumers think.

The outcome of a focus group depends heavily on the skill of the moderator. The moderator's responsibilities are to make sure that the most significant points are adequately covered and to follow up the most potentially useful ideas by asking insight-

ful, probing questions. That task requires the ability to think quickly in a complex and rapidly changing interview. It requires sensitivity and good judgment, and it demands an understanding of what the client needs to know. Moderators with those skills are scarce and are therefore in constant demand.

After the interview the moderator usually meets with the observers to discuss and evaluate what has gone on. In this discussion the moderator might contribute observations derived from other interviews or from other research in which the problem was somewhat the same.

The moderator may prepare a report that summarizes and evaluates the results obtained from a series of groups. Often such reports contain extensive quotations from the group interactions so that readers who were not in attendance can get some feel for how consumers reacted and for the language they used to express their thoughts. Such information can prove extremely helpful to writers who must understand the thoughts and feelings of their audience.

Focus groups provide direct contact with consumers. Compared with many other research methods, they are more intimate and more personal, and they can be fast and cheap. Although focus groups have many obvious limitations, they are becoming more and more popular.

hand remarks from a small sample of respondents, a copywriter, an art director, an account director, or a brand manager can become absolutely convinced that he or she had been on the right track all along. Sometimes even when better evidence presents itself at a later time these convictions can be very hard to alter.

In spite of the inevitable perils, however, the assets of diagnostic research outweigh its liabilities, and both individual in-depth interviews (sometimes called *one-on-ones*) and focus groups are widely used today. For a more detailed description of how focus groups are set up, conducted, and evaluated, see the Concepts and Applications box.

COMMUNICATION TESTS

The drawbacks of qualitative diagnosis have led many advertisers to use communication tests instead. These are one-on-one interviews, usually conducted in shopping malls that supply central interviewing facilities. Shoppers are recruited to fill out questionnaires on their age, sex, income, and product usage. They are asked to participate in a "study of consumers' opinions," and they are sometimes offered a small fee for their cooperation.

In the interviewing room respondents are shown advertisements one at a time and asked a standard list of questions such as:

- As you looked at the commercial, what thoughts or ideas went through your mind and what feelings did you have?
- In your own words, please describe what went on and what was said in the commercial.
- Besides trying to sell the product, what was the main point of the commercial?
- What was the name of the product advertised?
- Was there anything in this commercial that you found confusing or hard to understand?
- What, if anything, did you like or dislike about this commercial?

As the respondents answer the questions, the interviewer writes down the answers verbatim. The answers are later analyzed to determine how well respondents understood the message and how they reacted to the way the message was presented.

The verbatim comments are coded into categories such as:

- Main-point playback
- Spontaneous-claim recall
- Name recall
- Positive feelings
- Negative feelings
- Reactions to characters
- Believability
- Likes
- Dislikes

Communication-test samples are generally larger and usually somewhat more representative of the target audience than are the samples typically used for individual in-depth interviews or focus groups. Furthermore, although the coding of verbatim responses always requires a certain amount of judgment, it is not as casual and subjective as the interpretation of the more qualitative forms of diagnostic research.

Many communication tests also include a set of scales intended to capture a wide range of reactions. These scales, designed to include most of the ways consumers can respond to advertisements, supplement the answers to the open-ended questions. They also help less articulate respondents express their opinions, and they sometimes suggest ideas that respondents have not thought to mention.

Even though the communication test has some obvious limitations, it can usually provide answers to three fundamental questions:

1. Did the advertisement convey the message it was intended to convey?
2. Did the advertisement convey any messages it was not intended to convey?
3. How did consumers react to the characters, the setting, the message, and the tone of the advertising?

The answers to these questions are valuable because they come at a time when it is still relatively easy to make changes. Changes will be much more difficult and expensive to make later in the advertising development process. Early feedback is especially important, for example, in catching and weeding out plot lines that may involve stereotyping and other negative portrayals of some groups. It is much better not to have developed an advertisement fully than to have to pull it later—with apologies.

Although not all communication-test results are that clear-cut, these tests can reveal that an advertisement is failing to deliver the message it was intended to deliver, or that it is succeeding in delivering a message never intended. Such findings can avoid a lot of problems later on.

THE FUTURE OF ADVERTISING RESEARCH

There's a great deal of controversy about the value and direction of advertising research as we enter the twenty-first century. Recently, the American Academy of Advertising sponsored a content analysis of issues of *Advertising Age* and *Adweek*, the two primary trade publications in advertising. The result was a list of the five advertising research issues that loom as most important in the near future.[10]

TREND 1: RIGHT SIZING

In response to current profit pressures and organizational changes within the mass communication industry, both advertisers and advertising agencies are *right sizing*. In most cases, it has meant both across-the-board staff cuts and outplacement of staff functions—especially research functions. More work is now being done by fewer, less specialized professionals.

In response to client demands for less bureaucracy, many large advertising agencies are dividing themselves into small client-oriented teams that include rep-

---

[10]Karen McLaughlin, William D. Wells, Deborah K. Johnson, and James Crimmins, "Today's Most Important Advertising Research Issues," *Proceedings of the 1994 Conference of the American Academy of Advertising*.

resentatives from what were formally separate account management, creative, media, and (in some cases) planning or research departments. Some agencies have "spun off" entire departments—especially media and research departments—as separate profit centers. These events are fundamental and permanent changes in agency structure and management.

TREND 2: GLOBALIZATION

The advertising industry is increasingly global. Multinational American advertisers and their marketing communication agencies are expanding overseas. Expansion into Western Europe and much of the Pacific Rim is virtually complete. Indepth understanding of overseas economic and cultural conditions, government regulations, and communication media is now more important than ever before. Development of methods to solve global problems would establish a new and important advertising research tradition.

TREND 3: NEW MEDIA TECHNOLOGY

The change from three on-air television networks to 60 or more cable channels changed television programming, television program audiences, and television advertising throughout the United States. The next major development will be the merger of the telephone, the television set, and the computer. Changes in media technology will alter the meaning and consequences of almost all of our most familiar research constructs: involvement, brand equity, attitude toward the ad, emotional processing, and cognitive processing, for example. Advertising research today consists largely of full-page print ads and 30-second television commercials. As technology changes in the media unfold, that assumption will become increasingly invalid. (See the Issues and Controversies box for an additional example).

TREND 4: INTEGRATED MARKETING COMMUNICATION

The basic principle of integrated marketing communication (IMC)—that *all* marketing communication (including mass media, advertising, direct-response advertising, public relations, and sales promotion) should reinforce rather than contradict each other—is so obvious that all marketers try to apply it. However, implementation has proved surprisingly difficult. IMC casts a glaring spotlight on a basic research problem that has always been with us: How should an advertiser allocate limited resources across the cafeteria of available media? How much of the communication budget should go to four-color magazine ads, 30-second television commercials, 60-second radio commercials, public relations activities, and so forth? Future research methods must be designed in order to answer such questions.

TREND 5: INCREASED GOVERNMENT ACTIVISM

The change from Republican to Democrat administration has fueled activism throughout the federal government. The key issues are the impact of advertising (including the media) on health and crime. Government agencies are also newly active in controlling deceptive advertising, and in addressing the effects of advertising on children. On the positive side, governments at all levels—but especially the federal level—are turning to public service announcements and paid advertisements to advance their causes. Government officials are now more willing than in the recent past to solicit research-based counsel from private and public research organizations.

As we noted early in this chapter, information is the raw material out of which advertising campaigns are made. Although much of this information comes from the professional and personal experiences of those who are responsible for creating and approving the advertising, a great deal of it comes from research of one type or another. In the end, these sources of information are intricately and untraceably mixed. Examples like, "Does she or doesn't she?" and those in which one specific research finding led directly and unambiguously to one particular illustration or theme line are rare. And, even in those cases, many other considera-

THE REALITY OF RESEARCH

It's a hot, summer Saturday afternoon. Imagine you're at the local beer distributor to pick up a cold brew before tackling the day's worth of yard work that lies ahead. You park the car, cross the parking lot, and enter through the store's sliding, automatic doors. You pass a few cardboard displays and navigate three aisles until you find a six-pack of your favorite beer. You pick it up, check the price, and walk over to the cash register. A pretty typical afternoon . . . except that the entire experience took place on your computer screen—not at the local beverage outlet.

You've just experienced the future of market research according to Gadd International Research, Inc. The ten-year-old, Toronto-based firm is using virtual reality technology to make market research more accessible for companies without large budgets for expensive product testing campaigns and mockups. "There's a cost savings associated with the technology," says Glenn Saxley, research director at Gadd. "But for many companies this also means you don't have to disturb a store to conduct customer research."

Virtual reality refers to the practice of using technology to simulate real-world experiences. A user of virtual reality can navigate virtual worlds with only a desktop computer and mouse. Gadd has created a virtual reality environment called Simul-Shop, a market research tool that recreates shopping situations to see how consumers react to things like package designs, store layouts, product positioning, and ad strategies. The entire program exists on a CD-ROM.

If a cereal company wanted to test a new package design and the position of the product on store shelves, it would sit members of its test pool down behind standard desktop PCs. Users would first see the outside of the grocery store. To begin the virtual shopping spree, users would simply enter the virtual store using a mouse and be directed to the section of the store where the product has been placed. People can pick up the cereal boxes, rotate them, and turn around to see what is on the shelf behind them. Everything but open the box and try a sample. The entire experience includes sound, video, and a guide who directs you through the experience and answers your questions. "Once they move toward the item we want to test, you can look at different packaging, shelf layouts, and package colors," Saxley says.

Saxley says that this type of shopping experience benefits the companies in numerous ways. The company doesn't have to go through the expense of creating mockups for each different product color, shape, or size. And, he says, the results don't become skewed because of damaged mockups or the limitations of when and where a physical market research text can be conducted—the vertical tests can be run from any PC.

But experts say that there are drawbacks to relying on data derived from virtual reality tests. "Just because it's technically capable, that doesn't mean that when you put the average person behind a computer you're going to get true responses," says Michael Hammer, electronic communications manager with the American Marketing Association. "Any time you simulate an experience, you're not getting the experience itself. It's still a simulation."

Today, it would cost a company about $10,000 for the initial programming of Simul-Shop to fit the product. Beyond that companies can expect to pay between $10,000 and $15,000 for the actual market research with a sample size of between 75 and 100 people.

Sources: Tom Dellecave, Jr., "Curing Market Research Headaches," *Sales & Marketing Management* (July 1996):84–85; Scott G. Dacko, "Data Collection Should Not Be Manual Labor," *Marketing News* (July 18, 1996):31; and Kelly Shermach, "Research Firms Take Unusual Approach to Kids," *Marketing News* (April 28, 1995):20.

tions play important parts in the development of the campaign. In one way or another, research plays an important role in most advertising campaigns. Still, research is only *one source* of creative inspiration, as following chapters show.

*S*UMMARY

- Information is the basic ingredient from which all advertisements and all media purchases are made.

- A very important part of advertising information comes from the personal and professional experiences of the men and women who are responsible for developing and evaluating the advertising. Another part of this information comes from formal research. In the development of any campaign these two information sources interact in complex ways.

- Formal research is provided by government departments, trade associations, secondary research suppliers, primary research suppliers, and the research departments of advertisers and advertising agencies.

- In the development of an advertising campaign the problem is seldom too little information but too much. Someone must identify, collect, and organize the most useful information and present it in a useful form. That task usually falls to members of the advertising agency research department, or, in the absence of a research department, to the account group.

- The most important research information usually goes into a strategy document that is, in a rough sense, a plan for the campaign.

- The difficult decisions as to just what information should go into the strategy document and how that information should be interpreted call for interactive judgments on the part of the advertiser and its agency. Within the agency, these judgments involve all those responsible for making sure that the communication works. These judgments are never automatic or obvious, nor are they cut and dried.

- Once creative work has started, the developing advertising ideas may be checked for effectiveness with the intended audience through relatively qualitative and informal diagnostic research.

- Although diagnostic research provides exposure to real consumers, it also opens the possibility that potentially excellent ideas may be rejected or that previous prejudices may be confirmed. Despite these risks, diagnostic research provides a valuable safeguard against the possibility that the finished advertising will fail to convey the intended message or that it will contain some message it was not intended to convey.

QUESTIONS

1. Every year Copper Mountain must decide how much emphasis to put on front-range day skiers versus skiers from the Denver market who stay overnight versus skiers from outside Copper Mountain's geographic area. What research information would help Copper Mountain's managers make those decisions? Where would they get that information?

2. Suppose you had the opportunity to develop a research program for a new bookstore serving your college or university. What kind of exploratory research would you recommend? Would you propose both qualitative and quantitative studies? What specific steps would you take?

3. The research director for Angelis Advertising always introduces her department's service to new agency clients by comparing research to a road map. What do maps and research studies have in common? How does the analogy of a map also indicate the limitations of research for resolving an advertising problem?

4. Judging from the chapter discussions, would you expect the following databases to be developed from primary or secondary resources:

- **A.** national television ratings

- **B.** consumer brand's ad awareness scores
- **C.** household penetration levels for VCRs

5. Research professionals recommend using focus groups to help develop a campaign strategy or theme, but many are opposed to using focus groups to choose finished ads for the campaign. Is this contradictory? Why or why not?

6. A new radio station is moving into your community. Management is not sure how to position the station in this market and has asked you to develop a study with this decision.

- **A.** What are the key research questions that need to be asked?

- **B.** Outline a research program to answer those questions that uses as many of the research methods discussed in this chapter as you can incorporate.

7. In the course of diagnostic research, a few focus group respondents contradict an opinion based on years of professional and personal experience. Suppose that opinion is held by your client's top management. If you are a researcher, what do you do? Suppose that opinion is held by the creative director of your agency. What do you do? Suppose it is your opinion. What then?

SUGGESTED CLASS PROJECT

Run a focus group. Brainstorm to come up with something the class would like to advertise, for example, new audio equipment. Divide into researchers and the consumer group (you can run two groups and trade roles, if you like). Meet to decide on questions and format. Make assignments for note taking, facilitating, and collecting and organizing feedback. Write a report.

FURTHER READINGS

Day, George S., *Market-Driven Strategy: Processes for Creating Value* (New York: The Free Press, 1990).

Emory, C. William, *Business Research Methods*, 3rd ed. (Homewood, IL: Irwin, 1985).

Fletcher, Alan, and Thomas Bowers, *Fundamentals of Advertising Research*, 3rd ed. (Belmont, CA: Wadsworth, 1988).

Green, Paul E., Donald S. Tull, and Gerald Albaum, *Research for Marketing Decisions*, 5th ed. (Upper Saddle River, NJ: Prentice Hall, 1988).

Kerin, Roger A., Vijay Mahajan, and Rajan Varadarajan, *Contemporary Perspectives on Strategic Market Planning* (Needham Heights, MA: Allyn and Bacon, 1989).

Weiers, Ronald M., *Marketing Research*, 2nd ed. (Upper Saddle River, NJ: Prentice Hall, 1988).

It happens every holiday season: High demand for a particular toy triggers shortages, desperate searches by anguished parents—even fist fights. The ritual of a last-minute toy hunt has even turned into a hit movie starring Arnold Schwarzenegger. Over the past few years, "hottest toy" honors have been earned by Mighty Morphin Power Ranger action figures, Barney, a talking Simba from *The Lion King*, Doctor Dreadful Food Lab and, of course, Barbie. Tyco Toys was responsible for both Doctor Dreadful, the hit of 1994, as well as Tickle Me Elmo, the hottest toy of 1996.

Creating a new toy requires inspiration and a keen sense of current trends. Turning a new toy into a best-selling phenomenon requires careful research, solid marketing, and, often, a bit of luck. In the case of Doctor Dreadful, inventor Rick Gurolnick noticed that candy makers were promoting extreme flavors and colors, often in the form of body parts or secretions. Gurolnick linked the "gross food" trend to kids' perennial fascination with monsters, and the idea for a monster candy laboratory was born. Gurolnick and partner Bob Knetzger took their idea to Tyco, which in turn used focus groups to test the Doctor Dreadful concept with both kids and parents.

One concern was whether or not boys would consider mixing edible monster parts too much like cooking. Tyco executives were concerned that boys would dismiss the toy as "girl-oriented." (They didn't.) Another concern was whether or not gross-out food would be *too* gross for parents. (It wasn't.) By February, the two toys, Doctor Dreadful Food Lab and Drink Lab, were presented to toy retailers at the U.S. Toy Fair in New York City. Retailer reaction was enthusiastic, and Tyco promised to support the line with strong advertising and public relations. The result? A major hit in the marketplace.

The evolution of Tickle Me Elmo followed a similar pattern, although initial reaction from the market was less enthusiastic than it had been for Doctor Dreadful. Elmo, of course, is the popular figure from television's *Sesame Street*; the first time a child tickles the $30 doll, it giggles. A second tickle evokes a response of "Oh no, that tickles!" After a third tickle, Elmo vibrates and emits a peal of hysterical laughter. The idea for a ticklish doll came to Ron Druben after watching two children tickle each other while playing outside. Druben recalled that being tickled was one of childhood's purest joys, and, working with electronics expert Greg Hyman, he set about putting an electronic mechanism in a stuffed monkey. At the point in 1994 when Druben first presented his concept to a Tyco marketing executive, Tyco did not have a licensing agreement with Children's Television Network, owners of *Sesame Street*. There was talk of a Tickle Me Taz doll based on the popular Looney Toons character.

Tyco ultimately did acquire the licensing rights to create plush toys based on *Sesame Street* characters. As Stan Clutton, vice president of marketing at Tyco Preschool explained, Elmo was the perfect candidate for tickling. "He's fun loving. He's a little kid." Even as work on Elmo proceeded, there was little indication that shoppers would snap up 1 million of the dolls by Christmas 1996. As Greg Hyman observed, "You never know if you're going to have a hit. Once you've submitted a concept, it's a long way from the bank." Indeed, when Elmo was shown at the Toy Fair in February 1996, retail reaction to the $30 toy was cool. A focus group of moms was similarly unimpressed. Tyco executives forecast demand at between 300,000 and 400,000 units.

Throughout 1996, Tyco worked with Freeman Public Relations in an effort to create a buzz about Elmo. One tactic was to get the doll on Rosie O'Donnell's talk show. O'Donnell's 1-year-old son was sent Tickle Me Elmo, and the show's producers were sent 200. Then, on a show that aired in October, O'Donnell announced that whenever one of her guests said the word *wall*, an Elmo doll would be thrown into the studio audience. O'Donnell's viewing audience includes a high percentage of stay-at-home moms with preschool-aged children. Then, in November, *Today* show cohost Bryant Gumbel held Elmo on his lap during a segment on holiday gifts for kids. Thanks to the one-two publicity punch, the Elmo phenomenon took on a life of its own. To lure shoppers into stores after Thanksgiving, some stores discounted Elmo by $5 or more. As retailers sold out of the doll, they notified the local media, thereby generating additional publicity and fueling further demand.

Not surprisingly, a backlash set in. Tyco defended itself against claims by industry observers that the company had deliberately fed the frenzy by holding back production. As one toy buyer for an East Coast retailer commented, "Tickle Me Elmo is a study in mob mentality. People are looking for Elmo without even knowing what it looks like. They're in the stores because that's where everybody is." Although Tyco stopped running television ads for Elmo on December 6, Elmo's torrid sales pace continued. A radio station in West Palm Beach auctioned an Elmo for $3,500. Toy retailer Kay-Bee chartered a plane to bring a shipment of Elmo dolls direct from the factory in China. Hundreds of postings offering to buy or sell Elmo were posted on the Internet. Commenting on this turn of events, Ron Dubren, the man who started it all, said, "Six months from now, people could say, 'Tickle Me What?'"

Video Source: "The Business of Toys at Christmas Time," *Nightline* (December 22, 1994). *Additional Sources:* Kathy Balog, "Elmo's Evolution Is a Surprise to Those Involved," *USA Today* (December 11, 1996):1B, 3B; Joseph Pereira, "Toy Story: How Shrewd Marketing Made Elmo a Hit," *The Wall Street Journal* (December 16, 1996):B1, B8; and Kate Fitzgerald, "Publicity About Toy Shortages Feeds the Frenzy," *Advertising Age* (December 16, 1996):12.

QUESTIONS

1. What lessons can the Elmo story provide about the limitations of traditional research?
2. Do you believe it is possible for a marketer to engineer a product sellout?

Strategy and Planning

CHAPTER OBJECTIVES

When you have completed this chapter, you should be able to:

- Identify the key elements of a marketing plan and an advertising plan
- Understand how marketers allocate funds among advertising and other marketing functions
- Explain the difference between product-centered and prospect-centered strategies
- List the key elements of a creative platform

RADIOSHACK HAS THE ANSWERS

RadioShack was down in the dumps in 1993 when Leonard Roberts was hired to be its president and turn its fortunes around. The secret to the turnaround has been a new focus on the service side of the business. The hard-to-find cables, cords, diodes, and other electronic doodads are still the core of its business, but now you can also get a cellular phone or a radio and have it gift-wrapped and shipped.

The first step was to dump the company's longtime slogan, "America's Technology Store," in favor of the more service-oriented line, "You've got questions. We've got answers." An extensive employee training program has intensified the service mentality of the staff and helped them live up to the promise of answers to technical questions.

New programs like electronics repairs for RadioShack and other branded goods and a gift service were added to capitalize on new opportunities in the service side of RadioShack's business. Analysts estimate the repair and gift services, which were launched in 1994, delivered an electric $75 million in sales during their first year in 1995.

Another strategy is to move into more interactive and personalized communication with its customers by better using its 80-million-name database to do one-on-one target marketing.

The turnaround is evident in sales, which have increased 5 percent over previous years and are consistently higher than rival Circuit City, whose sales have been flat. Analysts estimate that after the first quarter in 1996 RadioShack's earnings were up 10.3 percent over the previous year. Focusing on service instead of technology has been the answer for RadioShack.[1]

STRATEGY AND PLANNING

Advertising is both an art and a science. The art comes from writing, designing, and producing exciting messages. The science comes from strategic thinking. Advertising is a disciplined art, and achieving the disciplined side of advertising is the focus of this chapter. Advertising messages aren't created by whimsy or a sudden flash of inspiration. Messages are formulated to accomplish specific objectives, and then strategies are developed specifically to achieve those objectives. This is all done through a process called *planning*.

STRATEGIC PLANNING: MAKING INTELLIGENT DECISIONS

PRINCIPLE Strategic thinking means weighing the alternatives and identifying the best approach.

Strategic planning is the process of determining *objectives* (what you want to accomplish), deciding on *strategies* (how to accomplish the objectives), and implementing the *tactics* (which make the plan come to life). All of this occurs within a specified time frame. Marketing and advertising strategies are chosen from an array of possible alternatives. Intelligent decision making means weighing these alternatives and sorting out the best approach. Often there is no *right* way, but there may be a *best* way to accomplish your objectives.

---

[1]Adapted from Bernhard Warner, "Leonard Roberts," *Superbrands '97* (October 7, 1996):115–17; Jeffery D. Zbar, "The Marketing 100; RadioShack," *Advertising Age* (June 24, 1996):S24; and Stephanie Anderson Forest, "RadioShack Looks Like a Palace Now," *Business Week* (May 13, 1996):153.

RadioShack, as indicated in the opening of this chapter, has apparently found the right strategy to market itself. Its answers campaign has effectively shifted the focus from technology to service.

It is sometimes difficult even for those experienced in advertising to tell the difference between an objective and a strategy. Both are important to the development of successful marketing and advertising plans; they are related to each other, but they are also different and serve different purposes. An objective is a *goal* or *task* to be accomplished. A strategy is the *means* by which the goal is accomplished.

For example, if the goal is to reinforce brand loyalty for the product, then any number of strategies could be employed to accomplish that task. Suppose, though, that the advertiser wants to create brand loyalty by emphasizing that the brand delivers more of the benefit than do competing brands. The number of tactics that could be used with that strategy is almost infinite. For instance, the brand could be compared with its leading competitor. Other possible tactics to carry out the strategy are a demonstration, a testimonial, an emotional or funny story, or a straightforward fact-based approach. Naturally, decisions related to media would be intertwined at both the strategic and tactical levels. Engaging in comparison advertising is only relevant if the message reaches the target audience at the right time and the medium reinforces the necessary credibility.

PLANNING DOCUMENTS

Business Strategic Plan: An overriding business plan that deals with the broadest decisions made by the organization.

Business strategic planning is usually a three-tiered operation beginning with the **business strategic plan,** moving on to functional plans, such as a *marketing plan* or a *financial plan*, and ending with specific plans for each element under that function, such as a *distribution plan* or an *advertising plan*. Naturally, each ensuing plan is dependent upon the plan that preceded it. It is possible, for example, that the business strategic plan for a particular business suggests that advertising is not necessary. Note how many products in your supermarket have no advertising support, for example, specialty items such as spices and ethnic foods. There are probably good business reasons for this situation.

The intent of this chapter is to provide you with a basic understanding of the advertising planning process. In order to do this, however, a brief overview of the business plan and the marketing plan is given. Note that many of the components of the marketing plan were introduced in Chapter 3 and will not be reexamined here.

THE BUSINESS PLAN

Typically, the business plan relates to a specific division of the company or a *strategic business unit* (SBU). These divisions or SBUs share a common set of problems and factors that can be identified. Although there are many ways of looking at this planning process, Figure 7.1 depicts a highly regarded model. It begins with a *business mission statement*. Such a statement is derived from the broader corporate mission and includes the broad goals and policies of the business unit. Does this business unit want to pursue long-term growth, short-term profits, or technological leadership? How does it feel about its customers, its employees, its stockholders?

The business next would examine its external environment for possible opportunities or possible threats. An *opportunity* is viewed as an area for the company's marketing process to move into where the company would enjoy a competitive advantage. Numerous mergers have occurred during the 1990s between related high-tech communication companies (for example, TCI and US West), whose managers felt that combining resources would allow the new company to take advantage of important opportunities. A *threat* is a trend or

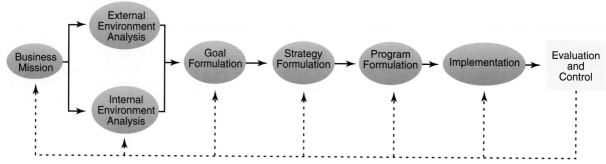

FIGURE 7.1

THE BUSINESS PLANNING PROCESS

Source: Philip Kotler, *Marketing Management: Analysis, Planning, Implementation, and Control,* 8th ed. (Upper Saddle River, NJ: Prentice Hall, 1993):79.

development in the environment that will erode the business position of the company unless purposeful marketing action is taken. Competition is a common threat, and international competition is increasingly a factor. U.S. automakers have begun to meet the threat of Japanese imports. When a business carefully prioritizes its opportunities and the threats against it, it arrives at a much better position for success.

There is also a need for the business to assess its internal competencies. What are the company's major *strengths* and *weaknesses?* Either of these could revolve around financial conditions, personnel issues, and technical expertise, to name but a few. Companies that are very production oriented often find they make great products but have nobody to buy them, or sell them, for that matter. The company may need to develop its consumer base and retrain its sales force. Based on this assessment the company weighs the relative importance of these internal strengths and weaknesses and the external threats and opportunities and prioritizes them, a procedure called a *SWOT* (strengths, weaknesses, opportunities, threats) *analysis.* (See Ad 7.1.)

After the business unit managers have defined the SBU's mission and examined its external and internal environment, they can proceed to develop specific objectives and goals for the planning period. Most businesses pursue several goals at the same time, for instance, sales growth, higher return on investment, higher quality, and market-share improvement. These goals should be prioritized; they should be stated quantitatively; they should be realistic; and they should be consistent.

Then specific programs are outlined that relate to each goal. For example, many corporations throughout the late 1980s and early 1990s viewed cost leadership as the best strategy regardless of the goal. CEOs were selected based on their reputation for ruthless cost cutting. Prominent examples are IBM and General Motors, fervent proponents of this strategy. Other companies, such as Microsoft, believe that technological innovation is the way to go, regardless of the costs. Still other companies, such as Conagra, maker of Healthy Choice, have decided to focus on one market—the health conscious in this example.

Once the business has developed its principal strategies for attaining its goals, it must work out supporting programs for carrying out these strategies. Thus, if the business has decided to attain technological leadership, it must run programs to strengthen its research and development (R&D) department, gather intelligence on the newest technologies that might affect the business, and so forth.

Even the best plans run the risk of failure if there is poor implementation. Although some businesses have wonderful planners, they simply cannot handle the hundreds of decisions that are required to implement that plan. Assuming that the new plan is implemented, the business needs to track the results and monitor late developments in the environment. Depending upon these findings, the company must determine what, if any, adjustments are necessary.

AD 7.1

REGIONAL COMPANIES HAVE
SOMETIMES FOUND THAT THEIR
GEOGRAPHICALLY FOCUSED
NAMES LIMIT THEIR BUSINESS
OPPORTUNITIES. IN THIS AD,
THE SOUTHERN COMPANY
MAKES THE POINT THAT IT IS IN
THE GLOBAL UTILITY BUSINESS.

How do 12 million people
get going every morning?

Whether it's tea in England or coffee in the U.S. we're probably the company that makes it happen. Because we're America's largest generator of low cost electricity and we're expanding. So from Bristol to Biloxi, our customers can look forward to a bill that's easier to swallow.

SOUTHERN COMPANY

Energy to Serve Your World

http://www.southernco.com

THE MARKETING PLAN

Marketing Plan: Document that proposes strategies for employing the various elements of the marketing mix to achieve marketing objectives.

A **marketing plan** is a written document that proposes strategies for employing the various elements of the marketing mix to achieve marketing objectives. It analyzes the marketing situation, identifies the problems, outlines the marketing opportunities, sets the objectives, and proposes strategies and tactics to solve these problems and meet objectives. A marketing plan is developed and evaluated annually, although sections dealing with long-run goals might operate for a number of years. Some companies are finding that the marketplace changes so rapidly today that plans have to be updated more frequently than once a year—perhaps even quarterly.

To a large extent, the marketing plan parallels the business strategic plan and contains many of the same components. This is shown in Figure 7.2. For advertising managers, the most important part of the marketing plan is the marketing strategy. It links the overall strategic business plan with specific marketing programs, including advertising. Also, the marketing plan is able to draw on much of the necessary preliminary research that the business plan has already supplied. Therefore, the marketing plan can start cleanly with a statement of objectives. Assessment of the external and internal environments is done on an as-needed basis.

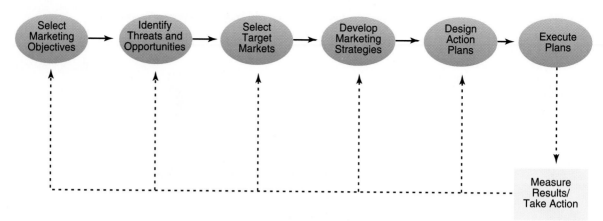

FIGURE 7.2

STEPS IN THE MARKETING PLAN

MARKETING OBJECTIVES

As indicated, the marketing planning process often begins with a selection of objectives. The objective may refer to a percentage of market share, unit sales, store traffic, or profit. In some companies the marketing planning process generates the company's corporate objectives; in others, marketing objectives are derived from the company's overall corporate objectives. In most successful companies, corporate objectives and marketing objectives influence each other.

Guided by the marketing objectives and market research, the marketer must then identify and evaluate market opportunities. Finding the cure for AIDS, for example, is a market opportunity for hundreds of pharmaceutical and research firms. Sometimes opportunities are identified by customers' complaints or suggestions. In the case of high-tech companies, opportunities are often little more than a new product looking for a problem. It took the marketing people at 3M over four years to find a profitable use for the adhesive that led to Post-it Notes. In either case, companies must have a mechanism for collecting information, examining trends, and assessing possible opportunities.

In order to capture more of the low-fat food market and continue the momentum from its highly successful launch, Nabisco's SnackWell's began launching a number of new products in 1995 and 1996 including breakfast snacks, chips, and chocolate yogurt. The chocolate yogurt won an award from the American Marketing Association for a new product that tapped into consumers' desires for healthy products that are "indulgent" and capitalized on the great-taste/no-guilt need.

MARKETING PROBLEMS AND OPPORTUNITIES

The heart of strategic planning is analysis—the process of figuring out what all the information and data mean. After you have studied what sometimes seems to be a mountain of information, the problems and opportunities begin to emerge. Spotting the key problem is often very difficult. It takes experience, marketing sophistication, an analytical mind, and a unique way of looking at things. It has been said that a well-defined problem is more than half of the solution. Obversely, an ill-defined problem may not be capable of being solved.

It has also been said that a problem is merely an opportunity in disguise. Some problems that are identified can be solved or overcome. Some have to be circumvented. Others can be turned into opportunities by those with creative minds.

Jergens used consumer research to understand consumers' gripes with standard soap. The company found that people don't like having to pick up a mushy bar out of the dish; they don't like the nasty film it leaves in the shower or bathtub; and they didn't like the way it dried out their skin. That created an opportunity for a new product, Jergens Body Shampoo, a creamy lather that rinses away easily and leaves the skin feeling moisturized.

SELECTING TARGET MARKETS

As we know, a *market segment* (the topic of Chapter 5) is a group of consumers having one or more similar characteristics. The dog food market, for example, is segmented according to age of the dog, its weight or breed, and activity level. Dog-owning consumers make choices among brands in these three or four segments. A company selects market segments that can be best served from a competitive point of view. The segments selected are the *target markets*.

MARKETING STRATEGIES

An important part of planning is identifying the key strategic decisions that will give the product or firm a competitive advantage in the marketplace. Strategy selection begins with several assumptions that the marketer makes about the market. These assumptions determine the relative emphasis to be given to each of the marketing mix components and lead to the next stage of the planning process.

The initial assumption deals with how the marketer views the composition and ensuing behavior of the marketplace. Two choices are evident. Either the marketer treats the market as *homogeneous*—that is, as a single, large unit—or as *heterogeneous*, as a group of separate, smaller parts known as segments. The former results in a market aggregation strategy, which calls for creating a single product supported by a single marketing program designed to reach as many customers as possible. Originally, Coke followed this single-product approach, until it was forced to consider segmentation. An assumption that the market contains much diversity, or is heterogeneous, results in a market segmentation strategy, which divides the market into several segments. Each segment tends to be homogeneous within itself in all significant aspects, and from these segments the marketer identifies, evaluates, and selects target markets. A company that uses this segmented approach aims to design products that match market demands and design advertising messages specifically aimed toward one or more target markets.

Regardless of whether the market is assumed to be homogeneous or heterogeneous, assumptions must be made about how to best differentiate the product. *Product differentiation* is twofold; it is a process, which consists of a series of strategic decisions, and it is a state or marketplace position in which the product offering is perceived by the consumer to differ from the competition. A product's perceived differences can be either physical or nonphysical product characteristics, including price. For many years, Miller Lite beer differentiated itself on two basic traits: "tastes great and less filling." Jell-O differentiates itself on the "fun" dimension. As a result, Jell-O also owns the "fun dessert" position in the minds of kids—it is perceived to be fun to eat.

Stated simply, *positioning* is how the marketer wants the consumer to view its product relative to the competition. Although product differentiation plays a role in creating a product position, product differences account for only part of a product's position. A positioning strategy also includes the manner in which a product's factors are combined, how they are communicated, and who communicates them. Under a new marketing chief in the mid-1990s, GM set about developing unique positions for each of its models. Oldsmobile becomes the model that Saturn buyers can step up to; Pontiac continues as GM's sport brand; Buick will compete strictly as an upscale sedan; Cadillac will become more of an import fighter in the luxury market to counter Lexus; GMC trucks will move to a more upscale position; and Saturn will continue as a cult brand that gains its loyalty from its value pricing and its strong customer relationships.

In order to develop specific action plans, each element of the marketing strategy must be dissected. Typically, at this stage, marketers specify plans for each aspect of the marketing mix. Simply using different proportions of these mix variables makes dramatic differences in marketing action programs possible. The goal is to design a marketing mix that will appeal to the target market and prove profitable, given the limitations imposed by available resources and the requirements of the marketing strategy.

EXECUTING PLANS

Implementing the typical marketing plan requires a great number of decisions. Making sure the product reaches the warehouse at the right time, that ads are run on schedule, and that salespeople receive the right support material represent just a sample of the details that must be tracked day by day, or even minute by minute. Poor execution has been the downfall of many excellent marketing plans. A case in point is Stouffer Foods Corporation's Right Course frozen dinner entrées. Relying heavily on its reputation for high quality, Stouffer decided to introduce an upscale, exotic set of offerings such as Chicken with Peanut Sauce and Fiesta Beef with Corn Pasta. These choices were made without any input from retailers. In addition, the advertising campaign didn't appear until four weeks after the products were introduced. The products did not sell well.

EVALUATING PLANS

Every marketing plan must include a control component that compares actual performance with planned performance. In most modern businesses, computerization allows access to several performance indicators that management can monitor daily or at any interval they choose. Usually, an annual review is a minimum. In addition to collecting performance data, managers must assess why these particular results have occurred. Finally, if the marketer determines that the gap between objectives and performance is significant enough, corrective action must be taken.

THE ADVERTISING PLAN

Advertising planning, which must dovetail with marketing planning, can occur at three levels. A firm may operate with an annual advertising plan. In addition to or instead of an annual advertising plan, a firm may develop a campaign plan that is more tightly focused on solving a particular marketing communication problem. Finally, a company may put together a copy strategy for an individual ad that runs independently of a campaign. The advertising plan and the campaign plan are similar in outline and in structure. The following discussion focuses on the elements of an advertising plan or a campaign plan. These are the responsibility of the account manager (see Weaver profile).

Advertising Plan: A plan that proposes strategies for targeting the audience, presenting the advertising message, and implementing media.

An **advertising plan** matches the right audience to the right message and presents it in the right medium to reach that audience. In other words, three basic elements summarize the heart of advertising strategy:

- *Targeting the audience:* Who are you trying to reach?
- *Message strategy:* What do you want to say to them?
- *Media strategy:* When and where will you reach them?

PETER WEAVER, ASSISTANT ACCOUNT EXECUTIVE, *Wunderman Cato Johnson Worldwide, New York City, New York*

Advertising is for people with the intuition, imagination, and spirit to position products, services, and ideologies in the forefront of consumers' minds. To fulfill this responsibility, advertising agencies recruit account managers with the facility for both the management and creative sides of the business: professionals with exceptional adaptability and communication skills, who can perceive what is important and interesting for solving problems and fulfilling objectives.

Before graduating in May 1996 from Boston University College of Communication, I had the opportunity to work with professors with diverse industry experience—account planning, media, account management, new media, and creative, and with students with various internship experiences from around the globe. Exposure to a wealth of ideas helped me to make sense of my marketing experiences and to position myself for postgraduate employment at an advertising agency.

I tested my first marketing ideas while in high school, when I launched Pasta Fantastico. Monitoring the craze in the general market, I decided to produce homemade fettuccini, linguine, angel hair, and ravioli pastas made from organically grown ingredients. I produced, packaged, and distributed my product to K.C. Becker's Deli Depot, a local deli with significant lunch and early-dinner business. While my effort was successful, what I learned about consumer behavior and perceptions was most helpful in my next endeavor.

During my sophomore-year summer internship at Smith Barney, a worldwide financial services firm in Washington, D.C., I learned how to formulate a segmentation strategy for outbound telemarketing initiatives. Writing telephone scripts and cold-calling prospects was part of my daily routine, along with researching investment opportunities for my brokers' clients.

The following summer, I was reacquainted with Raimund Stieger, a Washington metropolitan-area celebrity chef for whom I had apprenticed during high school. He had opened a contemporary seafood restaurant in the suburb of Fairfax called Fish Stories, and he needed some promotional support to increase the level of business. I began by outlining promotional opportunities and devising a communications plan. We utilized "above-the-line" media, such as radio and newspaper print ads, to showcase Raimund's talents and the restaurant's nouveau cuisine and "below-the-line" media, such as direct mail and personal appearances, to create awareness for special events and copromotions with our vendors. Raimund conducted food shows at Williams Sonoma, a chain of home-cooking–goods stores, and hosted cooking show programs on both spot and cable television. This exposure created awareness, which resulted in a feature article in *The Washington Post Magazine*, which helped increase business by over 150 percent in just the first two weeks after it ran.

I spent the summer before my senior year in Belgrade, Yugoslavia, interning for SMS Bates Saatchi & Saatchi Advertising. I had rotations in the account management, account planning, media, and creative departments, learning the unique chemistry inherent in the hypergrowth Balkans marketplace. My time was spent under the tutelage of Dragan Sakan, the agency's founder, with whom I worked for Johnson & Johnson, Procter & Gamble, and a host of roster accounts. We represented our clients throughout the 14 markets in the Balkans, each hosting indigenous social elements, which were often in contrast to their neighbors.

After returning to Boston University, I decided to approach a local computer hardware broker in South Boston about repositioning his company as a computer solutions provider, focused on platform-specific engineering and consulting. As we came to an agreement, I founded Idols & Friends Communications, a student-run communications consultancy. Because our collective advertising experience was so limited, we approached professors from Boston University College of Communication and John Connors at Hill, Holliday Advertising in Boston. Together we modeled a relationship in which students, with the aid of academia and Hill Holliday, aided a Boston-area small business. Our efforts yielded a World Wide Web site and direct-mail campaign that increased our client's market share and lifted employee morale with a strong corporate identity.

After graduation and the project's completion, I left for Cape Town, South Africa, to visit with several agencies. There was a boundless spirit that resonated in creative work throughout the country. I met with Ogilvy & Mather, BBDO, Young & Rubicam, Saatchi & Saatchi, J. Walter Thompson, and TBWA account managers to discuss employment opportunities. Due to the foreign exchange rate and difficulties in obtaining a work permit, I returned stateside and moved to New York City.

Here, in New York, I work for Wunderman Cato Johnson, an "action marketing" integrated communications agency that creates and manages profitable relationships, leading to increased sales and long-term customer equity for its clients. Using programs with built-in feedback, WCJ effects changes in consumer behavior where results are measurable and for which the agency stands accountable. Because the accounts I work on are fully integrated across all communication disciplines, it calls for my constant interaction among Y&R Inc. agencies to ensure utilization of integrated marketing solutions to meet our clients' objectives. As an assistant account executive, I work on AT&T WorldNet Service, Sears, United States Postal Service, and the New Business Team. My accounts span both public and private media, which is giving me invaluable exposure to this fascinating segment of the industry.

Nominated by Professor Dale Brill, Boston University

The outline that guides the development of an annual or campaign advertising plan is similar in some ways to that for a marketing plan. There is a situation analysis section and objectives and strategies are identified, for example, in both marketing and advertising plans. The most important differences are found in the sections that focus on message and media strategies. A typical advertising or campaign plan can be outlined as follows:

- **SITUATION ANALYSIS:**
  The advertising problem
  Advertising opportunities
- **KEY STRATEGY DECISIONS:**
  Advertising objectives
  Target audience
  Competitive product advantage
  Product image and personality
  Product position
- **THE CREATIVE PLAN**
- **THE MEDIA PLAN**
- **THE PROMOTION PLAN**
  Sales promotion
  Public relations
- **IMPLEMENTATION AND EVALUATION**
- **BUDGET**

SITUATION ANALYSIS

The first step in developing an advertising plan (as well as a marketing plan) is not planning but *backgrounding*—in other words, researching and reviewing the current state of the business in terms of its communication implications. This section details the search for and analysis of important information and trends affecting the marketplace, the competition, consumer behavior, the company itself, and the product or brand. The key word in the title of this section is *analysis*, and that means making sense of all the data collected and figuring out what the information means for the future success of the product or brand.

PROBLEMS AND OPPORTUNITIES

As in business and marketing planning, one way to analyze the situation is in terms of the problems that can be identified and the opportunities that can be created or maximized. Advertising exists to solve some kind of communication problem that affects the successful marketing of a product. Analyzing the situation and identifying the problem that can be solved with an advertising message are at the heart of strategic planning.

Different agencies employ different strategies. For example, BBDO uses a process called "Problem Detection" as the basis of its strategy building.[2] Problem Detection takes the question directly to consumers to find out what bothers them about the product or product category. DDB Needham searches for "Barriers to Purchase."[3] These barriers are reasons why people are not buying any or enough of a product. The American Dairy Association asked DDB Needham to find out why the consumption of cheese was declining. A study identified the major barriers to increased consumption and eventually directed the agency toward the one barrier that was most easily correctable through advertising: the absence of simple cheese recipes for homemakers.

[2]E.E. Norris, "Seek Out the Consumer's Problem," *Advertising Age* (March 17, 1975):43–44.
[3]Research for R.O.I.: 1987 Communications Workshop, DDB Needham, Chicago (April 10, 1987).

Flowers Direct is a long-distance floral delivery service that competes with FTD and 1-800-FLOWERS, both of which, it was discovered, have a major weakness that Flowers Direct can exploit. Flowers Direct connects the caller with a florist in the area where the customer is sending the flowers rather than placing the order with a neighborhood florist who then handles the communication. The advertising challenge was to explain this problem to the consumer and then capitalize on Flower Direct's opportunity to create a competitive advantage.

Advertising can only solve message-related problems such as image, attitude, perception, and knowledge or information. It cannot solve problems related to the price of the product or its availability. A message can speak, however, to the perception that the price is too high. It can also portray a product with limited distribution as exclusive. In other words, although advertising does not determine the actual price or availability of a product, it can affect the way price and availability are perceived by consumers.

ADVERTISING STRATEGY DECISIONS

There is a group of key decisions that is crucial to the development of advertising strategy: setting objectives and identifying the target audience, competitive advantage, product position, and establishing a brand image and brand personality.

ADVERTISING OBJECTIVES

The statement of advertising objectives evolves directly from the problem and opportunity analysis and answers the questions: What does this advertising message need to accomplish? What effect does it need to have on its audience? Basically advertising seeks to establish, modify, or reinforce attitudes, causing consumers to try a new product, buy more of it, or switch brands. Brand advertising seeks to create an image or personality for a product and carve out a unique position for it.

Hierarchy of Effects: A set of consumer responses that moves from the least serious, involved, or complex up through the most serious, involved, or complex.

Models of effects help analyze message impact and structure objectives as a series of steps called a **hierarchy of effects.**[4] One classic approach, the AIDA model, describes the impact on consumers as beginning with *attention*, then moving to *interest*, then *desire*, and finally *action*. A variation is a model developed by Colley, called the DAGMAR model (Defining Advertising Goals for Measured Advertising Results), which begins with *awareness*, moves to *comprehension*, then *conviction*, and ends with *action*.[5] It works like this: If you have skin allergies and Procter & Gamble advertises a new detergent for people with sensitive skin, the ad will probably catch your attention—you are aware of a possible desire for the product. If you are the person who buys detergent for your household, then you may find yourself interested in the idea of this new formulation—you have comprehended its value. You may want to try it and, therefore, when you receive a coupon in the mail, you may respond by picking up a trial package when you are at the store; in other words, you are spurred to action.

As Figure 7.3 demonstrates, simpler effects, such as awareness, are relatively easy to create and get high levels of response. The more complex the effect, the lower the level of response. In other words, a lot of people may be aware of the product, but far fewer will actually try it. The hierarchy model illustrates the relative impact of these various effects with the simplest, but broadest, impact at the bottom and the most complex, but smallest impact, at the top.

Michael Ray developed the *think-feel-do* model of message effects, which presumes that we approach a purchase situation using a sequence of responses.[6] In

[4]John D. Leckenby, "Conceptual Foundations for Copytesting Research," Advertising Working Papers, No. 2 (February 1976).

[5]Russell Colley, *Defining Advertising Goals for Measured Advertising Results* (New York: Association of National Advertisers, 1961).

[6]Michael L. Ray, "Communication and the Hierarchy of Effects," in *New Models for Mass Communication Research*, P. Clarke, ed. (Beverly Hills, CA: Sage Publications, 1973):147–75.

FIGURE 7.3

SETTING OBJECTIVES USING A
HIERARCHY-OF-EFFECTS MODEL

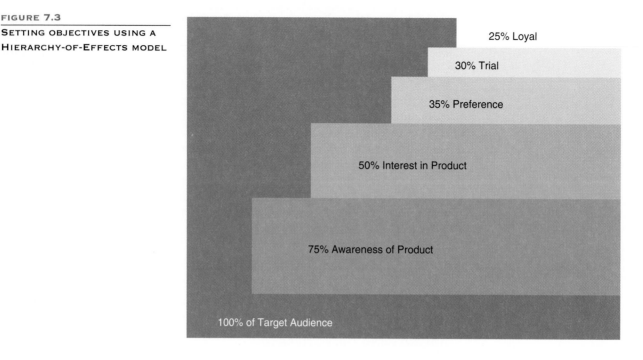

other words, we *(think)* about something, then we form an opinion or attitude about it *(feel)*, and finally we take action and try it or buy it *(do)*. This model identifies three categories of effects called *cognitive* (mental or rational), *affective* (emotional), and *conative* (decision or action). Robert C. Lavidge and Gary A. Steiner associate these categories with the hierarchy of effects in the model depicted in Figure 7.4.[7]

The think-feel-do model is also called the *high-involvement model* because it depicts a series of standard responses typically found with consumers who are ac-

[7]Robert C. Lavidge and Gary A. Steiner, "A Model for Predictive Measurements of Advertising Effectiveness," *Journal of Marketing* (October 1961):59–62.

FIGURE 7.4

THE THINK-FEEL-DO MODEL AR-
RAYED AS A HIERARCHY

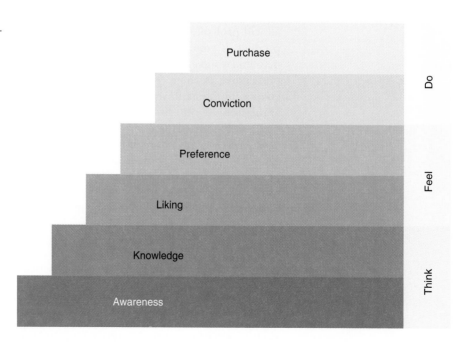

tive participants in the process of gathering information and making a decision; they are "active" thinkers. This standard hierarchy is likely to be found with product categories and situations where there is a need for information, such as high-priced or major purchases, or where there is a lot of product differentiation, as in industrial products and consumer durables. This type of advertising usually provides many product details and is very informative.

In contrast, the *low-involvement model* changes the order of responses to *think-do-feel*, with the idea that consumers learn about a product, try it, and then form an opinion. This situation occurs when there is little interest in the product or when there is minimal difference between the products, requiring little decision making. It also describes impulse purchasing. A third variation is the *do-feel-think* model, which explains how people try something and learn from the experience. It is called a *rationalization model* because consumers typically select from several alternatives and then rationalize their decision by developing strong positive feelings about the product.

TARGETING THE AUDIENCE

Target Audience: People who can be reached with a certain advertising medium and a particular message.

Advertising identifies a **target audience,** people who can be reached with a certain advertising medium and a particular message. The target audience can be equivalent to a target market, but it often includes people other than prospects, such as those who influence the purchase. For example, the target audience for an over-the-counter diet program might include doctors, pharmacists, dietitians, and government agencies concerned with health and nutrition, as well as consumers.

Target audiences are described in terms of their *demographic categories.* Because these categories often overlap, the process of describing an audience is also the process of narrowing the targeting. For example, you might use such descriptors as women 25 to 35 and suburban mall shoppers. These two categories would overlap because a certain percentage of women 25 to 35 are also in the suburban mall shopper category. Each time you add a descriptor, the targeted audience gets smaller because the group is more tightly defined. This kind of analysis lets the advertising planner pinpoint the target and zero in on the most responsive audience. Figure 7.5 illustrates how these descriptors zero in on a target. Demographic descriptions like these are particularly important to media planners who are comparing the characteristics of a targeted audience with the characteristics of the viewers, listeners, or readers of a particular medium.

FIGURE 7.5

TARGETING INVOLVES THE USE OF OVERLAPPING DESCRIPTORS TO IDENTIFY THE MOST RECEPTIVE AUDIENCE.

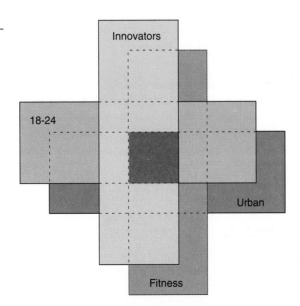

Audiences are also profiled in terms of the personality and lifestyle of the typical audience member. The attempt here is to identify a real person and make that person come to life for the creative people, who then try to write believable messages that will appeal to this person. For this reason, advertising planners usually redefine the target as a **profile** of a typical user of the product. Writers then associate that general profile with someone they know. Creatives have a hard time writing moving messages to a pile of statistics. They can write much more easily and believably to someone they know who fits the description.

The highly successful Red Dog beer launch was based upon an understanding of the personality and style of postmodern, young adult males. Using a broad, infectious humor the brand has made beer marketing fun again and reached out to the skeptical advertising-wary consumer of the 1990s with its antihero bulldog and the line, "Be your own dog."

Profile: A composite description of a target audience employing personality and lifestyle characteristics.

PRODUCT FEATURES AND COMPETITIVE ADVANTAGE

An important step in figuring out competitive advantage is to analyze your product in comparison to your competitors' products. **Feature analysis** is an easy way to structure this analysis. First make a chart for your product and competitors' products listing each product's relevant features. For example, taste is important for sodas, horsepower and mileage are important for cars, and trendiness is important for fashion watches. Next evaluate the lists in terms of how important each feature is to the target audience (based on primary research) and then evaluate how well the products perform on that feature. Your competitive advantage, as illustrated in Table 7.1, lies in that area where you have a strong feature that is important to the target and where at the same point your competition is weak. (See Ad 7.2.)

Feature Analysis: A comparison of your product's features against the features of competing products.

BRAND PERSONALITY

Creating a brand personality for a potato might sound like an impossible challenge, but that actually has been accomplished by Idaho Potatoes. The Idaho Potato Commission has been so successful that, while most people are aware of Idaho Potatoes and associate them with the highest quality, the Idaho Potato has almost gone generic. That is, most people refer to russet potatoes as Idaho Potatoes, regardless of what state they are grown in. However, the Idaho Potato® name is a federal registered trademark of the Idaho Potato Commission. In an award-winning campaign, the commission has taught consumers that Idaho Potatoes are unique and to look for the "Grown in Idaho" seal to ensure they are getting genuine Idaho Potatoes.

POSITIONING STRATEGIES

Positioning is a marketing strategy but the way it is created is through advertising. How a product is perceived by consumers relative to its competition is called **positioning.** Midwest Express Airlines, a national airline offering jet service to over 20 major business destinations from its bases of operations in Milwaukee and

Positioning: The way in which a product is perceived in the marketplace by consumers.

TABLE 7.1	FEATURE ANALYSIS				
FEATURE	IMPORTANCE TO PROSPECT	PRODUCT PERFORMANCE			
		YOURS	X	Y	Z
Price	1	+	−	−	+
Quality	4	−	+	−	+
Style	2	+	−	+	−
Availability	3	−	+	−	−
Durability	5	−	+	+	+

AD 7.2

TO TRY TO CREATE A POINT OF DIFFERENCE BETWEEN UNITED AND ITS OTHER U.S. COMPETITORS, THE AIRLINE ANNOUNCED THAT IT WAS PROVIDING SHOWERS FOR ITS FIRST- AND CONNOISSEUR-CLASS PASSENGERS.

B.Y.O. rubber ducky. Arrivals by United.®

Now First and Connoisseur Class® passengers on our overnight International and Transcontinental flights can refresh with a nice hot shower upon landing. And enjoy the use of valet services, business conveniences and other amenities. Some of the extras, however, are up to you. Arrivals by United.® Now available in 16 destinations throughout Europe, Asia and Latin America, and 8 locations throughout the U.S. Come fly our friendly skies.

UNITED AIRLINES
*Available only for paid and Mileage Plus® award travelers.

Omaha, has used a business strategy that offers comfort and luxury—two-across, wide leather seats, gourmet food, and truly friendly service—at a time when other airlines are cutting back on service and crowding in passengers. However, this "Best Care in the Air" theme did not position the airline completely, and research found that consumers thought the airline was more expensive at a time when the recession made travelers more price sensitive. A new theme, "Best Care. Same Fare," was implemented in the early 1990s in an award-winning campaign that extended the old position to include value as well as quality service.

Establishing as well as changing positions require a tremendous advertising effort. Both Marlboro cigarettes and Miller beer were originally sold to women at one time. Both were later repositioned as "macho" products through extensive and costly advertising campaigns, although recently the audience for beer is being widened to once again include women.

PERCEPTUAL MAPS

Perceptual Map: A map that shows where consumers locate various products in the category in terms of several important features.

Positioning research begins with the feature analysis described previously. From this research you should be able to describe the most relevant attributes of your product. You can then create a map of the marketplace that locates the position of your product relative to the positions of all the competitors. A sample two-dimensional (using two attributes) **perceptual map** based on the preceding feature analysis appears in Figure 7.6.

FIGURE 7.6

A TWO-DIMENSIONAL PERCEP-
TUAL MAP THAT EXAMINES TWO
PRODUCT ATTRIBUTES, PRICE
AND STYLE, ON A 1—10 SCALE.

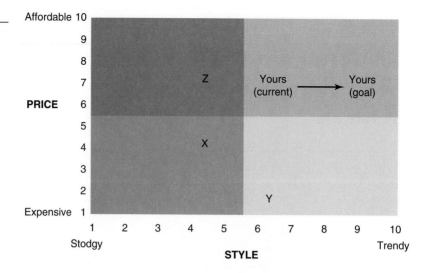

FIGURE 7.6

A TWO-DIMENSIONAL PERCEP-
TUAL MAP THAT EXAMINES TWO
PRODUCT ATTRIBUTES, PRICE
AND STYLE, ON A 1—10 SCALE.

Strategically, the first step is to identify the current position of the product, if one exists, using some form of perceptual mapping. For a new product, and for some existing ones, a position must be established. For ongoing product lines, the decision is either to reinforce a current position or to move it.

IMPLEMENTATION AND EVALUATION

The last section of an advertising plan contains details of the implementation strategy, including scheduling and determining the budget, as well as techniques for evaluating the success of the advertising plan. We will talk in more detail about schedules in the media-planning and media-buying chapters (Chapters 9 and 12). Evaluation is based on how well the plan meets its objectives; a variety of research techniques can be used to monitor effectiveness. One specific type of control is copy testing, a scientific evaluation of the effectiveness of an advertisement. Copy testing is discussed in more detail in Chapter 21.

THE ADVERTISING BUDGET

The advertising budget is established by the company and is usually broken out from the overall marketing communication budget in the marketing plan. In other words, a certain percentage of the *marketing budget* is allocated to marketing communication, and within that budget a certain percentage is allocated to advertising. Budget decisions are based on the emphasis given to marketing communication within the marketing mix and to advertising within the marketing communication program.

The budget level is important in terms of an advertising or campaign plan because it determines how much advertising the company can afford. In other words, a $50,000 budget will only stretch so far and will probably not be enough in most markets to cover the costs of television advertising. In addition to television costs, the budget level also determines how many targets and multiple campaign plans a company or brand can support. McDonald's, for example, can easily carry on multiple campaigns designed to reach different target audiences. Certain types of advertisers—industrial and business-to-business, for example—typically operate on smaller advertising budgets than do consumer packaged-goods companies. Their media choices and narrow targeting strategies reflect their budget and these companies often rely more on direct mail, trade publications, and telemarketing for their advertising.

The big question at each of these levels (marketing mix, marketing communication mix) is: How much should we spend?[8]

HISTORICAL METHOD

History is the source for a very common budgeting method. For example, a budget may simply be based on last year's budget with a percentage increase for inflation or some other marketplace factor.

TASK-OBJECTIVE METHOD

Task-Objective Method: A budgeting method that builds a budget by asking what it will cost to achieve the stated objectives.

The **task-objective method** is probably the most common method for determining the budget level. This method looks at the objectives set for each activity and determines the cost of accomplishing each objective; what will it cost to make 50 percent of the people in your market aware of this product? How many people do you have to reach and how many times? What would be the necessary media levels and expenses?

PERCENT-OF-SALES METHOD

Percent-of-Sales Method: A technique for computing the budget level that is based on the relationship between cost of advertising and total sales.

The **percent-of-sales method** compares the total sales with the total advertising (or promotion) budget during the previous year or the average of several years to compute a percentage. This technique can also be used across an industry to compare the expenditures of different product categories on advertising.

For example, if a company had sales figures of $5 million last year and an advertising budget of $1 million, then the ratio of advertising to sales would be 20 percent. If the marketing manager predicts sales of $6 million for next year, then the ad budget would be $1.2 million. The following explains how the percent of sales is computed and applied to a budget.

$$\text{Step 1:} \quad \frac{\text{Past advertising dollars}}{\text{Past sales}} = \text{\% of sales}$$

$$\text{Step 2:} \quad \text{\% of sales} \times \text{Next year's sales forecast} = \text{New advertising budget}$$

COMPETITIVE METHODS

Budgeting often takes into account the competitive situation and uses competitors' budgets as benchmarks. *Competitive parity* budgeting relates the amount invested in advertising to the product's share of market. In order to understand this method, you need to understand the *share-of-mind* concept, which suggests that the advertiser's share of advertising—that is, the advertiser's media presence—affects the share of attention the brand will receive, and that, in turn, affects the share of market the brand can obtain. The relationship can be depicted as follows:

$$\frac{\text{Share of}}{\text{media voice}} = \frac{\text{Share of}}{\text{consumer mind}} = \frac{\text{Share of}}{\text{market}}$$

You should keep in mind, however, that the relationships depicted here are used only as a rule of thumb. The actual relationship between share of media voice—an indication of advertising expenditures—and share of mind or share of market depends to a great extent on factors such as the creativity of the message and the amount of clutter in the marketplace. In other words, a simple increase in the share of voice does not guarantee an equal increase in share of market.

For example, Jolly Rancher is David taking on Goliath in the hard candy segment, where Life Savers has 85 percent of the market and a 99 percent share of voice. In other words it has done more than dominate the market, it has owned the media. In an early 1990s campaign that also won an Effie award, Jolly Rancher set out to overtake Life Savers in the rolled candy business. In one year, from 1990 to 1991, it moved its share of voice from 1 percent to 21 percent and gained a 39 percent market share increase as a result.

---

[8]John J. Burnett, *Promotion Management*, 3rd ed. (Boston: Houghton Mifflin, 1993).

THE CREATIVE PLAN AND COPY STRATEGY

So far we've been discussing advertising planning in terms of an annual plan or a campaign plan, but planning goes on at another level, too. A copy strategy can also be developed for an individual advertisement, and this document focuses directly on the message and the logic behind its development.

These plans go by various names—*creative* or *copy platform, creative work plan,* or *creative blueprint.* Not all agencies use such a document, but all copywriters work from some kind of systematic analysis of the problem to be solved. A **creative platform** is simply a way to structure this kind of analysis. It also serves as a guide to others involved in developing the advertisement so that everyone is working with the same understanding of the message strategy.

Most creative platforms combine the basic advertising decisions—problems, objectives, and target markets—with the critical elements of the sales message strategy, which include the selling premise, or main idea, and details about how the idea will be executed. Although outlines differ from agency to agency, the creative platform will include some or all of the following strategic decisions.

Creative Platform: A document that outlines the message strategy decisions behind an individual ad.

MESSAGE STRATEGIES

Advertisements can sell the product in a *generic* way, a strategy which works only when the product dominates the market, or they can sell the *brand,* a strategy which is usually considered to be more effective. Goodyear, for example, moved from its generic "Take Me Home" campaign to one that more aggressively set the brand apart from others. The ads end with a slogan that focuses on brand identification: "Nobody Fits You Like Goodyear."

Another message option considers the information content of the advertisement relative to its associational or emotional import. Information advertising is usually straightforward, fact filled, and often focused on news. This approach works for high-involvement products, or in a case where consumers are searching for information to make a decision. That situation, however, is not as common as the low-involvement situation in which consumers are making decisions about products that need minimal information and spend much less time in decision making. In those situations, advertising is more likely to focus on establishing an image or touching an emotion.

SELLING PREMISES

Every salesperson has his or her own idea of how to approach the prospect. Different people and different situations require different strategies, and salespeople are generally more comfortable with certain approaches than with others. The same is true in advertising. The various approaches to the logic of the sales message are called **selling premises.** The most common premises are categorized as either product centered or prospect centered.

Selling Premises: The sales logic behind an advertising message.

PRODUCT AND PROSPECT STRATEGIES

Product-centered strategies refer to advertisements that focus on the product itself. These ads look at the attributes, also called *features,* of the product and build a selling message around them; an example is the Jolly Rancher ad that dramatizes the candies' flavors. A **claim** is a statement about performance: how long the product lasts, how much it cleans, how little energy it uses. Torture tests, competitive tests, and before-and-after demonstrations can generate particularly strong claims. Often a scientifically conducted test provides support for the claim.

Claim: A statement about the product's performance.

Probably the least effective message strategy is one that focuses on the company and emphasizes the company's point of view, goals, and pronouncements with an overuse of the pronoun *we*. This kind of copy is boastful and egotistical. When you see copy with pompous headlines like "We're #1," "We've been in business for 50 years," or "We're reaching out in new directions," you know you are reading *brag-and-boast* advertising.

Prospect-centered strategies are very much in tune with the consumer-oriented marketing concept, which focuses on needs and wants rather than on what the company can produce. A number of message strategies are built on prospect-centered messages such as benefits, promises, reasons why, and unique selling propositions (USPs).

BENEFITS

In benefit strategies, the product is promoted on the basis of what it can do for the consumers. To develop a benefit strategy, you must be able to turn a feature or product attribute into a **benefit**. (See Ad 7.3.) Take a common product, like the shoe you're wearing. Ask yourself what each feature of that shoe does. Look at the sole—besides keeping your feet off the ground, what else does it do for you? Composition leather, for example, means it is durable and long-wearing; textured rubber may mean nonslip; different types of soles have shock-absorption features built in to help diminish the punishment of jogging or aerobics.

The following formula can be used to develop a benefit. First, identify a feature, and then tell what it means to you. Fill in the blanks and you will have developed a benefit statement.

The _(feature)_ feature is important because it will

do _____ for me.
                (benefit)

Benefits: Statements about what the product can do for the user.

AD 7.3

GM'S NEW ELECTRIC CAR IS A PRODUCT WITH A VERY DISTINCTIVE PRODUCT FEATURE—IT DOESN'T NEED GAS. TRANSLATING THE FEATURE INTO A BENEFIT, HOWEVER, IS A BIT MORE DIFFICULT. THE CAR'S LAUNCH AD TRIED TO EXPLAIN WHAT THAT FEATURE MEANT BY POINTING TO ITS LACK OF NOISE.

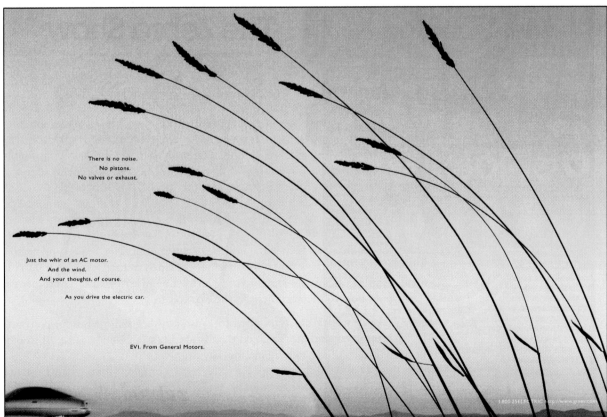

There is no noise.
No pistons.
No valves or exhaust.

Just the whir of an AC motor.
And the wind.
And your thoughts, of course.

As you drive the electric car.

EV1. From General Motors.

PRINCIPLE Focus on benefits, not features. Explain what the product can do for the prospect.

Note that the benefit is strictly in the mind of the consumer, not in the product. It is subjective. Some sample benefit statements are:

- Crest's stannous fluoride means you don't have to worry about cavities.
- Du Pont's cordura nylon means backpacks can be light and yet tough.
- Noxzema's Clear Pink formula brings deep cleaning to sensitive skin; its Clear Green formula brings deep cleaning to oily skin.
- Hampton shoe's Bio Glide provides extra foot stability in each phase of the walking motion.

PROMISES

A benefit statement that looks to the future is called a *promise*. It says something will happen if you use the advertised product. For example, if you use a certain type of toothpaste, then your breath will smell better, or your teeth will be whiter, or you will have extra cavity protection. Hershey's used a promise strategy to reinvigorate sales for its cocoa, which had picked up the image of being high in fat and bad for you.

To develop a promise, use the following formula. First, specify how you use the product, and then follow with a statement of what it will do for you.

When I use _____ *(product)* _____, I will get _____ *(what benefit)* _____.

As you can see from the formula, what you promise is a benefit, so the two are related. Following are several examples of promises:

When I use Dial deodorant soap, I will feel more confident than when I use other brands.

When I take Amtrak, I will be more comfortable, better treated, and more valued (than when I take a plane).

When I take Excedrin for my headache, I will be better able to cope with the stresses in my life.

When I stay at Ramada, I will have fewer hassles than when I stay at other hotels.

REASON WHY

Reason Why: A statement that explains why the feature will benefit the user.

A **reason why** you should buy something is another form of a benefit statement. It differs from a promise in that it clearly states a reason for the benefit gained. In many benefit strategies this reason is unstated, implied, or assumed. A reason-why statement is based on logic and reasoning. The development of this form is highly rational. A reason-why statement usually begins with a benefit statement, then follows with a "because" statement that provides the "proof" or "support."

An ad for Neutrogena Shampoo that asks, "Why your favorite shampoo will work better if you stop using it for 14 days," is an example of a reason-why ad. The copy goes on to provide all the reasons set up in the headline. To provide even more of an impression that the ad is fact based, it is designed to appear like the editorial matter in the women's magazines in which it appears. The following are some sample reason-why statements. Notice how the "because" statement is used to give support to the argument in the examples.

- When I take Amtrak from New York to Washington, I will feel more comfortable, better treated, and more valued than when I take a plane because Amtrak is a more civilized and less dehumanizing way to travel.
- When I use Dial deodorant soap, I will be more confident than when I use another brand because Dial has twice as much deodorant ingredient as the next-best-selling brand.

UNIQUE SELLING PROPOSITION

Unique Selling Proposition: A benefit statement about a feature that is both unique to the product and important to the user.

The concept of a **unique selling proposition,** or USP, is based on a benefit statement that is both unique to the product and important to the user. The heart of a USP is a proposition, which is a promise that states a specific and unique benefit you will get from using the product. If the product has a special formula, design, or feature, particularly if protected by a patent or copyright, then you are assured that it is truly unique. This is why a USP is frequently marked by the use of an "only" statement, either outright or implied. For example, the following is a USP taken from the ad copy for a camera:

> USP: This camera is the only one that lets you automatically zoom in and out to follow the action of the central figure.

SUPPORT

Regardless of which selling premise an advertiser uses, you should be able to analyze the logic behind the premise. Most selling premises demand facts, proof, or explanations to support the claim, benefit, reason, or promise. Support may be more important than any other part of the message strategy because it lends credibility to the premise. If the message is to be believable or have impact, it must have support. An example of a USP and its support is this excerpt from the strategy statement for Hubba Bubba bubble gum:

> USP: Hubba Bubba is the only chewing gum that lets you blow great big bubbles that won't stick to your face.
>
> Support: Hubba Bubba uses a unique and exclusive nonstick formula.

EXECUTION DETAILS

Execution of the strategy is the heart of the creative process in advertising. Developing the execution involves coming up with a creative idea variously called the *big idea*, or the *theme*, or the *creative concept*. This is where the creative people take the bare bones of a strategy statement and express that strategy in a way that is captivating and exciting. The execution is the creative team's "imaginative leap" that produces outstanding advertising that is both attention-getting and memorable. Creativity is discussed in detail in Chapter 13.

The details of the execution—how the advertisement looks and "feels"—are discussed in chapters on creating ads for various types of media (Chapters 14 through 17). What we are talking about here is the tone of the ad—is it serious, funny, concerned, or sympathetic?

Before you can begin to understand how this creative process works, however, you must know how advertising works, which is the subject of the next chapter.

SUMMARY

- Advertising messages are formulated to accomplish specific objectives, and then strategies are developed specifically to achieve these objectives. This is accomplished through strategic planning.
- Strategic planning is the process of determining objectives, deciding on strategies, and implementing tactics.

- Planning is usually a three-tiered operation containing interrelated operations: the business strategic plan, functional plans, and advertising plans.
- The business plan relates to a particular company division or strategic business unit. It begins with the mission statement and is followed by an analysis

of the external and internal environment, goal formulation, strategy formulation, and program formulation.

- A marketing plan (functional level) proposes strategies for employing the various elements of the marketing mix to achieve marketing objectives. It parallels the business plan. Its parts include selection of marketing objectives, identification of threats and opportunities, selection of target markets, development of marketing strategies, design of action plans, and evaluation of results.

- An advertising plan matches the right audience to the right message and presents the message in the right medium to reach the audience.

- A typical advertising plan includes the following components: situation analysis (problems and opportunities), key strategic decisions (objectives, target audience, competitive advantage, product image, product position), the creative plan, the media plan, the promotion plan, implementation and evaluation, and budgeting.

- The creative plan includes copy strategies that are used for individual ads.

- Message strategies determine what is going to be said about the product and how. This is reflected by the selling premise (sales logic). Possible premises include benefit, promise, reason why, and unique selling proposition.

QUESTIONS

1. What do advertisers mean by *strategy?* What are the key considerations in an advertising strategy?

2. Think of a product you have purchased recently. How was it advertised? Which strategies can you discern in the advertising? Did the advertising help to convince you to purchase the product? Why or why not?

3. Day-Flo products sold 400,000 units in 1993. The total category sales (all competitors) for 1993 was 3.5 million units. What was Day-Flo's share of sales in 1993? In 1994 Day-Flo's objective is to increase unit sales by 15 percent; projections for total category sales are estimated at 10 percent. If these projections prove to be correct, what would Day-Flo's share of the market be at the end of 1994?

4. Advertising strategies are particularly sensitive to marketers who follow benefit-segmentation targeting. If you were marketing a new line of denim jeans for women, what are some of the logical benefit segments that consumer research would identify? How would advertising creative strategy shift according to segment priorities? Be as specific as possible.

5. The following is a brief excerpt from Luna Pizza's situation analysis for 1993. Luna is a regional producer of frozen pizza. Its only major competitor is Brutus Bros. Estimate next year's advertising budgets for Luna under each of the following circumstances:

A. Luna follows a historical method by spending 40 cents per unit sold in advertising with a 5 percent increase for inflation.

B. Luna follows a method of a fixed percentage of projected sales dollars, using 7.0 percent.

C. Luna follows a share-of-voice method. Brutus is expected to use 6 percent of sales for its advertising budget in 1994.

	ACTUAL LAST YEAR	ESTIMATED NEXT YEAR
Units sold	120,000	185,000
$ sales	420,000	580,000
Brutus $ sales	630,000	830,000

6. A key to marketing advertising strategy is the ability to convert attributes into customer-oriented benefits. Look at these attributes for an automobile for the future and change them to benefit statements.

A. The "V" car computer-directed braking system that senses the exact pedal pressure needed for every road surface condition.

B. The "V" has a special battery with a separate section that is climate insulated against any temperature extreme.

C. The "V" has a programmed memory for the driver's seat that automatically positions height, distance from pedals, and steering wheel for each user.

SUGGESTED CLASS PROJECT

Select two print ads—one for a consumer product and one business-to-business. Working from the ad, determine the selling premise, the product position, the product image, the competitive advantage, and the specific target audience. What were the objectives? Were they achieved? Determine where the strategy was clear and where it was unclear.

FURTHER READINGS

Aaker, David, Rajeev Batra, and John G. Myers, *Advertising Management*, 4th ed. (Upper Saddle River, NJ: Prentice Hall, 1992).

Burnett, John J., *Promotion Management* (Boston: Houghton Mifflin Company, 1993).

Engel, James F., Martin R. Warshaw, and Thomas C. Kinnear, *Promotional Strategy*, 8th ed. (Homewood, IL: Irwin, 1993).

Schultz, Don E., and Stanley I. Tannenbaum, *Essentials of Advertising Strategy*, 2nd ed. (Lincolnwood, IL: NTC Business Books, 1988).

How do you go about selling an electric car to consumers who are in love with their big gas-guzzlers? General Motors launched its EV1 in December 1996 with help from Hal Riney & Partners, the advertising agency that helped revolutionize car marketing with its work on the Saturn launch.

GM's electric car is a tough sell. It goes only 70 to 90 miles before requiring 3 to 12 hours of recharging. It's smaller than the average economy car. And you can't buy it, you can only lease it with leasing costs ranging from $520 to $680 a month. The recharging device costs another $2,000 plus installation charges that run from $1,000 to $3,000. And when potential customers ask for information, they are told that the car isn't for everyone and they have to complete a questionnaire to determine if they are suitable candidates. So how do you market a car with such depressing sales features?

You're probably asking why bother with such a product when its sales seem so hopeless. One major reason is that California is requiring all automakers to have electric vehicles constitute 2 percent of its sales. Originally scheduled for 1998, the law has been postponed, but other states in the Northeast are also requiring that 10 percent of vehicles have zero emissions by 2003. All automakers understand that the clock is ticking and that a viable electric car must be in their line if the companies hope to continue selling cars in California or the Northeast after the start of the twenty-first century.

Even though GM is getting applause from government officials and environmentalists, it is still an expensive experiment with an initial launch investment costing approximately $350 million and six years in development. If sales go well, GM only expects to sell some 2,500 cars a year, so it will be a long time before the company recoups its investment.

But other automakers are also on the trail of an electric car. Honda, for example, intends to launch a four-passenger car in 1997 powered by a more advanced battery technology that will have a driving range of 125 miles. However, the battery costs $30,000 to $40,000 per car so Honda only expects to sell some 300 electric cars in its first three years. An engineering company, Unique Mobility, in Golden, Colorado, has also produced an electric car called the Ethos 3 EV. In a test drive, a *Denver Post* reporter found that it could zip up the mountain pass west of Denver at the maximum legal speed. The company says that if it could sell 20,000 Ethos a year, it could keep the price under $20,000 plus the cost of the batteries, which ranges from $3,000 to $7,000.

GM turned to Saturn, its marketing powerhouse division, for help with the launch of the new car. Available only from Saturn dealers, the car's lease means that GM will worry about resale value, battery replacement, and calculating the subsidies available for owners of electric vehicles from various government agencies. Although it will be leased at selected Saturn dealerships in Los Angeles, San Diego, Phoenix, and Tucson, EV1 will be the first vehicle marketed under the GM name alone, as GM EV1.

GM is only offering the car to a very select market with an exclusive profile: environmentally minded consumers with minimum $120,000 annual incomes and two other gas-powered cars. One of Saturn's specially trained EV1 specialists (not car salespeople) explains that GM doesn't want to screw up its experiment by selling cars to people who don't understand the drawbacks of battery-powered cars and then decide they hate them. Ideal candidates are people like Sylvester Stallone and Walt Disney CEO Michael Eisner. A six-page questionnaire is used to qualify prospects who then go through a training session so they know exactly what they are getting into. The idea is not to sell the car to someone who isn't prepared or doesn't understand how to make it work so there will be no disgruntled buyers.

Saturn's "EV1 specialists" will drive the vehicle to a prospect's home, explain its drawbacks, and demonstrate how it works. That is another technique to screen customers and make sure there is not a bad fit between car and owner.

In terms of advertising, Hal Riney's launch commercial for EV1 tries to associate the electric car to common household appliances. Dozens of electrical appliances come to life and stream out of the home to welcome their relative, the EV1 in the garage. The sustaining work, particularly the print ads, was more contemplative and tried to make an environmental appeal. (See Ad 7.3.)

Other launch events included a parade of celebrities arriving at Mann's Chinese Theater in EV1s for the premier of the Sylvester Stallone movie *Daylight*, which opened on December 5, the same day the EV1 went on sale. Jay Leno was one of the first to drive the EV1 off the lot. Outdoor boards were used heavily in Los Angeles and San Diego to reach the car-happy California consumers. And EV1's Web site (www.gmev.com) was launched first with a teaser page and then a full site with complete product information.

Sources: Adapted from Keith Naughton, "An Electric Car Propelled by Star Power?" *Business Week* (December 9, 1996); Tanya Gazdik, "Riney's EV1 Ads: Everything But the Kitchen Sink," *Adweek* (December 2, 1996):5; E. Scott Reckard, "Dealers Get First GM Electric Cars," *Denver Post* (December 6, 1996):3C; John Eaton, "Electric Ethos Charges Ahead," *Denver Post* (December 6, 1996):1C; Tanya Gazdik and Joan Voight, "Hal Riney to Target Upscale Buyers in Ads for GM EV1 Cars," *Adweek* (November 18, 1996):41.

1. You are asked to develop a message strategy for the next year of EV1's sales. You know the distribution will add more cities in the South, Southwest, and West. Study the message strategy discussion in this chapter and identify at least two approaches that might be useful for extending this campaign. Explain how the creative message would be developed for each strategy.

2. Develop a slogan for the GM car that will be memorable and signals the car's distinctive feature.

3. Besides advertising, identify two other promotional activities that might be used in the continuing promotion of this car.

4. You are the account manager for the advertising agency assigned to the new Honda electric car. You can learn from the EV1 experience and hopefully have an easier sell into the market. Develop a message strategy for the launch of the new Honda car, which goes faster but has higher battery costs.

5. The inventor of the Ethos believes that an electric car can be priced under $20,000 if 20,000 units per year could be sold. That is an entirely different strategy than what Saturn is using to launch the EV1. What changes would need to be made in the marketing and marketing communication strategy to begin to build this volume of sales?

For many companies, one of the goals of marketing and advertising is to build brand image. In the $50 billion U.S. beer market, for example, industry giant Anheuser-Busch spends huge amounts of money each year to create and present memorable ads designed to entertain and maintain the company's 44 percent market share. From taglines such as "Yes, I am" and "I love you, man" to the Budweiser frogs, Anheuser-Busch has a solid track record of using words and images to keep Budweiser on top. Lately, however, change has been sweeping through the industry. Beer drinkers have been searching for something different, and in the process they are forsaking mass-market beers whose annual production amounts to tens of millions of barrels. Instead, beer connoisseurs are turning from big brands in favor of hand-crafted, full-flavored brews from small, regional companies that may produce only a few thousand barrels each year. As a result of this change in tastes, upstart brands like Samuel Adams and Pete's Wicked now command shelf space alongside heavyweights such as Bud and Miller.

Targeted at a small segment of beer drinkers, a six-pack of craft brew can cost twice as much as Bud and other so-called premium brands. What many consumers may *not* know is that some of the companies that market craft beers have contracted with large companies to do the actual brewing. For example, Boston Beer Company contracts out much of the production of its Samuel Adams brand. Similarly, Pete's Wicked's various products are actually produced by Stroh Brewery, which also makes Old Milwaukee. This practice has angered some executives at the big breweries; now the Bureau of Alcohol, Tobacco, and Firearms is contemplating regulations that would require beer labels to indicate the identity of the company actually doing the brewing. As August Busch IV complained in an interview with *The Wall Street Journal*, "What we don't like are crafty marketers duping the consumers. If you're going to brew in somebody else's brewery, why don't you say so?" Mr. Busch gets support from microbreweries that do, in fact, actually brew their own beer.

Mr. Busch's interest is understandable: Although specialty beers are a true niche product, comprising a mere 2 percent of the market, they also represent the fastest-growing segment of the industry. Anticipating that demand for microbrews could reach 10 million barrels by the end of the decade, Anheuser-Busch, Miller, and Adolph Coors have launched their own specialty brands. They are sometimes referred to as *macrobrews* because several hundred thousand barrels are produced annually. For example, Miller introduced Red Dog and Icehouse; advertising for both brands mentions the Plank Road Brewery as the source. Coors's specialty brands include Killian's Irish Red and various flavors of Blue Moon. The big-name brewers are also growing via acquisition; for example, Anheuser-Busch recently purchased a 25 percent stake in Seattle-based Redhook. As Mr. Busch explains, "There is a certain mystique to smallness. Ours are not beers from a small place, but they offer a variety of tastes."

In advertising their niche brews, Anheuser-Busch, Miller, and Coors do not identify themselves as the corporate parent. Industry observers have called this a "stealth" strategy. (In some instances, however, the name of the parent brewery is included on the label of individual bottles.) Despite such criticism, one of the reasons the big brewers are attracted to the microbrew segment is because heavy investment in advertising or market research is not required. For example, Anheuser-Busch will not use television advertising for its Elk Mountain brand—even though such a strategy breaks with industry tradition. Notes Pamela Hinckley, vice president of marketing at Redhook, "Some of [Anheuser-Busch's] distributors expected to use the whole range of radio and TV tools, and to sell to all of their accounts. That's just the opposite of how we sell."

Still, it is too soon to tell whether or not consumers will develop long-term brand loyalty to microbrews served up by the big producers. Christopher Finch, author of a book on beer, dismissed Red Dog as "totally uninteresting." Moreover, some beer aficionados have reacted unfavorably to the stealth approach. Research conducted by Anheuser-Busch indicates that 50 percent of those surveyed are unhappy to learn that some so-called microbrews—Plank Road, for example—are simply brand names without a genuine small brewery affiliation. John N. MacDonough, chairperson of Miller, dismisses such criticism. "The only people annoyed are at AB [Anheuser-Busch]. The consumer doesn't care." If Mark F. Bozzini, president of Pete's Brewing Company, is concerned about competition from the major breweries, he isn't admitting it. "Anheuser, Miller, and Coors can make anything they want. The only thing they can't do is look like us, with the name, history, and goodwill. That's not something you can replicate in the market-data room," he says.

Video Source: "Stealth Marketing," *The Wall Street Journal Report* (October 1, 1995), #679. *Additional Sources:* Yumiko Ono, "Head of Marketing: Who Really Makes That Cute Little Beer? You'd Be Surprised," *The Wall Street Journal* (April 15, 1996):A1, A8; Richard A. Melcher, "From the Microbrewers Who Brought You Bud, Coors . . ." *Business Week* (April 24, 1995):66, 70; Marj Charlier, "Thinking Small: Specialty Beers' Success Prompts Big Brewers to Try Out the Niche," *The Wall Street Journal* (January 5, 1994):A1, A10; "Popular Microbreweries Accused of Misleading Labeling," *Morning Edition*, National Public Radio (February 13, 1996).

1. Do you agree with Anheuser-Busch's advertising strategy that downplays the corporate identity of its specialty beers?

2. Do you think microbrew brands that are brewed under contract should be labeled so that consumers know what company actually produces the beer?

ELIZABETH TAYLOR
BLACK PEARLS
EAU DE PARFUM SPRAY NATUREL
VAPORISATEUR
1.7 FL.OZ.

CHAPTER

How Advertising Works

CHAPTER OUTLINE

- Zapping the Ads
- Advertising Impact
- The Psychology of Advertising
- How Brand Images Work

CHAPTER OBJECTIVES

When you have completed this chapter, you should be able to:

- Understand the barriers that an effective advertisement must overcome
- Explain what *breakthrough advertising* is and how it works
- Be familiar with the different levels on which a viewer or reader will react to an ad
- Explain the importance of brand images and how advertising contributes to their development

ZAPPING THE ADS

Elizabeth Taylor's new perfume, Black Pearls, was launched with an unusual advertising strategy. On one night on CBS every show during a two-hour period featured the star as she wandered in and out of the various programs' storylines. She made appearances on everything from *The Nanny* to *High Society* looking for a missing string of black pearls. In this innovative product launch strategy, there's no actual commercial.[1] Why do you suppose such an unusual strategy was used?

The answer is: to defeat zapping. When people don't care for a commercial, they have a weapon to express their dislike—the remote control. Ever since its arrival in viewers' homes, this simple piece of technology has enabled viewers to avoid advertisements they dislike by pushing one button. Readers have been flipping past print ads for years by turning pages; with the remote control, viewers can just as easily flip past television commercials. Moreover, because the new viewing environment with more networks, independents, and cable channels offers so many attractive alternatives, viewers are zapping more frequently than ever before. And now industry research has found that there are more clickers than there are Americans.[2]

Zapping is one type of avoidance; another is zipping, which means fast-forwarding past the commercials on prerecorded videotapes. A related behavior is grazing or surfing, which means flipping around the channels, stopping now and then to look briefly at something, and then moving on. A person adept at grazing knows when a commercial break is about to begin and can time the cycle to return to the original program just as the break ends.

The Pretesting Company of Englewood, New Jersey, analyzes commercials to determine where in a commercial audience members are likely to zap it. By knowing when and what turns people off, the company can tell which commercials stand a better chance of not being zapped. For example, Pretesting found that the word *period* in commercials for sanitary pads and tampons was embarrassing for women viewers. In laboratory studies some 60 percent of the women viewers, upon hearing that word, zapped the commercial before it was complete.[3]

The Pretesting Company has found that comparative ads and ads that leave out the brand name until the end are prone to zapping, as are parodies of other commercials, especially if people don't like the originals. A number of agencies are using this service to isolate problems and to develop ads that will capture and hold viewers' attention. The key to zapproofing is to develop ads with "stopping power." Of course, once the ad arrests viewers' attention, it must continue to hold attention by addressing viewers' interests. This chapter will consider such behaviors as zapping, as well as other consumer and environmental factors that affect the impact of advertising.

ADVERTISING IMPACT

Do ads make a difference? Do they sell products? In 1996 one of the worst things that can happen to advertising happened. Video Storyboard Tests, which rates television commercials, rated the Budweiser commercials with its frogs and horses playing football first in eye measurement, likability, and memorability through the first three quarters of 1995. Not since Coca-Cola's Mean Joe Greene spot in 1979 has a series of ads received such high ratings. So why is that a problem? The prob-

---

[1] Mary Kuntz and Joseph Weber, "The New Hucksterism," *Business Week* (July 1, 1996):76–84.

[2] Kevin M. Williams, "Zappers Outnumber Americans," *Chicago Sun-Times* (April 7, 1996):2.

[3] Adapted from Jon Berry, "Zap Attack: How Audience Research Is Shaping Ads," *Adweek* (July 9, 1990):1; Carrie Heeter and Bradley S. Greenberg, *CableViewing* (Norwood, NJ: Ablex, 1988); and Sandra Moriarty, "Explorations into the Commercial Encounter," American Academy of Advertising Annual Conference, Reno, NV (April 1991).

lem is that Budweiser, even though it is still the best-selling beer in the United States with over 44 percent of the market, had sales decline 4.3 percent during the period the highly rated ads were running.[4] So the "best" ads in the country had a hard time selling the product.

A survey by *Parade* magazine found that when asked what prompts consumers to try new food products, coupons were the most effective and advertising was eighth. This result suggests that price promotions are important but people think advertising is far less effective. (Don't forget that those coupons have to be delivered somehow.) Although only 13 percent of the respondents confess that advertising is "very influential" on their own food purchases, nearly half (48 percent) believe it is very influential in motivating other people. In other words, people think it has impact, but they feel they themselves are relatively immune to the impact.[5]

Likewise, research by Yankelovich reported that *only* 25 percent of respondents said a television ad would induce them to try a new product. However, one might argue that convincing one out of four to try something new is actually a high level. An opposite view comes from the National Cancer Institute, which reports on a study of adolescents and concludes that advertising is effective in getting youngsters to start smoking.[6] The critics of advertising believe that it has a lot of power over people; advertisers, however, wonder if it has any impact at all.

In particular, advertisers ask if ads have impact on immediate sales or if ads are only useful in building long-term "soft" effects such as awareness and brand image. To answer that question, Syracuse University professor John Philip Jones has analyzed hundreds of ads using *single-source data* (information about media use as well as products purchased by a single household), and has concluded that consumers can in fact be persuaded to buy a product through advertising after seeing an ad only once *if the ad is effective*. So the question is: What makes an effective ad? According to Jones, effective ads have three qualities. "One, the ad itself has to be attractive enough for consumers to look at, it has to have likability; two, all effective advertising is totally visual; and three, you must have more than warm, fuzzy imagery."[7] In his book on this research, *When Ads Work*, Jones also concludes that the strongest ad campaigns can triple sales, while the weakest can cause sales to fall by more than 50 percent. So the next question is: What makes a strong ad different from a weak one?[8]

Keith Reinhard, president of DDB Needham, agrees with Jones that advertising can be effective if it is done right. His criteria for effective advertising is outlined in his introduction to a DDB Needham publication on its ROI philosophy: "Today, more than ever, if advertising is not relevant, it has no purpose. If it is not original, it will attract no attention. If it does not strike with impact, it will make no lasting impression."[9] Relevance, originality, and impact—ROI—are key elements of effective advertising, according to Reinhard and DDB Needham. Advertising that is relevant speaks to you about things you care about; advertising that is original catches your attention by its creativity; and advertising that has impact arouses your emotions and makes a lasting impression.

In order to understand the importance of these questions and what we know about how ads work, this chapter will focus on the psychology behind advertising. It is important for you to know how advertising works—and doesn't work—in order to understand why advertising is created the way it is. First, let's discuss the environment in which advertising operates, and the audience's interaction with the

---

[4]Rance Crain, "A Royal Pain for the King of Beers," *Advertising Age* (January 22, 1996):17.

[5]"Strongly Influenced by Ads?" *Adweek* (November 13, 1995):23.

[6]"The Power of Advertising?" *Advertising Age* (November 6, 1995):16.

[7]Kevin Sullivan, "A US $10 Million Study Is Underway to Find Out What Makes an Ad Effective," *Singapore Business Times* (July 5, 1996):3.

[8]John Philip Jones, *When Ads Work: New Proof That Advertising Triggers Sales* (New York: Lexington Books, 1995).

[9]Jeri Moore and William D. Wells, *R.O.I. Guidebook: Planning for Relevance, Originality and Impact in Advertising and Other Marketing Communications* (New York: DDB Needham, 1991).

advertisement. Then we will look at the psychology of advertising in terms of perception, awareness, understanding, persuasion, and memorability. Finally, we look at the special considerations of brand advertising.

THE ADVERTISING ENVIRONMENT

The advertising environment is extremely cluttered. Some 40,000 magazines and journals are published in the United States every year, and more than 10,000 radio stations crowd the airwaves. Since 1965, for example, the number of network television commercials has tripled from approximately 1,800 to nearly 6,000 commercials a week, up 50 percent since 1983. Prime-time television carries more than ten minutes of paid advertising every hour, roughly a minute more than at the beginning of the 1990s. Seventy percent of American homes are now wired for cable television, and the average household can view 35 channels. Tied to the explosion in media outlets is the monumental increase in the number of commercial messages. Networks often run five or six commercials in a row; during prime time commercials average 10.5 minutes per hour.[10]

In addition, advertisers must face an increasingly cynical generation of new consumers skeptical of sales messages from big corporations. Advertisers compete fiercely for the attention of people who are disinterested and disbelieving and their ads appear in an environment saturated with promotion and other information-laden messages. It is an extremely cluttered environment. Other media, other ads, news stories, outside distractions, and random thoughts also get in the way of an advertiser's very expensive and carefully constructed commercial messages.

THE AUDIENCE

Given this cluttered environment and general disinterest, most people give advertising only divided attention. A few ads may break through and receive total concentration, but not many. At best an ad gets half the mind and an occasional glance. Advertisers are also up against a short attention span. Human concentration happens in quick bursts. The actual information that gets attention is often nothing more than a quick impression or a message fragment.

INFORMATION PROCESSING

Besides problems with attention, viewers have problems making sense out of the mass of information that assaults them. Media messages become entangled in other thoughts and memories. Our minds are not tidy, and the approach we take to making sense of information is not predictable or thorough. For example, most people reading a newspaper or magazine look at both editorial information and advertisements. They browse, scan, jump back and forth, and find snippets of useful information in both categories. Ads and editorials are scanned or ignored; the information derived from both may well be fragmentary.

Similarly, every time you watch a television commercial, you decide whether to attend to it or not. The decision is always yours, even though you may not be aware you are making it. If you make a commitment, the commitment lasts only as long as the message maintains your interest. When you lose interest, your attention shifts and you move on to your own thoughts or to some outside distraction.

AVOIDANCE

The opening story focused on the fact that most people are very good at avoiding information that doesn't interest them. Bombarded with a huge number of commercials on television, you have no doubt become very good at avoidance. If you are like most people, you will either change the channel, mute the sound, leave the room, or turn your attention elsewhere. Typical viewers may note the first

---

[10]Kuntz and Weber, 1996:77; and Peter F. Eder, "Advertising and Mass Marketing," *The Futurist* (May–June 1990):38–40.

commercial in a cluster, then, depending on whether or not it catches their attention, they may or may not stick around for the remaining message. Actually, very few people watch all the way through a commercial break.

Furthermore, many consumers are scornful of advertising. A national survey found that 60 percent of consumers agreed that "advertising insults my intelligence," and over 70 percent said they "don't believe a company's products."[11] Disbelief, dislike, and irritation are important aspects of the consumer response to advertising. The Issues and Controversies box entitled "The Irritation Factor" takes a closer look at these aspects.

---

[11]Stephen J. Hoch and Young-Won Ha, "Consumer Learning: Advertising and the Ambiguity of Product Experience," *Journal of Consumer Research* (September 1986):221–33.

ℐSSUES AND 𝒞ONTROVERSIES

THE IRRITATION FACTOR

In a time of political campaigns, the headlines and airwaves are filled with complaints about negative advertising. People love to hate attack ads and yet political pros claim the ads work. Polls almost always track an immediate boost for the candidate who uses them.

But negative and irritating ads are used in product advertising as well as political advertising. Irritating ads are defined as those that cause displeasure and momentary impatience. The response is more negative than simple dislike. Why do advertisers use irritating ads? And why do people like some commercials and despise others? Research has found that disliked advertising might work because it generates high levels of attention and recall. Even if consumers dislike these commercials, when they get to the store they remember the product name and forget their irritation at the ad.

Most people say they hate negative ads, but the polls respond that the technique works. Some analysts believe negative political ads are effective because a sizable majority of voters are too detached, distrustful, or lazy to get involved. Also Americans have a dim view of politicians, so it may be easier to believe the worst than to accept good things about them.

An example of a candidate who tried to build a positive Mr. Nice Guy image was Lamar Alexander in the 1996 Republican presidential primary. His goal was to sell himself as something he's not, that is, not a negative campaigner.* The strategy worked to a point in that he rose from being an unknown to a strong third-place finish in the critical New Hampshire primary. In the end, however, he lost out to the aging, but more familiar, Senator Bob Dole, who also railed against negative advertising even as his campaign and his party received criticism for unfair charges made against the Democratic candidate, incumbent President Bill Clinton.

There also are political analysts who feel that attack ads actually sharpen the debate and that a negative ad isn't always a bad ad. False or misleading ads, of course, are not appreciated, but ads that address the credibility of candidates in a questionable area are important to the process. *Adweek* has noted that the trouble with negative political advertising is that it's clumsy in language and crude in production values.

"What we seldom see are political ads that are both negative and ingenious. That's just one respect in which brand advertising is miles ahead of its political counterpart." *Adweek* points to Apple's legendary "1984" commercial with its subtle attack on the unfriendliness of MS DOS system computers (i.e., IBM) as well as Pepsi's spoof of a Coca-Cola delivery man who tries to sneak a can of Coke only to have the cans in the display case fall out on the floor.

Still, it makes sense to assume that viewers' negative perceptions of the message may carry over to the product itself, particularly in product advertising, if it is heavy-handed. One wonders if those irritating commercials are successful in spite of the message strategy rather than because of it. They may deliver awareness for the short term as they smear the brand's image and reputation for the long term.

Research into irritating product advertising has found that a major source of irritation is the product itself; for example, feminine-hygiene products, underwear, laxatives, and hemorrhoid treatments. Regarding message strategy, irritation levels are higher when the situation is contrived, phony, unbelievable, or overdramatized. In the case of a sensitive product, the ads are more irritating when the product and its use are emphasized; indirect approaches seem to work better. Viewers also don't like to see people "put down" or forced into stereotypical roles. Neither do they like to see important relationships threatened, such as mother-daughter or husband-wife.

What do you think about the irritation factor in advertising? Can you remember any ads that you particularly disliked? Can you remember some that you liked? Why did you react that way? Are there products and situations where it isn't important for the commercial to be liked? If a particular commercial is irritating and unpopular but the product sells well, should that commercial be considered a success? Why or why not?

Sources: George Cantor, "Do Negative Ads Reflect Badly on the Electorate or Positively Sharpen Debate?" *The Detroit News* (August 11, 1996):B5; John Tierney, "Why Negative Ads Are Good for Democracy," *The New York Times* (November 3, 1996):sect. 6, p. 52; "When Negative Ads Are Positively Charming," *Adweek* (March 4, 1996):22; and William David A. Aaker and Donald E. Bruzzone, "Causes of Irritation in Advertising," *Journal of Marketing* (Spring 1985):47–57.

---

*Debra Goldman, "Red-Checkered Future," *Adweek* (February 26, 1996):16.

BREAKTHROUGH ADVERTISING

This discussion dramatizes how few advertisements actually are read or watched. You may scan the stories and ads in the newspaper, but with limited concentration. Less than half of all ads actually are noticed on a "thinking" level. Perhaps 20 percent are read a little, and very few are read thoroughly.

Advertising that makes any impact at all breaks through this inattention and mindless scanning; it helps consumers sort out and remember what they see and hear; and it overcomes avoidance and scorn. Such advertising is called *breakthrough advertising*. It is relevant and original, and it has impact. It speaks to the concerns of its audience on a personal level without being patronizing or phony.

THE PSYCHOLOGY OF ADVERTISING

How does advertising work? This is a very complex question. One thing we do know is that advertising may communicate a number of messages in a number of areas simultaneously. For example, at the same time you are understanding a copy point, you may also be forming a favorable or an unfavorable opinion of the product being advertised. The message's impact on both knowledge and liking can happen simultaneously.[12] The following discussion will analyze how advertising works in terms of five basic psychological categories: perception, awareness, understanding, persuasion, and memorability.

PERCEPTION: CREATING STOPPING POWER

When something has been perceived, the message has registered. One of the biggest challenges for advertisers is simply to get consumers to notice their messages. This is harder than it appears. Not only do consumers miss more than half the messages directed at them, other messages continuously compete for their attention. As an outdoor ad for the Los Angeles Fire Department, Ad 8.1 has stopping power.

EXPOSURE

The first step in perception is simple *exposure*. Exposure is primarily a media-buying problem. First the message has to be placed in a medium that your target sees, reads, watches, or listens to. Exposure is, therefore, the minimum requirement to perception. If your target never sees or hears the advertisement, or if your target skips the page or changes the channel, then no matter how great the message is, it will not be perceived.

ATTENTION

Once the audience has been exposed to the message, the next step is to keep their attention. *Attention* means the mind is engaged; it is focusing on something. Attention is aroused by a *trigger*, something that "catches" the target's interest. The trigger can be something in the message or something within the reader or viewer that makes him or her "lock onto" a particular message. In print it may be a sale price in large type, a startling illustration, or a strong headline. On television the trigger may be sound effects, music, a scene that is action oriented or visually interesting, or a captivating idea.

Getting attention involves more than just attracting the notice of the viewer or reader, however. When you are in the scanning mode, your attention is wan-

---

[12]Sandra E. Moriarty, "Beyond the Hierarchy of Effects: A Conceptual Model," in *Current Issues and Research in Advertising*, James H. Leigh and Claude R. Martin, Jr., eds. (Ann Arbor: University of Michigan Graduate School of Business, 1983):45–56.

AD 8.1

A STRIKING VISUAL IMAGE OF A
CHILD'S INJURED HAND, ALONG
WITH A TIGHTLY DIRECTED LINE
OF COPY, STOPS THE VIEWER
SHORT AND IMMEDIATELY CON-
VEYS THE MESSAGE: FIREWORKS
ARE DANGEROUS.

dering. Nailing down attention requires some kind of *stopping power.* Ads that stop the scanning are usually high in intrusiveness, originality, or relevance.

INTRUSIVENESS

Advertisements are designed to be attention getting. That means they sometimes have to be intrusive—in other words, they demand attention. Intrusiveness is particularly important for products that have a small "share of mind"—those that are either not very well known or not very involving or interesting. In many cases there is little difference between competing brands, so the product interest is created solely by the advertising message.

What can you do to create this kind of impact? Many intrusive ads use loud, bold effects to attract viewer attention—they work by shouting. Others use captivating ideas or mesmerizing visuals. For print ads, for example, research has found that contrast can attract viewer attention. If every other ad in the medium is big and bold, then be small, quiet, and simple—use a lot of white space. If everything else is tiny and gray (like type), then be bold and black or use color. If everything else is colorful, then use black and white. Identify the characteristics of the medium environment and then do something different.

ORIGINALITY

PRINCIPLE Originality is used to capture attention by presenting a unique or novel thought.

Creative advertising is interesting because it presents a unique or novel thought. The function of originality is to capture attention. People will notice something that is new, novel, or surprising. Creative advertising breaks through the old patterns of seeing and saying things without being irrelevant or bizarre. The unexpectedness of the new idea is what creates stopping power.

Advertising agencies go to great lengths to create intrusive advertising. The Young & Rubicam (Y&R) agency pushes its creative people to take more risks to make their ads more distinctive. For an Irish Spring ad the agency used a fully clothed man with a bar of soap in his hand. By all appearances, he is about to launch into a standard pitch. Suddenly the ad turns slapstick. He loses control of the soap. It squirts him in the face and lathers up in his pocket. Such unexpected approaches to mundane products are being used successfully by Y&R to sell things like toothpaste, coffee, and ice cream.

To encourage this kind of freewheeling thinking, Y&R set up a program called the Risk Lab that allows copywriters and art directors to have their ideas informally tested by researchers in the early stages of concept development. The director of creative research, Dr. Stephanie Kugelman, took the title "Dr. Risk" and moved to the creative floors to work closely with the creative people.

AWARENESS: MAKING AN IMPRESSION

Awareness: The message has made an impression on the viewer or reader.

Once a message has been perceived and has caught your attention, your perceptual process can move on to the next step, which is awareness of the message and the product. **Awareness** means that the message has made an impression on the viewer or reader, who can subsequently identify the advertiser. Note that although awareness of the advertising comes first, awareness of the advertising is not the ultimate objective. As far as the advertiser is concerned, the ultimate objective is awareness of the product, not the advertisement.

Attention is a message-design problem. The advertising message can, and must, compete with other messages in the same medium. Within a news medium, the advertising has to be able to compete with the intrinsically interesting nature of the news. In an entertainment medium like television, the advertising has to compete with the mesmerizing entertainment values of programming. Radio is almost always a background medium, and outdoor advertising is directed toward an audience whose attention, by definition, is directed elsewhere. Not only does outdoor advertising have to compete for attention, it also has to be able to win out over distractions such as other signs along the road, the car radio or tape deck, and conversations among passengers.

Relatively low levels of attention can create a minimal level of awareness. If the objective is simply brand or product reminder, then the attention level doesn't need to be as high as it does when the objective calls for the understanding of a copy point.

RELEVANCE

Most people want to hear or read about themselves and the things they care about. They want to know how to improve their skills, look better, live longer, make more money, or save themselves time and expense. People will pay attention to advertising only if it's worth their while to do so. They make a deal with the advertiser: "Make it worth my time and I'll pay attention to your message as long as it doesn't bore me."

Relevance: Ads that speak to our personal concerns or interests.

Selective perception, which we discussed in Chapter 5, is driven by **relevance.** We pay attention to ads that speak to our personal concerns and interests by providing information about such things as work, hobbies, roles, and relationships. Selection—being interested in one thing and not in something else—is also driven by changing conditions. When we are hungry or thirsty, for example, we pay more attention to food and drink ads.

INTEREST

Because there are different types of interest, there are many types of relevance. You might be interested in the product advertised or in some element in the ad itself—the model or star, the promise made in the headline or by the announcer, or an unusual graphic or production technique. Different topics, product categories, and products have different levels of built-in interest. Some products are just inherently more interesting than others. Food and vacations, for example, are more interesting to most people than are toilet cleaners. Some products are of interest to specific groups of people. A man might look at an ad for tires but avoid an ad for hair spray.

Interest is usually created by one of two things—personal involvement or curiosity. You have some predispositions that affect what interests you—getting through school, hobbies, a trip you want to take, or a career goal. If a message applies to any of these elements in your list, then it affects you personally and the message has personal relevance. Most people also respond to general human-interest items—a topic that strikes some universal chord, such as babies, kittens, and puppies, as well as tragedies and success stories.

Curiosity provides the "cognitive nudge" that engages your mind. Whenever you are confronted with something new, there is a period of curiosity, usually accompanied by doubt or some kind of questioning. New information is often greeted by phrases like "Can you believe it?" This confrontation of curiosity with doubt means you have entered the interested state. You are interested because the message might be personally relevant.

Advertisers who are trying to develop a message that stimulates interest will speak to the personal interests of their target audience as well as do something to elicit curiosity. Ads that open with questions or dubious statements are designed to build interest and create curiosity. For example, the Buick Regal used a teaser strategy to announce its new Web site. (See Ad 8.2.) We discussed getting attention as the stopping power of an advertisement; keeping attention is the pulling power of an ad—it keeps pulling the reader or viewer through to the end of the message.

MAINTAINING INTEREST

Interest is a momentary thing; it dies easily as attention shifts. A major challenge to advertisers is to maintain interest until the point of the message is reached. Because of the scanning and browsing behavior of many readers and viewers, maintaining interest is more difficult than arousing it.

If you are worried about maintaining interest in an advertisement, then you must consider the pulling power of your message. This is in part a sequencing problem: Does your copy pull the reader or viewer through to the end? How does the message develop? For example, if you start with a question, then the reader has to continue through the ad to find the answer. Storytelling is a good technique to hold the audience. Most people want to know how a story comes out. Suspense, drama, and narrative are good literary tools for maintaining interest.

Television has built-in sequencing because of the moving image. If skillfully used, the motion and action of a video message are hard to ignore. A layout in a print ad can do the same thing. A layout can be designed with strong direction or movement cues that keep the eye of the reader engaged.

INVOLVEMENT

Involvement: The intensity of the consumer's interest in a product.

Relevance is a key factor in the concept of **involvement,** which refers to the intensity of the consumer's interest in a product, medium, or message. *High involvement* means that a product—or information about it—is important and personally relevant. *Low involvement* means that the product or information is perceived as unimportant. Typically, people in a high-involvement situation—as when purchasing a new car, home, or European vacation—will be searching for information and critically evaluating it. Advertising for high-involvement products usually provides a lot of information about the product. In contrast, low-involvement purchases, such as chewing gum, toothpaste, and paper towels, are made without much searching and with little effort to think critically about the decision. Advertising for this type of product often focuses on simple slogans or images.

The word *involvement* is also used to describe an advertising technique that tries to get the audience to participate in how the message develops and evolves. Compelling readers or viewers to get involved in the message either physically or

AD 8.2

THIS TEASER AD IS FOR THE CAR'S NEW WEB SITE. IT IS DELIBERATELY AMBIGUOUS AND USED TO EXCITE CURIOSITY ABOUT THE WEB SITE.

mentally is a strong persuasive technique. For example, some ads start with a question in order to draw people into constructing the answer. An oil company advertisement displays a big picture of a beautiful forest and asks the reader to find the oil well hidden somewhere among the trees to dramatize the point that oil drilling can be respectful of nature. The more involved viewers or readers are in developing the message, the more impact the message has.

UNDERSTANDING: MAKING IT CLEAR

Being aware of the message is not enough. The message must be understood as well. *Understanding* refers to a conscious, mental effort to make sense of the information being presented. That is how we learn things. Whereas attention can be a relatively passive response, understanding demands an active response from the reader or viewer. It is an important part of the process of dealing with information. First we find ourselves interested, then we learn something about the subject of our interest, then we file it away in our memories. That is called *knowing*.

Informational Advertising: Advertising that presents a large amount of information about the product.

Understanding is particularly important for ads that present a lot of information—brand, price, size, how the product works, when and where to use it, and so on. When product differences exist, the features and how they translate into selling points are also important pieces of information to understand. An important requirement of **informational advertising** is that the explanation be clear and relevant to the prospect. Consumers have little patience with ads that are confusing, vague, or unfocused. The reader or viewer must be able to follow the logic, make discriminations, compare and contrast points of view, comprehend reasons and arguments, synthesize and organize facts, and, in general, make sense of things. If you are designing an advertising message where understanding is an objective, your ad must present the facts in a way that makes it easy for people to assimilate the information. Clarity is important.

Ads that don't work very well are ones that contribute to the consumer's confusion. An example is the battle between Tylenol and Advil. In 1996 the major television networks pulled commercials for both pills because they said the drug makers were unduly alarming consumers by overstating the dangerous side effects of each others' products.[13]

TEACHING, LEARNING, AND KNOWING

PRINCIPLE Learning is an important objective for new-product advertising.

Teaching is an important aspect of advertising because most advertisers want people to learn or know something after they have read, watched, or heard the message. Knowledge means the facts have been acquired through experience or study. In the case of new products, ads must bridge the gap in people's experience by teaching them how to recognize and use the product.

The literary tools of a message designed to stimulate understanding include definition, explanation, demonstration, comparison, and contrast. Definition and explanation are primarily verbal concepts, but demonstration, comparison, and contrast are often communicated in visuals. Any visual, whether print or video, can be used to compare two products or to show before-and-after scenarios. Television is particularly good for demonstration because it can show a sequence of operations.

ASSOCIATION

Association: The process used to link a product with a positive experience, personality, or lifestyle.

Another way to "know" something is to make a connection in your mind. When you link up two concepts—fall and football, or Coca-Cola and refreshment, for example—you have learned something. **Association** is used in advertising to build images. Advertisements that use association try to get you to know something by linking the product with something you aspire to, respect, value, or appreciate—like a pleasant experience or an envied lifestyle or person.

---

[13]Steve Sakson, "Tylenol, Advil Makers Wage Advertising Wars," *Daily Camera Business Plus* (March 26, 1996):11.

A metaphoric use of association appears in a campaign for the printer language called PostScript. This is a difficult concept to sell, so the creators of the advertising used a cherry inside a chocolate to represent "the best part" of the computer system.

PERSUASION: MAKING MOVING MESSAGES

Persuade: Establish, reinforce, or change an attitude, build an argument, touch an emotion, or anchor a conviction firmly in the prospect's belief structure.

In addition to providing information, advertisements must **persuade** people to believe or do something. A persuasive message will try to establish, reinforce, or change an attitude, build an argument, touch an emotion, or anchor a conviction firmly in the prospect's belief structure.

Believability is an extremely important concept in advertising. Do consumers believe the messages? Are the claims believable? Do spokespersons, particularly authority figures, have credibility? Consumers say they do not believe in advertising claims, but at the same time they find advertising helpful in making better decisions. Recent research has found that although consumers want proof of the validity of advertisers' claims, they do not require very convincing evidence to accept these claims.[14]

PRINCIPLE A persuasive message will shape attitudes, build a logical argument, touch emotions, and make the prospect believe something about the product.

In Chapter 6 you learned that support is an important element in the message strategy. Remember, support refers to everything in the message that lends credibility to the promise. If you want your message to be believable or to have impact, you must provide support, such as facts, convincing argument, or conclusive demonstrations.

APPEALS

Appeal: Something that moves people.

Persuasion in advertising rests on the psychological appeal to the consumer. An **appeal** is something that makes the product particularly attractive or interesting to the consumer. Common appeals are security, esteem, fear, sex, and sensory pleasure. Appeals generally pinpoint the anticipated response of the prospect to the product and message.

Advertisers also use the word *appeal* to describe a general creative emphasis. For example, if the price is emphasized in the ad, then the appeal is value, economy, or savings. If the product saves time or effort, then the appeal is convenience. A message that focuses on a mother or father making something for a child—like cookies or a rocker—might elicit an appeal to family love and concern. A status appeal is used to establish something as a quality, expensive product. Appetite appeal using mouth-watering visuals is used in food advertising.

Celebrities are also analyzed in terms of their appeal using a technique called Q scores. A Q score is an index used to gauge how "hot" a television program, performer, sports figure or team, brand name, or brand character is or isn't. In 1996, for example, research determined that the Budweiser frogs had more appeal than Mickey Mouse and that the Coca-Cola polar bears had pulled ahead of entertainment characters such as the Roadrunner, *The Lion King*, and Snoopy.[15]

ATTITUDES AND OPINIONS

Beliefs, attitudes, and values structure our opinions, which in turn reflect how negatively or positively we feel about something. This is how we evaluate the information we receive. People's opinions are built on a complex structure of attitudes. Every person has a different attitude structure based on individual experiences.

Advertising that seeks to affect this complex structure of attitudes will usually attempt to accomplish one of three things:

1. Establish a new opinion where none has existed before.
2. Reinforce an existing opinion.
3. Change an existing opinion.

---

[14]Hoch and Ha, "Consumer Learning," 221–33.
[15]Balir R. Fischer, "License to Sell," *Promo* (June 1996):42–50.

New opinions need to be created when a new product is introduced. Consumer opinion concerning the product or service, of course, will be modified or confirmed as the product is used. No matter how strong your advertising, a bad experience with a new product will negate all of the positive attitudes your message has implanted.

LIKABILITY

An important indicator of positive, as well as negative, attitudes, *likability* signals how people respond to a product or a message. An advertiser will try to build positive attitudes for new products and maintain existing positive attitudes for successful mature products. When a product is liked well enough by consumers to generate repeat sales, that is called **brand loyalty.**

Brand Loyalty: Positive opinions held by consumers about the product or service that make them want to repeat their purchase of this brand.

It is more unusual, and much harder, to try to change negative attitudes. If your product has a negative image—perhaps because the initial product or marketing strategy was faulty—then a major objective is to turn that consumer attitude around. Amtrak, for example, once suffered from an extremely negative image. Travelers assumed that long-distance trains would be late, that on-board service would be poor, and that equipment would be outdated and in bad condition. After these problems were corrected, Amtrak advertising focused on the task of persuading travelers to give Amtrak another try. While many travelers did return to Amtrak, with some routes becoming so popular that travelers must reserve space well in advance, some of the old impressions linger.[16] Once established, negative attitudes are extremely difficult to cure.

It is important to remember that advertising alone cannot repair a faulty product. If lack of brand loyalty is due to bad experience with the product itself, or with packaging, pricing, or some other element of the marketing program, advertising that persuades consumers to buy the product will only make matters worse. A product problem is a product problem, not an advertising problem. There is an old saying that the surest way to kill a bad product is with a lot of advertising because more people will try it and share their experiences with friends and relatives.

One likability technique, which was highlighted in the opening story on zapproofing, is the use of *entertainment.* Advertisers have found that commercials that look like shows and provide high entertainment values seem to be better liked by audiences than ads with high levels of information. The entertainment issue is one that has been debated by advertising experts because, although entertainment may get and keep attention, there are some who believe it doesn't sell the product very well.

ARGUMENTS

PRINCIPLE Advertising speaks to the head with arguments and to the heart with emotional appeals.

Persuasive messages deal with more than basic attitude structure. People are persuaded by argument or reasoning. Reasons are based on the logic of claims and the way the claims are supported or substantiated. Argument in this sense refers not to a disagreement, but to a line of reasoning where one point follows from another, leading up to a conclusion. Your ad must focus on logic and proof when you are dealing with reasons, as does the Jeep ad in Ad 8.3.

That is why the reason-why selling premise is a very common message strategy used in advertising. It is also why the support section of the creative strategy is so very important. There are legal implications to the substantiation issue. Competitors, as well as government regulators, review ads to find claims that are unsupported and can bring legal action against advertisers who have not adequately provided substantiation.

EMOTIONS

Persuasion is not only a logical process, it is also concerned with emotions. How someone "feels" about your product, service, brand, or company may be just as

---

[16]DDB Needham, "Amtrak Case Study," Prentice-Hall, 1991.

AD 8.3

THE JEEP AD DOCUMENTS ITS PERFORMANCE BY REFERRING TO THE FIVE TIMES IT HAS WON AN AWARD FROM AN INDUSTRY PUBLICATION. IN CONTRAST, THE HUMMER AD USES A GRITTY BLACK-AND-WHITE IMAGE TO SUGGEST THE EMOTION OF DOMINATING THE MEAN STREETS OF A CITY.

important as what that person knows about it. Feeling in this sense refers to an attitude, but it is an attitude surrounded by emotions. The intensity of the response—the impact—comes from the emotions. If you touch someone's emotions with your message, he or she is more likely to remember the message. The telephone and greeting-card companies have been very successful with emotional campaigns because, after all, they are selling sentiment—warm feelings, love, missing someone, nostalgia, and so on.

Many of our buying decisions are emotional ones. We buy shoes because we don't want to go barefoot, but we buy a closetful of shoes for other reasons: different styles for different occasions and different moods. We often use "logical" surface reasons to justify emotional decisions that we don't acknowledge, even to ourselves.

CONVICTION

Attitudes, reasons, logic, and emotion are all part of the persuasive package. What they lead to is belief. We believe something about every product we purchase; if we didn't, we wouldn't buy it. We believe it is good for us, it will make us look better or live better, or it will make us richer or healthier. Even low-involvement products like chewing gum involve some belief system. I buy this brand of gum rather than another one because I believe this gum will taste better, freshen my breath, or do less damage to my teeth.

Conviction: A particularly strong belief that has been anchored firmly in the attitude structure.

A **conviction** is a particularly strong belief that has been anchored firmly in the attitude structure. It is often built of strong, rational arguments that use such techniques as test results, before-and-after visuals, and demonstrations to prove something. Opinions based on convictions are very hard to change. An advertiser who can build conviction in the target audience achieves a strong competitive advantage.

Conviction may be based on convincing argument. It may be based on *demonstration*. According to the old adage, seeing is believing. Product performance that can be demonstrated tends to remove doubt and increase belief in the sales message.

LOCKING POWER: MAKING IT MEMORABLE

Whereas perception and attention are necessary for stopping power, and maintaining awareness is necessary for pulling power, ads that work effectively also have *locking power*—that is, they lock their messages into the mind. If you can't remember seeing the ad, or if you can remember the ad but not the brand, then you might as well not have seen it as far as the advertiser is concerned. When you go to the supermarket, it is important that you remember that soft drinks are on sale. It is also important that you remember the sale was for a certain brand. How does that process happen?

Our memories are like filing cabinets. You watch a commercial, extract those parts of it that interest you, and then find a category in your mental filing cabinet where you can store that fragment of information. The fragment, incidentally, may not look much like the original information as it was presented because your mind will change it to make it fit into your own system of concerns, preoccupations, and preconceptions.

A week later you may not remember that you have a fragment labeled "soft drink" filed away, or you may not be able to find it in the file. Most of us have messy mental filing systems. You have probably found yourself trying to remember something that you know. You can concentrate until your head hurts, and the thought just won't come to the surface. It does come back when it is cued, however. Maybe you remember the party you have planned for the weekend and that reminds you about the soft-drink sale. That is how the cueing process works to pull things out of the file and back onto the top of our minds. A pink bunny reminds you that you need batteries and that they should be the Energizer brand.

Advertising research focuses on two types of memory—**recognition** and **recall.** Recognition means you can remember having seen something before; in other words, it has achieved top-of-mind awareness. Recall is more complex. It means you can remember the information content of the message. These concepts and research methods are discussed in more detail in Chapter 21.

VAMPIRE CREATIVITY

One of the greatest challenges in the advertising world is to create memorability. However, it is easier to create a memorable advertisement than it is to create an advertisement that makes the product memorable. Testing has proved time and again that people often remember the commercial, but not the product. This problem, called **vampire creativity,** occurs primarily with advertisements that are too original, too entertaining, or too involving. The story of the commercial can be so mesmerizing that it gets in the way of the product. Celebrity advertising can have this problem. When major rock stars appear in song-and-dance extravagances for soft drinks, many viewers cannot remember which star is associated with which product. It is essential that the commercial establish a strong link between the message and the product so that remembering the advertisement also means remembering the brand.

REPETITION

You can do several things to ensure the memorability of your message. One technique is repetition. Psychologists maintain that you need to hear or see something a minimum of three times before it crosses the threshold of perception and enters into memory. **Jingles** are valuable memorability devices because the music allows the advertiser to repeat a phrase or product name without boring the audience.

Clever phrases are also useful not only because they catch attention, but also because they can be repeated to intensify memorability. Advertisements use **slogans** for brands and campaigns (a series of ads run under an umbrella theme).

Recognition: An ability to remember having seen something before.

Recall: The ability to remember specific information content.

PRINCIPLE An advertising message should make the product, not the advertisement, memorable.

Vampire Creativity: An advertising problem in which an ad is so creative or entertaining that it overwhelms the product.

Jingles: Commercials with a message that is presented musically.

Slogans: Frequently repeated phrases that provide continuity to an advertising campaign.

SLOGAN TEST

Here is a list of well-known slogans. How many can you identify? What does this test tell you about the role of slogans in establishing product memorability? How do slogans contribute to brand equity?

1. Somethin' for nothin.'
2. Most loved cars in the world.
3. Just do it.
4. Once you pop you just can't stop.
5. Get___ . It pays.
6. Smart. Very smart.
7. Head for the mountains.
8. Don't leave home without it.
9. Like a rock.
10. Gets the red out.
11. Breakfast of champions.
12. Smart money.
13. Let the good times roll.
14. You're in good hands.
15. Changing entertainment. Again.
16. Tastes great. Less filling.
17. It's your money. Demand better.
18. Quality is Job 1.
19. Own a piece of the rock.
20. It just feels right.

ANSWERS

A. Met Life
B. Oldsmobile
C. Busch
D. Chevy trucks
E. Allstate
F. Visine
G. MasterCard
H. Prudential
I. Domino's
J. Mazda
K. Ford
L. Nike
M. RCA
N. Miller Lite
O. Toyota
P. Volkswagen
Q. American Express
R. Wheaties
S. Magnavox
T. U.S. Army
U. Kawasaki
V. Pringles

Taglines: Clever phrases used at the end of an advertisement to summarize the ad's message.

How many slogans can you identify in the Slogan Test box? **Taglines** are used at the end of an ad to summarize the point of the ad's message in a highly memorable way such as: "Nothing outlasts the Energizer. They keep going and going and going." Both slogans and taglines are written to be highly memorable, often using mnemonic devices (techniques for improving memory) such as rhyme, rhythmic beats, and repeating sounds.

KEY VISUALS

In addition to verbal memorability devices, many print ads and most television commercials feature a **key visual.** This is a vivid image that the advertiser hopes will remain in the mind of the viewer. Remember that the memory's filing system usually stores fragments of information. Television is primarily a visual medium, and an effective commercial is built on some dominant scene or piece of action that conveys the essence of the message and can be easily remembered.

Key Visual: A dominant image around which the commercial's message is planned.

Logo: Logotype; a distinctive mark that identifies the product, company, or brand.

Signature: The name of the company or product written in a distinctive type style.

Superimpose: A television technique where one image is added to another that is already on the screen.

Memorability also has a structural dimension. Just as the beginning of an advertising message is the most important part for attracting attention, the end or closing of a message is the most important part for memorability. If you want someone to remember the product name, repeat it at the end of the commercial. Most print ads end with a **logo** (a distinctive mark that identifies the product or company) or a **signature** (the name of the company or brand written in a distinctive type style). Television commercials often conclude with a memorable tagline and **superimpose** the product name on the last visual, accompanied by the announcer repeating the brand name.

How Brand Images Work

Brand personalities and brand images create a feeling of familiarity with a known product. Because this product is familiar, the consumer is reassured that it is

Inside Advertising

TOM KUNTZ, ART DIRECTOR, *Kirshenbaum Bond & Partners, New York City*

Tom Kuntz is currently an art director at Kirshenbaum Bond & Partners (KB&P). He began his advertising career at Syracuse University where he earned his BFA in advertising.

His first job in advertising was at J. Walter Thompson, New York. From there he went on to work at KB&P, where he has produced campaigns for Snapple, Moet & Chandon champagne, Target stores, Operation Santa Claus (a probono account) as well as freelance work for Beachbum Tanning and Lucy's Surf Bar.

In addition to working at KB&P, Tom plays drums in two bands, runs a small independent record label, and teaches an advertising portfolio class at the School of Visual Arts.

Tom Kuntz, this is your life . . .

6:50 A.M. Awake 20 minutes late. Run to meet a photographer who picks me up in a Winnebago to go take shots of traffic jams for an outdoor campaign I'm doing for Target. Read *The New York Times* in the car heading out to Jersey. Spend the next few hours chasing traffic on the highways of Long Island and New Jersey.

9:30 A.M. Get dropped off by the Winnebago at the agency. Check voice mail messages. Return the important messages. Cancel lunch with a director's rep because it's looking like my day's going to be too busy. Flip through this week's *Adweek* and putz around with my copywriter/partner Mike for a couple of minutes.

9:35 A.M. Thank my lucky stars that I have a partner as brilliant as Mike.

9:45 A.M. Grab layouts of the outdoor campaign and run down to Bill Oberlander's (my creative director) office to get them in front of his face before he leaves for the day.

10:00 A.M. Hop on the computer to make some minor changes to the outdoor campaign when I get a page from my producer saying we have to make a couple changes to the edits of two television commercials we just did for Target. Mike (my copywriter) and I throw on our jackets and walk over to our editor's.

10:45 A.M. Arrive at editor's. Mike and I quickly sit down and order some expensive food for lunch. For the next two hours we sit and watch the editor. Mike, myself, and our producer go back and forth about how we want to make the edit work. Meanwhile, we're working on a print ad that needs to be done immediately. We throw around ideas and pick our three favorites. Then fax

them to our account executive so she can show the ideas to our creative director, then to the client.

12:30 P.M. Arrive back at the agency. Traffic people (the people who make sure jobs are running smoothly) are waiting for me to look at ads that are about to go to press. I look them over, give them my signature, then politely ask them to leave my office.

1:00 P.M. Meet with a new creative team that's working on some print ads for another client's campaign that Mike and I did. We evaluate their work and plan to meet again in two days.

1:30 P.M. Look at some photos that just came back from retouching. Make a few last minute changes to them. Then send them back out.

2:00 P.M. Mike and I take a quick walk a couple blocks away from the agency to see a billboard being painted for the agency (see photo). We swing by just to check that the colors are right and that the words are all spelled correctly.

2:30 P.M. Meet with a potential art director to look at her book.

3:05 P.M. Mike and I go out for a break.

3:30 P.M. Get back. Sit down. Start thinking about yet another ad that was due yesterday. Realize it never stops. Listen to Mike whine. Procrastinate. Suggest a few ideas to Mike. Mike suggests a few ideas. I suggest a few more. We work for about 20 minutes.

4:15 P.M. Check out a few directors' reels. Mostly for inspiration.

5:00 P.M. Meet with an agency public relations person to give her sound bites for an article being written about a public service campaign we just finished for Operation Santa Claus. She asks us why we chose the approach we did, etc.

5:30 P.M. Realize the day has flown by. Say this to Mike. He agrees with me. We start getting down to work after realizing we don't want to be here all night.

7:00 P.M. Get a call from the producer. It's back to the editor's to make a couple more changes as per Richard Kirshenbaum.

8:00 P.M. Arrive at editor's. Order an expensive dinner and break out a notepad and pen to write my day in the life for an advertising textbook.

9:00 P.M. Ask Mike to look it over, then type it up for me on his powerbook. He makes a few additions.

Nominated by Prof. Marcia Christ, Marist College

PRINCIPLE Branding creates the familiarity on which a relationship with a product can be built.

Transformation Advertising: Image advertising that changes the experience of buying and using a product.

appropriate to buy it again. That is the secret behind the phenomenal success of McDonald's over the years. The fast-food chain has a familiar and comfortable image, and consumers know from experience that it offers cleanliness, service, and dependable quality at reasonable prices. Branding creates memorability, but it also establishes preferences, habits, and loyalties. In other words, it creates a platform on which a *relationship* is built between a brand and its user.

Branding is particularly important for *parity products*—those products for which there are few, if any, major differences in features. The products are *undifferentiated* in the marketplace, but through the development of a brand image, they are differentiated in the minds of their users. Soaps are relatively indistinguishable. What enhances the difference between one soap and another is advertising. In such cases the distinction may be minor, but the *difference* is not—because the difference lies in the perceived image and personality of the product. Product personalities were discussed in Chapter 7. Personality is important both in positioning a brand and in developing a brand image.

Concepts and Applications

TRANSFORMATION ADVERTISING

Although most brands of jeans are physically very much alike, advertising has transformed Levi's 501s beyond the basic requirements of the category. Levi's has been endowed by advertising with the capacity to provide an experience different from the experience that comes from wearing any old pair of jeans. Advertising does more than tell consumers about product attributes. It actually transforms the consumer's experience when the consumer uses the product.

Experiences based on transformation advertising are very real. The experience of smoking a Marlboro is different from the experience of smoking a Pall Mall. The experience of using Coast is different from the experience of using Irish Spring or a generic bar of soap. If you doubt the reality of such differences, try giving your mother a watch for her birthday in a box that comes from K mart as opposed to giving the same watch in a box that comes from Tiffany. No doubt, you'll find the experiences of buying, giving, and wearing the watch are quite different.

Advertising provides information and at the same time transforms the experience of buying and using the product. Transformation is the secret to building a product personality and image. It is an expensive objective. In addition to consistency, one of the requirements for **transformation advertising** is frequent exposure. The process takes time because the effect is cumulative.

For transformation advertising to be effective in selling a product it should be positive. Its function is to make the experience richer, warmer, and more enjoyable. Wearers of Levi's jeans truly enjoy wearing Levi's more than they enjoy wearing jeans without the Levi's symbol (see Ad 8.4).

Transformation is not equally appropriate for every product. Upbeat advertising messages might not work for products related to drudgery or unpleasant experience because such a message would sound phony. It may not be possible to turn cleaning the oven, scrubbing the floor, or taking a laxative into a joyous occasion. When advertisements try to do this, they stretch credibility and sacrifice effectiveness.

However, it is possible to use transformation advertising to turn around perceived negatives. For example, the campaign for the financial company HFC, "People Use Our Money to Make the Most Out of Life," has taken some of the threat out of applying for a loan. The State Farm "agent" series, "Like a Good Neighbor, State Farm Is There," helped generate trust in a potentially brittle relationship. "The Friendly Skies of United" has, over the years, taken some of the anxiety out of flying.

Another requirement for transformation advertising is that it "ring true." Because transformation advertising deals with images, it may not be technically verifiable in a literal sense, but it must feel true. The characters must act as the real people in that situation would act, and they must use the product as people would use it in real life. A final requirement for transformation advertising is that it must link the brand so tightly to the experience that people cannot remember it without remembering the brand. One example where this did *not* occur involved a series of ads for a soap company that said:

"New blouse?"	"No, new bleach."
"New dress?"	"No, new bleach."
"New shirt?"	"No, new bleach."

That campaign created a strong link between the experience and the product category, but not the brand. Almost everyone remembered the line. Almost no one remembered the advertiser.

We know that most advertisements just "wash over" their audiences without any effect. Effective advertisements, in contrast, strike a responsive chord. In other words, they have impact, which means they overcome audience indifference and focus attention on the message. Furthermore, they catch attention without being irritating, and they keep attention while penetrating the mind. Advertisements that deliver impact have stopping power, pulling power, and lock the message into the mind of the target audience.

AD 8.4

THE LEVI 501 CAMPAIGN IS AN EXAMPLE OF TRANSFORMATIONAL ADVERTISING.

BRAND IMAGE

A brand identifies and represents a particular product, but it is much more than just a name. It is an image in customers' minds that reflects what they think and feel about a product—how they value it. A **brand image** is a mental image that reflects the way a brand is perceived, including all the identification elements, the product personality, and the emotions and associations evoked in the mind of the consumer. *Product personality*—the idea that a product takes on familiar human characteristics, such as friendliness, trustworthiness, or snobbery—is an important part of an image.

Brand Image: A mental image that reflects the way a brand is perceived, including all the identification elements, the product personality, and the emotions and associations evoked in the mind of the consumer.

A brand, then, has both physical and psychological dimensions. The physical dimension is made up of the physical characteristics of the product itself and the design of the package or logo—the letters, shapes, art, and colors that are used to define the graphics of the image. In contrast, the psychological side includes the emotions, beliefs, values, and personalities that people ascribe to the product. For example, when you talk about the brand image of Hershey's, you are talking about the chocolate itself, and also about the distinctive brown package, the lettering of the name, and the multitude of impressions and values conveyed by its slogan "the all-American candy bar."

PROMISE

A brand is also a promise of value. Because it seeks to establish a familiar image, a brand also creates an expectation level. Green Giant, for example, has built its franchise on the personality of the friendly giant who watches over his valley and makes sure that Green Giant vegetables are fresh, tasty, and nutritious. The name *Green Giant* on the package means there are no unexpected and unwanted surprises when you buy a Green Giant product. An accumulated reservoir of goodwill and good impressions is called **brand equity.**

Brand Equity: The value added to a product by a respected and well-known brand name.

BUILDING A BRAND

Brand equity is an increasingly important concept in the 1990s. The idea that a respected brand name adds value to a product goes back to the dawn of modern

AD 8.5

FERRARI AND FORD USE A VARI-
ATION ON THE SAME SYMBOL—
THE HORSE.

marketing and poses many questions: How much value is added? Can that value be enhanced? Can it be transferred? Castle & Cook, Inc., for example, extensively researched its well-known Dole brand and discovered that the Dole name stood for much more than pineapple. As a result, Castle & Cooke launched Dole Fruit & Juice bars and other frozen desserts. Cheerios has expanded to embrace a variety of Cheerios cereals, including Apple Cinnamon, Honey Nut, and Multi-Grain Cheerios. In contrast, Walt Disney Company discovered that any Disney film would be perceived as targeted to a young audience. Instead of looking for a way to extend the Disney name to films targeted at an adult audience, Disney launched Touchstone Films.

Branding is a way to assist the consumer's memory process. It identifies a product and also makes it possible to position the product relative to other brands. But more than that, branding transforms a product, as is described in the Concepts and Applications box, and makes it more valued because of the respect that has been created for the brand name. The tools used to transform products and lock brands into memory include distinctive names, slogans, graphics, and characters.

BRAND NAMES

Names have both denotative and connotative meanings. Denotative aspects tell what the brand is or does, like Head and Shoulders and Intensive Care. The connotative meaning contains a suggestion or association—a meaning that is supposed to carry over to the product, such as Bounce or Mustang. Some brand names don't say much, like Breck or Sony. Names like these take on meaning only through extensive advertising and the familiarity that comes from product use. Slogans work the same way, although they can carry more content than a simple name. Xerox, whose name has become practically synonymous with the copier product category, is repositioning itself with a new slogan: "The Document Company." It is broadening its image beyond that of copy machines.

Research into names considers linguistics as well as associations. How does the name sound? What does it sound like, and what does it remind you of? Manufacturers must also be certain that the name does not convey any unintended meanings. When Esso renamed itself Exxon, it conducted years of study to find a distinctive name that did not have any unwanted meanings.

Interbrand, a corporate image company that charges as much as $100,000 per name, came up with Polaroid's Spectra and the analgesic Nuprin. The San Francisco-based company Namelab takes a linguistic approach, building words from a table of 6,200 one-syllable sounds. Other namesmiths rely more on outside focus groups, which might include consumers, professional writers, or even Scrabble fanatics. Many firms also have computers that coin words by the bucketful or catalog millions of previous rejects.

GRAPHIC ELEMENTS

The brand's personality is displayed in distinctive graphics used in packaging and other forms of communication. A logo is a characteristic mark that identifies the maker. The graphic elements in the logo and the package design that define the graphic image include distinctive type, colors, and art.

Trademark: Sign or design, often with distinctive lettering, that symbolizes the brand.

A **trademark** is a distinctive visual brand that identifies a company's products. For example, distinctive detailing easily separates the bucking bronco used by Ford's Bronco from the prancing horse used by Ferrari. Trademarks are an important part of the brand image. (See Ad 8.5.)

Symbolic *characters* are used both to help identify a product and to associate it with a personality. The Marlboro cowboy and the Charlie woman are classic examples of symbols that represent an attitude with which the audience might want to identify. The Pillsbury Doughboy is a lovable character that associates warm, positive feelings with the company and its products. Mr. Goodwrench is the kind of friendly, helpful repairman you can trust. His image counters the stereotype of the auto repairman as a swindler. The Maytag repairman is not only friendly, he's lonely because Maytag washing machines are so dependable that he never gets to see customers. All these symbols convey subtle, yet complex, meanings about the products' values and benefits, in addition to serving as identity cues.

Because the effects of image advertising build up over time, consistency is critical to this process. You can't say one thing today and something different tomorrow. David Ogilvy, founder of Ogilvy & Mather, believed strongly in brand image advertising. He said that every ad should contribute to the image. The message should focus on what that image is supposed to be, and should be ruthlessly consistent.[17]

---

[17]David Ogilvy, *Confessions of an Advertising Man* (New York: Dell, 1964).

Summary

- An advertisement must compete with other advertisements, with surrounding editorial and entertainment stimuli, and with hundreds of other possible distractions for viewers' and readers' attention. To be effective, an advertisement must attract attention and hold it.

- In discussing how advertising works, this chapter focuses on five factors: perception, awareness, understanding, persuasion, and memorability.

- The first step in attracting and holding attention is to stop the viewer or reader. Advertisements that are intrusive—that demand attention—have the most stopping power and create high levels of awareness. Intrusiveness comes from the physical characteristics of the ad itself—its loudness, size, length, contrast, or color, for instance.

- In addition to stopping power, advertisements must have pulling power—they must hold as well as attract attention. Pulling power is achieved by being interesting and that relies on the personal relevance of the message.

- Information advertisements must be clear and factual to be understood. They work by providing information about the benefits of the brands they advertise. This information may change attitudes and opinions. It may also associate pleasant feelings and experiences with the brand, thereby making the brand more likable.

- When an informational advertisement works, it facilitates conviction—a firm belief that the brand is superior to its competitors. This belief, which is also influenced by ongoing personal experience with the brand, is known as brand equity. Brand equity is one of a marketer's most valuable and hardest-won achievements. It is the key factor in brand loyalty.

- Persuasive advertisements speak to the head with logic and to the heart with emotion. Reasoning and association are used to build arguments and link a brand with something positive or likable.

- Emotional associations with the brand also contribute to brand equity. Brand equity is not solely due to information, reason, and logic. It is in part a general, hard-to-pin-down, undifferentiated favorable disposition.

- In addition to attracting and holding attention, effective advertisements have locking power—they lock enduring impressions into memory. These impressions are strongest and most durable when the advertisement is original and personally relevant. They are strengthened by vivid, creative design and by frequent repetition.

- The sum of these impressions, combined with other experiences with the brand, constitutes the brand's image. A strong, favorable image is the most important property a brand can have. An unfavorable image is a handicap that must be overcome if the brand is to survive in free market competition.

- Advertising is one—but only one—of the factors that can help a marketer overcome an unfavorable image. If the unfavorable image is due to a defect in the product, or to a defect in a nonadvertising aspect of the marketing program, advertising alone cannot repair it.

- Transformation advertising transforms the consumer's experience of using the brand. It makes this experience warmer, richer, and more enjoyable than the experience would have been without the advertising. Transformation advertising can be and often is an important contributor to the brand's image.

- To be effective, transformation advertising must be consistent and frequent because the transformation process is cumulative. Furthermore, even though transformation advertising may not be technically verifiable in a literal sense, it must feel right. Transformation cannot take place when the feeling conveyed by the advertising and the experience of using the brand are incompatible.

- Effective advertisements strike a responsive chord. They overcome indifference and focus attention on the advertiser's message. They catch and hold attention without being irritating, and leave a lasting favorable impression. This impression may be factual, it may be emotional, or it may be a subtle combination of factual and emotional.

- Effective advertisements have stopping power, pulling power, and locking power. They attract and hold attention, and they make lasting impressions. They make significant contributions to the brand's equity by producing essential, favorable changes in the individual consumer's view of the brand's reputation.

QUESTIONS

1. What is meant by breakthrough advertising? How is this accomplished?

2. What are some common methods of attracting and maintaining consumer interest?

3. How does the pattern of perception-awareness-understanding-persuasion-memorability relate to advertising? What types of ads are appropriate at each level?

4. Mary Proctor is an associate creative director in an agency that handles a liquid detergent brand that competes with Lever's Wisk. Mary is reviewing a history of the Wisk theme "Ring Around the Collar." It is one of the longest-running themes on television, and Wisk's sales share indicates that it has been successful. What is confusing to Mary is that the Wisk history includes numerous consumer surveys that all show consumers find "ring around the collar" a boring, silly, and altogether irritating advertising theme. Can you explain why Wisk is such a popular brand even though its advertising campaign has been so disliked?

5. The chapter identifies five major operations in advertising creative strategy: perception, awareness, understanding, persuasion, and memorability. Emotional tactics are discussed under "persuasion," but emotion figures in the other operations as well. Identify how the creative use of emotion can enhance each operation. To bolster your position, select a current advertising campaign that supports your analysis.

6. Bill Thomas and Beth Bennett are a copywriter/art director creative team who often amuse themselves by arguing about famous ad campaigns. Their current subjects are the Energizer bunny and Budweiser frogs commercials. Bill says they are good examples of vampire creativity. Beth disagrees, stressing their strength through "interest" and "ambiguity." Who is right? Why?

SUGGESTED CLASS PROJECT

From current magazines, identify five advertisements that have exceptionally high stopping power, five that have exceptionally high pulling power, and five that have exceptionally high locking power. Which of these advertisements are primarily informational, and which are primarily transformational? How do the informational advertisements differ from the transformational advertisements in use of illustrations, headlines, body copy, and type style?

FURTHER READINGS

Aaker, David A., and Alexander I., Biez, *Brand Equity and Advertising* (Hillsdale, NJ: Lawrence Erlbaum, 1993), Chapters 5, 8, 11.

Bogart, Leo, *Strategy in Advertising: Matching Media and Messages to Markets and Motivation*, 2nd ed. (Chicago: Crain Books, 1984).

Burton, Philip Ward, and Scott C. Purvis, *Which Ad Pulled Best?* 7th ed. (Lincolnwood, IL: NTC Business Books, 1993).

Franzen, Giep, *Advertising Effectiveness* (Oxfordshire, United Kingdom: NTC Publications Ltd, 1994).

Jones, John Philip, *When Ads Work* (New York: Lexington Books, 1995).

Patti, Charles H., and Sandra E. Moriarty, *The Making of Effective Advertising* (Upper Saddle River, NJ: Prentice Hall, 1990).

Raymond, Miner, *Advertising That Sells: A Primer for Product Managers* (Cincinnati, OH: Black Rose, 1990).

Reeves, Rosser, *Reality in Advertising* (New York: Alfred A. Knopf, 1963).

Celebrities are used as endorsers for a brand because they are able to convey the product's message in a very persuasive fashion and anchor the message in memory more firmly than an anonymous spokesperson. When Bill Cosby talks about kids and Jell-O, mothers listen. The most persuasive communication is person-to-person and the celebrity not only delivers that contact, he or she brings a glamour that can intensify the association.

However, there is a downside and O.J. Simpson, Michael Jackson, and Burt Reynolds are the most visible examples. Celebrities are not predictable and they have been known to get into trouble or to say things in public that undermine the message they are delivering for a brand. And even if the celebrities are of impeccable character, there still may be confusion in the association if they speak on behalf of a number of products, as Bill Cosby does.

Michael Irvin pleaded no contest to a felony cocaine charge after being caught in a motel room with two dancers. Irvin made about $700,000 in 1996 but advertising executives estimate he would have been able to make more than $1 million in endorsement income as one of the NFL league's ten best players. After having been rumored to have been involved in a rape, industry experts doubt if any sponsor would touch him in 1997. Unfortunately Irvin's problems rub off on his team, the Dallas Cowboys, as well as other squeaky clean stars such as quarterback, Troy Aikman.

Created characters like the Maytag repairman and Betty Crocker and animated spokescritters like Tony the Tiger, the Pillsbury Doughboy, Fred Flintstone, Snoopy, Little Caesars' Pizza Man, or Coke's polar bears may not deliver the same personal communication, but they are a whole lot more dependable. Cartoon figures do, however, bring warmth and feeling to what might be seen as an otherwise boring product category, such as insurance, cereal, or vitamins. In 1995, the New York-based Video

Storyboard Tests company found that the top-rated commercial was Coca-Cola's polar bears, which attests to the power of spokescritters to create likability and memorability. The Brand Character Quiz gives you a chance to check the memorability of these characters for you personally.

Owens-Corning has used the Pink Panther for more than 15 years to dramatize its insulation. Since Owens-Corning is the only company in the United States making pink insulation, the association made sense. The important thing to remember from the Pink Panther example is that there has to be a connection that makes sense. In contrast, Metropolitan Life has used the highly recognizable Peanuts Gang as spokescharacters to bring some warmth and feeling to its insurance product. The response has been mixed because, although the characters enliven the company's image, their relevance to insurance is not clear. Experts claim that although Peanuts characters have created a great deal of awareness for Met, the characters haven't delivered sales. A *Business Strategy* article concludes that this is typical for characters—there is no way to directly tie an increase in profits to the use of a cartoon character. Awareness, yes. Revenues, no.

One of the longest running and most successful spokescharacters is the Jolly Green Giant. In 1926 a drawing of a giant appeared on the label of the Minnesota Valley Canning Company's extra-large sweet peas. Two years later the giant was colored green, and when Leo Burnett opened his ad agency, with Minnesota Valley Canning as his first client, he added the word *jolly*. Thus was born the Jolly Green Giant, the spokesperson and eventually the brand name for Pillsbury's Green Giant vegetables for over 65 years.

The Green Giant first appeared in print ads in the 1930s and was finally taken to television in the early 1960s. A man of few words, all the giant has ever uttered

BRAND CHARACTER QUIZ

Character	Brand
1. The Stag	A. Keebler
2. Nipper	B. Pillsbury
3. Speedy	C. Hartford Insurance
4. Tony	D. Camels
5. Poppin' Fresh	E. Green Giant
6. Elsie	F. Rice Krispies
7. Charlie	G. Alka Seltzer
8. Snap, Crackle, Pop	H. RCA
9. Joe	I. Borden
10. Uncle Ernie	J. Kellogg's Frosted Flakes
11. Sprout	K. Star Kist

1c; 2h; 3g; 4j; 5b; 6i; 7k; 8f; 9d; 10a; 11e

is the widely known phrase "Ho Ho Ho." To balance the Giant's silence, the Little Sprout was created, "chatting up a storm" and imparting his inside knowledge of the Green Giant products to consumers. The Sprout communicates the necessary product knowledge, allowing the Giant to retain his status as the strong, silent overseer of the valley. The giant is always in the background of the ads, his features obscured, and he moves and speaks very little. This portrayal is consistent across foreign markets, where the Giant receives the same positive response from consumers.

According to Gary Klengl, president of Green Giant Company in Minneapolis, "The giant gives consumers a reason to believe." The character is "bigger than life" and is able to connect with people's emotions, touching "the child within the consumer." The character also has years of consistency on his side and continues to stand for high quality and reasonable prices.

A study of food-product characters, however, indicates that the Giant's Q ratings (measures of overall appeal) are not as high as they could be. Of those consumers surveyed, 91 percent said they were familiar with

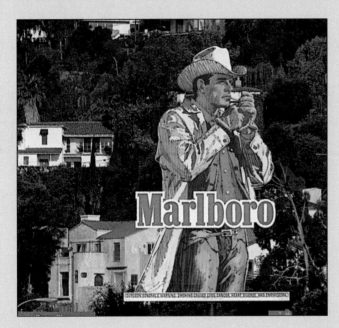

the Green Giant, but the character's Q rating was 19. (Little Sprout had a Q rating of 29.) This rating is average—the average food-product character had a familiarity rating of 72 percent and a Q score of 19—indicating that the Giant is a good fit for the product line but he doesn't generate a lot of enthusiasm. Higher Q scores went to Poppin' Fresh (36), the California Raisins (37), and Tony the Tiger (28).

Some suggest that the company needs to do something to make the Green Giant more modern, humanistic, authoritative, or educational. Greg Lincoln, director of advertising services at Pillsbury, disagrees. He feels the character's consistency is what appeals to consumers: "It's a known entity." The company is expanding on the Green Giant concept, however. In newer ads for Green Giant mushrooms, for example, Sprout is seen outside of the valley, and the Giant is absent altogether. But he'll be back, and the company does not intend to introduce any new characters.

But let's consider again the value of real people (assuming one believes that the personas projected by celebrities are real). If people like a celebrity, does that necessarily mean the celebrity is credible as a spokesperson? Everyone liked George Burns, but he had no success as a spokesperson for cat food because people couldn't imagine him as a doting cat owner. Research by New York-based Video Storyboard Tests finds a great deal of variability between likability and believability for different athletes and entertainers. Some celebrities have very high believability ratings such as Ray Charles (61 percent like, 60 percent believe) and Bill Cosby (69 percent like, 63 percent believe). Others, such as Cindy Crawford (51 percent like, 38 percent believe) and Cher (48 percent like, 32 percent believe) don't rate as highly.

Sources: Adapted from Andrea Gerlin, "Scandals Imperil Products Tied to the Cowboys," *The Wall Street Journal* (January 7, 1997):B1; "Liking vs. Believing," *Adweek* (November 6, 1995):23; Christine Unruh, "Snap, Crackle, Pop," *Journal of Business Strategy*, 16 (March 1995):39–43; Kevin Goldman, "Polar Bears and a Pizza Man Star in Most Popular Ads of 1994," *The Wall Street Journal* (March 16, 1995):B1; and Cyndee Miller, "The Green Giant: An Enduring Figure Lives Happily Ever After," *Marketing News* (April 15, 1991):2.

QUESTIONS FOR DISCUSSION

1. Do some research and find out how many different products Shaquille O'Neal has promoted. How many products can a spokesperson be associated with before confusion sets in? Does Shaq have a clear image as a spokesperson or is he in danger of overdoing the associations?

2. Who are the spokespersons for beverages such as Coca-Cola, Pepsi, and their diet versions? Are their associations clearly linked with the products or is there confusion? What could be done to anchor those associations more firmly in customers' minds?

3. So what would you do if you were in charge of the advertising for Hertz? Why did the O.J. Simpson character work so well for Hertz and how could, or did, his legal difficulties negatively reflect on Hertz? Would you find another celebrity? Would you buy rights to a character or create one of your own? Or would you move away from these types of associations altogether?

4. What would you suggest to the Green Giant brand manager that would reinvigorate the Green Giant character and help raise its Q score?

5. If IBM was considering using a spokescharacter for a new laptop personal computer line, what would you suggest? Would you use a celebrity or a created character? What personality would you recommend to associate with the computer company?

VIDEO CASE   TOOTHPASTE ADVERTISING: MORE THAN HYPE?

One of the most competitive categories of consumer products is toothpaste. Procter & Gamble dominates the market; P&G's Crest brand commands about 28 percent market share. Colgate-Palmolive's Colgate brand is number two, with an 18 percent share. P&G's domination of the market dates back to the mid-1950s, when ads for Crest began to emphasize fluoride content as a proven cavity preventative. That message had great appeal for parents during their children's early cavity-prone years. In the 1980s P&G and other manufacturers developed packaging innovations such as the pump dispenser and introduced new formulations such as gel-based products, tartar control formulas, and kid-friendly flavors. All the while, fluoride continued to be the basic selling point.

Today, however, widespread use of fluoride in public drinking water has offset the importance of brushing with fluoride. Also, with the population aging, the importance of cavity prevention is diminishing. As the baby boom generation enters middle age, whiteness, gum disease, and tooth loss are becoming bigger concerns. Manufacturers are responding by adding baking soda, peroxide, and other ingredients to toothpaste. Unilever's Mentadent contains both peroxide *and* baking soda; in just three years, Mentadent captured 12 percent of the U.S. market. In particular, Crest's market share has fallen since P&G was slow to bring a similar product to the market. Ironically, some experts say there is no evidence that either ingredient actually is beneficial in and of itself. Consumer enthusiasm for baking soda toothpaste is rooted in the vague—but unproved—notion that baking soda is good for teeth and gums. Likewise, the effervescent, bubbling sensation that accompanies brushing with a peroxide toothpaste can give people the impression of cleaner teeth and gums. That impression is reinforced by advertisers, but critics say it is not necessarily accurate.

Meanwhile, the number of toothpaste varieties continues to increase. The next phase of the toothpaste marketing wars in the United States will focus on gum disease, also known as gingivitis. Colgate is launching its newest brand, Total, in a concerted effort to take further market share away from Crest. Ads for the Total brand will make therapeutic claims based on an active ingredient, triclosan, that combats the bacteria that can lead to gingivitis. Total has already proven to be a winner outside the United States; its formulation, imagery, and ultimate consumer benefit were designed from the ground up to have global appeal. The product was tested in six countries, each with a different cultural profile: Australia, Colombia, Greece, the Philippines, Portugal, and the United Kingdom.

Faced with Total and other competitive products, Procter & Gamble is scrambling to shore up its market leadership in the toothpaste category. One reason behind P&G's market share slide is the fact that the company's research and development department did not believe a market would develop for baking soda and peroxide toothpaste. Instead, P&G created Crest Gum Care, a product that flopped because consumers didn't care for the taste. Also, the Food and Drug Administration would not allow P&G to make advertising claims that Gum Care controls gingivitis. Belatedly, P&G decided to launch its own entry in the baking soda and peroxide category. Meanwhile, in 1996, the company began supporting Crest Tartar Control with increased television ad spending. Overall, P&G spent $40 million on Crest in 1995; analysts estimate that $17 million of that amount was budgeted for Tartar Control. P&G was expected to spend twice that much to launch its new product.

Video Source: "Brushing Away the Hype," *20/20* (March 8, 1996). *Additional Sources:* Richard Tomkins, "Americans Face Dazzling Choice of Toothpaste," *Financial Times* (October 24, 1996):22; Pat Sloan "P&G Readies New Ads, Product to Bolster Crest," *Advertising Age* (August 5, 1996):4, 35; and Yumiko Ono and Raju Narisetti, "Toothpaste Makers Take Aim at Gums," *The Wall Street Journal* (August 29, 1996):B1, B14.

QUESTIONS

1. Propose a decision-making model that depicts a typical decision process for purchasing toothpaste.
2. Do you believe that toothpaste advertising presents more hype than truth?

Netscape - [You're in Dime Country]

e Edit View Go Bookmarks Options Directory Window Help

Back | Forward | Home | Edit | Reload | Images | Open | Print | Find | Stop

Netsite: http://www.sprint.com/college/index.html

What's New? | What's Cool? | Destinations | Net Search | People | Software

Sprint Services for Students -- Easy to choose, a value to use

Sprint wants you to be a happy customer so you'll want to

Document: Done

CHAPTER

Media Strategy and Planning

CHAPTER OUTLINE

- Where Are Those College Students?
- The Function of Media Planning in Advertising
- The Aperture Concept in Media Planning
- Media Planning Operations: Information Sources and Analysis
- Media Planning Operations: Setting Objectives
- Media Planning Operations: Developing Strategies
- Media Planning Operations: Media Selection Procedures
- Media Planning Operations: Staging a Media Plan

CHAPTER OBJECTIVES

When you have completed this chapter, you should be able to:

- Understand the central position of media planning in campaign development and how this function utilizes information from numerous sources, including product sales performance, competitor surveillance, and message creative strategy, to form the campaign design
- Understand the organization and purpose of the media plan, and see how each decision on selection and scheduling is coordinated with the client's sales objectives
- Explain how planners use communication aperture to give direction to media planning strategy
- Explain how the media's qualitative features (atmosphere and environment) are blended with their quantitative dimensions (reach, frequency, and efficiency) to provide the needed profile for selection

Where Are Those College Students?

Advertising to the college crowd soon may require a course in computer science for marketers looking to reach students where they live, study, and play—on their computers. College students still visit the usual haunts—bookstores, dorms, bars, campus events, sport venues, vacation spots, and the like—in massive numbers, but the newest hangout is cyberspace.

Marketers who can win over college students have a good chance of keeping them as customers, possibly for life. On their own for the first time, students are making independent purchasing decisions and forming preferences about products and services that, with a bit of marketing pressure, can turn into long-term brand loyalty.

The challenge of advertising to college students—whether via the Internet or more traditional media—is that their lifestyles put them out of range of most traditional media. Students watch less television (though they're addicted to certain prime-time, late night, and cable shows), listen to less radio, and read fewer periodicals than the rest of the population. That's why getting in their face with messages—from online offerings and special events to sampling—is the most effective way to reach them. "To impact students, marketers have to interact with them on a one-to-one basis," says Paul Tedeschi, president of Collegiate Advantage. Many marketers are betting that the Internet will enable them to do just that.

According to a recent survey by research firm Roper College Track, more than 35 percent of full-time students own personal computers, while even more have access through their schools to computers and online services. In the 1994–1995 period, the use of the Internet has doubled among college students.

One reason for this is that colleges and universities, the earliest institutions to use the Internet, are making it easier than ever to log on. The University of Wisconsin-Madison, for instance, installed voice, video, fax, and datajacks in 3,800 dorm rooms so students need only plug in their PC to be hooked up to the college network and the Internet.

The element of fun, plus intimate knowledge of the target audience, a big dose of creativity, and staying up-to-the minute are essential to the success of advertising online to students. With thousands of Web pages out there, there isn't much time to grab their attention.

Recognizing that the Internet has become the communication medium of choice for many students, marketers are looking to online research as a way to take the pulse of college culture and take their existing campus efforts to a new level. Their messages can then be honed with greater precision and advertisers can build relationships with students who respond across the two-way superhighway. Simply put, says Sprint's Mark Taylor, "College students are primary users of the Internet. If we want to be where they are, that's where we have to be."[1]

The Function of Media Planning in Advertising

Media Planning: A decision process leading to the use of advertising time and space to assist in the achievement of marketing objectives.

Media planning is a problem-solving process that translates marketing objectives into a series of strategic decisions. The ultimate goal is to place the advertising message before a target audience. The planning decisions involved include which audiences to reach, where (geographic emphasis), when (timing), for how long

---

[1] Carolyn Shea, "Hot Wiring the College Crowd," *PROMO* (July 15, 1995):61–64; John Nardone, "How to Develop an Internet Media Strategy," *PROMO* (September 1995):48–52; Larry Chase, "Crossroads: Advertising on the Internet," *Marketing Tools* (July/August 1994):60–61; and Eric Carrig, "Where to Reach Today's Young-Adult Generation," *Advertising Age* (September 19, 1994):23.

(campaign length), and how intense (frequent) the exposure should be. Media planning is a blend of marketing skills and familiarity with mass communication. Because it deals with the most significant portion of the advertiser's budget (cost for space and time), it is a crucial element in contemporary advertising.

Media planning was not always the sophisticated process it is today. In fact, it has undergone a substantial evolution in the last 25 years. What was once a clerical function of choosing media positions and contracting for them is now a central element in marketing strategy. Media department employees who once worked silently "behind the scenes" are now in the forefront directing marketing strategy.

If you were the media planner for a product targeted at college students, the opening vignette suggests your job would be quite easy by using online media. But this would be a mistake. The majority of college students still don't own computers, and many who do aren't interested in surfing the Net. Traditional media may still be very important. Moreover, if we employ an integrated approach, the media planner must consider all potential media that can reach our target audience, as well as how these media can be blended to create a harmonious message.

This chapter is an introduction to media planning, with particular emphasis on its integral role in merging the science of marketing with the art of advertising. As you will see, the planner's role is twofold: He or she must act as both a marketing analyst and an expert appraiser of media channel effectiveness.

THE APERTURE CONCEPT IN MEDIA PLANNING

Aperture: The ideal moment for exposing consumers to an advertising message.

Each customer or prospect for a product or service has an ideal point in time and place at which he or she can be reached with an advertising message. This point can be when the consumer is in the "search corridor"—the purchasing mode—or it can occur when the consumer is seeking more information before entering the corridor. The goal of the media planner is to expose consumer prospects to the advertiser's message at these critical points.

This ideal opening is called an **aperture.** The most effective advertisement should expose the consumer to the product when interest and attention are high. Aperture can be thought of as the home-run swing in baseball: The ball meets the bat at the right spot and at the precise instant for maximum distance.

Locating the aperture opportunity is a major responsibility of the media planner. The planner must study the marketing position of the advertiser to determine which media opportunities will do the best job of message placement. This is a complex and difficult assignment. Success depends on accurate marketing research, appreciation of the message concept, and a sensitive understanding of the channels of mass communication.

MEDIA PLANNING OPERATIONS: INFORMATION SOURCES AND ANALYSIS

Media department people often believe they are the "hub" in the advertising wheel, the central point where each campaign element (spoke) is joined. In part, this belief is based on the amount of data and information that must be gathered, sorted, and analyzed before media decision making can begin. Figure 9.1 illustrates the sources of the required information. This chapter will explore how this information is used at subsequent stages in media planning.

FIGURE 9.1

SOURCES OF INFORMATION IN
MEDIA PLANNING.

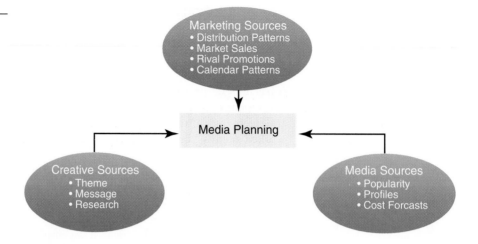

MARKETING SOURCES

Media analysis is described as the crucial bridge between product marketing and advertising strategy because so much of the activity in the marketplace has a direct bearing on media decisions.

AREA SALES PATTERNS

Virtually no company that sells products or services in multiple markets has balanced or equal sales across all territories. The sales activity and sales rank often are different for each area. Because a major role of advertising is to support sales activity, media plans usually vary the amount of advertising designated to each sales territory. As a consequence, each market's sales reports are used to determine geographic dollar allocations.

MONTH-BY-MONTH SALES PATTERNS

The timing of the advertising schedules is a vital strategy in media planning. Most sales for consumer products fluctuate. Media timing (when to start and stop a campaign) should reflect the sales calendar or seasonality for each advertiser. To do this accurately, planners carefully follow the consumer demand trends apparent from the monthly sales report.

DISTRIBUTION PATTERNS

The success of most brands is heavily dependent on how many of each market's retailers carry (stock) the product. Marketers with poor or just-developing distribution may be unable to exploit even good market potentials until they improve their distribution. Marketing people alert media planners to unsatisfactory distribution patterns so that ad spending can be modified accordingly.

COMPETITOR'S ADVERTISING PATTERNS

Rival companies may compete heavily for certain markets or regions, whereas other markets may only be lightly considered. A study of recent advertising history will give the planner some idea of how much advertising to expect from the competition. Heavy concentrations of competitive advertising may change a brand's spending strategy for a region or market. For more on this subject, see the "share of voice" (SOV) discussion later in this chapter.

CREATIVE SOURCES

Close cooperation between media planners and those responsible for the creative decisions can produce sales results. Sharing information influences a number of media strategies, including the choice of the creative theme, the media vehicle, and consumer research.

THEME CHARACTERISTICS

The recommended creative solution (what to say and how to say it) to an advertising challenge usually influences where the message should be placed. For example, complicated copy platforms, such as those for high-involvement products (running shoes or sports cars), might require the use of print media. Media planners must pay close attention to the thinking of the creative department.

MESSAGE CHARACTERISTICS

Creative tactics can also affect media vehicle choices. The tone of the message may indicate that one television program type is right and another one wrong for this creative approach. Media environments are discussed in more detail later in the chapter.

CREATIVE PERFORMANCE RESEARCH

Companies often monitor audience reaction to the advertising message (see Chapter 21). Although copy testing is primarily a measure of creative impact, media planners can use the data to make a number of decisions, including the number of messages to be used and the continuity pattern of the advertising.

MEDIA SOURCES

The eventual selection of a medium (a single form of communication, such as television) and specific media vehicles (a single program, radio station, magazine title, and so on) depends on the availability of media research and information supplied to media planners and buyers on the size and profile of the audience and the media costs for space or time.

MEDIA POPULARITY

Two obvious criteria for media selection are the size of the audience available for each media vehicle and how well the vehicle's audience matches the characteristics of the target market. Media planners and buyers have access to syndicated media audience research that estimates numbers of readers, viewers, and listeners from current audience studies. These data enable planners to forecast the popularity of most of the mass media. More important than the size of the audience are the social and economic profiles of audience members, including demographics, interests and lifestyles, purchasing patterns, and other characteristics that describe potential consumers.

MEDIA COST FORECASTING

Because media plans are developed long before the campaign begins, a careful and accurate estimate of what the advertiser will pay for space and time is vital to successful planning.

MEDIA CHARACTERISTICS

Information on the media is not all numbers, such as audience size. Planners also need to know about the qualities of the media. How influential are they with the audience? How believable? Do they involve the audience beyond entertainment or information? These and questions about media atmosphere are characteristics of each medium. The answers help planners estimate the impact the advertisement might have on the target audience. In the Concepts and Applications box we consider the characteristics of internet media.

In a traditional media model, most marketers are looking to get their message in front of the most consumers at an effective frequency for the lowest possible cost. In the Internet world, this is still partly true, but new dynamics are raised by the nature of self-selected advertising and the navigational structure of the World Wide Web.

There are two general objectives for media planning on the Web. First, as in traditional media, is to get your message to as much of your target audience as possible. The second is to associate your Web content with related and complementary content to enhance the impact and value of your marketing message. The ideal media plan effectively accomplishes both, creating maximum "surface area" for the advertising and multiple points of access for consumers.

Since advertising on the Internet is selected by the consumer, it's imperative to provide cues that encourage browsers to access your site. The typical setup for an Internet ad has two parts. First, the advertiser places a billboard within a content provider domain. This billboard provides an advertising message on its own, but also leads the consumer in some way to the content behind it. The billboard is then linked to the home page of the advertiser's own Web site. The consumer sees the billboard and if he or she chooses to click on it, he or she is immersed in the graphics, information, and utilities of the advertiser's home area. In effect, the advertiser makes use of the traffic flow of the content provider to herd consumers into the advertising. The more enticing the banner (from a creative standpoint) and the more traffic that sees it, the more consumers will likely be delivered to the advertiser's site.

Media placements in outside content provide links to the advertiser's site. In an ideal situation, the outside content is seamlessly integrated into the advertiser's site, but the advertiser's site is also integrated into the outside site. This is *distributed content*, meaning that the advertising content is distributed into other sites on the Web. This is accomplished by soliciting contribution and cooperation from content providers. The objective of this cooperation is to create *shared content* that meets the needs of the advertiser, but also fits snugly into the content environment. The beauty of the Web is that it does not matter on whose server the content resides. It can be seamlessly accessed from either the advertiser or content site because it simultaneously exists on both.

Planning and evaluating media placement opportunities on the Internet can be a fairly straightforward process. Just recognize the similarities and differences from traditional media planning, and be sure to consider the need to herd traffic to your site as well as the opportunity to associate the advertising with related content on the Web. Without too much extrapolation, you can compare the Web to your other media options, and make an educated cost-benefit efficiency decision about its place in your media mix based on familiar print and direct-mail benchmarks. Of course, your success will ultimately be determined by the specifics of your business, the target audience fit, and the quality of your creativity.

Source: John Nardone, "How to Develop an Interactive Media Strategy," *PROMO* (September 1995):48–50.

*M*EDIA *P*LANNING *O*PERATIONS: *S*ETTING *O*BJECTIVES

Each media plan has a series of objectives that reflect some basic questions, the answers to which comprise a strategic plan of action.

The basic questions that direct media strategy are whom to advertise to, which geographic areas to cover, when to advertise, what the duration of the campaign should be, and what the size or length of the ad should be.

FINDING TARGET AUDIENCES IN MEDIA OPPORTUNITIES

There are two major challenges facing media planners today in searching the media for target audience opportunities. Both of these challenges involve the type of research available to the media planner.

Marketers' profiles of valued customers and prospects are provided by company research. These profiles often contain descriptions of peoples' interests, activities, and attitudinal concerns—in all, a valuable insight into the company's target audience. The problem for media planners is that these profiles are not used by the mass media in describing *their* audiences. The result forces planners into translating the marketing research into a context that fits surveys of the mass media. This is not an easy job. Suppose the marketer was looking for prospects with strong ecological feelings. With no media measurement, the planner would have to find another indicator of environmental concerns.

Another challenge is the lack of compatible audience research for the many new and often unique media for advertising and sales promotion. New traditional media (e.g., magazines or cable networks) must wait some time before research companies can supply audience estimates. For innovative media (e.g., store-based advertising, special-event promotions), the existing research firms do not have compatible measurements available. While these opportunities have marketing value, it is very hard to judge their impact without research.

The following are the most common media audience measurements available to media planners. They are discussed in an order based upon availability.

DEMOGRAPHICS
Demographics represents the most common "name tags" given to people. People are described by their age, income (personal and household), education, occupation, marital status, family size, and several other tags. Ad 9.1 for NicoDerm, for

AD 9.1

THIS NICODERM AD IS TAR-
GETED AT CONSUMERS WHO
SMOKE.

example, is targeted at consumers who are trying to quit smoking. For a more detailed discussion of demographics, refer to Chapter 5.

PRODUCT-USE SEGMENTATION

Audiences can also be classified according to their consumption habits (usage). Media planners obtain information on which products readers, viewers, or listeners buy and how often they use or consume these products. For example, college students who are looking for information on local entertainment and spring break travel consider the college newspaper and bulletin boards as their primary media.

PSYCHOGRAPHICS

Psychographics looks for more sensitive measures of motivation and behavior. It attempts to classify people according to how they feel and act. For example, the lifestyle profile, one form of psychographic research, describes people by the way they view their careers and leisure recreation pursuits. A lifestyle profile provides perspective on people's *chosen* social and cultural environment. Preferences for products, services, and entertainment are identified from these consumer self-evaluations.

SALES GEOGRAPHY: WHERE TO ADVERTISE?

Sales geography is an important aspect of many advertising plans. As we mentioned earlier, although companies may distribute goods and services in many cities and states, sales are seldom consistent across areas. Even the most popular brands in sales leadership positions are not that way in every market. Differences affect which markets are used in the campaign and the dollars allocated. For the media planner a system is needed to accurately and fairly distribute the advertising dollars.

TIMING: WHEN TO ADVERTISE?

When is the best time to place the message before the target audience? The concept of aperture suggests advertising is most effective when people are exposed at a time when they are most receptive to the product information. This is easier said than done. Media planners might have to juggle a number of variables to make correct timing decisions: how often the product is bought, if it is used more in some months than others, and how heavily it is advertised by competitors month to month. Each combination of influences makes the timing strategy unique to each company and brand.

SEASONAL TIMING

Much of consumer demand for products and services is influenced by weather patterns. Recreation equipment, agricultural products, beverages, and foods all will reflect changes in season. Aperture exists when the target audience considers their calendar needs.

The strategic challenge for planners is locating the beginning aperture point and estimating how long the campaign should run to cover the demand. Because weather forecasting can be chaotic, media plans must have built-in flexibility.

HOLIDAY TIMING

The timing of advertising schedules can also be coordinated with holidays and other national celebrations. Just as with seasonal planning, media planners must exercise careful judgment regarding when to use advertising to take advantage of the consumer's interest. Nowhere is this judgment more critical than in advertising children's toys and gifts.

Holiday toys and gifts for children pose a fairly tricky problem for media planners. There are two target audiences involved—the child (user) and the adult (buyer). Are both targets making a brand decision at the same time? If not (which is often the case), the planner must decide which target takes priority.

DAY-OF-THE-WEEK TIMING

Retail advertisers know their customers' shopping patterns firsthand. Shopping patterns are dictated by needs, work schedules, and payroll calendars; each day of the week is not equal in shopping traffic. Retail advertising is often used to create traffic during the normally slower times. For example, stores often advertise price specials during the midweek, when shopping is slower, rather than on Friday or Saturday, when it is already heavier.

HOUR-OF-THE-DAY TIMING

Aperture is dictated by peoples' needs in the day. Advertising in selected media should be scheduled when product need is high.

Hour-of-the-day timing is used by companies that target special consumer groups, such as children and teens (after-school hours and Saturday mornings), or senior citizens (early morning rather than evening positions) and radio ads carry messages for restaurants having a large lunch business.

DURATION: HOW LONG TO ADVERTISE?

How many weeks of the sales year should the advertising run? If there is a need to cover most of the weeks, the advertising will be spread rather thin. If the amount of time to cover is limited, advertising can be more heavily concentrated. The selection of pattern depends on a number of factors, including the advertising budget, consumer use cycles, and competitive strategies.

THE ADVERTISING BUDGET

If their advertising allocations were unlimited, most companies would advertise every day. Not even the largest advertisers are in this position, as all advertising budgets are limited. Shorter schedules with stronger levels of advertising must be used instead.

CONSUMER-USE CYCLES

Continuity should match consumer-use cycles (the time between purchase and repurchase), especially for products and services that demand high usage rates, such as soft drinks, toothpaste, candy and gum, fast-food restaurants, and movies. The marketer views these cycles as the number of times customers can be gained or lost.

COMPETITIVE ADVERTISING

In crowded product categories (household products, food, and durable goods) few advertisers are willing to ignore the advertising activity of competitors. In such situations scheduling decisions are made in response to the amount of competitive traffic. The objective is to find media where the advertiser's voice is not suppressed by the voices of competitors. This concept, often called **share of voice** (percent of total advertising messages in a medium used by one advertiser), might mean scheduling to avoid the heavy clutter of competing advertising.

Share of Voice: The percentage of advertising messages in a medium by one brand among all messages for that product or service.

MEDIA PLANNING OPERATIONS: DEVELOPING STRATEGIES

To achieve the key plan objectives of who (target), where (location), when (time frame), how long (duration), and the size of the ad, media planners use a selection process of choosing the best alternatives and methods to satisfy the plan's needs.

The following section discusses some of the strategies used to meet company objectives.

TARGET AUDIENCE STRATEGIES: NEW TECHNOLOGY OF MEASUREMENT

Although media planners are captives of the audience research used in the mass media, there are valuable developments in the near future that may meet the challenges.

RETAIL SCANNERS

With the expansion of scanning at cashier stations and checkouts, marketing research is gaining much more knowledge about the individual consumer's purchasing behavior. Efforts are underway to match buyer activity with specific media preferences; a single source matching product and media likes and dislikes.

DATABASE DEVELOPMENTS

The computer has revolutionized the old-fashioned customer list. An individual's product preference can be stored by name and address. In logic it is only a small step to also store media choices on what individuals watch, hear, and read. More is said about databases in the direct-marketing chapter.

Inside Advertising

TOM JONAS, MANAGER OF STRATEGY DEVELOPMENT, CME • KHBB, *Minneapolis*

8:15–9:00 A.M. Arrive at office, check e-mail, voice-mail, and real mail for urgent messages and changes to the day's schedule. Return phone calls. Write list of what needs to be done today: Begin writing a presentation outlining the results of a strategy development case, meet with client and account executive to determine a new-products development plan, meet with new business coordinator to check on slide production and slide format, prepare for and attend a meeting on the repositioning of a cereal that is not achieving its sales objectives.

9:00–9:30 A.M. Meet with Sharon Guerre in her office to review different slide layouts and colors for the presentation of a strategy development case to about 150 people. Review alternatives, decide on three that she should develop a bit more, and agree to meet later in the day.

9:30–11:00 A.M. Have a conference call in my office with our snack-cakes client and the account executive about developing a strategic plan and planning process to determine where the snack-cake market is headed, how the overall business is changing, and ways in which the client can exploit those anticipated changes.

Reach agreement on the steps we want to take, discuss how the client is going to

need to sell-in the approach to her top management. We're in agreement as to the steps and what needs to be done. The account executive will summarize our conversation, write up what we've discussed, give it to me to review, and then forward to the client sometime late next week. We've agreed that we'll meet in two weeks to determine where to go from here, since there are immediate planning issues that our client needs to address in the meantime.

11:00–11:45 A.M. Work with management supervisor, account executive, and research supervisor to refine an outline for a new business presentation. Focus specifically on research findings from consumers and retailers to determine possible positioning opportunities for the brand, who the most critical target audiences are, and what some of the key positioning criteria should be.

11:45–12:15 A.M. Make "rounds" of creative and account floors to check on how people are coming with key assignments and see where I may be needed.

Talk with the creative team that's working with me on a new-product introduction for an "enthusiasm check" and see if they have any questions about the background of the assignment they've been

These person-specific sources of data could eventually make much of the industry's use of demographics and psychographics unnecessary and obsolete.

GEOGRAPHIC STRATEGIES: ALLOCATING MEDIA WEIGHT

When a regional or national marketer's sales patterns are uneven, it is often the media planner's task to balance sales with advertising investment market by market.

The formula used to allocate advertising dollars may use any or all of the following market statistics: target population, distribution strength, and media costs, in addition to company sales results. In Chapter 7, a marketing system called brand and category development was described. This is a popular method for low-involvement convenience product allocations.

The planner's ideal advertising allocation to a market will provide enough of the budget to fulfill each area's sales objectives. Heavy allocations in weak sales areas are not made unless there are strong marketing reasons to expect significant growth. Conversely, strong sales markets may not receive proportional increases in advertising unless there is clear evidence that company sales can go much higher. Allocation strategy needs the combined efforts of the media planner and marketing (sales) management to be successful.

---

given and any suggestions as I begin drafting positioning alternatives.

The account supervisor on cereals wants to talk to me about some changes in the creative blueprints that occurred while she was out of the office and with which she is not sure she is in agreement. Review whether the revisions are appropriate and really focus attention on what consumers apparently believe to be most compelling before a final recommendation is made to the client. In the end, we agree that the changes that have been made are consistent with the initial direction and have focused on the most important factors that are likely to motivate the consumer.

12:15–1:30 P.M.	Go to the health club to do some aerobics and Cybex circuit. Grab lunch.
1:30–2:30 P.M.	Learn that a meeting scheduled for 3:00 to 5:00 P.M. has been canceled! Review a memo my assistant just prepared, revise a fee estimate for a strategy development proposal. The management supervisor on a new business assignment stops by to discuss what role he would like me to play, and check my schedule between now and the presentation in two months. We agree which steps will be critical, block out some

time on my calendar and agree that he'll get me the briefing materials as soon as possible.

Place a call to a client regarding revised strategy development fee, leave a message.

2:30–3:00 P.M.	Review latest slide formats and colors with Sharon Guerre for the strategic presentation.
3:00–3:30 P.M.	Talk with others in the office about the implications of recently announced top-management changes and the reorganization of account services.
3:30–3:45 P.M.	Take a phone call from the office president and update him on the status of a strategy development and creative assignment we've been given for a new-product introduction.
3:45–5:00 P.M.	Review research on a new-product introduction we have been assigned. Begin outlining issues, targets, and possible positioning opportunities, which will lead to a presentation and creative blueprint. Determine if additional consumer research is likely to be required.
5:00–5:30 P.M.	Check messages, return phone calls, review calendar for tomorrow, and check that I'm either prepared or can wing it.
5:30 P.M.	Depart.

TIMING/DURATION STRATEGIES: CONTINUITY PATTERNS

Continuity: The strategy and tactics used to schedule advertising over the time span of the advertising campaign.

When to advertise can mean seasons, months, or parts of the day, but it all fits into the aperture concept. The strategy to accomplish these objectives involves a balancing of the advertising dollars available with the length of the campaign. A **continuity** strategy is a compromise to spread the advertising without sacrificing impact. Planners who cannot afford or do not want continuous scheduling have two other methods to consider: pulse patterns and flight patterns. (See Figure 9.2.)

PULSE (WAVE) PATTERNS

Pulsing: An advertising scheduling pattern in which time and space are scheduled on a continuous but uneven basis; lower levels are followed by bursts or peak periods of intensified activity.

Pulsing is a popular alternative to continuous advertising. It is designed to intensify advertising prior to an open aperture, and then to reduce advertising to much lighter levels until the aperture opens again. The pulse pattern has peaks and valleys.

Fast-food companies like McDonald's and Burger King use pulsing patterns. Although the competition for daily customers demands continuous advertising, they will greatly intensify activity to accommodate special events such as new menu items, merchandise premiums, and contests. Pulsed schedules cover most of the year, but still provide periodic intensity.

FLIGHT PATTERNS

Flighting: An advertising scheduling pattern characterized by a period of intensified activity called a *flight*, followed by periods of no advertising, called a *hiatus*.

The **flighting** strategy is the most severe form of continuity adjustment. It is characterized by alternating periods of intense advertising activity and periods of no advertising (hiatus). This on-and-off schedule allows for a longer campaign without making the advertising schedule too light. The hope in using nonadvertising periods is that consumers will remember the brand and its advertising for some time after the ads have stopped. Figure 9.3 illustrates this awareness change. The line represents the rise and fall of consumer awareness of the brand. If the flight strategy works, there will be a **carry-over effect** of the past advertising that will sustain memory of the product until the next advertising period begins. The advertiser will then have fewer worries about low share-of-voice conditions.

Carry-Over Effect: A measure of residual effect (awareness or recall) of the advertising message some time after the advertising period has ended.

THE SIZE OF THE AD

Timing of the media effort also involves determining the size and position of a particular message within a medium. Although a great deal of research has been conducted in this area, the results are not conclusive.

FIGURE 9.2

THE CONTINUITY TACTICS OF PULSING AND FLIGHTING.

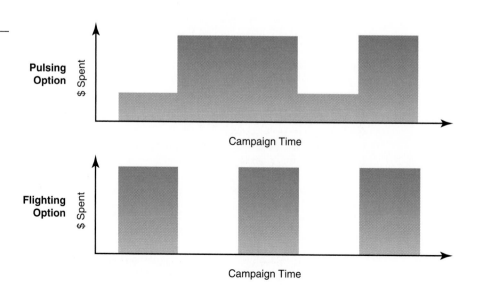

FIGURE 9.3

FLIGHTING TACTICS ARE SUP-
PORTED BY AWARENESS RE-
SEARCH THAT PROVES RECALL
DOES NOT DISAPPEAR ONCE AD-
VERTISING STOPS. AWARENESS
IS SHOWN BY THE SINGLE LINE.

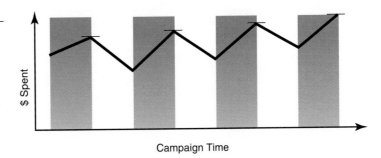

We do know that simply doubling the size of an ad does not double its effectiveness. Although a larger promotion creates a higher level of attraction and greater opportunity for creative impact, the extent is still undetermined. Equivocal results have been reported for print media of various sizes and for television and radio commercials of various lengths. Depending on what advertisers have to say and how well they can say it, a 30-second commercial may do the job much better than a 60-second commercial. Bigger or longer may not always be better. Still, the media planner must consider the possible positive effects. The size or length chosen should also be related to the objectives.

Guidelines regarding positioning are only slightly more enlightening. In general, there is some evidence to suggest that within a print medium (1) the inside cover and first few pages get a slightly better readership, (2) placement of compatible stories adjacent to an ad may enhance its effect, and (3) having many competing ads on the same page detracts from effectiveness. Findings related to broadcast media are almost nonexistent.

MEDIA PLANNING OPERATIONS: MEDIA SELECTION PROCEDURES

Setting objectives and recommending strategies help to focus the media plan, but other factors must be considered in selecting the advertising media and the specific vehicles that will carry the message. These "yardsticks" measure the number of different people exposed to the message (reach), the degree of exposure repetition (frequency), and the efficiency (cost per thousand or CPM) of the selected vehicles. Each of these major dimensions of media planning will be examined in detail. In order to understand their contribution, however, you must first be familiar with the basic audience terms planners use to measure media impact.

AUDIENCE MEASURES USED IN MEDIA PLANNING

In the same way that a carpenter uses feet and inches and a printer uses points and picas, the media planner uses special terms to evaluate a media plan.

GROSS IMPRESSIONS
Impression represents one person's opportunity to be exposed to a program, newspaper, or a magazine, or outdoor location. Impressions, then, measure the size of the audience either for one media vehicle (one announcement or one insertion) or for a combination of vehicles as estimated by media research.

If the *David Letterman Show* has an audience of 100,000 viewers, then each time the advertiser uses that program to advertise a product, the value in impressions is 100,000. If the advertiser used an announcement in each of four consecutive broadcasts, the total viewer impressions would be 100,000 times 4, or

TABLE 9.1	TOTAL TARGET IMPRESSIONS CALCULATION		
MEDIA VEHICLE	**TARGET IMPRESSIONS**	**NUMBER OF MESSAGES**	**TOTAL TARGET IMPRESSIONS**
Jeopardy	3,270,000	4	13,080,000
People Magazine	8,620,000	2	17,240,000
U.S.A. Today	1,700,000	2	3,400,000
			33,720,000

Gross Impressions: The sum of the audiences of all the media vehicles used within a designated time span.

400,000. In practice, planners discuss **gross impressions**—the sum of the audiences of all the media vehicles used in a certain time spot—when dealing with multiple vehicles in a schedule. The summary figure is called *gross* because the planner has made no attempt to calculate how many *different* people viewed each show. Gross values simply refers to the number of people viewing, regardless of whether each viewer saw one, two, or all of the shows. All the planner needs to do is find the audience figure for each vehicle used, multiply that figure by the times the vehicle was used, and add the vehicle figures to get the sum of gross impressions. See Table 9.1 for an example of impressions.

GROSS RATING POINTS

Gross impression figures become very large and difficult to remember. The rating (percentage of exposure) is an easier method of measuring the intensity of schedules because it converts the raw figure to a percentage. The sum of the total exposure potential expressed as a percentage of the audience population is called **gross rating points**.

Gross Rating Points: (GRP) The sum of the total exposure potential of a series of media vehicles expressed as a percentage of the audience population.

To demonstrate, in the previous example, *David Letterman* had 100,000 viewer impressions. Suppose there were a total of 500,000 possible viewers (total number of households with televisions, whether the sets are on or off) at that hour. The 100,000 viewers watching *Letterman* out of the possible 500,000 would represent 20 percent of viewers, or a 20.0 rating. The gross rating point total on four telecasts would be 80 (20 rating times 4 telecasts).

Total rating values are calculated just as total impressions are. The sum of rating points can be used to calculate the total of gross rating points for any schedule, whether actual or proposed. In Table 9.2 the impressions schedule is changed to gross rating points.

REACH AND MEDIA PLANNING

An important aspect of an advertising campaign is how many *different members of the target audience* can be exposed to the message in a particular time frame. Different, or unduplicated, audiences are those that have at least *one* chance for message exposure. Most advertisers realize a campaign's success is due, in part, to its ability to reach as many prospects as possible.

Reach: The percentage of different homes or people exposed to a media vehicle or vehicles at least once during a specific period of time. It is the percentage of unduplicated audience.

Reach is the percentage of the target population exposed at least once to the advertiser's message within a predetermined time frame. The reach of a schedule is produced according to research estimates that forecast the unduplicated audi-

TABLE 9.2	NATIONAL TARGET AUDIENCE GROSS RATING POINTS, SEPTEMBER 1993		
MEDIA VEHICLE	**TARGET RATING**	**NUMBER OF MESSAGES**	**TOTAL GROSS RATING POINTS**
Jeopardy	3.5	4	14.0
People Magazine	9.1	2	18.2
U.S.A. Today	2.0	2	4.0
			36.2

TABLE 9.3	VIEWING HOMES/WEEK FOR *THE DAVID LETTERMAN SHOW*

HOME	WEEK 1	WEEK 2	WEEK 3	WEEK 4	TOTAL VIEWINGS
1	📺	—	📺	📺	3
2	—	📺	—	📺	2
3	📺	—	—	—	1
4	—	📺	—	—	1
5	—	📺	📺	📺	3
6	—	—	—	—	0
7	—	—	—	📺	1
8	📺	📺	📺	—	3
9	📺	—	📺	—	2
10	—	—	—	—	0
Viewing/Week	4	4	4	4	16

ence. Most of the mass media are measured in this way, although for some media the estimate is only a statistical probability. This means the reach is not based on actual data but is calculated from the laws of chance. Reach can only be calculated when the planner has access to media audience research or projections from statistical models. It is not guesswork.

To see how the reach calculation could work in television activity, we use a very simplified situation. Our fictional television market of Hometown, U.S.A., has a total of only ten television households. Table 9.3 is a television survey that shows home viewing for *David Letterman* using a frequency analysis. The viewing survey is for four weeks during which the commercial ran once each week.

Each week four homes viewed *David Letterman*. Because there are ten homes in Hometown, the average program rating per week was four of ten or 40.0. This viewing was done by all homes except home 6 and home 10. To be counted as "reached," the household only has to view *one* episode, and eight of the ten homes did that. The reach is then eight of ten, or 80 percent.

This reach calculation can also be made in newspapers and magazines if the readership research can show the overlap or duplicated readers between two or more publications. If a planner wanted to figure the target reach between *Time* and *Newsweek* magazines, he or she needs the sole readers (i.e., reads only) of each publication along with the total readers for each one. The addition of the sole readers for each divided by total target population will calculate the reach.

FREQUENCY AND MEDIA PLANNING

Frequency: The number of times an audience has an opportunity to be exposed to a media vehicle or vehicles in a specified time span.

As important as the percentage of people exposed (reach) is the number of times they are exposed. This rate of exposure is called **frequency.** Whereas the reach estimate is based on only a single exposure, frequency estimates the number of times the exposure is expected to happen.

To measure the frequency of a schedule, planners use two methods: a shorthand summary called *average frequency* or the preferred frequency method that shows the percent of audience reached at each level of repetition (exposed once, twice, and so on). Both methods are illustrated next.

AVERAGE FREQUENCY

To figure the average frequency, you need only two numbers: the gross rating points (GRP) of a schedule and the reach estimate. The average frequency can also be calculated from the gross impressions and the unduplicated impressions if ratings are not available. Table 9.4 illustrates a situation involving a purchase of space in three magazines. For demonstration, the schedule is summarized in rating and impression values.

𝒥NSIDE 𝒜DVERTISING

AMY WARDROP, MEDIA SUPERVISOR, *Leo Burnett, Chicago*

My interest in the media side of advertising began when I took a media planning course during my junior year at the University of Colorado at Boulder. While my classmates were complaining and struggling through calculations, I was beginning to understand the various numerical relationships and how they related to marketing and advertising—and enjoying it! I was intrigued by both the concept of getting creative with numbers and determining the best means of delivering ads to prospective consumers.

Thus, upon graduation I sought out a job as a media planner/buyer and secured a position at the Leo Burnett Company in Chicago, the nation's largest advertising agency with over $5.6 billion in global billings! Little did I know that what I learned during that semester in college would cover just my first week on the job!

I was first placed on the Nintendo account as a media planner/buyer. After familiarizing myself with the product (oh, what a hardship!), I spent two years in this position working on various aspects of the planning and buying for this kid/teen-targeted product. There are many day-to-day maintenance-type projects involved in a media position. My responsibilities included writing POVs (point of view) for the client on new media opportunities; meeting with sales representatives to keep up-to-date on television programs, magazine readership, and alternative media; and stewarding and posting television buys, which ensure that the networks, syndicators, and stations were running our commercials correctly. It also shows that we are attaining the TRP (targeted rating points) levels they had guaranteed us. If these guarantees were not met, it was my responsibility to contact the appropriate sales representative to secure "makegoods" (spots at no charge that would make up the difference to the guarantee).

However, as a planner/buyer I was also given the opportunity to handle more in-depth projects, at times planning millions of dollars of advertising! During my first month in the planner/buyer position, I was given the task of developing a radio plan and coordinating promotions for the launch of Nintendo's Star Fox video game. After determining which station(s) best reached the target of 12- to 17-year-olds in each market (mostly Top 40 and dance stations), I negotiated the purchase of air time as well as the on-air promotions. These ranged from on-air cartridge/system giveaways during the stations' top-rated programs, to DJ remote broadcasts from Toys R Us stores upon product arrival.

Another particularly exciting moment during my tenure as a planner/buyer was being a member of the team that won *Mediaweek*'s Plan of the Year for the $1–10MM category in 1995. This media plan was developed for the launch of Nintendo's Donkey Kong Country during the fall/winter of 1994. With a new technology, the game was expected to be *the* newest, hottest thing in video gaming. We developed an integrated marketing campaign with two phases. Advertising prior to the launch was designed to generate excitement and presell the game. During the launch we executed brand contacts in as many venues as possible for Nintendo's target of young video game players. The campaign was multifaceted including direct mail, national print, national television, place-based advertising (Channel One in-school television and Channel M monitors in Aladdin's Castles) and promotions. In addition to being part of the media team that developed the objectives, strategies, and tactics, I specifically worked on securing ad time in each show during ABC's TGIF line-up the week of the launch for a vertical roadblock and determining the proper program allocations for the two versions of the commercial. One execution targeted kids under 12 and the other teens 12 to 17.

TABLE 9.4	AVERAGE FREQUENCY CALCULATION MAGAZINE SCHEDULE (ONE INSERTION EACH) TOTAL INSERTIONS THREE		
MAGAZINE	**READER/ISSUE**	**RATING (GRP)**	**UNDUPLICATED READERS**
Today's Happiness	50,000	50.0	30,000
News Round-Up	40,000	40.0	15,000
Yuppie Life	18,000	18.0	11,000
Totals	108,000	108.0	56,000
Target Population: 100,000			
Total Gross Impressions: 108,000			
Gross Rating Points: 108.0			
Unduplicated Readers: 56,000			
Reach: 56.0 (56,000/100,000)			
Average Frequency: 1.9 issues seen (108,000 ÷ 56,000 = 1.9) or (108 GRP ÷ 56 Reach = 1.9)			

Thus, I had to determine, based on the inventory we owned, which commercial would best fit which program. In the end, our plan was a huge success. The anticipation built up during the presell and the hype generated during the launch helped make Donkey Kong Country the biggest-selling game Nintendo had ever had at that time!

Other projects I executed during this time included planning and negotiating print space for adult Game Boy games in publications such as *Sports Illustrated, Time, Popular Science,* and *Discover;* developing a plan for a kid 6–11 game launch in publications like *Disney Adventures* and *Marvel Comics;* and negotiating annual gaming magazine rates and promotions.

After proving myself on Nintendo, I was promoted to media supervisor. Following a brief stint working on Tropicana Orange Juice, my current supervisory position is on the Walt Disney World account. I now oversee many of the same types of projects, from planning the annual Theme Park advertising to planning and negotiating print buys for the Disney Institute; from developing niche media plans for Disney's Fairytale Weddings, the Indy 200, and Disney's golf courses to creating newspaper plans to drive attendance during gap periods. I have had the opportunity to develop marketing plans aimed to boost awareness and inquiry for various Disney properties and to present them to some of Walt Disney's top management.

Internally at Burnett, I am also part of the Walt Disney World Lead Team, which is comprised of management representatives from client services, media, creative, planning, direct marketing, and database marketing. We meet weekly to review the various projects that are being worked on by the different departments as well as discuss any projects or situations that may require collective thinking. This interaction helps me see how specific projects I am working on fit into the bigger picture. It also ensures that the agency works as a team to provide Walt Disney World with the best, most cohesive plans possible.

The attitude in media, as in most of advertising, is "work hard/play hard." During planning, it is not unusual to work 10- to 14-hour days, including weekends. But it's well worth it. The opportunities you are given and the people you work with are second to none. Advertising is a great industry that attracts a lot of fun, creative people. This results in a very energized atmosphere that makes these long days bearable.

At Burnett, you are practically handed a built-in peer group. The transition from college to workplace is eased when you start out with approximately ten other people about your own age. You are with these people at least eight hours a day during your first two weeks on the job as you go through intensive media training. As a result, you find yourself making fast friends as you realize that they, too, are experiencing all this for this first time. After this training and your subsequent placement onto an account, the opportunity to socialize is enhanced through out-of-the-office activities such as the Chicago Ad Federation volleyball tournaments, lunch and dinner receptions, and movie previews hosted by various magazines, as well as department outings to Cubs games and other sporting events. (Unfortunately, Bulls tickets are not guaranteed!)

Marketing, advertising, and media have become a passion for me. I love the challenge of trying to come up with the Big Idea, finding the best way to achieve multiple marketing objectives with minimal dollars, or researching a new media vehicle to find out how my client can benefit from it. And I love the people, the energy, and the creative environment. As the dynamics of today's marketplace continue to change, the role of media is expanding from a once number-crunching, flow chart creating department into an essential, integrated partner in the marketing process. As such, the challenges that face us and the excitement surrounding us continue to grow every day.

Nominated by Professor Tom Duncan, University of Colorado at Boulder

The schedule involves three magazines: *Today's Happiness, News Round-Up,* and *Yuppie Life.* Each magazine is listed by its total readership, readers expressed as a percent (rating), and the number of unduplicated readers (those who do not read either of the other two magazines). Note the formula calculations at the bottom of the table. Average frequency is calculated as follows:

$$\text{Average frequency} = \frac{\text{Gross rating points}}{\text{Reach}(\%)}$$

or

$$\text{Average frequency} = \frac{\text{Gross audience impressions}}{\text{Unduplicated impressions}}$$

FREQUENCY DISTRIBUTION

Average frequency, however, can give the planner a distorted idea of the plan's performance. Suppose you had a schedule that could be seen a maximum of 20 times. If we figured the average from one person who saw 18 and another who saw two exposures, the average would be ten. But ten exposures isn't close to the experience of either audience member. Planners who consider frequency in a functional way will choose to calculate *frequency distribution* whenever possible. The distribution will show the number of target audience members.

Table 9.5 demonstrates the principle for a magazine schedule of three news magazines: *Time, Newsweek,* and *U.S. News & World Report.* Each publication is to receive two insertions for a total of six advertising placements. The minimum exposure would be one insertion, and the maximum would be six.

The planner evaluating this distribution might consider changing this schedule. First, 44 percent of the target audience would *not* be exposed. Then, only 23 (22.5) percent of the target would read more than half the scheduled issues (e.g., four, five, or six).

The frequency distribution method is more revealing, and thus more valuable, than the average frequency method of reporting repetition. However, frequency distribution data are only available from special research tabulations or from sophisticated math models, and this special research may be expensive.

Researcher John Phillip Jones in his book, *When Ads Work,* suggests that when an ad is targeted and on strategy, one frequency is enough. This proposition is addressed in the Issues and Controversies box.

COMBINING REACH AND FREQUENCY GOALS: EFFECTIVE FREQUENCY

PRINCIPLE Media are compared on the basis of their relative efficiency, which means cost and audience size.

Effective Frequency: A recent concept in planning that determines a range (minimum and maximum) of repeat exposures for a message.

As we have just seen, the reach of an audience alone is not a sufficient measure of an advertising schedule's strength. Many media planners now feel that there should be a threshold or minimum level of frequency before any audience segment can be considered exposed to the advertising message. In other words for anyone to be considered part of the "reached" audience, he or she must have been exposed *more than once.* This theory essentially combines the reach and the frequency elements into one. This combination is known as **effective frequency.**

What is this level of repetition? There is no single standard in media planning today, and it is doubtful there will ever be one. True, some observers say that two or three is the minimum, but to prove an ideal level, all the brand's communication variables must be known (aperture, message content, consumer interest, and competitor intensity).

Even without all the answers, planners can use their knowledge and experience to determine a probable range of effective frequency. The theory and technique behind these determinations is complex. Although the understanding of these questions is not complete, many planners are convinced that effective frequency is the essential planning dimension.

TABLE 9.5	MAGAZINE FREQUENCY DISTRIBUTION TABLE BASED ON THREE MAGAZINES, TWO INSERTIONS EACH	
ISSUES READ	**READERS**	**TARGET POPULATION (PERCENTAGE)**
0	44,000	44.0
1	7,000	7.0
2	6,500	6.5
3	20,000	20.0
4	10,600	10.6
5	8,200	8.2
6	3,700	3.7
Totals	100,000	100.0
56,000 read at least one issue. Reach = 56.0		

Issues and Controversies

HOW MUCH IS ENOUGH?

The age-old question of "how much advertising frequency is enough?" has just been answered . . . again. In his book *When Ads Work*, Professor John Phillip Jones states that all you need is a frequency of one. Intrigued by the notion of saving millions of dollars by cutting back advertising, might advertisers be taking an action that could be dead wrong?

Before slashing their ad budgets, advertisers should consider these points:

- *Weekly delivery.* Conceivably misleading, reach or frequency is often tabulated for a four-week period. Keep in mind that Jones suggests one hit each week, with continuity through the year. This equates to a 4.0 frequency over four weeks.
- *Diminishing returns.* For nearly all products there is a "magic range" of advertising pressure below which the sales effect is minimal, and above which advertising simply does not pay out. The same happens with reach and frequency. As more spots air, the rate of reach accumulation decreases and the rate of frequency increases.
- *Motivation.* Jones concentrated on packaged-goods brands where consumers do not need to be motivated. This is distinctly different from the challenge faced by other kinds of advertisers where the consumer must first be sold on the idea of doing something, then on the idea of buying a particular product.
- *Purchase cycle.* The cycle in which consumers buy something should affect how much frequency is needed to influence their decisions.

- *Purchase decision.* People think hard and long about buying a high-ticket item. During this consideration period, a reminder commercial or two makes sense.
- *Average brand.* Jones's research is for the average brand. One must question if any single brand is average.
- *Message complexity.* It's logical that a simple message could be understood after one exposure.
- *Commercial effectiveness and memorability.* According to recall tests, some commercials are more effective than others. Probably more hits are needed for less effective commercials.
- *Commercial length.* If a 10- or 15-second commercial has a lower recall score than its 30-second counterpart, is more than one hit needed?
- *Time of day and attention levels.* An advertiser that disperses commercials across multiple day parts needs to question if one hit could apply to all day parts.
- *Pragmatism.* It is unrealistic to assume that a media schedule could be purchased to achieve only a single frequency.
- *Your competitor is watching.* What if your competitor has not followed suit? Will you be outgunned? Will consumers be influenced more by your competitor because they "see" more advertising?

Source: Jim Surmanek, "One-Hit or Miss: Is a Frequency of One Frequently Wrong?" *Advertising Age* (November 27, 1995):17. Reprinted with permission from *Advertising Age.* Copyright Crain Communications Inc.

COST EFFICIENCY AS A PLANNING DIMENSION

The media plan is not only evaluated in terms of audience impressions. As we mentioned earlier, the cost of time and space determines the number of message units that can be placed. These costs also influence the selection of media or of media vehicles. Inherent in media planning is the notion that media should be selected according to their ability to expose the largest target audience for the lowest possible cost. The key to this notion is the *target* audience because the advertiser wants prospects and not just readers, viewers, or listeners. The *target audience* is that proportion of a media audience that best fits the desired aperture. Therefore, the cost of each media vehicle proposed should be evaluated in relation to the medium's delivered target audience. The process of measuring the target audience size against the cost of that audience is called *efficiency*—or more popularly, **cost per thousand** (CPM) and **cost per rating** (CPR).

Cost per Thousand (CPM): The cost of exposing each 1,000 members of the target audience to the advertising message.

Cost per Rating (CPR): A method of comparing media vehicles by relating the cost of the message unit to the audience rating.

COST PER THOUSAND

The CPM analysis is best used to compare vehicles within a medium (one magazine with another or one television program with another). It is also more valuable to base it only on that portion of the audience that has the target characteristics. To calculate the CPM you need only two figures: the cost of the unit (page or 30 seconds) and the estimated target audience. The target audience's gross impressions are divided into the cost of the unit to determine the advertising dollars needed to expose 1,000 members of the target.

$$CPM = \frac{\text{Cost of message unit}}{\text{Gross impressions}} \times 1,000$$

Here are some examples from print and broadcast vehicles to illustrate the formulas used in CPM analysis.

MAGAZINES An issue of *You* magazine has 10,460,000 readers who could be considered a target audience. The advertising unit is a four-color page and its rate is $42,000. The CPM is:

$$CPM = \frac{\text{Cost of page or fractional page unit}}{\text{Target audience readers}} \times 1,000$$

$$\frac{\$42,000 \times 1,000}{10,460,000} = .004015 = \$4.02$$

TELEVISION The show *Inside Gossip* has 92,000 target viewers. The cost of a 30-second announcement during the show is $850.

$$CPM = \frac{\$850}{92,000} \times 1,000 = \$9.24$$

COST PER RATING

Some planners prefer to compare media on the basis of rating points (ratings) instead of impressions. The calculation is parallel, with the exception that the divisor in CPR is the rating percentage rather than the total impressions used in CPM.

$$CPR = \frac{\text{Cost of message unit}}{\text{Program or issue rating}}$$

(*Note:* Because this is not on a per-thousand basis, the multiplication by 1,000 is not necessary.)

If the target audience rating for the program *Inside Gossip* were 12.0 and the cost were still $850, the CPR would be 850 ÷ 12, or $70.83.

Although both efficiency calculations are used, the CPR is favored by planners for its simplicity. Both the CPM and the CPR are relative values. The absolute numbers mean very little unless there are similar values to compare. A planner would not know if *Newsweek*'s CPM of $27.89 for the target audience were good or bad unless he or she had comparable figures for *Time* and *U.S. News & World Report.*

Although these efficiency analyses can be used across media (comparing one medium to another), such comparisons should be made with caution. When comparing the CPMs for radio and television, for example, you are comparing very different audience experiences, and if the experience is totally different, it is difficult to say that one medium is more efficient than the other. CPM and CPR are more valid when used to compare alternatives *within* a medium.

SELECTING ACCEPTABLE MEDIA ENVIRONMENTS

Success in media planning depends on more than knowledge of the audience size, reach, and cost per thousand. Success also involves some intangibles that can influence the target consumer's reception of the advertising message. Intangibles include both positive and negative communication conditions. To many readers, viewers, or listeners, the advertising message is seldom a desired intrusion. Although audiences only tolerate advertising (with the exception of shopping ads in newspapers), it is still risky for a company to run its advertising in an "alien" environment (a position of weaker communication potential). Three environmental areas deserve particular discussion: media content-product compatibility, media-created moods or atmospheres, and media clutter.

MEDIA CONTENT-PRODUCT COMPATIBILITY

Media content is said to be compatible with the product when the advertiser can find programming or editorial material that complements the message. Think of the sport and recreation magazines that are filled with advertisements for clothing and equipment. Think of televised golf and tennis matches, financial reports, hunting and fishing shows, cartoon adventures, and cooking shows. All offer advertisers a ready-made focus. One attraction of the opportunities is audience characteristics. The other attraction is the special communication between the customer and the content. When this environment is right, advertising becomes enjoyable rather than intrusive.

MEDIA-CREATED MOODS

Moods or atmospheres are created by the programming or editorial content of the media vehicle. Audience members react to content moods, and their emotional reaction is either good or bad for the advertising message that follows. Television situation comedies such as *Murphy Brown, Home Improvement,* and *Wings* are designed to produce laughter. Other programs create tension or anxiety (*NYPD Blue,* and made-for-television movies). Companies sensitive to these variations in atmosphere demand that their commercials be run in atmospheres that will support brand and advertising acceptance by the audience. For example, General Foods (Jell-O Products) will not allow its commercials to run during programming that is not fully suitable for family audiences. Other firms are very cautious about advertising on programs that deal with controversial subjects or social issues.

MEDIA CLUTTER

Most of the mass media allow too many promotional messages to compete for audience attention. Media planners cannot avoid all cluttered conditions, but they can reduce or limit the effect of clutter by isolating their messages from those of competitors and by advising against the use of the most cluttered media.

Judging medium clutter is a subjective process. Some people believe the commercial pod (a string of continuous broadcast messages run during program interruptions) is a severe form of clutter. Others feel that magazines that designate 50 percent of their pages to advertisements are cluttered. Every advertising media format is capable of becoming overcrowded to the point where communication is negatively affected.

MEDIA PLANNING OPERATIONS: STAGING A MEDIA PLAN

PRINCIPLE Media plans are interwoven with all other areas of advertising: the budget, the target audience, the advertising objectives, and the message demands.

To control the flow of information to the plan and to ensure that each component makes a logical contribution to strategy, the planner uses a sequence of decision stages to form the media plan. The plan is a written document that summarizes the recommended objectives, strategies, and tactics pertinent to the placement of a company's advertising messages. Plans do not have a universal form, but there is a similar (and logical) pattern to the decision stages. To illustrate a style of presentation in a real-life setting, we use an actual media plan (excerpted) from the National Dairy Board. The National Dairy Board's mission is to strengthen the dairy industry's position in domestic and foreign marketplaces. The example used relates specifically to the cheese portion of the National Dairy Board's challenge.

A systematic direction of media plans would begin with the general and work down to the more specific questions. Similarly, it would begin with the most important decisions and work down to those of lesser priority. The following section offers a brief description of each stage.

BACKGROUND/SITUATION ANALYSIS

The background/situation analysis is the marketing perspective discussed in the beginning of the chapter. The National Dairy Board summarized overview includes consumer target profiles, geographic considerations, and seasonality (see Figure 9.4).

MEDIA OBJECTIVES/APERTURE OPPORTUNITIES

A media objective is a goal or task to be accomplished by the plan. Objectives are pertinent to the brand's strategy, specifically detailed, and capable of being measured within a given time frame. The objectives listed in the media portion should be limited to goals that can be accomplished specifically from media directions (see Figure 9.5). Measurable media objectives usually focus on reach and frequency projections. Similarly, aperture guidance (though less specific) details the best opportunities of exposing the National Dairy Board's message. Observe that the objectives concentrate on target profile, geographic priorities, and scheduling requirements. Note the aperture importance of scheduling cheese advertising when consumers are most likely to grocery shop.

STRATEGY: SELECTION OF MEDIA

This section of the media plan explains why a single medium or set of media are appropriate for the campaign objectives. A sound strategy should be able to anchor each dimension to the recommendation.

Because planning occurs usually months before the campaign actually begins, some detail is omitted. For the television portion of the National Dairy Board campaign (Figure 9.6), the planner cannot be assured of the program availability or specific pricing in television. In such situations the recommendation must deal with the overall characteristics without identifying specific locations. This isn't guesswork, as the anticipated performance of the television activity is shown in detail.

FIGURE 9.4

NATIONAL DAIRY BOARD
OVERVIEW.

*(Courtesy of DDB Needham
Worldwide and America's
Dairy Farmers)*

Brand: National Dairy Board—Cheese	Media Budget: 18,700M
Marketing Objective:	To increase in-home consumption of domestic cheeses.
Demographic Target:	Women Age 25-54
	3+ Household Size
	Household Income of $30,000+
Target Universe:	22,710.0 (27% of all women)
Psychographics:	Middle class, sticks to basic foods, busy, active, family-oriented
Geographic Skew:	None
Seasonality:	Relatively flat, with increased sales in the November/December period.
Creative Executions:	Television: 15's
	Print Page 4/C Bleed

FIGURE 9.5

NATIONAL DAIRY BOARD MEDIA OBJECTIVES.
(Courtesy of DDB Needham Worldwide and America's Dairy Farmers)

MEDIA OBJECTIVES

Target advertising to medium/light cheese users, demographically defined as:
   Women Age 25-54
   3+ Household Size
   $30,000+ Household Income
Provide national advertising support
Schedule 12 months of support recognizing greater consumption during the
   November/December period
Achieve comparable monthly W25-54 GRP levels vs. year ago

Aperture being sought

Every-week support
   • Complements branded advertising activity
   • Recognizes every-week usage and purchase opportunities
Emphasize biweekly pay periods
   • Greater cheese sales opportunities due to increase in discretionary income
Best Food Day concentration
   • Complements the higher incidence of grocery shopping

FIGURE 9.6

NATIONAL DAIRY BOARD MEDIA STRATEGIES AND TACTICS.
(Courtesy of DDB Needham Worldwide and America's Dairy Farmers)

Audience Delivery

# Weeks:	52 weeks of television
Geography:	National, with emphasis in cable homes due to higher incidence of cheese usage and advertising cost efficiencies
Television:	40% Daytime
Daypart Mix:	25% Primetime
	20% Early Fringe
	15% Weekend

W25-54 GRPs
   Television: 7500
   Print: 1800
   Total: 9300
Average Monthly Audience Delivery (W25-54)

	Cable Households	Non-Cable Households
Reach/Avg. Freq.	98/10.1	89/4.3
Reach at 4+:	83%	42%

Media Buying Tactics

Daytime
   Minimum of 70% of weight in above average rated programs.
   Minimum of 75% of weight is soap opera programming.
   Not more than one commercial in a single program.
Early Fringe Syndication
   Emphasis on talk, sit-com, and entertainment type programs vs. court
   shows.
   A large mix of programs purchased on a weekly basis to maximize reach.
Primetime
   Drama and news programming is the priority to complement greater
   audience attentiveness.
Cable
   A large mix of networks purchased to maximize reach. Program
   sponsorships and billboards are highly desirable.
Magazines
   Position advertising on the right hand page in the food section opposite
   100% recipe edit.

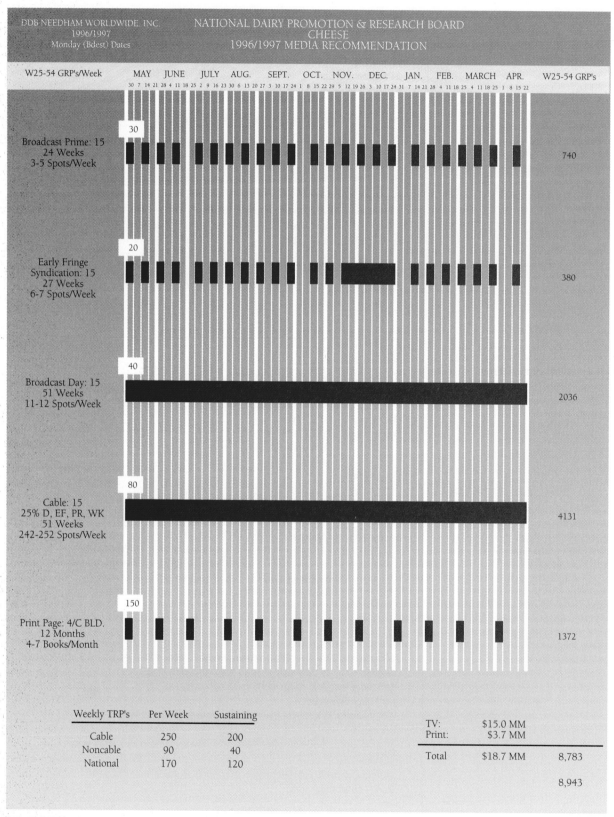

FIGURE 9.7

**NATIONAL DAIRY BOARD
CONSUMER PLAN.**

*(Courtesy of DDB Needham
Worldwide and America's
Dairy Farmers)*

THE FLOW CHART: SCHEDULING AND BUDGETING ALLOCATION

The graphic document depicted in Figure 9.7 on page 294 is designed to illustrate most of the media recommendations. It shows the month-by-month placement of messages, details the anticipated impact through forecasted levels of GRPs, and illustrates how the campaign budget is allocated by medium and by month. In a concise fashion a flow chart is the "blueprint" of the media plan.

The media plan is a recommendation and must be accepted before any further steps are taken. In fact, planning is only the first stage in the advertising media operations. Once the plan directions are set, the actual selection, negotiation, and contracting must be done for time and space. These duties, known as media buying, are the subject of Chapter 12, which examines how buyers convert objectives and strategies into tactical decisions. Before the role of buyer is examined, however, you need to learn more about the advertising media. Chapters 10 and 11 will provide the foundation for a better understanding of the "seller" side of the media business.

*S*UMMARY

- Media planning utilizes the company's full marketing intelligence to decide on the placement of advertising messages.

- The media planner's ultimate goal is known as *aperture*, placing a message before target consumers at the point when their purchase interest is high.

- Media planning objectives are directed by a series of key questions including: who (target), where (location), when (time frame), and how long (duration).

- The selection of media for the campaign is based on a number of factors including target size (impressions/reach), repeated exposure opportunities (message frequency), cost efficiency (CPM/CPR), and important qualitative features such as content moods and other compatible message environments.

- Media-related decisions are presented in a systematically organized document called a media plan. Plans are directed by media goals to be accomplished and the strategies and tactics needed to achieve each goal.

*Q*UESTIONS

1. Why is the media planning function considered the bridge between sales marketing and the creative function of advertising?

2. Allan Johnson is a graduating senior from a mideastern journalism program. He is seeking some career advice from one of his professors. Allan has an interest in advertising, and wants to know what an advertising-journalism major with a business minor in marketing has prepared him for. In addition to account management positions, the professor urges Allan to consider media planning as a logical entry-level position. Why does the professor advise this? Why is marketing study so important for media planners?

3. Susan Ellet has just begun a new job as senior media planner for a relatively new automobile model from General Motors. Facing a planning sequence that will begin in four months, Susan's media director asks her what data and information she needs for her preparation. What sources should Susan request? How will she use each of these sources in the planning function?

4. If the marketing management of McDonald's restaurants asked you to analyze the aperture opportunity for its breakfast entrees, what kind of analysis would you present to management?

5. The Pioneer account has accepted your recommendation for ten one-page insertions (ten issues) in a magazine known as the *Illustrated Press*. The magazine reaches an estimated 3,000,000 target readers per month, or a 10 percent rating per issue. The cost per page of the publication is $20,000. What are the total gross rating points delivered by this schedule? What is the cost per rating point and the CPM target readers?

6. If you were doing a frequency analysis composed of two magazines, a radio network schedule, and a national newspaper, would you rather use the average frequency procedure or a frequency distribution analysis? Defend your choice.

7. Explain why media planners try to *balance* reach, frequency, and continuity of proposed media schedules. What considerations go into this decision?

$\mathcal{S}$UGGESTED $\mathcal{C}$LASS $\mathcal{P}$ROJECT

In performing an aperture analysis, consider these products: video games (e.g., Nintendo), man's cologne (e.g., Obsession), computer software (e.g., Lotus), and athletic shoes for aerobics (e.g., Reebok). For each of the preceding products, find the answers to these questions:

1. Which media should be used to maximize aperture leverage?

2. How does aperture work in each of your recommendations?

3. Explain how timing and the duration of the advertising improves the aperture opportunity.

$\mathcal{F}$URTHER $\mathcal{R}$EADINGS

Barban, Arnold M., Steven M. Cristol, and Frank J. Kopeck, *Essentials of Media Planning: A Marketing Approach*, 2nd ed. (Lincolnwood, IL: NTC Business Books, 1987).

Bruvic, Allen, *What Every Account Executive Should Know About Media* (New York: American Association of Advertising Agencies, 1989).

Jugenheimer, Donald W., Peter B. Turk, and Arnold M. Barban, *Advertising Media Strategy and Tactics* (Dubuque, IA: Brown and Bookmark, 1992).

Sissors, Jack, and Lincoln Bumba, *Advertising Media Planning*, 3rd ed. (Chicago: NTC Business Books, 1989).

Since 1986 U S West had not supported its call-waiting service with advertising, nor had the company aggressively marketed this service to its customers. Consequently, in 1991, U S West's call-waiting service had the second-lowest household penetration of all the Regional Bell Operating Companies.

Research indicated that awareness of call waiting was high among U S West's customers. More than eight out of ten were familiar with the service. Research also indicated that the majority of U S West's nonsubscribers believed that the service was unnecessary. The problem, therefore, was to educate customers about the benefits of call waiting and to persuade customers to try it.

The target was middle-aged adults (18–54) with high incoming-call volumes. The consumers live in busy households within U S West's 14-state region.

The creative strategy focused on building awareness of the benefits of call waiting and building desire to try the service by positioning it as an effective way to avoid missing important phone calls. Using realistic, everyday scenarios, the advertising developed by CME·KHBB, U S West's advertising agency, portrayed situations in which typical consumers missed important calls while they were already on the phone.

The media strategy was designed to increase awareness through high levels of spot television, supported by newspaper and radio. Introductory six-week flights kicked off the campaign in 23 markets, and were followed by four-week flights designed to reduce the number of disconnections among customers who had agreed to try the service during the introductory period.

The introductory campaign included a 30-day free trial offer delivered via newspaper, free-standing inserts, direct mail, and tags on radio and television commercials. This promotion included a program that offered bonuses for call-waiting sales to U S West service representatives.

This integrated combination of advertising, consumer promotion, and sales promotion exceeded its goal. By the time the campaign concluded, it had added more than 300,000 new U S West call-waiting customers.

𝒬ᴜᴇꜱᴛɪᴏɴꜱ

1. Comment on how the media strategy for the U S West campaign supported the firm's advertising objective.

2. How was the target market reached?

3. Is there any aspect of the campaign that could have been omitted and the same result achieved?

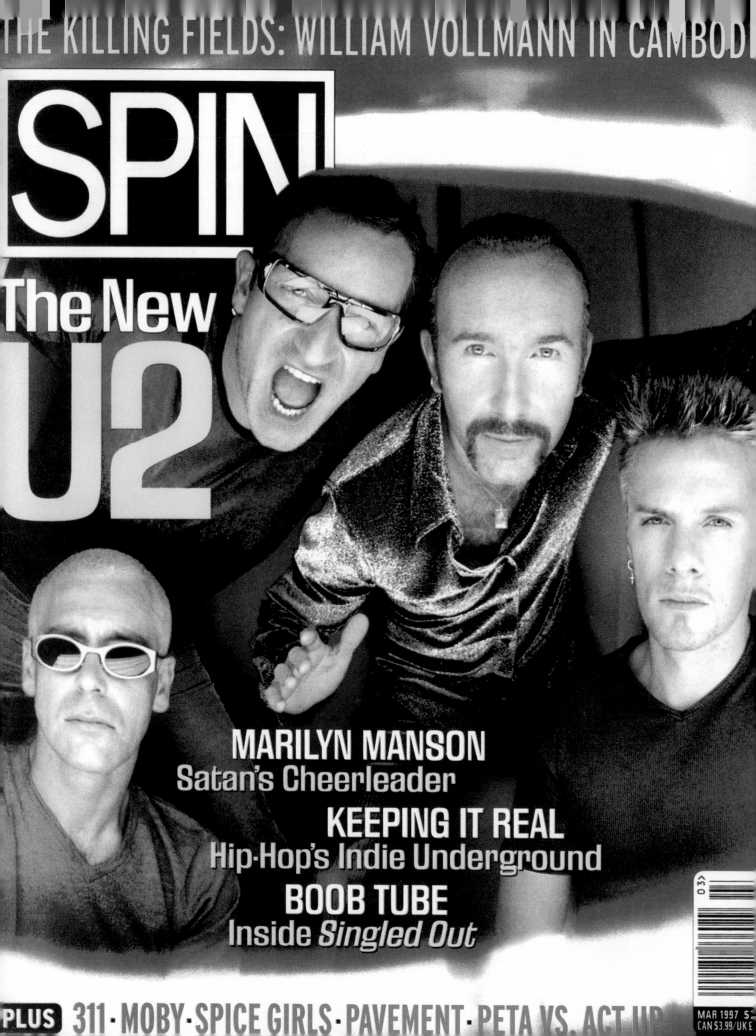

Print Media

CHAPTER OBJECTIVES

When you have completed this chapter, you should be able to:

- Understand the similarities and differences between newspapers and magazines
- Explain the advantages and disadvantages of newspaper, magazine, and other forms of media advertising
- Explain the major trends in print advertisements

Spinning Toward Generation X

Like any rising pop culture trend, alternative rock music has its own cultural lexicon. The scene's icons include Doc Martens shoes, snowboards, and bands like Smashing Pumpkins. One might also lump *Spin*, a magazine known for its alternative music coverage, with these symbols. But although its profile may have grown with the current interest in alternative rock, the 11-year-old monthly title's editorial focus always has been fixed steadfastly on pop culture. Further, *Spin* is zealous in covering the effect on the magazine's readership, centered on those aged 18 to 25 — Generation X.

This focus on the culture-reader connection has helped *Spin*, published by Camouflage Associates, record huge increases in circulation and advertising in 1995. "Our mission hasn't changed but it's organic," editor and publisher Bob Guccione, Jr. says. "We respond to the way the times change . . . One minute grunge is defining music of the movement, and we cover it comprehensively. Next minute there's a metamorphosis out of grunge, and we cover that."

Spin's music criticism and coverage have given it a reputation of being an insightful publication that's in tune not only with readers but also the artists it covers. Cover stars in 1995 included PJ Harvey, Michael Stipe, Rancid, and Green Day. On the cover of its tenth-anniversary issue was the late Kurt Cobain, lead singer of the former band Nirvana and a central figure in the explosion of alternative rock's popularity.

Even though alternative rock has become more popular in the last few years, with the number of radio stations carrying that format growing from 51 in 1994 to 129 in 1995, according to *M Street Journal*, *Spin* hasn't abandoned this area in search of the next cultural frontier.

Yet it's only recently that this connection between *Spin* and its readers has come to light among advertisers, smitten in recent years with the Generation X demographic of 18- to 29-year-olds. New *Spin* advertisers in 1995 included blue-chip marketers such as Sprint, Reebok International, IBM Corp., Apple Computer, General Motors Corp.'s Pontiac division, Eastman Kodak Co., and Calvin Klein. Also, its tenth-anniversary issue hit a perfect-bound 224 pages.

Spin spent 1995 not only cultivating advertisers but also working to develop a franchise through other media. Development of the *Spin* franchise includes a book deal, exposure on television and radio, and an online presence. *Spin* has a three-book contract with Vintage Books. *Spin* got some presence on television in 1995 through "The *Spin* on Fox," a series of 30-second segments on movie, television, and celebrity news aired on a split screen alongside show credits. In addition, *Spin* and Westwood One are assembling the *Spin* Radio Network, a series of two syndicated daily strips currently being pitched to stations and advertisers. The title also plans on developing its presence online from its America Online slot to a Web site scheduled to launch by June.

"I look at the magazine like a boat," notes Guccione. "If it looks like it's going up and down, left and right, it's not because that boat doesn't know where it's going, it's because it's moving with the wave. If you're doing your job right, you should be going in different ways a bit."[1]

The strategy followed by *Spin* is indicative of all traditional media that wish to survive into the next century. Print media is crossing into the realm of broadcast media and vice versa. Moreover, both are moving toward online media. Media planners must not only be familiar with the nuances of traditional media but also with how media have crossed over into other media and new technologies.

In this chapter we focus on the two primary print media — newspapers and magazines. In the next chapter we consider the major broadcast categories — tele-

---

[1] Junu Bryan Kim, "Putting '*Spin*' on Pop Culture," *Advertising Age* (March 11, 1996):58. Reprinted with permission from *Advertising Age*. Copyright Crain Communications Inc.

vision and radio. In both chapters we discuss the areas of overlap, especially the move to online technology.

PRINT MEDIA

Throughout most of the history of mass communication, print was the only readily accessible means of storing information and retrieving it at will. Print is the keeper of records, the vault of great literature, the storehouse of historic accomplishments. In advertising, it differs from broadcast media in several ways. For example, print media deliver messages one topic at a time and one thought at a time, whereas television and electronic media use a simultaneous approach, delivering a great deal of information in a rapid-fire manner. Furthermore, print advertising has a history and credibility unmatched by broadcast advertising. These differences have important consequences for advertisers and media planners to consider.

Advertisers benefit from the selective targeting print media provide as well. For example, those wishing to capture a college-age audience may be inclined to advertise in *U.* or one of the other popular college newspapers or magazines. For an advertiser trying to target college students, print is preferable because it utilizes a very structured information-processing style. Essentially, college students are constantly reading and absorbing information with intensity and credibility. Can we assume that this concentration carries over to print media? Probably. Can we assume that people tend to trust print more than broadcast and absorb it more carefully? Definitely.

Latest evidence of this phenomenon comes in research by New York-based Video Storyboard Tests (VST). While 7 percent of people surveyed said they sometimes find print ads in poor taste, 15 percent of them charged television spots with that offense. As VST's own analysis suggests, one reason for the disparity "might be that you can ignore a print ad more easily than a TV commercial." The same survey showed respondents saying they find print ads more enjoyable and informative than television commercials. If not for any other reason than it's easier to turn a page than to zip or zap around an unwanted commercial, people plainly feel more in control of what they see in print compared to television. Finally, 35 percent thought print ads were enjoyable, compared with 13 percent for television ads.[2]

Nevertheless, print media makers have had to recognize that their appeal is not universal. In general, we have become a broadcast-oriented society. Print does not work with all people. Consequently, it is not relevant to all advertisers. However, it is a viable alternative for certain advertisers under certain conditions. These conditions, along with the history, structure, and advantages and disadvantages of newspapers and magazines, will be the focus of this chapter. Table 10.1 summarizes the dollars spent on advertising for all the primary mass media. It is a useful reference device for this chapter and the one that follows.

NEWSPAPERS

Newspapers were once the nation's medium of choice. Today they compete with a wide range of media for audience share and advertising dollars. Advertisers can now choose between newspapers, point-of-purchase advertising, electronic media, and direct mail, to name but a few apart from broadcast. Audiences can get the

---

[2]Kevin Goldman, "Consumers Like Print Ads Better Than Those on TV, Study Says," *The Wall Street Journal* (June 6, 1995):B-9; and "Inoffensive Medium," *Adweek* (June 5, 1995):19.

TABLE 10.1   TOTAL MEASURED U.S. AD SPENDING BY CATEGORY AND MEDIA IN 1995

RANK 1995	RANK 1994	CATEGORY	TOTAL U.S. AD SPENDING 1995	1994	% CHG	CONSUMER MAGAZINE	SUNDAY MAGAZINE
1	1	Automotive	$10,625.9	$8,988.1	18.2	$1,333.2	$47.2
2	2	Retail	8,781.4	8,505.1	3.2	258.4	98.1
3	3	Business and consumer services	6,751.4	6,582.8	2.6	842.5	36.7
4	4	Entertainment and amusements	5,289.8	4,389.1	20.5	83.5	4.1
5	5	Foods and food products	4,033.1	3,915.1	3.0	675.3	50.6
6	6	Toiletries and cosmetics	2,950.5	2,835.4	4.1	888.1	18.4
7	7	Drugs and remedies	2,894.3	2,548.1	13.6	497.1	91.9
8	8	Travel, hotels and resorts	2,363.6	2,290.0	3.2	460.5	31.7
9	9	Direct response companies	1,633.0	1,652.8	−1.2	919.4	384.4
10	15	Computers, office equipment	1,626.9	932.5	74.5	875.3	8.4
11	11	Confectionery, snacks and soft drinks	1,429.9	1,435.9	−0.4	89.5	5.2
12	10	Insurance and real estate	1,394.1	1,446.0	−3.6	181.3	15.8
13	14	Publishing and media	1,261.4	1,085.5	16.2	290.8	6.9
14	12	Sporting goods, toys and games	1,177.5	1,134.2	3.8	247.7	3.2
15	13	Apparel, footwear and accessories	1,167.8	1,106.7	5.5	582.2	35.5
16	17	Household equipment and supplies	822.4	770.2	6.8	169.5	16.6
17	16	Beer and wine	806.8	798.1	1.1	27.4	0.9
18	18	Electronic entertainment equipment and supplies	723.1	689.1	4.9	149.6	18.7
19	19	Soaps, cleansers and polishes	596.4	591.7	0.8	80.6	2.9
20	20	Cigarettes, tobacco and accessories	504.4	455.8	10.7	317.5	10.7
21	22	Jewelry, optical goods and cameras	460.0	386.0	19.2	230.3	12.4
22	21	Bldg materials, equipment and fixtures	427.3	393.3	8.6	129.3	13.1
23	23	Household furnishings and supplies	340.5	349.0	−2.4	169.9	13.3
24	24	Gasoline, lubricants and fuels	313.9	343.1	−8.5	18.9	1.3
25	25	Horticulture and farming	283.2	255.3	10.9	28.2	16.0
26	26	Pets, pet foods, supplies and organizations	273.4	240.8	13.6	53.1	2.6
27	27	Liquor	233.5	207.0	12.8	192.6	7.6
28	28	Freight, industrial and agricultural	171.4	156.3	9.6	44.7	0.1
29	29	Industrial materials	146.4	139.3	5.0	56.7	0.3
30	30	Business propositions and recruitment	61.8	60.0	3.0	38.4	0.1
31	31	Airplanes (not travel)	32.5	22.4	45.0	14.5	0.1
		Other	309.3	317.3	−2.5	111.7	0.6
		Total	59,887.0	55,022.0	8.8	10,057.8	955.4

Notes: Dollars are in millions.

Source: Laura Petrecca, "Merged Agency West Wayne Has Nat'l Ambitions," *Advertising Age* (October 14, 1996):52. Reprinted with permission from *Advertising Age*. Copyright Crain Communications Inc. Competitive Media Reporting for all advertising.

news faster by turning on their television and radio; they can get the news in depth by watching all-news cable channels such as CNN. A new generation has grown up with this wider range of media options, and this generation is not in the habit of reading a daily newspaper. The consequences are evident. A century ago, there were 18 daily newspapers (dailies) published in New York City alone. As of 1990, only five existed; one was in Spanish, and three were tabloids that were fighting among themselves. Most U.S. cities are surviving now with only one daily paper.

The initial response of the newspaper industry to this fierce competition was to develop new technologies to alleviate the most glaring deficiencies of the medium, which were poor reproduction and lack of sound, movement, and color. Examples are the move from hot metal to cold, or computerized type, text editing, offset printing, on-line circulation information systems, electronic libraries, database publishing, and, most recently, satellite transmission and computerization. There have also been attempts to match the advantages offered by magazines and

LOCAL NEWSPAPER	OUTDOOR	NETWORK TV	SPOT TV	SYNDI-CATED TV	CABLE TV NETWORKS	NETWORK RADIO	NATIONAL SPOT RADIO	NATIONAL NEWS-PAPERS
$3,679.8	$118.6	$1,736.5	$2,937.1	$90.7	$361.8	$69.9	$134.5	$116.6
4,465.7	121.6	616.1	2,478.6	69.0	179.0	133.6	343.1	18.1
1,797.6	109.9	1,088.2	1,547.3	181.8	413.1	131.6	243.9	358.7
1,064.1	160.9	1,542.9	1,888.5	158.1	255.0	7.4	108.7	16.6
21.1	24.0	1,451.8	902.4	437.8	324.0	57.7	87.3	1.1
9.3	4.0	1,234.6	266.5	261.2	228.7	26.5	12.3	0.9
115.1	24.3	1,065.4	447.6	261.2	239.9	109.2	29.5	13.1
975.5	100.9	170.5	311.9	6.1	101.8	29.4	58.6	116.6
90.8	3.9	22.2	38.7	58.5	30.3	12.7	12.7	59.3
54.1	3.6	303.8	63.0	14.7	100.7	16.3	16.4	170.8
5.3	17.1	644.7	269.1	176.0	165.5	29.7	27.1	0.7
530.8	56.7	177.3	269.3	8.6	53.2	16.9	41.5	42.6
242.0	65.9	53.9	296.8	29.5	112.4	63.7	79.2	20.5
5.2	3.5	281.7	242.2	205.2	177.5	1.8	6.0	3.5
12.7	14.9	305.6	54.1	25.3	121.8	0.9	8.5	6.2
7.0	1.3	323.8	126.1	67.1	90.6	16.1	3.4	0.9
4.2	67.9	379.8	189.4	12.7	84.9	10.4	28.0	1.3
12.4	3.3	198.8	147.1	86.3	79.2	11.4	9.6	6.7
0.2	0.1	262.4	87.5	77.7	78.2	5.1	1.6	0.2
21.3	150.8	0.6	0.3	0.1	0.3	0.0	0.2	2.7
6.9	3.6	115.9	31.6	7.8	31.1	6.0	5.7	8.7
30.1	4.2	64.5	87.4	14.0	68.6	3.8	9.6	2.7
23.9	0.6	67.0	36.2	13.5	12.6	0.8	1.4	1.3
8.7	17.2	60.3	124.5	3.2	25.3	7.2	44.8	2.7
53.8	2.2	36.6	59.9	29.6	24.0	2.3	26.9	3.7
8.4	0.7	95.1	49.8	19.6	35.5	1.7	6.6	0.3
3.1	25.8	0.0	0.5	0.0	0.0	0.0	0.9	3.0
3.4	0.7	64.7	30.4	1.0	6.8	0.8	1.6	17.0
4.3	1.4	37.0	15.7	0.2	12.3	3.9	1.0	13.5
7.2	0.1	0.0	3.2	0.0	3.3	0.0	1.5	8.0
6.3	0.2	0.5	0.9	0.0	1.2	0.0	0.1	8.8
68.1	4.9	0.0	13.5	0.3	0.4	0.0	0.0	109.7
13,338.6	1,115.0	12,402.2	13,017.2	2,316.8	3,418.8	776.5	1,352.3	1,136.5

radio (market selectivity) and television (total market coverage). Examples of market selectivity are free-standing inserts and special-interest newspapers. The latter strategy is reflected in nationally distributed newspapers such as *The Wall Street Journal* and *USA Today*. Finally, the high cost of competition, combined with the increased costs of newspaper production, has resulted in a general consolidation in the newspaper industry. The major owners have become publishing empires, such as Gannett, Knight-Ridder, and Times-Mirror. Other newspaper conglomerates are Newhouse Newspapers, the Tribune Company, and the New York Times Company.

Since 1993, 256 of the nation's 1,550 daily papers have changed owners while the number of newspaper groups selling to other large publishers has increased steadily.

Statistics for 1995 indicated that the number of daily papers dropped again, to 1,532 from 1,538 a year earlier. The number of Sunday editions totaled 894, up five from the earlier year and up 57 percent since 1950, when there were only 549. Newspapers have learned that Sunday morning is one of the few times when they have their audience almost entirely to themselves. People usually aren't watching television then. Tables 10.2 and 10.3 provide additional facts related to newspapers.[3]

THE STRUCTURE OF NEWSPAPERS

Newspapers can be classified by three factors: frequency of publication, size, and circulation.

FREQUENCY OF PUBLICATION

Newspapers are published either daily or weekly. There are approximately 1,530 dailies and 8,000 weeklies in the United States. Daily newspapers are usually found in cities and larger towns.

Dailies have morning editions, evening editions, or all-day editions. Daily papers printed in the morning deliver a relatively complete record of the previous day's events, including detailed reports on local and national news as well as on business, financial, and sports events. Evening papers follow up the news of the

[3] Keith J. Kelly, "No Rest for 'N.Y. Post,' Other Sunday Papers," *Advertising Age* (April 29, 1996):S10.

| TABLE 10.2 | TOP NEWSPAPERS BY CIRCULATION |

Figures for the six months ended March 31, 1996, compared with the same period last year. Rank is based on Monday–Friday circulation, except where noted. When papers report separate circulations for some weekdays, the number used is the weighted average. In some cases, Sunday papers have different names.

RANK	NEWSPAPER	CIRCULATION	CHANGE	SUNDAY CIRCULATION	CHANGE
1	The Wall Street Journal	1,841,188	+1.0%	None	—
2	USA Today*	1,617,743	+3.0%	2,009,223	+1.5%
3	The New York Times	1,157,656	−1.1%	1,746,707	−1.3%
4	Los Angeles Times	1,021,121	−3.5%	1,391,076	−4.6%
5	Washington Post	834,641	−0.7%	1,140,564	−1.1%
6	Daily News	758,509	+4.5%	1,010,504	+3.7%
7	Chicago Tribune	667,908	−3.4%	1,066,393	−2.9%
8	Newsday	555,203	−17.1%	643,421	−13.7%
9	Houston Chronicle**	551,553	+33.3%	764,443	+25.6%
10	Dallas Morning News***	518,402	−3.8%	803,610	−2.2%
11	Chicago Sun-Times	501,115	+0.1%	469,161	−4.9%
12	San Francisco Chronicle	493,942	−1.1%	646,171	−2.1%
13	Boston Globe	486,403	−2.8%	777,902	−1.0%
14	Philadelphia Inquirer	446,842	−5.1%	901,891	−1.9%
15	Newark Star-Ledger	433,317	−3.8%	641,393	−5.1%
16	New York Post	418,255	+2.5%	None	—
17	Phoenix Republic A.B.	407,195	+1.9%	597,255	−2.4%
18	Cleveland Plain Dealer**	398,398	−1.5%	528,818	−2.9%
19	Minneapolis Star-Tribune A.B.	380,569	−6.0%	682,318	−1.9%
20	Miami Herald**	378,195	−5.0%	500,654	−4.0%
21	San Diego Union-Tribune**	376,511	−1.6%	453,891	−0.9%
22	St. Petersburg Times**	364,810	−2.1%	462,103	−1.9%
23	Orange Co. Register**	358,173	+0.1%	419,401	−0.3%
24	Portland Oregonian	349,193	−0.5%	445,293	−0.2%
25	Baltimore Sun A.**	337,292	+19.3%	488,562	−1.2%

*USA Today's Friday circulation is listed in Sunday column. **Rank based on Monday–Saturday circulation. ***Figures adjusted by *Ad Age* to indicate weekday average circulation. A = change in publication plan and/or frequency. B = figures adjusted by *Ad Age* to indicate comparable Monday–Saturday figures for 1996 compared to 1995.

Source: Keith J. Kelly, "Dailies Hold Their Own as Circulation Stabilizes," *Advertising Age* (May 6, 1996):52. Reprinted with permission from *Advertising Age.* Copyright Crain Communications Inc.

TABLE 10.3	TOP 25 ADVERTISERS

Top spending marketers in daily newspapers.* Dollars are in millions.

	ADVERTISER	1995 SPENDING
1	Ford Motor Co.	$498,055.4
2	General Motors Corp. (local dealers)	376,960.0
3	Federated Dept. Stores	340,086.3
4	May Dept. Stores	279,876.4
5	Toyota Motor Co. (dealers)	233,384.8
6	Valassis inserts	229,238.3
7	Circuit City Stores	206,174.7
8	Walt Disney Co.	201,631.4
9	Sears, Roebuck & Co.	184,004.7
10	Chrysler Corp. (dealers)	179,708.9
11	Time Warner	162,822.5
12	Nissan Motor Corp. (dealers)	160,150.1
13	Dayton Hudson Corp.	154,906.3
14	Sony Corp.	125,937.1
15	General Motors Corp. (dealer groups)	123,892.4
16	Honda Motor Co. (dealers)	117,938.9
17	K Mart Corp.	113,600.1
18	Viacom	110,218.4
19	Dillard Stores	108,314.2
20	J.C. Penney Co.	91,699.0
21	Seagram Co.	86,036.3
22	AT&T Corp.	75,759.9
23	Montgomery Ward & Co.	72,556.4
24	Turner Broadcasting System	68,734.4
25	News Corp.	66,563.4

*Does not include USA Today or The Wall Street Journal.

Source: Competitive Media Reporting and Publishers Information Bureau. Artist: John Hall, *Advertising Age* (April 29, 1996):S-10. Reprinted with permission from *Advertising Age.* Copyright Crain Communications Inc.

day and provide early reports of the events of the following day. Evening papers also tend to depend more on entertainment and information features than do morning papers. The *San Francisco Examiner* is an example of a daily evening paper. Approximately 30 percent of the dailies and a few of the weeklies also publish a Sunday edition. The *Chicago Sun-Times* is a daily paper that publishes both a morning and a Sunday edition. Sunday newspapers are usually much thicker and contain a great deal of news, advertising, and special features. The circulation of Sunday papers is usually greater than that of dailies because they contain more information and because they appear on a day when readers have more leisure time to spend reading a paper.

Weekly papers appear in towns, suburbs, and smaller cities where the volume of hard news and advertising is not sufficient to support a daily newspaper. These papers emphasize the news of a relatively restricted area; they report local news in depth but tend to ignore national news, sports, and similar subjects. Weeklies are often shunned by national advertisers because they are relatively high in cost, duplicate the circulation of daily or Sunday papers, and generate an administrative headache because ads must be placed separately for each newspaper. *Beverly Review* is an example of a weekly circulated in a Chicago neighborhood.

SIZE

Tabloid: A newspaper with a page size five to six columns wide and 14 inches deep.

Newspapers are typically available in two sizes. The first, referred to as the **tabloid,** consists of five or six columns, each about 2 inches wide, and a total length of approximately 14 inches. This form makes tabloids look similar to an

Broadsheet: A newspaper with a size of eight columns wide and 22 inches deep.

unbound magazine. The *Chicago Sun-Times* employs this size, as does the New York *Daily News*, the *National Enquirer*, and *The Star*. The *standard size*, or **broadsheet,** newspaper is twice as large as the tabloid size, usually eight columns wide and 300 lines deep, or 22 inches deep by 14 inches wide. For both pragmatic and aesthetic reasons, however, many standard-sized newspapers have recently reduced their layouts to six columns wide. More than 90 percent of all newspapers use standard size. *The New York Times* is an example of a standard-size newspaper.

The newspaper format is not fixed and frozen. The success of *USA Today* indicates that newspapers can and will adjust to changing consumer tastes. *USA Today* stories are brief and breezy, dressed up with splashy graphics and full color in every section, and include an array of charts and graphs to simplify the day's events for the reader. Ad 10.1 is an example of a newspaper with a novel format, influenced by the success of *USA Today*, and designed to attract young readers.

Advertisers' major criticism of the newspaper industry has not been as much about the lack of standardization of news format as about the standardization of ad-

AD 10.1

NEWSDAY REPRESENTS A NEW VERSION OF TRADITIONAL NEWSPAPERS.

vertisement format. Historically, national advertisers were discouraged from using newspapers because each paper had its own size guidelines for ads, making it impossible to prepare one ad that would fit every newspaper. This problem was resolved in 1981 with the introduction of the Standard Advertising Unit (SAU) system designed by the American Newspaper Publishers Association and the Newspaper Advertising Bureau. The present version was introduced in 1984 and is shown in Figure 10.1. It is now possible for an advertiser to select one of the 56 standard ad sizes and be assured this ad will work in every newspaper in the country.

CIRCULATION

Circulation: A measure of the number of copies sold.

For the most part, newspapers are a mass medium, attempting to reach either a regional or a national audience. Industry people use the word **circulation** to refer to the number of newspapers sold. A few newspapers have a *national* circulation, such as the *London Times* and *USA Today*; a far greater number are restricted to a *regional* circulation. Some newspapers, however, have attempted to reach certain

FIGURE 10.1

THE EXPANDED STANDARD ADVERTISING UNIT SYSTEM.

(*Source: Guide to Quality Newspaper Reproduction,* joint publication of the American Newspaper Publishers Association and Newspaper Advertising Bureau, 1986)

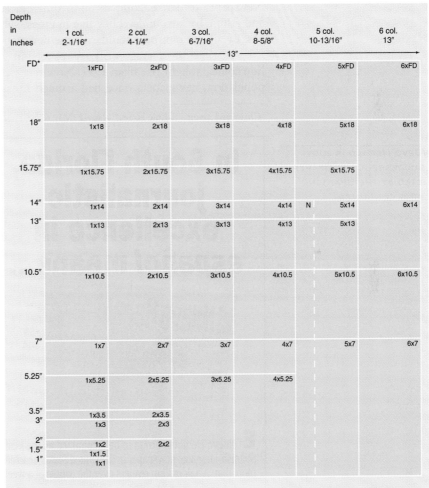

target audiences in other ways. Most common among these are newspapers directed at specific ethnic or foreign-language groups, such as *El Nuevo Herald*, a Spanish daily published in Miami (see Ad. 10.2). Over 200 newspapers in the United States are aimed primarily at black Americans. In New York City alone papers are printed in Chinese, Spanish, Russian, Yiddish, German, and Vietnamese.

AT&T uses black, Asian, and Hispanic papers to tout local corporate events; Honda, Canon, and Ricoh advertise in Japanese papers; and Carnation and GTE run ads in Hispanic papers in California and other regions. As is the case with mainstream newspapers, most advertisers are local retailers, especially ethnic restaurants, travel agents, banks, and stores.[4]

Special newspapers also exist for special-interest groups, religious denominations, political affiliations, labor unions, and professional and fraternal organizations. For example, *Stars and Stripes* is the newspaper read by millions of military personnel.

THE READERS OF NEWSPAPERS

Newspaper readers encompass all income brackets, educational levels, age groups, and ethnic backgrounds. They live in cities, suburbs, towns, resorts, and rural areas. By all demographic standards, the newspaper is a solid mass-market medium.

In 1992, the average weekday readership of newspapers increased to 115 million adults, a slight rise from 1991. Now representing about 68 percent of the adult population, newspapers once had a much broader base of support, as high as 80

---

[4]Christine Larson, "Ethnic Issues," *Adweek* (May 6, 1991):N.3.

AD 10.2

EL NUEVO HERALD IS JUST ONE SUCCESSFUL NEWSPAPER TARGETED AT THE SPANISH-SPEAKING CONSUMER.

In South Florida, journalistic excellence in *español* means...

El Nuevo Herald is proud to be recognized as the best Spanish-language newspaper in the United States, reaching more than a half million readers over the course of a week.

Your advertisement in any of our award-winning sections is the sure way to be on the spotlight of the nation's third and most affluent Hispanic market with a whopping buying power of $13 billion plus a year!

The fact is, no other daily newspaper has a higher penetration in a Hispanic market nationwide!

For current rates and information call our **Advertising Department at (305) 376-4951.**

percent in the 1960s.[5] Frequent readers of daily newspapers tend to be the most regular readers of the Sunday paper. Nearly half of all adults receive home delivery of a Sunday or weekend newspaper; delivery levels are highest in medium-sized cities and lowest in rural locations and the largest metropolitan areas.

Two-thirds of adults read the newspaper on an average Sunday. Over four Sundays, adult newspaper readership increases to 88 percent. The average reader spends 62 minutes reading the Sunday edition, compared with an average of 45 minutes on the weekday paper. Gender differences also exist. Men tend to read the "hard news" section of the Sunday paper, which includes the political, financial, and front-page sections. They also tend to read the sports section, whereas women do not have a particular preference. There are age differences as well. Those 35 and older are more likely than young readers to read news sections; those under 35 regularly read the comics, television booklet, entertainment and fashion sections, and inserts.[6]

Newspaper readership increases with age and with educational attainment. People aged 18 to 24 are 37 percent less likely than the average adult to be heavy newspaper readers (*heavy reading* is 25 or more papers in four weeks, or slightly more than one paper a day). Adults aged 25 to 34 are 17 percent less likely than average to be heavy readers, but those aged 35 to 44 are 17 percent more likely. The most faithful readers are aged 45 to 54, who are 24 percent more likely, and those aged 55 to 64, who are 22 percent more likely than average to be heavy newspaper readers. Probably the best single indicator of newspaper readership is education. College graduates are 65 percent more likely than the average adult to regularly read a newspaper, and those with postgraduate degrees are 87 percent more likely than the average adult to regularly read a newspaper.[7]

MEASURING THE NEWSPAPER AUDIENCE

The most useful way to assess newspaper readers is in terms of how they use the newspaper. In 1993 the Newspaper Association of America compiled a report from Simmons Market Research Bureau's Media & Markets studies of adults in 22,400 households. Of the readers surveyed, 65 percent scanned the entire paper in 1983, but only 54 percent scanned the entire paper in 1992. General news remained by far the most popular section of the newspaper among all types of readers. General news was looked at by 92 percent of all readers in 1992, down only slightly from 1979.[8]

THE AUDIT BUREAU OF CIRCULATIONS

Statements regarding newspaper circulation are verified by the Audit Bureau of Circulations (ABC), an independent auditing group that represents advertisers, agencies, and publishers. Members of the ABC include only paid-circulation newspapers and magazines. The ABC reports have nothing to do with setting the rates that a newspaper charges. They simply verify the newspaper's circulation statistics and provide a detailed analysis of the newspaper by state, town, and county. The newspaper can charge whatever it desires. Advertisers may decline to pay, however, if the rate is out of line with the paper's relative circulation figures as reported by ABC. Other companies, such as the Advertising Checking Bureau, provide newspaper research data and information on competitive advertising.

Newspapers that do not belong to an auditing organization must provide either a "publisher's statement" or a "Post Office statement" to prospective advertis-

[5]Kim Long, *The American Forecaster Almanac*, 1993 Business Edition.
[6]"The Sunday Newspaper and Its Readers," *Newspaper Advertising Bureau* (October 1988).
[7]Joe Schwartz and Thomas Exter, "The News from Here," *American Demographics* (June 1991):50–54.
[8]Christy Fisher, "Newspaper Readers Get Choosier," *Advertising Age* (July 26, 1993):5–21.

KENNETH O. HUSTEL, VICE PRESIDENT, *Newspaper Advertising Bureau, Inc.*

Organizations such as the National Advertising Bureau (NAB) are responsible for the economic health of the newspaper industry. As noted in this box, people like Kenn Hustel spend a very active life trying to make sure newspapers prosper. The following is a look at the morning schedule of a vice president of NAB.

Prior to the Thanksgiving holiday, I must meet with my newspaper Future of Advertising (FOA) teammates in Minneapolis—next Tuesday or Wednesday would be ideal. The FOA project is a team-selling project designed to convince a major advertiser to plan a sustaining newspaper program in a broad list of daily newspapers. The team involves a member of the NAB and two members of a specific newspaper—generally the senior marketing executive and the national advertising manager. The Bureau provides marketing services support, and in the event creative work is required, either the NAB or the creative services department of the member newspaper will be involved. Preparation of the advertising plan, presentation, et al. are in the hands of the three-person sales team.

Our category is ready-to-eat cereals (R-T-E). Following a thorough marketing review of this business we determined the category leader as our target account. The analysis includes not only secondary data sources, but also personal fact-finding sessions with appropriate advertising principles at each company and each of their agencies.

In our second presentation we encountered some resistance from the advertising agency, who suggested we target our effort toward the promotional budget rather than the consumer media budget. This means we need to see the client, since they control the promotional funds.

We have been persistently trying to schedule a meeting with the client's director of marketing services. We carefully explained our purpose and agenda as we requested a short 45 minutes of time. This morning we were "officially" advised that she has no interest in reviewing our concepts and ideas. I find this appalling. I always thought companies would be highly interested in learning of proposals/ideas that could conceivably move their business ahead. Most companies subscribe to this principle, but not all. I suppose we could go a level or two higher to force a meeting, but to what avail? That would only guarantee a hostile atmosphere and a negative response to our recommendation. Not to worry. We have another target that will be far more receptive.

I must remember to call the other major Chicago-based agency on the client's cereal business to review our complete proposal. These people provided us with helpful information during a fact-finding session, so it is appropriate for us to share the program with them. I'll try to schedule for mid-December. This also provides us with an opportunity to show the strong thinking and comprehensive program we can apply to other accounts controlled by the agency. You never know where business might emanate from, so it's important to take advantage of all opportunities.

Next week in the Twin Cities, our sales team will review our strategic sales plan for our new target. Because some time has elapsed since out initial fact-finding session with the client, we might well reexamine the status and direction of the client's cereal advertising program. If the client dictates, we will be prepared to visit with the New York-based ad agency responsible for the R-T-E cereal business within 2 weeks. Following those sessions, we will write the plan developing creative strategy, have NAB-NY prepare some conceptual creative units, and try to get back to the client in early January 1991.

As the R-T-E cereal project rolls ahead, I need to push ahead on a similar project for an Indianapolis-based major household cleaner/food protection company. The ad director of the consumer-products division listened to our target account proposal and quickly accepted our challenge. Since her company is under a mandate to search and examine media alternatives (to network television), our proposal struck a positive chord.

Our project has now reached the point where we are prepared to discuss it in detail with both agencies. I will call company ad director tomorrow to advise of our plans to meet with both agencies late the first week of December. I'll write the letters in Columbus and fax to my office for processing.

ers. The former is a sworn affidavit, and the latter is an annual statement given to the Post Office.

SIMMONS-SCARBOROUGH

The research firm Simmons-Scarborough Syndicated Research Associates provides a syndicated newspaper readership study that annually measures readership profiles in approximately 70 of the nation's largest cities. The study covers readership of a single issue as well as the estimated unduplicated readers for a series of issues. Scarborough is the only consistent measurement of popular audiences in individual markets.

ADVERTISING IN NEWSPAPERS

Although newspapers are not formally classified by the type of advertising they carry, this is a useful way of thinking about newspapers. There are three general types of newspaper advertising: classified, display, and supplements.

CLASSIFIED

Classified Advertising: Commercial messages arranged in the newspaper according to the interests of readers.

Historically, **classified advertising** was the first type of advertising found in newspapers. Classified ads generally consist of all types of commercial messages arranged according to their interest to readers, such as "Help Wanted," "Real Estate for Sale," and "Cars for Sale." Classified ads represent approximately 40 percent of total advertising revenue. *Regular classified* ads are usually listed under a major heading with little embellishment or white space. *Display classified* ads use borders, larger type, white space, photos, and occasionally, color. Often newspapers will include legal notices, political and government reports, and personals in the classified section.

To fight competition from specialty publications and audiotext, database, and online services, newspapers are launching their own specialty classified services. The move is designed to increase automotive, employment, and real estate classified revenues. For example, the *Chicago Tribune* introduced the *Auto Finder* in 1993, followed by *Truck Finder* in 1994. The two publications are available in about 2,000 outlets weekly for a cover price of $1.[9]

DISPLAY

Display Advertising: Sponsored messages that can be of any size and location within the newspaper, with the exception of the editorial page.

Display advertising is the dominant form of newspaper advertising. Display ads can be of any size and are found anywhere within the newspaper, with the exception of the editorial page. Display advertising is further divided into two subcategories—local (retail) and national (general) display advertising.

Local display advertising is placed by local businesses, organizations, or individuals who pay the lower, local advertising rate. The difference between what is charged for local display advertising and national display advertising is referred to as the *rate differential*. In a study conducted by the American Association of Advertising Agencies, it was determined that a national advertiser would be charged an average of 75 percent more than a local retailer for 1,000 inches of newspaper advertising, and 95 percent more for advertising in dailies having circulations of more than 250,000. That 75 percent differential is up 13 percentage points from a similar 1989 study; it marked the largest national/local rate differential since 1933.[10] National ads represent only 13 percent of the $30.4 billion in advertising placed in newspapers in 1991, as opposed to 52 percent for retail and 35 percent for classified. Approximately 85 percent of all display advertising is local, placed by local businesses.

This higher cost is justified by several factors. First, newspapers contend that national advertisers ask for more assistance from newspapers, especially with special promotions, such as coupons and free-standing inserts. Second, they argue that national advertisers are less reliable than local advertisers, often placing no ads for weeks or months at a time. Finally, newspapers believe that the national advertiser is unlikely to change the number of ads placed in a given newspaper regardless of whether the rate goes up or down.

As a result of these higher rates, national advertisers have been reluctant to use newspapers or have looked for ways to get around the rate differential. One alternative that allows the national advertiser to pay the local rate is cooperative (co-op) advertising with a local retailer. *Co-op advertising* refers to an arrangement between the advertiser and the retailer whereby both parties share the cost of

[9]Laura Loro, "Customized Info Leads Classified Rush," *Advertising Age* (April 24, 1995):S8.

[10]Christy Fisher and Joe Mandese, "4 As Hits Newspapers' National Rates," *Advertising Age* (June 1, 1992):40.

placing the ad. The exact share is negotiated between the two parties. Co-op advertising is discussed in more detail in Chapter 22. Some newspapers have created "hybrid" rates that are offered to regular national advertisers, such as airlines, car-rental companies, and hotels. Some newspapers discount for frequency or as an incentive to attract certain categories of advertising.

National display advertising is run by national and international businesses, organizations, and celebrities to maintain brand recognition or to supplement the efforts of local retailers or other promotional efforts.

SUPPLEMENTS

Supplements: Syndicated or local full-color advertising inserts that appear in newspapers throughout the week.

Both national and local advertising can be carried in newspaper supplements. **Supplements** refer to syndicated or local full-color advertising inserts that appear throughout the week and especially in the Sunday edition of newspapers. One very popular type is the magazine supplement, of which there are two kinds—syndicated and local.

Syndicated supplements are published by independent publishers and distributed to newspapers throughout the country. The logo for the publisher and the local paper appear on the masthead. The best-known syndicated supplements are *Parade* and *USA Weekend*. *Local supplements* are produced by either one newspaper or a group of newspapers in the same area. Whether syndicated or locally edited, magazine supplements resemble magazines more than newspapers in content and format.

Free-Standing Insert Advertisements: Preprinted advertisements that are placed loosely within the newspaper.

Another type of newspaper supplement is the **free-standing insert advertisement** (FSIA), or "loose insert." These preprinted advertisements range in size from a single page to over 30 pages and may be in black and white or full color. This material is printed elsewhere and then delivered to the newspaper. Newspapers charge the advertiser a fee for inserting the material plus a special rate for carrying the ad in a particular issue. This form of newspaper advertising is growing in popularity with retail advertisers for two reasons: (1) It allows greater control over the reproduction quality of the advertisement; and (2) the multipage FSIA is an excellent coupon carrier. Newspapers are not necessarily happy about the growth of free-standing inserts because they make less revenue from this form of advertising.

THE ADVANTAGES OF NEWSPAPERS

There are numerous advantages to advertising in newspapers. These include market coverage, comparison shopping, positive consumer attitudes, flexibility, and interaction of national advertising and local retailers.

MARKET COVERAGE

Undoubtedly the most obvious asset is the extensive market coverage provided by newspapers. When an advertiser wishes to reach a local or regional market, newspapers offer an extremely cost-efficient way to do so. Even special-interest groups and racial and ethnic groups can be reached through newspapers.

COMPARISON SHOPPING

Consumers consider newspapers valuable shopping vehicles. Many use newspapers for comparison shopping. Consumers can also control when and how they read the paper, as well as which papers they choose in the first place. As a result, they view newspaper ads very positively.

POSITIVE CONSUMER ATTITUDES

PRINCIPLE Newspaper advertising is viewed positively by consumers who use it for a shopping reference.

Consumers maintain positive attitudes toward newspapers in general. Readers generally perceive newspapers—including the advertisements—to be very immediate and current, as well as highly credible sources of information.

FLEXIBILITY

Flexibility is a major strength of newspapers. Newspapers offer great geographic flexibility. Advertisers using them can choose to advertise in some markets and not in others. Newspapers are often flexible in the actual production of the ads as well. Unusual ad sizes, full-color ads, free-standing inserts, different prices in different areas, and supplements are all options for a newspaper advertiser.

Inside Advertising

JENNIFER ZWIEF, ACCOUNT EXECUTIVE, *Cramer-Krasselt, Milwaukee*

8:15 A.M. It's Wednesday. I'm meeting a colleague before attending a client meeting. We need approval of a radio commercial which was recorded on Monday and finished on Tuesday. The commercial must be at Seattle radio stations tomorrow. We really need approval.

8:30 A.M. We play the radio commercial for client #1. Everyone listens attentively. The client approves the commercial with one minor change. The creative director and I are relieved and happy.

We discuss another project about to be produced, a direct-mail piece. It needs one addition to the copy. We promise new copy will be available tomorrow. I hope we can keep that promise.

10:00 A.M. I'm back at the office. My chair is full of mail, and my telephone is flashing with messages. I listen to voice mail messages first, amazed by how long that takes. Client #2 confirms meeting for next week. Traffic lets me know they need insertion instructions. Media has some new information. Pretty much routine business. I follow up by phone or in person.

10:30 A.M. Time to begin reviewing a document summarizing budgets for this year, as well as next year for client #2. Right now, we make sure we're on target with this year's budget. We also finalize plans and budgets for next year. There is no room for mistakes on a budget document. I go over every number twice, some three times. We'll be presenting this budget to the client early next week.

I talk with the media director about our status on preliminary media negotiations for next year. Since this affects budgeting, we'll want to review this information during next week's meeting. To date, the bottom line of our media negotiations totals less than what we budgeted. Good news.

11:40 A.M. We have an internal meeting with the account team for client #2. We review creative concepts for two print ads which will be presented to the client on Friday. We have multiple executions for each of the two ads; the client likes choices. The concepts meet the objectives and effectively communicate the product benefits and features. The layouts and copy are next. The creatives have a day and a half to do this, which isn't much time for them.

Noon It's the annual pumpkin-carving contest at Cramer-Krasselt—a record number of entries this year. Everyone gathers in the breakroom for the judging. It is hard to decide which is funnier—the entries or the awards. I hope the creative department didn't waste all its creative energy on pumpkins.

1:00 P.M. I write a creative work plan for a project that is needed next year for client #2. This project includes two ads, a direct-mail piece and a response card. The work plan details the background information, objectives, target audience, product benefits and features, and any other mandatories. After the management supervisor approves the work plan, it will be circulated to the entire account team and traffic will schedule a meeting to review the work plan. We need creative concepts in five weeks.

2:00 P.M. I have a couple of client phone calls. We discuss several upcoming projects and finalize some details.

2:30 P.M. It's time for production billing for client #1. Our new cost-control system at the agency makes this easier. I must review each project to make sure its description is accurate, that all invoices are correct and assigned to the appropriate category, and that the invoice total matches the production estimate. After review, these jobs go to the accounting department which processes the actual invoice. Now it's time to write a cover memo to be sent with the invoices.

4:00 P.M. The research director, management supervisor, and I have a meeting to decide how to best answer client #2's follow-up question from a benchmark research study we completed a month ago. We agree to the next steps and set a due date.

4:30 P.M. The management supervisor sits down to discuss the day's events. We need this time together to gather thoughts and make sure everything on today's agenda did get finished today. Then we prioritize what needs to be done before the end of the week.

4:45 P.M. I write a couple of memos and make a few more phone calls before attending a "going away" party for one of the art directors.

Newspapers are even willing to carry product samples. For example, Procter & Gamble recently delivered millions of sample sizes of either Vidal Sassoon Ultra Care Shampoo, Conditioner, or Finishing Rinse through Sunday newspapers in New England and the Midwest. The packet was either affixed to an advertising insert card or a sealed plastic bag. Papers charged 19 cents per sample delivered.[11]

INTRODUCTION OF NATIONAL AND LOCAL

Finally, newspapers provide an excellent bridge between the national advertiser and the local retailer. A local retailer can easily tie in with a national campaign by utilizing a similar advertisement in the local daily. In addition, quick-action programs, such as sales and coupons, are easily implemented through local newspapers.

Charlotte Weisinberger, J. Walter Thompson's media director, summarizes the benefits of advertising in newspapers: "There are a number of things—from representing a local retailer, to breaking a last-minute campaign, to couponing, to telling a detailed story that won't fit in a 30-second spot—that newspapers simply do better than any other medium."[12]

THE DISADVANTAGES OF NEWSPAPERS

Like every other advertising medium, newspapers also have their disadvantages. The issues that are most problematic in newspaper advertising are a short life span, clutter, limited reach of certain groups, product criteria, and poor reproduction.

SHORT LIFE SPAN

Although a great many people do read newspapers, they read them quickly and they read them only once. The average life span of a daily newspaper is only 24 hours.

CLUTTER

High clutter is a serious problem with most newspapers. This is particularly true on supermarket advertising days and on Sundays, when information overload reduces the impact of any single advertisement.

LIMITED COVERAGE OF CERTAIN GROUPS

Although newspapers have wide market coverage, certain market groups are not frequent readers. For example, newspapers traditionally have not reached a large part of the under-20 age group. The same is true of the elderly and those speaking a foreign language who do not live in a large city.

Because of the rate differential and the difficulty of making thousands of buys, newspapers often are not able to provide total market coverage for national advertisers. Recently, in an attempt to rectify this situation, newspapers in three states worked together to form a one-order/one-bill network tailored and priced to appeal to the national automobile dealer associations. The network is tailored to cover an association's trading area and does not include unwanted circulation.[13]

PRODUCT CRITERIA

Newspapers suffer the same limitations shared by all print media. Certain products should not be advertised in newspapers. Products that require demonstration would have a difficult time making an impact in the newspaper format. Similarly, products that consumers do not expect to find advertised in newspapers, such as

---

[11]Lorne Manly, "P&G Says Bag This," *Mediaweek* (July 22, 1993):1, 4.

[12]Warren Berger, "What Have You Done for Me Lately?" *Adweek* (April 23, 1990):13.

[13]Christy Fisher, "Newspapers Link to Attract Auto Groups," *Advertising Age* (November 30, 1992):36.

professional services (doctors, lawyers) and tradespeople (plumbers, electricians), might easily be overlooked.

POOR REPRODUCTION

With the exception of special printing techniques and preprinted inserts, the reproduction quality of newspapers is comparatively poor and limiting, especially for color advertisements, although color reproduction has improved thanks to the popularity of *USA Today*. Color reproduction is an expensive alternative to black and white, so advertisers want their money's worth. In addition, the speed necessary to compose a daily newspaper prevents the detailed preparation and care in production that is possible when time pressures are not so great.

THE FUTURE OF NEWSPAPERS

Tomorrow's newspapers will be different from today's newspapers. Some people predict newspapers will be read on a flat, tabloid-size hand-held screen. Others say color pages will evolve into faxed pages through high-speed machines. Still others think ink-on-paper will long remain the medium of choice for newspapers, although technology—such as audiotext, videotext, and fax—will provide ways to supplement the daily news product.

Though it is unclear exactly what the newspaper of the future will be, it is certain that newspapers will have to change to keep up with the needs of readers and advertisers and still retain a competitive edge against other forms of delivery and entertainment. As noted in the Issues and Controversies box, this problem is not unique to just newspapers in the United States.

A few examples will demonstrate what newspapers have done to date. The Media Laboratory at the Massachusetts Institute of Technology is doing research

---

Issues and Controversies

KEEPING READERS IN EUROPE

The remedy for Europe's hard-hit national dailies may not be black and white, but newspaper marketers are trying everything from cutting newstand prices to promotion binges to woo back advertisers and readers. Newspaper executives are fighting a triple whammy: Ad dollars are decamping to television, recession-bitten marketers still spend cautiously, and newsprint prices are soaring.

European newspapers are also taking their first steps in electronic publishing—with less gusto than their U.S. counterparts.

In the United Kingdom, a 10 percent drop in newspaper sales since 1988 has made circulation-boosting price cuts a way of life. Rupert Murdoch's News International first cut downmarket tabloid *The Sun*'s price to 32¢ from 40¢ in July 1993. This trial became a key strategy when he slashed *The Times of London* to 48¢ from 72¢ two months later. Its deadly rival, the Telegraph Group's *Daily Telegraph*, then cut its price to 48¢ from 77¢; *The Times* hit back with a slash to 32¢. "We were selling 360,000 copies a day before the price cuts; we're now selling 630,000 a day," said Alasdair MacLeod, marketing manager for *The Times* newspaper division.

"We were reluctant to cut prices because our policy has been to add value to our product and charge our readers for it," said David Pugh, the *Telegraph*'s marketing director. "But

had we done nothing, we would have allowed *The Times* to grow and attack our advertising market." The tactic did not come cheaply. "The move cost us $64 million in the first year," he said. "We did it to preserve our future."

The lower prices have boosted sales, but lost circulation revenue outweighs newspapers' gains, media experts said: "Only 5% of the people who buy newspapers increased the frequency of purchases," said CIA Media Labs Ray Jones. "And only 4% started to read other papers because of the price cuts."

The United Kingdom also leads European publishers' experimenting with electronic publishing. *The Daily Telegraph* has 85,000 subscribers to its ad-funded Electronic Telegraph. The *Times* is waiting for the online market to develop before placing its contents on the ad-free online service offered by News International Delphi. And the *London Evening Standard* started Business Day Interactive, an electronic version of its business section. "We are looking at the possibility of producing pages for the World Wide Web and making the accompanying advertisements more lively," said David Maude, the *Standard*'s systems editor.

Source: Juliana Koranteg, "European Papers Fight for Readers," *Advertising Age* (June 19, 1995):S-9.

on user modeling, a project which will allow for creation of *The Daily Me*, a paper tailored to an individual's interests. This newspaper could be available in various forms, such as on a personal computer screen, as a printout, on the TV screen, or by audio. Knight-Ridder is working on making general-interest newspapers, with individually requested supplemental news items, available via a portable, tabloid-sized screen. This system will allow the reader to turn pages, clip and save articles, and call up background information, all with a touch of an electronic pen.

For some papers, such as *The New York Times* and the *Los Angeles Times*, the object today is to use technology to repackage information the newspaper already offers and provide products to support core advertisers. The *Los Angeles Times* has user-paid audiotext lines and offers Financial Faxs, a service which tracks 10 to 15 requested stocks. It also sends a fax version of the paper to Moscow five days a week. *The New York Times* has TimesFax, a daily fax product offered to subscribers in Japan, hotels in Europe, and cruise ships.[14]

Audiotext is a phone-in service that provides information to the caller that is usually related to an advertised product or service. This is most often accomplished through the familiar 800- and 900-numbers system; the choice depends, of course, on who pays for the service.

In 1995, the Newspaper Association of America established its Newspaper National Network as a limited partnership to facilitate newspaper buys with a one-order/one-bill program. The program is intended to bring in more national advertisers that want to make a multiple-paper buy. In the past, national advertisers buying 150 newspapers would receive as many as 150 pieces of paper using 150 different accounting methods. And ad agency media buyers would grouse, about half of them failed to indicate the client for whom the ad was produced.[15]

Although newspapers have always been good at reaching a mass audience, many have discovered that their future relies on their ability to reach specific niches. The *Dallas Morning News*, for example, offers several niche vehicles such as a six-page weekly religion section and a bilingual Hispanic publication. *La Fuente* is mailed to 105,000 Hispanic households. The paper has enabled one advertiser, Nations Bank, to access an important market segment. Nations Bank has used the publication to launch new products, and educate the Hispanic population about the benefits of checking and saving accounts. The *Los Angeles Times* offers a comparable paper called *Nuestro Tiempo*.[16]

Undoubtedly the most significant change in the newspaper business is the adoption of online technology along with database marketing. The number of U.S. newspapers on the Web in 1996 was 215, with about 750 internationally. For example, New York Times Electronic Media Co., which launched *The New York Times* on the Web (http://www.nytimes.com) in early 1996, has signed Kraft Foods' Maxwell House coffee, Toyota Motor Corp., and Chemical Bank as charter partners, for $120,000 each per year.

"Online services offer a real ability to create a community and allow people to interact with each other and advertisers," says Henry Scott, vice president for new media/new products in the information services group at the Times Co. Most publishers acknowledge that newspapers won't live or die on revenue generated from online services, and they don't expect online profits to account for more than 10 percent of the total revenue over the next ten years. Still, newspapers must always position themselves as the premier information provider. Online is part of that image.[17]

[14]Christy Fisher, "Newspapers of Future Look to Go High-Tech as Experiments Abound," *Advertising Age* (October 5, 1992):S-3, S-8.

[15]Alice Z. Cuneo, "Drumming Up Demand for One Order/One Bill," *Advertising Age* (April 24, 1995):S-4.

[16]Michele Marchetti, "Extras," *Sales & Marketing Management* (March 1996):56–62.

[17]Jane Hodges, "Newspapers Plug Along in Quest for Web Answers," *Advertising Age* (April 29, 1996):S-6.

AD 10.3

THIS NEW YORK TIMES WEB
PAGE MAY REPRESENT THE
FUTURE OF NEWSPAPERS.

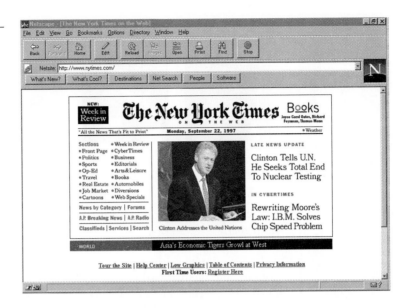

Newspapers are by no means obsolete, but the sales and marketing departments behind these newspapers require some adjustments. The traditional benefits to an advertiser are obvious, but today's customers expect more. Whether or not the industry as a whole can deliver on these expectations remains to be seen.

MAGAZINES

The earliest American magazines were local journals of political opinion. Most were monthly and did not circulate far beyond their geographic origins. Andrew Bradford's *American Magazine* was the first to appear in the colonies in 1741, arriving three days earlier than Benjamin Franklin's *General Magazine and Historical Chronicle*. Both publications folded within six months. Since that time, magazines have come and gone. All have been aimed at specific audiences; most sell advertising and are published monthly.[18] Figure 10.2 offers a pictorial view of the evolution of magazines throughout history. Despite the high risks associated with the magazine business, there appears to be no decline in the number of new magazines.

New magazine launches peaked in 1989, when 605 titles were introduced, more than double the number of titles launched in 1985. In 1991, the number of new magazines dropped to 541, with 1992 slightly higher.[19] Historically, over 50 percent of new titles fail. In addition, publishers are investing more money than ever in existing titles. Individual magazines have become bigger and brighter. Heavy paper stocks, lush photographs, and sophisticated graphics are used to create beautiful, eyecatching editorial environments that entice both readers and advertisers.

Upscale magazines seem to have an edge over mass consumer magazines in attracting advertisers. Upscale advertisers don't look to promotion spending as an alternative to advertising. Instead, they tend to turn to the image advertising that upscale magazines provide. For example, magazines such as *Gourmet*, *Architectural Digest*, and *Condé Nast Traveler* all have increased their ad pages since 1990. Steve Forbes, president and CEO of *Forbes* magazine, attributes this increase to gains in

---

[18]John McDonough, "In Step with History," *Advertising Age* (May 24, 1989):23.

[19]Laura Loro, "Heavy Hitters Gamble on Launches," *Advertising Age* (October 19, 1992):S-13.

FIGURE 10.2

THE EVOLUTION OF MAGAZINES
FROM 1883 THROUGH 1990.
*(Reprinted with permission from
Advertising Age, May 24, 1989.
Copyright 1989, Crain Communications,
Inc. 1989)*

the "luxury category" of advertising, such as Rémy Martin Amérique, Cadillac, and Jaguar.

The magazine industry has entered the "age of skimming," a time when readers acquire 80 percent of their information from the story titles, subheadings, captions, and pictures rather than from the editorial content. Although magazine advertising revenue in 1995 was $8.5 billion, magazines are still unsure of which format to adopt and which audiences to target.[20] This is a medium that advertisers tend to view cautiously. Table 10.4 on pages 320–321 lists the 1995 rankings of the top 25 magazines by advertising revenue.

THE STRUCTURE OF MAGAZINES

The Standard Rate and Data Service classifies magazines according to their frequency of publication and their audience. The magazine industry also classifies magazines by *geographic coverage, demographics,* and *editorial diversity.*

AUDIENCE

Three types of magazines are categorized by the audiences they serve. The first category, *consumer magazines,* is directed at consumers who buy products for their own consumption. These magazines are distributed through the mail, newsstands, or stores. Examples are *Reader's Digest, Lear's, Time,* and *People.* The second category is *business magazines.* These magazines are directed at business readers and are further divided into *trade papers* (read by retailers, wholesalers, and other distributors; for example, *Chain Store Age*), *industrial magazines* (read by manufacturers; for example, *Concrete Construction*), and *professional magazines* (read by physicians, lawyers, and others; for example, *National Law Review*). Business magazines are also classified as being vertical or horizontal publications. A *vertical publication* presents stories and information about an entire industry. *Women's Wear Daily,* for example, discusses the production, marketing, and distribution of women's fashion. A *horizontal publication* deals with a business function that cuts across industries, such as *Direct Marketing. Farm magazines* represent a third category. They go to farmers and those engaged in farm-related activities. *Peanut Farmer* is an example of a farm magazine.

GEOGRAPHY

Magazines generally cover certain sections or regions of the country. The area covered may be as small as a city (*Los Angeles Magazine* and *Boston Magazine*) or as large as several contiguous states (the southwestern edition of *Southern Living Magazine*). Geographic editions help encourage local retail support by listing the names of local distributors in the advertisement.

---

[20]Jon Berry, "Trade Magazines," *Adweek Supplement* (September 1, 1989):196.

DEMOGRAPHICS

Demographic editions group subscribers according to age, income, occupation, and other classifications. *McCall's*, for example, publishes a ZIP edition to upper-income homes. A ZIP edition is a special version of the magazine which is sent to subscribers who live in a specific zip code. A zip code presumably tells something about the people living in an area. They typically share common demographic traits, such as income. *Newsweek* offers a college edition, and *Time* sends special editions to students, business executives, doctors, and business managers.

EDITORIAL CONTENT

Various magazines emphasize certain types of editorial content. The most widely used categories are: general editorial (*Reader's Digest*), women's service (*Family Circle*), shelter (*House Beautiful*), business (*Forbes*), and special interest (*Ski*).

PHYSICAL CHARACTERISTICS

The structure of the magazine industry is also reflected in the terminology used to describe the physical characteristics of a magazine. The most common magazine page sizes are $8\frac{1}{2} \times 11$ and 6×9 inches.

DISTRIBUTION AND CIRCULATION

Traditional Delivery: Delivery of magazines to readers through newsstands or home delivery.

Nontraditional Delivery: Delivery of magazines to readers through such methods as door hangers or newspapers.

The method used to distribute a magazine partly reflects its structure. **Traditional delivery** is either through *newsstand purchase* or *home delivery* via the U.S. Postal Service. **Nontraditional delivery** systems include hanging bagged copies on doorknobs, delivery within newspapers, and delivery through professionals. Magazines distributed through nontraditional delivery systems are provided free. This is referred to as *controlled circulation* as opposed to *paid circulation*. Rodale Press, located in Pennsylvania, is one of the most active publishing houses in developing controlled circulation. Two Rodale Magazines, *Prevention* and *Men's Health*, are often placed in doctors' waiting rooms.

THE READERS OF MAGAZINES

Approximately 92 percent of all adults read at least one magazine per month. This is true of both males and females. On average, adults read nine different issues of magazines per month. The average magazine is read over a period of two days, for 54 minutes in total reading time, by an average of four adults per copy.[21] It is therefore safe to conclude that the American public has a voracious appetite for magazines and the unique and specialized information they provide. *Sports Illustrated* is an example of a magazine that is targeted at a specific audience.

Readers also appear to have a positive attitude toward magazine advertising. Approximately 79 percent of adults consider magazine advertising "helpful as a buying guide." Roughly 75 percent express positive attitudes toward various aspects of magazine advertising, including the amount of information carried, the use of color, and the provision of coupons. Women tend to have slightly more positive attitudes than men do. In general, people pay relatively more attention to magazine advertising than to television advertising.[22]

MEASURING MAGAZINE READERSHIP

Magazine rates are based on the number of readers, which correlates with the circulation that a publisher promises to provide—that is, the *guaranteed circulation*. As with newspapers, the ABC is responsible for collecting and evaluating these data to ensure that guaranteed circulation was obtained. The ABC audits subscrip-

---

[21]Mediamark Research Inc., *Doublebase 1988 Study:*19.

[22]"Study of Media Involvement," *Audits & Surveys* (March 1988).

| TABLE 10.4 | TOP 25 MAGAZINES: AD REVENUE AND PAID CIRCULATION |

RANK 1995	RANK 1994	MAGAZINE	HEADQUARTERS	TOTAL REVENUE	'95–'94 % CHG
1	1	*TV Guide*	Radnor, Pa.	$1,068,832	3.1
2	2	*People*	New York	801,153	5.5
3	3	*Sports Illustrated*	New York	697,381	6.7
4	4	*Time*	New York	672,626	5.3
5	5	*Reader's Digest*	New York	529,742	11.1
6	6	*Parade*	New York	515,591	15.2
7	7	*Newsweek*	New York	480,535	12.3
8	8	*Better Homes & Gardens*	Des Moines	406,573	15.0
9	9	*PC Magazine*	New York	391,341	13.2
10	10	*Good Housekeeping*	New York	339,000	7.5
11	11	*U.S. News & World Report*	Washington	316,390	0.4
12	12	*Business Week*	New York	313,478	12.3
13	14	*Woman's Day*	New York	288,045	17.5
14	15	*Ladies' Home Journal*	Des Moines	261,793	8.0
15	13	*Family Circle*	New York	255,199	−2.2
16	16	*Forbes*	New York	252,854	7.2
17	18	*Cosmopolitan*	New York	242,065	9.8
18	19	*USA Weekend*	New York	229,568	5.3
19	20	*Fortune*	New York	225,682	8.0
20	24	*National Geographic*	Washington	201,508	12.3
21	21	*PC Week*	Medford, Mass.	197,640	1.6
22	17	*National Enquirer*	Lantana, Fla.	195,646	−11.6
23	25	*Money*	New York	176,881	−0.7
24	29	*Computer Shopper*	New York	174,408	16.1
25	22	*Star Magazine*	Tarrytown, N.Y.	174,078	−6.2

Source: "Top 300 Magazines by Gross Revenue," *Advertising Age* (June 17, 1996):S-2. Reprinted with permission from *Advertising Age.* Copyright Crain Communications Inc.

tions as well as newsstand sales. It also checks the number of delinquent subscribers and rates of renewal.

Magazine circulation refers to the number of copies of an issue sold, not to the readership of the publication. A single copy of a magazine might be read by one person or by several people, depending on its content.

The Simmons Market Research Bureau (SMRB) goes one step further by relating readership patterns to purchasing habits. The bureau provides data on who reads which magazines and which products these readers buy and consume. Most advertisers and agencies depend greatly on SMRB estimates of magazine audiences. Other research companies, such as Starch and Gallup and Robinson, provide comparable information about magazine audience size and behavior. More is said about these research firms in Chapters 11 and 12.

MRI

A company known as MediaMark provides a service called MRI that measures readership for most popular national and regional magazines (along with other

AD REVENUE	AD PAGES	SUBSCRIBER REVENUE	NEWSSTAND REVENUE	PAID CIRCULATION	PARENT COMPANY
$406,945	3,228.84	$428,871	$233,016	13,175,549	News Corp.
437,663	3,328.21	170,151	193,338	3,321,198	Time Warner
435,710	2,627.71	245,615	16,057	3,157,303	Time Warner
404,462	2,322.55	242,182	25,982	4,083,105	Time Warner
186,588	1,099.64	319,830	23,324	15,103,830	Reader's Digest Association
515,591	740.12	0	0	37,268,000	Advance Publications
331,853	2,299.79	122,640	26,042	3,155,155	Washington Post Co.
274,445	1,653.98	122,154	9,974	7,603,207	Meredith Corp.
331,072	6,992.45	46,818	13,451	1,107,187	Ziff-Davis Publishing Co.
238,675	1,551.66	67,032	33,292	5,372,786	Hearst Corp.
222,420	2,171.22	86,151	7,818	2,220,327	Mortimer Zuckerman
267,632	3,816.36	39,437	6,409	882,583	McGraw-Hill
197,515	1,706.21	34,033	56,497	4,707,330	Hachette Filipacchi
158,469	1,454.50	87,675	15,649	5,045,644	Meredith Corp.
163,971	1,377.28	41,589	49,639	5,007,542	Bertelsmann (Gruner & Jahr)
205,704	4,542.13	41,661	5,490	779,901	Forbes Inc.
159,715	1,806.49	20,670	61,681	2,569,186	Hearst Corp.
229,568	694.89	0	0	19,217,360	Gannett Co.
179,524	3,184.37	40,421	5,736	758,171	Time Warner
52,295	350.22	149,046	167	7,768,071	National Geographic Society
196,435	6,517.14	1,205	0	6,179	Ziff-Davis Publishing Co.
29,242	740.31	17,745	148,659	2,613,647	American Media
105,341	1,256.12	60,020	11,520	1,922,737	Time Warner
145,933	7,911.78	7,630	20,846	541,830	Ziff-Davis Publishing Co.
20,152	602.44	14,877	139,049	2,406,150	American Media

media). Reports are issued twice a year and cover readership by demographics, psychographics, and product usage.

ADVERTISING IN MAGAZINES

Magazines are a valuable medium for reaching many demographic groups. By their nature, magazines must fill a niche with unique editorial content in order to satisfy specific groups of readers. As a result, they are extremely diverse in terms of their characteristics, readers, and reader interaction. In evaluating a magazine, it is important for advertisers to examine the full range of characteristics that distinguish one magazine from all others.

TECHNOLOGY

New technologies have enabled magazines to distinguish themselves from one another. For example, *selective binding*, and *ink-jet imaging* allow publishers to construct and personalize issues for individual subscribers one signature or insert at a time. Selective binding combines information on subscribers kept in a data base with a computer program to produce a magazine that includes special sections for subscribers based on their demographic profiles. Ink-jet printing permits a magazine such as *U.S. News & World Report* to personalize its renewal form so that each issue contains a renewal card already filled out with the subscriber's name, address, and so on. Personalized messages can be printed directly on run-of-book ads (the technology that is used for the entire magazine) or on inserts.

Desktop publishing is another mainline technology used by many magazines. This method, when combined with satellite transmission, allows magazines to close pages just hours before presstime—eliminating the long lead time that has traditionally been a serious drawback of magazine advertising. A final technology that has improved the advertising effectiveness of magazines is the adoption of sophisticated database management. This lets publishers combine the information available from exact subscriber lists with other public and private lists to create complete consumer profiles for their advertisers.

FORMAT

Each magazine or magazine category uses its own terminology to describe its format. Nevertheless, all magazines share some characteristics. For example, the front cover of a magazine is called its *first cover page.* The inside of the front cover is called the *second cover page*, the inside of the back cover the *third cover page*, and the back cover the *fourth cover page.* Normally the double-page spread is the largest unit of ad space sold by magazines. The two pages face each other. When a double-page ad is designed, it is critical that the *gutter* (the white space between the pages running along the inside edge of the page) be bridged or jumped— meaning that no headline words run through the gutter and that all body text is on one side or the other. A page without outside margins, in which the color extends to the edge of the page, is called a *bleed page.* Magazines can sometimes offer more than two connected pages (four is the most common number). This is referred to as a *gatefold.* Armstrong Floors has used a five-sided gatefold in the inside front cover of *Better Homes & Gardens* magazine for several years. The use of multiple pages that provide photo essays is really an extension of the gatefold concept. As noted in Chapter 2, Calvin Klein has employed this format. Photo essays also are becoming more common in magazines such as *Fortune* and *Business Week;* these magazines may present a 20-page ad for business in a foreign country, such as Japan or South Korea. Finally, a single page or double page can be broken into a variety of units called *fractional page space* (for example, vertical half-page, horizontal half-page, double horizontal half-page, half-page double spread, and checkerboard).

THE ADVANTAGES OF MAGAZINES

The benefits of magazine advertising include the ability to reach specialized audiences, audience receptivity, a long life span, visual quality, and the distribution of sales promotion devices.

TARGET AUDIENCES

PRINCIPLE Magazines are becoming more specialized.

The overriding advantage of magazines in the 1940s and 1950s was their ability to reach a wide, general audience. This is no longer true. As noted, the greatest areas of growth are expected to be in special-interest magazines and special editions of existing publications. The ability to reach specialized audiences has become a primary advantage. For example, a set of magazines published by the Hearst Corporation is referred to as the Seven Sisters and is clearly targeted to contemporary American women. These seven include *Better Homes and Gardens, Ladies' Home Journal, Family Circle, Redbook, Woman's Day, McCalls',* and *Good Housekeeping.* As noted in the Concepts and Applications box, custom publishing enhances targeting even more.

Concepts and Applications

THE PERFECT FIT: CUSTOM PUBLISHING

The leap from placing ads in magazines to creating magazines may appear to be a huge one to marketers just looking to sell product, but custom publishing is an increasingly popular tool that can achieve a range of marketing communication objectives, from generating sales to creating brand loyalty and ensuring corporate credibility—even educating customers about product developments and benefits.

Packaged-goods companies, couriers, nonprofit organizations, and health care firms are just a few of the categories using custom publishing to provide targeted consumers with informative or feel-good publications. The reason is that a custom publication, be it a cookbook, magazine, or resource guide, enables the sponsor to "own" both the message and the medium. Sponsorship of a custom publication gives the marketer control over the content that is simply not for sale with conventional commercial publications. The result is a highly targeted publication that matches—indeed, reinforces—a brand's image and positioning in an environment that is relevant to the lifestyle or interests of the reader.

No company is more committed to the strategy than Federal Express. The overnight courier's *Via Fed Ex* (220,000 circulation), *Service Guide* (500,000 circulation), *Fed Ex Global* (65,000 circulation) and PRPL (Personal Resource Planning Library) CD-ROM feature everything from new-product and service announcements and e-mail suggestions to service updates and answers to commonly asked questions. "Federal Express sees it as a very controlled way to build a relationship with key segments of its audience," notes William Wells, CEO of Wells/Hanley-Wood, the company that handles Fed

Ex's custom publishing. "A thirty-second TV spot has its place, but it's over in thirty seconds."

Via Fed Ex, which carries print ads from noncompeting companies like IBM and 3M, is mailed to secretaries—the gatekeepers of overnight delivery—while *Global Fed Ex* is mailed to corporate customers who ship internationally. Perhaps most discerning is Fed Ex's PRPL, a quarterly CD-ROM provided to 1,100 company sales reps that contains presentation materials and information.

Just as important as the information that custom publications provide and the speed with which they can be disseminated is the audience they target. Bayport, MN-based Andersen Windows mails a customized quarterly magazine called *Come Home* to consumers planning to remodel their homes. The company compiles its mailing list through 800-number responses to Andersen television and print ads. An Andersen Library insert placed inside *Come Home* allows prospective remodelers to receive free any one of six guides or brochures offering advice on window selection, choosing a contractor, and information about Andersen itself.

Custom publishing is a $3 billion category and Magazine Publishers of America reports that all of its major members now custom publish.

Sources: Alicia Lasek, "No Backing Out Now for Custom Publishing," *Advertising Age* (November 5, 1995):S-14; Blair Fischer, "Message and Medium," *PROMO* (November 1995):66, 107–109; and Keith Naughton, "Read All About It—In Marlboro Monthly," *Business Week* (November 18, 1996):179–80.

AUDIENCE RECEPTIVITY

The second advantage of magazines is their high level of audience receptivity. The editorial environment of a magazine lends authority and credibility to the advertising. Many magazines claim that advertising in their publication gives a product prestige. Clearly an ad in *Fortune* would impress business audiences, just as an ad in *Seventeen* would impress teenagers.

LONG LIFE SPAN

Magazines have the longest life span of all the media. Some magazines, such as *National Geographic* or *Consumer Reports*, are used as ongoing references and might never be discarded. Other publications, such as *TV Guide*, are intended to be used frequently during a given period of time. In addition, magazines have very high reach potential because of a large *pass-along*, or secondary, audience of family, friends, customers, and colleagues.

Finally, people tend to read magazines at a relatively slow rate, typically over a couple of days. Therefore, magazines offer an opportunity to use long copy. The magazine format also allows more creative variety through multiple pages, inserts, and other features.

VISUAL QUALITY

PRINCIPLE Magazines offer excellent reproduction of quality visual images such as color photographs.

The visual quality of magazines tend to be excellent because they are printed on high-quality paper stock that provides superior photo reproduction in both black and white and color. This production quality often reflects the superior editorial content. Feature stories are frequently written by well-respected writers.

SALES PROMOTIONS

Magazines are an effective medium through which to distribute various sales promotion devices, such as coupons, product samples, and information cards. A 1987 Post Office ruling allowed magazines to carry loose editorial and advertising supplements as part of the publication provided the magazine is enclosed in an envelope or wrapper.[23]

THE DISADVANTAGES OF MAGAZINES

Magazines are limited by certain factors. The most prominent disadvantages are limited flexibility, high cost, and difficult distribution.

LIMITED FLEXIBILITY

Although magazines offer many benefits to advertisers, long lead time and lack of flexibility and immediacy are two of their drawbacks. Ads must be submitted well in advance of the publication date. For example, advertisers must have engravings for full-color advertisements at the printer more than two months before the cover date of a monthly publication. As noted earlier, however, magazines that have adopted desktop publishing and satellite transmission are able to avoid this limitation and can close just hours before presstime. Magazines are also inflexible in respect to available positions. Prime locations, such as the back cover or inside front cover, may be sold months in advance. Some readers do not look at an issue of a magazine until long after it has reached their homes; therefore, impact builds slowly.

HIGH COST

The second disadvantage associated with magazines is their relatively high cost. In 1996 the cost for a full-page four-color ad in *Newsweek* magazine's national edition was $160,827. For a general-audience magazine such as *Newsweek*, the cost per thousand (CPM) is quite high, and magazines of this type do not compare favorably with other media on this score. However, magazines with carefully segmented audiences, such as *Byte*, can be very cost-efficient because a tightly targeted audience is more expensive to reach than a mass audience.

DISTRIBUTION

The final disadvantage associated with magazines is the difficulty of distribution. Many magazines, such as *Woman's Day* and *People*, are purchased primarily through newsstands. Yet there is no way that 2,500 different magazines can all appear on store racks. Some magazines are simply not available to all members of all possible target audiences.

THE FUTURE OF MAGAZINES

Just as with the case for newspapers, the future of magazines appears to rest on emerging technology—particularly, online technology. Also, as true for newspapers, magazine publishers are not sure whether this technology is imperative or whether participation is necessary simply to prove you are cutting edge. For example, *Salon* is a recent effort to create virtual magazines on the Internet: magazines without paper, postal mass and fuss, or limitations of length. Just ideas, images, and of course, ads.

However exciting the words, however beautiful the layout, critics contend that online magazines may never be able to overcome "the bathroom factor." "You can't take a computer to bed very comfortably. You can't read it from the tub.

---

[23]DDB Needham, *Media Trends* (1987):55.

There still will be some limitations," notes Russell Siegelman, vice president of the Microsoft Network.

Magazines and newspapers have existed for several hundred years in their current format because they provide interesting writing that's portable. The Web is most certainly not that, which begs the question: Will people really want their magazines online after the novelty has worn off?[24]

[24]Elizabeth H. Weise, "On-Line Magazines: Will Readers Still Want Them After the Novelty Wears Off," *The Marketing News* (January 29, 1996):1, 14.

$\mathscr{S}$UMMARY

- Print media are static and visual. They are superior to broadcast media in respectability, permanence, and credibility.

- Newspapers, which are still the leading local medium, have improved their technology owing to increased competition from broadcast and direct mail, but they are diminishing in number.

- The structure of newspapers is determined by frequency of publication, size, and circulation.

- Newspaper readers encompass all income brackets, educational levels, age groups, and ethnic backgrounds. However, readership varies by gender, age, and interests.

- Newspaper audiences are measured through two independent agencies: The Audit Bureau of Circulation (ABC) and Simmons-Scarborough.

- There are three general types of newspaper advertising: classified, display, and supplements.

- The greatest advantage of advertising in newspapers is extensive market coverage. The biggest disadvantages are a short life span, clutter, and poor reproduction.

- Magazines have the greatest ability to reach preselected or tightly targeted audiences. This selectivity is exhibited through the elaborate structure found in the industry.

- Magazines are categorized by audience, geography, demographics, and editorial content.

- Approximately 92 percent of all adults read at least one magazine per month. There are several other features that characterize magazine readers as well.

- Magazine readership is measured by the ABC, Simmons Market Research Bureau (SMRB), and MediaMark.

- Advertising in magazines does have drawbacks, including limited flexibility, high costs, and difficult distribution.

$\mathscr{Q}$UESTIONS

1. Discuss the various characteristics of newspaper readers. What are the implications for an advertiser considering newspapers?

2. You are the head media planner for a small chain of upscale furniture outlets in a top 50 market that concentrates most of its advertising in the Sunday magazine supplement of the local newspaper. The client also schedules display ads in the daily editions for special sales. Six months ago a new high-style, metropolitan magazine approached you about advertising for your client. You deferred a decision by saying you'd see what reader acceptance would be. Now the magazine has shown some steady increases (its circulation is now about one quarter of the newspaper's). If you were to include the magazine on the ad schedule, you'd have to reduce the newspaper linage. What would be your recommendations to the furniture store?

3. Many magazines have editorial environments that are well suited to certain products and services (home service, entertainment, sports, recreation, and financial magazines). Compatibility between the advertising and the reader's editorial interest is a plus. However, editorial "compatibility" will attract your competitors' ads too. Would having a number of competitors' ads in an issue where your ad appeared cause you to consider less compatible publications? Explain your reasons.

4. Discuss the advantages and disadvantages of advertising in newspapers and magazines from the viewpoint of the advertising directed for GE small appliances.

5. Peter Wilcox, a display salesman for the *Daily Globe*, thought he had heard all the possible excuses for not buying newspaper space until he called on the manager of a compact disc store that sold new and pre-owned discs. "I've heard about newspaper reader studies that prove how wrong the audience is for me.

Readership is too adult—mostly above 35 years of age," he said. "And besides, readers of newspapers are families with higher incomes—the wrong market for our used disc business," he continued. If the Globe is a typical metropolitan daily, could the store manager be correct? In any event, how should Wilcox try to counter the manager's views?

6. A terrific debate is going on in Professor Morrison's retail advertising class. The question is: "Why do national advertisers refuse to seriously consider newspapers in media plans?" The advertising manager for a home products company argues that despite newspaper's cre-

ative limitations, more firms would buy newspaper space if the medium did not practice rate discrimination against national companies. The sales manager for a small chain of newspapers admits the price difference, but says it is justified by the extra attention, and commissions (sales rep and agency) newspapers have to pay for each national order. The sales manager also claims the price issue is a "smokescreen" for advertisers to hide their continuing "love affair" with television. Which position would you accept? Is price difference an issue large enough to restrict marketer's interest? How does cooperative advertising figure into the debate?

Suggested Class Project

Contact a medium-to-large newspaper and magazine. Think of yourself as a potential advertiser. What do you need to know? Collect all the relevant information and services provided to advertisers. Ask as many questions as you need to. Compare the types of information and services available. Was the customer service helpful? Is this the right choice of media for your "company"? Analyze the results in a brief report: begin by stating your product and your advertising goals; then state what you might or might not accomplish by advertising in the publication. Make a decision.

Further Readings

Alson, Amy, "The Search for National Ad Dollars," *Marketing & Media Decisions* (February 1989):29–30.

Angelo, Jean Marie, "One Out of Four Mags Goes Off Rate Card," *Inside Print* (December 1988):21.

Damiano, Steve, "For Women, Business and Pleasure," *Marketing & Media Decisions* (April 1990):14.

Huhn, Mary, "Breaking the Black-and-White Habit," *Adweek Special Report—1988* (April 26, 1988):27.

Matovelli, John, "Toward an Age of Customized Magazines," *Adweek Special Report—Magazine World 1989* (February 13, 1989):36–37.

Perry, David, "Performance Advertisers Practice What They Preach," *Business Marketing* (March 1988):86.

Strauss, Steve, *Moving Images: The Transportation Poster in America* (New York: Fullcourt Press, 1984).

With the advent of numerous alternatives to traditional network television programming, such as cable, television stations across the country have been forced to use less orthodox techniques to generate acceptable revenues. One of the most notable examples of this trend is the increased use of "infomercials."

Infomercials are, in theory, informational videos featuring and sponsored by branded products or services. For example, Clorox produced an infomercial in the mid-1980s, which showed how its cleaning products could be used to clean up smoke damage after a fire. Originally conceived by advertisers as an acceptable way to slip product messages into a commercial-free environment of public television, infomercials have evolved to the point where they are now often merely 30- to 60-minute ads for products. However, for those viewers who tune in late or slip out of the room during the brief disclaimer that differentiates infomercials from true entertainment-based programming, infomercials can be mistaken for "normal" programs. Whether because of this confusion or because of the inherent effectiveness of infomercials as a marketing technique, they have been extremely successful.

Unfortunately for the unwary consumer, infomercials lack even the types of cursory guidelines and regulations that limit traditional advertising's use of false or deceptive claims. Nonetheless, the advertising community has thus far failed to single out infomercials for increased regulation.

Independent and network television also stand to lose in the long run if infomercials continue to proliferate. Just as advertisers fear that infomercials that make false claims could damage the credibility of advertising as a whole, television station owners must address the issue of whether infomercials that look like entertainment-based programming could damage the credibility of their regular programs. Television stations can profit from this type of advertising, however, because they can simply sell the entire 30- to 60-minute time period in which the infomercial runs to the infomercial producers rather than buying regular programming and trying to sell commercial space. Although this has obvious short-term benefits, if the credibility and authenticity of regular entertainment-based programming is questioned by the public, viewership will drop as will the price that stations can charge for commercial time.

The issue is more complex for advertisers. Anything that negatively affects the credibility of advertising can jeopardize that technique's long-term ability to sell products. However, the competitive nature of most industries is such that any new marketing tool that has proven itself effective cannot be summarily dismissed.

The infomercial format is well adapted for direct address to small market segments. Managers of vacation destinations, and marketers of automobiles and exercise equipment—among others—have found that videotaped infomercials mailed directly to prospective purchasers is an especially effective communication medium. In some cases prospective purchasers identify themselves by calling an 800 number or mailing a coupon for more information. In other cases marketers identify prospects from lists of previous purchasers, or lists of owners of related products.

Once the marketer has identified prime prospects, the marketer can develop an infomercial designed to appeal especially to that segment and can mail the videotape directly to members of the intended audience. Infomercials on videotape have all the motion and sound advantages of infomercials on television. In addition, consumers who receive videotapes pay closer attention to them than they do to infomercials on television, and many consumers who receive tapes give or lend them to others who have similar interests.

Although most consumers who receive infomercials on videotape find them interesting and useful, this method of communication is especially open to abuse, largely because the standing government and industry regulations that police truth in advertising are difficult to enforce. Thus, as infomercials on videotape become more common, advertisers can expect to be required to comply with new forms of regulation.

Source: "It's Really a Commercial," 20/20 (September 18, 1990).

---

*Q*UESTIONS

1. Explain how infomercials can actually be good for consumers.
2. As advertising costs have increased, advertisers have responded by producing shorter and shorter commercials. Given this trend, how can infomercials actually benefit advertisers?
3. **A.** Explain how and why infomercials should be regulated.
   B. Explain why infomercials should not be regulated.

Broadcast Media

CHAPTER OBJECTIVES

When you have completed this chapter, you should be able to:

- Understand the basic nature of both radio and television
- Describe the audience for each medium and explain how that audience is measured
- List the advantages and disadvantages of using radio and television commercials

MTV IN EUROPE: ONE COUNTRY AT A TIME

A hit with both viewers and advertisers as a pan-European satellite television channel, MTV Networks Europe sees its future growth coming from thinking locally. In two key moves, national ad buys are being created on the MTV Europe Channel that has plugged pan-European advertising since its 1987 introduction, and VH1, the company's baby boomer music channel, is rolling out in a format tailor-made for each country.

The new "think locally" strategy is already proving so effective that MTV Networks will apply it next in Asia.

MTV Europe's access to 59 million cable and satellite homes has made it one of the few successes in pan-European television. In 1995, the network served over 300 advertisers. Still, people at MTV are aware of aggressive, new competitors. Cologne-based Viva, an ad-supported German-language service introduced by record companies Warner Music Group, Sony Music Entertainment, Thorn EMI, Poly Gram, and German mail-order giant Otto, now reaches 90 percent of German cable television homes. Its operators have applied to set up a second, VH1-like service for older viewers, called Viva 2 to go on air in 1996.

Local spots are also available in Italy because of the fierce rivalry with Videomusic, a local rock-and-pop, over-the-air channel owned by the Marcucci Group. Videomusic earns an estimated $20 million from national advertising annually.

In September 1995, MTV Networks introduced VH1, its first channel with programs tailored to a local market. VH1 aims to complement MTV Europe, a plan that appeals to jeans marketer Levi Strauss & Co. "Although VH1 is for an older audience, we've learned that one-third of its audience is from the [jeans-buying] MTV age group," notes Steve Clar, group media manager at Levi Strauss's agency Bartle Bogle Hegarty, London.

The Media Centre, London, buying airtime for Anheuser-Busch's Budweiser beer, uses VH1 to circumvent regulatory obstacles that could be caused by advertising alcohol on a pan-European network. VH1 U.K. now claims more than 100 advertisers, including Procter & Gamble, Unilever, Nissan, Volkswagen, and Compaq. MTV's next move will be a tailor-made VH1 channel for Germany.

MTV Asia will be broadcast in English and aimed at India and Southeast Asia. It will also feature some programs in Hindi for viewers in India, South Asia, and the Philippines. MTV Mandarin is for Taiwan, China, Singapore, and Hong Kong. Experts acknowledge that advertising in this part of the world is quite complicated. Musical tastes differ, the national broadcast regulations are much more intricate, and distribution is also haphazard.[1]

The opening example clearly indicates that media are going global. Media planners and buyers must not only be familiar with media in their own country, but must also be cognizant of media differences from country to country. Most of this expansion is taking place with broadcast media, the topic of this chapter.

Broadcast media, the process of transmitting sounds or images, includes both radio and television. Advertising experts contend that creating commercials for broadcast media is quite different from creating advertisements for print media. Certainly broadcast media tap into different human senses: sight (through movement and imagery) and sound.

Print is a *space* medium that allows the reader to digest information and images at his or her own speed. Broadcast is a *time* medium that affects the viewer's emotions for a few seconds and then disappears.

---

[1]Juliana Koranteng, "MTV: Targeting Europe Market-By-Market," *Advertising Age* (March 20, 1995):I-13, I-20; and John Taguabue, "Local Flavor Rules European TV," *The New York Times* (October 14, 1996):C1, C4.

Chapter 10 introduced print media and its place in advertising. This chapter will explore broadcast media. The overview contained in these chapters will provide the necessary background for Chapter 12, Media Buying.

THE STRUCTURE OF TELEVISION

A great deal of change has taken place in the technical aspects of television. As a result, several different types of television systems are now available to advertisers for delivery of their messages to audiences.

WIRED NETWORK TELEVISION

Whenever two or more stations are able to broadcast the same program, which originates from a single source, a network exists. Networks can be "over-the-air" or cable. The FCC defines a network as a program service with 15 or more hours of prime-time programming.

Currently there are four national over-the-air television networks—the American Broadcasting Company (ABC), the Columbia Broadcasting System (CBS), the National Broadcasting Company (NBC), and Fox Broadcasting Company. The first three own 15 regional stations, and the remaining 600 regional stations are privately owned **affiliates** (each network has about 150 affiliates). An affiliate station signs a contract with the national network (ABC, CBS, NBC, or Fox) whereby it agrees to carry network-originated programming during a certain part of its schedule. For example, WDIV-TV is NBC's Detroit affiliate. These major networks originate their own programs and are compensated at a rate of 30 percent of the fee charged for programs in a local market. In turn, affiliates receive a percentage of the advertising revenue (12 to 25 percent) paid to the national network and have the option to sell some advertising time during network programs and between programs. This is the primary source of affiliate revenues.

In over-the-air *network scheduling* the advertiser contracts with either a national or a regional network to show commercials on a number of affiliated stations. Sometimes an advertiser purchases only a portion of the network coverage, known as a *regional leg*. This is common with sports programming where different games are shown in different parts of the country.

> **Affiliate:** A station that is contracted with a national network to carry network-originated programming during part of its schedule.

UNWIRED NETWORK TELEVISION

In contrast to the wired networks like ABC, NBC, CBS, and Fox, which do business directly with their affiliates in terms of programming, the unwired network station has nothing to do with programming and everything to do with advertising sales. Unwired networks are basically sales representative organizations that represent large market stations on a commission basis (15 percent). They simplify the buying process for the agency by designating one person at a network to handle the total buy. They also assist the client in media planning.[2]

PUBLIC TELEVISION: THE FIFTH NETWORK

Although many people still consider public television to be "commercial free," in 1984 the Federal Communications Commission (FCC) liberalized the rules, allowing the 341 PBS stations to interpret the line between underwriting and outright sponsorship that once seemed so absolute. The FCC says messages should

---

[2]Cara S. Trager, "Unwired Networks Work to Unplug Rivals' Shares," *Advertising Age* (April 14, 1986):S-8.

not make a call to action or make price or quality comparisons. Public television lobbied for advertising to compensate for the cutback in federal funding that first occurred during the Nixon administration and to compete more effectively with cable television. The House approved a 15 percent cut in 1996 and a 30 percent reduction in 1997. PBS is an attractive medium for advertisers because it attracts a large upscale audience and because it adopted a much more consistent programming schedule beginning in the 1980s.

Current FCC guidelines allow ads to appear on public television only during the local 2.5-minute program breaks. Each station maintains its own acceptability guidelines. Some PBS stations accept the same ads that appear on paid programming. A DeBeers Diamonds ad, showing a man presenting a diamond anniversary band to his wife, ran a lengthy schedule on eight public stations, including WLIW KERA in Dallas and WTTW in Chicago. Most of the spots that run on public television, however, are created specifically for public stations.[3]

Other PBS stations will not accept any commercial corporate advertising, only noncommercial ads that are "value neutral." Such messages may include non-promotional corporate and product logos and slogans, business locations and telephone numbers that are not used for direct-response selling, and brand names, service marks, and logos. In other words, there is no attempt to "sell" anything through these ads. Sponsors of PBS programming usually also are advertisers, but in a quite subtle fashion.

In the latest effort to compensate for lost funding, the Public Broadcasting Service initiated a total reorganization in 1995. The reorganization divides PBS into three operating divisions: programming services, learning ventures, and system services. PBS eventually could contemplate marketing some of its more popular children's programming such as *Sesame Street* and *Barney and Friends.*

In sum, PBS reaches affluent, educated households as well as minority and lower-end consumers. According to Nielsen data, during a typical week, 54 percent of U.S. households tune in to PBS sometime during the day. In addition, PBS still has a refined image and advertisers are viewed as good corporate citizens.[4]

CABLE AND SUBSCRIPTION TELEVISION

Cable Television: A form of subscription television in which the signals are carried to households by a cable.

The initial purpose of **cable television** was to improve reception in certain areas of the country, particularly mountainous regions and large cities. However, alternative programming, with an emphasis on entertainment and information, has been primarily responsible for the rapid growth of cable systems. Currently, two in three homes subscribe to cable through traditional coaxial cable delivery systems. Over 98 percent of the nation's 97.4 million households have television, and 66 percent of households subscribe to cable. This number is expected to grow to 72 percent by 2000. In 1981, cable television had less than 1 percent of the total television advertising pie. By 1994, its share had risen to nearly 9 percent, while broadcast network's share fell by the same amount.[5] Table 11.1 lists the top cable advertisers in 1995.

Some of these cable systems develop and air their own programs as well as pass along programs initiated by VHF stations, the 12 channels (2–13) located on the very high frequency band on the wavelength spectrum, or UHF (ultra-high frequency) stations, such as WTBS. *Pay programming* is an option available to subscribers for an additional monthly fee. Pay programming normally consists of movies, specials, and sports under such plans as Home Box Office, Showtime, and The Movie Channel. Pay networks do not currently sell advertising time. Homes

---

[3]Keith Dunnawant, "PBS: Dynamo or Dinosaur?," *Adweek* (February 24, 1992):18–26.

[4]Carrie Goerne, "Funding Losses, Competition Force PBS to Pitch Itself as a Marketing Company," *Marketing News* (May 11, 1992):1, 16.

[5]Rebecca Piirto, "Cable TV," *American Demographics* (June 1995):40–47.

TABLE 11.1	TOP 25 CABLE NETWORKS ADVERTISERS			
RANK 1995	ADVERTISER	CABLE TV NETWORKS ADVERTISING		
		1995	1994	% CHG
1	Procter & Gamble Co.	$177.5	$166.7	6.5
2	General Motors Corp.	90.0	82.2	9.5
3	Philip Morris Cos.	65.1	60.0	8.5
4	AT&T Corp.	55.1	77.2	−28.7
5	Kellogg Co.	50.8	43.1	18.1
6	MCI Communications Corp.	48.0	38.7	23.8
7	McDonald's Corp.	47.8	37.5	27.6
8	Unilever NV	45.5	29.5	54.1
9	Time Warner	44.9	42.0	6.9
10	Ford Motor Co.	43.9	33.8	29.7
11	PepsiCo	43.7	33.8	29.3
12	Chrysler Corp.	42.8	39.9	7.1
13	Hasbro Inc.	41.7	47.8	−12.6
14	Sprint Corp.	40.3	26.1	54.2
15	Johnson & Johnson	40.1	28.9	38.8
16	Anheuser-Busch Cos.	38.0	29.1	30.6
17	American Express Co.	37.6	27.6	36.1
18	General Mills	36.8	36.9	−0.5
19	Grand Metropolitan	35.6	23.3	52.7
20	Mattel	32.8	22.9	43.0
21	American Home Products Corp.	30.3	29.2	3.6
22	Mars Inc.	28.9	28.1	2.8
23	Pharmacia & Upjohn	26.9	14.7	83.3
24	Clorox Co.	26.7	28.6	−6.8
25	Coca-Cola Co.	26.4	24.8	6.8

Notes: Dollars are in millions.

Source: Competitive Media Reporting, *Advertising Age* (September 30, 1996):S44.

that do not subscribe to cable may purchase *subscription television* that is broadcast over the air with an electronically scrambled signal. Subscribers own a device that unscrambles the signal.

ORIGINS OF CABLE PROGRAMS

Most of the programming shown on cable television is provided by independent cable networks such as Cable News Network (CNN), the Disney Channel, the Nashville Network, Music Television (MTV), the Entertainment and Sports Programming Network (ESPN), and a group of independent superstations whose programs are carried by satellite to cable operators (for example, WTBS-ATLANTA, WGN-CHICAGO, and WWOR-NEW YORK). Although approximately 80 percent of cable programming is provided through these systems, the cable operators themselves are originating more of their own programs.

CABLE SCHEDULING

Cable scheduling is divided into two categories: network and local. The system is the same as for the noncable systems. Network cable systems show commercials across the entire subscriber group simultaneously. Local advertisers are able to show their commercials to highly restricted geographic audiences through **inter-connects,** a special cable technology that allows local or regional advertisers to run their commercials in small geographic areas through the interconnection of a number of cable systems. Interconnects are either "hard," in which different ads are distributed electronically by cable or microwave, or "soft," in which the same

Interconnects: A special cable technology that allows local advertisers to run their commercials in small geographical areas through the interconnection of a number of cable systems.

commercials are simply scheduled at the same time. Either way, they offer small advertisers an affordable way to reach certain local audiences through television.

MERGERS

Once considered a high-risk industry with little potential for profit, the cable industry is now in the maturity stage of its life cycle. Even small cable operations have been quite profitable, and it is apparent that cable television is here to stay. Even though the cable industry is still quite fragmented (see Figure 11.1), there is evidence that recent mergers and acquisitions will change this configuration by the year 2000. In essence, the battle is between the $183 billion telecommunications industry and the $20 billion cable industry. The battleground is the emerging technology: the next generation of televisions will be digital. Digitization—the transfer of analog pictures, text, and video into a series of ones and zeros—will allow information to flow into households just like electricity does today. As a result, tomorrow's viewers will see only what they want to see.

The question then becomes which industry, telecommunications or cable, is better able to deliver this new technology. The best alternative appears to be coaxial cable which is already used by cable television providers. Coaxial cable can carry much more information than the copper wires used by most telephone systems.

Today the cable industry is in a state of constant flux. Part of the change is due to new legislation. In 1992, the FCC abolished a ruling restricting telephone companies from carrying other types of signals. This not only opens the door for cable via telephone lines, it also prompts cable television companies to counter this competition by offering rival telephone service through coaxial cable originally installed to transmit television programming. Also, the *Financial Interest and Syndication Rules*, which limited the networks' ability to produce or own an equity stake in the shows they air, were abolished in 1995. This has prompted a series of mergers: Disney and ABC, Westinghouse and CBS, and Time Warner and Turner, just to name a few. This trend clearly puts the advantage on the side of the networks and greater pressure on cable to develop or buy programming. Finally, in 1996 the huge Telecommunication Act was passed, which essentially allowed all communication companies to engage in all aspects of business. Essentially, there will be little distinction between telephone, cable, and networks.

FIGURE 11.1

THE CABLE INDUSTRY IS HIGHLY FRAGMENTED.

(*Source:* Adapted from Andrew Kupper, "The No. 1 in Cable TV Has Big Plans," Fortune, June 28, 1993:97.)

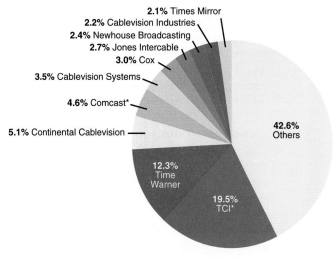

Share of Subscriber Households

2.1% Times Mirror
2.2% Cablevision Industries
2.4% Newhouse Broadcasting
2.7% Jones Intercable
3.0% Cox
3.5% Cablevision Systems
4.6% Comcast*
5.1% Continental Cablevision
12.3% Time Warner
19.5% TCI*
42.6% Others

* TCI and Comcast recently purchased by Storer Communications Cable Systems.

Various factors have contributed to the Big Three's decline in viewership, including the spread of the direct-broadcasting satellite business and the growth of the Fox Television Broadcasting Network. It is changes in the cable industry, however, that have been largely responsible for the decrease in network shares. Although some people maintain that the higher caliber of network programming will allow the networks to stay well ahead of cable, the networks need to be wary of federal changes in cable regulation and the increasing growth of the cable industry.

Some experts argue that cable's rise is certain to slow dramatically. Competition from new channels, fragmentation of the existing audience, a wave of new technology, and the threat of unfriendly legislation will all test cable's mettle over the next several years. Some of the difficulties cable faces are the industry's own making. For instance, video compression and fiber optics will enable cable systems to offer more channels and subject national cable networks to greater competition from within. A study by the brokerage firm Moran & Associates says 90 percent of all cable subscribers will have an average of 75 channels by 1997. The leading edge of that growth is already here. Time Warner Inc. is testing a 150-channel system in Queens, NY, and phone companies U S West and AT&T are trying out pay-per-view systems that will allow customers to choose from a vast array of movies at any time.[6]

LOCAL TELEVISION

Local television stations are affiliated with a network and carry both network programming and their own programs. Cost for local advertising differ, depending on the size of the market and the demand for the programs carried. For example, KHIO in Houston charges local advertisers $1,950 for a 30-second spot during prime time. This same time slot may cost $150 in a small town.

The local television market is substantially more varied than the national market. Most advertisers are local retailers, primarily department stores or discount stores, financial institutions, automobile dealers, restaurants, and supermarkets. Advertisers must buy time on a station-by-station basis. Although this arrangement makes sense for a local retailer, it is not an efficient strategy for a national or regional advertiser, who would have to deal individually with a large number of stations.

SPECIALTY TELEVISION

PRINCIPLE Network advertising schedules are dominated by large national advertisers.

Several alternative delivery systems have appeared recently. These systems attempt to reach certain audiences with television messages in a way that is more effective or efficient than network, cable, or local television. For example, low-power television (LPTV) was licensed by the FCC to provide television outlets to minorities and communities that are underserved by full-power stations or have signals that cover a radius of 15 miles, as opposed to full-power stations, whose signals can reach viewers in a 70-mile radius. The system can be picked up by homes through personal antennas and carries advertising for local retailers and businesses. Multipoint distribution systems (MDS) and subscription television (STV) both deliver limited programming without incurring the cost of cable installation. The former is used by hotels and restaurants to give guests access to special movies and other entertainment. The latter offers one-channel capabilities of pay-cable-type programming transmitted to individual homes through a signal decoder. Advertisers who use STV typically sell products related to the audience watching the STV program. All these specialty systems can carry advertisements. However, they represent a very minor delivery system.

[6]Stephen Battaglio, "The Rise and Fall," *Adweek* (April 6, 1992):10–16.

INTERACTIVE TELEVISION

After several false starts, interactive television may finally come of age by the end of the 1990s. *Interactivity* or *viewer control* can take one of three forms. The first type is video-on-demand (VOD), where viewers control what and when they watch. Pay-per-view (PPV) is a limited version of VOD that allows viewers to choose programs at predetermined two-hour intervals. The second type of interactivity is a system that stores information at the television set and allows viewers to choose programs with a box in the home, in much the same way VCRs and videotapes function today. The third type of interactivity is the *simulcast*, which transmits digital information in conjunction with an actual broadcast. Simulcast viewers can control the programming itself. By punching in their choices on a keypad, viewers can second-guess NFL quarterbacks or order more information during a documentary.[7]

To date, the interactive television concept, as originally envisioned, has not done well. ACTV, the industry leader, lost over $3 million from 1994 to 1995. Interactive Network lost $15 million during this same period. As a result, most interactive television companies have sought partnerships with existing cable companies. For example, ACTV is working with Prime Sports-West on customized interactive sports services. ACTV customers will pay $6 to $8 a month for unlimited access to on-demand instant replays, star-player camera coverage, and player statistics and facts.[8]

Recently, the cable industry has examined new ways to become an interactive television player. It is betting on high-speed modems that can be used with both televisions and personal computers. These devices would be capable of pulling pages off the World Wide Web at 1,000 times the speed of conventional modems. The industry still has to work out some problems, including the $500 price tag for each modem. Also, a lack of nationwide cable-network standards severely complicates efforts to come up with a universal device.[9]

TELEVISION SYNDICATION

Syndication: Television or radio shows that are reruns or original programs purchased by local stations to fill in during open hours.

The **syndication** boom has been fueled mainly by the growth of independent stations that require programming. Syndicated shows are television or radio programs that are purchased by local stations to fill in open hours. Today both networks and independents have been forced to bid on these shows, referred to as *strips* (like a comic strip, a syndicated strip is a show that appears daily at the same time) to fill the many open hours in the morning, late afternoon, early evening, and late night. This open time is the result of the prime-time access rule (PTAR), which forbids network affiliates in the 50 major U.S. television markets from broadcasting more than three hours of prime-time programming in any one four-hour slot.

Every winter hundreds of station directors attend the National Association of Television Program Executives (NATPE) meeting in order to bid on the many shows available for syndication. This is referred to as the *up-front buying process*, and a similar process exists for network program spots. *Mad About You* was the hottest show that moved into syndication in 1996. The top 25 syndicated advertisers are listed in Table 11.2.

OFF-NETWORK SYNDICATION

There are two primary types of syndicated programming. The first is *off-network syndication*, which includes reruns of network shows. Examples are *M*A*S*H*, *The Bob Newhart Show*, *Star Trek*, and *Seinfeld*. The FCC imposes several restrictions on such shows. Most important, a network show must produce 88 episodes before

[7]Rebecca Piirto, "Taming the TV Beast," *American Demographics* (May 1993):34–40.
[8]Mark Berniker, "Interactive TV Proves Slow Mover," *Broadcasting Cable* (May 22, 1995):41.
[9]Ronald Grover, "I-Way or No Way for Cable?" *Business Week* (April 8, 1996):75–78.

TABLE 11.2	TOP 25 SYNDICATED TELEVISION ADVERTISERS		
RANK		**SYNDICATED TV ADVERTISING**	
1995	**ADVERTISER**	**1995**	**1994**	**% CHG**
1	Procter & Gamble Co.	$203.1	$189.7	7.1
2	Philip Morris Cos.	131.5	155.5	−15.5
3	Kellogg Co.	87.1	75.0	16.1
4	Unilever NV	86.7	75.1	15.5
5	American Home Products Corp.	58.2	41.4	40.4
6	Hasbro Inc.	55.9	55.6	0.7
7	Mattel	52.2	52.1	0.1
8	Time Warner	50.4	71.5	−29.5
9	McDonald's Corp.	49.5	25.7	92.7
10	General Motors Corp.	45.3	38.6	17.3
11	AT&T Corp.	41.1	32.7	25.6
12	Grand Metropolitan	38.5	31.2	23.2
13	Johnson & Johnson	37.7	27.9	34.9
14	Mars Inc.	37.4	35.6	4.8
15	Wm. Wrigley, Jr. Co.	34.2	35.8	−4.4
16	Warner-Lambert Co.	31.2	34.2	−8.6
17	RJR Nabisco	30.9	35.6	−13.3
18	Regal Communications (Psychic Friends Network)	30.2	25.8	17.2
19	Sears, Roebuck & Co.	28.6	26.4	8.4
20	Novartis	26.4	22.8	16.0
21	Himmel Group	25.9	23.7	9.1
22	Walt Disney Co.	25.2	21.9	15.5
23	Sara Lee Corp.	24.4	25.6	−4.5
24	Bayer AG	24.1	22.9	5.0
25	Hershey Foods Corp.	22.9	26.2	−12.6

Notes: Dollars are in millions.

Source: Competitive Media Reporting, *Advertising Age* (September 30, 1996):S42. Reprinted with permission from *Advertising Age*. Copyright Crain Communications Inc.

it can be syndicated. The prime-time access rule prohibits large network affiliates from airing these shows from 7:30 P.M. to 8:00 P.M. Eastern time. These shows are often used as lead-ins to the local or network news.

The most expensive off-network show to date has been *The Cosby Show*, the most popular program in television history. Syndicator Viacom Enterprises did not have much difficulty selling the show to 174 stations for an estimated $500 million to $600 million for rerun rights covering four years. In return, each station received 11 30-second spots to sell in each episode.

In 1996, Columbia Tristar Television Distribution sold *Mad About You* to 200 stations with ad rates starting at $100,000 per 30-second spot. Stations are expected to air *Seinfeld* and *Mad About You* back-to-back. *Friends* will go into syndication in 1998 at an expected cost of $5 million per station.

FIRST-RUN SYNDICATION

Sometimes network shows that did not meet the minimal number of episodes, such as *Too Close for Comfort*, *It's a Living*, and *Rescue 911*, are purchased from the networks and moved into syndication even as they continue to produce new episodes. This is referred to as *first-run syndication*. Such shows are now produced strictly for syndication, an arrangement that allows them to avoid the FCC's prime-time access rule. Syndicators also produce their own original shows. Recent examples include *Kung Fu: The Legend Continues* and *Time Trax*. In 1993, 87 syndicated shows were offered. This included 22 new shows, including 13 daily (strip) series.

In negotiating the price a station will pay for a show, the syndicator can deal in cash, barter, or a combination of the two. A cash deal is simple: The syndicator grants the station the right to run a show for a specified period in return for a cash license fee. Cash syndication was once the only, and is still the largest, part of the $3.5 billion syndication industry: Station license fees are estimated at $1.8 billion to $2.0 billion annually. However, it is not growing very fast because stations have been relatively short of cash in recent years.

Beginning about 1980, faced with competition that was driving program prices up and revenues down, stations began paying for programming by giving back to the syndicator a portion of the commercial time in the show instead of cash. The syndicator then sold this time, packaged as national units, to national advertisers. This is the system known as advertiser-supported or *barter syndication*.

Trading programs for commercial time, rather than cash, is not a new idea: It is the way network television has always operated. But because syndicators generally back less commercial time in a show than the networks, the stations have more local time to sell and hence can make more money. For example, a half-hour show in syndication typically carries six commercial minutes. In a *full barter deal*, the syndicator will give the local station half the time, 3 minutes, to sell to spot advertisers and keep the remaining 3 minutes to sell to national advertisers. In a *cash/barter deal* (standard for many daily series), the syndicator takes back a smaller amount of time but charges a cash license fee as well.

There are several problems with bartering. One is that advertisers expect the syndicated show to be sold to enough stations to cover at least 70 percent of the market, with a preferred rate of 80 to 85 percent. New shows often don't reach this level. Also, guaranteed ratings are not always met. Furthermore, because of the tremendous competition, a 2-3 share is not uncommon, meaning the syndicated program is only delivering 2 to 3 percent of the audience watching television during that time period. Finally, contracts with some stations stipulate that the national commercials—the barter spots—must run in the more desirable time slots, even if the show itself no longer is carried in that time period.

Finally, the excessive supply of new shows offered for syndication during the next three to five years may mean that shows such as *Dr. Quinn, Medicine Woman* and *Hangin' with Mr. Cooper* will not receive the huge cash prices that *Cosby* and *Cheers* once did. Consequently, syndicators will be forced to either accept barter deals or not sell the shows. This heavy reliance on barter and old shows may have dire consequences to the syndication industry.[10]

*T*ELEVISION *A*DVERTISING

Like television programming, television ads can be aired through a number of different arrangements. Television advertisers can run their commercials through over-the-air network scheduling, local scheduling, cable scheduling, or unwired networks.

FORMS OF TELEVISION ADVERTISING

The actual form of a television commercial varies depending on whether a network, local, or cable schedule is employed (see Figure 11.2). Networks allow either *sponsorships* or *participations*, and local affiliates allow *spot announcements* and *local sponsorships*.

SPONSORSHIPS

Sponsorship: An arrangement in which the advertiser produces both a television program and the accompanying commercials.

In **sponsorships,** which characterized most early television advertising, the advertiser assumes the total financial responsibility for producing the program and pro-

---

[10]Kevin Goldman, "Sitcom Syndicators are Laughing Less," *The Wall Street Journal* (January 24, 1992):B1.

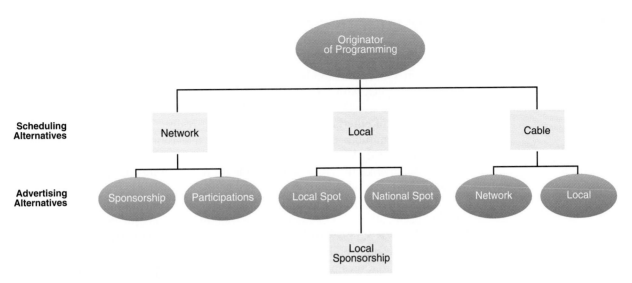

FIGURE 11.2

**THIS FIGURE ILLUSTRATES
THE CHOICES THAT FACE A
TELEVISION ADVERTISER.**
Reprinted with permission from
Advertising Age. Copyright Crain
Communications Inc.

viding the accompanying commercials. Examples of early sponsored programs are
Bonanza (sponsored by Chevrolet), *The Hallmark Hall of Fame,* and *The Kraft Music Hour.* Sponsorship has a powerful impact on the viewing public, especially because the advertiser can control the content and quality of the program as well as
the placement and length of commercials. However, the costs of producing and
sponsoring a 30- and 60-minute program make this option too expensive for most
advertisers today. An alternative is for several advertisers to produce a program
jointly. This plan is quite common with sporting events, where each sponsor receives a 15-minute segment.

Although not strictly a sponsorship, *infomercials* have come onto the scene
during the last decade and have many of the same characteristics of a sponsorship.

PARTICIPATIONS

Participations: An arrangement
in which a television advertiser
buys commercial time from a
network.

Sponsorships represent less than 10 percent of network advertising. The rest is
sold as **participations** in which advertisers pay for 15, 30, or 60 seconds of commercial time during one or more programs. The advertiser can buy any time that
is available on a regular or irregular basis. This approach not only reduces the
risks and costs associated with sponsorships but also provides a great deal more
flexibility in respect to market coverage, target audiences, scheduling, and budgeting. Participations do not create the same high impact as sponsorships, however,
and the advertiser does not have any control over the content of the program. Finally, the "time avails" (available time slots) for the most popular programs are often bought up by the largest advertisers, leaving fewer good time slots for the
small advertisers.

SPOT ANNOUNCEMENTS

Spot Announcements: Ads
shown during the breaks between
programs.

PRINCIPLE Spot buys are dominated by local advertising.

The third form a television commercial can take is the **spot announcement.**
(Note that the word *spot* is also used in conjunction with a time frame such as a
"30-second spot," and this usage should not be confused with spot announcements.) Spot announcements refer to the breaks between programs, which local
affiliates sell to advertisers who want to show their ads locally. Commercials of 10,
20, 30, and 60 seconds are sold on a station-by-station basis to local, regional, and
national advertisers. The local buyers clearly dominate spot television.

The breaks between programs are not always optimal time slots for advertisers because there is a great deal of clutter from competing commercials, station
breaks, public service announcements, and other distractions. Program breaks also
tend to be time when viewers take a break from their television sets.

THE TELEVISION AUDIENCE

With an estimated $52 billion in combined network, spot, and cable advertising revenue in 1995, television is big business.[11] Television has become a mainstay of American society, with 98 percent of American households having one or more television sets. People gather around the set day after day, night after night, to find a source of entertainment, an escape from reality. This dependency explains why a great number of advertisers consider television their primary medium. What do we really know about how audiences watch television? Are we a generation of zombielike television addicts? Or do we carefully and intelligently select what we watch on television?

A great deal of information describing the characteristics of television viewers has been gathered. For example, the total media hours for the average American in 1996 was 3,389, with 1,552 of those hours devoted to watching television.[12] In a recent Gallup poll, a majority of respondents believe television is getting worse, not better, on a number of key measures, and 65 percent said they don't believe disclaimers are effective. Meanwhile, 74 percent said violence on television contributes to real-life violence, while 68 percent say television encourages sexual activity among kids under age 18. In another survey, individuals were asked how many of the channels they receive do they actually watch. For those receiving 36 channels, they watch 13, and for those receiving 80 channels, 14 are watched.[13] Finally, as discussed in the Concepts and Applications box, the dreaded "channel surfer" is becoming more common.

---

[11]Keith J. Kelly and Chuck Ross, "Bright Prospects Seen for Cable TV, New Media," *Advertising Age* (August 19, 1996):8.

[12]"And It Doesn't Include Time Spent Deciphering Your VCR," *Adweek* (August 8, 1994):17.

[13]"Spending Tube Time," *Adweek* (February 28, 1994):18.

CONCEPTS AND APPLICATIONS

SURF TILL YOU DROP

Channel surfing is the closest many Americans come to a participatory sport. Virtually all new televisions come with remote controls that allow viewers to change channels without budging from their Barca-Loungers. With tens or hundreds of channels to choose from, two types of channel surfing have emerged. Some television viewers zip sequentially through channels when their attention begins to wander; others skip boring commercials by switching channels. The truly unhinged do both. Much to the chagrin of wives, sisters, and girlfriends, men are the kings of channel surfing. More than four in ten say their primary method for deciding what to watch on television is flipping channels, compared with 31 percent for women, according to a study by Roper Starch Worldwide for TVSM Inc., publisher of *Cable Guide*. Women prefer to use interpretive material for choosing programs. Forty-five percent say their primary method is a listing or guide, compared with 34 percent of men.

Americans aged 18 to 29 are significantly more likely than average to choose programs by surfing. Almost half do, compared with 37 percent of all adults. The urge to fly through the channel lineup decreases with age.

Channel surfers are the bane of the television networks, and the Big Four do everything they can to keep viewers' thumbs off the button. They have repositioned prime-time commercial breaks so that one show begins right on the heels of the previous one. Also, end-of-show credits have been relegated to a space on the side of the screen. The rest of the space is taken up with promos for upcoming shows, monologues by stars of the show just ending, trivia questions, or other filler designed to hold the viewers' attention. "This is a way to attract the poly-attentive viewer who channel surfs because he has no difficulty absorbing two or three activities on screen at the same time," says *TV Guide* managing editor Jack Curry.

Advertisers are also working to keep viewers from condemning their expensive commercials to remote-control purgatory. A 1991 survey conducted by Batr, Thomas Olney of Western Washington University and Morris Holbrook of Columbia University revealed that interesting and unique commercials that conjured a sense of pleasure and fun were zapped less often than messages that were utilitarian and factual in content. Advertisers may reduce the likelihood of viewers skipping their commercials by creating action-packed, fast-paced advertisements, and plot-based sequential ads.

Source: "Coping with Channel Surfers," *American Demographics* (December 1995):13–15. Reprinted with permission. Copyright © 1995, *American Demographics*, Ithaca, New York.

HOW PEOPLE WATCH TELEVISION

Further insights into the question of how people watch television were provided by a five-month study done by Peter Collett, research psychologist at the University of Oxford in England. Collett used a video camera to examine the viewing behavior of 20 families. After studying 400 hours of videotape, Collett concluded that viewers often do anything but view. They read, talk, knit, vacuum, blow-dry their hair, and sometimes fight over the remote control. The study found two major responses to commercials: A large segment (approximately 45 percent) watched less than 10 percent of a given commercial, and another segment (approximately 15 percent) watched more than 90 percent of a spot. Why this disparity? Collett believes it has to do with the following:

- The nature of the commercial, the way in which it is structured, or the nature of the product advertised.
- The makeup of the audience. Some viewers tend not to watch commercials at all; others are "commercial consumers."
- The positioning of commercials: What time of day they run, where spots fall in the commercial break.
- Viewer attention, perhaps related to the presence of others in the room. For example, the more people present, the fewer the commercials that are watched.
- The programming environment. If a break follows a popular, engaging program, viewers spend more time watching the commercial messages.

This study suggests that most people are not true television addicts. Actually, most people seldom give their full attention to the set. These facts must be kept in mind when considering television as an advertising medium.[14]

MEASURING THE TELEVISION AUDIENCE

Many of us have had our favorite television show taken off the air because of "poor ratings." Although we may have had some idea of how these ratings were derived, the "Nielsen family" and the rating process remain a mystery to most people.

Actually, the derivation of television ratings is a relatively simple process. Several independent rating firms periodically sample a portion of the television viewing audience, assess the size and characteristics of the audiences watching specific shows, and then make these data available to subscribing companies and agencies, which use them in their media planning. Currently, A.C. Nielsen dominates this industry and provides the most frequently used measure of national and local television audiences.

NIELSEN INDEXES

Nielsen measures television audiences at two levels: network (Nielsen Television Index, NTI) and spot (Nielsen Station Index, NSI). For local measurement, two measuring devices are used. The most famous is the Nielsen Storage Instantaneous Audimeter, or audimeter for short. The audimeter can record when the set is used and which station it is tuned to, but it cannot identify who is watching the program. Data on who is watching are provided by diaries mailed each week during survey months to sample homes in each of the 211 television markets—that amounts to approximately one million diaries a year.

PEOPLE METERS

Nielsen began to measure not only what is being watched but who is watching in the fall of 1987. People meters provide information on what television shows are being watched, the number of households that are watching, and which family

---

[14]Mary Connors, "Catching TV Viewers in the Act of Being Themselves," *Adweek* (March 9, 1987):30.

members are watching. In the fall of 1987 Nielsen replaced its Audimeter and diary system with *people meters* that provide information on what television shows are being watched, the number of households that are watching, and which family members are viewing. The type of activity is recorded automatically; household members merely have to indicate their presence by pressing a button. People meters have become the primary method for measuring national television audiences.

Nielsen Media Research has come under sharp criticism recently. Executives at Fox Broadcasting Co. and NBC Inc. have blasted the 45-year-old television rating operation for slipshod sampling and skewed results. NBC Television president, Neil S. Braun, has openly wondered whether or not broadcasters should accelerate plans to create a ratings service of their own. In Jackson, Mississippi, Fox says a local affiliate posted ratings when it wasn't on the air. Network executives say Nielsen chronically undercounts demographically significant kids, who typically don't bother to record their viewing habits. Nielsen acknowledges there are problems. "Anytime you deal with sampling like this, you're going to get errors," says Nielsen vice president Jack Loftus.[15]

CLUSTERPLUS   A.C. Nielsen is always looking for an opportunity to offer their subscribers something extra. Nielsen now provides data for the 47 ClusterPLUS geodemographic groupings developed by Donnelley Marketing Information Services. According to Nielsen, *geodemographic clusters* are distinct types of neighborhoods. Each of the nation's 250,000 census block groups is assigned to one of 47 cluster groups based upon its demographic and socioeconomic makeup. Cluster 1, the Established Wealthy, is composed of the most elite, affluent neighborhoods in places like Greenwich and Beverly Hills. Residents of Cluster 47, Lowest-Income Black Female-Headed Families, live in poverty-stricken areas such as the South Bronx or Watts.

One packaged-goods manufacturer used the ClusterPLUS Nielsen connection to market an ingredient used in baking cakes and cookies. The goal was to buy television commercials only for programs whose audience has a large proportion of consumers who regularly bake from scratch. By merging the ten highest-ranking clusters that fit the audience profile into one target group, the packaged-goods marketer got a detailed look at the product's best prospects. He decided to zero in on older, rural, and blue-collar viewers in the South and Midwest.[16]

Nielsen's audience measurement service covers every television market at least four times each year. These ratings periods, when all 211 markets are surveyed, are known as *sweeps*. In all markets Nielsen uses diaries to measure viewing. In 32 markets the service uses both household meters and diaries to measure TV set usage and audience identity.

Nielsen publishes its findings between four and seven times per year in a descriptive format called the Viewers in Profile (VIP) report. A **television market** is an unduplicated geographical area to which a county is assigned on the basis of market size. One county is always placed in just one television market to avoid overlap. Nielsen refers to its television markets in which local stations receive the majority of the viewing hours as Designated Market Areas (DMAs).

Television Market: An unduplicated geographical area to which a county is assigned on the basis of the highest share of the viewing of television stations.

ADVANTAGES AND DISADVANTAGES OF TELEVISION

ADVANTAGES

Advertisers would not invest large sums of money in television commercials unless these ads were effective. The major strength of television that make it appealing as an advertising medium are cost efficiency, impact, and influence.

[15]Ronald Grover, "Nielsen Schmielsen," *Business Week* (February 12, 1996):38–39.

[16]Jonathan Marks, "ClusterPLUS Nielsen Equals Efficient Marketing," *American Demographics* (September 1991):16.

COST EFFICIENCY

Many advertisers view television as the most effective way to deliver a commercial message. The major advantage of television is its wide reach. Millions of people watch some television regularly. Television not only reaches a large percentage of the population, it also reaches people who are not effectively reached by print media. For example, NBC's *Today* show would average approximately $18,500 for a 30-second spot, and the household CMP would be $4.50. This mass coverage, in turn, is extremely cost-efficient. For an advertiser attempting to reach an undifferentiated market, a 30-second spot on a top-rated show may cost a penny or less for each person reached.

PRINCIPLE Television advertising reaches mass audiences and is very cost-efficient.

IMPACT

Another advantage of television is the strong impact created by the interaction of sight and sound. This feature induces a level of consumer involvement that often approximates the shopping experience, including encountering a persuasive salesperson. Television also allows a great deal of creative flexibility because of the many possible combinations of sight, sound, color, motion, and drama. Television has tremendous dramatic capacity; it can make mundane products appear important, exciting, and interesting. In other words, television can create a positive association with the sponsor if the advertisement is "likable." The classic IBM "Little Tramp" campaign is viewed as one of the most likable ads ever.

INFLUENCE

The final advantage of television is that it has become a primary facet of our culture. For most Americans television is a critical source of news, entertainment, and education. It is so much a part of us that we are more likely to believe companies that advertise on television, especially sponsors of drama and educational programs such as IBM, Xerox, and Hallmark Cards, than we are to believe those that don't. Sometimes this influence comes from a tie-in with a popular celebrity, such as Tommy Lasorda for Ultra Slim-Fast (see Ad 11.1).

DISADVANTAGES

Despite the effectiveness of television advertising, problems do exist, including expense, clutter, nonselective targeting, and inflexibility.

AD 11.1

TOMMY LASORDA HAS BEEN A SUCCESSFUL SPOKESMAN FOR A DIET AID.

"I Lost 30 Pounds In 3 Months, And Never Felt Better In My Life."
Tommy Lasorda

EXPENSE

The most serious limitation of television advertising is the extremely high *absolute* cost of producing and running commercials. Although the cost per person reached is low, the absolute cost can be restrictive, especially for smaller and even mid-sized companies. Production costs include filming the commercial (several hundred to several hundred thousand dollars) and the costs of talent. For celebrities such as Bill Cosby, Candice Bergen, and Michael Jordan, the price tag can be millions of dollars (see Ad 11.2). The prices charged for network time are simply a result of supply and demand. Programs that draw the largest audiences can charge more for their advertising space. A 30-second prime-time spot averages about $185,000. Special shows, such as the Super Bowl, World Series, or Academy Awards, charge much more. Some experts estimate that only 50 U.S. companies can afford a comprehensive television media schedule at these costs. It has been said that television advertising is very cheap if you can afford it. (See Table 11.3).

CLUTTER

Television suffers from a very high level of commercial clutter. In the past, the National Association of Broadcasters (NAB) restricted the amount of allowable commercial time per hour to approximately 6 minutes. In 1982 the Justice Department found this restriction illegal. Although the networks now continue to honor the NAB guidelines, this could change as their needs for revenue increase. The Justice Department ruling could eventually increase the number of 30-second commercials, station-break announcements, credits, and public service announcements, which in turn would diminish the visibility and persuasiveness of television advertising. Although in recent years the growth of the 15-second spot (:15) has been responsible for much of the clutter in television advertising, 1990 marked the beginning of the decline of these shorter commercials since their introduction in 1983. Finally, much of the clutter is also a result of the many network and local stations promoting their own programming.

NONSELECTIVE AUDIENCE

Despite the introduction of various technologies that better target consumers, television remains nonselective. Network television still attracts about 75 percent of the U.S. audience. Although the networks attempt to profile viewers, their descriptions are quite general, offering the advertiser little assurance that appropriate people are viewing the message. Thus television advertising includes a great deal of *waste coverage*—that is, communication directed at an unresponsive (and often uninterested) audience that may not fit the advertiser's target market characteristics.

PRINCIPLE Television should be used as a primary medium when the objective is to reach a mass audience simultaneously with a visual impact.

AD 11.2

A FAMOUS CELEBRITY ENDORSE-MENT ENHANCES THE ADVERTIS-ING OF A PRODUCT, BUT THE EX-PENSE OF HIRING THE TALENT CAN BE LIMITING.

TABLE 11.3	TEN MOST EXPENSIVE PRIME-TIME SHOWS

SHOW	PER :30
1 *Seinfeld*	$550,000
2 *ER*	500,000
3 *Home Improvement*	455,000
4 *Friends*	450,000
5 *Monday Night Football*	400,000
6 *Spin City*	395,000
7 *Suddenly Susan*	370,000
8 *Single Guy*	315,000
9 *Ink*	300,000
10 *Cosby*	295,000

Source: Network and agency estimates, *Advertising Age,*
(September 16, 1996):1.

INFLEXIBILITY

Television also suffers from a lack of flexibility in scheduling. Most network television is bought in the spring and early summer for the next fall season. If an advertiser is unable to make this up-front buy, only limited time-slot alternatives will remain available. Also, it is difficult to make last-minute adjustments in terms of scheduling, copy, or visuals.

It should be noted that cable television has many advantages over network and spot television; especially important is the fact that cable is much more targeted and has far less waste. Conversely, it cannot cover a mass audience and probably is more cluttered than network.

THE STRUCTURE OF RADIO

Signals: A series of electrical impulses that compose radio and television broadcasting.

Frequency: The number of radio waves produced by a transmitter in 1 second.

Radio can be classified according to transmission and power. The actual range of the station depends on the height of the antenna, the quality of the equipment, and so forth. Radio is a series of electrical impulses called **signals** that are transmitted by *electromagnetic waves*. Radio signals have a height (amplitude) and a width. The width dictates the frequency of the radio signal. A **frequency** is the number of radio waves a transmitter produces each second. The wider the signal, the lower the frequency, and the narrower the wave, the higher the frequency. Frequency is measured in terms of thousands of cycles per second (kilohertz) or millions of cycles per second (megahertz). Thus a radio station assigned a frequency of 930,000 cycles per second would be found at 93 on your radio dial. The Federal Communications Commission (FCC) assigns these frequencies to ensure that station signals do not interfere with one another.

AM RADIO

Radio stations are designated either AM or FM. An AM, or *amplitude modulation*, station has the flexibility to vary the height of its electromagnetic signal so that during the daytime it produces waves, called *ground waves*, that follow the contour of the earth. At night the station transmits waves into the sky, called *sky waves*, that bounce back to earth and are picked up by receivers far beyond the range of the station's ground waves.

The actual power or strength of an AM signal depends on the power allowed by the FCC. Stations with a broadcast range of approximately 25 miles are considered *local stations*. Most local stations are allowed 100 to 250 watts of power. In contrast, *regional stations* may cover an entire state or several states. The most

INSIDE ADVERTISING

SHIRO KUROSAI, RADIO/TELEVISION DEPARTMENT, *Nihon Keizai Advertising, Tokyo*

Shiro Kurosai is positioned in Nihon Keizai Advertising's Media Headquarters Radio/Television Department and is in charge of television media planning and buying. He is a graduate of Rikkyo University in Tokyo and is in his fifth year at the agency.

8:40 A.M.	As usual, I board the train for the commute to work. I'm not much of a morning person so I listen to music on my Walkman to gradually wake myself up. Of my hobbies, music takes up the greatest part of my attention. And performing on weekends in a rock band with friends from my school days is the thing I enjoy most.
9:30–10:00 A.M.	The first thing to do at work is to look over yesterday's memos and confirm today's schedule. After that I am overrun with calls from each client's account manager. Because most of the workday is spent out of the office, every morning and evening is a constant exchange of phone calls. As this is the time for presentations for the November–December television spot campaigns, we talk briefly about the data that have been gathered. Several of the clients who have already had presentations are scheduled to give a decision this evening. So I relay a progress report to the people in charge at the television stations.
10:00–11:30 A.M.	We hold a meeting with section managers, department manager, and head office manager to examine plans for new television programs to start in April of next year in the commercial broadcast

time slots our company presently holds. The program now being shown in that slot is a golf tournament; its reviews are fair, but it is in its seventh year and has lost its central sponsor. There are about 20 possibilities for replacement, and there is hardly time to go through each one's features and problems.

11:30–1:00 P.M.	Mr. Hanamoto, TV Osaka Tokyo Branch's agency sales manager, paid me a visit. After briefly confirming the important areas with regard to a sponsoring client's television publicity during a program scheduled for next week, we go out to a nearby steak house for lunch together. During lunch we avoid discussing business as much as possible and enjoy a light private discussion. A relaxed meal tastes better than a so-called "power lunch."
1:00–1:30 P.M.	Mr. Kabashima, my section chief, Mr. Asakoshi, a client account manager, and I board the subway to head for TV Tokyo. On the subway I run my eyes across several hanging ads for the latest issues of magazines. This is the easiest way to quickly pick up on what the current topics are.
1:30–3:00 P.M.	At TV Tokyo we attended a meeting about a one-time golf program that will be broadcast at the end of the year. Those participating were program producer Mr. Wachi and the directors from Cross TV who will undertake production, Mr. Koseki and Mr. Yamamoto. This program

powerful stations are called *clear channel stations* and may use up to 50,000 watts (KMOX in St. Louis is an example). The relative power of each type of station will vary, depending on the frequency assigned. Generally, the lower the frequency, the farther the signal will travel.

FM RADIO

An FM, or *frequency modulation*, station differs from AM in that the bandwidth (frequency) is adjusted rather than the height (amplitude), which remains constant. Because the signal put out by an FM station follows the line of sight, the distance of the signal depends on the height of the antenna. Typically, 50 miles is the maximum signal distance. However, the tonal quality of an FM signal is superior to that of AM.

As radio's importance as a local medium increases, more of its programming will be satellite-delivered from radio network. Aaron Daniels, president of ABC Radio Networks, predicts that 30 percent of the country's 10,000 stations will use will be recorded on a golf course managed by the main client, a tourist/leisure-related company, and the world renowned golfer Gary Player will be participating. Recording will take place in mid-November, but the broadcast will be at the start of the year-end vacation on December 30, during which time the crucial audience, Japan's businessmen, will most likely be at home glued to their televisions. Meeting time is spent mainly discussing what is to be anticipated on the day of recording. What is decided today will be announced to the client in a presentation next week.

3:00–4:30 P.M. After the meeting we walk over to TV Tokyo's business section. First we confirm next week's presentation schedule with the manager. By maintaining a cooperative relationship with the television station, as opposed to proceeding independently, we can work with a much higher level of certainty. After we have finished conferring about that program we move on to meet with the spot CM manager's desk. It is also important to exchange information about client trends, and so on, in facing the latest spot CM demand period.

4:30–5:00 P.M. We board the subway to return to the office.

5:00–5:30 P.M. I return to my desk and return calls from the memos that came while I was out. From the information confirmed this morning, two good reports have come in.

However, one other decision we had been waiting for was put off until after tomorrow. I immediately put in calls to the television station's respective account managers to inform them of the news.

5:30–6:30 P.M. An automobile goods manufacturer who has already decided on a television spot campaign has expressed dissatisfaction with the time-slot proposal we had submitted, so the account manager and I meet for a discussion on the matter. If we don't resolve the differences in opinion we have between ourselves, it will be very difficult to convince our client of anything.

6:30–7:00 P.M. It has been a rigorous day, but now I begin preparing the materials for a presentation to a client tomorrow. The commercial time slots have already been decided on so I neatly put it in chart form on the word processor. I proofread it twice and, as there are no errors, today's work is done!

7:30 P.M. The other workers who have stayed late too head to a bar nearby, but I get on the train to go home. I pull out my Walkman again and this time listen to the tape my band recorded on the weekend. I've got to practice for next weekend. But this is ultimately a relaxed and enjoyable moment. In either case, it's something I can feel good about—that I accomplished something during a difficult day.

satellite-delivered programming by the middle of the 1990s. In addition, more stations will use satellite networks to reduce their programming costs.[17]

CABLE AND DAB RADIO

In addition to the dominant AM and FM radio delivery systems, cable radio was launched in 1990. The technology uses cable television receivers to deliver static-free music via wires plugged into cable subscribers' stereos. The thinking behind cable radio is that cable television needs new revenue and consumers are fed up with commercials on radio. The service typically is commercial-free and costs $7 to $12. An example is Digital Music Express, which offers CD sound in 30 formats around the clock.

DAB, or digital audio broadcast, exists in Europe and was introduced in the United States in 1995. DAB is essentially perfect quality audio delivery.

---

[17]Stephen Battaglio, "Radio," *Adweek* (September 11, 1989):185.

Potentially, it offers the capability for listeners to listen to the same station all the way across the country. It means better sound, less interference, and possible audience extension. In effect, it's a defense against other technologies, such as CDs.[18]

RADIO ADVERTISING

Network Radio: A group of local affiliates providing simultaneous programming via connection to one or more of the national networks through AT&T telephone wires.

Radio advertising is available on national networks and on local markets. **Network radio** refers to a group of local affiliates connected to one or more of the national networks through telephone wires and satellites. The network provides simultaneous network programming, which is quite limited compared with network television programming. Therefore many local or regional stations belong to more than one network, with each network providing specialized programming to complete a station's schedule. Ad 11.3 is an example of a radio network print ad.

[18]Melanie Rigney, "New Technology Brings Radio to Cutting Edge," *Advertising Age* (September 9, 1991):S1, S6.

AD 11.3

RADIO NETWORKS OFTEN PROVIDE SPECIALIZED PROGRAMMING, SUCH AS ABC RADIO NETWORKS.

Each station then sends out the network's signal through its own antenna. There are also regional networks (for example, Intermountain Network and the Groskin Group) that tend to serve a particular state or audience segment, such as farmers.

NETWORK RADIO

Complete market coverage combined with quality programming has increased the popularity of network radio. Over 20 national radio networks program concerts, talk shows, sports events, and dramas. Satellite transmission has produced important technological improvements. Satellites not only provide a better sound but also allow the transmission of multiple programs with different formats. Network radio is viewed as a viable national advertising medium, especially for advertisers of food, automobiles, and over-the-counter drugs.

In the 1980s network radio went through a period of consolidation that produced four major radio networks: Westwood One, CBS, ABC, and Unistar (see Ad 11.4). The Radio Advertising Bureau reported revenues of $414 million for network radio in 1995. Over $1 billion was spent on national spot advertising out of a total of $10.5 billion in advertising revenues. The growth of network radio is also attributed to the increase in syndicated radio shows and unwired networks.[19]

SYNDICATION

As the number of affiliates has boomed, so has the number of news syndicated radio shows, creating more advertising opportunities for companies eager to reach new markets. In fact, syndication and network radio have practically become interchangeable terms. Syndication has been beneficial to network radio because it offers advertisers a variety of high-quality specialized programs. Both networks and private firms offer syndication. Essentially a syndication offers a complete catalog of programming to the local affiliate. For example, Transtar Radio Network, located in Colorado Springs, claims about 600 affiliates. Its only direct competitor

---

[19]John McDonough, "Radio: A 75-Year-Roller-Coaster Ride," *Advertising Age* (September 4, 1995):22–23.

AD 11.4

THIS AD FOR UNISTAR LISTS ITS ADVANTAGES TO POTENTIAL ADVERTISERS.

is Satellite Music Network, Dallas, which claims 800 affiliates. Both networks offer 24-hour programming daily, which could provide a station with all its programming needs. With this kind of arrangement a broadcaster needs nothing but a satellite dish and a sales staff. The station remains, but much of the operating costs disappear.

UNWIRED NETWORKS

The final reason for the growth of network radio is the emergence of unwired networks. Network radio has always been at a disadvantage because of the difficulty of dealing with the many stations and rate structures available in large markets. This system was discussed earlier in connection with unwired television networks.

SPOT RADIO

Spot Radio Advertising: A form of advertising in which an ad is placed with an individual station rather than through a network.

PRINCIPLE Spot advertising dominates radio scheduling.

In **spot radio advertising** an advertiser places an advertisement with an individual station rather than through a network. Although networks provide prerecorded national advertisements, they also allow local affiliates open time to sell spot advertisements. Table 11.4 lists the leading spot radio advertisers. Spot radio advertising represents nearly 80 percent of all radio advertising. Its popularity is a result of the flexibility it offers the advertiser. With over 8,000 stations available, messages can be tailored for particular audiences. In large cities such as New York, Chicago, or Los Angeles, 40 or more radio stations are available. Local stations also offer flexibility through their willingness to run unusual ads, allow last-minute changes, and negotiate rates. Buying spot radio and coping with its non-standardized rate structures can be very cumbersome, however.

TABLE 11.4	TOP 25 NATIONAL SPOT RADIO ADVERTISERS			
RANK 1995	ADVERTISER	NATIONAL SPOT RADIO ADVERTISING		
		1995	1994	% CHG
1	News Corp.	$30.8	$23.5	31.1
2	AT&T Corp.	25.3	18.5	36.9
3	Montgomery Ward & Co.	21.3	16.2	31.6
4	General Motors Corp.	20.9	1.7	NA
5	Walt Disney Co.	20.3	15.2	33.4
6	MCI Communications Corp.	18.8	14.5	29.7
7	US West	18.5	14.3	29.0
8	CompUSA	18.0	12.2	47.5
9	Ito-Yokado Co. (7-Eleven)	16.9	22.7	−25.7
10	Tandy Corp.	16.4	13.5	21.8
11	Time Warner	15.7	11.7	34.3
12	Philip Morris Cos.	15.0	8.6	74.8
13	American Stores Co.	14.6	13.6	7.6
14	Grand Metropolitan	12.6	13.9	−9.4
15	Bell Atlantic Corp.	12.0	9.3	29.5
16	Viacom	11.4	6.1	88.3
17	U.S. Government	11.1	5.7	93.8
18	Kmart Corp.	10.8	11.4	−5.5
19	Allstate Insurance Group	10.8	8.0	34.9
20	PepsiCo	10.0	13.3	−24.6
21	TJX Cos.	8.9	10.4	−14.7
22	GTE Corp.	8.9	6.4	38.9
23	Amoco Corp.	8.7	7.3	18.8
24	Levitz Furniture Corp.	8.4	1.2	575.2
25	Charming Shoppes	8.3	1.8	359.1

Notes: Dollars are in millions.

Source: Competitive Media Reporting. *Advertising Age* (September 30, 1996):S47. Reprinted with permission from *Advertising Age.* Copyright Crain Communications Inc.

Radio advertising revenue is divided into three categories: network, spot, and local. Network revenues are by far the smallest category, accounting for approximately 5 percent of total radio revenues. National spot advertising makes up the remaining 5 percent.

The Radio Audience

PRINCIPLE Radio is a highly segmented medium.

Radio is a highly segmented medium. Program formats offered in a typical market include hard rock, gospel, country and western, "Top 40" hits, and sex advice. Virtually every household in the United States (99 percent) has a radio set (527 million radios in total, with an average 5.6 sets per household), and most of these sets are tuned in to a vast array of programs.[20]

Market researcher Michael Hedges separates radio listeners into four segments: station fans, radio fans, music fans, and news fans. Station fans make up the largest segment of radio listeners, at 46 percent. They have a clear preference for one or two stations and spend up to 8 hours or more each day listening to their favorite. Most station fans are women between the ages of 25 and 44. Radio fans represent 34 percent of the population. They may listen to four to five different stations per week, and they show no preference for one particular station. Most are under 35 years of age, though many women aged 55 and older are radio fans. Only 11 percent of the population are music fans—people who listen exclusively for the music being played. Men between the ages of 25 and 45 are most likely to be music fans, although many elderly adults also fit the profile. Finally, a percentage of radio listeners choose their station based on a need for news and information. They have one or two favorite stations, listen in short segments, and are almost exclusively aged 35 or older.[21]

Country music is the most prevalent format on the radio, but "talk" has the momentum. A survey by the Center for Radio Information showed that 73 stations became chatterboxes in 1995, and more than 12 percent of all stations are now in that genre. The number of news/talk outlets has tripled, from 400 to 1,200, since 1990, and the format has breathed new life into the AM band. This format may even be universal. A radio program produced by psychiatric patients recently won a prize at Argentina's top broadcasting awards ceremony.[22]

A traditional radio audience that seems to have gone through quite a transition lately is the teen audience. In the case of network radio, for example, audience levels for young adults aged 12 to 34 were down approximately 5.6 percent, or 400,000 listeners, according to RADAR data on page 352. Part of this decline is due to the fact that several network systems have abandoned the youngest segment of this market in favor of the 25- to 54-year-old format and the Oldies format.[23] Like many other markets, radio has followed the baby boomers. Portable tape and CD players with headsets have also played a part.

MEASURING THE RADIO AUDIENCE

Advertisers considering radio are most concerned with the number of people listening to a particular station at a given time. The radio industry and independent research firms provide several measures considered useful to the advertiser.

---

[20]Thomas Russell and Ronald Lane, *Kleppner's Advertising Procedure*, 11th ed. (Upper Saddle River, NJ: Prentice Hall, 1990):208.

[21]"Radio Days," *American Demographics* (November 1988):18.

[22]Allan Gottesman, "Lots to Talk About," *Adweek* (May 13, 1996):24.

[23]Stephen Battaglio, "Where Have All the Young Radio Listeners Gone?" *Adweek* (February 25, 1991):26.

The most basic measure is the station's *coverage*. This is simply the geographical area (which includes a given number of homes) that can pick up the station clearly, whether or not they are actually tuned in. A better measure is *circulation*, which measures the number of homes that are actually tuned in to the particular station. This figure is influenced by such factors as the competing programs, the type of program, and the time of day or night.

ARBITRON

Several major audience rating services operate in the advertising industry. One, the Arbitron Ratings Company, estimates the size of radio audiences for over 250 markets in the United States. The primary method used by Arbitron is a seven-day, self-administered diary that the person returns to Arbitron at the end of the week. Editors check that each diary has entries for every day and that the postmark shows the diary wasn't mailed before the week was over.

RADAR

A second radio rating service is Radio's All-Dimension Audience Research (RADAR). This service deals with local and network radio. For RADAR, Statistical Research calls 12,000 respondents for seven consecutive days and asks about network radio listening done the day before. The company contacts respondents before beginning data collection, so they can pay better attention to their listening habits. Final reports are based on data collected over 48 weeks.

BIRCH/SCARBOROUGH-VNU

Birch conducts 100,000 random phone interviews a month for its 273 markets, asking listeners aged 12 and older what they listened to yesterday and the day before yesterday. It also collects extensive demographic and product usage information for the Scarborough Report, an annual lifestyle report of the top 55 markets. The frequency of these reports varies according to the size of the market.

ADVANTAGES AND DISADVANTAGES OF RADIO

Radio is not for every advertiser, and it is important to understand the relative strengths and weaknesses of this medium.

ADVANTAGES

TARGET AUDIENCES

The most important advantage offered by radio is that it reaches specific types of audiences by offering specialized programming. In addition it can be adapted to different parts of the country and can reach people at different times of the day. Radio, for example, is the ideal means of reaching people driving to and from work. Known as *drive time*, these radio time slots provide the best audience for many advertisers.

SPEED AND FLEXIBILITY

The *speed and flexibility* of radio have been noted already. Of all the media, radio has the shortest *closing period*, in that copy can be submitted up to airtime. This flexibility allows advertisers to adjust to local market conditions, current news events, and even the weather. For example, a local hardware store can quickly implement a snow shovel promotion the morning after a snowstorm.

The flexibility of radio is also evident in its willingness to participate in promotional tie-ins. An example is the "Maalox Moments" that have successfully united a packaged-goods marketer, retailers, and radio stations ("Stuck in traffic?

The dog ate the notes you left out for the big presentation at 8:00 A.M.? Your kid did *what*, and you have to leave work early and see the principal?").[24]

COSTS

PRINCIPLE Radio offers high reach at low cost.

Radio may be the least expensive of all media. Because airtime costs are relatively low, extensive repetition is possible. In addition, the cost of producing a radio commercial can be low, particularly if the message is read by a local station announcer. Radio's low cost and high reach of selected target groups make it an excellent supporting medium. In fact, the most appropriate role for most radio advertising is a supportive one.

MENTAL IMAGERY

An important advantage of radio is the scope it allows for the listener's imagination. Radio uses words, sound effects, music, and tonality to enable listeners to create their own picture of what is happening. For this reason radio is sometimes referred to as the "theater of the mind." The script for John Moore Plumbing (Figure 11.3) demonstrates how radio effectively creates mental pictures.

HIGH LEVELS OF ACCEPTANCE

The final advantage of radio is its high acceptance at the local level. Partly because of its passive nature, radio normally is not perceived as an irritant. People have their favorite radio stations and radio personalities, which they listen to regularly.

---

[24]Howard Schlossberg, "Local Radio Tie-Ins Break Through Promotional Clutter," *Marketing News* (May 11, 1992).

FIGURE 11.3

THIS RADIO SCRIPT ILLUS-
TRATES THE USE OF HUMOR IN
CREATING A MEMORABLE SCENE
WITHOUT THE USE OF VISUALS.
From *Nielsen Newscast No. 4* (1985):6.
Copyright 1997 Nielsen Media
Research. Reprinted by permission.

John Moore Plumbing

    (*A telephone rings twice. A man groggily answers:*)

He: John Moore Plumbing.

She: It's 2 A.M. and I'm not asleep...

He: I'm not either.

She: Are you having insomnia too?

He: No, I'm having a phone conversation.

She: When I can't sleep I read the Yellow Pages. Do you ever do that?

He: No.

She: Anyway, I saw that John Moore Plumbing is open 24 hours a day. So I thought I'd call...

He: Well, John Moore Plumbing has a 24-hour emergency service. Do you have an emergency?

She: Well, I'm desperate. Does desperate count?

He: Are you desperate about plumbing?

She: Sometimes.

He: How 'bout tonight?

She: Sorry, I have plans for tonight.

He: No, no. I mean do you have leaking pipes or a backed-up toilet or something?

She: Hold on a second, I'll check.

Announcer: When you have a plumbing emergency in the middle of the night or middle of the day, call John Moore. Call 590-5555. 24 hours a day. And you'll always get prompt service when you call John Moore Plumbing. Even at 2 A.M.

She: Toilets are fine. I can't see the pipes.

He: Why not?

She: They're underwater.

He: I'll be right over.

She: I'll set a place for you...

Announcer: John Moore Plumbing. 590-5555. Call John. And get more.

RADIO WON'T RELENT

In the mid-1960s, Stan Freberg created a radio campaign for the National Association of Broadcasters that touted the power of radio versus that of television. In the spots, Freberg made a herd of elephants run through the studio, dodged an oncoming train, and built a huge ice-cream sundae in Lake Michigan, complete with a 10-ton maraschino cherry. The point: Radio stretches the imagination beyond the limits of the television screen. While television commercials' screen averages 19 inches, radio's screen is a person's entire mind.

Why then is radio so vastly underused as an advertising medium? If an advertiser can hire the USC marching band for a radio spot at a cost of $10,000, why would it pay between $200,000 and $250,000 for a television spot with actors in band uniforms? And the significantly lower production cost of a radio spot does not compromise the effectiveness of the message. In fact, it has been shown that message recall is no different between a television and radio commercial.

In 1995, radio advertising spending was $2.1 billion, compared to $27.7 billion on television. Radio's limited use can be attributed only to media buyers' and planners' lack of understanding of its impact in a campaign. Radio has been an integral part of many successful marketing efforts by such companies as Molson beer, Dial-A-Mattress, Snapper, and NutriSystems Weight Loss Centers. Television (excluding cable) is not as demographically selective or cost-efficient as radio is in reaching defined segments of the population. Radio can be aimed at different segments based on age, sex, residence, interests, and hobbies, as well as psychological traits.

Radio also offers the greatest value in terms of price and efficiency. In the last decade, radio has experienced minimal price increases while other media have witnessed very dramatic ones. For example, where the CPM for newspapers has risen consistently and is now about $20, radio's CPM has been steady at about $3.

Though reaching as many people as possible is the main goal of most campaigns, the message needs to be reinforced again and again before the average person responds. By using radio, an advertiser can achieve very high frequency in a short time without spending a small fortune. A consumer will be exposed to a radio message 25 times more than a television commercial produced for the same price. Frequency also contributes to brand building.

It has been proven that consumers easily can picture the visual aspects of a television commercial when exposed to a radio spot with similar audio track. This allows an advertiser's dollars to go twice as far as they would if newspaper or outdoor advertising were used.

For one reason or another, radio is considered a second-tier medium by both advertisers and their agencies. Concepts for radio spots don't seem to generate the same excitement as do concepts for television. However, radio's ability to deliver an advertising message to consumers is just as great, if not greater, than that of other media. The advertising world needs to realize that, though every campaign does not need radio, radio at least needs to be considered.

Source: Gerry McGoldrick, "Marketers Ignore Radio, But It's a Better Ad Buy," *Marketing News* (October 7, 1996):4. Reprinted by permission of American Marketing Association.

Messages delivered by these are more likely to be accepted and retained. More is said about the power of radio in the Issues and Controversies box.

DISADVANTAGES

INATTENTIVENESS

Radio is not without its drawbacks. Because radio is strictly a listening medium, radio messages are fleeting and commercials may be missed or forgotten. Many listeners perceive radio as pleasant background and do not listen to it carefully.

LACK OF VISUALS

The restrictions of sound may also hamper the creative process. Clearly, products that must be demonstrated or seen to be appreciated are inappropriate for radio advertising. Creating radio ads that encourage the listener to see the product is a difficult challenge. Experts believe that the use of humor, music, and sound effects may be the most effective way to do this.

PRINCIPLE Radio should be used as a support medium when the target audience is clearly defined and visualization of the product is not critical.

CLUTTER

The proliferation of competing radio stations, combined with the opportunity to engage in heavy repetition, has created a tremendous amount of clutter in radio advertising. Coupled with the fact that radio listeners tend to divide their attention among various activities, this clutter greatly reduces the likelihood that a message will be heard or understood.

SCHEDULING AND BUYING DIFFICULTIES

The final disadvantage of radio is the complexity of scheduling and buying radio time. The need to buy time on several stations makes scheduling and following up on ads very complicated. The bookkeeping involved in checking nonstandardized rates, approving bills for payment, and billing clients can be a staggering task. Fortunately, computers and large-station representatives have helped alleviate much of this chaos.

SUMMARY

- Broadcast media include both radio and television. Whereas print media are bound by space, broadcast media convey transient messages and are bound by time.

- Among the different television systems that an advertiser can use are network, cable, subscription, local, specialty, and public television. Network television is still the dominant form.

- The size of the television audience is measured in a number of ways, including the use of diaries and people meters.

- Television offers advertisers cost efficiency, impact, and influence.

- Advertisers have a choice of scheduling their commercials on a network, local, or cable scheduling basis.

- Television commercials can take the form of sponsorships, participations, or spot announcements.

- Radio is classified as either AM or FM according to transmission and power.

- The audience for radio can be measured in terms of a station's coverage or its circulation.

- The advantages of radio include specialized programming, speed and flexibility, low cost, the use of mental imagery, and high levels of acceptance. Its disadvantages include inattentiveness, lack of visuals, clutter, and scheduling and buying difficulties.

QUESTIONS

1. What are the major differences between broadcast and print media? How are the two media similar?

2. Describe television syndication. Contrast off-network syndication with first-run syndication. What is barter syndication? How does syndication affect the advertiser?

3. What are the primary advantages and disadvantages offered to advertisers by cable television? How do interconnects affect the decision to advertise on cable?

4. You are a major agency media director who has just finished a presentation to a prospective client in convenience food marketing. During the Q and A period a client representative asks you this question, "We know that television's viewer loyalty is nothing like it was ten or even five years ago with cable and VCRs. There are smaller audiences per program each year, yet television time-costs continue to rise. Do you still believe we should consider commercial television as a primary medium for our company's advertising?" How would you answer?

5. Local market radio audiences are primarily measured by the diary (Arbitron) and the telephone inter-

view (BIRCH). If you, as a media sales director for a radio station, had to choose one service to measure station popularity, which one would you subscribe to? Assume that the cost of each service is roughly the same.

6. Message clutter affects both radio and television advertising. Advertisers fear audiences react to long commercial pods by using the remote control for the television set or the push button on the radio. Some have proposed that advertisers should absorb higher time costs to reduce the frequency and length of commercial interruptions. Others argue that broadcasting should reduce the number of commercials sold and also reduce program advertising even if it means less profit for broadcasters. Which of these remedies would be the best to take in the 1990s?

7. One of the interesting ways to combine the assets of radio and television is to use the sound track of television commercials for the radio creative. Why would an advertiser consider this media/creative strategy? What limitations would you mention?

Suggested Class Project

As a group, make a chart for five radio stations, of the type of station (easy listening, top 40, classical, and so on), the products commonly advertised, and the probable target markets for these products. Note the time of the day these products are advertised. Try to get three or four times as many products as there are people in your group. Now put all of the products in a hat and have everyone draw one. Each student now is responsible for advertising his or her product. He or she needs to allocate a budget of $2,500 among the five stations for a week's worth of programming. It costs $250 for 30 seconds of air time.

Further Readings

Broadcasting/Cable Yearbook 1992 (Washington, DC: Broadcast Publications, Inc.)

Kalish, David, "Bad Reception," *Marketing & Media Decisions*, August 1988, pp. 63–65.

Television: The Critical View, 4th ed. (New York: Oxford University Press, 1987).

Whetmore, Edward J. *Mediamerica*, 4th ed. (Belmont, CA: Wadsworth Publishing Co., 1989).

William, Martin, *TV: The Casual Art* (New York: Oxford University Press, 1982).

INFOMERCIALS IN THE 1990S: MORE SLICING AND DICING

Thomas Burke, president of Saatchi & Saatchi's infomercial division, calls infomercials "the most powerful form of advertising ever created." Infomercials are a form of paid television programming in which a particular product is demonstrated, explained, and offered for sale. Advertisers produce the infomercials and pay cable and satellite systems and local television channels to air them. According to estimates compiled by the National Infomercial Marketing Association (NIMA), 1995 worldwide sales revenues from infomercials and home shopping totaled $8.2 billion. More than one third of that amount—$3.1 billion—was generated outside the United States. In the United States alone, some 500 infomercials were produced in 1995 at a cost of up to $3 million for a single program.

As these figures suggest, the infomercial industry has grown tremendously in recent years. Although originally associated with household products such as those from legendary direct-response pitchman Ron Popeil, infomercials have been embraced by well-known multinational corporations. Philips Electronics was in the name-brand vanguard with a groundbreaking infomercial to help launch its $700 CD-i multimedia player in the United States. Other companies that have gotten on the infomercial bandwagon are Microsoft, Lexus, Sears, AT&T, and Apple Computer. Infomercials are also a viable advertising format outside of the United States. They are growing in popularity in Japan, Singapore, China, Indonesia, and other Asian countries.

Why are advertisers attracted to infomercials? Unlike regular commercials that are sandwiched between programming, viewers consciously choose to watch infomercials. The demographic profile of the typical infomercial customer is also quite attractive. According to a recent survey conducted by *TV Guide*, 72 percent of television viewers have watched at least one infomercial, and 29 percent of those have purchased a product featured in an infomercial. Another poll suggested that the average infomercial customer was a married homeowner between the ages of 36 and 45 with a college education and a household income of $26,000 to $35,000. Advertisers also like the fact that the response to a particular

infomercial can be measured quite accurately. For example, Lexus generated more than 40,000 telephone inquiries after launching its used-car program with an infomercial; 2 percent of those who called ultimately bought a Lexus automobile.

Since infomercials are typically 30 minutes in length and often feature studio audiences and celebrity announcers, many viewers believe they are watching regular talk-show-type programming. (In fact, infomercials are sometimes referred to as *program-length commercials*, or PLCs). It is precisely this blurring between commercial and regular programming that concerns some industry observers. Despite the potential for abuse, the Federal Communications Commission only requires that television stations airing infomercials clearly identify the programs as advertisements. A spokesperson for the FCC's mass media bureau recently explained why the commission is reluctant to impose standards or controls on infomercials. "The commission believed guidelines could stifle broadcasters in their presentation of programs desired by their audiences," he said.

Critics of infomercials also point out the format's potential to deceive consumers when advertisers make false or misleading product claims. Such criticism is often directed at traditional infomercial fare such as money-making schemes and baldness treatments. Currently, the industry relies on self-regulation to address such concerns. NIMA has 350 members in the United States and Europe who agree to adhere to voluntary standards for infomercial content. As Jack Schember, editor of *Response TV*, noted, "[Advertisers] realize that, in order to attract the audience and grow in the industry, they can't mislead people."

Video Source: "Infomercials Go Mainstream," *The Wall Street Journal Report* (April 1, 1995), #653. *Additional Sources:* Kevin Whitelaw, "Not Just Slicing and Dicing," *U.S. News and World Report* (September 9, 1996):43–44; Darren McDermott, "All-American Infomercials Sizzle in Asia," *The Wall Street Journal* (June 25, 1996):B6; Andrew Miller and Michael Zapolin, "Does Your Product Have Infomercial Potential?" *Boston Business Journal* (June 14, 1996):15; and Tim Triplett, "Big Names Crowd the Commercial Airwaves," *Marketing News* (March 28, 1994):1.

$\mathcal{Q}$UESTIONS

1. Have you ever watched an infomercial? Have you ordered a product featured on an infomercial? What affected your decision to buy or not to buy?

2. Do you believe the FCC should step up its efforts to regulate the infomercial industry?

3. Do you think self-regulation is sufficient to prevent serious abuses by infomercial advertisers?

CHAPTER

Media Buying

CHAPTER OUTLINE

- Ads May Show Up Anywhere
- Media-Buying Functions
- Special Skills: Expert Knowledge of Media Opportunities
- Special Skills: Knowledge of Media Pricing
- Special Skills: Media Vehicle Selection and Negotiation
- Special Skills: Maintaining Plan Performance

CHAPTER OBJECTIVES

When you have completed this chapter, you should be able to:

- Explain how media buying is different from media planning and how it complements media planning
- Understand the major duties of media buyer: research analyst, expert evaluator, negotiator, and troubleshooter
- Explain how buyers translate media plan objectives into target-directed advertising schedules
- Understand why negotiation skills are more important today to advertising strategies than ever before

Ads May Show Up Anywhere

As drivers on Atlanta's busy downtown freeway approached the Olympic Village during the summer of 1996, they had the option of following an interstate exit sign onto Red Brick Ale Boulevard. That street name may sound quaint, but it isn't a link to Atlanta's past. It's the name of the best-selling product of Atlanta Brewing Co., a local microbrewer. It's also an example of a fast-growing phenomenon: the packaging and selling of Hometown, USA.

Across the country, cash-strapped cities, counties, school boards, and other institutions are offering companies the opportunity to plaster the public domain with corporate messages. In the past year, local governments in California, Illinois, and Indiana have authorized plans to display advertising on police cruisers. A dozen or more public school systems from Big Harbor, Washington, to New York City are pursuing plans to sell advertising space on the sides of yellow school buses, in the corridors of school buildings, or on the jerseys of school athletic teams.

Buffalo, New York, has agreed to endorse paint manufacturer Pratt & Lambert United Inc. as the city's "official corporate partner" in return for an annual supply of latex and oils. City officials are trying to sell advertising on parking meters, garbage trucks, and other vehicles.

In the case of Red Brick Ale Boulevard, Atlanta Brewing Co. is offering to buy, for $50,000, the right to rename a section of Williams Street, which was named in 1846 to honor a pioneer real estate developer. The deal would give Red Brick Ale a highly identifiable location, free publicity, and, the company hopes, billing on an interstate exit sign. The $50,000 would be earmarked for city antidrunk-driving efforts.

Proponents of so-called municipal marketing say advertising on public spaces is inevitable—and harmless—in an era of shrinking support among taxpayers. "You've got to look for ways to raise money," agrees Sheriff Mearl J. Justus, whose squad cars in St. Clair County, Illinois, carry the name, phone number, and logo of a local security-alarm company on their fenders. The price is $6,500 per vehicle for three years. "It's tasteful, it's simple, and we're at the present time talking to some other companies," he says. "I think you're going to see more and more of it."

But critics say the trend blurs the line between crediting civic contributions and crassly commercializing public property and the public trust. "A government allowing advertising on public property sort of implies that a government can be bought," says Susan Monaco, research director at the center for the Study of Commercialism in Washington. "If you don't draw [the line] here, we're going to encourage a society where advertisements and advertising are everywhere, and there's no place where one could go to escape."

Martha Anderson, a member of the Osceola County, Florida, school board, voted against a proposal to sell advertising in school hallways. To explain her decision, she points to all the peer pressure children face because of television commercials. If the schools allow ads, she says, children "have not only the pressure of the TV telling them they're going to be cool if they wear 'Nikes'; they're going to have the schools telling them, too."[1]

The growth of municipal advertising media suggests that the task of media buying is going to become more complicated. Grocery store carts, painted city buses, interactive mall kiosks, e-mail, restroom stalls, and baseball caps all represent the *splintering* of media. Media buyers are supposed to be the guides who skillfully traverse in and around all the media choices and combine the most efficient mix to reach advertising goals.

---

[1]Douglas A. Blackman, "New Ad Vehicles: Police Car, School Bus, Garbage Truck," *The Wall Street Journal* (February 20, 1996):B1, B6. Reprinted by permission of *Wall Street Journal*. Copyright © 1996 Dow Jones & Company, Inc. All rights reserved worldwide.

In addition to media knowledge, media buyers need to be involved as early as possible in the marketing plan. This is the time to explain to the advertisers who have their hearts set on a certain medium that it isn't feasible within their budget or in their marketing area. This is also the time to plan for promotional involvement and merchandising. An experienced media buyer knows what it takes to make an impact and the equation involves more than a certain number of gross rating points; how they're placed and where they're placed are just as critical as the overall media mix.

MEDIA-BUYING FUNCTIONS

A media buyer has a number of distinct responsibilities and duties, which we will describe here in an operational sequence. We will discuss some of the most important buyer functions in more detail later in the chapter.

PROVIDING INSIDE INFORMATION TO THE MEDIA PLANNER

Media buyers are close enough to day-to-day changes in media popularity and pricing to be a constant source of inside information to media planners. For example, a newspaper buyer discovers that a key newspaper's delivery staff is going on strike, a radio-time buyer learns a top disk jockey is leaving a radio station, or a magazine buyer's source reveals that the new editor of a publication is going to seriously change the editorial focus. All of these things can influence the strategy and tactics of current and future advertising plans. (See Ad 12.1.)

MEDIA VEHICLE SELECTION

One essential part of buying is choosing the best media vehicles to fit the target audience's aperture. The media planner lays out the direction, but the buyer is

AD 12.1

THIS *ROLLING STONE* AD EMPHASIZES A WIDE AUDIENCE APPEAL.

PRINCIPLE Media buyers must know everything there is to know about media vehicles and their performance.

responsible for choosing the specific vehicles. Armed with the media plan directives, the buyer seeks answers to a number of difficult questions. Does the vehicle have the right audience profile? Will the program's current popularity increase, stabilize, or decline? How well does the magazine's editorial format fit the brand? Does the radio station's choice of music offer the correct atmosphere for the creative theme? How well does the newspaper's circulation pattern fit the advertiser's distribution? The answers to those questions bear directly on the campaign's success. *Alternative Press* (Ad 12.2) clearly matches Generation X.

As we move closer to global advertising, the possibility of making a global media buy becomes a more important issue. The Concepts and Applications box discusses the likelihood that this will happen.

NEGOTIATING MEDIA PRICES

Aside from finding aperture-related target audiences, nothing is considered more crucial in media buying than securing the lowest possible price for placements. Time and space charges make up the largest portion of the advertising budget so there is continuing pressure to keep costs as low as possible. To accomplish this, buyers operate in a world of transaction or negotiation. In the case of the municipal media, both parties must jointly determine the value of school bus media.

AD 12.2

ALTERNATIVE PRESS DEDICATES ITSELF TO THE LIFESTYLE OF THE TWENTYSOMETHINGS.

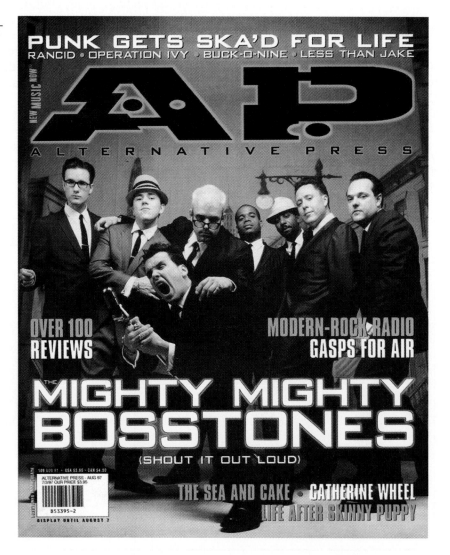

*C*ONCEPTS AND *A*PPLICATIONS

GLOBAL MEDIA BUYING

If there's one phrase that seems to sum up the state of the global media buy, it is "When, if ever, will global media buys be possible?" Once heralded as the wave of the future, global media buying has suffered serious setbacks. The lingering worldwide recession hasn't helped, but the biggest problem seems to be clients' reluctance to shift from the proven strategy of tailoring buys to individual markets despite growth of cross-border marketing.

Still, major global media buyers and publishers say they have not given up. *Advertising Age International* asked several dozen ad agency media directors, newspaper and magazine publishers, television network sales executives, and other experts, "Is the idea of a global media buy dying?" The following comments represent a sample of responses.

John Perriss, chairman, Zenith Media Worldwide, London: Global media buying is waiting for some encouragement from media owners . . . Until more media make interesting buys, available clients will not alter their own structures to exploit the opportunities.

Ron de Pear, executive media director, J. Walter Thompson Europe, London: It's not a matter of global media buys dying or not—it's a matter of whether they have relevance to the total communications needs of clients . . . Very few genuine global deals exist, the reason being that very few media owners, agencies and clients are structured in a way that, once agreed, allows it to happen.

Mike Drexler, president, BJK&E Media Group, New York: Global media per se is not a reality. Regional buys are being made on a multinational basis—many also involve more than one continent. Pan-regional buys are also being combined on a so-called global basis.

Michael D. Moore, executive VP-worldwide media director, D'Arcy Masters Benton & Bowles, New York: No, it is not dying. The concept has simply felt the effects of a dose of reality which as usual follows hype. The facts are that there are relatively few media companies that can supply a truly global buy and relatively few companies that can effectively make use of such opportunities.

James McLeod, advertising director, International Herald Tribune, Paris: The concept of media buy is alive and well. Consider the plethora of print and broadcast media which have entered this arena over the last few years. Clearly, this would not be happening unless there was a demand.

Harvey Ganot, executive VP-advertising and promotion sales, MTV Networks, New York: To make it effective you need to take the idea of the global network to the next level: It must be delivered through a brand that is recognized and accepted as part of the culture in diverse parts of the world. When you combine a trademark like MTV with a world-renowned product in an electrifying way, it can galvanize consumers like no other medium.

Source: Todd Pruzan, "Global Media Buying and Planning," *Advertising Age International* (July 18, 1994):I-11, I-14. Reprinted with permission from *Advertising Age.* Copyright Crain Communications Inc.

MONITORING VEHICLE PERFORMANCE

In an ideal world every vehicle on the campaign schedule would perform at or above expectations. Likewise, every advertisement, commercial, and posting would run exactly as planned. In reality, underperformance and schedule problems are facts of life. The buyer's response to these problems must be swift and decisive. Poorly performing vehicles must be replaced or costs must be modified. Production and schedule difficulties must be rectified. Delayed response could hurt the brand's sales.

POSTCAMPAIGN ANALYSIS

Once a campaign is completed, the buyer's duty is to review the plan's expectations and forecasts against what actually happened. Did the plan actually achieve GRP, reach, frequency, and CPM objectives? Did the newspaper and magazine placements run in the positions expected? Such analysis is instrumental in providing the guidance for future media plans. For a full discussion of postcampaign research see Chapter 21.

These five tasks provide highlights of media buying. For a better understanding of buying operations, however, we need to look at some of these duties in closer detail.

SPECIAL SKILLS: EXPERT KNOWLEDGE OF MEDIA OPPORTUNITIES

If you were to ask media buyers what they need to know in order to do their jobs, they would probably say "Everything I can." Buying media has a great many dimensions. Network and local television stations are constantly changing and rearranging programs. Radio stations alter their music formats. Media audiences change their habits. Media prices are fluid and increase or decrease at different times.

Knowledge means keeping up with changes. Media buyers need experience to anticipate how changes will affect the advertiser's plans. Many media buyers concentrate on a single medium. For example, television buyers do nothing but buy television time. Whereas media planners work with a broad range of opportunities, media buyers develop narrow but deep expertise in one medium.

MEDIA CONTENT

As we emphasized in Chapter 9, media placement strategy is more than a popularity contest of choosing the media vehicles with the largest target audience. Often the buyer must also judge the message environment. Does it have the right mood or style for the advertiser's message? Is the media vehicle overcrowded with other ads or commercials? Is it careful in its production of messages? The answers to these questions cannot be found in reader surveys or broadcast ratings. Buyers monitor sample copies of publications, listen to off-the-air tapes, and study analyses of media content.

AUDIENCE HABITS

People's media preferences are neither stable nor consistent. Audiences are fickle about how they spend their leisure time. Their interests change with the seasons. They grow tired of one entertainment mode and shift to another. Buyers cannot afford to wait until the shift is obvious; they must sense it coming and select accordingly. Fresh and interested media options provide the best opportunities for aperture. Buyers who can judge where media audiences are headed will be waiting. In Ad 12.3 *Good Housekeeping* is stressing reader loyalty and trust. What products would particularly value this?

RESEARCH EVALUATION

Besides their constant exposure to standard audience research (such as Arbitron and SMRB), media buyers are inundated with research and special analyses by media salespeople. This information may be special interpretations of standard research, or it may be a special research study ordered by the station or publication. Because such research is less than objective, buyers must carefully judge it. Did it follow sound statistical guidelines? Was the sample size adequate? Buyers are responsible for deciding if sales-presented research is valuable to the client.

SPECIAL SKILLS: KNOWLEDGE OF MEDIA PRICING

Marketers bear many costs in the advertising campaign. They pay for the talent that develops the message, the production to create the message, and the media costs to place the message before the target audience. With few exceptions, media costs are the largest area of advertising investment.

AD 12.3

IN THIS AD *GOOD HOUSEKEEP-
ING* STRESSES THE VALUE OF
BELIEVABILITY IN ADVERTISING.

SHE THINKS YOU'RE LYING.

This is about truth in advertising.
Over 60% of the people think there isn't any.* That's an all-time low for advertising credibility.

And the hard truth is—if they don't believe your ad, they may not buy your brand. In a recent Roper study, 76% of women agree that in the '90s, women aren't going to put up with claims about products which the

manufacturer can't prove.
That's why it is time for marketers to take another long, hard look at the power of the Good Housekeeping Seal.

For 83 years, the Seal has meant that Good Housekeeping will refund or replace products advertised in its pages if they prove defective.** No other magazine can make that claim.

Fully 62% of all women, and 72%

of Good Housekeeping readers have positive things to say about the Seal. They say the Seal gives them greater confidence in the products that they buy.

In the New Traditionalist '90s, shoppers are seeking honest value above all else. So make sure that your brand has earned the Good Housekeeping Seal.

It's your brand's best offense in a skeptical world.

AMERICA BELIEVES IN GOOD HOUSEKEEPING

MEDIA COST RESPONSIBILITIES

Media buyers should be experts in all aspects of media pricing, not only in price negotiations but also for gathering historical price experience.

The buyer's cost training begins with an understanding that the advertiser and the media are adversaries. Marketers want the lowest possible price, and the media try to charge as much as they can. As the marketer's representatives, the buyers are expected to use all skills and leverage to secure the lowest prices. They must not, however sacrifice target audience profiles or reach objectives. The price paid must be balanced against the size and quality of the audience delivered.

Media buyers must develop skills in three costs areas: charting media cost trends, learning to use media rate cards, and balancing audience to price (CPM). The following discussion describes each of these areas in more detail.

AVERAGE COST TRENDS

The prices paid for advertising in the recent past are carefully monitored. These are called **cost trends.** Cost changes can be compiled in a number of ways includ-

Cost Trends: A history of changes in the average unit (per message) prices for each medium that is used in cost forecasting.

FIGURE 12.1

MAGAZINE RATE CARD

(FREQUENCY DISCOUNT)

BLACK/WHITE RATES					4-COLOR RATES				
	1 ti	3 ti	6 ti	12 ti		1 ti	3 ti	6 ti	12 ti
1 Page	21,000	20,400	19,175	18,025	1 Page	32,000	31,050	30,120	28,915
1/2 Page	13,000	12,610	12,230	11,850	1/2 Page	19,200	18,625	18,060	17,340
1/4 Page	7,800	7,600	7,400	7,180	1/4 Page	11,500	11,270	11,045	10,715
Spread	43,000	40,850	38,810	37,250	Spread	67,000	64,320	61,100	58,660

ing: national averages for each medium, for particular media vehicles (i.e., sports events), and for individual markets.

MEDIA PRICE FORMATS (RATE CARDS)

Each media company has its own way of charging for its advertising positions. Some, such as national cable and network television, prefer not to use set pricing at all. They allow complete negotiation with each advertiser to determine the price. (Open pricing will be discussed in more detail later in the chapter.) Others present price schedules through a published format called a *rate card*, which includes the price for each message unit (size or length), the types of incentive discounts available, and scheduling and production requirements.

Although rate cards follow general formats, there is no standard for prices or discounts. Each rate card is unique. The variety of rate cards and formats may seem overwhelming to beginners. Through steady experience, however, the buyer learns to master each approach. To give you some idea of how the rate cards are organized, here are two illustrations—one for magazines and one for television.

CONSUMER MAGAZINES

Figure 12.1 illustrates a common style of rate card that offers discounts based upon the number of insertions used within the contract year. The more insertions (an ad in an issue) used per publication the lower the cost for each insertion. To illustrate, the excerpt in Figure 12.1 shows a one-time "4-Color" cost for a page advertisement as $32,000. If the marketer was to contract for 12 one-page units, the individual price for each one would drop to $28,915 (a 10 percent discount).

Advertisers can receive these discounts in advance (before they run the full schedule) or as a lump sum at the end of the schedule contract (a *rebate*). If discounts are taken in advance and the advertiser does *not* complete the schedule, the advertiser has to pay the difference between the discount taken and the discount earned (called a *short rate*).

LOCAL TELEVISION

Television station sales departments would have a very hard time trying to publish an individual price for each television program, or for spots between programs. Each program has a different size and type of audience, and each month there are program changes that affect popularity.

The stations' solution to this problem of finding a fair price for each position is illustrated in Figure 12.2. Notice that rates are defined for hours of the day (dayparts). Each day segment offers four different prices (F to P3). The F is the highest rate an advertiser can pay. It also means the position belongs to the advertiser as long as the advertiser wants it. The P rate means it is *preemptible*, meaning

FIGURE 12.2

LOCAL TELEVISION RATE CARD

DAYPART	F	P1	P2	P3
Day 6 AM–3 PM	65	60	55	40
Evening 5–8 PM ...	110	100	90	75
News	230	220	200	185
Prime 8–11 PM	250	200	170	145
Late Evening	85	70	60	45

MEDIA BUYERS DON'T LOSE TOUCH

Two new computer systems could bring spot television sales into the electronic future from their paper wasteland. These systems won't replace the process of negotiating or planning ad-time sales, but they should help stations reduce paperwork errors and receivables, and better handle last-minute sales. "We hope to achieve a basically paperless communications process between the station and the agency," says Ray Heacox, director of sales at KNBC-TV, Los Angeles.

Technology advocates have wanted to lure television stations and their reps directly to ad agency media buyers for years. Though there have been technical obstacles in the past, there's also been institutional resistance to change.

Ad sellers don't want to lose face-to-face dialog with their customers. Reps fear being knocked out of the loop by a direct electronic line between stations and ad agencies. And all parties have resisted being forced to use a proprietary system designed by a potential competitor. Still, supporters say, the efficiencies of those systems are too grand to ignore.

According to a study by Group W, the television station group of Westinghouse Broadcasting Co., about 70 percent of the invoices that pass between the stations and the agency have some discrepancy in them. "This is annoying and time consuming," says David Graves, president of Ad Value Media Technologies, which markets its Ad Value Network system linking buyers and sellers. He estimates 40 percent of the revenue lost to errors could be eliminated by a third-party system that handles transaction tracking.

Mr. Graves says the system's major savings are in sales credits—the 1 percent to 3 percent of inventory a station can't bill because of an error or a dispute. In those situations, the station generally writes off the time. But with a computerized system, Mr. Graves claims, "You never run a spot you don't get paid for."

Using the system also speeds up the payment of receivables, which now averages more than 70 days. "In most industries, that would get your comptroller fired," says Mr. Graves, who claims Ad Value can bring stations a ten-day improvement in speed.

Despite having seen sales technology promises go unfulfilled, station sales managers are looking forward to incorporating these innovations into their sales procedures. "I think the need on the part of this business to automate is enough to make it happen," notes Ray Heacox. But some things must still be done the old-fashioned way, he says. "I'm a firm believer that the selling process will never fundamentally change," he notes. "It's two people talking about what the best deal for the customer and the station is. There's no reason to want to eliminate the rep. They still have efficiencies of supply and demand."

Sources: Jon Lafayette, "Escape from Waste," *Adweek* (June 13, 1994):S-26, S-29; and Joe Mandese, "Drowning Media Buyers Continue Their Pleas for Technological Help," *Adweek* (June 13, 1994):S-26, S-29.

movable. If another advertiser is willing to pay a higher rate for the advertiser's position, the station will take the position away from the company paying the lower price. The numbers P1–P3 refer to how much notice you have before preemption. The price selected by the buyer should reflect how needed that position is. The risk is clear; clients can save money by using lower rates but risk losing a valuable audience. Buyer experience pays off with these rates cards because they can balance the risk with the cost saving.

COST-PER-THOUSAND PATTERNS (CPM)

CPM Trends: Longitudinal (long-term) history of average cost-per-thousand tendencies of advertising media that is used to assist in forecasting future CPM levels.

Experienced buyers keep a careful record of the **CPM trends** for local media in each market. Changes in CPM trends may signal shifts in media popularity or shifts in advertising demand. This information prepares buyers beginning negotiation. It also helps media allocations market-to-market. As noted in the Issues and Controversies box, the task of simply making all the necessary media buys can be overwhelming.

SPECIAL SKILLS: MEDIA VEHICLE SELECTION AND NEGOTIATION

PRINCIPLE Negotiation involves getting the best schedule at the best price.

A buyer's knowledge and expert preparation are tested when he or she represents the client in the media marketplace. It is here that execution of the plan takes place. The key questions are: Can the desired vehicles be located, and can a satisfactory schedule be negotiated?

THE BOUNDARIES: WORKING WITHIN PLAN REQUIREMENTS

The boundaries of media negotiation are usually set by the advertising plan (Chapter 7). How many dollars are available? Who is the target audience? When does the advertising run? What atmosphere is desired? What is the duration of scheduling? Question after question must be answered to construct the advertiser's schedule. The following paragraphs detail some of the critical considerations.

DOLLAR ALLOCATIONS

Allocations: Division or proportions of advertising dollars among the various media.

The budget in an advertising campaign limits the dollars available to achieve plan objectives. **Allocations** include all the other money decisions concerning how to divide the budget. Allocations of dollars will determine how much money each medium will receive, how much will be spent per month or per week, how many dollars each geographic area will receive, and so on. Media buyers follow the allocation recommendations as closely as possible.

TARGET AUDIENCES

The media plan will try to give the buyer a clear profile, with media-sensitive characteristics, of the target prospect. Research services, such as Simmons, offer data on particular audience markets, such as the media preferences of children (see Ad 12.4). If multiple targets are specified by the plan, the plan should also specify a weight or priority for each characteristic.

Airline advertising offers a good illustration. Suppose an airline profiled a key prospect as an adult traveler, between 25 and 54 years old, with a sales/managerial occupation. This profile specifies two elements: age and occupation. But which dimension is more important?

Target audience research from the media plan will often reveal the *relative* importance of each profile characteristic. If the audience research for the airline indicated that although both the age and the occupation of prospects were important, occupation (professional or managerial) was twice as important as age, the buyer would assign these audience priorities as value weights. For each media vehicle evaluated, the portion of the media audience having the goal occupation

AD 12.4

CHARACTERISTICS OF TARGET AUDIENCES ARE USED TO DETERMINE WHICH VEHICLE IS MOST APPROPRIATE FOR ADVERTISING CERTAIN PRODUCTS OR SERVICES.

A New Simmons Release...

The Kids Study

The only comprehensive research survey of kids, ages 6-14.

Powerful Data

✔ Media habits: Newspapers, Sunday Comics, Magazines, Comic Books, Television, Cable TV and Radio
✔ Product usage, brand volume and purchase influence
✔ Household demographics of Baby Boomer parents as reported in the Simmons Study of Media and Markets

Simmons

For more information contact, Pamela Baxter: 212-916-8970

...Another Simmons Media & Marketing First!

Weighted Audience Values:
Numerical values assigned to different audience characteristics that help advertisers assign priorities when devising media plans.

would be doubled (X2), whereas the age segment would be used as it appears (X1). Once the **weighted audience values** are calculated, they would be added together to determine the highest audience score.

TIMING AND CONTINUITY

Many schedules must work within a tight time frame. Buyers are expected to follow any flight or pulse pattern required by the media plan (see Chapter 9). The buyer must adjust the number of message placements to reflect the desired campaign calendar. The greater the changes in intensity and in advertising periods, the more difficult the scheduling is for the buyer.

GROSS RATING POINT LEVELS

Many plans dictate weighting messages according to goals based on desired repetition (frequency) or exposure (reach). Often the rating point levels are used pri-

Inside Advertising

DANIEL J. CAHILL, MEDIA BUYER/PLANNER,
Wolf Blumberg Krody, Cincinnati

8:00–9:00 A.M.	Breakfast meeting with a sales representative from *Ladies' Home Journal.* The magazine has come to us with a proposal for White-Westinghouse. We take some time to go over our corporate discount and some merchandising opportunities. It's a great deal, but we can't commit until we square budgets with the client.
9:00–10:15 A.M.	My morning meeting has put me slightly behind. I need to finish a media plan for a campaign in Ashland, Kentucky for King's Daughters' Medical Center. The client has decided to extend their schedule until the end of the year, and I have to crunch numbers and prepare flowcharts for an 11:00 A.M. meeting. As I'm printing out a rough draft of the schedule, the account supervisor tells me the campaign has been put on hold.
10:15–11:45 A.M.	I need to check up on some work we've been coordinating with Kohler's distributors. I make follow up phone calls to the distributors to make sure they have all necessary materials for their upcoming promotions. The production manager and I find some problems with one of a distributor's materials, and we need to put a rush on the creative. I call to let the distributor know where we stand.
11:45 A.M.–12:30 P.M.	Luncheon at the Advertising Club of Cincinnati reviewing local television stations and their importance to the market. I run into some old friends from an agency where I used to work.
1:30–2:00 P.M.	Quick meeting with an account executive on the White-Westinghouse team to review changes for a trade plan proposal.
2:00–2:30 P.M.	Phone calls from media sales representatives have piled up and need to be returned. Many of the reps want to know the state of the plan for King's Daughters'. Also, there are some makegoods from the current flight. Others are interested in White-Westinghouse's plans for fourth quarter.
2:30–3:00 P.M.	We are working on a pro bono project for Juvenile Diabetes, and they need some suggestions for cheap, alternative media opportunities.
3:00–4:30 P.M.	The agency has a new business opportunity resulting from a pitch made earlier in the week. Management briefs me on goals, budgets, and so on and tells me they would like to see a media plan late tomorrow morning. I make phone calls and leave messages with reps so I can get the information I will need in the morning. I will be in here early tomorrow.
4:30–5:30 P.M.	Kohler has asked for some big ideas for an upcoming promotion. We organize a group to come up with incentive programs for distributors and contractors. We come up with some good ideas, but everyone is a little braindead so we decide to regroup tomorrow morning around 8:00 A.M.
5:30–6:00 P.M.	Fax over some proofs to a Kohler distributor in Colorado for approval. We talk about the changes, and I get them to the production manager as she is leaving.
6:00–6:45 P.M.	Get a jump on the new business media plan due tomorrow morning. I crunch as many numbers as possible to get ahead before tomorrow. Record my hours for the day and try to get out of the office for an 8:00 softball game.

marily for budget guidance. These levels are then translated by the buyer into insertion frequencies (print) or into announcement frequencies (broadcast). The buyer's task is to use the GRP guides (with the dollar allocation) to develop schedules that can also match frequency and reach objectives.

For example, imagine this situation for a clothing retailer. The plan calls for a special month-long schedule for October. The buyer's instruction might look like this:

- Desired GRP Level: 460/month
- Medium: Spot Television
- Dayparts: 25 percent of GRP in Evening-Fringe (5 – 7:30 P.M.) and
- 75 percent in Prime Evening (8:00 – 11:00 P.M.)

The buyer for each market would negotiate schedules for 4 weeks at an average target GRP of 115 per week (4 weeks × 115 AVG. GRP = 460). The placements must follow the dayparts and the proportions. Evening fringe should have 115 (25 percent of 460). Prime evening should have 345 (75 percent of 460 GRP).

NEGOTIATION: THE ART OF A BUYER

Just as a labor union transacts with management for pay raises, security, and work conditions, so does a media buyer pursue special advantages for clients. The following are some of the key areas of negotiation.

VEHICLE PERFORMANCE

Selection through negotiation is especially important when the medium offers many options and when the buyers might need to use forecasted audience levels. One serious example is network television.

Nighttime programming is particularly fluid or changeable. Because of the dollars at risk, networks are very quick to rearrange programs, to cancel them and replace them with new ones, and to make other sorts of shifts. Buyers of time in network television are usually faced with selecting programs that (1) are new, (2) are not new but have been scheduled on a different night, or (3) have new lead-in programs. Under these conditions, little, if anything, stays the same. Selection must be made with little or no guarantee of audience popularity. Buyers deal with these uncertainties through careful research on the type of program (action, situation comedy), the rating history of the time slot, the audience flow patterns of competing programs, and other factors.

UNIT COSTS

Open Pricing: A method of media pricing in which prices are negotiated on a contract-by-contract basis for each unit of media space or time.

Getting a low price has always been a goal for media buyers, but today it is mandatory. The published price is no longer acceptable to advertisers. **Open pricing,** in which each buyer or buying group negotiates a separate price for each vehicle, is gaining favor. Open pricing makes buyer negotiation both important and risky. The balance or trade-off between price and audience objectives must be fully understood before an all-out pursuit of open pricing is attempted. Some media experts fear that pricing will replace all other values, and media will eventually be treated like a bag of grain or a barrel of oil. These experts know that there is a very important balance to maintain between cost and value. No matter what pressure the buyer is under for low prices, he or she must balance a vehicle's quality with its cost.

PREFERRED POSITIONS

In magazines there are assumed readership advantages in having the advertising message placed next to well-read pages or in special editorial sections. These

Preferred Positions: Sections or pages of magazine and newspaper issues that are in high demand by advertisers because they have a special appeal to the target audience.

placements are known as **preferred positions.** Imagine the value to a food advertiser of having its message located in a special recipe section that can be detached from the magazine for permanent use by the homemaker. How many additional exposures might that ad get? An ideal position in newspapers might be opposite the editorial page or a location in the food, financial, or sports section. With so many competing "voices," buyers are very anxious to find the most widely read sections.

Because they are so visible, preferred positions often carry a premium surcharge, usually 10 to 15 percent above standard space rates. In these days of negotiation space buyers are not hesitant about requesting that such charges be waived. Buyers will offer publications a higher number of insertions if the special positions are guaranteed without extra cost.

EXTRA SUPPORT OFFERS

In this time of strong emphasis on all sorts of promotional emphasis besides advertising, buyers are not shy about demanding additional assistance from the media beside space and time. These activities, sometimes called *value-added* services,

AD 12.5

IN ADDITION TO PROVIDING ADVERTISING SPACE AND TIME, THE MEDIA MUST OFFER MERCHANDISING AND SALES SUPPORT TO ADVERTISERS.

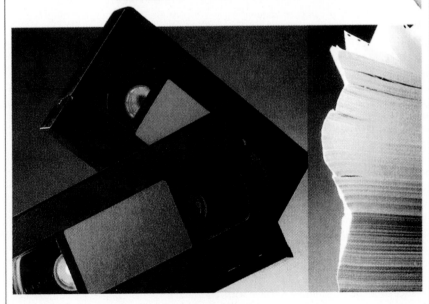

A WORLD OF MEREDITH MERCHANDISING/SALES SUPPORT OPPORTUNITIES

We can also help create a customized merchandising/sales support program that maximizes the effectiveness of your advertising with your sales staff, distributors and dealers. Some of the many possibilities:

▲ Producing special videos for promotional use.
▲ Using consumer direct mail lists (35 million names in all) for specialized direct marketing.
▲ Creating special publications to maintain contact with your customers or with your distribution network.
▲ Using Meredith books as consumer premiums or in sales incentive programs.
▲ Conducting quantitative or attitudinal marketing research.
▲ Using our real estate network to reach homebuyers.

These and other programs can be used individually or in combination.

can take on any number of forms including: contests, special events, merchandising space at stores, displays, and trade-directed newsletters. The "extra" depends on what facilities each media vehicle has, and how hard the buyer can bargain with the dollars available.

Some media companies have decided to actively solicit marketers' budgets by integrating or packaging multimedia activities. At this time when integrated marketing communication programs are being favored, these plans are receiving serious consideration by marketing managements and media buyers alike. In Ad 12.5 (on page 371) the Meredith Company promotes a number of their available operations.

---

*I*NSIDE *A*DVERTISING

CHRISTINA MURRAY, DIRECTOR OF CONTENT AND DISTRIBUTION, *Jones Internet Channel*

My company, Jones Internet Channel, is an entrepreneurial startup within a large corporation (Jones International, Ltd.). We are affiliated with the eighth largest cable company in the United States (Jones Intercable, Inc.) and we were the first cable company in the United States to offer consumers Internet-over-cable access.

Our subscribers in Alexandria, Virginia can surf the Web over fiber/coax cable at speeds up to 10 megabits per second. In addition to high-speed Internet access, Jones Internet Channel offers subscribers community content that is "speed enabled," or designed specifically for the cablemodem platform. Examples of speed-enabled content include: 3D Chat, multiplayer networked games, audiostreaming and VOD (video on demand).

My job as head of the content and distribution team is to manage content licensing, development, installation, distribution, and maintenance. *Content* includes third-party content, original content, user-generated content, and online local and global advertising.

My background is in interactive advertising. I studied television and radio with a concentration in advertising and public relations as an undergraduate at Ithaca College. As a student at Ithaca, I was heavily involved in starting a student chapter of the American Advertising Federation (AAF) on campus and in leading two years of teams competing in the AAF National Student Advertising Competition (we won the National Championship my senior year).

During college I interned at the Walt Disney Company and BBDO New York (where I was an assistant account executive on the Häagen-Dazs account). My junior year, I took a leave of absence and participated in a program abroad called Semester At Sea where I studied marketing and advertising in 11 countries around the world—via steamship. My studies included an "Apartheid in Advertising" conference at Foote, Cone & Belding in Cape Town, South Africa and a discussion of freedom of speech with national soap

opera stars in Taipei, Taiwan. After completing my semester abroad, I relocated to Paris to work on the opening of the EuroDisney Theme Park, where I was, among other things, a multimedia trainer.

It was upon my return to college to complete my Bachelor of Science degree that I learned of an obscure, but blossoming, niche of the computing industry called interactive media. I enrolled in graduate school at NYU's Interactive Telecommunications Program to study new media application development for two years while working full-time at Ogilvy & Mather Direct's Interactive Marketing Group on interactive kiosk, diskette, and CD-ROM projects and teaching second and third grade using nontraditional teaching modalities like computers and video—in an inner-city K–12 program.

Upon completion of graduate school, I relocated from New York to Denver where I worked on postproduction of interactive television ads and production of advertising World Wide Web templates for US West's Interactive Services Group. After US West, I started at Jones Internet Channel.

Working for a company with 14 employees allows me a flexible schedule that is full of impromptu brainstorms and collaborative approaches to problem solving. Much of the new media industry is embryonic. Day-to-day business challenges include procuring revenues from content.

Here is a synopsis of a typical day in my life:

5:45 A.M. Wake up, shower, drink breakfast while paging through March issue of *WIRED* magazine. Scribble URL for new shopping site onto Post-It note. Stick note to front of briefcase.

6:45 A.M. Head off to work.

7:30 A.M. Start-of-day rituals—check e-mail, voice mail, snail mail, and FedEx delivery.

7:40 A.M. Paperwork: Review travel expense form with director of finance; sign going-away card for group president who is leaving Jones to start his own videoconferencing-over-the-Web company.

8:01 A.M. Executive assistant tells me that meetings scheduled from 8–11 A.M. have been postponed.

Special Skills: Maintaining Plan Performance

Today a media buyer's responsibility to a campaign does not end with the signing of space and time contracts. Buys are made in advance on *forecasted* audience levels—the expectation that the audience for a vehicle will be at a certain level. What if vehicles underperform? What happens if unforeseen events affect scheduling? What if newspapers go on strike, if magazines fold, if a television show is canceled? Buyers must fix these problems.

8:10 A.M.	Phone call from new business manager at LYCOS/Point. Wants to meet with me in Denver on his way to Internet World in L.A. next week. Schedule meeting with him.
8:15 A.M.	Review art files on CD-ROMs to make sure all are intact.
8:45 A.M.	Call designer to confirm receipt of discs.
8:50 A.M.	Reply to two e-mails. Return three voice mail messages.
9:00 A.M.	Receive fax from executive vice president with suggested changes to Reuters new media content licensing agreement.
9:15 A.M.	Impromptu meeting with director of finance to discuss content and distribution operating budget for 1997. Discuss list of questions about budget. Agree to meet later in the day to discuss business model for new content brokering idea I am championing.
9:45 A.M.	Offsite brunch meeting with director of sales and marketing. Reviewed content plan for 1997. Talk for 40 minutes about how to define *local advertising* versus *national advertising* in affiliate agreement with Jones cable company. Spent 30 minutes debating about whether newspaper advertising model is the best analogy to Internet advertising (his view) or whether the cable advertising model more closely parallels what we are trying to do on the Net (my view).
11:45 A.M.	Returned to office. Listened to six voice mail messages. Returned three.
12:00 P.M.	Conference call with The Shopper's Source wholesale distributor who wants to provide content to me for Alexandria Community Web site. Decide to speak again next week.
12:45 P.M.	Look up shopping Web site from Post-It note (http://www.dreamshop.com). Bookmark page. Jot contact name and phone number into phone log for future reference.
1:30 P.M.	Shuffle through in-box, reading first few sentences of five trade articles clipped by colleagues.
1:40 P.M.	Impromptu Web site production meeting with Webmaster that needs original Java script from Alexandria Community site. Phone designer together to ask him (for the tenth time) to FTP code to our server so we can build launch schedule for Web site redesign.
2:00 P.M.	Edited press release from Internet Shopping Network, newly signed content partner.
2:30 P.M.	Seven new e-mail messages.
3:00 P.M.	Meet with director of Internet services, director of sales and marketing, and director of finance to discuss network management consulting and content and distribution opportunity in South America for big South/Central America cable operator.
3:20 P.M.	Meet with director of finance to build content brokering business model. Long discussion on whether Jones keeps a portion of ad revenues.
5:15 P.M.	Leave work early to visit car dealership and test drive new automobile.
8:00 P.M.	Order pizza at dealer (while purchasing paperwork goes through).
9:30 P.M.	Before bed, read this week's *Interactive Week*, *Ad Age*, and rest of *WIRED* magazine. Earmark pages with interesting articles (for future distribution to team) and Web site evaluations (for hotlink pages).
10:00 P.M.	Call from former colleague at McCann Erickson who wants to work for new interactive division of DDB Needham. Wants advice on Internet advertising models. Debate whether CPM model works in interactive (nonmeasurable) media.
10:45 P.M.	Leave two voice mails for colleagues about *WIRED* article.
11:00 P.M.	Go to bed.

Nominated by Prof. Howard Cogan, Ithaca College.

MONITORING AUDIENCE RESEARCH

When campaigns begin, the forecasts in the media plan are checked against actual performance. Whenever possible, buyers check each incoming research report to determine whether the vehicle is performing as promised.

BROADCAST RESEARCH

Change is the foundation of broadcast buying. Forecasting future popularity or target audience interest is full of risk. Once the schedule is running, buyers make every attempt to get current audience research. It is the only way to assure that schedules are performing according to the forecast.

PUBLICATION RESEARCH

Newspaper and magazine readership reports are produced less frequently than broadcast ratings, but print buyers are still concerned over changes in circulation. If a circulation audit shows a drop, it may indicate serious readership problems. Furthermore, buyers also check the publication issues to verify if advertisements have been correctly placed.

OUT-OF-HOME MEDIA CHECKING

Major users of outdoor advertising understand it is necessary to visually check sign and billboard positions. The condition of the ad, the presence of obstructions (buildings or trees), and any other situation that would reduce the expected audience exposure must be checked.

SCHEDULE AND TECHNICAL PROBLEMS

Temporary snags in scheduling and in the reproduction of the advertising message are usually unavoidable. For missed positions or errors in handling the message presentation, buyers must be alert to make the needed changes to reconcile difficulties. Most adjustments involve either replacement positions at no cost or money refunds. This policy of various forms of substitution is called *making good on the contract*. The units of compensation are known as **makegoods.** Here are some examples.

Makegoods: Compensation given by the media to advertisers in the form of additional message units that are commonly used in situations involving production errors by the media and preemption of the advertiser's programming.

Program Preemptions: Interruptions in local or network programming caused by special events.

PROGRAM PREEMPTIONS

Special programs or news events often interrupt regular programming. When this happens, the commercial schedule is also interrupted. **Program preemptions** occur nationally and locally. In the case of long-term interruptions—for example, congressional hearings or war coverage—buyers may have difficulty finding suitable replacements before the schedule ends.

MISSED CLOSINGS

Magazines and newspapers have clearly set production deadlines, called *closings*, for each issue. Sometimes the advertising materials do not arrive in time. If the publication is responsible, it will make some sort of restitution. If the fault lies with the client or the agency, there is no restitution by the publication.

TECHNICAL PROBLEMS

Technical difficulties are responsible for the numerous "goofs," "gliches," and "foul-ups" that haunt the advertiser's schedule. In a classic example the buyer for a major airline received a call from the sales representative of the *Washington News*. The makeup staff at the newspaper had missed the intended position for the airline's ad and had run it instead on the *obituary page*. Damage done, makegood was forthcoming. In an extreme case the buyer for a new consumer brand learned that someone at a television station had inserted a "super" (an optical phrase superimposed on the film or tape) informing viewers that the product was *only* available in two small area towns. In truth, those towns accounted for less than 10 percent of the brand's distribution. The damage was serious, and the station did more than make good. It settled out of court.

Most technical problems are not quite so disastrous. *Bleed-throughs* and out-of-register colors for newspapers, torn billboard posters, broken film, and tapes out of alignment are more typical of the problems that plague media schedules.

SUMMARY

- Media buying involves a series of duties and functions that are separate from media planning.

- Media buyers are responsible for executing the media plan recommendations. To do this they must find and select the media vehicles that best fulfill the advertiser's needs.

- The media buyer must observe activity in the media marketplace, analyze audience research, negotiate for positions and price, and monitor schedule performance.

- Price negotiation has become more important as media have shifted from fixed to flexible pricing. Buyers are under strong pressure to get the lowest possible rates without sacrificing desired audience values.

- Buyers are also responsible for maintaining the performance standards established by the media plan throughout the campaign. Changes that lower the value of the message placements must be rectified quickly and efficiently.

QUESTIONS

1. Explain the job-related differences between media planning and media buying. Which job do you feel would be more challenging and satisfying? Assume that both positions offer equal compensation.

2. Mavis Cord is the senior buyer-negotiator for network television for her agency. Through "insider" production contracts she has learned that a key program in the upcoming Willow Foods campaign is having serious production problems (star-director conflict). The start of the schedule is still two months away. Because this new program is projected to be one of the hits of the fall season, Willow management has been very excited about merchandising opportunities using the show's star. What should Mavis do, if anything, about this situation? How should she use her confidential information?

3. Your client is a major distributor of movie videotapes. Its yearly plan for magazines has been settled and you are in negotiation when you learn that a top publishing company is about to launch a new magazine dedicated to movie fans and video collectors. Although the editorial direction is perfect, there is no valid clue as to how the magazine will be accepted by the public. Worse, there won't be solid research on readership for at least a year. The sales representative offers a low charter page rate if the advertiser agrees to appear in each of the first year's issues (monthly). There is no money to add the publication to the existing list. To use it you will have to remove one of the established magazines from your list. Is the risk worthwhile? Should the client be bothered

with this information considering that the plan is already set? What are your recommendations?

4. Bob Maples is the head buyer on the Killer Cola account. One portion of the soft drink's media plan involves a news programming buy in Columbus for radio advertising. The plan's primary goal is to develop frequent exposure against the target audience. Below are the highlights of two competing proposals. Only one can be selected. Which station should Bob recommend and why?

STATION	MONTHLY COST ($)	ANNOUNCE-MENTS PER MONTH	TARGET IMPRESSIONS PER MONTH
WOOK	2000	50	307,000
KLOD	1992	83	285,000

5. *Environmental Weekly* is one of the fastest-growing publications in the consumer sector. It has just announced that it will adopt an open-pricing program for space rates. The sales manager of *EW* has warned, however, that each magazine buy will be negotiated separately (if one of the agency clients gains a low page rate, it will not set a standard for others). As the head of the magazine buying group, what problem(s) does this approach suggest to you? What will you recommend to the department's director?

6. Discuss the difference between open and fixed media pricing. How does the use of these price policies affect the buying process?

𝒮UGGESTED 𝒞LASS 𝒫ROJECT

Identify the best media buys that are *locally* available to expose a twentysomething audience. Set them in priority and discuss ranking. Specifics, such as newspaper name, station call letters, and cable channel are necessary.

𝒻URTHER 𝓡EADINGS

Arnold, M., Donald W. Jugenheimer, and Peter B. Turk, *Media Research Sourcebook and Workbook* (Lincolnwood, IL: NTC Business Books, 1989).

Wall, Robert W., *Media Math: Basic Techniques of Media Evaluation* (Lincolnwood, IL: NTC Business Books, 1987).

LOOK! UP IN THE SKY! IT'S A BIRD! IT'S A PLANE! IT'S AN—ADVERTISEMENT!

It's a truism in advertising that ads need to be noticed if they are to be effective. Ads on television, radio, and in print media compete with other ads for attention. To boost the visibility of their ads, Fuji, Goodyear, PepsiCo, Sea World, Metropolitan Life Insurance, and other companies use aerial advertising in their media mix. There are several aerial media to choose from, including blimps and banners towed by airplanes.

Goodyear was a major blimp manufacturer in the early twentieth century; the company has used a fleet of blimps as airborne advertising vehicles for more than 70 years. Today Goodyear blimps are fixtures at major sporting events, where they are seen both by spectators at the event and by television audiences. Mickey Whitman, Goodyear's airship coordinator, explains the connection. "The demographics of sports are the demographics of tire buyers. It's a match made in heaven—or 1,500 feet over the stadium. Blimps are the greatest billboards in the world." Moreover, as Joe Olma, vice president of a blimp company in Oregon, observes, "Blimps are one of the few advertising media that people never get tired of."

Most major corporations lease blimps on a long-term basis. Airship Management Services is one of several companies in the United States that provide leasing services. The company charges $350,000 per month for a 190-foot blimp. Because blimps provide an ideal, stable platform for television cameras, they can provide breathtaking, bird's-eye-view perspectives of sports events. In return, sportscasters and other commentators mention the blimp and its sponsor several times on the air while a camera on the ground provides an on-air shot of the blimp.

Met Life uses characters from the popular "Peanuts" comic strip in its ads; Met Life's two blimps are dubbed Snoopy One and Snoopy Two. Met Life's blimps are often seen at major golf tournaments. Tim King, regional director of external relations for Met Life, explains why his company uses blimps. "If we were to pay for the equivalent amount of advertising exposure using more traditional means . . . suffice it to say that the blimps are a very profitable venture for us, even when

you include the cost of leasing them," he says. Scott Bennett, the public relations director for Airship International, estimates that the monthly leasing fee for a blimp generates the equivalent of $1 million in traditional media advertising.

Advertisers can also take to the air with advertising messages on banners towed by an airplane. For about $1,000 per day, record companies, fast-food restaurants, and beverage companies can use aerial advertising to reach people at sporting events, beaches, malls, or amusement parks. Personal messages such as marriage proposals can also be taken aloft for about $275. As the aerial medium has increased in popularity, however, some controversies have arisen. In 1995, for example, fans at a New York Giants game complained after a plane towing an ad for Ramses brand condoms flew over Giants Stadium. The complaints came to the attention of the Federal Aviation Administration; the following week, the pilot for Aerial Advertising was ordered to land his airplane after he informed an air traffic controller that the 75-foot banner attached to his plane was another condom ad. Not surprisingly, Paul Calabro, owner of Aerial Advertising, objected. "The FAA's job is just to make sure we fly safely and the people in the stadium are safe and not to decide for us what advertising is correct." John Blutenthal, marketing vice president for the company that markets Ramses, says aerial ads "get people talking about a serious message. The major networks do not allow condom advertising on TV and I think it's shocking . . . We have to find some way of advertising."

Video Source: "Billboards in the Sky," *Wall Street Journal Report* (December 16, 1995). *Additional Sources:* Carol R. Richards, "The Writing on the Wall Is Up in the Sky," *Newsday* (October 27, 1996):A42; Todd Shapera, "Big Spenders Attracted by the Battle of the Blimps," *Financial Times* (January 6, 1997):12; Luther Turmelle, "Blimps Sell from on High," *Gannett News Service* (July 28, 1995); Jodi Duckett, "Majestic Airships Take Back an Honored Place in the Skies," *Los Angeles Times* (January 5, 1995):E5; Ellen Yan, "Ad Ban in Unfriendly Skies," *Newsday* (October 17, 1995):A29; and Jodi Wilgoren, "High-Flying Messenger: It's Always a Banner Day in the Aerial Advertising Business," *Los Angeles Times* (July 4, 1994):B1.

QUESTIONS

1. What are the pros and cons of using aerial advertising in the media mix?
2. If you were a spectator at an outdoor sporting event, would you be offended by an airborne condom ad?

CHAPTER

The Creative Side of Advertising

CHAPTER OUTLINE

- How Ideas Evolve: The "Got Milk?" Campaign
- The Creative Concept
- Creative Thinking
- The Creative Process

- Creative Strategy
- Creative Executions
- Effective Creativity

CHAPTER OBJECTIVES

When you have completed this chapter, you should be able to:

- List various characteristics of creative people
- Explain what advertisers mean by a creative concept
- Describe the various stages involved in creating an advertisement
- Understand how the various elements in an advertisement work together to create impact
- Distinguish between effective copywriting and adese

How Ideas Evolve: The "Got Milk?" Campaign

What do you drink when you're eating a chocolate chip cookie, a bowl of cereal, or a pancake? Although you might reach for a soft drink after a game of softball or iced tea on a sunny afternoon sitting on your patio, when you're eating a cookie there's nothing that tastes better than milk. But milk is something most people generally don't even think about, unless they are ready for a bowl of cereal or a cookie and don't have any milk in the refrigerator.

Those two insights drive the big idea behind California's award-winning "Got Milk?" campaign. Jeff Manning, executive director of the California Milk Processor Board, had a hunch that people drink milk primarily in combination with other foods. Certain foods, in other words, are the driver.

Previous campaigns had focused on trying to change people's perceptions about milk to make it "sexier," like cola. With slogans like "Milk Does a Body Good," and "America's Favorite Health Kick," previous campaigns had tried to give milk a healthy image showing beautiful people in great condition dancing and singing its praises. Unfortunately average milk consumption around the country continued to decline throughout the 1980s, and the problem was even worse in California. By 1993 the average Californian drank 24 gallons a year, compared to 29 gallons in 1980, and the overall volume of milk sold in California declined by an average of 2 to 3 percent per year between the late 1980s and the early 1990s.

The California Milk Board hired Goodby, Silverstein from among 32 agencies competing for the account, and gave the agency four months to execute an advertising campaign that would turn these trends around. The goal was not more image enhancement but increased milk sales. Goodby, Silverstein decided to target people who were already milk consumers and encourage them to drink more rather than to focus on nonusers.

Manning's hunch about the food connection was proved true by research that found that milk is usually accompanied by other foods. Most frequently, that food is cereal. Other foods include cookies, pastries, peanut butter and jelly sandwiches, pancakes, brownies, and cake.

In-home observations and focus group research also found out that milk is a peripheral item in most people's food menu. Analysis by an account planning group arrived at a particularly telling insight: The only time people thought about it was when they were out of it. In certain situations, milk deprivation is very real. In an unusual approach to research, Goodby, Silverstein asked focus group participants not to drink any milk for a week before the next session. Participants then described what it was like to wake up at 7 A.M. and pour a bowl of cereal, only to find no milk in the fridge. Others contributed their experiences, and from these real-life anecdotes, Goodby, Silverstein crafted a series of lively television commercials emphasizing the discomfort that awaits those who run out of milk.

In one spot a man agonizes over a bowl of cereal, trying to decide whether to rob from his baby's bottle or his pet's bowl. In a Christmas spot, Santa enters a home, eats a brownie, finds no milk, and takes his presents away. In another commercial, a ruthless young executive dies and goes to "eternity." He questions whether he's in heaven or hell when he finds a plate of oversized chocolate chip cookies and a refrigerator full of empty milk cartons. Each spot ends with the campaign's slogan, "Got Milk?"

The campaign achieved incredibly high awareness. In January 1994 after just three months on the air, total awareness in California of "Got Milk?" was already at 62 percent. It reached 91 percent by January 1996 with nine out of ten Californians being able to recall either the commercials or the slogan. But the acid test is sales. The campaign appears to have stopped the decline in milk consumption experienced in the 1980s and early 1990s. In 1994, the first year of the campaign, sales rose 1.8 percent instead of continuing at the average decline of 3.5 percent. If the 1.8 percent increase is added to the 3.5 percent decline, then the impact of the campaign translates into 40 million gallons, or $100 million in sales. The sales continued to be stable in 1995, but first quarter sales were about 2 percent higher in 1996 than they were in 1995, which suggests the campaign continues to have impact.[1]

The Creative Concept

Creative Concept: A "big idea" that is original and dramatizes the selling point.

Behind every good advertisement is a **creative concept,** a big idea that makes the message distinctive, attention-getting, and memorable. In the California Milk Board campaign, the big idea is the idea that people drink milk with certain foods, and if milk is not available when they are eating those foods, they are discomforted.

Finding the brilliant creative concept involves what advertising giant Otto Kleppner called "the creative leap."[2] To come up with the big idea, you have to move beyond the safety of the *strategy* statement and leap into the creative unknown. The creative team's mission is to find a novel and unexpected way to showcase a sales point. In its business language the idea might sound like a dull statement of strategy, but in an advertisement this same idea is expressed in a way that grabs the audience's mind. The creative leap dramatizes the strategy behind the message, captures attention, and makes the advertisement memorable. An example is Goodby, Silverstein's translation of the idea of being out of milk by applying it to unexpected situations such as the ruthless business executive with his plate of chocolate chip cookies and a fridge full of empty milk cartons, which signaled that he wasn't in heaven after all.

The springboard for the leap is the strategy. Advertising has to be creative, but it also has to be strategic. However, there is a big difference between the creative brief, usually written in marketing language, and the creative concept, which is another term for the big idea. The difference represents the "leap," which is not merely a step away from that which existed before, but miles away.

Execution: The form taken by the finished advertisement.

The creative concept then becomes the springboard for the execution of the advertisement and that also must be handled creatively. The word **execution** refers to all the details and decisions involved in production of the advertisement—the casting, staging, setting, action, lighting, props, colors, sounds, typography, and so forth. The Concepts and Applications box illustrates some award-winning creative concepts and executions.

WHAT MAKES AN IDEA CREATIVE?

Creative ideas aren't limited to advertising. People such as Henry Ford, who created and then advertised his Model T, and Steven Jobs, the cofounder of Apple Computer, are highly creative. They are idea people, creative problem solvers, and highly original thinkers. Creative people are found in business, in science, in engineering, as well as in advertising. But in advertising, creativity is both a job description and a goal. Different agencies approach the cultivation of creativity in different ways. We'll consider the approach used by DDB Needham Worldwide and then consider the relationship between creativity and strategy in advertising.

---

[1] Adapted from Paula Mergenhagen, "How 'Got Milk?' Got Sales," *Marketing Tools* (September 1996):4–7.

[2] Thomas Russell and Glenn Verrill, *Otto Kleppner's Advertising Procedure*, 11th ed. (Englewood Cliffs, NJ: Prentice Hall, 1990):457.

*C*ONCEPTS AND *A*PPLICATIONS

THE ENVELOPE, PLEASE

There are a number of award shows that identify the best advertisements in any given year, including the Effies, which measure an advertisement's creative approach against its sales impact. In addition, the industry trade press, as well as research companies like Video Storyboards, which publishes its list of the Top 15 most popular campaigns, also identify their best ads. *Adweek* publishes a list of its top 50 ads. The following is a compilation of ads that appeared in at least two of these three lists in 1996. Only the Budweiser campaign made it on all three lists.

Budweiser, "Frogs," "Ants," "Clydesdales;" DMB&B, St. Louis and DDB Needham, Chicago. One of the most popular and memorable commercials of the year featured three frogs that croaked out "Bud-"weiser"-"er." Another spot showed industrious ants hauling a Bud to their anthill for a wild disco party. Another well-liked execution featured two teams of Clydesdales playing football. The ads retain the long-running, "This Bud's for You" tagline but repositioned the idea completely presenting the brand as more fun, entertaining, and contemporary. The new spin more than halved the long-term erosion in Bud's sales, and in many states halted it completely, which was seen by the Effies judges as a tremendous victory in the highly competitive beer wars. (Effies, Video Storyboards, *Adweek*)

Little Caesars, "Training Camp;" Cliff Freeman, New York. The long-running Little Caesars humorous spots feature the animated Little Caesars man. One spot shows delivery boys being in a training camp where they are learning how to properly deliver the pizza fast. (Video Storyboards, *Adweek*)

Coca-Cola, "Summer Sun;" Creative Artists Agency, Beverly Hills. Part of the long-running "Always Coca-Cola" campaign, this commercial featured an animated sun setting up a spot on the beach complete with umbrella and popping a Coke. (Video Storyboards, *Adweek*)

Bud Light, "Fishing;" DDB Needham, Chicago. Featuring the lovable but conniving Johnny who professes in the now famous phrase, "I love you, man," this campaign takes up from a fishing scene to a high-end party where Johnny gets the put-down of his life by Charlton Heston. (Video Storyboards, *Adweek*)

California Milk Board "Got Milk" campaign; Goodby, Silverstein, San Francisco. This regional campaign is built on the idea that there are certain foods that you always drink milk with, such as chocolate chip cookies. Milk isn't on the top of anyone's mind until you are ready for a bowl of cereal and find out you don't have any milk in the fridge. (Video Storyboards, *Adweek*)

Nike, "Pee Wee Football—Running Backs," "Pippen/Supernatural," "The Wall;" Wieden & Kennedy, Portland, Oregon (Video Storyboards, *Adweek*) "The Wall" depicts soccer players in various cities delivering kicks that bounce around the world, eventually shattering a brick wall.

Comedy Central, "Baby," In house, and Korey, Kay & Partners, New York. For several years Comedy Central has been a winner in a number of award shows both for its effectiveness as well as its creativity. In a humorous (what else?) trade campaign to convince cable system operators to add Comedy Central to their lineups, a typical cable manager was invented named Herb Langley, who became a local hero for picking up the channel. Print ads showed Herb having statues erected in his honor and children named after him. The campaign appealed to operators on a personal level and they responded with 125 new systems picking up Comedy Central, an increase of 1.5 million subscribers. (Effies, *Adweek*)

IBM, "French Guys," Ogilvy & Mather, New York. Shaking off its long-time inertia, IBM sought to reinvent itself in the mid-1990s with a more human persona, even while stressing its global reach. Thus was born the "Subtitles" campaign, which eliminated spoken English altogether. Instead, a group of nuns, fashion models, or French guys conversed in their native tongues about their information processing problems and the solutions offered by IBM technology. The idea was to show how IBM was making the world smaller as it put a human face on the monolithic "Big Blue" corporation. This campaign continued to reinforce the "Solutions for a Small Planet" theme line. (Effies, *Adweek*)

Old El Paso, "Nacho Man," Leo Burnett, Chicago. Having recently acquired Old El Paso, Pillsbury wanted to breathe new life into the tired brand. Leo Burnett came up with a memorable campaign, the "Nacho Man," featuring a silly, loud-shirted, college-frat-boy type shaking his booty to the Village People's vintage 70's hit, "Macho Man," as he pops his nachos into his mouth. The campaign became a cult hit and moved from a regional run in the spring to a national blitz in the fall as it also helped Old El Paso increase its market share. The character has also been used in promotions, particularly for the introduction of new products. (Effies, *Adweek*)

Sources: Adapted from "Adweek's Best of 1995," *Adweek* (February 5, 1996):36–41; *Brandweek* Magazines Salutes The 1996 Effies, *Brandweek* (June 10, 1996) Special Supplement; and Sally Goll Beatty, "Omnicom Menagerie Tops Poll of Most Popular TV Ads," *The Wall Street Journal* (March 11, 1996):B1.

ROI

The creative philosophy of DDB Needham is summarized in a play on the bottom-line concerns of business as ROI: relevance, originality, and impact. These three characteristics help describe what makes ideas creative in advertising.

Advertising is a disciplined, goal-oriented field that tries to deliver the right message to the right person at the right time. The goal is persuasion that results in

Relevance: That quality of an advertising message that makes it important to the audience.

PRINCIPLE If it doesn't conform to strategy, reject it.

either a change of opinion or a sale. Ideas have to mean something important to the audience. In other words, they must have **relevance.**

Advertising is directed at convincing people to do something. Unlike a painting, a building, or a technological breakthrough, creativity in advertising requires empathy, a keen awareness of the audience: how they think and feel, what they value, and what makes them take notice. A creative idea has to speak to the right audience with the right sales message. No matter how much the creative people or the client or the account executive may like an idea, if it doesn't communicate the right message or the right product personality to the right audience, then it won't work.

An advertising idea is considered creative when it is novel, fresh, unexpected, and unusual. **Original** means one of a kind. Any idea can seem creative to you if you have never thought of it before, but the essence of a creative idea is that no one else has thought of it either.

Original: One of a kind; unusual and unexpected.

In classes on creative thinking, a teacher will typically ask students to come up with ideas about, for example, what you can build with ten bricks. Some ideas—such as a wall—will appear on many people's lists. Those are obvious and expected ideas. The original ideas are those that only one person thinks of.

An unexpected idea can be one with a twist, an unexpected association, or catchy phrasing. A familiar phrase can become the raw material of a new idea if it is presented in some unusual or unexpected situation. An ad for Bailey's Irish Cream, for example, shows the product being poured into a wine glass over ice cubes. The twist is in the headline that reads: "Holiday on Ice." A play on words is also a good way to develop something unexpected, as is an analogy. Harley-Davidson compared the legendary sound of its motorcycles to the taste of a thick juicy steak in Ad 13.1.

Cliché: A trite expression, an overused idea.

Unoriginal advertising is not novel or fresh; it is the common or obvious idea. Look-alike advertising copies somebody else's great idea. Unfortunately, a great idea is only great the first time around. When it gets copied and overused, it becomes a **cliché.** Even though professionals continually disparage copycat advertising, it remains a dominant advertising form.

One of the most copied advertising ideas in history is the Perception/Reality campaign for *Rolling Stone* magazine created by the Fallon McElligott agency. The campaign, which began running in 1985, pairs people's "perceptions" of the magazine as a publication for hippies with the reality of who the early hippie readers of

AD 13.1

THIS AD BY HARLEY-DAVIDSON ILLUSTRATES HOW PICTURE AND WORDS COME TOGETHER TO PRODUCE A POWERFUL CREATIVE CONCEPT.

TREAT YOUR EARS
TO A THICK JUICY STEAK.

Rolling Stone have become, using visual and verbal puns. The campaign has become so popular within the advertising community that every time a creative team has an assignment that asks them to change a perception, they are tempted to create a copycat ad. An example of the *Rolling Stone* campaign is shown in Chapter 5.

Impact: The effect that a message has on the audience.

To be creative, the ideas must also have **impact.** Most advertisements just "wash over" the audience. A commercial with impact can break through the screen of indifference and focus the audience's attention on the message and the product. An idea with impact helps people see themselves or the world in a new way. The classic campaign for V-8 vegetable juice demonstrates the impact of a creative idea when the various characters hit themselves on the forehead in the familiar gesture that says "Why didn't I think of that" while saying aloud, "I could have had a V-8." That ad dramatizes the impact and power of a relevant, new idea.

An ad with impact has the stopping power that comes from an intriguing idea—something you have never thought about before. An example of how a startling thought can stop you and make you think is an ad for Compaq that uses a visual of a chained butterfly to illustrate the concept of freedom in computer workstations. (See Ad 13.2.)

STRATEGY AND CREATIVITY

Let's look at the relationship between strategy and the creative concept. A creative concept in advertising has to dance to the tune of two different masters—originality and strategy. To be creative, an idea must be both original (different, novel, unexpected) and right for the product and target. Good advertising is both cre-

AD 13.2

A CHAINED BUTTERFLY IS
USED BY INTEL TO DRAMATIZE
THE FREEDOM OFFERED BY ITS
COMPUTER CHIP.

YOUR RELIANCE ON CONVENTIONAL WORKSTATIONS
IS ABOUT TO CHANGE FOREVER.

ative and strategically sound—it is both an art and a disciplined solution to a communication problem. Creative people in advertising must answer to both masters, and this makes creative advertising extremely difficult to do. Cleverness is not enough. Jim Osterman, *Adweek* editor, explained in his column, "I get ample opportunity to see the work students are doing. It's fresh and has attitude, but some of it wouldn't sell because it's not strategic. That doesn't mean it's bad work, but it does mean that just being clever is not enough. To me, great creative has to be targeted creative as well."[3] The Issues and Controversies box discusses ethical problems that arise when the creative is too risky.

Positioning is as important as targeting and very much reflected in the way the advertising is developed. Under the guidance of the BBDO advertising agency, Pepsi advertising has evolved strategically over time as a reflection of its generational positioning. The recent "Be Young. Have Fun. Drink Pepsi." slogan was developed to reaffirm its connections with its youthful target audience and restate the Pepsi attitude connects with a youthful attitude. The previous "Gotta Have It" slogan replaced the "Choice of a New Generation" theme that had worked so well since Michael Jackson and the Pepsi Generation began in the early 1980s. "Gotta Have It" was replaced by the "Be Young" line because it wasn't seen as reflecting Pepsi's long-held position of owning the "young and hip" franchise. The client wanted to get that position back.

The Leo Burnett agency has developed an approach to analyzing the message design that keeps both strategy and creativity in perspective. Called *structural analysis*, it first looks at the power of the narrative or story line and then evaluates the strength of the product claim. Finally, it looks at how well the two aspects are integrated—that is, how the story line brings the claim to life. The creative team checks to see if the narrative level is so high that it overpowers the claim or if the claim is strong but there is no memorable story. Ideally, these two elements will be so seamless that it is hard to tell whether the impact derives from the power of the story or strength of the claim.

---

[3]Jim Osterman, "Whatever's Clever Is Never Enough," *Adweek* (October 25, 1993):54.

*I*SSUES AND *C*ONTROVERSIES

SLEEPING YOUR WAY TO THE TOP

How far can you go to make your point? Westin Hotels found out it was teetering on the edge of good taste with its "Who's He Sleeping With?" campaign. A typical ad in the campaign by DDB Needham features a driven businessperson described by the announcer as "Broke his neck to get this job, then broke the corporate sales record. Even broke the corporate 'no jeans' rule. Who's he sleeping with?" The tagline: "Choose your travel partner wisely."

The vice president of advertising and public relations for Seattle-based Westin Hotels & Resorts says Westin's customers are "people who are climbing the corporate ladder two steps at a time. We wanted to be provocative to get the attention of readers and viewers. It's a clever double-entendre."

The campaign features three men and one woman and, as you might guess, it's the commercial about the woman that's generating the most protest. Angry viewers have responded that showing a businesswoman staying in a beautiful suite on a business trip and concluding with the line "I wonder who she's sleeping with" just perpetuates the notion that successful women get there by sleeping their way to the top. The campaign theme is also carried out in direct mail with promotional mailings that feature women and men saying, "Who are they sleeping with?"

The Westin advertising and public relations executive says she is proud of the commercial because "it shows images of successful business executives, women and men, rather than traditional hotel advertising."

What do you think? Is this a clever double-entendre that speaks to the hip young businessperson or is it another example of insensitive and sexist advertising? Should Westin worry about the fact that some people in the audience might be offended? On what basis should the decision to run or not run this campaign be made?

Sources: Adapted from Carol Kleiman, "Criticism of Westin Ad," *Daily Camera Business Plus* (December 24, 1996):26; and "Sleeping Around with Westin," *Advertising Age* (May 6, 1996):1.

CREATIVE THINKING

AD 13.3

WRIGLEY'S USES AN ANALOGY
TO CREATE A "MIND-SHIFT"
THAT CAUSES READERS TO
THINK OF CHEWING GUM AS
CARRY-ON LUGGAGE FOR AN
AIRPLANE TRIP ON A NONSMOK-
ING ROUTE.

Free Association: An exercise in
which you describe everything
that comes into your mind when
you think of a word or an image.

Convergent Thinking: Thinking
that uses logic to arrive at the
"right" answer.

Divergent Thinking: Thinking
that uses free association to uncover all possible alternatives.

How do you get creative ideas? One of the myths of the advertising business is
that only certain people are creative. Actually, creativity is a special form of problem solving, and everyone is born with some talent in that area.

Furthermore, creativity is not limited in advertising to the "creative side."
Advertising is a very creative business that demands imagination and problem-
solving abilities in all areas. Media planners and researchers, for example, are just
as creative as copywriters and art directors in searching for innovative solutions to
the problems they face.

An idea, according to James Webb Young, a legendary advertising executive,
is "a new combination" of thoughts. In his classic book *A Technique for Producing
Ideas*, Young claimed that "the ability to make new combinations is heightened by
an ability to see relationships."[4] An idea is a thought that is stimulated by placing
two previously unrelated concepts together. The juxtaposition sets up new patterns and new relationships and creates a new way of looking at things. This phenomenon has been described as making the familiar strange and the strange familiar. A creative idea involves a "mind-shift." Instead of seeing the obvious, a
creative idea looks at something in a different way, from a different angle as in
Ad 13.3, which associates a package of gum with carry-on luggage.

Creative thinking uses a technique called **free association.** Young's definition of a new idea calls for the juxtaposition of two seemingly unrelated thoughts.
That is what happens in associative thinking. In free association you think of a
word and then describe everything that comes into your mind when you imagine
that word. Associative thinking can be visual or verbal—you can start with a picture or a word. Likewise, you can associate by thinking of either pictures or words.

An example of how free association works is the campaign for the state of
Texas by GSDM advertising agency. The agency's famous "Don't Mess with
Texas" antilitter campaign is a takeoff on a common pseudo-macho phrase, but it
has a twist because of the double meaning of the word *mess.*

Actually researchers say there are two basic approaches to getting ideas: *creative* approaches using techniques such as brainstorming and free association and
analytical approaches based on techniques such as market analysis and consumer
research. Creative techniques tend to generate more new-product ideas compared
with the analytical, but both are needed for effective creativity.

DIVERGENT THINKING

Creative thinking is different from the way you think when you try to balance
your checkbook or develop an outline for an essay in English class. Most of the
thinking that students do in classrooms is rational and is based on a linear logic
whereby one point follows from another, either inductively or deductively.

Creative thinking uses an entirely different process. J.P. Guilford, a well-
known cognitive psychologist, distinguished between convergent thinking and divergent thinking.[5] **Convergent thinking** uses linear logic to arrive at the "right"
conclusion. **Divergent thinking,** which is the heart of creative thinking, uses associative thinking to search for all possible alternatives.

RIGHT AND LEFT BRAIN

In current neurophysiology these two types of thinking have been associated with
different hemispheres of the brain. Left-brain thinking is logical and controls
speech and writing; right-brain thinking is intuitive, nonverbal, and emotional.
Most people use both sides of their brains, depending on the task. An artist is gen-

---

[4]James Webb Young, *A Technique for Producing Ideas*, 3rd ed. (Chicago: Crain Books, 1975).

[5]J.P. Guilford, "Traits of Personality," in *Creativity and Its Cultivation*, H.H. Anderson, ed. (New York:
Harper & Brothers, 1959).

erally more oriented to right-brain thinking, whereas an accountant is more left-brained. A person who is left-brain dominant is presumed to be logical, orderly, and verbal. In contrast, a person who is right-brain dominant deals in expressive visual images, emotion, intuition, and complex interrelated ideas that must be understood as a whole rather than as pieces.[6]

THE CREATIVE PERSON

Is creativity a personality trait we are born with or a skill we can develop? Geneticists studying the issue contend that we are all born with creative potential—the ability to solve problems by combining complex and sometimes unrelated ideas. You probably know people in your school and circle of friends who are just naturally zany, coming up with crazy off-the-wall ideas. In terms of being creative, these people start off with a little advantage. But that's all it is. And it may be a disadvantage if they can't tame their craziness to fit into an office environment or the world at large.

As a matter of fact, a lot of the traits that lead to creative thinking—being nonconforming and unconventional, for example—are smothered in the educational process, which is more concerned with teaching children to be "well behaved." Both education and society can punish children for being different and that, of course, is the springboard for creative thinking.

Research by the Center for Studies in Creativity and the Creative Education Foundation, both in Buffalo, New York, has found that most people can sharpen their skills and develop their creative potential, just as most people can learn to play the piano. But first you need to know what makes a person creative and then you can work on developing those skills.

PERSONAL CHARACTERISTICS

Although everyone has some problem-solving abilities, certain traits seem to be typical of creative problem solvers. The first is that they soak up experiences like sponges. They have a huge personal reservoir of material: things they have read, watched, or listened to, places they have been and worked, and people they have known.

Research has found that creative people tend to be independent, self-assertive, self-sufficient, persistent, and self-disciplined, with a high tolerance for ambiguity. They are risk takers, and they have powerful egos. In other words, they are internally driven. They don't care much about group standards and opinions. They are less conventional than are noncreative people and have less interest in interpersonal relationships.

Creative people typically have an inborn skepticism and very curious minds. They are alert, watchful, and observant, and reach conclusions through intuition rather than through logic. They also have a mental playfulness that allows them to make novel associations. They find inspiration in daydreams and fantasies, and they have a good sense of humor.

In general, creative people tend to perform difficult tasks in an effortless manner and are unhappy and depressed when they are not being creative. In addition to having many positive characteristics, however, they have also been described as abrasive, hard to deal with, and withdrawn.

What characteristics do creative thinkers not exhibit? They are not dogmatic (although they can be stubborn), and they have little patience with authoritarian people. These people don't follow the crowd, and they like being alone. They aren't timid, and they don't care much about what other people think.

---

[6]Betty Edwards, *Drawing on the Right Side of the Brain* (Los Angeles: Tarcher, 1979).

VISUALIZATION SKILLS

Most copywriters have a good visual imagination as well as excellent writing skills. Art directors, of course, are good visualizers, but they can also be quite verbal. Stephen Baker, in his book *A Systematic Approach to Advertising Creativity*, describes "writers who doodle and designers who scribble" as the heart of the advertising concept team.[7]

Writers as well as designers must be able to visualize. Good writers paint pictures with words; they describe what something looks like, sounds like, smells like, and tastes like. They use words to transmit these sensory impressions. Most of the information we accumulate comes through sight, so the ability to manipulate visual images is very important for good writers. In addition to seeing products, people, and scenes in their "mind's eye," good writers are able to visualize a mental picture of the finished ad while it is still in the talking, or idea, state.

Visualization, the ability to imagine how the ad or commercial will look, is critical to people on the creative side of advertising. For example, imagine you are creating an advertisement for Chevy trucks that associated the vehicle with the U.S. Ski Team. How would you visualize that connection? Ad 13.4 shows how the creative people working on the Chevy Truck account made that connection.

Creative advertising people are zany, weird, off the wall, and unconventional, but they are not eccentric. In other words, they are still very centered on doing effective advertising. Some try to be eccentric in style and appearance and

Visualization: The ability to imagine how an advertisement or commercial will look.

[7]Stephen Baker, *A Systematic Approach to Advertising Creativity* (New York: McGraw-Hill, 1979).

AD 13.4

THIS CHEVY TRUCK AD COMPARES THE TRUCK'S MANEUVERABILITY TO DOWNHILL SKIING.

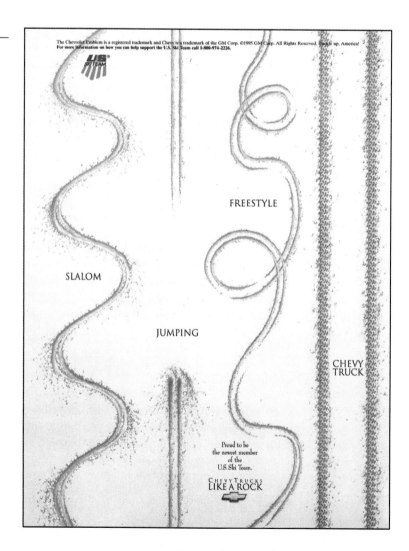

wear it as a badge to announce their creativity. But advertising is a business and businesspeople, however creative, still have to be in touch with the forms and style of business. If you are so eccentric that your agency is afraid to let you make the presentation of your ideas to the client, then your style gets in the way of your productivity and that can damage a career as well as kill a campaign presentation.

Creative people in advertising also have to live with deadlines—a factor that separates the fine artist from the advertising creative. You have to be able to push ideas together when you are under pressure and tired. Some creative people say it's the pressure that makes them perform; the more pressure, the better their work. Advertising is a tough, problem-solving field where you don't have the luxury of waiting for a creative concept to appear. According to former advertising executive Gordon White, "It is creativity on demand, so to speak. Creating within strict parameters. Creativity with a deadline."[8]

In order to force group creativity against a deadline, some agencies have special rooms and processes for brainstorming—rooms, for example, with no distractions and interruptions, such as telephones, and walls that can be papered over with tissues covered with ideas. Other agencies rent a suite in a hotel and send the creative team there to immerse themselves in the problem, again without distractions from the office. When GSDM, for example, was defending its prized Southwest Airlines account, president Roy Spence ordered a 28-day "war room" death march that had staffers working around the clock, wearing Rambo-style camouflage, and piling all their trash inside the building to keep any outsiders from rummaging around for clues to their pitch.

PERSONAL DEVELOPMENT

For many years conventional wisdom was that, like Einstein, you were either born creative or you were not. Today research demonstrates that almost anyone can learn to develop his or her innate creativity. Creativity is not a talent, it is a way of operating, a mode of behavior. Learning how to operate more creatively, then, is possible for anyone. The Portfolio Center ad discusses the way the school identifies creative talent. (See Ad 13.5.)

People who are successful in the creative world have learned how to get into the mood and how to proceed. That is, they have developed a way of operating that stimulates their innate creative abilities. Sometimes it's ritualized: One writer may ride the elevator up and down or take a walk along a certain route as a mental signal to the creative mode; another writer may sharpen pencils as a way to jumpstart the creative process.

Attitude is a big part of it. Research into the personalities of creative people has found that the primary personality difference between those who are creative and those who are not is that creative people *believe* they are creative. So, for someone who wants to be more creative, understanding the importance of that basic mind-shift is the first step in unleashing creative potential.

The opposite of that principle is that negative thinking is the single most destructive factor for a creative person. Being in a bad mood, depressed, or not confident almost always sets you up for a bad creative day. Professionals, of course, sometimes get depressed and have bad moods, so how do they continue to be productive? They develop ways to put the bad mood aside when they move into their creative mode. They do it instinctively because most of them realize that their job responsibilities rise above the daily difficulties of life. When they are on the job, the other stuff gets filed in a back compartment of the mind.

Research also shows that wide *experience* is a prerequisite to creativity. Creative people need mental fodder to work with, a lot of material stewing in the

---

[8]Gordon E. White, "Creativity: The X Factor in Advertising Theory," in *Strategic Advertising Decisions: Selected Readings*, Ronald D. Michman and Donald W. Jugenheimer, eds. (Columbus, OH: Grid, Inc., 1976):212.

AD 13.5

THIS AD FOR THE PORTFOLIO
SCHOOL FOCUSES ON WAYS
OF IDENTIFYING CREATIVE
TALENT.

mind's melting pot. Anything you can do to build up your reservoir of life experiences helps. Working, particularly in an environment foreign to your upbringing, such as picking peas in the fields during summer vacation or working in a cannery when you grew up in an upper-middle-class suburban home, brings you in touch with people whose lives and concerns are different from yours. Being around people who see the world differently, which also comes from travel, always broadens the experiences of open-minded people.

LEONARDO DA VINCI, ALBERT
EINSTEIN, AND GEORGIA
O'KEEFE EXCELLED IN DIFFER-
ENT FIELDS, BUT ALL THREE
QUALIFY AS CREATIVE
GENIUSES.

Likewise, reading and staying in touch with a variety of mass media such as publications and programs aimed at different audiences add to your reservoir. Every advertising creative person interviewed for a study on how they work mentioned their voracious reading habits and compulsive need to know everything on television, in the movies, and on the radio. Being tuned in, plugged in, and in touch with popular culture are very important.

Understanding how the creative process works is the biggest step in learning to be more creative. Most people who think they aren't creative simply don't work at it hard enough. The mental digestion process takes time and effort. Develop your own getting-started techniques like doodling with words and pictures. Creative people often fill pads with what seems to be aimless doodling. They even sleep with notepads by their beds. In fact, these half-sketched ideas and phrases are the raw materials of ideas. This stage often leads to what seems to be a blind wall. Don't give up too easily; take a walk instead. Too many people give up too soon.

Another way to become more creative is to develop your associative thinking skills. You can practice free association by yourself. Just look around the room, pick out an object, relax, open your mind, and see what thoughts come into it. The more often you do this, the more comfortable you will be with the process. You will find that the number and variety of associations increase. Strive for the funniest, silliest, craziest associations you can think of—that is how you develop the ability to come up with original associations.

Analogies are also useful exercises. Look around the room and pick out something. Ask yourself what that item is like—what it resembles either physically or functionally. Functional analogies compare processes such as how something works or how something is used. A vacuum cleaner is like . . . an anteater, the tentacles of an octopus, a swimmer gasping for air. Keep playing with the images—once again, the crazier the better. The creative mind is a muscle that can be strengthened through exercises like making associations and analogies, but it takes practice.

CREATIVE ROLES

All agencies have *copywriters* and *art directors* who are responsible for dreaming up the creative concept and crafting the execution. They frequently work in teams of two, are sometimes hired and fired as a team, and may successfully work together for a number of years. The creative director manages the creative process and plays an important role in focusing the strategy of ads and making sure the creative concept is strategically on target.

Usually both members of the creative team come up with concept ideas as well as word and picture ideas. Their writing or design specialties come into play more in the crafting of the idea once it is agreed upon. The concept may come to mind as a visual, a phrase, or a thought that uses both visual and verbal expression. If it begins as a phrase, the next step is to try to visualize what the concept looks like. If it begins as an image, the next step is to come up with words that express what the visual is saying.

ART DIRECTION

Art Director: The person who is primarily responsible for the visual image of the advertisement.

The person who is primarily responsible for the graphic image of the advertisement is the art director. The **art director** "composes" the visuals in both print and video and "lays out" the ad elements in print. Artists may do the specific illustrations or renderings, but the art director is the chief arranger of these elements. He or she is responsible for the visual "look" of the message.

One of the primary decisions made by an art director is whether to use photography or artwork (animation in television). Photography is the mainstay of the advertising business because it is "real" and adds credibility to the message. Seeing

Inside Advertising

DEIONNA WILBURN, ADVERTISING ART DIRECTOR, *Leo Burnett, Chicago*

As an art director at Leo Burnett U.S.A., my workday can be so jam-packed. To cope with it, I have to slap an "S" on my chest and call myself Superwoman. Following is the a description of a typical hectic day. Enjoy.

7:00 A.M.   My alarm sounds. I don't listen to it.

8:00 A.M.   Okay, okay. I'm up!

8:30 A.M.   I'm on the bus doing what I do best, people watching. I consider it food for thought. Some of my best ideas come to me while on the bus listening in on conversations that have nothing to do with me.

9:00 A.M.   I received a call from my account executive. He has made major changes to the creative strategy, a document that gives creatives specific guidelines for creating ads. The client decided that they did, in fact, need a tagline, unlike last week when they were *sure* that they didn't. But wait. There is good news! We do have more time to work on the ad. Oh, what sweet music!

9:30 A.M.   My partner and I look over the television spots for the Creative Review Committee (CRC) meeting this afternoon. Of course, there are changes to be made. The paradox. My partner needs to cut words, but I need to draw two extra frames for the television spot. You figure it out.

10:30 A.M.   Capps Studio, Burnett's print production subsidiary, sends down a low-resolution print ad for me to approve. I call the print production manager and the studio's traffic manager to schedule a meeting for 1:00 to view what I hope are the final changes to the previous final changes for this print ad. *Final changes* is a term loosely used in the advertising business. Pride yourself on being flexible.

11:45 A.M.   I meet with my creative director to show her the two spots for the television campaign. I also discuss with her the changes made to the print ad at Capps Studio. I get notice that the CRC is changed from 5:00 P.M. to 2:30 P.M. So much for more time, and I'm slowly beginning to lose my mind.

12:30 P.M.   Lunch? What lunch. It's soup and a sandwich at my desk.

1:30 P.M.   I meet with my creative director to get the official approval for the print ad to go to high resolution. I get it . . . God does answer prayers.

2:00 P.M.   Final additions are made to the presentation. My partner and I practice the delivery of our ideas and decide on the best way to sell our ideas.

2:30 P.M.   The CRC begins. Blah. Blah. Drama. Drama.

5:30 P.M.   The CRC ends. And it wasn't too long this time!

5:45 P.M.   I place a call to Capps Studio to check on the progress of the print ad in its high-resolution format. Capps tells me I'll see something to look at tomorrow morning. I place a call to my print production manager to review the timetable for the distribution of the ad to the client.

6:00 P.M.   My partner and I begin to make the necessary changes suggested at the CRC to our television spots and print ads. Everything will be sent to the client tomorrow afternoon for review.

8:00 P.M.   And what's my reward for this long and hard day? A print campaign and two great television spots soon to be seen by millions!

Deionna Wilburn received a B.S. in Advertising from the University of Texas at Austin and then completed the school's three-semester creative program in 1996. In the fall of 1996 she was offered a position as associate art director at Leo Burnett and has been there ever since.

Nominated by Professor John Murphy, University of Texas-Austin.

is believing, after all. Probably three-fourths of all advertising visuals are photographic. Of the photographs, around 80 percent are realistic. Illustrations in print and animation on television are used for fashion, fantasy, and exaggerated effects.

If the decision is to use photography, then there are different styles of images from which to choose. A reportorial style uses dramatic black-and-white images to try to imitate photojournalism. Documentary style also uses black and white or sepia (a brown tone), but the style is more stark. Most products and product scenes, however, are shot in realistic full color, either in a studio, on a set, or on location.

Different photographers specialize in different types of shots. Some are great with fashion, others shoot buildings, some are good at landscapes, others know all the difficulties of shooting food, and still others specialize in photographing babies or animals. Each area demands specialized knowledge of how to handle lighting, staging, props, and models.

If the layout calls for illustrations, the art director must decide which artist to use. Every artist has a personal style, although most good artists are able to shift styles somewhat to reflect the nature of the message. There is a big difference between a loose style, which is somewhat rough, primitive, or casual in appearance, and a tight style, which is detailed, perhaps even technical. Some artists are good at realistic effects, whereas others are better at abstract or highly stylized effects, as in fashion advertising. Some are good cartoonists.

COPYWRITING

Copywriter: The person who writes the text for an ad.

Advertising writing is called *copy*, and the person who shapes and sculpts the words in an advertisement is called a **copywriter.** Copywriters are preoccupied with language. They listen to how people talk. They read everything they can get their hands on, from technical documents to comic books. They are tuned in to current expressions and fads.

Versatility is the most common characteristic of copywriters. They can move from toilet paper to Mack trucks and shift their writing style to match the product and the language of their target. Copywriters don't have a style of their own because the style they use has to match the message and the product. Some veteran copywriters specialize in certain types of writing, but beginners find themselves advertising all types of products. Except in a few rare cases, advertising copy is anonymous, so people who crave a by-line generally would not be very happy as copywriters.

There is good writing and there is bad writing in advertising, just as there is in every other area of expression. Some of the characteristics discussed here are features of good advertising writing, although all ads are not written this way.

PRINCIPLE Keep it simple.

Advertising has to win its audience, and usually it is in competition with some other form of programming or editorial matter. For that reason, the copy should be as easy to understand as possible. Unless the rewards are exceptional, most people will shun advertising copy that taxes them. Simple ads avoid being gimmicky or too cute. They don't try too hard or reach too far to make a point. The long-running Soloflex campaign is a good example of a simple concept simply expressed. The visual is of a well-built man taking off his shirt. There is no headline, but the short body copy is set in large type and serves as a long headline. The copy reads: "To unlock your body's potential, we proudly offer Soloflex." The short slogan is a play on words: "Body by Soloflex."

ARTISTIC CREATIVITY IS ESSENTIAL TO SUCCESSFUL ADVERTISING.

Advertising copy uses short, familiar words and short sentences. You will probably notice in print advertising that some of the paragraphs are only one sentence long. Every attempt is made to produce copy that looks or sounds easy to understand. Long blocks of copy in print, which are too "gray" or intimidating for the average reader, are broken up into short paragraphs with many subheads. The equivalent of a long copy block in television advertising is a long speech by the announcer. Television monologues can be broken up by visual changes, such as shots of the product. Sound effects can also be used to break up the heaviness of the monologue.

Advertising copy is very tight. Every word counts because both space and time are expensive. There is no time or room for ineffective words. Copywriters will go over the copy a hundred times trying to make it as concise as possible. The tighter the copy is, the easier it is to understand and the greater its impact will be.

The more specific the message, the more attention-getting and memorable it is. The better ads won't say "cost less" but will spell out exactly how much less the product costs. There isn't a lot of time to waste on generalities.

The best advertising copy sounds natural, like two friends talking to one another. It is not forced; it is not full of generalities and superlatives; it does not brag or boast. Conversational copy is written the way people talk. It uses incomplete sentences, fragments of thoughts, and contractions.

In order to get the right tone of voice, copywriters usually move away from the target audience description and concentrate on the typical user. If they know someone who fits that description, then they write to that person. If they don't, then they may go through a photo file, select a picture of the person they think fits the description, and develop a profile of that personality. They may even hang that picture above their desk while they write the copy.

One way that advertising copy differs from other writing is in the use of direct address. It is perfectly acceptable in copywriting to use "you" in direct address. In fact, a conscious attempt to use "you" will force copywriters to be more natural and less affected in their writing. It also forces them to think about the product in terms of the prospect and benefits.

Brag-and-Boast Copy: Advertising text that is written from the company's point of view to extol its virtues and accomplishments.

"We" copy is advertising that is written from the company's point of view. It tends to be more formal, even pompous. It is also called **brag-and-boast copy.** Research has consistently found that this is the weakest form of ad writing. "I" copy is used occasionally in testimonials or in dramas such as slice of life where a leading character speaks about a personal experience.

Adese: Formula writing that uses clichés, generalites, stock phrases, and superlatives.

Unfortunately, advertising does have a style that is so well known that it is parodied by comedians. It is a form of formula writing, called **adese,** that violates all the preceding guidelines. Adese is full of clichés, superlatives, stock phrases, and vague generalities. For example, imagine saying things like this to a friend: "Now we offer the quality that you've been waiting for—at a price you can afford." "Buy now and save." Can you hear yourself saying that aloud?

An ad by Buick for its Somerset line is full of adese. The headline starts with the stock opening: "Introducing Buick on the move." The body copy includes superlatives and generalities such as:

"Nothing less than the expression of a new philosophy."

"It strikes a new balance between luxury and performance; a balance which has been put to the test."

"Manufactured with a degree of precision that is in itself a breakthrough."

The problem with adese is that it looks and sounds like what everyone thinks advertising should look and sound like. Because people are so conditioned to screen out advertising, messages that use this predictable style are the ones that are the easiest to notice and avoid.

This section has been a review of how creative people work and think and the jobs they do in advertising. Now let's look at the creative process itself and how advertising tries to manage the process so it is productive and results in strategic ideas that solve very specific advertising problems.

THE CREATIVE PROCESS

There is a tendency to think of a creative person as someone who sits around waiting for an idea to strike. In comic books that is the point where the light bulb comes on above the character's head. In reality, most people who are good at thinking up new ideas will tell you that it is hard work. They read, they study, they analyze, they test and retest, they sweat and curse and worry, and sometimes they give up. Major breakthroughs in science or medicine may take years, decades, even generations. The unusual, unexpected, novel idea doesn't come easily.

Certainly, any individual is capable of coming up with an idea or two, but in reality, as Osterman, *Adweek* editor, pointed out, many of those ideas are either lacking in potential, impractical to produce, or outside the product's strategy. This is especially true of the ideas that arise without the aid of disciplined procedures. Random ideas come mainly by chance but in a disciplined systematic approach, such as that diagrammed in Figure 13.1, ideas are generated through an organized procedure. Rarely do the ideas just come from "out of the blue."

FIGURE 13.1

THE CREATIVE PROCESS IN ADVERTISING.
(*Source:* Reprinted from *Marketing News*, March 18, 1983:22, published by the American Marketing Association. Bruce Vanden Bergh, *"Take this 10-Lesson Course on Managing Creatives Creatively."*)

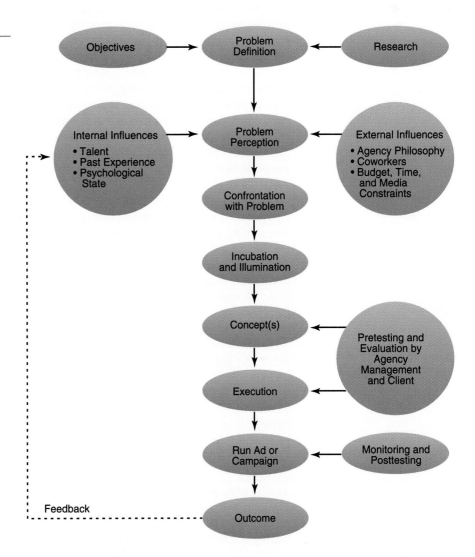

Despite differences in terms and emphasis, there is a great deal of agreement among the different descriptions of the creative process. The creative process is usually portrayed as following sequential steps. As long ago as 1926 an English sociologist named Graham Wallas first put names to the steps in the creative process. He called them: *preparation, incubation, illumination,* and *verification.*[9]

A more comprehensive process is suggested by Alex Osborn, former head of the BBDO agency, who established the Creative Education Foundation in upstate New York, which runs workshops and publishes a journal on creativity:

1. Orientation: pointing up the problem
2. Preparation: gathering pertinent data
3. Analysis: breaking down the relevant material
4. Ideation: piling up alternative ideas
5. Incubation: letting up, inviting illumination
6. Synthesis: putting the pieces together
7. Evaluation: judging the resulting ideas[10]

Although the steps vary somewhat and the names differ, all creative strategies seem to share several key points. Researchers consistently have found that ideas come after the person has immersed himself or herself in the problem and worked at it to the point of giving up. Preparation and analysis is that essential period of hard work when you read, research, investigate, and learn everything you can about the problem.

Next comes ideation, a time of playing with the material, of turning the problem over and looking at it from every angle. This is also a period of teasing out ideas and bringing them to the surface. Most creative people develop a physical technique for generating ideas, such as doodling, taking a walk, jogging, riding up and down on the elevator, going to a movie, or eating certain foods. It is a highly personal technique used to "get in the mood," to start the wheels turning. The objective of this stage is to generate as many alternatives as possible. The more ideas that are generated, the better the final concepts.[11]

The processes of analysis, juxtaposition, and association are mentally fatiguing for most people. You may hit a blank wall and find yourself giving up. This is the point that James Webb Young describes as "brainfag." It is a necessary part of the process.

Incubation is the most interesting part of the process. This is the point where you put your conscious mind to rest and let your subconscious take over the problem-solving effort. In other words, when you find yourself frustrated and exasperated because the ideas just won't come, try getting away from the problem. Go for a walk, go to a movie, do anything that lets you put the problem "out of your mind" because that is when the subconscious will take over.

Illumination is that unexpected moment when the idea comes. Typically, the solution to the problem appears at the least expected time: not when you are sitting at the desk straining your brain, but later that evening just before you drop off to sleep or in the morning when you wake up. At an unexpected moment, the pieces fit together, the pattern is obvious, and the solution jumps out at you.

One of the most important steps is the verification or evaluation stage, where you step back and look at the great idea objectively. Is it really all that creative? Is it understandable? Most of all, does it accomplish the strategy? Most people working on the creative side of advertising will admit that many of their best creative ideas just didn't work. They may have been great ideas, but they didn't

---

[9]Graham Walls, *The Art of Thought* (New York: Harcourt, Brace & World, 1926).

[10]Alex F. Osborn, *Applied Imagination*, 3rd ed. (New York: Scribners, 1963).

[11]Bruce G. Vanden Bergh, Leonard N. Reid, and Gerald A. Schorin, "How Many Creative Alternatives to Generate," *Journal of Advertising*, 12(1983):4.

solve the problem or accomplish the right objective. Copywriters will also admit that sometimes the idea they initially thought was wonderful does not project any excitement a day or week later.

Part of evaluation involves the personal go/no go decision which every creative person has to be able to make. Craig Weatherup, Pepsi president/CEO explained, "You must have a clear vision . . . and have the nerve to pull the trigger." Weatherup is willing to pull the trigger on ideas for Pepsi advertising strategies, as is BBDO's Dusenberry. "On Pepsi, the kill rate is high," Dusenberry says. "For every spot we go to the client with, we've probably killed nine other spots."

IDEATION

Ideation is the process used to come up with an original or creative idea. Ideation sessions are used for new-product development and naming, positioning, strategic planning, cost cutting, and reengineering, as well as the development of advertising big ideas. William Miller, president of Global Creativity in Austin, Texas, says everybody falls into one of four innovation styles:[12]

- *Envision:* Those who envision focus on the end result and work toward a vision of what they want to create.
- *Modify:* Those who modify prefer to take things one step at a time, examine components of problems, and build on what they already know.
- *Experiment:* People who experiment like to troubleshoot, test, and answer questions about their products or target markets.
- *Explore:* People who explore thrive on the unknown and have a sense of adventure.

Brainstorming: A creative-thinking technique using free association in a group environment to stimulate inspiration.

PRINCIPLE In brainstorming, seek quantity but defer judgment.

Brainstorming is an ideation technique developed in the early 1950s by Alex Osborn of BBDO. Brainstorming uses associative thinking in a group context. Osborn would get a group of six to ten people together in his agency and ask them to come up with ideas. One person's ideas would stimulate someone else, and the combined power of the group associations stimulated far more ideas than any one person could think of alone. The secret to brainstorming is to remain positive. The rule is to defer judgment. Negative thinking during a brainstorming session can destroy the informal atmosphere necessary to achieve a novel idea.

Another type of divergent thinking uses such comparisons as analogies and metaphors, as in the Wrigley's ad (Ad 13.3). Young's definition of an idea also called for the ability to see new patterns or relationships. This is what happens when you think in analogies. You are saying that one pattern is like or similar to another totally unrelated pattern. William J.J. Gordon, a researcher in the area of creative thinking, discovered in his research that new ideas were often expressed as analogies. He has developed a program called Synectics that trains people to approach problem solving by applying analogies.[13]

MANAGING THE CREATIVE PROCESS

Management styles and the agency atmosphere are both very important factors in nurturing creativity and they vary tremendously across agencies. Some are rule-by-fear shops with threats of firing, barracuda-like colleagues swimming on your flanks, and screaming bosses who try to terrorize you into brilliant thinking. Needless to say, that approach doesn't work very well. Some agencies are businesslike, with endless rules and rigid work procedures. While that may impress clients, rigid procedures don't add much to the creative process either. The Inside Advertising box explains the philosophies of creative directors who manage this process.

---

[12]Chad Rubel, "Brainstorming Not the Only Path to Ideas," *Marketing News* (March 25, 1996):2.
[13]W.J.J. Gordon, *The Metaphorical Way of Learning and Knowing* (Cambridge: Penguin Books, 1971).

THE CD: DEN MOTHER, COACH, AND DICTATOR

If an agency's product is its creative work, then it follows that its most important player is the director in charge of that product—the creative director (CD)—who is the person responsible for the care and feeding of an agency's creative talent. Success at the job is fairly clear-cut: to create ads whose success is judged by the number of award show trophies in the agency's showcase as well as by sound sales figures, and the praise of clients. It may be clear-cut, but it's not easy.

Adweek described this person as "den mother, psychologist, cheerleader, arbiter of taste, basketball coach, team player, dictator, historian, jack-of-all-trades, showman, social chairman, architect, designer and Renaissance man [woman]" and continued that today's CD is also required to be "strategist, businessman, planner, financier, and new product developer." The following is a collection of viewpoints by some of the leading creative directors in the business:

- Jay Schulberg, vice chairperson and chief CD at Bozell, believes great creativity only comes from great people. He advises, "Hire not only talented people, but nice, decent people who you would like to be around eight hours a day, who will bond together as a team. Avoid strutting egomaniacs who think they are terrific and everyone else is a pair of hands; stifle office politics; jettison back stabbers and malcontents quickly. Real teamwork transcends the writer, art director, and producer. It's the whole team—account management, creative, media and strategic planning."

- When Bill Westbrook, Fallon McElligott, took over as CD, one of the first things he did was to emphasize the importance of strategy. "If it's not a great strategy, it's not a great campaign." Westbrook also believes that to advance a client's business, creatives must understand integration. "Nine out of 10 prospects want to know about our agency's integrated capabilities." He explained, "The CD used to just consider TV and print ads. Today, managing an integrated campaign is different from just doing ads. It requires a whole new way of thinking."

- Lee Clow, chairperson and chief creative officer of TBWA Chiat/Day, Los Angeles, says integration is important but points out that Chiat/Day has been doing it for years. "When we worked for Apple, we did everything from write the manual to design the ads." He feels that integration "is only now evolving into an actual discipline." What's more important for a CD to understand, he feels, is account planning. "As creative directors, we've become joined at the hip with planners."

- Ron Berger, creative partner at Messner Vetere Berger McNamee Schmetterer/Euro RSCG, says that CDs also have to work more closely with account management. In his agency, the creatives even share offices with account executives. "It's symbolic," he explains. "It says to the client, we have a shared viewpoint and responsibility."

- Bill Oberlander, executive creative director at Kirshenbaum and Bond, has set up a series of mini-agencies within his agency, creating teams that have total responsibility over their own accounts, including the bottom line.

- And more from Mike Rogers who is less concerned about his creative people understanding the bottom line, "I'm constantly reminding people about the role of the copywriter and art director." He explains, "They're the creative engineers who build the ads. But what's happening is they're getting more involved with strategy, and they shouldn't be used as account executives. I tell them, 'Your job is to create ads, not do client service.'"

- Mike Rogers, executive vice president and CD at DDB Needham, "There's a swirling vortex of fear that sucks creative people right in, and one of my jobs is to protect my people and allow them to do their jobs."

- Nina DiSesa, executive vice president and executive CD at McCann-Erickson, "Often, people get the job because they're creatively brilliant. But the qualities you have as an award-winning copywriter or art director are completely different from those of a creative director."

Jeff Goodby, partner and CD at Goodby, Silverstein & Partners, has often been identified as one of the best CDs in the business. Here's what others had to say about him:

- "Jeff and Rich were good at keeping the place chaotic to allow spontaneous and different kinds of thinking. It was almost a non-CD approach. They hired people who hated advertising as much as they did." (David O'Hare, CD at Hal Riney)

- "Part of Goodby's attraction is he's one of the best writers we've ever had. And he's one of the best social observers. He's like our very own Tom Wolfe. He does interesting work that has cultural resonance." (Make Hughes, president and CD of the Martin Agency)

And from the legendary Bill Bernbach, founder of Doyle Dane and Bernbach (now DDB Needham) probably the most respected CD ever, "Our job is to sell our clients' merchandise . . . not ourselves. Our job is to kill the cleverness that makes us shine instead of the product. Our job is to simplify, to tear away the unrelated, to pluck out the weeds that are smothering the product message."

Sources: Adapted from Ann Cooper, "Bernbach's Children Come of Age," *Adweek* (March 25, 1996):33–37; and Jay Schulberg, "Sell the Client's Product, Not Just the Creativity: Bozell at 75," *Advertising Age* (April 8, 1996):c18–c20.

Many agencies are experimenting with new ways to manage the creative process, encouraging whatever it takes to develop ideas and yet keep the work on schedule and on target. Chiat/Day is recreating itself as a "virtual office," which means an office that can be anywhere. The creative people can work wherever they want to work—at home, on a mountaintop, in the middle of a busy city. As long as they are attached to the office by a fax machine and phone line, they can do their work however and wherever they work best.

BBDO's experiments with small, independent creative teams is one way to break down the anonymity and bureaucracy of a big agency and bring the creative people to the front line of the business. The Pepsi campaign is a testimony to the system institutionalized by BBDO chairperson/CEO Phil Dusenberry to ensure that creativity does not get lost in the corridors of the giant agency. Dusenberry has devised a remarkably fluid mechanism for sculpting advertising.[14] Essentially, the agency is constructed as if there were ten or so separate, small advertising shops instead of just one large one. The arrangement allows for radical changes in direction, for on-the-spot invention, and for what Dusenberry calls "terrific accidents."

The creative system at BBDO, refined over time, is designed to protect the fragile creative process, although not fragile egos. Rejection, Dusenberry says, is part of the game. Intense competition among the small, mobile creative teams is blended with an almost complete lack of bureaucracy within the agency. Creative and strategic review boards no longer exist, dropped by Dusenberry to help eliminate the mediocrity that plagued BBDO's work in the 1970s. A direct link between creative teams and the client is nurtured. Pepsi's director of advertising, Marina Hahn, spends the better part of her time in liaison with the agency. And top management at Pepsi talks with top management at BBDO. Because the work is not shrouded in mystery and clients are made a part of the process, they seem to trust the agency. That translates into a latitude to experiment.

CREATIVE STRATEGY

There are two dimensions to the creative side of an advertisement: the creative concept and its execution. Creative strategy determines *what* the message says and the execution details *how* it is said. Creative strategy, however, is based on the overall advertising strategy, which was discussed in Chapter 7, so you might review that chapter as a reminder of how the creative work dovetails with other critical aspects of advertising planning.

What is said in an advertisement is determined by a strategic platform called a *creative brief, work plan,* or *blueprint.* This document presents and explains the logic behind the ad message, the creative concept, and the executional details that bring the idea to life. Since effective advertising is built on strategy, it is important to understand how different strategies affect the creative options and how the creative idea mirrors the strategy. A long-running campaign by New York's Goldsmith/Jeffrey for Everlast targets series fitness fanatics who wear Everlast clothing and takes punches at those in the lightweight fitness crowd who are more comfortable drinking a cup of cappuccino. (See Ad 13.6.)

It is also important to understand how strategy can get in the way of creative thinking. There is a real danger in focusing too heavily on the marketing objectives and ignoring the need for original, novel ideas. Strategy hypnosis, an extreme concentration on strategy, can stifle creative thinking. The environment can also block creative thinking. Bureaucracy, specialization, and time clocks can all hinder the spirit of exploration and playfulness necessary for creative thinking.

---

[14]Betsy Sharkey, "Super Angst," *Adweek* (January 25, 1993):24–33.

AD 13.6

GOLDSMITH/JEFFREY TARGETS
SERIOUS ATHLETES FOR ITS
EVERLAST SPORTS CLOTHING.

To claim that only tough guys wear Everlast is probably a generalization.
However, it's doubtful many start the day with a croissant and a cup of cappuccino.

EVERLAST

TYPES OF MESSAGES

Different types of strategies take different types of message design—figuring out what to say and how to say it. The strategy is first of all a reflection of the product and its product category. Some kinds of products such as clothes, jewelry, and cosmetics are fashion items, and their advertising often makes its own fashion statement. Some products are just naturally difficult to advertise such as hemorrhoid treatments and feminine hygiene products.

Fishing line is another product that most people would find uninspiring; however, the creative people at Carmichael Lynch have built an award-winning campaign for Stren fishing line using the line in a variety of situations—sewing up dungarees, pulling a tooth, lassoing a calf, and holding pants up over a beer belly—complete with a nice bow. Everything except fishing is featured in this campaign, which demonstrates the fishing line's durability in very novel and unexpected ways.

PACKAGED-GOODS ADVERTISING

Other kinds of advertising are for products used in the home (cleansers, light bulbs), for personal care (toothpaste, toilet paper and tissue, laxatives, cold remedies), or for sustenance (food of all kinds including snacks and soft drinks). In Europe these are described as *fast-moving consumer goods* (fmcg); in the United States they are called *packaged goods*. Advertising for these products can range from the basic problem solution (ring around the collar, toilet bowl, or sink) to fun (the Pepsi Generation and the Pillsbury Doughboy).

In explaining the difference that the product category makes in the type of advertising used—and in defense of the Chicago School of advertising with its "family values" approach—Ralph Rydholm, chairperson/CEO of Tatham Euro RSCG, said, "Seventy percent of what we advertise in Chicago, we put in our mouths. You want warm wholesome images for things you put in your mouth, not cold, angular, sharp, fast images for things you put in your mouth."[15]

By "things you put in your mouth," Rydholm means food. Other "in your mouth" categories include beverages, beer, fast food, vitamins, over-the-counter medicines, cigarettes, and toothpaste. The Chicago-based Leo Burnett agency is a good example of an agency that handles both product categories and "family value" creative ideas. It has created the Jolly Green Giant, the Pillsbury Doughboy, Tony the Tiger, and Charlie the Tuna as well as that giant icon of Americana,

---

[15]Beth Heitzman, "For Chicago Advertising: School's Out," *Adweek* (November 1, 1993):18–20.

the Marlboro cowboy. "We don't have a lot of clients in the categories that look for the cutting edge work—travel, high tech, fashion, and automotive," Rydholm explained. "We work for leading companies that make things for everybody and we write ads for people, not just for people in the ad business."

Some packaged-goods advertising is considered dull because it delivers a message about products that aren't considered very exciting, but Marshall Ross, executive creative director CME-KHBB, explains that is what makes a creative challenge. He also feels that's where the Chicago School is strong. "When you see a spot that's well done for a can of peas—and some agencies are doing good work here for those kinds of products—you realize it can be done, and that's what we need to strive for as an agency community."

PUBLIC SERVICE ADVERTISING

Public service advertising and pro bono ads involve a different, more emotional or punchier style. *Pro bono ads* are done for free or for a very small fee for nonprofit groups and firms too small to have much of an advertising budget. Agencies like such clients because they will usually let the agency be as free and creative as it can be, unfettered by the restrictions of strategy statements and budget approvals. These ads are showcased in award shows. Some agencies, like Fallon-McElligott in Minneapolis, have built their creative credentials on such work. The agency is very frank in admitting it originally set out to win as many awards as possible in order to get the attention of major advertisers outside of Minneapolis. The strategy worked and the agency has helped to build the reputation of Minneapolis as a center for creative advertising.

Not all public service advertising is for small clients and many times the creative ideas, given the heart-tugging message platform, are very strong. One campaign that has won many creative awards over the years is "The Truth" campaign for the Massachusetts Department of Public Health's Tobacco Control Program. The campaign targets teenagers and 20-somethings with an appeal to their vanity. In one ad, Pamela Laffin, a Massachusetts woman who started smoking at 10, tells of her struggles with lung disease and surgery. In the gritty black-and-white photography, she looks at least 45 years old. At the end, she reveals she is only 26. "I started smoking to look older," she says. "And I'm sorry to say, it worked."[16]

An example of an industry-related public service advertisement is the one explaining misleading ads, which was developed by Bozell for the National Advertising Division of the Council of Better Business Bureaus (see Ad 13.7).

HARD AND SOFT SELL

In addition to the product category, there are other message design decisions that affect how the execution is shaped. Advertisements are designed to touch either the head or the heart. These two approaches are also called *hard sell* and *soft sell*. A **hard sell** is a rational, informational message that is designed to touch the mind and create a response based on logic. The approach is direct and emphasizes tangible product features and benefits. Hard-sell messages try to convince the consumer to buy because the product is very good, better, or best. An example of this approach is a commercial for Cheer laundry detergent, which shows a mother and her teenage son arguing about the laundry. The son concedes to his mother when he sees how All-Temperature Cheer removes the dirt from his shirts of different colors and different fabrics.

Soft sell uses an emotional message and is designed around an image intended to touch the heart and create a response based on feelings and attitudes. The subtle, intriguing, and ambiguous commercials Jordache, Calvin Klein, and Guess jeans produce illustrate how advertisers sell moods and dreams more than

Hard Sell: A rational, informational message that emphasizes a strong argument, and calls for action.

Soft Sell: An emotional message that uses mood, ambiguity, and suspense to create a response based on feelings and attitudes.

[16]"Telling 'The Truth' About Smoking," *Adweek* (November 25, 1996):12.

AD 13.7

PUBLIC SERVICE ADS CAN BE
JUST AS CREATIVE AS PRODUCT
ADVERTISING.

MISLEADING ADS CAN RUN BUT THEY CAN'T HIDE.

Member of Congress_____
Signature_____
Address_____
_____
Name of Advertiser_____
When Advertising Appeared_____
Where Advertising Appeared (TV, Magazine, Etc.)
_____
Why You Consider the Advertising Misleading_____
_____
_____
_____
_____
_____
_____
_____
_____
_____
_____
_____
_____

Mail to: The Director, NAD, 845 Third Avenue, New York, N.Y. 10022

The National Advertising Division of the Council of Better Business Bureaus continues to invite members of Congress to help us identify national advertisers who run misleading or false advertising.

Since 1971, the NAD has resolved more than 2,500 complaints. In over half of the cases, the advertising investigated has been modified or discontinued as a result.

If the NAD fails to achieve a resolution, the case is appealed to the National Advertising Review Board. In almost 20 years of operation, the NARB has never failed to resolve a case.

If you encounter an ad you believe is misleading, send us the information in writing. Your complaint will receive a quick reply and will be handled at no cost to the taxpayer. You will be informed of the results.

Let's continue to work together to protect the public. And to protect advertisers who tell the truth.

THE NATIONAL ADVERTISING DIVISION OF THE COUNCIL OF BETTER BUSINESS BUREAUS

product features. A soft sell can be used for hard products. For example, if you were designing an ad for an auto-parts store, you might be inclined to take a rational, informative approach. However, NAPA auto parts ran an emotional ad that showed a dog sitting at a railroad-track crossing, forcing a truck to break hard to avoid hitting him as a train bears down on the scene. The slogan puts the heart-stopping visual story into perspective: "NAPA because there are no unimportant parts."

The research firm McCollum/Spielman has found that although the emphasis today is on soft-sell advertising, hard-sell messages have not become extinct. In a random two-hour viewing of afternoon soap operas, researchers counted 36 hard-sell commercials out of a total of approximately 42 commercials run during the period. In a different study the company found that although hard-sell commercials might be less arresting than soft sell, nearly two-thirds of those studied enjoy acceptable levels of brand awareness. They also discovered that hard sell was clearly more persuasive than soft sell.

Lecture: Instruction delivered verbally to present knowledge and facts.

LECTURES AND DRAMAS

Most advertising messages use a combination of two basic literary techniques: lecture and drama. A **lecture** is a serious, structured instruction given verbally by a

Drama: A story built around characters in a situation.

teacher. A **drama** is a story or play built around characters in some situation. Both techniques are used in advertising.

Lectures are a form of direct address. Stylistically, the speaker addresses the audience from the television or written page. The audience receives the message "at a distance." The speaker presents evidence (broadly speaking) and employs such techniques as an argument to persuade the audience. Some lectures work by borrowing expertise from authority figures or experts in certain technical areas, such as Michael Jordan for Nike, and Chuck Yeager (a former test pilot) for Delco automobile parts. Compared with unknown presenters, such "authorities" are more likely to attract audience respect and attention.

Because advertising lectures work by presenting facts, they face the same kinds of problems schoolteachers face. The audience often becomes distracted by other matters, discounts part or all of the evidence, makes fun of the source, or disputes every point. In many cases these responses dilute or even cancel the message the advertiser wants to convey. Lectures do not have to be dull, however.

One advantage of lectures is that they cost less to produce. Another is that they are more compact and efficient. A lecture can deliver a dozen selling points in seconds, if need be. Because the current trend is toward shorter commercials, lectures may become more common because they are so efficient—it takes time to set up a dramatic scene and introduce characters. A third advantage of lectures is that they get right to the point. A lecture can be perfectly explicit, whereas drama relies on the viewer to make inferences.

A drama is a form of indirect address, like a movie or a play. In a drama the characters speak to each other, not to the audience. In fact, they usually behave as though the audience were not there. Members of the audience observe and sometimes even participate vicariously in the events unfolding in the story. They are "eavesdroppers." Like fairy tales, movies, novels, parables, and myths, advertising dramas are essentially stories about how the world works. Viewers learn from these commercial dramas by inferring lessons from them and by applying those lessons to their everyday lives. Packard Bell used a drama format to play off the old Stanley and Livingston rescue story to introduce its videoconferencing feature. The headline, which used an antique looking typeface, said, "Stanley plodded through the equatorial jungle risking malaria, venomous spiders and ankle-biting pygmies just for the face-to-face greeting, 'Dr. Livingstone, I presume?'"

A commercial drama can be very powerful. The source of the power is the viewer's involvement in the story development. When a drama rings true, the viewer "joins" in it, draws conclusions from it, and applies those conclusions to his or her own life. From the viewer's perspective, conclusions drawn from dramas are "mine," whereas conclusions urged in lectures are "ideas that other people are trying to impose on me."

PRINCIPLE Stress the inherent drama of the product.

One important thing to remember is that the drama should be inherent to the product. In other words, don't tell a cute or funny story just to be entertaining. There is a drama in every product, and the product must be central to the drama. The tendency in using drama is to forget or downplay the point of the ad. Even with dramatic forms, you still need a solid selling premise.

Many television commercials combine lecture and drama. One common format begins as a drama, which is then interrupted by a short lecture from the announcer, after which the drama concludes. An example of this is the classic Charlie the Tuna ads. Charlie is a cartoon character who is always being placed in some situation where he aspires to "good taste." The commercials then turn to real-life product shots of tuna fish being used in meals while the announcer explains the quality of Starkist tuna. The commercials close with Charlie once again realizing he is not good enough for Starkist, but vowing to keep trying.

CREATIVE EXECUTIONS

We have discussed the creative concept and how creative ideas are born; now let's move on to the execution factors that also contribute to the relevance, originality, and impact of the advertising. The execution details are the specifics about how the message is designed in the advertising. Although doing anything in a standardized way is not likely to lead to breakthrough advertising, there is still a set of fairly standard ways to discuss the way the messages are presented. These are formulas or formats. In addition, the tone of the advertising is also a function of its execution. Finally, we will look at the way the words and pictures are handled in the execution in order to demonstrate how these two dimensions work together in effective advertising.

ADVERTISING FORMATS

Advertisers use a number of common format formulas for advertising messages. These include straightforward and factual messages, demonstrations, comparisons, humor, problem solution, slice of life, and spokesperson.

In a *straightforward factual* message, the advertisement usually conveys information without using any gimmicks or embellishments. Such ads are rational rather than emotional. Cigarette advertisements that make claims about low tar, for example, are usually presented in a straightforward manner. Business-to-business advertising also is generally factual in tone.

Volvo, BMW, and Saab use straightforward factual copy for their cars. For example, in one BMW ad, the headline simply reads: "How purists tell a future classic from a contemporary antique." In contrast, other car companies use beauty shots of their cars against pretty backgrounds such as mountains, deserts, or beaches.

Two other types of message formats that are usually straightforward and rational in tone are *demonstrations* and *comparisons*. The demonstration focuses on how to use the product or what it can do for you. The product's strengths take center stage. In demonstration seeing is believing, so conviction is the objective. Demonstration can be a very persuasive technique.

A comparison contrasts two or more products and usually finds the advertiser's brand to be superior. The comparison can be direct, in which a competitor is mentioned, or indirect, with just a reference to "other leading brands." Advertising experts debate the wisdom of mentioning another product in comparative advertising, particularly if it is a category leader. A direct comparison has to be handled carefully, or you may find your expensively purchased time or space is simply increasing your competition's awareness level.

Substantiation is critical in *comparative advertising*, which positions one product against another. Companies have gone bankrupt and agencies have been fired for the sloppy use of comparative information. The following factors identified by law expert Douglas Wood in his book, *Please Be Ad-Vised*, are considered by the Federal Trade Commission (FTC) in challenges against advertisers and agencies for false and deceptive advertising:[17]

1.   *The type of product advertised:* The level of substantiation is higher in advertising for drugs, foods, or other potentially hazardous consumer products.
2.   *The type of claim made:* A higher level of substantiation is required for ads that make health, medical, dietary, or safety claims, rather than generalized statements regarding product performance.
3.   *The benefits of a truthful claim:* If a product is beneficial to consumers, such as

---

[17]Douglas Wood, "Protect Yourself," *Brandweek* (September 18, 1995):30–37.

a very low interest rate on a mortgage, the FTC will tolerate a lower level of substantiation.

4.   *The ease of developing substantiation:* The FTC considers how costly and difficult it is to obtain substantiation, particularly in conjunction with factor 3.

5.   *The consequences of a false claim:* The FTC requires a high level of substantiation if personal injury, property damage, or extensive monetary loss may result from relying on the claim.

6.   *The amount of substantiation:* The FTC tries to determine what the experts in the industry—the drug industry and the FDA, for example—consider to be a reasonable level of substantiation.

In the *problem-solution* technique, also known as the *product-as-hero* technique, the message begins with a problem, and the product is presented as the solution to that problem. This is a common technique used with cleansers and additives that make things run more smoothly. Automotive products often use problem solution. The Wrigley's ad (Ad 13.3) highlights a problem for smokers on airplanes—smoking is prohibited—and proposes a solution: Chew gum instead. A variation is the problem-avoidance message where the problem is avoided because of product use. This is a form of threat appeal. It is often used to advertise insurance and personal care products.

The *slice of life* commercial is an elaborate version of a problem-solution message presented in the form of a little drama. It uses a commonplace situation with "typical people" talking about the problem. Procter & Gamble (P&G) is particularly well known for its reliance on the slice-of-life technique. The P&G version puts the audience in the position of overhearing a discussion wherein the problem is stated and resolved. There is something very compelling about listening in on a conversation and picking up some "tip." The tip, of course, is a P&G product. Kathleen Sullivan, a former network news reporter, began a series of testimonial ads for Weight Watchers that had her going through the Weight Watchers regime. The idea was that if a former beauty queen and television celebrity could benefit from the Weight Watchers program, then anyone could. The ads followed her through the weeks of diet planning and "weigh-ins" to track her success.

PRINCIPLE The spokesperson should not overpower the product.

Using a person to speak on behalf of the product is another popular message technique. *Spokespersons* and *endorsers* are thought to build credibility. They are either celebrities we admire, experts we respect, or someone "just like us" whose advice we might seek out. One of the problems with a spokesperson strategy is that the person may be so glamorous or so attractive that the message gets lost. Although anyone can be a spokesperson, endorsers usually fall into one of four categories:

1.   A created character like the Pillsbury Doughboy or the Energizer bunny
2.   A celebrity like Ray Charles for Diet Pepsi or Bill Cosby for Jell-O
3.   An authority figure like a doctor for an over-the-counter drug product
4.   A typical user who represents as closely as possible the targeted audience

Testimonial: An advertising format in which a spokesperson describes a positive personal experience with the product.

A **testimonial** is a variation of the spokesperson message format. The difference is that people who give testimonials are talking about their own personal experiences with the product. Their comments are based on personal use, which has to be verifiable or the message will be challenged as deceptive.

TONE

PRINCIPLE Write to someone you know and match the tone of voice to the situation.

Because it is written as if it were a conversation, advertising copy can also be described in terms of *tone of voice*. In developing a statement of message strategy, copywriters are often asked to describe the tone of the ad. Most ads are written as if an anonymous announcer were speaking. Even with anonymity, however, there may be an identifiable tone of voice. Some ads are angry, some are pushy, some are friendly, others are warm or excited.

ATTITUDE

Message tone, like tone of voice when you speak to someone, reflects the emotion or attitude behind the ad. Ads can be funny, serious, sad, fearful. Recently *attitude* has become a synonym for a style of advertising that is in your face, or even abrasive. Pepsi used a series of attitude commercials featuring some Generation X personalities and their wacky, irreverent lifestyles to reclaim its ties to a young, hip generation. In one a sociologist muses about youth in the serious nineties. As he spins out theories of introspection, moderation, and the return to "quiet elegance," the camera grabs kids in various states of excess proving that every wacky thing that has been said about Generation X is true.

Although most of the 1980s and early 1990s were fairly serious and stimulated generally conservative and inoffensive advertising, that seems to be changing in the mid-1990s, when attitude is creeping into advertising in a backlash against the self-righteous enforcers of correct thinking. The in-your-face style of Rush Limbaugh and Howard Stern have opened the door for freer expression on some previously taboo—politically incorrect—topics.

Advertising is usually slow to pick up on such cultural trends, but an ad for Rib Ticklers barbecue sauce by Seattle-based Cole & Weber is sure to offend both the animal rights movement and vegetarians. With a children's choir singing in the background, the commercial begins with an ode to barnyard animals—the cow, the chicken, the lamb. Then a barbecue grill appears silhouetted against a brilliant blue sky and the announcer says, "Let's eat them."

HUMOR

PRINCIPLE Humor should focus attention on the selling point.

The copy strategy behind using humor is the hope that people will transfer the warm feelings they have as they are being entertained to the product. Humor is hard to handle, however. Although everyone appreciates a good joke, not everyone finds the same joke funny. Some advertising experts advise against using humor because of the danger it will overpower the brand identification—people will remember the punch line and forget the product name. This was the long-time philosophy of David Ogilvy, founder of the Ogilvy & Mather agency, although he has changed his opinion in recent years and is now saying some humor, if deftly handled, is acceptable.

For a humorous ad to be effective, the selling premise must center around the point of the humor. Humor should never be used to poke fun at the product or its users. One campaign character who consistently scores well with the public is the Energizer bunny who shows up in the middle of other television spots, parody programs, and vintage movies.

WORDS AND PICTURES

PRINCIPLE What you show can speak more effectively than what you say.

Two of the most important factors in the execution are the words and the pictures—and that's true in both print and broadcast advertising. Even radio can evoke mental pictures through suggestive or descriptive language and sound effects. Typically advertising planners and researchers focus on the words when they consider the effectiveness of advertising (through copy testing), and yet there is substantial evidence that the vast majority of all advertising communication received occurs nonverbally. An increasing number of advertising effectiveness studies focus on the visual imagery in the advertising.

Research has proven that well-integrated advertising where the words and pictures work together to present the creative concept is most effective. But within the frame of the creative concept, keep in mind that words and pictures also do different things.

Visuals are thought to be better at getting attention, although words can be strong if they are bold and don't have to compete with the visual. Pictures also communicate faster than words. A picture is seen instantaneously, but verbal communication must be deciphered word by word, sentence by sentence, line by line.

Visuals are also thought to be easier to remember, although some verbal phrases can make a long-term impression, such as "I love you, man"—which is why slogans are so important. Many people remember messages as visual fragments. These are key images that people lock into their minds. You probably remember the word *home* in terms of the image of a specific house in which you have lived. Most of us remember a print ad in terms of how it looked. A television commercial is remembered for some key visual image that is just a section or fragment of the entire commercial. It is the power of this visual image that makes an ad easy to remember and creates effective impact.

Before deciding whether to emphasize words or pictures, a creative team has to consider the underlying strategy for the ad. For example, if the message is complicated, if the purchase is deliberate and well considered, or if the ad is for a high-involvement product, then the more information the better, and that means using words. If you are doing reminder advertising or trying to establish a brand image, then you may want to put less emphasis on words and more on the visual impression. Undifferentiated products with low inherent interest are often presented with an emphasis on the visual message.

THE POWER OF THE VISUAL

An ad for Saab demonstrates the power of the visual by deliberately avoiding nearly all copy. The picture is taken from inside a car on a winding highway, looking over the driver's hands. The headline reads: "What we could tell you about the Saab 900 in the space below is no substitute for ten minutes in the space above." The "space below" where the body copy would normally be found was left blank in the layout.

The Benetton ads are great examples of strong visuals that make a lasting impression as well as an editorial statement. Benetton has used a controversial campaign that features a picture of a white man's hand and a black man's hand handcuffed together as well as a nun and a priest kissing, and a dying AIDS patient surrounded by his family.

The global marketer is known for using strong visuals to draw symbolic parallels between its multicolor and multicultural apparel and larger world issues, such as racial harmony. These parallels are confirmed through the company's slogan, "United Colors of Benetton." In the early 1990s Benetton toned down the campaign with a series of ads that promoted brotherhood. The campaign used more subtle and safe imagery, such as cute black and white children and a white dog paw-in-paw with a black cat. Later that year Benetton ads became less subtle, however. One ad showed test tubes filled with blood, labeled with the names of world leaders, to show that all people are the same. Benetton's more recent campaigns have moved back into other issue-oriented areas such as AIDS and overpopulation, as the company continues to make a statement about being socially conscious.

Different people respond to words and pictures in different ways. When you think of a car, do you think of an image or a word? Some people are highly visual and automatically think and remember in images; others are more verbal and would respond with a word like *Ford* or *Ferrari*.

Research involving print advertising has found that more than twice as many magazine readers are captured by a picture in an ad as by the headline. Furthermore, the bigger the illustration, the higher the attention-getting power of the advertisement. Ads with pictures are noticed more than are ads composed entirely of type. Ads with pictures also tend to pull more readers into the body copy. In other words, the initial attention is more likely to turn to interest with a strong visual. Similar research with television has found that the pictorial elements of a television commercial are better remembered than are the words.

EFFECTIVE CREATIVITY

Advertising also has to be effective; in other words, the creative ideas are used in support of the strategy and the selling message. Advertising can be considered effective only after it has been evaluated in some way. The McCollum Spielman research firm has determined the characteristics of effective creative messages based on 25 years of research (see Table 13.1).

Evaluating the effectiveness of their work is a problem for some creatives in advertising who may lack an understanding of strategy and an ad's objectives. They are frequently at a loss for words when asked how well their advertising fared in the marketplace. They are more interested in winning awards than in achieving sales objectives. The legendary Bill Bernbach reminds the creative person to make the product—not the author—shine:

> Merely to let your imagination run riot, to dream unrelated dreams, to indulge in graphic acrobatics and verbal gymnastics is not being creative. The creative person has harnessed his imagination. He has disciplined it so that every thought, every idea, every word he puts down, every line he draws, every light and shadow in every photograph makes more vivid, more believable, more persuasive the product advantage.[18]

One problem is the risk-averse nature of many large organizations—both agencies and clients. It is difficult to evaluate a new idea because you don't have any benchmarks; it is easier to evaluate ideas that have been used before because you know how they were received. Consequently, a manager will use a proven formula for an ad, knowing that the approach is safe and the ad probably won't fail, even though it may not be highly successful either. A new approach is always a gamble. The creative person who tries a new idea may be dismissed as lucky if the ad is successful or incompetent if it fails. In such an environment creative people often choose to play it safe when working with a multimillion-dollar investment.

[18]Bill Bernbach, *Bill Bernbach Said* (New York: Doyle Dane Bernbach International).

TABLE 13.1	TWELVE CREATIVE HOT BUTTONS

What is good creative? Here are the 12 recurring qualities found in the most sales-effective advertising McCollum Spielman has measured, 25 years and some 25,000 copy tests later.

1. Brand rewards/benefits are highly visible through demonstration, dramatization, lifestyle, feelings, or analogy.
2. The brand is the major player in the experience (the brand makes the good times better).
3. The linkage between brand and execution is clear (scenario revolves around and highlights the brand).
4. The execution has a focus (there's a limit to how many images and vignettes the consumer can process).
5. Feelings (emotional connectives) are anchored to the needs and aspirations of the targeted consumer.
6. Striking, dramatic imagery is characteristic of many successful executions, enhancing their ability to break out of clutter.
7. An original, creative signature or mystique exists in many of the best commercials, to bond the consumer to the brand and give it a unique personality.
8. In food and beverage advertising, high taste appeal is almost always essential.
9. The best creative ideas for mature brands frequently employ fresh new ways of revitalizing the message.
10. Music (memorable, bonded tunes and lyrics) is often integral to successful executions for many brands.
11. When humor is used, it is relevant, with clear product purpose.
12. When celebrities are employed, they are well matched to brands, have credibility as users/endorsers and their delivery is believably enthusiastic.

Source: McCollum Spielman Worldwide, *Topline* (October 1993):2.

Another problem in evaluating the contribution of the creative dimension is the attitude of some managers who scorn the use of the word *creative* because they feel it deflects people's attention away from the purpose of the advertising, which is to persuade and sell. Most copy testing, which reflects this viewpoint, is focused on persuasiveness and recall (awareness) measures. A hint that there might be another factor appeared in a study by the Advertising Research Foundation.[19] It was found that liking may be just as important, if not more so, than persuasion and recall. This finding has been treated as heresy by the hard-nosed persuade-and-sell managers. It did open the door, however, to a broader view of what makes an advertisement effective and makes it possible to do a more thorough evaluation of what the creative dimension really contributes to advertising effectiveness.

Good creative people know that every advertising message is up against a cluttered environment and a generally indifferent audience. The only way to break through is to express the selling message in an original, fresh way. In other words, dull advertising can be persuasive but it will rarely get the attention of the audience. Breakthrough advertising, to be effective, has to be both persuasive and creative.

---

[19]Russell I. Haley, "The ARF Copy Research Validity Project," *Journal of Advertising Research* (April/May 1991):11–32; Cyndee Miller, "Study Says 'Likability' Surfaces as Measure of TV Ad Success," *AMA Newsletter* (January 1, 1991):6.

$\mathscr{S}$UMMARY

- The big idea is the creative concept around which the entire advertising campaign revolves and behind the creative concept is the execution of the idea, which also has to be handled creatively.

- A creative concept must have relevance, originality, and impact.

- All people are born with creative skills.

- Creative people tend to be right-brain, rather than left-brain, dominant. These differences correspond roughly to divergent versus convergent thinking.

- The two basic sales approaches used in advertising are hard sell and soft sell.

- The two basic literary techniques used in advertisements are lectures and dramas. Some ads use a combination of the two.

- Common advertising formats include humor, problem solution, slice of life, spokesperson, straightforward factual, and comparisons and demonstrations.

- Effective copywriting is informal, personal, conversational, and concise. Forced, unnatural writing is referred to as *adese*.

- Advertising has to be effective. That means creativity is used to enhance the strategy of the message.

$\mathscr{Q}$UESTIONS

1. What are some of the major traits of creative people? Which characteristics of the advertising world do you think enhance creativity? Which discourage it?

2. Find a newspaper or magazine advertisement that you think is bland and unexciting. Rewrite it, first to demonstrate a hard-sell approach, and then to demonstrate a soft-sell approach.

3. One of the challenges for creative ad designers is to demonstrate a product whose main feature cannot be seen by the consumer. Suppose you are an art director on an account that sells shower and bath mats with a

patented system that ensures the mat will not slide (the mat's underside is covered with tiny suction cups that grip the tub's surface). Brainstorm for some ways to demonstrate this feature in a television commercial. Find a way that will satisfy the demands of originality, relevance, and impact.

4. Peter Madison, a sophomore in advertising, is speaking informally with a copywriter from a local advertising agency following the writer's class presentation. Peter states his strong determination to be some sort of creative professional once he gets his degree.

"My problem is that I'm a bit shy and reserved. I'm interested in all sorts of stuff, but I'm not really quick in expressing ideas and feelings. I'm not sure my personality is suited for being an advertising creative. How do I know if I've picked the right career direction?" What advice should that writer give Peter?

5. Some time ago a copywriting analyst warned writers that they should be aware of the "ignorance distance" between the writer and the audience. He meant avoiding copy that is either over the heads of the audience or well below the audience's knowledge of the product. What are the copy dangers in speaking above the audience's frame of reference? What are the dangers of underestimating the audience's knowledge? Which of the elements discussed in the "copywriting" section of the chapter would reduce these threats of "ignorance distance"?

SUGGESTED CLASS PROJECT

Divide the class into groups of eight to ten. Each group should find an area to work apart from other groups. Here's the problem: Your community wants to encourage people to get out of their cars and use alternative forms of transportation. How many different creative concepts can your team come up with to express that idea in an advertisement? Brainstorm for 15 minutes as a group, accumulating every possible idea regardless of how crazy or dumb it might initially sound. Have one member be the recorder and list all the ideas as they are mentioned. Then go back through the list as a group and put an asterisk next to the ideas that seem to have the most promise. When all the groups reconvene in class, each recorder should list his or her group's ideas on the blackboard. Cover the board with all the ideas from all the groups. As a class, pick out the three ideas that seem to have the most potential. Analyze the experience of participating in a brainstorming group and compare the experiences of the different teams.

FURTHER READINGS

Baker Stephen, *A Systematic Approach to Advertising Creativity* (New York: McGraw-Hill Book Co., 1979).

De Bono, Edward, *Lateral Thinking: Creativity Step by Step* (New York: Harper and Row, 1970).

Gordon, W.W.J., *The Metaphorical Way of Learning and Knowing* (Cambridge, MA: Penguin Books, 1971).

Marra, James L., *Advertising Creativity: Techniques for Generating Ideas* (Upper Saddle River, NJ: Prentice Hall, 1990).

Michalko, Michael, *Tinkertoys* (Berkeley, CA: Ten Speed Press, 1991).

Young, James Webb, *Technique for Producing Ideas*, 3rd ed. (Chicago: Crain Books, 1975).

Every advertiser knows that consumers respond to vivid images. In the environmental arena, one of the most vivid images of the late 1980s was that of a gigantic, ominous garbage barge traveling up and down the East Coast of the United States seeking a place to disgorge its unwanted cargo. The garbage barge's odyssey, covered every evening on the network news, drove home the size of America's solid waste problem.

The image of the homeless barge helped convince Americans that solid waste disposal is a critical, immediate national issue—more critical and immediate than litter, for example. This rearrangement of national priorities prompted Keep America Beautiful, a nonprofit environmental organization, to reconsider the creative content of its public service announcements. Through the 1970s and 1980s, these announcements had featured Iron Eyes Cody, a Native American. Few could forget the tear running down his cheek as he surveyed once-beautiful lands defiled by litter.

Keep America Beautiful's communication problem was to evoke an image that would be as relevant as the garbage barge and as powerful as Iron Eyes Cody. To help define this new image, Rotando, Lerch & Iafelice, Keep America Beautiful's volunteer advertising agency, commissioned a series of individual, in-depth interviews with a cross section of Americans from a variety of backgrounds. The interviews sought respondents' views on environmental issues, especially the solid waste problem, and their reactions to environmental messages.

The interviews disclosed that, while many Americans were keenly aware of environmental degradation, many felt helpless as individuals. One common reaction was, "Yes, these problems are immediate and serious, but they are overwhelming. I'm just one person. What can I do about them?"

Another common reaction, often from the same respondents, was a peculiar sort of complacency. The reaction was, "Someone else is taking care of it," or "I'm recycling. What more can I do?"

The interviews reinforced the premise that a new, powerful image was needed. The interviews also suggested that while the new image must elicit strong emotional reaction, it must not be totally negative. It must not promote hopelessness or cynicism, but rather offer a ray of hope for the future. Finally, the interviews indicated that concerned citizens wanted specific detailed information. They wanted to know what more they as individuals can do to protect the environment.

The need to convey a powerful but positive image and the need to convey more information than can be covered in a 30-second television commercial led Rotando, Lerch & Iafelice to create a public service announcement that combines a powerful, future-oriented image with an invitation to call or write for action-oriented information. The announcement opens on a closeup of an attractive, happy baby. As the camera pulls back to show that the baby is surrounded by trash, the narration, read by actor Michael Douglas, says, "For future generations, our country is leaving behind our knowledge, our technologies, our values . . . and 190 million tons of garbage every year. Recycling alone just can't do it. Keep America Beautiful is an organization that can do something. We have solutions that have worked in cities and towns across the country. What can you do? More than you think!" The announcement concludes with an invitation to write to Keep America Beautiful or call an 800 number to request a free booklet that explains how individuals can help solve the problem it portrays so graphically.

Adapted from Joseph Rydholm, "Here's Looking At You, Kid," *Quirk's Marketing Research Review*, 7, No. 3 (March 1993):6–7, 28–29.

*Q*UESTIONS

1. One creative option would have been to continue to use Iron Eyes Cody. What are the arguments for and against extending this vivid and familiar image?

2. Another option would have been to use the wandering garbage barge. What are the arguments for and against this possible solution?

3. What do you think of Rotando, Lerch & Iafelice's answer to the image question? Can you think of a better way to address these complex issues?

4. Suppose Keep America Beautiful were to consider Iron Eyes Cody, the garbage barge, the baby, and your idea. How would they be able to tell which was the most effective?

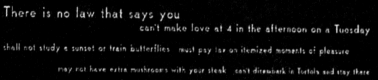

There is no law that says you

        can't make love at 4 in the afternoon on a Tuesday

shall not study a sunset or train butterflies must pay tax on itemized moments of pleasure

    may not have extra mushrooms with your steak can't disembark in Tortola and stay there

must pack worry along with your luggage can't learn about life from a turtle

      must contribute to the GNP every single solitary day of your life

   absolutely must act your chronological age not your shoesize shall contain strict amounts of emotion

can't make love again at 5 in the afternoon on the Tuesday we spoke of earlier

because the laws of the land do not apply the laws are different out here

It's

differ-

out

here.

⊠NORWEGIA

Creating Print Advertising

CHAPTER OUTLINE

- Slow Down and Dream
- Print Advertising
- Writing for Print
- Designing for Print
- Print Production

CHAPTER OBJECTIVES

When you have completed this chapter, you should be able to:

- Distinguish between the key features of newspaper and magazine advertising
- List the various elements of a print ad and their function
- Understand the process by which print ads are created
- Distinguish between letterpress, offset, gravure, and silk-screen printing

SLOW DOWN AND DREAM

In today's frenetic media marketplace, most ads try to get attention by screaming and outyelling each other. An example of a campaign that used print to capture the pace of leisure was one for Norwegian Cruise Lines (NCL) created by Goodby, Silverstein & Partners.

The cruise line's campaign built its strategy on the core ideas of escape and fantasy, rather than on showgirls and mountains of food used by competitors. On a steady decline for several years, NCL not only wanted to recapture market share, it also wanted to attract younger, more upscale people to its cruises.

From focus groups, Goodby, Silverstein found that good service and food were expected on a cruise but were not distinctive since all cruise lines made that promise. What this more upscale target audience wanted was escape, the fantasy of taking an "out of the ordinary" vacation.

The agency created a campaign with the slogan "It's Different Out Here," which delivered the emotional sense of elegance and luxury that comes from living life—and appreciating it—at a slower pace. The tranquility, as Richard Kirshenbaum, executive creative director at Kirshenbaum & Bond, explains is indigenous to print advertising. As a busy executive, he responded to the appeal of the ads because they promised the freedom to stop time: "That's really appealing for somebody like me who's in desperate need of a vacation." (See Ad 14.1.)

The campaign also helped NCL create a brand personality that let the company become the most recognizable cruise line next to Carnival, a competitor that

AD 14.1

A LEADING CREATIVE DIRECTOR POINTS TO THIS NORWEGIAN CRUISE LINE CAMPAIGN AS A GOOD EXAMPLE OF A CREATIVE, BUT YET STRATEGIC, ADVERTISEMENT.

outspent NCL by an 8-to-1 margin. NCL was pleased that the average customer age on its cruises also went down with bookings up 5 percent for the targeted 35–44 age group. In a tough market, NCL reversed its decline with this campaign and filled all its berths for the first time in years.[1]

Print Advertising

This chapter will introduce you to print advertising, which actually covers a variety of forms of advertising—everything from matchbooks to catalogs. In order to focus on the principles of print, however, we concentrate on newspaper and magazine advertising. First, we will look at how the type of print medium interacts with the creative message, as well as the limitations each medium creates.

The foundation of modern advertising message strategy and design lies in the early print formats. The earliest mass-produced commercial messages either appeared in newspapers or as handbills. Thus, many advertising guidelines originated with print, and print techniques, such as headline writing, are still considered basic concepts. Many things have changed over the years. Television has had a tremendous impact on advertising. Visuals, which were limited in the early press to infrequent woodcuts, are now as important as words. Print advertising continues to be important, however, and still serves as a foundation in that its techniques are the easiest to understand and analyze. We will therefore begin our discussion of media and their creative characteristics with newspapers and magazines.

The key elements of print advertising are divided between copy and art. The **copy** elements include headlines, underlines, overlines, subheads, body copy, captions, slogans, and taglines. **Art** refers to the visual elements, which include illustrations or photography, the type, logotypes (logos) and signatures, and the layout itself, which is the arrangement of all the elements.

Copy: The written elements in an ad, including headlines, underlines and overlines, subheads, body copy, captions, slogans, and taglines.

Art: The visual elements in an ad, including illustrations, photos, type, logos and signatures, and the layout.

NEWSPAPER ADVERTISEMENTS

Most people see newspaper advertising as a form of news. In fact, when newspapers have gone on strike, people say what they miss the most are the ads—they have other sources of news—but newspapers are the primary source of local advertising. Newspaper advertising is one of the few forms of advertising that is not considered intrusive. People consult the paper as much to see what is on sale as to find out what is happening in City Hall. For this reason, newspaper advertisements do not have to work as hard as other kinds of advertising to catch the attention of an indifferent audience.

In addition, because the editorial environment of a newspaper is generally more serious than entertaining, newspaper advertisements don't have to compete as entertainment, as television ads do. Therefore, most newspaper advertising is straightforward and newslike. Local retail advertising announces what merchandise is available, what is on sale, how much it costs, and where you can get it.

PRODUCTION CHARACTERISTICS

Newsprint: An inexpensive, tough paper with a rough surface, used for printing newspapers.

Daily newspapers are printed at high speed on an inexpensive, rough-surfaced, spongy paper called **newsprint** that absorbs ink on contact. The demands of speed and low cost have traditionally made newspaper reproduction rather low-quality printing. Newsprint is not a great surface for reproducing fine details, especially photographs and delicate typefaces. Most papers offer color to advertisers,

---

[1]Adapted from Chad Rubel, "Out of Ideas? Try Thinking 'Out of the Dots,'" *Marketing News* (November 6, 1995):19; *Brandweek* Magazine Salutes The 1996 Effies, *Brandweek* Special Advertising Supplement (June 11, 1996):24; and Richard Kirshenbaum, "I Wish I'd Done That Ad," Magazine Publishers of America advertising campaign.

In Register: A precise matching of colors in images.

PRINCIPLE Illustrations reproduce better than photos in newspapers.

Freelance Artists: Independent artists who work on individual assignments for an agency or advertiser.

but because of the limitations of the printing process, the color may or may not be **in register** (aligned exactly with the image).

We are accustomed to seeing news photographs that are somewhat "muddy," but most of us expect better quality in advertising. Although photographs are used in newspaper advertising, illustrations generally reproduce better. Illustrations in newspaper advertisements are bold, simple, and specifically designed to reproduce well within the limitations of the printing process.

Most newspapers subscribe to an artwork service called a *mat service* that sends general and seasonal illustrations directly to the advertising department. This generic art satisfies the needs of most local advertisers. Larger newspapers may have their own graphic artists who are available to local advertisers. Some major advertisers have their own art services through their trade associations, such as banks and savings and loan associations. Large department stores often have an in-house advertising staff that includes artists. Stores also hire **freelance artists,** who provide original art for the store's ads.

This scene is changing, however. *USA Today* has pioneered better-quality reproduction for daily newspapers. Because the paper itself is of better quality, pho-

AD 14.2

BECAUSE OF IMPROVEMENTS IN NEWSPAPER PRINTING TECHNOLOGY, IT IS POSSIBLE TO OFFER MUCH BETTER QUALITY COLOR REPRODUCTION THAN IN THE PAST.

tographs and color reproductions are considerably better than are those found in most newspapers. Significant use of color is an important part of the *USA Today* formula. Many newspapers are upgrading their technology to catch up with *USA Today*, so quality color is more easily available to advertisers now as can be seen in the Ericsson personal telephone ad, which ran as a full-page in *The Wall Street Journal* (see Ad. 14.2).

Even fancy printing techniques are now possible. Some newspaper advertisements include decals and logos that have been printed with a special heat-transfer ink. These can be cut out of the paper and then ironed onto T-shirts. These techniques will be discussed in more detail later in the chapter.

MAGAZINE ADVERTISEMENTS

PRINCIPLE In magazine advertising, speak to readers' special interests.

Advertising that ties in closely with the magazine's special interest may be valued as much as the articles. For example, skiers read the ads in the ski magazines to learn about new equipment, new technology, and new fashions. Readers of professional publications may cut out and file ads away as part of their professional reference library. For this reason, magazine ads are often more informative and carry longer copy than do newspaper ads. Still, despite this built-in interest, ads must catch the attention of the reader who may be more absorbed in an article on the opposite page. To do that, magazine advertising is often more creative than newspaper advertising, using beautiful photography and graphics with strong impact. Magazines are also particularly useful for image advertising, as noted in the opening story on the Norwegian Cruise Line campaign. The Issues and Controversies box explores another technique used by magazine advertisers to catch reader's attention.

PRODUCTION CHARACTERISTICS

PRINCIPLE Color reproduction is better in magazines than in newspapers.

Magazines have traditionally led the way in graphic improvements. The paper is better than newsprint; it is slick, coated, and heavier. Excellent photographic reproduction is the big difference between newspapers and magazines. Magazines do use illustrations, but they employ them to add another dimension, such as fantasy, to the visual message.

Magazine advertisements are also turning to more creative, attention-getting devices such as pop-up visuals, scent strips, and computer chips that play melodies when the pages are opened up.

*W*RITING FOR *P*RINT

Display Copy: Type set in larger sizes that is used to attract the reader's attention.

Body Copy: The text of the message.

In Chapter 13 we talked in general about advertising copywriting. In this chapter we will examine the specific demands of print advertising, both words and pictures. There are two categories of copy: display and body copy, or text. **Display copy** includes all those elements that the reader sees in his or her initial scanning. These elements, usually set in larger type sizes, are designed to get attention and to stop the viewer's scanning. **Body copy,** the text of the message, includes the elements that are designed to be read and absorbed.

HEADLINES

Headline: The title of an ad; it is set in large type to get the reader's attention.

Most experts on print advertising agree that the headline is the most important display element. The **headline** works with the visual to get attention and communicate the creative concept. This big idea is usually best communicated through a picture and words working together. For example, the ads for Microsoft's Internet Explorer kit dramatizes the Microsoft slogan, "Where do you want to go today?" (See Ad 14.3.) The ad only works if you put the words and pictures together. The copy, which is a Web address for an exotic location in India, mirrors the "screen grab" images from the computer. A third page explains how the Microsoft Internet Explorer starter kit makes it easy to surf the Web.

Issues and Controversies

OBSCENITY AND FASHION

Advertisers often joke that they know their ads have made it in the popular culture when spoofs begin to show up in comic strips and comedians' jokes. So when a *Cincinnati Post* editorial cartoonist depicts a bare-legged guy in a trench coat exposing himself to a couple of women walking by and the women respond, "Another Calvin Klein ad," then one might suppose that Calvin Klein is happy. And a series of letters-to-the-editor in *Marketing News* complaining about obscenities in Guess? jeans campaigns might generate a similar response.

The Calvin Klein cartoon spoof was in response to a campaign featuring young teenagers in various suggestive postures with a liberal display of crotch and cleavage that raised an uproar of protest. One observer noted the wood paneling background and the dirty purple carpet, and fluorescent light: the visual connotations (peep shows, back offices, basements, cheap motel rooms) "are too powerful and grim." Characterized as "kiddie porn," readers argued whether or not the ads were exploiting children. Some believed the pictures of the young girls with their skimpy tops, belly buttons showing above their jeans, and white panties were actually not as erotic as the boys in short shorts who are being projected in a crude way as sex pets.

Teenagers, however, often found a different meaning. They noted that their friends often wear pants exposing their underwear. And if you have the body, why not?

From the days of Brooke Shields and her breathy line that nothing comes between her and her Calvins, the company has built a fashion empire by relating to the cultural unease about youthful sexuality.

In defense of the Generation X-rated campaign, Calvin Klein himself explained why the company decided to withdraw the ads. In an interview, he said the ads were completely misunderstood and explained, "People don't get that it's about modern young people who have an independent spirit and do the things they want to and can't be told or sold. None of that came through." The company subsequently released a statement as an ad that tried to defend the advertising strategy on the basis of the kids' "strength of character" and "great ability to know who they are and who they want to be." The ad also salutes the "media savvy" of the younger generation and informs us that "glamour is an inner quality."

Adweek editorializes that the Calvin Klein statement, seen in black and white in a newspaper ad, "just looks stupid." It continues, "Neither a bold defense nor a contrite apology, the Statement expresses nothing more heartfelt than an eagerness to escape from a messy situation."

The Guess? ads use a slightly out-of-focus photo of a model wearing blue eye makeup and bright red lipstick. At first glance she looks as if she's been beaten up. A defender observed that, although the ads are crude and "they have no positive merit in the world of advertising," they do fall short of outright pornography. Tasteless and overly provocative, maybe, but not pornographic, which the writer defines as drawing one to an imagery of nudity, casual sex, and blatant lack of morality.

Adweek closes its attack on Calvin Klein's ads by admitting that even though the ads are cheesy, they do speak a certain truth: "Many a teenager does aspire to be the star of someone else's sexual fantasy."

What do you think: Was this really an out-of-bounds ad campaign or was Calvin Klein right that adults just didn't get it? Should youthful sexual fantasies be used as the stuff of advertisements? Or are these really adult fantasies and are they appropriate for a campaign targeted to teenagers? What are the arguments both for and against the Calvin Klein approach? On what grounds should the go/no go decision be made in a situation such as this?

Sources: Adapted from Kirk Davidson, "Guess? Ads Cross Line from Fashion Art to Pornography," *Marketing News* (October 21, 1996):13; Barbara Lippert, "The Naked Untruth," *Adweek* (September 18, 1995):26; Michele Ingrassia, "Calvin's World," *Newsweek* (September 11, 1995):60–66; and "Pleading Not Guilty on Grounds of Inanity," *Adweek* (September 4, 1995):17.

PRINCIPLE Tell as much of the story in the headline as possible.

The headline, however, is a very important element in print advertising because it pulls the concept together and in most ads carries the responsibility for helping people make sense of the message and get the point of the ad. It's important for another reason. For people who are scanning, they may read nothing more, so the point has to be clear from the headline or the combination of headline and visual. Researchers estimate that only 20 percent of those who read the headline go on to read the body copy.[2] Because headlines are so important, there are some general guidelines for their development and particular functions that they serve. A headline must select the right prospect, stop the reader, identify the product and brand, and start the sale by luring the readers into the body copy.

THE HEADLINE'S FUNCTION

Ideally, a good headline will attract only those who are prospects; there is no sense in attracting people who are not in the market for the product. A good headline selects target audience members by speaking to their interests. An old advertising

---

[2]Philip Ward Burton, *Which Ad Pulled Best?* (Chicago: Crain, 1981).

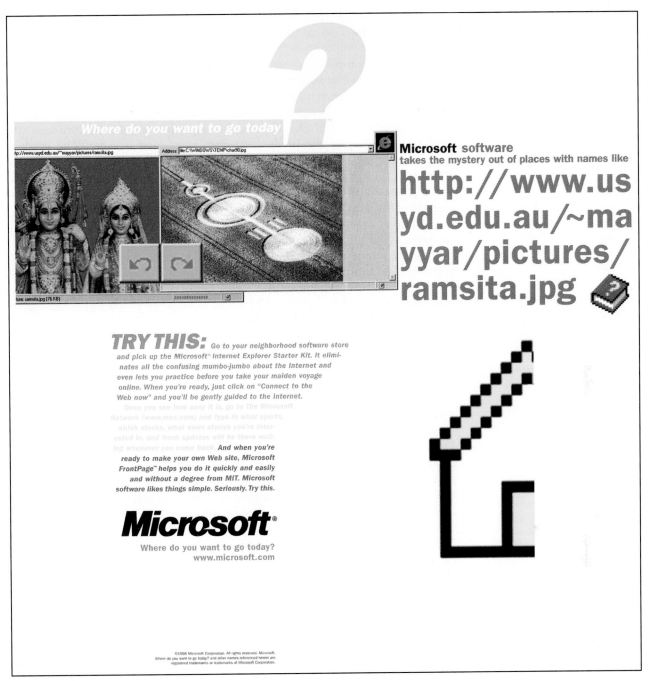

AD 14.3

THIS AD FOR MICROSOFT'S
INTERNET EXPLORER KIT
DEMONSTRATES HOW TO PUT
THE WORDS AND PICTURES
TOGETHER.

axiom is: "Use a rifle, not a shotgun." An example of signaling the target is the long-running Nike women's campaign that uses headlines that begin, "A woman is often measured, . . ." or "You were born a daughter."

Once the prospects have been selected, stopping and grabbing their attention are critical. As discussed in Chapter 8, this responsibility, shared with the visual, is a measure of the strength of the creative concept. An advertisement by Range Rover shows a photo of the car parked at the edge of a rock ledge in Monument Valley with the headline, "Lots of people use their Range Rovers just to run down to the corner."

One way to stop and grab readers is to promise them something. A headline for American Express says "Pressure is off. Weekend is on." The thought is continued in the tagline at the end of the ad, "Now you've got weekend privileges."

Another way is to involve them in completing the message. Involvement techniques can have tremendous impact. Questions can be puzzling, make you think, and invite you to participate in the development of the message. Furthermore, you feel compelled to read on to find out the answer. One of the award-winning ads in the Norwegian Cruise Lines campaign started with a headline that ran on to become the first line of the body copy: "There is no law that says you can't make love at 4 in the afternoon on a Tuesday."

PRINCIPLE Name the brand, if you can, in the headline.

Product and brand identification is very important. At the very least, the headline should make the product category clear to the reader. The headline should answer the question: "What kind of product is this?" The more the brand is tied into the concept, the more likely you are to leave some minimal identification with the 80 percent of the audience who look at the ad, read the headline, and then move on.

PRINCIPLE Telegraph the selling premise in the headline.

Another function of a good headline is to introduce the selling premise. If the strategy calls for a benefit, a claim, a unique selling proposition (USP), a promise, or a reason why, that message should be telegraphed in the headline. If you have a strong sales point, lead with it. For example, even though the execution for an Alpo ad uses soft humor with its picture of a bunch of kittens asleep on an office desk, the headline—"New ALPO Cat Food is the product of exhaustive research"—is still focused solidly on the product.

Finally, a good headline will lead the reader into the body copy. In order for that to happen, the reader has to stop scanning and start concentrating. This need to change the perceptual mode—the "mind-set"—is the reason only 20 percent of scanners become readers.

TYPES OF HEADLINES

Headlines can be grouped into two general categories: direct and indirect action. Direct headlines are straightforward and informative, such as the Tylenol headline about "The Power to Stop Pain." They select the audience with a strong benefit, promise, or reason why. They identify the product category, and they link the brand with the benefit. Direct headlines are highly targeted, but they may fail to lead the reader into the message if they are not captivating enough.

Action techniques include news announcements, assertions, and commands. News headlines obviously are used with new-product introductions, but also with changes, reformulations, new styles, and new uses. An assertion is used to state a claim or a promise. A command headline politely tells the reader to do something. The headline used in an ad for Nike starts out "The body you have is the body you inherited, but YOU MUST DECIDE WHAT TO DO WITH IT." It's an unusual graphic technique since the headline, as indicated by the capital letters, actually falls at the end of the sentence, but it's a good example of a command headline.

Indirect headlines like those used with the Norwegian Cruise Line campaign are not as selective and may not provide as much information, but they may be better at luring the reader into the message. They are provocative and intriguing, and they compel people to read on to find out the point of the message. Indirect headlines use curiosity and ambiguity to get attention and build interest.

Techniques for indirect headlines include questions, how-to statements, challenges, and puzzlements. Challenges and puzzling statements are used strictly for their provocative power. All these techniques require the reader to examine the body copy to get the answer or explanation. Sometimes these indirect headlines are referred to as "blind" because they give so little information. A blind headline is a gamble. If it is not informative or intriguing enough, the reader may move on without absorbing any product name information.

HEADLINE WRITING

Writing a headline is tremendously challenging. Writers will cover notepads with hundreds of headlines and spend days worrying about the wording. Headlines are also carefully tested to make sure they can be understood at a glance and that they communicate exactly the right idea. Split-run tests (two versions of the same ad) in direct mail have shown that changing the wording of the headline, while keeping all other elements constant, can double, triple, or quadruple consumer response. That is why the experts, such as David Ogilvy, state that the headline is the most important element in the advertisement.[3]

OTHER DISPLAY COPY

In addition to headlines, copywriters also craft the subheads and captions that continue to help lure the reader into the body copy. These are considered display copy in that they are usually larger and set in different type (bold or italic) than the body copy. Subheads are sectional headlines and are also used to break up a mass of "gray" type (or type that tends to blur together when one glances at it) in a large block of copy. Captions are very useful in explaining what's happening in photos, since people often find such visuals confusing. Captions also have very high readership.

Slogans and taglines are used for memorability. Product and campaign slogans are repeated from ad to ad. A tagline is a particularly memorable phrase that is used at the end of the ad to wrap up the idea.

Copywriters employ a number of literary techniques to enhance the memorability of slogans and taglines. Some slogans use a startling or unexpected phrase; others use rhyme, rhythm, alliteration (repetition of sounds), or parallel construction (repetition of the structure of a sentence or phrase). This repetition of structure and sounds contributes to memorability. Notice the use of these techniques in the following slogans:

- BMW: "The Ultimate Driving Machine"
- Army: "Be all that you can be"
- *The Wall Street Journal:* "The daily diary of the American dream"

BODY COPY

Like poetry, body copy is very well crafted. Copywriters will spend hours, even days, on one paragraph. They will write a first draft, revise it, then tighten and shorten it. After many revisions the copy gets read by others, who critique it. It then goes back to the writer, who continues to fine-tune it. Body copy for most major ads is revised over and over again. (See Concepts and Applications box.)

PRINCIPLE The headline catches the readers' eye, but the copy wins their heart.

The body copy is the text of the ad, the paragraphs of small type. The content develops the sales message and provides support, states the proof, and gives the explanation. This is the persuasive heart of the message. You excite consumer interest with the display elements, but you win them over with the argument presented in the body copy.

The relationship between the headline and the body copy is important and determines how effective the ad is in arousing interest and stopping the reader's scanning.

TYPES OF BODY COPY

There are as many different kinds of writing styles as there are copywriters and product personalities. Some body copy is straightforward and written in the words of an unknown or unacknowledged source. A narrative style may be used to tell a story, which may be either in the first person or the third person. A dialogue style lets the reader "listen in" on a conversation.

One of the most difficult writing style challenges involves translating technical information, like that written for the high-technology and medical industries,

---

[3]David Ogilvy, *Ogilvy on Advertising* (New York: Vintage Books, 1985).

Concepts and Applications

PACKED WITH IMPACT

An example of the craftsmanship involved in copywriting is the "You were born a daughter" ad from Nike's women's campaign, which reads as if it were a poem. As you read it, notice the use of natural language, personal address, parallel structure, and alliteration and the familiar tagline at the end that ties it back in to Nike's other campaigns:

> *Sooner or later, you start taking yourself seriously.*
> *You know when you need a break. You know*
> *when you need a rest. You know what to get worked*
> *up about, and what to get rid of.*
> *And you know when it's time to take care*
> *of yourself, for yourself. To do something that makes*
> *you stronger, faster, more complete.*
> *Because you know it's never too late to have a life.*
> *And never too late to change one.*
> *Just do it.*

A campaign for Canon Copiers celebrates colors and the way the copier is able to reproduce them. Across a picture of a jungle with lots of ferns and hanging Spanish moss, the copy, which is artfully arranged like a poem across the image, reads:

> *between yellow and green*
> *there's olive.*
>
> > *between olive and gray*
> > *there's fern green.*
> *between fern green and gray*
> *there's slate green.*
>
> > > *and if you*
> > > *keep finding the colors*
> > > *between the colors*
> > > *you get to a color called*
> > > *Moss.*

Good copy can also deliver a selling point about a product feature. In the "Solutions for a Small Planet" campaign, IBM features people at work in faraway places who rely on computers and computer data. With a picture in the background of an archaeological dig in Casablanca, Morocco, the copy said:

> *IN CASABLANCA, A SLIVER OF BONE REVEALED A CHUNK OF HISTORY when Dr. Jean-Jacques Hublin*

unearthed a few fossilized skull fragments. Then Hublin and a team of IBM scientists fed this shattered 3-D jigsaw puzzle into a unique program called Visualization Data Explorer.™ The tiny pieces helped form an electronic reconstruction of our early ancestor, the first Homo sapiens. The new IBM technology has turned time back 400,000 years, uncovering clues to the origins of mankind. What can visualization technology reveal to you?*

In contrast to lyrical writing or writing that dramatizes a selling point, ad copy can also speak in the language of the target. An ad for Adidas that features 18-year-old NBA star, Kobe Bryant, introduces him in the context of a young star wondering how good he really is. The copy makes it easy to associate with him because he is so clearly presented as a work in progress. The copy reads:

> Can I beat my sister?
> Can I beat my cousin?
> Can I beat my dad?
> Can I make JV?
> Can I make varsity?
> Play in college?
> Make the NBA?
> First Round?
> All-Star Game?
> Championship ring?
> MVP?

An ad for Trojans condoms makes a very pointed argument on a very touchy subject for its young, single-person target audience by combining headline with body copy:

> *"I didn't use one because I didn't have one with me."*
>
> **Get Real**
>
> *If you don't have a parachute, don't jump, genius.*

Good writing in advertising is carefully crafted. People spend hours working and rewriting a single phrase. The tools vary—prose, poetry, conversation, street language—but the objective is to create a message packed with impact.

---

into understandable language. The Concepts and Applications box addresses this problem.

STRUCTURE OF BODY COPY

Two paragraphs get special attention in body copy: the lead-in and the close. The first paragraph of the body copy is another point where people test the message to see if they want to read it. Magazine article writers are particularly adept at writing lead paragraphs that pull the reader into the rest of the copy.

Closing paragraphs in body copy are difficult to write because they have to do so many things. Usually the last paragraph refers back to the creative concept and wraps up the big idea (see Chapter 13). Often the closing will use some kind

Read poetry. Make peace with all except the motor car.

Schwinns' are red, Schwinns are blue. Schwinns are light and agile too. Cars suck. The end.

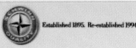

Established 1895. Re-established 1994.

AD 14.4

THE ANTICAR MESSAGE BUILDS
IN THIS AD BY SCHWINN UNTIL
IT EXPLODES AT THE END OF
THE BODY COPY.

of "twist," an unexpected tie-in with the concept. In addition, direct-action messages include some kind of *call to action* with instructions on how to respond. Even indirect-action advertisements, such as brand-reminder ads in magazines, may use some kind of call to action, perhaps a reminder of where the product can be found. The Schwinn ad demonstrates how powerful the closing can be (Ad 14.4).

DESIGNING FOR PRINT

Architects design buildings in their minds and then translate the details of the structure onto paper in a form known as a blueprint. The blueprint guides the construction of a building. It tells the builder what size everything is and what goes where.

The same thing happens in advertising. The art director takes the creative concept that has been developed with the copywriter and visualizes in his or her mind how the final ad will look. This visual inventiveness is characteristic of good designers.

PRINCIPLE The layout imposes structure on chaos.

Art directors manipulate the elements on paper to produce a **layout,** which is a plan that imposes order and at the same time creates an arrangement that is aesthetically pleasing. A layout is a map, the art director's equivalent of a blueprint. The art director positions and sizes the elements. These include the visual or visuals, the headline and other supplemental display copy, copy blocks, captions, signatures, logos, and other details such as boxes, rules, and coupons.

Layout: A drawing that shows where all the elements in the ad are to be positioned.

A layout has several roles. First, it is a communication tool that translates the visual concept for others so that the idea can be discussed and revised before any money is spent on production. After it has been approved, the layout serves as a guide for the production people who will eventually handle the typesetting, finished art, photography, and pasteup. In some cases the layout acts as a guide for the copywriter who writes copy to fit the space. It is also used for cost estimating. Figures 14.1A through 14.1D on pages 426 and 427 demonstrate some of the major steps involved in creating a print ad.

LAYOUT STYLES

The most common layout format is one with a single dominant visual that occupies about 60 to 70 percent of the area. Underneath it is a headline and a copy block. The logo or signature signs off the message at the bottom. A variation on that format has a dominant visual and several smaller visuals in a cluster. A panel or grid layout uses a number of visuals of certain sizes.

Less frequently you will see layouts that emphasize the type rather than the art. Occasionally you will see an all-copy advertisement where the headline is treated as type art. A copy-dominant ad may have art, but it is either embedded in the copy or positioned at the bottom of the layout.

The truth is there are many ways to lay out an ad and different layouts can create an entirely different feeling about the product. For example, look at two different ads for work boots below and the way they are designed. The Timberland ad is part of a campaign that features what Barbara Lippert, in her critique of this campaign in *Adweek*, calls Big Mama Weather—snow, ice, water, and mud (which is illustrated in Ad 14.5A). In another ad in that campaign, the shot of what looks like a woman's eyes peering between a leather and fur hat and a snowcaked muffler is explained by the headline in a turn-of-the-century typeface, "In the Iditarod, the idea that there are only snowmen is abominable." Also appealing to explorers who master Mother Nature is an ad showing clumps of ice floating at the end of a melting glacier somewhere in the Antarctic headlined, "How to Survive a Meltdown."

Contrast that ad with the Dunham boot ad (Ad 14.5B), which looks like a work of fine art. The reflective attitude of the serene outdoor scenes say this boot

AD 14.5A

THE LAYOUT IN THE TIMBER-
LAND AD VISUALLY EXPRESSES
TOUGH BOOTS FOR ROUGH
WEATHER.

AD 14.5B

THE LAYOUT FOR THE DUNHAM
BOOT—IN CONTRAST TO
TIMBERLAND—SPEAKS TO
THE CRAFTSMANSHIP AND
THE BEAUTY OF NATURE.

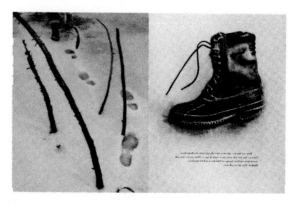

is for people who appreciate the beauty of nature. Likewise, a picture of a steel-driving man balanced on a crosspiece of girders, which is depicted in another ad in the campaign, is an artful arrangement. Even the copy is poetic. But the difference clearly lies with the visual impact that comes from the picture, the type, and the ads' layouts.

DEVELOPING LAYOUTS

There are several steps in the normal development of a print layout and they are depicted in the series showing the development of a Maybelline ad (Figure 14.1). Most art directors—and sometimes copywriters at this stage—work with a form known as **thumbnail sketches.** These are quick miniature versions of the ad, preliminary sketches (more like doodles) that are used for developing the concept and judging the positioning of the elements. In the early stages of development an art director may fill page after page with these thumbnail sketches, trying to decide what the ad will look like and where the elements will be positioned.

Thumbnail Sketches: Small preliminary sketches of various layout ideas.

The second step is a *rough layout.* Roughs are done to size but not with any great attention to how they look. Once again, a rough layout is for the art director's use in working out size and placement decisions. It is sometimes called a visualization. In newspaper ads the rough may be the only step before the layout goes to production.

In order to show the idea to someone or test various concepts, the art director will usually move to the next step, which is a **semicomp** ("comp" is short for comprehensive). A semicomp is done to the exact size of the ad, and all the elements are exactly sized and positioned. It is done by hand, but because it is going to be presented to others, extra care is taken to make it look good.

Semicomp: A layout drawn to size that depicts the art and display type; body copy is simply ruled in.

In a semicomp the art is sketched in, usually with felt-tip markers. Color is added where appropriate. Shading for black and white is done with various gray markers to indicate tonal variations. The display type is lettered in to resemble the style of type in the final ad. The body copy is indicated by ruling in parallel lines that indicate the size of the body type and the space it will fill. Most advertising layouts are presented in either the rough layout or semicomp stage. The semicomp is used for most routine presentations.

On special occasions a full-blown **comprehensive** may be developed. This is an impressive presentation piece. Type may be set, particularly for the display copy. Body copy is often just nonsense type (also called *Greeking* type), either commercially available or cut out of another publication. It is supposed to be the right size and resemble the actual typeface specified for the ad. The art may be a rendering by an artist who specializes in realistic art for comps, or it may be cut out of another publication. The idea is to make the comp look as much as possible like the finished piece. It is used for presentations to people who cannot visualize what a finished ad will look like from a semicomp. It is also used in important situations like new business presentations and agency reviews.

Comprehensive: A layout that looks as much like the final printed ad as possible.

The last stage in the production process is the development of **mechanicals,** also called *keylines.* These are meticulously prepared pasteups intended for the printer or reproduction-quality printouts from the computer if the ad has been created electronically. They are strictly for production use. Pasteup mechanicals are disappearing as more agencies and printers move to electronic publishing. With computer composition and layout, everything is done on the screen and the computer prints out an electronically assembled image—or sometimes a page negative that is one step closer to printing plates.

Mechanicals: A finished pasteup with every element perfectly positioned that is photographed to make printing plates for offset printing.

DESIGN PRINCIPLES

A layout begins with a collection of miscellaneous elements, usually a headline and other display copy, one or more pieces of art, maybe some accompanying captions, body copy complete with subheads, a brand or store signature, and perhaps a trademark, a slogan, or a tagline. Local retail advertising will also include reminder information such as address, hours, telephone number, and credit cards accepted. Arranging all of these elements so that they make sense and attract attention is a challenge. These decisions are both functional and aesthetic. The

FIGURE 14.1A

THUMBNAILS. THE ARTIST TRIES DIFFERENT WAYS TO LAY OUT THE ELEMENTS IN AN AD. THIS IS AN ARTIST'S CONCEPTION OF AN ARTIST'S CONCEPTION.

FIGURE 14.1B

A ROUGH LAYOUT. THE ROUGH CONTAINS LITTLE DETAIL (NOTE THE NONSENSE TYPE) AND IS USED FOR SIZE AND PLACEMENT.

FIGURE 14.1C

THE MECHANICAL (ON OPPOSITE PAGE). USED IN OFFSET PRINTING, THE MECHANICAL IS A PHOTO-READY ORIGINAL WITH ALL OF THE ELEMENTS PROPERLY PLACED. VARIOUS INSTRUCTIONS ARE PRINTED ON TRANSPARENT OVERLAYS.

FIGURE 14.1D

THE FINAL PROOF (ON OPPOSITE PAGE).

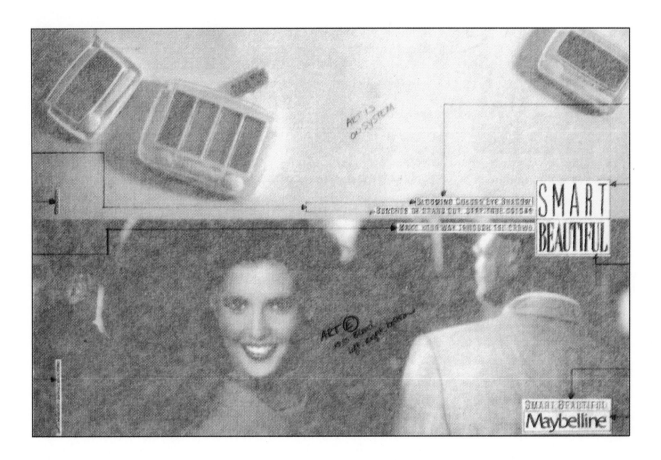

functional side of a layout makes the message easy to perceive; the aesthetic side makes it attractive and pleasing to the eye.

There are a number of design principles that help structure the way elements are arranged in a layout. The first is organization. We know from research into perception that organized visual images are easier to recognize, perceive, and remember than are visual images without any order. By order, we mean *visual organization*—imposing some pattern on the placement of the elements. If you take a piece of tracing paper, as we have done here with the Mustang ad in Figure 14.2, and convert the major elements of any good ad to geometric shapes, a pattern will emerge. A layout without any order lacks visual coordination of the elements.

The next thing you will notice when you study the tracing paper is that your eye follows some kind of *visual path*, or *direction*, when it scans the elements. This path is determined by the ordering of the elements. In Western countries most readers scan from top to bottom and from left to right, a process tagged the **Gütenberg Diagonal** by graphics expert Edmund Arnold. The tissue paper on the Mustang ad in Figure 14.2 illustrates with the black line how the eye progresses from the upper left to the lower right. Most layouts try to work with these natural eye movements, although directional cues can be manipulated in a layout to cause the eye to follow an unexpected path. The biggest problem occurs when the visual path is unclear.

Most good layouts have a starting point, called the *dominant element*. Within the design process, someone must determine the relative importance of the various elements in order to decide which one should be dominant. Normally the dominant element is a visual as in the Nike "Dan O'Brien" ad (Ad 14.6). But it can be a headline if the type is sufficiently big and bold to overpower the other ele-

Gütenberg Diagonal: A visual path that flows from the upper left corner to the lower right.

PRINCIPLE If everything is bold, then nothing is bold.

FIGURE 14.2

EVEN WITHOUT THE HIGHLIGHT-ING, YOU CAN TRACE THE EYE-FLOW OF THIS FORD AD.

AD 14.6

THIS AD IN THE NIKE CAMPAIGN
USES STRONG, DOMINANT
VISUALS AS THE FOCAL POINT
OF THE LAYOUT.

Focal Point: The first element
in a layout that the eye sees.

PRINCIPLE Think unity. Keep
things together that go together.

PRINCIPLE Keep things together
that go together.

ments. By definition there can be only one dominant element; everything else
must be subordinate. This element is the **focal point** of the ad; it is the first thing
you see.

A layout begins with a collection of discrete elements and culminates in a
design with *unity*. All the elements fuse into one coherent image: The pieces become a whole. On a visual level the content of the message must fuse with the
form of the presentation. The ad's appearance should match its message. You
wouldn't use delicate letters for an ad about Mack trucks, nor would you use fanciful art for an ad targeted to truck drivers. Using one typeface rather than several is
a good technique for creating unity, particularly for display copy. If there is a
dominant artistic style, stick to it. Ultramodern type doesn't fit with an illustration
that looks Victorian.

Neighboring elements that touch and align are another important aspect of
unity. An old axiom states the importance of grouping things: "Keep things together that go together." Captions need to adjoin the pictures to which they refer.
Headlines lead into the text, so the headline should be over the body copy. Pictures providing a different view of the same thing should be grouped.

White space is not simply an area where nothing happens. It can be massed
and used as a design element. It works in one of two ways: It either frames an element, which gives it importance, or it separates elements that don't belong together. Because it sets things apart and frames them, white space is used as a prestigious cue in layouts for upscale stores and products.

PRINCIPLE Contrast makes the important elements stand out.

Contrast indicates the importance of the various elements. Contrast makes one element stand out because it is different. People notice opposites, the unexpected. Contrast is also used to separate an ad from its surroundings. Because the newspaper environment is mostly black and white, an ad that uses color will stand out in contrast. In magazines, where most of the ads and editorial materials use color, a black-and-white ad might stand out. Black-and-white ads, by definition, are high in contrast. They can create dramatic, high-contrast images. A small ad or illustration can dominate if it contrasts effectively with its surrounding. Size is important in establishing contrast.

When an artist decides where to place an element, he or she is manipulating *balance.* A layout that is not in a state of visual equilibrium seems to be heavier on one side than the other. A layout that is out of balance looks like a mistake. There are two types of balance—formal and informal. *Formal balance* is symmetrical, left to right. Everything is centered. Formal balance is conservative and suggests stability. *Informal balance* is asymmetrical and creates a more visually exciting or dynamic layout. Informal balance is much harder to achieve because it requires manipulating and counterbalancing visual weights around an imaginary **optical center.** Counterbalancing uses the teeter-totter principle: Larger figures are positioned closer to the fulcrum than are smaller figures. (See Ad 14.7.)

Optical Center: A point slightly above the mathematical center of a page.

Proportion is both an aesthetic and a mathematical principle that concentrates on the relative sizes of the elements. The basic idea is that equal proportions are visually uninteresting because they are monotonous. Two visuals of the same size fight with one another for attention, and neither provides a point of visual interest. Copy and art, for example, should be proportionately different. Usually the art dominates and covers two-thirds to three-fifths of the page area.

PRINCIPLE Less is more, so when in doubt, delete.

The architect's axiom applies to *simplicity:* Less is more. The more elements that are crowded into a layout, the more the impact is fragmented. Don't over-

AD 14.7

ACG IS AN AD WITH AN ASYMMETRICAL LAYOUT THAT EFFECTIVELY USES A COLOR ACCENT.

load the layout. The fewer the elements, the stronger the impact. *Clutter* is the opposite of simplicity. It comes from having too many elements and too little unity.

COLOR

Color is used in advertising to attract attention, provide realism, establish moods, and build brand identity. Research has consistently shown that ads with color get more attention than do ads without color. In newspapers, where color reproduction may not be very accurate, *spot color*, in which a second accent color is used to highlight important elements, has proved to be highly attention-getting. The ACG ad uses the color red as a spot color that accents the product and brand name (Ad 14.7).

Realism is important for certain message strategies where full-color photographs may be essential. Some things just don't look right in black and white: pizza, flower gardens, beef stroganoff, and rainbows, for example. Color is needed to do justice to the content.

Color has a psychological language that speaks to moods and symbolic meanings. Warm colors, such as red, yellow, and orange, are bright and happy. Pastels are soft and friendly. Earth tones are natural and no-nonsense. Cool colors, such as blue and green, are aloof, calm, serene, reflective, and intellectual. An award-winning campaign for Levi Strauss Co.'s Dockers was built on the mood value of different colors. Ad 14.8 shows the "brown" ad; other ads featured gray, tan, blue, and black.

Yellow and red have the most attention-getting power. Red is used to symbolize alarm and danger, as well as warmth. Yellow combined with black is not only attention-getting but also dramatic because of the stark contrast in values between the two colors. Black is used for high drama and can express power and elegance.

Color association can be an important part of a brand image. Johnnie Walker Red has built a long-running campaign on all the warm associations we have with red, such as sunrises and sunsets, a fireplace, even an Irish setter. Kool cigarettes has used the color green so extensively that you can recognize the ad even when the product image is obliterated. IBM uses the color blue so extensively that the company is referred to as "Big Blue."

AD 14.8

THE DOCKERS CAMPAIGN FOR ITS MEN'S PRODUCTS USED THE MOOD ASSOCIATION OF VARIOUS COLORS AS ITS THEME.

ℐNSIDE ᴀDVERTISING

CATHERINE BEW, PRINT PRODUCTION ASSISTANT, *The Martin Agency,*
Richmond, Virginia

Most people could probably tell you a plethora of ways to land a job at a top advertising agency. For instance, they may say do your homework, surf the Net, and know the values of the agency. Or they might urge you to be unusual and mail in a tape of Mom telling them why you are so great and deserve a job there. Or if you are really daring, you could dress as a chicken in order to congratulate your agency of choice on winning its latest poultry account. Which is all good and true, but above all, I implore you to be creative and be persistent. After all, if at first you do not succeed, pool your brain power and attempt it again. Agency people ignore quitters.

I first thought about a career in advertising as a junior in college while at the University of Richmond. I was studying business administration and was not quite sure what facet of the business world was for me. I had filed documents for a life insurance company, collected money from delinquent credit card customers, and sold endless amounts of clothing in an upscale clothing store. Surely more electrifying jobs existed, and I was open to suggestions, but had not stumbled onto anything truly tantalizing.

Shortly thereafter, my global marketing professor passed out some flyers for a student workshop at The Martin Agency, an interactive program that involved the development of a campaign for a real client. After deliberating for a couple of days, I dragged my Phi Beta Kappa roommate down to the Career Development Center to pick up applications and apply with me. At the time we only had two days before the applications were due. We would update our résumés, answer their brief questions, and mail them off without any problems. Unfortunately, about one month later we were thanked for our applications, told that the selection process had been very competitive, and were back at square one. Although the agency's response disappointed me, I rechanneled my efforts toward academics.

The next spring with plans beyond graduation not finalized, I decided to apply to the workshop again. However, this round I took the advice of a friend who had completed the workshop. His advice was simple: Be creative. The Martin Agency, ranked consistently as one of the top creative agencies in the country, did not want a run-of-the-mill, carbon-copy piece of paper. This is essentially who you are until you distinguish yourself from the rest of the pack. Otherwise, you will remain a rough draft in line for the recycling bin. Therefore, I challenged my strong liberal arts curriculum, took his advice, and sent in a six-page bound book. Not only did it contain my normal résumé but a creative résumé as well. I did a take-off of Leonardo da Vinci's embryo and fetus "Studies of Influences on an Individual and the Brain." And if it sounds complex, that is because it really was a piece of art.

Basically, I analyzed the right and left sides of the brain interjecting my attributes. Plus I had a handful of sardonic retorts to match their inquiries. At the time it seemed like I was taking a big chance because it was 180 degrees from a "typical application." However, my marketing professor encouraged me to use ingenuity and self-expression, and it eventually paid off because I was accepted for the June session. Now not everyone has to go to these extremes, but in order to ensure myself a spot, I went the extra mile.

Once accepted I made valuable connections that helped me to obtain a job. During the workshop we had free roaming power within the agency. Even though we could not waltz into meetings with "Mr. Twenty Million Dollar Client," many students like myself utilized our breaks to network. We spoke with art directors, account managers, and others in various departments who sparked our interests. I was extremely fortunate that one kind soul mentioned an opening in print production to me. And you had better believe that I heeded this advice. Unfortunately, the departmental head was only in the initial stages of creating a position for an additional print production assistant. Nonetheless, I contacted my current boss and expressed my interest in such a position; at this point, she invited me in for an interview.

After thinking about the position, interview, and student workshop, I now knew that I really wanted to be a part of The Martin Agency. I proceeded with the proper follow-through process of thank-you notes and phone calls. However, I also knew that the position had still not been approved by personnel, and hiring from within the company was still a potential roadblock for me.

At this point I want to digress and say that this process can be extremely lengthy. However, it is vital to continue to show your aggressiveness—on a professional level, of course, not to the point of being obnoxious. After all, advertising is a cutthroat business and can be linked to Darwin's theory known as "survival of the fittest."

Besides the barrage of phone calls and letters, I wanted to make a lasting impression. O.K., so maybe I did not resort to the chicken mentioned previously. However, my current boss did wind up with a three-dimensional photographic box on her desk; and after one final interview, I was offered the job.

Looking back I can say how proud I am to have landed an entry-level position at such a prestigious agency. Anywhere you start can be used as a springboard. Internships and workshops are always great places to test the field because they allow you to gain a basic understanding of agencies and their functions. In addition, they give you the opportunity to make connections. Remember that it takes perseverance and imagination, and you must be willing to start anywhere just to be on the inside. In the end, your reward lies with admittance into the club, and getting in is a reward in itself.

Nominated by Prof. Dana Lascu, University of Richmond

*P*RINT *P*RODUCTION

Getting a print ad produced involves a bit of knowledge of the graphic arts industry. Courses are available to help you learn more about that industry; however, we will briefly review some aspects of production that you may need to be able to discuss or manage. (See Bew profile).

TYPOGRAPHY

Words in a print ad are presented as either hand-drawn letters or handwriting or the characters are officially typeset by computer or photocomposition equipment.

Most people don't even notice the letters in an ad, which is the way it should be. Good typesetting doesn't call attention to itself because its primary role is functional—to convey the words of the message. As George Lois, chairperson and creative director at Lois Pitts Gershon Pon/GGK, stated: "It's important the typography doesn't get in the way of an idea."[4]

PRINCIPLE Typefaces have distinctive personalities.

Type also has an aesthetic role, however, and the type selection can, in a subtle way, contribute to the impact and mood of the message. The ACG ad (see Ad 14.7) is a good example of an ad that uses the typography as art. In this case, the heavy, bold type has an attitude and makes a statement about the durability of the product.

TYPEFACE SELECTION

Font: A complete set of letters in one size and typeface.

The basic set of typeface is called a **font.** A type font contains the alphabet for one typeface in one size plus the numerals and punctuation (see Figure 14.3). The alphabet includes both capital letters, called *uppercase*, and small letters, called *lowercase*. You may want to specify *all caps*, which means every letter is a capital, or *U&lc* (upper and lower case), which means the first letter is capitalized and the others are lowercase.

Most people don't realize that designers must choose among thousands of typefaces to find the right face for the message. Within each category of type are type families, which are made up of typefaces of similar design. Two of the major categories are serif and sans serif. The **serif** is the little flourish that finishes off the end of the stroke. "Sans" means "without" in French, which is how **sans serif** letters are identified: They are missing the serif. Most of the sans serif typefaces are clean, blocky, and more contemporary in appearance (see Figure 14.4).

Serif: A typeface with a finishing stroke on the main strokes of the letters.

Sans Serif: A typeface that does not have the serif detail.

Italic: A type variation that uses letters that slant to the right.

The posture, weight, and width of a typeface also vary, as shown in Figure 14.5. Posture can vary from the normal upright letters to a version that leans to the right, called **italic.** The weight of the typeface can vary depending on how heavy

[4]Noreen O'Leary, "Legibility Lost," *Adweek* (October 5, 1987):D7.

FIGURE 14.3

THIS IS AN EXAMPLE OF THE WIDELY USED TIMES ROMAN TYPEFACE.

14 pt
ABCDEFGHIJKLMNOPQRSTUV
abcdefghijklmnopqrstuvwxyz
1234567890

FIGURE 14.4

THE TOP LINE IS PRINTED IN SERIF LETTERS; THE BOTTOM LINE IN SANS-SERIF.

ABCDEFGHIJKLMNOPQRSTUVWXYZ ABCD
ABCDEFGHIJKLMNOPQRSTUVWXYZ   ABCD

FIGURE 14.5

COMMON TYPEFACE VARIATIONS.

This is set in a light typeface.
This is set in a normal weight.
This is set in a boldface.
This is set in italic.
This is set in an expanded typeface.
This is set in a condensed typeface.

the strokes are. Most typefaces are available in boldface or light, in addition to the normal weight. Variation in width occurs when the typeface is spread out horizontally or squeezed together. These variations are called extended or condensed.

PRINTERS' MEASURES

To understand type sizes, you must understand the printers' measuring system. Type is measured in **points,** which are the smallest unit available (see Figure 14.6). There are 72 points in an inch.

Most designers consider type set in 14 points or larger to be display copy and type set 12 points or smaller to be body copy. The width of columns, also called *line length*, is measured in picas. The **pica** is a bigger unit of measurement than the point. There are 6 picas in an inch and 12 points in a pica. So 12-point type is exactly 1 pica high, or one-sixth of an inch.

JUSTIFICATION

One characteristic of typeset copy as opposed to typewriter copy is the forced alignment of the column edges. With **justified** copy, such as you are reading here, every line ends at exactly the same point. Other options are available to advertisers. One variation is to let the right line endings fall where they will. This is called *ragged right*, as our definitions in the margin illustrate. You can also specify the opposite, *ragged left*, although that is a very unusual way to set type. If you want to specify that either edge be justified, then the phrase *flush left* or *flush right* is used. Another option is to set everything *centered*, which means neither the right nor the left edges align, but instead everything is centered around a vertical midpoint axis.

LEGIBILITY

As previously mentioned, type selection is primarily functional. The objective of *legibility* is to convey the words as clearly as possible. Because reading is such a complex activity, the type should make the perceptual process as easy as possible.

Point: A unit used to measure the height of type; there are 72 points in an inch.

Pica: A unit of type measurement used to measure width and depth of columns; there are 12 points in a pica and 6 picas in an inch.

Justified: A form of typeset copy in which the edges of the lines in a column of type are forced to align by adding space between words in the line.

FIGURE 14.6

EXAMPLES OF DIFFERENT SIZES AVAILABLE FOR TIMES ROMAN TYPEFACE.

6 POINT

ABCDEFGHIJKLMNOPQRSTUVWXYZABCDEFGHIJKLMNOPQRSTUVWXYZABCDEFGHIJKLMNOPQRSTUVWXYZAB

abcdefghijklmnopqrstuvwxyzabcdefghijklmnopqrstuvwxyzabcdefghijklmnopqrstuvwxyzabcdefghijklmnopqrstuvwx   1234567890

12 POINT

ABCDEFGHIJKLMNOPQRSTUVWXYZ ABCDEFGHIJKLMN
abcdefghijklmnopqrstuvwxyz abcdefghijklmnopqrstu 1234567890

18 POINT

ABCDEFGHIJKLMNOPQRSTUVWXYZ

abcdefghijklmnopqrstuvwxyz   abcdefghijkl

1234567890

If the type is difficult to read, most people will turn the page. Research has discovered a number of type practices that can hinder the reading process.[5] All capital letters, for example, can create legibility problems, as can reverse type (white or light-colored against a black or darker background), unusual typefaces, and surprinting the type over a photo or some kind of patterned background.

THE ART

The word *art* refers to the graphics, whether an illustration or a photograph. Although art directors lay out the ad, they rarely do finished art. If an illustration is needed, then an artist is hired, usually freelance. Fashion illustration is different from cartooning, for example. If a photo is needed, then a photographer is hired. Both artists and photographers tend to have personal styles or specialties, and the right person has to be found for the visual.

ART REPRODUCTION

There are two general types of images that are reproduced in print. A simple drawing is called **line art** because the image is just solid black lines on a white page. Photographs, however, are much more complicated because they have a range, or shades, of gray tones between the black and white. The phrase *continuous tone* is used to refer to images with this range of gray values.

Because printing is done with a limited number of inks, printers must be able to create the illusion of a range of grays. Continuous-tone art and photos must be converted to **halftones** in order to be printed. In the *halftone process*, the original photograph is shot through a fine screen (see Figure 14.7). Areas on the original that are dark will create large dots that fill the space; if the original is light, then a tiny dot will be surrounded by empty white space. The image, in

Line Art: Art in which all elements are solid with no intermediate shades or tones.

Halftones: Images with a continuous range of shades from light to dark.

FIGURE 14.7
THIS FIGURE CONTRASTS THE SAME IMAGE REPRODUCED AS LINE ART (LEFT) AND A HALFTONE (RIGHT).

[5] Rolf Rehe, *Typography: How to Make It Most Legible* (Indianapolis: Design Research Publications, 1974).

other words, is converted to a pattern of dots that gives the illusion of shades of gray. If you look at a photograph in most newspapers, you may be able to see the dot pattern with your naked eye.

The quality of the image depends on how fine the screen is that is used to convert the original picture to a dot pattern. Because of the roughness of newsprint, newspapers use a relatively coarse screen, usually 65 lines per inch. (This is referred to as 65-line screen.) Magazines use fine screens, which may be 90, 110, 120, and on up to 200 lines per inch. The higher the number, the finer the screen and the better the quality of the reproduction.

Screens are also used to create various *tint blocks*, which can either be shades of gray in black-and-white printing or shades of color. A block of color can be printed solid or it can be screened back to create a shade. These shades are referred to as a range of percentages such as 100 percent (solid) down to 10 percent (very faint). Examples of screens are found in Figure 14.8.

COLOR REPRODUCTION

Besides reproducing halftones, the other major problem for printers is the reproduction of full color. When you look at a slide, you see a full range of colors and shades. It would be impossible to set up a printing press with a separate ink roller for every possible hue and value. How, then, are these colors reproduced?

The solution to this problem is to use a limited number of base colors and mix them to create the rest of the spectrum. Full-color images are reproduced using four distinctive shades of ink called **process colors.** They are magenta (a shade of pinkish red), cyan (a shade of bright blue), yellow, and black.

Printing inks are transparent, so when one ink overlaps another, a third color is created. Red and blue create purple, yellow and blue create green, yellow and red create orange. The black is used for type and, in four-color printing, adds depth to the shadows and dark tones in an image.

The process used to reduce the original color image to four halftone negatives is called **color separation.** The negatives replicate the red, yellow, blue, and dark areas of the original. The separation is done photographically, beginning with original full-color images on slides. (Slides, or transparencies, produce the most accurate and grain-free images.) Color filters are used to screen out everything but the desired hue. A separate color filter is used for each of the four process colors. Lasers are now used to scan the image and make the separations. Figure 14.9 illustrates the process of color separation.

New technologies have made it possible for a color piece to go directly from computer to film. Some agencies don't create mechanicals at all anymore. Instead, ads are created on the computer and transmitted to a service bureau or color separation house by modem or floppy disks. There they can go directly to film.

Using computers for illustrations is creatively simple. The difficulty is in photography. In theory, a transparency can be scanned into a traditional high-end prepress system, then data can be sent to a Macintosh, for example, and assembled

Process Colors: Four basic inks—magenta, cyan, yellow, and black—that are mixed to produce a full range of colors found in four-color printing.

Color Separation: The process of splitting a color image into four images recorded on negatives; each negative represents one of the four process colors.

FIGURE 14.8

THESE SPECTRA SHOW THE DIF-
FERENT SCREENS FOR BLACK
AND FOR A COLOR.

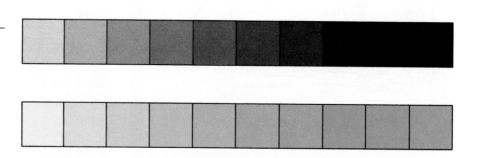

FIGURE 14.9A

YELLOW PLATE. THE SIX PHOTOS STARTING HERE ILLUSTRATE THE PROCESS OF FOUR-COLOR SEPARATION.

FIGURE 14.9B

RED (MAGENTA) PLATE.

into an ad and then returned to the system for output on film. In reality, such files use up huge amounts of memory and time, and color calibration is not yet sophisticated enough to guarantee that what you see is what you get. What actually happens is that art directors work with low-resolution scans for positioning purposes only. The prepress operators then assemble the ad electronically, replacing the position-only scans they've made from transparencies in the traditional way.

As these methods are perfected, the time-consuming, labor-intensive assembling of ad pieces will be replaced with desktop color imaging. Color matching can be expensive, but it can also save companies money in stripping costs and typesetting, and the industry is optimistic about the continuing refinement of computerized color graphics.

PRINTING PROCESS

There are a number of printing processes used in advertising such as *letterpress*, which is used for numbering and specialty printing effects; *offset lithography*, which is the most popular type of printing for newspapers and most magazines; *rotogravure*, which is used for long print runs with quality photographic reproduction; *flexography*, which prints on unusual surfaces; and *silk screen*, which is used to print posters, T-shirts, and point-of-sale materials.

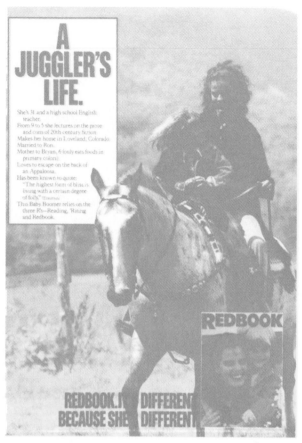

FIGURE 14.9C

YELLOW AND RED PLATES.

FIGURE 14.9D

BLUE (CYAN) PLATE.

Tip-Ins: Preprinted ads that are provided by the advertiser to be glued into the binding of a magazine.

If an ad is going to run in a number of publications, there has to be some way to distribute a reproducible form of the ad to all of them. For letterpress, a *mat* made from a kind of papier-mâché is sent, along with a *proof* made from the original engraving. For gravure printing, *film positives* are sent to the publications. The duplicate material for offset printing is a "slick" proof of the original mechanical. These proofs are called *photoprints* or *photostats*, which are relatively cheap images. *Veloxes* or *C-Prints* are better-quality proof prints.

A number of special printing effects are created at the end of the production process. These are mechanical techniques that embellish the image using such methods as embossing or foil stamping. The last step in production is the binding, where the pages of a publication are assembled.

Newspapers are folded, and the fold holds the sheets together. Magazines are folded, stapled or sewn, and trimmed. Sometimes a separate cover is glued on. During this binding process separate preprinted ads provided by the advertiser can be glued in. Such ads are called **tip-ins.** They are used when an advertiser wants particularly fine printing or wishes to include something that can't be accommodated in the normal printing process. Most perfume manufacturers, for example, are tipping in perfume samples that are either scratch-and-sniff or scented strips that release their fragrance when pulled apart.

NEW TECHNOLOGY

A new technology, based on computers and transmission by phone line using fiber optics or by satellite, has generated a revolution in print media. Computerized

FIGURE 14.9E

BLACK PLATE.

FIGURE 14.9F

**THE FINISHED AD WITH ALL
FOUR PROCESS COLORS.**

(Courtesy of Redbook)

typesetting now makes it easy to transmit type electronically. Art can be *digitized* (broken into tiny grids, each one coded electronically for tone or color) and then transmitted. Fiber optics can send type, art, or even complete pages across a city for local editions of newspapers. Satellites make national page transmission possible for regional editions of magazines and newspapers such as *USA Today*.

Printing by personal computer, utilizing easy-to-use software, is taking over the low end of the typesetting function. In addition to typesetting, page layouts as well as advertising layouts can be done on a personal computer. This approach to typesetting and layout is called *desktop publishing*. Graphics that can be drawn and modified on computers are now being used in many newspapers.

At the higher end of the typesetting function, many quality typesetting systems use some kind of computer-based *pagination* equipment that combines sophisticated computer typesetting with page layout capabilities.

Inkjet printing, which is a type of printing directed by computer, is becoming more common. It can speed up the entire printing process by eliminating many of the technical steps in printing, such as negatives and plate making. It will soon be possible to go directly from the computer to a printed publication. This may make it feasible to customize the content of a publication, advertising as well as articles, to the interest of the reader, thus creating a new world of one-on-one publishing and, eventually, personalized target marketing. *Time* magazine used this to print subscribers' names on each cover.

Summary

- The key elements of a print ad are divided between copy—the headlines, text, and other verbal elements—and art, which refers to the visual elements including illustrations, photographs, type, and layout. In an effective advertisement, all these elements work together to create impact.

- While newspapers are focused on news, the ads they carry usually also announce something and provide useful information to the paper's readers. Magazines are usually more tightly targeted than newspapers to readers' special interests and have better-quality reproduction, which means the advertisements can use better color, more finely detailed photographs, and more detailed artwork.

- Headlines target the prospect, stop the reader, identify the product, start the sale, and lure the reader into the body copy. Body copy provides the persuasive details such as support for claims, proof, and reasons.

- A layout arranges all the elements to provide a visual order that helps the reader to process the information in the ad; at the same time it is aesthetically pleasing and makes a visual statement for the brand. Layouts are built in stages starting with thumbnails and moving through rough comprehensives and full comprehensives to the production stage where they are turned into mechanicals.

- Color is used in advertising to attract attention, provide realism, establish mood, and build brand identity. Color is reproduced in print using a process that photographically separates full nature color into four negatives that can be reproduced in four colors of ink. These will overlap to create the illusion of full color.

- The most common printing process for newspapers and most magazines is offset lithography. Other types of printing occasionally used in advertising include letterpress, rotogravure, flexography, and silk screen.

Questions

1. What are the major features of a print ad? What is the purpose of each one?

2. Collect a group of ads for department and discount stores. Compare their layouts. What does the layout "say" about the type of store and the merchandise it carries?

3. Think of ads you have seen in newspapers and magazines over the past ten years. What trends, if any, do you notice? How do you account for these trends?

4. We read from left to right and top to bottom. This pattern forms the natural "Z" shape. What does the chapter call this pattern of direction? Now look at some advertising in a favorite magazine. Do any of the ads not follow this pattern? Trace the visual direction used. What shape does it take? Why would the designer choose this direction pattern?

5. A student struggles with a layout assignment involving informal balance. She has a dominant vertical illustration element placed at the right side of her page. Her difficulty is finding some other element (copy block or small illustration) to balance the size and strength of the key visual. When she asks her instructor for help, he tells her, "You've forgotten one of the simplest principles of equilibrium: You don't always need other copy and design pieces to balance the dominant object." What does he mean?

6. Search your area newspapers for ads for clothing stores. Sort these into expensive stores and those that feature lower-priced apparel. Now compare the design aspects of each type of store. How many differences do you see in design, art, type, and other elements? Do any of these differences produce a store personality or image? Identify those print concepts in the ad that provide a special "signature" for the store.

Suggested Class Project

If you are making a pitch to get an athletic shoe account, what approach would you consider? What is there left to do? This is the problem McCann Erickson faced when it won the estimated $4 million Brooks Sports' athletic shoe account. That's a relatively small budget compared to the huge Nike budgets. The assignment is to name, position, and launch the new brand. The advertising is mostly print and will run in both men's and women's magazines as well as fitness and trade publications. You are part of the art director/copywriter team. Develop the "spec" work (speculative) for the presentation. Develop an idea for the campaign and rough out two sample ads.

FURTHER READINGS

Baird, Russell N., Duncan McDonald, Ronald H. Pittman, and Arthur T. Turnbull, *The Graphics of Communication* (New York: Harcourt, Brace, Jovanovich, 1993).

Bendinger, Bruce, *The Copy Workshop* (Chicago: The Copy Workshop, 1993).

Burton, Philip Ward, *Which Ad Pulled Best?* (Lincolnwood, IL: NTC, 1981).

Keding, Ann, and Thomas H. Bivins, *How to Produce Creative Advertising* (Lincolnwood, IL: NTC, 1991).

Moriarty, Sandra E., *Creative Advertising* (Upper Saddle River, NJ: Prentice Hall, 1991).

Nelson, Roy Paul, *The Design of Advertising* (Madison, WI: Brown & Benchmark, 1994).

Major league baseball (MLB) suffers from an image problem. The labor dispute that ended the 1994 season halfway through continues to linger in public memory. That compounded by the fact that owners still hadn't worked out a collective bargaining agreement with players as of the end of the 1996 season makes both players and owners look greedy and disrespectful of fans. The problem? How can you recreate America's love affair with the boys of summer?

In contrast the National Basketball Association (NBA) has engineered a turnaround that baseball managers envy. In the mid-1980s games were routinely played before half-empty arenas and players were known more for their drug records than their scoring or rebounding records. The final indignity came in 1984 when the championship finals were relegated to a tape-delay broadcast against *The Tonight Show*. By 1996, however, the NBA has become a merchandising miracle. Sales of merchandise (T-shirts, caps, anything with a team logo) have reached as high as $3 billion worldwide. People who think a dribble is an eating accident have not heard of superstars like Michael Jordan, Shaquille O'Neal, and Dennis Rodman.

During the 1996 season the baseball association began a $2 million consumer campaign, tagged "What a Game." An ad celebrating "Opening Day" was headlined "About this time every year a strange phenomenon occurs." Under the headline is a large photo of a baseball with the payoff line printed across its middle: "The earth revolves around this."

In addition Sports Marketing & Television International (SPTI) created sponsorship agreements with Borden, Coca-Cola, Quaker's Gatorade, Gillette, MCI, and Sherwin Williams to buy more than $50 million in ad time during baseball broadcasts on Fox and NBC.

Unfortunately, the 1996 season continued to be one of half-filled stadiums, except in a few cities like Denver where the Rockies continue to play to sell-outs.

Television, however, is costly and the industry needs to get more at-bats from its bucks. Baseball is also a local game so a partnership with local newspapers makes sense financially as well as strategically. Even with a limited budget, it is possible to dominate local newspapers.

Sources: Adapted from Jeff Jensen, "Baseball Starts Without New Marketing Slugger," *Advertising Age* (April 1, 1996):2; and Bob Ryan, "Hoop Dreams," *Sales & Marketing Management* (December 1996):48–53.

QUESTIONS FOR DISCUSSION

1. Given baseball's image problems, which advertising approach would you recommend—using national television, local spot television, or local newspapers?

2. What message strategy would you recommend to turn around the public's disgust with major league baseball?

3. If the association decides to emphasize local newspapers, what kind of print campaign would you recommend? Develop a proposal for the association that would maximize impact and localize the appeal. What would the ads say and look like?

For years The Gap was a retailing steam engine that no one could stop. With casual attire the uniform-of-choice of baby boomers, their parents, and children, sales of The Gap's denim jeans, khaki pants, all-cotton shirts and sweats, and wool sweaters catapulted the earnings of the San Francisco-based retailer into the financial stratosphere. By the end of 1991, sales had reached $2.5 billion, up 30 percent from the year before.

The Gap's strategy was to sell "good style, good quality, good value"—a mission it undertook with the help of a unique, magazine-based advertising campaign that communicated the primacy of consumer taste. In 1988, The Gap launched its "Individuals of Style" campaign—a series of dramatic black-and-white photos, featuring such well-known celebrities as Spike Lee, Kim Basinger, and Miles Davis. Each celebrity wore a single item of basic Gap apparel as well as clothes from his or her personal wardrobe. The visual message of classic simplicity combined with individual style helped convince consumers that Gap clothes were cool. Not wanting to overdo a good thing, The Gap eventually discontinued the ads, at least for a while.

Buoyed by the campaign's success, The Gap seemed invincible for about six years. Its concept of selling well-made, moderately priced basics in an attractive, trendy setting was the right merchandising approach for the times. However, The Gap's success was due only in part to its merchandising genius. The inability of competitors to produce comparable apparel at lower costs than The Gap gave the retailer a near monopoly on the kinds of clothes Americans wanted to wear.

This changed when the economic recession forced consumers to look for bargains and when companies such as JCPenney and Kmart began selling back-to-basics apparel at prices consumers could not ignore. Adding to The Gap's problems was the discontent of female customers who began to tire of the no-frills look. As a result of competitive pressure and changing tastes, The Gap's profits declined in 1992, the first time since 1984.

Recognizing the need to revise its merchandising strategy, The Gap introduced more fashionable, higher-priced items in the fall of 1993. Along with denim jeans and rugby shirts, shoppers also found stretch pants and leather vests. Persuading consumers that The Gap had a wider variety of merchandise was the challenge of the company's new print advertising campaign. Not surprisingly, the campaign featured more than just the basics. In a series of magazine ads, waiflike model Kate Moss wore Gap form-fitting sleeveless turtlenecks, a far cry from the Individuals of Style campaign.

Does this mean that the Gap's Individuals of Style campaign and back-to-basics look are dead? Certainly not. The Gap just reincarnated them in another form. In the fall of 1993, the retailer unveiled a six-week print campaign, running in three national magazines, to sell its casual, khaki pants to a larger, somewhat older audience. The campaign featured archival photos of 13 celebrities wearing their own khakis. At the bottom right-hand corner of the black-and-white photos is The Gap logo. Each photo is also accompanied by copy likening khakis sold by The Gap to those worn by "legendary writers, actors, adventurers with style." Featured celebrities include Humphrey Bogart, Marilyn Monroe, and Pablo Picasso.

After the first Individuals of Style campaign ended, Maggie Gross, The Gap's senior vice president for advertising and marketing, made the prediction that the campaign would be back "when the time is right" but with a different slant. An appeal to the nostalgia of older baby boomers seems to be the strategy of the 1990s, combined, of course, with a second set of ads that tells consumers that the basics look is only part of the picture.

Sources: Christina Duff, "Gap's New Line Goes Beyond the Basics," *The Wall Street Journal* (August 12, 1993):B1; "Gap Ads to Feature Celebrities in Khakis," *The New York Times* (August 18, 1993):D17; Michael Janofsky, "Advertising: Imitation May Be Flattery, But Conehead Ad Is Alien to The Gap," *The New York Times* (July 15, 1993):D21; Russell Mitchell, "A Bit of a Rut at The Gap," *Business Week* (November 30, 1992):100; Russell Mitchell, "How the Gap's Ads Got So-o-o Cool," *Business Week* (March 9, 1992):64; Russell Mitchell, "A Humbler Neighborhood for The Gap," *Business Week* (August 16, 1993):29; and Russell Mitchell, "The Gap: Can the Nation's Hottest Retailer Stay on Top?" *Business Week* (March 9, 1992):58–64.

Questions

1. How would you assess the effectiveness of The Gap's dual ad campaigns—one featuring Kate Moss and the other looking at adventurers who wore khakis—to communicate the retailer's broadened variety of merchandise?

2. The Gap uses black-and-white photos in many of its print campaigns. How effective is this technique in selling the product?

3. In what ways are The Gap's newest print ads right for the times?

Creating Broadcast Advertising

CHAPTER OUTLINE

- Promoting the Big Screen on the Little Screen
- The Video Environment
- Characteristics of Television Commercials

- Producing a Television Commercial
- The Radio Commercial
- Producing a Radio Commercial
- Message Trends

CHAPTER OBJECTIVES

When you have completed this chapter, you should be able to:

- Understand the roles of the various people associated with television commercials, including the producer, director, and editor
- List the various stages in the production of a television commercial
- Identify the critical elements in radio and television commercials
- Read and understand a radio script and a television script
- Compare and contrast radio ads and television commercials

PROMOTING THE BIG SCREEN ON THE LITTLE SCREEN

MGM/United Artists launched its latest James Bond movie, *GoldenEye*, with a 30-minute infomercial. The long-format commercial also launched the James Bond home video library. Much of the success of the Bond infomercial is due to the very popular format it used—a "behind the scenes" look at the making of the movie.

Beth Bornhurst, vice president of market development for MGM/UA Home Entertainment, who had been with the company only two months when she got the idea of launching *GoldenEye* with an infomercial, explained that she initially faced a mixed reaction. She had to convince her boss and senior studio management that the old image of the late-night infomercial for a vegetable chopper wasn't what she was proposing. She put together a presentation that pointed out that a lot of big respected brand names were doing infomercials and examples of their videos demonstrated that they could be entertaining. Eventually she found herself presenting the idea to Frank Mancuso, MGM/UA chairperson, who saw the potential and thought it was worth the risk.

Movies had not been advertised before using infomercials, so Bornhurst created a format for her project. The "MGM/UA Presents . . ." concept made the video look more like an entertainment show and less like a commercial. She interviewed five or six production houses to get help with the project and finally choose In-Finn-Ity Direct because they understood what she meant when she said she wanted an *Entertainment Tonight* approach. Using a news set with male and female anchors, the half-hour infomercial wove together scenes from the previous 007 flicks with glimpses from *GoldenEye*, plus selected interview clips from the newest Bond, actor Pierce Brosnan. The same format will be used for other launch videos for new MGM/UA movies.

The infomercial also offers viewers the chance to become a member of the James Bond Video Collection club, receiving a new digitally remastered Bond video each month. If viewers failed to join the club during the infomercial broadcast, they could also join through participating local video retailers. So in addition to selling the videos, the infomercial was also used to drive traffic into retail stores.

GoldenEye was a big success with the movie grossing more than $100 million in the United States while in theatrical release and another $200 million in international sales. But Bornhurst found out her projections on the sales of the videos were completely wrong. "Once we started testing we realized we'd underestimated just how effective this campaign would be. All of this worked in our favor because there were so many more orders, but the downside was we didn't plan our inventory properly."[1]

The *GoldenEye* infomercial was a focus of Hollywood talk and opened the door for an entirely new form of movie advertising. This chapter will discuss infomercials and other types of videos used in marketing communication but the focus will be on more traditional broadcast advertising for both television and radio.

THE VIDEO ENVIRONMENT

Like most Americans, you probably have a love-hate relationship with television commercials. On the one hand, you may have a favorite commercial or campaign. The Budweiser frogs commercials have been amazingly successful using frogs and

[1]Adapted from "MGM's Breakthrough Infomercial," *Infomercial 96*, Supplement to *Adweek, Brandweek,* and *Mediaweek* (1996):14–18; "Half-Hour Show for 007 Is a License to Sell for MGM/UA," Infomercials Special Advertising Section, *Advertising Age* (March 11, 1996):8a; and Helene Blake, "New Challenges Ahead for Infomercials," Infomercials Special Advertising Section, *Advertising Age* (March 11, 1996):4A.

lizards, who croak the brand's name, because the characters are so captivating. On the other hand, you can probably identify a dozen commercials that you resent so much you turn the channel or leave the room the minute they appear. You might hate the product or see the characters in the commercial as stupid and the message as insulting. Your reaction may be personal—different people like different things; strategic—you are not in the target for that particular product and the message isn't addressed to you; or factual—there are, after all, a number of dreadful commercials on television. Questionable television advertising is discussed in the Issues and Controversies box.

But the use of video in marketing communication is much broader than the familiar 30-second commercial you see on television. In addition to infomercials, video is also used for product literature and direct marketing, as well as public relations news releases and training films. The first two of these uses are really extended commercials but they usually have less resistance because they don't interrupt programming.

For example, WLIT-FM in Chicago used an 8.5-minute video as a direct-response mailer to 250,000 local residents. In contrast to a 15-, 30-, or even 60-second spot, the video gave the station time to tell its story and build a relationship with its listeners. Because the station is also owned by Viacom, sister retailer Blockbuster also distributed the video for customers to borrow free of charge. The station saw its Arbitron ratings jump from sixth to fourth place after the mailing was received.[2] Likewise, to introduce the Donkey Kong Country video game, Nintendo distributed a teaser video explaining the game's features. The car industry has been using videos for years as product "literature" to give potential customers a "test drive" on their television screen. The World Wildlife Fund has sent videos in membership renewal kits and Du Pont used a video to tell farmers the complex story of its Synchrony STS soybean seed/herbicide system.

Although videos of all types play an important part in integrated marketing communication programs, this chapter will focus primarily on creating broadcasting commercials, since the basic planning and production techniques are the same.

CHARACTERISTICS OF TELEVISION COMMERCIALS

A tremendous effort goes into creating an effective television commercial. In fact, a 30-second spot that flies by you as you watch your favorite television show represents hundreds of hours of careful planning and execution. In earlier chapters we discussed the pros and cons of broadcast media. In this chapter we present an overview of how television and radio commercials are developed and produced.

PRINCIPLE Television commercials should be intriguing as well as intrusive.

Effective television commercials can achieve audience acceptance if they are well done, and they can minimize viewers' patterns of avoidance if they are intriguing as well as intrusive. People do like to watch commercials if the ads are well done. They watch excerpts from the annual Clio awards given for television advertising when they appear on news broadcasts or as a program. Television shows on famous ads and advertising bloopers consistently get high ratings. Lines from commercials can even take on a life of their own, such as "Do you know me?" from the American Express campaign, "Thanks, I needed that" from a Mennen Skin Bracer commercial, and "I love you, man" from a Bud Light campaign.

Most people pay more attention to television than they do to radio programming. People watching a program they enjoy are frequently absorbed in it. Their absorption is only slightly less than that experienced by people watching a movie in a darkened theater. Advertising is considered an unwelcome interruption because it disrupts concentration. This intrusiveness can be disconcerting and can cause the viewer to be even less receptive to the commercial message. Another

[2]"Video Helped the Radio Star," *Promo* (April 1996):10.

Issues and Controversies

SPIRITS ON THE TUBE

The distilled spirits industry has had a voluntary ban on broadcast advertising since 1936, the earliest days of television. In mid-1996, Seagram broke the ban and its agency, Grey Advertising, began running a 30-second Crown Royal whiskey spot first on a local NBC affiliate in Corpus Christi, Texas, and then in dozens of major television markets along with television ads for Seagram's Chivas Regal and radio ads for Lime Twisted Gin.

DISCUS (Distilled Spirits Council of the United States), the trade association that represents the spirits industry, points out that 1.5 ounces of liquor, 5 ounces of wine, and 12 ounces of beer are equal in alcoholic content. DISCUS feels that liquor should be treated like any other alcoholic beverage, advertising included. If beer and wine can be advertised on television, then why not liquor?

The industry would also like to be able to counter the public perception that spirits are stronger or more dangerous than beer and wine and thus deserve stricter controls. As DISCUS president explained, "In truth, alcohol is alcohol is alcohol." Typical servings of wine, beer, and spirits all contain roughly the same amount of alcohol.

President Clinton denounced the decision in the name of protecting the nation's youth and, as the story goes, asked Seagram president Edgar Bronfman, Jr. at a fundraiser not to advertise his liquor products on television. Bronfman's refusal only raised the intensity of the debate.

Government efforts by the Federal Trade Commission (FTC) and the Federal Communications Commission (FCC) to restrict liquor advertising are seen by the industry as violating its rights of free speech. In order to successfully regulate this advertising, the FTC will have to make the argument that these ads not only target underage consumers but have a harmful effect on them, such as inducing them to drink, which is a difficult argument to make. The FCC under its powers to make sure that broadcasters serve the public interest, has some leeway to propose a broad rule limiting commercials for alcohol.

Critics of the plan feel that television is the most youth-oriented advertising medium and the ads will naturally be seen by young people. U.S. Rep. Joe Kennedy, D-Mass., charged that Seagram targeted youth in its first ad for Crown Royal. The commercial shows two canines trotting out to the strains of "Pomp and Circumstance." The first carries a newspaper in its mouth (the obedience school graduate); the second carries a fifth of Crown Royal (the valedictorian). Kennedy charges that this is a blatant attempt to appeal to young people by identifying high school success with alcohol.

Plans to advertise have been slow to develop given the deafening protests by government and special-interest groups. Another reason to go slow is limited budgets. Since 1980, liquor sales have been steadily declining. Although television advertising might engineer a turnaround in the industry's dismal record, it is also expensive. The president of Carillon Importers, marketer of Stolichnaya vodka, says television doesn't make sense for financial as well as strategic reasons. He says, "If you want to be on TV, you want to be on TV like Bud or Miller, and you need the money to do that."

The other barrier may be the networks who also have bans against liquor advertising. Furthermore, the beer industry is considerably larger and its advertising is more lucrative, so there may be financial reasons for the networks to restrict liquor advertising and to protect its other clients. The cable industry, of course, would be hungry for new ad dollars.

Adweek editorializes satirically that liquor advertising may even be good for society because most liquor advertising depicts a drink as a reward for working hard; "In other words, the category's ads have been built largely around a positive treatment of deferred gratification." In *Adweek*'s view, that's a socially useful concept that may outweigh the negatives of having liquor promoted more widely than it is now.

Meanwhile Seagram's $700 media buy for its 30-second ad on the Corpus Christi NBC affiliate got an avalanche of free publicity. Seagram estimates that the ad appeared at least three dozen times on network newscasts alone, which is roughly equivalent to more than $1 million to gain equal exposure by buying air time.

DISCUSSION QUESTIONS

1. In your view, are distilled spirits in the same category as beer and wine and should they be allowed to advertise on television?

2. Do you feel that a ban on liquor advertising violates the industry's rights of free speech?

3. Your agency handles Bailey's Original Irish Cream liquor. Your team has been assigned to come up with an idea for a television commercial should the client decide to move to television advertising. What are the pros and cons of television advertising for this brand and what would you recommend?

Sources: Adapted from Sally Goll Beatty, "A Peek at the Best and Worst of 1996," *The Wall Street Journal* (January 2, 1997):10; Ian P. Murphy, "Competitive Spirits: Liquor Industry Turns to TV Ads," *Marketing News* (December 2, 1996):1, 17; Owen Ullmann, "The Spirited Brawl Ahead Over Liquor Ads on TV," *Business Week* (December 16, 1996):47; "In Which We Explain Why Liquor Advertising Is Good for Society," *Adweek* (November 18, 1996):30–31; Eleftheria Parpis, "Separate But Equal?" *Adweek* (December 16, 1996):23–30; Cristina Merrill and Judy Warner, "Spirited Debate," *Adweek* (November 4, 1996):28–31; Todd Pruzan, "Seagram Serves Up Crown Royal 'Message,'" *Advertising Age* (April 29, 1996):4; and Bruce Ingersoll, "FTC Opens Investigation of TV Alcohol Advertising," *The Wall Street Journal* (November 27, 1996):A5.

problem confronting television advertisers is the tendency of viewers to switch channels or leave the room during commercial breaks. Because of television viewers' strong patterns of avoidance, commercials have to be intriguing as well as intrusive.

MESSAGE STRATEGY

Every advertising medium is different, and copywriters are adept at writing messages that take advantage of each medium's particular set of strengths. Television is unlike radio or print in many ways—in the most important way, it is a medium of moving images.

ACTION AND MOTION

PRINCIPLE Television uses motion and action to create impact.

Television is a visual medium, and the message is dominated by the impact of visual effects. But, you might observe, newspapers and magazines also use visuals. So what makes the difference in impact between television and print visuals? It is the moving image, the action, that makes television so much more mesmerizing than print. When you watch television you are watching a walking, talking, moving world that even gives the illusion of being three-dimensional. Good television advertising uses the impact of action and motion to attract attention and sustain interest.

STORYTELLING

Stories can be riveting if they are well told, and television is our society's master storyteller. Most of the programming on television is storytelling. The long-running Energizer bunny campaign has featured the pink bunny with its drum who materializes in a variety of unexpected settings. In a recent commercial, the bunny is the focus of a "sighting" by a group of followers who search with much anticipation for the event. One of the characters says reverently, "I feel very fortunate to be here because when we're all gone, it'll still be out there."

Commercial stories have to be imaginative to hold their own against the programming that surrounds them. An example is "Drugstore," a Levi's commercial by London's Bartle Bogle Hegarty that won a Gold Lion at Cannes. (See Ad 15.1.) The plot features a teenager entering a drugstore to buy condoms. When he meets his date, he discovers it was her father who sold him the condoms.

But stories do more than just entertain—they express values, teach behavior, and show us how to deal with our daily problems. Television shows such as *Roseanne, Friends,* and *Grace Under Fire* all include discussions of ethics, morals, or personal values. Commercials, too, can present bigger issues in their stories. Commercials for the IKEA furniture store have received praise because they featured an interracial couple and a gay couple trying to furnish their homes.

PRINCIPLE Television uses stories to entertain and to make a point.

Effective television advertisements use storytelling both for entertainment value and to make a point. These little stories can be funny, warm, silly, or heart-rending, just as in real life. Emotion is best developed and expressed in a narrative form. *Slice-of-life* advertising is simply instruction in a soap opera format.

EMOTION

More than any other advertising medium, television has the ability to touch emotions, to encourage people to feel things. This ability to touch the feelings of the viewer makes television commercials entertaining, diverting, amusing, and

AD 15.1

A TEENAGER MEETS HIS DATE AND HER DAD WHO SOLD HIM CONDOMS AT THE LOCAL DRUGSTORE.

absorbing. Real-life situations with all their humor, anger, fear, pride, jealousy, and love come alive on the screen. Humor, in particular, works well on television. These emotions are pulled from natural situations that everyone can identify with. Hallmark has produced some real tear-jerker commercials about those times of our lives that we remember by the cards we get and save. Kodak and Polaroid have used a similar strategy for precious moments that are remembered in photographs.

One humorous commercial that critics either loved or hated was the "Doctors" spot by Foote, Cone & Belding for Levi's Wide Leg jeans. Described as a cross between Monty Python and MTV, the spot shows a near-dead guy being wheeled into an operating room where he starts singing the 80's number, "Tainted Love." As he passes through a near-death experience, the doctors join in the maniac dance number. (See Ad 15.2.) Older people think it is the ultimate in bad taste, but Levi's is betting that the audience for wide leg jeans will be Gen Xers who will think the spot is hilarious.[3]

DEMONSTRATION

PRINCIPLE Demonstrations are persuasive on television because we believe what we see.

Demonstration was discussed in Chapter 7 as an important message strategy. If you have a strong sales message that lends itself to demonstration, then television is the ideal medium for that message. Its realism makes the demonstration persuasive. Believability and credibility are high because we believe what we see with our own eyes. Demonstration is also a good reason for considering the use of an infomercial because the longer format makes it possible to better deliver a demonstration. Car videos are particularly useful for that type of marketing communication.

SIGHT AND SOUND

PRINCIPLE Sight and sound should reinforce one another.

Television is an audiovisual medium—that is, it uses both sight and sound—and an effective television commercial fuses the audio and visual elements. One of the strengths of television is its ability to reinforce verbal messages with visuals or visual messages with verbal.

However, television is predominately a visual medium. The Coors campaign uses scenes of people playing warm weather sports such as volleyball and frisbee

---

[3]Marc Shattner, "Visitor's View," *Adweek* (December 16, 1996):43; Barbara Lippert, "Anesthetically Pleasing," *Adweek* (December 16, 1996):54; and Harry Berkowitz, "Levi's Jeans Ad Flat-lines for Some TV Viewers," *Denver Post* (December 2, 1996):2E.

AD 15.2

LEVI'S USED AN IRREVERENT SURGERY SCENE FOR ITS WIDE LEG JEANS, WHICH ARE TARGETED TO A GEN X AUDIENCE.

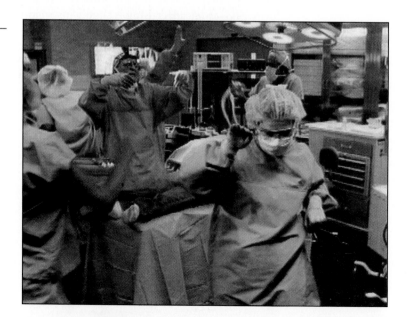

with a dog merged into a mountaintop setting with spraying snow used as visual punctuation. It's an interesting attempt at juxtaposing in an unexpected way the product's lifestyle cues with the brand's imagery.

Hooper White, who has been making television commercials since the 1950s, says in his book *How to Produce an Effective TV Commercial* that "The idea behind a television commercial is unique in advertising." He explains that it is a combination of sight and sound: "The TV commercial consists of pictures that move to impart fact or evoke emotion and selling words that are not read but heard." He concludes: "The perfect combination of sight and sound can be an extremely potent selling tool."[4]

The point of audio-visual fusion is that words and pictures must work together or else commercials will show one thing and say something else. Researchers have found that people have trouble listening and watching at the same time unless the audio and visual messages are identical. A Mountain Dew spot is a takeoff on a James Bond adventure with 007 in grunge on snowboards and mountain bikes. The storyline is reinforced by the Bondlike music and the tagline, "Shaken, not stirred."

ELEMENTS

Various elements work together to create the visual impact of television commercials. Audiovisual elements do not stand alone. They must be put into the right setting and surrounded by appropriate props. The right talent must be chosen, and appropriate lighting and pacing are critical, along with other elements.

VIDEO

The visual dominates the perception of the message in television, so copywriters use it as the primary carrier of the concept. The video elements include everything that is seen on the screen. Copywriters use visuals, the silent speech of film, to convey as much of the message as possible. Emotion is expressed most convincingly in facial expressions, gestures, and other body language. Good television writers try not to bury the impact of the visual under a lot of unnecessary words.

A tremendous number of visual elements must be coordinated in successful television ads. Because television is theatrical, many of the elements, such as characters, costumes, sets and locations, props, lighting, optical and computerized special effects, and on-screen graphics, are similar to those you would use in a play, television show, or movie. Because of the number of video and audio elements, a television commercial is the most complex of all advertising forms.

AUDIO

The audio dimensions of television and radio ads are the same—music, voices, and sound effects—but they are used differently in television commercials because they are related to a visual image. An announcer, for example, may speak directly to the viewer or engage in a dialogue with another person who may or may not be on-camera. A common manipulation of the camera-announcer relationship is the **voice-over,** in which some kind of action on the screen is described by the voice of an announcer who is not visible. Sometimes a voice is heard *off-camera,* which means it is coming from either side, from behind, or from above.

Voice-Over: A technique used in commercials in which an off-camera announcer talks about the on-camera scene.

TALENT

A television commercial has all the ingredients of a play. The most important element is people, who can be announcers (either on- or offstage), presenters, spokespersons, "spokesthings" (like talking butter dishes), character types (old woman, baby, skin diver, police officer), or celebrities, such as Shaquille O'Neill who came to the NBA with a complete marketing plan in hand outlining his

---

[4]Hooper White, *How to Produce an Effective TV Commercial* (Chicago: Crain Books, 1981).

Talent: People who appear in television commercials.

endorsement strategy, assuming he made it as a basketball star. People in commercials are called **talent.** Some commercials use just parts of people, such as hands, feet, or the back of the head.

Depending on what kind of people are being used, *costumes* and *makeup* can be very important. Historical stories, of course, need period costumes, but modern scenes may also require special clothing such as ski outfits, swim suits, or cowboy boots. The script should specify which costumes are essential to the story. Makeup may be important if you need to create a skin problem or to change a character from young to old.

PROPS

PRINCIPLE The most important prop is the product.

In most commercials the most important prop is the product. The ad should reflect the essential properties of the product. Does it come in a package? Does it have a distinctive logo? How should it be depicted? Can you show it in use? What other props are necessary to make the story come together? Sometimes props are critical to the action, like a tennis racket in a tennis scene. Sometimes they are used just to set the scene, like the patio table and tray of drinks in the background behind the tennis players. The script should identify every important element in the scene.

SETTING

Set: A constructed setting where the action in a commercial takes place.

The setting is where the action takes place. It can be something in the studio—from a simple table top to a constructed **set** that represents a storefront. Commercials shot outside the studio are said to be filmed *on location.* In these cases the entire crew and cast are transported somewhere. The location could be an alley or a garage down the street, or it could be some exotic place like New Zealand.

LIGHTING

Lighting is another critical element that is usually manipulated by the director. Special lighting effects need to be specified in the script. For example, you might read "Low lighting as in a bar," or "Intense bright light as though reflected from snow," or "Light flickering on people's faces as if it were reflecting from a television screen."

GRAPHICS

Crawl: Computer-generated letters that move across the bottom of the screen.

There are several types of visuals that are filmed from a flat card or generated electronically on the screen by a computer. Words and still photos are shot from a card. Words can also be computer-generated right on the screen. The **crawl** is computer-generated letters that appear to be moving across the bottom of the screen.

Stock footage is a previously recorded image, either video, still slides, or moving film, that is used for scenes that aren't accessible to normal shooting. Examples are shots from a satellite or rocket, historical scenes such as World War II scenes, or a car crash.

PACING

The speed of the action is another important factor in a television commercial. Pacing describes how fast or how slow the action progresses. Some messages are best developed at a languid pace; others work better when presented at an upbeat and fast pace. If the pacing is an important part of the message, then it needs to be explained in the script.

FILMING AND TAPING

Producing a major national commercial may take the work of hundreds of people and cost as much as half a million dollars. The "1984" commercial for Apple Computer that ran only once during the 1985 Super Bowl used a cast of 200 and is estimated to have cost half a million dollars. Since that time even more expensive commercials have been produced. The expense only makes sense if the ads will reach large numbers of people.

There are a number of ways to produce a message for a television commercial. It can be filmed live or it can be prerecorded using film or videotape. It can also be shot frame by frame using animation techniques.

LIVE

In the early days of television most commercials were shot live. The history of advertising includes numerous stories about refrigerator doors that wouldn't open and dogs that refused to eat the dog food. These traumatic experiences explain why most advertisers prefer to prerecord a commercial rather than gamble on doing it live.

Even in cases where an activity is live, such as a sporting event, a three- to seven-second delay is built into the televising process. This allows a commercial delivered by a sports announcer, for instance, to be stopped before it goes on the air if there was an error. Thus, there are very few instances when a commercial is actually live.

FILM

Today most television commercials are shot on 16 mm or 35 mm film. The film is shot as a negative and processed, after which the image is transferred to videotape. This transferring technique is called film-to-tape transfer.

Film: A strip of celluloid with a series of still images called frames.

Film consists of a series of frames on celluloid that, for advertising, is usually 35 mm wide. Actually, each frame is a still shot. The film passes through a projector, and the small changes from frame to frame create the illusion of motion. Film is shot at 24 frames per second. In film-to-tape transfer the film has to be converted to videotape that uses 30 frames per second.

Editing on film is done by cutting between two frames and either eliminating a segment or attaching a new segment of film. The term **cut,** which comes from this editing procedure, is used to describe an abrupt transition from one view of a scene to another.

Cut: An abrupt transition from one shot to another.

VIDEOTAPE

Until the 1980s **videotape** was thought of as an inferior alternative to film. It was used primarily by the television news industry because it records sound and images instantly, without a delay for film processing, and the videotape can be replayed immediately, Videotape's "cheap cousin" image has changed dramatically in the last decade. First of all, the quality of videotape has improved. The film-to-tape transfer has seen significant improvements. Also, a number of innovations in editing have made the process more precise and faster; computer editing has improved accuracy and made special effects possible. Thus, a director can look at one version of a television ad (including editing) minutes after it is shot and make immediate modifications.

Videotape: A type of recording medium that electronically records sound and images simultaneously.

ANIMATION

Animation, which uses film rather than videotape, records drawn images one at a time, frame by frame. Cartoon figures, for example, are sketched and then resketched with a slight change to indicate a small progression in the movement of an arm or a leg or a facial expression. Animation is traditionally shot at 12 or 16 drawings per second. Low-budget animation uses fewer drawings and, consequently, the motion looks jerky.

Animation: A type of recording medium in which objects are sketched and then filmed one frame at a time.

Because of all the hand work, animation is labor intensive and expensive. It takes a long time to create an animated commercial because of the drawing time, though the introduction of computers is speeding up the process. Now illustrators need draw only the beginning and the end of the action sequence; the computer plots out the frames in between.

One award-winning animation commercial created by TBWA Chiat/Day for Nissan is the "Toys" spot that used a remote-controlled toy red sportscar to

Stop Motion: A technique in which inanimate objects are filmed one frame at a time, creating the illusion of movement.

Claymation: A technique that uses figures sculpted from clay and filmed one frame at a time.

sell the Nissan 300ZX. The commercial became so popular that licensing deals with toy makers took the toy car to market, as well as the real one.[5]

A variation on animation is called **stop motion,** a technique used to film inanimate objects like the Pillsbury Doughboy, which is a puppet. The little character is moved a bit at a time and filmed frame by frame. The same technique is used with **claymation,** which involves creating characters from clay and then photographing them. The dancing raisins in the "Heard It Through the Grapevine" commercial by the California Raisin Advisory Board are the product of the claymation technique.

PLANNING AND PRODUCING COMMERCIALS

In planning a television commercial, there are many considerations. Producers of the commercials must plan how long the commercial will be, what shots will appear in each scene, what the key visual will be, and where to shoot the commercial.

LENGTH

As we discussed in Chapter 11, the most common length for a commercial on broadcast television today is 30 seconds. Because of the increasing costs of air time, 60-second commercials are becoming rare. Some network commercials now run in 20-second and 15-second formats. An advertiser may buy a 30-second spot and split it in half for two related products in the line. If the two messages are interdependent, the strategy is called *piggybacking*. An example of piggybacking is a 15-second cake mix ad sharing a 30-second spot with a 15-second frosting ad. Infomercials, because of their need for longer segments of time, are usually purchased for half-hour time slots in late evening, although there are some 5-minute formats being purchased by companies such as MCI, Healthrider, and Volvo that can work into commercial breaks.

SCENES

A commercial is planned in scenes. These are segments of action that occur in a single location. Within each scene there may be a number of shots from different angles. A 30-second commercial is usually planned with four to six scenes, though a fast-paced commercial may have many more.

KEY FRAMES

Key Frame: A single frame of a commercial that summarizes the heart of the message.

The writer and art director begin the planning together. The television equivalent of a thumbnail sketch is called a **key frame.** Because television is a visual medium, the message is developed from a key visual that contains the heart of the concept. The last frame in a Mastercard commercial, which shows the company logo, is the key frame. The various concepts are devised, tested, and revised as key visuals. When a concept seems promising, the writer and art director move to a rough *script* and *storyboard*, which we will discuss later.

LOCAL PRODUCTIONS

Most local retail commercials are simple, relatively inexpensive, and are shot at the local station or production facility on videotape. The sales representative for the station may work with the advertiser to write the script, and the station's director handles the filming of the commercial. These commercials may not have extravagant production techniques, but they can be just as effective as any big-budget production.

SCRIPTS AND STORYBOARDS

A print advertisement is created in two pieces: a copy sheet and a layout. Commercials are planned with two similar documents. A script is the written version

---

[5]Michael McCarthy and Bernhard Warner, "Nissan's Toy Story," *Adweek* (November 11, 1996):6.

*C*ONCEPTS AND *A*PPLICATIONS

CREATING INFOMERCIALS

Infomercials are different than traditional commercials and the infomercial industry, which has only been around since the mid-1980s, is learning how to deliver more effective messages in this format. The infomercial industry reached $1 billion in sales in 1994 and continues to increase every year since then, according to the Washington, DC-based National Infomercial Marketing Association (NIMA). The following is a collection of what producers have learned from various infomercial projects.

- Riding on the success of Soloflex and HealthRider, fitness products have solidified their hold as the leading infomercial product category.
- Upjohn's Rogaine was the first prescription product to use an infomercial. The long format made it possible to explain complicated products to consumers and provide the supporting medical information required by the Federal Drug Administration.
- Greg Renker, a partner in Guthy-Renker Corp., believes that an infomercial is an extremely cost-effective way to launch a new product. "If I want to launch a new brand the traditional way, it will cost me about $8 million in development and marketing costs." In contrast, he says you can spend $400,000 to launch a new brand using direct marketing and infomercials and find out immediately if people want your product.
- Lexus dealers are using an infomercial to sell their inventory of reconditioned, used Lexus cars as they come off lease. The goal is to generate leads for local Lexus dealerships and drive traffic at the dealerships by preselling prospects on the idea that the reconditioned car was still a luxury car, but just as reliable, and much more attractively priced.
- Lexus also discovered the value of inserting clips from regular Lexus television commercials to provide reinforcement of the Lexus image.
- Nissan's "The Art of Buying a Car" was test marketed in Dallas and Phoenix, running nearly a hundred times in each market in a wide mix of time slots. Nissan found that no advance advertising was necessary because viewers found the infomercials via routine channel surfing.
- Nissan also found that impact was aided by inserting calls to action, which were designed as 2- to 2.5-minute recaps of benefits and features. In other words, the infomercial was strengthened by these "ads" embedded in the longer format.
- An infomercial for Sony's high-end Surround Sound home system was produced in two versions, one offering consumers a chance to buy the Maximum Television System direct and another offering them information about the prod-

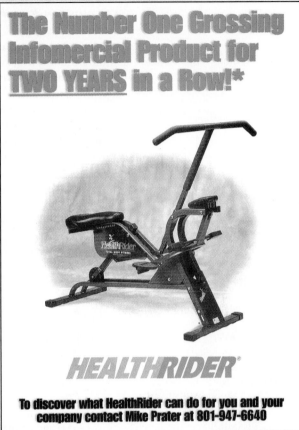

The Number One Grossing Infomercial Product for TWO YEARS in a Row!*

HEALTHRIDER®

To discover what HealthRider can do for you and your company contact Mike Prater at 801-947-6640

*SOURCE: Infomercial Marketing Report

uct and the names of nearby retailers. The company found that the infomercial that drove retail received a higher response than the one that offered to sell the system direct. In the case of a high-end product, people want to go to a store, hear the system, and have its operation demonstrated.

- Infomercials can be extremely cost-effective. A half-hour Kal-Kan program promoting its Pedigree Puppy Food drove retail sales increases as much as 270 percent in markets where it aired. Nissan's infomercial "The Art of Buying a Car," targeted to female viewers, delivered an extremely low cost per lead, and reached many male viewers as well as females.

Sources: Adapted from "In a Changing Infomercials Marketplace," a supplement to *Advertising Age* (March 11, 1996):1A–12A; and *Infomercial 96*, a supplement to *Adweek, Brandweek,* and *Mediaweek* (1996).

with all the words, dialogue, lyrics, instructions, and description; the storyboard shows the number of scenes, the composition of the shots, and the progression of the action.

TELEVISION SCRIPTS

A television **script** is a detailed document. It includes the visual plan of the commercial plus all the descriptions necessary to assist the director or producer in finding the location or building the set, the talent agency in casting the talent, the composer/arranger in creating the music, and the producer in budgeting and scheduling the entire project.

Script: A written version of a radio or television commercial.

The script is written in two columns with the audio on the right and the video on the left. Ad 15.3 for State Farm Insurance is an example of a television script with key frames from the commercial. The key to the structure of a television script is the relationship between the audio and the video. The video is typed opposite the corresponding audio. Sometimes these are numbered to correspond to the frames on the storyboard.

AD 15.3

EXAMPLE OF A TELEVISION SCRIPT AND KEY FRAMES.

STATE FARM INSURANCE
9/18/89
RURAL
:30 TV

    "Hoffrogge/Rural"

VIDEO

OPEN ON RURAL MINNESOTA
FARM.- DAWN
CUT TO SCENES OF AGENT WITH:
    LOCAL RESIDENTS,
    FAMILIES
    TOWN SHOPKEEPERS
INTERCUT WITH SCENES OF:
    FAMILY LIFE
    CHILDREN PLAYING
    LEAF RAKING ETC.

CUT TO DENNIS IN HIS OFFICE, CU
AT DESK

CUT TO WIDE SHOT OF TOWN
FROM EXTREME HIGH ANGLE

AUDIO

AGENT: I grew up on a farm just down the road. I know 'most everybody in town, and handle the insurance for quite a few.
I'm their State Farm agent... Dennis Hoffrogge.
My job is to help my neighbors. To help 'em protect their families, and the things they've worked for.
It's a job I take seriously.
Every State Farm agent does.
Y'know, State Farm started out in small towns just like this.... people trying to help their neighbors.
We're _still_ helpin'.

SING: LIKE A GOOD NEIGHBOR,
STATE FARM IS THERE.

I'm their State Farm Agent . . .

SOLO SINGER (VO): AND LIKE A GOOD NEIGHBOR,

STATE FARM IS THERE.

STORYBOARDS

Storyboard: A series of frames sketched to illustrate how the story line will develop.

The **storyboard** is the visual plan, the layout, of the commercial. It uses selected frames to communicate how the story line will develop. It depicts the composition of the shots as well as the progression of action and the interaction of the audio with the video. A 30-second commercial will be planned with six to eight frames. These frames, of course, are stills. They don't show action; they can only suggest it by a pictorial progression. The art director must determine which visuals convey the most information. Underneath the frame will be a short version of the audio, just enough to locate the dialogue in relation to the video. The storyboard is a very important tool for showing the basic concept of the commercial to the client and other agency members.

ANIMATICS AND PHOTOBOARDS

Animatic: A preliminary version of a commercial with the storyboard frames recorded on videotape along with a rough sound track.

Photoboard: A type of rough commercial, similar to an animatic except that the frames are actual photos instead of sketches.

As the concept is revised and finalized, the script becomes more detailed and the storyboard art more finished. A finished storyboard is equivalent to a comprehensive in print. To make the storyboard even more realistic, the frames may be shot on slides for presentation to the client. If the frames are recorded on videotape along with a rough sound track, the storyboard is called an **animatic.** Animatics are frequently used for client presentations and market research sessions. If frames are actual photographs of the action, which are more realistic, they are called **photoboards.** You have been looking at photoboards in many of the ads depicted throughout this book.

THE TEAM

A locally produced commercial uses the station's personnel for most of the production roles. In addition to a lot of time and a great deal of money, however, producing a major national advertisement requires a number of people with specialized skills. The agency crew usually includes the copywriter, art director, and producer. The outside people include a production house, a director and shooting crew, a talent agency, a music arranger/director plus musicians, and a film or video editor. The client's advertising manager is also involved throughout the planning and production.

The copywriter, art director, and possibly a creative director and producer work together to develop the idea and translate it into a script and a storyboard. The copywriter writes the actual script, whether it involves dialogue, narrative, lyrics, announcement, or descriptive copy. The art director develops the storyboard and establishes the "look" of the commercial, whether realistic, stylized, or fanciful.

Producer: The person who supervises and coordinates all of the elements that go into the creation of a television commercial.

The **producer,** usually an agency staff member, is in charge of the production. He or she handles the bidding and all of the arrangements, finds the specialists, arranges for casting the talent, and makes sure the budget and the bids all come in together.

The production house usually coordinates the entire shoot, working closely with the agency staff. The production house normally provides the director, but may choose to use a freelance director instead, particularly if that director's special "look" is desired for the commercial. The production house provides most of the technical expertise and equipment needed to produce the commercial. The **director** is in charge of the actual filming or taping: the look of the set and lighting; how long the scenes and pieces of action are; who does what and moves where; and how the lines are spoken and the characters played. The director manages the flow of action and determines how it is seen and recorded by the camera.

Director: The person in charge of the actual filming or taping of the commercial.

Composer: The person who writes the music.

Arranger: The person who orchestrates the music, arranging it for the various instruments, voices, and scenes.

Editor: The person who assembles the best shots to create scenes and who synchronizes the audio track with the images.

The music **composer** writes original music; the music **arranger** orchestrates that music for the various instruments and voices to make it fit a scene or copy line. The copywriter usually writes the lyrics or at least gives some idea of what the words should say. A composer who does a lot of commercials, such as Barry Manilow, might write the lyrics along with the music. Musicians are hired as needed, from a complete orchestra to a marching band to a vocalist.

In a film production the **editor** becomes involved toward the end of the process and puts everything together. Film is shot from a number of different cameras, each representing a different angle. The audio is recorded on multiple tracks. The editor's job is to decide which are the best shots, how to assemble the scenes, and how the audio tracks work best with the assembled video.

PRODUCING A TELEVISION COMMERCIAL

Commercials for local stores are relatively inexpensive to produce because they use the facilities and staff of the local station. The production process for a major national television commercial, however, is long and expensive. It is also involved and complex. The script and storyboard are reviewed and approved by the client and become the basis for the production planning. The producer and staff first develop a set of production notes, describing in detail every aspect of the production. These are important for finding talent and locations, building sets, and getting bids and estimates from the specialists.

PREPRODUCTION

Before the commercial can be filmed or taped, a number of arrangements need to be handled. Once the bids have been approved, a preproduction meeting of the creative team and the producer, director, and other key players is held. The meeting attempts to outline every step of the production process and anticipate every problem that may come up. A detailed schedule is also finalized and agreed to by all parties.

The talent agency is in charge of casting, which is accomplished through a series of auditions. A location has to be found and arrangements made with owners, police, and other officials to use the site. If sets are needed, then they have to be built. Finding the props is a test of ingenuity, and the prop person may wind up visiting hardware stores, second-hand stores, and maybe even the local dump. Costumes may have to be made.

THE SHOOT

Although the actual filming takes a rather short time, the setup and rehearsal can take incredible amounts of time. It may seem as though nothing is happening when actually everyone is busy setting up and checking specialized responsibilities.

The film crew includes a number of technicians, all of whom have to know what is happening and what they are supposed to do. Everyone reports to the director. If the sound is being recorded at the time of shooting, the recording is handled by a *mixer*, who operates the recording equipment, and a *mic* or *boom* person, who sets up the microphones. For both film and video recording, the camera operators are the key technicians.

Other technicians include the *gaffer*, who is the chief electrician, and the *grip*, who moves things such as the sets. The grip also lays track for the dolly on which the camera is mounted and pushes the camera on the dolly along the track at the required speed. The *script clerk* checks the dialogue and other script details and times the scenes. All of the technicians are supported by their own crew of assistants. A set is a very busy, crowded place. The box entitled "Television Termi-

TELEVISION TERMINOLOGY

- *Distance* (camera to image): Long shot (LS), full shot (FS), medium shot (MS), wide shot (WS), close-up (CU), extreme close-up (ECU or XCU).

CAMERA MOVEMENT

- *Zoom in or out:* The lens on the camera manipulates the change in distance. As you zoom in, the image seems to come closer and get larger; as you zoom back, it seems to move farther away and get smaller.
- *Dolly in and out:* The camera itself is wheeled forward or backward.
- *Pan right or left:* The camera is stationary but swings to follow the action.
- *Truck right or left:* The camera itself moves right or left with the action.
- *Boom crane shoot:* Camera mechanism moves over a scene.

TRANSITIONS

- *Cut:* An abrupt, instantaneous change from one shot to another.

- *Dissolve:* A soft transition where one image fades to black while another image fades on.
- *Lap dissolve:* A slow dissolve with a short period in which the two images overlap.
- *Superimposition:* Two images held in the middle of a dissolve so they are both on-screen at the same time.
- *Wipe:* One image crawls across the screen and replaces another.

ACTION

- *Freeze frame:* Stops the scene in mid-action.
- *Stop motion:* Shots are taken one at a time over a long period. Used to record animation, claymation, or something that happens over a long period of time, like a flower blooming.
- *Slow motion:* Suspends the normal speed of things by increasing the number of frames used to record the movement.
- *Speeded-up motion:* Increases the normal speed by reducing the number of frames used to record the movement.
- *Reverse motion:* The film is run backward through the projector.

---

nology" offers a concise definition of terms commonly used in television commercial production.

The commercial is shot scene by scene, but not necessarily in the order set down in the script. Each scene is shot and reshot until all the elements come together. If the commercial is filmed in videotape, the director plays it back immediately to determine what needs correcting. Film, however, has to be processed before the director can review it. These processed scenes are called *dailies*. **Rushes** are rough versions of the commercial assembled from cuts of the raw film footage. They are viewed immediately after the filming to make sure everything necessary has been filmed.

Rushes: Rough versions of the commercial assembled from unedited footage.

If the audio is to be recorded separately in a sound studio, it is often recorded after the film is shot to **synchronize** (sync) the dialogue to the footage. Directors frequently wait to see exactly how the action appears before they write and record the audio track. If the action occurs to music, then the music may be recorded prior to the shoot and the filming done to the music.

Synchronize: Matching the audio to the video in a commercial.

POSTPRODUCTION

For film, much of the work happens after the shoot. That is when the commercial begins to emerge from the hands and mind of the editor. Editing can condense time, extend time, and jumble time. Condensing time might show a man getting off from work, cut to the man showering, then cut to the man approaching the bar. Extending time is the train approaching the stalled car on the tracks. By cutting to various angles it may seem the train is taking forever to reach the car. To jumble time, you might cut from the present to a flashback of a remembered past event or flash forward to an imagined scene in the future.

Rough Cut: A preliminary edited version of the commercial.

Interlock: A version of the commercial with the audio and video timed together, although the two are still recorded separately.

In film a **rough cut** is a preliminary edited version of the story. The editor chooses the best shots and assembles them to create a scene. The scenes are then joined together. After the revision and reediting are completed, an **interlock** is

Answer Print: The finished version of the commercial with the audio and video recorded together.

Dubbing: The process of making duplicate copies of a videotape.

Release Prints: Duplicate copies of a commercial that are ready for distribution.

made. The audio and film are separate, but they are timed, and they can be listened to simultaneously. The final version with the sound and film mixed together is called an **answer print.**

In order for the commercial to run at hundreds of stations around the country, duplicate copies have to be made. This process is called **dubbing,** and the copies are called **release prints.** Release prints are distributed on 16 mm film or videotape. Because the industry now uses the film-to-tape transfer process, most production is done on videotape, thereby avoiding much of the film-laboratory work.

RULES OF THUMB FOR PRODUCING TELEVISION COMMERCIALS

A great many questions must be answered in creating a television spot. How much product should there be in your commercial? Should the action be fast or slow? Is it wise to defy tradition and do unusual ads that create controversy? Every producer and director will respond to these questions differently depending on his or her personal preferences. Nevertheless, there are a few general principles that correspond to all successful television commercials:[6]

1.   Gain the interest of your viewer at the beginning—the first three seconds are critical.
2.   Look for a key visual—a scene that encapsulates your entire selling message into one neat package.
3.   Be single-minded. Tell one important story per commercial. Tell it clearly, tell it memorably, and involve your viewer.
4.   Observe the rules of good editing. Make it easy for the viewer to get into the idea for the commercial.
5.   Always try to show the product in close-up at the end.

The Concepts and Applications box describes video innovations that have affected television production by combining computer technology with video.

THE RADIO COMMERCIAL

Imagine you are writing a musical play. This particular play will be performed before an audience whose eyes are closed. You have all the theatrical tools of casting, voices, sound effects, and music available to you, but no visuals. Imagine having to create all the visual elements—the scene, the cast, the costumes, the facial expressions—in the imagination of your audience. Could you do it?

PRINCIPLE Radio creates images in the imagination of the listener.

This is how radio works. It is a theater of the mind in which the story is created in the imagination of the listener. The listeners are active participants in the construction of the message. How the characters look and where the scene is set come out of their personal experience. Because of this personal involvement, radio is the most personal of all media.

CHARACTERISTICS OF THE RADIO ENVIRONMENT

Of all advertising media, radio is the one that relies most heavily on the special talents of the copywriter. Production budgets tend to be comparatively low; there is no need to choose type styles or layout formats. Radio urges the copywriter to reach into the depths of imagination and cunning to create an idea that rouses

---

[6]A. Jerome Jewler, *Creative Strategy in Advertising*, 4th ed. (Belmont, CA: Wadsworth Publishing, 1992):264–265.

$\mathscr{C}$ONCEPTS AND $\mathscr{A}$PPLICATIONS

THE MORPHING OF TELEVISION

One of the most creative video techniques is called *morphing* where one object magically changes into another. As we approach the end of the millenium, industry experts are predicting a similar change for television because of digitization, which experts believe is the most important technological innovation to hit the communication industries. When images are digitized, they can be transmitted and manipulated via a computer.

As the digitizing standards are ironed out and the technology developed, television as we know it will be replaced by a hybrid television/computer that will allow consumers to access land-based, cable, and satellite television signals, as well as the Internet. And this PCTV will have a keyboard that will turn it into an interactive communication medium.

The Federal Communications Commission (FCC) has been working since the 1980s to establish a standard for digital broadcasting, a new system of broadcasting that would work by breaking images into bits and bytes that can be reproduced by computers. When the commission thought it had finally worked out a standard, Microsoft's Bill Gates and his colleagues and competitors from Intel, Compaq, Apple, and Dreamworks SKG insisted that the new standard also had to work on personal computers. Otherwise, with the FCC standard, it could cost as much as $500 a computer to convert it to the FCC standard. Realizing the importance of the newly emerging and merging video and computer technologies, the FCC went back to the drawing board and came up with a PC-compatible digital broadcasting standard.

The technology to make this type of broadcasting work is still developing. Sony and Phillips Electronics make the $300 set-top gadget that is needed to convert the television images, and WebTV Networks offers a new service that connects the television to the Web for $20 a month. Offered for the first time as the hot product of Christmas 1996, WebTV didn't make much of a splash. The industry estimates that there are only 15 million U.S. homes with personal computers capable of tapping into the Web, but more importantly 97 million homes have television sets.

What does that mean for television as we know it? It means that the television we have watched since we were kids can be hooked up to a personal computer and reincarnated as a two-way, interactive medium. What shall we call it? WebTV? PCTV?

Who's driving this convergence? The new medium is evolving in the midst of a free-for-all involving media networks, cable companies, consumer electronics companies (television manufacturers), telecommunication companies (both wired and wireless), and the computer industry including Silicon Valley startups like WebTV Networks, which has

just come out with a set-top box that takes your television set online. There's big money here and even bigger egos.

What does it mean for entertainment? It means that actors have to learn how to act for computer vignettes, as Detective Mike Kellerman (played by actor Reed Diamond) from *Homicide* found out when he was interviewed in character but without a script by an NBC Interactive reporter. In this new medium, which uses both the World Wide Web and an experimental technology called Intercast, NBC Interactive not only shows the program, it has the capability to take audiences backstage for interviews with the characters and other backgrounding experiences.

What does it mean for television programming? So what will be the "killer app" (application) in this new format: the WebTV equivalent of *The Hit Parade* or *The Honeymooners?*

What does it mean to the professionals who are pioneering this new converging medium? The executive producer of NBC Interactive says, "We're peeing in our pants every day." Another staff member explains, "It's just like the Forties, when television was starting out live."

What does it mean to the typical viewer? It means we are now on the cutting edge of becoming Web potatoes. The questions are: Will we watch television on big-screen home computers? Or will we surf the Web on our Trinitrons with the help of a WebTV box available from Sony, Magnavox, or Philips? Will we get our programming from a satellite, a cable hook-up, or a phone line? What will happen to our familiar networks when the 60 or 70 channels currently available on cable morph into a million or more on the World Wide Web?

And more importantly from our viewpoint, what will happen to advertising when interactive WebTV or PCTV systems take off? What do you think will be the role of commercial communication in this new environment? And how will advertising be changed by the merging of television and computers?

DISCUSSION QUESTIONS

1. Imagine that your computer and your television are combined into one unit. How would that affect your life?
2. How would you promote the new PCTV? What are the advantages of this new electronic medium and what creative strategies would you use to sell it?

Sources: Adapted from Thomas E. Weber, "Why WebTV Isn't Quite Ready for Prime Time," *The Wall Street Journal* (January 2, 1997):9; Frank Rose, "The End of TV As We Know It," *Fortune* (December 23, 1996):58–62; Stewart Alsop, "The Birth of a Web Potato," *Fortune* (December 9, 1996):231–232; and Alan Gottesman, "Special D," *Adweek* (December 9, 1996):14.

the apathetic listener. The radio writer cannot hide behind props and techniques. Radio forces the writer to write better, to revise, to take more time with his or her craft. In radio, you are alone with your imagination.

Writing for radio is fun, but it is also very challenging because of the need to create an imaginary visual. Successful radio writers and producers have excellent visualization skills and a great theatrical sense. In addition, radio has some unique characteristics that make it a challenging medium for advertisers.

PERSONAL

PRINCIPLE Like a friend, radio speaks to us one on one.

Radio is the most intimate of all media. It functions as a good friend in our culture, particularly for teenagers. Radio has one wonderful advantage over print media and that is the human voice, whether it is a newscaster's, a sportscaster's, a talk-show announcer's, or a singer's. The "boombox" on the shoulder or the earphones on a jogger reflect this intimate relationship. Programming is oriented toward the tastes of particular groups of people. In that sense radio is a very specialized type of medium.

INATTENTION

There is one serious problem, however. Although radio is pervasive, it is seldom the listener's center of attention. Most people who are listening to the radio are doing something else at the same time, like jogging or driving. The listener's attention can focus on radio, particularly during programming that demands concentration like news and weather, but generally radio is a background medium.

Even though most people listen to radio with divided attention, strategists in radio advertising have employed three tactics that usually heighten the listener's attention level. The first is to engage in heavy repetition. During a 30-minute drive home, a driver can listen to the same jewelry store ad four times. Almost unconsciously, the listener becomes aware of the three facts detailed in the ad. A second tactic is to present the radio copy in the context of music or humor. Both are consistent attention getters, and they inspire memory as well. Finally, timing the radio ad to correspond to an immediate need works quite well. Restaurant ads played while the listener drives home and special weekend-event announcements on Friday evenings and Saturday mornings are two examples. Ultimately, radio advertisers must intrude upon the inattention of the listener yet not be so intrusive as to anger the listener. More will be said about these tactics in the next section.

MOST PEOPLE WHO ARE LISTENING TO THE RADIO ARE DOING SOMETHING ELSE AT THE SAME TIME.

MESSAGE STRATEGY

The radio message is ephemeral—it is here one moment and gone the next. You cannot tune in to the middle of an ad and then go back to the headline, as you can with print. You cannot reread a radio message. The key to the success of radio advertising is to evoke visual images based on what the listener hears. Writers creating ads for radio need to capitalize on its intimacy and the imagination of the listener. For example, one award-winning radio ad is titled "Hubble Telescope," sponsored by Nike Flight basketball shoes. It begins with the deadpan delivery of a basketball player in a sports arena. He thumps the ball on the floor a few times and then says his shoes are propelling him upward. His words begin to echo as he nears a ventilation duct, then his voice takes on the quality of one communicating from space as he leaves the confines of the arena. When he spots the Hubble Telescope in space, he says, "Nike, it's so beautiful, pal."

Creating vivid images is what makes radio copywriting so challenging. Ogilvy & Mather's Peter Hockstein offers these rules for making better radio commercials:[7]

1. Identify your sound effects. Tell listeners what they're hearing, and they'll be more likely to hear it.
2. Use music as a sound effect.

---

[7]Peter Hochstein, "Ten Rules for Making Better Radio Commercials," Ogilvy & Mather's *Viewpoint* (1981).

3. Build your commercial around a sound: the sound of a crisp new cracker, for example, or thunder to represent the power of a solid bank account.

4. Give yourself time. Fight for 60-second spots. It is often impossible to establish your sound effects in 30 seconds and still relate them to product benefits.

5. Consider using no sound effects. A distinctive voice or a powerful message straightforwardly spoken can be more effective than noises from the tape library.

6. Beware of comedy. It's rare when you can sit down at your computer and match the skill of the best comedians. On the other hand, well-written and relevant humor can be a powerful advertising technique.

7. If you insist on being funny, begin with an outrageous premise: Lake Michigan will be drained of water and refilled with whipped cream. A man puts on his wife's nightgown at 4 A.M. and goes out to purchase *Time* magazine—and the cops catch him.

8. Keep it simple. Radio is a wonderful medium for building brand awareness. It's a poor medium for registering long lists of copy points or making complex arguments. What one thing is most important about your product?

9. Tailor your commercial to time, place, and specific audience. If it is running in Milwaukee, you can tailor it for Milwaukee. You can talk in the lingo of the people who will be listening and to the time of day in which your commercial will be broadcast. Talk about breakfast at the breakfast hour or offer a commuter taxi service during rush hour.

10. Present your commercial to your client on tape, if possible. Most radio scripts look boring on paper. Acting, timing, vocal quirks, and sound effects make them come alive.

There is one element this list does not address—the problem of retention. Because radio is a transitory medium, the ability of the listener to remember facts, such as the name of the advertiser, along with the address and phone number, is constantly challenged. To help the listener remember what you are selling, you must mention the name of the product emphatically. An average of three mentions in a 30-second commercial and five mentions in a 60-second commercial may not be too frequent, as long as the repetition is not done in a forced and annoying manner. Since the last thing listeners hear is what they tend to remember, you will also want to mention the key selling idea and the brand name at the close of the commercial.

WRITING FOR AUDIO

Writing radio copy requires a particular style and certain tools. Like television scripts, radio copy is written for a certain time frame and according to a particular form and code.

PRINCIPLE For radio, write as you speak, not as you write.

Radio copywriters write in a conversational style using *vernacular* language. Spoken language is different from written language. We talk in short sentences, often in sentence fragments and run-ons. We seldom use complex sentences in speech. We use contractions that would drive an English teacher crazy. Spoken language is not polished prose.

Word choice should reflect the speech of the target audience. Slang can be hard to handle and sound phony, but copy that picks up the nuances of people's speech sounds natural. Each group has its own way of speaking, its own phrasing. Teenagers don't talk like 8-year-olds or 80-year-olds. A good radio copywriter has an ear for the distinctive patterns of speech that identify social groups.

TOOLS

Radio uses three primary tools to develop messages: *voice*, *music*, and *sound effects*. These can be manipulated to create a variety of different effects.

VOICE

Voice is probably the most important element. Voices are heard in jingles, in spoken dialogue, and in straight announcements. Most commercials have an announcer, if not as the central voice, at least at the closing to wrap up the product identification. *Dialogue* uses character voices to convey an image of the speaker—a child, an old man, an executive, a Little League baseball player, or an opera singer. The absence of pictures demands that the voices you choose help listeners "see" the characters in your commercial.

MUSIC

Music is another important element of radio. It has been found to be more effective in persuasiveness than celebrity endorsements, product demos, or hidden-camera techniques. It falls just a little under kids, kittens, or puppy dogs. It's not only persuasive, it's also very important for memorability since we remember information when we sing along with it.

PRINCIPLE The simpler the jingle, the higher the memorability.

So-called "jingle houses" are companies that specialize in writing and producing jingles for radio and television. The people who work in this side of the music industry prefer the term *commercial music.* A custom-made jingle—one that is created for a single advertiser under strict specifications—can cost $10,000 or more. In contrast, many jingle houses create "syndicated" jingles made up of a piece of music that can be applied to different lyrics and sold to several different advertisers in different markets around the country. These jingles may only cost around $1,000 or $2,000.

In Chapter 8 we mentioned the use of jingles—catchy songs about a product that carry the theme and product identification. These finger-snapping, toe-tapping songs have tremendous power because they are so memorable. Jingles are good for product identification and reminder messages, but they do not effectively convey complex thoughts and copy points.

Jingles can be used by themselves as a musical commercial, or they can be added to any other type of commercial as a product identification. A straight announcer commercial, for example, might end with a jingle. Musical forms can be easily adapted to the station's programming. Most major campaigns that use radio produce a number of different versions of the jingle, each one arranged to match the type of music featured in the programming, whether it is country and western, rock, reggae, or easy listening.

Music can also be used behind the dialogue to create mood and establish the setting. Any mood, from that of a circus to that of a candle-lit dinner, can be conveyed through music. Music can be composed for the commercial or it can be borrowed from a previously recorded song. There are also a number of music libraries that sell stock music. This music is not copyrighted, however, so there is no guarantee that other ads will not use the same music.

SOUND EFFECTS

Sound Effects (SFX): Lifelike imitations of sounds.

Sound effects (SFX) are also used to convey a setting. The sound of sea gulls and the crash of waves, the clicking of typewriter keys, and the cheers of fans at a stadium all create images in our minds. Sound effects can be original, but more often they are taken from records. As with anything else, restraint is a good rule of thumb with sound effects. Use only those you need unless the genuine purpose is to bombard the listeners with sounds.

SCRIPTING

As we discussed in Chapter 11, radio commercials are written for a limited time frame. The common lengths are 10, 20, 30, and 60 seconds. The 10-second and 20-second commercials are used for reminders and product or station identification. More elaborate messages are usually 30 or 60 seconds. The 60-second spot is quite common in radio, although it has almost disappeared in television, where the more common length is 30 seconds.

As a rule of thumb, you can estimate that about two words a second is average for a well-placed commercial. You can go as high as 135 words in a 30-second commercial. If you exceed these limits, chances are your speaker will have to rush through the copy with little or no time for those pauses and special inflections that add color and dimension to the spoken word.

FORMS

Like television scripts, radio scripts use a common form and code. The scripts are typed double-spaced with two columns. The narrow column on the left describes the source of the sound, and the wider column on the right gives the actual content of the message, either words or a description of the sound and music. The typing style is important because typed cues tell the producer and announcer instantly what is happening. For example, anything that isn't spoken is typed in capital letters. This includes the source identification in the left column and all instructions and descriptions that appear in the right column. Underlining is used to call attention to music and sound effects in the right column so the announcer can see instantly that those instructions are not to be read over the microphone as if they were copy. If you write radio scripts often, you will probably use a preprinted form that sets up the columns and the identification information for the commercial at the top.

PRODUCING A RADIO COMMERCIAL

Radio commercials are produced in one of two ways. They are either taped and duplicated for distribution, or they are recorded live. The more common form is the taped radio commercial.

TAPED COMMERCIALS

The radio *producer* is in charge of getting the commercial casted, recorded, mixed, and duplicated. All the sound elements are recorded separately or laid down in stages. Voices can be double- and triple-tracked to create richer sounds. There may be as many as 24 separate tracks for an ad. **Mixing** occurs when the tracks are combined, with appropriate adjustments made in volume and tone levels.

Mixing: Combining different tracks of music, voices, and sound effects to create the final ad.

National radio commercials are produced by an advertising agency, and duplicate copies of the tape are distributed to local stations around the country. Commercials for local advertisers might be produced by local stations, with the station's staff providing the creative and production expertise. The recording is done in house using the station's studio.

Many such commercials are designed to run five seconds short of the time purchased to give the local announcer time to add a *live local tag* (where to buy the product, sales dates, and so on). Copy for the tag is included with the produced tape.

LIVE SPOTS

By their nature, live spots are usually composed of straight announcer copy. The inclusion of sound effects, music, or additional speaking parts would require studio production. The live script is advantageous to the local retailer who must get a message on the air in a matter of hours.

An unusual experiment in live radio was conducted in Chicago when the *Chicago Tribune* hired two of the city's top radio personalities to ad-lib commercials while they bantered on the air. The approach was the idea of Hal Riney & Partners. Media columnists criticized the ads for not sounding like ads. The "extemporaneous ad-lib announcement" involved reading an item—whether personal ad, column, or news story—from the *Tribune* and mentioning the paper's name. The ads were paid for and listed as 60-second commercials in the station's program log.

MESSAGE TRENDS

What does the future have in store for broadcast advertising? Cable and videocassettes are having a tremendous impact on television commercials. The nature of the advertising message has changed dramatically, and the percentage of the audience that watches and listens to the commercials has diminished. Clutter on the networks, the increasing costs of commercials, and smaller audiences have forced television commercials to become more competitive than ever before.

There are two observable trends in the length of television messages. As previously explained, network commercials are getting shorter, with 15-second spots becoming more and more common. In alternative media such as cable, videocassettes, and movie theaters, advertising messages are getting longer—often lasting 2 to 5 minutes. **Infomercials** are even longer commercials—some lasting 30 minutes—and provide extensive product information.

Infomercial: A long commercial that provides extensive product information.

ZAPPING

The threat of zapping commercials, or zipping (editing out ads when replaying a prerecorded video), makes the creative side of the message even more important. To survive in this new era when control over the message is in the hands of a viewer holding a remote-control device requires an awesome creative effort that will make the commercials even better than the programs. See the Concepts and Applications box for a discussion of techniques being developed to create commercial messages that people won't want to zap.

Another technique used to beat the zipping and zapping is to embed the commercial message in some kind of programming. For example, during the Texas Sesquicentennial, Media Drop In Productions produced a series of true tales about Texas featuring Willie Nelson. Included within the 45 vignettes were commercials for Wrangler jeans. In this instance Willie Nelson delivered the stories to the audience, while a voice-over delivered the advertising messages. However, it is not unusual for an actor to deliver the ad message. This was quite common in the early days of network television when advertisers sponsored an entire program, such as *The Dinah Shore Chevrolet Show*.

Another threat to television advertising, which has been a characteristic of radio listening for many years, is *surfing* or *grazing*. Combine the many choices offered by cable systems with the television remote control and you have grazing. Men are particularly guilty of constantly switching channels, often when the commercial comes on. Grazing is much easier than zapping and may prove to be a more serious problem.

THE VCR VOICE PROGRAMMER CAN ZAP THROUGH COMMERCIALS ON COMMAND.

IMAGE MANIPULATION

Sophisticated computer graphic systems, such as those used to create the *Star Wars* special effects, have pioneered the making of fantastic original art on computers. At the same time, MTV has generated some of the most exciting video techniques to be seen anywhere on television. The messages are filled with action, unexpected visuals, and, most of all, imaginative special effects.

*C*ONCEPTS AND *A*PPLICATIONS

ZAPPROOFING THE ADS

The opening story in Chapter 8 described "stealth advertising" by Elizabeth Taylor's Black Pearls perfume. The product and star appearances were designed to be ads that couldn't be zapped. In other words, the promotional message was embedded in a program. As more people get remote controls and become more impatient with commercials, zapping is becoming a serious issue and the search is on for ways to zapproof ads. *Zapproofing* commercials means designing them to be entertaining—dramatic, funny, puzzling, or emotional.

The Pretesting Company has found that the key to zapproofing is to develop ads with "stopping power." Of course, once the ad arrests viewers' attention, it must continue to hold attention by addressing viewers' interests. Len Sugarman, executive vice president and creative director at Foote, Cone & Belding, says that zapproofing calls for "advertising that is more intriguing up front . . . more intriguing and beautiful."

Arthur Meranus, executive vice president and creative director at Cunningham & Walsh, separates ads into those that use a traditional tell-it-up-front approach, sometimes referred to as the P&G (Procter & Gamble) approach, and those that use "some sort of likability in the beginning." The traditional commercials start by telling the viewer what the product is and what it promises. Meranus feels, however, that the trend is toward commercials that start with likability devices, such as the Bud Light sight gags. What that is leading to is fast-moving ads that are intended to catch the eye of someone grazing through the channels and hold his or her attention. They have to immediately catch the eye or they are lost in the blur.

But there are even more unavoidable techniques being developed. In addition to Elizabeth Taylor's appearance in programs, the technology exists to insert logos or other short messages right into the image-creating commercials that can't be zapped. Primarily used in sports marketing, Princeton Electronic Billboard (PEB) has invented a way to insert live video images, such as a logo or slogan, in such prime locations as behind the batter's box or above the basketball rim. Called "L-vis" for short, live video insertions can be used to block out somebody else's sign on the wall of a stadium as a way to replace a local sign for a national broadcast. Players can move in front of these virtual signs, and television viewers can't tell the difference.

Watch how you watch television. Have you ever stopped for a commercial as you surfed through the channels? What caught your attention? What about the commercial stopped

your surfing? Compile your ideas and those of your classmates to create a profile of a zapproof commercial.

DISCUSSION QUESTIONS

1. What one ad has caught your attention recently? What makes it attention-getting? Would it stop you if you were surfing through the channels? Why?

2. If you were designing an ad for Gap clothing stores, what would you do to make sure that it is zapproof?

Sources: Adapted from Mary Kuntz, Joseph Weber, and Heidi Dawley, "The New Hucksterism," *Business Week* (July 1, 1996):76–84; Ronald B. Lieber, "Here Comes the TV Commercial No Remote Control Can Zap," *Fortune* (October 16, 1995):31; Kevin M. Williams, "Zappers Outnumber Americans," *Chicago Sun-Times* (April 7, 1996):2; "Can Ad Agency Creativity Combat Zapping, Zipping?" *Television/Radio Age* (November 11, 1985):63–65.

In the new computer-animated world, television images are changing dramatically. Already the Quantel Paint Box system is being used by computer graphics specialists to create and manipulate video images. Eventually, as costs decrease, these systems will find their way into the art director's office and will expand the graphic capabilities of the agency and production houses—both for print and for video.

Computer graphics artists brag that they can do anything with an image using a computerized "paintbox"—they can make Mel Gibson look 80 or Bob Dole look 30. They can look at any object from any angle or even from the inside out. Photographs of real objects can be seen on television as they change into art or animation and then return to life.

An example of computer graphics is a commercial by the computer production company Charlex for Pringles potato chips that shows six children munching on Pringles that appear to come out of their computers. The set is a collection of real elements, including desks, chairs, computers, students, and bookcases, but the scene is "perfectly colorized, cloned, and totally paintboxed, right down to shadows and lighting effects." The wide-angle pan reveals six children plucking Pringles from their computer screens. However, two of those youngsters were created via paintbox. Likewise only three computers actually existed in the original scene; the rest were cloned by paintbox.

INTERACTIVE MEDIA

Another technological change that may affect the way broadcast ads are created in the future is interactive media. Recall from our discussion in Chapter 11 that interactive media will allow the consumer to select from a myriad of choices within a commercial. In the case of an auto manufacturer, for example, the company may dispatch a sales representative to a viewer's home to offer a test drive after the viewer simply presses a button. Or a catalog could be sent electronically to a printer placed beside a television set in the viewer's living room. Want more information on a Ford vehicle? Push a button and a videotape could be mailed to your house. Interactive advertising also may involve activities that attempt to draw consumers' attention to a specific commercial. Viewers may be asked to respond to elements in a spot in order to receive, say, a $2 coupon. For example, a viewer may be asked to hit a button as soon as he or she understands the message in a commercial so that the viewer can get the coupon.

How will interactive media influence broadcast advertising? The keynotes of the new era are sponsorship, embeds, and target marketing. There likely will be many more *full sponsorships*; this means that the viewer won't be able to take advantage of a service without sitting through an ad. Consequently, there will be times when viewers won't be able to tell the difference between the advertising and the programming. With embedded advertising the ad becomes part of the program, or vice versa. As media companies learn more about viewers, interactive ads will become more and more targeted. Add the interactive component, and the problem becomes designing commercials that contain (on demand) all the components that might interest all the viewers.

*S*UMMARY

- A television commercial is characterized as acceptable if it is well done, intrusive, and if it can gain the attention of the viewer without annoying.

- The most common message strategies employed in television commercials are combining action and motion, storytelling, the use of emotion, demonstration, and combining sight and sound.

- There are several possible elements in a typical television commercial: video, audio, talent, props, setting, lighting, graphics, and pacing.

- A number of ways to produce a message for a television commercial exist: live film, prerecorded film or videotape, or animation techniques that include shooting frame by frame.

- Planning and producing television commercials require a number of decisions involving the length, the number of scenes, key frames, whether or not to use local production, the appropriate point of view, and the creation of scripts and storyboards.

- Producing a television commercial usually includes a team consisting of a director, producer, composer, and editor. Production goes through a variety of stages: preproduction, the shoot, rushes, and postproduction.

- A radio commercial relies heavily on the special talents of the copywriter; it is characterized as being more personal but requiring less listener attention.
- Like television scripts, radio copy is written for a certain time frame and according to a particular form and code. The style tends to be vernacular. The primary creative tools are the proper voice, music, and appropriate sound effects.

- Radio commercials can be live or taped.
- There are several trends that will affect the creation of broadcast commercials in the future: Commercials will get shorter, but infomercials will provide lengthy commercials; commercials that reduce zapproofing and grazing will be produced; and commercials will be embedded into programming, especially in the case of interactive media.

QUESTIONS

1. Think of an effective television commercial you have seen recently. Why was it effective? What types of creative efforts do you think went into producing this commercial? How long do you think it took to produce? How much do you think it cost?

2. How has the emergence of cable television and VCRs affected the nature of commercials? How might they affect advertising in the future?

3. What are the major characteristics of radio ads? How do these characteristics reflect the use of voice, music, and sound effects?

4. Professor Strong has set up a lively debate between the advertising sales director of the campus newspaper and the manager of the campus radio station, which is a commercial operation. During the discussion the newspaper representative says that most radio commercials sound like newspaper ads, but are harder to follow. The radio manager responds by claiming that radio creativity works with "the theater of the mind," something that no newspaper ad can do. Can you explain what these creative positions mean? Do you agree with either one?

5. Jingles are a popular creative form in radio advertising. Even so, there are probably more jingles that you don't want to hear again than ones that you do. Identify several short musical bits that you really dislike. Consider the reasons why you do not like them. Do they reflect on the advertiser? Write some descriptive statements on why these jingles don't work in your case.

6. Rough ideas for television commercials are often tested on selected members of the target audience. Sometimes tests use key visuals or storyboards; other times they use photoboards or even animatics. If you were deciding which testing style to use, would the type of product help you decide? Give some examples of products that would be better tested with animatics than with storyboards.

7. Television is primarily a visual medium. However, very few television commercials are designed without a vocal element (actors or announcers). Even the many commercials that visually demonstrate products in action use an off-screen voice to provide information. Why is there a need to use the voice to provide continuity and information?

SUGGESTED CLASS PROJECT

Select a product that is exclusively advertised through print. Examples of such products are alcohol, cigarettes, many industrial products, school supplies, and several canned food items. Develop a 30-second television spot for this product, providing a complete schedule of activities beginning with the creative component and ending with a completed ad. (You can stop with the storyboard.) Include all the key decisions a producer and director would make.

FURTHER READINGS

Baldwin, Huntley, *Creating Effective TV Commercials* (Chicago: Crain Books, 1972).

Heighton, Elizabeth J., and Don R. Cunningham, *Advertising in the Broadcast Media* (Belmont, CA: Wadsworth Publishing Co., 1976).

Orlik, Peter B., *Broadcast Copywriting* (Boston: Allyn and Bacon, 1982).

Terrell, Neil, *The Power Technique of Radio-TV Copywriting* (Blue Ridge Summit, PA: Tab Books, 1971).

White, Hooper, *How to Produce an Effective TV Commercial* (Chicago: Crain Books, 1981).

It's a sign of the times: Employees laid off because of technological advances that are part of the computer-driven information age. For example, the number of bank tellers fell dramatically from the mid-1980s through the mid-1990s as ATMs became popular. The trend has even affected musicians, particularly those who earn their livings by recording jingles for the advertising industry and work on record projects and motion picture soundtracks. Today, thanks to a technique called *sampling*, a single musician using a digital synthesizer can reproduce the sounds of violins, horns, drums, and virtually any other instrument. Moreover, using special software known as a sequencer, the musician can record the fully orchestrated composition directly onto a computer hard drive or digital tape. This eliminates the need to pay hourly rates at a conventional recording studio. The new technology means that the total cost of creating a jingle that will air nationally has fallen from $10,000 a few years ago to $2,000 or less today.

Not surprisingly, this trend has hit musicians right where it hurts, namely, in their pocketbooks. Musicians who provide freelance performance services are known as session players; the two most important markets for session players are Los Angeles and New York City. Until recently, top session players could expect to earn as much as $100,000 each year, including hourly fees for actually playing music in the recording studio and subsequent payments (known as residuals) based on the number of times the ad was aired. Now more than half of the commercials shown on television feature music created with synthesizers. Many session players trained on traditional acoustic instruments have watched helplessly as the number of bookings for jingles sessions, records, and film sessions has dwindled. Membership in the New York chapter of the American Federation of Musicians has fallen from 18,000 in 1982 to 10,000 in 1996.

Dave Tofani is a 25-year veteran of the New York recording scene. A graduate of the prestigious Juilliard School, he earns a living as a saxophone and woodwind player. During the heyday of the jingles scene in the 1970s, Dave played on hundreds of national television spots for companies such as Coca-Cola, Pepsi, and TWA. In those days, union scale for musicians was in the $50 to $60 range; the current rate is $90 per hour plus residuals. A long-running ad can generate considerable income from residuals; over time, a musician could earn $500 to $2,000 or more from a single date. Dave continues to receive payments for a Dunkin' Donuts spot he recorded 20 years ago that is still being aired today.

How would a musician like Dave hook up with a session? The agency responsible for an ad—McCann-Erickson, for example—would contract with a music house to provide a producer, a composer/arranger, and musicians. Herman Edel Associates was one of the dozen or more large music houses that hired top session players to ensure the best possible sound in the session. "It wouldn't be uncommon to do three jingles sessions per day, say from 10 to 11 in the morning, another from noon to 1 pm, and then maybe a two-hour session from 2 to 4," Dave says. The sessions took place in major recording studios such as CBS Studios, A&R Recording, and the Power Station. Studios typically charged the ad agency rates of $200 to $250 per hour.

The computer revolution means there are only two or three sessions per week requiring the services of classically trained musicians like Dave. Others in the industry have been negatively affected as well. Technology has opened opportunities for smaller music houses such as New York's Schneider Music; in the early 1990s, pressured by competition from newcomers, Herman Edel went out of business. Gone too are some of the famous studios; CBS Studios has closed, as has A&R. The Power Station was on the brink of closing but received a last-minute reprieve when it was sold to a Japanese company.

Of course, not everyone has been hurt by the computer revolution in the jingles industry. One former studio musician, John Giaier, has created more than 1,000 jingles using a unique approach: He inputs musical notes and chords from well-known hit songs into his computer. The computer then recombines the music and, thanks to powerful music notation software, generates sheet music for a new jingle. Giaier then composes lyrics and handles vocals; an assistant creates instrumental backing tracks for the jingle using a synthesizer. Finished jingles, many of which are for car dealers, sell for about $8,000. Not everyone approves of computer-generated jingles, however. Ray Barnette, a Nashville-based jingle writer, says, "It is ultimately not real music." But Barnette acknowledges, "The work is becoming highly competitive and the advertisers want it done as cheaply as possible."

Source: "Music: Man vs. Machine," *The Wall Street Journal Report* (July 13, 1996) #720. *Additional Sources*: Oscar Suris, "Jingle Man Retreads Pieces of Pop Hits in Car-Dealer Ditties," *The Wall Street Journal* (June 11, 1996):A1, A8; Joan E. Rigdon, "Retooling Lives: Technological Gains are Cutting Costs, and Jobs, in Services," *The Wall Street Journal* (February 24, 1994):A1, A5; Barbara March, "Small Companies Hope Music Is the Food of Success," *The Wall Street Journal* (April 8, 1991):B2; and Michael Walker, "The Plight of the Session Player," *The New York Times* (November 18, 1990):30, 39, Sec. 2.

QUESTIONS

1. Summarize the variety of ways in which computer technology helps advertising agencies to cut costs when creating music for ads.

2. Do you think the quality of the music that is used in ads has suffered as a result of the computer revolution?

First Hilton HHonors Brought You The Best Hotel Reward Program.

Now We Give You The World. Introducing

Hilton HHonors® Worldwide. Now the best hotel reward program* just got better.

HHonors members can earn both hotel points and airline miles at more than 400

Hilton hotels worldwide. HHonors points can also be earned and redeemed at Vista

and Conrad International hotels. With Hilton HHonors Worldwide, the world is within

your reach. For reservations, call your professional travel agent. Or, you can make

reservations and enroll online at http://www.hilton.com or by calling 1-800-HILTONS.

*Voted Hotel Program of the Year by the readers of *InsideFlyer* magazine, 1994, 1995 and 1996. Membership, earnings and redemption of points is subject to HHonors Terms and Conditions. Airline mileage earnings subject to rate restrictions. ©1997 Hilton HHonors Worldwide.

HILTON
HHONORS
WORLDWIDE

CHAPTER

Creating Direct-Response Advertising

- They Keep Coming Back
- Direct Marketing
- The Direct-Response Industry
- Integrated Direct Marketing
- Managing Direct Marketing
- Managing the Database
- The Media of Direct Response
- Online Marketing
- The Future of Direct Marketing

CHAPTER OBJECTIVES

When you have completed this chapter, you should be able to:

- Define direct-response advertising
- Distinguish between direct-response advertising, direct marketing, and mail order
- Evaluate the various media that direct-response advertising can utilize
- Explain how today's technology has transformed the nature of direct response

They Keep Coming Back

Marriott began the hotel customer loyalty program in 1983 with Honored Guest. Hyatt followed in 1985 with its Gold Passport. By 1987 the Hilton chain realized it also needed a competitive program to protect its market share. Here's why: In only five years (1983–1987) there was a 23 percent increase in hotel rooms available in the United States but only a 10 percent increase in volume.

Instead of directly copying the competition, Hilton surveyed its best customers—the business travelers who book only 15 percent of the hotel's rooms per night but who are responsible for 60 percent of Hilton's annual business. The responses to the survey gave Hilton information on how to tailor its Hilton Honors program. Nearly 350,000 of these business travelers joined the program "practically overnight," said Perryman Maynard, vice president of the Hilton Hotel marketing program.

These valued customers received points for each stay toward future rewards: free hotel rooms, rental car savings, and more. Membership jumped to 1 million in one year. Results: These members nearly doubled their room stays from 2.5 percent of the chain's business in 1987 to 4.5 percent in 1988.

Hilton keeps changing and expanding the program, for example, by introducing a "double-point" program in partnership with American Express. When you charged your room to American Express, you received twice as many points. That extra benefit doubled Hilton's reservations.

But what about those folks who joined but never used their card? Hilton wrote and offered them upgrades the next time they stayed at a Hilton. Nearly 13 percent responded. Today Hilton Honors has more than 3 million members.

Question: Was this direct-marketing program expensive? Answer: Yes. When the program first began, Hilton's return on investment was 10 to 1. Today it's 31 to 1—or, for every dollar Hilton spends on this program, it receives $31 back. In a short time, Hilton traced more than $423 million in sales directly back to its Hilton Honors program.[1]

Direct Marketing

PRINCIPLE Traditional advertising targets groups of people; database advertising targets the individual.

Databases: Lists of consumers with information that helps target and segment those who are highly likely to be in the market for a certain product.

Direct Marketing: A type of marketing that uses media to contact a prospect directly and elicit a response without the intervention of a retailer or personal sales.

A revolution is taking place in marketing and advertising as marketers are moving to more direct forms of communication with their customers. In the past marketing communication was a monolog, with advertisers talking to anonymous consumers through the mass media. Now communication is becoming a one-on-one dialogue through computers, the mail, video, and the touch-tone telephone.

With the advent of computers and the development of extensive **databases**—files of information that include names, addresses, telephone numbers, and demographic and psychographic data—it is becoming possible for an advertiser to develop one-on-one communication with those most likely to be in the market for a certain product. This is the ultimate in "tight" targeting because the information allows advertisers to understand consumers more thoroughly and zero in on primary prospects. In other words, although traditional advertising targets groups of people, database advertising targets the individual.

According to the Direct Marketing Association, **direct marketing** "is an interactive system of marketing which uses one or more advertising media to effect a measurable response and/or transaction at any location."[2] Pete Hoke, Jr., publisher of *Direct Marketing* magazine, adds one element to this definition: "In direct

---

[1]Howard Schlossberg, "Sheraton Checks in with Club Program," *PROMO* (March 1994):23; and Murray Raphel, "How to Make Sure There's No Room at the Inn," *Direct Marketing* (September 1996):42–44.
[2]*Direct Marketing* (October 1990):22.

marketing, a database—a customer file—must exist." Embedded in this definition are five components.

First, direct marketing is an *interactive system;* that is, the prospective customer and the marketer engage in two-way communication. This allows for a much more precise feedback, typically a behavior on the part of the consumer—compared to the surrogate or more vague measures of effectiveness available for image advertising.

A second characteristic of direct marketing is that a *mechanism for the consumer to respond* to the offer is always made available. Making a measurable response available suggests that the characteristics of respondents and nonrespondents can be assessed.

A third characteristic of direct marketing is that the *exchange between the buyer and the seller is not bound by a retail store or salesperson.* Location is not an issue—the order can be made at any time of the day or night and product delivery can be made to the consumer's home.

A fourth trait and the element that suggests the primary strategic advantage offered by direct marketing is that the *response is measurable.* That is, direct marketing allows the marketer to calculate precisely the costs of producing the communication effort and the resulting income. Some posit that the ability for a type of marketing to be held accountable is the reason for the tremendous growth of direct marketing.

The final element of direct marketing is the necessity for a *database of consumer information.* Through the information in databases, the direct marketer can target communications to an individual consumer or a specific business customer who has been identified as a viable prospect. To marketers, direct marketing offers the ability to reach appropriate target audiences with the right benefits.

If this discussion still seems diffuse, let's look at a few primary, easily identified divisions within direct marketing: direct mail, telemarketing, and electronic-response media. The differences among these three lie in *how* the message is transmitted from the marketer to the consumer—and, ideally, back again. In the case of direct mail, generally the U.S. Postal Service transmits the message; in telemarketing, it's the telephone, and with electronic media, the television and radio usually predominate. These divisions are not clean, however, because one single direct-marketing project may use one or even all of the ones just mentioned. For example, you receive a catalog from Land's End in the mail. That's direct marketing. You decide to order items from the catalog by completing the order blank and returning it via mail. That's direct marketing. Or, say you decide to take advantage of the company's 800 number to place your order. That, too, is direct marketing.

The general benefits direct marketing offers to consumers are: convenience, efficiency, and compression of decision-making time. One can see how these benefits are derived when a consumer purchases a product through one of the video shopping systems such as QVC. Mrs. Smith calmly sits in front of her television and watches the various merchandise explained, demonstrated, and modeled. She notes an item she likes, places an order via the toll-free number, pays with her Visa card, and receives delivery in 48 hours. The item costs considerably less than retail, has a money-back guarantee, and she never left home.

TYPES OF DIRECT MARKETING

Direct marketing takes many different forms, although three basic categories exist: the one-step process, the two-step process, and the negative option. The *one-step process* allows the consumer to respond to an ad in a media vehicle and receive the product by mail. Often, the consumer will receive a *bounce-back* brochure promoting related merchandise with the order. The *two-step process* requires that the consumer must first be qualified before ordering the product. This might mean a required physical exam in the case of an insurance company, or a credit check before the purchase of an expensive piece of jewelry. Several catalog companies will charge a nominal fee for the catalog and apply the fee to the purchase price. Finally, the *negative option* requires that the consumer joins a plan, such as those offered by video or book clubs, that automatically sends unrequested merchandise unless the consumer mails a response card by a specific date. As an incentive to join, the initial merchandise is often offered with a free gift, extra merchandise, or a discount price.

THE DIRECT-RESPONSE INDUSTRY

Direct response has been an important advertising area for over a century. The first major venture by an important national company into mail order was the publication of the Montgomery Ward catalog in 1872.[3] The Direct Mail/Advertising Association was founded in 1917. Currently known as the Direct Marketing Association (DMA), it has long been active in industry research and professional training programs. One of DMA's most successful programs is a seminar for college students sponsored by its Direct Marketing Educational Foundation.

Direct response has been a fast-growing segment of the advertising industry in recent years. In the early 1980s annual growth averaged 30 percent. Total 1990 U.S. direct-response volume rose 18.3 percent. The current state of the industry is depicted in Figure 16.1. In 1996 it was estimated that approximately $170 billion was spent on direct-response advertising.[4]

Direct marketing is one of the selling methods applied in virtually every consumer and business-to-business category. For example, direct marketing is used by IBM, Digital Equipment, Xerox, and other manufacturers selling office products. It is used by almost every bank and insurance company. It is used by airlines, hotels, and cruise lines, as well as by resorts and government tourist agencies. It is used by packaged-goods marketers, such as General Foods, Colgate, and Bristol Myers; by household product marketers, such as Black and Decker; and by automotive companies, such as Ford, Buick, and Cadillac. Direct marketing is also employed for membership drives, fund raising, and solicitation of donations by nonprofit organizations such as the Sierra Club, Audubon Society, and political associations.

An example of a company that has become interested in integrated marketing communication vis-à-vis direct marketing is Safeway Stores. Essentially, Safeway has signed up manufacturers such as Quaker Oats Co. and Stouffer Food Corp. for a database mail program that trades incremental trade dollars for top-notch data. The program exemplifies the convergence of two trends: Grocers are looking for manufacturers to supplement their own shrunken marketing budgets, and manufacturers eager to allocate new field-marketing support dollars are shopping for local deals. Up to seven manufacturers will fund Safeway's quarterly mailings in exchange for in-store support and sales data. Safeway's mid-Atlantic division piloted "Families with Children" mailings in Baltimore, targeting 250,000 households from its 1.2 million Savings Club members.[5]

REASONS FOR GROWTH

Direct-response advertising is growing for both social and technological reasons. The influx of women into the work force in recent decades and the rise in

---

[3]Kenneth C. Otis II, "Introduction to Direct Marketing," DMMA Manual Release 100.1 (April 1979):1.

[4]"Direct Marketing—An Aspect of Total Marketing," *Direct Marketing* (September 1996):3.

[5]Betsy Spethmann, "Safeway Signs Up Marketers in New Deal," *Adweek* (May 8, 1995):9.

FIGURE 16.1

THE ORGANIZATION AND
REVENUE FOUND IN DIRECT
MARKETING.

Source: Direct Marketing, 224 Seventh
Street, Garden City, New York
11530-5771, p. 3. Reprinted with permission from Hoke Communications,
Inc., Garden City, NY USA 11530,
(516)746-6700.

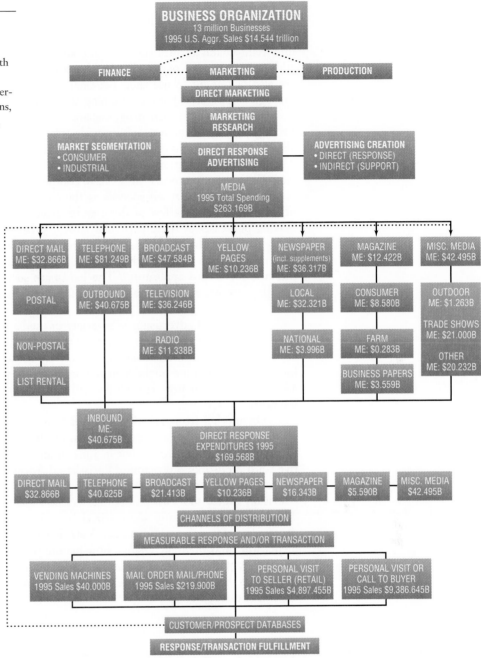

the number of single-parent homes are two societal factors. Furthermore, both
men and women are very busy today and find shopping a nuisance. They would
rather not spend their precious leisure time looking for a place to park at the
mall.

Technological advances have made direct response more efficient for marketers and more beneficial for shoppers. Zip codes and toll-free numbers have
made it easier for consumers to respond. Another major factor has been the credit
card. With an automated billing system, a customer can call in an order and give a
number for billing. The order is filled immediately; the company does not have to
wait for a check to be mailed and cleared by the bank. These technological improvements have created the "armchair shopper" who would just as soon shop
from the easy chair at home as drive to a store.

THE COMPUTER

The technology that has had the biggest impact on direct marketing is the computer. Advertisers use the computer to manage lists of names, sort prospects by important characteristics such as zip code or previous ordering patterns, handle addressing, and feed personalized addresses into the printing process. Consumers are also beginning to use their personal computers at home to reach marketers through computerized home-shopping services.

Computers and their programs are getting smarter. Online services, such as Prodigy, run by Sears, not only provide the user with online buying services but also remember purchases and, over time, build a purchase profile of each user. This kind of information is very valuable to marketers, resellers, and their agencies. Already some grocery stores have computerized their grocery carts with displays that show advertised specials as the customer moves from one aisle to another. Customers at a few of these stores have been issued bank cards to use in making purchases at these particular stores. When a customer makes a purchase using the card, the store's computer provides an item-by-item list of that customer's purchases and adds this to the demographic and income information on the customer's card application. The banks are so interested in this information that they are willing to waive the usual fees and charges to the store in trade for the data.

Personalized advertising in a variety of media may become the norm in the near future. Smart computers, used with videotext systems and cable broadcast facilities, will be able to tailor messages precisely to each of us as individuals. Imagine hitting a milestone birthday or obtaining a new job and finding that all of the advertisements you now receive are tailored to these new characteristics about yourself.

On another front, AT&T and Ford Motor Company's Lincoln-Mercury division signed on for the launch of *Newsweek* Interactive, a CD-ROM version of the newsweekly being rolled out in June in an IBM-compatible format. And Active Card Networks, a division of Paris-based Adventure SA, is helping to roll out in the United States an interactive device that allows consumers to play along with television games and earn points that can be redeemed at participating retailers. The situation is cogently summarized by Ellen Oppenheim, senior vice president/media director at FCB/Leber Katz Partners. "We believe that interactive media will fundamentally change how people will use their televisions and think it's important that our clients have an opportunity to understand this at an early stage of its development."[6] More will be said about online services under the discussion of direct media.

INTEGRATED DIRECT MARKETING

Throughout this text we have been extolling the benefits of integrated marketing as a managerial approach. Historically, direct marketing is the first area of marketing communication that has adopted this philosophy. In fact, it would be appropriate to rename direct marketing as *integrated direct marketing*. To be concise, instead of treating each medium separately, integrated direct marketing seeks to achieve precise, synchronized use of the right medium at the right time, with a measurable return on dollars spent. Here's an example: Say you do a direct-mail campaign, which commonly generates a 2 percent response, a percentage long viewed as a good or average return. If you include a toll-free 800 number in your mailing as another option to the standard mail-in reply—with well-trained, knowledgeable, tightly scripted individuals handling those incoming calls—you

---

[6]Scott Donaton, "Interactive Ventures Sign First Ad Deals," *Advertising Age* (May 24, 1993):4.

will achieve a response of 50 percent to 100 percent over and above the base return of 2 percent. You will go to a 3 percent to 4 percent response rate.

If you follow up your mailing with a phone call—within 24 to 72 hours after your prospect receives the mailing—you can generate a response 100 percent to 700 percent higher than the base rate. So, by adding your 800 number, you bring the rate from a 2 percent response to 3 percent or 5 percent. By following up with phone calls, you add another 2 percent to 14 percent, bringing your response rate as high as 5 percent to 18 percent. This example has integrated only two marketing channels, direct mail and telemarketing.

The principle behind integration is that not all people respond the same way to direct mail. One person may sit down and very carefully fill out the order form. Someone else may immediately reach for the phone to call the 800 number. Most people, however, if an ad has grabbed them at all, tend to think to themselves, "Looks interesting, but I'm not sure it's for me. Let me put it in my pending pile." That pile grows and grows—and then goes into the garbage at the end of the month. The phone call, however, may get them off the fence and take a suggested action.

Hewlett-Packard, AT&T, Citibank, and IBM have all used integrated direct marketing to improve their response rates dramatically. In this economy, with markets shrinking because of competition and market budgets flat, integration is the smartest option.

PROBLEMS WITH DIRECT MARKETING

Tremendous growth and poor early management have created serious problems in the direct-marketing industry. Many of the troubles are symptoms of managerial nearsightedness, a failure to consider long-term goals, and the organization as a whole.

One initial problem stems from the trade-off between short-term versus long-term strategies. Several direct-marketing techniques are characterized as "one-shot" strategies. Examples of the short-term approach crop up daily in consumer mailboxes: mailings that look like telegrams, air-express packages, legal communications, or government documents. Short-term direct marketing does get a response—for a while, until customers become wary. Telemarketing techniques have proven to be even a greater irritant to consumers. Calls that disturb meals or an evening of relaxation, or play a voice recognition recording, prompt 2 to 7 percent of consumers to buy. But at what price? This type of direct market consists of short-term, disloyal customers who were really fooled or coerced into responding. It also reinforces the "junk messages" image that many consumers hold of direct marketing.

A second problem with direct marketing is its tendency not to mesh well with a company's operations, its distribution systems, communications, research, overall strategy, or even culture. For example, direct marketers have been part of programs that have failed because they are so successful: Catalog companies have run out of inventories, costing them not only short-term sales but long-term goodwill; financial firms have generated too many leads for their salespeople to follow up. Another common failure in integration involves direct marketing and advertising. Direct-marketing messages and advertising messages often do not reinforce each other because, organizationally, the people who do direct-response advertising usually are not integrated with people who do advertising. Nor is the advertising agency integrated with the direct-marketing agency or in-house group. This is changing, however.

A final problem with direct marketing is its relatively high cost per thousand. Although it is hard to accurately document a general figure, experts posit that direct-response advertising has a higher CPM than image advertising. A direct-mail campaign, for example, still can cost between $200 and $500 per thousand households. The cash differential will likely continue to rise as the costs of both postage and paper increase. Bulk mailing, although cheaper than first class, offers no guarantees on time of delivery, and delays are common. Thus, sale mailers by retailers may arrive after the sale is over.

DIRECT-RESPONSE ADVERTISING

No doubt, creative approaches and placement strategies in direct-response advertising are far different for each type of product or service for sale. The one common thread that seems to run through all types of direct-response advertising is that of action. That is, **direct-response advertising** seeks to achieve an action-oriented objective—such as an inquiry, a visit to a showroom, an answer to a questionnaire, or the purchase of a product—as a result of the advertising message and without the intervention of a sales representative.

Ad 16.1 for Ford Escort, for example, looks like a traditional advertisement except that it is featuring an 800 number and a Web page to encourage inquiry. Direct-response advertising can use any medium—magazines, newspapers, radio, television, or direct mail. The focus on the objective contrasts with *brand or image advertising*, where the desired response to the advertising message is typically awareness, a favorable attitude, or a change of opinion. With brand or image advertising, the actual sale is made by a retailer in a store or a sales representative who calls at the office or home.

Direct-Response Advertising: A type of marketing communication that achieves an action-oriented objective as a result of the advertising message.

AD 16.1

ESCORT PROVIDES BOTH AN 800 NUMBER AND A WEB PAGE IN THIS AD.

Obviously direct response can be a very efficient form of sales communication because it eliminates that second sales step. Historically, however, it has been seen as less efficient because it didn't reach as many people as did mass-media advertising or, if it did, the cost of reaching them individually was very high. Today this argument is being reconsidered. Direct response is now seen as reaching a prime audience—people who are more likely than the average person, for some reasons related to their demographics or lifestyles, to be interested in the product. In other words, although it costs more per impression, direct-response advertising has less waste than mass-media advertising. It is better targeted. Furthermore, although it lacks personal contact, which is an important element in closing some types of sales, the newer forms of interactive media are beginning to solve that problem as well.

DATABASE MARKETING

As we mentioned earlier, the growth of extensive databases has contributed to more targeted communication with consumers. CCX, for example, is a database program that stores more than 1 billion names and allows list users to mix and match information.

Based on recent research conducted by John Cummings & Partners DBM/scan, database marketing usage increased 30 percent from 1993 to 1995, with 3,207 database programs noted in the packaged-goods industry alone. Moreover, the companies committed to using database marketing for the long term is approximately 42 percent.[7] This new development is also referred to as *database marketing, relationship marketing,* or *"MaxiMarketing."*[8] More and more marketers are moving to this new form of direct marketing as a way to develop a deeper and longer-lasting relationship with their customers. Auto companies, for example, are using database marketing systems to link national marketing, service, and dealer organizations with customers. Databases allow companies to call new customers within 30 days of delivery of their cars to get their impressions of the product and to take care of any problems. Such systems can also be used to profile customers and research their purchasing behaviors.

List brokers have thousands of lists tied to demographic, psychographic, and geographic breakdowns. They have classified their data on America's households down to the carrier routes. For instance, one company has identified 160 zip codes it calls "Black Enterprise" clusters, inhabited by "upscale, white-collar, black families" in major urban fringe areas. If you want to target older women in New England who play tennis, most major firms would be able to put together a list for you by combining lists, called **merging,** and deleting the repeated names, called **purging.**

Merging: The process of combining two or more lists of prospects.

Purging: The process of deleting repeated names when two or more lists are combined.

Nintendo has a 2-million-name database it uses when it introduces more powerful versions of its video game system. The names and addresses were gathered from a list of subscribers to its magazine, *Nintendo Power.* The company believes that many of its current customers will want to "trade up" and this direct communication will make it possible for Nintendo to speak directly to its most important target market about new systems as they become available. Nintendo began its database in 1988 and credits database marketing with helping it to maintain its huge share of the $4.7 billion video game market.

As discussed in the Issues and Controversies box, the evolution of massive databases is not without its problems. The "right to privacy" alarm has been sounded since shows like *60 Minutes* and *48 Hours* have featured the sharing and selling of databases.

---

[7]B.G. Yovovich, "Database 'Stealth' Adds to Marketing Arsenal," *Advertising Age* (October 16, 1995):26.

[8]Stan Rapp and Tom Collins, *MaxiMarketing* (New York: McGraw-Hill Book Co., 1987).

INTERACTIVE TECHNOLOGY

The new interactive technology, however, is what makes this area of direct marketing so exciting. Interactive means the consumer can respond back to the message. The telephone is the prime example of a media vehicle that both delivers and receives messages. For example, Pepsi planned a call-in sweepstakes for the 1991 Super Bowl but postponed the effort because it feared the nation's telecommunication capacity could not handle the response. Interactive technology is being developed, possibly using toll-free 800 numbers or 900 pay-for-call numbers, that will be able to generate 30,000 simultaneous calls and take detailed messages, like answers to a trivia quiz or a credit card order. Such systems will be capable of handling up to 300,000 phone calls in 30 minutes. At present, this system still envisions using a bank of clerks to transcribe names and addresses spoken by callers, but computer voice recognition will eliminate that need when that technology becomes available.

The secret to the success of database marketing is the power of the computer to manage the incredible wealth of descriptive data that are now being accumulated along with prospect lists. Most list brokers have standard lists for sale, but in addition they can sort, merge, and purge lists to custom-design one to fit a particular prospect profile.

Managing Direct Marketing

Direct marketing employs the same general planning framework suggested for advertising earlier in this text. It is unique, however, because of certain elements considered crucial to its success. For example, direct marketing is dependent on the quality of its database. It also uses special media to deliver messages. Many of these components have been covered in earlier chapters. The discussion that follows highlights elements unique to direct marketing. We begin with a brief description of the key players in direct marketing.

Three main players are involved in direct-response marketing: *advertisers* who use direct response to sell products or services by phone or mail; certain *agencies* that specialize in direct-response advertising; and *consumers* who are the recipients of direct-mail and phone solicitations.

THE ADVERTISERS

There are more than 12,000 firms engaged in direct-response marketing whose primary business is selling products and services by mail or telephone.[9] This number does not include the many retail stores that use direct marketing as a supplemental marketing program. Traditionally, the product categories that have made the greatest use of direct marketing have been book and record clubs, publishers, insurance, collectibles, packaged foods, and gardening firms.

In a recent study sponsored by the DMA, the following was learned:

In 1995, when direct-response advertising was used to solicit a direct order, generate a lead, or generate retail store traffic, it resulted in nearly $600 billion in sales.

In 1995, business-to-business sales from direct orders, lead generations, and traffic generation were estimated to have reached nearly $500 billion.

Compounded annual growth rates of sales over the next five years will be 7.2 percent for consumer; 10.2 percent for business-to-business.

---

[9]Mary Lou Roberts and Paul D. Berger, *Direct Marketing Management* (Englewood Cliffs, NJ: Prentice Hall, 1989).

ISSUES AND CONTROVERSIES

THEY KNOW WHO YOU ARE!

The privacy issue is going public as consumers complain and direct marketers fight for their right to conduct business. Many industry insiders expect the issue to get more attention from the Clinton administration. Consumers' privacy problems with direct marketers involve two key issues. The first is fairly basic: Some consumers simply feel they shouldn't have to deal with pitches flooding their mailboxes and telephones. The second issue is far more complex. It involves sophisticated databases and other wonders of modern technology that allow marketers to mine a wealth of information about consumers: everything from the names and ages of their children to what kind of socks they prefer.

That type of information is invaluable to direct marketers, allowing them to zero in on prime targets for their products and services. But increasing numbers of consumers are voicing concern that there's too much personal information floating around in those databases, and they want to know how it got in there.

Today, consumers are more willing to take an active role in protecting their own privacy, with about 59 percent reporting cases where they've refused to provide requested data, up from 42 percent since 1990, according to the Equifax Harris Mid Decade Consumer Privacy Survey. In a parallel study by Louis Harris & Associates, of 1,006 people, 82 percent said they were "very" (47 percent) or "somewhat" (35 percent) concerned about threats to personal privacy, and 80 percent said they feel "consumers have lost all control over how personal information about them is circulated and used by companies," up from 71 percent in 1990.

In 1992, more than 1,000 bills on privacy issues were presented in state legislatures. At least ten bills made an appearance at the federal level. Consumer advocates are also pushing for protection of the consumer's right to privacy. The American Civil Liberties Union has said that while direct marketing can be valuable to marketers and consumers, there's a need for a watchdog group to protect personal privacy rights.

The direct-marketing industry has effectively argued that there is no need for legislation and that self-regulation is working. As proof, it points to the Direct Marketing Association's Mail Preference Service (MPS) and Telephone Preference Service. Consumers who do not wish to be contacted by direct marketers can register with one or both of the services. The DMA puts these names into a file and makes them available to direct marketers four times a year.

In 1996, the Telecommunications Competition and Deregulation Act (commonly referred to as the Reform Bill) was enacted. This bill makes human privacy—as consumer, business, and government agency—far more important. It ensures that consumers are able to use the wide array of information and distribution media available to them without fear of being unduly exploited.

"It's a very complicated issue. Privacy means a lot of different things to different people. Mere mention of the word privacy and you have a reaction," said Steve Cone, chairman of Epsilon, a database marketing subsidiary of American Express. "My read on the American public is that it's not a top-of-the-mind issue," said Cone. "People say they get too much mail, but when you ask them if they want all mail stopped, they say 'no, but why can't people send things I want?' which is why we have databases." What concerns consumers is that companies trade personal information, he said, but what much of the public doesn't understand is that when a company buys a list, it only has one-time use of names and addresses. "Believe it or not, companies are not in business to irritate the consumer by doing bad or improper things with the data," he said.

Adapted from Cyndee Miller, "Privacy vs. Direct Marketing," *Marketing News* (March 1, 1993):1, 14, 15; Gary Levin, "DMA Speakers Caution Use of Databases," *Advertising Age* (April 5, 1993):37; James Morris-Lee, "It's Everyone's Business Now," *Direct Marketing* (April 1996):40–43; and Laura Loro, "Privacy Concerns Have Consumers Guarding Data," *Advertising Age* (December 11, 1995):40.

One of every 13 jobs in the United States today is the result of direct-marketing sales activity.[10]

Some of the largest direct-marketing firms are well known because they are major retail firms that use national advertising, but others are not as familiar because they only engage in direct marketing. Among the largest U.S. direct marketers are Sears, J.C. Penney, Time-Warner, and the American Automobile Association.[11]

THE AGENCIES

Three types of firms are involved in direct-response advertising: advertising agencies, independent direct-marketing agencies, and service firms.

[10]"WEFA Study Measures Direct Response Ad," *Direct Marketing* (November 1995):6–9.
[11]Arnold Fishman, "The 1986 Mail Order Guide," *Direct Marketing* (July 1987):40.

A WOMAN ORDERING
MERCHANDISE DIRECTLY
FROM A CATALOG.
(Teri Stratford)

ADVERTISING AGENCIES

First are the *advertising agencies*, whose primary business is general media advertising. These agencies either have a department that specializes in direct response or they might own a separate direct-response company. Many major advertising agencies that want to provide integrated, full-service promotional programs for their clients are buying direct-response companies because this is such an important part of the corporate promotional program.

The ability of traditional advertising agencies to integrate direct marketing into their operation has proven very challenging for many. Apparently, the differences between direct and traditional advertising are greater than first envisioned.

INDEPENDENT AGENCIES

The second category is the *independent, full-service, direct-marketing agency.* These companies specialize in direct response, and many of them are quite large. Table 16.1 lists the top ten direct-marketing agencies. The largest direct-marketing agencies include some firms that specialize only in direct response and others that are affiliated with major agencies.

SERVICE FIRMS

The third category is made up of the *service firms* that specialize in supplying such services as printing, mailing, and list brokering.

A type of service firm that is vital to the success of many direct-marketing strategies is the *fulfillment house.* Essentially these businesses are responsible for making sure consumers receive whatever they request in a timely manner, be it a catalog, additional information, or the product itself.

THE CONSUMERS

Most people have a love-hate relationship with direct-response advertising. They complain about the "junk mail" that clutters their mailbox. They hate to get tele-

TABLE 16.1	DIRECT-RESPONSE AGENCY RANKINGS BY BILLINGS					
AGENCIES	**TOTAL BILLINGS (IN MILLIONS)**		**U.S. BILLINGS (IN MILLIONS)**		**INTERNATIONAL BILLINGS (IN MILLIONS)**	
	1993	**1994**	**1993**	**1994**	**1993**	**1994**
1. Ogilvy & Mather Direct	$928.7	$973.0	$440.0	$413.0	$488.7	$560.0
2. Rapp Collins Worldwide (1)	833.2+	934.4	390.0	461.0	443.2	473.4
3. Wunderman Cato Johnson	708.5	910.5	393.4	430.6	315.1	479.9
4. Kobs & Draft Advertising, Inc.	438.0	493.7	201.2	259.8	236.8	233.9
5. Bronner Slosberg Humphrey, Inc.	305.1	333.5	305.1	333.5	NA	NA
6. Grey Direct International	287.0	312.3	161.0	184.3	126.0	128.0
7. DIMAC DIRECT, Inc. (1) (2)	176.1	271.4	176.1	271.4	NA	NA
8. Barry Blau & Partners, Inc.	204.3	261.6	204.3	261.6	NA	NA
9. McCann Direct	203.0	215.0	53.0	50.0	150.0	165.0
10. Customer Development Corp. (1)	151.3	172.4	151.3	172.4	NA	NA

Source: "DM Special Report," *Direct Marketing* (November 1995):58. Reprinted with permission from Hoke Communications, Inc., Garden City, NY USA 11530, (516) 746–6700.

phone calls at dinnertime asking for donations, no matter how good the cause. They ridicule the salesperson on television who is demonstrating a new screwdriver. However, they respond. They buy through direct-mail letters and catalogs, they listen to the personal sales pitch over the telephone, and they call in orders after watching television ad pitches.

NEW SHOPPERS

Although people might dislike the intrusiveness of direct-response advertising, they appreciate the convenience. Former Postmaster General Preston Tisch observed that it is "a method of purchasing goods in a society that is finding itself with more disposable income but with less time to spend it."[12]

PRINCIPLE The push-button shopper is self-confident and willing to take chances on a product that can't be seen, touched, or tried on.

Stan Rapp described this new consumer in his speech to the annual DMA conference a few years ago as "a new generation of consumers armed with push-button phones and a pocket full of credit cards getting instant gratification by shopping and doing financial transactions from the den or living room." He pointed to the tremendous success of Domino's Pizza, with its home-delivery service, as the fastest-growing sector of the $12 billion pizza market.[13]

Relative to merchandising history, the push-button shopper is a new breed. It takes some daring to order a product you can't see, touch, feel, or try out. It is not like shopping at a retail store. This new breed of consumer is self-confident and willing to take a chance but doesn't like to be disappointed.

CREATING LOYALTY

One of the historical truths about the direct-marketing industry was that merchandisers tended to view the relationship with the consumer as a short-term one, with the assumption that losing one unhappy consumer is not a disaster since another sucker is right around the corner. While there are some direct marketers that still employ this philosophy, most have realized that maintaining a long-term relationship with the consumer is crucial.

Changing the attitude of the consumer toward direct marketing has not been easy. The question is: How do you create consumer loyalty? Several attempts are evident. For example, companies like Sprint are taking an innovative approach to sales force training in order to enhance loyalty. In one case, for customer Siptech Display, a Sprint representative recognized a phone number which might have been mistakenly disconnected. The simple act of calling to verify the discon-

---

[12]"Outlook '87," *Target Marketing* (January 1987):25–28.

[13]"Looking into the Future of Direct Marketing," *Direct Marketing* (May 1987):144–145, 153.

nect order so impressed the customer that Siptech decided to move its entire phone system to Sprint.[14] Similarly, Saks Fifth Avenue identified a group of customers who accounted for half of all sales and offered the group exclusive benefits through a program called Saks First. The benefits include fashion newsletters and first crack at all sales.

Perhaps the most ambitious attempt to create consumer loyalty is through a concept called *lifetime customer value* (LCV). LCV is simply a measure, over time, of how much purchase volume you can expect to get from the various purchase segments. To put it scientifically, LCV is "the over-time volume/financial contribution of an individual customer or customer segment, based on known consumption habits plus future consumption expectations, where contribution is defined as return on investment, i.e., revenue gains as a function of marketing costs."[15] In simple terms, by knowing a consumer's past behavior, you can decide how much you want to spend to get him or her to buy your product—and you can track your investment by measuring the response.

MANAGING THE DATABASE

As noted earlier, the database is the very essence of direct marketing. According to the Direct Marketing Association, a marketing database has four primary objectives:[16]

1.   To record names of customers, expires (names no longer valid), and prospects;
2.   To provide a vehicle for storing and then measuring results of advertising (usually direct-response advertising);
3.   To provide a vehicle for storing and then measuring purchasing performance; and
4.   To provide a vehicle for continuing direct communication by mail or phone.

Managing this process is extremely difficult, and it is growing in complexity along with improved technology. The initial decision a company must make is whether it will gather data from internal sources, external sources, or both. Internal, or in-house, databases are derived from customer receipts, credit card information, or personal information cards completed by customers. The internal approach is cost-effective as long as the company has the expertise and resources. If either expertise or resources are lacking, a company can obtain commercial databases from firms whose sole purpose is to collect, analyze, categorize, and market an enormous variety of detail about the American consumer. Companies such as National Decision Systems, Persoft, and Donnelly Marketing Information Systems are only a few of these firms. For example, Donnelly recently took the wraps off Hispanic Portraits, a database of households that segments the U.S. Hispanic population into 18 cluster groups.[17]

DESIGNING A DIRECT-MARKETING PIECE

Although there are differences depending on the medium used, all direct-marketing pieces have five equal components. Moreover, there are certain sound princi-

[14]Margery Tippen, "Building Customer Loyalty through Quality Telemarketing," *Direct Marketing* (September 1996):14–15.

[15]Barbara Jack, "There's No Rocket Science to 'Lifetime Customer Value,'" *PROMO* (October 1992):27.

[16]Fred R. McFadden and Jeffrey A. Hoffer, *Data Base Management* (Menlo Park, CA: Benjamin/ Cummings, 1985):3.

[17]Glenn Heitsmith, "New Hispanic Marketing Tools Announced," *PROMO* (March 1993):33.

ples of design and strategy that apply. The five elements are: (1) the offer, (2) the medium, (3) the message, (4) timing and sequencing, and (5) customer service.

The *offer* constitutes all the variables that together are intended to satisfy the needs of the consumer. Because of the unique benefits provided through direct marketing, the offer may contain the following elements—a price, the cost of shipping and handling, optional features, future obligations, availability of credit, extra incentives, time and quantity limits, and guarantees or warranties.

Selecting the *medium* and the *message* are decisions that go hand-in-hand with direct marketing. The message strategies discussed in earlier chapters are equally applicable to direct marketing. The media used in direct marketing have been specially developed to accommodate the unique advantages of direct marketing and will be discussed later in this chapter.

There is a great deal of similarity between the *timing* and *sequencing* of direct marketing and of advertising. The direct marketer must consider questions about repetition, seasonality, flighting versus pulsing, and one-shot programs versus campaigns. One difference, however, is the greater emphasis placed on the strategic aspect of direct marketing. In advertising, creative execution receives most of the attention; the key to the success of direct marketing, however, is reaching the right person at the right time.

Direct marketing owes its evolution from junk-mail status to credibility to the introduction of *customer service.* The types of customer service offered, such as toll-free telephone numbers, free limited-time trial, and acceptance of several credit cards, for example, are important techniques for overcoming customer resistance to buying through direct-response media. The Concepts and Applications box demonstrates how one company has successfully implemented a direct-marketing plan.

THE MEDIA OF DIRECT RESPONSE

Direct response is a multimedia field. All conventional advertising mass media can be used, as well as others that you might not think of as advertising media, such as the telephone and the postal service. Sometimes media are used in combination. A mail offer, for example, may be followed up with a telephone call. Advertising is allocating increasing sums of money to direct-response media.

Telemarketing is clearly the growth area in direct response. It includes both incoming and outgoing calls—in other words, any telephone call related to direct marketing comes under this category, including offers, orders, inquiries, and service calls. The calls placing orders may be in response to ads in any of the media. Direct mail through television is expensive because of the costs of production and airtime. Figure 16.2 summarizes how the media of direct marketing is employed by its users.

DIRECT MAIL

Direct mail provides the historical foundation for the direct-response industry. A direct-mail piece is a complex, self-standing advertising message for a single product or service. It may be as simple as a single-page letter or as complex as a package consisting of a multiple letter, a brochure, supplemental flyers, and an order card with a return envelope.

Direct mail continues to be the main medium of direct-response messages. It accounted for nearly 60 percent, or $3.8 billion, of total direct-response media spending in 1990.[18]

---

[18]Laura Loro, "Mail Favorite Tool in Direct Marketing Circles," *Advertising Age* (June 1996):S-16.

$\mathscr{C}$ONCEPTS AND $\mathscr{A}$PPLICATIONS

GTE DOES IT DIRECT

How does a phone company communicate the fact that a new directory offers significant benefits over existing products? That was the question GTE Directories tackled as it launched an ambitious marketing campaign to introduce a new edition of The Everything Pages® Yellow Pages. The book was the first to combine the metropolitan areas of Portland, Oregon, and Vancouver, Washington, into one easy-to-use book. The phone company needed to show area businesses that this was not a parity product—that it was a new concept that could play a major role in their marketing efforts.

The challenge was to fuel revenue growth with existing sales personnel, so GTE needed to cut through the clutter with attention-getting marketing vehicles. GTE launched a team effort, which included key managers and administrators from advertising, public relations, field marketing, and sales. The goal was to craft a memorable, integrated effort with all of the components reinforcing one another. One of the key elements was the direct-mail piece.

To assist in measuring the success of the direct-mail piece, the following objectives were agreed upon: to introduce the benefits of GTE's new Portland/Vancouver directory to potential advertisers; to contribute to the sales team's ability to hit aggressive revenue targets by building awareness of the product and by increasing advertisers' propensity to purchase space in a first-year product; and to encourage trial among targeted audiences through the use of a promotional offer.

The major question was how to communicate the primary benefit (advertise in one directory to reach two markets) to potential advertisers. Although GTE was committed to an integrated approach that included radio advertising, public relations, and promotions, the company determined that the

cornerstone of the campaign would be a direct-mail piece targeted to potential advertisers.

The direct-mail piece was designed to complement an existing nationwide media campaign that featured famous historical figures. GTE built its local marketing efforts, including the direct-mail piece, around the theme of trail blazing and called on the famous Oregon trail blazers, Lewis and Clark, to help introduce the book.

To maximize existing budget dollars, the program was divided into high-potential and low-potential advertisers. The former received an attention-getting box containing a brochure and trail mix. Copy on the outside of the box read, "If you're scouting for customers in the Portland/Vancouver area, we're the right mix." Inside, a bag of trail mix accompanied a brochure describing the new directory and its many benefits. The mailer also contained a $300 gift certificate to Circuit City. Low-potential advertisers received a self-mailer, which mirrored the illustrations and messages of the brochure in the high-potential mailing. This allowed recipients to take advantage of the promotional offer but reduced GTE's cost per unit.

Feedback from advertisers indicated that they were overwhelmingly impressed with the uniqueness of the campaign. In addition, more than 70 percent of the advertisers that signed contracts purchased larger space or more items than were required to qualify for the incentive offer. The campaign was particularly effective in tying a national creative umbrella campaign with characters of unique local appeal. And its segmented approach allowed budget dollars to be used cost effectively and efficiently.

Source: Doug Knight, "Direct Marketing Campaign Sparks Interest, Spurs Action," *Direct Marketing* (September 1996):38–41.

Most direct mail is sent using the third-class bulk mail permit, which requires a minimum of 200 identical pieces. Third class is cheaper than first class, but it takes much longer to be delivered. Estimates of nondelivery of third-class mail run as high as 6 to 8 percent.

FIGURE 16.2

DIRECT-MARKETING TOOLS.
Source: Laura Loro, "Mail Favorite Tool in Direct Marketing Circles," *Advertising Age* (June 1996):S-16. Reprinted with permission from *Advertising Age.* Copyright Crain Communications Inc.

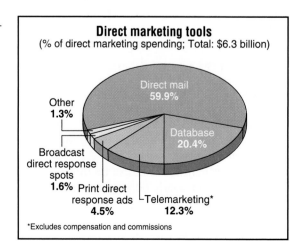

Direct marketing tools
(% of direct marketing spending; Total: $6.3 billion)

Direct mail 59.9%
Database 20.4%
Other 1.3%
Broadcast direct response spots 1.6%
Print direct response ads 4.5%
Telemarketing* 12.3%
*Excludes compensation and commissions

CHARACTERISTICS

Direct mail, more than any other medium, demonstrates how a message can sell a product without the help of a salesperson. Because direct mail is a self-contained sales message, it has to deliver all the information and all the incentives necessary to make a sale. If it didn't work, it wouldn't have been used all these decades. Response rates for direct mail are generally higher than those for any other medium used in direct marketing.[19]

There are a number of advantages associated with direct mail as compared to traditional mass media. First, the medium offers a variety of formats and provides enough space to tell a complete sales story. Second, since direct mail has little competition when received, it can actually engage the reader's attention. Third, it is now possible to personalize direct mail across a number of characteristics, such as name, product usage, and income. Fourth, direct mail is particularly conducive to marketing research and can be modified until the package matches the desired target audience. Finally, direct mail allows the marketer to reach audiences who are inaccessible by other media.

The primary drawback of using direct mail is the widespread perception that it is junk mail. According to the 1991 Harris-Equifax Consumer Privacy Survey, about 46 percent of the public still sees direct-mail offers as a nuisance, and 90 percent considers them an intrusion of privacy.[20] A second disadvantage of direct mail is the high cost per prospect reached. A great deal of this high cost is a result of postage. In fact, a technique that some direct-mail organizations use to cut postage costs is called *remailing*. Simply, direct marketers send their materials to the United States from foreign countries. Remailers typically ship prepared mailings in bulk to a Central American country such as Panama or Honduras, where postal rates to U.S. addresses are much lower than in the United States.[21] The postal service is attempting to stop this practice. A final disadvantage of direct mail is the heavy reliance on the quality of the mailing list.

MESSAGE FORMAT

Direct mail can be anything and look like anything, but most pieces follow a fairly conventional format. The packaging usually includes an outer envelope, a letter, a brochure, supplemental flyers or folders, and a reply card with a return envelope.

PRINCIPLE The critical decision whether to read or toss is made on the basis of the outer envelope.

THE OUTER ENVELOPE   One of the most important elements in direct mail is the outer envelope. The critical decision by the target is whether to read the mailing or throw it out, and that decision is made on the basis of the outer envelope. Actually, the industry estimates that three-fourths of the pieces do get read. Ad 16.2 gives examples of outer envelopes.

Advertisers use a number of techniques to get people to open the envelope. One is to state the offer on the outside: "Save $50 on a set of china." If an incentive is part of the offer, then that might be used: "Order now and get a free telephone." An envelope that looks very much like it contains a check is another type. A *teaser* statement or question might be used to spark curiosity: "What is missing from every room in your house?" A "peek-through window" may be used to show part of the product; a "show-through envelope" can call attention to the message design of the brochure and the quality and colorfulness of its graphics. Teaser copy is especially valuable when advertisers are mailing third class to a new or unknown list.

PRINCIPLE Direct-response letters have to do the work of hundreds of people.

THE LETTER   The letter is second in importance because it is the next thing seen after the envelope. The letter highlights and dramatizes the selling premise and explains the details of the offer. Most letters are two to four pages long,

---

[19]Katzenstein and Sachs, *Direct Marketing*, p. 118.

[20]Carrie Goerne, "Direct Mail Spending Rises, But Success May Be Overblown," *Marketing News* (March 2, 1992):6.

[21]Ibid.

AD 16.2

EXAMPLES OF DIRECT-MAIL ENVELOPES. WHAT CHARACTERISTICS OF THESE ENVELOPES WOULD ENCOURAGE RECIPIENTS TO EXAMINE THE CONTENTS?

although many are longer. Research has found that people with any interest in the product will read everything in the letter. The letter has to carry the full weight of the marketing, advertising, and sales effort.

Bill Jayme, one of the best copywriters in direct-response advertising, has commented that people "often ask why we in direct marketing are so verbose. Letters that can run to eight pages. Brochures the size of a bedsheet." He explains why: "Because a single mailing package must in one fell swoop do the work, in more conventional selling, of many hundreds of people."[22]

[22]John Francis Tighe, "Complete Creative Checklist for Copywriters," *Advertising Age* (February 9, 1987):24, 69.

---

*I*NSIDE *A*DVERTISING

ANN RAMOS, SENIOR ACCOUNT EXECUTIVE, *Topp Direct Marketing, Harlingen, Texas*

While there are some who call current marketing trends revolutionary, I say that they have come full circle.

There was a time when marketing was confined to your neighborhood—a one-on-one "sales call" by a neighbor asking for your business, a flyer on an upcoming sale or grand opening of a store down the street that is personally handed to you by an industrious young man (probably the son of a neighbor), signs hanging off buildings or painted on fences. With the great technological leaps made in communication, the neighborhood grew into a part of the city, into a city, into a part of the state, into a state, into a region, into a nation and beyond, into the rest of the world.

With the growth of the neighborhood and the growth in technological progress, the business and industrial world turned to mass media to communicate messages to the population. This proved to be the most efficient and effective means of capturing the attention of prospects and soliciting their business . . . until now.

With the rise of mass media advertising costs and the even faster rise of computer technology that aids in building extensive databases, more and more businesses are returning to neighborhood marketing. But the neighborhood is no longer necessarily a geographical area. It may also incorporate such demographics as a group of people with the same range of annual household income or the number of children under age 18 at home, or such psychographics as similar buying habits or interests.

One way that business may reach such a neighborhood is by direct-mail marketing. As account executive for Topp Di-

rect Marketing, a 13-year-old direct-mail marketing agency located in the southern tip of Texas called the Rio Grande Valley, I help Valley businesses communicate with the neighbors of their choice.

Our full line of services includes creative (art, copy, and composition of the elements of a direct-mail package), printing, mailing lists, addressing, data processing, mailing, binding, warehousing, and fulfillment. In the history of our business, clients have included community colleges, car dealers, political candidates, banks, mobile phone systems, commercial real estate agencies, fast-food restaurants, evangelical ministries, and insurance agencies.

My first priority for a client that has either come to us with a marketing problem or that has expressed an interest in direct-mail marketing is to determine the precise nature of the target audience. While some advertising agencies or professional marketers are sophisticated enough to know this information already, many small businesses must be talked through the process of identifying their marketing objectives and then narrowing down the description of their prospects.

The basic mailing job includes the purchase of the list, the application of labels to a provided mailing piece, and delivery to the applicable post office. Other direct-mail jobs include the creation and printing of the mailing piece, the creation of a direct-response package that may include a custom outer envelope, a personalized letter, a brochure, and a response piece that can be mailed alone or in a provided envelope, and the development of a regularly scheduled or follow-up mailing program.

The style of the letter is personal. It usually begins with a personal salutation that includes the target's name. The tone is a little different from that of traditional media advertising. It points out things about the offer as a friend might. The first paragraph works like a headline to convince the reader to stay with the message all the way through. It may dramatize the selling premise, spark curiosity, or make some incredible statement as a way to build interest. Often the first paragraph will also introduce a task, such as finding a personalized sticker, that will provide the consumer with additional benefits or prizes.

The body of the letter provides support, explanation, proof, documentation, and details. This is serious hard-sell copy. One critical part of the letter is the postscript (P.S.). Because the postscript is highly attention-getting, most writers use it to wrap up or restate the offer.

THE BROCHURE   Accompanying the letter may be a brochure that features the product in glowing color. The letter uses words; the brochure uses graphics to create impact. The product is displayed in as many attractive settings as possible. Demonstrations and how-to-use visuals are included, if appropriate. These can be one-page flyers, multipanel folders, multipage brochures, or spectacular **broadsheets** that fold out like maps to cover the top of a table. Smaller, supplemental pieces may also be used as postscripts or for additional details or incentive offers.

Broadsheets: Large brochures that unfold like a map.

THE RESPONSE DEVICE   The response device is the order form, often including a toll-free phone number. It should summarize the primary selling points and be

---

Once we have identified the group or groups of people who would be most interested in purchasing the products or services of, or donating funds to, or voting for our client, then we turn to our resources for the ideal list or combination of lists that best meets the objectives and the budget of the client. Such resources include companies that rent their own mailing lists, like magazines or credit card companies, list compilers that accumulate data from public records or surveys, and list managers that rent the lists of an accumulated group of companies that don't wish to market their lists themselves.

Prior to the rental, the list resources will provide for budgeting purposes a count of the total number of addresses on a particular list and the base cost per thousand, along with any additional charges, such as those for specific ages or geographical boundaries. With the count in hand, we can determine the cost of ordering and receiving the list into our office, processing the application of labels, and mailing the pieces at the lowest possible rate. We then provide the client with a quotation.

With the implementation of the restructured postal rates as of July 1, 1996, ignorance is costly while compliance pays. The United States Postal Service is streamlining the mail delivery system and rewards the compliant user with the best rates.

By adhering to postal requirements for addressing that may include barcoding, bundling that includes the proper use of the post office's provided trays or bags, and addresses that include Zip+4 and approved abbreviations and formats, we can ensure our clients lower postal expenses. That means getting the most mailing for the money. In addition, we can en-

sure higher rates of delivery. After all, what good is a mailing piece that doesn't reach the target audience?

This is how we work for our clients. But why does direct marketing work? The concept has changed from mass marketing through mass media to *maximarketing* through targeted media. The term was coined by direct-marketing experts Stanley Rapp and Thomas L. Collins to describe the marketing methods that have developed in response to the demassification of today's society. Our new neighbors need not be down the street, but they do need to share some attribute or interest that is important to the marketing effort of a business.

According to the Direct Marketing Association's *1996 Statistical Fact Book*, the average consumer receives 21.31 pieces of mail per week and they read 54.3 percent of all advertising mail. That's why advertising expenditures on direct mail have more than doubled in the ten years from 1984 to 1994, from $13.8 billion to $29.6. With the fragmentation of the mass media audience, direct mail makes sense for business.

Even though the maximarketing concept was introduced to the business world more than ten years ago, smaller businesses like the kind that dominate the Rio Grande Valley are still learning to make the most of their marketing budget through direct marketing. With my deep background in small-market newspaper advertising and promotional products sales, I find it rewarding to see the independent businessperson grow and prosper in the marketplace. My goal with Topp Direct Marketing is to prepare our Valley businesses and organizations for the twenty-first century through smarter marketing.

Nominated by Prof. Salma Ghanem, University of Texas Pan-American

simple to read and fill out. Finally, since the order form is a legal document, it is important that the firm's legal department clear all wording.

THE RETURN DEVICE   The return device is any mechanism that allows the consumer to return the necessary information. It can be an information request form, an order form, or a payment. Typically, a response envelope is provided unless a card is used as a response device. The envelope serves as an incentive and is convenient, especially if the postage is prepaid.

MESSAGE FUNCTIONS

The functions of a direct-mail message are similar to the steps in the sales process. The mailing plays many roles. First, it has to get the attention of the targeted prospect. Then it has to create a need for the product, show what it looks like, and demonstrate how it is used. Furthermore, it has to be able to answer questions like a good salesperson and reassure the buyer. It might have to provide critical information about product use. It must inspire confidence, minimize risk, and establish that the company is reputable. Finally, it has to make the sale, which involves explaining how to buy, how to order, where to call, and how to pay or charge the purchase. There may even be an incentive to encourage a fast response.

THE LIST

Direct-mail advertising can only be effective if the mailing list targets the appropriate customers. If the prospects are not in the market for the product, then even the best direct-mail package will be thrown away. The biggest problem with computer-generated lists is accuracy. Updating mailing addresses is a constant problem in a mobile society. Other errors include addressing a woman as a man (and vice versa) and misspelling names.

The mailing list is really a segmentation tool. The list is usually categorized in terms of certain consumer characteristics, such as demographics (young mothers), professions (accountants, hair stylists, engineering professors), interests (sailing, jogging, cat or dog owner), or buying behavior (buys from upscale catalogs). As with all other forms of advertising, the more selective and upscale the list, the more it will cost.

Lists can be purchased or rented from *list managers,* people who work for companies that offer lists of group memberships that they want to market, or from list brokers. A *list broker* handles a variety of lists from many different sources and can act as a consultant to help you find a list or compile your own list from several different sources.

There are three types of lists: house lists, response lists, and compiled lists. *House lists* are lists of customers maintained by a company, store, or association. Most retailers know that their most important target audience is their own customers, so it is important to identify these people and keep in touch with them. Stores offer their own credit plans in order to maintain this link. They also offer things like service plans, special sale announcements, and contests that require customers to sign up. Some stores fill in the customer's name and address at the cash register on the sales slip, and the carbon copy becomes a source of names for the list. This is probably the most valuable list available to a store or company.

A *response list* is derived from people who respond to something such as a direct-mail offer or solicitation from a group whose members are similar to the advertiser's target audience. For example, if you sell dog food, you might like a list of people who have responded to a magazine ad for a pet identification collar. These lists are usually available for rent from the original direct-mail marketer. This type of list is very important because it indicates a willingness to buy by direct mail.

A *compiled list* is one that is rented from a direct-mail list broker who represents a company that has a house list for sale or who works for a direct-mail company that is in the business of building lists. These are usually lists of some specific category, such as sports car owners, new home buyers, graduating seniors, new mothers, association members, or subscribers to a magazine, book club, or record club.

Lists can be further combined using a computer that has the ability to merge several lists and purge the duplicate names. For example, you may want to develop a list of people who are in the market for upscale fine furniture in your city. You could buy a list of new home buyers and combine that with a list of people who live in a desirable census tract. These two lists together would let you find people who have bought new homes in upscale neighborhoods. The merge/purge capability is very important to avoid using several lists that have the same names, in which case people may receive multiple copies of the same mailing. This is annoying to the recipient and expensive to the mailer.

THE CATALOG MARKETPLACE

A catalog is a multipage direct-mail publication that shows a variety of merchandise. The big books are those produced by such retail giants as Montgomery Ward and J.C. Penney. The Spiegel company is a major catalog merchandiser that doesn't have a retail outlet. Saks Fifth Avenue, Neiman-Marcus, and Bloomingdale's are major retailers that support their in-store sales with expensive catalogs.

The catalog business went through a decade of explosive growth, increasing 25 to 30 percent in the mid-1980s, but the industry has settled down in the 1990s and is coming to grips with saturated markets. The postal rate increase in 1991 was one factor in the slowdown. A slowing economy is another. Catalog experts estimate that sales in 1994 totaled $76 billion to $80 billion and are now growing only at a rate of 8 to 12 percent a year.

SPECIALTY CATALOGS

The real growth in this field is in the area of specialty catalogs. There are catalogs for every hobby, as well as for more general interests, such as men's and women's fashions, sporting goods, housewares, gardening, office supplies, and electronics. There are catalogs specifically for purses, rings, cheese and hams, stained-glass supplies, garden benches, and computer accessories—to name just a few. For example, Balducci's fruit and vegetable store in Greenwich Village, New York City, produces a catalog promising overnight delivery of precooked gourmet meals.

Some of these retailers have their own stores, such as L.L. Bean, Williams-Sonoma, and Banana Republic. Others, such as Hanover House and FBS, offer their merchandise only through catalogs or other retailers. Levi's, for example, has always depended on other retailers to distribute its products, but it is now planning a catalog that will make the entire Levi's line available to its customers. Some of the merchandise is relatively inexpensive, like the Hanover line, which is usually $10 or less. Others are much more upscale.

There are even examples in the catalog industry of targeting specific races. Essence by Mail is a partnership with Hanover Direct that features apparel and collectibles, and annually reaches over 11 million African-American households. Hanover has uncovered some differences in the way that Essence by Mail customers shop. They spend more time with the telemarketing reps than general market customers, for example. Another key difference is that black consumers "don't respond to traditional seasons the way the general market does—African-Americans buy closer to the season and their needs."[23]

---

[23]Cyndee Miller, "Catalogers Learn to Take Blacks Seriously," *Marketing News* (March 13, 1995):8.

Catalogs are the chief beneficiaries of the social changes that are making armchair shopping so popular. In fact, catalogs are so popular that direct-response consumers receive mailings offering them lists of catalogs available for a charge. People pay for catalogs the way they pay for magazines: An increasing number of catalogs can now be purchased at newsstands.

DESIGNING THE CATALOG MESSAGE

The most important part of the catalog message is the graphics. Products are displayed in attractive settings showing as many details and features as possible. People scan through a catalog, looking at the pictures. Only after they have been stopped by the visual do they read the copy block. Thus copy is usually at a minimum and provides such details as composition, fabric, color, sizes, and pricing.

Some catalogs are low-budget, particularly those in special-interest areas such as hobbies and professional supplies. A catalog for woodworkers or plumbers might be printed on cheap paper in black and white. Most general-interest catalogs, however, are moving to quality reproduction with slick paper and full-color printing. The fashion catalogs are often shot at exotic locations, and the reproduction values are excellent.

Some catalogs are designed to create an image, such as the Banana Republic and Caswell-Massey catalogs, which come in unusual sizes and use distinctive illustrative styles. Caswell-Massey is an apothecary that dates back to Colonial days and carries an unusual assortment of soaps, brushes, after-shave lotions, and colognes. Banana Republic specializes in the "jungle look" in fashion, and each of its catalogs features a story about some expedition to an exotic location.

ELECTRONIC CATALOGS

Catalogs are becoming available in videocassette and computer disk formats. Buick developed an *electronic catalog* on computer disk. The message is interactive and features animated illustrations. It presents graphic descriptions and detailed text on the Buick line, including complete specifications, and lets you custom-design your dream car.[24] The electronic catalog has been marketed to readers of computer magazines.

Video catalogs are being considered by a number of advertisers. Video offers a dynamic live presentation of the product, its benefits, and its uses. With more than half of American homes owning VCRs, this medium is becoming increasingly important. Cadillac developed a video brochure for Allante, its new luxury car. Air France and Soloflex have also investigated videos for in-home promotions.

PRINT MEDIA

Ads in the mass media are less directly targeted than are direct mail and catalogs. However, they can still provide the opportunity for a direct response. Ads in newspapers and magazines can carry a coupon, an order form, an address, or a telephone number for customers to respond to. The response may be either to purchase something or to ask for more information. In many cases the desired response is an inquiry that becomes a sales lead for field representatives.

One of the most interesting experiments with personal targeting using magazines was *Time* magazine's cover in 1990 that incorporated each reader's name into its cover design. The covers read, "Hey (*subscriber's name here*) don't miss our really interesting story on the junk mail explosion" (see Ad 16.3). Newsstand copies read: "Hey, you at the newsstand." The article, incidentally, noted that 92 million Americans responded to direct-marketing in 1989, a 60 percent increase in six years.

---

[24]"Software Beats Hard Sell at Buick," *Advertising Age* (November 24, 1986):59.

AD 16.3

MAGAZINES HAVE EXPERI-
MENTED WITH PERSONAL TAR-
GETING TO ATTRACT SPECIFIC
AUDIENCE MEMBERS.

In *MaxiMarketing* Rapp and Collins discuss the power of *double-duty adver-tising* that combines brand-reinforcement messages with a direct-response cam-paign to promote a premium, a sample, or a coupon. Giorgio perfume, Cuisinart, and Ford all use multifunctional advertising in magazines that works two or more ways, including direct response.[25]

American Express is using this double-duty concept in its attempt to com-bine magazine and direct marketing. The company has launched *Your Company,* a quarterly mailed to more than 1 million American Express corporate card mem-bers who own small businesses. *Your Company* was launched by four sponsors—IBM, United Parcel Service, Cigna Small Business Insurance, and American Express Small Business Services. American Express also mails a magazine, *Connections,* to college students. Such efforts combine the editorial direction of a magazine with direct advertising's ability to target a narrow audience based on de-mographics and lifestyle. Magazines have been trying to do this with demographic editions and selective bindings as well.

REPLY CARDS

In magazines the response cards may be either *bind-ins* or *blow-ins.* These are free-standing cards that are separate from the ad. Bind-in cards are stapled or glued right into the binding of the magazine adjoining the ad. They have to be torn out to be used. Blow-in cards are blown into the magazine after it is printed by special machinery that "puffs" open the pages. These cards are loose and may fall out in distribution, so they are less reliable.

BROADCAST MEDIA

Television and radio have also become involved in direct-marketing advertising.

---

[25]Rapp and Collins, *MaxiMarketing,* p. 171.

TELEVISION

Television is a major medium for direct marketers who are advertising a broadly targeted product and who have the budget to afford the ever-increasing costs of television advertising. Direct-response advertising on television used to be the province of the late-night hard sell with pitches for vegematics and screwdrivers guaranteed to last a lifetime. As more national marketers such as Time-Warner move into the medium, the direct-response commercial is becoming more general in appeal.

In a departure from its traditional reliance on magazine ads and its door-to-door sales force, Avon aired a series of television commercials in 1992 encouraging women to buy its products via a toll-free number. One 30-second commercial featured a woman using Anew, a skin product Avon is touting for wrinkles. So far, sales are up 13 percent and sales leads have increased by 33 percent.[26]

CABLE TELEVISION   Cable television lends itself to direct-response commercials because the medium is more tightly targeted to particular interests. For example, ads on MTV for products targeted to the teenage audience can generate a tremendous response. Sales are soaring on the Home Shopping Network (HSN), a cable network that displays merchandise in living color. The QVC network, a home-shopping channel, and HSN reported more than 57 million subscribers in 1990.

The infomercial, discussed earlier, is a heavy user of cable television. The infomercial for AbFlex, for example, runs 3,000 times a month, and sells approximately 11,500 units every day.

J.C. Penney is the first major retailer to go on air via a cable hookup. The company invested $40 million in its new interactive home-shopping service called Teleaction. Through this "video catalog" service, customers can order the merchandise on screen by using their push-button phones.[27]

RADIO

Radio has not been a dynamic medium for direct-response advertising because most experts believe the radio audience is too preoccupied with other things to record an address or a telephone number. Home listeners, however, are able to make a note and place a call, and local marketers have had some success selling merchandise this way.

Radio's big advantage is its targeted audience. Teenagers, for example, are easy to reach through radio. There has even been some success selling products such as cellular phones and paging systems specifically to a mobile audience.

TELEMARKETING

Telemarketing: A type of marketing that uses the telephone to make a personal sales contact.

The telephone system is a massive network linking almost every home and business in the country. More direct-marketing dollars are spent on telephone ads using **telemarketing** than on any other medium. The telephone combines personal contact with mass marketing, which is an important factor in relationship marketing.

COSTS

Personal sales calls are very expensive but very persuasive. Telemarketing is almost as persuasive, but a lot less expensive. A personal sales call may cost anywhere from $50 to $100 when you consider time, materials, and transportation. A telephone solicitation may range from $2 to $5 per call. That is still expensive,

---

[26]Jeffrey A. Trachtenberg, "Avon's New TV Campaign says, 'Call Us,'" *The Wall Street Journal* (December 28, 1992):B1.

[27]"Penney Says Teleaction to Start by September," *Advertising Age* (June 8, 1987):82.

though, if you compare the cost of a telephone campaign to the cost per thousand of an advertisement placed in any one of the mass media. Telemarketing is four to five times as expensive as direct mail.[28]

If this medium is so expensive, why would anyone use it? The answer is that the returns are much higher than those generated by mass advertising. Telemarketing has to be efficient to be justifiable. The revenue has to justify the bottom-line costs.

CHARACTERISTICS

Telemarketing is personal; that is its primary advantage. The human voice is the most persuasive of all communication tools. Although many people regard a telephone solicitation as an interruption, there are still large numbers who like to talk on the telephone. Some people are flattered by receiving a telephone call, even if it is just a sales pitch.

TWO-WAY

Telephone conversations are also two-way. There is a conversation in which the prospect can ask questions and give responses. This conversation can be tailored to individual interests. Furthermore, if the person isn't a prospect, the caller can find out immediately and end the call.

There are two types of telemarketing: inbound and outbound. An *inbound* or incoming telemarketing call originates with the customer. Calls originating with the firm are outgoing or *outbound.* (See Figure 16.3 for top 10 outbounders.)

---

[28]Laura Loro, "Players Changing in Telemarketing Industry," *Advertising Age* (October 23, 1996):32.

FIGURE 16.3

TOP 10 OUTBOUND TELE-MARKETING FIRMS.

Source: Laura Loro, "Players Changing in Telemarketing Industry," *Advertising Age* (October 23, 1996):32.

'95 rank	'94 rank	Company	Call center locations	Specialization
1	2	**ITI Marketing Services** Omaha, Neb. (402) 393-8000	18	Financial services (including insurance), telecommunications, publishing
2	4	**Sitel Corp.** Omaha, Neb. (800) 25-SITEL	28	Insurance, financial services, telecommunications
3	3	**West Telemarketing Outbound** San Antonio, Texas (210) 690-6900	2	Financial services, insurance, various product/service sales
4	5	**Matrixx Marketing Inc.** Cincinnati, Ohio (800) 628-7499	13	Customer service, increasing sales, 800-number response
5	6	**APAC TeleServices** Deerfield, Ill. (708) 945-0055	16	Financial, insurance, telecommunications
6	9	**ProMark One Marketing Services** Phoenix, Ariz. (800) 933-0233	6	Telecommunications, financial services, high tech
7	7	**Edward Blank Associates** New York, New York (212) 741-8133	5	Financial services, telecommunications, publishing
8	14	**Results Telemarketing** Dania, Florida (305) 921-2400	34	Financial services, credit-card acquisition, insurance services
9	11	**FutureCall Telemarketing West** Colorado Springs, Colorado (808) 489-5134	2	Telecommunications, financial, publishing
10	10	**TeleService Resources** Ft. Worth, Texas (800) 325-2580	4	Customer service, reservations, sales & marketing

Source: Telemarketing magazine

Inbound calls are customer responses to a marketer's stimulus, whether a direct-mail piece, a direct-marketing broadcast, a catalog, or a published toll-free number. Since it is almost impossible to schedule customer calls, every effort must be made to ensure that the lines are not blocked. Although most inbound telemarketing occurs via toll-free 800 numbers, the 1-900 number has also grown in popularity. The popularity is a result of the interactive capacity of 1-900 numbers, which enables callers to respond to questions and leave information via touch-tone phones.

Outbound telemarketing is used by direct marketers whenever they take the initiative for a call—for opening new accounts, qualifying, selling, scheduling, servicing, or profiling consumers. Wide Area Telephone Service (WATS) is often used as an economic long-distance vehicle.

TELEMARKETING FIRMS

Most companies that use telemarketing hire a specialized company to handle the solicitations and order taking. They do this because most of the activity occurs in bunches. If a company advertises a product on television, for example, the switchboard will be flooded with calls for the next 10 minutes. Companies that do occasional direct-response advertising don't have the facilities to handle a mass response. A service bureau that handles a number of accounts is more capable of coping with the bursts of activity that follow promotional activities.

THE MESSAGE

The most important thing to remember about telemarketing solicitations is that the message has to be simple enough to be delivered over the telephone. If the product requires a demonstration or a complicated explanation, then the message might be better delivered by direct mail.

The message also needs to be compelling. People resent intrusive telephone calls, so there must be a strong initial benefit or reason-why statement to convince prospects to continue listening. The message also needs to be short; most people won't stay on the telephone longer than 2 to 3 minutes for a sales call. That, of course, is still a lot longer than a 30-second commercial.

ONLINE MARKETING

The latest and newest form of direct media is interactive online. Despite the relative uncertainty associated with the profitability of the interactive online medium, companies are spending millions of dollars to become a player in cyberspace.

Commercial Online: Private companies that provide online information for a fee.

There are two types of online channels. The first is labeled **Commercial Online,** and includes companies that have set up online information and marketing services, which can be accessed by those who have signed up and pay a monthly fee. The best-known online services are CompuServe, America Online, and Prodigy. Such companies provide subscribers with four primary services: e-mail, shopping services and dialogue opportunities (bulletin boards, forums, chat boxes), information (news, libraries, education, travel, sports, references), entertainment (fun and games).

Internet: A global web system of computer networks.

The **Internet** is the second online alternative. The Internet is a global web of some 45,000 computer networks. Originally established to facilitate research and exchanges among scholars, the Internet is now available to a much broader audience of some 30 million people. Users can send e-mail, exchange views, shop for products, and access real-time news, food recipes, art, and business information.

AD 16.4

THE L.L. BEAN HOMEPAGE PRO-
VIDES MANY INFORMATION
OPTIONS.

Direct marketers can use the Internet in four ways: create an electronic storefront; place direct-response ads online; participate in forums, newsgroups, and bulletin boards; and communicate via e-mail. For example, if a person types in L.L. Bean's home page address (http://www.lbean.com), L.L. Bean's home page appears in full color along with a multitude of options (see Ad 16.4). The key is to entice browsers to visit and then to respond to the company's home page. Web shopping malls are indexes of many product and service providers. Consumers or business shoppers can visit the malls, search via product or service, and link to a company's electronic storefront. The shopper can browse offerings and access the service or product with the click of a mouse.

Companies and individuals can place ads on commercial online services in three different ways: (1) online services offer an ad section for listing classified ads, (2) ads can be placed in certain newsgroups that are basically set up for commercial purposes, and (3) ads can be put on online billboards. The ad for Deja News illustrates a newsgroup company (see Ad 16.5).

THE FUTURE OF DIRECT MARKETING

It is clear that the relationship between advertising and direct marketing will become more intense. It is not a coincidence that a medium offering measurable levels of response has grown while others have shriveled. Direct mail, and the proliferation of infomercials with toll-free numbers, are clear signals for the future of

AD 16.5

DEJA NEWS IS AN EXAMPLE OF
AN ONLINE NEWSGROUP.

advertising. Successful marketers are investing more creativity in ads that create a response instead of just conjuring an image. Moreover, these responses can be swift, measured, and catalogued for future use. Unlike most traditional brand advertising, direct-response advertising actually builds an infrastructure from a customer database.

As for specific developments in direct marketing, experts predict that there will be a proliferation of new home-shopping systems, interactive television, and Internet retail applications. In addition, consumers will become empowered with information, and the industry will have to increase level of customer service, speed of fulfillment, and quality control. Finally, despite the constraints some would apply, technology is exploding. As the cost of managing information continues to plummet, the options continue to grow. This means that it will take a great deal of experimentation to find the right media for a particular product or service. Moreover, the same creativity that has led to innumerable clubs, infomercials, and consumer interactive promotions will be challenged to create competitive advantage in emerging interactive media.

Direct-response advertising inherently understands that wallet share and purse share is just as important as mind share. The implications of an advertising industry built around direct response are profound.

Summary

- Direct marketing always involves a one-on-one relationship with the prospect. It is personal and interactive.
- The growth in direct-response advertising has been stimulated by technologies such as computers, zip codes, toll-free numbers, and credit cards.
- Direct-response advertising can use any advertising medium, but it has to provide some type of response or reply device.
- Direct-response advertising has benefited from the development and maintenance of a database of customer names, addresses, telephone numbers, and demographic and psychographic characteristics.
- The new push-button consumer is busy and appreci-

ates the convenience of shopping at home or at the office.
- A direct-mail advertising piece is a complex package using an outer envelope to get attention, a cover letter, a brochure, an order card, and a return envelope.
- Catalogs are so popular that some consumers will pay to get their names on the mailing lists.
- Telemarketing is the biggest direct-response area; it combines the personal contact of a sales call with mass marketing.
- Online media provides direct access to product information as well as ordering and payment via the computer.

Questions

1. What are the major advantages of direct response compared to other forms of advertising? The major disadvantages?

2. What types of firms produce direct-response advertising?

3. Hildy Johnson, a recent university graduate, is interviewing with a large garden-products firm that relies on television for its direct-response advertising. "Your portfolio looks very good. I'm sure you can write," the interviewer says, "but let me ask you a serious question. What is it about our copy that makes it more important than copy written for Ford, or Pepsi, or Pampers?" How should Hildy answer that question? What can she say that would help convince the interviewer she understands the special demands of direct-response writing?

4. We know that copy and illustration are vital parts of a successful direct-mail campaign, but there must be

some priorities. Review the Chapter 13 section on "What Makes an Idea Creative." All of the components are important, but which one is the first consideration for direct-response creativity? Defend your choice.

5. One of the smaller privately owned bookstores on campus is considering a direct-response service to cut down on its severe in-store traffic problems at the beginning of each semester. What ideas do you have for setting up some type of direct-response system to decrease "traffic overload"?

6. Suppose you are the marketing director for a campus service organization dedicated to assisting needy people and families in the immediate area. What are your ideas for developing a telemarketing program to promote campus fund raising? Would it be better to solicit money directly or indirectly by having people attend specially designed events? Your primary targets are students, faculty, and staff.

Suggested Class Projects

1. Select a consumer product that is not normally sold through direct marketing. Create a direct-marketing campaign for this product. Be sure to specify your objectives and indicate the parts of the offer as well as the medium and the message.

2. Notice what sort of direct-mail advertising you and your family receive. Extrapolate what sort of database you are likely to be part of. Refer to Chapter 7 to get a

precise characterization of the groups and subgroups to which you might belong. Keep in mind age, geography, past buying habits, and so on. Evaluate your reactions: Do you mind being on such lists? Why or why not? Are you likely to order products as a result of receiving a direct-mail advertisement? If so, how frequently? Write a brief report.

FURTHER READINGS

Katzenstein, Herbert, and William S. Sachs, *Direct Marketing* (Columbus, OH: Merrill Publishing Co., 1986).

"Looking into the Future of Direct Marketing," *Direct Marketing*, May 1987, pp. 144–45, 153.

Rapp, Stan, and Tom Collins, *MaxiMarketing* (New York: McGraw-Hill Book Co., 1987).

Rapp, Stan, and Tom Collins, *The Great Marketing Turnaround* (Upper Saddle River, NJ: Prentice Hall, 1990).

Roberts, Mary Lou, and Paul D. Berger, *Direct Marketing Management: Text and Cases* (Upper Saddle River, NJ: Prentice Hall, 1989).

At a troubled time in retailing, analysts are watching the phenomenon of home shopping become a glimmer of hope—a savior of sorts—to fix industry ills. Still in its infancy, home shopping has grown from a base of zero in 1986 to over $2 billion in 1992, and sales are expected to keep growing by at least 20 percent a year. At the heart of this explosion are the QVC and Home Shopping Networks, both of which advertise an array of products, ranging from clothing to gold jewelry, from cosmetics to throw pillows, and make sales when consumers order merchandise via toll-free phone lines.

Although, according to *Business Week*, home shopping's image is now so lowbrow that it conjures up thoughts of "selling tacky figurines to the more woebegone denizens of trailer parks," its horizons are expanding rapidly into classier territory. Here are some examples of home shopping's new world:

- In just 90 minutes, socialite designer Diane Von Furstenberg sold $1.2 million in dresses on QVC and also plans to market her jewelry, fragrance, and home furnishings collections in the same way. One of the advantages of home shopping, said Von Furstenberg, is that "when you sell on TV, you do the selling and the advertising all at once."
- Tony Fifth Avenue retailer Saks Fifth Avenue has also adopted the home shopping approach to advertising. When the retailer ran its first one-hour show on QVC in 1993, it sold $570,000 worth of merchandise in its Real Clothes Collection. When designer Arnold Scaasi aired his clothing on QVC, he had a similar response. "I was just thrilled that I was reaching a consumer who doesn't have anywhere to shop," said Scaasi. "People call in saying there are no stores in their area that have this kind of clothes—better clothes selling for $135 to $225 with more styling."

Upscale retailers such as Nordstrom, Williams-Sonoma, Bloomingdale's, Spiegel, and Sharper Image are attracted to what home shopping will become as the number of cable channels approaches 500, thereby allowing marketers to target specific consumers. "The expansion of the number of cable channels will be the critical difference for a lot of specialty retailers like Sharper Image and Brooks Brothers," said Richard Thalheimer, Sharper Image's chairperson.

Using electronic superhighways, consumers will be able to take personal shopping trips via cable television. The industry envisions shoppers choosing the store, department, or type of product they want to purchase via interactive menus on their television screens.

Shrinking leisure time is largely responsible for home shopping's phenomenal growth. Working women no longer have time to spend hours browsing at the mall and prefer the convenience of shopping at home. The home shopping networks also plan to target frequent catalog shoppers who are already in the habit of shopping from home. Realizing the move from print catalogs to cable television may leave them behind, cataloguers like Spiegel Inc. are turning to the tube themselves. "We're in the retail business to provide consumers with a convenient way to shop," said Debbie Koopman, a Spiegel spokesperson.

Despite the sophistication of the technology, retailers still need a solid advertising approach to reach home shoppers and elicit orders. Experience has taught home shopping pioneers that there are key elements in a successful home shopping pitch. Among these are:

- An air of exclusivity; consumers want merchandise they perceive as limited or hard to get
- "Bargain" prices to make up for hefty shipping and handling costs
- Celebrity spokespersons who glamorize inexpensive merchandise

Analysts believe that retailers who master these techniques and learn to travel the right roads on the electronic superhighway have a strong future in home shopping. As for consumers, they're just waiting for the chance to forget the mall.

Sources: Scott Donaton, "Home Shopping Networks Bring Retailers on Board," *Advertising Age* (April 19, 1993):98; Annetta Miller and Seema Nayyar, "Highbrow Goes Lowbrow," *Newsweek* (April 5, 1993):48–49; Pat Sloan and Kate Fitzgerald, "Macy's Rings Up Home Shopping," *Advertising Age* (June 7, 1993):8; and Laura Zinn, "Retailing Will Never Be the Same," *Business Week* (July 26, 1993):54–60.

$\mathscr{Q}$UESTIONS

1. What did Diane Von Furstenberg mean when she said, "When you sell on TV, you do the selling and the advertising all at once"?

2. Why is increasing the number of cable channels to 500 important to specialty retailers?

3. Do you envision home shopping working in conjunction with other forms of direct-response advertising, including direct mail and catalogs?

When the Medium Is a Mode of Transportation

Want to break through the clutter of urban life with your marketing message? Super-Graphics will wrap your ad around a 40-foot bus with a special perforated vinyl that lets your message be seen while allowing passengers to see out. The cost: $8,000 to $10,000 per bus. The Sunnyvale, California, firm does about 50 per month.

ED QUINN—SABA (3)

Creating Directory and Out-of-Home Advertising

CHAPTER OBJECTIVES

When you have completed this chapter, you should be able to:

- Understand how consumers use the Yellow Pages to search for information about stores, products, and services
- Describe the characteristics of a well-written and well-designed Yellow Pages ad
- Understand the effect of a moving audience on the design of a billboard
- Explain the difference between interior and exterior transit advertisements
- Identify innovative media to use to deliver sales, reminders, and action messages

DELIVERING THE GOODS

Buses, trucks, and even airplanes are becoming the hottest way to reach people on the move. Buses have carried posters for decades; however, the latest rage is to paint the whole bus. A new company in Sunnyvale, California, called Super Graphics has developed a vinyl wrapping that can be wrapped around a 40-foot bus to deliver messages with huge impact. The company uses a special perforated vinyl that lets the message be seen while allowing passengers to still see out the window. The costs range from $8,000 to $10,000 per bus.

When the movie *Independence Day* was released on video, its studio dressed up a number of buses in New York City for the announcement. The same technique was used by Mitsubishi Motors to unveil the new Eclipse Spyder. The New York-based TDI company provided Avon with six fully-wrapped minibuses to support the "Just Another Avon Lady" campaign. These moving billboards have been found by their sponsors to deliver tremendous brand and product visibility in a highly memorable form.

Other companies have had luck buying their own buses and painting them for a tour. Coca-Cola used a brightly painted Fruitopia bus on a 30-city sampling tour. The Body Shop, which does no traditional advertising, uses its own painted 18-wheeler containing a miniature Body Shop, which travels across the United States stopping at malls, college campuses, and various cause-related events such as the March of Dimes walk-a-thon. Salespeople on the truck give out coupons and catalogs and will do makeovers and massages to demonstrate the products.

But for the real high-flyers, planes are the media vehicle of choice. Southwest Airlines was the first to put a *logo-jet* in the air in 1988 when it painted Shamu the killer whale on one of its jets to promote its Sea World partnership. Southwest and America West also paint planes to honor the states they serve and to promote sports sponsorships. For $2 million a year, Fox Broadcasting launched two Western Pacific Airlines planes painted with *The Simpsons* characters. Western Pacific has also partnered with Thrifty Rent-A-Car System on another logo-jet. AirOutdoor, the Spokane, Washington, company that sells space on airplanes, delivery trucks, and buses, says that a lighted film technology created by 3M is used on airplanes. At two-thirds the weight of the average 3,000 pounds of paint, the new paint job also saves airplanes fuel costs.[1]

This chapter will discuss the use of out-of-home media such as outdoor billboards and transportation vehicles, as well as directory advertising, and advertising using innovative alternative media.

OUT-OF-HOME ADVERTISING

Out-of-Home Advertising: All advertising that is displayed outside the home—from billboards, to blimps, to in-store aisle displays.

Not so very long ago, a media planner would base a schedule around newspaper, radio, television, and outdoor advertising. The outdoor portion was easy—there were 8- and 30-sheet posters and painted bulletins. Not so any more. Even the name of the medium has changed. No longer called outdoor advertising, it is now **out-of-home advertising**, and it includes everything from billboards to hot-air balloons. There are still 8- and 30-sheet poster panels and giant painted bulletins, but now there are also fully painted buses, painted walls, telephone kiosks, painted semitrucks, taxi signs, transit/rail platforms, airport/bus terminal displays, bus shelter displays, bus benches, shopping mall displays, grocery store carts, bath-

---

[1]Adapted from Michael Wilke, "Kiwi Climbing Aboard High-Flying Promo Trend," *Advertising Age* (April 29, 1996):21; Pam Weisz, "Body Shop, in Lieu of Ads, Hits the Road," *Brandweek* (April 24, 1995):42; and Julie Ralston, "Bath Shops Work Up Lather," *Advertising Age* (June 19, 1995):1, 14.

room walls, skywriting, and in-store clock and aisle displays. And don't forget blimps and airplanes towing messages over Yankee Stadium and the scoreboard inside.

Another change is in the advertisers. In the 1980s, tobacco companies dominated outdoor advertising. Today packaged-goods advertisers are using outdoor to build up their brands and reinforce their mass-media advertising.[2]

Out-of-home advertising also has taken giant steps to target specific people with specific messages at a time when they are most susceptible to its impact. A sign at the telephone kiosk reminds you to call for reservations at your favorite restaurant, a sign on the rail platform suggests you enjoy a candy bar while riding the train, and a bus card reminds you to listen to the news on a particular radio station.

Yet these steps are really history repeating itself. Public communication has fulfilled a human need from the Stone Age onward, and humans have communicated visual ideas openly for others to admire. Over 5,000 years ago, hieroglyphics on obelisks directed travelers, and Egyptian merchants chiseled sales messages into stone tablets and placed them along public roads. By the fifteenth century, bill posting was an accepted practice in Europe. In the mid-1880s, outdoor advertising became a serious art form.

There are many success stories from the early outdoor advertising days, but the most notable was a little company that tried giving products away on approval and hoped the consumer would pay for it. When this didn't work, the managers tried a series of signs that took 18 seconds to read at 35 miles per hour and the series of signs became such a hit that they created a national pop culture with rhymes like: "He Played The Sax/Had no B.O./But His Whiskers Scratched/So She Let Him Go/Burma Shave." There were some 600 jingles, such as: "His face was smooth/And cool as ice/And oh, Louise/He smelled so nice." They worked well for nearly 40 years, from 1925 to 1963, until the national interstate system made the signs obsolete. Almost 7,000 sets of 40,000 individual tiny signs dotted the roads from Maine to Texas. Most recently Albuquerque has used the old format to encourage drivers to reduce their speeds along Interstate 40 through a four-mile construction zone. Using the rhyme: "Through this maze of machines and rubble/Driving fast can cause you trouble/Take care and be alert/So no one on this road gets hurt."[3]

Out-of-home advertising has enjoyed great success during the decade of the 1990s. Today total spending on outdoor media is estimated to be over $1.5 billion. Yet this has not been without change, opposition, and self-discipline. As mentioned earlier, as much as 50 percent of poster panel and painted bulletin space used to be filled with cigarette and liquor advertising. Social pressure and lifestyle changes have decreased these categories to less than 20 percent, forcing the outdoor companies to find new sources of revenue. Entertainment and amusements, travel, media, health care, and apparel have taken up most of the slack. The other major shift has been from predominantly national advertisers to local companies and national companies with a local message.

OUTDOOR ADVERTISING

Outdoor advertising is used by a variety of marketers. Table 17.1 lists the top 25 outdoor advertisers. There are two kinds of standardized or commercially sold billboards: poster panels and painted bulletins. In addition there are also free-form posters and signs erected locally by advertisers or organizations.

---

[2]Mukesh Bhargava, Naveen Donthu, and Rosanne Caron, "Improving the Effectiveness of Outdoor Advertising," *Journal of Advertising Research* (March/April, 1994):46–54.

[3]Sandra Dallas, "Road to Pave? Remember Burma-Shave!" *Business Week* (December 30, 1996):8.

TABLE 17.1	TOP 25 OUTDOOR ADVERTISERS			
		OUTDOOR SPENDING		
RANK	ADVERTISER	1992	1991	% CHG
1	Philip Morris Cos.	$59.9	$70.1	−14.5
2	RJR Nabisco	29.1	51.7	−43.7
3	Loews Corp.	26.4	35.0	−24.7
4	McDonald's Corp.	12.5	6.9	79.8
5	American Brands	11.7	12.5	−6.1
6	Anheuser-Busch Cos.	10.9	11.6	−6.2
7	B.A.T. Industries	10.5	24.3	−57.0
8	Grand Metropolitan	5.7	7.7	−26.0
9	Seagram Co.	5.2	7.7	−32.2
10	BankAmerica Corp.	5.1	5.7	−9.8
11	Brown-Forman Corp.	4.5	4.4	4.1
12	S&P Corp.	4.1	2.0	103.4
13	PepsiCo	3.8	2.9	30.9
14	General Motors Corp.	3.7	6.4	−42.7
15	Brooke Group	3.2	2.1	51.7
16	CBS Inc.	3.0	2.2	36.0
17	Bass PLC	3.0	3.3	−10.0
18	Hospitality Franchise Systems	2.8	3.5	−20.0
19	Matsushita Electric Industrial Co.	2.8	3.3	−15.7
20	Adolph Coors Co.	2.7	3.2	−13.8
21	Delta Air Lines	2.5	2.2	13.8
22	Walt Disney Co.	2.5	0.4	593.1
23	Guinness PLC	2.4	5.9	−59.0
24	Wendy's International	2.3	1.9	21.5
25	Imasco	2.2	2.0	6.6

Notes: Dollars are in millions. *Source:* Competitive Media Reporting

Source: Reprinted with permission from *Advertising Age* (September 29, 1993):54. Copyright, Crain Communications, Inc., 1993.

POSTERS

Posters are lithographed or silkscreened by a printer and shipped to an outdoor advertising company. They are then prepasted and applied in sections to the poster panel's face on location. Early posters and signs were primarily pictorial or symbolic because most of the population couldn't read. A sculptured wooden shoe over the door indicated a shoemaker; a sign of a lady with a crown indicated the Queens Crown pub. Graphics remain central to the design of posters as well as other forms of outdoor advertising. Even if a poster is predominantly type, the type will be designed artistically for maximum impact. The key to most posters, however, is a dominant visual with minimal copy.

The design for an outdoor board is supplied by the advertiser or agency. For poster panels, the art is printed on a set of large sheets of paper. Thousands of copies can be printed and distributed around the country. The sheets are then pasted like wallpaper on existing boards by the local outdoor advertising companies that own the boards. The standard sizes of poster boards are the 30-sheet poster, with a printed area 9 feet 7 inches by 21 feet 7 inches surrounded by margins of blank paper; and the bleed poster, with a printed area 10 feet 5 inches by 22 feet 8 inches that extends all the way to the frame. Smaller 8-sheet posters are 5 feet high and 11 feet wide. These "junior posters" are used by groceries and local advertisers and are generally placed for exposure to pedestrian traffic as well as vehicular traffic.

If people are moving, then the design needs to be simple and easy to read instantly. If people are waiting, then the advertiser has a captive audience, and the poster can present a more complicated message.

PRINCIPLE Because viewers are traveling past the billboard, outdoor billboards must deliver the message with "quick impact."

PRINCIPLE The huge horizontal format of outdoor affects the design of the message.

Extensions: Embellishments to painted billboards that expand the scale and break away from the standard rectangle limitations.

Cutouts: Irregularly shaped extensions added to the top, bottom, or sides of standard outdoor boards.

The format of all out-of-home advertising has a tremendous impact on its message design. The format is extremely big and horizontal, and visuals and layouts are forced to accommodate these dimensions. Television screens are slightly horizontal, and magazine and newspaper pages are vertical. A design for a magazine or newspaper page doesn't transfer very well to a billboard because of the elongated horizontal dimension.

Extensions can be added to painted billboards to expand the scale and break away from the limits of the long rectangle. The extensions are limited to 5 feet 6 inches at the top and 2 feet at the sides and bottom. These embellishments are sometimes called **cutouts** because they present an irregular shape that reflects something like a mountain range or a skyscraper.

As part of a campaign against drunk driving by MADD (Mothers Against Drunk Driving), a billboard was created using the smashed remnants of an actual car in which a family of four was killed by a drunk driver. (See Ad 17.1.) This billboard is distinctive and memorable both because of its message and because of the way it is communicated outside the confines of the flat surface of the billboard.

PAINTED BULLETINS

Painted bulletins are prepared by artists working for the local outdoor advertising company. They are hand-painted either on location or in the shop on removable panels that can be hoisted up and attached to the billboard frame. All three of the standardized poster panel sizes maintain a basic 2-1/4:1 proportion. The painted bulletin used for local advertising is even more horizontal than poster panels; the proportion is 3-1/2:1. The standard size of painted bulletins is 14 feet by 48 feet. Some use a rotary plan and are moved to different places every 30, 60, or 90 days for greater exposure. Others are permanent and remain at one location.

Painting a large-scale image takes an unusual eye because the details are so much larger than life. Up close the work looks like an impressionistic painting because the colors, contrasts, and shading patterns are so exaggerated. From a distance the details blend together to create a recognizable image. For advertisers who maintain a more stable message and image, the painted bulletin is more impressive and is less likely to be affected by weather, vandalism, and so on. As to cost effectiveness, this seems to be a function of the objectives of the advertiser. Table 17.2 lists the advantages and disadvantages an outdoor advertiser should consider.

MESSAGE DESIGN

Outdoor messages differ from other advertising messages. Some of the key elements are discussed next.

AD 17.1

MOTHERS AGAINST DRUNK DRIVING (MADD) USED A POWERFUL 3-D IMAGE TO GET ITS MESSAGE ACROSS IN THIS BILLBOARD.

TABLE 17.2	ADVANTAGES AND DISADVANTAGES OF OUTDOOR ADVERTISING

ADVANTAGES	DISADVANTAGES
■ *Impact:* Outdoor is big, colorful, hard to ignore, and larger than life.	■ *Message:* Because the message must be simple and brief, you can't develop an involved story or copy points.
■ *Strategy:* An excellent reminder medium, outdoor can also be used to trigger an impulse.	■ *Exposure:* The average driver is exposed to an outdoor message for only a few seconds.
■ *Message:* Outdoor can showcase a creative concept.	■ *Criticism:* Some critics feel outdoor advertising is visual pollution.
■ *Cost:* Outdoor is the least expensive of all major advertising media based on CPMs.	■ *Availability:* Because of criticism of outdoor advertising, some areas restrict or ban billboards.
■ *Long Life:* Outdoor is good for messages that need to be repeated.	

CONCEPT

Effective outdoor advertising is built on a strong creative concept that can be instantly understood. The idea needs to be creative because the message has to get attention and be memorable. Most of all, it has to make the point quickly. For example, a billboard for a doughnut store announcing that it now sells cookies featured a huge, one-word headline filling the entire board that read: "Goody." The two O's in the middle were both round cookies. The underline read: "Winchell's has gone cookies." The concept was expressed in both words and visuals.

COPYWRITING

PRINCIPLE Outdoor advertising uses short, catchy phrases and very few words.

The copy on a billboard is minimal. Usually there is one line that serves both as a headline and as some kind of product identification. The most important characteristic is brevity. The words are short, the phrases are short, and there are no wasted words. Some books suggest that no more than six to seven words be used. The headline is usually a phrase, not a sentence. There is nothing equivalent to the body found in a print ad. The best copy for outdoor is a short, catchy phrase. It needs to catch attention, but it also needs to be captivating in order to be memorable. Often the phrase will be a play on words or a twist on a common phrase. For example, a billboard for Orkin pest control showed a package wrapped up with the word "Orkin" on the tag. The headline read: "A little something for your ant." A billboard for Best Foods mayonnaise showed a butcher block with tomatoes, lettuce, cheese, and rye bread sitting next to the mayonnaise bottle. The headline read: "Best on the block."

THE DESIGN

PRINCIPLE Effective outdoor advertising is built on a strong creative concept that can be understood instantly.

Because billboards must make a quick and lasting impression, design is critical to their effectiveness. The integration of art and headline is critical for the development of a strong concept. The layout is compact, with a very simple visual path, usually beginning with a strong graphic, followed by a catchy headline, and ending with some kind of product identification. The relationships should be so clear and so integrated that the elements are perceived as one whole concept. Ad 17.2 for "Erase Illiteracy" is an example of a good layout.

GRAPHICS   The most important feature of billboard design is high visibility. Visibility means that a billboard is conspicuous; it is noticeable; it bursts into view. The illustration should be an eye-stopper. What makes something visible? Size is one factor. It offers a grand scale, much larger than life and, therefore, can create tremendous impact. You can depict a 25-foot-long pencil or a pointing finger that is 48 feet long. The product or the brand label can be hundreds of times larger than life. Most elements on a billboard are big and bold—the type as well as the illustrations.

AD 17.2

THIS BILLBOARD USES WORDS
AND VISUALS TOGETHER IN A
VERY EFFECTIVE MANNER.

Bold, bright color is another characteristic of impact. The outdoor industry has done significant research on color and color combinations. It has found that the greatest impact is created by maximum contrast between two colors. The strongest contrast, for example, comes from dark colors against white or yellow. Yellow adds tremendous impact as well as contrast. Other bright colors also add impact. The visibility problem is compounded by the fact that outdoor boards are seen at all times of the day and night under all kinds of lighting conditions. The most visible billboards use bright, contrasting colors.

Another aspect of visibility is the clarity of the relationship between foreground and background. In outdoor advertising the best practice is to make this distinction as obvious as possible. A picture of a soft drink against a jungle background will be very hard to perceive when viewed from a moving vehicle at a distance. The background should never compete with the subject.

TYPOGRAPHY

Type demands unusually sensitive handling. It has to be easy to read at a distance by an audience in motion. The outdoor industry has researched type legibility on billboards. Among its conclusions is to avoid all-capital letters because that is the hardest typographical form to read. Ornamental letters, depending on how fanciful they are, can also be hard to read, as can script and cursive letters. Anything that is unusual can create legibility problems. Experts in outdoor advertising advise using simple, clean, and uncluttered type.[4]

DISTANCE

Planning for reading at a distance is an important aspect of billboard design. The Institute for Outdoor Advertising has developed a poster distance scale viewer that designers use in planning the layout. Designers realize that a layout on a desk has a very different impact than on a billboard by the side of a highway. The viewer lets designers evaluate the design as it would be seen at a distance from a moving car.

PRODUCT IDENTIFICATION

Product identification is another important aspect of the design of outdoor advertising. Most billboards focus attention on the product. The distinctive label on a

[4]*A Creative Guide to Outdoor Advertising* (New York: OAAA Marketing).

cold, dripping Perrier bottle filled the entire space on one billboard. Underneath was the headline: "It's only natural." The red Smirnoff label with its distinctive typeface appeared on another board next to an olive and a lemon peel. The headline was a play on words: "Olive 'R Twist." The Marlboro billboards with their familiar cowboy figures are a good example of strong product identification.

The Concepts and Applications box outlines other factors to be considered in creating outdoor advertising.

PRODUCTION OF OUTDOOR ADVERTISING

As a result of modern technology, outdoor ads can now utilize a number of special effects.

LIGHTING

Spectaculars: Billboards with unusual lighting effects.

Lighting is a very important aspect of outdoor advertising. Illuminated billboards against a nighttime sky can create a compelling visual. In urban areas, illuminated billboards may be combined with special lighting effects that blink and change colors. Neon may even be added. These displays are called **spectaculars.** Las Vegas and Times Square in New York display many examples of lighted spectaculars.

Holography: A technique that produces a projected three-dimensional image.

A new backlighting technique used for nighttime showings appears to make the background of the board disappear so that the image pops out against the black sky. Another experiment involves the use of an internally illuminated transparent polyvinyl that gives the appearance of a luminous image projected onto a screen. Some advertisers are experimenting with **holography,** which can project a three-dimensional image from a board or onto a board.

SHAPE

Designers have been searching for decades for techniques to break away from the rectangular frame of most boards. Extensions help, but advertisers are also experi-

---

$\mathcal{C}$ONCEPTS AND $\mathcal{A}$PPLICATIONS

FACTORS THAT MAKE OUTDOOR ADVERTISING EFFECTIVE

A Canadian research study based on a large sample of actual outdoor advertising campaigns developed a comprehensive analysis of factors that make outdoor advertising more successful. Following are the findings.

MESSAGE FACTORS

- A brand-differentiating message is significantly related to a high recall score. (However, only 6.7 percent of the campaigns in the study were judged to have a brand-differentiating strategy.)
- A product's performance also is significantly related to high recall. (Only 14.5 percent showed the product performance.)
- Communicating the benefit also generated high recall. (Only 32.3 percent of the campaigns were judged to have a clear communication of the benefit.)
- The study found that a single-minded focus was more effective. As the number of concepts increases, the recall scores decrease and this relationship is significant. (The average number of concepts across all the outdoor ads was 2.89.) In other words, a more complex presentation using more concepts is negatively related to recall.

DESIGN FACTORS

- The amount of text had a strong relationship with recall. Increasing the copy length is related significantly to a decrease in recall. (The average number of words in the sample was 9.8.)
- The legibility of the message is significantly related to recall.
- Surprisingly, the size of the visual did not have a relationship to recall. (On an average, 59.8 percent of the outdoor board is devoted to the illustration.)

DISCUSSION QUESTIONS

1. Find examples of outdoor boards in your community that are good and bad examples of both message factors and design factors. Explain why they work or don't work.

2. Are there any other factors that you have noticed that impact the effectiveness of the outdoor boards you have investigated?

Adapted from Mukesh Bhargava, Naveen Donthu, and Rosanne Caron, "Improving the Effectiveness of Outdoor Advertising: Lessons From a Study of 282 Campaigns," *Journal of Advertising Research* (March/April 1994):46–55.

AD 17.3

EXTENSIONS, SUCH AS THIS
WINDOW ON AN ANDERSON
WINDOWS RENEWAL OUTDOOR
BOARD, ARE USED TO CATCH
ATTENTION.

menting with designs that create the illusion of three-dimensional effects by playing with horizons, vanishing lines, and dimensional boxes.

Inflatables are even closer to three-dimensional. Giant inflatable liquor bottles and cigarette packs made of a heavyweight-stitched nylon inflated by a small electric fan have been added to outdoor boards. An especially impressive billboard for Marineland shows a three-dimensional creation of Orca, Marineland's killer whale, bursting through the board. Campbell Mithun Esty developed a three-dimensional board for its client Andersen Windows, which came complete with a window that projected above the board. (See Ad 17.3.)

Kinetic Boards: Outdoor advertising that uses moving elements.

MOTION

Revolving panels, called **kinetic boards,** are used for messages that change. These two-, three-, or four-sided panels can contain different messages for different products or they can be used to develop a message that evolves. Two- or three-sided stationary panels can be used to create a message that changes as the viewer passes by—different angles giving different versions of the message.

Motors can be added to boards to make pieces and parts move. Disklike wheels and glittery things that flicker in the wind have all been used to create the appearance of motion and color change. Special effects include techniques to make images squeeze, wave, or pour.

A public service promotion by Target for the Minnesota Zoo used the headline "Fishing Cats. Now at the Minnesota Zoo." To illustrate the idea, the designer placed two huge cat's eyes in the middle of the board surrounded by fleeing fish. To make the board even more animated, the cat's eyes rolled back and forth following the fish. (See Ad 17.4.)

New technology is creating hologramlike images on outdoor boards that also move. Called high-definition volumetric display, the Matthew Outdoor company and Dimensional Media Associations have built demonstration units

AD 17.4

ANIMATION, SUCH AS THESE
MOVING CAT EYES, IS ANOTHER
ATTENTION GETTING DEVICE.

showing a revolving Chanel bottle and a Budweiser can. A small version of the hologram concept can also be used for point-of-purchase displays.[5]

BUYING OUTDOOR SPACE

During the last decade, the outdoor industry has taken steps to increase its professional standards—and thereby be more competitive with other media. The industry has adopted a system based on the gross rating points (GRPs); it has gathered more data on audience segments; and organizations such as Out-of-Home Media Services (OHMS) have emerged. OHMS conducts research on the industry and provides a national buying service for outdoor and transit advertising.

The GRP system provides a quantifiable measurement for exposure by defining a standardized unit for space sales. If an advertiser purchases 100 GRPs daily, the basic standardized unit is the number of poster panels required in each market to produce a daily effective circulation equal to 100 percent of the population of the market. (Note: This formally was called a 100-showing.) As used by the outdoor industry, a rating point is 1 percent of the population one time. GRPs are based on the daily duplicated audience as a percentage of a market. If three posters in a community of 100,000 people achieve a daily exposure to 75,000 people, the result is 75 GRPs.

Advertisers can purchase any number of units, although 75, 50, or 25 GRPs daily are common. The number of panels required for 100 GRPs varies from city to city. Posters are rented for 30-day periods. Painted bulletins and spectaculars are bought on an individual basis, usually for one, two, or three years.

THE AUDIENCE

As one would expect, accurately measuring the mobile audience for outdoor advertising is very difficult. Media that cannot verify their audience size or composition usually have a slim chance of being selected by advertisers. In the case of outdoor advertising, this assessment process is still under revision. Currently, however, the audience reach-frequency of outdoor advertising is reported nationally by Simmons Market Research Bureau (SMRB) and locally by Audience Measurement by Market of Outdoor (AMMO). It all begins with a series of local market surveys that the outdoor industry conducts periodically in specific U.S. markets. These are called calibration surveys. Purposes are (1) to measure respondents' actual frequencies of exposure and (2) to relate these frequencies to respondents' demographic characteristics and travel behavior.

Frequency of exposure to a 100-GRP advertisement, in a week, is measured by the map recall method in which the respondent recalls each trip out of home in the past seven days and physically draws his or her travel route on a separate map for each trip. In the home office, a transparent sheet is laid over each map, showing the location of panels in a 100 GRP, and trained office coders tally the number of exposures (if any) for each respondent trip. Although a bit more complicated, this information is sampled and verified by SMRB at the national level and by AMMO at the local level. As noted earlier, there are flaws in this mechanism that are being rectified. One problem is accounting for all the people and possible travel patterns. This issue is discussed in a somewhat different context in the Issues and Controversies box.

---

[5]Michael Wilke, "Outdoor Ads Go to New Depths," *Advertising Age* (April 15, 1996):24.

THE OUT-OF-HOME MEASUREMENT DILEMMA

One of the problems facing media experts is how to count people who are experiencing media away from home. People read magazines at the doctor's office, listen to the radio while shopping at the mall, and watch television at their favorite bar. It is in the category of television where the controversy looms largest.

And the out-of-home problem is only exacerbated by the overall difficulty of media measurement. Media expert Erwin Ephron has observed about magazine measurement, "There is a great deal of evidence that our total audience measurement misses the act of reading by a wide margin. The limits of memory, title confusion, the desire to please, or appear smart, or sophisticated, or caring, or moral, the pressures of time, the tediousness of the interview, et. al., all affect response."

In a series of meetings in New York, Chicago, and Los Angeles, Nielsen Market Research asked its advertising and television clients for input on developing a plan to integrate out-of-home viewing into regular syndicated ratings reports. But the request brought an outcry from agency executives concerned that the networks may use out-of-home data to inflate the price of advertising. Out-of-home estimates would increase network television ratings by 25 percent overall, adding about 20 million viewers each week to the Big 3's share figures.

Traditionally, Nielsen has counted only viewing inside television sample households. Viewers in such venues as bars, hotels, offices, and on college campuses have historically been considered an implicit part of television buys. But in recent years, the Big 3 have sought to make the value of out-of-home viewing a key part of their negotiations. Nielsen has already conducted three customized studies for the Big 3 to measure out-of-home viewing via personal diaries that viewers use whenever they watch television. The first two studies, in 1989 and 1991, showed overall television viewing levels are

about 2 percent higher than current estimates, and as much as 25 percent higher for specific television shows and dayparts. The third study, conducted in 1992, shows that, on average, network television audiences are 4 percent higher than those reported in Nielsen's regular syndicated ratings reports when out-of-homes are included. The study found a wide range of out-of-home viewership among adults, depending on the show. For example, *Love and War* had no statistically measurable out-of-home viewers among adults, while *Letterman* had a nearly 10 percent boost in its audience size from people viewing outside the home, and *Nightline* had a boost of 16 percent. Overall, Nielsen found that 28 million adults watch television in out-of-home locations each week and that 23 percent of their viewing exceeds five hours each week.

Ultimately, nobody disputes that there are out-of-home viewers who are currently not being measured. The real question, however, is not how to measure them, but whether or not to measure them, whom to measure, and how it will impact the buying and selling of television time.

DISCUSSION QUESTIONS

1. Can you measure your own exposure to out-of-home media? Keep a diary for one day that records all the commercial messages you see as you go about your daily business.

2. If you are a marketer trying to reach college students, which is a very difficult audience to reach with conventional media, what out-of-home media might you consider?

Adapted from Erwin Ephron, "The Natives Are Restless: Hunting for the Elusive Total Audience Is a Wild Boar Chase," *Inside Media* (May 29, 1966):54; Joe Mandese, "Out-of-Home TV: Does It Count?" *Advertising Age* (January 18, 1993):53; and Joe Mandese, "What People Watch Away from Home," *Advertising Age* (March 29, 1993):43.

Transit Advertising

Transit advertising is primarily an urban advertising form that uses vehicles to carry the message to people. The message is on wheels, and it circulates through the community. Occasionally you might see trucks on the highway that carry messages. Many semitrailer trucks carry graphics to identify the company that owns them. Some of these graphics are striking, such as the designs on the sides of the Mayflower Moving trucks and the Steelcase trucks. In addition to this corporate identification, the sides of trucks may also be rented out for more general national advertising messages. Trucks are also becoming moving billboards on our nation's highways.

Transit advertising also includes the posters seen in bus shelters and train, airport, and subway stations. They are targeted at commuters and travelers. Most of these posters must be designed for quick impressions, although posters on subway platforms or bus shelters are often studied by people who are waiting and thus may present a more involved or complicated message.

Transit advertising is reminder advertising; in other words, it is a high-frequency medium that lets advertisers get their names in front of a local audience at critical times such as rush hour and drive time. Frito-Lay used a transit campaign to promote its Smartfoods, the white cheddar cheese popcorn. The campaign's objective was to demonstrate that Smartfood is everywhere and to make the image a powerful presence in a local market. Other companies are making more and more use of this type of advertising as well.

THE TRANSIT AUDIENCE

There are two types of transit advertising—interior and exterior. **Interior transit advertising** is seen by people riding inside buses, subway cars, and some taxis. **Exterior transit advertising** is mounted on the sides, rear, and top of these vehicles, and it is seen by pedestrians and people in nearby cars.

Transit messages can be targeted to specific audiences if the vehicles follow a regular route. Buses that are assigned to a university route will expose a higher proportion of college students, whereas buses that go to and from a shopping mall will expose a higher population of shoppers.

To support Infection Control Week, Kimberly-Clark developed a batch of posters for use in terminals and kiosks like the one in Ad. 17.5, which shows salt and pepper shakers with the warning, "Remember: Everything you touch has been touched by someone else. Thanks for washing your hands."

Interior Transit Advertising:
Advertising posters that are mounted inside vehicles such as buses, subway cars, and taxis.

Exterior Transit Advertising:
Advertising posters that are mounted on the sides, rear, and top of vehicles.

AD 17.5

TRANSIT POSTERS, SUCH AS THIS PUBLIC SERVICE AD, ENTICE THEIR AUDIENCES TO THINK ABOUT THINGS.

Remember: everything you touch has been touched by someone else. **Thanks for washing your hands.**

MESSAGE DESIGN

Car Cards: Small advertisements that are mounted in racks inside a vehicle.

Interior advertising in buses and subways uses a format called **car cards.** These cards are mounted in racks above the windows and in panels at the front and back of the vehicle. The car cards are horizontal, usually 11 inches high by either 28, 42, or 56 inches wide.

Interior advertising is radically different from exterior transit advertising. People sitting in a bus or subway car are a captive audience. Their ride averages 20 to 30 minutes. Some read books or newspapers, but most watch other riders, look out the window, and read and reread the ads. In addition, most people who commute on mass transit ride both ways, so the messages get studied twice.

PRINCIPLE Interior transit advertising uses longer and more complex messages because it can be studied.

As a result, car cards can have longer and more complex messages than outdoor or exterior panels. The only problem with length is visibility. The messages are read from a distance and frequently at an angle. The type must be big enough to be legible given this seating problem.

Car cards offer other opportunities for extending the message. Many cards come with *tear-offs* and *take-ones.* Tear-offs are pads of coupons or other information that are glued to the car card. Take-ones are pockets filled with flyers or leaflets. Both can be used for coupons, recipes, or just to provide more in-depth information.

EXTERIOR TRANSIT

PRINCIPLE Exterior transit advertising is designed like small billboards with simple, bold, and catchy messages.

Exterior advertising panels are very similar to outdoor boards and the same guidelines are used in their design. The only difference is that the vehicle carrying the message, as well as the reader, may be in motion. This makes the perception of the message even more difficult. Exterior panels are designed like small billboards: simple, bold, catchy, and legible. A new advertiser for transit ads has been marketers with Web sites. Pepsi-Cola promotes its Pepsi World (http://www.pepsi.com) site and C/net has a campaign running that urges commuters to "Get On" its Web site (http://www.cnet.com).[6] People who are sitting on a bus or subway train or waiting at a station have the time to write down the Web address so this has become a new way to reach a new audience.

[6]Jane Hodges, "Outdoor Sets Sights on Web Marketers," *Advertising Age* (April 1, 1996):36.

AD 17.6

POSTERS FOR EVENTS ARE FOUND ON KIOSKS, BULLETIN BOARDS, AND OTHER PUBLIC POSTING SITES.

The Great American Beer Festival.
208 breweries. 950 Beers. Plenty of restrooms.

OLD CHICAGO

Station posters are mini-billboards that are located at bus, railroad, subway, and air terminals. The most common units are the two-sheet poster (46 inches by 60 inches) and the one-sheet poster (46 inches by 30 inches).

OTHER POSTERS

Kiosks: Multisided bulletin board structures designed for public posting of messages.

In Europe and on university campuses special structures called **kiosks** are designed for public posting of notices and advertisements. Some of these locations are places where people walk by; others are places where people wait. The location has a lot to do with the design of the message. Kiosks are appearing in more U.S. locations, and there are also some out-of-home media that serve the same function as the kiosk, such as the ad-carrying bus shelter and the sign subway riders encounter coming up the exit stairs.

These other types of posters are designed primarily for local display and are used in a variety of locations other than transit locations. Posters for movies, plays, and other kinds of special events can be seen on kiosks and bulletin boards all over town. These are frequently highly creative, as the poster for the Old Chicago restaurant chain's "Great American Beer Festival" demonstrates. (See Ad 17.6.)

DIRECTORY ADVERTISING

Directories are books that list the names of people or companies, their phone numbers, and their addresses. In addition to this information, many directories publish advertising from marketers that want to reach the people who use the directory. The most common directories are produced by a community's local phone service. Of course, the Yellow Pages is also a major advertising vehicle, particularly for local retailers. The Yellow Pages revenues total more than $12 billion, making it the fourth-largest advertising medium.

But that is just the beginning of the directory business. There are an estimated 7,500 directories available, and they cover all types of professional areas and interest groups. In advertising, for example, the *Standard Directory of Advertisers and Advertising Agencies* (known as the red books) take advertising targeted at potential advertisers, as does *The Creative Black Book*, which takes ads for photographers, illustrators, typographers, and art suppliers. Similar publications are available in cities that have large advertising communities.

The ads in trade and professional directories are usually more detailed than those in consumer directories because they address specific professional concerns, such as qualifications and scope of services provided. Trade directories also use supplemental media such as inserts and tipped-in cards (glued into the spine) that can be detached and filed. Although many different kinds of directories take advertising, this section will focus on Yellow Pages advertising.

YELLOW PAGES ADVERTISING

As noted in the chronology displayed in Ad 17.7, the design of Yellow Pages ads has changed during the last 60 years. The Yellow Pages directory lists all local and regional businesses that have a telephone number. In addition to the phone number listing, retailers can also buy display space and run a larger ad. The industry's core advertisers are service providers—restaurants, travel agents, beauty parlors, and florists, for example—rather than retailers, which have been hard hit by the economic slowdown of the late 1980s and early 1990s. For some small businesses, the Yellow Pages is the only medium of advertising. Approximately 88 percent of Yellow Pages advertising is generated from local businesses.

Directional Advertising: Advertising that directs the buyer to the store where the product or service is available.

Yellow Pages advertising is described as **directional advertising** because it tells people where to go to get the product or service they are looking for. There

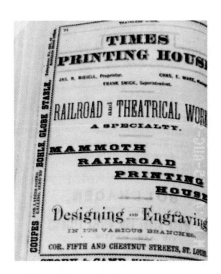

AD 17.7

THIS SERIES OF YELLOW
PAGES ADS SHOWS THE
CHANGES OVER THE YEARS.
CLOCKWISE FROM UPPER
LEFT: 1882, 1920S, 1930S,
1940S.

is one important difference between this kind of advertising and brand-image advertising, which attempts to create a desire to buy: Directory advertising reaches prospects—people who already know they have a need for the product or service. If you are going to move across town and you want to rent a truck, you will consult the Yellow Pages. Directory advertising is the primary media form that is actively consulted by prospects who need or want to buy something and have decided to buy.

Although there has always been a certain amount of competition among businesses in the same category listings, the competition has become more intense and complex since the breakup of AT&T in 1984. With deregulation, the local Bell companies and their directories are faced with competition from many independent sources. Most major cities now have a number of alternative and competing local directories.

Some 200 publishers produce more than 6,500 Yellow Pages directories. And because AT&T never copyrighted the term *Yellow Pages*, any publisher can use the term. In many cities, there are competing directories, giving advertisers a choice and an opportunity to target their messages. (In fact, there are so many competing directories in some areas that publishers of Yellow Pages have taken to advertising to build customer loyalty.)

Many of these are aimed at general consumers, but there are also books that specialize by providing listings for certain regions or neighborhoods or by targeting certain consumer groups, such as the Silver Pages for senior citizens or Spanish-language books for Hispanics.

TYPES OF DIRECTORY SEARCH BEHAVIORS

When thinking about the audience for Yellow Pages ads, industry experts suggest that there are two basic categories.[7]

THOSE WHO KNOW YOU:
- Current and former customers
- Recommended customers
- Those who have seen your ads
- Passersby
- Credit card customers

THOSE LOOKING FOR WHAT YOU OFFER:
- Customers new to the market
- Emergency buyers
- Those dissatisfied with your competitors
- Infrequent buyers
- Competitive shoppers
- Transients (browsers)

Some coastal areas have their own boater's directories. There's even a commercial marine directory. In addition to telephone numbers and advertisements for every imaginable product and service relating to pleasure boating and commercial shipping, these directories contain information on tides, harbor descriptions, U.S. Coast Guard regulations, and other important boating information.

THE AUDIENCE

PRINCIPLE Yellow Pages advertising is not intrusive because the audience is looking for the information in the ad.

The behavior of consumers using the Yellow Pages is considerably different from that of consumers using other forms of mass-media advertising. For this reason directory advertisements are designed differently than other ads. As stated earlier, the Yellow Pages are consulted by consumers who are interested in buying something. They know what they want, they just don't know where to find it. Almost 90 percent of those who consult the Yellow Pages follow up with some kind of action. Because a Yellow Pages ad is the last step in the search for a product or service by a committed consumer, the ads are not intrusive.

Studies have found that the heaviest consumer user of the Yellow Pages continues to be a person who is young to middle-aged, well educated, professional or managerial, living in a metropolitan suburban area, and enjoying a relatively high income. The heavy user reads magazines and newspapers, is exposed to outdoor advertising, and listens to the radio. Television viewing is relatively low.

According to a survey by the Gallup organization, the Yellow Pages are used primarily for comparison shopping. Of the consumers surveyed, 40 percent said they use the Yellow Pages to compare different stores and suppliers. Another 32 percent use the directory to find the business closest to their residence, 10 percent use it to check store hours, and 6 percent use it for local maps. Of the more affluent consumers, 47 percent said that the larger display advertisements are most useful to them.

CREATING THE YELLOW PAGES AD

Although unlike other forms of advertising that have to attract the attention of an indifferent audience, Yellow Pages ads still have to stand out in a cluttered environment. Once they locate the category, most consumers tend to "browse" through the listings. The decision about which store to call or visit will be based on certain criteria, the first being the size of the ad. Larger ads typically get more attention than smaller ads.

Another decision factor is convenience, especially location and hours, which means this type of information must be given prominence. Most people prefer to shop at the nearest store. Large directories in major metropolitan areas often

[7]Alan D. Fletcher, "Target Marketing Through the Yellow Pages," Yellow Pages Publishers Association (1991):24.

group businesses by geographical area. Other factors that affect the consumer's decision are the scope of the services or product lines available and the reputation or image of the store.

Finally, when a consumer is unfamiliar with a product category or has no particular selection criteria in mind, the business listed first alphabetically may get the call.

INDEX AND HEADINGS

PRINCIPLE The headings are the key to searching for something in the Yellow Pages.

The most important feature of Yellow Pages advertising is the category system. Because consumers must be able to find the product, store, or service in the directory, category headings are extremely important.

NYNEX used a sweepstakes promotion to anchor these headings in its consumers' memories. Cash prizes were given to residents who knew both the advertised "heading of the day" and its corresponding page number in the Yellow Pages. NYNEX also won awards for its creative commercials that featured visual puns built on headings such as "Civil Engineers." The commercial showed a group of railroad engineers in overalls with caps and bandanas sitting in a parlor setting and having tea. The NYNEX ad in Ad 17.8 uses that same concept to attract advertisers.

If there is any doubt about where people would be likely to look, then the best practice for an advertiser is to use multiple ads that cover all possible headings. For example, a store selling radios may be listed under "Appliances" or even under "Television." It is critical for an advertiser to know how people search for the store or service and to make sure information is found under every possible heading that might be used.

CRITICAL INFORMATION

Certain pieces of information are critical to a Yellow Pages ad. In addition to location and hours of operation, the telephone number, of course, must be included. The Yellow Pages, after all, is a directory of phone numbers, and many consumers will call to see if the product is available before making a trip. Note the multiple telephone numbers listed in Ad 17.9 for IBM.

WRITING

Yellow Pages specialists advise using a real headline that focuses on the service or store personality rather than a label headline that just states the name of the store. The ad should describe the store or the services it provides, unless the store's name is a descriptive phrase like "Overnight Auto Service" and "The Computer

AD 17.8

NYNEX ADS USED A SERIES OF PUNS IN THEIR HEADINGS.

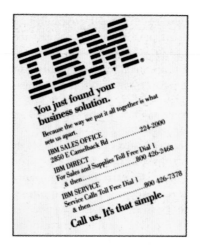

AD 17.9

THIS AD FOR IBM CONTAINS
A GREAT DEAL OF VALUABLE
INFORMATION, INCLUDING
SEVERAL TELEPHONE NUMBERS
FOR VARIOUS SERVICES.

AD 17.10

THIS AD DEVELOPS A STRONG
BRAND IMAGE.

Exchange." In Ad 17.10, because "Great Bear" gives no clue to the product, the advertiser uses descriptive phrases and a drawing to signal both the product category and the company name.

Complicated explanations and demonstrations don't work very well in the Yellow Pages. Any information that is timely or changeable can become a problem because the directory is only published once a year.

THE DESIGN

Among the key design elements of Yellow Pages ads are size, image, and graphics. When people browse through the ads in a category, their choice of a company or product is often influenced by the size of the ad. One study reported that the larger the ad, the more favorable the consumer perception. Nevertheless, deciding on the best sizes and format can be difficult. The advertiser should begin by reviewing competitors' advertisements that may appear under different headings in the same directory. Depending on the nature of an advertiser's business and sales objectives, the best ad size and format can range from a simple, one-line listing up to one a size larger than the largest ad under a heading.

People make decisions based on the reputation and image of the store. This unique personality should be reflected in the design of the ad. Is it a high-quality,

---

THE RASCIL APPROACH TO YELLOW PAGES ADVERTISING

Within the Yellow Pages industry and among sales representatives, basic copy factors for Yellow Pages ads are summarized by the term *RASCIL*. This acronym suggests that, depending on the company, ads might stress:

- Reliability: years in business, references, connection with well-known firms or associations, and safety.
- Authorized Sales and Service: national brand names.
- Special Features: credit cards and 24-hour service.

- Completeness of Lines or Services: range and variety, special type, and quality.
- Illustrations: emblems and slogans.
- Location/Large, Clear, Easy-to-Read Phone Number: maps, landmarks, and major intersections.

Adapted from Alan D. Fletcher, "Target Marketing Through the Yellow Pages," Yellow Pages Publishers Association (1991):24.

upscale, expensive store? Is it nostalgic or classy or exclusive? When you look through the Yellow Pages for restaurants, women's clothing stores, or hair stylists, can you tell something about the personality of the store from the ad? This personality is communicated through the headline, the illustration, the layout, and the use of type (see Ad 17.11).

In addition to communicating a store image, the design performs several other functions. In a competitive market, design helps an ad stand out. An illustration, for example, can make an ad more visible. The attention-getting elements should also be big and bold. Spot color, which is becoming available at an additional cost, contributes tremendously to the impact of the ad.

Simplicity is very important. Specialists advise advertisers to keep the number of elements to a minimum. If you must use a lot of pieces, then organize the layout carefully so that the visual path is clear and things that belong together are grouped together. A fanciful display type may be used for the headline to communicate an image, but try to avoid using a variety of faces in a variety of sizes. Use a list with bullets (a series of dots) rather than an extended block of body copy to list important points.

Photographs don't reproduce well in phone books, given the quality of the paper and printing. Line drawings work better, although a high-contrast photo may be acceptable. Avoid any graphic that has a lot of detail. Full-color art also does not reproduce well. Maps are very important, but they need to be simplified to show only major streets in the immediate neighborhood.

AD 17.11

FLOWERS ARE THE FOCUS OF THIS FLORAL DELIVERY SERVICE THAT OPERATES AS AN 800-NUMBER SERVICE.

INSIDE ADVERTISING

JOSH BAZE, ASSISTANT ACCOUNT EXECUTIVE, *Valentine Radford,*
Kansas City, Missouri

Believe it or not, I cut my teeth in the advertising world at the tender age of seven. I had, along with my twin brother and two other classmates, abandoned my GI Joes to publish a newspaper for our second grade class. *Kid Kapers* was a great success, and before very long we had our first edition ready to go to press. We were, however, faced with a serious dilemma. Lacking a steady source of income (as most 7-year-olds do), we needed a way to raise the capital necessary to make copies. It was not long until my mom gave me a suggestion, and my first lesson in media sales: Sell ads to cover copying costs. This was my job, and I loved it. While most 7-year-olds probably saw the creation, production, approval, and placement of 1/4-page ads a perverse source of entertainment, I couldn't get enough.

In spite of my early exposure and experiences, my career goals shifted from wanting to become an architect to playing center field for the Kansas City Royals without ever settling on advertising. I don't remember consciously wanting to pursue a career in advertising until my freshman year in college. Having always had an insatiable interest in popular culture, I enrolled in two electives in the journalism school: principles of advertising, and mass communication in society. It didn't take long for me to see the error of my business school ways, and I promptly transferred into the college of journalism and mass communication to study advertising.

While in college, I tried to gain as much exposure to the field as possible. I enrolled in many extra advertising electives, participated in the ad club, even traveled to other universities to see their guest speakers. It didn't take long for me to realize the importance of gaining experience through an internship. I picked up a copy of *The Kansas City Business Journal*, which annually publishes a list of the top 25 area agencies. In March, I fired off a cover letter and résumé to each of the 25 agencies, hoping to find a position as a summer intern. When all 25 agencies had notified me that there were no available internships, I took my old summer job as a maintenance worker at a check printing plant.

After three and a half weeks of painting, planting, pruning, and polishing, I'd had it. I walked out 45 minutes after lunch one Tuesday, not sure what I'd do, but knowing I wouldn't be cleaning the factory's truck driver bathroom ever again. I went home, grabbed my list, and called all 25 agencies again. After getting yet another 25 rejections, I hung up the phone and sat stunned, trying to decide how I was going to explain my actions to my parents, let alone how I would fund my next semester at school. Just as I began to contemplate returning to the plant and groveling for the job I had so brusquely quit, the phone rang. It was the personnel director for Valentine Radford, Kansas City's second largest agency. He said that he'd just received a call informing him that one of his interns would be unable to work this summer, and since I'd just called, my résumé was at the top of the stack. Was I still interested?

I started at Valentine Radford four days later as an account service intern. Over the course of that summer I learned what life in an agency was like; how traffic is handled, how bills are paid—the things you can't learn in any classroom. I ended up coming back to serve as an intern that winter, and again the following summer, both times for the same account. The more familiar I became with the account and the people working on it, the more I wanted to return.

My last semester at school I remained in close contact with my boss at Valentine Radford, and I was constantly skimming the business journals and newspapers, trying to stay up to speed with account activity not only at Valentine Radford, but all around Kansas City. I spoke with my boss often to see how things were going with the account, and I arranged to have lunch with him shortly after graduation.

Over the course of that lunch, we discussed events that had transpired since graduation, what was new around the agency, and a new position that had been created at Valentine Radford. When we got back to his office, he offered me the position of an assistant account executive on the account I had worked on as an intern. Thrilled, I returned home to think it over before accepting the offer at the end of the day.

I started work a little over a month ago, exactly one month to the day after graduation. On a daily basis, I am responsible for tracking and forecasting projects, managing communications both internally and with the client, and developing conference reports, among other tasks. The pace is fast and the days are long, but it is the most fun I can imagine having eight (or ten, or more) hours a day.

If I were to offer advice to someone preparing to dedicate himself or herself to advertising, I would say simply to be tenacious and observant. Keep your eyes peeled for events you can turn into opportunities. Read every piece of advertising you can, from billboards to bumper stickers to T-shirts. Build and maintain relationships with as many people as you can. And start early. The earlier you begin, the better your chances are of staying ahead of the pack.

Nominated by Prof. Charles Pearce, Kansas State University

TRENDS IN DIRECTORIES

The Yellow Pages industry has made many important changes in order to become a more viable media alternative. For example, audiotext combined with Yellow Pages is now available in approximately 175 cities in the United States and Canada. After referring to the appropriate section of the Yellow Pages directory, the consumer dials an access number and a code for the individual advertiser and listens to a message about business hours, special services, special promotions, or other helpful information. The Talking Yellow Pages also offers news, sports, weather, and financial information. Yellow Pages publishers have also begun offering a variety of merchandising services. Many carry coupon pages and samples. Telephone subscribers in Orange County, California received with their Yellow Pages a 16-page set of discount coupons for Pizza Hut pizza, Reese's Pieces, Peter Pan peanut butter, and other food and nonfood items.

A recent development in directories is the electronic Yellow Pages, a database accessed by computer. These databases are used primarily in business-to-business communication, although the idea is becoming popular among consumers who have computers hooked up to telephone modems and who subscribe to such online services as America OnLine.

The concept of electronic directories was pioneered in France by Minitel, which provides consumers there with access to telephone listings, news, and sports through a network of 5 million small video terminals located throughout the country. As of spring 1991, the regional Bell companies were prohibited from entering into this type of electronic publishing. The U.S. government maintains that a dominant carrier of information (technical transmission) should not also be the source of information because that would give it too much control (although this is changing). These services therefore were primarily provided by independent publishers that were actively exploring the possibilities for this new type of information and advertising.

Other Innovative Advertising Media

MOVIE ADVERTISING

Trailers: Advertisements that precede the feature film in a movie theater.

Most movie theaters will accept filmed commercials to run before the feature. Called **trailers,** these advertisements are similar to television commercials but are generally longer and better produced. Theater messages are usually 45 seconds or 1 minute in length. This gives more time for message development than the typical 30-second television spot. There is even talk of 2-minute mini-films for theater showings.

PRINCIPLE Theater advertising is the most compelling form of advertising because of the impact of larger-than-life images in the dark on the big screen.

There may be some limited targeting of these messages in terms of location and the type of audience attracted by various kinds of movies. The important audience factor, however, is the attention and concentration generated by the theater environment. The projection of larger-than-life images in a darkened theater is totally unlike the experience of watching television. The impact of the large screen makes for a compelling image that commands total attention. It is very difficult for the audience to turn off or tune out whatever is happening on that screen.

MESSAGE DESIGN

The critical feature of theater advertising is that it must function as entertainment. People in theaters have a low tolerance for hard-sell messages. Dramas and MTV techniques, with their music and intense imagery, have been particularly effective with theater advertising.

THE CONTROVERSY

Movie advertising isn't universally appreciated. Moviegoers have been known to picket outside movie theaters to express their displeasure that advertisements are being shown before the feature movies. Walt Disney refuses to let its movies be shown in movie houses that run commercials before the films. People have also been known to boo and hiss in the theater when these commercials come on. Most people who resent these ads explain that they have paid money to attend the movie and, therefore, they shouldn't be subjected to commercials.

The decision to run ads is usually not up to the individual theater but is made by the motion picture companies and the distributors that handle the films. Theaters typically limit the commercials to no more than three per film. Ads will be run for everything from cars to credit cards to the Marine Corps, but the mix usually depends on the type of audience perceived as watching that particular film. Movies thought to appeal to teenagers, for example, will often open with MTV-like advertisements. As with most advertising, some theater ads are irritating and some are entertaining.

OTHER ALTERNATIVE MEDIA

New and novel media are constantly being utilized as vehicles for advertising messages. Pay telephones are beginning to carry advertising space. This can be a highly targeted medium. If you want mall shoppers, then you can reach them at telephone booths in malls; if you want travelers, use the airport telephones; if you want college students, advertise on campus pay telephones.

Indicia: The postage label printed by a postage meter.

Companies that have their own postage meters use the **indicia** for printed messages on the envelopes of the correspondence. Some people have even suggested that the government sell space on postage stamps for advertising messages.

Even garbage and trash cans on the city streets are being used for short messages. These advertisements can carry short copy lines and product symbols. Bus-stop benches are also available for short copy such as slogans, although visuals don't work well on benches.

REMINDER MESSAGES

Blimps have been around for decades and, of course, the Goodyear Blimp is a classic example of brand-reminder advertising. Planes pulling banners have been used over major outdoor events such as fairs and football games. More recently, hot-air balloons have carried commercial messages.

Athletic competition makes heroes, and heroes are good message endorsers. Consequently, almost every sports event is a display for special-interest advertising. All the tennis, skiing, swimming, and golf equipment manufacturers prominently display their brands on the course or on the athletes' clothing.

Other sponsors, such as beer companies, simply like to affiliate with an attention-getting event such as the Indy 500 or the Super Bowl. The Indy cars are covered with decals for the sponsors that underwrite the cost of getting the car into the race and onto the track.

ACTION MESSAGES

Grocery carts now have placard space that can be rented. These are reminder messages, but they function like point-of-purchase advertising (see Chapter 18). They confront the shopper at the moment when he or she is ready to make a purchase.

Coupons are printed on the back of tickets to major events like college football games. Coupons are also showing up on the back of grocery store receipts. As discussed in Chapter 15, there are even advertisers that are producing their own video cassettes. Two Buick regional ad groups provide personalized videocassette messages about the dealerships' cars to prospects who call a toll-free number. Each video includes a 2-minute talk by a local dealer as well as an on-screen video letter addressed to the consumer, inviting him or her to call the dealership with questions.

SUMMARY

- The Yellow Pages is the most universal advertising medium.
- Yellow Pages ads focus on the service offered or the store personality.
- Posters are the oldest form of advertising.
- Posters are graphic, and the focus of the message is the visual.
- Out-of-home advertising delivers messages to moving audiences using "quick-impact" techniques such as strong graphics and short, catchy phrases.
- A billboard is the largest advertising medium.

- National billboards are distributed as preprinted posters; local billboards are original, hand-painted art.
- Interior transit messages can be studied; exterior messages must be seen in a glance.
- Theater advertising is the most compelling form of advertising because of the impact of larger-than-life images on the big screen; it is controversial, however.
- Innovative media include a wide variety of techniques that either deliver a sales message, a reminder message, or an action message. Examples include ads on telephones, garbage cans, blimps, and grocery carts.

QUESTIONS

1. Why is Yellow Pages advertising described as "directional"?

2. Out-of-home advertising is described as "quick impact." What does that mean? How do you design effective messages for this medium?

3. Since his freshman year in college, Phil Dawson, an advertising major, has waited on tables at Alfredo's, a small family-operated restaurant featuring excellent food and an intimate atmosphere. The owner has been approached by a Yellow Pages representative to run a display ad. He asks Phil for advice on whether or not a display would help, and if so, what the ad should look like. What should Phil recommend?

4. You are constantly exposed to poster advertising all over your campus. If you had authority over all poster advertising, what would you do to improve the effectiveness of poster advertising on campus?

5. There is some extraordinary outdoor billboard technology under development that will allow advertising images to be projected onto the board space. The same technology could also provide public information (in addition to the advertising) from each board location. The creative possibilities of computer-controlled projection are obvious, but what about the ability to convert each location into a special message board? What sort of services could key locations provide that would contribute to public service? Do you feel that such ideas would improve public opinion toward outdoor billboards?

6. One of the most logical opportunities for new advertising methods is to expand the communication options found inside stores. What are some store-level activities that could be used in (a) supermarkets and (b) department stores?

SUGGESTED CLASS PROJECT

Test the following research hypothesis about directory advertising by either surveying advertisers, customers, or both.
- Hypothesis 1: Larger ads produce more sales than smaller ads.

- Hypothesis 2: Ads later in the alphabet create more sales.
- Hypothesis 3: Ads with some color produce more sales.

FURTHER READINGS

The Big Outdoor (New York: The Institute of Outdoor Advertising).

A Creative Guide to Outdoor Advertising (New York: The Institute of Outdoor Advertising).

Fletcher, Alan D., *Yellow Pages Advertising* (Chesterfield, MO: American Association of Yellow Pages Publishers, 1986).

Henderson, Sally, and Robert Landau, *Billboard Art* (San Francisco: Chronicle Books, 1981).

The Balloonist's Prayer

The winds have welcomed you with softness.
The sun has blessed you with his warm hands.
You have flown so high, and so well,
that God has joined you in your laughter
and set you gently back again
into the loving arms of Mother Earth.

Everyone loves hot-air balloons, and that includes bottom-line corporate advertising executives who understand the balloon's nearly unparalleled ability to generate publicity and draw crowds. Corporate giants like the Cadillac Motor Car Division of General Motors, Disney, Coca-Cola, and Kodak as well as small companies like Herring Gas in Naches, Mississippi, Houser Asphalt Company in Dayton, Ohio, and Mr. Rubbish, a garbage hauler in Ann Arbor, Michigan fly balloons emblazoned with their corporate messages to create open-air spectacles featuring their companies as the stars.

"There's no better way to touch people around the country than with hot-air balloons," said Larry P. Anderson, manager of dealer marketing for Cadillac. Tucker Comstock, president of Cameron Balloons, a custom-balloon manufacturer based in Ann Arbor, agrees. "Balloons make large companies real for people. They turn cold corporate identities into joyful, personal experiences."

Cadillac's commitment to hot-air ballooning began in 1989. Today, the 70-foot-high Cadillac balloon, equipped with a rattan, birch, and suede basket that carries three, appears in 18 major balloon and corporate events as well as 35 dealer promotions nationwide. These events, including the Albuquerque International Balloon Fiesta and the Colorado Springs Balloon Classic, draw 3 million on-site spectators. National, regional, and local media coverage spreads Cadillac's corporate image to an additional 45 million potential buyers. The reward for Cadillac has been a sixfold return on investment, based on these events generating 60 incremental vehicle sales. The current value of the program exceeds $1 million.

A cornerstone of Cadillac's program is dealer-based participation. For a fee of $700 a day, the Cadillac hot-air balloon can either be tethered or launched from a dealership. To maximize the promotional impact, dealers issue press releases, inviting the media and public to attend the ballooning event and enjoy no-cost balloon flights. The program has been so popular that dealer demand now exceeds balloon availability and has created an army of devoted followers. Daniel Jobe, a Cadillac dealer from Greenbelt, Maryland, is one. "Please put me down for our balloon event every year," said Jobe.

Print collateral pieces bolster the program's impact. In 1993 alone 500,000 calendars, postcards, balloon race brochures, travel and tourism brochures, and major event publications were distributed to spread the impact of the various ballooning events.

Why is ballooning such a successful promotional technique? Because people love balloons and because balloons create thousands of impressions as they fly over a community. Indeed, the late Malcolm Forbes, arguably the ultimate capitalist and a hot-air balloon aficionado, believed that the cost of a corporate balloon is returned 100 times in its publicity value.

Sources: Cadillac Hot-Air Balloon/Cold-Air Balloon Programs: Sponsorship Impact, 1993; Cadillac Hot-Air Balloon Program, 1993 Promotional Materials; Telephone Interview with Larry P. Anderson, manager dealer marketing, Cadillac Motor Car Division, General Motors Corporation, March 4, 1993; and Telephone Interview with Tucker Comstock, president Cameron Balloons, March 3, 1993.

QUESTIONS

1. How effective are hot-air balloons as brand-reminder advertising?

2. In your opinion, is the promotional impact of the corporate hot-air balloon greatest on the local, regional, or national level?

3. Why are local dealership tie-ins so crucial to the success of the Cadillac program?

A Thank You from

Helpful Hints and a
Great New Book
for Philadelphia- area parents

PLUS MONEY-SAVING COUPONS INSIDE!

CHAPTER

Sales Promotion

CHAPTER OUTLINE

- Happy Meals—Happy Opportunities
- Defining Sales Promotion
- The Size of Sales Promotion
- The Role of Sales Promotion in Marketing
- The Relationship between Sales Promotion and Advertising
- Types of Sales Promotion
- The Future of Sales Promotion

CHAPTER OBJECTIVES

When you have completed this chapter, you should be able to:

- Distinguish between sales promotion and advertising
- Explain how promotion and advertising work together within the marketing mix
- List several types of promotions, both for consumers and for resellers
- Understand why advertisers are spending increasing sums of money on sales promotion
- Explain the advantages and disadvantages of sales promotion as compared to advertising

Happy Meals—Happy Opportunities

McDonald's is evaluating use of its Happy Meal packages to deliver coupons and other value-added incentives aimed at parents as part of an experiment in targeted marketing. A nine-market test, developed in conjunction with the Parent-Source division of Targeted Marketing Solutions, involves gluing eight-page booklets to Happy Meal bags.

The experiment is an extension of the fast-food leader's seldom discussed Mc-Moms affinity program, which launched in 1994 and now has built up a mailing list of close to 1 million names, insiders say. "Our goal is to understand McDonald's customers and increase the value perception for their core customer base," says Nick Carter, national director of Parent Source. Mr. Carter emphasized that McDonald's senior management has not yet committed to go national with the program.

During the ten-day test, which began November 1, 1996, Happy Meal purchasers in cities including Boston, Chicago, Cincinnati, Minneapolis/St. Paul, and Philadelphia found a booklet glued to the bag, containing family-oriented editorials on subjects such as making a home first-aid kit, playground safety, and dealing with parental stress. The booklets also contained coupons for Fuji Photo Film, USA's Fuji film, three brands from Mars Inc., Uncle Ben's Country Inn rice dishes, Pedigree dog food, Whiskas cat food, and a $5-off coupon on ordering a $14.95 *Parent Source Resource Directory* targeting that market.

Parents were offered a cash incentive to submit parenting observations and tips for possible inclusion in a future McMoms newsletter. The test featured distribution of 2.8 million copies.

Officials at Mars Inc.'s Kal Kan unit said the company bought into the program in September. "We haven't evaluated results yet, so we're not sure if we'll repeat" the promotion, said one official. Another Mars official said the fit was natural, given the high incidence of pet owners among families with small children.

In addition, Targeted Marketing Solutions produces a biannual *Parent Source* magazine sent to the McMoms mailing list. The magazine also includes coupons and bound-in copy of the *McMoms* newsletter.

The chain compiled the list via in-store promotions in select markets and mail-in campaigns tied to films and premium promotions. The next phase of the test will be to use the outserts to acquire names for the McMoms program, with a sample of the editorials, additional coupons, and the opportunity to sign up for the mailing list.[1]

Recall from Chapter 1 how McDonald's has attempted to appeal to the adult market through its new line of Arch Deluxe products. Yet McDonald's also recognizes that the heart of its business still lies with families with young children. The McMoms program represents an effort by McDonald's to offer this target market extra incentives to buy. Whenever a marketer increases the value of its offering, it is engaging in sales promotion, the topic of this chapter.

Defining Sales Promotion

Sales Promotion: Those marketing activities that add value to the product for a limited period of time to stimulate consumer purchasing and dealer effectiveness.

The evolution of **sales promotion** has also changed the way experts define the practice. At one point, the official definition of sales promotion proposed by the American Marketing Association (AMA) was: "Marketing activities, other than personal selling, advertising, and publicity, that stimulate consumer purchasing and dealer effectiveness, such as displays, shows, exhibitions, demonstrations, and various nonrecurrent selling efforts not in the ordinary routine."[2]

---

[1] Bill McDowell and Judann Pollack, "McD's Serves Up Coupon Trail," *Advertising Age* (November 25, 1996):1, 26.

[2] American Marketing Association, *Marketing Definitions: A Glossary of Marketing Terms* (Chicago, 1960):20.

In 1988 the AMA offered a new definition: "Sales promotion is media and nonmedia marketing pressure applied for a predetermined, limited period of time in order to stimulate trial, increase consumer demand, or improve product quality."[3] The Council of Sales Promotion Agencies offers a somewhat broader perspective: "Sales promotion is a marketing discipline that utilizes a variety of incentive techniques to structure sales-related programs targeted to consumers, trade, and/or sales levels that generate a specific, measurable action or response for a product or service."[4] All these definitions present sales promotion as a set of techniques that prompts members of the target audience to take action—preferably immediate action.

PRINCIPLE Sales promotion offers an extra incentive for consumers to take action.

We can refine the definitions by examining what sales promotion does today. Sales promotion offers an "extra incentive" for consumers to act. Although this extra incentive is usually in the form of a price reduction, it may be additional amounts of the product, cash, prizes, premiums, and so on. Furthermore, sales promotions usually include specified limits, such as an expiration date or a limited quantity of the merchandise. Finally, sales promotion has three somewhat different goals, which relate to its three target audiences: (1) to increase immediate *customer* sales, (2) to increase support among the marketer's *sales force*, and (3) to gain the support of *intermediaries* (resellers) in marketing the product.

THE SIZE OF SALES PROMOTION

Determining the actual size of the sales promotion industry is difficult; estimates vary according to which agency or research firm collects the data.

For example, Table 18.1 lists the gross revenues for the various consumer sales promotion categories, as collected by *PROMO* magazine, the industry trade publication. Note that premium incentives and P-O-P displays led the way with $20.8 billion and $12 billion, respectively. Total 1995 expenditures were over

---

[3]Russ Brown, "Sales Promotion," *Marketing & Media Decisions* (February 1990):74.

[4]"Shaping the Future of Sales Promotion," Council of Sales Promotion Agencies (1990):3.

TABLE 18.1	PROMOTION INDUSTRY GROSS REVENUES ($ MILLIONS)		
	1995	**1994**	**% CHANGE**
Premium Incentives	$20,800.0	$20,000.0	+4.0%
P-O-P Displays	12,024.0	11,098.0*	+8.3
Advertising Specialties	8,037.0	7,008.0*	+14.7
Couponing	6,950.0	6,995.0	−0.6
Specialty Printing	5,250.0	4,870.0*	+7.8
Promotional Licensing	4,850.0	4,900.0	−1.0
Sponsored Events	4,700.0	4,250.0	+10.6
Promotion Fulfillment	2,160.0	2,180.0	−0.9
Interactive	1,540.0	1,126.0*	+36.8
Research	941.0	856.8	+9.8
Promotion Agencies	999.9	833.0	+20.0
In-Store Marketing	990.4	828.8	+19.5
Product Sampling	774.0	703.9	+10.0
	$70,016.3	$65,649.5	+6.7%

*Adjusted figure. Copyright © 1996 by PROMO Magazine. All Rights Reserved.
Source: PROMO (July 1996):36.

$70 billion, with annual growth averaging over 8 percent. This $70 billion represents 24 percent of the total amount spent on promotion and marketing communication. Over 50 percent, or $142 billion, is spent on promotions directed at the trade (resellers), with the remaining dollars ($72 billion) spent on mass media. Current trends suggest that more dollars are now spent on sales promotion than on advertising (roughly 75 percent versus 25 percent, per Figure 18.1).[5]

Finally, with the growth of sales promotion has come the growth of organizations supporting sales promotion. Virtually all major advertising agencies have acquired a sales promotion subsidiary or have brought sales promotion in-house.

REASONS FOR THE GROWTH OF SALES PROMOTION

The statistics presented thus far pose one question: Why are companies spending more and more money on sales promotion? The chief reasons are the pressure for short-term profits, the accountability factor, economic factors, changes in the marketplace, and the increasing power of retailers.

SHORT-TERM SOLUTIONS
Most U.S. companies have a drive for immediate profits and progress, which sales promotion satisfies. Vincent Sottasanti, president and CEO of the consulting firm Comart-KLP, states: "There's pressure on the brand manager and senior management as well for short-term profits as well as long-term goals."[6] Others agree that product managers are under pressure to generate quarterly sales increases. Because advertising's benefits are often apparent only in the long term, companies are investing more money in sales promotion, which generates immediate results.

NEED FOR ACCOUNTABILITY
Another reason for the growth is the accountability of sales promotion techniques. It is relatively easy to determine whether a given sales promotion strategy accomplished its stated objectives. Moreover, this assessment can be done rather quickly. Providing accountability is critical at a time when marketers want to know exactly what they are getting for their promotional dollars.

FIGURE 18.1

DOLLARS ALLOCATED TO SALES PROMOTION VERSUS ADVERTISING.
"Carol Wright Survey: Trade Promotion Still Dominates," PROMO (June 1996):107.

[5]"Carol Wright Survey: Trade Promotion Still Dominates," *PROMO* (June 1996):107.
[6]"Sales Promotion: What's Ahead?" *Advertising Age* (May 8, 1989):38.

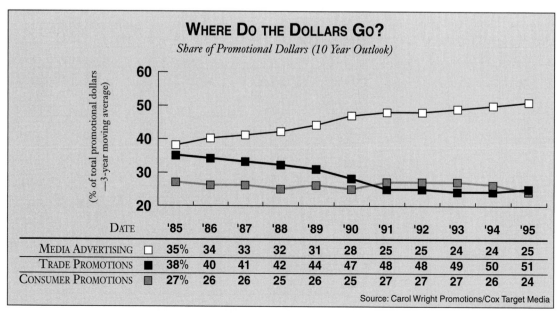

WHERE DO THE DOLLARS GO?
Share of Promotional Dollars (10 Year Outlook)

(% of total promotional dollars —3-year moving average)

DATE	'85	'86	'87	'88	'89	'90	'91	'92	'93	'94	'95
MEDIA ADVERTISING ☐	35%	34	33	32	31	28	25	25	24	24	25
TRADE PROMOTIONS ■	38%	40	41	42	44	47	48	48	49	50	51
CONSUMER PROMOTIONS ▨	27%	26	26	25	26	25	27	27	27	26	24

Source: Carol Wright Promotions/Cox Target Media

ECONOMIC FACTORS

Advertisers also cite economic reasons for the shift. Media costs have escalated to the point where alternatives must be thoroughly explored. The cost of mass-media advertising increased approximately 5 percent in 1996, compared to sales promotion cost increases of only 2 percent. But as the networks have been raising their prices, their share of prime-time television viewing has been dropping (to approximately 50 percent in 1996 from 92 percent in 1979). Advertisers therefore are exploring fresh new media forms that cost less and produce immediate, tangible results, and sales promotion is able to produce the desired results.

CONSUMER BEHAVIOR

Other reasons for the move toward sales promotion reflect changes in the market-place. For instance, shoppers today are better educated, more selective, and less loyal to brand names than in the past. In addition, many new markets are developing because of demographic shifts. The affluent "gray" market, the "new man," the "yuppie," and the working woman are all markets that appear responsive to the benefits of sales promotion.

From the consumer's perspective, sales promotion reduces the *risk* associated with purchase because promotions typically offer the consumer "more for less." This attitude was reinforced during the recession of the 1970s, when people were desperately looking for opportunities to save. That economic downturn introduced many consumers to the benefits of sales promotion, and they apparently enjoyed the experience.

LACK OF NEW-PRODUCT CATEGORIES

Although we are constantly bombarded with the terms *new* and *improved*, very few entirely new product categories have emerged since World War II. Today's marketplace is characterized by mature product categories and considerable consumer experience and knowledge. In most industries, the battle is for market share rather than general product growth. In many instances advertising remains the best tool for launching new products, especially when the need for brand awareness is important. However, sales promotion is often the most effective strategy for increasing share and volume for an existing product.

THE PRICING CYCLE

Retail pricing has also been influential in creating opportunities for the increased use of sales promotion, particularly in the highly volatile supermarket environment. Prices soared during the inflationary 1970s as the result of increased costs of labor, raw materials, and manufacturing. This situation led to the growth of low-priced private-label brands and the emergence of generic products. Having adjusted to these lower-priced goods, consumers have come to expect constant short-term price reductions such as coupons, sales, and price promotions.

THE POWER OF THE RETAILER

The final reason for the growth of sales promotion is the increasing power of the modern retailer. Dominant players, such as Safeway, Wal-Mart, Toys 'R' Us, and Home Depot, demand a variety of promotional incentives before allowing products into their stores. Obtaining desirable shelf location requires special in-store merchandising support. Procter & Gamble, for example, estimates that 25 percent of sales time and approximately 30 percent of brand-management time are spent in designing, implementing, and overseeing promotions.[7]

---

[7]Robert D. Buzzell, John A. Quelch, and Walter J. Salmon, "The Costly Bargain of Sales Promotion," *Harvard Business Review* (March–April 1990):141.

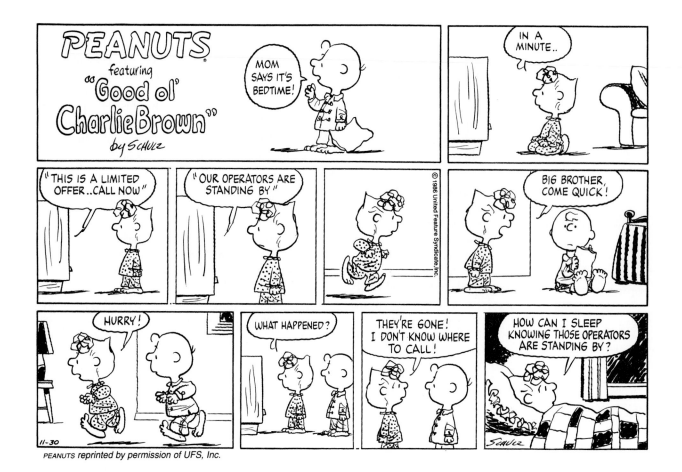

PEANUTS *reprinted by permission of UFS, Inc.*

THE ROLE OF SALES PROMOTION IN MARKETING

As explained in Chapter 3, sales promotion is just one element of the marketing communication mix available to the marketer, the other three being personal selling, advertising, and public relations. Because of its unique characteristics, however, the various sales promotion techniques we just discussed can accomplish certain communication goals that the other elements cannot.

For example, research suggests that there are certain things that sales promotion can and cannot do. Promotion alone cannot create an image for a brand. It cannot compensate for low levels or lack of advertising. It cannot do much to change negative attitudes toward a product, overcome product problems, or reverse a declining sales trend. But promotion can help introduce a new product as well as build a brand over time by reinforcing advertising images and messages, by generating positive brand experiences among buyers in many places along the purchase continuum, by creating an affinity between brands and buyers, and by providing new channels for reaching audience segments.

Promotion can offer consumers an immediate inducement to buy a product, often by the simple step of making the product more valuable. Promotion can cause consumers who know nothing about your product to try it, and it can persuade them to buy again.[8]

---

[8]J. Brian Robinson, "Promotion Is a New Way to Make Brand Contact With Buyers," *The Marketing News* (April 12, 1993):2, 16.

Sales promotion should be incorporated into the company's strategic marketing planning, along with advertising, personal selling, and public relations. This means establishing sales promotion goals and selecting appropriate strategies. A separate budget should be set up for sales promotion. Finally, management should evaluate the sales promotion performance.

Although all these elements are important, setting promotional objectives is particularly important. Our definition of sales promotion implied three broad objectives:

1. To stimulate demand by industrial users or household consumers
2. To improve the marketing performance of resellers
3. To supplement and coordinate advertising, personal selling, and public relations activities

The more specific objectives of sales promotion are quite similar to those of advertising. For example, in order to *get customers to try a new product*, companies such as Del Monte, Ralph Lauren, Wilkinson Sword, and VLI's Today sponge distribute over 500,000 free samples in Daytona Beach each spring break. To *encourage increased spending during the holiday season*, Kraft food products and Hasbro toys participated in a joint promotion through a nationally distributed free-standing newspaper insert that included cents-off coupons and rebates on toys. To *encourage present customers to use the product more often* in France, Orangina sales rocketed when the tangerine-flavored soft drink tied in with a fast-food chain to offer music-related premiums to consumers who ordered the drink.

Thus, sales promotion has become an important element in the strategy of many marketers. Like advertising, it is not right for everyone, however, and it will be effective only if it is carefully managed.

THE RELATIONSHIP BETWEEN SALES PROMOTION AND ADVERTISING

As we mentioned earlier, advertising and sales promotion are two of the elements that make up the promotional mix. These two elements have a number of similarities and often work together toward a common goal, but they also differ in many ways.

DIFFERENCES AND SIMILARITIES

DIFFERENCES

The major differences between advertising and sales promotion concern their methods of appeal and the value they add to the sale of the product or service. Whereas advertising is interested in creating an image and will take the time to do so, sales promotion is interested in creating immediate action, preferably a sale. In order to accomplish this immediate goal, sales promotion relies heavily on rational appeals, whereas advertising relies on emotional appeals to promote the product's image. Advertising also tends to add intangible value to the good or service and makes a moderate contribution to profitability. In contrast, sales promotion adds tangible value to the good or service and contributes greatly to profitability (see Table 18.2).

SIMILARITIES

Advertising and sales promotion also have much in common. According to Leonard Lodish, an international expert on sales promotion, the two share the

TABLE 18.2	THE DIFFERENCES BETWEEN ADVERTISING AND SALES PROMOTION	
ADVERTISING		**SALES PROMOTION**
■ Creates an image over time		■ Creates immediate action
■ Relies on emotional appeals		■ Relies on rational appeals
■ Adds intangible value to the product or service		■ Adds tangible value to the product or service
■ Contributes moderately to profitability		■ Contributes greatly to profitability

same roles: to increase the number of customers and to increase the use of the product by current customers. Both tasks attempt to change audience perceptions about the product or service, and both attempt to make people do something.[9] Of course, the specific techniques used to accomplish these tasks differ.

INTRODUCING A NEW PRODUCT

One area in which advertising and promotion work well together is the introduction of new products and services. Suppose we are introducing a new corn chip named Corn Crunchies. Our first challenge is to create awareness of this product. This is the real strength of advertising. However, sometimes advertising should be combined with an appropriate sales promotion device calling attention to the advertising and the brand name. Possibilities are colorful point-of-purchase displays, a reduced introductory price, and a special tie-in with a well-known chip dip company.

Creating awareness will only take the product so far, however. Corn Crunchies must also be perceived as offering some clear benefit compared to the competitors to convince consumers to purchase it. Advertising promotes this perception through informational and transformational executions. Recall from Chapter 8, informational advertising provides meaningful facts to the consumer when needed, whereas transformational advertising moves the consumer emotionally to a point of greater acceptance. Sales promotion enhances the message by offering coupons as part of the ad (known as an *overlay* ad), mailing free samples of Corn Crunchies to households, and conducting a contest in conjunction with the product introduction during the July 4th holiday. Ad 18.1 for Arm & Hammer cat litter is an example of an overlay ad. If we have successfully implemented this *pull strategy*, consumers will be convinced of the value of Corn Crunchies and go to their supermarkets and demand that the product be stocked. By asking for it, they will *pull* it through the channel of distribution.

Unfortunately, creating awareness and desire means nothing unless the product is available where the consumer thinks it should be. Somehow resellers (the trade) must be convinced that the product will move off the shelves before they will stock it. Therefore, a *push promotional strategy* is used to convince members of the distribution network to carry and market Corn Crunchies. We literally *push* the product through the channel. This is accomplished through two devices, *trade advertising* and *trade sales promotion*. Trade advertising directed at wholesalers and retailers can be effective in providing resellers with important information. In addition, trade sales promotion techniques, especially price discounts, point-of-purchase displays, and advertising allowances, help to gain shelf space.

In reality, most marketers use some combination of push and pull strategies. Using one to the exclusion of the other would usually prove risky, given the need to appeal to both customers—reseller and consumer. (See Figure 18.2.)

---

[9]Leonard M. Lodish, *The Advertising and Promotion Challenge* (New York: Oxford University Press, 1986):18.

AD 18.1

AN EXAMPLE OF AN OVERLAY AD
CONTAINING A TRADITIONAL AD
PLUS A COUPON.

After the initial purchase we want the customer to repeat purchase, and we also want retailers to allocate more shelf space to Corn Crunchies. This means that advertising copy is changed to remind customers about the positive experience they had with the product, and sales promotion is used to reinforce their loyalty with coupons, rebates, and other rewards. Retailers will be rewarded as well, with a predictable customer who will not only buy the product being promoted but will also purchase other products while in the store.

FIGURE 18.2

PUSH, PULL, AND A
COMBINATION.

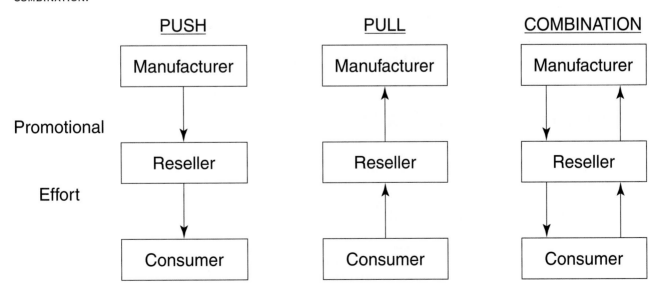

CAN SALES PROMOTION BUILD BRANDS?

For several years now there has been a heated debate between the advertising industry and the sales promotion industry concerning brand building. Advertisers claim that the strength of advertising is creating and maintaining brand image and that sales promotion negates all their hard work by diverting the emphasis from the brand to the price. The result is a brand-insensitive consumer. Critics of sales promotion cite the price-cutting strategies followed by Coke and Pepsi as an example of two brands that are now interchangeable in the minds of many consumers. On any given weekend, especially holiday weekends, Coke and Pepsi product displays are located on end-of-the-aisle caps or island displays featuring per-case prices as low as $4 and six-pack prices as low as $1.29, down from the regular price of $5.50 and $2.69, respectively. Procter & Gamble's division manager of advertising and sales promotion, V.O. "Bud" Hamilton, describes the situation as follows: "Too many marketers no longer adhere to the fundamental premise of brand building, which is that franchises aren't built by cutting price but rather by offering superior quality at a reasonable price and clearly communicating that value to consumers. . . . The price-cutting patterns begun in the early 1970s continue today, fostering a short-term orientation that has caused long-term brand building to suffer."[10] Critics point to a general decline in consumer brand loyalty as just one negative consequence caused by sales promotion.

Experts in sales promotion respond to this criticism in two ways. First, they argue that the claim that sales promotion destroys brand image is greatly exaggerated. They refer to many cereal brands, rental car companies, airlines, and hotels that have used a variety of well-planned sales promotion strategies to enhance their brand image. Hertz, for example, uses price promotions regularly, yet they have increased sales and market share both during and after these promotions. Second, they acknowledge that *continuous* promotion—particularly continuous price promotion—does not always work. They point to situations in which an entire advertising/promotion budget has been committed to a single promotion technique, causing the brand to self-destruct. Sears's predictable price reductions are a classic example of a company that destroyed its brand name through poor promotion planning. Conversely, continuous sales promotion can and does work if it is part of a well-analyzed and well-executed strategy. Furthermore, such promotion works most efficiently when it is part of a well-integrated advertising/promotion plan.

Finally, the criticism that sales promotion destroys brand loyalty appears to be exaggerated. In a 17-year tracking survey of brand equity conducted by HPD Group, the results show that loyalty to top brands has been steady since 1987.[11] Besides, notes Michael Schrage, "traditional advertising no longer has the responsibility of maintaining brand equity. Product value is no longer created through advertising imagery, it is determined by the price/performance relationship.[12]

TYPES OF SALES PROMOTION

PRINCIPLE Consumer sales promotion is most effective if the product or service is presold by advertising.

Sales promotion strategies are divided into three primary types: end-user or consumer, reseller or trade, and salesforce strategies. The first two have direct implications for advertising and will be discussed in some detail. Salesforce sales promotions are simply activities directed at the firm's salespeople to motivate them to strive to increase their sales levels. These activities are classified in two ways. The

[10]Scott Hume, "Rallying to Brands' Rescue," *Advertising Age* (August 13, 1990):3.
[11]Scott Hume, "Brand Loyalty Steady," *Advertising Age* (March 2, 1992):19.
[12]Michael Schrage, "Reinventing the Wheel," *Adweek* (April 6, 1993):23.

first set of activities includes programs that better prepare salespeople to do their jobs, such as sales manuals, training programs, and sales presentations, as well as supportive materials like films, slides, videos, and other visual aids. The second set of activities is concerned with promotional efforts or incentives that will motivate salespeople to work harder. Contests dominate this category.

CONSUMER SALES PROMOTION

Consumer sales promotions are directed at the ultimate user of the good or service. They are intended to "presell" consumers so that when people go into a store they will look for a particular brand. Most often, consumer sales promotions are the responsibility of the product manager, along with the advertising campaign planner, the advertising department, or a sales promotion agency or advertising agency.

The primary strengths of consumer sales promotions are their variety and flexibility. There are a large number of techniques that can be combined to meet almost any objective of the sales promotion planner. This flexibility means that sales promotion can be employed by all kinds of businesses.

PRICE DEALS

Price Deal: A temporary reduction in the price of a product.

A temporary reduction in the price of a product is called a **price deal.** Price deals are commonly used to encourage trial of a new product, to persuade existing users to buy more or at a different time, or to convince new users to try an established product. They are effective only if price is an important factor in brand choice or if consumers are not brand loyal.

There are two principal types of consumer price deals: cents-off deals and price-pack deals. A *cents-off deal* is a reduction in the normal price charged for a good or service (for example, "was $1,000, now $500," or "50 percent off"). Cents-off deals can be announced at the point of sale or through mass or direct advertising. Point-of-sale announcements include the package itself and signs near the product or elsewhere in the store. Advertising includes sales flyers, newspaper ads, and broadcast ads. Both types of cents-off deals can be initiated by the manufacturer, the wholesaler, or the retailer. (See Ad 18.2.)

Price-pack deals provide the consumer with something extra through the package itself. There are two types of pack deals: bonus packs and banded packs. *Bonus packs* contain additional amounts of the product free when the standard size is purchased at the regular price. For example, Purina Dog Food may offer 25 percent more dog food in the bag. Often this technique is used to introduce a new large-size package of the product. When one or more units of a product are sold at a reduced price compared to the regular single-unit price, a *banded pack* is being offered. Sometimes the products are physically banded together. The Pillsbury Company has been banding three cans of their biscuits together for many years. Bar soap, such as Dial, often is offered this way. In most cases the products are simply offered as two-for, three-for, five-for, and so on.

COUPONS

Coupons: Legal certificates offered by manufacturers and retailers that grant specified savings on selected products when presented for redemption at the point of purchase.

Legal certificates offered by manufacturers and retailers that grant specified savings on selected products when presented for redemption at the point of purchase are called **coupons.** *Manufacturer-sponsored coupons* can be redeemed at any outlet distributing the product. *Retailer-sponsored coupons* can only be redeemed at the specified retail outlet. The primary advantage of the coupon is that it allows the advertiser to lower prices without relying on cooperation from the retailer. In 1995, over 325 billion coupons were distributed.

There are several disadvantages associated with coupons, however. Distribution volume of coupons has slipped by at least 1 percent each year since 1995, and redemption rates have fallen to less than 2 percent, saving consumers $3.9 billion, under $4 billion for the first time since 1990. There are several reasons offered for

AD 18.2

THIS AD NOT ONLY INCLUDES
A PRICE DISCOUNT, BUT ALSO
SEVERAL OTHER DEALS.

the decline in coupon usage. Shorter expiration dates (now 3.5 months) and the plateauing of face values (now 58 cents) are mentioned most often.

Another is so-called bonus couponing. By offering shoppers double and triple the face value of manufacturers' coupons, but limiting the offer to those worth 55 cents or less, bonus-couponing retailers have been able to draw high-value manufacturers' offers downward. Cost increases are another serious problem. As noted in Figure 18.3, the face value of the coupon represents only 52 percent of the cost of a coupon. All the other cost factors, especially postage and distribution, have increased steadily during the last five years. Some of these cost factors can be reduced through technology. For example, misredemption (accidentally or intentionally misredeeming coupons) can be lessened as more supermarkets and other retailers employ scanners at the checkout. Distribution costs can be reduced in a number of ways. Improved databases will mean that coupons can be better targeted. It will reduce waste as well as clutter, since fewer consumers will be inundated with irrelevant coupons. *Clipless* or *paperless* coupons reflect a new cost-saving technology. Clipless coupons often work this way: A retailer and manufacturer agree to promote a product by discounting to the retailer's frequent-shopper customer base. The discount, which is normally advertised via flyers and shelf-talkers, is given to all consumers who purchase the product and have their store cards scanned at checkout. A final way to save money is to engage in co-op couponing by combining several noncompeting marketers in a single coupon mailing.

Perhaps the biggest problem facing couponing is accountability. Procter & Gamble recently dealt a serious blow when it announced that it would eliminate

FIGURE 18.3

THE COSTS OF COUPONING.
Source: PROMO (July 1996):38.

1995 EXPENDITURES
($Millions)

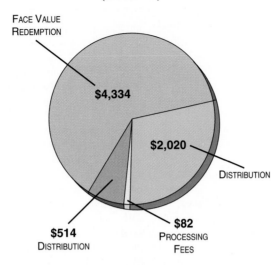

FACE VALUE
REDEMPTION

$4,334

$2,020

DISTRIBUTION

$514
DISTRIBUTION

$82
PROCESSING
FEES

coupons altogether from three upstate New York markets in a drive to spend its promotion dollars more effectively (see the Issues and Controversies box). This move by P&G could prove to be the end of couponing as we know it.

Manufacturer-sponsored coupons can be distributed directly (direct mail, door-to-door), through media (newspaper/magazine ads, free-standing inserts), in or on the package itself, or through the retailer (co-op advertising). Manufacturers also pay retailers a fee for handling their coupons. According to a 1993 study conducted by the Food Marketing Institute, coupon usage does vary:

- Shoppers who live in the East and Midwest are most likely to use coupons.
- One-person households are the most infrequent users of coupons.
- The most avid coupon users are those with a high school education or less and those in the $15,000 to $25,000 annual income bracket.
- Only 32 percent of shoppers under age 24 use coupons.[13]

CONTESTS AND SWEEPSTAKES

The popularity of contests and sweepstakes grew dramatically during the 1980s. These strategies create excitement by promising "something for nothing" and offering impressive prizes. **Contests** require participants to compete for a prize or prizes on the basis of some sort of skill or ability. **Sweepstakes** require only that participants submit their names to be included in a drawing or other chance selection. A **game** is a type of sweepstake. It differs from a one-shot drawing-type of sweepstake in that the time frame is much longer. A continuity is established, requiring customers to return several times to acquire additional pieces (such as bingo-type games) or to improve their chances of winning.

A good contest or sweepstakes generates a high degree of consumer involvement, which can revive lagging sales, help obtain on-floor displays, provide merchandising excitement for dealers and salespeople, give vitality and a theme to advertising, and create interest in a low-interest product. Contests are viewed favorably by advertising designers because the copy tends to write itself as long as it is supported by background enthusiasm and excitement.

Contests: Require that the participant exhibit some sort of skill or ability in order to win.

Sweepstakes: Require only that the participant supply their name as part of a random drawing.

A game: Is a type of sweepstake.

[13]Bob Gatty, "Consumers Using Fewer Coupons," *PROMO* (June 1993):85.

ISSUES AND CONTROVERSIES

P&G OPTS FOR NO COUPONS

When Procter & Gamble announced in the spring of 1996 that it was abandoning coupons, the wake-up call was loud and clear: Manufacturers and coupon suppliers could no longer ignore the steady five-year decline in coupon distribution and redemption.

Proctor & Gamble's zero-coupon market test is the first known effort to look at the elimination of couponing. P&G's test started February 1, 1996 and ran through 1996. It affected all P&G brands in Buffalo, Rochester, and Syracuse, New York. P&G, which spends an estimated $5 billion annually on marketing, has reduced national coupon spending by 50 percent since 1990. Given its leadership in categories ranging from toothpaste to laundry care, observers believe it's best positioned to test coupon elimination and plow the savings back into value pricing and brand building.

Since the test began, area supermarkets have reported solid sales of P&G brands. P&G president and chief operating officer Durk Jager was so emboldened by initial tests results that he reportedly said at the National-American Wholesale Grocers' Association meeting that "About 40% of total coupon spending never reaches the consumer. We decide what coupons have to go." A P&G spokeswoman refused to comment on Mr. Jager's speech but said P&G's studies show coupons are an "inherently inefficient way to promote products."

Supermarkets are on board with P&G's program and are equally interested in getting rid of the costly operational aspect of processing coupons in exchange for programs oriented around the retailer's needs and product mix. "Everybody's fallen out of bed with national coupons because marketer spending has shifted to niches and retailers don't want to hassle with coupons that don't address their specific strategies," said Frank Everett, president, DEO of Reach Marketing, Westport, Connecticut.

Now Clorox Co. and other marketers are also paring their coupon use in the area, says analysts, who expect the tactic to spread among more marketers and to other regions as part of a growing move to replace national coupons with account-specific and in-store promotional efforts. "Clorox has cut back its couponing on bleach and cleaning products in upstate New York and General Mills is experimenting there with replacing national coupons for cereal with Catalina Marketing's electronic in-store coupons, all with good results," notes Burt Flickenger, analyst with Price Waterhouse & Co.'s Management Horizons.

Despite the movement away from heavy reliance on national couponing, marketers and analysts agree the coupon remains an important tool when used strategically for new-product trial and brand conversion.

Sources: Kate Fitzgerald, "P&G's Zero-Coupon Move Sparks Related Cutbacks by Competitors," *Advertising Age* (March 18, 1996):3; Pat Sloan, "P&G Tops Rivals in No-Coupon Push," *Advertising Age* (January 15, 1996):3, 40; and Ina B. Chadwick, "Pushing the Envelope," *PROMO* (October 1996):33–40.

While contests and sweepstakes can be effective for many promotion objectives, they seem to work particularly well when a product or brand is not living up to its potential or expectations and needs a shot in the arm to stimulate sales. The *New York Daily News* is a case in point. The newspaper created a "Scratch 'n' Match" game, with pieces inserted into each issue, to increase circulation and frequency of readership. One $75,000 prize and hundreds of cash awards were given each week of the ten-week-long promotion. With subway advertising and television and radio spots, plus much space in the paper itself devoted to trumpeting the campaign, response rates have hovered in the area of 32 percent.[14]

Sweepstakes and contests are one of the most frequently used tools to drive people to marketers' Internet sites. Dulles, Virginia-based American Online, for instance, has conducted numerous prize promotions to drive users to its advertisers' areas—the latest gives visitors a chance to win a $1 million drawing and one of the dozens of daily prizes including merchandise emblazoned with the online service's logo. To participate, members log on to the service and click on a number of icons. Entrants can also enter both the daily drawings by calling an 800 number.

---

[14]Carolyn Shea, "Playing to Win," *PROMO* (August 1996):53–62.

REFUNDS AND REBATES

Refund: An offer by the marketer to return a certain amount of money to the consumer who purchases the product.

Simply stated, a **refund** is an offer by the marketer to return a certain amount of money to the consumer who purchases the product. Most refunds encourage product purchase by creating a deadline. The details of the refund offer are generally distributed through print media or direct mail. General information may be delivered through broadcast media. Refunds are attractive because they stimulate sales without the high cost and waste associated with coupons. The key to success is to make the refund as uncomplicated and unrestrictive as possible. The refund may take the form of a cash *rebate* plus a low-value coupon for the same product or other company products, a high-value coupon alone, or a coupon good toward the brand purchased plus several other brands in the manufacturer's line.

PREMIUM OFFERS

Premium: A tangible reward received for performing a particular act, such as purchasing a product or visiting the point of purchase.

A **premium** is a tangible reward received for performing a particular act, usually purchasing a product or visiting the point of purchase. The toy in Cracker Jacks, glassware in a box of detergent, and a transistor radio given for taking a real estate tour are examples of premiums. Premiums are usually free. If not, the charge tends to be quite low.

In 1995, almost $21 billion was spent on premiums.

DIRECT PREMIUMS   There are two general types of premiums: direct and mail. *Direct premiums* award the incentive immediately, at the time of purchase. There are four variations of direct premiums:

1.   Store premiums: given to customers at the retail site
2.   In-packs: inserted in the package at the factory
3.   On-packs: placed on the outside of the package at the factory
4.   Container premiums: the package is the premium

Cereal manufacturers are among the biggest users of in-packs. In 1996, Kellogg's distributed millions of "special anniversary promotions" across minibrands, including Corn Flakes, Rice Krispies, and Froot Loops to celebrate the company's ninetieth anniversary. The cereal boxes offer consumers commemorative Matchbox trucks, utensils, and other collectible items. In addition, Kellogg's Special K cereal teamed with Reebok and Polygram to offer an on-pack special-edition Reebok Versa Training exercise video. And a recipe and coupon offer good for free Sun Maid Dried Fruit appeared on packages of Kellogg's Low Fat Granola cereal.

MAIL PREMIUMS   In contrast, *mail premiums* require the customer to take some action before receiving the premium. The original mail premium is called a *self-liquidator.* Self-liquidators usually require that some proof of purchase and payment be mailed in before receiving the premium. The amount of payment is sufficient to cover the cost of the item, handling, mailing, packaging, and taxes, if any. The food industry is the largest user of self-liquidating premiums. Country Pride Fresh Chicken, for example, offers an apron in exchange for the proof-of-purchase of their product. The *coupon plan* or *continuity-coupon plan* is the second type of mail premium. It requires the customer to save coupons or special labels attached to the product that can be redeemed for merchandise. This plan has been used by cigarette and diaper manufacturers. The final type of mail premium is the *free-in-the-mail* premium. In this case the customer mails in a purchase request and proof of purchase to the advertiser. For example, Procter & Gamble offered a discount on a down comforter premium with proof of purchase of White Cloud toilet paper.

One advantage of premiums is their ability to enhance an advertising campaign or a brand image. The best examples of this strategy are those brands or companies that are symbolized by characters such as the Campbell Soup Kids,

Charlie the Tuna, Tony the Tiger, Cap'n Crunch, Ronald McDonald, and the Pillsbury Doughboy.

SPECIALTY ADVERTISING

Advertising specialties are similar to premiums, except that the consumer does not have to purchase anything in order to receive the specialty item. These items normally have a promotional message printed on them somewhere. Although specialties are often given away as year-end gifts (the calendar hanging in the kitchen), they can be used throughout the year in particular sales situations. For example, some specialties, including pens, pencils, and organizers, are ideal for desktops. Other items work well because they are attention-grabbing novelties. Balloons, fans, litter bags, and tote bags fall into this category. The ideal specialty item is something that is kept out in the open where a great number of people can see it, such as a calendar or penholder displaying the company's name. Most notably, the cost of specialty advertising is often quite high, especially in comparison to the actual value derived. A specialty silkscreened baseball hat may cost as much as $11.00.

The 15,000-plus specialty items that are manufactured by companies are used for a variety of marketing purposes: thanking customers for patronage, reinforcing established products or services, generating sales leads. Specialty advertising has numerous advantages, but it also has some disadvantages.

Some people question the value of specialty advertising. A study sponsored by Specialty Advertising Association of Greater New York, however, suggests the contrary. Consider this: (1) 83 percent of consumers use such products; (2) 94 percent appreciate receiving them; (3) 94 percent have a positive attitude toward the advertiser.[15]

CONTINUITY PROGRAMS

Continuity Program: A program that requires the consumer to continue purchasing the product or service in order to receive a reward.

A **continuity program** requires the consumer to continue purchasing the product in order to receive the benefit or reward. The purpose of any type of continuity program is to tie consumers to the organization by rewarding them for their loyalty. Typically, the higher the purchase level, the greater the benefits. In the 1950s and 1960s the popular type of continuity program was trading stamps. Today continuity programs are synonymous with the word "frequent." Frequent-flier clubs sponsored by airlines are the model of a modern continuity program. They offer a variety of rewards, including seat upgrades, free tickets, and premiums based on the number of frequent-flier miles accumulated. Continuity programs work in

---

[15]"Consumers Notice Specialty Items," *PROMO* (June 1992):74.

SPECIALTY ITEMS CAN BE EFFECTIVE MEMORY DEVICES IF THEY ARE USEFUL AND REASONABLY WELL MADE. *(Teri Stratford)*

very competitive situations where the consumer has difficulty perceiving real differences between brands.

Most continuity programs are long-term, point-based incentive programs in which the more money customers spend with a vendor, the more benefits or rewards they receive. One way that AT&T is differentiating itself—and attempting to promote loyalty among its small business customers—is through its Global Contacts loyalty program. The program is simple: Customers spending more than $200 a month on AT&T Business International Long Distance Service can sign up for free and receive discounts from AT&T and its program partners. The program is constantly reviewed and upgraded; sponsors change with the changing needs of AT&T customers. Currently, program rewards include 10 percent off on classes at AT&T School of Business, discounts on air travel with Delta Airlines, on hotel stays at Sheraton Hotels, on car rentals from Avis, and on such business services as HQ Business Centers and UPS.[16]

CONSUMER SAMPLING

Allowing the consumer to experience the product or service free of charge or for a small fee is called **sampling.** It is a very effective strategy for introducing a new or modified product or for dislodging an entrenched market leader. To be successful, the product sampled must virtually sell itself on the basis of a certain uniqueness and ability to create a strong positive impact with minimal trial experience.

Samples can be distributed to consumers in several ways. The most common method is through the mail. An alternative is to hire companies specializing in door-to-door distribution. Advertisers can design ads with coupons for free samples, place samples in special packages, or distribute samples at special in-store displays. Ad 18.3 for Sampling Corporation of America suggests how targeted a sampling program can be.

Quaker Oats provides an interesting example of product sampling. The program involved their new Quaker Oat Cups shelf-stable oatmeal cereal. In Chicago, sample crews took to the streets during the morning rush hours handing

Sampling: Is allowing the consumer to experience the product at no cost.

PRINCIPLE Sampling, which allows the consumer to try the product or service free, is effective for new-product introductions.

---

[16]Ginger Colon, "True Romance," *Sales & Marketing Management* (May 1996):85–90.

AD 18.3

THIS AD IS TARGETED AT COMPANIES THAT MIGHT WANT TO SAMPLE TO SCHOOL CHILDREN.

Your Apples* Can Reach Kids Where They Do The Most Good – IN SCHOOL!

TEEN CO-OPS —5MM April & 5MM September, non-duplicating, gender specific

ELEMENTARY SCHOOL CO-OP —7 MM October, household income 25M or greater

1993 CUSTOM PROGRAMS —Reach up to 16MM age 6-12, 14MM teens — through schools

*Your apples might be cereal, candy, shampoo, or gym shoes! Give our proven vehicles a chance to produce tasty results for your brand! Call us today — we'll polish one up for you.

CALL **708/296-7032**
SAMPLING CORPORATION OF AMERICA

TARGETED IN-SCHOOL COUPONING/SAMPLING PROGRAMS

out free Quaker Oat Cups to workers outside office buildings and near train stations. Because the product was already premixed with water, workers could then zap Quaker Oat Cups in the office microwave to enjoy a hot oatmeal breakfast.[17]

In general, retailers and manufacturers maintain that sampling can boost sales volume as much as five to ten times during a product demonstration and 10 to 15 percent thereafter. Sampling is generally most effective when reinforced on the spot with product coupons. Most consumers like sampling because they do not lose any money if they do not like the product.[18]

In a recent survey, Target Marketing sought to determine the method of greatest impact for delivering product samples from national brand marketers. The survey involved intercept interviews with more than 2,000 consumers in 13 U.S. cities. The results state the case for sampling as a powerful promotion strategy to boost sales, increase market share, and create top-of-mind awareness. Among the findings: (1) For a product they have not tried, nine out of ten consumers prefer a free sample over a cents-off coupon. (2) Two out of three respondents wanted to be handed a sample, rather than delivery by mail or through the newspaper. (3) More than two-thirds are more likely to use a sample delivered by hand as opposed to a sample delivered by mail or newspaper. (4) Nine out of ten respondents said a positive experience with a sample product would cause them to switch brands.[19]

Although all of these consumer sales promotion techniques can be effective alone, they can also be combined to create a tremendous impact. This is demonstrated in the Concepts and Applications box that follows.

SPONSORSHIPS

The role of sponsorships in marketing communication is a bit confusing. As noted in Figure 18.4, sponsorships include a number of different activities, including sports; entertainment tours and attractions; festivals, fairs, and annual events; cause marketing; and arts. Many of these activities would be the responsibility of the public relations manager. In other instances, they would be a sales promotion activity. In addition, the term *event marketing* has emerged in the last decade. For a company like Reebok, there is a director of events marketing.

Regardless of title or place in the organization, when a company sponsors a sports event, concert, or charity with its resources, it is attempting to increase the perceived value of the sponsor's product in the mind of the consumer. IBM, General Motors, and Sony spent millions of dollars becoming an official sponsor of the 1996 Summer Olympics. Lipton Tea sponsors golf tournaments, Texaco sponsors car races, Siuemens sponsors international men's tennis, and 7-11 sponsors the Jerry Lewis Annual Telethon.

Corporations are finding that sponsoring high-profile events, such as the Olympics, as well as professional teams and their leagues, is not enough to sustain their marketing efforts. Jim Andrews, spokesperson for IEG Sponsorship Report, notes that increased sponsorship actually is at the local level: "A consumer at home watching TV sees Coca-Cola as an official sponsor and it's not that big a deal. But if a company is sponsoring a hockey clinic in someone's local area, then it has [added] meaning to the consumer. It might become a place to go with the kids when they get to hang out with the athletes."

Examples of corporation sponsors are McDonald's, which sponsors the World Cup as well as the regional Chicago's Mayor's Cup soccer tournament, and John Hancock's sponsorship of the U.S. Olympic hockey team, which is anchored by involvement with numerous local hockey clinics. John Hancock has also

[17]Glenn Heitsmith, "Try It, You'll Like It," *PROMO* (September 1992):6.
[18]*The Wall Street Journal* (August 28, 1986):19.
[19]Kate Fitzgerald, "Survey: Consumers Prefer Sampling Over Coupons," *Advertising Age* (January 29, 1996):9.

*C*ONCEPTS AND *A*PPLICATIONS

THE CD SAMPLER: A WAY OF REACHING GENERATION X

Record companies and marketers can make beautiful music together as long as the venue, the audience, and the promotion are in sync with each other's sales objective. Music blends perfectly with many promotions by setting a mood that instantly establishes and reinforces a brand's image with the intended core audience.

Why, then, are musical tie-ins so rarely attempted? Answer: Established acts receive plenty of free exposure on radio and all-music cable television, and the performers don't want commercialism to target their "product." Plus, companies don't want to market a CD featuring an unknown artist. Enter the CD sampler: a compilation of tracks from various recording artists—some already known, some soon-to-be discovered—packaged solely for use as a premium incentive. With a wide array of performances from which to choose, consumers are more likely to find something to their liking.

Starbucks, for one, will let coffee buyers purchase an exclusive hodge-podge of '60s rhythm and blues artists on 850 locations; Sony is giving away a double disc CD sampler featuring exclusive tracks from Modern Rock Lives weekly radio show with the purchase of a Sony Discman or Sony CD Boombox. And Dr. Martens is giving consumers a 21-track Capital Records CD sampler with the purchase of a pair of shoes. In each case, the targeted customers are the elusive (but musically inclined) Generation X through the thirty-something generation.

"If you want to influence the youth and culture of tomorrow, you have to be a part of the culture that makes it today," says John Walbrecht, marketing strategist of Dr. Martens. Recently, the Portland, Oregon-based manufacturer distributed 200,000 CD samples featuring such alternative artists as Everclear, Radiohead, Ioo Fighters, and Supergrass, with the purchase of its footwear.

The company is so pleased with its sales results that it plans to execute two sampler giveaways every year. "[Music tie-ins] aren't right for every brand," adds Walbrecht. "For us, it's right because that's what the consumer expects of us." Over the years, Dr. Marten's has provided musicians with free apparel in exchange for subtle product placement on stage and in music videos.

Depending on how the deal is structured, marketers can expect to shell out between $1 and $3 per CD unit. However, the perceived value of the final product is between $12 and $18. K-Swiss paid $1.50 for each CD sampler featuring alternative and hip-hop artists from Geffen and A&M Records.

SHOE MONEY: Dr. Martens and K-Swiss to record sales with sampler giveaway.

The two-month program was structured similarly to Dr. Martens's promotion, and reportedly cost the company less than $10,000 to support.

"Music defies fashion and we have a strong appeal in the inner city and suburbs," notes K-Swiss assistant category manager Ramen Ramhormozi, explaining the purpose of the program and music genre selections.

Source: Blair R. Fischer, "Perfect Pitch," *PROMO* (October 1996):86.

sponsored the New York City and Boston marathons as well as running clinics. These events give sales representatives the opportunity to interact with people for the first time in a social environment as opposed to a less relaxed business environment.[20]

---

[20]"Sponsorship to Hit $5.4 Billion in '96," *PROMO* (March 1996):12.

FIGURE 18.4

1996 SPONSORSHIP SPENDING IN NORTH AMERICA BY TYPE OF PROPERTY ($MILLIONS/PROJECTED)

Source: PROMO (March 1996):12.

1996 SPONSORSHIP SPENDING IN NORTH AMERICA BY TYPE OF PROPERTY ($MILLIONS/PROJECTED)

TOTAL: $5.4 BILLION

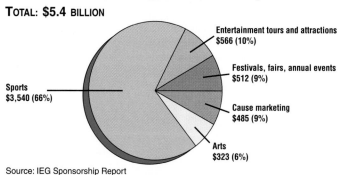

Entertainment tours and attractions $566 (10%)

Festivals, fairs, annual events $512 (9%)

Cause marketing $485 (9%)

Sports $3,540 (66%)

Arts $323 (6%)

Source: IEG Sponsorship Report

TIE-IN PROMOTIONS

Tie-ins are proving to be an effective strategy for marketers that are using associations between and among complementary brands to make one plus one equal three. The reason for the many success stories is that brands can leverage similar strengths to get a bigger and quicker impact in the marketplace.

Packaged-goods companies, financial institutions, and entertainment marketers are all part of the mix. Typically, marketers align themselves with partners that provide numerous complementary elements, including common target audiences, purchase cycle patterns, distribution channels, retailer penetration, and demographics to drive their products and promotions through retail channels and into the minds of consumers.

One company that is tasting the sweet benefits of a tie-in strategy is Westlake Village, California-based Dole Foods Company. The manufacturer uses Easter and other holiday-teamed tie-ins to increase display space and market share for its canned pineapple juice, canned pineapple, raisin, and mandarin orange products.

Dole used a two-pronged approach in 1996 during its month-long Easter promotion. The big-ticket sweepstakes included 50 cruises for two abroad American Hawaii Cruises, plus airfare from anywhere in the U.S. mainland. The trade was also invited. Retailers could give away a cruise if they put at least 100 cases of product on display. This provided a local sweepstakes component to complement the national-level program and generated widespread retailer support during a period when displays are tough to get.

The second element was a cooking video that tied in with Dole brands by focusing on Hawaiian and Pacific Rim dishes. The cruise line got exposure since the video was shot on board an American Hawaiian ship and featured its head chef. The video cost consumers only $4.95 plus two proofs of purchase.

Dole's percentage share of the canned pineapple market is usually in the low forties. The four-week period surrounding the 1996 Easter holiday saw the company's market share in the category hit 50 percent, with a sales increase of 20 percent.[21]

INTERACTIVE

The interactive sales promotion industry encompasses prepaid phonecards, telemarketing 800- and 900-number programs, and Internet-based promotions. The most talked about segment of the industry—the Internet—generated about $750 million in 1996. But cybermarketing is far from an exact science with most marketers still in the experimentation phase. Generally, little pressure is applied to get a respectable return-on-investment as marketers dabble with online formulations

[21]Glenn J. Kalinoski, "Forgiving a Winning Combination," *PROMO* (August 1996):79–83.

that will hopefully attract consumers. Selling products or services to Net surfers remains a hypothetical notion.

The prepaid phonecard market represents $770 million in revenue. Its primary appeal is free long-distance calls. Thanks to the passage of the Congressional Telecom bill, this product will be simplified. One breakthrough: A manufacturer is now making an audio-based phonecard that eliminates consumer number-punching of the toll-free and P.I.N. numbers.

RESELLER (TRADE) SALES PROMOTION

Resellers, or intermediaries, are the 1.3 million retailers and 338,000 wholesalers who distribute the products made by manufacturers to other resellers and ultimate users. The manufacturer usually is certain the product is acceptable only if resellers are willing to carry and *push* it. Sales promotion is used to bring resellers to that point of conviction.

Reseller sales promotions are intended to accomplish four overall goals:

1.   Stimulate in-store merchandising or other trade support (for example, feature pricing, superior store location, and/or shelf space)

2.   Manipulate levels of inventory held by wholesalers and retailers

3.   Expand product distribution to new areas of the country or new classes of trade

4.   Create a high level of excitement about the product among those responsible for its sale

The ultimate gauge of a successful reseller promotion is whether sales increase among ultimate users.

The actual size/worth of trade promotions is difficult to accurately determine. Although this category represented nearly 50 percent of total promotional spending, this varies by industry and size of business. Moreover, there are millions (or perhaps billions) of trade dollars that are difficult to trace. There does appear to be a shift, however, away from trade promotion toward consumer promotions.

A great many promotional devices that are designed to motivate resellers to engage in certain sales activities are available to the manufacturer. The major ones are discussed in the following paragraphs.

POINT-OF-PURCHASE DISPLAYS

Point-of-Purchase Display (P-O-P): A display designed by the manufacturer and distributed to retailers in order to promote a particular brand or line of products.

PRINCIPLE Point of purchase brings all the elements of the sale together: the consumer, the product, and the money.

A **point-of-purchase display (P-O-P)** is designed by the manufacturer and distributed to retailers in order to promote a particular brand or group of products. Although the forms vary by industry, P-O-P can include special racks, display cartons, banners, signs, price cards, and mechanical product dispensers. Point of purchase is the only advertising that occurs when all the elements of the sale—the consumer, the money, and the product—come together at the same time. As we move toward a self-service retail environment in which fewer and fewer customers expect help from sales clerks, the role of point of purchase will continue to increase. According to the Point of Purchase Advertising Institute (POPAI), 66 percent of purchase decisions are made in the store rather than before entering the store.[22]

Point of purchase is a big-business effort ($12 billion in 1996) that must be well thought out if it is to be successful.[23] Advertisers must consider not only whether P-O-P is appealing to the end user but also whether it will be used by the reseller. Retailers will use a P-O-P only if they are convinced that it will generate greater sales.

A P-O-P should be coordinated with the theme used in advertisements. This not only acts as a type of repetition, it also creates a last-minute association between the campaign and the place of decision.

---

[22]Cyndee Miller, "P.O.P. Gains Followers as 'Era of Retailing' Dawns," *Marketing News* (May 14, 1990):2.

[23]"Growth in P-O-P Spending Slows," *PROMO* (May 1992):16.

To survive, smart P-O-P suppliers are concentrating on developing not just relationships with manufacturers but also with retailers that are driving in-store displays. Partnering between brand marketers and retailers is becoming more common. Therefore, brand marketers are seeking out P-O-P suppliers that have an expertise with the retailer.

DEALER CONTESTS AND SWEEPSTAKES

As in the case of consumer sales promotion, contests and sweepstakes can be developed to motivate resellers. Contests are far more common, primarily because contest prizes are usually associated with the sale of the sponsor's product. A sales quota is set, for example, and the company or individual who exceeds the quota by the largest percentage wins the contest.

The need to create the desired amount of excitement and motivation has forced designers to develop spectacular contests with very impressive prizes. It is also important to offer the right incentive. According to a survey sponsored by *Business & Incentive Strategies* magazine, 46 percent of women and 51 percent of men would opt for cold cash, followed by merchandise worth $1,000 or more, and travel.[24] Frequent contests quickly lose their excitement, however. Contests are effective only if they take place periodically. If conducted properly, contests can provide short-term benefits and can improve the relationship between the manufacturer and the reseller.

TRADE SHOWS AND EXHIBITS

Many industries present and sell their merchandise at trade shows and exhibits that allow demonstrating the product, providing information, answering questions, comparing competing brands, and writing orders. In turn, trade shows permit manufacturers to gather a great deal of information about their competition. In an environment where all the companies are attempting to give a clear picture of their products to potential customers, competitors can easily compare quality, features, prices, and technology.

Because of the tremendous importance of trade shows, the Center for Exhibition Industry Research estimates that collectively companies annually spend $16.5 billion on trade show exhibiting in the United States, and the trade show industry has an $80 billion direct impact annually on the U.S. economy. Participating in a trade show is not cheap. Dell Deaton, marketing trade show expert, posits that a company spends about $10 for every second of the trade show.[25]

TRADE INCENTIVES

There is an alternative for instances when a contest is not appropriate or the goal may be to gain extra shelf space or to increase use of promotional material rather than to increase sales. In such cases trade incentives for accomplishing certain tasks are offered to the reseller by the marketer. The only requirement is that the reseller demonstrate in some way that the object was displayed. For example, a retailer might send the manufacturer a photograph of the display he or she promised to use. Incentive programs are very common when attempting to introduce a new product into a market, gain shelf space, or get retailers to stock more of a product. For example, a manufacturer may offer a substantial prize of cash or merchandise to a retailer who orders a certain amount of product or a certain product. Most incentive programs are customized for each reseller and each situation. However, there are two types of trade incentive programs that are somewhat standard—push money and dealer loaders.

Push Money: (spiffs) A monetary bonus paid to a salesperson based on units sold over a period of time.

PUSH MONEY　**Push money,** or *spiffs,* is a monetary bonus paid to a salesperson based on units sold over a period of time. For example, a manufacturer of air con-

[24]"Our Favorite Incentives," *Adweek* (October 19, 1992):20.
[25]Chad Kaydo, "Wait a Minute," *Sales & Marketing Management* (November 1996):85–89.

ditioners might offer a $50 bonus for the sale of model EJ1, $75 for model EJ19, and $100 for model EX3 between April 1 and October 1. At the end of that period each salesperson sends in evidence of total sales to the manufacturer and receives a check for the appropriate amount.

Dealer Loader: A premium given to a retailer by a manufacturer for buying a certain quantity of product.

DEALER LOADER   A **dealer loader** is a premium (comparable to a consumer premium) that is given to a retailer by a manufacturer for buying a certain amount of a product. The two most common types of dealer loaders are *buying loaders* and *display loaders*. Buying loaders award gifts for buying a certain order size. Budweiser offered store managers a free trip to the Super Bowl if they sold a certain amount of beer in a specified period of time before the event. Display loaders award the display to the retailer after it has been taken apart. For example, Dr Pepper built a store display for the July 4th holiday, which included a gas grill, picnic table, basket, and so forth. The store manager was awarded these items after the promotion ended. Both techniques can be effective in getting sufficient amounts of a new product into retail outlets or in getting a point-of-purchase display into a store. The underlying motivation for both arrangements is to sell large amounts of the product in a short period of time.

TRADE DEALS

Trade Deals: An arrangement in which the retailer agrees to give the manufacturer's product a special promotional effort in return for product discounts, goods, or cash.

Trade deals are the most important reseller sales promotion technique. A retailer is "on deal" when he or she agrees to give the manufacturer's product a special promotional effort that it would not normally receive. These promotional efforts can take the form of special displays, extra purchases, superior store locations, or greater promotion in general. In return, retailers sometimes receive special allowances, discounts, goods, or cash.

No one knows exactly how much money is spent on trade deals; experts estimate approximately $8 billion to $12 billion annually.[26] In some industries, such as grocery products, electronics, computers, and automobiles, trade deals are expected. A manufacturer would find it impossible to compete in these industries without offering trade discounts. In fact, the requirement to "deal" has become so prevalent that many advertisers fear it is now more important in determining which products receive the greatest promotion than either the value of the product or the expertise of the manufacturer. In the grocery field, for example, approximately 60 percent of all manufacturers' sales are accompanied by a trade deal averaging about 12 percent of the asking price.[27] The requirement to deal has been a point of contention between manufacturers and retailers for many years.

BUYING ALLOWANCES   There are two general types of trade deals. The first is referred to as *buying allowances* and includes situations in which a manufacturer pays a reseller a set amount of money for purchasing a certain amount of the product during a specified time period. All the retailer has to do is meet the purchase requirements. The payment may be given in the form of a check from the manufacturer or a reduction in the face value of an invoice.

ADVERTISING ALLOWANCES   The second category of trade deals includes advertising and display allowances. An *advertising allowance* is a common technique employed primarily in the consumer-products area in which the manufacturer pays the wholesaler or retailer a certain amount of money for advertising the manufacturer's product. This allowance can be a flat dollar amount or it can be a percentage of gross purchases during a specified time period. *Cooperative advertising* involves a contractual arrangement between the manufacturer and the resellers whereby the manufacturer agrees to pay a part or all of the advertising expenses incurred by the resellers (as examined in Chapters 3 and 4). A *display allowance* involves a direct payment of cash or

[26]Kevin T. Higgins, "Sales Promotion Spending Closing in on Advertising," *Marketing News* (July 4, 1986):8.
[27]Keith M. Jones, "Held Hostage by the Trade?" *Advertising Age* (April 27, 1987):18.

AD 18.4

THIS IS JUST PART OF THE
TRADE PROMOTION GENERAL
MILLS PRESENTED IN SUPPORT
OF ITS BASIC 4 CEREAL.

goods to the retailer if the retailer agrees to set up the display as specified. The manufacturer requires the retailer to sign a certificate of agreement before being paid.

Ultimately, the willingness of retailers to carry and support a manufacturer's brands depends on both direct incentives offered to the retailers along with the promotions offered to consumers. The latter suggests that the brand is adequately supported by the manufacturer and ensures the product will prove profitable to the retailer. Ad 18.4 shows an example of a program that the General Mills salesperson would present to supermarket managers.

THE FUTURE OF SALES PROMOTION

It should be obvious by now that sales promotion is a very diverse area. Trying to become an expert on all aspects of sales promotion may be unrealistic, and special skills in certain areas may be best learned on the job.

Certainly, when we talk about integrated marketing communication, sales promotion skills remain the most difficult for advertisers to learn. Of course, this difficulty may be due partly to the historical division in the creative philosophies between the two. As long as advertisers feel that sales promotion is denigrating the brand and stealing dollars from them, cooperation and synergy are unlikely.

It is apparent that sales promotion will continue to grow as a promotional alternative. Whether it will diminish the importance of advertising is still debatable, but certainly the varieties and styles of sales promotion are changing the world of advertising.

Summary

- Sales promotion offers an "extra incentive" to take action. It gives the product or service additional value.

- Sales promotion is growing rapidly for many reasons. It offers the manager short-term solutions; the extent to which sales promotion has achieved objectives can be assessed; sales promotion is less expensive than advertising; it speaks to the current needs of the consumer to receive more value from products; and it responds to the new power acquired by modern retailers.

- Sales promotion has three broad roles: to stimulate demand by users or household consumers; to im-

prove the marketing performance of resellers; and to supplement and coordinate advertising, personal selling, and public relations activities. In turn, sales promotion can move the consumer to purchase.

- Sales promotions directed at consumers include price deals, coupons, contests and sweepstakes, refunds, premiums, specialty advertising, continuity programs, and sampling.

- Reseller sales promotion includes point-of-purchase displays, contests and sweepstakes, trade shows, trade premiums, and trade deals.

Questions

1. What is sales promotion? What are the broad goals of sales promotion in terms of its three target audiences, and how do these goals differ from those of advertising? How are they the same? Discuss when sales promotion and advertising should be used together.

2. One agency executive was quoted as saying the following: "Advertising is on its way out. All consumers want is a deal. Sales promotion is the place to be." What do you think this executive meant? Do you agree or disagree?

3. You have just been named product manager for Bright White, a new laundry detergent that will be introduced to the market within the next 6 months. What type of sales promotion strategy would work best for this product? What types of advertising would enhance this strategy?

4. The chapter discussion says that sales promotion has made significant strides in marketing investment at the expense of advertising. Many companies show more confidence in direct sales stimulation. Why has this happened? Try to identify which explanations fit in each of these categories: (a) changes in advertising, (b) changes in consumer needs/wants, and (c) changes in marketing strategy. Does some change in any of these signal a shift back to more advertising emphasis?

5. Tom Jackson's promotional strategy professor is covering some sales promotion methods, explaining

that, in selecting the consumer sales promotion, planners must know the brand situation and objectives *before techniques* are chosen; some ways are for increased product usage, and some are for getting new consumers to try the product. "Which methods belong with which objective and why?" the professor asks. How should Tom answer this question?

6. Janice Wilcox is a brand manager for a very new line of eye cosmetics. She is about to present her planning strategy to division management. Janice knows her company has been successful in using sales promotion plans lately, but she has strong misgivings about following the company trend. "This new line must create a consumer brand franchise—and promotion isn't the best way to do that," she thinks to herself. What is a weakness of sales promotion in "brand franchising"? Should Janice propose no promotion or is there a reasonable compromise for her to consider?

7. Jambo Product's promotion manager, Sean Devlin, is calculating the cost of a proposed consumer coupon drop for March. The media cost (FSI) and production charges are $125,000. The distribution will be 4 million coupons with an expected redemption of 5 percent. The coupon value is 50 cents, and Devlin has estimated the handling and compensation (store) to be 8 cents per redeemed coupon. Based on these estimates, what will be the cost to Devlin's budget?

Suggested Class Projects

1. Observe your local newspaper and identify a retailer who is engaging in co-op advertising. Interview the store manager and determine the specific arrangements that exist between the advertiser and the retailer. What is the attitude of the retailer toward this arrangement? Write a two-page report.

2. Select a print ad for a national marketer. Redesign the ad, including at least two types of consumer sales promotion techniques. Show both before version and after version to five people. Assess whether the second version has increased their intention to buy.

FURTHER READINGS

Babakus, Emin, Peter Tat, and William Cunningham, "Coupon Redemption: A Motivational Perspective," *Journal of Consumer Marketing* (Spring 1988):40.

Fitzgerald, Ken, "Ad Support Builds for Tools," *Advertising Age* (August 28, 1989):20.

Haley, Douglas F., "Industry Promotion and Advertising Trends: Why Are They Important?" *Journal of Advertising Research* (December 1987–January 1988):RC-6.

Hume, Scott, "Premiums & Promotions: After Buying-Binge, What?" *Advertising Age* (September 12, 1988):S1–S5.

Lodish, Leonard M., *The Advertising and Promotion Challenge* (New York: Oxford University Press, 1986).

McCann, Thomas, "Promotions Will Gain More Clout in the '90s," *Marketing News* (November 6, 1989):4, 24.

Quelch, John A., *Sales Promotion Management* (Upper Saddle River, NJ: Prentice Hall, Inc., 1989).

Lens Express, a Deerfield Beach, Florida, marketer of contact lenses, had created an advertising presence through television and magazine ads that features Lynda Carter, television's "Wonder Woman." However, compared to its competitors, its use of advertising is relatively limited. Instead, the company relies on telemarketing, generated through toll-free telephone numbers. After viewing an ad, interested consumers call the number and set into motion Lens Express's telemarketing response. Customers needing a prescription are referred to a local doctor. Otherwise calls are handled by a telephone representative who takes orders and tells customers about special sales promotions entitling them to use the services of an eye-care professional.

An increasing number of companies are using the phone to sell everything from cruises to mufflers to municipal bonds to health insurance with the result that the value of goods and services sold via telemarketing skyrocketed from $56 billion in 1983 to $300 billion in 1992. The number of telemarketers also increased from 175,000 in 1983 to more than 5 million in 1994.

In the case of Lens Express, contact between the telemarketer and the customer was generated by the customer. In other cases, the company calls first, a technique many people consider intrusive. Despite the annoyance level these calls sometimes generate, they also generate a return that makes the effort worthwhile. "While a segment of people complain about telemarketing, it's still supereffective," explains Robert Blattberg, a marketing professor at Northwestern's business school. "You only need a 1 percent to 2 percent success rate for telemarketing to be effective."

Another company that has used telemarketing successfully in sales promotion is Olan Mills Inc., the largest portrait photography firm in the United States. "We got to be number one because we never gave up on telemarketing," said co-owner Olan Mills, II who hires 7,000 telemarketers to operate the phones in search of business and only 1,500 photographers. The company started telemarketing in 1952 as a way of spreading business throughout the year, instead of seeing customers only at Christmas. Co-owner Charles George Mills explains: "Back in 1952 Dad had this idea to get on the phone and sell a package of three sittings for $3, taken over a 12-month period. Invariably, customers arriving for the second or third sitting would buy additional photos, increasing the cash flow throughout the year." Although it now costs $15, the same sales promotion package is used today. As a direct result of its telemarketing efforts, Olan Mills's sales have grown 8 to 10 percent a year over the past five years compared to half that amount for its competitors.

Often, telemarketing is most effective when used in conjunction with other media, including direct mail. Telemarketing consultant Bernie Goldberg explains: "Your relationship to the customer is the key to everything. If you announce your program in a letter to customers and set the relationship, the phone call is easy. The best offer will have a yes/no response."

Despite its success as a sales promotion tool, telemarketing has an image problem with consumers who consider telemarketers uninvited dinner guests. Many people are also concerned about unscrupulous behavior. A case in point: Telemarketers working for long-distance carriers, including U.S. Sprint, offered consumers special sales promotions if they agreed to switch phone companies. Although most of the switches were handled correctly, some switches were made without customer approval; no written authorization was needed to process the change. Sprint realized what was happening only when consumer complaints began pouring in. Since then it uses a variety of safeguards, including random confirmation calls to customers who have switched.

Sprint is not alone in realizing that its image is on the line with every call. Although the potential to close sales is there, the potential to turn people off is also present—a realization that has convinced many companies that telemarketing's success is linked to the skill and professionalism of those delivering the message.

Sources: Martin Everett, "Your Job Is On the (Phone) Line," *Sales & Marketing Management* (May 1993):66–71; John Greenwald, "Sorry, Right Number," *Time* (September 13, 1993):66; Linda J. Neff, "Six Myths About Telemarketing," *Sales & Marketing Management* (October 1992):108–111; Roger Peterson, "Uninvited Dinner Guests," *Newsweek* (March 23, 1992):18; Ernan Roman, "More for Your Money," *Inc.* (September 1992):113–116; Aimee L. Stern, "Telemarketing Polishes Its Image," *Sales & Marketing Management* (June 1991):107–110; and William M. Stern, "We Got On the Phone," *Forbes* (March 1, 1993):94–95.

QUESTIONS

1. Why is telemarketing an effective sales promotion tool?
2. Why is telemarketing most effective when used in conjunction with other media?
3. What can companies do to overcome telemarketing's image problem?

CHAPTER

Public Relations

CHAPTER OUTLINE

- Food Lion Roars Back
- The Challenge of Public Relations
- Comparing Public Relations and Advertising
- The Components of Public Relations

- Public Relations Techniques
- Nonprofit Public Relations
- Evaluating Public Relations

CHAPTER OBJECTIVES

When you have completed this chapter, you should be able to:

- Understand what public relations is, how it differs from advertising, and what its advantages are
- Explain how public relations, advertising, and other marketing communications can work together to achieve greater benefit for an organization
- Identify the areas in which public relations operates and some of the activities performed in those areas
- Understand the value and importance of measuring the results of public relations efforts

Food Lion Roars Back

In 1992 *PrimeTime Live*'s Diane Sawyer showed up with a hidden camera at a North Carolina Food Lion supermarket. When the program aired, it showed a hidden-camera exposé charging that Food Lion sold rotting meat, fish dipped in bleach to kill the odor, cheese nibbled on by rats, and even produce that had been retrieved from fly-infested dumpsters.

Following the broadcast, the company's profits fell from $178 million in 1992 to a mere $3.9 million in 1993. In an attempt to stem the red ink, the company curbed its expansion plans and closed 88 stores.

Food Lion responded by suing ABC for $2.47 billion, charging that it had been smeared by unethical television producers working undercover in the store in partnership with a hostile labor union. In 1996, some four years after the broadcast, Food Lion finally got its day in court. And won.

Late in December 1996, a jury found ABC guilty of fraud, trespass, and breach of employee loyalty in the undercover investigation. The chance for a big punitive award declined, however, when the judge ruled that Food Lion couldn't prove that the producers faked the footage for the broadcast.

The question remains as to whether or not the company handled the crisis in the best possible manner. An article in *Fortune* suggested that regardless of whether or not the company won, Food Lion handled the crisis badly by focusing its attentions on the lawsuit. As *Fortune* observed, "The company spent more time attacking ABC than trying to calm jittery shoppers by assuring them that they were buying food that was fresh, clean, and safe to eat." Public relations experts say that when you know somebody is planning a bad story, there are two ways to handle it: Admit the problem, fire the people involved, and explain what you're doing to solve the problem, or hire an independent expert to conduct an investigation which will exonerate the company. Either way, people see a concerned company responding responsibly.

Rather than speaking to customer concerns, Food Lion found a third way to handle the crisis and blamed the messenger. The problem with a lawsuit, however, is that it opens up the nightmare all over again and brings a replay of the charges and the hidden-camera footage that sent the chain reeling in 1992.[1]

Handling a crisis calls for extraordinary public relations skills and a well-thought out plan in advance. This chapter will discuss crisis planning, as well as all the other specialty areas, activities, and tools of public relations.

The Challenge of Public Relations

The goodwill of the public is the greatest asset any organization can have. A public that is well informed and holds a positive attitude toward the organization is critical to its survival. If Food Lion had a professional public relations program, one expert in both issues management and crisis management, it might have been able to design a public relations strategy that would have been able to handle the charges without furthering the damage to its image. This chapter considers the role of public relations in a company and in a marketing communication program, its organization, its tools, and its practices. A basic understanding of public relations can help managers to avert the kinds of problems that face companies like Food Lion, and to better handle public relations crises when they do occur.

---

[1]Adapted from Marc Gunther, "Yikes, Diane Sawyer's Downstairs!" *Fortune* (December 23, 1996):231–234; "ABC Must Pay $1,402 to Food Lion in 1st Phase," *Chicago Tribune* (December 31, 1996):3; "Food Lion Award Damages from ABC," *The New York Times* (December 31, 1996):D4; Joseph Menn and Cynthia Adams, "Jury Awards Food Lion $1,402 in ABC Lawsuit," *Austin American-Statesman* (December 31, 1996):D3.

The art of public relations is very old. Historians tell us that Caesar and Alexander had their publicists. Kings and emperors staged special events to enhance their images. Counselors, heralds, bards, and even court artists sometimes assumed the functions we will later ascribe to public relations. Edward L. Bernays, considered the father of public relations, was the first to call himself a public relations counsel. In 1923, he wrote the first book on the subject, *Crystallizing Public Opinion,* and he taught the first college course on public relations at New York University. Despite this lengthy tradition, however, there is confusion about the nature of public relations.

Public Relations: A management function enabling organizations to achieve effective relationships with their various audiences through an understanding of audience opinions, attitudes, and values.

Although there is no universally accepted definition of **public relations,** the First World Assembly of Public Relations Associations in Mexico City offered the following definition in 1978: "The art and social science of analyzing trends, predicting their consequences, counseling organizational leaders, and implementing planned programs of action which will serve both the organization and the public interest." A much simpler definition is offered by Dilenschneider and Forrestal in the *Public Relations Handbook:* "Public relations is the use of information to influence public opinion."[2]

Both definitions treat public relations as a management function that is practiced by companies, governments, trade and professional associations, nonprofit organizations, the travel and tourism industry, the educational system, labor unions, politicians, organized sports, and the media. Its audiences (publics) may be external (customers, the news media, the investment community, the general public, the government) and also internal (investors, employees). The Concepts and Applications box discusses the management dimensions of the new media.

[2]Robert L. Dilenschneider and Dan J. Forrestal, *Public Relations Handbook*, 3rd rev. ed. (Chicago, IL: The Dartnell Corp, 1987):5.

CONCEPTS AND APPLICATIONS

WHERE'S THE PROPER HOME FOR THE HOME PAGE?

One management issue is whether the Internet is a responsibility of the management information services (MIS) or information technology (IT) departments or a tool to be used for communication and managed through some area with a public relations sense. In the survey of the top 50 U.S. companies, the *pr reporter* found that the survey responses suggest that the MIS and IT personnel are setting the rules for management of communication in this realm. From the pattern of no answers to the questionnaire, it was obvious that building relationships wasn't their main concern in managing their Web site.

For those companies that manage their Internet sites as a communication tool, another debate focuses on whether it is an advertising medium, a direct-marketing medium, the key to a corporate identity, or a public relations tool. Paul Holmes, editor of *Inside PR* says, "We believe the Internet is primarily about those things public relations does well: dialogue rather than monologue; education rather than promotion; relationship-building rather than transaction; all a company's audiences rather than its customers only. But a quick survey of the firms clients are calling in to create and manage their Internet sites reveals that PR is not currently winning this battle." He points to the annual Thomas Harris survey, which found in 1996 fewer than one-third of clients are turning to public relations firms for online communication assistance.

A culture war between MIS departments and public relations (or other communication) departments for informa-tional control was also identified in a study by the Institute for Public Relations Research and Education. "The implications are critical," say the authors. "Most organizations are missing a fundamentally important opportunity to use the unprecedented capability of the Internet and the Web to effectively manage relationships with their most important publics: those with an active interest in the organization." Chevron's Web site is an example of how these turf battles can be successfully worked out. The IT department is responsible for site security and day-to-day operations, but the corporate public affairs department coordinates content.

DISCUSSION QUESTIONS

1. What is the difference in the content of the home page when it is managed by MIS or IT rather than public relations departments? Would it be different if the home page were managed by the marketing department?

2. Pick a business category and inventory the home pages that you can find on the Internet. What ones do you think are well designed and what ones are not? Why?

Sources: Adapted from "Study Details Bumps to Watch Out For on Info Superhiway," *pr reporter* (August 5, 1996):2–3; Paul A. Holmes, "Going Unarmed Into a Battle for Corporate Image," *Inside PR* (September 8, 1996):2; and "The Battle Between MIS and PR for Internet Control," *Inside PR* (July 28, 1996):8.

Public relations is a growing industry. It is estimated that the public relations industry employs 145,000 people and that its billings are increasing by 18 to 20 percent annually. Virtually every city in the United States contains at least one public relations practitioner serving clients of every size and interest. Annual fees paid by these clients range from a few hundred dollars to several million. Table 19.1 lists the 25 largest public relations firms and their annual fees. In addition, many companies, such as Texas Instruments and IBM, have their own in-house public relations departments and do not contract with public relations agencies. Others, such as Exxon, consult with agencies only about specific activities.

Public relations, advertising, sales promotion, and direct marketing together present the marketing communication strategy of an organization. What a company's advertising says, how it says it, and what medium it uses have a direct bearing on the company's public relations strategy and vice versa. Thus, advertising agencies need to understand what public relations is and how it works with advertising to benefit both public relations and advertising. Furthermore, advertising strategists, especially copywriters and media specialists, often play a major role in the design and placement of public relations messages in mass media. Accordingly, this chapter attempts both to provide an overview of public relations and to show its direct applications to advertising. Before we enter into this discussion, however, we must distinguish advertising from public relations.

TABLE 19.1	TOP 25 PR FIRMS	
RANK	**COMPANY**	**NET FEES**
1	Burson-Marsteller	$211,864,434
2	Shandwick	171,128,000
3	Hill and Knowlton (A)	141,200,000
4	Fleishman-Hillard	89,544,000
5	Edelman Public Relations Worldwide	89,521,480
6	Ketchum Public Relations	64,325,000
7	Porter/Novelli	45,872,061
8	Manning, Selvage & Lee	43,858,688
9	Ogilvy Adams & Rinehart	12,876,000
10	GCI Group	40,088,090
11	Robinson Lerer/Sawyer Miller/Bozell	40,000,000
12	Rowland Worldwide	35,400,000
13	Ruder Finn	33,084,552
14	Cohn & Wolfe	19,900,000
15	Financial Relations Board	16,347,652
16	Morgen-Walke Assocs.	13,876,000
17	Powell Tate	12,432,782
18	The Weber Group	12,304,381
19	Cunningham Communication	11,284,000
20	Stoorza, Ziegaus & Metzger	9,312,179
21	Gibbs & Soell	9,113,200
22	The Kamber Group	8,780,931
23	MWW/Strategic Communications	8,426,000
24	Pacific/West Communications Group	7,627,298
25	Dewe Rogerson	7,198,000

Source: Adapted from "Profiles of the Top 25 PR Firms," *O'Dwyer's PR Services Report* (May 1996). Reprinted with permission of *O'Dwyer's Directory of PR Firms*, New York.

COMPARING PUBLIC RELATIONS AND ADVERTISING

Developing strategies, designing ads, preparing written messages, and buying time or space for their exposure are the primary concerns of advertising people. If we believe in an integrated approach to mass communication, advertising and public relations should be complementary.

In many companies they are separate uncoordinated functions. Partly this is due to tradition and partly to differences in functions. With respect to the former, public relations has historically been physically separated from advertising. This separation has been a result of the nature of the work performed by public relations as well as the people working in public relations. The public relations function operates at two different levels in most companies. On one level, you have the technical people who write news releases and produce brochures and newsletters; on another level you have the public relations counselor who advises senior management on public opinion and the anticipated impact of corporate actions. An example of an upper-level advisor who faced unfriendly fire is the Volkswagen public relations chief who was brought in to turn around the image of the company. Unfortunately his remarks on the Beetle's links to the Nazi regime got almost as much negative publicity as the book that reported the connection.[3]

Since public relations is not considered a direct profit generator and has difficulty verifying its accomplishments, individuals working in advertising are sometimes reluctant to incorporate public relations into their planning. Conversely, individuals working in public relations are often unwilling to work with others outside their field, particularly people involved in marketing or selling. Public relations people are often trained as journalists, with little background in marketing or advertising.

One area where the two overlap is corporate advertising. Corporate advertising is advertising designed to promote a corporate image or viewpoint. For that reason, the ad may originate in the public relations department. The Mobil ad in Ad 19.1 is an example of a corporate ad that explains the company's contribution to the economy.

Public relations and advertising differ in the way certain tasks are performed. Specifically, they differ in the way they employ the media, the level of control they have over message delivery, and their perceived credibility.

MEDIA USE

Publicity: Public relations that relates messages through gatekeepers, such as the news media.

To begin with, public relations practitioners have a different approach to the media than do advertisers. Whenever possible, they avoid purchasing time or space to communicate messages. Instead, they seek to persuade media *gatekeepers* to carry their information. These gatekeepers include writers, producers, editors, talk show coordinators, and newscasters. This type of public relations is labeled **publicity** and is characterized as cost free because there are no direct media costs. There are indirect costs, however, such as production expenses and getting the cooperation of the gatekeepers.

Corporate/Institutional Advertising: Advertising used to create a favorable public attitude toward the sponsoring organization.

Even when public relations uses paid-for media, the nature of the message tends to be general or focused on the organization with little or no attempt to sell a brand or product line. The goal is to change the attitudes of the public in favor of the sponsoring organization. This type of advertising is referred to as **corporate** or **institutional advertising.**

An example of corporate advertising used to counter an image problem and the bad publicity that it stimulated was Denny's Restaurants' response to the racism charges that surrounded the organization in the early 1990s. It came to a

---

[3]Gabriella Stern and Brandon Mitchener, "Volkswagen PR Chief Accelerates Controversy," *The Wall Street Journal* (January 3, 1997):B1.

AD 19.1

THE LONG-RUNNING MOBIL CAMPAIGN IS AN EXAMPLE OF CORPORATE ADVOCACY.

An interesting industry

When ripples make waves

Even the proverbial drop in the bucket will cause water to ripple to the bucket's edge. It's a principle that also works with money.

But that doesn't mean the money that circulates through Mobil represents just a drop in the bucket of the American economy. It's a lot more than that. After all, we're a large company, and we have a substantial impact. In the U.S. alone last year, Mobil gross revenues were over $22 billion—and more than $106 billion in the last five years.

Obviously, we don't hold on to all of that, what with our employees and shareholders and the vendors we do business with deserving their share of the wealth. So, the money moves around in what some call the "ripple effect."

And ripples do make waves.

Take us, for instance. We market our petroleum and chemical products throughout the United States, and we have facilities of one sort or another in most states in the country. Which means we help fuel the economies of a lot of different communities.

Here's a partial listing of how some of the dollars you spent at the pump, at the supermarket or in heating your homes over the past five years were fed back into your local economies.

■ Nearly $10 billion was paid as salaries to our employees working in their own corners of the country from Maine to California and to federal and state governments on our employees' behalf in unemployment and Social Security taxes.

■ $2.3 billion went to our retired employees as pension payments.

■ $6 billion was paid out in dividends to our 194,000 individual shareholders and pension and mutual funds holding nearly 400 million shares of our common stock—95 percent of which are in the U.S.

■ $15.8 billion went to federal and state governments in excise taxes and in property, production, payroll and other taxes.

■ $3.8 billion was spent on environmental activities associated with our plants and operations around the country.

■ $9.3 billion went for goods and services to vendors across the country, who in turn paid their employees, paid taxes and generally did all of the above. That number, by the way, does not include monies spent for crude oil and product purchases.

■ And, we made some $1.2 billion in interest payments to American lenders to finance many of our projects.

Then, include the estimated $2 billion we paid in royalties to individuals and to the federal and various state governments, and it's not hard to see how the foregoing items represent a significant contribution to the nation's economy. And that's only in the U.S. The story, although not the size of the numbers, is echoed in the more than 100 countries around the world where we do business.

And keep in mind, we're just one company in this one industry.

Understandably, economics can, at times, be a daunting subject. And too often we have tended to think of it as having little impact on our daily lives.

Not so.

Every time a cash register rings in this country, it creates a ripple in the U.S. economy that eventually builds into a tidal wave of activity.

Mobil

© 1995 Mobil Corporation

head in 1993 with reports that Denny's required cover charges and prepayment of meals from minorities. On May 24, 1993, a lawsuit was filed by six African-American Secret Service agents, who claimed they were denied equal service at Denny's in Annapolis, Maryland, because of deliberately slow service. In response, Denny's aired an unprecedented 60-second spot nationwide that featured Caucasian, African-American, Hispanic, and Asian employees of Denny's endorsing a solemn promise that all customers would be treated with respect, dignity, and fairness. Posters with visuals from the "pledge" ad and employee signatures were displayed in the restaurants. A print campaign followed using the same creative approach. Corporate advertising will be discussed in more detail later in the chapter.

The American Association of Retired Persons (AARP), the nation's largest organization of people aged 50 and older, also engages corporate advertising. The

AARP has recently attempted to develop a national program to reduce health care costs without sacrificing the quality of the care. Part of this program involves educating older consumers about these issues. To reach this large audience the AARP advertises its program—that is, it creates print advertisements and purchases space in newspapers and magazines to carry the ads. This special type of corporate advertising tends to be targeted and delivers a pointed message. It is labeled **advocacy advertising.** The organization also persuades television talk shows to invite AARP spokespersons to appear and encourages radio call-in programs to air the association's views of the issues.

Advocacy Advertising: A type of corporate advertising that involves creating advertisements and purchasing space to deliver a specific, targeted message.

CONTROL

Amount of control is the second inherent difference between advertising and public relations. In the case of news stories, the public relations strategist is at the mercy of the media representative. There is no guarantee that all or even part of the story will appear. In fact, there is the real risk that the story may be rewritten or reorganized so that it no longer means what the strategist intended. In contrast, advertising is paid for, so there are many checks to ensure that the message is accurate and appears when scheduled.

AD 19.2

CORPORATE ADVERTISING IS OFTEN FOCUSED ON IMPROVING THE VALUE OF A COMPANY OR BRAND IMAGE.

The difficulty in measuring the results of public relations is another problem. It may take months or even years to change public opinion. In addition, it is hard to measure accurately the components that reflect public opinion.

CREDIBILITY

Public relations efforts that are successful offer a credibility not usually associated with advertising. For example, a two-minute story delivered by Tom Brokaw on the *NBC Evening News* about an Eli Lilly Drugs medical breakthrough is far more credible than a print ad sponsored by Eli Lilly. And that, of course, was the problem created for Food Lion by Diane Sawyer's *PrimeTime Live* exposé.

Consumers assume that the media are trustworthy and that they wouldn't deliver a story that was not true. Adding to this credibility is the amount of information provided by the media. A feature story on General Electric that appears in *Forbes* magazine may be six to eight pages long, compared to a print ad containing 100 words of copy. Being able to tell a more complete and objective story about a company or product is something advertising cannot do.

Ultimately, the difference between advertising and public relations is that public relations takes a longer, broader view of the importance of reputation as a competitive asset. Although advertising must also be cognizant of a client's reputation, the focus is on reaching brand-related communication goals within a much shorter time frame. However, with the emphasis on integrated marketing communication, the separation between advertising and public relations is beginning to diminish. Ad 19.2 is an attempt to link corporate image with the value of a brand, or its brand equity.

THE COMPONENTS OF PUBLIC RELATIONS

As noted, the emerging partnership of public relations and advertising is moving rapidly toward a focused interaction with all individuals who are in a position to influence the fortunes of an organization. Public relations must increasingly become a management discipline, like advertising, involved in the earliest stages of corporate strategy. As mentioned, every company has a corporate image, although sometimes not quite by design. Managing a public relations image begins with a plan. The plan should complement the marketing and advertising strategies so the organization communicates with one clear voice. Public relations should also align the organization's interests with the public interest so that both are served. These public interests are expressed as public opinions.

TRACKING PUBLIC OPINION

Publics: Those groups or individuals involved with an organization, including customers, employees, competitors, and government regulators.

Traditionally in public relations, the term **publics** has been used to describe any group that has some involvement with an organization, including customers, employees, competitors, and government regulators. Another term for *public* is *stakeholders*, groups of people with a common interest who are affected by or can affect the success of an organization.

Public Opinion: People's beliefs, based on their conceptions or evaluations of something rather than on fact.

The public relations strategist researches the answers to two primary questions about public opinion. First, which publics are most important to the organization, now and in the future? Second, what do these publics think? In identifying important publics, public relations follows the same process as advertising does in identifying a target audience, which is simply the group of people or institutions we wish to receive our message (see Chapter 7). Determining what these publics think, however, is often quite challenging. **Public opinion,** the label used to denote what people think, is defined as "a belief, based not necessarily on fact but on the conception or evaluation of an event, person, institution, or product."[4]

The power of public opinion cannot be denied. It created the dictatorial influence of Adolf Hitler, made a hero of John F. Kennedy and a villain of politician Gary Hart, and has prompted countries to go to war. However, as many celebrities, politicians, and major corporations have found, public opinion is very fickle because of its fragile base in perceptions. Such perceptions are difficult to control, and often the public keys in on cues that are either negative or easily misinterpreted. Hot words and phrases, such as *abortion, taxes, misuse of power,* and *equal rights,* can be taken out of context or overshadow the real message. Physical appearance, mannerisms, or one poorly handled event can influence public opinion.

Despite the critical need to understand public opinion, there is still no one system of measurement of the climate of public opinion. Polls only measure public opinion on a particular issue at a given time. Different people maintain different values; likewise, a person's values can change over time. Clients of public relations agencies may rely on the research capabilities of the firm to evaluate public opinion, but they are more likely to rely on professional pollsters such as Louis Harris, George Gallup, and the Opinion Research Corporation.

One renowned expert on measuring public opinion is Daniel Yankelovich. In his book *Coming to Public Judgment,* he contends that public opinion evolves through seven stages, and unless one knows an opinion's stage of development on an issue, poll numbers will usually mislead.[5] Furthermore, public opinion on any issue develops slowly over time—at least ten years for a complex issue. The seven stages follow:

STAGE 1

Dawning awareness. Here people become aware of an issue or some aspect of it. At this stage most people remain largely unaware of the more specific issues and may express strong but unsettled opinions on the problem.

STAGE 2

Greater urgency. People now acquire a sense of real urgency about the issue, with the dominant sentiment being "Do something!" Real "consciousness raising" has occurred.

STAGE 3

Discovering the choices. In the third stage the public begins to focus on alternatives for dealing with issues. The timing of Stage 3 varies by issue. For some issues, choices become clear almost immediately, but for most issues they do not. This stage begins the process of converting the public's free-floating concern about the need to do something into proposals for action.

STAGE 4

Wishful thinking. This is where the public's resistance to facing trade-offs kicks in. Most of the time on most issues, the public raises a barricade of wishful thinking that must be overcome before people come to grips with issues realistically. To make sacrifices ungrudgingly, people must understand why these sacrifices are needed, and they must have some say in the types, forms, and conditions of sacrifices they are asked to make.

STAGE 5

Weighing the choices. Here the public weighs the pros and cons of alternatives for dealing with the issue. In practice Stages 4 and 5 overlap, with people thinking through how they feel at the same time that they continue to resist coming to grips with the hard choices.

---

[4]Doug Newsom, Alan Scott, and Judy Van Slyke Turk, *"This Is PR: The Realities of Public Relations,"* 4th ed. (Belmont, CA: Wadsworth Publishing Co., 1989):99.

[5]Daniel Yankelovich, "How Public Opinion Really Works," *Fortune* (October 5, 1992):102–108.

STAGE 6

Taking a stand intellectually. This works in conjunction with Stage 7.

STAGE 7

Making a responsible judgment morally and emotionally. As the stages of resolution, these last two can be considered together. People are quicker to accept change in their minds than in their hearts. Intellectual resolution requires people to clarify fuzzy thinking, reconcile inconsistencies, consider relevant facts and new realities, and grasp the full consequences of choices. Emotional resolution requires people to confront their own ambivalent feelings, adjust to unwelcome realities, and overcome an urge to procrastinate (see Ad 19.3).

We can illustrate Yankelovich's seven-stage process with a look at the current health care debate and its hopeful resolution. The process will begin when the public learns that more than waste and greed are involved in driving costs higher (Stage 1). People's sense of urgency will grow less panicky and more tightly concentrated on controlling and reducing costs (Stage 2). Voters will focus particularly on choices entailing a larger role for government (Stage 3). Resistance will grow as people learn more about the options and the extent to which each involves higher costs and less choice for the individual. Resistance will focus particu-

AD 19.3

THIS AD APPEALS TO A PERSON WHO HAS REACHED THE SIXTH AND SEVENTH STAGES OF PUBLIC OPINION ON THE ISSUE OF THE ENVIRONMENT.

THE NEW TRADITIONALIST.

SHE WANTS MUCH MORE THAN A CLEAN HOUSE. SHE WANTS A CLEANER WORLD.

Our readers, the New Traditionalists who feel a renewed commitment to improving the environment, look to Good Housekeeping to help lead the way.

Here is what we're doing to guide the millions of people who want to do their part:

• Good Housekeeping US and UK have joined forces to create a landmark, two-nation publishing venture, "Green Watch - the World of Good Housekeeping" to appear in March, 1991.

• The Good Housekeeping Institute established the Bureau of Chemistry and Environmental Studies.

• The Good Housekeeping "Green Watch" awards have been established to honor those making significant contributions to the environment.

• The Good Housekeeping "Green Watch" pages - a monthly editorial section.

• "The Environmental Moments" - special public service announcements on cable TV.

Healing the earth is a responsibility we all share. Good Housekeeping will make it our continuing priority throughout the "Decency Decade" of the 90's.

THE EARTH BELIEVES IN GOOD HOUSEKEEPING

larly on options requiring employees to pay more, limits on technology, rationing of health care, and any efforts that otherwise restrict choice and access (Stage 4). If the debate genuinely engages the voters, then the public, in Stage 5, should be ready to consider the merits of proposals concerning some degree of federal regulation of costs, extending coverage to those who lack it, or curtailing heroic measures applied to those who are dying. A few choices may even make their way to Stage 6. If the national debate is productive, Americans will support, at least intellectually, proposals for drastically reducing the incentives for malpractice lawyers to drive up settlement costs. It is unlikely that Americans can reach Stage 7, the public judgment stage, on such a vexing issue in a short time.

ISSUES MANAGEMENT

An important role of a public relations counselor is to advise companies and senior management on how public opinion is coalescing around certain issues. This advice is provided by senior public relations professionals for large companies that need to monitor public opinion, such as car manufacturers and chemical companies, as well as by outside agencies that employ experts in issues management. These people monitor public opinion research by independent research companies and commission research for their own companies and clients on particular topics. Getting the information is important, but knowing how to assess it and build recommendations on it is an even bigger challenge.

Recognizing the important role of information about public attitudes to its clients, the Porter/Novelli public relations agency does an annual tracking of the credibility of American institutions. Its 1996 survey found that the credibility of institutions such as government, the media, and corporations is continuing to decline. The agency interpreted these findings to mean that America "is deeply mired in the Age of Cynicism."[6]

An annual survey of the food industry conducted by CMF&Z Public Relations of Des Moines found that for the fourth consecutive year, most editors felt public concern over food handling was declining, while the number of consumers who expressed concern over such issues continued to rise.[7] Another study by Porter/Novelli investigated consumers' concerns about health, nutrition, and their lifestyles. The company analyzed the findings in terms of seven different personality types from Hard-Living Hedonists (people who smoke, drink, and eat cheeseburgers without even a twinge of guilt) to Decent Dolittles (people who pay attention to health issues but can't bring themselves to do much about it). The agency believes such information is useful in identifying people's orientation to health messages.[8]

A CASE STUDY: THE TOBACCO INDUSTRY

Few issues are more controversial in the United States than smoking. The tobacco industry is continually under fire from citizen's groups, the government, the media, and legislators. Public opinion seems to be solidly behind those who wish to restrict cigarette advertising and marketing.

And yet, cigarettes are legal to sell and smoke in the United States and many in the marketing communication and public relations industries feel that abridging a cigarette company's right to advertise is a serious challenge to the First Amendment and free speech rights. And people who smoke continue to remind us that they have rights, too. The smokers' group, which claims three million members, believes smoking is a civil rights issue, as well as a free speech issue.[9]

---

[6]"Survey Highlights 'Age of Cynicism' But Finds Most Keep an Open Mind," *Inside PR* (July 15, 1996):1, 3.

[7]"Food Safety: Editors Underestimate Consumers' Concern for Second Year," *Inside PR* (July 29, 1996):1, 7.

[8]"Porter/Novelli Research Seeks to Identify Health Styles," *Inside PR* (March 11, 1996):8.

[9]Jim Motavalli, "Tobacco Truths," *The Public Relations Strategist* (Summer 1996):50–53.

ISSUES AND CONTROVERSIES

TOBACCO ISSUES CONTINUE TO SMOKE

Marketing 101: Tobacco Ads Influence Children

Tobacco companies spend billions annually on cartoon ads, free clothing and other youth-oriented marketing. Yet they claim this has no effect on children. Research confirms what common sense tells us:

- Teens are twice as likely to be influenced by cigarette advertising as they are by peer pressure.[1]
- Teens are three times more sensitive to cigarette advertising than are adults.[2]
- 85% of kids who smoke (vs. just 35% of smokers overall) choose the three most advertised brands.[3]

Why are tobacco companies allowed to get away with marketing that clearly influences kids? They flood politicians with cash to block measures that would protect America's children.

To keep tobacco companies away from our kids, get tobacco cash out of politics. Ask your elected officials and all candidates to reject tobacco contributions. Tell them our children aren't for sale.

To contact your Members of Congress or to learn more, call **1-800-284-KIDS.**

This ad sponsored by the National Association of Elementary School Principals, National Coalition of Hispanic Health and Human Services Organizations (COSSMHO), National Association of Secondary School Principals, National Association of County and City Health Officials, National Black Child Development Institute, Intercultural Cancer Council, and American Society of Addiction Medicine.

CAMPAIGN for TOBACCO-FREE Kids

[1] Pierce, L.P., *Journal of the National Cancer Institute*, October 18, 1995.   [2] Pollay, R.W., *Journal of Marketing*, April 1996.
[3] U.S. Centers for Disease Control and Prevention, August 1994.

The social marketing campaign is targeting 10- to 13-year-olds who are on the brink of making a decision to smoke. The campaign has found out that 90 percent of adult smokers begin smoking as children, and most kids who smoke start at 13. The campaign is using a number of strategies to counter the impact of tobacco advertising including:

- *A Truth Squad:* The campaign tries to respond with facts every time the tobacco industry speaks out against FDA proposals or other control initiatives.
- *Peer Initiatives:* A group of eighth graders has been mobilized to carry the message to what the campaign calls its Smoke-Free Class of 2000.
- *Coalitions:* The campaign is hooking up with researchers and the ads are cosponsored by ten prestigious medical organizations.
- *Attacks on Influence Money:* Working with Common Cause, the campaign is publicizing tobacco industry contributions to members of Congress. Ads used to publicize these connections carry an 800 number, which can patch callers to the office of their political representatives via phone, fax, or letter to send an antismoking message to members of Congress.
- *Geographical Targeting:* Working with the Center for Disease Control and one of its studies that analyzes tobacco use in individual states, special programs, such as press conferences featuring local teens, were designed for problem areas. West Virginia, for example, ranks number one in teen smoking.
- *Celebrities:* The campaign will recruit roving ambassadors—athletes and celebrities that kids look up to—to speak to them on this issue.

The Campaign for Tobacco-Free Kids uses public policy initiatives, research, opinion leaders, and face-to-face communication, as well as media support and public service advertising, to battle the tobacco industry. The effort was designed to win public and legislative support for a successful Food and Drug Administration (FDA) proposal in 1996 banning vending machines, where most kids get their cigarettes. The proposal also prohibits billboards and other cigarette ads within 1,000 feet of schools and playgrounds and ads in publications read by children.

An effort by the privately funded National Center for Tobacco-Free Kids raised $30 million in startup funds and appointed ex-public relations firm head Bill Novelli as president. This is the largest tobacco control initiative. According to media director, Brian Ruberry, however, "it doesn't compare to the billions of dollars the tobacco industry spends on marketing its products to kids. But we have the facts and public opinion on our side. We think we can make a difference."

DISCUSSION QUESTIONS

1. What more efforts might the campaign make to deliver its message to kids?

2. Who else besides kids should be targeted with this message? Can you think of any target audiences that the campaign hasn't reached yet, but should?

3. If you worked for a cigarette company, how would you advise it to respond to this campaign?

Sources: "Tobacco-Free Kids Campaign Is Test for PR Strategies," *pr reporter* (March 25, 1996):1–2; Stuart Elliott, "Trade Groups Square Off Against Tobacco Restrictions, But Not All Agencies Agree," *The New York Times* (August 23, 1996):C6; and Bill Novelli, "Philip Morris Is the Mommar Quaddafi of PR," letter to the editor, *Inside PR* (June 17, 1996):3.

Within the advertising community, most of the professional associations such as the American Association of Advertising Agencies, the American Advertising Federation, the Association of National Advertisers, the Magazine Publishers Association of America, the Direct Marketing Association, and the International Advertising Association come down four square in favor of the right to advertise a legal product.[10]

As an example of how the debate is being carried out within the public relations community, Paul Holmes, editor of *Inside PR*, wrote an editorial praising Philip Morris for its leadership in upholding commercial free speech and its willingness to meet President Clinton halfway on his efforts to reduce the sale of cigarettes to minors. In response, Bill Novelli, former head of the large Porter/Novelli agency and now director of the antismoking campaign for Tobacco-Free Kids, compared Philip Morris to Mommar Quaddafi, saying that not all "leaders" deserve respect and praise.[11] The Issues and Controversies box reports on the Campaign for Tobacco-Free Kids.

REPUTATION MANAGEMENT

With an understanding of public opinion and the issues related to a company's business, public relations professionals can better design a reputation management program. An organization's policies and actions determine its reputation—in other words, reputation is built on practices, not press releases or corporate image ads.

The overriding goal of reputation is to strengthen the trust that stakeholders have in an organization.[12] That's particularly important in an era of public cynicism when business has a worse erosion of trust, according to a Roper study, than even politicians.[13]

---

[10]Stuart Elliott, "Trade Groups Square Off Against Tobacco Restrictions," *The New York Times* (August 23, 1996):C6.

[11]Paul A. Holmes, "Tobacco: Is It Leadership Or Is It Propaganda?" *Inside PR* (June 17, 1996):2–3; and William D. Novelli, "Philip Morris Is the Mommar Quaddafi of PR," *Inside PR*, letter to the editor (June 17, 1996):3.

[12]"Reputation Management Not PR, But Sound PR Key to It," *pr reporter* (February 5, 1996):1.

[13]"Trust, Today's Basic Issue, Reaches Far Beyond Government," *pr reporter* (February 12, 1996):1.

REPUTATION RED FLAGS

In Building Your Company's Good Name, Davis Young identifies eight red flags that a company can use to analyze its reputation. He suggests that before being able to communicate positively and proactively, a company must measure at least 35 out of a potential 40 points on the following test:

		STRONGLY DISAGREE				STRONGLY AGREE
1.	When there is a problem, we try to fix both the problem and its cause.	1	2	3	4	5
2.	We stand behind our products and services.	1	2	3	4	5
3.	We are loyal to our stakeholders.	1	2	3	4	5
4.	We operate within both the letter and the spirit of the law.	1	2	3	4	5
5.	We are truly involved in and care about our communities.	1	2	3	4	5
6.	We are more concerned with tomorrow than today.	1	2	3	4	5
7.	We emphasize what's right over what's expedient.	1	2	3	4	5
8.	People can count on us.	1	2	3	4	5

Source: Adapted from Davis Young, *Building Your Company's Good Name* (New York: AMACOM, 1996).

Public Relations Tools and Techniques

The arsenal of tools available to the public relations practitioner is vast and diverse. One way of organizing the available material is to divide it into two categories: controlled media and uncontrolled media. Controlled media include house ads, public service announcements, corporate (institutional) advertising, in-house publications, and visual presentations. These techniques are paid for by the sponsoring organizations. In turn, the organization maintains total control over how and when the message is delivered. The two exceptions to the paid-for criteria are house ads and public service announcements. Uncontrolled public relations media include the press release, the press conference, and crisis management.

PUBLIC RELATIONS AND CONTROLLED MEDIA

HOUSE ADS

A house ad is an ad that is prepared by the organization for use in its own publication or a publication over which it has some control. Consequently, no money changes hands, even though a particular organization may use some sort of billing mechanism. For instance, a local television station may run a house ad announcing its new fall programming.

PUBLIC SERVICE ANNOUNCEMENTS

Public Service Announcement (PSA): A type of public relations advertising that deals with public welfare issues and is typically run free of charge.

Public service announcements (PSAs) are designed by charitable and civic organizations to broadcast on television or radio or to be placed in print media free of charge. The United Way, American Heart Association, and the local arts council all rely on public service announcements. These ads are prepared just like commercials, and in many instances ad agencies donate their expertise to the design of PSAs.

The Advertising Council is a private, nonprofit organization that creates public service advertising campaigns in the public interest. The Advertising Council follows a prescribed procedure in evaluating and producing PSA campaigns (see Figure 19.1). Essentially, all public service announcements appearing on network television have been produced by the Advertising Council.

Unfortunately, networks and publishers have been so inundated with requests to run public service announcements that many are never aired or are run during very low viewing times or printed at the end of magazines. This severe competition has forced nonprofit organizations to do a better job designing PSAs or to run them as paid-for commercials.

CORPORATE (INSTITUTIONAL) ADVERTISING

As we mentioned earlier, corporate advertising is designed and paid for by the organization to enhance or change the image of the firm. There is no attempt to sell a particular product. This type of advertising sometimes takes the form of position statements directed at the public.

Companies seeking public support for corporate policies and programs have begun to invest more in a type of corporate advertising called *advocacy advertising*. For example, during the breakup of AT&T in the early 1980s, the Pacific Telesis Group had a negative image with the financial community, which viewed the firm as a high-risk investment. Among its other problems, Pacific Telesis had the lowest earnings record of the seven Regional Bell Holding Companies that began operation independently on January 1, 1984. In preparation for the AT&T divestiture, however, Pacific Telesis embarked on a strategic plan to turn the firm around. Convinced that the strength of the plan, combined with the company's vastly improved financial condition, would more than compensate for poor earnings in the past, the company believed that all that remained to be accomplished was to communicate these changes to the financial community. Pacific Telesis did

FIGURE 19.1

THE ORGANIZATION OF THE
ADVERTISING COUNCIL.
*Source: The Advertising Council Report to
the American People, 1988–1989.*
Reprinted by permission of The Ad-
vertising Council, Inc.

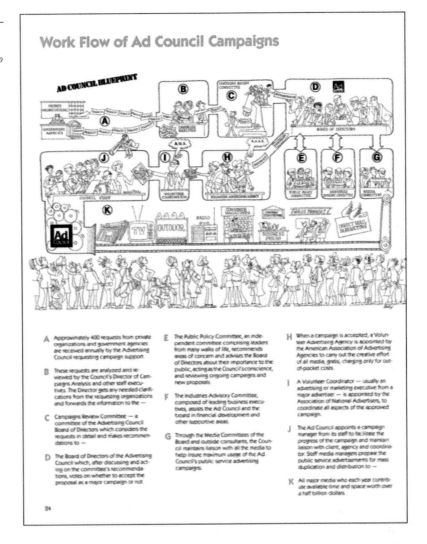

this through institutional advertising. The first print ad laid out the whole story—
from the company's financial health, to its marketing strategy, to the strength of
its top-management team.

Corporate identity advertising is another type of advertising used by firms
that want to enhance or maintain their reputation among specific audiences or to
establish a level of awareness of the company's name and nature of its business.
Johnson & Johnson targeted its Healthy Start institutional campaign at pregnant
women in an attempt to position itself as a concerned company. Companies that
have changed their names, such as Nissan (formerly Datsun) and Exxon (formed
from Esso, Humble Oil, and Standard Oil of New Jersey), have also employed
corporate identity advertising.

Corporate Identity Advertising:
A type of advertising used by firms
to establish their reputation or
increase awareness.

IN-HOUSE PUBLICATIONS

There is an almost endless list of publications provided by organizations to their
employees and other publics. Examples are pamphlets, booklets, annual reports,
books, bulletins, newsletters, inserts and enclosures, position papers, and information racks. In-house publications differ from house ads in that the latter are not
distributed in-house. Rather, house ads are carried by a medium owned by the organization that conveys information outside the organization. For example, NBC
might broadcast a commercial about a new television program or *Sports Illustrated*
might run an ad about its swimsuit edition. An example of an in-house publication
is the free booklet Corning Fiberglass Insulation offers on home insulation "do's

and don'ts" as an integral part of its promotion effort, which is highlighted in its advertising campaign. A company's financial report, especially the annual report, may be the single most important document the company distributes. Millions of dollars are spent on the editing and design of annual reports.

SPEAKERS, PHOTOGRAPHS, AND FILMS

Maintaining visual contact with the various publics is a big part of public relations. Many companies have a speakers' bureau of articulate people who are made available to talk about topics at the public's request. Apple Computer, Harvard University, and the Children's Hospital in Houston, Texas, all have speakers' bureaus.

Pictures of people, products, places, and events may all be desired by some publics. It is important for an organization that receives such requests to maintain a picture file and make sure these photographs are accurate, in good condition, and delivered promptly. Even the permissions for ads in this book were provided because they present the advertisers in a positive light. Companies seldom give permission for ads that are to be criticized.

Films, especially videotapes, have become a major public relations tool for a great many companies. At $1,000 to $2,000 per minute, these videos are not cheap. However, for a company like Cunard Cruise Line, mailing videotapes that show the beauty of a newly developed Caribbean paradise to 10,000 travel agents is a worthwhile investment.

DISPLAYS, EXHIBITS, AND STAGED EVENTS

There is no clear distinction between displays, exhibits, and staged events, though display is thought of as the simplest technique of the three. A picture of a new store being built and a presentation of a company's product line at a regional fair are examples of displays. Exhibits tend to be larger, may have moving parts, sound, or video, and are usually manned by a company representative. Booth exhibits are very important at trade shows, where many companies take orders for a majority of their annual sales. Parade floats, museum exhibits, and historic exhibits are other common types.

There are various kinds of staged events, such as open houses and plant tours. However, the use of more elaborate staged events has seen the most growth. Corporate sponsorship of various sporting events has evolved as a favorite public relations tactic.

For example, *Sports Illustrated* magazine has developed an elaborate events strategy in order to attract new advertisers. The centerpiece of that strategy is the Sports Festival, a 70,000-square-foot exhibition that tours Time-Warner's Six Flags theme parks during the summers, spending ten days at each park. The exhibition will include interactive games allowing participants to slam dunk a basketball or simulate a race against Carl Lewis. Eventually, 15,000-square-foot versions will start touring college campuses and shopping malls.

MEDIA RELATIONS

As we mentioned earlier, there are instances when an organization has no direct control over how the media will report on corporate activities, such as the opening story on the ABC investigation of the Food Lion grocery store chain. Sometimes the company will initiate the publicity and even provide pertinent information to be used by the media. In other cases the media will report a news event (good or bad) without guidance from the company. For either scenario to turn out favorably for the company, the public relations practitioner must become an expert at media relations, as is described in the profile of Peter Duckler on page 576.

When you say *public relations*, most people immediately think about *publicity* or *media relations*, which is an indication of the importance of this tool.[14] The rela-

---

[14]Carole M. Howard, "Ten Media Lessons Learned the Hard Way," *The Public Relations Strategist*, 2:2 (Summer 1996):45–48.

tionship between the public relations person and the media representative is tenuous at best and sometimes adversarial. The reporter is motivated by the public's right to know, and the public relations practitioner's loyalty is to the client or company. A successful relationship between public relations and the media is built on a reputation for honesty, accuracy, and professionalism. Once this reputation is tarnished or lost, the public relations person cannot function.

THE NEWS RELEASE

News Release: Primary medium used to deliver public relations messages to the media.

The **news release,** or press release, is the primary medium used to deliver public relations messages to the various media editors and reporters. Although the news release is under the control of the company distributing it, how it is used by the media is their decision. That's why we consider publicity to be uncontrolled.

News releases must be written differently for each medium, accommodating space and time limitations. The more carefully the news release is planned and written, the better the chance it has of being accepted and published as written. Being a good writer is considered a prerequisite for going into public relations. The news release is the primary reflection of this skill. Note the tight and simple writing style in the news release from the Plumbing-Heating-Cooling Information Bureau, the official spokesperson for that industry.

THE PRESS CONFERENCE

Press Conference: A public gathering of media people for the purpose of establishing a company's position or making a statement.

One of the riskiest public relations activities is the **press conference.** Although some companies, such as Polaroid and Chrysler Motors, have been very successful in introducing new products through press conferences, there have been many disasters. For example, in the fall of 1990 Victor Kiam, president of Remington Razors and owner of the New England Patriots football team, called a press conference concerning the allegations against his players over the improper treatment of a female reporter in the locker room. Protesters were refusing to buy

AN EXAMPLE OF A NEWS RELEASE. THE LANGUAGE IS CONCISE AND SIMPLE.

NEWS RELEASE

PLUMBING • HEATING • COOLING
INFORMATION BUREAU

303 East Wacker Drive • Chicago, Illinois 60601 • Phone (312) 372-7331

CONTACT: Susan Birkholtz or Lynette Duncan

FOR IMMEDIATE RELEASE
October, 1989

Is Your Home Ready For Winter?

PRECAUTIONS KEEP PIPES FROM FREEZING

Is your plumbing ready for the icy blasts of subzero wind chill factors?

The combination of low temperatures and high winds can freeze pipes in your home, possibly causing them to burst. However, preventing this common winter problem is not difficult, according to David Weiner, executive director of the Plumbing-Heating-Cooling Information Bureau.

"If a pipe has frozen in the past, keep heat close to it," he advised. "Leave the cabinet door open to let warm air from the house get in.

"People who use wood-burning stoves to save on heating bills during cold snaps often have problems with frozen pipes because the outside walls don't get enough heat," Weiner continued. "Don't shut off your furnace or boiler completely. Fuel costs less than a major plumbing repair."

-more-

FROZEN PIPES -- add 1

If a pipe does freeze, an electric hair dryer will defrost it. For safety, be sure the dryer is grounded and never hold the pipe while operating an electric appliance.

Larger pipes will probably require professional attention. To prevent them from bursting, turn off the water supply. However, if you have hydronic heat, remember the boiler must have a continual water supply while operating.

Another way to prevent freezing is to keep faucets in problem areas running in a low-to-moderate stream during a cold snap. If all else fails, the Bureau recommends having a licensed plumbing contractor relocate the pipes.

The Plumbing-Heating-Cooling Information Bureau is the consumer information arm of the plumbing-heating-cooling industry.

-30-

PETER DUCKLER, MEDIA RELATIONS MANAGER, *HLB Communications, Chicago*

It's great to have a job where every day I wonder where the day went. That's because every day is a different problem. It's deadline driven; it's frantic and hectic; but most of all it's fun.

I've worked in public relations for seven years after getting my masters in 1990 at the University of Wisconsin—Madison in communication. I moved to Chicago and worked at two different PR jobs after I got my degree, each for about a year. I've been here at HLB Communications now for five years. The reason I changed jobs in those first two years is that although I was really excited to get my first job, it's hard to get a job that matches your interests.

I learned a number of important skills in school, such as how to write, how to research, and how to contact the media, but I still didn't understand what a day-to-day media relations job would entail until I actually got the position. I learned a lot more about how the media actually works once I got to work.

Writing and research are terribly important in your education. If you can't write, you shouldn't be in PR. Students today are more proficient in research and looking up information on the computer than I was.

The hardest thing is getting your foot in the door; everyone wants people with experience. I had some internships and a good book of writing samples; you always need something to show. But an internship is really important. You may even have to take a job without pay in order to fulfill the requirement for experience.

GETTING THE JOB

How I got this job is an interesting story because it also illustrates what I do for my clients. There is a PR newsletter called the *Bulldog Reporter* that reports on the media. One issue featured a reporter who is particularly difficult for PR people to contact—she writes two syndicated columns, she's incredibly busy, and she doesn't have time for a PR person to call and ask if she got their release. In the interview article she mentioned me as having handled the contact right—i.e., I wrote her a one-page letter pitching a story that involved one of my clients. HLB saw that story, tracked me down, and offered me a job.

The point is, that's what I do for my clients—I contact the media with story ideas and arrange coverage of their projects or ideas. My agency represents a lot of clients and offers them a number of services, such as arranging for and writing speeches, writing white papers on a particular topic, writing and designing annual reports, helping design Web pages, and setting up special events. Some clients are always in a crisis mode so we try to help them manage this pressure.

WHAT I DO

I specialize in media relations. An example of what I do is the coverage I get for KPG Peat Marwick which has several executives who want to be known as thought leaders. In other words, whenever a reporter needs to interview someone in one of their areas of specialty, he or she will call me to arrange the interview.

That means, however, that I have to have a good relationship with reporters. When I first started I had to deal with the problem of busy reporters who don't take calls. In order to break through this barrier, I do research on reporters. I look up their stories and try to determine what they want and the kind of stories and information they like. I have built a database with all this information I collect on reporters. Now that I've been doing this for five years, I know a lot of reporters and I can call them with story ideas. I couldn't do that originally.

In other words, you can't contact a reporter with information that reads like an ad. You need to identify a current trend where your client can provide expert commentary or a case study. For example, one of our clients is a super-regional travel agency. We are constantly looking for "news pegs" to help raise awareness of the company. The firm's president, for example, likes to talk about the impact of technology on the productivity of the business, the "value added" services they offer their clients, and how their customers (travelers) are reaping the benefits. Because the spokesperson is accessible to the media, prepared in advance for all interviews, and has something interesting ("newsworthy") to say, he is frequently quoted by national business reporters. Last week his commentary appeared on the front page of *USA Today*. Because of the national coverage he receives, the company is considered in the industry to be a "major player" even though its size is significantly smaller than its competitors.

It's more than sending a press release. I was in a professional seminar and a *Tribune* editor dumped a whole bag of letters on the table. I thought that must be a week's worth but he said it was that day's letters. In other words, it's hard to break through.

Remington products, and questions raised by reporters and answers given by Kiam had serious negative repercussions on the sale of his razors.

Companies worry about various issues when planning a press conference. Will the press show up? Will they ask the right questions? Will they ask questions the company cannot or will not answer? One way to avoid some of these problems is to design an effective *press kit*. A press kit, normally in a folder form, provides all the important background information to members of the press either before they arrive or when they arrive at the press conference. The risk in offering press kits is that they give reporters all the necessary information so that the press conference itself becomes unnecessary.

Our agency is structured into account teams and each team works on five or six clients. The team is made up of people with a variety of different skill sets. I'm a good writer, but I do mostly press releases and work with the media. Another woman on my team is a technical writer and handles things like product literature. We also do a lot of authored articles for clients, i.e. ghost-writing. The team approach is great because we can have a really flat organization with fewer layers and less politics. The emphasis is on our skills and we focus on what people do best and like to do.

A TYPICAL DAY

I'm going to describe a typical day in terms of some of my general categories of work:

7:30–9:00 A.M.	I scan local papers, *The Wall Street Journal*, *New York Times*, *Fortune*, *Business Week*, and other business publications and make notes in my database on reporters and their stories. I track all my contacts with the media so that if one returns a call to me a week or two later I can see on my computer what I sent them or called them about. Then I take care of voice mail and e-mail. I also get on screen all the articles with references to any of my clients when I turn on my computer. I never know what will be there. If it's a problem, then I know that will affect the rest of my day. Some days are quiet but there are also days when all five clients are in a crisis. That means you have to be able to juggle and shift gears because every one wants your attention.
9:00 A.M.–12:00 P.M.	I spend the rest of the morning on the phone calling my targets, if I'm not in meetings. The trick is learning when to call; most writers for daily publications are working on stories in the afternoon and won't

take calls. Business publications are different. The point is you don't call Crain's business magazine on a Thursday, which is its deadline day. If possible, never call reporters when they are working against deadline. The first question a PR practitioner should ask at the beginning of every call is "are you on deadline?" or "is this a bad time?"

Lunch	I often don't have time for lunch, although I do bring a lunch and sometimes eat at my desk while I'm on the computer or on hold. Our company, like many others, has a kitchen and a collection of frozen meals that we all eat. If I go out for lunch, I usually go to my health club. It's a good time to do some thinking or reading while I ride an exercise bike.
Midafternoon	I close the door and try to get some writing done. We also have lots of client meetings at various times during the day, but particularly in the afternoon. Sometimes it's frustrating because I spend all day in meetings and don't feel like I have gotten anything done.
End of the Day	So much of our job is deadline driven, that I sometimes reach a burnout point, however, that also ties in to natural breaks. After everything is out, the phone calls have been made, the meetings have been arranged, it's time to wind down and go home. That can be 5:30 or it can be 8:00. And then there's the evenings when you try to get away at 5:30 and a client calls with a crisis. I turn around and start writing.

Nominated by Professor Jacqueline Hitchon, University of Wisconsin–Madison

CRISIS MANAGEMENT

The 1980s and 1990s seemed to be two decades of corporate disasters. Insider trading scandals, oil spills, plane crashes, and management improprieties made it difficult not to characterize American business as corrupt and poorly managed. This image is due in part to our efficient mass-communication system and in part to the media's desire to publish sensational news. There is no greater test for any organization than dealing with a crisis. The key is to be prepared.[15] Handling bad news such as the *PrimeTime Live* exposé of Food Lion is the responsibility of

---

[15]Robin Cohn, "Learning from Crisis: As the Curtain Rises," *The Public Relations Strategist*, 2:2 (Summer 1996):26–43.

PRESS CONFERENCES ARE
HIGH RISK ACTIVITIES, BUT
CAN PAY OFF IN A BIG WAY
IF MANAGED CORRECTLY.

public relations. A proactive public relations strategist will anticipate the possibility of a crisis and establish a mechanism for dealing with it.

Johnson & Johnson demonstrated the correct way to handle a crisis when in 1982 an unknown person contaminated dozens of Tylenol capsules with cyanide, causing the deaths of eight people and a loss of $100 million in recalled packages for Johnson & Johnson. In 1986 a second poisoning incident forced J&J to withdraw all Tylenol capsules from the market at a loss of $150 million. The company abandoned the capsule form of medication and consequently had to redesign its production facilities. It also ran a series of ads informing the consumer of these changes, gave away free packages of the new product, and endeared the consumer through its honesty and quick action.

In contrast, Jack-in-the-Box restaurants may never recover from the public relations disaster it faced in 1993. The tragedy began with a $2.69 "Kid's Meal." On January 11, Michael Nole, 2, happily tore into the dinnertime cheeseburger bought for him at the Jack-in-the-Box restaurant on South 56th Street in Tacoma, Washington. The next night, the boy was admitted to Children's Hospital & Medical Center in Seattle. Ten days later, Michael died of kidney and heart failure. Soon reports came in that over 300 people had been stricken with the same *E. coli* bacteria responsible for Michael's death. Most victims had eaten recently at Jack-in-the-Box outlets in Idaho, Nevada, and Washington. Others apparently got sick after contact with restaurant customers.

The company's 12-person crisis team, working from a plan devised in the mid-1980s, quickly scrapped nearly 20,000 pounds of hamburger patties prepared at meat plants where the bacteria was suspected of originating. It also changed meat suppliers, installed a toll-free number to field consumer complaints, and instructed employees to turn up the cooking heat to kill the deadly germ. But it took nearly a week for the company to admit publicly its responsibility for the poisonings. Even then, the admission seemed half-hearted. At a Seattle news conference, Jack-in-the-Box president Robert J. Nugent attempted to deflect blame—first criticizing state health authorities for not telling his company about new cooking regulations, then pointing a finger at Vos Companies, which supplied the meat. Sales dropped off 20 percent the first week.

Sometimes a company handles a crisis poorly at the onset and makes good decisions later. This is what happened to Sears, Roebuck and Co. when a scandal emerged in response to several of its automotive service departments. Apparently several stores were engaging in a variety of illegal activities, including charging for work not performed, charging for parts not replaced, and installing used parts. Sears's initial response was to deny the allegations. When it became clear that the reports were true, Sears changed its position and accepted responsibility.

Sometimes, in the case of natural disasters, prevention is not possible. However, there are instances when a carefully planned strategy is appropriate. When Hurricane Andrew struck Louisiana and Florida in 1992, businesses had a choice as to how they would respond to this terrible disaster. Some supermarkets decided to take advantage of people in crisis by charging exorbitant prices for food, batteries, bottled water, and so forth. Insurance companies also hurt their reputations by their slow response in adjustments and payments. Conversely, several companies did the right thing:

- AT&T provided 200 coinless public phones and donated to shelters 2,000 TeleTickets usable for free local and long-distance calls.
- American Express pledged $100,000 and relief supplies to the American Red Cross Disaster Relief Fund.
- Campbell Soup shipped approximately 5,000 cases of food to southern Florida. Another 5,000 cases were sent to Lafayette, Louisiana.
- Coors shipped 80,000 quarts of drinking water to both states.
- Toyota Motor Sales USA donated $250,000 to the Red Cross.
- Ford Motor Company provided more than $800,000 in cash contributions and goods and services to the relief efforts, including more than 100 vehicles for use by nonprofit organizations in both states.

ELECTRONIC COMMUNICATION

The biggest change in the communication landscape is being sculpted by new electronic media—e-mail, intranet systems that connect people within an organization, Internet advertising, Web sites that offer home pages—all of which open up new avenues for public relations activities. Table 19.2 lists how public relations professionals use online services.

E-mail, for example, is a great way for people in separate sites to communicate. It is quick and you can get fast return if people on the other end are checking their mail regularly. It is also an inexpensive way to send one message to many people. It has limited reach, however, since only about 10 percent are online.

Internal networks, called local area networks (LANs) or intranets, use personal computers to allow coworkers to easily send e-mail and documents to other

TABLE 19.2	PR PROS GO ONLINE

Survey of how PR pros use online services—by Creamer Dickson Basford	
Assessing news services	94%
Communicating with media	87%
Releasing information to the public	79%
Accessing marketing or competitive information	66%
Monitoring the "buzz"	65%
Post new-product notices	62%
Conduct surveys	60%
Target special user groups	56%
Create special-interest groups	34%
Locate experts or spokespeople	25%
Games/fun	23%

Source: "Survey: 411 PR Pros Say How They Value On-Line Services," *PR Reporter* (July 29, 1996):3. Reprinted by permission of Creamer Dickson Basford.

people in the organization. It permits the sharing of common databases such as customer records and client information.

Web sites and home pages are the hottest new online development. A survey of the top 50 U.S. companies found that 48 of them have their own Web sites.[16]

---

[16]"Study Details Bumps to Watch Out For on Info Superhiway," *pr reporter* (August 5, 1996):2–3.

*I*SSUES AND *C*ONTROVERSIES

TAMING THE WILD WEB

Paul Holmes, editor of *Inside PR*, has said, "The Internet is the most powerful vehicle yet for companies to truly relate to the publics with which they interact." He continues, "The greatest value of the Internet lies not in the ability to use it for full-page ads or hypertext versions of company brochures, but rather in the ability to use it to create virtual communities, places where people of like mind or interest . . . can congregate and discuss issues of importance." Unfortunately the Web raises more issues than advantages for public relations professionals to consider.

The Web is also a wild and lawless legal frontier for many organizations. The legal challenges faced by communication managers include liability for the Web activities of employees, intellectual property rights, and copyright, libel, privacy, and piracy issues. Anyone can create an unofficial site and there are even problems with the registration of company or brand names for Web sites by people unaffiliated with the company.

Employee relations professionals worry about "the loose cannon" employee or disgruntled ex-employee, who can go online and say anything. Acting on such concerns, courts have given legal permission to employers to monitor employees' online activity.

Public mobilization is another area of concern to public relations managers who deal with crises management and issues management. Educated and active publics are capable of rapid and powerful issue-based mobilization, domestically and internationally—influencing everything from votes in the U.S. Congress to organizational decisions. The problem with Intel's Pentium chip was announced on the Internet and generated a tremendous barrage of complaints around the world even as Intel tried to argue that the problem was minor. American Association of Retired People (AARP) is particularly successful at spreading news about legislative actions and mobilizing immediate response from the organization's membership on issues that seniors feel are important.

Companies are particularly concerned about criticism—whether justified or ill founded—that may appear on the Web. McDonald's fanned the flames by reacting strongly to an obscure site lampooning the company. In response, a Webmaster created McSpotlight, which invites Web surfers around the world to post their criticisms of McDonald's. Many sites on the Web are dedicated to criticizing companies, from the alt.destroy.microsoft group to the Kmart Sucks home page. These critics can't be silenced easily through litigation. Judges have already ruled that the Internet is an area where free speech is honored.

Public debate over the verdict in the lawsuit by Grady Carter and wife Millie against Brown & Williamson Tobacco Corp. became even more visible when a public relations company representing the law firm for the Carters set up a Web page on the trial (http://www.bottary.com). Visitors to the Web site will find a case overview, the actual verdict, legal team biographies, a look at what the tobacco companies knew, what they were telling the public, what the medical research showed, and information about the warning labels.

Another issue is the use of the Web for marketing activities. The Internet is an organic living entity: The minute a software package is developed that allows companies to place advertising on every page of the Internet, another program will be developed by college students and made available free as shareware that allows Internet users to strip out those ads.

The International Chamber of Commerce has established a voluntary code of ethics for online marketers: The most important suggestion is not to force commercial messages down the throats of people who have not been given the opportunity to avoid them, no free trade in confidential consumer information, and no corporate bullying in newsgroups.

If you were in charge of public relations for a company that's in the public eye a lot, what would you recommend to the CEO to include in the organization's Web policies? What is your position on the privacy of e-mail? How should criticism be handled online? Is it okay for your company to engage in online advertising? What are the pros and cons of all three of these issues?

DISCUSSION QUESTIONS

1. As a public relations director for a company, how many different ways can the Internet affect or be affected by your public relations program?

2. You have a boss who has gone ballistic over a new Web site that was set up by a disgruntled ex-employee to criticize your company. What position would you take with your boss about handling this problem? Outline the reasoning behind your argument.

3. Do some proactive planning for ways that your public relations office can work with the marketing department to manage the company's online marketing effort in a Web-sensitive way. What are the issues? How would you handle them?

Sources: "Study Details Bumps to Watch Out For on Info Superhiway," *pr reporter* (August 5, 1996):2–3; Paul A. Holmes, "Don't Mess with the Culture of the Internet," *Inside PR* (June 24, 1996):2; "Tobacco Trial Documents Now at PR Firm Web Site," *Inside PR* (September 23, 1996):7.

Another study found that 77 percent of U.S. companies are on or plan to be on the Net within two years; of that number 38 percent already have Internet sites. The study also found that the information to be provided includes corporate news (84 percent), product/service information (61 percent), customer support/educational information (37 percent), and employment listings (33 percent). On the Web sites, 58 percent also have e-mail addresses; only 16 percent use their sites to capture data.[17] The Issues and Controversies box discusses the ethical problems being created by the growing use of the Internet.

$\mathcal{N}$ONPROFIT $\mathcal{P}$UBLIC $\mathcal{R}$ELATIONS

Noncommercial Advertising: Advertising that is sponsored by an organization to promote a cause rather than to maximize profits.

Thus far we have discussed public relations activities employed by corporations and organizations that are motivated to increase profits or create a positive company image. This is not the only type of public relations advertising. **Noncommercial advertising** is sponsored by businesses or organizations that are not motivated by the maximization of profits. The emphasis in this type of advertising is on changing attitudes or behaviors relative to some idea or cause. This is not to say that these organizations operate without costs or are staffed by all volunteers. There are often pleas for donations in order to keep the organization going, but acquiring money is not the ultimate goal. Noncommercial advertising is typically sponsored by nonprofit organizations.

NONPROFIT ORGANIZATIONS

Placing an organization in the nonprofit category is not simple. Although the Red Cross and the Salvation Army are clearly considered nonprofit, organizations such as the U.S. Postal Service are not as easy to classify. Ultimately, the only important classification dimension is a legal one. Section 501 of the Revenue Code grants tax-exempt status to 23 categories of organizations. Thirty-nine percent of these are covered under Section 501(c)(3), which includes charitable, religious, scientific, and educational institutions. Section 501(c)(4) of the tax code includes civic leagues; Section 501(c)(6) covers business leagues; and Section 501(c)(7) includes social clubs.

The government's rationale for giving these organizations special status is twofold. First, the concept of *public goods* argues that nonprofit organizations provide services, such as health care, education, and basic research, which would not be provided were it not for the tax subsidy. Second, nonprofit organizations provide *quality assurance* in that they furnish services in areas in which consumers are ordinarily ill-equipped to judge quality, such as health care and education.

In their book *Strategic Marketing for Nonprofit Organizations*, Philip Kotler and Alan Andreasen contend that all advertising sponsored by nonprofit organizations falls into one of six categories:[18]

1. Political advertising (local, state, federal)
2. Social-cause advertising (Drug-Free America, Planned Parenthood)
3. Charitable advertising (Red Cross, United Way)
4. Government advertising (parks and recreation departments, U.S. Armed Forces)
5. Private nonprofit advertising (colleges, universities, symphonies, museums)
6. Association advertising (American Dental Association, The American Bankers Association)

---

[17]"A Reasonably Balanced View of Electronic Communication," *pr reporter* (January 8, 1996):2–3.

[18]Philip Kotler and Alan R. Andreasen, *Strategic Marketing for Nonprofit Organizations*, 3rd ed. (Englewood Cliffs, NJ: Prentice Hall, 1987):544–545.

Each of these six categories reflects a slightly different approach toward advertising. Political advertising, for example, has reached a very high level of sophistication and is guided by in-depth research and highly creative minds. Conversely, charitable and private organizations have limited funding and expertise and rely heavily on outside assistance and public service announcements. An example of nonprofit advertising is the television spot Dave Thomas, founder of Wendy's and an adopted child himself, did for the Adopt-A-Child organization.

EVALUATING PUBLIC RELATIONS

Measuring the effectiveness of public relations has been a problem, which is a major reason that public relations generally has not been accepted as an efficient and effective approach to behavior change. We need better standards for gauging the effectiveness of public relations efforts.

Evaluating public relations differs in several ways from evaluating advertising. One major difference relates to the lack of control public relations practitioners exercise over whether or not their message appears in the media and what it will look like if it does appear. Advertisers at least know the exact nature of their messages and the schedule of exposure to target audiences. Public relations practitioners must devote significant effort just to identifying and tracking the output of a campaign.

Public relations measurement may be divided into two categories: process evaluation (what goes out) and outcome evaluation (effect on the audience).

PROCESS EVALUATION

Process Evaluation: Measuring the effectiveness of media and nonmedia efforts to get the desired message out to the target audience.

Process evaluation examines the success of the public relations program in getting the message out to the target audiences. It focuses on media and nonmedia approaches with such questions as:

- How many placements did we get? (See Ad 19.4.) For example, how many articles were published? How many times did our spokesperson appear on talk shows? How much airplay did our public service announcements receive?
- Has there been a change in audience knowledge, attitudes, or reported behavior (as measured in the pre- and posttracking)?
- Can we associate actual behavior change (for example, product trial, repeat purchase, voting, or joining) with the public relations effort?

OUTCOME EVALUATION

There are several difficulties in evaluating the outcome of public relations efforts. As with advertising, it is hard to assess the public relations contribution within a larger marketing communications mix. In fact, because public relations programs have smaller budgets and, presumably, more modest effects, results are even more difficult to isolate and measure than they are for advertising. In addition, unless the program is directly aimed at changing a specific audience behavior, such as product purchase, success is ambiguous and hard to ascertain.

This is also true of image campaigns, such as corporate communications or community relations. How do you determine whether or not a public relations campaign has changed popular attitudes toward a product or an organization? And even if a positive change in awareness and attitudes is achieved, it is difficult to know whether or not these changes will lead to desired behaviors, such as receptivity to salespeople, donations, or a purchase.

MEASUREMENT PROBLEMS

Results and *measurement* are two of the hottest buzz words in public relations today. The current emphasis by senior management and shareholders on quarterly

AD 19.4

TRACKING PRESS COVERAGE IS A
SERVICE OFFERED BY COMPA-
NIES SUCH AS BURRELLE'S.

OK hotshot. So you ran a sensational PR campaign and the clips are pouring in. Now what do
you do? Your bosses want to know what it all
means. What do you show them...a big box
of clips?

Not bad for a start, but what do they **really**
mean? What is the true impact of your public
relations effort...in terms of exposure, circulation, audience? What is the quality of the pickup
you're getting? Which products or services are
getting covered? Is the tone favorable, or neutral?

What is the advertising equivalence in real
dollars? There's more...but we think you get
the idea.

It's time you received NewsClip Analysis from
Burrelle's. Burrelle's can create detailed, accurate, and visually stimulating reports that give
you a true evaluation of your public relations
effort. Burrelle's NewsClip Analysis reports are
timely, and they won't break your budget.

So call today for more information. Then, next
time you're rolling in the clips, instead of saying
"Now What?" you'll be saying "Look At This!"

NewsClip Analysis

Burrelle's Information Services
75 East Northfield Road, Livingston, NJ 07039
Telephone: 1-800-631-1160, In NJ: 201-992-6600

BURRELLE'S
Intelligence through media monitoring.

earnings as the main measurement of a company's success has accelerated the pressure on public relations to contribute directly to the bottom line. Historically, the success of publicity was measured by the number of news clips the public relations professional generated or simply the number of people who attended a special event, not by their attitudes or behavior change.

Evaluating more broad-based public relations calls for more sophisticated research. There is a variety of research techniques that can be used to develop and evaluate a company's public relations program and its contribution to the bottom line. The right mix of research can help determine audience receptivity to the message, their information needs, their concerns that relate to the company and its products, and ultimately whether or not the communication effort is having the desired effect. Public opinion surveys, focus groups, and secondary data research are some of the ways to collect information and evaluate an organization's communications efforts. They give the practitioner statistical validation for programs.

Public opinion surveys should be conducted by a firm that specializes in providing such a service. A research expert will help develop the questionnaire, identify potential respondents, administer the survey, and provide an analysis and interpretation. The company should work closely with the research firm and give as much information as possible about company objectives and how the information will be used. Results are useful when first developing a public relations program, launching new products, or making business decisions around public policy issues.

Focus groups are a qualitative research method in which a group of individuals representing a company's target audience is recruited for a guided discussion. The information gathered in focus groups is not quantifiable—it cannot be applied or projected to the whole target audience—but it often yields a vast amount of information about how effective a communication strategy might be or how receptive an audience might be to a specific public relations effort.

Numerous studies (secondary research) are being done around the country and the world. The results of many of these studies are available through online databases such as Lexis/Nexis. This is a much less costly way to get quantifiable data to use in public relations planning. However, the information generally will not be specific to a secondary situation. So a thorough evaluation of the data, as they relate to the company's information needs, is necessary to make the data of real value.

Despite the problems associated with evaluating public relations, there is little doubt that carefully planned public relations works. The key here is to move public relations into the realm of professional management. Major public relations firms leave nothing to chance. They carefully identify target markets, establish appropriate objectives, and design and implement public relations strategies that are equivalent to the best advertising strategies. It is under these conditions that public relations complements advertising and vice versa.

SUMMARY

- Public relations is a management function practiced by companies, governments, trade and professional associations, and nonprofit institutions.

- Advertising and public relations are separate activities, but the two work best when they are integrated.

- Both advertising and public relations use a number of different media. Public relations practitioners often have less control over their messages than do advertisers, but offer more credibility.

- Public relations activities can be performed by a department within a large organization or by a public relations agency.

- Public relations techniques can be divided into controlled media and uncontrolled media.

- Corporate advertising is implemented by organizations to enhance or change the firm's image.

- Managing crises is the responsibility of public relations.

- Public relations is similar to advertising in that it must be evaluated, although its direct effects on the audience are difficult to establish.

QUESTIONS

1. How does public relations differ from advertising? Does public relations offer advantages not available through advertising? Explain.

2. Define the concept of public opinion. Why is it so important to the success of public relations?

3. Dynacon Industries is a major supplier of packaging containers for industrial and food-service companies. Its research labs have developed a foam-polymer container with revolutionary environmental characteristics. The public relations department learns the trade and consumer press is unwilling to give the product the coverage the company needs. Public relations proposes that paid space (news and trade magazines) be used. The message will feature product background and the story about the environmental implications. Public relations argues that half the media and creative costs should be shared from the advertising budget. If you were in charge of these budgets, what would you recommend?

4. Prescription drug companies are supposed to be forbidden by law to advertise directly to consumers. However, Upjohn has run a campaign on hair loss on commercial television. Similarly, CIBA-GEIGY has promoted an oral medication as an alternative to gall bladder surgery in daily newspaper ads. Is this considered legal because it is public relations (despite using paid space and time)? What difference should it make whether the consumer is reached through advertising or public relations?

5. Wendy Johnson and Phil Draper are having a friendly career disagreement before class. Wendy claims that she is not interested in advertising because she dislikes the "crass commercialism" of promoting products and services that many people don't need. Phil counters by saying that public relations is doing the same thing by "selling ideas and images," and its motives are usually just as economic as advertising. If you overheard this discussion would you take Wendy's or Phil's side? Could you offer advice on ethical considerations for both careers?

6. Suppose your fraternity, sorority, or other campus group was planning a special weekend event on campus to raise public support and funds for a local charity.

This will cost your organization time and money. Although contributions at the event will be some measure of the effectiveness of your public relations program, what other things could you do to evaluate the success of the public relations activities?

Suggested Class Projects

1. Locate library materials on two organizational crises, one whose outcome was positive and the other negative. Evaluate how these outcomes resulted.

2. Adopt a local cause that operates on a low budget and needs public relations help. Develop a public relations plan for that nonprofit organization.

Further Readings

Dilenschneider, Robert L., "Marketing Communications in the Post-Advertising Era," *Public Relations Review*, 17 (Fall 1991):227–236.

Gronstedt, Anders, "Integrating Marketing Communications and Public Relations: A Stakeholder Relations Model," in *Integrated Communications: The Search for Synergy in Communication Voices*, Esther Thorson and Jacki Moore, eds. (Hillsdale, NJ: Lawrence Erlbaum, 1996).

Harris, Thomas L., *The Marketer's Guide to Public Relations* (New York: John Wiley & Sons, 1993).

Holmes, Paul A., "Reputation Management: Earning a Reputation and Leveraging It for Success," *Reputation Management* (January/February 1995):9–16.

Moriarty, Sandra, "PR and IMC: The Benefits of Integration," *Public Relations Quarterly*, 39 (Fall 1994):38–44.

Sexual harrassment charges can be a company's nightmare, particularly if not handled with public relations sensitivity. When Swedish pharmaceutical giant, Astra, received reports that the head of its U.S. subsidiary was accused of harrassment and "other activities considered inappropriate" by an investigation by senior company officials, the executive was immediately suspended.

In contrast, when Mitsubishi Motor Company was notified that as many as 700 female employees at its Normal, Illinois, manufacturing plant may have been exposed to sexual harrassment, the company not only denied the allegation, it paid a day's wages to 3,000 employees to travel to Chicago to picket the U.S. Equal Employment Opportunity Commission.

The *Chicago Tribune* wrote, "Mitsubishi lit the fuse rather than snuffed it out by such theatrics as busing workers to the EEOC in Chicago to protest the suit." A Chicago stockbroker observed, "The feeling among some analysts and brokers is that Mitsubishi has got something to hide and that this is why they are handling the situation this way."

Fears among employees that Mitsubishi sales might drop were increased when the Rev. Jesse Jackson and the National Organization for Women called for a nationwide boycott against the company, a move that only aggravated the fact that the Normal plant was losing money.

Furthermore, statements to the EEOC by Mitsubishi employees suggested that they believed that anything that stopped short of physical contact was acceptable. In other words, they had received no instruction on the sexual harrassment law.

Public relations experts speculate that Mitsubishi's problems stem from a lack of public relations sensitivity. In reporting on the need for public relations staff to keep in touch with employees and what they are thinking and doing, Paul Holmes, editor of *Inside PR*, observed that, "If Mitsubishi, for example, had a public relations staff that spent time on the product line, talking with workers and observing their work habits, might that PR staff have predicted and perhaps helped to avoid the problems the company experienced with the charges?"

The plant's management finally began to understand the seriousness of the situation when pressure from the company's Japanese headquarters motivated it to take a more conciliatory tone. The pressure came from the numerous other companies that carry the Mitsubishi name and feared damage to their image, as well as sales, because of the motor company's behavior and hard-line response.

Both *Inside PR* and *pr reporter* suggest that the problem was aggravated by the fact that the person who serves as general counsel is also public relations director. He orchestrated the busing that led public relations expert Otto to state, "Some say that a lawyer should never be placed in charge of public relations because lawyers tend to be confrontational." Whether it stemmed from a lawyer mentality or not, it was definitely a public relations problem that needed to be handled with more sensitivity.

Sources: Otto Lerbinger, "Mitsubishi Uses Wrong Proactive PR Measures in Combatting Sexual Harrassment Charges," *purview*, a supplement of *pr reporter* (May 20, 1996):1; Paul A. Holmes, "Mitsubishi Response to Sex Charges Creates More Problems Than It Solves," *Inside PR* (May 4, 1996):1, 8; Paul A. Holmes, "PR Needs to Get Closer to the Care Business," *Inside PR* (May 25, 1996):2; Jim Mateja, "Mitsubishi Toughness Was a Mistake," *Chicago Tribune* (May 6, 1996):C-7; and Peter Elstrom and Edith Hill Updike, "Fear and Loathing at Mitsubishi," *Business Week* (May 6, 1996):35.

$\mathcal{Q}$UESTIONS FOR $\mathcal{D}$ISCUSSION

1. You have been hired as the new public relations director for Mitsubishi, develop an action plan for rebuilding this company's reputation.

2. You work for a company that sells auto parts in a chain of 145 retail stores throughout the country. Your assignment is to develop a sexual harrassment training program for all the employees. How would you present this to employees and get them to buy into the program?

Video Case

"Whose Side Are You On?" Creating a Public Service Ad Campaign

After Alex Kroll resigned the chair of the Young & Rubicam advertising agency at the end of 1994, there was much speculation about his future plans. A legend in the industry, Kroll had joined Y&R as a copywriting trainee in 1962. He became chairperson in 1986 and, during the next ten years, Y&R's annual billings tripled to $8 billion. As it turned out, Kroll did not take much of a break from the advertising business. He became chairperson of the Advertising Council, the nonprofit group that creates public service advertising with funding provided by some of America's biggest corporations. Some of the Ad Council's slogans have become ingrained in America's consciousness, including "Friends Don't Let Friends Drive Drunk," "Only You Can Prevent Forest Fires," and "A Mind Is a Terrible Thing to Waste." After less than two years in his new position, Kroll has already created what is sure to be his legacy: an advertising campaign designed to create awareness of, and support for, urban parents who are struggling to raise children in tough neighborhoods.

The slogan for the new campaign is "Whose Side Are You On?" The campaign's tone was shaped by focus group research that revealed the belief among the general public that irresponsible parents were contributing to the plight of urban kids. After hearing comments such as "What's wrong with parents who let this happen? I would never let this happen!" researchers were convinced that the campaign would only work if it helped viewers see past their stereotyped attitudes about urban parents. But the researchers also wanted viewers to emphasize and identify with urban parents who were doing their best under difficult circumstances. In fact, that empathy did materialize in the focus group when researchers read the following statement: "We hear a lot of news about welfare cheats, but what the news doesn't cover is all the millions of parents and kids who are struggling hard, often under circumstances that are so difficult they would wear down the best of us." As Mr. Kroll commented, "When [focus group participants] hear of these stories of people trying to help themselves, it's like the ice block melts."

With the concept for the campaign established, the Ad Council set about actually creating the first group of spots. Tom Shortlidge of Young & Rubicam helped in the effort. Actual neighborhood residents appear in the ads rather than professional actors. An effort was made to present universal images of caring parents, such as a mother looking through a screen door to check on her children. As Shortlidge explained, "You're going to care about your neighbors' kids, and if you feel they're threatened by whatever, you're going to do something about it. And, in a way, that was what we were trying to do. We were trying to make these cases all somebody's neighbor, and, as a result, have you feel for these people." To break stereotypes, one spot featured former gang members who had joined together in a neighborhood patrol group called Mad Dads.

Mr. Kroll has committed the Ad Council to support the campaign for ten years—an unusually long time in the world of public service announcements. In addition to television and print ads, a Web site on the Internet and a toll-free telephone number are sources of further information and practical, specific suggestions for activities supporting children. The council supplies its ads to the media, which air or print them for free when time or space is available. Mr. Kroll hopes that the equivalent of $1 billion worth of media time will be devoted to the campaign each year. However, he acknowledges that the campaign's success depends on the willingness of the media to do their part by running the ads. "To make sure they do," Mr. Kroll explains, "we have to create enough advertising, and have enough money to create advertising, that will keep them interested." He concludes, "What's at stake is the future of a lot of innocent kids. We're talking about the future of America."

Source: The "Whose Side Are You On?" Ad Campaign, *Nightline* (August 19, 1996). *Additional Source:* Joseph Hanania, "Campaigning to Give All Kids a Fair Chance," *Los Angeles Times* (December 3, 1996):F5.

Questions

1. How did focus group research contribute to the creation of the "Whose Side Are You On?" campaign?
2. Why do AT&T and other companies support the Ad Council?

The Campaign Plan

CHAPTER OUTLINE

- Where's Your Mustache?
- The Structure of a Plan
- Situation Analysis
- Campaign Strategy
- Marketing Communication Activities
- Phases of a Campaign
- Evaluation

CHAPTER OBJECTIVES

When you have completed this chapter, you should be able to:

- Understand the role of the situation analysis in identifying key problems to be solved by the advertising
- Understand how the basic strategy decisions are developed for an advertising campaign
- Analyze how the message strategy solves the key problem
- Explain how the media plan relates to advertising objectives and message needs
- Explain how the effectiveness of an advertising campaign is evaluated

Where's Your Mustache?

The opening story in Chapter 13 focused on the California Milk Advisory Board's "Got Milk" campaign as an example of a very successful regional campaign for milk. The other success story is the national "Milk Mustache" campaign created by the Bozell agency for the National Fluid Milk Processor Promotion Board, or MilkPep as the board calls itself.

In spite of a small ad budget, a declining sales pattern for the industry, and a product considered by many to be boring, this campaign begun in January 1995 has captured the imagination of the world. It has been featured in news stories, spoofed, parodied, and mentioned around the globe, even though it has only run in the United States.

The idea behind the campaign was to associate glamour with a product that was seen as plain and, at the same time, weave in a health message. It was done by enlisting a team of celebrities who would sport the mustache above their upper lips left by drinking deeply from a glass of milk.

The campaign was developed as a print campaign because with just $36 million for the initial launch, the creative director, Jay Schulberg, vice chairperson and chief creative officer at Bozell Worldwide, feared that television would gobble up the budget before the campaign had a chance to make an impact. By using magazines, the agency was able to spread the original campaign plan over a 15-month period.

This chapter will use the Milk Advisory Board "Milk Mustache" campaign as an extended case study in campaign planning. It will explain how all the pieces of this complex marketing communication program are managed under the umbrella theme of a mustache of milk on celebrities.[1]

The Structure of a Campaign Plan

Advertising Campaign: A comprehensive advertising plan for a series of different but related ads that appear in different media across a specified time period.

In Chapter 7 we talked about the use of military metaphors for advertising planning. The *campaign* is another military term adopted by the advertising industry. An **advertising campaign** is a complex set of interlocking, coordinated activities. A campaign results from a comprehensive advertising plan for a series of different but related ads that appear in different media across a specified time period. The campaign is designed strategically to meet a set of objectives and to solve some critical problem. It is a short-term plan that usually runs for a year or less.

Many of the advertisements you see are *single-shot* ads; in other words, they are free-standing ads unrelated to ads that preceded or followed them. Companies that create one ad at a time and constantly change the core message are not involved in a campaign process.

However, much of the advertising national advertisers use is developed as a campaign with an umbrella theme that extends across time, different audiences and stakeholders, and different advertising vehicles and marketing communication opportunities. A campaign may focus on one specific product attribute or one audience, or it may cover all the attributes and reach all the audiences. For example, in 1997 the Walt Disney Company used a campaign created by Leo Burnett to freshen up the image of Disneyland, the first theme park created more than 40

---

[1]Adapted from Jay Schulberg, "Sell the Client's Product, Not Just the Creativity: Bozell at 75," *Advertising Age* (April 8, 1996); "Takes: Mixed Blessings," *Adweek* (November 25, 1996):22; Stuart Elliott, "Milk Mustaches Jump Off the Page and Onto the Side of Buildings," *The New York Times* (October 4, 1996):D5; Chad Rubel, "Mustache Ads Change Attitude Toward Milk," *Marketing News* (August 26, 1996):2; Carole Sugarman, *The Washington Post* (August 21, 1996):E01; Stuart Elliott, "Milk Mustaches Are Sticking Around, But Can They Stay Fresh?" *The New York Times* (July 10, 1996):D6; Mark Gleason, "Men Are Newest Target for 'Milk Mustache' Ads," *Advertising Age* (July 1, 1996):10; and Bud Shaw, "Rodman to Reach Youth With Milk," *The Plain Dealer* (December 25, 1996):1D.

FIGURE 20.1

CAMPAIGN PLAN OUTLINE

Situation Analysis
    Consumer Research
    Company/Product Research
    Competitive Research

SWOT Analysis
    Internal Factors: Strengths and Opportunities
    External Factors: Weaknesses and Threats
    Analysis
        Key Problems
        Market Analysis
        Competitive Advantage

Campaign Strategy
    Objectives
    Targeting
    Positioning
    Appropriation

Advertising and Marketing Communication Activities
    Creative Theme
    Creative Strategy and Executions/ Tactics
    Media Plan
    Other Marketing Communication Activities

Phases of a Campaign

Evaluation

years ago. The campaign includes television, print, outdoor, and radio. After extensive research with visitors, the theme park selected the "Let's Go Play" slogan, which will try to reestablish the preeminence of Disneyland in people's minds, hearts, and lives. A related campaign will target the Hispanic market.[2]

As you can see in Figure 20.1, a campaign plan summarizes the marketplace situation; the underlying campaign strategy; the tactics for the primary areas of creative and media, as well as the other marketing communication areas of sales promotion, direct marketing, and public relations; and it concludes with a plan for the evaluation of the effectiveness of the effort. The campaign plan is presented to the client in a formal business presentation. It is also summarized in a written document called a *plans book*. The profile of Mark Thomson discusses the work of someone who specializes in designing presentations.

SITUATION ANALYSIS

The first section of most campaign plans is a situation analysis that summarizes all the relevant information available about the product, the company, the competitive environment, the industry, and the consumers. Sometimes called a business review, this information is obtained using primary and secondary research techniques. The three most important research areas are:

1.   *Product/Company Research:* This is a review of the product in terms of its uses, packaging, quality, price, unit of sale, brand image, distinctive features, distribution, positioning, and product life cycle as well as the company behind the

---

[2]Michael McCarthy, "Mickey's Message: Let's Play," *Adweek* (November 25, 1996):2.

INSIDE ADVERTISING

MARK THOMSON, PRESIDENT, *Thomson Productions, Inc., Des Moines, Iowa*

One of the most remarkable aspects of a career in advertising is that it can lead to something completely unexpected. If you keep an open mind, you may find work in an area that you never even knew existed. This happened to me. Here's my story of how I ended up in *business theater.* I hope this story helps you get into whatever part of the advertising business that interests you.

When I was a freshman at Iowa State University, I did not know exactly what I wanted to do, so I selected a general business curriculum and earned a B.S. in business. However, after an introductory advertising class, I discovered that I much preferred "hanging out" with the journalism and communications crowd rather than taking statistics classes.

Although I didn't receive a degree in advertising, I spent most of my junior and senior years involved with the journalism/advertising department. To this day, I can tell you that this involvement was the key to breaking into the advertising industry. For example, as president of the advertising club, I learned leadership skills and how to get things done. I participated in other clubs and campus activities by serving in publicity or communications roles, sold advertising space in the college newspaper (a great way to pay the bills), and so on. One of the most memorable college experiences, which resulted in lifelong friendships and a better understanding of the world, was a summer European media studies trip. I think that unique experiences like these differentiate you from other job candidates and make you more valuable to a potential employer.

I was also an account executive for the American Advertising Federation (AAF) student competition where I learned advertising skills and how to work as a member of a team. I highly recommend this AAF experience to you. In fact, it must be working; all of my fellow team members went on to great advertising careers. For example, one team member started as a secretary at an advertising agency but today is an account supervisor on a major automotive account. One student used a direct-mail campaign with a "money-back guarantee if not completely satisfied" to land a copywriting job at a Young & Rubicam advertising agency. Today he is a very busy and successful freelance copywriter. Another team member started at a local television affiliate in the promotions department and went on to be a writer/producer for a nationally syndicated television show.

It seems to me that a frequently overlooked method to get into the business is to find a mentor (usually a professor) who will sponsor an independent study project for you. You can select a segment of the field that interests you and set out on a project for college credit. I had always enjoyed producing slide shows, so my project was a multi-image sales presentation (multiple slide projectors synced to a sound track) for a corporation's exhibit at a robotics trade show in Chicago. When I arrived in Chicago with a truck full of slide projectors and "scenic" set pieces, I found out that my set was too big for the exhibit space. I had to saw the set in half so it would fit. Obviously, there was some miscommunication between the client and me. Well, you can't beat the real-world education; as painful as it may be!

product and its corporate reputation and image, resources, philosophies, mission, and culture.

2. *Consumer and Market Research:* The consumer should be described demographically and psychographically in order to answer questions such as: Who buys the product? When do they buy it? How frequently do they buy? How do they use the product? What are their attitudes and perceptions about the product? What decision process do they go through in making their decision to buy (or not buy) a product?

3. *Competitive Situation:* This involves tracking the activities of competitors (direct and indirect) with respect to market share, product features, new products, positioning and targeting strategies, as well as competitors' current and past advertising strategies, media expenditures, and advertising schedules.

For the milk campaign, research was used to determine consumer concerns and find out why they were not drinking milk and who might be the most likely target for increased milk consumption. The market research conducted for the board showed that the major reasons people gave for giving up milk were that they saw it as a complement to high-fat foods (cookies), they mistakenly believed lower-fat milk contains fewer nutrients than regular milk, and that it was not "cool" compared to other beverages.

At the same time that the campaign was being planned, osteoporosis, a debilitating bone disease, was also getting headlines. It affects more than 25 million

Along the way with these projects and campus activities, something very interesting happened. A door opened to an advertising career. I began to discover what I loved to do. I also became acquainted with the faculty, which resulted in an opportunity to attend a Direct Marketing Association (DMA) conference.

While at that conference, I got my first job as a sales trainee in the envelope division of a large corporation. When I graduated during a recession, I was very glad to have this job. But apparently the recession was a little too tough for the envelope business. This 30-year old division folded within six months after I had started. Luckily, my professor gave me a lead on an account coordinator job at a large New York City advertising agency. I pretty much got the job because of the strong reference from my professor. It was my first real ad agency job. I worked 70-hour weeks for $16,000 a year, but it was the best training I could ever get.

A few months later, I got a yearning to produce slide shows again (although no more trips to Chicago trade shows for me!). I contacted my independent study advisor who, with her husband, runs a small agency in the Midwest. I joined this agency as an account executive and serviced accounts, produced print ads, television, and radio spots, and a zillion other things. A smaller agency gives you more breadth of experience. This agency also permitted something a larger agency would not. I was allowed to start a "nontraditional" advertising agency service of multi-image shows. I began to produce large, wide-screen, multimedia shows and started using lasers and other media in these productions. I discovered that there was a market for what I truly loved to do.

What had started as a college interest in slide shows led to bigger productions. I struck out on my own to start Thomson Productions, Inc. Today Thomson Productions produces *business theater* for *Fortune* 500 corporations and national associations. The term *business theater* loosely means using live, Broadway-style productions to unveil new corporate products, motivate and recognize salespeople at national meetings, or kick off big conventions with "opening ceremonies." My company hires choreographers, dancers, singers, orchestras, celebrities, and motivational speakers. Depending on the client's objectives, the productions can also include a variety of media such as video, computer graphics, lasers, pyrotechnics, megaprojections, illusions, lighting, interactive technologies, and all kinds of unique staging and special effects. I travel throughout the United States, Europe, and Asia producing these shows for audiences of 400 to 4,000 people.

If you would like to work for a business theater production company, most opportunities are in places like New York City, Chicago, or Los Angeles. You can also work for one of their suppliers: lighting, sound, video, entertainment, and many other types of support companies.

If I knew back in college what I know now, it would be this: Follow your dream. Find out what you really love to do and start doing it. Find a mentor to help you discover your opportunities along the way.

If you just follow your dream, everything else usually falls into place.

Nominated by Prof. Tom Groth, University of West Florida

people in the United States and is the major cause of bone fractures in postmenopausal women and the elderly. The calcium in milk increases bone mass during youth, helps to maintain it during adulthood, and helps to prevent its loss as one ages. And nutritionists believe that most Americans don't get nearly enough of it. The calcium connection is a nugget of information provided in Ad 20.1.

SWOT ANALYSIS

SWOT Analysis: A study of the Strengths, Weaknesses, Opportunities, and Threats that will impact upon the successful promotion of the product, the service, or the company.

The concluding section of the situation analysis evaluates the significance of the research. Some plans include a section called "Problems and Opportunities;" others call it a SWOT analysis and look at the plan's strengths, weaknesses, opportunities, and threats. During the situation analysis, you are compiling all the information you can about the brand and its competitive situation, marketplace factors such as the health of the category, and the behavior of consumers relative to this brand. In order to make sense of what you find, some planners recast this information in terms of *internal factors*—strengths that lead to opportunities—and *external factors*—weaknesses that make the brand vulnerable to threats from outside.

Once the information is gathered and sorted into SWOT categories, then the analysis begins. In this stage you are trying to make sense of all the information you have gathered and identify key areas on which you will build your campaign strategy. Three types of analyses need to be conducted: problem, target market, and competitive advantage analysis.

AD 20.1

RHEA PERLMAN AND DANNY
DEVITO BRING A TOUCH OF
COMEDY TO THE CALCIUM
MESSAGE.

To us, looks are everything. Obviously. Which is why we eat well
and drink so much skim milk. The calcium helps prevent osteoporosis–
you know that thing that weakens your bones and can make you look
like a human camel. And besides, it's got good taste, just like us.

MILK
Where's your mustache?

NOW APPEARING IN
Matilda

PROBLEM ANALYSIS

From the SWOTs, you should be able to conclude that there are a small set of serious communication problems that this campaign must address. For example, a campaign for Hewlett-Packard sought to soften the company's image by poking fun at the clash between high-tech engineers and "normal people."[3]

For the milk board, Bozell's assignment was to alter milk's long-standing negative image. Milk sales had been in decline for nearly three decades, and the product had little appeal for consumers above the age of 12. The Florence Griffith Joyner and Michael Johnson ads were designed to spread that appeal (see Ads 20.2 and 20.3).

These problems differ from year to year and situation to situation. For example, in one year's marketing plan, a brand may be launching a line extension, which means the advertising will address the problem of launching a new product under a familiar brand name. The next year, the marketing plan may focus on increasing distribution, so the advertising will probably be focused on opening up new territories where the brand is unknown. Each type of problem calls for a different advertising and marketing communication strategy. Different audiences are reached with different messages; different marketing communication tools may be used; and different communication objectives are set.

An example of problem analysis is the campaign that broke in mid-1996 for Rogaine. Previously a prescription product, the Pharmacia & Upjohn company had to redesign the product for over-the-counter sales. Previously protected by government regulations, the new opportunity also came with a more intense competitive situation as the company's market exclusivity vanished.[4]

[3]Joan Voight, "Ads Soften Hewlett-Packard Image," *Adweek* (November 18, 1996):41.

[4]Carolyn Shea, "Rogaine Campaign Covers All Bases," *PROMO* (July 1996):6.

ADS 20.2 AND 20.3

THESE ADS USING ATHLETES
FLORENCE GRIFFITH JOYNER
AND MICHAEL JOHNSON ARE
DESIGNED TO EXTEND THE
APPEAL OF DRINKING MILK
BEYOND ITS TRADITIONAL CHIL-
DREN'S MARKET.

MARKET ANALYSIS

This involves finding the best markets for the product by determining who and where the best prospects are with respect to demographic characteristics, geographic location, sociopsychological groupings (lifestyles, interests, attitudes), and degree of product usage (heavy, light, nonuser, switcher, loyal user). It also includes an assessment of the accessibility of the market. In the case of a direct-action advertising campaign, for instance, the availability of an extensive and accurate database is critical if messages are going to reach the target market.

COMPETITIVE ANALYSIS

The focus of this analysis is to determine competitive advantage. What are the distinctive features of this product and competitors' products—and how important to consumers are these features? In other words, this analysis seeks to identify an area that's important to consumers and where the product has an advantage over its competitors.

CAMPAIGN STRATEGY

After the situation analysis and the SWOT analysis, most advertising campaign plans focus on the key strategic decisions that will guide the campaign. The strategy section of a campaign plan identifies the advertising objectives that will solve the key problems identified at the end of the SWOT analysis. It will also specify the target audience and how the strategy will handle competitive advantage and the product's position.

These decisions were discussed in detail in Chapter 7. They are fundamental decisions that are relevant for all areas of marketing communication planning, from the creative plan to the media, sales promotion, and public relations plans. In addition the strategy must consider the appropriation and how it will limit or open up marketing communication opportunities.

OBJECTIVES

Objectives are used to guide the development of the campaign's strategy by stating its goal. Since objectives provide the goal, they can then be used at the end of the process to measure the results of the campaign. These objectives are established based on an understanding of the hierarchy of effects and the various ways advertising can impact on its audience (see Chapters 7 and 8).

The milk campaign's short-term goal was to change consumer attitudes that caused the decline in milk consumption and to increase public awareness of its nutrition. The long-term goal was to ultimately reverse the decline.

TARGETING

During the process of analyzing consumer behavior and possible markets, potential *target markets* are identified and segmented into groups identified by certain demographic or psychographic characteristics, such as environmentalists, bike riders, mall teens, or, to use an expression from the last election, soccer moms. In other words, within those markets, certain groups of people are more likely than others to be targeted for advertising and other marketing communication messages.

These *target audiences* (i.e., groups of people to whom a marketing communication message is directed) shift with each campaign, its situation, key problems, and objectives. For example, if you are launching a line extension, then you will probably target current users of the brand. If, however, you are opening up new territory, then there aren't current users, so you will have to target competitors' users. For both audiences, however, the objective may remain the same, which is to convince the target audiences to try a new product.

Women ages 25 to 44 were originally chosen as the target market for the milk campaign because they are a relatively large market with a real need for milk and the calcium it provides. They also buy food products for the household and influence others to drink milk. By initially emphasizing skim milk, the campaign was able to appeal to women who were diet conscious.

POSITIONING

Although objectives and targeting differ from campaign to campaign, the product's positioning—at least for existing products—generally remains the same. It does have to be accounted for, however, in the strategy. In other words, identify the product's position and then analyze that position relative to this campaign's strategy—the key problem, objectives, and targeting decisions. Does the position mean the same thing to familiar brand users considering a new line extension? What would it mean to entirely new users in a new market territory who are unfamiliar with the brand? They may not respond to the position in the same way, which means that the way the position is presented in the message strategy may need to be adjusted to the target audience's needs, interests, and level of knowledge.

The milk campaign was a repositioning campaign. Its mission was to move the position of milk from being something that children drink to a healthful drink for adults. The Al Michaels, Frank Gifford, and Bob Costas ad associates milk with adults who have their own images as interesting people (Ad 20.4).

THE APPROPRIATION

The amount of money available governs all strategic decisions. If you are working on a campaign for a major marketer like Coke or Pepsi, you may have plenty of

AD 20.4

THIS AL MICHAELS, FRANK GIF-
FORD, AND BOB COSTAS AD
ASSOCIATES MILK WITH ADULTS
WHO HAVE THEIR OWN IMAGES
AS INTERESTING PEOPLE.

money for the most expensive form of television advertising. However, if you are working for a nonprofit, you may need to focus on inexpensive marketing communications such as publicity and try to stimulate as much word of mouth as possible. Most campaigns are somewhere in between and their planners rarely have as much money as they feel they need to do the job right. Once the appropriation is set, then the money can be allocated among the various advertising and marketing communication activities.

MARKETING COMMUNICATION ACTIVITIES

A campaign is a complex communication program that is tightly interwoven with all of an organization's marketing efforts. This total communication program reaches all stakeholders, all audiences, and all publics with the same promotional theme. Message variations related to that theme speak to the interests of the different audiences. In other words, even though a campaign may be directed at a consumer audience, there may be subsections of the campaign plan that focus on the sales force, dealers, or retailers.

CREATIVE THEME

A campaign is a series of ads built around one central theme. The creative plan includes a theme, or *creative concept*, and variations, or *executions*, for different media, situations, audiences, and times of the year. The various ads are designed to be different in order to speak to different audiences or address different copy points.

The campaign theme, then, must be a strong concept that can hold all these diverse efforts together. When Pepsi, for example, created the classic "Pepsi Generation" theme, a new position and an entirely new type of lifestyle advertising were created. That theme continues to be expressed in subsequent campaigns through the years even though the specific campaigns change. (See opening story in Chapter 13.)

The milk mustache is a simple idea but visually powerful. Who would think that beautiful people would agree to have their pictures plastered on outdoor boards and in the pages of magazines with a milk mustache above their upper lip? The idea was to make this symbol of milk drinking as hip as the celebrities who agreed to sport the mustache. And the unexpected appearance of these glamorous people was reinforced with the campaign's slogan: "Milk. What a surprise!"

A strong umbrella theme holds the various ads together and creates the *synergy* that comes from using different messages for different audiences in different media that are still linked to some central image or position. Synergy is important because it intensifies the impact, but that impact is created by repetition. In order for a message to be repeated, it has to be interesting. Maintaining interest is the reason variation is built into a campaign.

Continuity devices, such as the Jolly Green Giant and the Pillsbury Doughboy, are also used in campaign planning to create the link from ad to ad. Slogans are another important type of continuity device. Such phrases as "Reach Out and Touch Someone" (AT&T), "It's the Real Thing" (Coke), and "Let the Good Times Roll" (Kawasaki) are corporate slogans that serve like a "battle cry." A good slogan generates its own excitement but, more importantly, it is highly memorable and can be used in a variety of different situations.

Image transfer, which means a presentation in one medium such as radio stimulates the hearer to think about the presentation in another medium such as television, is another concern of campaign planners. When image transfer works successfully, then a cheaper medium (radio, outdoor) can be used to remind people of a message delivered in a more expensive way, and the links between the two help to create a more powerful synergy. An example is the "Fast Fruit" campaign from SunMaid Raisins, which uses artwork in print and animation in television to strengthen the visual association.[5]

CREATIVE STRATEGY AND TACTICS

The creative work on a campaign can be divided into two steps: first is determining the *creative strategy*—what the message says—and the second is determining the *tactics*—how the message will be executed. The creative strategy flows from an understanding of the key communication problems and the objectives. It outlines the impressions the campaign intends to convey to the target audience. For example, Kraft Miracle Whip Salad Dressing's key problem is to devise ways to increase product usage. As a result, ads must emphasize new uses for the product.

In terms of the creative strategy for the milk campaign, Bozell's Schulberg knew people would tune out long, factual copy about nutrition, so he designed the copy to offer little "milk nuggets" about why people should be drinking milk. For example, in the Spike Lee ad, the director says, "Here's the direction. You thought milk was just a kid thing. But the plot thickens and you discover your bones are still growing until you're 35. You're on a mad quest for calcium." The little nugget is the piece of information about bones growing until age 35—something most people don't realize. That ad was also one of the first to run the address of the National Milk Board's Web site (http://www.whymilk.com).

CREATIVE TACTICS

The means for carrying out the creative strategy are outlined in the creative tactics. For Kraft, the tactics might include the sponsorship of two Kraft Music Hall

---

[5]"What's New Portfolio," *Adweek* (November 11, 1996):48.

television specials, including 12 separate spots with voice-overs by long-time announcer Ed Herlihey. Each ad would emphasize new recipes tied in some way to the programs using the product as an important ingredient, at the same time continuing to emphasize the tradition of Kraft Salad Dressing and its product quality.

The milk campaign's magazine layouts were designed to look like posters, an idea taken from the "Portraits" campaign for American Express, which featured pictures of celebrity card holders taken by photographer Annie Liebovitz. Bozell also recruited Liebovitz to shoot the "Milk Mustache" celebrity photos.

To lure the celebrities into participating, Bozell's creative director, Jay Shulberg, teased them with pictures of milk mustaches drawn on their photos. Some 29 celebrities have signed on for the project. They play to their natural audiences with their own views on why milk was good for them. Models emphasized milk for bone structure and skim milk for low-fat diets. Athletes talked about milk's rejuvenating abilities after a workout. The collection of celebrities was diverse, including athletes (Gabriela Sabatini, Steve Young, Patrick Ewing), models (Iman, Christie Brinkley, Kate Moss), actors (Lisa Kudrow and Jennifer Aniston from *Friends*, Joan Rivers, Isabella Rossellini, and Lauren Bacall), a Miss America (Heather Whitestone), letter turner Vanna White, a singer (Tony Bennett), and a country music star (Billy Ray Cyrus).

PRODUCTION

Having a great idea is important, but getting it produced can either make or break it. The production problem for the milk campaign centered on the creation of the mustache.

It has been a fascinating experience for food stylist, Norman Stewart, milkman to the stars, who has gotten to work with well-regarded photographer Annie Liebovitz as he has smeared his white dairy delight on all of those celebrity upper lips. Most of all, he's mastered the fine art of making "dairy" mustaches that won't wilt under the lights of a photo session. What most people really want to know about the campaign is how the mustache is created. Is it Elmer's Glue? White-Out? Plaster? Actually the milk mustache is a photo-friendly concoction created by Stewart of heavy cream, vanilla essence, and milk. The mixture varies with the weather and the person's skin tone. There is also an endurance problem. The mustache will last for about three-quarters of a roll of film and Liebovitz generally takes 20 rolls of each celebrity. In the beginning, Stewart has the stars actually swig the mixture to coat their upper lips.

Many advertisers expect to see that both strategies and executions are *pretested* to predict their effectiveness and eliminate approaches that don't work. Advertising pretesting helps avoid costly mistakes, predicts the relative strength of alternative approaches, and generally improves the efficiency of the advertising.

MEDIA PLAN

The media plan is just as important as the creative plan and is developed simultaneously with it. The media plan, which contains the campaign's budget, is driven by the advertising appropriation. Initial decisions about which media to use usually reflect the availability of a budget big enough to use television, which is the most costly of all media.

The *media mix* is created by selecting media vehicles that are best able to reach the target audience and solve the communication problem. If a product has an awareness problem, then widespread mass media will probably be used to increase the general level of awareness. If the problem is one of trial, then sales promotion may be the most important tool. However, if the product only appeals to a small target, such as martial arts clothes for aikido devotees, then direct mail (assuming, of course, that you can find a list or build one) and the Internet may be more effective ways to reach them.

The word *reach* in the last sentence is very important to media planners who allocate media dollars in terms of their two objectives: *reach* and *frequency*. In a high-reach campaign, money is spent to get the message to as many people as possible. In a high-frequency campaign, the money is spent on fewer media reaching fewer people but repetition of the message is increased.

The media plan section in a campaign plan, then, includes media objectives (reach and frequency), media strategies (targeting, continuity, timing), media selection (the specific vehicles), geographic strategies, schedules, and the media budget. Usually a *pie chart* is used to show how the budget is allocated to the various media activities. A *flow chart* depicts the timing strategies and scheduling. A *spreadsheet* identifies the key expenditures and their budget figure total.

Primarily a print campaign in women's publications and general-interest magazines, nearly the entire advertising budget for the milk campaign was spent buying pages in magazines during the campaign's first phase—more than 50 books in 1995 and nearly 100 in 1996. In 1996 the campaign also included *Men's Health* and *Sports Illustrated*.

OTHER MARKETING COMMUNICATION ACTIVITIES

In most cases, advertising campaigns are supported by other forms of marketing communication such as sales promotion and public relations. In *integrated marketing communication programs (IMC)*, advertising is just one of many tools that work together to deliver a comprehensive package of communication messages. Either way, subsections of the plan will be devoted to these other important marketing communication areas.

Sales promotion was used to support the milk campaign. A contest entitled "Milk. Where's *your* mustache?" was announced in the fall of 1996 to increase involvement in the campaign. The contest's poster uses the Spike Lee photograph from the campaign and offers to the winner a trip to Australia and a moment of fame in a milk-mustache ad in *Rolling Stone*. Contestants have to send in a photo of someone wearing a milk mustache, along with a register receipt for the purchase of a gallon of milk, and an entry form available in stores to the Milk Mustache Photo Contest.

PHASES OF A CAMPAIGN

Timing and scheduling are an important part of the media plan and are also tied into the overall strategy of the campaign. Many campaigns have phases—the launch, the continuing campaign, the close—for example. In some cases, particularly with campaigns that continue for a number of years, such as the milk campaign, the campaign may be launched with one strategy that evolves into another strategy as the campaign matures.

Originally running with the slogan, "Milk. What a surprise!," the campaign came of age in mid-1995 when the slogan was changed to "Milk. Where's your mustache?" That was the point where the milk board could see evidence that the campaign was working in terms of dramatic changes in the image of milk, so it entered its second phase with new celebrities, new ads, and a larger budget. The total budget in 1995 of $52 million, which was originally for a 15-month campaign, doubled in 1996 to $110 million.

The increased ad spending was linked to two new strategies: appeal to a wider target and shift to a harder sell. Therefore, 1996 also saw a change in targeting from women ages 25 to 44 to a broader audience that included girls, young men, and college students. The "Where's your mustache?" line was seen as a more direct invitation to consumers but yet one that wasn't too heavy-handed. It was intended to deliver a harder sell than the more image-oriented original theme line: "What a surprise!" The ads for Jeff Gordon and Spike Lee demonstrate the widening of the appeal to men (Ads 20.5 and 20.6).

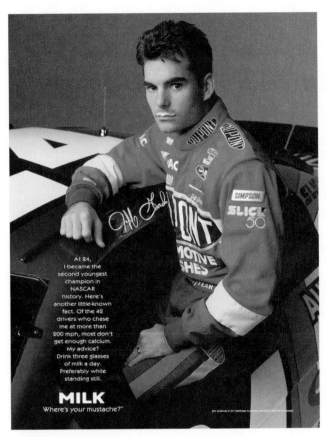

ADS 20.5 AND 20.6

**THESE ADS FOR JEFF GORDON
AND SPIKE LEE BROADEN THE
MARKET TO MEN.**

Long-married Hollywood funny couple Danny DeVito and Rhea Perlman appear as characters they portrayed in *Matilda*, a film based on a children's book. Model Tyra Banks was also added to the line-up for 1997, as were sportscasters Bob Costas, Frank Gifford, and Al Michaels, and athlete Florence Giffith Joyner. Other men the MilkPep group is looking to include are John Travolta and Arnold Schwarzenegger.

In keeping with its relaunch strategy, the campaign also added outdoor boards and posters to its media mix in 1996. An additional $18 million was budgeted for the first half of 1997 to cover the expenses of outdoor boards and transit posters. The Bozell media director explains that out-of-home media make sense because they are location specific. "We can meet people at points where they're thinking of quenching their thirst," such as supermarkets and convenience stores. Another reason to use out-of-home media is the prevalence of ads for soft drinks and sports drinks. Bozell must create the impression of milk as a refreshing drink in that competitive environment.

The posters feature Spike Lee, the film maker, and Kate Moss, the model. Lee's poster will include the line, "Do the right thing. Three glasses a day," and the headline for the Moss poster, who is best known for her work for Calvin Klein apparel and fragrances, reads, "Calcium? It's my obsession."

In addition to magazine ads and outdoor boards and posters, the milk campaign also moved to a Web site (http://www.whymilk.com), postcard ads, and schoolbook covers. Other additions to the campaign include cross promotions with consumer brands in categories such as cereal, coffee, and soup. Mattel is even offering a milk mustache version of Barbie.

THE NEXT PHASE

The campaign has not been as effective yet in reaching the younger generation, particularly males. None of the athletes used to date—Steve Young, Pete Sampras, Patrick Ewing, Kristy Yamaguchi, among others—has helped position milk as a hip drink for Generation X. For that reason, the milk board turned to Dennis Rodman wearing a milk mustache in 1997 to get a more hip image. Calling him "wonderfully rebellious," the milk board hopes he will have more of an appeal for teenagers. Certainly his green, red, and yellow hair attests to that image. "I'm not the boy next door," the copy goes. "I'm the baddest rebounder the game has seen. And my body? It's a temple and milk is the drink of the gods."

The question the advertising industry is asking is how long the campaign can continue. Successful campaigns that last for years can have tremendous impact, but they can also wear out if the idea behind the campaign isn't freshened. Ken McCarren, senior partner at Bozell Worldwide in charge of the campaign, is monitoring the wear-out problem constantly. That's one reason the theme line was changed and new celebrities and media were added to the mix. In addition, the tie-in promotions will give consumers ideas about how to add more milk to their diets. But still, as McCarren admits, "as you can imagine, with the stakes being high, we're keeping an eye on it to make sure we're staying fresh."

EVALUATION

Evaluation is the final and, in some respects, the most important step in an advertising campaign. If not done formally through a research project, some sort of evaluation is always done informally to determine if the effort was successful.

A formal evaluation builds a research effort around the campaign's objectives to see if it reached them. This information is concerned with questions of effectiveness: Does the campaign work? Does it do what needs to be done? What were the results? It is also concerned with questions of taste and judgment: Is the campaign fair and accurate? Does it build the brand or corporate reputation? Does it mislead?

The milk campaign has won many awards and has been listed by *USA Today* as one of the country's top-ten favorite advertisements, the only print campaign in that distinguished group. In 1995 Video Storyboards Tests, based on its survey of 20,000 consumers, identified "Milk Mustache" as the number-one campaign in the United States, the first time a print campaign has received that kind of recognition without the support of television.

Stories about the mustachioed celebrities have appeared in publications all over the world. Jay Leno has done several monologues on them and Schulberg himself has appeared on *Entertainment Tonight* three or four times. Schulberg has found that kids are actually saving the ads and trading them.

More importantly, Bozell claims the campaign has changed the way people think about milk by associating the product with glamorous stars, athletes, and other celebrities. It has achieved more impact for the milk industry than any other milk campaign and has prompted Americans to buy more milk for the first time in 25 years. Ten months into the 15-month milk campaign, Bozell measured dramatic improvement with significant attitude shifts in awareness of milk and its nutritional benefits.

Although total consumption in 1995 was flat, Bozell's objective initially was to stop the decline, and the campaign seemed to have done that. Furthermore, in the first six months of 1996, milk volume rose seven-tenths of a percent compared to the corresponding period in 1995. While that may seem like a tiny gain, milk board executives feel that it is a major increase for the milk industry given that consumption had been declining for decades.

SUMMARY

- The situation analysis includes primary and secondary research findings about the organization, its product, the competition, the marketplace, and consumers.
- The SWOT analysis summarizes the situation in terms of key strengths, weaknesses, opportunities, and threats.
- The strategy section of a campaign plan identifies the key problems to be solved and the advertising objec-

tives that will accomplish those tasks, the target audience, the competitive advantage, and the position.

- The creative plan includes a theme, or creative concept, and variations, or executions, for different media, situations, audiences, and times of the year.
- The media plan includes media objectives, media selection, geographic strategies, timing schedules, and a budget.

QUESTIONS

1. Explain how the strategy behind the "Milk Mustache" campaign has evolved and changed during its first three years. What other strategic directions might the campaign take in subsequent years?

2. The "Milk Mustache" campaign is a print campaign, primarily because of the initial size of the budget. Now that more money is becoming available from the milk board, would you recommend that the agency move the idea to television? Justify your recommendation. In your consideration of this decision, rough out a proposal for how the idea would be executed in a television commercial and critique its effectiveness.

3. Who else besides Dennis Rodman might be an appropriate celebrity to attract the teenage market?

4. You are the national account director for the National Fluid Milk Processor Promotion Board. For the

next advertising year, would you stay with the "Milk Mustache" campaign or bring in the new California "Got Milk" campaign and move it national? How would you know if the "Milk Mustache" idea was beginning to wear out? Compare the advantages of staying with a successful campaign versus trading off for something new.

5. Your agency just got the account for the National Egg Producers Advisory Board. The board wants to do advertising that is as effective as the "Milk Mustache" or the California "Got Milk" campaign. Brainstorm in a team and come up with at least three different ideas for a campaign that heightens the visibility and promotes more use of eggs.

SUGGESTED CLASS PROJECTS

1. Interview a local advertiser about a local campaign and write a report on how and why it was developed, its strategy, its creative theme, its media plan, and its evaluation.

2. Develop a research proposal in outline form for a program that you would recommend to evaluate the effectiveness of the most current campaign for Pepsi, Coca-Cola, Burger King, Wendy's, or McDonald's.

3. You have been asked by the Milk Advisory Board to study its total communication program and develop a plan to move it into a more integrated marketing communication program. What needs to be done? What are the key recommendations you would propose to make this an IMC campaign?

FURTHER READINGS

Heibing, Roman G., and Scott W. Cooper, *How to Write a Successful Marketing Plan* (Lincolnwood, IL: NTC Business Books, 1990).

Schultz, Don E., and Beth Barnes, *Strategic Advertising Campaigns*, 5th ed. (Chicago: Crain Books, 1995).

Taylor, James W., *How to Develop a Successful Advertising Plan* (Lincolnwood, IL: NTC Business Books, 1993).

*Excludes other GM products. ©1997 GM Corp. Buckle up, America.

The kids aren't going to listen
to you anyway.

Save your breath. The all-new Chevy *Venture* is the only minivan*

available with a Dual Mode Sound System that lets you listen to the radio in the front seat

and lets them listen to a CD of whatever they call music in the back. And vice versa.

Which means they won't roll their eyes when you sing, and you won't have to listen to something

that sounds like bees attacking a hippo. And that should help keep every trip in harmony.

Chevy Venture ⌁ Let's Go!

For a free brochure and video, call toll free **1-888-950-VENTURE** or visit us at **www.chevrolet.com**

Things we've noticed about Americans:

Going places is
a national obsession.

Been there, 1969 ◄——— CASE IN POINT ———► The reliable
new Chevy Malibu.

• Up to 100,000 miles before its first scheduled tune-up.*   • 5-year/150,000-mile coolant life.†

• Lubed-for-life chassis.*   • Lifetime transmission fluid.*   • Have a nice trip.

• Look! It even won the Motor Trend 1997 Car of the Year award! Pretty neat, huh?

• 1-800-New Malibu • www.chevrolet.com/malibu • $15,995**

The All-New Malibu

The Car You Knew America Could Build. ⌁ Genuine Chevrolet

**MSRP includes dealer prep and destination charge. Tax, license and optional equipment additional. *Maintenance needs vary with use and driving conditions. See owner's manual for more information. †Whichever comes first. See your dealer for terms of this limited warranty. Chevy and Malibu are trademarks of the GM Corp. ©1997 GM Corp. Buckle up, America!

RIDE ALL 255 HORSES AT ONCE.

Vortec.™ The Most Powerful Line of Engines Ever In a Chevy™ Truck.
    If you like powerful horses and you like lots of them, you've come to the right place.
Saddle up a Chevy Full-Size Pickup with an available Vortec 5700 V8 engine and hold on tight —
255 horses are rarin' to go.
    But power is only part of the Vortec story. Patented Sequential Central-Port Fuel Injection

helps deliver maximized power *and* efficiency. And every Vortec engine is designed to go
    100,000 miles before its first scheduled tune-up.* So get going — 255 horses are waiting
for you. Chevy. The most dependable, longest-lasting trucks on the road.†

1-800-950-2438 or www.chevrolet.com

Chevy Trucks
⌁
LIKE A ROCK

CHEVROLET

CHAPTER

Evaluative Research

CHAPTER OBJECTIVES

When you have completed this chapter, you should be able to:

- Explain why advertisers devote time and money to evaluative research
- Distinguish between evaluative and diagnostic research
- Identify the eight major evaluative research methods and what each one claims to test
- Evaluate the strengths and weaknesses of various forms of testing
- Understand the concerns surrounding the issues of validity and reliability

EVERYONE IS THE SAME AT GM

Recently, General Motors has broken with a long-standing tradition and decided to standardize the way it assesses advertising by its six vehicle dimensions, a move that will put competitive pressure on agencies and help pave the way for incentive-based compensation. The move was driven by a desire to share information among divisions, and was accelerated by the company's shift to a brand management structure. The underlying benefits were expressed by Philip Guarisco, vice president, general manager/marketing and advertising, "It's a process that's going to enable us to understand the best practices in terms of advertising. We can then transfer the learning because we're creating a common dialogue within the organization on the subject of organization."

While GM, the nation's third largest advertiser, didn't develop the process to evaluate agencies, it could provide a way to issue grades. It should improve the fairness of any incentive that might be based on advertising and marketplace performance because it will use a broader base of experience. Agencies are typically paid on a commission and fee system, with compensation said to average about 9 percent of billings.

Currently, GM has 36 brand managers who have broad marketing responsibility for specific models. They also determine ad strategy for their models, though divisional ad managers still work with agencies on execution. Still, a major goal is for GM to have a consistent message for each vehicle brand.

The new across-the-board assessment process covers strategic development, copy testing, and market tracking. "In a broad sense, we'll be looking at whether advertising is on strategy, whether it is unique to the brand character and whether it resonates against its targets," notes Mr. Guarisco. "Effectiveness will primarily be measured by credibility, by the ability to connect emotionally and on the persuasiveness level of advertising, as opposed to recall."[1]

Major advertisers, such as General Motors, as well as your smallest retailer, are interested in the answer to one question: Does advertising work? In this chapter we address the research technologies used by advertisers to answer this question. Specifically, the testing techniques used in evaluative research are discussed. Here, the term **evaluative research** means research used to make final go/no-go decisions about finished or nearly finished ads, as distinguished from the *strategic research* described in Chapter 6, which is used to test strategies and different versions of a concept or approach. Advertisers who use evaluative research hope that it will provide a valid measure of effectiveness, and that it will eliminate the risks and conflicts inevitable when decisions are based on judgment alone.

The stakes are high. By the time an average 30-second commercial is ready for national television, it has cost about $200,000. If it is run nationally, its sponsor invests several million dollars in air time. Furthermore, careers are on the line. Brand managers and advertising managers are rewarded for successes and punished for failures. Among the agency creatives, the reel or the portfolio—a collection of advertisements "authored" by an individual writer, art director, or producer—is both the key to salary increases and the passport to professional respect.

Ideally, the results of evaluative research would be available before large sums of money have been invested in finished work. Failing that, advertisers want a test that predicts effectiveness before millions of media dollars have been spent in purchasing space or time. Test results may even be useful after an advertisement has been placed. Sales may fall, or they may not increase as rapidly as expected. Is the advertising at fault? Would sales be better if the advertising were "working harder"? Advertisers may feel a need to test their advertising anywhere along the line.

Evaluative Research: Research intended to measure the effectiveness of finished or nearly finished advertisements.

---

[1]Raymond Serafin, "GM Will Standardize Assessment of Ad Work," *Advertising Age* (December 18–25, 1995):1, 30.

FIGURE 21.1

CURRENT MEASURE OF COM-
MERCIALS' EFFECTIVENESS.
Source: "Humor Remains Top Tool for
Ad Campaigns," *USA Today* (Septem-
ber 30, 1996):3B. Copyright © 1996
USA TODAY. Reprinted by permis-
sion.

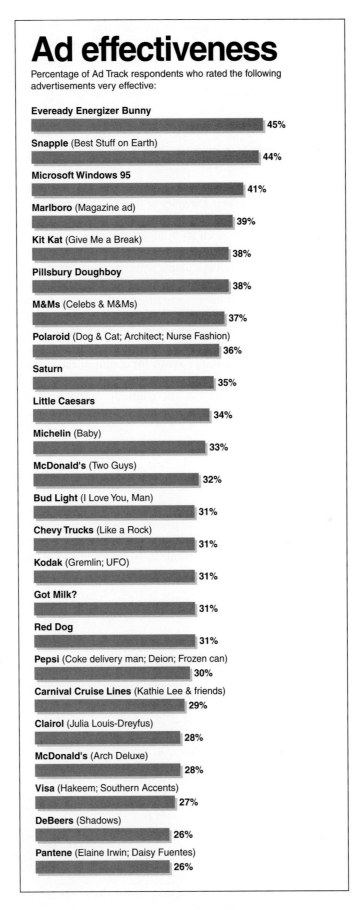

Ad effectiveness

Percentage of Ad Track respondents who rated the following advertisements very effective:

Eveready Energizer Bunny — 45%

Snapple (Best Stuff on Earth) — 44%

Microsoft Windows 95 — 41%

Marlboro (Magazine ad) — 39%

Kit Kat (Give Me a Break) — 38%

Pillsbury Doughboy — 38%

M&Ms (Celebs & M&Ms) — 37%

Polaroid (Dog & Cat; Architect; Nurse Fashion) — 36%

Saturn — 35%

Little Caesars — 34%

Michelin (Baby) — 33%

McDonald's (Two Guys) — 32%

Bud Light (I Love You, Man) — 31%

Chevy Trucks (Like a Rock) — 31%

Kodak (Gremlin; UFO) — 31%

Got Milk? — 31%

Red Dog — 31%

Pepsi (Coke delivery man; Deion; Frozen can) — 30%

Carnival Cruise Lines (Kathie Lee & friends) — 29%

Clairol (Julia Louis-Dreyfus) — 28%

McDonald's (Arch Deluxe) — 28%

Visa (Hakeem; Southern Accents) — 27%

DeBeers (Shadows) — 26%

Pantene (Elaine Irwin; Daisy Fuentes) — 26%

This chapter deals with tests of advertising effectiveness that are somewhat formal and scientific. Sometimes, as is the case illustrated in Figure 21.1, outside agencies, such as *USA Today*, conduct surveys that are equivalent to advertising popularity contests. While not scientific, they do give winning advertisers a certain amount of status.

EVALUATIVE RESEARCH SUPPLIERS AND METHODS

Evaluative research suppliers are listed in the American Marketing Association's *International Directory of Marketing Research Companies and Services*, which we described in Chapter 6. Most major advertisers have a favorite supplier and a favorite research method; a few use proprietary methods of their own (methods that have been developed by, and are used exclusively by, one advertiser). Some of the best-known evaluative research suppliers are listed in Table 21.1.

This list is not exhaustive. Many other research companies offer some form of copy testing, including qualitative, in-depth interviews, and focus groups. The question is: Which (if any) of the evaluative research methods really work?

Although every supplier is in some way unique, all use copy-testing methods that fall into eight major categories: (1) memory tests, (2) persuasion tests, (3) direct-response counts, (4) communication tests, (5) focus groups, (6) physiological tests, (7) frame-by-frame tests, and (8) in-market tests. Of these eight types, memory, persuasion, communication, and focus groups are the most widely employed.[2]

MEMORY TESTS

Memory tests are based on the assumption that an advertisement leaves a mental "residue" with the person who has been exposed to it. One way to measure an advertisement's effectiveness, therefore, is to contact consumers and find out what they remember about it. Memory tests fall into two major groups: *recall tests* and *recognition tests*.

[2]William A. Cook and Theodore F. Dunn, "The Changing Face of Advertising Research in the Information Age," *Journal of Advertising Research* (January/February 1996):55–63.

TABLE 21.1	SUPPLIERS OF EVALUATIVE RESEARCH	
SUPPLIER	**MEDIUM**	**METHODS**
ASI Market Research, Inc. New York, NY	Television, print	Recall; Persuasion
Bruzzone Research Co. Alameda, CA	Television	Recognition
Burke Marketing Research Cincinnati, OH	Television, print	Recall; Persuasion; In-market sales
Communications Workshop, Inc. Chicago, IL	Television, print, radio	Communications test
Diagnostic Research, Inc. New York, NY	Television, print, radio	Communications test
Gallup and Robinson, Inc. Princeton, NJ	Television, print	Recall; Persuasion
Information Resources, Inc. Chicago, IL	Television	In-market sales
Starch INRA Hooper, Inc. Mamaroneck, NY	Print	Recognition

RECALL TESTS

Recall Test: A test that evaluates the memorability of an advertisement by contacting members of the advertisement's audience and asking them what they remember about it.

The supplier most commonly associated with day-after recall (DAR) tests is Burke Marketing Services. Gallup and Robinson's In-View Service is another recall test designed to show which ads best capture and hold attention. In a traditional **recall test** a finished commercial is run on network television within a regular prime-time program. The next evening, interviewers in three or four cities make thousands of random phone calls until they have contacted about 200 people who were watching the program at the exact time the commercial appeared. The interviewer then asks a series of questions:

- Do you remember seeing a commercial for any charcoal briquettes?
- (If no) Do you remember seeing a commercial for Kingsford charcoal briquettes? (Memory prompt)
- (If yes to either of the above) What did the commercial say about the product? What did the commercial show? What did the commercial look like? What ideas were brought out?

The first type of question is called *unaided recall* because the particular brand is not mentioned. The second question is an example of *aided recall*, where the specific brand name is mentioned. The answers to the third set of questions are written down verbatim. The nature of these questions is important. Interviewers do not ask, "Please tell me about all the commercials you remember seeing on television last night" or "Please tell me about any charcoal briquette commercials you remember." The test requires that the respondent link a specific brand name, or at least a specific product category, to a specific commercial. If the commercial fails to establish a tight connection between the brand name and the selling message, the commercial will not get a high recall score.

The traditional recall test has many variations. In one variation interviewers prerecruit people to watch a specified program and recontact only those respondents the following day. This method saves research costs and eliminates the need to make thousands of phone calls to find 200 viewers who happen to have been watching the program on which the test commercial appeared. Another method exposes respondents to commercials in a theater setting. The respondents are then telephoned at home 24 or 72 hours later. In a third variation respondents are pre-recruited to watch a program telecast on local cable television. The latter two methods are popular because, unlike recall tests that employ network television, they can be used to test rough executions.

ANALYZING TEST RESULTS

Recall test results are analyzed by examining the verbatim responses (verbatims) to determine how many viewers remembered something specific about the ad. If an answer indicates that the viewer was merely guessing, or remembering other advertising, that viewer is not counted toward the recall score. Furthermore, even though some recall test verbatims are surprisingly detailed, many are so sketchy that it is hard to be sure the respondent was remembering a specific ad. Here are your typical verbatims. Which prove recall of the specific commercial being tested?

1. The guy was in his backyard, I think, and he was using them. I'm not really sure about that. The guy was using them in his grill.
2. I think they grilled a steak. I just remember it was Kingsford. They were grilling a steak.
3. They showed the bag of charcoal. It was fast lighting. I think it said it burned evenly.
4. I remember numerous grills in the commercial.
5. I remember, I think it was the one with big letters, with reference to the professionals, what the professionals use. I thought it was a pretty good advertis-

ing scheme. Amateur chefs like to think they're professionals. It was mostly the big letters. I remember a guy with a chef's hat on, smiling real big. I think the guy had dark hair. It was sort of a quick, not a subliminal thing but everything flashed real quick, the big letters, sort of a rapid fire approach. Just all I remember was that line, what the pros use.

Typically, anywhere from zero to 60 to 70 percent of viewers are able to prove recall. The average recall score for a 30-second commercial across a range of product categories is about 20 percent. In other words, about one in five of those who view a commercial can recall something about it the following day.[3]

PRINT AD RECALL TESTS

When recall tests are used to evaluate magazine advertisements, respondents who have read the magazine go through a deck of cards containing brand names. If the respondent says, "Yes, I remember having seen an advertisement for that brand," the interviewer asks the respondent to describe everything he or she can remember about the ad. As in a television recall test, answers are taken down verbatim and studied later to determine how many respondents remembered the specific advertisement being tested.

ASSESSING RECALL TESTS

Recall tests have several advantages over other memory methods. First, they have been around for a long time, almost since the beginning of national advertising. Advertisers are accustomed to using them—for some advertisers, they have become part of the corporate culture, an ingrained tradition.

Second, because recall tests have been so popular, research companies that conduct them have accumulated *norms*—records of results that serve the same purpose as batting averages. Norms allow the advertiser to tell whether a particular advertisement is above or below the average for either the brand or its product category. Without norms the advertiser would not know whether a score of 23, for example, is good or bad. Like students, commercials are graded with reference to others in the category being tested.

Reliability: A characteristic that describes a test that yields essentially the same results when the same advertisement is tested time after time.

RELIABILITY   A third advantage of recall tests is **reliability.** In this context, the term *reliable* means that the commercial gets essentially the same score every time it is tested. Reliability is important because, like all tests scores, recall test scores incorporate a certain amount of random measurement error. Measurement errors are due to differences among interviewers and among the programs or magazines that carry the advertisement, as well as a host of other factors that vary from time to time. When the amount of measurement error is high, as it is in some of the more qualitative methods of evaluating advertisements, scores vary from test to test—a high score this time, a low score the next time, a medium score the time after. When results are inconsistent, the test obviously is not dependable.

Although recall tests are not perfectly reliable, they are more reliable than most tests. That fact alone helps to explain why they remain popular with advertisers.

VALIDITY   Reliability is only one measure of the value of a copy test. An advertiser who uses a recall score is assuming that the score reflects the ad's ability to sell the product. At first glance, it might seem obvious that the most effective advertisements would make the most indelible impressions. Yet everyone can remember advertisements for brands they never use, and everyone uses some brands without being able to remember any advertising for them. The real question is whether there is a strong positive relationship between the ad's overall score and some later assessment of its sales effectiveness.

---

[3]David W. Stewart and David H. Furse, *Effective Television Advertising* (Lexington, MA: DC Heath & Co., 1986).

Validity: The ability of a test to measure what it is intended to measure.

The technical term for what we are discussing is **validity.** When an advertiser uses a recall test, the advertiser is assuming that the recall score is a valid indication of the advertisement's sales effectiveness. Many researchers and most of advertising's creative leaders believe that this assumption is incorrect. Here is what one well-known researcher said about the validity of day-after recall tests:

> We know that recall data are inherently weak. We know that the theory on which recall data are based is shaky. We know that the evidence for the validity of recall is—to be charitable—checkered. We may not know the answer to the longest playing controversy in all of marketing research, but we know what the answer is not—and it's not recall.[4]

COST   Recall tests are not inexpensive. On the average, television recall tests cost from $9,000 to $17,000 per commercial; and print recall tests cost from $7,000 to

---

[4]Lawrence D. Gibson, "If The Question Is Copy Testing, The Answer Is Not Recall," *Journal of Advertising Research*, 23 (1983):39–46.

FOREIGN AND DOMESTIC CAR OWNERS

A nationwide study on car ownership revealed some basic data about the population of car owners. The study found that 72 percent of Americans owned domestic cars only, 19 percent possessed foreign cars only, and just 9 percent owned both types of cars at the same time. What do the personal opinions, activities, purchasing styles, media habits, and background characteristics of these people tell us about the differences between foreign and domestic car owners?

Research reveals quite a few surprises about the foreign car owner. This person is apt to be female, under 35, and either single or divorced. Not only has she graduated from college, but she has most likely attended graduate school as well. Most probably, she lives in a large metropolitan area in the Pacific region. She sees herself as a career woman and works full time in a professional or managerial position, earning a pretty good salary. Two out of three of these women earn at least $30,000 a year, and one out of two has an income over $40,000. Being more affluent than the typical domestic car owner does not mean that she necessarily feels content with her salary. However, she does assume that in the future she will probably be more financially comfortable than she is at present. In fact, she has a pretty positive outlook on life in general and is convinced that her greatest achievements are yet to come.

The foreign car owner's buying style is not a cautious one. She will be the first to buy that new electronic product, perhaps even on a whim, although she is far more careful about buying major items. She would by no means restrict either small or large purchases to American-made products. She has no compunctions about using a bank credit card; unlike the domestic car owner, she doesn't feel she should necessarily pay cash for her purchases.

This woman is willing to take calculated risks in the investment realm. High interest rates are considerably more appealing to her than is the sheer safety of an investment. She relishes the speed of the sports car, but she is neither a wild driver nor a wild purchaser. On the contrary, she is a thorough shopper, searching for the best price. She is also far more concientious about using her seat belt than is the domestic car buyer. Although she will probably have mufflers, shock absorbers, and spark plugs changed at a specialty shop, she's not adverse to doing some of this work herself.

She is generally more liberal than the American car buyer. For instance, she thinks television advertising for contraceptive products is quite desirable, and she is in favor of legalized abortion. Moreover, she does not agree with the domestic car owner that the government should exercise more control over television content. As you might predict, the foreign car owner is not a believer that a woman's place is in the home. She is all for the woman's liberation movement.

Not surprisingly, the foreign car owner likes to travel and to see foreign places, and she travels more frequently than do domestic car owners. Television is not her primary mode of entertainment, but she does like to watch rented movies on her VCR. She enjoys all types of music, with the exception of country-western. Active sports, such as cycling and swimming, appeal to her, and she is likely to attend exercise classes or work out at a health club. No matter what her chronological age, she has a youthful, adventurous, and optimistic outlook.

EXERCISE

If you were marketing auto parts or auto services, how would you tailor your advertising specifically to female foreign-car owners? How would you evaluate its effectiveness?

Source: Adapted from DDB Needham Worldwide, *A Lifestyle Profile of Foreign and Domestic Car Owners* (July 1989).

$13,000 per ad. These costs limit the number of advertisements that an advertiser can afford to test.

RECALL TESTS AND DECISION MAKING

PRINCIPLE In spite of much re-search, the relationship between day-after recall scores and sales effectiveness is still unknown.

If recall tests are costly and if their validity is unknown (to say the least), why do so many advertisers use them? One reason is that recall is a relatively reliable measure of *something*, and many advertisers believe—despite evidence to the contrary—that recall must be related to effectiveness. It just seems logical that a well-remembered advertisement will, on average, be more effective than an advertisement that leaves little impression in the viewer's mind.

But the most fundamental reason that advertisers use recall tests is that test scores help them make decisions. As we noted earlier, the decision to run or not to run an advertisement affects the careers of everyone involved and triggers the expenditure of very large marketing resources. Aware of the consequences, and beset on all sides by doubts and conflicting opinions, decision makers need something to help them justify the decisions they make. In so tense a setting, a recall test—or any other test that has been approved by corporate tradition—can play a decisive role even when no one is really sure that the test predicts sales effects.

RECOGNITION TESTS

Recognition Test: A test that evaluates the memorability of an advertisement by contacting members of the audience, showing them the ad, and asking if they remember it.

Another way to measure memory is to show the advertisement to people and ask them if they remember having seen it. The latter kind of test is generally called a **recognition test.** Like recall tests, recognition tests were first used to evaluate print advertising. One of the earliest, and still one of the most popular recognition tests, is named after its inventor, Daniel Starch.

THE STARCH TEST

The Starch test can test only print ads that have already run. After verifying that the respondent at least looked through the magazine being studied, the interviewer proceeds page by page, asking whether the respondent remembers having seen or read each ad.

In the magazine used in the interview, each ad is assigned an item number and is broken down into component parts (such as illustration, headline, logo, or main body of print) that are identified by codes. Figure 21.2 shows the various components as they are measured by the Starch test. If the respondent says he or she remembers having seen a specific ad in that particular issue, the interviewer then asks a prescribed series of questions to determine exactly how much of the ad the respondent saw or read. The Starch procedure produces three scores:

1. *Noted:* The percentage of respondents who say they noticed the ad when they looked through the magazine on some previous occasion.
2. *Associated:* The percentage of respondents who said they noticed a part of the ad that contains the advertiser's name or logo.
3. *Read Most:* The percentage of respondents who reported reading 50 percent or more of the ad copy.

ASSESSING THE STARCH TEST

Compared with a recall test, the Starch test has some valuable advantages. First, because the questions are easier, the Starch interview proceeds more rapidly. A faster interview allows more advertisements to be tested, which in turn lowers the cost per advertisement. Starch tests cost $600 per ad, much less than the cost of recall tests. Lower cost implies a better investment of the advertiser's research resources.

NORMS   Like recall tests, the Starch test has been in use for many years, and the research supplier has accumulated norms that help interpret individual test scores. The Starch test's norms now include many different product categories. This specificity makes interpretation more precise.

FIGURE 21.2

THIS REPRESENTS A STARCH
REPORT SHOWING THE THREE
SCORES.

Rolex Oyster Perpetual Air-King in stainless steel with matching Oyster bracelet.

RELIABILITY   The Starch procedure is very reliable. Repeated evaluations have shown that Starch scores are remarkably consistent. In fact, in the print medium Starch tests are substantially more reliable than are recall tests.

VALIDITY   In experiments on the Starch method some respondents have claimed recognition of unpublished advertisements they could not possibly have seen. These false claims show that claimed recognition is not a perfectly valid measure of memory and that something else is probably at work.

Subsequent investigations have suggested that when a Starch respondent says, "Yes, I looked at that ad when I went through the magazine," he or she is really saying, "Ads like that usually attract my attention." When the Starch respondent says, "I didn't look at that ad," he or she is saying, "I usually ignore that kind of advertising." If that interpretation is correct, a Starch score actually represents a kind of consumer vote on whether that advertisement is worth more than a passing glance.[5] Given that the ability to attract and hold attention is a quality most advertisers want in their advertising, the Starch procedure is probably well worth its relatively modest cost.

THE BRUZZONE TEST

A television analogue of the Starch test is offered by the Bruzzone Research Company (BRC). The Bruzzone test is conducted through the mail. Consumers receive questionnaires that show scenes from television commercials along with the scripts, but minus the brand names (see Figure 21.3). The questionnaire asks whether they remember having seen each commercial before. If the answer is "yes," the respondents are asked to identify the brand and to rate the commercial on the basis of a

---

[5]Herbert K. Krugman, "Point Of View: Limits Of Attention To Advertising," *Journal of Advertising Research*, 38 (1988):47–50.

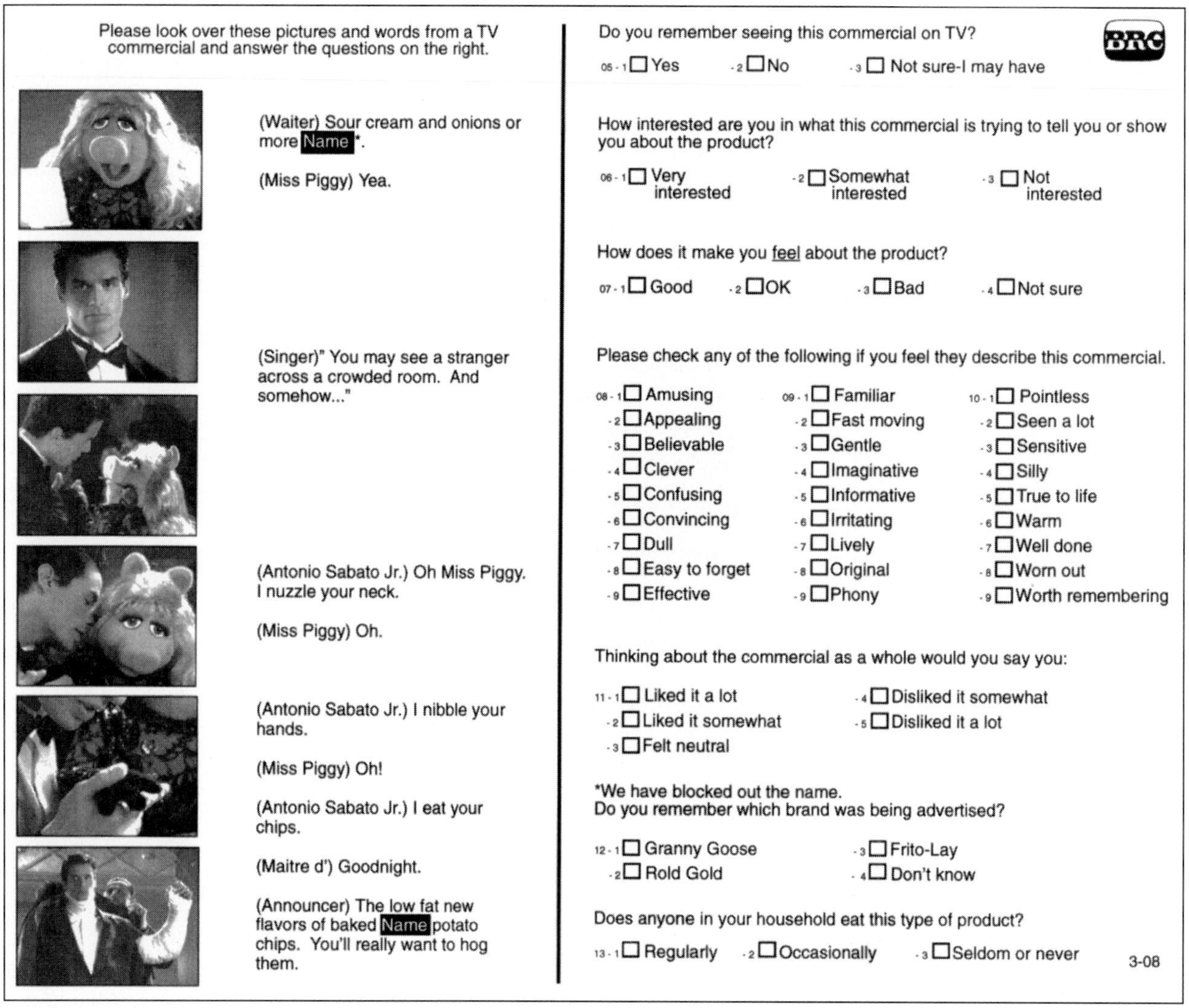
Please look over these pictures and words from a TV commercial and answer the questions on the right.

(Waiter) Sour cream and onions or more Name*.

(Miss Piggy) Yea.

(Singer)" You may see a stranger across a crowded room. And somehow..."

(Antonio Sabato Jr.) Oh Miss Piggy. I nuzzle your neck.

(Miss Piggy) Oh.

(Antonio Sabato Jr.) I nibble your hands.

(Miss Piggy) Oh!

(Antonio Sabato Jr.) I eat your chips.

(Maitre d') Goodnight.

(Announcer) The low fat new flavors of baked Name potato chips. You'll really want to hog them.

BRC

Do you remember seeing this commercial on TV?

05-1 ☐ Yes -2 ☐ No -3 ☐ Not sure-I may have

How interested are you in what this commercial is trying to tell you or show you about the product?

06-1 ☐ Very interested -2 ☐ Somewhat interested -3 ☐ Not interested

How does it make you feel about the product?

07-1 ☐ Good -2 ☐ OK -3 ☐ Bad -4 ☐ Not sure

Please check any of the following if you feel they describe this commercial.

08-1 ☐ Amusing	09-1 ☐ Familiar	10-1 ☐ Pointless
-2 ☐ Appealing	-2 ☐ Fast moving	-2 ☐ Seen a lot
-3 ☐ Believable	-3 ☐ Gentle	-3 ☐ Sensitive
-4 ☐ Clever	-4 ☐ Imaginative	-4 ☐ Silly
-5 ☐ Confusing	-5 ☐ Informative	-5 ☐ True to life
-6 ☐ Convincing	-6 ☐ Irritating	-6 ☐ Warm
-7 ☐ Dull	-7 ☐ Lively	-7 ☐ Well done
-8 ☐ Easy to forget	-8 ☐ Original	-8 ☐ Worn out
-9 ☐ Effective	-9 ☐ Phony	-9 ☐ Worth remembering

Thinking about the commercial as a whole would you say you:

11-1 ☐ Liked it a lot -4 ☐ Disliked it somewhat
-2 ☐ Liked it somewhat -5 ☐ Disliked it a lot
-3 ☐ Felt neutral

*We have blocked out the name.
Do you remember which brand was being advertised?

12-1 ☐ Granny Goose -3 ☐ Frito-Lay
-2 ☐ Rold Gold -4 ☐ Don't know

Does anyone in your household eat this type of product?

13-1 ☐ Regularly -2 ☐ Occasionally -3 ☐ Seldom or never

3-08

FIGURE 21.3
BRUZZONE TEST QUESTIONNAIRE.
(Courtesy of Bruzzone Research Company)

short checklist of adjectives. This procedure produces a recognition score for each commercial, along with a brief assessment of how many respondents liked it and how many thought it said something relevant to their needs.

The Bruzzone test has many of the same advantages as the Starch test. The scores it produces are quite reliable. Compared with other television copy-testing methods, it is relatively inexpensive—about $1,450 per ad. The research supplier also has accumulated norms that help the advertiser interpret scores. The Bruzzone test also shares the Starch test's principle drawback, however: It cannot be used until after all the costs of final production and placement in the media have already been incurred.

PERSUASION TESTS

Persuasion Test: A test that evaluates the effectiveness of an advertisement by measuring whether the ad affects consumers' intentions to buy a brand.

The basic format for a **persuasion test,** or attitude-change test, is this: Consumers are first asked how likely they are to buy a specific brand. They are exposed to an advertisement for that brand. After exposure, they are again asked about what they intend to purchase. Results are analyzed to determine whether intention to buy has increased as a result of exposure to the advertisement.

TYPES OF PERSUASION TESTS

Research companies that conduct persuasion tests often invite consumers to a theater to see a "preview of a new television show." They use this pretense because they do not want respondents to pay undue attention to advertising before coming to the testing session and because they want to minimize artificial attention to the commercials once the testing session has begun.

Before the audience members see the program, they fill out a questionnaire that asks about their preferences for various brands. They then watch a television program, complete with commercials, after which they answer questions concerning their reactions to the entertainment. They then respond to the brand-preference questions again.

At the beginning of the session most members of the audience believe that their major task will be to evaluate the entertainment. Before the session is over, however, most respondents have figured out that the commercials are the object of the test. Although some respondents react negatively when they realize their cooperation has been secured through false pretenses, most go along with the instructions and evaluate the different ads.

Like recall tests, persuasion tests come in several different versions. In one variation, respondents are telephoned at home and requested to watch a program at a certain time. During the course of the recruitment interview they are asked about their brand preferences. After the program has been telecast, they are recontacted and asked about their brand preferences again. Another method exposes respondents to commercials only, without program material. The procedure is basically the same in all such variations: pretest-exposure-retest, with a comparison of purchasing intentions before and after exposure to the advertisement.

ASSESSING PERSUASION TESTS

AUDIENCE COMPOSITION

The validity of a persuasion test depends in part on whether participants in the experiment constitute a good sample of the prospects the advertiser is trying to reach. A dog-food advertiser, for example, would not be interested in responses from people who do not own dogs. That requirement creates a problem because, unless the audience has been specially recruited to contain only dog owners, many of the responses in a typical persuasion test audience will come from people who are not really interested in the product.

Audience composition becomes especially important when the target audience is relatively small. Denture wearers, heavy users of pain relievers, and potential buyers of luxury automobiles will be tiny minorities of the audience in any normal persuasion test. Yet their reactions are the only reactions the advertiser really wants.

To control costs, persuasion test suppliers usually evaluate five or six commercials in different product categories during the same testing session. This means that even if the audience has been recruited to match the requirements of one product category—dog food, for example—it will not match the requirements of the other commercials being tested. An audience of dog owners will not necessarily be denture wearers, heavy users of pain relievers, and potential buyers of expensive European cars.

Because perfectly appropriate samples are so difficult to get, advertisers are tempted to ignore audience composition and to take findings from the entire group, regardless of how many respondents are really potential buyers. An understandable decision, but to anyone concerned with validity, wrong.

THE ENVIRONMENT

Because respondents are in a strange environment and because they may feel that they themselves are being tested, they are likely to be more alert, attentive, and critical than they would be at home. These characteristics of the theater environment may produce artificially high levels of attention and may exaggerate rational, as distinguished from emotional, response.

BRAND FAMILIARITY

PRINCIPLE For well-known brands the change produced by one exposure to one advertisement may be too small to measure accurately.

When the advertisement being tested is for a well-known brand, the amount of change created by one exposure to one commercial is almost always very small. Small changes tend to be unreliable. The advertiser cannot tell whether small differences among commercials are real or due to some random combination of factors that accidentally affected the results.

The small size and consequent unreliability of persuasion test scores for well-known brands is an important limitation. Advertisers of well-known brands are heavy users of persuasion testing. Yet the better known the brand, the less dependable the results.

COST

Persuasion tests are unusually expensive. A typical persuasion test costs between $11,000 and $15,000, and if special efforts to recruit a hard-to-find sample are required, the cost can go much higher. One justification for this large expenditure is that persuasion test suppliers typically provide recall scores and attitude scores, along with persuasion scores, when reporting their findings. Another even more important justification is that persuasion is what advertisements are all about. Because an unpersuasive advertisement is nearly worthless, even a rough indication of persuasive power is evidence that the message will have its intended effect.

PROTEST

Naturally, creative directors do not like persuasion tests any more than they like recall tests. When, for example, the Carnation company decided to compensate its agencies through a formula based in part on persuasion test scores, creative directors predicted dire consequences. One said, "It's the end of creativity, the end of anything meaningful or right in the advertising business if this isn't laughed out of the business quickly." Another said, "I think it's insane. There's going to be a lot more commercials that are good for [research companies] and less that are good with the consumer."[6]

Research executives have been less vehement. Although audience composition, the environment, and brand familiarity pose serious threats to persuasion test validity, evidence has shown that, when persuasion tests are competently conducted, scores are positively related to sales effectiveness—especially for advertisements that have something new and important to say about the brand.[7]

Despite all the arguments against persuasion tests, advertisers continue to use them for the same basic reason they continue to use recall tests: The tests help them make difficult and important decisions. Advertisers reason that even though the tests may not be perfect, they provide some objective information. When conflicting arguments intrude from every side, some objective information is a lot more reassuring than none at all.

DIRECT-RESPONSE COUNTS

Some television commercials request direct response via an 800 number. Some print ads request direct response via an 800 number, a coupon, or an offer embed-

[6]Marcy Magiera, "Admen Question Carnation Plan," *Advertising Age* (March 13, 1989):4.

[7]Anthony J. Adams and Margaret Hendersen Blair, "Persuasive Advertising and Sales Accountability: Past Experience and Forward Validation," Advertising Research Foundation 35th Annual Conference, New York City, April 1989.

Direct-Response Counts: Evaluative tests that count the number of viewers or readers who request more information or who purchase the product.

ded in the body copy. Responses to these requests provide direct measures of effectiveness. Instead of depending on memory or persuasion or some other indirect and possibly misleading indication of effectiveness, the advertiser simply counts the number of viewers or readers who request more information or buy the product. **Direct-response counts** are sometimes called *inquiry tests*. This name is not quite accurate, however, because increasingly the counts are of actual sales rather than inquiries.

In some cases, direct-response advertisements are split run—the advertisements being tested are bound into alternate copies of newspapers or magazines. Because each advertisement has its own code on the reply coupon or its own box number in the return address, the advertiser can tell exactly which ad produced the best results. Compared with recall tests and persuasion tests, few reliability or validity problems plague this type of evaluative research.

Of course, direct-response counts cannot be used to test all advertisements. Most ads are intended to encourage purchase at a retail outlet—an automobile showroom, a supermarket, or a department store, for example. When the product is distributed through retail outlets, the direct connection between ad and purchase is lost, and no one can tell which purchaser responded to which, if any, of the advertiser's ads. In the Concepts and Applications box, the methods employed by John Jones to relate advertising and sales are discussed.

CONCEPTS AND APPLICATIONS

DOES ADVERTISING PRODUCE SALES?

In his book *When Ads Work*, John Philip Jones, a professor at the Newhouse School of Public Communication at Syracuse University, uses "pure single-source" data gathered by the Chicago-based research firm A.C. Nielsen Co. to provide concrete information on the link between advertising and sales. Jones finds that a consumer can in fact be persuaded to buy a product through advertising—after seeing an effective ad just once.

His approach differs from those of the traditionalists, who typically measure the effect of ads based on long-term objectives, such as brand equity, or how consumers value brands to an increasing degree. A major reason for this long-term preference, writes Jones, is that it is difficult to measure advertising's short-term effectiveness except through direct response.

Jones's approach breaks new ground in using a statistical device called the short-term advertising strength (STAS) differential, which is a measure of the immediate effect of advertising on sales. In taking this approach, Jones demonstrates that:

- The strongest ad campaigns can triple sales, while the weakest campaigns cause sales to fall by more than 50 percent.
- Ads that don't have immediate success won't have long-term success.
- Short-term sales success can be translated into long-term success.

Such research makes it possible for manufacturers to identify winning campaigns. And it enables them to pull the losers because to run a campaign that has no short-term effect, said Jones, means a "total waste of advertising dollars."

Jones's research is based on a technique that concentrates on individual households and relates each household's exposure to identified television advertising for named brands and to its purchases of those same brands shortly after the advertising. He uses Nielsen research that draws upon three streams of data collected from each household:

- The household's purchases of brands.
- A record in each household based on information collected by an electronic meter hooked up to their television sets, which monitors the time when the set is on.
- The names of these brands advertised on those television channels during the time period in question.

Jones uses Nielsen data for 1991 and 1992 that are based on a sample of 2,000 households. It tracks the effect of advertising on the sales of 142 brands, 80 of which were advertised and 62 were not.

He categorizes brands according to their short-term advertising strength (STAS) differential. A positive STAS demonstrates a campaign is having a short-term effect. A negative STAS means campaigns are so weak that they are vulnerable to the stronger effects of a positive differential of a rival brand.

He concludes that the key to turning short-term sales success into longer-term advantage lies in media continuity—advertising week after week. In addition, he shows a strong correlation between advertising and sales promotion—or price reductions—when both activities work cooperatively.

Sources: Marilyn Much, "New Research Quantifies the Effect of Ads," *Investor's Business Daily* (April 24, 1995); and John Philip Jones, *When Ads Work* (New York: Lexington Books, 1995).

COMMUNICATION TESTS

The communication test described in Chapter 6 is sometimes used for final evaluation as well as for diagnostic research. Advertisers who are not convinced that recognition, recall, or persuasion are adequate measures of an ad's effectiveness, and who can't rely on direct-response counts, may settle for answers to the three basic communication questions: Did the ad deliver the message it was intended to deliver? Did the ad deliver any messages it was *not* intended to deliver? How did the representatives of the target audience react to the message, the characters, the situation, and the tone? Although the answers to these questions are a far cry from definitive measures of sales effectiveness, they obviously are important. Because these answers are important and because communication tests are relatively inexpensive, some major advertisers have decided that communication tests are about the best evaluation tests they can get.

Memory test scores, persuasion test scores, and direct-response counts are final grades that can be quickly interpreted as good, bad, or indifferent, pass or fail. In contrast, communication tests do not give single scores, but rather patterns of findings, which require detailed analysis and interpretation of consumers' reactions to the advertisement. This quality is both a disadvantage and an advantage. On the one hand, it increases the unreliability caused by subjective interpretation. On the other hand, it provides richer, more detailed information about how consumers reacted to the ad.

FOCUS GROUPS

Some advertisers use focus groups to make final go/no-go decisions about television commercials and print ads. This practice is popular because—compared with memory tests, persuasion tests, and even communication tests—focus groups can provide quicker feedback and can be less expensive.

However, this practice has an important downside: When used to make final go/no-go decisions, focus groups are notoriously unreliable. Because so much can happen in the course of a group discussion, different groups of respondents and different moderators often produce dramatically different evaluations.

When focus groups are used to gather background information, as described in Chapter 6, respondents' reactions are treated as clues to be weighed and evaluated, accepted or rejected, in the context of information from many other sources. But when focus groups are used as juries, respondents' reactions are liable to be taken literally, and accepted at face value. When that happens, the fate of an expensive creative product is determined by a complex set of semi-accidental happenings. Advertisers who use focus groups to make final go/no-go decisions are placing far too much weight on extremely unreliable results.

PHYSIOLOGICAL TESTS

Physiological Tests: Tests that measure emotional reactions to advertisements by monitoring reactions such as pupil dilation and heart rate.

All of the methods discussed thus far require consumers to make verbal responses: Do you remember seeing a commercial for a detergent? As you were looking at the commercial, what thoughts or ideas went through your mind? Which brand do you intend to buy? The value of those questions depends on the respondents' ability to observe their own reactions and to report those responses accurately.

Aware of the shortcomings of verbal response, investigators have tried to use **physiological tests** to evaluate emotional reactions to ads. They reasoned that physiological measurements might pick up responses that the person was unable or unwilling to report. Some physiological measurements that have been tried are:

- *Heart rate:* The heart speeds up during an emotional response.
- *Pupil dilation:* The pupil of the eye dilates when a person sees something especially interesting.
- *Galvanic skin response:* Emotional reactions produce measurable changes in the electrical conductivity of the skin.
- *Electroencephalographic (EEG) response:* Electrical activity in the brain changes as the brain processes information.

ASSESSING PHYSIOLOGICAL TESTS

Despite their apparent advantages, physiological measurements have not yet come into general use. Validity has been a problem because physiological reactions are often caused by minor changes in the testing environment, changes in a commercial's brightness or color, or even random thoughts. Such instability leads to questions about what is being measured and to inconsistent findings when the same ad is tested more than once.

THE TEST ENVIRONMENT

Most physiological tests require that respondents report to a laboratory, a setting that is hardly conducive to natural responses. Also, many of the tests require that respondents be attached to unfamiliar laboratory instruments, sometimes for extended periods of time. These requirements reduce the representativeness of samples because many consumers cannot be persuaded to submit to such unusual and possibly threatening procedures. They also reduce the representativeness of the environment in which the advertisement is shown.

Furthermore, no one is entirely sure how to interpret any of the physiological reactions. A change in emotional response may mean that the consumer likes the advertisement or the product. Then again, it may mean that the consumer is irritated or upset by something in the advertisement or by something in the testing situation itself. Researchers have had a hard time deciding what bearing any of that might have on the advertisement's intended effect.

PRINCIPLE Many physiological tests are so sensitive to outside influences that their test-retest reliability is unacceptably low.

PHYSIOLOGICAL TESTS MEASURE EMOTIONAL RESPONSES TO ADVERTISING.
(Tim Davis/Photo Researchers)

INSIDE ADVERTISING

SOME THINGS I THINK I KNOW ABOUT STUDYING TELEVISION COMMERCIALS *John S. Coulson*

Courtesy of John S. Coulson

John Coulson is a former vice president in charge of research at the Leo Burnett agency and a partner in Communication Workshop, Inc., a creative and marketing research company that specializes in developing and evaluating new products and corporate communications. In both capacities he has evaluated numerous television commercials. The following observations are based on his research experiences.

1. No single set of measurements will serve to evaluate all commercials. A commercial is a very complex communication with many different goals. It is part of a total advertising program that is part of a total marketing program. Studying it out of context can produce highly irrelevant information.

2. A key element in the results of a commercial test is the type of people among whom the commercial is being studied. Some people are more receptive to a particular brand's advertising than are others. For example, product and brand users are generally more receptive to a message about that brand than are nonusers. Trier-rejecters show even less interest and acceptance. Generally women are more accepting than men, older adults are more accepting than younger adults, and children are more accepting than adults.

3. The most basic rule for achieving a successful commercial is that its viewers be able to identify the product and brand being advertised. Occasionally a competitive brand is misidentified as the advertiser. To be sure that the brand is correctly identified, it must be an integral part of the story line of the commercial rather than an element that is out of synch with the rest of the commercial.

4. The commercial's ability to create brand or product recall is largely independent of its effect on the viewer's atti-

tudes toward the brand or product. Recall is a measure of how well the commercial is communicating its message. It is related to the commercial's *efficiency* rather than to the *effectiveness* of its communication.

5. One effective commercial format is to provide news that is relevant and important to viewers. Information about a product can be news to the public for a long time, particularly if it can be given a fresh twist. Advertisers frequently feel that news is stale long before the public does.

6. When the objective of the commercial is to provide news, the news should be seen as important and relevant to the way the consumer uses the product, it should be believable, and it should be unique to the brand being advertised. Otherwise the commercial will be less effective.

7. The measurement of believability is tricky. If there is no news in the commercial, it tends to be rated as believable. Also, the believability of the message in the commercial is not always important to the commercial's success. If the product is relatively low priced, consumers might purchase it just to test the claim that they found difficult to believe in the commercial.

8. A basic problem of advertising with the goal of providing news is trying to cover too many ideas. It is more than twice as difficult to deliver two ideas as it is to deliver one, and the attempt to deliver three or four ideas almost always produces a jumble that is quickly forgotten.

9. An attractive spokesperson who is appropriate for the product or brand attracts attention and makes the message more believable and compelling.

10. Viewers are wary about the use of celebrity spokespeople in advertising. If the spokespeople are not appropriate to the commercial, viewers do not believe them and reject the message.

11. In addition to informative commercials, another widely used approach to television advertising is a mood or emotional commercial designed to create greater awareness of, and favorable reaction to, the product or the brand. Many commercials successfully combine the two approaches.

12. When a commercial is delivering news of real interest to its viewers, liking the commercial or empathizing with its situation is generally not critical to its effectiveness. Instead, clarity and simplicity are important. For mood commercials, on the other hand, likability and empathy are far more important than clarity and simplicity.

13. Appropriate music can enhance the mood of a commercial. Music can make a commercial more memorable and improve consumer attitudes toward the product.

Because physiological measurements show so much theoretical promise, investigators have gone back to them again and again. However, every attempt to put them into commercial practice has run aground on the reliability and validity difficulties just described. As a result, although physiological tests continue to attract intermittent attention and interest, they are not now a major factor in evaluative research.

FRAME-BY-FRAME TESTS

Frame-by-Frame Test: Tests that evaluate consumers' reactions to the individual scenes that unfold in the course of a television commercial.

A great deal goes on while a television commercial unfolds. Even though the commercial may be very brief, it is always made up of separate parts. As those episodes progress, viewers' responses to the commercial change as well.

Researchers have attempted to track those changes in several different ways. In one form of **frame-by-frame test,** viewers turn a dial or press numbers on an electronic keypad to indicate their moment-to-moment reactions to what they are seeing on the screen. That procedure produces a *trace*—a continuous record of ups and downs. When the trace is correlated with the commercial frame by frame, it provides a record of which parts of the commercial increased attention (or liking of whatever is being measured) and which parts reduced it.

One of the best-known frame-by-frame tests is VIEWFACTS' PEAC test, in which respondents in a minitheater setting press buttons on hand-held keypads to indicate how much they like or dislike what they are seeing on a television screen. The test commercial is embedded in a series of commercials, and respondents indicate their reactions to each one. As respondents are reacting, a computer collects and averages the responses and translates them into a continuous trace line keyed to the commercial's scenes.

After respondents give their initial reactions, they use their keypads to answer a set of questions that resemble those asked in a communication test. The computer collects the answers and tabulates them for discussion later on.

In the second half of a PEAC session the computer superimposes the response line over the test commercial on the screen (see Figure 21.4). An interviewer stops the commercial at key turning points and asks the audience members why their evaluations went up or down. Toward the end of the sessions the inter-

FIGURE 21.4

THE PEAC TEST.

(Courtesy of VIEWFACTS and VMI)

viewer reviews the communication questions and asks the respondents to explain why they reacted the way they did.

Thus the PEAC test combines the advantages of moment-to-moment response with an opportunity to ask and discuss questions about the respondents' reactions. Although the PEAC test is relatively expensive, this combination provides useful diagnostic information that cannot be accumulated in any other way.

In another form of frame-by-frame test viewers wear tiny electrodes that measure the electrical conductivity of the skin. As various parts of the commercial provoke an emotional reaction, electrical conductivity changes, producing an "emotional response" trace line. Unlike the PEAC test, which produces a voluntary measure of liking, electrical conductivity tests measure involuntary, emotional reactions. Although this method is still in the early stages of development, it shows considerable promise. It combines the advantages of frame-by-frame analysis with the advantages of involuntary emotional response.

ASSESSING FRAME-BY-FRAME TESTS

Frame-by-frame tests can be useful because they provide some guidance as to how the commercial might be improved. When a commercial gets a low recall score or a low persuasion score, no one can really be sure what will bring that score up. In contrast, because the trace line in frame-by-frame tests goes up in response to some scenes and down in response to others, it provides direct clues as to which parts of the commercial need further work.

As usual, reliability and validity are difficult to establish. Traces can be unstable from person to person and from group to group, especially when physiological measures are involved. Furthermore, the relationship between the trace's form or level and the advertisement's ultimate effect is uncertain. Even when the trace can be shown to be reliable, the question remains: Exactly what is the trace a reliable measurement of?

Nevertheless, frame-by-frame tests bring something to advertising research that other methods do not. They provide an opportunity to look inside a commercial, and they offer clues as to what scenes produce what kind of response. Because that is such a valuable advantage, the PEAC test and its direct competitors are becoming more widely used.

In-Market Tests

In-Market Tests: Tests that measure the effectiveness of advertisements by measuring actual sales results in the marketplace.

In-market tests evaluate advertisements by measuring their influence on sales. In view of all the problems discussed thus far, a sales-impact measurement might appear to be the only measurement that an advertiser should accept. However, the practical difficulties of conducting in-market tests are so great that full-scale in-market tests are seldom attempted in evaluating individual ads.

One problem is that sales are produced by a tightly interwoven net of factors, including economic conditions, competitive strategies, and all of the marketing activities in which the advertiser is engaged. Within that complicated set of interrelationships the effect of any single advertisement is extremely difficult to detect. Even with the benefit of a carefully designed, large-scale (and therefore costly and time-consuming) experiment, the effect of a single advertisement may be entirely lost.

Another reason that in-market tests are not popular is that by the time sales figures become available, most of the important investments have already been made: The advertisement has been produced, and media costs have all been incurred. For purposes of evaluating an advertisement, in-market test results become available very late in the game.

SIMULATED TEST MARKETS

Simulated Test Market:
Research procedure in which respondents are exposed to advertisements and then permitted to shop for the advertised products in an artificial environment where records are kept of their purchases.

Some of those problems can be avoided by using **simulated test markets.** In a simulated test market the research company conducting the test exposes respondents to advertising and then asks them to choose among competing brands. Later the researchers contact respondents who have used the advertiser's brand to ask if they would purchase the same brand again. The two numbers produced by that pair of interviews are *trial*—the proportion of respondents who chose to try the brand after seeing an advertisement for it—and *repeat*—the proportion of respondents who, having tried the product, chose to purchase the same brand again.

Despite the artificiality of simulated test markets, research companies have developed trial-and-repeat formulas that have proved to be remarkably accurate predictors of later in-market success. One of the reasons for this accuracy is that the trial-and-repeat numbers are much closer to what happens in the real marketplace than are the numbers provided by memory or *persuasion* tests.

In a simulated test market, however, the advertisement's effect is combined with the effects of packaging and pricing, and of course with reactions to the product itself. Therefore, although simulated test markets can predict the success of a marketing program as a whole, they cannot give more than a rough indication of the advertisement's independent influence on sales.

In principle, this problem could be solved by conducting multiple simulated test markets in which only the advertisements were varied and everything else remained the same. This solution runs into the problem of cost. The cost of conducting a single simulated test market runs from $50,000 to $75,000. The cost of conducting multiple experiments is higher than most advertisers believe they can afford.

SINGLE-SOURCE DATA

In another major substitute for a full in-market test, the research company conducting the test arranges to control the television signal received by the households in a community. The company divides the households into equivalent matched groups. It then sends advertisements to one group of households but not to the other and collects exact records of what every household purchases. Because advertising is the only variable being manipulated here, the method permits an unambiguous reading of cause and effect. The data collected in this way are known as *single-source data* because exposure records and purchasing records come from the same source.

PRINCIPLE The most realistic tests of an advertisement's effectiveness are too expensive for routine use.

Single-source data can produce exceptionally dependable results. Real advertisements are used, and they are received under natural conditions in the home. The resulting purchases are real purchases made by real consumers for their own use. The method is very expensive, however—$200,000 to $300,000 per test. Furthermore, the method usually requires more than 6 months to produce usable results. It is therefore not acceptable for routine testing of individual ads.

ℐMPLICATIONS OF ℰVALUATIVE ℛESEARCH

In evaluative copy testing, the advertiser must make trade-offs. In-market tests, which come closest to duplicating the most important features of the natural environment, are too expensive and too time-consuming to be used on a regular basis. Tests that are fast and affordable have so many obvious flaws. Added to all that, creative "experts" within the company and—especially—within the advertising agency fight all kinds of evaluative research at every step. Faced with such problems, advertisers must either depend on unaided judgment, which may be less reliable and less valid than even the least reliable and least valid research, or supple-

DOES ONLINE WORK OR NOT?

Thanks to researchers in traditional media, marketers can more or less tell how many and what kinds of people will see the message, based on circulation, viewership, or traffic. The Internet, however, combines elements of all the foregoing media. As nothing less than the integration of print and broadcast—an interactive text-and-picture magazine, catalog, or billboard delivered on-screen at the consumer's request—it's no wonder the advertising and publishing communities are having trouble pinning it down. But without a standardized method of tabulating audience exposure and impact, much less a way for marketers to know who's on the other end of the mouse, companies that advertise on the Net still do so largely on the basis of trust.

"There has to be some standardization for the Internet to move forward," says Alison Smith, a spokesperson for Next Century Media, a Web-audit service. "It's going to be an advertiser-supported medium, and it needs to have more advertiser support. Look at it from an advertiser's perspective. You want to know what rate of return you are getting and how you can actually make money from this."

In addition to Next Century Media, audit services that have stepped up to report Web traffic include WebTrack, NetCount, and Internet Profile's I/Pro. None has emerged to be a Nielsen or Arbitron yet, probably due to disagreement on what to count. Collecting raw data on Web site use is easy. When users log on to an Internet server, software tracks "hits" and "click-throughs." Sometimes it even tracks time spent at a site. But counting alone can be misleading, and the fact that much of the data are collected by Internet providers themselves makes its worth questionable as a basis for rate assessment. Internet providers already set rates according to the available figures, even based on number of hits. "We haven't gotten any further on quantifying the Web," says Charles D'Oify, director of online research at Yankelovich Partners. "There are companies out there that manage to sell ad space using CPMs. *Playboy* charges something like $5 per thousand hits. Figures like that encapsulate the need for the third-party auditing."

Will the Internet require independent third-party audits? "We don't believe you can audit something you don't understand," notes Stephen Klein, I/Pro vice president of marketing. "ABC and CNN may speak the same language as the conventional publishing company, but they don't understand the Web or have a technology of their own to measure it."

Source: Ian P. Murphy, "On-line Ads Effective? Who Knows for Sure?" *Marketing News* (September 23, 1996):1, 38.

---

ment judgment with research findings that, although far from perfect, are likely to be better than no help at all.

In this dilemma the advertiser joins the government official, the military leader, the business executive, the economist, the physician, and the educator. When decisions are difficult, important, and controversial, research cannot tell the decision maker what to do. However, it can provide guidance, and when that guidance is used reasonably, decisions generally turn out better than they would have if based on intuition alone.

The same principles apply to selection and purchase of advertising media. Whereas research can be a valuable guide, decisions as to how much to spend—and when, where, and how to allocate those funds—always include an element of hard data and an element of hunch. Of course, with new media, hard data that are valid and reliable may be hard to come by (see Issues and Controversies box).

SUMMARY

- Creative experts disagree with one another, and agencies disagree with their clients. Faced with these conflicts of opinion, advertisers often resort to evaluative research in the hope that it will provide a reliable and valid prediction of an advertisement's sales effectiveness.

- The major evaluative research methods fall into eight major groups: (1) memory tests, (2) persuasion tests, (3) direct-response counts, (4) communication tests, (5) focus groups, (6) physiological tests, (7) frame-by-frame tests, and (8) in-market tests.

- Although memory tests have a long history in advertising research, no one knows whether they predict sales. Many creative leaders and many research leaders believe that they do not.

- Persuasion tests are relatively good predictors of effectiveness when the ad has something new and interesting to say. However, when brands are well known, and when all messages are similar, persuasion findings may be largely due to chance.

- Direct-response counts show exactly how many consumers responded to each ad. Although this method is highly accurate, it can be used only with advertisements that request a direct response. It cannot be used with television commercials or print ads intended to encourage purchases at retail stores.

- Communication tests do not produce simple pass-fail results. Rather, they provide a detailed analysis of consumers' subjective reactions to the advertisements being tested. This quality makes them less useful for go/no-go decisions but more useful for understanding how the advertisement works.

- Focus groups are the least reliable of the major evaluative research methods. Advertisers who use them for this purpose are leaving too much to chance.

- Although physiological tests show considerable theoretical promise, low reliability and high cost have excluded them from routine use in evaluative research.

- Frame-by-frame tests allow advertisers to examine viewers' reactions as a television commercial unfolds. Because they link reactions to specific scenes, frame-by-frame tests provide especially useful clues as to how a commercial may be improved.

- When properly conducted, in-market tests are the most valid of all types of evaluative research. However, they are so expensive and so time consuming that they are not practical options for testing individual ads.

- Each evaluative method has its own unique pattern of costs, assets, and liabilities. In the end, advertisers must make trade-offs in deciding which method or methods to use. Advertisers make this decision in the same way they make any other business decision: They ask themselves, "which alternative, including unaided judgment, provides the most benefit, given its cost?"

QUESTIONS

1. Make a list of the assets and liabilities of each of the copy-testing methods reviewed in this chapter. Considering this list, if you were an advertiser with a $100 million advertising budget, which method would you use? Why? Would your answer change if you had a $1 million budget? In what way?

2. Suppose you are in charge of advertising a student production of a Broadway play and that an advertising class has developed several quite different ads. How would you decide which ad to use? How would you know whether you made the right choice?

3. The problems an advertiser encounters in trying to evaluate an individual advertisement resemble the problems a college administrator encounters in trying to evaluate an individual college course. In what ways are the two sets of problems similar? In what ways are they different?

4. Professor Fletcher is illustrating research principles by describing a case in which he was involved. A marketer of men's cologne was testing its advertisement for recognition. Ten sample groups of men aged 25 to 40 were tested, and the recognition scores for each sample were in the 25 to 35 percent range. Fletcher tells the class that the data were clearly reliable but very likely invalid. Then he asks the class two questions: Why must a result be reliable in order to be valid? Why was the cologne testing probably invalid? What would your answers be?

5. One of the methods used for testing television commercial impact is the theater test. Approximately 100 people are invited to view television programs being considered by the networks, and the commercials are embedded in the programs. Prior to the viewing, the audience is asked to select products that they would like to receive if they were a door-prize winner. After the viewings (and drawings), the audience repeats its choices. The tested products (and competing brands) are on the selection lists. What dimension of consumer effect is being tested in this way? Is this a valid method of testing for this effect?

6. The chapter discusses one weakness of physiological testing by pointing out that results from these experiments are very hard to interpret for eventual sales effectiveness. A number of researchers claim the same sort of weakness affects many recall and attitude procedures used in copy testing. Why would these very popular tests be criticized this way? What is the best way to measure the persuasion of an advertising message?

7. Through advanced technology (UPC scanning), research companies are able to speed up results from field tests on advertising effectiveness. Although companies do not have to wait several months for results, many are still fearful of real-life field testing. In part, this fear explains the continued popularity of simulated test market studies. What is this fear about? What serious validity threat to test marketing can be relieved by a market simulation?

Suggested Class Project

Following the description of the Starch test in this chapter, test recognition of five advertisements from a recent edition of the college newspaper. What do the *noted, associated*, and *read most associated* scores tell about the advertisements' effectiveness?

Further Readings

Clancy, Kevin J., and Lyman E. Ostlund, "Commercial Effectiveness Measures," *Journal of Advertising Research*, (1976):29–34.

Fletcher, Alan D., and Thomas A. Bowers, *Fundamentals of Advertising Research*, 3rd ed. (Belmont, CA: Wadsworth Publishing Co., 1988).

Kalwani, Manohar U., and Alvin J. Silk, "On the Reliability and Predictive Validity of Purchase Intention Measures," *Marketing Science*, 1 (1980):243–86.

Stewart, David W., "Measures, Methods, and Models in Advertising Research," *Journal of Advertising Research*, 29 (1989):54–60.

Stewart, David W., and David H. Furse, *Effective Television Advertising* (Lexington, MA: D.C. Heath and Co., 1986).

Walker, David, and Michael F. von Gonten, "Explaining Related Recall Outcomes: New Answers from a Better Model," *Journal of Advertising Research*, 29 (1989):11–21.

Young, Shirley, "Copy Testing Without Magic Numbers," *Journal of Advertising Research*, 12 (1972):3–12.

The women's fragrance category accounts for over $2 billion and has experienced annual growth rates of approximately 4 percent. Unlike traditional consumer products, however, the women's fragrance category has hundreds of competitors, many with fractional shares. The category is, extremely fragmented and is further segmented by "mass versus class" channels of distribution. Approximately half of the women's fragrances are sold through broad (mass) distribution channels, such as drug and mass merchandisers. The remaining products are sold through higher priced, more exclusive (class) locations, such as department and specialty stores.

Cover Girl developed the Navy fragrance for introduction in Spring of 1990. The product was designed for mass-distribution outlets. In such a highly fragmented category full of brands with short life expectancies, strong initial success is considered critical for long-term success. Cover Girl's ultimate goal for advertising was to achieve sales and share for Navy among the top ten brands in mass distribution within 3 years. The objective of the resulting "Perfect" campaign for Navy was to communicate strongly a highly desirable brand personality. Cover Girl also established objectives related to awareness, trial, purchase intent, and brand image/personality. The specific image/personality goal was to create an "aspiration" brand image that would establish Navy as a clean, classic fragrance, with a personality that would be stylish, smart, sexy, and confident—"perfect" for any occasion.

Because Cover Girl wanted women to consider Navy appropriate for all-day, year-round usage, the main promise for the new campaign was "You always feel perfect in Navy."

Demographically, Navy's target audience was identified as women 18 to 34 years of age who are regular users of fragrance, who currently include mass-market brands among their "wardrobe" of personal fragrances, and for whom fashion is an important consideration. Navy's introductory media spending amounted to approximately 7.5 percent of the total media expenditures in the women's fragrance category. Media vehicles included a 30-second television commercial and four-color, full-page magazine ads with scent strips.

Navy's initial success surpassed the objectives. After 3 months of introductory advertising, the brand's share of unit volume established it as the number two mass-distributed brand in the category, trailing the number one brand by only a narrow margin. It ranked third in terms of dollar sales, behind two well-established major brands. Consumer awareness of Navy's advertising immediately following the launch of the campaign was in the same range as the strongest brands in the category, whose campaigns had run for several years. Further consumer tracking study data indicated that Navy easily exceeded all of its awareness, trial, purchase intent, and attitudinal objectives. Among the brand's target group, Navy's purchase intent scores ranked second in the category, and its advertising ranked first in terms of recall. Cover Girl also reported that the advertising successfully communicated its brand image objectives, as consumers characterized the product as "stylish, confident, and sexy," a scent that can be worn at any time.

Source: Courtesy of Lotas Minard Patton McIver, Inc.

$\mathcal{Q}$UESTIONS

1. With the shortened product life cycles common in the women's fragrance category, why do you think it is essential for brands to establish strong rapid trial and awareness during their introductory periods?

2. Manufacturers of women's fragrances have successfully positioned their products as similar to apparel styles. Fragrances, like clothes, should be unique, ever-changing, and always up-to-date. How has this success heightened new product competition, shortened product life cycles, and increased product development and advertising costs?

3. What problems and difficulties described in this chapter apply to evaluating the effectiveness of the "Perfect" Navy campaign? Which measures of this campaign's effect might be unreliable? Which might be invalid?

SEE WHAT THE INTERNET HAS IN STORE FOR YOU.

Wouldn't it be cool if you could buy more than just computer stuff on the net? Now you can, at the Internet Shopping Network. Sure, we have over 22,000 computer products including programs from companies like Lotus, Symantec and Microsoft—but that's just the beginning. It's also a place where you can

order flowers from FTD Online and see the arrangements before you buy them. If tea is your thing, you can browse and buy a whole selection from Celestial Seasonings. Look through the Hammacher-Schlemmer catalog on-line, and find everything from footballs to footwear, even a home sauna for two. Imagine using the net to catch fresh steak and lobster from Omaha Steak International. Sample thousands of music titles. Check out thousands of software programs. Get more information,

on more products, than anywhere else on the net. And if you ever have a question about our services or products, simply ask Dave, one of our service gurus, for help.

The Internet Shopping Network is more than a cool stop on an otherwise overheated highway, it's the last place you'll ever expect to find business as usual on the net.

Free membership
http://shop.internet.net
1-800-677-SHOP
For more information,
e-mail: info@internet.net

ISN

The Internet Shopping Network

©1995 Home Shopping Network, Inc. All rights reserved. Internet Shopping Network is a trademark of Home Shopping Network, Inc. All others are trademarks or copyrights of their respective companies. Another cool thing about the Internet is the lack of all this legal fineprint...for now.

CHAPTER 22

Retail and Business-to-Business Advertising

CHAPTER OUTLINE

- A Store Without a Store
- Retail Advertising
- Buying and Selling Local Media
- Business-to-Business Advertising
- Business-to-Business Advertising Media

CHAPTER OBJECTIVES

When you have completed this chapter, you should be able to:

- Understand how local retail advertising differs from national brand advertising
- Understand how cooperative advertising works
- Explain business-to-business advertising objectives
- List the different markets in the business arena and the various media used in business advertising

A Store Without a Store

Would you buy a computer from an online shop? Such a computer may be cheaper but you can't get a demonstration or try it out yourself. And what about after-sales support? If you need help, who do you call? On the other hand, many people don't have a lot of time to cruise stores shopping around and it can be a frustrating experience to wander the aisles in a superstore and not find a salesperson. So would *you* buy a computer from the Web?

The fact is: The biggest new wave in retailing is digital shops that sell through the Internet. The Internet Shopping Network is an online version of the Home Shopping Network and offers computer programs, as well as a cornucopia of products from a variety of retailers such as FTD (flowers), Celestial Seasonings, Hammacher-Schlemmer, and Omaha Steak International.

Amazon.com is leading the pack of Web stores that are invading established retailing with online outlets. Way back in 1994, Jeff Bezos was a young senior vice president at a Wall Street fund company. After drawing up a list of 20 products that he figured could be sold online—including books, music, magazines, and computers—he settled on books. Two years later he was CEO of the fast-growing Internet bookstore Amazon.com and stealing real-world customers from traditional bookstores. He named the new store Amazon, after the world's largest river, because he believed the store would carry many more books than conventional stores. He sold his first book in July 1995.

A multimillion-dollar virtual storefront, Amazon employs some 110 people, however, there's no store and very little inventory. Customers connect to Amazon's Web site and search a database of 1.1 million books by title, author, subject, or keyword. An online form is used to order the book and payment is by credit card submitted via telephone or the Web. (The Web transaction is safeguarded by encryption.) Then Amazon requests the books from distributors and publishers that deliver them to the company's Seattle warehouse. The order is then packed and shipped. On average, customers get books five days after ordering. Amazon's success is driven by its comprehensive selection: The goal is that "If it's in print, it's in stock." The company also offers 10 to 30 percent discounts on most books.

For the first full year of 1996, analysts estimate revenues at well over $10 million. Bezos admits that orders increased through the year by 34 percent a month. And 44 percent of Amazon's sales are to repeat customers.

Cyberstores are coming online but some are also becoming traditional. The computer retailer, Gateway 2000, for example, has recently opened showrooms in Charlotte, North Carolina and New Haven, Connecticut where shoppers can compare models before ordering.[1]

Retailing is a fast-changing industry and marketing communications are a big part of the change. This chapter will focus on retailing, both traditional forms and new forms, and business-to-business marketing, where companies sell to other companies rather than to consumers.

Retail Advertising

This chapter deals with two special types of advertising—retail and business-to-business—that are not known for producing great advertising. Ads found in these two categories are sometimes described as dull and uninspiring. Such descriptions are unfair, however, given the limitations and special circumstances with which

---

[1]Adapted from Peter Burrows, "Let Your Fingers Do the Walking," *Business Week* (November 4, 1996):154–159; Machael H. Martin, "The Next Big Thing: A Bookstore?" *Fortune* (December 9, 1996):168–170.

both types of advertising must cope. These factors, as well as the special adjustments necessary to create effective business-to-business and retail advertising, will be discussed in this chapter.

Most discussions of advertising focus on commercials that run on the Super Bowl, full-page ads in *Time* magazine, and copy strategies used by companies like Procter & Gamble to reach their product's users. Often overlooked is **retail advertising,** which is used by local merchants to sell their products and services directly to consumers and which accounts for nearly half of all the money spent on advertising. Just as advertising is part of the marketing mix for nationally promoted products and services, it also plays an important role in the marketing or merchandising mix for retailers. Therefore, to understand retail advertising, it is first necessary to see how it differs from national brand advertising.

RETAIL ADVERTISING VERSUS NATIONAL ADVERTISING

Retail advertising is often called local advertising because the target market is frequently local in nature. However, institutions that may advertise locally, such as banks, financial services, and real estate organizations, are not considered part of the retail trade by the Bureau of the Census. Moreover, some retailers, such as Sears and J. C. Penney, advertise nationally. Thus, when we talk about retail advertising, we are referring to advertising disseminated by retail institutions. Although retailers try to create a local presence, a great deal of retail advertising is standardized across regions of the country or even nationally. Retail advertising is designed to perform several universal functions: sell a variety of products, encourage store traffic, deliver sales promotion messages, and create and communicate a store image or "personality."

Retail advertising differs from national advertising in various ways. First, retail advertising, whether sponsored by a national chain or a local retailer, is usually targeted at people living in the local community. Such advertising is customized to match the needs, wants, culture, and idiosyncrasies of these people. In comparison, national advertisers must deliver a standardized message that often deals with consumer generalities. Second, national advertising supports the brand(s) of the sponsor, whereas retail advertising may promote several different brands or even competing brands. The retailer's loyalty gravitates to whichever brand is selling best. An example of a retailer advertising a supplier's product line is the Foley's ad for Liz Claiborne. This is a long-running campaign featuring "52 Weeks of What to Wear" and the weekly ads try to creatively relate to the lives of the target audience. (See Ad 22.1.)

Retail advertising also has an inherent urgency. Everything about the ad pushes the consumer toward a behavior, typically visiting the store. Consequently, the retail ad includes price information, conditions of sales, colors, sizes, and so on. National advertising is more concerned with image and attitude change. As a result, there tends to be less copy and fewer specifics. The third difference is that retail advertising is customized, to some extent, to reflect the local store. Usually it includes basic information such as the store's name, address, telephone number, business hours, and so forth, as the Foley's ad (Ad 22.1) illustrates.

To build and maintain store traffic, a retailer must meet four objectives: build store *awareness*, create consumer *understanding* of items or services offered, *convince* consumers that the store's items and services are high quality or economical, and create *consumer desire* to shop at this particular store. In addition, most retailers use advertising to help attract new customers, build store loyalty, increase the amount of the average sale, maintain inventory balance by moving out overstocks and outdated merchandise, and help counter seasonal lows.

With a few exceptions, retail advertising is less sophisticated and more utilitarian than national advertising. There are several reasons for this. First, retail

Retail Advertising: A type of advertising used by local merchants who sell directly to consumers.

AD 22.1

WEEKLY ADS TRY TO CRE-
ATIVELY RELATE TO THE LIVES
OF THE TARGET AUDIENCE.

advertising is short term compared to national advertising. Most retail ads deal with price and run for only a few days, whereas a national ad may be used for months or years.

In addition, retailers can't justify high production costs for advertising. National advertisers can easily justify spending $5,000 to produce a newspaper ad when they are paying $200,000 to run it in 100 large markets. A local retailer that places an ad in the local newspaper might have a media cost of only $400, making it difficult to justify spending $5,000 on production.

Most retailers have little formal training in advertising and, therefore, are often uncomfortable making professional advertising decisions. Consequently, they rely on their media sales representatives to design and produce their ads. Most media advertising departments turn out several dozen ads a day, rather than working on one ad for several days (or weeks) as ad agencies do. Also, print media generally use *clip art* rather than custom art. Clip art services provide books of copyright-free pieces of art, which can be clipped and used as the advertiser sees fit. The ads work, but they are seen as generally less "creative" than national brand advertising.

COOPERATIVE ADVERTISING

Cooperative Advertising: A
form of advertising in which the
manufacturer reimburses the
retailer for part or all of the
advertising expenditures.

One way retailers can compensate for their smaller budgets and limited expertise is to take advantage of **cooperative advertising,** in which the manufacturer reimburses the retailer for part or all of the advertising expenses. Most manufacturers (or franchisers) have some type of ongoing promotional program that provides retailers with advertising support in the form of money and advertising materials. Funds for cooperative advertising are available subject to certain guidelines and are generally based on a percentage of sales to the retailer.

Co-op funds, which are sometimes referred to as *ad allowances*, are no longer just "a little something extra" from the manufacturer. Ad allowances have become so widespread, in fact, that most retailers won't even consider taking on a new brand, especially one in a heavily advertised category, without receiving some support. (This was also discussed in Chapter 18.)

Ad money, as it is also called, generally comes to retailers in one of three ways. An ad allowance is an amount that can change from month to month for each unit of purchase. The higher the amount, the more the retailer is expected to do. With an *accrual fund* the manufacturer automatically accrues, or sets aside, a certain percentage of a retailer's purchases that the retailer may use for advertising at any time within a specified period.

Vendor support programs are developed by retailers themselves. Large drug and discount chains, for example, will periodically schedule a special advertising supplement. Their suppliers are offered an opportunity to "buy" space in this supplement. Suppliers are generally promised that no competing brands will be included.

To receive co-op money retailers must send the manufacturer a **tear sheet**, which is proof that the ad ran, and an invoice showing the cost of the advertising. For broadcast ads, stations will provide the retailer with a letter, or affidavit, stating when the ad ran.

Manufacturers also make artwork available, which can be used for preparing catalogs and other print ads. Some manufacturers also provide a **dealer tag**, in which the store is mentioned at the end of a radio or television ad. Also available are window banners, bill inserts, and special direct-mail pieces, such as four-color supplements that carry the store's name and address.

The Robinson-Patman Act prohibits a manufacturer from offering one retailer a price or promotion incentive that will give that retailer an advantage over competitors in the same trading area. This restriction becomes especially delicate in food and drug store retailing, where almost all advertising is price advertising.

Tear Sheet: The pages from a newspaper on which an ad appears.

Dealer Tag: Time left at the end of a broadcast advertisement that permits identification of the local store.

TYPES OF RETAIL ADVERTISING

Despite the great diversity in retailing, the nature of the advertising employed can be placed in one of two categories: product or institutional. *Institutional retail advertising* sells the store as an enjoyable place to shop. Through institutional advertising, the store helps to establish its image as a leader in fashion, price, and wide merchandise selection, as well as superior service, or quality, or whatever image the store chooses to cultivate.

Product advertising presents specific merchandise for sale and urges customers to come to the store immediately to buy it. This form of advertising helps to create and maintain the store's reputation through its merchandise. Product advertising centers around themes relating to merchandise that is new, exclusive, and of superior quality and designs (called *nonpromotional advertising*), as well as around themes relating to complete assortments and merchandise events (called *assortment advertising*). Sales announcements, special promotions, and other immediate-purpose ads are other forms of product advertising. When the sale price dominates the ad, it is called promotional or *sales advertising*. When sales items are interspersed with regular-priced items in the ad, it is referred to as semipromotional advertising.

PRICE ADVERTISING

In recent years retail advertising has focused on price—more specifically on sale or discounted prices. Many retailers now use any reason they can find to have a sale (Presidents' Day, Tax Time, Over-stocked). There are also EOM (end-of-month) sales and even hourly sales (Ayre's 14-Hour Sales, K mart's Midnight

Madness Sale). This trend has led to retailers' complaints about the disappearance of consumer loyalty as people move from store to store searching for the best price.

As strange as it may seem, the items that retailers advertise at reduced prices are often not the ones they really want to sell. In order to offer a reduced price, retailers generally have to sacrifice part of their profit on each of these products. Sometimes stores even offer items for less than they paid for them merely to attract customers to the store. These items are called **loss leaders.**

Loss Leader: Product advertised at or below cost in order to build store traffic.

TRENDS IN RETAILING

The good old days of the mom-and-pop retailers who knew all their customers personally and who could count on their continued loyalty are gone for most retailers. During the last 40 years there have been dramatic changes in retailing, many of which have had a direct impact on retail advertising.

IN-STORE MARKETING

As competition and clutter have hit the aisles in many retail establishments, more and more attention is being focused on in-store marketing, also called *merchandising.* In-store marketing is the area that specializes in designing materials that communicate sales messages at the point where the consumer is ready to make a purchase. A growth area, in-store merchandising accounts for approximately $660 million, according to a 1996 industry annual report.[2]

Obviously this overlaps with such sales promotion tools as point-of-purchase displays. But other tools, which are primarily signage, also are important. Banners, posters, *shelf talkers* (signs attached to a shelf that let the consumer take away some piece of information or a coupon), end-aisle displays, shopping cart ads, among other things, are all the tools used in merchandising to remind customers of brands and stimulate sales. And new interactive electronic kiosks complete with a touch-screen computer, CD-ROM-based databases, full graphics, and product photos are moving into the aisles in many stores where they provide more information about more products than the store can ever stock on its shelves.[3] The turmoil in this area of marketing communication is discussed in the Issues and Controversies box.

Merchandising firms and in-store marketing specialists have developed as manufacturers have eliminated or downsized their sales forces. Retailers have even less time, money, labor, and interest in installing in-store marketing communication programs. These companies help to handle the increasing crush of in-store promotional materials. As *PROMO* magazine observed, "Virtually all in-store promotions require staffing levels that are beyond manufacturers' capabilities." And that's the reason for the in-store specialists.[4]

In a form of two-level communication, these programs involve both trade and consumer marketing programs—the trade arranges for the messages to be seen and the consumer responds to them. As Dan Ailloni-Charas, chairperson of a New York company that specializes in in-store marketing, points out, "No marketing vehicle delivers better or faster results in launching new products or enhancing the franchise of existing ones."[5]

---

[2] "A Virtual Staff," *PROMO* (November 1996):75–76.

[3] Jim Killam, "Interactive Kiosks Score In-Store," *Sales and Marketing Strategies & News* (March 1996):19.

[4] "A Virtual Staff," p. 75.

[5] Dan Ailloni-Charas, "Beyond the Upheaval in In-Store Marketing," *Brandweek* (September 23, 1996):18.

The supermarket aisle is also a marketing battleground with in-store marketing pioneers throwing up beachheads and limping away from the field. In-store sampling companies have been particularly hard hit as Advo sold its Marketing Force division at what's been reported to be a significant loss. Likewise Time Warner is trying to sell its Media One and Smart Demo companies after only a few years in this business and Supermarketing and Sunflower are either being sold or going under.

The knock-down, drag-out battle, however, is between Norwalk, Connecticut-based ActMedia, the dominant player in on-shelf coupon-dispensing machines, and News America In-Store, a newly formed unit of New York-based News America, which has also introduced to the trade its own on-shelf, paper-based instant couponing machine. (News America is the marketing arm of Rupert Murdoch's news empire.) ActMedia had enjoyed a lock on this highly profitable vehicle. The battle will likely be waged on price (marketers currently pay roughly $45 per store per machine per month) for exclusive rights in roughly 20,000 prime supermarket sites. ActMedia has its Instant Coupon Machines (ICMs) in more than 11,000 outlets, including Vons, Kroger, Safeway, Certified Grocers, Price Chopper, and Fred Meyer. New America reportedly has agreements for its launch with A&P, Jewel, Acme, Farmer Jack, Waldbaum's, Food Emporium, and Schnuck's.

ICMs first appeared in supermarket aisles in 1990. They now account for most of ActMedia's $346 million in revenues, a figure that has been increasing dramatically throughout the mid-1990s. A *PROMO* magazine study of in-store marketing preferences among consumers found that 46 percent used coupons from shelf dispensers and 67 percent said they expect to use them in the future.

ActMedia's success also reflects its ability to offer other in-store promotions—cart ads, aisle signs, in-store demos—which can be used to extend the impact of the coupon program.

But why is there so much stress in the aisles? One expert speculates that rampant price competition has marginalized income to the point where costs exceed income and these promotions are, therefore, no longer cost-effective. That added to the increased use of *slotting allowances* (charges that retailers make to manufacturers in return for putting the product on the shelf) have reduced budgets for in-store promotional activities and made them much more competitive among themselves.

The importance of in-store marketing, however, should not be discounted just because it's become such a competitive arena. The race is on to find even more creative ways to reach shoppers with messages to which they will respond.

DISCUSSION QUESTIONS

1. Observe the amount of in-store promotion in your favorite supermarket, discount store, and department store. Do the aisles seem more cluttered or less?

2. Are any of the merchandising efforts more effective in your view than others?

Sources: "Store Wars," *PROMO* (November 1996):73–74; Dan Ailloni-Charas, "Beyond the Upheaval in In-Store Marketing," *Brandweek* (September 23, 1996):182.

NONSTORE RETAILING

Nonstore retailing is when the exchange between the manufacturer/retailer and the consumer takes place outside the traditional retail store. In the case of Mary Kay Cosmetics and Lands' End, the companies produce the product and sell it through door-to-door and catalog selling, respectively. Lillian Vernon, in contrast, purchases products from a variety of manufacturers and sells the products through its catalog. The opening story discussed the newest area of nonstore retailing on the Web.

Nonstore retailing has grown in popularity for a variety of reasons. Most notably, the time-conscious consumer is no longer inclined to spend hours shopping for goods and services. Simultaneously, the quality and selection of the merchandise sold through nonstore retailing have greatly improved. Warranties and guarantees remove the risk associated with purchasing unseen merchandise. Finally, improvements in mailing lists have better matched the marketer with potential customers. The use of nonstore retailing has shifted a great deal of retail advertising toward direct marketing and direct mail.

LOYALTY PROGRAMS

Frequent-flyer programs in the airline industry developed this category of loyalty-building programs. Actually one of the earliest loyalty programs was the local retail stores' credit programs where customers could either use the store's credit card or simply charge to an open bill. The growth of the large credit card companies such as Visa and Mastercard have made many of these retailer cards obsolete. This is both a blessing to the stores who no longer have to maintain the credit database, but it is also a loss in that the stores have lost this very important link with their customers and are largely unable to identify their "regular" customers anymore.

Other relationship-building, frequent-shopper programs are being designed, however, to recreate that link to the "regulars." Many grocery stores are implementing card-based programs that reward shoppers who present the card at the cash register with discounts and special sale prices. When scanned electronically (*swiped*), the cards also register customer identification as well as shopping information into the store's database.[6]

CONSOLIDATION

Ownership consolidation, especially among department stores and specialty chains, has brought mass merchandising to many stores that formerly operated on a smaller scale. This consolidation of power among fewer retailers has changed the nature of the relationship between manufacturers and retailers. Retailers now dictate terms of sale, delivery dates, and product specifications. Wal-Mart, for example, has so much clout that Procter & Gamble has placed some 70 employees near Wal-Mart's Arkansas headquarters to quickly service the account. Consolidation has also given retailers a much greater interest in mass advertising. For example, Pier 1 Imports, a once-small specialty retailer, now spends $40 million annually on billable media. Retailers such as Wal-Mart have also been able to dictate the creative strategy of many manufacturers. In addition, they have created tremendous growth in the use of different media, such as *free-standing inserts* (FSI), in lieu of traditional newspaper space.

DEMOGRAPHICS

Several demographic changes in our society have a bearing on retail advertising. These changes include time compression, the aging of the population, geomarketing, and market fragmentation. For families in which both spouses work, time is a valuable commodity. As a result, creative avenues must be found to reach consumers with messages that are short and sweet.

Contemporary women, for example, have broken out of the stereotyped homemaker role and are now being featured in a number of different lifestyle cues, such as depicted earlier in the Liz Claiborne ad (see Ad 22.1).

The population is made up of more elderly people, who are knowledgeable and adept at shopping and have definite opinions on the value of brand names and the relationship between price and quality. Advertising copy must facilitate such comparisons.

PRINCIPLE The primary factor in retail targeting is geography.

In targeting consumers, a retailer's first concern is geography: Where do my customers live? How far will they drive to come to my store? The next concern is consumer taste. *Geomarketing* is a phenomenon geared to the increasing diversity in tastes and preferences. Retailers are attempting to develop offers that appeal to consumers in different parts of the country as well as in different neighborhoods in the same suburb. For example, H.E.B. Supermarkets operates its stores in both central and south Texas. In San Antonio, the stores located in Mexican-American neighborhoods carry a very different merchandise assortment than do those located in neighborhoods dominated by upscale apartments and condominiums. In contrast, national advertising targeting is more concerned with other factors such as age, income, education, and lifestyle.

Markets will continue to decrease in size as competitors segment them according to values, lifestyles, demographics, geographics, and product benefits. Advertising strategies must place greater emphasis on developing the appropriate image to match the consumer's lifestyle and less emphasis on price promotions.

[6]"Card-Carrying Loyalists?" *PROMO* (November 1996):69–72.

Ultimately, consumers want to be assured that the quality, value, service, and price are all there.

CATEGORY SPECIALIZATION

Many retailers have begun to specialize in merchandising products, such as electronics, running shoes, tennis equipment, baked potatoes, toys, and the like. The largest of these retail specialists are referred to as *superstores*. Examples include HQ Office Supplies, Sportmart, Home Base, and Circuit City. The idea behind the superstore is fairly simple: Provide customers with the ultimate assortment in a product category—say, hardware—and they will come. In these cases retail advertising has become more like manufacturer advertising in that fewer products are highlighted and the emphasis is on image rather than a quick sale. Benetton, a clothing company that specializes in Italian sportswear, is an example of this type of retailing. Its ads often feature founder Luciano Benetton touting two or three of his new designs. Originality, quality, and image are always emphasized over price. However, as will become apparent in the discussion that follows, price copy is still prevalent because of growing competition in retailing and an uncertain economy.

CREATING THE RETAIL AD

The primary difference between national and retail ad copy is the emphasis retail advertising places on prices and store name. Store image should be as important to a retailer as brand image is to a manufacturer. In order to build store traffic, ads are designed either to emphasize a reduced price on a popular item or to promote the store image by focusing on such things as unusual or varied merchandise, friendly clerks, or prestige brands.

IMAGE OR PRICE

For retail operations that sell products and services where there is little product differentiation, such as gasoline, banking, and car rentals, a positive, distinctive image is a valuable asset. The retailer can only convey this image through advertising. The Johnson Controls ads in the Concepts and Applications box try to create an image for a hard-to-describe product.

Price also can be a factor in establishing a store's image. Most discount stores signal their type of merchandise with large, bold prices. Several specialty retailers emphasize price by offering coupons in much of their print advertising. Featuring prices doesn't necessarily apply only to ads that give the store a bargain or a discount image, however. Price can help the consumer comparison-shop without visiting the store. Many customers appreciate this basic information.

EXECUTING RETAIL ADS

Because the main objective of retail ads is to attract customers, store location (or telephone number, if advertising a service) is essential. For merchandise that is infrequently purchased, such as cars, furniture, wallpaper, and hearing aids, the ad should include a map or mention a geographical reference point (for example, three blocks north of the state capitol building) in addition to the regular street address.

A creative mistake some retailers make is wanting to be the star or key spokesperson in their advertising. This is especially noticeable in broadcast commercials, where a presenter needs acting talent or training. Although hiring the acting superstars of advertising is beyond the budgets of most retailers, competent and affordable actors abound in most cities. In fact, local celebrities typically have greater attention-getting potential than does imported talent.

Small- and medium-sized retailers often save money by using stock artwork. All daily newspapers subscribe to clip art services that provide a wide range of photographs and line drawings. Larger retailers or upscale specialty retailers, such

CONCEPTS AND APPLICATIONS

AIR CONDITIONING FOR THE PARTHENON?

An award-winning campaign for Johnson Controls explains how the company's services help to manage building environments. The company offers services from mail services to heating, ventilation, air conditioning, structural maintenance, landscaping, painting, cleaning, security, and even food service. In other words, the company offers an integrated facility management program for the entire building.

That's a complicated product to advertise. It's also not one that inspires creative people to run to their computers with breakthrough creative ideas. The creative people at Milwaukee-based Cramer-Krasselt rose to the challenge and turned the mundane into monuments.

THIS CAMPAIGN BY JOHNSON CONTROLS IS AN EXAMPLE OF CREATIVE ADVERTISING USED IN BUSINESS-TO-BUSINESS MARKETING.

The ads not only explain that Johnson Controls can put all necessary building systems together for an end result of comfort, as well as performance satisfaction, they won awards for their creativity. The Kelly awards are given to the best magazine ads and this campaign, even though it is a business-to-business campaign rather than consumer advertising, is a winner.

The ads use beautiful images of historical sites like the Parthenon, the Leaning Tower of Pisa, a Canyon de Chelly pueblo, and El Castillo in Chichen Itza to explain what environmental building controls can do. For example, the ad for the Anasazi pueblo high on its cliff is headlined, "Building se-

as The Denver Hardware (see Ad 22.2), generally have their art custom-designed, which gives all of their ads a similar look and helps confer a distinctive image. Retailers have also found ways to make their television production more efficient by using a "donut" format in which the opening and closing sections are the same, whereas the middle changes to focus on different merchandise.

The recent trend in shopping center advertising is to produce a slick four-color "magazine" that carries editorial material, such as recipes, a calendar of local events, and other topics of local interest, in addition to ads for the retail stores in curity is quite good, but we'd recommend some improvements in dust filtration." It's a relevant message with a touch of humor. For the Parthenon, the headline reads, "The ventilation is fine, but we'd work on the cold zones in the lobby and north-facing rooms." The copy continues to provide the necessary detail about the company's specialty areas, but the headline brings the whole story into comic relief.

DISCUSSION QUESTIONS

1. As this campaign continues, the creative people on the account wonder if they should move to images of modern architecture. What do you think?

2. You work for Ramsey Corporation, a competitor that would like to build a bigger practice in this same area of environmental building controls; however, your company is losing business because of the effectiveness of the Johnson Controls campaign. How would you compete against this campaign? Develop a proposal for an advertising strategy that would turn around your company's business and make it equally as competitive in this market.

Sources: Alice Z. Cueo, "The Last Laugh Belongs to Goodby, Silverstein," *Advertising Age*/Creativity Special Supplement (May 1995):K6–K17; Lee Kovel, "Print," *Creativity* (August 1994):22.

WINDOWLESS DESIGN SAVES ENERGY. *However,* LET'S CONSIDER REGULAR & *Thorough* INSPECTIONS *for* STRUCTURAL FATIGUE.

EACH BUILDING *may* be unique in its own right, yet there are certain critical elements that every truly great one possesses.

Comfortable temperature and humidity levels. Soft, balanced lighting. Nicely maintained appearance. And, of course, superior structural integrity.

At Johnson Controls, our mission is to create this ideal building environment.

Outsourcing is a prime way to make this happen. It's a tool whereby you contract with an outside company to perform typically in-house services that are often quite distinct from your core business. Outsourcing helps lower operating costs while allowing you to tap into a resource of specialized skills.

With over 40 years experience in integrated facility management, we have the skills to manage an entire building. Everything from the physical plant to landscaping.

We can offer services like vibration analysis and infrared imaging inspection. Services that can predict structural problems before they occur. And allow you to schedule maintenance so your building works right all the time.

As the experienced leader, we realize that any building can become a more productive environment. There's no reason why your building can't as well.

With help from Johnson Controls. People committed to improving life in the great indoors. To learn more, please call 1-800-972-8040 ext. 134.

JOHNSON CONTROLS

[LEANING TOWER OF PISA, *Pisa, Italy*]

the shopping center. Centers interested in projecting a status image to upscale consumers make the greatest use of this magazine concept.

WHO DOES THE CREATIVE WORK?

Most retail advertising is created and produced by one or a combination of the following: in-house staff, media, ad agencies, and freelancers. The larger the retail operation, the more likely it is to have an in-house advertising staff. An in-house agency can guarantee a consistent look and can react on short notice. One disad-

AD 22.2

WELL-DESIGNED ADS CAN
DELIVER AN IMAGE TO THE
STORE, AS THIS AD FOR AN UP-
SCALE HARDWARE STORE ILLUS-
TRATES.

vantage of the in-house agency is lack of creativity, as many good creative people prefer working for a multiclient agency where the work is more diversified and the pay is often higher.

All local media create and produce ads for retailers. With the exception of television, most provide this service free. The medium- and larger-sized newspapers and stations often have people whose only job is to write and produce ads.

Although some professional retail ads are created by agencies, this is the most costly way to produce ads. Also, because agencies work for many different clients, they cannot always respond as quickly as an in-house agency can. Few agencies are prepared to handle the large number of day-to-day copy changes that are characteristic of major retail advertising. What an agency can best do for a retailer is develop an image or position and some ad formats that the store's in-house creative people can use for fast-breaking advertising. Television spots, particularly if they are more image oriented than product or price focused, may be created by outside agencies.

Freelancers often provide a good compromise between an in-house staff and an ad agency. They generally charge a lower hourly rate than do ad agencies because they work out of their homes and, therefore, have minimal overhead.

BUYING AND SELLING LOCAL MEDIA

Perhaps the most rapidly changing area in retail advertising is the buying and selling of local media time and space. On the buying side, retailers are becoming more sophisticated about media as they are being forced to work with tighter budgets, are getting more advertising help and advice from their suppliers, are being exposed to more media ideas at association workshops and seminars, and are being educated by a growing number of media salespeople.

At the same time, local media competition has significantly increased. Nearly all major markets now have, in addition to network affiliates, at least one local independent plus a public television station (which now solicits underwriting, a type of soft-sell advertising). These stations, along with local advertising that is now being sold by the national cable networks, have created many more television opportunities for the retailer. Most of the top 50 markets have at least one local magazine offering retailers high-quality, four-color ads to reach the up-scale consumer. Examples are *Los Angeles Magazine*, *Palm Springs Life*, and *Colorado Homes & Lifestyle*.

The increase in competition for the retailers' advertising dollar has resulted in a different type of selling. Salespeople increasingly emphasize advertising and promotion ideas rather than just rate cards and circulation figures. Unfortunately, many retailers still buy advertising strictly on price or number of spots. Some retailers don't realize that five spots during morning-drive time on the market's leading radio station can sometimes reach more people than can 50 spots that run between 2:00 A.M. and 4:00 A.M.

RETAIL MEDIA STRATEGY

PRINCIPLE Local retail advertisers usually prefer reach over frequency.

Unlike national advertisers, retailers generally prefer reach over frequency. A retailer with a "1/3 Off All Women's Casual Shoes" ad doesn't have to tell this more than once or twice to women interested in saving money on a pair of casual shoes. In contrast, a national advertiser with an image campaign like Coke continually needs to remind soft-drink users that "Coke Is It."

Because retailers can choose from many local media, they must be careful not to buy a lot of wasted circulation (see Chapter 9). Take, for example, an ordinary bakery in an area of dominant interest (ADI) like Des Moines, Iowa, which has approximately 380,000 households and 24 other competing bakeries. Over 80 percent of this bakery's business could come from within a three-mile radius that contains only 6 percent of the ADI's households. If this bakery uses television advertising that covers the total ADI, the bakery will be wasting over 90 percent of its advertising dollars.

Successful retailers use media that minimize waste. Direct mail, which is narrowly targeted, is now the second-largest advertising medium used by retailers. Also, many newspapers can zone the delivery of advertising circulars and inserts, offering geographical targeting to neighborhoods, counties, or even zip codes. Outdoor, of course, is particularly well suited to geographic or location-specific targeting. A Massachusetts bank, Springfield Institution for Savings, used outdoor to advertise its competitive advantage over larger rivals in this award-winning campaign. (See Ad 22.3.)

MEDIA ALTERNATIVES

Retailers may choose from the entire arsenal of media alternatives. Both local and national retailers may use an identical media mix to reach a particular local target market. In general, however, local retailers are interested only in local media and stay clear of media that reach an audience beyond their immediate markets. There are several media that are more relevant to retailers.

NEWSPAPERS

Newspapers have always made up the bulk of the retailer's advertising, probably because the local nature of newspapers fits the retailer's desire for geographic coverage, prestige, and immediacy. In addition, newspapers are a participative medium that people read in part for the advertising. In fact, many people use newspapers as a shopping guide. Also, retailers can gain some measure of audience selectivity by advertising in specific sections of the paper, such as the sports, society, and financial pages.

Most retailers that advertise regularly make space contracts with the newspaper. In the contract the retailer agrees to use a certain amount of space over the

AD 22.3

A MASSACHUSETTS BANK,
SPRINGFIELD INSTITUTION FOR
SAVINGS, USED OUTDOOR TO
ADVERTISE ITS COMPETITIVE AD-
VANTAGE OVER LARGER RIVALS
IN THIS AWARD-WINNING CAM-
PAIGN.

year and pay a certain amount per line, which is lower than the paper's open rate for the same space. The lower rate is simply a quantity discount.

In addition to special rates, newspapers have developed several other products or services to remain competitive. Many newspapers will provide retail advertisers with their zip/postal code circulation reports, which identify the circulation level for that newspaper in the various zip codes. This information, combined with zone editions of the paper (certain versions of the paper go to certain counties, cities, and so on), greatly reduces the wasted circulation often associated with large newspapers. Special advertising sections, such as preprints, can be inserted in these various papers. Specialty-type papers, such as shoppers, have also emerged.

SHOPPERS AND PREPRINTS

Free-distribution newspapers (shoppers) that are dropped off at millions of suburban homes once or twice each week are becoming increasingly popular advertising outlets for retailers. More than 3,000 such papers are published in the United States, such as *Center Island Pennysavers*, distributed in Long Island, New York.

Preprints are advertising circulars furnished by a retailer for distribution as a *free-standing insert (FSI)* in newspapers. In recent years preprinted inserts have also become popular with retailers striving for greater market coverage. For example, preprints account for more than 80 percent of Wal-Mart's advertising budgets.

MAGAZINES

Many magazines have regional or metropolitan editions. They enable local retailers to buy exposure to the audience within their trading area only. Sears, Kmart, and J. C. Penney advertise in monthlies targeted to particular audience segments and in weeklies to accommodate short-term sales patterns. Local retailers use magazines primarily for institutional or image ads.

BROADCAST MEDIA

Local retailers advertise on television and radio as well, but broadcast media are used primarily to supplement newspaper advertising. Both offer important advantages over print media. Radio has a relatively low cost and a high degree of geographic and audience selectivity. It also provides high flexibility in spot scheduling, and this flexibility carries over into creativity. Radio will help retail advertisers write the ads, provide live hookups from the store or any other location, and is able to take advantage of last-minute events. For example, a station in Colorado Springs helped a hardware store sell hundreds of snow shovels when an unexpected storm dumped 7 inches of snow one April morning.

Many of the same advantages are found in local television. The cost of television is higher, however, as is the creative expertise needed to produce satisfactory commercials. Television stations will produce commercials for a fee. The expense problem has been reduced somewhat by the advent of cable television with its ability to show a retail commercial in the local market only. Cable also offers the retailer the kind of selectivity that network television cannot. Undoubtedly, as more and more homes are hooked up to cable, retailers will view television as an affordable, effective media alternative.

DIRECTORIES

Telephone directories (the Yellow Pages) are important advertising media for retailers. In the Yellow Pages the retailer pays for an alphabetical listing (and a larger *display ad*, if desired) within a business category. The overwhelming majority of retailers advertise in the Yellow Pages (refer to Chapter 17). The advantages are widespread customer usage and long life (one year or more). The disadvantages included limited flexibility and long lead times for new ads. Retailers that don't get their ads to the Yellow Pages in time (for example, a camera-ready ad must often be mailed by May or June for the September directory) will have to wait an entire year.

DIRECT RESPONSE

Direct response is a medium retailers use extensively to communicate their product offerings to a select group of consumers. In direct-response advertising, the retailer creates its own advertisement and distributes it directly to consumers either through the mail or through the personal distribution of circulars, handbills, and other printed matter. Although direct-response advertising is expensive in terms of cost per thousand, it is actually the most selective medium because the ads are read only by people the retailer selects. It is also a personal form of advertising and extremely flexible. Direct-response advertising can include pictures, letters, records, pencils, coins, coupons, premiums, samples, and any other gifts the retailer chooses.

RETAIL MARKET RESEARCH

Information about the local market is becoming more and more valuable to retailers. Although retail stores that belong to a national chain often receive research findings from their parent company, most independent retailers must depend on the media and their suppliers for local marketing research information. Many commercial research companies like Simmons and PRIZM provide information on the top markets.

One of the most valuable, yet inexpensive, types of research a retailer can conduct is to identify its customers. This can be done by analyzing credit card files or by sponsoring a contest or sweepstakes. Businesses that issue their own credit cards report that two-thirds of their sales come from their credit card customers. Smart retailers send up to a dozen direct-mail pieces to these customers each year in addition to their regular advertising. Sweepstakes use an entry form that asks for customer name, address, age, income, or whatever information is desired.

Retailers can also conduct focus groups to help determine their store's image. These are best if arranged and conducted by an outside, trained research service. To help test ad copy, one furniture retailer had a direct-mail piece made up for a mattress sale and sent it to a limited number of households. When he found it had a relatively good response, he then placed the same copy and artwork in a newspaper ad.

Just as most retailers can't justify spending large sums on ad production, neither can they for marketing research. Retailers have direct consumer contact and can quickly determine which ads work. That's one advantage they have over national advertisers.

BUSINESS-TO-BUSINESS ADVERTISING

Advertising directed at people in business who buy or specify products for business use is called **business-to-business advertising.** A recent study found that

Business-to-Business Advertising: Advertising directed at people who buy or specify products for business use.

business-to-business marketers captured $51.7 billion or 37.4 percent of the total spent by U.S. businesses on marketing and communications.[7] Table 22.1 lists the tools used by business-to-business marketers to promote their services and products. The sales force is the most important marketing communication area followed by advertising, then direct marketing and sales promotions.

As Figure 22.1 shows, these people work in a variety of business areas, such as commercial enterprises (retailing and manufacturing), government agencies (federal, state, and local), and nonprofit institutions (universities and hospitals), and purchase many different types of products. Table 22.2 breaks down the business-to-business marketing communication spending by industries. Services is the largest marketing area, followed by wholesale, then finance/insurance/real estate.

Although personal selling is the most common method of communicating with business buyers, business advertising is used to create product awareness, enhance the firm's reputation, and support salespeople and other channel members. A purchaser in the business market, just as a consumer, goes through a search process beginning with gathering information about alternatives, processing this information, learning about available products, determining which alternatives match the perceived needs most closely, and carrying through by making a purchase.

[7]Char Kosek, "Business-to-Business Grabs $51.7 Billion," *Advertising Age* (June 1996):S3–S4.

TABLE 22.1	BUSINESS-TO-BUSINESS CATEGORY SPENDING	
	1995	
	($ BILNS)	**%**
Sales force management*	11.9	22.9
Advertising	11.3	21.9
Direct marketing	6.3	12.3
Sales promotions	6.3	12.2
Trade shows	5.5	10.7
Public relations	2.6	5.1
Market research	2.5	4.7
Other	2.0	3.9
Premiums/Incentives	1.9	3.7
Online	1.4	2.6
Total	51.7	100.0

*Excludes compensation and commissions

Source: Outfront Marketing study. Reprinted with permission from *Advertising Age.* Copyright Crain Communications Inc.

Graphic by John Hall

TABLE 22.2	BUSINESS-TO-BUSINESS COMMUNICATIONS SPENDING BY INDUSTRY	
	($ MILNS)	**% OF TOTAL MARCOMM**
Services	17,432	59.5
Wholesale	8,439	69.4
Finance, insurance & real estate	6,329	48.9
Computers—software[1]	3,309	56.8
Industrial machinery (no computers)	2,885	73.2
Transportation[2]	2,808	73.9
Electronic/electric equipment	1,717	76.5
Chemicals & allied products	1,590	56.3
Computers & hardware	1,494	59.3
Metals	1.456	59.5
Instruments & related products	1,348	74.1
Rubber	809	71.6
Furniture & fixtures	732	67.7
Communications/utilities	518	20.9
Food & beverage	496	39.2
Construction	382	54.7
Printing & publishing	348	42.9
Textile & apparel	247	40.5
Computers—services[1]	190	91.4
Lumber & wood	180	71.4
Paper & allied products	133	48.7
Mining	131	66.3
Agriculture	131	32.3
Stone/clay, glass & concrete	94	70.8
Petroleum & coal	90	61.1
Average (per company; all industries)	4.6	59.9

[1]Subset of total services category
[2]SIC 3700, 3799; 4000, 4789

FIGURE 22.1

THE DIVERSITY OF BUSINESS
MARKETS AND PRODUCTS PUR-
CHASED.

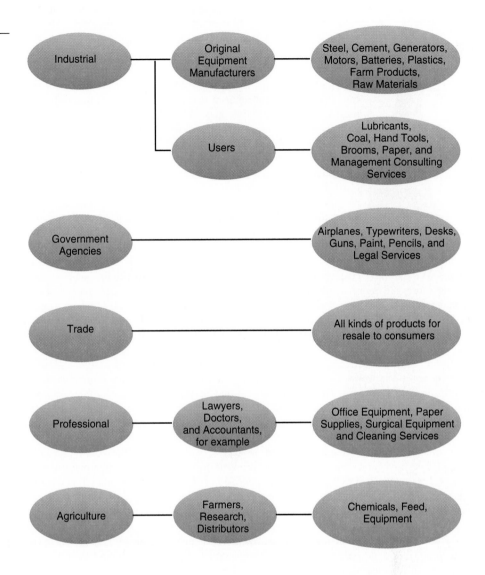

In the business arena, however, many people can be involved in the purchasing decision—people from different functional areas, such as marketing, manufacturing, or purchasing, who have varying information needs. For example, when a purchasing decision might result in a product change, such as altering the product's materials or packaging, marketing interest centers on product salability; manufacturing interest centers on production costs. Thus, business advertising is also used to (1) reach the various influencers involved and (2) communicate the different information needs. The profile of Jean Oursler describes the work of someone who specializes in pharmaceutical advertising, a particular type of business-to-business advertising.

TYPES OF BUSINESS-TO-BUSINESS ADVERTISING

Information needs also depend on the type of business market the business advertiser is trying to reach. The business arena is comprised of five very distinct markets, each of which tends to purchase products and services quite differently. These markets are most frequently referred to as the *industrial, government, trade, professional,* and *agricultural* markets.

Pharmaceutical advertising? Haven't you heard of it? If you haven't, think about investigating this rapidly growing industry. Start by looking at health care and what is happening in that industry. As the population gets older, prescription drug usage is expected to continue to make dramatic increases. New pharmaceutical products will continue to be introduced into the marketplace as medical technology becomes more sophisticated. Additionally, many prescription products currently on the market will start losing their prescription patents by the turn of the century and will try to switch to over the counter. Some products are doing this already, like acid blockers and nicotine patches. With all these changes, pharmaceutical companies are turning more and more to pharmaceutical agencies to help them develop brand strategies so they can increase marketshare for their products. That means more business for pharmaceutical advertising agencies, which translates into more jobs.

My name is Jean Oursler. I work as an account manager at CommonHealth USA, the largest pharmaceutical communications agency in the world. I didn't start off in pharmaceutical advertising. My career started on Madison Avenue in consumer advertising. I worked on several consumer product launches, and it was always exciting to see my product on television or in a popular magazine. However, after a couple of years of consumer advertising, I started to feel it wasn't enough. I wanted more than just hawking products to consumers; I wanted to work on products that help people. I decided to conduct some research on different advertising industries where I could best use my skills. Where did my research take me? It took me to the pharmaceutical advertising industry.

Pharmaceutical advertising agencies traditionally promote prescription or health products to professionals like physicians or pharmacists rather than the general population. Some accounts are very high science; examples are HIV and cancer drugs. Other accounts are more consumer oriented, such as antacids or baby formula.

I'm sure you are thinking, "That's great, but isn't pharmaceutical advertising very different from consumer? Isn't it boring? And doesn't it require advanced scientific knowledge to understand how a product works?" Perhaps you were someone who hated science in school. I fit that description. But that has not been a problem. In fact, I find pharmaceutical advertising to be very similar to consumer advertising. The main difference is the type of product you are promoting. Instead of promoting soda, you are promoting an antihistamine.

In pharmaceutical advertising, you still need to develop strategies to position your product, and you are still marketing a product to a target audience. However, instead of thinking of your target audience in terms of male 18 to 24 or female 35 to 54, your target audience consists of family physicians, neurologists, pharmacists, or physician assistants, just to name a few. Also, research doesn't come from Nielson. It comes from IMS or Scott Levin.

As an account manager, I'm involved in developing marketing plans and annual objectives that help increase product usage. We also work closely with our clients to develop brand character and long-term positioning strategies. I'm still responsible for guiding my creative team to develop advertising that is impactful and on strategy. That isn't really very different from what I was doing in consumer advertising.

What I find to be really different between the two industries is how the strategy is executed. When you work in consumer advertising, you usually can see your commercial on television, read it in a magazine, or hear it on the radio. In pharmaceutical advertising, while you see your ad in a medical journal, you also use a variety of other vehicles to deliver your message to your target audience. There are direct mail campaigns, sales aides, flash cards, training videos, convention materials, booth graphics, and product monographs, etc. Every day pharmaceutical advertisers are finding new ways to reach professionals, so there are many new tactics to learn.

If you are not convinced that pharmaceutical advertising is totally for you because you are determined to work in consumer advertising, there is an area that combines both worlds. It is called direct-to-consumer advertising or DTC. A DTC campaign is prescription drug advertising to the general population rather than professionals. These campaigns generally appear in traditionally consumer vehicles, such as television, radio, and magazines. In DTC advertising, you develop the same tactics as in consumer advertising, but at the same time you are exposed to the pharmaceutical side of the product. Many people who are making the transition into pharmaceutical advertising really enjoy DTC because it offers a little of both worlds. In my experience, many of these people, after working on DTC for a while, make the transition to a strictly pharmaceutical drug.

Let me tell you some of the best things about working in the pharmaceutical advertising industry. First, pharmaceutical advertising companies are more stable than consumer agencies. One of the reasons for this is that clients are much more likely to stay at one pharmaceutical advertising agency than move their business to another. In contrast, with consumer advertising, you are always reading about clients leaving one advertising agency for another one. That just doesn't happen very often in the pharmaceutical business. Additionally, there are always new business opportunities in pharmaceutical advertising as new pharmaceutical products are developed. Existing clients often increase their current business at the agency as their products grow. That's great because there is always something new and exciting to work on, so your interest level stays high. Another bonus is that due to the stability of the industry, you will probably always have a job.

Finally, what I like most about working in pharmaceutical advertising is that it gives me a great feeling of satisfaction. It is wonderful to listen to physicians speak about my product and how it helped patients get better. I also enjoy hearing patients talk in focus groups about how my product makes a difference in their lives.

I would strongly encourage any student who is interested in marketing to explore pharmaceutical advertising. It is a stable field that is growing very rapidly and is looking for new people. It is not as difficult to learn as you think, even if you didn't like science in school. It provides you with the same marketing experiences as consumer advertising, yet gives you a sense of helping other people, not just hawking a product. From account to creative, media to traffic, there is a place for you in the pharmaceutical advertising industry.

AD 22.4

THIS AD STRESSES THE TECHNI-
CAL ADVANTAGES OF DALY &
WOLCOTT'S INTEGRATED MAN-
AGEMENT SOFTWARE TO POTEN-
TIAL BUSINESS USERS.

Imagine Your Company Working Like This.

Application Plus® is the integrated enterprise
software that makes all your systems work as one.
Smoothly, and toward a single objective.
  Application Plus turns complex functions into
a simple operation. So that everyone in your
organization can get the information they need,
when and how they need it, and share it with those
who need to know.
  Application Plus gets to work quickly,
managing your enterprise with proven, trouble-free
reliability, no matter what your hardware, operating
or database system.
  Managing software has suddenly gotten a lot
easier. Now what more could you ask?

Daly&Wolcott
INTEGRATED MANAGEMENT SOFTWARE

Daly & Wolcott, Inc., 21st Floor, One Hospital Trust Plaza, Providence, RI 02903
Telephone: (800) 343-2414, ext. 336, Fax: (401) 351-8484
Or visit us at http://www.dalywolcott.com
ATLANTA • CHICAGO • DALLAS • LOS ANGELES • PROVIDENCE

INDUSTRIAL ADVERTISING

Original equipment manufacturers (OEMs), such as IBM and General Motors, purchase industrial goods and/or services that either become a part of the final product or facilitate the operation of their businesses. Information needs, then, depend on the reason for the purchase of the product.

Industrial Advertising: Advertising directed at businesses that buy products to incorporate into other products or to facilitate the operation of their businesses.

     Industrial advertising is directed at such businesses. *Business Week*, *Auto World*, and *Fortune* may all be used for industrial advertising. For example, when General Motors purchases tires from Goodyear, information needs focus on whether or not the purchase will contribute to a quality finished product. When Goodyear purchases packaging material to ship the tires it manufactures, information needs focus on prompt, predictable delivery. Ad 22.4 stresses the technical advantages of Daly & Wolcott's integrated management software to potential business users.

GOVERNMENT ADVERTISING

The largest purchasers of industrial goods in the United States are federal, state, and local governments. These government units purchase virtually every kind of good—from $15 hammers to multimillion-dollar Polaris missiles. Such goods may be advertised in *Federal Computer Week*, *Commerce Business Daily*, or *Defense News*. Interestingly, however, you seldom see advertisements targeted directly to government agencies. Perhaps this is because government agencies normally use advertising to notify potential suppliers that they are in the process of taking bids. Supplier reputation, however, plays an important role in the selection decision. Because government buyers are responsible to, and influenced by, numerous interest groups that specify, legislate, evaluate, and use the goods and services that governments purchase, corporate image advertising is one way of influencing the government market. Such interest groups include Congress, the Office of Management and Budget, and external watchdogs, such as the Consumer Union.

TRADE ADVERTISING

Trade advertising is used to persuade resellers, wholesalers, and retailers in the consumer market to stock the products of the manufacturer. *Chain Store Age*, *Florist's Review*, and *Pizza and Pasta* are examples of trade publications. Because resellers purchase products for resale to ultimate consumers, they want information on the profit margins they can expect to receive, the product's major selling points, and what the producer is doing in the way of consumer advertising and other promotional support activities.

PROFESSIONAL ADVERTISING

Professional Advertising: Advertising directed at people such as lawyers, doctors, and accountants.

Professional advertising is directed at a diverse group of mostly white-collar people such as lawyers, accountants, management consultants, doctors, teachers, funeral directors, and marketing research specialists. Advertisers interested in attracting professionals advertise in publications such as the *Music Educator Journal* or *Advertising Age*. Information needs depend on both the advertiser's product and the desired audience. The Blessing White "Rocket Launcher" advertisement (Ad 22.5) explains the employee motivation services that it provides to other companies.

AD 22.5

THE BLESSING WHITE COMPANY USES ADS LIKE THIS ONE TO SELL ITS PROFESSIONAL SERVICES TO OTHER COMPANIES.

Agricultural Advertising: Advertising directed at large and small farmers.

AGRICULTURAL ADVERTISING

Agricultural advertising promotes a variety of products and services, such as animal health products, seeds, farm machinery and equipment, crop dusting, and fertilizer. Large and small farmers alike want to know how industrial products can assist them in the growing, raising, or production of agricultural commodities. They turn to publications such as *California Farmer* or *Trees and Turf* for such assistance.

BUSINESS VERSUS CONSUMER MARKETING

There are several inherent characteristics that differentiate business marketing from consumer marketing, including the market concentration, decision makers, strategy, and purchasing objectives. As a result, the process of creating business-to-business advertising, as well as the expertise of the people involved, differs from that involved in consumer marketing. For example, Blessing White's "Rocket Launcher" ad (Ad 22.5) has to explain what the company's services can do to help focus employees on their employer's goals.

MARKET CONCENTRATION

The market for a typical business good is relatively small compared to the market for a consumer good. In some cases, particularly where an original equipment manufacturer (OEM) is concerned, the market may even be geographically concentrated. For example, the auto industry is located primarily in Detroit, the steel industry in Pennsylvania and Illinois, and the furniture industry in North Carolina. These concentrations have direct ramifications for media selection and the ability to target media. For example, businesses selling special computer hardware and software used in stock-and-bond purchases can run their ads in media concentrated in cities, such as New York and Chicago, or zone editions of magazines that reach these markets.

In addition to geographic concentration, businesses can be grouped according to the *Standard Industrial Classification (SIC) System.* The U.S. government established the SIC system in order to group organizations on the basis of major activity or major product or service provided. It enables the federal government to publish the number of establishments, number of employees, and sales volume for each group, designated by a commercial code. Geographic breakdowns are also provided where possible. The SIC system classifies more than 4 million manufacturers into ten major categories that are each subdivided into more specific groups. For example, food SIC is 20, meat products is 201, and canned food is 2032. The SIC system permits a business advertiser to find the SIC codes of its customers and then obtain SIC-coded lists that also include publication usages by SIC classifications. This publication usage information allows the advertiser to select media that will reach the businesses in a certain SIC.

DECISION MAKERS

In general, those involved in making decisions for businesses are professionals who utilize rational criteria when comparing choices. Many times these professionals possess technical knowledge and expertise about the products and services being advertised. Moreover, it isn't uncommon for as many as 15 to 20 people to be involved in a particular purchase decision. Unfortunately, little is known about the inner workings of the decision process or the people involved. Dillard B. Tinsley, a professor of marketing at Stephen F. Austin State University, suggests that we must understand a firm's organizational culture before we can know how decisions are made at that firm. *Organizational culture* includes the stories and anecdotes employees tell about their company, how they feel about their competitors, and how they feel about being (for example) the industry leader, as well as company procedures, policies, rules, job descriptions, and other formalized guidelines for employee activities.[8]

---

[8]Dillard B. Tinsley, "Understanding Business Customers Means Learning About Its Culture," *Marketing News* (March 14, 1988):5, 15.

According to a study sponsored by the newspaper *Australia Post*, there are four types of business decision makers: (1) *information seekers* (25 percent), who are very receptive to both advertising and sales representatives; (2) *hesitants* (19 percent), who are concerned about the quality of both the advertising and the sales representatives; (3) *innovators* (31 percent), who are particularly positive toward advertising efforts, but negative toward sales representatives; and (4) *doubters* (25 percent), who are negative toward both the advertising and sales representatives.[9] Advertisers may create separate messages and media strategies to reach each of these diverse groups.

STRATEGIC ORIENTATION

Unlike the typical consumer who makes decisions based on partial information and sometimes irrational criteria, businesses tend to be guided by a specific strategy. This strategy eliminates much of the autonomy available in other kinds of decision making. Factors such as cost pressures, measures of advertising effectiveness, the agency-client partnership, company-customer linkages, and distribution may dictate what a business must do regardless of the advertising message. Therefore, advertisers must understand the components of a business's strategy and adjust their own strategies accordingly.

One major adjustment is simply accepting the time frame of a typical business strategy. Buying decisions, as well as advertising decisions, are often made by committees and are influenced by others within the organization. This process can take days, weeks, or months. Furthermore, creative efforts and media buys may no longer be valid when approval is finally given. Each of the other functional areas may also have its own timetable. The product-development people will not be willing to introduce the product until test results have achieved certain scores; finance won't fund the effort until certain conditions prevail; and the marketing director will closely monitor the chosen market segment, looking for strategic opportunities that signal a successful product launch.

PURCHASING OBJECTIVES

As you can see in the AIG advertisement (Ad 22.6), purchasing objectives in the insurance and financial services market for the most part center on rational, pragmatic considerations such as price, service, quality of the product or service, and assurance of supply. The AIG ad assures business purchasers that the company offers customized coverage to help the clients deal with governmental regulations.

1.   **Price** Buyers in the business arena are more concerned than ordinary consumers are with the cost of owning and using a product. Most notably, the large volume of a particular product purchased, or the high per-unit cost, means that businesses spend thousands or millions of dollars with each purchase decision. In evaluating price, therefore, businesses consider a variety of factors that generate or minimize costs, such as: What amount of scrap or waste will result from the use of the material? What will the cost of processing the material be? How much power will the machine consume?

2.   **Services** Business buyers require multiple services, such as technical assistance, availability of spare parts, repair capability, and training information. Thus, the technical contributions of suppliers are highly valued wherever equipment, materials, or parts are in use.

3.   **Quality** Organizational customers search for quality levels that are consistent with specifications. Thus, they are reluctant to pay for extra quality or to compromise specifications for a reduced price. The crucial factor is uniformity or consistency in product quality that will guarantee uniformity in end products, reduce the need for costly inspections and testing of incoming shipments, and ensure a smooth blending with the production process.

---

[9]Tony Rambaut, "Getting Through to Business Consumers," *Direct Marketing* (March 1989):78–81.

AD 22.6

GOVERNMENT REGULATIONS IM-
PACT UPON MANY BUSINESSES
AND AIG HELPS COMPANIES
DEAL WITH THEM.

Tire Dump

California

5 October
1600 hrs

**DUMP THEM, YOU BREAK THE LAW. RECYCLE IMPROPERLY, YOU BREAK THE LAW.
MEANWHILE, MORE TIRES JUST CAME IN.**

Whether your company produces waste, tries to recycle it or depends on a steady supply of raw materials, your business is bound to be affected by environmental controls.

There are thousands of regulations, both in the U.S. and overseas, designed to protect the environment. These environmental standards are in a constant state of flux, and can have far-reaching risk implications for all kinds of businesses.

Fortunately, AIG specializes in designing the kind of custom coverages you need to cope successfully with changing conditions. In fact, AIG is the only worldwide insurance and financial organization that helps manage your business risks with a broad range of customized services. Services like environmental remediation coverage, hedging and market-making in commodities and stop-loss protection. And we've got the top financial ratings to back us up. So we'll be there to help keep your business rolling along.

AIG

WORLD LEADERS IN INSURANCE AND FINANCIAL SERVICES
American International Group, Inc., Dept. A, 70 Pine Street, New York, NY 10270

4.   **Assurance of Supply** Interruptions in the flow of parts and materials can shut down the production process, resulting in costly delays and lost sales. To guard against interruptions in supply, business firms rely on a supplier's established reputation for delivery.

BUSINESS-TO-BUSINESS ADVERTISING OBJECTIVES

The average cost of an industrial sales call is nearly $250.00. Business-to-business advertising enables a business marketer to reach a large portion of the market at a lower cost. For example, according to one study, the adjusted cost per thousand for ads by Minolta, IBM, and Toshiba in the same issue of *Time* magazine ran from $49.71 to $51.78, which is considerably cheaper than a sales call.

Although business advertising is an economical means of reaching large numbers of buyers, it is primarily used to assist and support the selling function. Thus, business advertising objectives center on creating company awareness, increasing overall selling efficiency, and supporting distributors and resellers.

CREATING COMPANY AWARENESS
Effectively planned business advertising assists the industrial salesperson by increasing customer awareness of, and interest in, the supplier's product. When buy-

ers are aware of a company's reputation, products, and record in the industry, salespeople are more effective.

INCREASING OVERALL SELLING EFFICIENCY

Salespeople most often deal with purchasing agents or buyers and are frequently unaware of people within a firm who are in a position to exert influence on a purchasing decision. Such influencers could be engineers who design the product, production experts who manufacture the product, or financial people who maintain cost controls. These influencers, however, do read trade magazines and general business publications, and they can be reached through advertising. By responding to these ads, unknown influencers often identify themselves, making it possible for salespeople to contact them. Such advertising, therefore, generates leads for the salesforce. Furthermore, for some producers, particularly those of industrial suppliers, advertising may be the only way of reaching broad groups of buyers and influencers efficiently.

SUPPORTING CHANNEL MEMBERS

Business advertising frequently provides an economical and efficient supplement to personal selling by providing information to distributors and resellers as well as to end users. It can reassure intermediaries that the end users are aware of the company's products. At the same time, it can answer the most common resellers' questions, such as what profit they can expect on a product and what the producer is doing in the way of consumer advertising and other promotional support. Rarely can a salesforce be deployed to reach all potential distributors and resellers often enough to satisfy all of these information needs.

AD 22.7

JUST BECAUSE IT IS A BUSINESS-TO-BUSINESS AD DOESN'T MEAN IT CAN'T BE CREATIVE. THIS AD FOR FRUIT OF THE LOOM IS DESIGNED TO ARREST THE ATTENTION OF PURCHASING AGENTS.

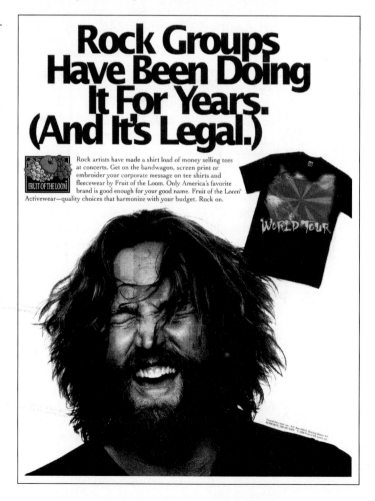

CREATING BUSINESS-TO-BUSINESS ADS

As in consumer advertising, the best business-to-business ads are relevant, understandable, and strike an emotion in the prospective client. There are, however, adjustments that must be made in light of the differences discussed earlier. According to Steve Penchina, creative director of Penchina, Selkowitz of New York, effective business-to-business ads must establish an emotional connection between the product and the prospective client and the ad should sell to people, not to companies. Penchina is bothered by boring or ridiculous visuals, trite taglines, and irrelevant or insulting metaphors.[10] The Fruit of the Loom ad for its T-shirts uses a creative approach to catch the attention of busy purchasing agents. (See Ad 22.7.)

Another expert, Sandra Tenney, says that the two keys to successful business-to-business advertising are headlines and art. "Headlines should demonstrate specific benefits in language readers understand. Excellent photography and clear illustrations increase readership while strengthening headlines or elaborating on them," she notes.[11]

Finally, John Graham, president of John R. Graham, a public relations/advertising agency, provides three guidelines for business-to-business advertising: (1) Make it easy for the prospect to respond or to pursue further information; (2) send reprints of ads with a personal letter to current customers and prospects explaining why you are advertising and where your ads will appear; and (3) combine advertising with media stories and a newsletter and mail these to prospects.[12]

BUSINESS-TO-BUSINESS ADVERTISING MEDIA

Although some business advertisers use traditional consumer media, most rely on general business or trade publications, industrial directories, direct marketing, or some combination thereof. Table 22.3 breaks down the outside vendors and suppliers or tools used in business-to-business marketing. Advertising leads the list, followed by trade shows, then research.

GENERAL BUSINESS AND TRADE PUBLICATIONS

Horizontal Publications: Publications directed to people who hold similar jobs in different companies across different industries.

Vertical Publications: Publications directed to people who hold different positions in the same industries.

General business and trade publications are classified as either horizontal or vertical. **Horizontal publications** are directed to people who hold similar jobs in different companies across different industries. For example, *Purchasing* is a specialized business publication that is targeted to people across industries who are responsible for a specific task or function. The magazines read by accountants or computer programmers are other examples of horizontal publications.

In contrast, **vertical publications,** such as *Iron Age and Steel*, are targeted toward people who hold different positions in the same industries. Some general business publications, such as *Fortune, Business Week*, and *The Wall Street Journal*, tend to be read by business professionals across all industries because of the general business news and editorials they provide. Advertisers select publications on the basis of whom they want to reach and what their goals are. Other specialized business publications, such as *Iron Age and Steel*, however, are targeted to people in a specific industry and are therefore classified as vertical publications.

---

[10]Patricia Winters, "Business-to-Business: Trite Is Blight," *Advertising Age* (August 28, 1989):48.

[11]Sandra M. Tenney, "For Good Business Ads, Apply Some Simple Rules," *Marketing News* (March 14, 1988):12.

[12]John R. Graham, "Business-to-Business Ads Can Work," *Marketing News* (March 13, 1989):7.

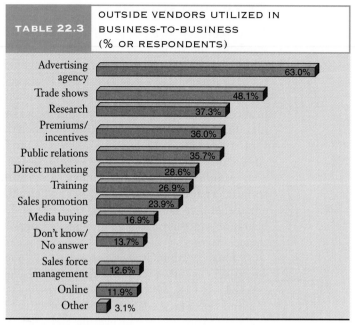

TABLE 22.3	OUTSIDE VENDORS UTILIZED IN BUSINESS-TO-BUSINESS (% OR RESPONDENTS)
Advertising agency	63.0%
Trade shows	48.1%
Research	37.3%
Premiums/ incentives	36.0%
Public relations	35.7%
Direct marketing	28.6%
Training	26.9%
Sales promotion	23.9%
Media buying	16.9%
Don't know/ No answer	13.7%
Sales force management	12.6%
Online	11.9%
Other	3.1%

Source: Outfront Marketing study   Graphic by John Hall

DIRECTORY ADVERTISING

Every state has an industrial directory, and there are also a number of private ones. One of the most popular industrial directories is the New York-based *Thomas Register.* The *Register* consists of 19 volumes that contain 60,000 pages of 50,000 product headings and listings from 123,000 industrial companies selling everything from heavy machine tools to copper tubing to orchestra pits.

DIRECT MARKETING

Data Sheets: Advertising that provides detailed technical information.

In addition to trade magazines and general business publications, business advertisers use various other vehicles, such as direct mail, catalogs, and **data sheets,** to reach their markets. Business advertisers often use direct mail to prepare the groundwork for subsequent sales calls. Catalogs and data sheets support the selling function by providing technical data about the product as well as supplementary information concerning price and availability.

Direct mail emerged as a primary medium for several business-to-business advertisers during the last decade. Thanks to the evolution of computer software, direct mail can be designed in a manner that personalizes the message to specific customers, includes highly technical information, and provides top-notch photography and designs. Long copy, illustrations, diagrams, or any other device can be carried through direct mail. In addition, dramatic improvements in the accuracy of mailing lists have reduced the waste historically associated with direct mail. Direct mail has the capacity to sell the product, provide sales leads, or lay the groundwork for subsequent sales calls.

CONSUMER MEDIA

Consumer media, despite their wasted circulation, can sometimes be very effective owing to the lack of competition from other business advertisers. Because the message exposure occurs away from the office, it also encounters less competition from the receiver's other business needs. Although consumer media are also an excellent means of reaching a market where market coverage is limited geographically, they are still not used much. In general, consumer publications received less than 5 percent of the total dollar amount spent on business-to-business advertising, and spot radio, spot television, and network television each receive less than 1 percent. Sometimes businesses advertise in consumer magazines (such as *Better Homes and Gardens* or *Newsweek*) in hopes of influencing consumers to ask for specific brands when they go to a business.

In addition to the use of traditional consumer media, there has been a tremendous growth in business television programming that is targeted at both businesspeople and consumers who are interested in business-related topics. For example, FNN not only produces its own business shows, it also provides the syndicated business shows *This Morning's Business* and *First Business*. Introduced in 1989, CNBC was conceived with the consumer in mind, and its programming focuses more on personal finances.

RECENT TRENDS IN MEDIA SERVICES

Today there are more media choices available to the business-to-business advertiser than ever before. Consequently, media that can offer advertisers a competitive advantage in reaching their customers will be quite appealing. In some instances an existing medium has developed a unique service unmatched by its competitors. For example, *Business Week* offers a Federal Express service so subscribers can get their issues on Friday instead of waiting for the Monday mail. New media have also emerged. Of course, the role of interactive media technology on business-to-business media still is evolving. Clearly, businesses that are far more comfortable with computers will accept interactive alternatives much more quickly than will individual consumers.

The videocassette industry has also entered the fray as a reliable business-to-business medium. Videocassettes can be sent to customers requesting product information or a product demonstration. They can also be mailed unsolicited as an exciting selling tool. Entire catalogs called "video logs" can be put on video. This is affordable owing to the development of disposable videocassettes that have a life of 10 to 12 plays and cost just pennies to produce.

DOES BUSINESS ADVERTISING SELL?

Although few business marketers today rely exclusively on their salesforce to reach potential buyers, many people have questioned the effectiveness of business advertising. However, the Advertising Research Foundation (ARF) and the Association of Business Publishers (ABP) undertook to study the link between business advertising and industrial product sales and profits.[13] The researchers monitored product sales and the level and frequency of their advertising schedules for a period of one year. To ensure that the study's findings could be applied to a wide range of industries and products, three very different products were monitored: a portable safety device that sold for less than $10, a commercial transportation component package that sold for around $10,000, and highly specialized laboratory equipment priced between $5,000 and $10,000. Despite the diversity in price, product life, purchase complexity, and distribution channels, the study found that, for all three products:

- Business-to-business advertising created more sales than would have occurred without advertising.
- Increased advertising frequency resulted in increased product sales.
- It paid to advertise to both dealers and end users when the product was sold through dealers.

[13] "From a Reporter to a Source: A New Survey of Selling Costs," *Sales & Marketing Management* (February 16, 1987):12.

- Increased advertising frequency increased sales leads and generated higher profits.
- It took four to six months to see the results of the advertising program.
- The use of color in the advertising made a dramatic difference.
- The advertising campaign was effective long after the campaign had ended.
- Advertising favorably affected purchasers' awareness of, and attitudes toward, industrial products.

Business-to-business advertising has a reputation for dull advertising. The future of business-to-business, however, is dependent upon how well it adapts to the following trends:[14]

- More accountability and efficiency in marketing communications programs are being required of business-to-business marketers.
- Since advertising efficiency is not easy to measure, ad programs and staff, seen as marginal expenses in many business-to-business companies, are being pared down or eliminated.
- Business-to-business marketing itself is becoming more people oriented, with the best television and print ads addressing a product's solution to human problems.

With scaled-down in-house marketing departments and more outsourcing of the various functions, the role of business-to-business advertising is going to change. Business-to-business marketing is like trying to move a battleship; consumer marketing is like turning a corner. Change will not come easily, but it will come.

---

[14]Lynn G. Coleman, "The Crunch Has Come," *Marketing News* (March 4, 1991):16.

$\mathscr{S}$UMMARY

- Business-to-business advertising is used to influence demand and is directed at people in the business arena who buy or specify products for business use. Its objectives include creating company awareness, increasing selling efficiency, and supporting channel members.
- Compared to the consumer market, the market for business goods is relatively limited, decision making tends to be shared by a group of people, and purchasing decisions center around price, services, product quality, and assurance of supply.

- Business-to-business media consist of general business and trade publications, directories, direct mail, catalogs, data sheets, and consumer media.
- Compared to national advertising, retail advertising is less concerned with brand awareness and more concerned with attracting customers.
- Retail advertising uses various media alternatives, from shoppers and preprinted inserts to television and radio.
- Identifying customers is one of the most valuable kinds of research a retailer can conduct.

$\mathscr{Q}$UESTIONS

1. You are developing an ad to reach chemists in the oil industry. Would you place this ad in a general business magazine or in a trade publication? Why?

2. How does retail advertising differ from national advertising?

3. Think of a restaurant in your community. What types of people does it target? Would you recommend that its advertising focus on price or image? What is (or should be) its image? Which media should it use?

4. Biogen Corporation's corporate mission is to become a leading company in genetic research and devel-

opment for health industries. Privately held at time of incorporation, it has decided to go public and have its stock traded. How would corporate advertising assist Biogen in its mission? What audience targets should be priorities for its communication programs? Should it develop more than one campaign?

5. Although personal selling is a vital marketing tool for industrial (business-to-business) companies, advertising also has a significant role in many marketing situations. What if a limited budget means expanding one at the sacrifice of the other, however? Suppose you were making a decision for a company that is beginning a marketing effort for a new set of products; you'll need approximately six new salespeople. If an advertising campaign to introduce the firm would mean hiring four salespeople instead of six, is the advertising worth it? Explain the strengths and weaknesses of this idea.

6. Tom and Wendi Promise have just purchased a frozen-yogurt franchise. They found a good lease in a neighborhood shopping center, but the cost of franchising, leasing, and other charges have left them very little for advertising. With limited dollars, Tom and Wendi can only afford one of the following options: (a) Yellow Pages display ad, (b) a series of advertisements in the area's weekly "shopper" newspaper, (c) advertising in the area's college newspaper (the campus is six blocks from the store). Which of these opportunities will best help Tom and Wendi get the awareness they need?

7. Abby Wilson, the advertising manager for a campus newspaper (published four times per week) is discussing ways to increase advertising revenues with her sales staff. She asks opinions on using sales time to promote a co-op program to interest campus-area businesses. One salesperson says the retailers won't be bothered with all the "paperwork." Another explains that newspaper reps really have to understand co-op to sell it, and that none of Wilson's staff has experience. Would you be persuaded that promoting cooperative advertising is more trouble than it is worth?

Suggested Class Project

Select a print ad directed to a business-to-business consumer. Think about how this ad could be converted into a television commercial. Indicate examples of when this broadcast ad would be aired.

Further Readings

Beisel, John L., *Contemporary Retailing* (New York: Macmillan, 1987).

Bolen, William H., *Contemporary Retailing*, 3rd ed. (Upper Saddle River, NJ: Prentice Hall, 1988).

Diamond, Jay, and Gerald Pintel, *Retailing Today* (Upper Saddle River, NJ: Prentice Hall, 1988).

Hall, S. Roland, *Retail Advertising and Selling* (New York: Garland Publications, 1985).

Mahen, Philip W., *Business-to-Business Marketing* (Boston: Allyn & Bacon, 1991).

Mason, J. Barry, and Morris L. Mayer, *Modern Retailing: Theory and Practice*, 4th ed. (Plano, TX: Business Publications, Inc., 1987).

Stern, L. W., Adel I. El-Ansary, and James R. Brown, *Management in Marketing Channels* (Upper Saddle River, NJ: Prentice Hall, 1992).

In 1993 Fort Worth–based RadioShack was the ubiquitous electronics store that sold gadgets and gizmos to nerds and techies. The new president, Leonard Roberts, who was hired in 1996 because of his marketing savvy, not his knowledge of consumer electronics, has turned the chain around. Its image has been polished and upgraded and its sales are up.

Turning around a company with $3.5 billion in sales and some 6,800 units was a challenge. His strategy was to exploit its ubiquity. After all there are more RadioShack stores than there are Wal-Marts, K marts and Sears combined. More than 84 percent of all Americans live or work within five minutes of a RadioShack store.

The turnaround was engineered by dropping the emphasis on the store's depth of inventory as "America's Technology Store" in favor of an emphasis on customer service. Roberts believed that customers were average consumers who were seeking a nonintimidating place to buy electronic products rather than techies.

The repositioning strategy was hammered out by image consultants Landor Associates, ad agency Lord, Dentsu & Partners, New York, and a 140-person in-house ad staff. The idea was to focus less on products and more on service and the store's educated salesforce.

The repositioning was anchored by a new slogan, "You've Got Questions. We've Got Answers," to promote the new service philosophy. That was supported by an in-depth training program for the company's employees to turn them into answerers. As the campaign evolved, Roberts systematically added reasons why consumers should turn to their local store for solutions to their problems. He also inaugurated gift-giving and repair services.

The strength of the Shack's new success is its philosophy of customer service. His first day on the job, Roberts gathered a group of the company's top executives and ordered them to tear up their job descriptions. He told them, "There will be two job descriptions: those who serve our customers directly, and those who serve someone who does."

In an unusual partnership RadioShack signed a deal with Sprint Spectrum that puts the chain in the middle of the telecommunications business. Under the agreement, the stores are to devote 15 percent of their floor space to a Sprint phone center featuring Sprint-branded phone products and services, from prepaid calling cards to desktop phones to Internet access.

Building on the chain's locations, Roberts also negotiated partnerships with respected big brands: IBM in personal computers, Casio watches, Primestar home satellite systems, and ADT home-security devices. RadioShack has a strong value-added promise for manufacturers in the area of distribution—"We're in every neighborhood." Furthermore, the store brings the most technologically savvy sales staff in the business. RadioShack ads mention the brands, and the manufacturers like Primestar refer potential customers to RadioShack as the place to go for its products. These partnerships allowed RadioShack to grab 15 percent of the home digital satellite system market in less than a year and 10 percent of the market for cellular phones.

To get the message out, RadioShack has boosted its advertising spending since 1993 by $30 million to a current level of $200 million. It has also changed the mix from radio and print—both predominately local—to national television (good for image building) and direct marketing (used to build customer relationships).

The repositioning effort seems to be worth it. While the other chains in parent company Tandy's are floundering, RadioShack's sales and profits are up smartly. One analysts estimates the repair and gift services, launched in 1994, racked up a cool $75 million in sales during 1995. RadioShack recorded an increase in same-store sales of 5 percent in the first quarter of 1996 compared to flat sales at rival Circuit City and 1 percent at Best Buy. In 1996 another analyst estimated these earnings were up 10.3 percent over the previous year.

CASE QUESTIONS

1. Outline the nature of the repositioning effort made by RadioShack. How much of the effort was marketing and how much was marketing communication?

2. What other dimensions of the store's business might be showcased in advertising? In other words, are there other business opportunities that the company might be able to use to better advantage to build more business?

3. If you were the ad manager for RadioShack, how would you extend this campaign? What message strategy would you use in the next year that maintains a link with the "We've Got Answers" theme but freshens it and extends its meaning in new ways?

Sources: Adapted from Bernhard Warner, "Leonard Roberts," *Superbrands '97* (October 7, 1996):115–117; Jeffery D. Zbar, "The Marketing 100; RadioShack," *Advertising Age* (June 24, 1996):S24; and Stephanie Anderson Forest, "RadioShack Looks Like a Palace Now," *Business Week* (May 13, 1996):153.

As the largest grocery retailer in the Kansas City area Price Chopper continually faced increasing competition from both new and existing retail grocery operations. As the volume leader, Price Chopper stood to lose the most in terms of market share, particularly because the Kansas City area was experiencing no significant population growth.

To combat this increased competition, Noble & Associates, Price Chopper's advertising agency, recommended a new creative strategy for its client in 1989. The principle campaign objective was to maintain Price Chopper's share of market leadership while fighting off the increased competition from new and existing retail grocery competitors in the Kansas City market. The creative strategy itself offered shoppers the dual benefits of low price and high quality. Thus, it positioned Price Chopper as the retail grocery that sold the best and the freshest perishable foods.

Price Chopper and Nobel & Associates summarized the consumer benefits of this creative strategy as follows: Price Chopper brings consumers the best and the freshest food at the best price. All effective creative strategies include "support" statements that justify the consumer benefit and, thus, enhance its credibility. The support for Price Chopper's consumer benefit include the following: 1) Price Chopper buys and makes the best food in Kansas City; 2) Price Chopper buys more food than any other retail grocery operation in Kansas City; 3) Price Chopper's large volume purchasing results in the lowest prices in Kansas City; and 4) Price Chopper's large volume purchasing and high turnover results in the freshest food.

Price Chopper primarily targeted women between the ages of 18 and 54 and identified men between 18 and 54 as a secondary target. This is a fairly traditional retail grocery target audience because women still represent the most common grocery shoppers. The target audiences were further defined as men and women who are concerned about both good value and good quality. Noble & Associates also knew from syndicated data that Price Chopper held the largest share of voice in the Kansas City Area of Dominant Influence (ADI). Specifically, this put Price Chopper in the best position to create or modify consumer's perceptions.

Within the first year of the campaign's introduction in October 1989, Price Chopper's market share had increased by 5 points to 36 percent, more than double the share increase experienced in the prior year. This was achieved during a period of flat population growth in the Kansas City area and less than a 1 percent increase in all-commodity grocery sales volume (ACV) and no new Price Chopper store openings.

Research results indicated that consumer recall of the campaign tagline "Best Food/Best Price" was 80 percent among Price Chopper customers and 43 percent among total Kansas City residents. Research conducted just 2 months after the campaign started indicated that the "Jammin Nanas" spot successfully communicated the overall message of "Price Chopper sells more quality fruit at a lower price than any other store."

Source: Courtesy of Noble & Associates.

QUESTIONS

1. Typically grocery retailers emphasize either food price or food quality in their advertising. Explain what additional demographic factors besides age and sex should be included in a grocery retailer's target audience definition for a price-based advertising strategy and for a food quality-based advertising strategy.

2. Explain why it would be difficult for a smaller grocery retailer in the Kansas City market to successfully employ a "Best Food/Best Price" advertising strategy.

3. Based on your existing knowledge of traditional retail grocery advertising, what general characteristics in addition to those discussed above make "Jammin Nanas" different from the bulk of existing grocery advertising?

WRIGLEY COMPANY (Hong Kong) LTD.

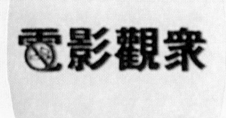

1. (SFX: FANFARE MUSIC)
MVO: I smoke, but now in the cinema . . .

(ROMANIZATION of Cantonese):
Gao dzi ho jin ga, daan hai ji ga hai hei jyn . . .

2. (SFX: THUMP!)

3. MVO: . . . smoking is illegal.

(ROMANIZATION): . . . Dzi jin hai wai faat ge.

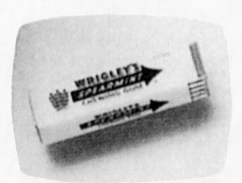

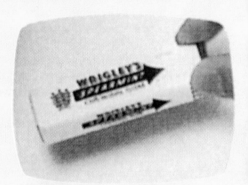

4. MVO: No problem, I have . . .

(ROMANIZATION): Mou man tai, gao jau . . .

5. MVO: . . . White Arrow Chewing Gum.

(ROMANIZATION): . . . Baak zin heung hau gao.

6. MVO: Chewing White Arrow gives me . . .

(ROMANIZATION): Baak zin daai bei gao . . .

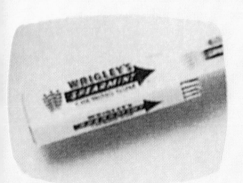

7. MVO: . . . pure relaxing and satisfying enjoyment.

(ROMANIZATION): . . . Soen hing sung mun dauk ge hoeng sau.

8. MVO: When (I) can't smoke . . .

(ROMANIZATION): Ng dzi dak jin ge si hau . . .

9. MVO: . . . (I) chew White Arrow (for that) perfect relaxing feeling.*

(ROMANIZATION): . . . Dziu baak zin hing sung mou dak tuan.

SUPER: CHEW WHITE ARROW FOR PERFECT RELAXING FEELING.

International Advertising

CHAPTER OBJECTIVES

When you have completed this chapter, you should be able to:

- Distinguish among local, regional, international, or global brands
- Explain how international advertising is created and executed
- Understand how international agencies are organized
- List the special problems that international advertisers face
- Watch with greater understanding the growth of global advertising

TROUBLESOME TRANSLATIONS

The Internet is full of jokes and one area that seems to fascinate Web surfers is the problem big international companies have translating their products, product names, and advertising into a local language. We can't vouch for the truth of these stories, but here is a collection that's circulating on the world of the Web.

Chevrolet is the focus of a classic story about translating into Spanish: When General Motors introduced the Chevy Nova in South America, it was apparently unaware that "no va" means "it won't go." Ford had a similar problem in Brazil when the Pinto flopped. The company found out that Pinto was Brazilian slang for "tiny male genitals."

Other Spanish stories from the Net include: When Parker Pen marketed a ballpoint pen in Mexico, its ads were supposed to say "It won't leak in your pocket and embarrass you." The company thought the Spanish word "embarazar" meant embarrass. Instead the ads said that "It won't leak in your pocket and make you pregnant." A Miami t-shirt maker printed shirts that promoted the Pope's visit. Instead of the desired "I Saw the Pope" in Spanish, the shirts proclaimed "I Saw the Potato." Chicken-man Frank Perdue's slogan, "It takes a tough man to make a tender chicken," got mangled when billboards all over Mexico proclaimed "It takes a hard man to make a chicken aroused."

The American slogan for Salem cigarettes, "Salem–Feeling Free," got translated in the Japanese market into "When smoking Salem, you feel so refreshed that your mind seems to be free and empty."

Chinese, however, is particularly difficult for international companies to adapt to names and product slogans. The name Coca-Cola in China was first rendered as Ke-kou-ke-la. Unfortunately, the Coke company did not discover until after thousands of signs had been printed that the phrase means "bite the wax tadpole" or "female horse stuffed with wax" depending on the dialect. Coke then researched 40,000 Chinese characters and found a close phonetic equivalent, "ko-kou-ko-le," which can be loosely translated as "happiness in the mouth."

In Taiwan, the translation of the Pepsi slogan "Come alive with the Pepsi Generation" came out as "Pepsi will bring your ancestors back from the dead." Also in Chinese, the Kentucky Fried Chicken slogan "finger-lickin' good" came out as "eat your fingers off." That's why Wrigley's, to avoid a difficult translation for its campaign that promoted chewing gum when smoking isn't allowed, used the universal "no" symbol (a circle with a diagonal bar) rather than trying to say it in Chinese.

European languages also have their share of stories: Colgate introduced a toothpaste in France called Cue, the name of a notorious porno magazine. Hunt-Wesson introduced its Big John products in French Canada as Gros Jos before finding out that the phrase, in slang, means "big breasts." In this case, however, the name problem did not have a noticeable effect on sales. In Italy, a campaign for Schweppes Tonic Water translated the name into Schweppes Toilet Water.

The problem is not limited to English-language companies in foreign markets, customers in the United States have even seen an occasional blooper. Scandinavian vacuum manufacturer Electrolux, for example, used the following in an American ad campaign: "Nothing sucks like an Electrolux." And Japan's second-largest tourist agency was mystified when it entered English-speaking markets and began receiving requests for unusual sex tours. Upon finding out why, the owners of Kinki Nippon Tourist Company changed its name.

ℐNTERNATIONAL ℳARKETING

Since Wendell Willkie coined the phrase "One World" in his 1940 presidential campaign, the distance between the concept and the reality has narrowed. The top worldwide marketers began spending more than 50 percent of their advertising dollars outside the United States in the early 1990s. The non-U.S. gross income of the top 500 agencies reached $8 billion in 1996, a 9.7 percent increase over 1995.[1]

Of the top 25 agencies, ten were headquartered in the United States, seven were from Japan, four from London, and no other country had more than two. Table 23.1 lists the top 25 international advertisers of 1996.

The subject of this chapter is the evolution of advertising from the home country to a foreign country to regional blocs to a worldwide audience. Included in this discussion are the tools of international management, the means of organizing for international advertising, creating and planning international advertising campaigns, and special problems in the international arena.

[1]"53rd Annual Agency Report," *Advertising Age* (April 21, 1997) S1.

TABLE 23.1	WORLD'S TOP 25 ADVERTISING ORGANIZATIONS							
RANK				**WORLDWIDE GROSS INCOME**			**CAPITALIZED VOLUME**	
1996	**1995**	**AD ORGANIZATION**	**HEADQUARTERS**	**1996**	**1995**	**% CHG**	**1996**	**1995**
1	1	WPP Group	London	$3,419.9	$3,125.5	9.4	$24,740.5	$22,688.4
2	2	Omnicom Group	New York	3,035.5	2,708.5	12.1	23,385.1	20,805.4
3	3	Interpublic Group of Cos.	New York	2,751.2	2,465.8	11.5	20,045.1	17,621.8
4	4	Dentsu	Tokyo	1,929.9	1,999.1	−3.5	14,047.9	14,597.2
5	6	Young & Rubicam	New York	1,356.4	1,197.5	13.3	11,981.0	9,857.4
6	5	Cordiant	London	1,169.3	1,203.1	−2.8	9,739.9	10,021.9
7	9	Grey Advertising	New York	987.8	896.6	10.2	6,629.4	6,005.5
8	8	Havas Advertising	Levallois-Perret, France	974.3	924.4	5.4	7,295.1	6,931.4
9	7	Hakuhodo	Tokyo	897.7	958.6	−6.3	6,677.0	6,909.3
10	10	True North Communications	Chicago	889.5	805.9	10.4	7,040.9	6,358.1
11	11	Leo Burnett Co.	Chicago	866.3	805.9	7.5	5,821.1	5,386.7
12	12	MacManus Group	New York	754.2	713.9	5.6	6,830.3	6,247.1
13	13	Publicis Communication	Paris	676.8	624.8	8.3	4,617.7	4,270.5
14	14	Bozell, Jacobs, Kenyon & Eckhardt	New York	473.1	404.5	17.0	3,675.0	3,050.0
15	15	GGT/BDDP Group	London	398.1	380.6	4.6	3,149.1	2,977.5
16	16	Daiko Advertising	Osaka, Japan	256.7	263.6	−2.6	1,853.4	1,998.3
17	17	Asatsu Inc.	Tokyo	242.0	254.2	−4.8	1,904.8	1,958.8
18	19	Carlson Marketing Group	Minneapolis	222.0	189.0	17.5	1,880.8	1,574.5
19	18	Tokyu Agency	Tokyo	214.0	231.1	−7.4	1,844.6	1,926.1
20	20	TMP Worldwide	New York	194.6	177.4	9.7	1,297.0	1,182.8
21	21	Dai-ichi Kikaku	Tokyo	164.5	168.4	−2.3	1,249.0	1,291.0
22	22	Dentsu, Young & Rubicam Partnerships	Tokyo/ Singapore	164.2	161.6	1.6	1,245.5	1,201.8
23	24	Chell Communications	Seoul	152.0	124.9	21.7	1,005.1	869.8
24	28	Abbott Mead Vickers	London	137.1	106.5	28.7	1,079.0	926.0
25	23	Yomiko Advertising	Tokyo	125.9	133.0	−5.3	1,106.3	1,149.5

Notes: Figures are in millions of U.S. dollars. Companies hold minority equity in each other as follows: True North owns 49% of Publicis Communication; Omnicom owns 46.67% of Clemenger/BBDO; Young & Rubicam and Dentsu each own nearly 50% of Dentsu, Young & Rubicam Partnerships.

Source: Advertising Age, April 21, 1997, p. 814.

EVOLUTION OF GLOBAL MARKETING

Local Brand: A brand that is marketed in one specific country.

Regional Brand: A brand that is available throughout a regional trading bloc.

International Brand: A brand or product that is available in most parts of the world.

PRINCIPLE Marketing emerged when the focus changed from importing products to exporting them.

International Advertising: Advertising designed to promote the same product in a number of countries.

In most countries, markets are composed of local, regional, and international brands. A **local brand** is one marketed in a single country. A **regional brand** is one marketed throughout a region, for example, North America or Europe. An **international brand** is available virtually everywhere in the world. This chapter deals with regional and international brands, products, and services, and with the advertising that supports them.

Marketing emerged when the emphasis changed from importing products (tea, spices, silk, gold, and silver) to exporting products. Advertising was used to introduce, explain, and sell the benefits of a product—especially a branded product—in markets outside the home country. The current patterns of international expansion emerged largely in the twentieth century. Understanding these trading patterns helps us appreciate both how they operated in the past and some of the restrictions that custom and history have imposed on them through the years.

International advertising is a relatively recent development within international commerce. It did not appear in any organized manner until the late nineteenth century. Ancient records in Egypt, Persia, Greece, and Rome refer to metals, spices, fabrics, gemstones, and other materials of value that were exchanged over great distances. Except for tribute or taxes, this commercial intercourse was based on the trading of goods from one region to another.

By the Middle Ages, Holland was trading tulip bulbs internationally in exchange for various products and services. English, French, Spanish, and Dutch companies procured spices, tea, and silk in the Orient for European consumers. This was not considered marketing as we define it, however, because the old *trading companies* were not developing products for the European market, nor were producers in Turkey, China, the Philippines, and Indonesia seeking to stimulate demand for their goods in Europe.

HOME-COUNTRY PRODUCTION

Figure 23.1 illustrates the development of product marketing from companies such as S. C. Johnson, Nestlé, and Stanley Tools outside the home market. It starts with product that begins to reach the saturation point in its home market and cannot grow faster than the population. At this point, management seeks to recapture the sales gains of the growth period. This can be accomplished in one of two ways. The company can introduce new products in its home market, or it can expand into foreign markets.

It is not the saturation of the home-country market alone that causes com-

FIGURE 23.1

THE TYPICAL S-CURVE LIFE CYCLE OF A PRODUCT.

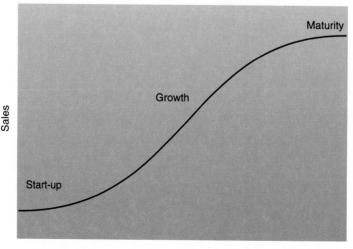

panies to move products outside home markets. After World War II, market research was used to evaluate market potential and find pockets of demand for products. Merger and acquisitions put companies into new national markets and added products to company lines whose potential could be exploited in neighboring countries. Companies also moved into other markets to preempt development by competitors. By studying the historical sequence, we can get a better understanding of the growth and intensity of international marketing and advertising.

EXPORT

The next step, exporting a product, requires a means of inserting this product into the distribution system of another country. The exporter typically appoints a distributor or an importer who assumes responsibility for marketing and advertising in the new country. As volume grows, the complexity of product sizes, product lines, pricing, and local adaptation increases. The exporter might send an employee to work with the importer to handle details, to verify that promised activities are being carried out, and to solve communication problems. This employee serves as a facilitator between the exporter and the importer. Some companies prefer to appoint a local distributor who knows the language and the distribution system and can, therefore, handle customers and the government better than a foreigner could.

Exporting is still the first step in international marketing. In 1989, for example, Lands' End tested the European and Japanese markets by shipping directly from its home office in Dodgeville, Wisconsin. The company generated orders by placing small space advertising in English in both Japan and Europe, encouraging Americans to order their products by fax. By 1993, Lands' End had opened a distribution center in the United Kingdom and was hiring staff in Japan to expand marketing there. (See the Concepts and Applications box for more discussion of the internationalization of Japanese advertising.)

---

*C*ONCEPTS AND *A*PPLICATIONS

THE DEVELOPMENT OF JAPANESE INTERNATIONAL ADVERTISING

The Japanese followed the export route to international marketing in their export drive after World War II. Although they set up their own companies in some major countries, they relied heavily on local, particularly U.S., ad agencies, which built relationships with Japanese managers and learned Japanese business customs. For example, McCann-Erickson serves Canon in Europe and Asia. FCB Publicis works for Mazda Motors in North America and in five other nations. Grey Advertising handles Sony in eight markets, while Young & Rubicam handles the advertiser in 13 others. Saatchi & Saatchi handles Toyota in North America and in 15 other countries. The agency has a senior executive at Toyota headquarters to coordinate international advertising whose advertising budget for Toyota is said to be more than $150 million worldwide. Dentsu has partnered with Young & Rubicam and uses the Dentsu Y&R name for its international operations outside Japan.

The large Japanese agencies typically have not been given global assignments to extend their services for clients outside the home islands, but Japanese agencies are emulating Western global agencies in their expansion plans. However, they also bring a more comprehensive approach to marketing communication. Kouichi Segawa, director of Dentsu's overseas operations planning division, has said, "Our concept of a communications service company outside Japan is a little different from the usual pattern of a Western-style agency (and) could include sports events, designing restaurants or showrooms, space planning, corporate identity, packaging and product design."

Both Dentsu and Hakuhodo, the leading Japanese agencies, are examining opportunities to expand or to establish joint ventures in Europe, North America, and Latin America. Hakuhodo, one of the largest advertising agencies in the world, celebrated its 100th anniversary in 1995. Known as the creator of the award-winning campaign for Nissin Cup Noodles, the ads are built around hapless cavemen whose problem is trying to capture a mammoth for dinner. Using a variety of visual sight gags, the one-word punch line, "Hungry?" is followed by a picture of the product's familiar styrofoam cup.

Sources: Adapted from Adam Lashinsky, "Making Japanese Advertising More Universal," *Advertising Age* Special Issue: Hakuhodo at 100 (June 19, 1995):H6–H8; David Kilburn, "Densu Expanding to Mideast, Europe," *Advertising Age* (September 7, 1992):4.

It's important to note that international marketing and advertising are not the exclusive province of large companies. Bu Jin, an innovative company in Boulder, Colorado, creates and markets martial arts products. With only eight full-time employees, its products fill a high-end, international niche market worldwide. Most of Bu Jin's business is driven by its catalog.[2]

As airlines move outside their home market, they are in effect exporting a service. American Airlines' "Smiles" campaign ran in Europe, basically changing only the language. See Ad 23.1.

TRANSFER OF MANAGEMENT AND NATIONALIZATION

As the product or product line grows in export markets, it receives greater attention from the exporter. This process may involve sending someone from management to work in the importer's organization or to supervise the importer from an office in the importing country. At this point, the company still considers itself a domestic producer, exporting products to other markets. As long as this is true, the transferred employee must secure approval of plans, obtain funds for operations, and defend sales forecasts to a company management that is primarily concerned with its domestic market.

As the local importer-distributor grows with the imported line, the exporter may want greater control over the product or a larger share of the profits. As a result, the exporting company may buy back the rights contracted to the importer or set up assembly (or even manufacturing) facilities in the importing country. The result is the transfer of management and manufacturing to what was the importing country. The resourceful transferee will seek means of increasing sales and profits.

At this point, key marketing decisions focus on acquiring or introducing products especially for the local market. For example, Japanese car makers now are developing cars specifically for the United States from design studios in California to be built in their "transplants" in America. Ford's new "world car," named the Mondeo, was developed primarily in Europe for adaptation and manufacture in plants in the United States, Latin America, and Asia.

REGIONALIZATION

As the exporter's operations become nationalized in one of the regional blocs, the company establishes an international regional management center and transfers responsibilities for day-to-day management from the home country to the regional office. The regions are the major trading areas of Europe, Latin America, Asia-Pacific, and North America. Numerous American companies followed this pattern after World War II: exporting, establishing local subsidiaries, and acquiring local companies. Corporations such as ITT, S. C. Johnson, Procter & Gamble, and IBM all had European management centers by the 1960s, and most major companies have management centers now for Latin America, usually directed from Miami, and the Asia-Pacific region, directed from Hong Kong, Singapore, Sydney, or Tokyo. When a company is regionalized, it may still focus on its domestic market, but international considerations become more important. In the 1980s, Ford Motor Company lost money on North American automobile operations but was profitable and growing in Europe, which sustained the whole organization.

THE GLOBAL PERSPECTIVE

After a company has established regional operations with a management structure in Europe, Latin America, and the Pacific, if it is still managing its North American operations as well as the regional activities from North America, it faces the ultimate decision: Should it establish a world corporate headquarters? That is,

[2]Karen Mitchell, "Samurai Spirit Lives in Boulder Company," *Business Plus* (January 7, 1997):3.

AD 23.1

WITH THIS "SMILES" CAMPAIGN, AMERICAN AIRLINES PROJECTED ITS WELCOMING IMAGE IN EUROPEAN MARKETS, SPECIFI- CALLY (CLOCKWISE) THE UNITED KINGDOM, SWEDEN, FRANCE, AND SPAIN.

Global Perspective: A corporate philosophy that directs products and advertising toward a worldwide rather than a local or regional market.

should North American and global operations be separated and a new global headquarters created? Once this decision has been made, a truly **global perspective** will emerge, one not tied to any geographic area. Change to such an international or global management structure has been made by companies such as Unilever and Shell (both of which have twin world headquarters in the United Kingdom and the Netherlands), Arthur Andersen, IBM, Nestlé, and Interpublic.

The achievement of a global perspective requires internationalizing the management group. As long as management is drawn exclusively from one country, a global perspective is difficult to achieve in a manufacturing company—or in an advertising agency. Table 23.2a depicts the top 10 U.S. agencies in terms of their worldwide gross income. To see which ones are more international than others in terms of their revenue streams, compare this table with Tables 23.2b and c.

TABLE 23.2A   WHO'S ON TOP IN LATIN AMERICA

RANK	AGENCY	1992 LAT. AM. GROSS INCOME BY EQUITY	% CHANGE FROM 1991	1992 LAT. AM. BILLINGS BY EQUITY	1992 GAAP GROSS INCOME
1	McCann-Erickson Worldwide	$108,912	27.8	$726,072	$108,912
2	Lintas: Worldwide	70,164	−14.6	467,990	69,710
3	J. Walter Thompson Co.	61,895	26.5	376,920	56,894
4	Young & Rubicam	50,584	58.2	289,959	50,557
5	Ogilvy & Mather Worldwide	50,335	47.8	293,720	48,099
6	Leo Burnett Co.	45,137	39.9	307,412	46,130
7	BBDO Worldwide	33,705	59.6	155,638	42,352
8	Grey Advertising	29,022	42.7	174,385	27,845
9	Duailibi, Petit, Zaragoza	28,000	−29.0	106,830	28,000
10	Foote, Cone & Belding Communications	24,810	31.4	165,187	28,492

Figures are in thousands. GAAP = Generally Accepted Accounting Principles: Equity less than 50% excluded; if an agency owns 50% or more equity, 100% of gross income included. Agency omitted because it lacks an office outside the home country is Salles/Interamericana de Publicidade.

Source: Reprinted with permission from *Advertising Age* (May 17, 1993):I-22. Copyright, Crain Communications, Inc., 1993.

TABLE 23.2B   WHO'S ON TOP IN ASIA/PACIFIC

RANK	AGENCY	1992 ASIA/PACIFIC GROSS INCOME BY EQUITY	% CHANGE FROM 1991	1992 ASIA/PACIFIC BILLINGS BY EQUITY	1992 GAAP GROSS INCOME
1	Dentsu	$1,283,432	−4.4	$9,668,350	$1,285,012
2	Hakuhodo	578,288	0.7	4,548,365	579,967
3	Daiko	175,901	0.9	1,330,860	175,901
4	Asatsu	153,815	8.9	1,182,920	153,815
5	Dai-ichi Kikaku	123,700	−5.5	892,381	125,779
6	McCann-Erickson Worldwide	115,504	8.2	770,411	170,254
7	I&S Corp.	107,412	2.5	854,447	107,412
8	Dentsu, Young & Rubicam Partnerships	105,968	6.2	735,983	107,320
9	J. Walter Thompson Co.	104,088	26.2	695,131	105,485
10	Chell Communications	103,330	4.1	377,983	104,561
11	Backer Spielvogel Bates	103,215	6.6	685,780	106,697
12	Leo Burnett Co.	83,672	6.2	557,831	81,582
13	Ogilvy & Mather Worldwide	72,842	−10.4	506,235	63,032
14	Foote, Cone & Belding Communications	57,579	6.4	357,970	53,969
15	Lintas: Worldwide	56,424	12.4	376,338	60,549

Figures are in thousands. GAAP = Generally Accepted Accounting Principles: Equity less than 50% excluded; if an agency owns 50% or more equity, 100% of gross income included. Agencies omitted because they lack an office outside their home country include Tokyu Agency, Tokyo; Yomiko Advertising, Tokyo; Asahi Advertising, Tokyo; Man Nen Sha, Osaka, Japan; Nikkeisha Inc., Tokyo.

Source: Reprinted with permission from *Advertising Age* (May 17, 1993):I-22. Copyright, Crain Communications, Inc., 1993.

| TABLE 23.2c | WHO'S ON TOP IN EUROPE | | | | |

RANK	AGENCY	1992 EUROPEAN GROSS INCOME BY EQUITY	% CHANGE FROM 1991	1992 EUROPEAN BILLINGS BY EQUITY	1992 GAAP GROSS INCOME
1	Euro RSCG	$775,494	−2.6	$5,355,014	$775,494
2	Publicis FCB	560,437	12.6	3,746,425	557,727
3	McCann-Erickson Worldwide	417,995	13.0	2,788,028	418,429
4	Young & Rubicam	372,220	−2.6	2,563,193	412,546
5	Backer Spielvogel Bates Worldwide	339,515	18.1	2,270,738	366,288
6	Saatchi & Saatchi Advertising Worldwide	335,823	7.8	2,336,228	340,827
7	Ogilvy & Mather Worldwide	323,967	0.7	2,336,687	312,694
8	Lintas: Worldwide	323,854	4.5	2,160,111	322,242
9	J. Walter Thompson Co.	321,796	7.1	2,314,833	311,719
10	Grey Advertising	312,171	13.3	2,109,466	335,383
11	DDB Needham Worldwide	296,673	18.2	2,125,447	293,521
12	BBDO Worldwide	263,378	13.5	1,835,829	346,186
13	D'Arcy Masius Benton & Bowles	251,597	8.1	1,916,220	254,149
14	BDDP Worldwide	213,931	6.5	1,294,010	213,931
15	Leo Burnett Co.	173,278	13.7	1,155,242	173,766
16	Lowe Group	167,279	31.6	1,115,262	171,134
17	N W Ayer	96,485	35.9	686,419	109,602
18	TBWA	95,512	9.4	690,055	107,974
19	FCA Group	76,258	13.3	571,913	78,472
20	Armando Testa Group	73,303	12.2	559,597	69,424

Figures are in thousands. GAAP = Generally Accepted Accounting Principles: Equity less than 50% excluded; if an agency owns 50% or more equity, 100% of gross income included.

Source: Reprinted with permission from *Advertising Age* (May 17, 1993):I-22. Copyright, Crain Communications, Inc., 1993.

As mentioned earlier, virtually every product category can be divided into local (or national), regional (trading bloc), and international brands. *International brands* are those that are marketed in two or more of the four major regional market blocs: North America, Latin America, Europe, and Asia-Pacific. (China is becoming a major part of the Asia-Pacific bloc.) Although the Eastern European bloc will exist as a trading region for years, the Western-most countries in this group seem likely to be subsumed into the European bloc, while Russia and the Asian republics of the former Soviet Union may coalesce into a smaller fifth bloc. The sixth bloc—Africa, the Middle East, and Southern Asia—is so much smaller economically than the others that it is usually attached to Europe or Asia-Pacific in the way in which it is managed as a regional bloc.

GLOBAL BRANDS

Global Brand: A brand that has the same name, same design, and same creative strategy everywhere in the world.

Substitute the word *global* for *international* and the controversy begins. A **global brand** is one that has the same name, design, and creative strategy everywhere in the world and is marketed in most of the major regional market blocs. The product that is almost always used as an example of a global brand is Coca-Cola. The global definition breaks down slightly, however, because Classic Coke appears only in the United States and a few other markets. Elsewhere Coke is Coke, and it is marketed virtually the same way everywhere.

Other global brands are emerging as well: Revlon, IBM, Apple, Marlboro, Xerox (including Rank Xerox and Fuji Xerox), Avis, Hertz, Chanel, Gillette, BMW, Mercedes-Benz, products from Pepsi-Cola Foods, McDonald's, Rolex, Toyota, Nissan, Ford, and Henkel all have global brands in their product lines, or their company name is considered a global trademark. The controversy arises not so much over the concept of a global brand, as defined, but how and whether or not it will be realized.

THE GLOBAL DEBATE AND ADVERTISING

The global controversy was ignited by an article in the May/June 1983 issue of *Harvard Business Review* by Theodore Levitt, professor of business administration and marketing at Harvard Business School. In his article, Levitt argued that companies should operate as if there were only one global market. He stated that differences among nations and cultures were not only diminishing but should be ignored altogether because people throughout the world are motivated by the same desires and wants. Furthermore, Levitt argued, businesses will be more efficient if they plan for a global market. In other words, we should see the world market as one.

The London-based Saatchi & Saatchi company adopted this philosophy in a bid to become the first global advertising agency. In 1984 the agency ran a two-page ad in both *The New York Times* and the *Times* of London with the headline, "The Opportunity for World Brands." This ad applied Levitt's global proposition to advertising and to the service to be expected of global agencies.

Under the subheading, "Impact on Agency Structure," Saatchi & Saatchi stated in its ad:

What are the implications of these trends for the advertising industry? . . .

Most observers believe that the trend to pan-regional or global marketing will have a marked impact on the structure of advertising agencies . . . because world brands require world agencies.

A HANDFUL OF WORLDWIDE AGENCY NETWORKS WILL HANDLE THE BULK OF $140 BILLION IN WORLD ADVERTISING EXPENDITURE FOR MAJOR MULTINATIONALS.[3]

Other agencies tried to incorporate the global concept as well. A typical response was that of Grey Advertising, which took the position "Global Vision with Local Touch." As one of Grey's presentations states:

Every idea needs a champion and Global Vision with Local Touch needs several at both the client company and its agencies . . . . The role of these Grey champions is to:

- Provide the global vision
- Look for the positive signals that point to global applications
- Ward off the NIH (not invented here) factor and develop mutual trust and respect with local client managers
- Employ all of Grey's tools, knowledge, and considerable resources to achieve global application.[4]

Philip Kotler, marketing professor at Northwestern University, disagreed with Levitt's philosophy. According to Kotler, Levitt misinterpreted the overseas success of Coca-Cola, PepsiCo, and McDonald's. "Their success," he argued, "is based on variation, not offering the same product everywhere."[5] Eight years later, in 1992, Levitt remained committed to his position, "I haven't backed away from the theory of globalization. It's a big mistake for advertisers to think that everything is becoming narrow. The challenge is to effectively come up with ways to communicate the same message to a homogenized audience all over the world."[6]

The focus of this section is on global perspective. Levitt and Kotler are theorizing; neither is totally correct. Global advertising is restricted by language, reg-

PRINCIPLE Ideas are global; products or services that embody those ideas might not be.

[3]Courtesy of Saatchi & Saatchi.

[4]Courtesy of Grey Advertising.

[5]"Colleague Says Levitt Wrong," *Advertising Age* (June 25, 1984):50.

[6]Kevin Goldman, "Professor Levitt Stands by Global Ad Theory," *The Wall Street Journal* (October 13, 1992):B7.

ulation, and lack of global media. The direction toward global markets, however, is inescapable. Will true global advertising ever be achieved? Probably not. At least probably not soon. Ideas are global. Management thinking is increasingly global. The challenge in advertising is the careful and sophisticated use of Kotler's "variations" nationally or regionally under a basic Levitt-style global plan.

OPEN MARKETS AND REGULATIONS

As the Eastern bloc shed the stifling weight of a planned economy, abolishing regulations and freeing businesses to compete, the opposite trend appeared in the Common Market and North America. New regulations were proposed, more restrictions were written into law, and draft provisions for a unified Common Market after 1992 alarmed the advertising industry. While comparative advertising, for example, is banned in Germany (although cleared recently for use in Greece), comparative ads are still frowned upon in many European countries. Piracy is an issue everywhere but some countries are less interested in regulating the practice. (See the Issues and Controversies box.)

These concerns came to a head at the International Advertising Association (IAA) world convention in Hamburg, Germany, in June 1990. Philip Geier of Interpublic challenged the attendees by stating that no organization adequately represented the three segments of the industry—the advertisers, the media, and the agencies. The IAA, under the leadership of its director-general, Norman Vale, former Grey Advertising executive, successfully pulled the warring or disaffected elements together by convincing the parties that the IAA was best suited for the task. It then began a coordinated effort to maintain more freedom and individual rights in consumer markets, in Europe and elsewhere.[7]

From this start, the IAA developed an advertising campaign that has been run in virtually every country in the world. A benchmark research project was conducted for the IAA by Gallup International in 22 countries in Europe, Asia-Pacific, Africa, and Latin America. Some 22,000 respondents were asked to agree or disagree with eight statements. The IAA cited four answers to its members:

1. **ADVERTISING HAS AN IMPORTANT ROLE TO PLAY IN THE HEALTH OF A MODERN ECONOMY.** Agreement with this statement was high with 75 percent among Western Europeans, 76 percent in Asia-Pacific, and 71 percent in the Baltic republics. Bulgaria and South Africa (82 percent) plus Uruguay (81 percent) were in exceptionally high agreement. Egypt was the only country to disagree, with 77 percent of the population overall and 32 percent disagreeing completely. Majorities clustered around the midpoint in the United Kingdom (62 percent), Finland (59 percent), Japan (56 percent), and New Zealand (50 percent).

2. **IF A PRODUCT IS LEGAL TO SELL, IT SHOULD ALSO BE LEGAL TO ADVERTISE.** In all countries, majorities in excess of 65 percent agreed. Estonia (91 percent) and Bulgaria (88 percent) exhibited the highest level of agreement. Countries where a third or more of the population agreed completely were Switzerland (32 percent), Estonia (47 percent), South Africa (55 percent), Latvia (38 percent), Bulgaria (55 percent), Finland (34 percent), Turkey (32 percent), Australia (32 percent), and Uruguay (38 percent).

3. **ADVERTISING HELPS IMPROVE THE QUALITY OF GOODS AND SERVICES BY CAUSING COMPANIES TO COMPETE MORE DIRECTLY WITH ONE ANOTHER.** Approximately 70 percent of respondents agree with this statement, with the highest level of agreement from Bulgaria (87 percent), South Africa (84 percent), Uruguay (80 percent), Australia, New Zealand, and Finland (78 percent).

4. **WITHOUT ADVERTISING, NEWSPAPERS AND MAGAZINES WOULD BE MORE COSTLY OR UNAVAILABLE IN SUCH A WIDE VARIETY.** Overall, there was over-

---

[7]*International Advertising Association Perspectives* (November 20, 1990).

*I*SSUES AND *C*ONTROVERSIES

MODERN-DAY PIRATES

You're traveling in Southeast Asia and have an opportunity to visit the outdoor market in Chinatown in Kuala Lumpur, Malaysia. Covering many city blocks, the market is a shopper's fantasy with stalls selling everything from Calvin Klein T-shirts and jeans to Ralph Lauren's signature Polo shirts, Coach bags, and Rolex watches. The question is: Would you buy? The problem is that many of these products are counterfeit.

Marketers with big brands, worried more about their loss of image than monetary loss, are battling with international pirates who steal their logos, packages, and sometimes counterfeit their products. In negotiations with the Chinese, the U.S. trade representative held up two boxes of Microsoft Word—one legitimate, one a copy. There was no way to tell the difference, other than the price.

China has been indifferent to its citizens' unauthorized copyright and trademark use of international marketers' software, music, film, apparel, and sporting goods. However, it agreed to enforce its own laws against piracy and undertook a nationwide crackdown in 1995 in order to be awarded the 1996 Olympiad trademark licenses. The Chinese are not the only marketing pirates. The International Intellectual Property Alliance (IIPA) also cites Turkey, Bulgaria, and Indonesia on its list of priority-watch countries.

The IIPA also estimates that Japan and Germany were the leading sources of monetary loss to piracy. The Software Publishers Association (SPA), representing 1,200 business, education, and consumer software marketers, estimates that the Singapore market cost U.S. software marketers $33 million last year, small potatoes compared to markets like Germany with an estimated $1.1 billion loss and Japan where the SPA estimates U.S. industry losses at $1.3 billion a year, the world's highest rate. And that's only one industry. Germany, as concerned as the United States about the piracy problem, has passed a tough new law called the Brand Law that enables marketers to protect not only their brand logo but also the logo's colors and the product's packaging design.

As piracy has escalated, marketers and industry trade associations worldwide have increased their vigilance in lobbying lawmakers, instigating local police seizures, and even ad campaigns. International marketers, such as Reebok and Levi Strauss, are fighting their battles with public relations campaigns. Reebok, fighting piracy in China and South Korea, reaches its trade audience with its message about supporting legitimate brands through articles in business and trade publications.

The Motion Picture Association is running an ongoing cinema and videocassette trailer campaign in Belgium, Germany, Italy, and the United Kingdom. In Latin America, the group has targeted Venezuela, a growing piracy market, for an antipiracy poster campaign. A spokesperson for the association said, "The video trailer in Europe is working very well, with a toll-free hot line [for consumers reporting piracy]."

Washington-based Software Publishers Association this month broke a Singapore antipiracy campaign in both Singapore and Malaysia. The education-and-enforcement campaign is the association's first outside the United States. Previously the association has distributed ads in Spanish for Mexico and Costa Rica, in Portuguese for Brazil, and in Hebrew for Israel.

The bottom line is that piracy hurts brands and consumers of brands. If Ralph Lauren's Polo brand gets copied so much that the original brand is unrecognizable, then why buy Polo? As the marketplace becomes more and more international, the problem only becomes greater. Regardless of where you live, the money you invest in buying a brand is wasted if the brand loses its cachet. How can that message be communicated through advertising and other forms of marketing communication? What message makes that point?

So go back to your imaginary trip through the marketplace in Kuala Lumpur (or walk down a street in New York City). Would you buy the incredibly cheap Rolex watch?

Sources: Adapted from "Modern Day Pirates a Threat Worldwide," *Advertising Age* (March 20, 1995):I3; "Halting the World's Pirates," *Advertising Age* (March 20, 1995):I26.

whelming agreement in all countries. Most noticeably, agreement was particularly strong (more than 80 percent) in the United Kingdom. The Netherlands, Luxembourg, Switzerland, Germany, Finland, Japan, Australia, New Zealand, and Uruguay were also in agreement. The newly democratized countries of Central and Eastern Europe, although in agreement with this statement (ranging from 51 percent to 76 percent), were in less agreement than the other countries. This lower awareness of advertising's contribution to print media could be attributed to government control of media and lack of advertising in these countries before the fall of communism.[8]

Gallup found widely differing opinions on a fifth statement: *If advertising were banned tomorrow, I would miss it.* As Figure 23.2 shows, 79 percent disagreed with that statement in Egypt, and would not miss advertising, while 78 percent in

---

[8]*IAA Hotline Bulletin* (October 11, 1993).

Responses to the statement, "If advertising were banned tommorrow, I would miss it."

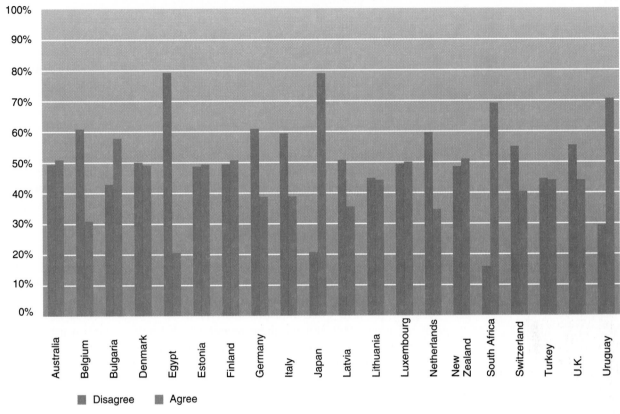

FIGURE 23.2

GLOBAL ATTITUDES TOWARD ADVERTISING.

Note: Percentages do not necessarily total 100% due to non-response or answer of "Don't know."

Source: Gallup International

Japan, 71 percent in Uruguay, and 68 percent in South Africa said they would miss advertising.

Michael Reinarz, director of visual communications at Nestlé, explains the dichotomy between the breakdown of the restrictive communist system in the Eastern countries and the increase in legislative control and censorship in the West:

> For both the West and the East it is the loss of power to the people. Once people are informed—have tasted freedom and can choose freely their religion, political party, newspaper, TV channel, supermarket, or spaghetti brand—that freedom cannot be taken away. And if people have the choice and therefore the power, one must "sell" them a specific ideology, religion, newspaper, TV channel, supermarket, or spaghetti brand. This means politicians, religious leaders, media owners, distributors, and manufacturers all have to do "marketing."[9]

Consequently, Reinarz states, competition is the key to any successful economic system. A free market economy not only is preferable, it is mandatory. His solution to the growing changes in Eastern and Western thought is simple: "All goods and services which are legally in the marketplace should enjoy the same freedom of commercial speech. Now that the Eastern countries have begun to acknowledge this philosophy, we must make sure that the West does not forget it."

[9]Michael Reinarz, "Will the West Liberate Itself After the East?" *IAA Perspectives* (August 24, 1990).

International Management

As soon as a second country is added to a company's operations, management practices begin to change. Experience has shown that regardless of the company's form or style of management, internationalization requires new management disciplines or tools. These tools include one language (usually English), one control mechanism (the budget), and one strategic plan (the marketing strategy).

LINGUA FRANCA

It is not difficult to understand why English would be the language of choice. Because the expansion of international marketing was accomplished chiefly by American companies within the Common Market, language was not an issue. To succeed within the company, and sometimes even to be hired, a person needed a working knowledge of English.

The American companies brought with them standardized forms of accounting, law, and banking. As a result, local lawyers, accountants, and bankers found it necessary to speak English in order to serve international clients and to have a hope of securing business from local companies owned or operated by Americans.

Language also affects the creation of the advertising itself. English normally requires the least space in printed material or air time. The range of words (estimated at over 900,000) and the ease with which English adopts words from other languages make it more exact and more economical than other languages. This creates a major problem when the space for copy is laid out for English and one-third more space is needed for French or Spanish.

Headlines in any language often involve a play on words, themes that are relevant to one country, or slang. The images called to mind in the originating language are distorted or poorly communicated in another. Unintentional meanings, slang, and national styles must be removed from the advertising unless the meaning or intent can be recreated in other languages. For this reason, international campaigns are not translated, they are rewritten by a copywriter into a second language.

As demonstrated in the opening story, every international advertiser has an example of how a word translated into another language produced a disaster. An example is Coca-Cola's use of "Coke adds life" in China. The Chinese translation reportedly came out "Coke brings your ancestors back from the dead." On the same note, translations of languages into English have the same problems. From a Japanese hotel: "You are invited to take advantage of the chambermaid." From a Bangkok dry cleaners: "Drop your trousers here for best results." From an ad for a Rome laundry: "Ladies, leave your clothes here and spend the afternoon having a good time." And from a Moscow weekly: "There will be a Moscow Exhibition of Arts by 15,000 Soviet Republic painters. These were executed over the past two years."

Some languages simply do not have words equivalent to English expressions. Computer words and advertising terms are almost universally of English derivation. There are even problems translating English to English as the following dictionary of BritSpeak illustrates.[10] There are, however, some unexpected commonalities between the United Kingdom and the United States as Ad 23.2 about road rage points out.

The French since 1539 have had legislation to keep their language "pure" and now have a government agency to prevent words, especially English words, from corrupting the French language. *Marketing* and *weekend*, unacceptable to the French government agency, are translated literally as "study of the market" or in another attempt "pertaining to trade," and "end of the week," respectively. Nei-

---

[10]"A Pitch With a New Angle," *Brandweek* (November 11, 1996):20.

AD 23.2

AN AD FROM THE U.K.
ADDRESSES ROAD RAGE.
BECAUSE OF THE POWER OF THE
VISUAL, IT IS UNDERSTOOD EAS-
ILY IN OTHER COUNTRIES THAT
HAVE HIGHWAY CONGESTION.

DO YOU GO INTO REVERSE EVERY TIME YOU DRIVE?

Don't drive like a dipstick.

ther captures the essence of the English word. As if to prove how difficult it is to dislodge the most appropriate word, the French functionary who announced the preceding equivalents for *marketing* and *weekend* was pressed at the news conference why the agency head was not present. Without thinking, he replied "Monsieur is gone for *le weekend.*"

BILINGUAL COPYWRITING

Experience has shown that the only reasonable solution to language problems is to employ bilingual copywriters who understand the full meaning of the English text and can capture the essence of the message in the second language. It takes a brave and trusting international creative director to approve copy he or she doesn't understand but is assured is right. A *back translation* into English is always a good idea, but it never conveys a cultural interpretation. The language problem is intensified in bilingual countries such as Canada or Belgium, and even more in Switzerland which has three main languages, or in China which has more than 20 dialects. Multiple back translations can produce sharply different messages in English, even if they have the desired strategic focus in the language used.

STRATEGIC PLAN

The strategic plan is prepared in conjunction with the budget. Basically, the plan outlines the marketing strategy, whereas the budget allocates the funds. If one is changed, the other must change as well. This principle is especially important in international management. Two major models of assessing how to advertise in foreign cultures have developed, one market oriented, the other culture oriented.

AN ENGLISH-TO-ENGLISH DICTIONARY

Rubber: an eraser	Estate car: station wagon
Ladder: a run in a stocking	Hoover, Hoovering: vacuum cleaner, to vacuum
Bonnet: a car's hood	Wind-up: a practical joke
Queue: to stand in line	Taking a piss: to make fun of someone or something
Freephone: a toll-free number	
Fag: cigarette	Adapted from "A Pitch With a New Angle," *Brandweek* (November 11, 1996):20.

THE MARKET-ANALYSIS MODEL

This model is based on data and observation from several countries. It recognizes the existence of local, regional, and international brands in almost every product category. The two major variables are the share of market of brands within a category and the size of the category. For example, the brand's percentage share of the category market might vary substantially in four countries:

	COUNTRY A	COUNTRY B	COUNTRY C	COUNTRY D
Global Brands	25%	30%	50%	20%
Regional Brands	60	30	10	55
Local Brands	15	40	40	25

According to this example, Country C looks very valuable for the global brand. Considering the size of the market changes the picture, however. Assume that the category market in the four countries is as follows:

	COUNTRY A	COUNTRY B	COUNTRY C	COUNTRY D
Category Units	200,000	100,000	50,000	300,000
Global Brands	25%	30%	50%	20%
Global Market Size	50,000	30,000	25,000	60,000

When the market-analysis model is used, Country C actually is much less important. Half of this smaller market is already in global brands. Country D not only is a larger global brand market but also is a much larger total market. A headquarters marketing manager must look not only at share but also at market size, growth rates, and opportunities for growth through new products or increased expenditures.

For example, cola-flavored soft drinks are not nearly as dominant in Germany as they are in the United States. To generate sales in Germany, therefore, a soft-drink company would have to develop orange and lemon-lime entries. McDonald's serves beer in Germany, wine in France, a local fruit-flavored shake in Singapore and Malaysia, and even a Portuguese sausage in Hawaii, in addition to the traditional Big Macs, fish sandwiches, and French fries in order to cater to local tastes.

Such "variations" to the uniform global-brand strategy are adjusted by market, by season, and by company. Wise global companies employ a flexible global strategy and allow management to test new local brands. They realize that almost every successful global or multinational brand started as a local brand somewhere. In contrast, in 1990, after extensive research and development, Gillette launched the Sensor razor virtually worldwide without first establishing it in one country. The product was so successful that Gillette had difficulty fulfilling early demand.

The largest advertising agencies have benefited from the increasing volume of global planning. In the 13 years from 1976 to 1989, the market share of the multinational agencies rose from 14 percent to 30 percent of worldwide billings, as advertisers aligned brand advertising with the same agencies across Europe, Asia, and North America. By 1992, top ten agency networks' combined share of global ad spending had risen to more than 48 percent.[11]

See Table 23.3 for the 25 largest global advertising agencies. Compare this with Table 23.2 to see how many non-U.S. agencies are on this list. Note that the biggest agency in the world is Tokyo's Dentsu. In the top five, three are U.S. based and two are Japanese. The first agency from a different country is Saatchi & Saatchi, which comes eleventh, followed by Euro RSCG and Publicis Communication of France.

---

[11]"The Global Decade of Alignment," *Advertising Age* (September 20, 1993):1–10.

TABLE 23.3	WORLD'S TOP 25 AGENCY BRANDS			
RANK			**WORLDWIDE GROSS INCOME**	
1995	**1994**	**AGENCY**	**1995**	**1994**	**% CHG**
1	1	Dentsu	$1,930.0	$1,583.7	21.9
2	2	McCann-Erickson Worldwide	1,153.9	1,037.0	11.3
3	3	J. Walter Thompson Co.	1,007.1	887.7	13.4
4	4	Hakuhodo	958.6	774.2	23.8
5	5	BBDO Worldwide	857.5	736.5	16.4
6	7	Leo Burnett Co.	803.9	677.5	18.7
7	8	DDB Needham Worldwide	785.7	661.7	18.7
8	6	Grey Advertising	777.3	703.0	10.6
9	9	Ogilvy & Mather Worldwide	714.1	611.4	16.8
10	10	Foote, Cone & Belding Communications	679.0	605.2	12.2
11	11	Saatchi &Saatchi Advertising	676.9	602.7	12.3
12	12	Euro RSCG	643.4	568.6	13.2
13	14	Publicis Communications	606.3	543.2	11.6
14	15	Bates Worldwide	575.2	510.3	12.7
15	13	Ammirati Puris Lintas	568.3	545.7	4.1
16	16	Young & Rubicam	555.8	498.1	11.6
17	17	D'Arcy Massius Benton & Bowles	497.0	483.5	2.8
18	18	TBWA International	318.2	287.3	10.7
19	19	Lowe Group	310.3	280.9	10.5
20	21	Bozell Worldwide	279.9	224.7	24.6
21	20	BDDP Group	278.5	263.3	5.8
22	23	Asatsu Inc.	254.1	210.1	20.9
23	22	Tokyu Agency	238.5	212.1	12.4
24	24	Daiko Advertising	211.1	202.7	4.1
25	26	Wunderman Cato Johnson	209.5	167.5	25.1

Notes: Figures are in millions of U.S. dollars. Each worldwide agency brand excludes U.S. branded subsidiary shops ranked elsewhere in this report. Included are international networks associated with the agency.

Reprinted with permission from *Advertising Age*. Copyright Crain Communications Inc.

THE CULTURE-ORIENTED MODEL

The second model of international advertising emphasizes the cultural differences among peoples and nations. This school of thought recognizes that people worldwide share certain needs, but it also stresses the fact that these needs are met differently in different cultures.

Although the same emotions are basic to all humanity, the degree to which these emotions are expressed publicly varies from culture to culture. The camaraderie typical in an Australian business office would be unthinkable in Japan. The informal, first-name basis relationships common in North America are frowned upon in Germany, where coworkers often do not use first names. In Japan, the gulf between management and staff is submerged in uniforms and group dynamics but is actually wider than in most Western nations. Likewise, the ways in which we categorize information and the values we attach to people, places, and things depend on the setting in which we were raised.

HIGH-CONTEXT VERSUS LOW-CONTEXT CULTURES

How do cultural differences relate to advertising? According to the high-context/low-context theory, although the *function* of advertising is the same throughout the world, the expression of its message varies in different cultural settings.[12] The major distinction is between *high-context cultures*, in which the mean-

---

[12]The high-context/low-context distinction is adapted from two books by Edward T. Hall, *The Silent Language* (New York: Doubleday, 1973) and *Beyond Culture* (New York: Doubleday, 1977).

ing of a message can be understood only within a specific context, and *low-context cultures*, in which the message can be understood as an independent entity. The following is a list of cultures from high to low context, with Japanese being the highest-context culture: Japanese, Chinese, Arabic, Greek, Spanish, Italian, English, French, North American, Scandinavian, and German.

As mentioned earlier, an issue that cannot be overlooked in international advertising involves language concerns. The differences between Japanese and English are instructive. English is a low-context language. English words have very clearly defined meanings that are not highly dependent on the words surrounding them. In Japanese, however, a word can have multiple meanings. Listeners or readers will not understand the exact meaning of a word unless they clearly understand the preceding or following sentences, that is, the context in which the word is used.

Advertising messages constructed by writers from high-context cultures might be difficult to understand in low-context cultures because they do not get right to the point. In contrast, messages constructed by writers from low-context cultures may be difficult to understand in high-context cultures because they omit essential contextual detail.

In discussing the Japanese way of advertising, Takashi Michioka, president of DYR, joint-venture agency of Young & Rubicam and Dentsu, put it this way: In Japan, differentiation among products does not consist of explaining with words the points of difference among competing products as in America. Differentiation is achieved by bringing out the people appearing in the commercial—the way they talk, the music, the scenery—rather than emphasizing the unique features and dissimilarities of the product itself.

BUDGET CONTROL

The budget has become almost another language—in this instance, one of control. Centralized companies distribute budget responsibility to branch operations. As a result, techniques of forecasting, currency fluctuation, hedging against swings in exchange rates, and monitoring have improved, especially with the development of advanced computer techniques. Companies have refined budget steps, standardized budget philosophies, and now tie performance to achievement. Local managements negotiate final budgets.

STRUCTURE OF INTERNATIONAL ADVERTISING

Although the United States still dominates world advertising spending, advertising growth rates outside the United States, reinforced by a weaker dollar since 1985, have outstripped U.S. growth. Table 23.4a and b identifies the top ten U.S. cities and non-U.S. cities in terms of their advertising volume. Although big markets still dominate most of advertising's creative work, smaller agencies in cities not known as hotbeds of advertising excellence are also still hard at work. For example, South Africa's largest agency, Ogilvy & Mather Rightford, was named International Agency of the Year by *Advertising Age* in 1996.

Most international advertisers can be analyzed according to the model presented in Figure 23.3. Most companies fall on the axis from similar products and centralized managements (quadrant 1) to different or localized products and decentralized managements (quadrant 3). There are exceptions, however. For example, McDonald's products are largely standardized, and its international management is decentralized (quadrant 2). Nestlé allows some local autonomy but markets a large number of products (quadrant 4). Each company develops its own policy to guide its application of resources in regional or global marketing.

TABLE 23.4A TOP 10 U.S. CITIES BY VOLUME

RANK 1995	MARKET	TOTAL LOCAL SHOP BILLINGS			SHOPS REPORTING	TOP OFFICE IN MARKET BY LOCAL VOLUME	VOLUME 1995
		1995	1994	% CHG			
1	New York	$29,929.8	$27,053.2	10.6	143	Grey Advertising	$1,871.9
2	Chicago	9,496.3	8,152.0	16.5	73	Leo Burnett Co.	2,484.8
3	Los Angeles	6,231.9	5,575.9	11.8	53	TBWA Chiat/Day	602.2
4	Detroit	5,720.9	5,180.6	10.4	24	Campbell-Ewald (Detroit, Mich.)	843.6
5	San Francisco	3,629.9	3,106.5	16.8	31	Foote, Cone & Belding Communications	620.0
6	Minneapolis	2,535.0	2,169.7	16.8	19	Gage Marketing Group	723.8
7	Boston	2,373.1	1,965.2	20.8	27	Bronner Slosberg Humphrey	450.2
8	Dallas	2,364.6	2,163.3	9.3	22	DDB Needham	623.0
9	Connecticut	1,348.7	1,173.0	15.0	17	Barry Blau & Partners (Fairfield)	332.7
10	Atlanta	1,174.7	1,154.8	1.7	24	BBDO Worldwide	214.3

Notes: Billings (capitalized volume) are in millions of U.S. dollars. U.S. markets are limited to local billings. Totals are based on nearly 800 offices of 621 U.S. agencies.
Reprinted with permission from *Advertising Age*. Copyright Crain Communications Inc.

TABLE 23.4B TOP 10 NON-U.S. CITIES BY VOLUME

RANK 1995	MARKET	TOTAL LOCAL SHOP BILLINGS			SHOPS REPORTING	TOP OFFICE IN MARKET BY LOCAL VOLUME	VOLUME 1995
		1995	1994	% CHG			
1	Tokyo	$35,839.1	$30,668.5	16.9	50	Dentsu Inc.	$12,412.9
2	London	12,447.4	10,790.6	15.4	76	Saatchi & Saatchi Advertising Group	1,071.8
3	Paris	9,917.2	8,373.5	18.4	50	Euro RSCG France	1,706.6
4	Frankfurt	4,454.2	3,577.9	24.5	18	Ogilvy & Mather	964.5
5	Düsseldorf	3,691.3	3,014.7	22.4	16	BBDO Group Germany	916.6
6	Madrid	3,601.6	3,099.3	16.2	30	Bates Holding	322.0
7	São Paulo	3,494.7	2,907.3	20.2	26	McCann-Erickson	556.9
8	Seoul	3,010.2	2,190.9	37.4	16	Chell Communications	869.8
9	Sydney	2,978.9	2,485.3	19.9	35	George Patterson Pty. (Bates)	615.5
10	Milan	2,906.8	2,837.1	2.5	35	Young & Rubicam Italia	369.6

Reprinted with permission from *Advertising Age*. Copyright Crain Communications Inc.

Agencies have to develop techniques to service brands that are marketed around the world. Some agencies exercise tight control, while others allow more local autonomy. All of these techniques fall into three groups: tight central international control, centralized resources with moderate control, and matching the

FIGURE 23.3

THE PRODUCT MANAGEMENT AXIS.

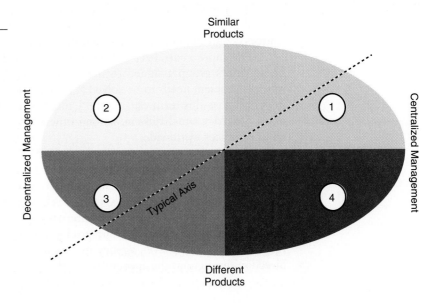

client. Henkel, a large German manufacturer of household and cleaning products, provides an example of how centralized management with similar products works. Henkel's international strategy was designed to accomplish three goals: to eliminate duplication of effort among its national companies, to provide central direction for new products, and to achieve efficiency in advertising production and impact. It included these steps:

- Identifying the need to be fulfilled or the function of a product.
- Determining the commonality of that need or its benefit in Europe or a larger area.
- Assigning that specific need or benefit to one product with one brand name.
- Assigning that brand to one brand manager and one advertising agency to develop and market.
- Not allowing the benefit, the name, or the creative campaign of that brand to be used by any other brand in the company.

ORGANIZING FOR INTERNATIONAL ADVERTISING

Agencies that handle global campaigns operate either with a tight central control or with centralized resources and moderate control that allow some local initiatives. In many cases agencies are organized to match the structure of their clients. McCann-Erickson, a subsidiary of Interpublic Group, relies on tight central international control. Among its clients, McCann-Erickson handles Coca-Cola. The Leo Burnett Company uses a very similar system, especially for Marlboro cigarettes. Agencies such as BBDO Worldwide, Grey Advertising, and DDB Needham centralize their resources for clients but allow their agencies local autonomy in creatively executing centrally planned strategies.

Table 23.5 is a listing of the top 25 world advertising organizations. These are conglomerates that own a number of different agencies. Omnicom Group, for example, includes the BBDO as well as DDB Needham agency systems.

MATCHING THE CLIENT

Matching the client's organization must be part of any international support system for a client. Companies with few international clients can easily offer each one personalized services. Those with more clients must decide whether each client will receive tailored service or whether some features will be standardized to establish a pattern of service.

What is emerging in international marketing is a flexible system, responsive to local or national needs, tailored to client needs, a melding of centralized resources deployed to match client requirements.

The more centralized the client, the more likely the agency is to have a headquarters group assigned to the client with a tactical team ready to fly anywhere a problem needs to be solved. In the future, international agencies increasingly will base this team outside the United States and will have multiple centers of service. McCann-Erickson, among others, uses tactical teams to support local national offices worldwide.

In analyzing how clients work, the J. Walter Thompson agency, a unit of WPP Group PLC, identified three strata of support for international campaigns: exchange, encouragement, and enforcement. At the first level, the agency office at client headquarters (the lead agency) exchanges information, advertising campaigns, and material with its other international offices. At the next level, agency management more actively encourages local offices to follow the international direction. At the third level, agency management is asked to enforce international direction throughout the agency's network.

| TABLE 23.5 | WORLD'S TOP 25 ADVERTISING ORGANIZATIONS |

| RANK | | | | WORLDWIDE GROSS INCOME | | |
1995	1994	AD ORGANIZATION	HEADQUARTERS	1995	1994	% CHG
1	1	WPP Group	London	$3,129.7	$2,778.1	12.7
2	2	Omnicom Group	New York	2,576.7	2,207.5	16.7
3	3	Interpublic Group of Cos.	New York	2,337.2	2,127.3	9.9
4	4	Dentsu	Tokyo	1,998.6	1,641.5	21.8
5	5	Cordiant	London	1,377.8	1,236.1	11.5
6	6	Young & Rubicam	New York	1,197.5	1,046.9	14.4
7	9	Hakuhodo	Tokyo	958.6	774.2	23.8
8	7	Havas Advertising	Levallois-Perret, France	909.4	813.3	11.8
9	8	Grey Advertising	New York	896.5	808.7	10.9
10	10	Leo Burnett Co.	Chicago	803.9	677.5	18.7
11	11	True North Communications	Chicago	758.7	674.7	12.4
12	12	D'Arcy Masius Benton & Bowles	New York	645.6	608.4	6.1
13	13	Publicis Communications	Paris	606.3	543.2	11.6
14	14	Bozell, Jacobs, Kenyon & Eckhardt	New York	404.5	329.6	22.7
15	15	BDDP Group	Paris	278.5	263.3	5.8
16	17	Asatsu Inc.	Tokyo	254.1	210.1	20.9
17	16	Tokyu Agency	Tokyo	238.5	212.1	12.4
18	18	Daiko Advertising	Tokyo	211.1	202.7	4.1
19	20	Dai-Ichi Kikaku Co.	Tokyo	168.4	139.3	20.9
20	19	Dentsu, Young & Rubicam Partnerships	Tokyo/Singapore	160.6	139.9	14.8
21	22	TMP Worldwide?	New York	152.7	131.5	16.2
22	21	Ketchum Communications	Pittsburgh	126.9	134.2	−5.4
23	25	Chell Communications	Seoul	124.9	111.6	11.9
24	26	I & S Corp.	Tokyo	124.9	109.6	13.9
25	24	Yomiko Advertising	Tokyo	116.5	114.7	1.5

Notes: Figures are in millions of U.S. dollars. Companies hold minority equity in each other as follows: True North owns 49% of Publicis Communication; Omnicom owns 46.67% of Clemenger/BBDO; Young & Rubicam and Dentsu each own nearly 50% of Dentsu, Young & Rubicam Partnerships.

Reprinted with permission from *Advertising Age*. Copyright Crain Communications Inc.

INTERNATIONAL ADVERTISING CAMPAIGNS

PRINCIPLE Every sale is local, although the persuasion that led to the sale might have been part of an international campaign. The plan will fail if the individual buyer is not motivated or cannot find a way to take action.

According to an old axiom, "All business is local." This proverb should be modified to read "Almost all *transactions* are local." Although advertising campaigns can be created for worldwide exposure, the advertising is intended to persuade a reader or listener to do something (buy, vote, phone, order). That something is a transaction that is usually completed at home, near home, or usually in the same country if by direct mail. Even this will change as multinational direct-mail campaigns will be possible in a unified common market.

There are a number of ways to approach international advertising campaigns. One is the tightly controlled global campaign with minimum adaption for local markets. At the other end is the international marketer that develops local campaigns in every major market. Most companies are somewhere in the middle with a global campaign and a standardized strategy that is partially adapted as needed. The Concepts and Applications box discusses how these decisions about whether or not to standardize are made.

CENTRALLY CONTROLLED CAMPAIGNS

How are the campaigns, which can have near-global application, created? For international advertising campaigns, the two basic starting points are: (1) success in

Concepts and Applications

HOW TO MANAGE A GLOBAL BRAND IMAGE

Companies engaged in global marketing have to decide whether to standardize the marketing communication or adapt it for every market. The issue is: Will the creative approach cross cultural borders or are the cultural differences so great that the message has to be changed? The global consistency problem haunts advertising; however, it is also a problem for signage, packaging, promotions, and all other areas of the marketing program.

Global brands need consistency of image, as Pepsi found when it analyzed its brand presentation in various countries. *The Wall Street Journal* reported on the problem, "Overseas, some Pepsi billboards are more than 20 years old—and its image is all over the map: A grocery store in Hamburg uses red stripes, a bodega in Guatemala uses '70s-era lettering, and a Shanghai restaurant displays a mainly white Pepsi sign." In describing Pepsi's advertising, the paper said, "A hodgepodge of commercials feature a variety of spokespeople, ranging from cartoons and babies to doddering butlers." But the biggest problem, the paper concluded, was the product itself: "Worse yet, consumers say the cola tastes different in different countries."

What began in 1994 as a merchandising project ballooned into a total corporate image overhaul and product relaunch. The result was "Project Blue," an effort to revamp manufacturing and distribution to get a consistent-tasting drink, as well as an overhaul of all marketing communication. As part of the effort, Pepsi scratched its red-white-and-blue colors in favor of electric blue and introduced a new blue can throughout Europe in the summer of 1996.

Similarly, Belgium beer Stella Artois used a repackaging under the slogan "Launch of the Red Crate" to attract new customers and get the product out of the red. The new packaging, which focused on the splashes of red in its design, was part of a comprehensive brand relaunch supported by television advertising, a sampling program, a contest, coupons, and direct-mail brochures. An executive at Karamba, the agency that created the program, reported that more than 12 percent of the coupon recipients visited local stores to see if they had won and 46 percent used the coupons to buy crates of Stella Artois. The executive said, "The new packaging was very well accepted by consumers and sales stopped declining once we changed the color."

For marketing communication managers on global products, the challenge is to know what can be standardized in order to maintain consistency of image and what needs to be changed. There really are a number of options including aspects of the marketing mix (the product design and brand name/identification, the price, the distribution) as well as the product's strategy (target, position) marketing communication mix, and within that, the creative theme and all the executions.

The brand identification is one area where consistency is almost always possible, although there may need to be some change in the language. Packaging is another element that of- ten transfers from one culture to another with only language changes needed. In Europe, for example, many packages for pan-European brands are standardized; however, they are designed with messages in four or five languages. In advertising, there are a few products that maintain strategic consistency across borders such as Marlboro and Silk Cut, a European cigarette advertised nonverbally throughout Europe with visual puns. More often, however, the theme and selling strategy may be the same although the executions differ to reflect the lifestyle, dress, and appearance of people in local markets. In some cases, the brand's marketing is totally localized and the creative theme and selling strategy are adapted for the individual markets.

An example of how that decision is made comes from Thailand where a global brand of toothpaste targeted at children was having trouble with its advertising. The highly successful ad campaign was being used in the United States, Canada, Europe, and Australia. In Bangkok, however, viewers were saying it was "too American." As politely as their Eastern culture would allow them, they were telling the brand manager that the campaign would not work in their country. Why? It had to do with the pat on the head used at the end of the commercial as a visual tagline. Designed to express the parents' appreciation for the good brushing behavior of their child, the act ran up against cultural mores. One does not touch the head of another person in many Asian countries.

Does that mean that this cannot be a global campaign? Since the pat on the head was used to express the parental approval, then the campaign and its strategy can still be global. However, in Eastern cultures a different symbol may need to be used. Jacques R. Chevron, a consultant who specializes in international marketing and advertising explained, "If, in a particular market, a communication device does not work as well as in other markets, it can (and should) be replaced with one that communicates the intended set of values or 'brand character' that forms the backbone of a global brand strategy."

The important thing, Chevron warns, is that communicators understand exactly what creates the character of the brand. He explains, "It requires an absolute consistency of purpose which one can only achieve by having, at the onset of the communication planning, a very clear idea of the set of values to be linked to the brand." It is also important that managers understand all the different levels and dimensions of standardization and know which ones can be standardized and which need to be adapted for local markets.

Sources: Adapted from Steven Gundersen and Jeff Cahn, "Specialize, Globalize . . . or Vaporize," *PROMO* (April 1996):36; Robert Frank, "Seeing Red Abroad, Pepsi Rolls Out a New Blue Can," *The Wall Street Journal* (April 2, 1996):B1; "Global Conquest," *Sales Management and Marketing* (November 1996):100–101; Jacques R. Chevron, "Global Branding Married to the World," *Advertising Age* (May 15, 1955):23–24; "New Packaging Shows the Color of Money," *PROMO* (November 1996):84.

one country; or (2) a centrally conceived strategy, a need, a new product, or a directive.

A NATIONAL SUCCESS STORY

In the first case, a successful advertising campaign, conceived for national application, is modified for use in other countries. Impulse, the body spray, started in South Africa with a campaign showing a woman being pleasantly surprised when a stranger hands her flowers. That strategic idea has been used all over the globe but in most markets, the people and the setting are localized. Wrigley, Marlboro, IBM, Waterman Pen, Seiko Watches, Philips Shavers, Procter & Gamble, Ford, Hasbro, and many other companies have taken successful campaigns from one country and transplanted them around the world. A strong musical theme, especially typical of Coke and Pepsi, makes the transfer even smoother because music is an international language.

CENTRALLY CONCEIVED CAMPAIGNS

The second form, a centrally conceived campaign, was pioneered by Coca-Cola and is now used increasingly in global strategies. Although the concept is simple, the application is difficult. A work team, task force, or action group (the names vary) is assembled from around the world. Usually a basic strategy is presented. The strategy is debated, modified if necessary, and accepted (or imposed) as the foundation for the campaign. Some circumstances require that a strategy be imposed even if a few countries object. Primarily, cost is a factor. If the same photography and artwork can be used universally, this can save the $10,000 or more each local variation might cost. Or, if leakage across borders is foreseen, international management may insist on the same approach. Colgate, among others, faced this problem before its red dentifrice package and typography were standardized when distributors in Asia bought shipments from the United States or Europe, depending upon currency rates and shipping dates. A variety of packages for the same product is confusing to the consumer.

A variation on this procedure occurs when a promising new product is being developed. The team is assembled and might begin its work by developing a common global strategy. Once the strategy is developed, the members of the team responsible for creative execution go to work. In the case of one Coke campaign, the multinational group was sequestered until a campaign emerged. In other cases, the team may return to its home country, develop one or more approaches or prototype campaigns, reassemble in a matter of weeks, review all the work, and decide on one or two executions to develop into a full campaign. Such a campaign would include television, radio, newspaper, magazine, cinema, and outdoor advertising, and collateral extensions (brochures, mailings, counter cards, in-store posters, handouts, take-one folders, or whatever is appropriate). The team can stay together to finish the work, or it can ask the writer or developer of the campaign to finish or supervise the completion of the entire project.

In order to communicate their positions clearly and cope with rapidly changing conditions, several major advertisers gather their agencies for strategy sessions. McDonald's does this every year in August or September to announce the forthcoming year's plans. Eastman Kodak called its agencies together in early 1990 to discuss needs to economize and "get more bang for the buck." Nestlé convened its five major agencies—J. Walter Thompson, Ogilvy & Mather, McCann-Erickson, Lintas: Worldwide, and Publicis-FCB—to discuss agency alignments by product group, how a more market-driven and consumer-driven Nestlé is responding to change. Barry Day, Lintas's assistant to the CEO and an attendee, said "I believe agencies have to match the client organization. They must mold to (the client) philosophy and respond in kind."[13]

VARIATIONS ON CENTRAL CAMPAIGNS

Variations of the centrally conceived campaign do exist. For example, Rank Xerox may handle its European creative development by asking the European offices of Young & Rubicam to develop a campaign for a specific product—telecopiers, copiers, or whatever. The office that develops the approved campaign would be designated the *lead agency*. That agency office would then develop all the necessary pattern elements of the campaign and the relationship of the various elements to one another, shoot the photography or supervise the artwork, and prepare a standards manual for use in other countries. This manual would include examples of layouts, patterns for television (especially the treatment of the logo or the product), and design standards for all elements. Individual offices could either order the elements from the lead agency or produce them locally if this were less expensive. Because photography, artwork, television production, and color printing are very costly, performing all of these in one location and then overprinting typography or rerecording the voice track in the local language saves money. But advertisers must be careful to look local. In Ad 23.3, note how Pioneer subtly changed its U.S. ad to run in French Canada.

McDonald's, Coca-Cola, and others record basic music for campaigns and make various sound tracks available for local use. This work is not necessarily done in the home country. Superb sound studios and musicians are available, for example, in Spain, where costs are significantly lower than in the United States.

[13]Laurel Wentz, *Advertising Age* (September 10, 1990):87.

AD 23.3

IN ORDER TO LOOK LOCAL AND USE BASICALLY THE SAME LAYOUT—IN CASE A READER SAW BOTH VERSIONS—PIONEER HI-BRED CHANGED THE CONTENTS OF THE ATTACHÉ CASE. THE ENGLISH VERSION RAN IN THE UNITED STATES; THE FRENCH VERSION IN FRENCH-SPEAKING QUEBEC AND ONTARIO, CANADA.

LOCAL APPLICATION AND APPROVAL

Beyond central approval is local application and approval. Every ad in every country cannot come back to regional and world headquarters for approval. Local application is simplified when common material originates from a central source. Within a campaign framework, most companies allow a degree of local autonomy. Some companies want to approve only *pattern ads* (usually the two or three ads that introduce the campaign) and commercials and allow local approval of succeeding executions. Others want to approve only television commercials and allow local freedom for other media. In any case, free-flowing communication is necessary. Senior officers travel, review work, and bring with them the best of what is being done in other countries. Seminars, workshops, and annual conventions all serve to disseminate campaign strategies, maintain the campaign's thrust, and stimulate development of new ideas. Today, companies must balance the globalization of concepts and strategy with the localization of application.

The evolution in this globalization/localization process was described by Stanley Bendelac, president of Backer Spielvogel Bates-Europe at the IAA Latin American Advertising Congress in Caracas, Venezuela, in 1993. Bendelac started with the basic split.

Bendelac then analyzed the steps that have occurred:

1. Globalization
2. Localization
3. Concentration of market share among fewer companies
4. Specialization in business
   By geography
   By category
   By channels of distribution
5. Harmonization within the global companies
   By product line
   By name
   By formula
   By price
6. Adaptation of harmonized brands
   To local tastes
   To local customs
   To local sizes and containers
7. Centralization
   Of management
   Of production
8. Devolution of defined authority for execution
9. Coordination of plans, budgets, and strategies
10. Innovation in meeting local needs, customs, or market niches

As companies learn to move faster and give national managers more latitude for innovation, Step 10 feeds back to Step 1 as a successful local product is adopted by a global company as a global brand. Oil of Olay, a successful product acquired by Procter & Gamble in the United States, moved from a national to a global brand in fewer than five years. P&G took a campaign for Pantene shampoo with vitamins developed by its agency in Taiwan to Latin America, changing the commercial only to accommodate regional hair types; sales for the already distributed product soared.

HOW WELL DOES ADVERTISING CROSS BORDERS?

One of the most interesting studies on this question was conducted in 1990 by Alice, a French advertising agency, and IPSOS, a French research group. Rather than measuring what is acceptable in all markets (and possibly lowering creative standards), the agency took the most competitive advertising in each local market and found out how competitive it remains in the other markets.[14] Top commercials from France, Germany, Holland, Italy, Spain, and the United Kingdom were judged by 100 consumers in each of those countries. Each commercial was adapted into each of the six languages. At the end of each commercial, an explanation or further translation appeared. The conclusions of this research were:

1.   *Local nationality characteristics dominate in a market.* The most competitive commercials in each market, those that garnered the strongest responses, are from local commercials.

2.   *There exist genuine national advertising cultures.* Local creation and production recognize these local cultures. What makes a commercial strong in its home market also makes understanding difficult outside the local market.

3.   *A basic creative approach explains the capacity of some commercials to cross frontiers.* The key determinants of commercials both "liked" and "convincing" were the strength of their emotional appeal, the quality of their entertainment value, and the simplicity of the human situations they portray.

As the report states in its final page, "decentralized advertising appears to be the most competitive approach because of the importance of national cultures [however] globalization is possible but in the most extreme way, benefiting [from] the strongest ideas. Supra-national can only be creative."

MEDIA FOR INTERNATIONAL CAMPAIGNS

As we have seen, advertising practitioners can debate the applications of global theories to their profession, but one fact is inescapable: Global media do not currently exist. Television can transmit the Olympics around the globe, but no one network controls this global transmission. Therefore, an advertiser seeking global exposure would have to deal with different networks in different countries. Satellite transmission now places programs with advertising into many European homes, but its availability is not universal because of the *footprint* (coverage area of the satellite), the technical limitations, and the regulations on transmission by the various governments. As other satellites have been launched, they beam signals to more than one country in Europe, the Asian subcontinent, North America, and the Pacific, but they will be regional, not global. Most recently, the new international medium of choice for many companies is the Internet.

For example, as a series of events seized the world's attention in the late 1980s, Cable News Network (CNN) became the medium for the exchange of news for most of the world. Advertisers were quick to see this network as a means of reaching influential consumers even before CNN was available in homes. The 1991 Gulf War heightened CNN's recognition and increased its influence. By 1993, it was a nearly global electronic medium, reaching 141 million households in more than 100 countries. However, its coverage was in English, a language understood by less than 20 percent of the world's population. CNN has competition from the BBC and from MTV, now available in many satellite transmissions. Music is a more universal language than English, even though the language of pop culture is English. (See Figure 23.4 for data on satellite viewership.)

Global campaigns are becoming more and more common and successful. At a rate of seven or eight per month, new global campaigns are being launched. To handle this surge, advertising agencies have had to find ways to execute concepts globally. Of the 40 largest agencies in the United States and Britain, 39 have global networks compared to fewer than one-third in the late 1980s.

EXECUTION OF INTERNATIONAL CAMPAIGNS

Media planning for an international campaign does follow the same principles used for reaching a national target audience. The execution, however, is more complex.

---

[14]"Europe: Can Creative Advertising Cross Frontiers?" Alice and IPSOS (1990).

FIGURE 23.4

EUROPEAN VIEWERS PREFER SATELLITE AND CABLE.
Source: Pan European Television Audience Research. Reprinted with permission from *Advertising Age International* (April 19, 1993):1–4. Copyright, Crain Communications, Inc., 1993.

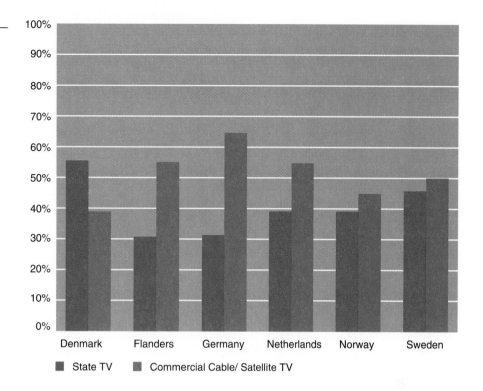

International campaigns are not always centrally funded. The global corporation has operating companies locally registered in most major countries. Advertising might have to be funded through these local entities for maximum tax benefits or to meet local laws of origination. Therefore, the media planner might only be able to establish the media definition of the target audience, lay down a media strategy, and set the criteria for selecting media. Greater latitude is allowed in media application than in creative variation. For example, a media campaign in the southern hemisphere, especially for consumer goods and seasonal items, requires major changes from a northern hemisphere campaign. In the southern hemisphere, summer, Christmas, and back-to-school campaigns are all compressed from November through January. National media directors must examine local research on audience characteristics and use judgment in executing media strategies.

MEDIA CHOICES

Once the basic global media strategy and plan have been created and approved, the central media planner will look for regional or multinational media. If magazines are part of the plan, advertising space in *Time, Newsweek, The Economist, Reader's Digest,* and other magazines with international editions may be bought. With the exception of *Reader's Digest,* these publications are available in English only. The *International Herald Tribune* and *The Wall Street Journal* are published simultaneously in a number of major cities using satellite technology. See Table 23.6 for a listing of global media circulation.

Magazines published by international airlines for their passengers are another option. Multinational satellites, such as British Satellite Broadcasting in Europe and Star in Hong Kong, provide opportunities to place the same message before a target audience at the same time across national boundaries. If the audience is targeted for a consumer product, local planning and purchase are required. This is accomplished in one of two ways: through an international advertising agency (or international consortium of agencies) or an international media-buying service. If these two methods are not used, the media executive must execute the plan through a multitude of local, national, or regional media-buying services or advertising agencies.

| TABLE 23.6 | INTERNATIONAL GLOBAL MEDIA (DISTRIBUTION BY CIRCULATION AND HOUSEHOLD REACH) |

	TOTAL DISTRIBUTION 1993	NORTH AMERICA	CENTRAL/ SOUTH AMERICA	EUROPE	MIDDLE EAST/ AFRICA	ASIA/ PACIFIC	AUSTRALIA/ NEW ZEALAND
DAILIES							
Financial Times, London	290,124	26,942	1,172	252,029	2,861	6,848	272
International Herald Tribune, Neuilly, France	195,075	8,988	1,489	134,118	6,438	43,624	418
USA Today, Arlington, VA	2,064,808	1,996,952	—	47,811	—	20,045	—
The Wall Street Journal, New York	1,994,863	1,894,248	—	57,505	—	43,110	—
WEEKLIES							
Business Week, New York	1,013,602	896,139	18,296	63,048	—	36,119	—
The Economist, London	534,122	236,665	9,115	219,985	14,238	42,061	12,058
The Guardian Weekly, Manchester, England	105,910	42,149	1,376	48,558	2,779	2,142	8,906
Newsweek, New York	3,845,000	3,100,000	70,000	285,000	55,000	225,000	110,000
Paris Match, Paris	187,033	30,594	1,610	132,656	21,495	678	—
Time, New York	5,510,000	4,350,000	95,000	560,000	85,000	270,000	150,000
MONTHLIES							
Cosmopolitan, New York	5,812,085	2,705,224	517,343	1,728,434	151,862	393,000	316,222
Esquire, New York	1,174,558	713,960	—	110,598	—	350,000	—
Good Housekeeping, New York	5,657,739	5,012,159	199,361	446,219	—	—	—
Harper's Bazaar, New York	1,028,198	715,680	76,354	155,164	—	81,000	—
National Geographic, Washington, DC	9,560,741	8,164,959	97,599	841,945	68,369	145,588	242,281
Reader's Digest, Pleasantville, NY	27,925,000	17,965,000	1,157,000	6,680,000	400,000	1,080,000	643,000
Redbook, New York	3,941,694	3,367,778	—	433,916	—	—	140,000
Runner's World, Emmaus, PA	512,000	430,000	—	70,000	12,000		—
Scientific American, New York	626,157	518,847	7,944	73,100	1,801	8,700	15,765
The WorldPaper, Boston	1,230,000	3,000	298,300	560,000	10,000	359,000	—
OTHER PRINT							
Fortune, New York	870,000	740,000	10,000	65,000	—	55,000	—
TV							
BBC World Service TV, London	19,500,000	6,500,000	—	1,800,000	—	11,200,000	—
CNN, Atlanta	141,300,000	68,000,000	1,300,000	60,000,000	4,000,000	8,000,000	—
Cartoon Network, Atlanta	24,000,000	9,000,000	1,000,000	14,000,000	—	—	—
MTV: Music Television, New York	154,100,000	58,300,000	26,000,000	58,300,000	—	11,500,000	—
TNT, Atlanta	75,983,000	59,983,000	2,000,000	14,000,000	—	—	—

Source: Reprinted with permission from *Advertising Age International* (February 21, 1994):1–11. Copyright, Crain Communications, Inc., 1994.

INTERNATIONAL ADVERTISING AGENCIES

If the campaign is being handled by one of the international advertising agencies, the senior media officer in the office that works for client headquarters will be in charge. He or she will supervise the efforts of that agency's offices in cities around the world in executing the media plan. Media orders will be placed locally, with copies sent to the coordinating agency office for review and compilation. In other cases, the plan will be reviewed centrally and placement will be handled locally without reporting to headquarters.

International networks of independent agencies have been formed to provide their members with global reach and to prevent the loss of clients to the international corporate agencies. Examples include Affiliated Advertising Agencies International, Advertising and Marketing International Network, and International Federation of Advertising Agencies. Similar groups are forming in regional blocs, such as the National Advertising Agency Network in the United States and the Association for European Marketing, Advertising, and Public Relations in Europe. These groups provide multinational media buying for their clients.

INTERNATIONAL MEDIA-BUYING SERVICES

The other primary option of media placement is to use international media-buying services. These services usually work for smaller international companies that do not have well-developed agency relationships in each country in which they operate. Regional media-buying services, such as Carat of France, are gaining great strength in Europe. International Production The Wace Group PLC, the world's largest producers of color separations used in printing, provides advertisers and media with a satellite-linked network of printing facilities. This allows for global print advertising transmission in the same way satellites have made multinational television commercials possible in most parts of the world.

SPECIAL INTERNATIONAL CONSIDERATIONS

International advertising has a worldly glamour about it—extensive travel, cultural opportunities, exotic places and cuisines, and the excitement of spending a weekend half a world away from home. It is also tough work, with long days, jet lag, insomnia, and dysentery. The business itself has some peculiar problems. We already discussed the problems that language creates. Other concerns relate to laws, customs, time, inertia, resistance, rejection, and politics.

International advertisers do not fear actual laws; they fear not knowing those laws. For example, a marketer cannot advertise on television to children under 12 in Sweden or Germany, cannot advertise a restaurant chain in France, and cannot advertise at all on Sunday in Austria. Until recently, a model wearing lingerie could not be shown on television in the United States. In contrast, nudity is acceptable in France. In Malaysia jeans are considered to be Western and decadent, and are prohibited. A commercial can be aired in Australia only if it is shot with an Australian crew. A contest or promotion might be successful in one country and illegal in another.

CUSTOMS AND CULTURE

Customs can be even stronger than laws. When advertising to children age 12 and over was approved in Germany, local custom was so strong that companies risked customer revolt by continuing to advertise. In many countries naming a competitor is considered bad form.

Customs are often more subtle and, therefore, easier to violate than laws. Quoting an obscure writer or poet would be risky in the United States, whose citizens would not respond to the unknown author. In Japan, the audience would respect the advertiser for using the name or become embarrassed at not knowing a name they were expected to recognize. Thus, in the United States the audience might be turned off, whereas in Japan consumers might search for the meaning in the message. In one case, the communication might be terminated, and in the other case, reinforced.

The Middle East is an exciting new market for many companies as the peace process between Israel and its neighbors has been hammered out. The problem, however, is that marketers will have to learn new selling methods because the region is so devoutly religious. There are major restrictions, for example, on how women are presented in advertising.

Cultural differences affect all aspects of doing business, including advertising. Ad 23.4 illustrates, for example, the emphasis on relationships that dominates business in Eastern countries.

MARKETING IMPERIALISM

Countering the move to a global perspective is concerns about the homogenizing of cultural differences. *Marketing* or *cultural imperialism* are terms used to describe what happens when Western culture is imposed on others, particularly cultures like those in the East and Africa that are considerably different. Countries in Southeast Asia have advertising codes. Singapore has an ad code determined to prevent Western-influenced advertising from impairing Asian family values.

AD 23.4

THE HONGKONG BANK EMPHA-SIZES THE IMPORTANCE OF PERSONAL RELATIONSHIPS IN ASIAN BUSINESS DEALINGS.

Everything has changed. Except the relationship, and the barbecued duck.

In Asia, there are always new markets and new opportunities. And there are always new ideas, new products and new technologies. But there are also old ties and long relationships.

HongkongBank
The Hongkong and Shanghai Banking Corporation Limited
Member HSBC Group

Malaysia requires that all ads be produced in the country, which cuts back dramatically on the number of foreign ads seen by its public.

Bob Garfield, ad critic for *Advertising Age*, uses an eight-country pan-European ad for Japanese car maker Honda to illustrate the "horrifying result" of Americanizing other consumer societies.[15] The ad uses The Addams Family who walk around a Honda dealership and deliver their typically ghoulish and contrarian reactions: on the practicality, "horrible;" on the mileage, "monstrous;" on the handling, "depressing." In the end, they look at the camera and advise: "Don't buy it." Garfield says the premise that telling consumers the opposite of what they expect to hear may be sound, but that it would have been more refreshing if the ad's creators hadn't resorted to American film adaptions of American television characters to make the point.

The French with its Academie Française that protects the French language and culture is an example of cultural defense. But there are also differences in cultural styles that have to be accounted for in advertising, even in the developed Western world. Uli Wiesendanger, a principal and chief creative director in TBWA International, Paris, points out that Americans are clear; the French are ambiguous. Which means that in France there is "no praise for ideas that are round and flawless and understandable and clear and logical and acceptable and testable and sellable." He explains, "We don't support that way of thinking." Instead he praises ideas that "have weird edges, are out of whack, have obvious dark sides and are elliptic, that polarize, confuse, are uneasy and above all open, and therefore ambiguous."[16]

TIME

PRINCIPLE Everything takes longer internationally—count on it.

Time is the enemy in international advertising. Everything takes longer. The New York business day overlaps for only three hours with the business day in London, for two hours with most of Europe, and for one hour with Greece. Normal New York business hours do not overlap at all with Japan, Hong Kong, the Middle East, or Australia. Overnight parcel service is dependable to most of Europe, if the planes are able to take off and land. For these reasons, telecopy transmission is now the mode for international communication. Facsimile or fax numbers have become as universal as telephone numbers on stationery and business cards in international companies. No matter what the activity, it always seems to take longer in another country, even if that second country is the United States.

Time is an enemy in other ways. France and Spain virtually close down in August for vacation. National holidays are also a problem. U.S. corporations average 14 to 15 paid legal holidays a year. The number escalates to over 20 in Europe (with over 30 in Italy). Some countries have patron saints for industry sectors. For example, Spain should be avoided on St. Barbara's Day. St. Barbara is the patron saint of advertising and artillery.

INERTIA, RESISTANCE, REJECTION, AND POLITICS

Inertia, resistance, rejection, and politics are sometimes lumped together as "not invented here" situations. Advertising is a medium for change, and change may frighten people. Every new campaign is a change. A highly successful campaign from one country might or might not be successful in another country. (Experience suggests the success rate in moving a winning campaign to another country is about 60 percent.) Creative directors often resist advertising that arrives from a distant headquarters rather than advertising created within the local agency. This resistance is partially the result of a very real problem in local offices of

---

[15]Bob Garfield, "A Horrifying Result of Crossing Borders," *Advertising Age* (May 15, 1996):I23.

[16]Uli Wiesendanger, "In Praise of Ambiguity," *Adweek* (January 16, 1995):44.

international agencies: an inability to develop a good creative team or a strong creative reputation when most of the advertising emanating from the office originates elsewhere.

Government approval of television commercials can also be difficult to secure in some countries. Standards may seem to be applied more strictly to international than to national products.

Flat rejection or rejection by delay or lack of support must be anticipated with every global strategy and global campaign. Typical responses may be, "We do not do it that way here," or "You do not understand how different we are in this country," or "We tried that once and it did not work." The best solution is to test a locally produced version of the advertising against an original ad both based on the global pattern advertising. As mentioned, the global strategy usually wins 60 percent of the time. If the locally produced advertising of the global strategy wins, the victory must be decisive or the costs of the variation may not be affordable. Or, a new campaign may have been found. These are times that try the will and the tact of global advertising managers. Global companies must remain flexible enough always to adopt a new winner if it emerges. This is the case with the Wrigley Spearmint campaign that used the no-smoking symbol used in the chapter opening. The U.S. campaign has been adapted for use in Hong Kong and Singapore in Chinese.

OVERCOMING INERTIA AND RESISTANCE

At times the resistance and rejection are political. These may be the result of office politics or an extension of international politics. Trying to sell a U.S. campaign in a foreign country, for example, can be difficult if relations between the two nations are strained. Being politic in the diplomatic sense of the word is the only practical way to overcome local resistance. International advertising involves the forging of consensus. This cannot be accomplished by mail. Successful international companies have frequent regional and world conferences, maintain a constant flow of communication, transfer executives, and keep their executives well informed through travel, videotapes, teleconferences, and consultation.

They have learned that few actions are as flattering as asking for advice. When local managements are asked to comment on a developing strategy or campaign, their involvement often turns into support. Another proven axiom is always go to a problem, do not bring it to headquarters. Solutions worked out in the country that has the problem are seldom what either party anticipated and are frequently better than either could have hoped. The adrenalin that precedes an "international confrontation" can often be directed to very positive solutions.

Despite its complexities and difficulties, international advertising is growing and will continue to grow in an increasingly interconnected world economy. Two of the largest agency groups are British-owned Saatchi & Saatchi and WPP; and one of the largest single agencies is Japanese (Dentsu), indicating that international advertising is no longer under American control. Students in the United States need to understand how international advertising works if they wish to succeed in this ever-changing industry. In fact, the United States is the only major country that still distinguishes between business and international business. Most of the Western world has made the transition.

UMMARY

- International business and trade now account for more than 10 percent of domestic production in almost every industrialized country and the percentage is growing.

- Another way to look at this is that more than 10 percent of the products and services in the industrialized

countries are either very similar (localized versions) or the same everywhere.

- The communication of the benefits and characteristics of products and services are much the same; as the world's various regional blocs have become more homogenized, consumers in these regions are becoming more similar in taste and outlook.

- Advertising provides a valuable function and the dominant structure for providing advertising is the advertising agency, whose importance on a global stage is increasing.

- An understanding of the origin, role, and function of advertising as the commercial voice of the global marketplace will help students understand better the currents of world trade and international marketing.

QUESTIONS

1. What are the differences among a local, regional, and international brand?

2. When did marketing emerge in international trade?

3. What pattern did Japanese companies follow in introducing their products in new markets?

4. Why would an exporter of goods nationalize its operations in another country?

5. Give three examples of global brands.

6. What belief does Professor Levitt hold? Which agency adopted his theory?

7. What are the tools of international management?

8. Is English a high-context or low-context language?

9. Name some impediments to international advertising.

SUGGESTED CLASS PROJECT

To demonstrate the problems of language in advertising, divide the class into teams of five or six. Each team should choose a print advertisement it believes would have universal appeal. Take the headline and one paragraph of body copy to a language professor or someone who is proficient in a language other than English. See if you can do this for up to five different languages. Next take that translation to another professor or native language speaker of the same language and ask for a back translation into English. Compare and report on whether the concept traveled easily or with difficulty.

FURTHER READINGS

Axtell, Roger E., *The Do's and Taboos of International Trade* (New York: John Wiley & Sons, Inc., 1994).

Cateora, Philip R., *International Marketing*, 8th ed. (Place: Irwin, 1993).

DeMooij, Marieke K., *Advertising Worldwide*, 2nd ed. (London: Prentice Hall International, 1994).

Global Management, 1994 (London: Sterling Publishing Group, PLC, 1994).

Griffin, Tom, *International Marketing Communications* (London: Butterworth Heinemann, 1993).

Eurostar trains, painted a handsome navy and canary yellow, can be identified by their sleek bullet noses like their T.G.V. French cousins. The Eurostar sprints from Paris to Calais then dives under the English Channel and pops up on the other side in Dover, England. Three hours after leaving Paris, it arrives in central London's Waterloo Station. Coming back, you can go from London to Paris or London to Brussels, a route that takes 3.5 hours to go from city center to city center. French passengers can change trains and reach a number of other cities; service from Manchester, Birmingham, and Glasgow on the U.K. side is being added in 1997.

There are really three products here. The Eurotunnel is the quasi-government agency that built and maintains the 31-mile tunnel under the English Channel. Eurotunnel spent more than double its $7.5 billion on the project and has never been able to crawl out of the red. Popularly called the Chunnel, the Eurotunnel is run by a British-French group that leases its rails to the Eurostar railroad company. In service since 1994, Eurostar, the product of a British-French-Belgian railroad consortium, is the train that runs through it. The same British-French group that owns and operates the tunnel also runs the separate car transport system, a company known as LeShuttle.

The Eurostar trains run a dozen times a day through the famous Chunnel connecting France and England. Speeding along at up to 200 mph on the French side and 100 mph on the English side, the ride is noticeably quiet—there is none of the "clickety click" sounds common to other trains. The train zips through the Chunnel in less than 20 minutes. The train offers a quick, simple check-in, preassigned seats, and a separate terminal space with lounge, cafe, and shops. One advantage over flying is that there is spacious seating in both standard and first-class sections with more room to work and relax. There is food service in both classes (although the food doesn't win rave reviews), on-board phones, and on-board immigration and customs. The trip is far easier than the traditional train-ferry-train shuttle between London and Paris and eliminates many of the hassles of flying. The terminals are conveniently located close to subway stops in the center of each city.

The voyage is particularly attractive to tourists and other curious travelers who pay $67 for a one-way tourist-class ticket. For standard or first class, the tickets are comparable to flying, which is around $150 to $180 for one way. Eurostar has seen growth, from 3.9 million to 6.4 million passengers in the year ending August 1996, an increase of 64 percent. Most of the growth, however, has been in the leisure market, which has lower profit margins.

For people with claustrophobia, the trip only got more impossible in late 1996 when a freight train caught fire inside the tunnel. No one died, but 34 truck drivers and the train crew had to walk to safety through thick smoke. The accident caused Eurostar to run at less than half normal capacity while the damaged tunnel was repaired. The question is: Is a tunnel accident scarier than a plane accident?

As the novelty wears off, Eurostar finds it must begin doing a better job of marketing. To get help with that project, the Eurostar management partnered with Virgin Airlines to take over its marketing. In particular, Eurostar knows it must lure large numbers of frequent business travelers to try Eurostar rather than just automatically making plane reservations.

CASE QUESTIONS:

1. What are the advantages and disadvantages to business travelers of using the Chunnel?

2. What kind of advertising should Eurostar use to announce the resumption of its services? How should it deal with the accident?

3. Develop a proposal for an advertising campaign focused on business travelers. Would it be a standardized campaign or would you do different campaigns for different countries?

Sources: Adapted from Steven Keenan, "Eurostar Finally Gets Up to Speed," *The Times* (October 15, 1996):15; Kim Campbell, "Goodbye London, Bonjour Paris in Three Hours," *The Christian Science Monitor* (October 24, 1996):B2; Stephen Armstrong, "Tunnel Reverberations," *The Guardian* (November 25, 1996):T13; Charles Batchelor, "Eurotunnel Reintroduces Limited Shuttle Service," *Financial Times* (December 9, 1966):8; Todd Pruzan, "Chunnel Surfing With Eurostar," *Advertising Age* (June 12, 1995).

As noted in this chapter's opening story, attempts by U.S. firms to break into international markets are littered with horror stories of translational gaffes and unintentional cultural slurs. When Perdue Chicken attempted to translate its famous tagline "It takes a tough man to make a tender chicken" into Spanish for Hispanic markets, the phrase was literally translated as "It takes a sexually aroused man to make a chick excited."

Such examples are all too common as companies attempt to master the marketing strategies necessary not only to overcome language barriers but to address cultural differences. Some of the hard-won lessons of international advertising and marketing include the hiring of local marketing and advertising staff to develop and implement the plans to achieve the broader business objectives defined by the corporate parent. Consequently, if domestic sacred cows, such as long-used advertising taglines or positionings, are inappropriate for use in foreign countries, they should not be considered unless budgetary considerations mandate it.

Despite the promise of multinational, mega-merger agencies resulting from the acquisition frenzy of the 1980s, few domestic campaigns have translated into truly international efforts to date. Only very simple graphic images for fashion and other intangibly based product benefits have succeeded in developing international appeal, such as the "United Colors of Benetton" campaign.

Given these obstacles, when McDonald's secured the rights to open its first restaurant in the Soviet Union after decades of negotiations, it was committed to doing it right. With competition escalating and domestic fast-food sales flattening, the international market represents one of the most promising areas for revenue expansion in the industry. So, when McDonald's began planning its largest restaurant for Pushkin Square in Moscow, it devoted a great deal of time to studying the culture, hiring and training local staff, and procuring local sources of ingredients. In some cases, when the quality of local ingredients was below McDonald's standards, arrangements were made to contract-produce an adequate supply of ingredients exclusively for McDonald's use.

Although state-run restaurants in the Soviet Union were famous for bad food and service, their prices were extremely low. Without state subsidization, McDonald's recognized that a typical meal at the Golden Arches would require a princely fee from Soviet citizens. Consequently, they focused on the other critical elements of successful fast-food operations: quality and service. Thoroughly screened Soviet youths were hired and trained to be courteous to all patrons, a novelty in Moscow restaurants. With over 700 seats, the Moscow Golden Arches location would be among the first to offer fast food with consistent quality and friendly service.

To date, McDonald's sales in Moscow have exceeded expectations, with Muscovites continuing to endure lengthy waits for a chance to dine on a Big Mac and fries and to sample capitalist enterprise at close range. Despite 400 percent increases in food prices, sales have scarcely been affected. In fact, waiting in line at McDonald's has become the premiere people-watching spot in Moscow, with youths emulating western fashions seen in fashion magazines from Europe and the United States.

Source: ABC News, *Prime Time Live* (January 24, 1990).

$\mathscr{Q}$UESTIONS

1. Traditionally, international marketers identify current cultural norms and attempt to mimic them in the presentation of their product or service in other countries. Why did McDonald's choose to deviate from the existing cultural norms for restaurant service in Moscow?

2. What characteristics common to Soviet shopping practices actually offer advantages for McDonald's over its domestic operations?

3. The basic elements of food-service success are quality, service, cleanliness and value. Without state subsidies, McDonald's could not address the value component via meal prices as effectively as state-run restaurants. Why was the company still able to create a high perceived value among Soviet consumers?

APPENDIX

Careers in Advertising

The American Association of Advertising Agencies publishes a brochure entitled "Go For It: A Guide to Careers in Advertising," which provides detailed job descriptions and advice for pursuing a career in advertising. The material found in this appendix provides a more in-depth look at agency positions, their requirements and career opportunities, as well as helpful information on preparing a résumé and for a job interview.

JOBS IN AN ADVERTISING AGENCY

As you have seen in these chapters, agencies handle a broad range of tasks requiring people with experience and ability in overall management as well as specialized fields. In a small agency, one person may wear several hats, such as media planner and buyer, whereas at a large agency some people will tend to specialize, such as a network television buyer. In all agencies, however, the jobs usually fall into five categories:

- Account management
- Creative
- Media
- Market research
- Support services and administration

ACCOUNT MANAGEMENT

At an agency, the client and its business are usually called "the account." One advertiser may offer many products or services and ask separate agencies to handle each one. Another may use a single agency to handle several products or services. No matter what the particular situation, the account management department is where the resources of the agency and the needs of the client connect.

The account manager oversees the advertising business that has been assigned to the agency and is ultimately responsible for the quality of service the client receives. The account manager serves as the client's representative at the agency and the agency's representative at the client's organization. It is his or her job to get the client its money's worth—to get the best possible work from the agency for the client—but at a profitable return for the agency. This means knowing how to handle people at the agency so that they give the client their best effort without spending more time than the income from the client's business justifies.

The effective account manager develops a thorough knowledge of the client's business, the consumer, the marketplace, and all aspects of advertising, including creative, media, research, and commercial production. As team leader and strategist, the account person must communicate the client's needs clearly to the agency team, plan effectively to maximize staff time and energy, and present the agency's recommendations candidly to the client. He or she must also know all about the agency: who are the most qualified people in each department and how to get their attention when it is needed.

The account manager must also know all about the client, enthusiastically learning every aspect of the client's business—ideally, from product development through the entire marketing operation—well enough to command the client's respect when presenting the agency's recommendations. In the final analysis, the account person must be able to foster productive communication between client and agency staffs, identify common goals, and make sure that the final product is profitable and effective for the client and the agency.

ENTRY-LEVEL POSITIONS

ASSISTANT ACCOUNT EXECUTIVE (MANAGER) The typical assistant account executive reports directly to an account executive and has a wide range of responsibilities. Some common duties include reporting client billing and forecasting agency income, analyzing competitive activity and consumer trends, writing conference reports from meetings, and coordinating creative, media, research, and production projects.

Successful candidates have strong general business skills: the ability to write and spell effectively, demonstrated leadership experience, a capability for statistical analysis, and developed organizational skills. In addition, it is important to be able to work well under pressure, handle a variety of tasks simultaneously, and coordinate the work and energy of diverse types of people, as well as to have creative sensibility and an intense interest in advertising and marketing.

Candidates for this position should have a bachelor's degree and, in some cases, a master of business administration. A degree in advertising or marketing is not a prerequisite. Within the agency business, agency account management and media departments hire the greatest number of entry-level candidates. Some of the large agencies offer entry-level training programs in account management.

CAREER OPPORTUNITIES An entry-level position in account management usually leads to account executive and then to more senior positions, with responsibility for more than one account and for the work of several account executives. Ultimately, account management can assume broader office and corporate positions. Currently the largest percentage of top agency management positions are filled from the ranks of the account management department.

CREATIVE

The creative department of an advertising agency is responsible for developing the ideas, images, and words that make up commercials and ads. Although many people contribute to the process, the invention and production of advertising is mainly the responsibility of copywriters and art directors.

When a copywriter and art director are assigned to an account, they must learn about the product or service to be advertised, marketing strategy, consumer or potential consumer, media to be used, advertising by competitors, production budget, and the client personnel (such as brand managers) with whom the agency deals. The research, account management, and media departments provide basic information on all these topics. However, the creative people will most likely want to gain first-hand experience with the client's product.

After the creative people assimilate as much information as possible, they agree on a general direction. The art director and copywriter work as a team trying out ideas first on each other, on the creative director, and on the other agency groups working on the account. These executions are reviewed by senior members of the agency (including legal counsel), sometimes called the review board, to evaluate whether they match the goals of the marketing and advertising strategy.

The reviewed creative executions are presented to the client for approval. Once the client approves, the art director and copywriter work with print and broadcast production people to produce the final version of the advertisement.

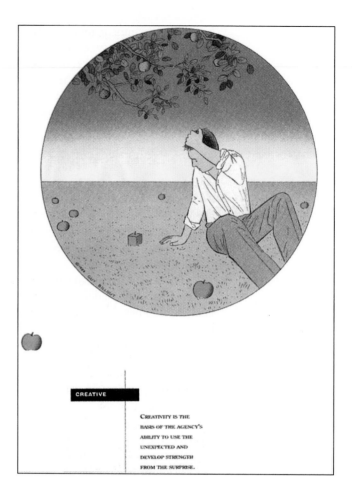

CREATIVE

CREATIVITY IS THE
BASIS OF THE AGENCY'S
ABILITY TO USE THE
UNEXPECTED AND
DEVELOP STRENGTH
FROM THE SURPRISE.

Magazines and newspapers require camera-ready copy. To prepare such print advertisements, agencies rely on outside services, from photographers to typesetters. Agency specialists in print production oversee this contracted work. Television stations require videotape; radio stations must have audio tape. Broadcast commercials often involve a large cast of outside specialists. Agency producers oversee the completion of television and radio commercials. They hire directors, production studios with film crews, and actors. In addition, producers administer the budget, work with composers and musicians, and participate in the review and editing of the rough film or videotape into the final version.

ENTRY-LEVEL POSITIONS

JUNIOR COPYWRITER   A junior copywriter assists one or more copywriters in editing and proofreading ad copy, writing body copy for established print campaigns, and developing merchandising and sales promotion materials. With proven ability and experience, assignments might include generating ideas for product or company names and writing dialog for television commercials and scripts for radio ads.

A successful candidate not only has outstanding skills in writing but has a "love affair" with words and symbols and their use in communication. Interest in a wide range of subjects and an insatiable sense of curiosity are assets. Candidates should have some knowledge of marketing and how words and visuals have been used in advertising.

Agencies expect job candidates to demonstrate their talent by showing portfolios of previous creative work, seminal ideas, and "rough" designs of potential campaigns, even if they were done in the classroom or on your own. Although a bachelor's degree is not required, most agencies look for candidates with proven intellectual ability and emotional maturity. Degrees in English, journalism, or advertising and marketing can be helpful. Opportunities for candidates who have no writing experience are limited. Some of the largest agencies offer entry-level training programs in copywriting.

JUNIOR OR ASSISTANT ART DIRECTOR The junior art director assists one or more art directors in preparing paste-ups, rough lettering, and layouts for print ads and television storyboards, developing visual concepts and designs, and overseeing photo sessions and the filming of television commercials.

A successful candidate will have strong visual concept skills and good basic drawing and design ability. Although an assistant art director must be capable of handling day-to-day lettering and matting tasks, agencies are also interested in identifying candidates with visual imagination and an interest in applying that ability to marketing and advertising problems.

Agencies expect candidates to show portfolios displaying their basic drawing skills and roughs of ideas for potential advertising campaigns. Although a bachelor's degree is not required, most agencies look for candidates with at least a two-year degree from an art or design school. Entry-level opportunities are very limited for candidates with only some related business experience, such as in a retail advertising department.

CAREER OPPORTUNITIES An entry-level position as junior copywriter leads to copywriter. An entry-level position as a junior art director leads to art director. In these more senior positions, each is given more responsibility and freedom in developing the visual and copy ideas for campaigns and may work on more than one account or on accounts that make special demands.

The position of art director or copywriter can lead to creative supervisor, the professional responsible for the work of a group of copywriters or art directors. More senior positions usually include creative group head, responsible for supervising teams of art directors and copywriters as well as production functions; creative director, responsible for all creative work produced by the agency for either all clients or a group of clients; and chief or executive creative director, responsible for overall creative work in a division, region, or company-wide. Senior creative people are important to the overall management of an agency. Many of them reach top agency management positions.

MEDIA

Even the most innovative and highly creative advertising in the world can fail if it is presented to the wrong audience or if it is presented at the wrong time or in the wrong place. The media department of an advertising agency is responsible for placing advertising where it will reach the right people in the right place and do so in a cost-effective way.

To bring advertising messages to the public, agencies must use a carrier, called a medium of communication or simply a medium. The four most commonly used media are television, radio, magazines, and newspapers. Some other media include billboards, posters, printed bulletins, and even skywriting.

Planning and buying media at an advertising agency is exciting and challenging because ways of communicating are constantly changing and becoming more complex. Such technological advances as cable television or videotext make an impact on what media are available for advertising and how viewership is calculated. A recent increase in the number of specialty publications enables more precise targeting of consumers. Today, more than ever, agencies and clients are recognizing the importance of creative and innovative media planning and buying.

When working on a particular advertising campaign, the media planners discuss, with the client and other agency people, the goals of the marketing strategy as well as a description of the potential consumer. As planners, they think about the kinds of media the target group might read, listen to, or watch. They compare the content, image, and format of each medium with the nature of the product or service, its image, and the goals of the advertising campaign. In discussions with the creative department and account team, planners suggest which media can be used most effectively to reach the target audience.

The media department is responsible for developing a plan that answers the question: How can the greatest number of people in the target group be reached often enough to have the advertising message seen and remembered—and at the lowest possible cost? Once the media plan has been developed, presented to the client, and approved, the department's media buyers start negotiating for space and time. Buyers purchase space in which to display their messages in print media. They buy time in the broadcast media.

Buyers must not only find and reserve available space and time, but also negotiate the best price. Will a station offer a lower price if more time slots are bought? Will prime time be discounted if the buyer is willing to purchase, in addition, some less desirable time in the morning or late at night? Buyers who have outstanding negotiating skills are valuable assets to any agency's media department.

After the space and time have been purchased, the department must monitor the media to make sure that the advertising actually appeared, in the proper form and at the proper time as it was ordered. If a discrepancy occurs, the department negotiates an adjustment to the billing or accepts a credit for additional time or space.

ENTRY-LEVEL POSITIONS

ASSISTANT MEDIA PLANNER   The typical assistant media planner reports to a media planner and gathers and studies information about people's viewing and reading habits, evaluates editorial content and programming of various media vehicles, calculates reach and frequency for specific target groups and campaigns, learns all there is to know about the media in general (magazines, newspapers, radio, television) and about media vehicles in particular *(Time, The Wall Street Journal)*, and becomes thoroughly familiar with media data banks and information sources.

Accomplishing these tasks requires the ability to find and analyze data, apply computer skills, ask innovative questions, and interpret or explain findings with attention to quantitative and qualitative considerations. In short, a planner must gain knowledge of what information is important and where to find it. By assisting in gathering statistics to support a variety of plans, he or she eventually becomes familiar with broader characteristics and trends in all media.

ASSISTANT MEDIA BUYER   The typical assistant media buyer reports directly to a media buyer and knows when and where space and time are available for purchase, reconciles agency media orders with what actually appears, calculates rates, usage, and budget, learns buying terminology and operating procedures, develops skills in negotiation and communication with media sales representatives, and becomes familiar with the media market. Accomplishing these tasks requires ease at working with numbers and budgets, outstanding communication skills, and the ability to work under pressure. Skills in negotiation and sales are especially advantageous.

Successful candidates have strong general business skills: the ability to write and speak effectively, developed organizational skills, aptitude for working with numbers and statistics, and basic computer skills. in addition, other important attributes are working well under pressure, maintaining priorities while handling a variety of tasks simultaneously, the ability and desire to interact with a wide range of personalities at the agency, the client, and within the media industry, an intense curiosity and interest in all types of media and their role in the marketing process, and understanding of sales and negotiation concepts (leverage, timing, and positioning), and a winning personal attitude.

Candidates should have a bachelor's degree. A degree in advertising or marketing is not a prerequisite. In most agencies, the media department, along with account management, hires the greatest number of entry-level candidates. Most larger agencies offer entry-level training programs in media.

The organization of a media department varies with the size of the agency. In large agencies, a person may specialize by medium, whereas in small and medium-sized agencies each person may handle all media. The media function is headed by a media director, who usually reports to the highest level of management.

CAREER OPPORTUNITIES   An entry-level position as an assistant media planner usually leads to media planner, the person responsible for developing a media plan. An entry-level position as an assistant media buyer usually leads to media buyer, responsible for negotiating time and space. It is common for the planner and buyer to develop expertise in specific media categories, such as magazine or network or spot television. In a small agency, the two jobs may be combined.

The next step is supervisory. The media planning supervisor coordinates the work of planners and presents recommendations to the account group and client. The broadcast buying supervisor oversees buying operations.

With greater knowledge and experience, media people advance to any of several positions—associate media director, manager of media research, network supervisor, director of spot broadcast, groups media director, director of programming and negotiations, and media director. Many agencies have top media people represented in senior management and as members of their boards of directors.

MARKET RESEARCH

The basic role of the market research department in an advertising agency is to understand the wants, desires, thoughts, concerns, motivating forces, and ideas of the consumer. By researching secondary information, conducting focus groups or one-on-one interviews, testing people's reactions to new advertising copy, tracking sales volume, or studying buying trends, the advertising agency researcher becomes an expert on consumer behavior.

Most researchers are assigned to specific accounts and work as advisors to the account, creative, and media people. They help develop, refine, and evaluate potential strategies and are called on to react to possible creative approaches based on their understanding of the consumer. This might be done with the creative team during the process or with account managers as evaluators of creative alternatives.

Some agencies also employ researchers who specialize in specific areas of quantitative or qualitative research. Consumer trends and lifestyle research are two ares in which most large agencies maintain continuing studies. Findings from these specialized studies tend to have an impact on all agency clients as well as on the process of creating advertising. In addition, the research department oversees projects that are subcontracted to "out-of-house" research firms. A typical example is surveys of shoppers at malls. The agency researchers design the questionnaire and interpret results, but a private firm conducts the interviews and summarizes the data so the researcher can write a report on the survey.

ENTRY-LEVEL POSITIONS

ASSISTANT RESEARCH EXECUTIVE   The typical assistant reports directly to a research executive. Duties usually include compiling data from secondary resources, following the progress of research projects, assisting in the development of primary research tools, and learning to analyze facts and numbers, interpreting and explaining what these really mean.

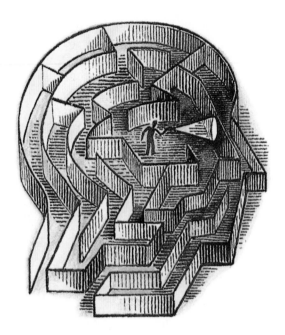

Successful candidates have strong quantitative skills and the aptitude for analyzing and interpreting qualitative as well as quantitative data. Computer literacy is also advantageous. In addition, candidates should be able to write and speak effectively, work well under pressure, and organize work priorities. They should have an interest in forecasting trends and patterns and a fascination with human behavior and motivation.

A bachelor's degree is the minimum requirement, but it is not unusual to find people who have master's or doctorate degrees employed in agency research departments. Although a specific major is not a prerequisite, many employers are attracted to candidates whose coursework is related to research. Some academic disciplines fitting this category are sociology, psychology, marketing, marketing research, economics, journalism, quantitative methods, anthropology, and mass communications.

Entry-level positions in agency research departments are relatively rare, especially in medium- and small-sized agencies. Candidates who have only bachelor's or master's degrees and no experience might find some opportunities at the largest agencies or at research firms.

CAREER OPPORTUNITIES   An entry-level position as an assistant research executive usually leads to a supervisory position with responsibility for managing research on individual accounts or brands overseeing the work of assistant research executives. During this stage a person might identify a personal interest in a specific research area and seek to specialize. The next step is management of a specialized research function or responsibility for all research on more than one account. Ultimately, a research person may have the opportunity to move into more general corporate management or marketing functions.

SUPPORT SERVICES

Like any well-run business, the advertising agency must maintain a full complement of people who handle accounting, personnel, clerical, and office services. In addition, agency traffic managers make sure that, once started, an ad or commercial moves smoothly through the agency, additions and corrections are obtained, and the whole job arrives at the publication or the broadcast station on time.

Cost controllers monitor agency costs, making sure that work stays within budget or that everyone is aware of, and approves, any needed changes in the budget. Other agency employees may include lawyers, librarians, and certain specialists. For example, agencies with big food or packaged-goods accounts sometimes keep nutritionists and home economists on staff. Those with health products or medical accounts may employ physicians. Such diversity is one more aspect that makes agency work such a fascinating and rewarding career choice.

PREPARING FOR A CAREER IN ADVERTISING

Breaking into advertising is not easy. Most jobs require a college degree. Internships and related work experience can be helpful. Retail selling experience is also excellent preparation. In addition to all this, however, getting a job in an advertising agency requires determination for two reasons. First, there are few job openings, and second, a lot of other bright people, like yourself, want those jobs, too. This year alone many agencies will receive thousands of inquiries for entry-level opportunities. Of this number, a very large agency might hire only 30. In short, there are many more people interested in working at agencies than there are openings. Nothing guarantees a job with an agency, but there are seven basic steps you should consider.

1. EDUCATE YOURSELF ABOUT THE BUSINESS

Find out as much as possible about the advertising business, what an agency does, and the career area or department in which you would like to work. Read every bit of relevant material you can find—articles, books, and such trade journals as *Advertising Age, Mediaweek,* and *Adweek.*

Talk to people. Track down any contacts or friends you have in the business. Sit down with your college instructors and career counselors. Make inquiries at such professional organizations as the American Association of Advertising Agencies, Advertising Women of New York, the American Advertising Foundations, or your local advertising club. Find out about seminars and attend them. One source of information can lead you to ten others. The more you know about your chosen area, the better you can present yourself as a first-rate candidate.

2. TARGET YOUR PROSPECTS

Decide what factors are important to you about a company and evaluate prospective employers on that basis. Make use of the *Standard Directory of Advertising Agencies,* popularly known as the "Agency Red Book." It is available at most libraries and lists all the agencies worldwide. It gives names and titles of key people, size of the agency (in dollar billings, number of offices, and total personnel), the agency's accounts, and a breakdown of the media in which the agency invests its client' money.

Read the trade press to learn more about specific agencies you want to target. For example, Advertising Age prints a special issue each year that provides profiles of individual agency business activity during the previous 12 months. It also selects an "agency of the year" and publishes an in-depth description.

3. DEVELOP A STRATEGY

With all the competition for jobs in advertising, you must develop your own "unique selling proposition" to communicate your own unique qualities. It is not enough that you are interested in advertising, or that you made dean's list eight times, or that you wrote for the school newspaper. So did most of your competition. You have to connect what you have done in the past, in a unique way, to what you will do for the agency in the future. Developing a strategy gets your commitment, imagination, and analytical thinking out in the limelight. It is the key to making you stand out from other candidates.

4. CREATE A GOOD RÉSUMÉ

The primary purpose of a résumé is to get you an interview. Used correctly, it can open doors. Used incorrectly, it slams them shut. A good résumé connects your experience to your job goal. Support your candidacy by highlighting relevant skills, such as writing, speaking, managing, and so on. Include any activities, jobs, or internships directly related to advertising. Did you sell space for the school's newspaper? Were you yearbook editor? Or stage manager for the college theater group? Add less related activities only if they are outstanding. Be selective. Your résumé is a selling tool, not a life history. Keep it neat, clear, precise, and all on one page. Try to make it unique and interesting but not gimmicky.

5. TAKE PAINS WITH EACH COVER LETTER

A cover letter works hand in hand with your résumé. Together they create a first impression of you. Your cover letter should work as a connecting tool between you and the agency you are writing to. Don't let it read like a form letter. Instead, include real knowledge of the agency, its clients, its work, and its position in the industry. Tell the agency why you are interested in them and why you think you'd be right for them. Then make sure that you are prepared to discuss in your interview whatever you say in the cover letter. Remember, you are being judged on communicative skill. Watch spelling, grammar, and typing. Most importantly, be clear, crisp, and brief.

6. ASSEMBLE A PORTFOLIO

To help you get a job in an agency creative department, you must prepare a portfolio that shows your thinking and imagination. If you are an aspiring art director, this clearly has to include ample demonstration of your design ability and graphic sense. If you want to be a copywriter, visuals are less critical than is demonstration of your writing ability and marketing sense.

In either case, show your very best work. If you have not had any experience, pick some currently running campaigns, determine their objectives, and interpret them in your own way. It doesn't matter if your "ads" are not professional. Your prospective employer wants to see fresh concepts and new ideas that prove you have potential. Then keep making changes to improve your portfolio. For more specific suggestions, see Maxine Paetro's book on building portfolios, entitled *How to Put Your Book Together and Get a Job in Advertising*.

7. PREPARE FOR YOUR INTERVIEW

At most agencies, an invitation to be interviewed reflects more than casual interest in a candidate. If you have made it this far, you're at least in the quarterfinals. And if you've done your homework, you should have nothing to worry about.

Before the interview, organize your thinking. Review your résumé and the cover letter you sent the agency. Decide what key selling points you should communicate about yourself. Think how you can best do this. Review the information you have about the agency. Be aware of its current campaigns and any fast-breaking developments. Commenting on these can help you make an immediate connection with the interviewer.

Be ready to discuss your point of view on advertising in general and your area of interest in particular. Be articulate. Be self-confident and enthusiastic, but relax and do it naturally. Don't try to recite everything you know. Selectivity shows you are thinking.

Remember, someone is interested enough in your background to invest 30 minutes or more in you. That person wants you to succeed.

Source: Courtesy of The American Association of Advertising Agencies.

GLOSSARY

A

Account management (p. 125)   The function within an advertising agency that acts as liaison with the client and supervises day-to-day work and development of recommendations and plans.

Account planner (p. 201)   The person responsible for the creation, implementation, and modification of the strategy on which creative work is based.

Adese (p. 394)   Formula writing that uses clichés, generalities, stock phrases, and superlatives.

Advertiser (p. 16)   The individual or organization that initiates the advertising process.

Advertising (p. 13)   Paid nonpersonal communication from an identified sponsor using mass media to persuade or influence an audience.

Advertising campaign (p. 590)   A comprehensive advertising plan exists to accomplish a communication goal or goals, usually over a relatively short period of time.

Advertising plan (p. 224)   A plan that proposes strategies for targeting the audience, presenting the advertising message, and implementing media.

Advocacy advertising (p. 565)   A type of corporate advertising that involves creating advertisements and purchasing space to deliver a specific, targeted message.

Affiliate (p. 331)   A station that is contracted with a national network to carry network-originated programming during part of its schedule.

Agricultural advertising (p. 648)   Advertising directed at large and small farmers.

Allocations (p. 368)   Division or proportions of advertising dollars among the various media.

Animatic (p. 456)   A preliminary version of a commercial with the storyboard frames recorded on videotape along with a rough sound track.

Animation (p. 453)   A type of recording medium in which objects are sketched and then filmed one frame at a time.

Answer print (p. 460)   The finished version of the commercial with the audio and video recorded together.

Aperture (p. 273)   The ideal moment for exposing consumers to an advertising message.

Appeal (p. 255)   Something that moves people.

Arranger (p. 458)   The person who orchestrates the music, arranging it for the various instruments, voices, and scenes.

Art (p. 415)   The visual elements in an ad, including illustrations, photos, type, logos and signatures, and the layout.

Art director (p. 391)   The person who is primarily responsible for the visual image of the advertisement.

Association (p. 254)   The process used to link a product with a positive experience, personality, or lifestyle.

Attitude (p. 173)   A learned predisposition that we hold toward an object, person, or idea.

B

Benefits (p. 235)   Statements about what the product can do for the user.

Body copy (p. 417)   The text of the message.

Brag-and-boast copy (p. 394)   Advertising text that is written from the company's point of view to extol its virtues and accomplishments.

Brainstorming (p. 397)   A creative-thinking technique using free association in a group environment to stimulate inspiration.

Brand equity (p. 262)   The value added to a product by a respected and well-known brand name.

Brand image (p. 262)   A mental image that reflects the way a brand is perceived, including all the identification elements, the product personality, and the emotions and associations evoked in the mind of the consumer.

Branding (p. 90)   The process of creating an identity for a product using a distinctive name or symbol.

Brand loyalty (p. 256)   Positive opinions held by consumers about the product or service that makes them want to repeat their purchase of this brand.

Broadsheet (p. 306)   A newspaper with a size of eight columns wide and 22 inches deep.

Broadsheets (p. 491)   Large brochures that unfold like a map.

Business strategic plan (p. 219)   An overriding business plan that deals with the broadest decisions made by the organization.

Business-to-business advertising (p. 644)   Advertising directed at people who buy or specify products for business use.

Business unit (p. 123)   A cluster of related products or services that functions as if it were a company within a larger corporation.

Cable television (p. 332)   A form of subscription television in which the signals are carried to households by a cable.

Car cards (p. 517)   Small advertisements that are mounted in racks inside a vehicle.

Carry-over effect (p. 282)   A measure of residual effect (awareness or recall) of the advertising message some time after the advertising period has ended.

Cease-and-desist order (p. 66)   A legal order requiring an advertiser to stop its unlawful practices.

Channel of distribution (p. 90)   People and organizations involved in moving products from producers to consumers.

Circulation (p. 307)   A measure of the number of copies sold.

Claim (p. 234)   A statement about the product's performance.

Classified advertising (p. 311)   Commercial messages arranged in the newspaper according to the interests of readers.

Claymation (p. 454)   A technique that uses figures sculpted from clay and filmed one frame at a time.

Cliché (p. 383)   A trite expression, an overused idea.

Cognitive dissonance (p. 169)   A tendency to justify the discrepancy between what a person receives relative to what he or she expected to receive.

Color separation (p. 436)   The process of splitting a color image into four images recorded on negatives; each negative represents one of the four process colors.

Commission (p. 132)   A form of payment in which an agent or agency receives a certain percentage (historically 15 percent) of media charges.

Composer (p. 458)   The person who writes the music.

Comprehensive (p. 427)   A layout that looks as much like the final printed ad as possible.

Consent decree (p. 66)   An order given by the FTC and signed by an advertiser, agreeing to stop running a deceptive ad.

Consumers (p. 151)   People who buy or use products.

Contests (p. 543)   Sales promotion activities that require the participants to exhibit some skill or ability in order to win.

Continuity (p. 282)   The strategy and tactics used to schedule advertising over the time span of the advertising campaign.

Continuity program (p. 546)   A program that requires the consumer to continue purchasing the product or service in order to receive a reward.

Control group (p. 207)   A control group does not receive the treatment.

Convergent thinking (p. 386)   Thinking that uses logic to arrive at the "right" answer.

Conviction (p. 257)   A particularly strong belief that has been anchored firmly in the attitude structure.

Cooperative advertising (pp. 92, 633)   A form of advertising in which the manufacturer reimburses the retailer for part or all of the retailer's advertising expenditures.

Copy (p. 415)   The written elements in an ad, including headlines, underlines and overlines, subheads, body copy, captions, slogans, and taglines.

Copywriter (p. 393)   The person who writes the text for an ad.

Corporate identity advertising (p. 573)   A type of advertising used by firms to establish their reputation or increase awareness.

Corporate/institutional advertising (p. 563)   Advertising used to create a favorable public attitude toward the sponsoring organization.

Corrective advertising (p. 66)   A remedy required by the FTC in which an advertiser that produced misleading messages is required to issue factual information to offset these messages.

Cost per rating (CPR) (p. 289)   A method of comparing media vehicles by relating the cost of the message unit to the audience rating.

Cost per thousand (CPM) (p. 289)   The cost of exposing each 1,000 members of the target audience to the advertising message.

Cost trends (p. 365)   A history of changes in the average unit (per message) prices for each medium that is used in cost forecasting.

Coupons (p. 541)   Legal certificates offered by manufacturers and retailers that grant specified savings on selected products when presented for redemption at the point of purchase.

CPM trends (p. 367)   Longitudinal (long-term) history of average cost-per-thousand tendencies of advertising media that is used to assist in forecasting future CPM levels.

Crawl (p. 452) Computer-generated letters that move across the bottom of the screen.

Creative concept (p. 381) A "big idea" that is original and dramatizes the selling point.

Creative platform (p. 234) A document that outlines the message strategy decisions behind an individual ad.

Cultural and social influences (p. 155) The forces that other people exert on your behavior.

Culture (p. 155) The complex whole of tangible items, intangible concepts, and social behaviors that define a group of people or a way of life.

Cut (p. 453) An abrupt transition from one shot to another.

Cutouts (p. 509) Irregularly shaped extensions added to the top, bottom, or sides of standard outdoor boards.

Databases (p. 474) Lists of consumers with information that helps target and segment those who are highly likely to be in the market for a certain product.

Data sheets (p. 654) Advertising that provides detailed technical information.

Dealer loader (p. 553) A premium given to a retailer by a manufacturer for buying a certain quantity of product.

Dealer tag (p. 633) Time left at the end of a broadcast advertisement that permits identification of the local store.

Demography (p. 159) The study of social and economic factors that influence human behavior.

Diagnostic research (p. 205) Research used to identify the best approach from among a set of alternatives.

Directional advertising (p. 518) Advertising that directs the buyer to the store where the product or service is available.

Direct marketing (p. 474) A type of marketing that uses media to contact a prospect directly and elicit a response without the intervention of a retailer or personal sales.

Director (p. 457) The person in charge of the actual filming or taping of the commercial.

Direct-response advertising (p. 480) A type of marketing communication that achieves an action-oriented objective as a result of the advertising message.

Direct-response counts (p. 617) Evaluative tests that count the number of viewers or readers who request more information or who purchase the product.

Discretionary income (p. 164) The money available for spending after taxes and necessities are covered.

Display advertising (p. 311) Sponsored messages that can be of any size and location within the newspaper, with the exception of the editorial page.

Display copy (p. 417) Type set in larger sizes that is used to attract the reader's attention.

Divergent thinking (p. 386) Thinking that uses free association to uncover all possible alternatives.

Drama (p. 403) A story built around characters in a situation.

Dubbing (p. 460) The process of making duplicate copies of a videotape.

Early feedback (p. 205) Preliminary reactions to alternative creative strategies.

Editor (p. 458) The person who assembles the best shots to create scenes and who synchronizes the audio track with the images.

Effective frequency (p. 288) A recent concept in planning that determines a range (minimum and maximum) of repeat exposures for a message.

Evaluative research (p. 606) Research intended to measure the effectiveness of finished or nearly finished advertisements.

Exchange (p. 79) The process whereby two or more parties give up a desired resource to one another.

Execution (p. 381) The form taken by the finished advertisement.

Exploratory research (p. 194) Informal intelligence gathering, backgrounding.

Extensions (p. 509) Embellishments to painted billboards that expand the scale and break away from the standard rectangle limitations.

Exterior transit advertising (p. 516) Advertising posters that are mounted on the sides, rear, and top of vehicles.

Evaluative research (p. 193) Research that determines how you did.

Family (p. 158) Two or more people who are related by blood, marriage, or adoption and live in the same household.

Feature analysis (p. 230) A comparison of your product's features against the features of competing products.

Federal Communications Commission (FCC) (p. 69) A federal agency that regulates broadcast media and has the power to eliminate messages, including ads, that are deceptive or in poor taste.

Federal Trade Commission (FTC) (p. 60)   A federal agency responsible for interpreting deceptive advertising and regulating unfair methods of competition.

Fee (p. 136)   A mode of payment in which an agency charges a client on the basis of the agency's hourly rates.

Film (p. 453)   A strip of celluloid with a series of still images called frames.

Flighting (p. 282)   An advertising scheduling pattern characterized by a period of intensified activity called a *flight*, followed by a period of no advertising, called a *hiatus*.

Focal point (p. 429)   The first element in a layout that the eye sees.

Focus group (p. 193)   A group interview that tries to stimulate people to talk candidly about some topics or products.

Font (p. 433)   A complete set of letters in one size and typeface.

Food and Drug Administration (FDA) (p. 69)   A federal regulatory agency that oversees package labeling and ingredient listings for food and drugs.

Frame-by-frame tests (p. 621)   Tests that evaluate consumers' reactions to the individual scenes that unfold in the course of a television commercial.

Free association (p. 386)   An exercise in which you describe everything that comes into your mind when you think of a word or an image.

Freelance artists (p. 416)   Independent artists who work on individual assignments for an agency or advertiser.

Free-standing insert advertisements (p. 312)   Preprinted advertisements that are placed loosely within the newspaper.

Frequency (p. 285)   The number of times an audience has an opportunity to be exposed to a media vehicle or vehicles in a specified time span; also, (p. 345). The number of radio waves produced by a transmitter in 1 second.

Full-service agency (p. 114)   An agency that handles all of a client's advertising efforts and offers four major staff functions—account management, creative services, media planning and buying, and research.

Game (p. 543)   A type of sweepstakes that requires the player to return to play several times.

Global brand (p. 669)   A brand that has the same name, same design, and same creative strategy everywhere in the world.

Global perspective (p. 667)   A corporate philosophy that directs products and advertising toward a worldwide rather than a local or regional market.

Gross impressions (p. 284)   The sum of the audiences of all the media vehicles used within a designated time span.

Gross rating points (GRP) (p. 284)   The sum of the total exposure potential of a series of media vehicles expressed as a percentage of the audience population.

Gütenberg diagonal (p. 428)   A visual path that flows from the upper left corner to the lower right.

Halftones (p. 435)   Images with a continuous range of shades from light to dark.

Hard sell (p. 401)   A rational, informational message that emphasizes a strong argument, and calls for action.

Headline (p. 417)   The title of an ad; it is set in large type to get the reader's attention.

Hierarchy of effects (p. 227)   A set of consumer responses that moves from the least serious, involved, or complex up through the most serious, involved, or complex.

High-involvement decision process (p. 177)   Decisions that require an involved purchase process with information search and product comparison.

Holography (p. 512)   A technique that produces a projected three-dimensional image.

Horizontal publications (p. 653)   Publications directed to people who hold similar jobs in different companies across different industries.

Household (p. 158)   All those people who occupy one living unit, whether or not they are related.

Impact (p. 384)   The effect that a message has on the audience.

Indicia (p. 526)   The postage label printed by a postage meter.

Industrial advertising (p. 646)   Advertising directed at businesses that buy products to incorporate into other products or to facilitate the operation of their businesses.

Infomercial (p. 466)   A long commercial that provides extensive product information.

Informational advertising (p. 254)   Advertising that presents a large amount of information about the product.

In-house agency (p. 20)   An advertising department on the advertiser's staff that handles most, if not all, of the functions of an outside agency.

In-market tests (p. 622)   Tests that measure the effectiveness of advertisements by measuring actual sales results in the marketplace.

In register (p. 416) A precise matching of colors in images.

Integrated marketing communication (p. 36) The concept or philosophy of marketing that stresses bringing together all the variables of the marketing mix, all the media, all the actions with which a company reaches its publics, and integrating the company's strategy and programs.

Interconnects (p. 333) A special cable technology that allows local advertisers to run their commercials in small geographical areas through the interconnection of a number of cable systems.

Interior transit advertising (p. 516) Advertising posters that are mounted inside vehicles such as buses, subway cars, and taxis.

Interlock (p. 459) A version of the commercial with the audio and video timed together, although the two are still recorded separately.

International advertising (p. 663) Advertising designed to promote the same product in different countries and cultures.

International brand (p. 663) A brand or product that is available in most parts of the world.

Involvement (p. 253) The intensity of the consumer's interest in a product.

Italic (p. 433) A type variation that uses letters that slant to the right.

Jingles (p. 258) Commercials with a message that is presented musically.

Justified (p. 434) A form of typeset copy in which the edges of the lines in a column of type are forced to align by adding space between words in the line.

Key frame (p. 454) A single frame of a commercial that summarizes the heart of the message.

Key visual (p. 259) A dominant image around which the commercial's message is planned.

Kinetic boards (p. 513) Outdoor advertising that uses moving elements.

Kiosks (p. 518) Multisided bulletin board structures designed for public posting of messages.

Layout (p. 423) A drawing that shows where all the elements in the ad are to be positioned.

Lecture (p. 402) Instruction delivered verbally to present knowledge and facts.

Lifestyle (p. 158) The pattern of living that reflects how people allocate their time, energy, and money.

Line art (p. 434) Art in which all elements are solid with no intermediate shades or tones.

Local brand (p. 662) A brand that is marketed in one specific country.

Logo (p. 259) Logotype; a distinctive mark that identifies the product, company, or brand.

Loss leader (p. 634) Product advertised at or below cost in order to build store traffic.

Low-involvement decision process (p. 177) Decisions that require limited deliberation; sometimes purchases are even made on impulse.

Makegoods (p. 374) Compensation given by the media to advertisers in the form of additional message units that are commonly used in situations involving production errors by the media and preemption of the advertiser's programming.

Manipulation (p. 207) Control of the variable of interest.

Market (p. 81) An area of the country, a group of people, or the overall demand for a product.

Marketing (p. 78) Business activities that direct the exchange of goods and services between producers and consumers.

Marketing plan (p. 221) Document that proposes strategies for employing the various elements of the marketing mix to achieve marketing objectives.

Marketing research (p. 193) Research that investigates all the elements of the marketing mix.

Market research (p. 193) Research that gathers information about specific markets.

Mechanicals (p. 427) A finished pasteup, with every element perfectly positioned, that is photographed to make printing plates for offset printing.

Media (p. 21) The channels of communication used by advertisers.

Media-buying service (p. 117) A company that offers to buy media directly for advertisers and performs basically only this service.

Media planning (p. 272) A decision process leading to the use of advertising time and space to assist in the achievement of marketing objectives.

Merging (p. 481) The process of combining two or more lists of prospects.

Mixing (p. 465) Combining different tracks of music, voices, and sound effects to create the final ad.

Motive (p. 170) An unobservable inner force that stimulates and compels a behavioral response.

Needs (p. 171)   Basic forces that motivate you to do or to want something.

Network radio (p. 348)   A group of local affiliates providing simultaneous programming via connection to one or more of the national networks through AT&T telephone wires.

Newsprint (p. 415)   An inexpensive, tough paper with a rough surface, used for printing newspapers.

News release (p. 575)   Primary medium used to deliver public relations messages to the media.

Noncommercial advertising (p. 581)   Advertising that is sponsored by an organization to promote a cause rather than to maximize profits.

Nontraditional delivery (p. 319)   Delivery of magazines to readers through such methods as door hangers or newspapers.

Norms (p. 155)   Simple rules for behavior that are established by cultures.

Open pricing (p. 370)   A method of media pricing in which prices are negotiated on a contract-by-contract basis for each unit of media space or time.

Optical center (p. 430)   A point slightly above the mathematical center of a page.

Original (p. 383)   One of a kind; unusual and unexpected.

Out-of-home advertising (p. 506)   All advertising that is displayed outside the home—from billboards, to blimps, to in-store aisle displays.

Participations (p. 339)   An arrangement in which a television advertiser buys commercial time from a network.

Perceived value (p. 105)   The value that a customer or buyer intrinsically or subjectively attaches to a brand or service. It is the image or personality that differentiates one product from a virtually identical competitor.

Percent-of-sales method (p. 233)   A technique for computing the budget level that is based on the relationship between cost of advertising and total sales.

Perception (p. 167)   The process by which we receive information through our five senses and acknowledge and assign meaning to this information.

Perceptual map (p. 231)   A map that shows where consumers locate various products in the category in terms of several important features.

Personality (p. 174)   Relatively long-lasting personal qualities that allow us to cope with, and respond to, the world around us.

Persuasion test (p. 614)   A test that evaluates the effectiveness of an advertisement by measuring whether the ad affects consumers' intentions to buy a specific brand.

Photoboard (p. 456)   A type of rough commercial, similar to an animatic except that the frames are actual photos instead of sketches.

Physiological tests (p. 618)   Tests that measure emotional reactions to advertisements by monitoring reactions such as pupil dilation and heart rate.

Pica (p. 434)   A unit of type measurement used to measure width and depth of columns; there are 12 points in a pica and 6 picas in an inch.

Point (p. 433)   A unit used to measure the height of type; there are 72 points in an inch.

Point-of-purchase display (P-O-P) (p. 551)   A display designed by the manufacturer and distributed to retailers in order to promote a particular brand or line of products.

Population (p. 207)   Everyone included in a designated group.

Positioning (p. 230)   The way in which a product is perceived in the marketplace by consumers.

Preferred positions (p. 371)   Sections or pages of magazine and newspaper issues that are in high demand by advertisers because they have a special appeal to the target audience.

Premium (p. 545)   A tangible reward received for performing a particular act, such as purchasing a product or visiting the point of purchase.

Press conference (p. 575)   A public gathering of media people for the purpose of establishing a company's position or making a statement.

Price deal (p. 541)   A temporary reduction in the price of a product.

Primary research (p. 196)   Information that is collected from original sources.

Process colors (p. 435)   Four basic inks—magenta, cyan, yellow, and black—that are mixed to produce a full range of colors found in four-color printing.

Process evaluation (p. 582)   Measuring the effectiveness of media and nonmedia efforts to get the desired message out to the target audience.

Producer (p. 457)   The person who supervises and coordinates all of the elements that go into the creation of a television commercial.

Professional advertising (p. 648)   Advertising directed at people such as lawyers, doctors, and accountants.

Profile (p. 230)   A composite description of a target audience employing personality and lifestyle characteristics.

Program preemptions (p. 374)   Interruptions in local or network programming caused by special events.

Promotion (p. 94)   That element in the marketing mix that communicates the key marketing messages to target audiences. Also called marketing communication.

Promotion mix (p. 95)   The combination of personal selling, advertising, sales promotion, and public relations to produce a coordinated message structure.

Psychographics (p. 166)   All the psychological variables that combine to shape our inner selves, including activities, interests, opinions, needs, values, attitudes, personality traits, decision processes, and buying behavior.

Publicity (p. 563)   Cost-free public relations that relates messages through gatekeepers.

Public opinion (p. 566)   People's beliefs, based on their conceptions or evaluations of something rather than on fact.

Public relations (p. 561)   A management function enabling organizations to achieve effective relationships with their various audiences through an understanding of audience opinions, attitudes, and values.

Publics (p. 566)   Those groups or individuals who are involved with an organization, including customers, employees, competitors, and government regulators.

Puffery (p. 46)   Advertising or other sales representation that praises the item to be sold using subjective opinions, superlatives, and similar mechanisms that are not based on specific fact.

Pulsing (p. 282)   An advertising scheduling pattern in which time and space are scheduled on a continuous but uneven basis; lower levels are followed by bursts or peak periods of intensified activity.

Purging (p. 481)   The process of deleting repeated names when two or more lists are combined.

Push money (p. 552) *(spiffs)*   A monetary bonus paid to a salesperson based on units sold over a period of time.

Qualitative data (p. 201)   Research that seeks to understand how and why people think and behave as they do.

Quantitative data (p. 201)   Research that uses statistics to describe consumers.

Randomization (p. 207)   Everyone has a known and equal chance of being selected.

Reach (p. 284)   The percentage of different homes or people exposed to a media vehicle or vehicles at least once during a specific period of time. It is the percentage of unduplicated audience.

Reason why (p. 236)   A statement that explains why the feature will benefit the user.

Recall (p. 258)   The ability to remember specific information content.

Recall test (p. 609)   A test that evaluates the memorability of an advertisement by contacting members of the advertisement's audience and asking them what they remember about it.

Recognition (p. 258)   An ability to remember having seen something before.

Recognition test (p. 612)   A test that evaluates the memorability of an advertisement by contacting members of the audience, showing them the ad, and asking if they remember it.

Reference group (p. 157)   A group of people that a person uses as a guide for behavior in specific situations.

Refund (p. 545)   An offer by the marketer to return a certain amount of money to the consumer who purchases the product.

Regional brand (p. 662)   A brand that is available throughout a regional trading bloc.

Release prints (p. 460)   Duplicate copies of a commercial that are ready for distribution.

Relevance (p. 383)   That quality of an advertising message that makes it important to the audience.

Reliability (p. 610)   A characteristic that describes a test that yields essentially the same results when the same advertisement is tested time after time.

Retail advertising (p. 631)   A type of advertising used by local merchants who sell directly to consumers.

Rough cut (p. 459)   A preliminary edited version of the commercial.

Rushes (p. 459)   Rough versions of the commercial assembled from unedited footage.

Sales promotion (p. 532)   Those marketing activities that add value to the product for a limited period of time to stimulate consumer purchasing and dealer effectiveness.

Sample (p. 207)   A selection of people who are identified as representative of the larger population.

Sampling (p. 547)   An offer that allows the customer to use or experience the product or service free of charge or for a very small fee.

Sans serif (p. 433)   A typeface that does not have the serif detail.

Script (p. 455)   A written version of a radio or television commercial.

Secondary research (p. 195)   Information that has been compiled and published.

Selective distortion (p. 168)   The interpretation of information in a way that is consistent with the person's existing opinion.

Selective exposure (p. 168)   The ability to process only certain information and avoid other stimuli.

Selective perception (p. 167)   The process of screening out information that does not interest us and retaining information that does.

Selective retention (p. 168)   The process of remembering only a small portion of what a person is exposed to.

Selling premises (p. 234)   The sales logic behind an advertising message.

Semicomp (p. 427)   A layout drawn to size that depicts the art and display type; body copy is simply ruled in.

Serif (p. 433)   A typeface with a finishing stroke on the main strokes of the letters.

Set (p. 452)   A constructed setting where the action in a commercial takes place.

Share of voice (p. 279)   The percentage of advertising messages in a medium by one brand among all messages for that product or service.

Signals (p. 345)   A series of electrical impulses that compose radio and television broadcasting.

Signature (p. 259)   The name of the company or product written in a distinctive type style.

Simulated test market (p. 623)   Research procedure in which respondents are exposed to advertisements and then permitted to shop for the advertised products in an artificial environment where records are kept of their purchases.

Slice of life (p. 405)   A problem-solution message built around some common, everyday situation.

Slogans (p. 258)   Frequently repeated phrases that provide continuity to an advertising campaign.

Social class (p. 156)   A way to categorize people on the basis of their values, attitudes, lifestyles, and behavior.

Societal marketing concept (p. 70)   A concept that requires balancing the company, consumer, and public interest.

Soft sell (p. 401)   An emotional message that uses mood, ambiguity, and suspense to create a response based on feelings and attitudes.

Sound effects (SFX) (p. 464)   Lifelike imitations of sounds.

Spectaculars (p. 512)   Billboards with unusual lighting effects.

Sponsorship (p. 338)   An arrangement in which the advertiser produces both a television program and the accompanying commercials.

Spot announcements (p. 339)   Ads shown during the breaks between programs.

Spot radio advertising (p. 350)   A form of advertising in which an ad is placed with an individual station rather than through a network.

Stereotyping (p. 49)   Presenting a group of people in an unvarying pattern that lacks individuality and often reflects popular misconceptions.

Stop motion (p. 454)   A technique in which inanimate objects are filmed one frame at a time, creating the illusion of movement.

Storyboard (p. 455)   A series of frames sketched to illustrate how the story line will develop.

Strategic research (p. 193)   All research that leads to the creation of the ad.

Subliminal message (p. 56)   A message transmitted below the threshold of normal perception so that the receiver is not consciously aware of having viewed it.

Superimpose (p. 259)   A television technique where one image is added to another that is already on the screen.

Supplements (p. 312)   Syndicated or local full-color advertising inserts that appear in newspapers throughout the week.

Survey research (p. 207)   Research using structured interview forms that ask large numbers of people exactly the same questions.

Sweepstakes (p. 543)   Sales promotion activities that require participants to submit their names to be included in a drawing or other type of chance selection.

SWOT analysis (p. 593)   A study of the Strengths, Weaknesses, Opportunities, and Threats that will impact upon the successful promotion of the product, the service, or the company.

Synchronize (p. 459)   Matching the audio to the video in a commercial.

Syndication (p. 336)   Television or radio shows that are reruns or original programs purchased by local stations to fill in during open hours.

T

Tabloid (p. 305)   A newspaper with a page size five to six columns wide and 14 inches deep.

Taglines (p. 259)   Clever phrases used at the end of an advertisement to summarize the ad's message.

Talent (p. 452)   People who appear in television commercials.

Target audience (p. 229) People who can be reached with a certain advertising medium and a particular message.

Task-objective method (p. 233) A budgeting method that builds a budget by asking what it will cost to achieve the stated objectives.

Tear sheet (p. 633) The pages from a newspaper on which an ad appears.

Telemarketing (p. 496) A type of marketing that uses the telephone to make a personal sales contact.

Television market (p. 342) An unduplicated geographical area to which a county is assigned on the basis of the highest share of the viewing of television stations.

Testimonial (p. 405) An advertising format in which a spokesperson describes a positive personal experience with the product.

Thumbnail sketches (p. 427) Small preliminary sketches of various layout ideas.

Tip-ins (p. 438) Preprinted ads that are provided by the advertiser to be glued into the binding of a magazine.

Trade deals (p. 553) An arrangement in which the retailer agrees to give the manufacturer's product a special promotional effort in return for product discounts, goods, or cash.

Trademark (p. 263) Sign or design, often with distinctive lettering, that symbolizes the brand.

Traditional delivery (p. 319) Delivery of magazines to readers through newsstands or home delivery.

Trailers (p. 525) Advertisements that precede the feature film in a movie theater.

Transformation advertising (p. 261) Image advertising that changes the experience of buying and using a product.

True experiments (p. 207) A research method that manipulates a set of variables to test hypotheses.

Unique selling proposition (p. 237) A benefit statement about a feature that is both unique to the product and important to the user.

Validity (p. 611) The ability of a test to measure what it is intended to measure.

Value and Lifestyle Systems (VALS) (p. 175) Classification systems that categorize people by values for the purpose of predicting effective advertising strategies.

Values (p. 155) The source for norms, which are not tied to specific objects or behaviors.

Vampire creativity (p. 258) An advertising problem in which an ad is so creative or entertaining that it overwhelms the product.

Vendors (p. 21) Institutions that provide certain expertise that advertisers and agencies cannot perform.

Verbatims (p. 206) Spontaneous comments by people who are being surveyed.

Vertical publications (p. 653) Publications directed to people who hold different positions in the same industries.

Videotape (p. 453) A type of recording medium that electronically records sound and images simultaneously.

Visualization (p. 388) The ability to imagine how an advertisement or commercial will look.

Voice-over (p. 451) A technique used in commercials in which an off-camera announcer talks about the on-camera scene.

W

Weighted audience values (p. 369) Numerical values assigned to different audience characteristics that help advertisers assign priorities when devising media plans.

CREDITS

CHAPTER 1

2 (Ad) © 1996 McDonald's Corporation; 5 (Ad) Courtesy of BBDO; 8 (Ad) Courtesy of THE CALIFORNIA RAISINS™ © 1987 CalRab, licensed by Applause Licensing; 8 (Ad) Courtesy of Little Caesars; 9 (Ad) Courtesy of Apple Computer, Inc.; 11 (Ad) © 1981 Federal Express Corporation; 25 (Ad) Source: Alex Groner, *The American Heritage History of American Business and Industry* (New York: American Heritage Publishing Co., 1972): 19. Courtesy of Bodleian Library, Oxford, U.K.; 26 (Ad) Courtesy of Warshaw Collection, Smithsonian Institution; 27 (Photo) Courtesy of FBC/Leber Katz Partners; 27 (Photo) Courtesy of FBC/Leber Katz Partners; 28 (Ad) Courtesy of Foote, Cone, & Belding; 29 (Ad) Courtesy of U.S. Army; 30 (Ad) Courtesy of William Heinemann; 31 (Ad) Courtesy of General Electric; 33 (Ad) Courtesy of William Heinemann; 34 (Ad) Courtesy of Personal Products; 35 (Ad) Courtesy of Dreyfus Fund Inc.; 35 (Ad) Courtesy of Xerox Corporation.

CHAPTER 2

40 (Ad) Courtesy of Volvo; 44 (Ad) Courtesy of Toyota Motor Sales, U.S.A., Inc.; 49 (Ad) Courtesy of Christian Dior Perfumes, Inc.; 50 (Ad) Reprinted with the permission of AMP; 52 (Ad) Courtesy of the Quaker Oats Company; 53 (Cartoon) Courtesy of Bill Whitehead; 57 (Ad) Courtesy of American Association of Advertising Agencies.

CHAPTER 3

84 (Ad) Courtesy of American Honda Motor Co., Inc./Rubin Postaer and Associates; 86 (Ad) Courtesy of Porsche; 91 (Ad) Courtesy of Famous Footwear.

CHAPTER 4

102 (Ad) © 1996 GM Corp. Used with permission GM Media Archives; 106 (Ad) Reproduced with permission from the April 13, 1994 issue of *Advertising Age*. Copyright, Crain Communications Inc., 1994; 108 (Ad) Illustration: Copyright © 1995 by The New York Times Co. Reprinted by permission. Leo Burnett logo. Courtesy of Leo Burnett Co., Inc.; 109 (Ad) Courtesy of CKS; 115 (Ad) Courtesy of Price/McNabb Focused Communications; 127 (Ad) Courtesy of Young & Rubicam, Inc.; 129 (Ad) Courtesy of DoubleClick

CHAPTER 5

154 (Ad) Courtesy of Apply Technology, L.L.C. Scholarship search provided by fastWEB, a registered service mark of Student Services, Inc.; 156 (Ad) Courtesy of Good Housekeeping; 157 (Photo) Courtesy of Dennie Cody/FPG; 158 (Ad) Copyright 1993 Sony Electronics; All rights reserved; 168 (Ad) Courtesy of Rolling Stone; 171 (Ad) Courtesy of Energizer Corporation; 174 (Ad) Courtesy of Rolex Watch U.S.A., Inc.; 184 (Ads) Courtesy of DDB Needham Worldwide; 184 (Ad) Courtesy of Marty Horn, Associate Director of the Delta Group, DDB Needham Worldwide.

CHAPTER 6

203 (Ad) Courtesy of MTV Networks. © 1991 MTV Networks. All rights reserved. The MTV music television logo is a registered trademark of MTV Networks, a division of Viacom International Inc.; 208 (Photo) © 1987 by Prentice Hall, Inc.

CHAPTER 7

216 (Ad) Courtesy of RadioShack; 221 (Ad) Courtesy of the Southern Company; 231 (Ad) Courtesy of United Airlines; 235 (Ad) Courtesy of General Motors.

CHAPTER 8

251 (Ad) Courtesy of the Los Angeles Fire Department; 253 (Ad) Courtesy of General Motors; 257 (Ad) Courtesy of Chrysler Corporation; 262 (Ad) Courtesy of Levi Strauss & Company; 263 (Ad) Courtesy of Ferrari North America and Ford Motor Company.

CHAPTER 9

270 (Screen capture) Courtesy of Sprint Communications Company; 277 (Ad) Courtesy of Nicotrol, a registered trademark of Pharmacia AB, © 1996 SmithKline Beecham Consumer Healthcare LP.

CHAPTER 10

298 (Photo) SPIN Magazine March 1997; 306 (Ad) Source: Claritas 1996; American Demographics, January 1996; 308 (Ad) Courtesy of *el Nuevo Herald*; 310 (Photo) Courtesy of Kenneth O. Hustel; 317 (Screen capture) Courtesy of *The New York Times*.

CHAPTER 11

328 (Ad) Courtesy of MTV Networks Europe; 343 (Ad) Courtesy of Slim•Fast; 344 (Ad) Courtesy of DDB Needham

Worldwide, Courtesy of General Mills and Michael Jordan; 348 (Ad) Courtesy of ABC Radio Networks; 349 (Ad) Courtesy of Unistar.

CHAPTER 12

361 (Ad) Courtesy of *Rolling Stone;* 362 (Ad) Courtesy of Alternative Press; 365 (Ad) Courtesy of *Good Housekeeping;* 368 (Ad) Courtesy of Simmons Market Research Bureau; 371 (Ad) © Copyright by Meredith Corporation 1988. All rights reserved.

CHAPTER 13

378 (Ad) © 1996 National Fluid Milk Processor Promotion Board; 383 (Ad) Courtesy of Harley-Davidson; 384 (Ad) © 1996 Compaq Computer; 386 (Ad) Courtesy of William Wright, Jr. Company; 388 (Ad) Courtesy of the General Motors Corporation; 390 (Photos) Leonardo da Vinci, Albert Einstein, and Georgia O'Keefe, courtesy of The Bettmann Archives; 393 (Photo) Courtesy of Stock/Boston; 400 (Ad) Courtesy of Everlast; 402 (Ad) Courtesy of the Council of Better Business Bureaus, Inc. and Bozell Worldwide.

CHAPTER 14

412 (Ad) Courtesy of Norwegian Cruise Lines; 414 (Ad) Courtesy of Magazine Publishers of America, Norwegian Cruise Lines and Kirshenbaum, Bond & Partners; 416 (Ad) Courtesy of Ericsson Mobile Phones USA; 419 (Ad) © 1996 Microsoft Corporation. all rights reserved; 422 (Text from ad) Reprinted with permission from Carter-Wallace, Inc. © Carter-Wallace, Inc. All Rights Reserved. 423 (Ad) Courtesy of Schwinn Cycling & Fitness Inc.; 426 (Ad) Courtesy of the Timberland Company; 426 (Ad) Courtesy of the Dunham Company; 429 (Ad) Courtesy of the Nike Corporation; 431 (Ad) Courtesy of the Nike Corporation; 431 (Ad) Courtesy of Levi Strauss & Co.

CHAPTER 15

444 (Still shot) Still courtesy of MGM Consumer Products. Reprinted with permission of Pierce Brosnan; 449 (Ad) Courtesy of *Adweek*/March 25, 1996; 450 (Ad) Courtesy of Levi Strauss & Co.; 456 (Ad) Source: Infomercial Marketing Report; 457 (Ad) Courtesy of State Farm Insurance Companies and DDB Needham Worldwide.

CHAPTER 16

472 (Ad) Courtesy of Hilton HHonors Worldwide; 480 (Ad) Courtesy of Ford Motor Co.; 490 (Ad) Courtesy of Time-Life Music; Reader's Digest Association, and Crest Fruit; 495 (Ad) Copyright 1990 The Time Inc. Magazine Company. Reprinted with permission; 499 (Ad) Courtesy of L.L. Bean; 500 (Ad) Courtesy of Deja News.

CHAPTER 17

504 (Ad) *Fortune* December 9, 1996; 509 (Ad) Courtesy of MADD, MN; 511 (Ad) Courtesy of the Literacy Council of America; 513 (Ad) *Adweek*/September 25, 1995; 513 (Ad) *Adweek*/September 25, 1995; 516 (Ad) Courtesy of Kimberly-Clark; 517 (Ad) Courtesy of Old Chicago; 519 (Ad) Courtesy of *Link* magazine; 521 (Ad) Courtesy of Yellow Pages Associ-

ation; 522 (Ad) Courtesy of IBM; 522 (Ad) Courtesy of Great Bear Spring Co.; 523 (Ad) Courtesy 1-800-Flowers.

CHAPTER 18

530 (Pamphlet on bag) Courtesy of the McDonald's Corporation; 536 (Cartoon) *Peanuts* reprinted by permission of UFS, Inc.; 539 (Ad) Courtesy of Arm & Hammer; 542 (Ad) Courtesy of Pearle Vision; 547 (Ad) Courtesy of Sampling Corporation of America; 554 (Ad) Courtesy of General Mills.

CHAPTER 19

558 (Video image) Courtesy of Lee Van Grack; 564 (Ad) © 1995 Mobile Corporation; 565 (Ad) Courtesy of Dow Jones/Wall Street Journal; 568 (Ad) Courtesy of Good Housekeeping, a publication of Hearst Magazines, a division of the Hearst Corporation; 570 (Ad) Pierce, L.P., Journal of the National Cancer Institute, October 18, 1995, Pollay, R.W., *Journal of Marketing*, April 1996, U.S. Centers for Disease Control and Prevention, August 1994; 583 (Ad) NewsClip Analysis, Burrelle's Information Services.

CHAPTER 20

588 (Ad) Cal Ripken, Jr. © 1996 National Fluid Milk Processor Promotion Board; 594 (Ad) Danny Devito & Rhea Perlman as Harry & Zinnia Wormwood. © 1996 National Fluid Milk Processor Promotion Board; 595 (Ad) Florence Griffith Joyner. © 1996 National Fluid Milk Processor Promotion Board; 595 (Ad) Michael Johnson. © 1997 National Fluid Milk Processor Promotion Board; 597 (Ad) Al Michaels, Frank Gifford, & Bob Costas. © 1996 National Fluid Milk Processor Promotion Board; 601 (Ad) Jeff Gordon. © 1997 National Fluid Milk Processor Promotion Board; 601 (Ad) Spike Lee. © 1996 National Fluid Milk Processor Promotion Board.

CHAPTER 21

604 (Ad) Courtesy of Chevrolet Motor Division.

CHAPTER 22

628 (Ad) Copyright 1995 Home Shopping Network, Inc. All rights reserved. Internet Shopping Network is a trademark of Home Shopping Network, Inc. All others are trademarks or copyrights of their respective companies; 632 (Ad) Courtesy of Foley's; 638 (Ad) © 1994, Johnson Controls, Inc.; 639 (Ad) © 1994, Johnson Controls, Inc. 640 (Ad) Courtesy Denver Hardware; 642 (Ad) Courtesy *Brandweek* June 12, 1995; 647 (Ad) Courtesy of Daly & Wolcott; 648 (Ad) Courtesy of Blessing/White; 651 (Ad) Courtesy of American International Group, Inc.; 652 (Ad) © 1996 Fruit of the Loom, Inc.

CHAPTER 23

660 (Ad) Courtesy of the Wm. Wrigley Jr. Company; 666 (Ad) Courtesy of American Airlines and DDB Needham; 674 (Ad) Courtesy of J. Walter Thompson London, "Anti-Aggressive Driving" Campaign, 1996; 684 (Ad) Courtesy of Pioneer Hi-Bred and Meyocks Benkstein Associates; 686 (Ad) © 1996 Compaq Computer Corporation. All rights reserved; 690 (Ad) Courtesy of The Hongkong and Shanghai Banking Corporation Limited.